CTA

Awareness Paper Workbook
Finance Act 2009
Study Text September 2009 Edition

For exams in May and November 2010

Contents

Second edition September 2009

Printed Text ISBN 9780 7517 6798 8

e book ISBN 9780 7517 7767 3

British Library Cataloguing-in-Publication Data

A catalogue record for this book is available from the British Library

Published by

BPP Learning Media Ltd
BPP House, Aldine Place
London W12 8AA

www.bpp.com/learningmedia

Printed in the United Kingdom

All our rights reserved. No part of this publication may be reproduced, stored in a retrieval system or transmitted, in any form or by any means, electronic, mechanical, photocopying, recording or otherwise, without the prior written permission of BPP Learning Media Ltd.

Whilst every care has been taken in the preparation of this text to ensure its accuracy, no responsibility for loss occasioned by any person acting or refraining from acting as a result of any statement made herein can be accepted by BPP Learning Media or Kaplan Financial.

© BPP Learning Media Ltd 2009

This text is printed on paper sourced from sustainable, managed forests

A note about copyright

Dear Customer

What does the little © mean and why does it matter?

Your market-leading TQT books, course materials and e-learning materials do not write and update themselves. People write them: on their own behalf or as employees of an organisation that invests in this activity. Copyright law protects their livelihoods. It does so by creating rights over the use of the content.

Breach of copyright is a form of theft – as well as being a criminal offence in some jurisdictions, it is potentially a serious breach of professional ethics.

With current technology, things might seem a bit hazy but, basically, without the express permission of BPP Learning Media:

- Photocopying TQT materials is a breach of copyright.

- Scanning, ripcasting or conversion of TQT digital materials into different file formats, uploading them to Facebook or e-mailing them to your friends is a breach of copyright.

You can, of course, sell your books, in the form in which you have bought them – once you have finished with them. (Is this fair to your fellow students? We update for a reason.)

Page

The Exam Structure

E Assessments	iv
The Awareness Paper	v
The Advisory Papers	vi
The Application and Interaction Paper	vii

Approaching your studies

The Awareness Modules	viii
Syllabus	ix
TQT talks to the Examiners	xxxvi
Using the Home Study Programme	xlii
The Revision Phase	xliv

Modules

Taxation of Individuals	1
IHT, Trusts and Estates	95
Unincorporated Businesses	177
Corporation tax	251
VAT and Stamp Taxes	317

Sample Paper

Questions	373
Answers	403

Tax Rates and Allowances

429

Review form

The exam structure

Under the syllabus, candidates must pass four three-hour written papers on taxation which can be taken separately or in any combination. The four taxation papers are as follows:

- One awareness paper
- Two advisory papers
- One application and interaction paper

In addition there are two one-hour e-assessments, one on Professional Responsibilities & Ethics and the other on Law.

E-assessments

The e-assessments can be sat separately or together. Candidates can sit the assessments at a time of their choosing at examination centres throughout the UK. It will, however, be a condition that these assessments must be **passed** before the examination entry closing date for the last tax paper that a candidate will sit (if sitting in a modular way) or before the examination entry closing date if a candidate is taking all the written tax papers at the same sitting.

Candidates must answer **60 questions** from a variety of multiple choice and multiple response questions. Multiple choice questions are where a candidate must identify one correct response from a choice of four. Multiple response questions are where a candidate must identify several correct responses from a choice of up to six.

Candidates must answer 60 questions within the hour permitted for each assessment. **A candidate must provide a total of 40 correct responses out of the 60 questions to pass each e-assessment.** The questions for an e-assessment are randomly selected before candidates start the test and therefore each individual assessment is unique.

A short section is provided before the start of the hour long assessment in order to allow candidates to familiarise themselves with the format of the examination.

Objective

The objective of the Professional Responsibilities and Ethics e-assessment is to test candidates' understanding of the obligations of a Chartered Tax Adviser in the areas of professional responsibilities & ethics. Examinable documents are available for download without charge from the Institute's website www.tax.org.uk.

The objective of the Law e-assessment is to test candidates' knowledge of law within the relevant areas of tax. Questions are drawn from the CIOT's manual Essential Law for the Chartered Tax Adviser (fifth edition examinable to 28 February 2010, sixth edition examinable from 1 March 2010) which is available for purchase from the Institute. Candidates are not expected to demonstrate a high level of application and interpretation of law in order to satisfy the requirements to pass the assessment. Candidates who have studied Scots law are allocated alternative questions compliant with that jurisdiction, where required.

TQT materials

To assist your studies TQT have written **market leading i-pass CD Roms** which contain plenty of **questions** including the CIOT's sample questions. We believe that the best way for you to practice for this E-assessment, is to work through these questions provided to you in an E-format. In addition, in order to aid your revision TQT also supply **pocket sized passcards**. These are a handy set of revision cards designed to reinforce, and help you remember, the key examinable topics.

TQT strongly recommends that you purchase the law manual 'Essential law for the Chartered Tax Adviser' from the CIOT as it has been updated for the new syllabus exams and it defines the syllabus. You can purchase this manual by telephoning the CIOT on 020 7340 0550 or 0844 579 6700. The sixth edition (examinable from 1 March 2010) is available from October 2009.

The Awareness paper

Objective

One of the strengths of the CTA examination is the requirement for candidates to show an understanding of a broad range of taxes. The objective of the Awareness paper is to examine core areas of the various taxes which candidates may not deal with on a daily basis and which do not form part of their chosen Advisory papers.

Detail

The Awareness paper comprises one three-hour paper covering five modules. Candidates must choose **three out of the five modules** and answer all the questions on each of their chosen modules. All Awareness modules must be attempted at the same sitting.

The five modules in the Awareness paper are:

- Taxation of Individuals
- Inheritance Tax, Trusts and Estates
- Taxation of Unincorporated Businesses
- Corporation Tax
- VAT Including Stamp Taxes

Candidates choose three modules from the Awareness paper – BEWARE – these cannot be the same as the corresponding Advisory papers chosen, for example candidates who have decided to sit the taxation of Owner-Managed Businesses Advisory paper are precluded from selecting the Taxation of Unincorporated Businesses module at Awareness level.

Each module contains 12 short-form questions. Each question is worth five marks. To obtain a credit, candidates must obtain 50% or more of the total marks awarded for the whole paper at the same sitting. There is no requirement to obtain 50% of the marks in each individual module.

The Awareness paper takes place on the morning of the second day of the examinations.

TQT materials

To assist your studies TQT has prepared an **Awareness Paper Study Text** which you should use in conjunction with the **Awareness Paper Workbook**. These products are completely focussed on the exam you will be facing. Together they contain all the technical material you need plus plenty of questions to practise. In addition, to give you a really good idea of what the paper is like, the CIOT's sample paper is included. Finally, in order to aid your revision TQT also supplies **pocket-sized passcards**. These are a handy set of revision cards designed to reinforce, and help you remember, the key examinable topics.

The Advisory papers

Objective

The objective of the Advisory papers is to test candidates' knowledge at an advisory level, on the areas of taxation which they choose, in accordance with the defined syllabus for each paper.

Detail

Candidates choose **two** Advisory papers. TQT produces material for each of the following four Advisory papers:

- Taxation of Owner-Managed Businesses
- Taxation of Individuals
- Inheritance Tax, Trusts and Estates
- Advanced Corporation Tax

The Advisory papers form the first day of the examinations and are divided into two sessions. The grouping is as follows:

Morning session	Afternoon session
Taxation of Owner-Managed Businesses	Taxation of Individuals
Inheritance Tax, Trusts & Estates	Advanced Corporation Tax

It is considered that the groupings as shown accommodate the choices of the majority of candidates who wish to sit the examination in a single sitting. There is no restriction on a candidate choosing two advisory papers from the same group. In such circumstances, however, the candidate cannot sit both papers at the same examination sitting.

Each Advisory paper is a 'stand alone' paper. Candidates receiving a mark of 50% or more of the total marks will receive a credit in that paper.

TQT materials

TQT's innovative approach to the Advisory level is to provide three technical study texts:

- Business Taxes
- Capital Taxes
- Personal Taxes

Which of these technical texts you need depends on which Advisory paper you are taking as shown in the table below:

Advisory paper	Technical texts required
Taxation of Owner-Managed Businesses	Personal Taxes Capital Taxes Business Taxes
Advanced Corporation Tax	Business Taxes
Inheritance Tax, Trusts and Estates	Capital Taxes
Taxation of Individuals	Personal Taxes Capital Taxes

All of the texts are signposted to ensure that you only study the material that is relevant to the paper you are sitting.

In addition to the technical texts, there is a workbook for each paper. This workbook guides you through the technical texts. In addition it contains plenty of questions and answers relevant to the paper that you will be sitting. The questions range from introductory to exam standard. Some of the answers to questions in the workbook include marking schemes so that you really can gauge how well you are doing.

The Application and Interaction paper

Objective

The objective of the Application and Interaction paper is to test candidates' ability, to apply to a practical case study, the knowledge gained in sitting the Advisory and Awareness papers and to demonstrate how the various taxes interact.

Detail

The paper consists of a case study, which candidates must answer in three hours. Candidates must answer **one** Application and Interaction case study question. TQT provides material for you to study for any of the following case study questions:

- Taxation of Individuals, Trusts & Estates
- Taxation of Companies
- Taxation of Owner-Managed Businesses

Each case study question is worth 100 marks. The pass mark is 50%.

The subject matter of the case study may include any of the items specified at Advisory level for those topics. It may also include elements of any subject within any of the Awareness modules. For example, the case study on the Taxation of Companies will be mainly corporation tax based but may also include areas such as shareholder issues, VAT and SDLT. Issues involving consideration of professional responsibilities, ethics and/or law should also be expected to feature in the case studies.

This is not a 'time pressured' case study. The emphasis is on allowing the candidates the time to submit a complete answer, thus demonstrating their ability to deal with practical situations.

The Application and Interaction paper takes place on the afternoon of the second day of the examinations.

TQT materials

TQT's material is outstanding. We produce a study text for the application and interaction paper which includes a chapter on **how to use your legislation** (essential for this examination); **guidance on how to approach the case study; guidance on how to use your time in the examination hall; guidance on how marks will be awarded; guidance on how to write reports** as well as **recap of some major technical points** that you will need for this examination. There are some questions in the Study Text for you to attempt at the initial phase of your studies. The pilot paper question and answer is included together with all important guidance on how this question would have been best approached.

Revision phase

Practice and revision kits

For your revision phase TQT publishes practice and revision kits for the Awareness, Advisory and Application and Interaction papers. These practice and revision kits will be available in January 2010.

The practice and revision kits are the **key to your success** in your CTA exams. They are packed full of questions, together with **helpful hints on how to approach the questions**. The answers are **clearly structured** and **supported by hints on how you can maximise your marks in an examination situation**. In addition some answers have **marking schemes** so that you can really gauge how well you are doing. The May and November 2009 questions and answers are also included.

Approaching your studies

The Awareness Modules

We will be introducing the topics in each module to you from first principles. If you have any previous knowledge, perhaps as a result of work experience, or as a result of having studied for other papers within this, the ATT or any other syllabus, you can modify the amount of time you spend on each topic to take account of your knowledge. The main areas of knowledge required for each of the modules given below.

1   TAXATION OF INDIVIDUALS

This module tests three main areas of knowledge:

(a) The **income tax liability** arising in connection with various types of income including employment income, income from property and investment income.

(b) The **national insurance** position of employees and their employers.

(c) The **capital gains tax** issues arising when an individual sells both business and non business assets.

2   INHERITANCE TAX, TRUSTS AND ESTATES

This module tests three main areas of knowledge:

(a) The preparation of **inheritance tax computations** for both lifetime and death transfers of value.

(b) The understanding of the legal issues surrounding **trusts** and the preparation of computations of tax due by trustees.

(c) The preparation of computations of tax for deceased persons, their executors and beneficiaries of their estates.

3   TAXATION OF UNINCORPORATED BUSINESSES

This module tests three main areas of knowledge:

(a) The **income tax and national insurance liabilities** arising in connection with an unincorporated business for its owner.

(b) The **capital allowance** position of an unincorporated business.

(c) The **capital gains tax** issues arising on the sale of business assets including the relief available when a business is incorporated.

4   CORPORATION TAX

This module tests three main areas of knowledge:

(a) The **computation of a company's taxable profits** from trading and other activities, such as investments and renting out property.

(b) The **capital allowance** position of a company.

(c) The basic **chargeable gains** issues arising on the sale of assets by a company.

5   VAT INCLUDING STAMP TAXES

This module tests four main areas of knowledge:

(a) The **scope** of VAT and the meaning of **supply**.

(b) Calculating the **VAT liability** in simple and more complex situations involving land and buildings, and international transactions.

(c) Accounting for and the administration of VAT.

(d) The **stamp duty** and **stamp duty land tax** implications of the transfer of business assets.

TQT note: At the time of printing this text the CIOT had not updated the syllabus for FA 2009. The syllabus below was the most recent version at the time of printing: you should refer to the CIOT website for an updated version in due course.

Syllabuses for the Advisory Papers

2009 Examination

Taxation of Individuals

INCOME TAX

Administration
Self-assessment system
General Provisions – ITTOIA part 10
The operation and application of the PAYE system
Personal reliefs
Taxation of income of spouses

Employment Income
Status – employed or self-employed
Charge to tax – excluding IR35
Earnings and benefits treated as income
Exemptions
Deductions allowed from earnings
Payments to and from non-approved pension schemes
Payments and benefits on termination of employment
Income & exemptions relating to shares and securities (excl EMI, SAYE Options & Priority Share Allocations)
SAYE Options and Priority Share Allocations
Enterprise Management Incentives
Former employees: deduction for liabilities
Excluded: Sections 28, 42, 43, 211-215, 290-306, 351, 352, 360, 372, 378-392, 549-554, 713-715 ITEPA 2003

Pension income
Part 9 ITEPA 2003
Excluded: Sections 605-637 ITEPA 2003

Social security income
Part 10 ITEPA 2003

Property Income
Part 3 ITTOIA 2005
Rent-a-Room relief
Anti-avoidance – transactions in land
Excluded: Sections 315-319 and 335-343 ITTOIA 2005

Savings and Investment Income
Interest
Dividends from UK resident companies
Dividends from non-UK resident companies
Stock dividends from UK resident companies

Release of loan to participator in a close company
Profits from deeply discounted securities (excluding s.443 – s.459 ITTOIA 2005)
Gains from life assurance – overview only required
Company purchase of own shares
Excluded: Sections 422-426 and 547-573 ITTOIA 2005

Miscellaneous Income
Receipts from intellectual property
Amounts treated as income of settlor
Beneficiaries' income from estates in administration
Annual payments not otherwise charged
Income not otherwise charged
Excluded: Sections 609-618, 671-678 and 803-828 ITTOIA 2005

Exempt Income
Part 6 ITTOIA 2005
Excluded: Sections 713-748, 751-756 and 769-782 ITTOIA 2005

Foreign Income
Part 8 ITTOIA 2005
Residence, Ordinary Residence & Domicile
Double tax relief
Transfer of assets abroad
Remittance Basis

Sundry Matters
Enterprise Investment Scheme
Venture Capital Trusts
Relief for interest paid
Gift Aid
Pension Contributions – post 6 April 2006
Anti-avoidance – transactions in securities
Anti-avoidance – transfer of assets abroad
Pre-owned assets
Interaction with CGT
Disclosure of avoidance schemes
Impact of tax credits on tax planning (awareness only)

NATIONAL INSURANCE

Class 1
Class 1A and 1B
Internationally mobile employees

CAPITAL GAINS TAX

Capital Gains Tax and Corporation Tax on Chargeable Gains
The charge to tax and persons chargeable (s.1 to s.8 TCGA 1992)
Entrepreneur's relief (including schedule A1 TCGA 1992)
Residence
Calculation of tax liability for individuals

Excluded: s.11 TCGA 1992

Computation of Gains and Acquisitions and Disposals of Assets
Computation of gains and losses
Use of losses
Transactions treated as made at market value
Transactions between connected parties
Disposal in a series of transactions
Assets and disposals of assets (s.21 to s.28 TCGA 1992)
Value Shifting (excluding s.31 to s.34 TCGA 1992)
Rebasing to 1982
Allowable deductions
Wasting Assets
Miscellaneous computational provisions (s.48 to s.52 TCGA 1992)
Indexation Allowance

Individuals, Partnerships, Trusts and Collective Investment Schemes
Husband and wife
Partnerships and Limited Liability Partnerships
Nominees and bare trustees
Death
Excluded: Section 61, 99-103 TCGA 1992. Section 63 TCGA 1992 (included for Scottish law candidates)

Shares, Securities, Options etc
Share pooling, identification of securities and indexation
Gilt edged securities and qualifying corporate bonds
Exemption for government non-marketable securities
Capital distribution in respect of shares
Disposal of a right to acquire shares or debentures
Transfer of asset at undervalue to shareholders of a close company
Reorganisation or reduction of share capital
Conversion of securities
Company reconstructions
Stock dividends
Options (s.144 – s.144A TCGA 1992)
Employment related securities (s.149A to s.149C TCGA 1992)
Enterprise Investment Scheme
Venture Capital Trusts
Excluded: Sections 118-120, 124, 140E-140G, 150, 151C, 151D TCGA 1992

Transfer of Business Assets
Replacement of business assets
Gifts of business assets

Other Property, Businesses, Investments etc
Private residences
Share schemes
Leases of land and other assets
Furnished holiday lettings
Part disposals
Compulsory acquisition

Debts
Charities and gifts of non-business assets
Chattels exemption
Other exemptions
Excluded: Sections 227-236, 237, 239A, 239B, 249, 250, 263ZA-271 TCGA 1992

Supplemental
Supplemental matters contained in s.272 to s.291 TCGA 1992
Post transaction valuations
Marren v Ingles

INHERITANCE TAX

Miscellaneous and Supplementary
Interaction with capital gains tax

Inheritance Tax, Trusts & Estates

INCOME TAX

Administration
Self-assessment system
General Provisions – ITTOIA part 10

Miscellaneous Income
Amounts treated as income of settlor
Beneficiaries income from estates in administration
Estates of deceased persons in course of administration
Excluded: Sections 671-678 ITTOIA 2005

Sundry Matters
Pre-owned assets
Taxation of income of settlements
Interaction with CGT
Disclosure of avoidance schemes

CAPITAL GAINS TAX

Capital Gains Tax and Corporation Tax on Chargeable Gains
The charge to tax and persons chargeable (s.1 to s.8 TCGA 1992)
Entrepreneur's Relief (including schedule A1 TCGA 1992)
Residence
Calculation of tax liability for individuals, trusts and estates
Excluded: s.11 TCGA 1992

Computation of Gains and Acquisitions and Disposals of Assets
Computation of gains and losses
Use of losses
Transactions treated as made at market value
Transactions between connected parties
Disposal in a series of transactions
Assets and disposals of assets (s.21 to s.28 TCGA 1992)
Rebasing to 1982
Allowable deductions
Wasting Assets
Miscellaneous computational provisions (s.48 to s.52 TCGA 1992)
Indexation Allowance

Individuals, Partnerships, Trusts and Collective Investment Schemes
Husband and wife
Nominees and bare trustees
Death
Expenses of administration of estate
Tax liability of trustees and personal representatives
Settlements (s.68 to s.98A TCGA 1992)

Excluded: Section 61, 99-103 TCGA 1992. Section 63 TCGA 1992 (included for Scottish law candidates)

Shares, Securities, Options etc
Share pooling, identification of securities and indexation
Gilt edged securities and qualifying corporate bonds
Exemption for government non-marketable securities
Capital distribution in respect of shares
Disposal of a right to acquire shares or debentures
Transfer of asset at undervalue to shareholders of a close company
Reorganisation or reduction of share capital
Conversion of securities
Company reconstructions
Excluded: Sections 118-120, 124, 140E-140G, 150, 151C, 151D TCGA 1992

Transfer of Business Assets
Gifts of Business Assets
Gifts to settlor interested trusts
Excluded: Sections 163-164N TCGA 1992

Other Property, Businesses, Investments etc
Private residences
Leases of land and other assets
Part disposals
Chattels exemption
Other exemptions
Excluded: Sections 227-236, 237, 239A, 239B, 249, 250, 263ZA-271 TCGA 1992

Supplemental
Supplemental matters contained in s.272 to s.291 TCGA 1992
Post transaction valuations
Marren v Ingles

INHERITANCE TAX

General
Main charges and definitions
Rates
Dispositions that are not transfers of value

Exempt Transfers
Exemptions
Conditional exemptions
Allocation of exemptions
Excluded: Sch 4 IHTA 1984

Settled property
Preliminary provisions
Interests in possession, reversionary interests and settlement powers
Settlements without interests in possession
Miscellaneous

Excluded: Sections 55A, 57A, 70, 73, 74, 76-79A and 87 IHTA 1984. Pre 27 March 1974 settlements
Close companies

Reliefs
Business property relief
Agricultural property relief
Woodlands relief
Transfers in the seven years before death
Successive charges
Changes in distribution of deceased's estate
Pension schemes
Armed forces
Non-residents bank accounts
Double taxation relief
Excluded: Sections 148-150, 153-156 IHTA 1984

Valuation
General provisions
Estate on death
Sale of shares from deceased's estate
Sale of land from deceased's estate
Excluded: Sections 186A, 186B IHTA 1984

Liability
General rules
Special cases
Burden of tax, etc

Administration and Collection
Excluded: Sections 230-232 IHTA 1984

Miscellaneous and Supplementary
Miscellaneous provisions (Sections 262-278 IHTA 1984)
Disclosure of avoidance schemes
Gifts with reservation
Lex situs
Intestacy
Liabilities
Interaction with capital gains tax

Taxation of Owner-Managed Businesses

INCOME TAX

Administration
Self-assessment system
General Provisions – ITTOIA part 10
The operation and application of the PAYE system
Personal reliefs
Taxation of income of spouses

Employment Income
Status – employed or self-employed
IR35 and Managed Service Companies
Earnings and benefits treated as income
Exemptions
Deductions allowed from earnings
Payments and benefits on termination of employment
Income and exemptions relating to shares and securities (excl EMI, SAYE Options and Priority Share Allocations)
Enterprise Management Incentives
Excluded: Sections 28, 42, 43, 211-215, 290-306, 351, 352, 360, 372, 378-392, 549-554, 713-715 ITEPA 2003

Trading Income
Badges of Trade
Income taxed as trade profits and basic rules
Rules restricting deductions
Rules allowing deductions
Receipts
Gifts to Charities
Valuation of Stock and Work in Progress
Unremittable Amounts
Basis Periods
Adjustment Income (except for barristers)
Post-Cessation Receipts
Losses
Partnerships including LLPs

Property Income
Anti-avoidance – transactions in land

Savings and Investment Income
Release of loan to participator in a close company
Company purchase of own shares

Sundry Matters
Enterprise Investment Scheme
Venture Capital Trusts
Relief for interest paid

Pension Contributions – post 6 April 2006
Anti-avoidance – transactions in securities
Anti-avoidance – transfer of assets abroad
Interaction with CGT
Disclosure of avoidance schemes
Impact of tax credits on tax planning (awareness only)

Specialist trades and professions
Except where indicated, candidates are only required to be aware that special rules exist and will not be required to have a knowledge of those rules or be able to apply them:
Mines & quarries, Divers, Construction Industry, Lloyds Underwriters, Farmers Herd Basis and Averaging of Profits, Non resident entertainers and sportsmen, Barristers, Artists & Authors, Films and sound recordings, Ministers of Religion, MPs, Armed Forces.

NATIONAL INSURANCE

Class 1
Classes 1A and 1B
Classes 2, 3 and 4

CAPITAL GAINS TAX

Capital Gains Tax and Corporation Tax on Chargeable Gains
The charge to tax and persons chargeable (s.1 to s.8 TCGA 1992)
Entrepreneur's Relief (including schedule A1 TCGA 1992)
Residence
Calculation of tax liability for individuals
Excluded: s.11 TCGA 1992

Computation of Gains and Acquisitions and Disposals of Assets
Computation of gains and losses
Use of losses
Transactions treated as made at market value
Transactions between connected parties
Disposal in a series of transactions
Assets and disposals of assets (s.21 to s.28 TCGA 1992)
Value Shifting (excluding s.31 to s.34 TCGA 1992)
Rebasing to 1982
Allowable deductions
Wasting Assets
Miscellaneous computational provisions (s.48 to s.52 TCGA 1992)
Indexation Allowance

Individuals, Partnerships, Trusts and Collective Investment Schemes
Husband and wife
Partnerships and Limited Liability Partnerships
Nominees and bare trustees
Excluded: Section 61, 99-103 TCGA 1992. Section 63 TCGA 1992 (included for Scottish law candidates)

Shares, Securities, Options etc
Share pooling, identification of securities and indexation
Gilt edged securities and qualifying corporate bonds
Exemption for government non-marketable securities
Capital distribution in respect of shares
Disposal of a right to acquire shares or debentures
Transfer of asset at undervalue to shareholders of a close company
Reorganisation or reduction of share capital
Conversion of securities
Company reconstructions
Stock dividends
Options (s.144-s.144A TCGA 1992)
Enterprise Investment Scheme
Excluded: Sections 118-120, 124, 140E-140G, 150, 151C, 151D TCGA 1992

Transfer of Business Assets
Replacement of business assets
Stock in Trade
Transfer of a business to a company
Gifts of business assets
Excluded: Sections 163-164N TCGA 1992

Companies
Groups and transactions within groups
Anti-gain buying
Companies leaving groups
Recovery of tax otherwise than from taxpayer company
Substantial shareholding exemption
Excluded: Sections 193-221 TCGA 1992

Other Property, Businesses, Investments etc
Share schemes
Leases of land and other assets
Furnished holiday lettings
Part disposals
Compulsory acquisition
Debts
Charities and gifts of non-business assets
Know how
Other exemptions
Excluded: Sections 227-236, 237, 239A, 239B, 249, 250, 263ZA-271 TCGA 1992

Supplemental
Supplemental matters contained in s.272 to s.291 TCGA 1992
Post transaction valuations
Marren v Ingles

CORPORATION TAX

Accounting Standards
Impact of accounting standards on taxable profits

Administration
Corporation Tax Self-Assessment system
The charge to corporation tax
Small companies rate
Deduction of income tax

Computation of Taxable Profits
Computation of trading profits
Intangibles
Loan relationships – basic principles
Deductions for share schemes
Investment companies
Double tax relief – basic principles
Schedule A
Other investment income
Charges on income
Losses
Research and Development

Distributions
Distributions excluding demergers

Groups and Consortia
Groups excluding consortia

Close companies

Miscellaneous Matters
IR35
Liquidation, receivership, administration

Anti-avoidance
Change in ownership of company
Disclosure of avoidance schemes
Sale and leaseback – basic principles
Transfer pricing – basic principles

CAPITAL ALLOWANCES

Part 1 CAA 2001

Plant & Machinery Allowances
Introduction (s.11 to s.14 CAA 2001)
Qualifying activities
Qualifying expenditure
First year qualifying expenditure
Annual Investment Allowance
Other Allowances and charges
Hire purchase etc and plant provided by lessee
Computer software

Cars etc
Short life assets
Fixtures
Assets provided or used only partly for qualifying activities
Additional VAT liabilities and rebates (s.234 to s.240 CAA 2001)
Giving effect to allowances and charges
Partnerships and successions
Use of plant or machinery for business entertainment
Excluded: Sections 34-38, 40-43, 127-171, 209-212, 254-261, 270

Flat Conversion Allowance

Research and Development Allowances

Know How Allowances

Patent Allowances

Contributions

Supplementary Provisions
Effect of partnership changes
Successions
Miscellaneous – s.562-570A CAA 2001
Final Provisions – s.571-581 CAA 2001
Excluded: Sections 544-545, 552-556, 560

General Exclusions:
Industrial Buildings Allowances
Agricultural Buildings Allowances
Mineral Extraction Allowances
Dredging Allowances
Assured Tenancy Allowances

INHERITANCE TAX

Reliefs
Business property relief

Valuation
General provisions

Miscellaneous and Supplementary
Interaction with capital gains tax

Advanced Corporation Tax

INCOME TAX

Trading Income
Badges of Trade

Property Income
Anti-avoidance – transactions in land
Excluded: Sections 315-319 and 335-343 ITTOIA 2005

Savings and Investment Income
Company purchase of own shares

Sundry Matters
Venture Capital Trusts
Anti-avoidance – transactions in securities
Disclosure of avoidance schemes

CAPITAL GAINS TAX

Capital Gains Tax and Corporation Tax on Chargeable Gains
The charge to tax and persons chargeable (s.1 to s.8 TCGA 1992)
Residence
Excluded: s.11 TCGA 1992

Computation of Gains and Acquisitions and Disposals of Assets
Computation of gains and losses
Use of losses
Transactions treated as made at market value
Transactions between connected parties
Disposal in a series of transactions
Assets and disposals of assets (s.21 to s.28 TCGA 1992)
Value Shifting (s.31 to s.34 TCGA 1992)
Rebasing to 1982
Allowable deductions
Wasting Assets
Miscellaneous computational provisions (s.48 to s.52 TCGA 1992)
Indexation Allowance

Individuals, Partnerships, Trusts and Collective Investment Schemes
Nominees and bare trustees

Shares, Securities, Options etc
Gilt edged securities and qualifying corporate bonds
Exemption for government non-marketable securities
Capital distribution in respect of shares
Disposal of a right to acquire shares or debentures
Reorganisation or reduction of share capital
Conversion of securities

Company reconstructions
Transfers concerning companies of different member states
Stock dividends
Options (s.143 – s.148C TCGA 1992)
Excluded: Sections 118-120, 124, 140E-140G, 150, 151C, 151D TCGA 1992

Transfer of Business Assets
Replacement of business assets
Stock in Trade
Excluded: Sections 163-164N TCGA 1992

Companies
Groups and transactions within groups
Losses attributable to depreciatory transactions
Anti-gain buying
Companies leaving groups
Non-resident and dual resident companies
Recovery of tax otherwise than from taxpayer company
Demergers
Substantial shareholding exemption
Excluded: Sections 193-221 TCGA 1992

Other Property, Businesses, Investments etc
Share schemes
Leases of land and other assets
Part disposals
Compulsory acquisition
Debts
Know how
Other exemptions
Excluded: Sections 227-236, 237, 239A, 239B, 249, 250, 263ZA-271 TCGA 1992

Supplemental
Supplemental matters contained in s.272 to s.291 TCGA 1992
Post transaction valuations
Marren v Ingles

CORPORATION TAX

Accounting Standards
Impact of accounting standards on taxable profits
Deferred tax

Administration
Corporation Tax Self-Assessment system
The charge to corporation tax
Small companies rate
Permanent establishment/branch
Company residence
Deduction of income tax

Computation of Taxable Profits
Computation of trading profits
Intangibles
Loan relationships
Deductions for share schemes
Investment companies
Double tax relief
Schedule A
Other investment income
Charges on income
Losses
Research and Development

Distributions
Distributions
Demergers

Groups and Consortia
Groups
Consortia

Close companies

Miscellaneous Matters
Double tax treaties – OECD model
Corporate Venturing scheme
Liquidation, receivership, administration
Financial instruments
Joint Ventures
Property Derivatives
Stamp Taxes and Groups of Companies

Anti-avoidance
Controlled foreign companies
Change in ownership of company
Migration of company
Disclosure of avoidance schemes
Sale and leaseback
Transfer pricing

CAPITAL ALLOWANCES

Part 1 CAA 2001

Plant & Machinery Allowances
Introduction (s.11 to 14 CAA 2001)
Qualifying activities
Qualifying expenditure
First year qualifying expenditure
Annual Investment Allowance
Other Allowances and charges

Hire purchase etc and plant provided by lessee
Computer software
Cars etc
Short life assets
Long life assets
Overseas leasing
Fixtures
Assets provided or used only partly for qualifying activities
Anti-avoidance
Additional VAT liabilities and rebates (s.234 to s.246 CAA 2001)
Giving effect to allowances and charges
Use of plant or machinery for business entertainment
Excluded: Sections 34-38, 40-43, 127-171, 209-212, 254-261, 270

Research and Development Allowances

Know How Allowances

Patent Allowances

Contributions

Supplementary Provisions
Successions
Transfers – s.561, 561A CAA 2001
Miscellaneous – s.562-570A CAA 2001
Final Provisions – s.571-581 CAA 2001
Excluded: Sections 544-545, 552-556, 560

General Exclusions:
Industrial Buildings Allowances
Agricultural Buildings Allowances
Mineral Extraction Allowances
Dredging Allowances
Assured Tenancy Allowances

Syllabuses for the Awareness Papers

Taxation of Individuals

INCOME TAX

Administration
Self-assessment system
General Provisions – ITTOIA part 10
The operation and application of the PAYE system
Personal reliefs
Taxation of income of spouses

Employment Income
Status – employed or self-employed
Charge to tax – excluding IR35
Earnings and benefits treated as income
Exemptions
Deductions allowed from earnings
Payments to and from non-approved pension schemes
Payments and benefits on termination of employment
Income and exemptions relating to shares and securities (excl. EMI, SAYE Options and Priority Share Allocations)
SAYE Options and Priority Share Allocations
Enterprise Management Incentives
Former employees: deduction for liabilities

Pension income
Part 9 ITEPA 2003

Social security income
Part 10 ITEPA 2003

Property Income
Part 3 ITTOIA 2005
Rent-a-Room relief
Anti-avoidance – transactions in land

Savings and Investment Income
Interest
Dividends from UK resident companies
Dividends from non-UK resident companies
Stock dividends from UK resident companies
Release of loan to participator in a close company
Company purchase of own shares

Miscellaneous Income
Annual payments not otherwise charged
Income not otherwise charged

Exempt Income
Part 6 ITTOIA 2005

Foreign Income
Part 8 ITTOIA 2005
Residence, Ordinary Residence and Domicile
Double tax relief
Transfer of assets abroad
Remittance Basis

Sundry Matters
Enterprise Investment Scheme
Relief for interest paid
Gift Aid
Pension Contributions – post 6 April 2006

NATIONAL INSURANCE

Class 1
Class 1A and 1B

CAPITAL GAINS TAX

Capital Gains Tax and Corporation Tax on Chargeable Gains
The charge to tax and persons chargeable (s.1 to s.8 TCGA 1992)
Entrepreneur's relief (including sch. A1 TCGA 1992)
Residence
Calculation of tax liability for individuals

Computation of Gains and Acquisitions and Disposals of Assets
Computation of gains and losses
Use of losses
Transactions treated as made at market value
Transactions between connected parties
Disposal in a series of transactions
Assets and disposals of assets (s.21, s.22, s.23, s.24 and s.28 TCGA 1992)
Rebasing to 1982
Allowable deductions
Wasting Assets
Indexation Allowance

Individuals, Partnerships, Trusts and Collective Investment Schemes
Husband and wife

Shares, Securities, Options etc
Gilt edged securities and qualifying corporate bonds
Exemption for government non-marketable securities

Capital distribution in respect of shares
Disposal of a right to acquire shares or debentures
Transfer of asset at undervalue to shareholders of a close company
Reorganisation or reduction of share capital
Conversion of securities
Company reconstructions
Options (s.144-s.144A TCGA 1992)
Employment related securities (s.149A-s.149C TCGA 1992)
Enterprise Investment Scheme

Other Property, Businesses, Investments etc
Private residences
Share schemes
Leases of land and other assets
Furnished holiday lettings
Part disposals
Charities and gifts of non-business assets
Chattels exemption

Supplemental
Supplemental matters contained in s.272 to s.291 TCGA 1992
Marren v Ingles

Inheritance Tax, Trusts & Estates

INCOME TAX

Miscellaneous Income
Amounts treated as income of settlor
Beneficiaries' income from estates in administration
Estates of deceased persons in course of administration

Sundry Matters
Pre-owned assets
Taxation of income of settlements
Interaction with CGT

CAPITAL GAINS TAX

Capital Gains Tax and Corporation Tax on Chargeable Gains
The charge to tax and persons chargeable (s.1 to s.8 TCGA 1992)
Entrepreneur's relief (including schedule A1 TCGA 1992)
Residence

Computation of Gains and Acquisitions and Disposals of Assets
Computation of gains and losses
Use of losses
Transactions treated as made at market value
Transactions between connected parties
Disposal in a series of transactions
Assets and disposals of assets (s.21, s.22, s.23, s.24 and s.28 TCGA 1992)
Rebasing to 1982
Allowable deductions
Indexation Allowance

Individuals, Partnerships, Trusts and Collective Investment Schemes
Nominees and bare trustees
Death
Tax liability of trustees and personal representatives
Settlements (s.68 to s.98A TCGA 1992)

Other Property, Businesses, Investments etc
Part disposals

Supplemental
Supplemental matters contained in s.272 to s.291 TCGA 1992

INHERITANCE TAX

General
Main charges and definitions
Rates
Dispositions that are not transfers of value

Exempt Transfers
Exemptions
Conditional exemptions
Allocation of exemptions

Settled property
Preliminary provisions
Interests in possession, reversionary interests and settlement powers
Settlements without interests in possession
Miscellaneous

Reliefs
Business property relief
Agricultural property relief
Transfers in the seven years before death
Successive charges

Valuation
General provisions
Estate on death
Sale of shares from deceased's estate
Sale of land from deceased's estate

Liability
General rules
Special cases

Miscellaneous and Supplementary
Miscellaneous provisions (Sections 262-278 IHTA 1984)
Gifts with reservation
Lex situs
Intestacy
Liabilities

Taxation of Unincorporated Businesses

INCOME TAX

Administration
Self-assessment system
General Provisions – ITTOIA part 10
Personal reliefs
Taxation of income of spouses

Employment Income
Status – employed or self-employed

Trading Income
Badges of Trade
Income taxed as trade profits and basic rules
Rules restricting deductions
Rules allowing deductions
Receipts
Gifts to Charities
Valuation of Stock and Work in Progress
Basis Periods
Adjustment Income (except for barristers)
Post-Cessation Receipts
Losses
Partnerships including LLPs

Sundry Matters
Relief for interest paid

NATIONAL INSURANCE

Classes 2, 3 and 4

CAPITAL GAINS TAX

Capital Gains Tax and Corporation Tax on Chargeable Gains
The charge to tax and persons chargeable (s.1 to s.8 TCGA 1992)
Entrepreneur's relief (including schedule A1 TCGA 1992)
Residence
Calculation of tax liability for individuals

Computation of Gains and Acquisitions and Disposals of Assets
Computation of gains and losses
Use of losses
Transactions treated as made at market value
Transactions between connected parties
Disposal in a series of transactions
Assets and disposals of assets (s.21, s.22, s.23, s.24 and s.28 TCGA 1992)
Rebasing to 1982

Allowable deductions
Indexation Allowance

Individuals, Partnerships, Trusts and Collective Investment Schemes
Partnerships and Limited Liability Partnerships

Transfer of Business Assets
Replacement of business assets
Stock in Trade
Transfer of a business to a company
Gifts of business assets

Other Property, Businesses, Investments etc
Part disposals

Supplemental
Supplemental matters contained in s.272 to s.291 TCGA 1992

CAPITAL ALLOWANCES

Part 1 CAA 2001

Plant & Machinery Allowances
Introduction (s.11 to s.14 CAA 2001)
Qualifying activities
Qualifying expenditure
First year qualifying expenditure
Annual Investment Allowance
Other Allowances and charges
Hire purchase etc and plant provided by lessee
Computer software
Cars etc
Fixtures
Giving effect to allowances and charges
Partnerships and successions

Corporation Tax

INCOME TAX

Employment Income
IR35 and Managed Service Companies

CAPITAL GAINS TAX

Capital Gains Tax and Corporation Tax on Chargeable Gains
The charge to tax and persons chargeable (s.1 to s.8 TCGA 1992)
Residence

Computation of Gains and Acquisitions and Disposals of Assets
Computation of gains and losses
Use of losses
Transactions treated as made at market value
Transactions between connected parties
Disposal in a series of transactions
Assets and disposals of assets (s.21, s.22, s.23, s.24 and s.28 TCGA 1992)
Rebasing to 1982
Allowable deductions
Indexation Allowance

Companies
Groups and transactions within groups
Anti-gain buying
Companies leaving groups
Non-resident and dual resident companies
Substantial shareholding exemption

Other Property, Businesses, Investments etc
Part disposals

Transfer of Business Assets
Replacement of Business Assets
Stock in Trade

Supplemental
Supplemental matters contained in s.272 to s.291 TCGA 1992

CORPORATION TAX

Accounting Standards
Impact of accounting standards on taxable profits

Administration
Corporation Tax Self-Assessment system
The charge to corporation tax
Small companies rate

Permanent establishment/branch
Company residence
Deduction of income tax

Computation of Taxable Profits
Computation of trading profits
Intangibles
Loan relationships – basic principles
Deductions for share schemes
Investment companies
Double tax relief – basic principles
Schedule A
Other investment income
Charges on income
Losses
Research and Development

Distributions

Groups and Consortia
Groups

Miscellaneous Matters
IR35

Anti-avoidance
Controlled foreign companies
Change in ownership of company
Transfer pricing – basic principles

CAPITAL ALLOWANCES

Part 1 CAA 2001

Plant & Machinery Allowances
Introduction (s.11 to s.14 CAA 2001)
Qualifying activities
Qualifying expenditure
First year qualifying expenditure
Annual Investment Allowance
Other Allowances and charges
Hire purchase etc and plant provided by lessee
Computer software
Cars etc
Short life assets
Fixtures
Giving effect to allowances and charges

VAT including Stamp Taxes

VAT

Scope of VAT and the charge to tax
Taxable person
Business/economic activity
Transactions within the scope of VAT (i.e. supplies, importations, and intra-Community acquisitions)
Territorial scope of VAT
VAT rates

Taxable person
Business and non-business activities
Employment status
Single taxable persons (VAT groups)

Supply & consideration
Meaning of supply
Meaning of consideration
Single v multiple supplies
Supply of goods v supply of services
Deemed supplies
TOGCs and other non-supplies
Outputs and output tax

Valuation
Value of supplies – general provisions (s.19 VATA 1994)
Bad debt relief

VAT registration
Registration and deregistration
Group registration
Registration of partnerships
Registration of unincorporated bodies

Tax points
Time of supply – general provisions (s.6 VATA 1994)
Time of supply – specific provisions (Regulations 81 - 95)

Right to deduct
Scope of the right to deduct input tax
Inputs and input tax
Disallowed and "blocked" input tax
Exceptional claims for VAT relief (Regulation 111)
Partial exemption
Capital goods scheme

Place of transactions
Place of supply of goods
Place of supply of services
Place of "belonging"
Scope and application of the reverse charge within ss.8 and 9A VAT A 1994

Reliefs and exemptions
Exempt supplies
Zero-rated supplies
Reduced-rated supplies
Exports

Accounting and administration
Accounting and record-keeping requirements
Assessments
Default surcharge
Invoicing and other accounting documentation
Penalties
Repayment supplement
Special VAT accounting schemes (e.g. margin schemes, flat-rate scheme)
VAT returns
Voluntary disclosures

Miscellaneous
Disclosure of avoidance schemes
HMRC powers in respect of VAT

Application in specific circumstances
Acquisitions, disposals and other corporate transactions
Charities and other non-profit-making bodies
Works to immovable property
Financial services
International Trade
Intra-Community Trade
Transactions in immovable property
TOGCs

STAMP DUTY

Administration
Stocks & shares
Rates of charge
Groups of companies

STAMP DUTY LAND TAX

Administration
Chargeable interests, transactions consideration
Rates of charge
Group relief
SDLT rules relating to the sale and letting of immovable property

TQT talks to the Examiners

1 **Prospective legislation**

   Question   When is prospective / new legislation examinable?

   Examiner Response: Legislation enacted at least 5 months prior to the exam is examinable in any given exam even if it has yet to come into force ie the legislation may still be prospective at the date of the exam. In relation to FA09 changes, the following items will therefore be examinable in 2010:

   New administration and compliance rules

   Harmonised interest rules

   Changes to personal allowances where income exceeds £100,000 and higher rate of income tax

   VAT cross border changes

   Disclosure of tax avoidance schemes in relation to SDLT

   World-wide debt cap

2 **Availability of actual student scripts**

   Question   Would the CIOT be prepared to issue actual scripts from the Application & Interaction exams to offer students additional guidance as to the standard that needs to be achieved to pass. Perhaps one first quartile and one marginal pass script could be released?

   Examiner Response: Education Department will publish a 'reasonable script' subject to obtaining candidate's permission.

3 **Marking guides**

   Question   Would the CIOT consider publishing its marking guides for all papers again?

   Examiner Response: There are no plans to make these guides available...all marking guides are flexible and credit will always be given to candidates who make relevant comments not within the marking guide/model answer.

4 **Interest rates for unpaid / late tax**

   Question   Will rates be given in the exam? And where the rate is 0% (eg IHT and repayment supplement) presume no point in examining?

   Examiner Response: Rates of interest on unpaid and overpaid tax due vary from time to time and in some cases the calculation will span a change of rate date so it would not be appropriate to assume there is no point in examining merely because the current rate is nil. Where relevant the rates will usually be supplied in the question.

5 **New compliance rules**

   Question   Many of the new compliance rules will not come into effect until April 2010 – are they going to be examined now?

   Examiner Response: Questions may be set on prospective legislation passed more than five months prior to the examination date even if coming into force in the future. It would be examined on the basis of that legislation rather than on any subsequent changes.

   TQT Comments: Following the CIOT's response, the material for the 2010 examinations was prepared (in August 2009) on the basis that the administration changes in FA 2009 apply even where their implementation date was unknown at the time.

6 New harmonised interest regime

Question: As the new harmonised regime for interest on overdue/overpaid tax introduced by FA 2009 does not apply until Royal Assent at the earliest can we assume that it will not be examined in the 2010 exams?

Examiner Response: The rules will be examinable in 2010.

7 Historic compliance rules

Question: Can we assume that any compliance rules which ceased to apply from April 2009 are no longer examinable? Eg penalties for incorrect returns for IT, CT and VAT (misdeclaration penalty)?

Examiner Response: We will not examine the historic rules in 2010.

8 Chattels – Advisory level

Question: Are chattels rules for P&M examinable in the Taxation of Individuals paper? Seems more of a Taxation of Owner-Managed Businesses topic, but chattels are excluded from that syllabus.

Examiner Response: Yes they are examinable in so far as they may relate to a non-residential property. However, as capital allowances are not in the syllabus candidates would be advised as to whether allowances had been claimed. As you suggest, chattels should be in the Taxation of Owner-Managed Businesses paper and will therefore explicitly be in that paper in the updated syllabus for 2010.

9 Share pooling

Question: Given the recent changes to the share pooling rules in FA 2008 is it reasonable to assume that the detailed share pooling rules for companies will not be examined?

Examiner Response: Not examinable.

10 Intra-spouse transfers & indexation

Question: Where an intra-spouse transfer has been made would candidates be given the indexed cost to the spouse or be expected to calculate the relevant amounts from the tables?

Examiner Response: Candidates need to calculate the indexation.

11 Incorporation relief – Advisory level

Question: Is incorporation relief on the Taxation of Individuals syllabus - it wasn't, then it was ,and now we cannot see it in the syllabus document?

Examiner Response: It is examinable in the Taxation of Owner-Managed Businesses paper but not the Taxation of Individuals paper.

12 Rollover relief – Advisory level

Question: Rollover relief is on the Taxation of Individuals syllabus – but not all candidates for this paper will have studied for the Taxation of Owner-Managed Businesses paper. Can we expect therefore, that the questions will concentrate more on the other reliefs such as PPR, gift relief and EIS.

Examiner Response: Rollover relief could be tested on the Taxation of Individuals paper.

13 Rollover relief – Awareness level

Question: Rollover relief is not examinable in the Corporation Tax module of the Awareness paper, but groups and transactions within groups are. Can we assume that questions about groups would not include rollover relief? Would this include the potential for rollover of a de-grouping charge?

Examiner Response: Correct.

14 Gift relief – Awareness level

Question: Gift of business assets is only examinable in the Taxation of Unincorporated Businesses module – would this exclude gifts of shares in view of the fact that disposals of shares in general is only examinable in the Taxation of Individuals Awareness module?

Examiner Response: The syllabus includes all forms of business asset.

15 Entrepreneurs' relief – Advisory level

Question: Can we assume that entrepreneurs' relief is only examinable in the Taxation of Owner-Managed Businesses paper?

Examiner Response: Entrepreneurs' relief will be in Taxation of Owner-Managed Businesses, Individuals and also in IHT, Trusts and Estates.

16 March 1982/April 1965 assets

Question: Are assets held at 31 March 1982 / 6 April 1965 examinable in the Awareness paper?

Examiner Response: 31 March 1982 - yes
6 April 1965 - no

17 CGT administration

Question: To what extent is CGT administration examinable in the Awareness papers?

Examiner Response: We would not expect candidates to have a detailed knowledge of the administration of CGT. The thrust of the Awareness papers is to enable candidates to spot issues rather than to be able to deal with the detailed administration of the tax.

18 IHT

Question: Does the syllabus for IHT, Trusts and Estates Advisory include double grossing up?

Examiner Response: Yes

19 IHT planning

Question: We assume that the more complex planning schemes for IHT such as double flip-flops are not included in the Advisory syllabus for Inheritance Tax, Trusts & Estates.

Examiner Response: We do not specifically expect candidates to be aware of the various complex planning schemes which have been marketed – to do so may unfairly penalise candidates from smaller firms who may be less likely to come across such schemes. However, we would expect candidates to be aware of schemes if they are part of a tax case so that they are then widely known.

20 NIC

Question: NIC is included in the syllabus for the Taxation of Individuals Awareness module. What is the position with regard to Class 1A and Class 1B NIC as these are not paid by the individual. Would these be excluded from this paper?

Examiner Response: This includes Class 1A and Class 1B. Please also note that the operation of the PAYE system is included in this paper.

21 PAYE

Question: The operation and application of the PAYE system is examinable in Taxation of Individuals Awareness module. Can we assume this is from the individual's perspective and so things like due dates for the employer submitting forms, details re PSAs would not be examinable?

Examiner Response: No, this also covers employer aspects.

22 Unincorporated businesses – Awareness level

Question: Are we correct to assume that just basic income tax computations involving trading income would be examinable in this paper?

Examiner Response: Yes

23 Restricted securities

Question: The syllabus is not clear as to whether the rules on restricted securities are examinable and in which Advisory level papers. Can this please be clarified?

Examiner Response: Yes they are examinable, but only in the Taxation of Individuals paper. Since the rules are so complex, we will not require a detailed knowledge of the rules nor require candidates to prepare detailed calculations. We would expect them to be aware of the concept of restrictions which may attach to shares, to be aware that this affects the value, to be aware of the broad impact this may have in terms of the timing of the tax and to be aware that a s.431 election could be made.

24 Pension forestalling rules

Question: Are the pension forestalling rules examinable?

Examiner Response: Yes.

25 Overseas issues – Advisory level

Question: The previous Paper IIA exam did not examine overseas issues. Can we assume that this will also be the case for the Taxation of Owner-Managed Businesses paper?

Examiner Response: The syllabus includes, for example transfers of assets abroad and DTR on companies. However, overseas issues will really only feature in passing rather than as a core element of a question. The in depth testing of overseas issues will be in the other papers.

26 World-wide debt cap

Question: Is the new world-wide debt cap examinable at Awareness level?

Examiner Response: Not examinable at Awareness level, but will be examinable for both the Taxation of Owner-Managed Businesses paper (at a basic level) and Advanced Corporation Tax (in depth) Advisory papers.

27 Foreign dividends

Question: To what extent are the old rules examinable for receipt of foreign dividends prior to 1 July 2009?

Examiner Response: For Awareness level, foreign dividends received prior to 1 July 2009 are not examinable. At Awareness level it is acceptable to assume that all foreign dividends received are exempt from tax in the UK and that the exclusions from exemption are not examinable.

For Advisory level Advanced Corporation Tax, questions may be set in 2010 which require consideration of the treatment of pre 1 July 2009 foreign dividends. Thus, EUFT and onshore pooling are still examinable in 2010 (it will be removed from the syllabus in 2011).

For Advisory Taxation of Owner-Managed Businesses paper, EUFT and onshore pooling is not on the syllabus. Any questions relating to dividends received prior to 1 July 2009 would thus be restricted to basic DTR principles only.

28 CFC ADP and exempt activities holding companies transitional rules

Question: To what extent are the transitional rules examinable?

Examiner Response: The rules are examinable in detail for Advisory level Advanced Corporation Tax.

29 Cars transitional rules – leases and capital allowances

Question: To what extent are the transitional rules for cars in relation to capital allowances and leases examinable?

Examiner Response: Transitional rules are examinable. Existing expenditure on pre April 2009 cars is therefore examinable as are leases entered into before April 2009.

30 Capital allowances changes

Question: To what extent are the old rules examinable?

Examiner Response: Pre April 2008 first year allowances, the old long life asset pool, and pre April 2008 rates are no longer examinable.

31 Industrial buildings allowance

Question: Can you confirm that IBA/ABA/Hotels are outside the syllabus.

Examiner Response: Yes

32 Share schemes

Question: Are the examiners prepared to give more guidance to students with regard to the perspective that the exams will take, eg with regards to share schemes (in both Taxation of Owner-Managed Businesses & Taxation of Individuals Advisory papers) is it the intention that Taxation of Owner-Managed Businesses paper will be from the perspective of the employer and the Taxation of Individuals from the perspective of the individual employee?

Examiner Response: This is generally true. The main thrust of a shares question in the Taxation of Individuals paper would be from the employee's perspective whilst the main thrust in the Taxation of Owner-Managed Businesses paper would be from the employer's or owner's perspective.

33 **Owner-Managed Businesses**

Question: What does the CIOT consider to be an owner-managed business? Is it primarily going to be sole traders and partnerships or is it just as likely to be companies? Are groups going to be significant? Small groups only? What about a £100m group owned by wealthy chairman?

Examiner Response: It can be sole traders, partnerships, LLPs and companies. Groups may be tested, but will not form a significant part of this paper. It is not possible to give hard and fast rules about what is and what is not an OMB and size alone will not mean that that the subject matter is more or less complex. As you will know from practice, often the greatest complexities come from relatively small transactions.

Using the Home Study Programme

1 Introduction

This TQT Home Study Programme will guide you through the September 2009 edition of the TQT Study Text. If your Study Text does not have that date on the cover, please contact your course provider.

The September 2009 edition of the study text has been thoroughly and reliably updated for the Finance Act 2009 and Corporation Tax Act 2009. These Acts will be examined in the May 2010 and November 2010 exams. If you are not taking your exams in 2010 please contact your course provider.

2 Using the Home Study Programme

This Home Study Programme is made up of a number of **Study Periods**, for each of the FIVE Awareness modules. **You must only study for THREE of the Awareness modules**. Identify which modules you will study now and then use the study periods for those modules to take you through the learning phase of your studies.

As every individual studies at a different pace, there is no definitive time period over which the learning phase is designed to be completed. Ideally you should aim to complete the learning phase within six to twelve months, depending on your own learning pace.

Once your 'learning phase' is complete you should move onto the Revision Phase. More detail is given later in this Workbook.

Each Study Period has been graded as high or medium priority and consists of the following elements:

Exam Guidance

This gives you **important** information of how your exam is likely to focus on the particular area you are studying

Introduction to the session

Here you are **introduced** to the subject and the **main issues** that you should understand when you have finished your study of this session.

Guidance through the Study Text

This provides you with **important instructions** on how to work through the TQT Study Text. You must follow the guidance in this table for time efficient study, as you will be told which areas of each chapter must be worked through in detail and which can be skimmed over. It contains **key points**, summarising the most vital areas of the Study Period.

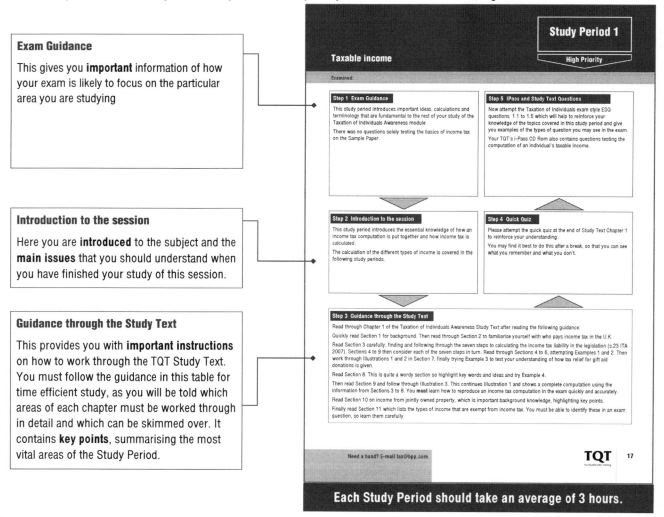

Each Study Period should take an average of 3 hours.

Progress Tests

Some of the Study Periods are '**Progress Tests**' which you can use to assess the work you have done on a limited number of Study Periods. You should mark the tests yourself using the solutions in this Workbook.

Course Examinations

If you are a home study student your TQT material contains **Course Examinations**. These should be attempted at the points suggested within the Study Programme (they cover the preceding Study Periods). If you are attending a taught course your course provider may use these exams or they may use different exams. You should follow the instructions given to you by your course provider regarding the sitting and marking of any exams you are told to sit.

To gain the greatest benefit from the exams, you must set aside a period of three hours during which you will have no interruptions.

> By sitting these exams, you will increase your chances of passing the real exams by 30%.

Please note that course exams are only available as part of the home study package. They are not available to purchase individually.

Sample Paper

When you have studied all three of the CTA Awareness modules attempt the CTA Awareness Sample Paper. Set aside a period of three hours and attempt the exam in exam conditions. This will help you to assess how you would perform in the real exam.

The Revision Phase

Congratulations

If you've got this far. Well done!

It might not feel like it at the moment, but the hard work you've already put in is about to pay off. You have about a month to go before the exam and you now need to focus your attention on even more question practice.

The final steps

The key to passing this examination is to work as many questions as possible during the revision phase of your studies. You should initially re-work any questions in the Workbook that you may have struggled with in the learning phase of your studies. You will then be ready to make the transition to practising the questions on in the **TQT Practice and Revision Kit**.

The TQT **Practice and Revision** Kit contains:

Exam Standard Questions and Answers. Now is the time to practise as many questions as you can and TQT's material certainly gives you plenty of opportunity to do just that.

Marking schemes: A number of the questions in the Practice and Revision Kit have marking schemes. You should use these when marking your own answers to obtain an idea of your progress in the particular topics being tested. Remember, you do not need full marks to pass!

Passcards are not just a condensed text. Each card is separately designed for clear presentation of the facts. The topics are self contained in a highly visual format, including diagrams and boxes to highlight important points. The Passcards focus on the exam and contain helpful hints to help you pass each chapter.

Revision course

We strongly recommend you book on a revision course – these courses will give you valuable support and guidance on how to approach the questions in the **TQT Practice and Revision Kit** and on how to maximise your marks in the examination hall. **The ability of a tutor to help you prioritise your studies at this stage is vitally important**. Tutors have a wealth of experience of these examinations and they are there to help you. They'll be happy to go through any problem areas and to support you in any other way they can.

Work smart (and hard)

Don't fall into the trap of assuming that if you work for 5 hours a night for the next six weeks, then you will pass the exam. Your brain doesn't work that way – so make sure you factor in the following when creating your revision plan:

- Make sure you get enough sleep – a tired mind won't pass the exam
- Make sure you build in time to relax (your brain needs the time to process the information you're trying to squash in to it)
- You are more likely to retain knowledge if sessions are short and there is a recap session built in to the plan later on
- Keep disruptions to a minimum, and take regular short breaks where possible
- Try to reproduce exam conditions for timed question practice

Stick with it!

There is not long to go now. Don't give up. Remember these exams are hard for everyone and when you finally pass you'll be really pleased that you kept going.

Awareness Paper
Taxation of individuals

Study Period Planner
Taxation of Individuals

Use this schedule and your exam timetable to plan the dates on which you will complete each Study Period. The letters 'H' and 'M' tell you whether the topic is high or medium priority.

Study Period	Topic		Due Date
1	Taxable income	H	
2	Savings and dividend income	H	
3	Income from UK land and buildings	H	
4	Tax efficient investments	M	
5	The employed earner	H	
6	Share remuneration	M	
7	Pensions	H	
8	Overseas matters	M	
9	National Insurance Contributions/PAYE	M	
10	Administration of income tax	M	
11	**Progress Test 1**	H	

Study Period	Topic		Due Date
12	Outline of CGT	H	
13	Computing gains and losses	H	
14	Shares and securities	H	
15	Chattels and wasting assets	M	
16	Principal private residence relief	M	
17	Other CGT reliefs	H	
18	Administration of CGT	M	
19	**Progress Test 2**	H	

COURSE EXAM 1

A practice exam covering Study Periods 1 to 10.

COURSE EXAM 2

A practice exam covering all Study Periods.

REVISION PHASE

Your revision phase will begin when **Course Exam 2** is complete. This should ideally be four months before the final exam.

TQT Note: The Course Exams contain questions for all FIVE of the awareness paper modules. In your exam you must answer questions from THREE modules. We suggest that you identify the THREE modules you will study and then work through the Study Period Planners for each of those modules until the point where you are told to take Course Exam 1. When you have completed all THREE modules to that point, sit Course Exam 1. Similarly, you should complete all THREE modules before you sit course exam 2. Course Exam 2 covers all of the Study Periods, although it is weighted towards the second half of your studies.

Study Period 1

Taxable income — High Priority

Step 1 Exam Guidance

This study period introduces important ideas, calculations and terminology that are fundamental to the rest of your study of the Taxation of Individuals Awareness module.

The basics of income tax were tested in:
- Question 2 of the Sample Paper and
- Question 5 of the May 2009 exam

Step 2 Introduction to the session

This study period introduces the essential knowledge of how an income tax computation is put together and how income tax is calculated.

The calculation of the different types of income is covered in the following study periods.

Step 3 Guidance through the Study Text

Read through Chapter 1 of the Taxation of Individuals Awareness Study Text after reading the following guidance:

Quickly read Section 1 for background. Then read through Section 2 to familiarise yourself with who pays income tax in the U.K.

Read Section 3 carefully, finding and following through the seven steps to calculating the income tax liability in the legislation (s.23 ITA 2007). Sections 4 to 9 then consider each of the seven steps in turn. Read through Sections 4 to 6, attempting Examples 1 and 2. Then work through Illustrations 1 and 2 in Section 7, finally trying Example 3 to test your understanding of how tax relief for gift aid donations is given.

Read Section 8. Highlight key words and ideas and try Example 4.

Then read Section 9 and follow through Illustration 3. This continues Illustration 1 and shows a complete computation using the information from Sections 3 to 8. You **must** learn how to reproduce an income tax computation in the exam quickly and accurately.

Briefly read Section 10 and note those benefits which are taxable and those which are exempt from tax.

Read Section 11 on income from jointly owned property, which is important background knowledge, highlighting key points.

Finally read Section 12 which lists the types of income that are exempt from income tax. You must be able to identify these in an exam question, so learn them carefully.

Step 4 Quick Quiz

Please attempt the quick quiz at the end of Study Text Chapter 1 to reinforce your understanding.

You may find it best to do this after a break, so that you can see what you remember and what you don't.

Step 5 iPass and Workbook Questions

Now attempt the exam style questions (ESQs) 1.1 to 1.5 which will help to reinforce your knowledge of the topics covered in this study period and give you examples of the types of question you may see in the exam.

Your TQT's i-Pass CD Rom also contains questions testing the computation of an individual's taxable income.

Module 1: Taxation of Individuals

Study Period 2

Savings and dividend income

High Priority

Step 1 Exam Guidance

It is unlikely that you will be able to avoid calculating income tax for individuals in the exam.

The tax rates differ depending on whether the income being taxed is savings, dividend or non-savings income.

You must be able to identify the different types of income and calculate tax at the appropriate rate.

The taxation of dividend income was tested in:

- Question 5 of the May 2009 exam

Step 2 Introduction to the session

Now that we understand how a basic income tax computation is put together, we need to look in more detail at the different rates of tax that can apply to different types of income.

In the income tax computation, we need to be able to split taxable income into savings, dividend income and non savings income, understand the order in which income is taxed and the tax rates that apply.

Step 3 Guidance through the Study Text

Read through Chapter 2 of the Study Text after reading the following guidance:

Read Section 1 quickly as background information. Refer to the Institute's tax tables at the front of the Study Text as you go along so that you know what rates and allowances will be given to you in the exam.

Read through Section 2 and note that interest can be received both gross and net (of 20% tax). Then read Section 3, which covers dividends and items that are treated as dividends. These all come with a 10% *deemed* tax credit. Attempt Examples 1 and 2. You **must** understand that all figures are included **gross** in the income tax computation.

Read through Section 4 on the order in which savings and non-savings income should be taxed and the appropriate tax rates to use. Pay particular attention to the three column format of the computation. Attempt Examples 3 to 6 to check your understanding.

Review the illustration in Section 5 to check your understanding of what has been covered in this study period and how savings and non savings income fit into the income tax computation. Attempt Example 7.

Finally, quickly read Section 6 on other income.

Step 5 iPass and Workbook Questions

Now attempt ESQs 2.1 to 2.7 which will help to reinforce your knowledge of the topics covered in this study period and give you examples of the types of question you may see in the exam.

Your TQT's i-Pass CD Rom also contains questions on the taxation of savings income.

Step 4 Quick Quiz

Please attempt the quiz at the end of Study Text Chapter 2 to reinforce your understanding.

You may find it best to do this after a break, so that you can see what you remember and what you don't.

Module 1: Taxation of Individuals

Study Period 3

Income from UK land and buildings

High Priority

Step 1 Exam Guidance

In the exam, you may be required to calculate the amount of taxable property income or you may be asked factual questions, such as the conditions for a furnished holiday letting or for rent a room relief to apply.

This topic was tested in:

- Question 7 of the Sample Paper
- Question 7 of the May 2009 exam

Step 2 Introduction to the session

In this study period we learn to calculate how much to include as taxable property income from UK land and buildings in the income tax computation.

Step 5 iPass and Workbook Questions

Now attempt the ESQ 3.1 to 3.8 which will help to reinforce your knowledge of the topics covered in this study period and give you examples of the types of question you may see in the exam.

Your TQT's i-Pass CD Rom also contains questions on property income.

Step 4 Quick Quiz

Please attempt the quiz at the end of Study Text Chapter 3 to reinforce your understanding.

You may find it best to do this after a break, so that you can see what you remember and what you don't.

Step 3 Guidance through the Study Text

Read through Chapter 3 of the Study Text after reading the following guidance:

Read Section 1 quickly for background then concentrate on Section 2 which covers how to calculate the property income figure. Pay attention to the deductions available, in particular the 'wear and tear' allowance in Section 2.2 and attempt Example 1. Read Section 3 on property losses and the restricted ways in which they can be used.

Section 4 on lease premiums is an important topic, so work through Illustration 1 and then attempt Example 2 to test your understanding.

Read Section 5 on 'furnished holiday lettings' but do not waste time learning the conditions, instead learn where to find them in the legislation. Then read Section 6 which deals with the rent a room scheme. Locate the rent limit in the Institute's tax tables that you will be given in the exam.

Read quickly through Section 7 on non-resident landlords then read Section 8, which deals with Real Estate Investment Trusts (REITs). Contrast how dividends from a REIT are taxed compared to normal dividends. Follow through Illustration 2.

Finally read through Section 9 on transactions involving land, following through the relevant part of the legislation.

Study Period 4

Tax efficient investments

Medium Priority

Step 1 Exam Guidance

You must be able to identify tax free investments so that you do not include them in an income tax computation. Do, however, always tell the examiner why you have not taxed the income.

You also need to understand the conditions for, and the tax consequences of, investing in the Enterprise Investment Scheme (EIS). Questions could examine the qualifying conditions for the scheme, the tax implications of an investment or the calculation of an investor's tax position.

There are no questions in the sample paper or the May 2009 exam dealing solely with the income tax issues of EIS investments.

Step 2 Introduction to the session

In this Study Period the aim is to understand how individuals can make tax efficient investments that can reduce the amount of tax they have to pay.

The investments considered are:

- Tax free investments, including ISAs
- The enterprise investment scheme.

Step 3 Guidance through the Study Text

Please read Chapter 4 of the Study Text after reading the guidance below:

Read quickly through Section 1 so that you can identify the main sources of tax free investments in the exam. The point to note here is that income arising from these investments is tax free.

Read through Section 2 on ISAs, highlighting the key points and terminology.

Concentrate your study during this period on Section 3 on the Enterprise Investment Scheme (EIS). This is another area where you can rely heavily on your legislation in the exam, so take this opportunity to locate the relevant part of the ITA 2007 and highlight the key conditions, rules, rates of relief and limits as you read through the section. Attempt Example 1.

Step 4 Quick Quiz

Please attempt the quiz at the end of Study Text Chapter 4 to reinforce your understanding.

You may find it best to do this after a break, so that you can see what you remember and what you don't.

Step 5 iPass and Workbook Questions

Now attempt the ESQs 4.1 and 4.3 which will help to reinforce your knowledge of the topics covered in this study period and give you examples of the types of question you may see in the exam.

Your TQT's i-Pass CD Rom also contains questions testing tax efficient investments.

Module 1: Taxation of Individuals

Study Period 5

The employed earner

High Priority

Step 1 Exam Guidance

You must be able to calculate the amount of income to include in the income tax computation of an employed earner.

Questions can focus on many different aspects of the employed earner, for example:

- The basis of assessment
- Identifying and calculating taxable employment income including the value of benefits received
- Understanding the taxation of termination payments.

Employment income and benefits were tested in:

- Question 3 of the Sample Paper
- Question 2 of the May 2009 exam

Step 2 Introduction to the session

In this study period we look at the rules for calculating the amount of employment income to include in the income tax computation.

You must be able to identify what is taxable and in which tax year.

A fundamental element of this study period is to learn the rules for calculating the taxable value of benefits. We also need to know how to deal with payments on termination of employment.

Step 3 Guidance through the Study Text

Please read Chapter 5 of the Study Text after reading the guidance below:

Read through Section 1 for background. This is quite a wordy section so highlight key words and terminology only. Attempt Example 1.

Sections 2 and 3 are the core elements of this study period so read through carefully. Section 2 deals with benefits that are taxable on all employees, regardless of their income level, while Section 3 covers those benefits that are only taxable on directors and employees earning £8,500 pa or more. Work through Examples 2 to 10 carefully to ensure you have understood the rules.

You must also be able to identify benefits that are not taxable on any employees so read through the list of tax-free benefits in Section 4 carefully. The most important tax-free benefits are in **bold** so concentrate on learning these.

Read Section 5 to ensure you understand what can be deducted from employment income. There are not many things! Try Example 11.

Read Section 6 which covers the different types of payment that can be received when employment ends ('termination payments'). Do you understand which payments are taxable and which are exempt from tax? Work through Example 12.

Step 4 Quick Quiz

Please attempt the quiz at the end of Study Text Chapter 5 to reinforce your understanding.

You may find it best to do this after a break, so that you can see what you remember and what you don't.

Step 5 iPass and Workbook Questions

Now attempt the ESQs 5.1 to 5.9 which will help to reinforce your knowledge of the topics covered in this study period and give you examples of the types of question you may see in the exam.

Your TQT's i-Pass CD Rom also contains questions on the taxation of the employed earner.

Study Period 6

Share remuneration

Medium Priority

Step 1 Exam Guidance

An employed earner may receive part of his remuneration in the form of shares or may be entitled to join his employer's share scheme(s). This can be a tax efficient way of rewarding employees particularly if the value of the shares increases.

You must understand the conditions that apply for the different share schemes, identify the tax efficiency, or otherwise, of such schemes for the employee and calculate how such remuneration is treated for tax purposes.

Employee share schemes were tested in:

- Question 5 of the Sample Paper
- Question 4 of the May 2009 exam

Step 2 Introduction to the session

Now that we understand how to calculate employment income we can look at how employees can be rewarded in a tax efficient way. Usually this is by taking advantage of an approved share scheme. We need to be able to identify when a share scheme is approved and the conditions for approval.

We also need to be able to understand the tax implications for the employee of both approved and unapproved share schemes.

Step 3 Guidance through the Study Text

Read through Chapter 6 of the Study Text after reading the guidance below:

Read quickly through Section 1 for background.

Sections 2 and 3 deal with employers providing shares and share options to their employees other than through an approved scheme. Read through these sections, highlighting key ideas and terminology (such as 'restricted shares'). Do you understand the difference between an employer giving shares **directly** to employees and granting them share **options**? Attempt Example 1 to check your understanding of the tax treatment of shares received from an unapproved scheme.

Section 4 on the approved share schemes is essential for the exam. Read through the information on the four main approved share schemes and make notes ensuring that you know how each scheme works, the conditions for approval and the tax implications of each scheme.

Finally, read through Section 5 which deals with the National Insurance Contribution (NIC) implications for the various share schemes.

Step 5 iPass and Workbook Questions

Now attempt the ESQs 6.1 to 6.4 which will help to reinforce your knowledge of the topics covered in this study period and give you examples of the types of question you may see in the exam.

Your TQT's i-Pass CD Rom also contains questions on share schemes.

Step 4 Quick Quiz

Please attempt the quiz at the end of Study Text Chapter 6 to reinforce your understanding.

You may find it best to do this after a break, so that you can see what you remember and what you don't.

Module 1: Taxation of Individuals

Study Period 7

Pensions

High Priority

Step 1 Exam Guidance

New pension rules only came into force from 6 April 2006, so they are still highly examinable.

You may be asked to calculate the amount of pension contributions that an individual can make, to either an occupational or a personal pension scheme, on which tax relief is available and to explain how the tax relief is given. You may also be asked about drawing the pension once retirement has taken place.

Tax relief for pension contributions was tested in:

- Question 6 of the May 2009 exam.

Step 2 Introduction to the session

In this study period, we learn how pension contributions made both to occupational schemes run by employers and to personal pension schemes are treated for tax purposes. Tax relief will be given for pension contributions made up to certain limits.

We also need to understand how pension income will be taxed on retirement.

Step 3 Guidance through the Study Text

Read through Chapter 7 of the Study Text after reading the following guidance:

Read through Section 1 for background knowledge. Make sure you can distinguish between occupational and personal pension schemes and understand that one of the main benefits of saving in a pension is that the fund grows free of any tax.

Read through Section 2 on pension contributions. Make sure you can calculate the maximum amount that an individual can contribute to a pension scheme for which tax relief is available. Note that the limit is the same for both occupational and personal pension schemes.

Then read Section 3 which deals with giving tax relief for contributions to occupational and personal pension schemes. Organise your notes so that you can compare the different way of making of contributions to occupational and to personal pension schemes. Are they made net or gross of tax? Do you understand how both ways of obtaining tax relief fit into the income tax computation you have learnt? Attempt Example 1.

Finally, read through Section 4 to understand how the pension fund can be taken out of the pension on retirement.

Step 5 iPass and Workbook Questions

Now attempt the ESQs 7.1 to 7.4 which will help to reinforce your knowledge of the topics covered in this study period and give you examples of the types of question you may see in the exam.

Your TQT's i-Pass CD Rom also contains questions on pensions.

Step 4 Quick Quiz

Please attempt the quiz at the end of Study Text Chapter 7 to reinforce your understanding.

You may find it best to do this after a break, so that you can see what you remember and what you don't.

Study Period 8

Overseas matters

Medium Priority

Step 1 Exam Guidance

So far we have considered the income tax position of UK resident individuals. However, you could also be examined on the overseas aspects of income tax, for example, determining the residence status of an individual, to decide if and how they are liable to UK income tax, or how overseas income is taxed.

You should bear in mind that if an individual is taxed both in the UK and another country on the same source of income that double tax relief (DTR) may be available.

The tax position of a non-UK domiciled individual was tested in:

- Question 4 of the Sample Paper
- Question 3 of the May 2009 exam

Step 2 Introduction to the session

In this study period we learn the definitions of residence, ordinary residence and domicile and how these concepts affect an individual's income tax position.

We also learn how to calculate DTR, which reduces the tax liability where income is taxed in both the UK and overseas.

Finally we look at the provisions that apply to stop individuals attempting to avoid UK income tax by transferring their assets overseas.

Step 3 Guidance through the Study Text

Read through Chapter 8 of the Study Text after reading the following guidance:

Begin by looking back at Section 2.4 of Chapter 1 to refresh your memory on the UK tax implications of residence and domicile status.

Then read Sections 1 and 2 of Chapter 8. Highlight the key issues and terminology used in this area. It is possible that you will see an individual either leaving or coming to the UK in a question, so make sure you understand how residence, ordinary residence and domicile affect individuals in these situations. Work example 1 and see if you can reproduce the summary diagram in Section 2. Section 2.3 covers overseas income. Note the similarity of treatment in many cases to UK income.

Then read Section 3 on the remittance basis whereby individuals who are not domiciled or not ordinarily resident in the UK may only be taxed in the UK on foreign income and gains remitted to the UK. The flowchart in section 3.7 is a useful summary of the rules.

Quickly read through Section 4 and note the impact of residency status on the availability of personal allowances.

Then read Section 5 on DTR. Focus on 'unilateral' relief in 5.3 and attempt Example 4 to check that you have understood the topic.

Finally read through Section 6 on the anti-avoidance rules that apply when an individual tries to avoid UK tax by transferring their assets abroad to a non-UK resident trust or company. Do not waste time trying to learn the details. Instead locate the provisions in your legislation as you are reading through the section so that you can easily find them in the exam.

Step 5 iPass and Workbook Questions

Now attempt the ESQs 8.1 to 8.3 which will help to reinforce your knowledge of the topics covered in this study period and give you examples of the types of question you may see in the exam.

Your TQT's i-Pass CD Rom also contains questions testing the overseas aspects of income tax.

Step 4 Quick Quiz

Please attempt the quiz at the end of Study Text Chapter 8 to reinforce your understanding.

You may find it best to do this after a break, so that you can see what you remember and what you don't.

Module 1: Taxation of Individuals

Study Period 9

National Insurance Contributions and PAYE

Medium Priority

Step 1 Exam Guidance

NICs are payable by employed and self employed earners. In addition, individuals who no longer have earned income can make voluntary NI contributions.

You will **only** be examined on NIC for employees in the Taxation of Individuals Awareness module.

So far we have considered the income tax and national insurance position of employees. You may be examined on the PAYE system which is used to collect income tax and NIC from employees.

NICs for an employee was tested in:
- Question 8 of the Sample Paper
- Question 8 of the May 2009 exam

Step 5 iPass and Workbook Questions

Now attempt ESQs 16.1 to 17.2 which will help to reinforce your knowledge of the topics covered in this study period and give you examples of the types of question you may see in the exam.

Your TQT's i-Pass CD Rom also contains questions on NIC for employees and employers.

Step 2 Introduction to the session

In this Study period we look at National insurance Contributions (NIC). You must be able to identify and calculate the different classes of NIC payable by an employee and his employer.

Look at the Institute's tax tables as you work through this chapter so that you know what information you will be given in the exam.

In this study period we also look at the PAYE system. You could be examined on both the employee and employer aspects of the system.

Step 4 Quick Quiz

Please attempt the quick quiz at the end of Study Text Chapter 9 to reinforce your understanding.

You may find it best to do this after a break, so that you can see what you remember and what you don't.

Step 3 Guidance through the Study Text

Read through Chapter 16 of the Study Text after reading the following guidance:

Read Sections 1 and 2 carefully and work through the example and illustrations. Look at the Institute's tax tables to see what NIC information you will be given in the exam.

Read Section 3 on Class 1A contributions which are **only** payable by employers on benefits provided to employees. Again, locate the information in the tax tables. Then try Example 2. In the exam, you may need to calculate the amount of the benefit and then the Class 1A liability.

Read Section 4 on Class 1B contributions which, again, are only payable by employers, this time on items included in a PAYE Settlement Agreement (PSA). Note the rate and the date the liability is due.

Read through Chapter 17 of the Study Text after reading the following guidance:

Read Section 1 for background information. Read Section 2 noting when PAYE is payable. Read Sections 3 and 4 noting the type of payments on which PAYE is applied. Quickly read Section 5 (especially Section 5.2 on PAYE code numbers. Try Examples 1 and 2). Read Section 6 noting the key forms and submission deadlines. Finally read Sections 7 to 11 (the most important is Section 10.1 which you will deal with in detail in the next study period).

Module 1: Taxation of Individuals

Study Period 10

Administration of income tax

Medium Priority

Step 1 Exam Guidance

The administrative provisions are essential knowledge for the exam. They can form part of a question or could be an entire question.

Learning where to find the relevant provisions in your legislation is crucial. Do not waste time learning details that you can easily locate in your open book.

The administration of income tax was tested in:

- Question 1 of the Sample Paper
- Question 1 of the May 2009 exam

Step 2 Introduction to the session

In this study period our aim is to understand the administrative requirements of the income tax system. Chapter 15 of the Study Text covers the administration rules for both income tax and capital gains tax. You only need to focus on income tax in this period.

We look at the returns of income tax that must be made to HMRC, the due date for submission of these returns and the due date for the payment of tax due and HMRC's powers with regard to returns and payment of tax.

Step 3 Guidance through the Study Text

Read the relevant sections of Chapter 15 of the Study Text, after reading the following guidance:

Chapter 15 considers the administrative aspects of both income tax and capital gains tax (CGT). As you have not learnt CGT yet, only study the income tax aspects of this chapter at this stage. We will come back to CGT administration in a later study period.

Skim read Section 1 for background. Then read Section 2 carefully, noting the deadline for notifying HMRC of chargeability to income tax (and CGT). Locate the rules in your legislation so that you can easily find and refer to them in the exam.

Read Section 3. Familiarise yourself with the contents of an income tax return then locate the deadlines for submitting tax returns in the legislation. Note the new rules for penalties for late filing of returns from April 2010. Read Sections 4 and 5 on incorrect returns and the time limits for making claims for reliefs, with your legislation, highlighting the key areas.

All of Section 6 (*except* Section 6.5) is essential reading in this period. Highlight key income tax dates and ensure you understand how payments on account are calculated and reduced. Attempt Example 1 (you can leave Example 2 for now).

Read Sections 7 to 9 to understand the powers of HMRC to enquire into returns, the interest and penalty regime and the appeals system. Again, the legislation is your friend here so use it wisely.

Step 5 iPass and Workbook Questions

Now attempt the ESQs 15.1 to 15.2 and 15.4 and 15.5 which will help to reinforce your knowledge of the topics covered in this study period and give you examples of the types of question you may see in the exam.

Your TQT's i-Pass CD Rom also contains some questions testing the administration of income tax. It also contains questions on the capital gains tax (CGT) aspects, so you may wish to wait until you have also covered CGT before you attempt this module.

Step 4 Quick Quiz

Please attempt questions 1 to 5 of the quiz at the end of Study Text Chapter 15 to reinforce your understanding.

You may find it best to do this after a break, so that you can see what you remember and what you don't.

Progress Test 1

Study Period 11 — High Priority

In order to reinforce what you have learnt so far, answer the following questions. Try to answer them without referring to your Study Text or notes. The test should take you no longer than one hour and covers Study Periods 1-10. Solutions begin on page 27.

1 Ian received dividends of £2,700 in 2009/10. He also had other taxable income of £36,000.

   Calculate the tax payable by Ian on his dividend income for 2009/10.

2 Elizabeth has a furnished property. She wants to know what she would have to do to make her property qualify as a furnished holiday let.

   State the conditions that must be satisfied for a letting to be classified as a furnished holiday let.

3 Doug let a furnished property in 2009/10. His statement of rental income and expenses was as follows:

	£
Rental income	24,000
Less expenses:	
New kitchen	10,000
Buildings insurance	1,000
Lettings agents fees	1,000
Council tax	1,650

   You are required to calculate Doug's property income profit for 2009/10.

4 Dorian has the following income in 2009/10:

   (a) Bank interest
   (b) NS & I Savings Certificates interest
   (c) NS & I Savings account interest
   (d) Lottery winnings
   (e) Employment income
   (f) Gross rental income of £2,500 from letting out a room in his house
   (g) Dividends from an Enterprise Investment Scheme (EIS) company
   (h) Inheritance from great-aunt Maud

   You are required to advise Dorian if each item is taxable and, if so, whether it receive net or gross.

5 James was employed by X plc. On 6 June 2009 his employer made available to James for private use a company car. The car has a list price of £30,000 and has a diesel engine and CO_2 emissions of 170g/km. James was also provided with private fuel for the car from 6 June 2009 onwards.

   James paid his employer £10 per month towards the private use of the car.

   Calculate James' taxable benefit for 2009/10 in respect of the car and car fuel.

6 Ruth received share options in her employer's unapproved share option scheme in 2009/10. The options received were as follows:

   5,000 options granted to Ruth on 10 January 2010 at a cost of 50p per option. The market value of one share at 10 January 2010 was £2.

   Ruth will exercise the options in March 2010 for a further cost of 50p per option. It is estimated that the market value of each share will have risen to £2.15 by March 2010.

   Calculate the amount subject to income tax on the grant and exercise of the share options.

Module 1: Taxation of Individuals

Study Period 11

Progress Test 1 (continued)

High Priority

7. Albert is 40 years old and has salary of £50,000 in 2009/10.

   What is the maximum pension contribution he can pay into his personal pension scheme, on which tax relief will be available and how will he receive tax relief for these payments?

8. Roscoe is a client of yours and needs some advice. He files a paper self assessment income tax return and wants to know when this should be filed for the 2009/10 tax year. He would also like advice about when he should pay any tax due. In 2008/09 he had income tax payable by self assessment of £10,000. In 2009/10 he expects that once his tax return has been submitted the income tax due under self assessment will be approximately £15,000.

   Advise Roscoe:

   - **By what date his paper self assessment return for 2009/10 should be submitted to HMRC.**
   - **The dates and amounts of tax payable both as payments on account and balancing payments for his 2009/10 self assessment tax liability.**

9. Ernie has the following employment income:

   Salary of £30,000 per annum
   Bonus of £55,000 paid in March 2010 in respect of the year ended 31 March 2009.
   Bonus of £60,000 paid in March 2011 in respect of the year ended 31 March 2010.

   Ernie is not a director and has no other sources of income.

   You are required to calculate Ernie's income tax liability for 2009/10.

10. An individual is usually either resident or not resident in the UK for income tax purposes for a complete tax year.

    You are required to set out the rules for determining an individual's residency position for income tax purposes and explain when it is possible to 'split' the tax year (ie be treated as UK resident for only part of the year) if the individual is leaving the UK.

11. Bertie is aged 55 and is employed by Bask Ltd. Bertie is paid a salary of £900 per week. He also receives annual private medical insurance under a company insurance scheme which costs the company £450 in December each year. On 31 December 2009 Bertie received a performance related bonus of £250.

    You are required to calculate the national insurance payable by Bertie and Bask Ltd for 2009/10.

12. Ned earns £36,000 a year. His employer provides him with a company car, which produces a taxable benefit of £2,465. He pays for his own private petrol. His employer also provides private medical insurance which costs his employer £410.

    Ned has underpaid tax from 2008/09 of £225.

    You are required to calculate Ned's PAYE tax code for 2009/10.

You will find the answers to this test on page 27. If you answer more than 6 questions correctly, your performance is satisfactory; if you answer more than 8 correctly, you are doing well. Once you have reviewed how you have performed, go back over topics where you feel your understanding is poor.

Module 1: Taxation of Individuals

Study Period 12

Outline of CGT

High Priority

Step 1 Exam Guidance

In the exam you must be able to identify transactions that require you to calculate a gain (or loss) for an individual and those that are exempt disposals.

The topics in this study period were not examined in isolation in the Sample Paper or the May 2009 exam.

Step 2 Introduction to the session

This study period covers the basic CGT knowledge that underpins any gains question in the exam.

We need to understand who pays CGT and on what?

In addition, we look at the overseas issues affecting the UK CGT liability. We have already considered the meaning of residence, ordinary residence and domicile in Study Period 8.

Step 3 Guidance through the Study Text

Read through Chapter 9 after reading the following guidance:

Read Section 1 for essential CGT background knowledge. Try Example 1 to test your basic understanding.

Then read through Section 2, which deals with chargeable and exempt persons, disposals and assets.

Quickly read Section 3 on the administration of CGT, noting the payment date for CGT. This will be dealt with in more detail later, in the 'Administration' Study Period.

Read Sections 4.1 and 4.2 on the impact of residence and domicile status on the chargeability of an individual to UK CGT on the disposal of UK and overseas assets. Attempt Example 2 to check your understanding. Read Sections 4.3 to 4.5 quickly and attempt Example 3 on double taxation relief. Finally, learn the rules in Section 4.6 for determining the location of assets for CGT purposes.

Step 5 iPass and Workbook Questions

Now attempt ESQ 9.1 which will help to reinforce your knowledge of the topics covered in this study period.

Your TQT's i-Pass CD Rom also contains questions on the basics of CGT.

Step 4 Quick Quiz

Please attempt the quiz at the end of Study Text Chapter 9 to reinforce your understanding.

You may find it best to do this after a break, so that you can see what you remember and what you don't.

Study Period 13

Computing gains and losses

High Priority

Step 1 Exam Guidance

The calculation of capital gains tax, on a full or part disposal, is fundamental to your CGT studies.

Ensure that you can set out a basic gain computation quickly and accurately. You must also have a good grip of how capital losses can be used.

Various computational aspects are examinable such as:
- Part disposals
- Assets acquired before 31 March 1982
- Transfers between connected persons or husband and wife.

Question 9 of the Sample Paper tested the calculation of CGT after the offset of losses. One part of Question 11 tested losses and connected persons.

Step 2 Introduction to the session

In this study period we learn how to calculate a capital gain and a capital loss in a number of circumstances.

This session introduces a number of computational aspects. It may take longer than any of your previous study periods, but do not rush as you must have a good grasp of all the topics covered.

Step 3 Guidance through the Study Text

Read through Chapter 10 after reading the following guidance:

Section 1 is fundamental to your study of CGT. Learn the proforma for calculating a capital gain. Attempt Example 1.

Read Section 2 on capital losses. Do you understand how current year losses and brought forward losses can be set off differently? Attempt Examples 2 to 6. Then read through Section 3, which deals with assets acquired before 31 March 1982 and attempt Example 7. You can read through Section 4 on the valuation of assets quickly but make sure you try Examples 8 and 9.

Read Sections 5 and 6, which set out the rules for dealing with disposals between 'connected' persons and married couples or civil partners respectively and attempt Example 10. Then work carefully through Section 7 on part disposals. Can you calculate the cost to use? Try Examples 11 and 12.

Finally you should read Section 8 on compensation (ie insurance proceeds) received for damaged and destroyed assets, attempting Examples 13 and 14.

Step 5 iPass and Workbook Questions

Now attempt ESQs 10.1 to 10.7 which will help to reinforce your knowledge of the topics covered in this study period and give you examples of the types of question you may see in the exam.

Your TQT's i-Pass CD Rom also contains questions testing the computation of gains and losses.

Step 4 Quick Quiz

Please attempt the quiz at the end of Study Text Chapter 10 to reinforce your understanding.

You may find it best to do this after a break, so that you can see what you remember and what you don't.

Study Period 14

Shares and securities

High Priority

Step 1 Exam Guidance

There are special rules for calculating gains on the sale of shares (which includes 'securities' for the purpose of this study guide).

Try and keep the concepts in this study period (such as 'paper for paper' treatment on a takeover of a company) clear in your head. A question can only be worth five marks so a question on shares should not be too complicated at the Awareness level.

Takeovers were tested in both Question 12 of the Sample Paper and Question 10 of the May 2009 exam.

Step 2 Introduction to the session

In this study period we are now in a position to take the CGT computation further and look at the special rules that apply when there is a disposal of shares.

We need these special 'matching' rules for shares to help us identify which shares are actually being disposed of in a transaction.

We build on these basic rules to understand the treatment of shares acquired via bonus issues, rights issues and takeovers.

Step 3 Guidance through the Study Text

Read through Chapter 11 of the Study text after reading the following guidance:

Read Section 1 for background and to understand why we need special rules for dealing with disposals of shares.

Read through Sections 2 and 3 carefully, attempting Examples 1 and 2 to test your understanding. At the end of these two sections you should be able to deal with a basic calculation of a capital gain (or loss) on the sale of shares. This computation forms the basis of all questions involving shares, so make sure you understand it before you move on.

Take your time with Section 4 on 'reorganisations'. The concepts in this section may be completely new to you. First work through Sections 4.1 and 4.2 and try Example 3 on bonus issues. Then read Section 4.3 and try Example 4 on rights issues, and Section 4.4 on capital distributions. Attempt Example 5. Only once you are happy with these sections should you move onto Section 4.5 on the re-organisation of shares and try Examples 6 and 7. Using your knowledge from this section, now read Section 4.6 on takeovers. Try Example 8. Then read Section 4.6.2 on the different ways to receive consideration on a share disposal. Try Example 9.

Only once you are happy with these rules should you move onto Section 5 on transactions involving gilts and QCBs and try Example 10. Finally read quickly through Section 6 on the treatment of disposals by close companies and Section 7 on employee shares.

Step 4 Quick Quiz

Please attempt the quiz at the end of Study Text Chapter 11 to reinforce your understanding.

You may find it best to do this after a break, so that you can see what you remember and what you don't.

Step 5 iPass and Workbook Questions

Now attempt ESQs 11.1 to 11.7 which will help to reinforce your knowledge of the topics covered in this study period and give you examples of the types of question you may see in the exam.

Your TQT's i-Pass CD Rom also contains questions on disposals involving shares and securities.

Module 1: Taxation of Individuals

Study Period 15

Chattels and wasting assets

Medium Priority

Step 1 Exam Guidance

There are special rules for dealing with the disposal of chattels (broadly personal property) and 'wasting' assets, including leases.

You must understand and be able to use the terminology used in this chapter.

The rules for the disposal of short leases were examined in the May 2009 exam (Question 12).

Step 2 Introduction to the session

In this study period we again build on our knowledge of the CGT computation and look at the special rules that apply for calculating a gain or loss on the disposal of certain assets.

The terminology can make the topic seem difficult but try to 'translate' what you are reading into language that you can understand (eg when you read the word 'chattel', try and think of the phrase 'personal property', when you see the word 'assignment' think of the word 'sale', and so on).

Step 3 Guidance through the Study Text

Read through Chapter 12 after reading the following guidance:

Read through Section 1 on chattels (personal property) and work through Examples 1 to 3. When dealing with a chattel disposal there is usually some restriction that applies to reduce the loss or the gain. Make sure you are comfortable with the calculations.

Quickly read Section 2.1 on the general treatment of wasting assets and try Example 4. Then carefully work through Section 2.2 on options (a particular type of wasting asset). Make sure you can deal with the grant, exercise (ie the purchase of the underlying asset) and disposal of an option. Attempt Examples 5 to 9.

Take your time working through Section 3 on leases. Do you understand the difference between assigning (ie the sale of) a lease and granting a lease (ie subletting)? Can you define a short and a long lease? Work through the five different scenarios and try Examples 10 to 14. The most effective way of learning the rules for leases is to attempt the questions, noting the different tax treatment in each scenario.

Step 4 Quick Quiz

Please attempt the quiz at the end of Study Text Chapter 12 to reinforce your understanding.

You may find it best to do this after a break, so that you can see what you remember and what you don't.

Step 5 iPass and Workbook Questions

Now attempt ESQs 12.1 to 12.7 which will help to reinforce your knowledge of the topics covered in this study period and give you examples of the types of question you may see in the exam.

Your TQT's i-Pass CD Rom also contains questions testing chattels and wasting assets, including leases.

Study Period 16

Principal private residence relief

Medium Priority

Step 1 Exam Guidance

Reliefs and exemptions are very important in any tax exam.

In the Taxation of Individuals Awareness module the main CGT exemptions and reliefs you may be tested on are Principal Private Residence (PPR) relief (including letting relief) and the Enterprise Investment Scheme (EIS) CGT reliefs. In this study period we focus on PPR relief, which can exempt the gain on the disposal of someone's home.

Questions will rarely focus on a property that is entirely exempt from tax. Instead you will probably need to consider a scenario where a property is only partly exempt because it has not been lived in by the owner throughout the ownership period.

Question 10 of the sample paper and Question 11 of the May 2009 test the PPR rules.

Step 2 Introduction to the session

In the last few study periods we have learnt how to calculate and tax chargeable gains. In this and the next study period we are introduced to some CGT reliefs that can be given to either exempt (or defer) CGT.

In this Study Period we look at PPR relief. The exemption itself is pretty straight forward. Our focus, therefore, is to identify situations when the exemption will only apply to part of the property or part of the period of ownership and how to deal with such a scenario.

Step 3 Guidance through the Study Text

Read through Chapter 13 of the Study Text after reading the following guidance:

Read carefully through Section 1.1 which establishes the basic principles for when the relief applies. The rest of the Chapter relies on your understanding of these fundamental rules. Find the periods of 'deemed' occupation in your legislation so that you can easily find them in the exam. Attempt Example 1. Then quickly read Section 1.2.

Do not spend too much time on Section 2 which sets out the rules where an individual owns more than one residence. Just highlight key ideas in this section.

When a property is let out the full exemption is not available. This is covered in Section 3. Read this section carefully, making sure that you can identify when letting relief is available (ie when a property is let out and the period is not covered by a period of 'deemed' occupation) and the maximum relief available. Try Example 2 to check your understanding.

The full exemption is also not available is where there is some business use of a home. Attempt Example 3 in Section 4 to ensure you can deal with this scenario.

Step 5 iPass and Workbook Questions

Now attempt the ESQs 13.1 to 13.5 which will help to reinforce your knowledge of the topics covered in this study period and give you examples of the types of question you may see in the exam.

Your TQT's i-Pass CD Rom also contains questions on PPR relief.

Step 4 Quick Quiz

Please attempt the quiz at the end of Study Text Chapter 13 to reinforce your understanding.

You may find it best to do this after a break, so that you can see what you remember and what you don't.

Other CGT reliefs

Study Period 17

High Priority

Step 1 Exam Guidance

The other CGT reliefs that you are examinable on are Entrepreneurs' relief, those connected with the Enterprise Investment Scheme (EIS) and gift relief.

You have already seen the EIS scheme in an earlier study period covering income tax relief on investments in EIS shares.

The CGT aspects of the EIS scheme were tested in Question 6 of the Sample Paper.

Entrepreneurs' relief is a new CGT relief available on certain business disposals after 6 April 2008. It is a valuable relief and is a high priority for your studies. It was tested in Question 9 of the May 2009 exam.

Gift relief is available in specific circumstances.

Gift relief was tested in question 11 of the sample paper.

Step 2 Introduction to the session

In this Study Period we conclude our study of CGT reliefs by looking at Entrepreneurs' relief, gift relief and EIS CGT reliefs.

There are two CGT EIS reliefs: an exemption on the disposal of EIS shares in certain circumstances, and a deferral of a gain arising from the disposal of **any** asset when the taxpayer subscribes for EIS shares.

Entrepreneurs' relief is specifically available for individuals who are withdrawing from a business. Gift relief applies to gifts of business assets or gifts where IHT is chargeable.

Step 3 Guidance through the Study Text

Read through Chapter 14 of the Study Text after reading the following guidance:

Read through Section 4 of Chapter 10 of the '**Taxation of Unincorporated Businesses**' section of the text on Entrepreneurs' relief. Ensure you understand the type of disposals to which the relief applies and how the relief is calculated. Try Example 4.

Now turn back to Chapter 14 of the Taxation of Individuals section of the text.

Read through Section 2 carefully. Ensure you understand the implications of selling EIS shares at both a gain and a loss. Attempt Example 1.

Read through Sections 3.1 and 3.2 to understand the deferral relief that is available on the disposal of any asset if the gain is reinvested in EIS shares. Try Example 2 to ensure you understand the amount of relief available. Read through Sections 3.3 and 3.4 and locate the conditions for relief and the events when the deferred gain will crystallise in the relevant legislation.

Finally read through Section 4 on gift relief. Sections 4.2 and 4.3 explain the circumstances in which it is available. Try Example 3 to make sure you follow how gift relief works.

Step 5 iPass and Workbook Questions

Now attempt the ESQs 14.1 to 14.6 which will help to reinforce your knowledge of the topics covered in this study period and give you examples of the types of question you may see in the exam.

Your TQT's i-Pass CD Rom also contains questions testing CGT reliefs.

Step 4 Quick Quiz

Please attempt the quiz at the end of Study Text Chapter 14 to reinforce your understanding.

You may find it best to do this after a break, so that you can see what you remember and what you don't.

Study Period 18

Administration of CGT

Medium Priority

Step 1 Exam Guidance

The administrative provisions are essential knowledge for the exam. The main aspect of CGT administration that differs from income tax is the possibility of paying CGT in instalments.

CGT administration was tested in Question 1 of the May 2009 exam.

Step 2 Introduction to the session

We have already covered the administrative provisions for income tax in an earlier study period. In this study period our aim is to understand the administrative requirements for the capital gains tax system.

This study period is in some ways revision of our earlier study of income tax administration as many of the same rules apply to both income tax and CGT.

Step 3 Guidance through the Study Text

Read the relevant sections of Chapter 15 of the Study Text, after reading the following guidance:

This chapter considers the administration aspects of both income tax and CGT. You have already studied income tax in an earlier study period and, in most cases, the rules are identical. This period is mainly revision with emphasis on areas where the rules for income tax and CGT differ.

Read Sections 1 to 5 quickly. This should be revision for you as you have already read these sections.

Read Section 6 carefully, focusing on the payment date for CGT, contrasting this with the dates for income tax. You must understand how payments on account are calculated where there is both income tax and CGT due for a period. Try Example 2 to test your understanding. Read Section 6.5 carefully so that you can identify the situations when CGT can be paid by instalments.

Revise Sections 7 to 9 on the powers of HMRC to enquire into returns, the interest and penalty regime and the appeals system.

You have now completed your study of the **Taxation of Individuals Awareness** module.

Step 5 iPass and Workbook Questions

Now attempt ESQs 15.3, 15.6 and 15.7 which will help to reinforce your knowledge of the topics covered in this study period and give you examples of the types of question you may see in the exam.

Your TQT's i-Pass CD Rom also contains questions on all aspect of income tax and CGT administration.

Step 4 Quick Quiz

Please attempt question 6 of the quiz at the end of Study Text Chapter 15 to reinforce your understanding.

You may find it best to do this after a break, so that you can see what you remember and what you don't.

Study Period 19

Progress Test 2

High Priority

In order to reinforce what you have learnt so far, answer the following questions. Try to answer them without referring to your Study Text or notes. The test should take you no longer than one hour and covers Study Periods 12-18. Solutions begin on page 31.

1. Sophie is UK resident but not UK domiciled.

   State the basis on which she will be charged to UK CGT on any capital gains she makes and whether she will be able to use her capital losses against other capital gains.

2. Martin was left a pair of paintings by his uncle. His uncle died in July 2003.

   The probate value of the pair of paintings was £100,000.

   Martin sold one of the paintings to a dealer in May 2009 for £75,000. The value of the remaining painting at that date was £50,000.

   Calculate, showing all your workings, the gain on sale.

3. Brian sold some shares in 2009/10, realising a gain of £25,000. He made no other disposals in 2009/10.

   Calculate Brian's Capital Gains Tax Liability for 2009/10 and state when it is payable.

4. Katy sold an asset for £95,000 on 1 January 2010. She originally bought the asset on 10 October 1999 for £50,000. She sold another asset in December 2009 on which she made a capital loss of £30,000. She had capital losses brought forward from 2008/09 of £20,000.

   Calculate Katy's taxable gain for 2009/10.

5. William bought a commercial building to use in his trade on 21 January 1981 for £15,000. By 31 March 1982 the asset was worth £50,000. He spent £7,500 on capital improvements to the building in June 2001.

   William ceased to trade in October 2009 and sold the building to his sister on 25 October 2009 for £250,000, when the building was worth £350,000 on the open market.

   Calculate William's chargeable gain on disposal assuming he claims entrepreneurs' relief but not gift relief.

6. Mary bought a plot of land for £30,000 in May 1999. In June 2007 she sold half the land for £50,000, when the remaining half of the land was worth £30,000. In August 2009 she sold the remaining half of the land for £95,000.

   Mary has sold no other assets in 2009/10.

   Calculate Mary's capital gains tax liability for 2009/10.

7. Amy had the following transactions in the shares of X plc:

Date		No of shares	Cost/Disposal proceeds £
10/1/99	Bought	5,000	5,000
12/6/02	Bonus issue (1 for 2)	2,500	Nil
15/8/09	Sold	4,500	22,500
20/8/09	Bought	1,000	3,000

   Calculate Amy's capital gain on the sale of X plc shares in 2009/10.

Module 1: Taxation of Individuals

Progress Test 2 (continued)

Study Period 19 — High Priority

8   Jamie owned 10,000 shares in Twizzler plc. He had bought the shares for £3 each in June 2002.

In January 2010 the board of Twizzler plc agreed to a takeover by Turkey plc. Twizzler plc shareholders were to receive £5 cash and 2 ordinary shares in Turkey plc for every 5 shares in Twizzler plc. Turkey plc shares were worth £10 each immediately after the takeover.

Calculate the amount of capital gain that will be chargeable on Jamie on takeover and the base cost of the Turkey plc shares for any future share disposal.

9   Gordon sold the following assets in 2009/10:

(a)   In January 2010 he sold a racehorse for £35,000. He had bought the racehorse as a foal for £10,000 in July 2005.

(b)   In February 2010 he sold a painting for £4,500. He had bought the painting for £9,000 in August 2003.

(c)   In March 2010 he sold an antique chest of drawers for £8,500. They had cost him £5,500 in August 2006.

Calculate the amount of capital gain or loss arising from each of the above disposals.

10   Ainsley bought his main residence on 1 March 2002 for £200,000. He lived in the house for the first three years and then on 1 March 2005, Ainsley moved abroad to take up a new job. He came back to the UK in March 2006, but chose to return home to live with his mum rather than re-occupy the house. The property was empty throughout his absence. He never returned to live in the house and sold the house on 1 December 2009 for £500,000.

Calculate Ainsley's gain on the sale of his house, after claiming principal private residence relief.

11   The following individuals subscribed for shares in qualifying EIS companies. They each claimed the maximum available income tax relief:

Gary: Subscribed for £80,000 shares in Kelly Ltd in May 2008. He disposed of the shares in October 2009 for £60,000.

Helen: Subscribed for £50,000 shares in Napier Ltd in May 2005. She disposed of the shares in June 2009 for £70,000.

Mary: Subscribed for £60,000 shares in Collingwood Ltd in April 2008. She disposed of the shares in May 2009 for £90,000.

You are required to set out, with explanations, the capital gains tax position of each of the above disposals.

12   On 1 June 2009 Carl sold a factory for £1,100,000 which he had acquired in May 1983 for £150,000. He had used the factory in his unincorporated business until he ceased to trade on 1 May 2007.

On 1 June 2007 Carl commenced employment with Richmond Ltd. He acquired a 20% shareholding in the company on 1 July 2007 for £80,000. On 1 July 2009 he gave half of his shares to his daughter when they were worth £100,000. A gift relief election will not be made.

You are required to calculate Carl's taxable gain for 2009/10 assuming he makes any beneficial claims (apart from gift relief).

You will find the answers to this test begin on page 31. If you answer more than 6 questions correctly, your performance is satisfactory; if you answer more than 8 correctly, you are doing well. Once you have reviewed how you have performed, go back over topics where you feel your understanding is poor.

Progress Test 1 — Solutions

Module 1: Taxation of Individuals

1. Ian

   Tax payable on dividend income 2009/10:

   Dividends taxed as the top slice of his income. Tax bands remaining for the dividend income = £1,400 of basic rate band (£37,400 - £36,000).

   Dividends taxable £2,700 × 100/90 = £3,000

	£
Taxable in basic rate band 1,400 × 10%	140
Balance at higher rates 1,600 × 32.5%	520
Total tax due	660
Less: tax credit	(300)
Tax payable	360

2. The conditions to be satisfied for a letting to be classified as a furnished holiday let are:

   (a) The property must be furnished and situated in the UK or the European Economic Area.

   (b) The letting must be on a commercial basis with a view to a profit.

   (c) The property must be available for commercial letting to the public for not less than 140 days in a year and actually let for at least 70 days in that period.

   (d) Not more than 155 days may fall during periods of longer term occupation. Longer term occupation is a continuous period of more than 31 days during which the accommodation is in the same occupation.

   Elizabeth should be aware that the tax advantages for furnished holiday lets have been withdrawn from the 2010/11 tax year.

3.

	£
Rental income	24,000
Less: expenses	
Buildings insurance	(1,000)
Letting agents fees	(1,000)
Council tax	(1,650)
	20,350
Less: wear & tear allowance	
10% × £(24,000 – 1,650)	(2,235)
Property income 2009/10	18,115

   The expenditure on the new kitchen was capital in nature and so not deductible from the property income.

Solutions

Progress Test 1

4   Dorian

(a)	Bank interest	Taxable – received net of 20% tax
(b)	NS & I Savings Certificates interest	Exempt
(c)	NS & I Savings account interest	Taxable – received gross
(d)	Lottery winnings	Exempt
(e)	Employment income	Taxable – tax deducted via PAYE system
(f)	Gross rental income of £2,500 from letting out a room in his house	Exempt as gross rental income is less than the rent-a-room limit of £4,250 unless elect to ignore the rent-a-room exemption when income less expenses would be taxable –rental income received gross
(g)	Dividends from an Enterprise Investment Scheme (EIS) company	Taxable – received net of 10% non-refundable tax credit
(h)	Inheritance from great-aunt Maud	Exempt

5   James

Car benefit percentage 15% + (170 – 135/5) = 22% + 3% diesel supplement = 25%

	£
Car benefit (30,000 x 25% x 10/12)	6,250
Less Contributions by James (£10 x 10 months)	(100)
	6,150
Fuel benefit (£16,900 x 25% x 10/12)	3,521
	9,671

6   As this is an unapproved share option scheme there will be a charge to tax once the share options are exercised. (There will be no charge to tax on grant of the options).

	£
Market value of shares at exercise (5,000 x £2.15)	10,750
Less: price paid at grant (5,000 x 50p)	(2,500)
Less: price paid at exercise (5,000 x 50p)	(2,500)
Amount liable to income tax	5,750

7   Albert can pay into his personal pension schemes up to 100% of his relevant earnings for 2009/10. This would mean he could make contributions of up to £50,000 in 2009/10. This is below the annual allowance of £245,000.

Contributions to personal pension schemes are made net of basic rate tax and the pension scheme will recover the basic rate tax from HMRC. So, for every £80 contributed to a personal pension scheme a further £20 will be contributed by the Government.

For higher rate taxpayers like Albert, the basic rate tax band is extended by the amount of the gross pension contribution made to ensure that they receive higher rate relief for their contributions.

Progress Test 1 — Solutions

8 Roscoe should:

Submit his paper self assessment return by 31 October 2010

The tax due will be as follows:

Payments on account:

(a) 31/1/10 50% x 2008/09 liability £5,000
(b) 31/7/10 50% x 2008/09 liability £5,000

Balancing payment £15,000 – less payments on account = £5,000 due 31 January 2011

9 Ernie

Ernie's employment income is taxed on the receipts basis:

	£
Salary	30,000
Bonus (received in 2009/10)	55,000
Total	85,000
Less: PA	(6,475)
Taxable income	78,525
Tax:	
£37,400 @ 20%	7,480
£41,125 @ 40%	16,450
Tax liability	23,930

10 Residency

For an individual to be treated as resident in the UK they must either:

(a) Be present in the UK for at least 183 days (ie more than half the year), or
(b) Make visits totalling more than 91 days on average over a four year period.

It is possible to 'split' the tax year if the individual leaves the UK part way through the year and is caught by the above rules, but:

(a) They intend to leave the UK permanently, or
(b) They are leaving to take up full time employment abroad for a period that covers a complete tax year.

Progress Test 1

11   Bertie – NIC 2009/10

Class 1 earnings: £900 per week for 51 weeks
                            £1,150 for 1 week

Class 1A benefits: Medical insurance £450

	£
Bertie - Class 1 NIC primary	
(£844 – £110) × 11% × 52	4,198
(£900 – £844) × 1% × 51	29
(£1,150 – £844) × 1% × 1	3
	4,230
Bask Ltd	
Class 1 NIC secondary	
(£900 – £110) × 12.8% × 51	5,157
(£1,150 – £110) × 12.8% × 1	133
	5,290
Class 1A	
£450 × 12.8%	58
	5,348

12   Ned - Tax code 2009/10

	£	£
Basic personal allowance		6,475
Less: deductions for		
Company car	2,465	
PMI	410	
Underpaid tax (W2)	1,125	(4,000)
Available allowances		2,475

Ned's PAYE code is 247L

Working

Underpaid tax

Ned is a basic rate taxpayer so his underpaid tax must be grossed up by 20%

£225 × 100/20 = £1,125

Solutions

Progress Test 2

1 Sophie

Sophie will be charged to tax on the disposal of assets situated in the UK. In respect of the disposal of assets situated overseas she can claim to only be charged to tax to the extent that the gains are remitted to the UK.

If Sophie does not claim the remittance basis she will get full relief for her capital losses (including losses realised on assets situated overseas). If Sophie claims the remittance basis she will not get relief for losses realised on assets situated overseas unless she irrevocably elects into a regime which allows relief for foreign capital losses in any years where she chooses to be taxed on an arising basis.

2 Martin

	£
Proceeds	75,000
Less: cost $\dfrac{75,000}{75,000 + 50,000} \times £100,000$	(60,000)
Gain	15,000

3 Brian

	£
Gain	25,000
Less: annual exempt amount	(10,100)
	14,900
Capital gains tax @ 18%	£2,682

Payable: 31 January 2011.

4 Katy

	£
Asset 1:	
Sale proceeds	95,000
Less: cost	(50,000)
Gain	45,000
Current year loss	(30,000)
Losses b/fwd (restricted to preserve AE)	(4,900)
	10,100
Annual exempt amount	(10,100)
Taxable gain	-

5 William

	£
Sale proceeds (deemed = MV)	350,000
Less: MV'82	(50,000)
Less: enhancement expenditure	(7,500)
	292,500
Less: entrepreneurs' relief (£292,500 × 4/9)	(130,000)
Chargeable gain	162,500

Solutions

Progress Test 2

6 Mary

	£
Sale proceeds	95,000
Less cost (W1)	(11,250)
Gain	83,750
Less: annual exempt amount	(10,100)
Taxable gain	73,650
CGT liability @ 18%	£13,257

Working

Cost used on first sale in June 2007

£30,000 x 50,000/30,000 + 50,000 = £18,750

Cost remaining for second sale = £11,250 (£30,000 - £18,750)

7 Amy

(1) Purchase in next 30 days

	£
Sale proceeds 1,000/4,500 × £22,500	5,000
Less: cost	(3,000)
Gain	2,000
Sale proceeds 3,500/4,500 × £22,500	17,500
Less Cost (W)	(2,333)
Gain	15,167
Total gains	17,167

Working

Share pool:

Date		No	Cost £
10/1/99		5,000	5,000
12/6/02		2,500	Nil
		7,500	5,000
Sale			
15/8/09	3,500/7,500 × 5,000	(3,500)	(2,333)
		4,000	2,667

Module 1: Taxation of Individuals

Progress Test 2 — Solutions

8   Gain chargeable on takeover:

	£
Consideration for takeover	
Cash £5 × 10,000/5	10,000
Shares £10 × 2 × 10,000/5	40,000
	50,000

Gain chargeable immediately = gain relating to cash

	£
Sale proceeds	10,000
Less cost: 30,000 × 10/50	(6,000)
	4,000
Base cost of Turkey plc shares:	
Cost of Twizzler plc shares	30,000
Less used vs cash consideration	(6,000)
Cost left for shares	24,000

9   Gordon:

(a) Sale of racehorse exempt as wasting chattel.

(b) Sale of painting:

	£
Proceeds – deemed	6,000
Less cost	(9,000)
Restricted capital loss	(3,000)

(c) Sale of antique chest of drawers:

	£
Sale proceeds	8,500
Less cost	(5,500)
	3,000

Restricted to a maximum of 5/3 £8,500 - £6,000 = £4,167

Gain therefore £3,000

10   Ainsley

	£
Sale proceeds	500,000
Less: cost	(200,000)
Gain	300,000
Less PPR (W)	
300,000 × 72/93	(232,258)
	67,742

Progress Test 2 — Solutions

Working

Period of ownership

1/3/02 – 1/12/09 = 7 years 9 months (93 months)

Period of actual and deemed occupation:

Actual:
1/3/02 – 1/3/05 = 3 years (36 months)

Deemed:
Last 36 months:

1/12/06 – 1/12/09 = 36 months

The period from 1/3/05 to 1/12/06 cannot be treated as deemed occupation, as, although Ainsley went abroad for his employment, he never re-occupied the property, even though he could have done. There is no letting relief as the property was never let.

11 Gary

Disposed of shares within 3 years realising a capital loss of £20,000 (£60,000 - £80,000). The loss is an allowable loss for CGT purposes but is reduced by the amount of EIS income tax relief given and not withdrawn.

Income tax relief given 2008/09: £80,000 × 20% = £16,000

Income tax relief withdrawn £60,000 × 20% = £12,000

Allowable loss is therefore:

	£	£
Proceeds		60,000
Cost	80,000	
less IT relief not withdrawn (16,000 – 12,000)	(4,000)	
		(76,000)
Allowable loss		(16,000)

Helen

No income tax relief withdrawn as sold more than 3 years after acquisition.

Gain on disposal is exempt.

Mary

Normal capital gains computation as shares sold within three years. All of the income tax relief is withdrawn.

Capital gain:	£
Proceeds	90,000
Cost	(60,000)
	30,000

12 Carl – Capital gains computation 2009/10

	£	£
Factory:		
Proceeds	1,100,000	
Cost	(150,000)	
Gain	950,000	
Less Entrepreneurs' relief £950,000 × 4/9	(422,222)	527,778
Shares:		
Proceeds (Deemed MV)	100,000	
Cost (£80,000 × 50%)	(40,000)	
Gain	60,000	
Less Entrepreneurs' relief £50,000 × 4/9 (Max £1,000,000 lifetime limit)	(22,222)	37,778
Total gains		565,556
Less: Annual exempt amount		(10,100)
Taxable gain		555,456

Exam style questions

1.1 Roger (aged 69) is married to Vicky (aged 76) and is registered blind.

Roger's net income for 2009/10 was £23,980, made up of rental income (£16,980) and bank interest (£7,000). Vicky's only income is her pension of £4,500.

You are required to calculate Roger and Vicky's allowances and tax reductions for 2009/10. Also give brief advice on how they could improve their joint tax position.

1.2 Charles earned £59,500 from his employment in 2009/10. He paid tax of £13,800 under PAYE.

In 2008 he took out a personal loan of £6,250 to buy a laptop and printer which he uses only for work purposes. He is paying interest at a rate of 8% per annum on this loan.

He paid £12,000 (net) to Oxfam via Gift Aid in the year.

You are required to calculate his tax payable/repayable for 2009/10.

1.3 George, a 76-year-old retired journalist, received the following income during the year ended 5 April 2010:

	£
Income from writing and lecturing	7,700
Net income distributed from his grandfather's discretionary trust	1,650
Interest on an ISA	800

George entered into a civil partnership with Paul on 1 March 2010. Paul is 63 years old and has net income of £5,000.

You are required to calculate George's tax payable/repayable for 2009/10.

1.4 Julie had the following income during 2009/10:

	£	
Earnings	34,000	(PAYE deducted £7,200)
Lottery winnings	10,000	
Legacy from late grandfather	15,000	

In July 2007 she had gifted some shares to her daughters, Philippa (age 19) and Jessica (age 17). The daughters each received a dividend of £1,800 in 2009/10.

On 8 September 2009, Julie subscribed £20,000 for shares in Brack Ltd, a company qualifying under the Enterprise Investment Scheme.

You are require to calculate Julie's income tax payable/repayable for 2009/10 and explain the income tax treatment of the dividend income received by her daughters.

1.5 **You are required to explain how income tax relief is given for the following payments (if at all) made by an individual in 2009/10:**

(a) A gift of shares in ICI plc, valued at £10,000, to Oxfam.

(b) Interest payable at 4% per annum on a loan taken out in August 2002 to buy printing machinery used within a partnership.

(c) Non-trade related patent royalties paid of £1,560.

(d) A gift of £2,000 cash to NSPCC, a registered charity.

(e) Maintenance payments from a 35 year old man to his ex-wife aged 33.

2.1 Mr Fairbanks took early retirement in 2004 when he was 55. He now works part-time. In 2009/10 his gross earnings were £6,000 and he paid tax under PAYE of £250. He received £900 in dividends and £800 of building society interest. He received interest on his Midwest Savings Bank account totalling £80.

You are required to calculate his tax payable/repayable.

2.2 Jonty, aged 38, is a married man whose wife has no income. The following information is relevant for the year ended 5 April 2010:

(1) His salary was £45,000 (PAYE deducted £7,400)

(2) His other income was:

	£
Building society interest received	80
Dividends received	63

(3) In March 2010 Jonty closed down his NS&I investment account which he had kept for many years. Interest of £142 was credited.

(4) He made a donation of £396 (net of basic rate tax) to Oxfam in May 2009 under Gift Aid.

(5) Jonty won £100 on the Grand National.

You are required to compute the tax payable by Jonty for 2009/10.

2.3 Archie (76) is married to Belinda (61). Archie received the following income in 2009/10:

	£
Rental income	23,900
Building society interest	4,400
UK Treasury Stock interest	290

Belinda has no income.

You are required to calculate Archie's tax payable for 2009/10.

2.4 Fiona, who is 35, lives on her own. She has been running her own business for many years. Her taxable trading profits for 2009/10 are £34,000.

During 2009/10 she received the following investment income:

	£
UK dividends	8,000
Bank interest held with a Jersey bank (gross amount)	4,300
Premium bond winnings	13,000

Fiona borrowed £24,000 in March 2008 to invest in shares in a close company. She pays interest at 4% per annum. She repaid £10,000 of the loan when she received her Premium Bond winnings on 5 December 2009.

She makes an annual donation to charity of £1,600.

You are required to calculate Fiona's tax payable for 2009/10.

2.5 Mildred, who is aged 76, has the following income for 2009/10:

	£
State pension	11,047
Interest from bank account in Guernsey (gross amount)	13,450

Mildred also owns 1,200 shares in Bassett Ltd. The company paid a dividend of 60p per share on 15 May 2009 in respect of the year ended 31 December 2008. Shareholders were offered the option to take shares in lieu of the dividend, valued at £6.50 per share, at a rate of one share for every 10 held. Mildred chose to take the stock dividend.

Mildred pays £500 each year to the NSPCC (a registered charity) under Gift Aid.

You are required to calculate Mildred's tax payable/repayable for 2009/10.

2.6 On 15 November 2007, Tennyson Ltd, a close company, makes a loan at commercial interest rates of £80,000 to Sylvia who owns 30% of the shares in Tennyson Ltd. The company has a 31 December year end.

On 20 October 2009 the company decides to write off the entire loan.

You are required to explain the consequences of the loan and subsequent waiver for the company and Sylvia. You should assume that the company is not 'large' for corporation tax purposes and that Sylvia is a higher rate taxpayer.

2.7 Petra works one day a week at her local internet café. She earned £2,080 during the 2009/10 tax year. No tax was deducted via PAYE.

She can afford to work so little as she has a large investment portfolio that she inherited on the death of her grandmother four years ago.

During 2009/10 she received the following income from the portfolio:

	£
Dividends	122,850
Treasury stock interest (gross)	54,650
Bank interest (net)	1,300
NS&I account interest	600
NS&I Certificate interest	900

Petra donated £10,000 via gift aid to the NSPCC.

You are required to calculate Petra's income tax payable for 2009/10

3.1 Ben owns a house which he lets out furnished to earn extra income. He purchased this with the aid of an interest only mortgage of £60,000 at 7%.

In 2009/10 the property was let for the whole year at a rate of £1,500 per month (although he only received rental income of £16,500 as one month was paid late).

He incurred the following expenses

	£
Agent's fee (6 April 2009 – 5 April 2010)	1,800
Water rates	120
Cost of building new porch	2,500
Insurance	500

You are required to calculate Ben's taxable property income and explain the alternative ways in which tax relief may be obtained for the cost of furnishing the property.

3.2 Lizzie is employed by a firm of accountants, earning a salary of £45,000 per annum. She recently bought a cottage in Devon which she intends to let out to visitors to the area at a rate of £500 a week. Lizzie expects to let the property out through the period from April to October each year, with new tenants in occupation every 2 to 3 weeks. She has spent around £10,000 on furnishing the cottage.

You are required to explain how you would determine whether the cottage will be treated as a 'Furnished Holiday Letting' for income tax purposes.

Assuming that it does satisfy the 'Furnished Holiday Letting' definition, you are required to explain:
- **how relief for the expenditure on furnishing would be given.**
- **how relief would be given if Lizzie makes a loss on the letting in 2009/10.**

3.3 Randall owns three properties which are let on the following terms, all rents being payable quarterly in advance on (31 March, 30 June, 30 September and 31 December). Randall is responsible for repairs on all properties; the rents on properties A, B and C are full rents.

A   Let at £620 a year on a 20 year lease which commenced in 1988.

B   Let at £348 a year on a lease which expired on 30 September 2009, then empty until 31 December 2009 when let at £440 a year.

C   Let at £100 a year throughout the year.

Expenditure by Randall on these properties in the year was as follows:

	A £	B £	C £
Agent's commission	20		
Advertising for tenants		76	
Repairs: while let	142		119
while empty		255	

You are required to calculate the property income assessment for Randall for 2009/10.

3.4 Sebastian owns two properties:

A   5 Arnhem Avenue
B   27 Cannae Road.

Both are let out unfurnished.

A   This was let until 24 June 2009 at an annual rental of £2,400. On 29 September 2009, it was let out to a new tenant on a 10-year lease agreement. The annual rental is £1,600. The tenant paid a premium of £5,000 on 29 September 2009.

B   This was let from 24 June 2009 at an annual rental of £600.

All the rents are payable quarterly in advance on the normal quarter days and are sufficient to cover the landlord's outgoings.

Property A was acquired in 1981; property B was purchased on 15 April 2009.

Expenditure in connection with the properties was as follows:

	A £	B £
Agent's commission: 1 May 2009	25	10
1 November 2009	25	10
Repairs (note)	–	1,800
Advertising for new tenants 10 July 2009	50	–

Note. The repairs in respect of property C are analysed as follows:

	£
Installation of new kitchen equipment	300
Retiling part of the roof after damage in May 2009	1,500
	1,800

You are required to compute Sebastian's property income assessment for 2009/10.

3.5 On 1 October 1999, Adam granted a lease over a building to Brian for a period of 30 years at a premium of £20,000. On 1 October 2009 Brian granted a 5 year sublease to Claire, who paid a premium of £8,000.

You are required to calculate:

(a)   **Brian's property income assessment in 2009/10 in respect of the premium received;**

(b)   **the deduction available to Claire in 2009/10, assuming she uses the building for the purposes of her trade. Claire's year end is 31 December and she has been trading for many years.**

3.6 Judy begins to let out a room in her home to a lodger with effect from 1 April 2009, at a rate of £600 per month payable in advance.

She has calculated that in 2009/10 the following expenditure may be attributed to the room which is let out:

	£
Electricity	1,200
Gas	1,400
Cost of new furnishings	2,000

You are required to explain (with supporting calculations):

(a) the alternative bases under which Judy's property income may be assessed; and

(b) the time limit for any election which she should make in order to achieve the more favourable basis in 2009/10, and the impact of this election on future tax years.

3.7 Seraphina bought a warehouse on 1 June 2009 for £685,000. She took out a loan for 50% of the cost, paying annual interest at 5.25%.

On 1 July 2009 she granted a 15 year lease over the building to Jet Ltd for a one off premium of £50,000, and an annual rent of £42,000, paid monthly in advance.

Although the property could have been rented out immediately, Seraphina spent £7,895 on repairs before Jet Ltd took occupation in July.

Seraphina also paid a management company 15% (inclusive of VAT) of the monthly rent. Jet Ltd paid all other expenses in connection with the property.

You are required to calculate Seraphina's property income assessment for 2009/10.

3.8 Seraphina bought a warehouse on 1 June 2009 for £685,000.

On 1 July 2009 she granted a 15 year lease over the building to Jet Ltd for a one off premium of £50,000, and an annual rent of £42,000, paid monthly in advance.

You are required to calculate the chargeable gain or allowable loss arising in 2009/10 assuming that the value of the reversion on 1 July 2009 was £565,000.

4.1 Patricia Jones had the following income during 2009/10:

	£	
Earnings from employment	95,000	(PAYE £27,000)
Interest on NS&I Saving Certificates	3,700	
Dividends from Black Ltd (a qualifying EIS company)	3,000	(net)

Patricia subscribed £20,000 for ordinary shares in Blanche Ltd in November 2009 and £30,000 for ordinary shares in Rouge Plc (an AIM listed company) in May 2010. Both companies qualify under the Enterprise Investment Scheme.

You are required to calculate Patricia's 2009/10 income tax payable or repayable assuming that she makes any necessary elections to claim the maximum possible EIS relief in 2009/10.

4.2 Madeleine, aged 45, is interested in investing in an ISA in 2009/10.

You are required to advise on the following:

(a) The types of investment available and maximum subscriptions;
(b) The tax treatments of income and gains within the ISA;
(c) Any requirements regarding the individual investor.

4.3 Maggie is a higher rate taxpayer.

During 2009/10 she invested the maximum possible into an ISA share account.

She also subscribed for 25,000 shares in LiteHead Ltd, an unquoted trading company run by her friend, Lucy, for £25,000. LiteHead Ltd is a very small company with only 10 employees and gross assets of £500,000.

On 1 October 2010 Maggie withdrew half of the funds from her ISA, which had increased in value by £450, and sold half of her shares in LiteHead Ltd to a third party for their market value of £4.50 a share.

You are required to calculate Maggie's total chargeable gains for 2009/10 in respect of these two transactions.

5.1 Penny, a full time employee, was made redundant by her employer in June 2009. She received the following redundancy package:

	£
Statutory redundancy pay	3,800
Ex gratia cash payment	45,000
Market value of company car – ownership transferred to Penny	12,000
Outplacement counselling	4,500

Penny spent 10 years out of her 30 years' service with the company working abroad, her last 2 years of service being spent in the UK.

You are required to calculate what amount will be taxable on Penny in 2009/10.

5.2 In 2009/10 Jim, a director of a wine importing company, is paid £10,000 per annum and is given the use of a new 2-litre car with a list price of £16,000 and an emission rate of 200g/km, plus wine costing £1,000. Jim's 20-year old student daughter, Jane, also works for the company on Saturdays, is paid £15 per day and has the use of a new 1,150cc car with a list price of £12,000 and an emission rate of 163g/km. Jim uses £600 of the wine promoting the company's products. Private petrol is paid for by the company in respect of Jim's car but not his daughter's.

You are required to calculate Jim's earnings for 2009/10.

5.3 Mr Thomas is a director of a private company; his remuneration for 2009/10 was £30,000.

During the year ended 5 April 2010, the following benefits were provided to him:

Accommodation in a four bedroom house, owned by the company.

	£
Original cost 1995	80,000
Cost of extension 1999	25,000
Annual value	750

Mr Thomas moved in on 1 March 2004, at which time the house was valued at £125,000. He pays a nominal rent of £1,200 per annum for use of the house.

Expenses paid directly by company 2009/10:	£
Council tax	1,400
Electricity	750
Gas	250
Telephone	350
Redecoration (internal)	700
Gardener	1,500

You are required to calculate Mr Thomas's earnings for 2009/10. Assume that the official rate of interest charged throughout 2009/10 was 4.75%.

5.4 Raymond received the following benefits from his employer as part of this remuneration package in 2009/10:

(1) Interest-free loan for a non-qualifying purpose – first advance 6 June 2009

			£
6.6.09	advance		10,000
6.8.09	advance		5,000
6.12.09	repaid		7,500
6.2.10	advance		4,000
6.3.10	repaid		2,500

(2) Car

– Mercedes, list price £21,500, purchased 1 June 2006. The emission rate is 150g/km.

– 1,600 cc Escort, list price £10,000, purchased 5 August 2009, used by Raymond. The emission rate is 165g/km.

No petrol was provided for either vehicle.

You are required to calculate the benefits assessable on Raymond for 2009/10.

Assume that the official rate of interest charged throughout 2009/10 was 4.75%.

5.5 You have been consulted by Alf, one of the directors of your company, who has no shareholding in the company, concerning the taxability of emoluments and benefits received. The following information is provided for the tax year 2009/10.

(1) Alf's salary is £32,600 (PAYE £5,755).

(2) An expenses allowance of £2,500 for 2009/10 spent as follows:

	£
Business travelling	1,800
Entertainment:	
Overseas customers	400
Overseas suppliers	100
United Kingdom customers	200

(3) Benefits for the year were as follows:

(i) The company purchased hi-fi equipment for Alf's personal use at a cost of £800. The company retained ownership of the equipment.

(ii) Alf had exclusive use of a new 2.5 litre petrol engined car with a list price of £15,000. The emission rate is 180g/km. No petrol was provided for private motoring.

(iii) Medical insurance was provided for £300. Alf would have had to pay £450 to take out the insurance personally.

(iv) Alf visited Saville Row for 5 tailored shirts, which cost the company £400.

You are required to calculate Alf's earnings for 2009/10, giving brief explanatory notes on the treatment of his benefits and expenses.

5.6 Mr Bjork is chairman and chief executive of Peepop Ltd.

He receives a salary of £46,000 per annum and during the income tax year 2009/10 he is provided with the following benefits:

The company provided him with the use of a 2,100 cc petrol Jaguar motor car with a list price of £20,000 from 6 April 2009. The emission rate is 220g/km.

On 31 July 2009 he was involved in a serious road accident and the car was written off.

While he had use of the Jaguar, he contributed 50% of the cost of his private fuel.

When he resumed work on 1 October 2009, he was provided with a Mercedes car with a list price of £30,000 and the use of a chauffeur. This car is used solely for business purposes. The emission rate is 190g/km.

He is given a computer by Peepop Ltd on 6 October 2009, when it has a market value of £200. He has had use of that computer since 6 October 2007 when its market value was £6,000.

You are required to compute the total amount of benefits assessable on Mr Bjork for 2009/10.

5.7 Giles has worked for HiTech Computers Plc for many years and he has recently been promoted to sales manager, receiving a £5,000 pay rise from 1 July 2009. His revised salary is £36,000. He has continued to pay contributions into the company's registered occupational pension scheme of 5% of his salary and bonus. He has received sales commission as follows:

Year ended 31 December 2008   £3,000 received 28 February 2009
Year ended 31 December 2009   £4,000 received 28 February 2010

As a result of his promotion, he has been provided with a flat in London, due to being required to spend increasing amounts of time in London. The company pays £5,000 annual rent on the property, which has an annual value of £2,400. He is required to contribute £100 per month towards this.

Giles also receives £100 per month payment towards the provision of crèche facilities for his child who attends a private nursery.

You are required to calculate Giles's earnings for 2009/10.

5.8 Arnold has a salary of £30,000. He drives his own car to work, taking his two year old daughter to crèche on the way. Arnold's employer pays the cost of the crèche which is £200 per week. Arnold is provided with a designated parking space at his employer's premises. This costs his employer £1,000 pa. Sometimes Arnold has to drive to clients and his employer reimburses him for his business mileage at 60p per mile.

In 2009/10 Arnold did 5,000 business miles.

Arnold incurred the following expenses in 2009/10:

- a subscription of £250 to his local golf club, where he sometimes plays with clients.
- a subscription of £800 to a club in London where he stays when his work necessitates an overnight stay in London.

You are required to calculate Arnold's earnings for 2009/10.

5.9 Sally has worked for Generality Ltd for the last three years. Her current annual salary is £52,000.

Due to a downturn in the economy she was made redundant on 6 December 2009. As part of her redundancy package she received the following:

	£
Statutory redundancy	990
Payment in lieu of notice period provided for in her contract	13,000
Discretionary payment	28,000

Sally has had her company car, a BMW 320i SE, since she started working for Generality Ltd. It had a list price of £23,000 when it was originally provided to her and CO_2 emissions of 189g/km. Generality Ltd also paid all of her private and business petrol costs. Sally will pay £8,000 to Generality Ltd to keep the car, even though its market value is £10,000.

Sally has decided to take six months to find her ideal replacement job.

You are required to calculate Sally's employment income figure for 2009/10.

6.1 Ray is a director of Sun Ltd, who earns a salary of £60,000 in 2009/10. PAYE of £15,000 was deducted. Ray was granted an Enterprise Management Incentive option in July 2006 to acquire 10,000 shares in Sun Ltd for £1.50 each. The shares were worth £2 each at the date of grant. He exercised the option in July 2009 when the share price was £4.75.

Ray's only other income in 2009/10 was interest received of £1,500 on his NS&I Easy Access Savings Account.

You are required to calculate Ray's 2009/10 income tax payable, explaining the treatment of the option on grant and exercise, assuming all the conditions for a qualifying EMI option are met.

6.2 Sue has been a director of Porchester Ltd for three years. In order to reward her performance to the company on 1 January 2010, she was granted 5,000 ordinary share options under an approved Enterprise Management Incentive scheme to buy shares at £4.00 at any time in the next 10 years. The market value of the shares at January 2010 was £3.96. She is planning to buy the shares in 8 years time when she estimates that the share price will have risen to £10.00. She plans to sell them shortly afterwards (assume share price at date of sale = £10.40).

You are required to:

(a) **Explain the tax consequences of the granting of the share options and the subsequent sale by Sue.**

(b) **Explain how your answer would change if the scheme was unapproved and the exercise price was £3.00.**

6.3 Sharon is employed by Bruiser Ltd. The company is proposing to offer her some form of share incentive and are considering the following possibilities:

(i) The company could issue her with 10,000 ordinary shares worth £5 per share. Sharon would pay £2 per share.

(ii) The company could grant Sharon an option to buy 10,000 ordinary shares in three years' time at an exercise price equal to £2 per share. It is estimated that in three years the company's shares will be valued at £8 per share.

(iii) The company could issue her with 10,000 preference shares, currently valued at £2 per share, for which Sharon would pay the market value price. The preference shares carry the right to conversion into ordinary shares in 3 years' time on a 1 for 1 basis. The preference shares have limited rights and are not expected to rise in value.

You are required to explain the amounts on which income tax would be payable in each of the above situations. You should assume that Bruiser Ltd will not be willing to set up any form of approved share scheme.

6.4 Janet earns an annual salary of £75,000 and already holds options over the maximum value of shares in her employer's Company Share Option Plan.

Her employer granted her options over an additional 10,000 shares at a cost of 12p per option on 1 October 2007. The market value of the shares at that date was £5.00 per share and the exercise price was set at £2.75.

On 15 March 2010 Janet exercised 5,000 of the October 2007 options when the shares were worth £12.50 per share. She sold the shares one week later, by which time the share price had increased to £13.95.

You are required to calculate Janet's:

(i) income tax and
(ii) capital gains tax liabilities

in respect of the exercise of the options and sale of the shares.

You may assume that the shares are not readily convertible assets

7.1 Jeremy who is finance director of a large public company, has the following earnings in 2009/10:

Salary and bonuses	£380,000
Medical insurance	£1,500
Company car benefit	£12,000

He is also given free parking in a car park next to his office which costs his employer £750. Jeremy pays an annual subscription of £500 to the ICAEW.

You are required to advise Jeremy on the maximum contribution he can make to a registered pension scheme in the tax year and obtain tax relief, and the tax consequences of contributing this amount.

7.2 Ed Tommy and Joan Ball are in partnership running a design studio, with profits being shared in the ratio 4:1. They both wish to start saving for their retirement and would like to make maximum contributions to a pension. The partnership's trading profit for 2009/10 is £175,000. Neither Ed or Joan has any other income.

You are required to:

(a) Advise Ed and Joan of the maximum amount they can each contribute to a pension for 2008/09 and 2009/10.

(b) Explain the method by which Ed and Joan will be given tax relief for their pension contributions.

(c) Explain how they will be able to continue to contribute to their pensions if the partnership ceases trading on 5 April 2010 and they no longer have earnings.

7.3 Dwaine is the sales director of a small central heating and plumbing company based in the Midlands. The company draws up accounts to 31 December each year.

Dwaine's salary (paid monthly) for the year ended 31 December 2009 was set at £40,000 per annum. This was raised to £44,000 at the Board meeting on 20 January 2010. PAYE deducted in 2009/10 came to £6,000.

Dwaine also receives half yearly bonuses dependent on the performance of his sales team. These have been as follows:

Bonus period	Bonus	Awarded	Received
6 m/e 31.12.08	£2,000	31.3.09	30.4.09
6 m/e 30.6.09	£6,881	30.9.09	31.10.09
6 m/e 31.12.09	£6,990	31.3.10	30.4.10

The company does not have an occupational pension scheme and therefore agreed to make payments into Dwaine's personal pension. Dwaine pays £150 per month – the company add on an extra £100 per month.

You are required to calculate the income tax payable/(repayable) by Dwaine for the year ended 5 April 2010.

7.4 Alfred earns an annual salary of £200,000. The value of his taxable benefits is a further £44,000.

Alfred owns two investment properties that he rents out. One is let furnished and the taxable rental income (net of expenses) is £18,000 a year. The other qualifies as a furnished holiday let and the net taxable income from this property is £25,000 for 2009/10.

Alfred's other income for 2009/10 is £112,500 interest from a bank account that he holds jointly with his wife and dividends of £363,330 from UK companies.

You are required to calculate Alfred's income tax payable assuming he makes the maximum contribution to his personal pension.

8.1 Ricardo Garcia is resident and domiciled in Spain.

He has recently married a British woman and will be coming to live in London when he retires; he has advised you that he would, however return to Spain in the event that his wife should predecease him.

He has a large pension from the Spanish company that he used to work for, which he will need to bring into the UK for living expenses. He will keep his Spanish bank account and his large portfolio of Spanish investments.

You are required to explain the income tax treatment of Mr Garcia's different sources of income. You should also note the basic planning which should be implemented with regard to Mr Garcia's existing funds before he comes to the UK.

8.2 Marco, an Italian client, arrived in the UK on the 5 August 2008 to work for the UK branch of his Italian employer for 2 years.

In 2009/10 he received the following income:

	£
Salary – Paid in the UK	60,000
– Paid in Italy	15,000
Company car benefit (UK)	5,200
Bank interest – UK (net)	35
– Italy (gross)	500

No element of the income received in Italy was remitted to the UK. 20% of Marco's working time was spent in Italy.

You are required to:

(a) **Identify Marco's residence, ordinary residence and domicile for UK income tax purposes in 2009/10.**

(b) **Comment on the date from which any changes to his residence status as a result of coming to the UK would have taken place.**

(c) **Calculate Marco's taxable income for 2009/10 assuming he makes all beneficial claims.**

8.3 Steffen was born in Germany and spends most of his time living there, but for the last few years has been making regular visits to the UK, as follows:

2005/06	75 days
2006/07	98 days
2007/08	92 days
2008/09	104 days
2009/10	100 days

During 2009/10, Steffen's received interest of £80,000 (net of 45% foreign withholding tax) on his offshore bank account and brought £28,600 of this net interest into the UK. Steffen also received rental income of £57,800 (net of 15% withholding tax) from letting out his villa in Utopia and transferred all of this income to the UK.

You are required to:

(a) **Determine, with explanation, at what point (if any) Steffen will be treated as having become UK resident, assuming that he had no previous intention to make this level of visits.**

(b) **Calculate Steffen's UK income tax payable in 2009/10 assuming he makes all beneficial claims.**

9.1 Matilda, who had previously lived in the UK all her life, left the country on 11 January 2005 and moved to France to work at a vineyard in Bordeaux. Having mastered the trade, she then returned to the UK on 22 May 2009 with a view to setting up her own vineyard in East Anglia. During her absence from the UK, Matilda made the following chargeable gains/ allowable losses.

Asset	Date acquired	Date sold	Chargeable gain/losses
Painting	June 2004	August 2008	£55,000
Holiday cottage	September 2005	January 2009	£38,000
Land	June 2002	December 2007	£(15,000)

You are required to:

(a) Explain the basis on which gains made while Matilda was non UK resident may be subject to UK CGT.
(b) Calculate Matilda's total chargeable gains for 2009/10.

10.1 In May 2009 Mark made a gain of £17,900 on the sale of shares in an unquoted trading company (owned for 3 years). He also made a loss of £7,000 on the sale of a painting at auction and a further loss of £26,000 on the sale of a cottage to his brother. He has losses brought forward of £5,000.

You are required to calculate the losses to carry forward to 2010/11.

10.2 Dorrit has been trading for many years and has produced the following recent results:

Year ended	£
31 December 2009	15,000 profit
31 December 2010	(28,000) loss

He has UK property income of £3,000 per annum and in 2009/10 realised a chargeable gain of £16,000 on an asset which was originally acquired on 2 May 1998.

You are required to compute Dorrit's revised net income and chargeable gains, before the annual exempt amount for 2009/10 assuming earliest possible relief is sought for the loss.

10.3 Ambrose made the following chargeable disposal in 2009/10:

	Asset
Purchase date	31.12.81
Purchase price	£4,500
31.3.82 Market value	£7,500
Enhancement date	1.5.98
Enhancement cost	£1,000
Proceeds	£28,800
Disposal date	1.1.10

You are required to calculate the capital gains tax payable by Ambrose for 2009/10. State the due date for payment.

10.4 Emily made the following disposals in 2009/10:

(1) *Factory*

Acquired 1 July 2005 for £150,000. Emily let out the factory to Teds R Us Ltd, a soft toy manufacturer. The factory was sold for £225,000 on 10 July 2009.

(2) *Painting*

This had been acquired by Emily's husband Arthur on 1 March 1999 for £50,000. Arthur had given the painting to Emily on 1 July 2001 when it was worth £60,000. Emily sold the painting for £73,000 on 2 May 2009.

You are required to calculate the capital gains tax payable by Emily for 2009/10

10.5 Kidson purchased a plot of land on 1 January 1983 for £8,000. On 31 August 2009, he sold part of the land for £45,000 but declined an offer of £50,000 for the rest.

You are required to calculate the capital gains tax arising on the sale assuming this is the only capital transaction Kidson has in 2009/10.

10.6 Cyril buys an asset for £40,000 in June 1999. It is damaged by fire in August 2000. Its unrestored value was £50,000. The asset was restored in September 2000 at a cost of £14,000 and this sum was received from the insurance company in November 2000. Cyril sells the asset on 10 July 2009 for £85,000.

You are required to show Cyril's chargeable gain on the sale in July 2009 if he did not make a claim under s.23(1)(a) in 2000/01.

10.7 Jake buys an asset for £7,500 in February 1986, and it is completely destroyed by fire in February 2010. Insurance recoveries immediately amount to £17,000. He bought a replacement asset for £16,000 within six months and made a claim under s.23(5) TCGA 1992.

You are required to show Jake's CGT position.

11.1 James bought 1,000 shares in G plc for £2,954 in April 1985 and another 1,000 for £6,000 in May 2005. He disposed of 500 shares in August 2009 for £15,000.

You are required to calculate the chargeable gain arising on the disposal in August 2009.

11.2 Mr Smith acquired 5,000 shares in S plc in April 1985 for £5,605. In July 1999 S plc made a bonus issue of one ordinary share for every five held. In December 2009 Mr Smith sold 3,500 of his shares for £6,250.

You are required to calculate the gain arising on the sale of shares in December 2009.

11.3 Peter made the following disposals in 2009/10:

(i) He purchased a building for £50,000 on 1 January 1971 which he let commercially as offices to an unquoted company. On 10 April 2009 he sold the building for £600,000. The value on 31 March 1982 was £200,000.

(ii) He held 20,000 shares in Forum Follies plc which he purchased in May 1986 for £50,000. In March 2010, Exciting Enterprises plc acquired all the share capital of Forum Follies plc. Under the terms of the take-over for every two shares previously held in Forum Follies plc shareholders received three ordinary shares in Exciting Enterprises plc plus £1 cash. Immediately after the take-over the ordinary shares in Exciting Enterprises plc were quoted at £3 each.

You are required to calculate Peter's taxable gain in 2009/10.

11.4 Giles purchased shares in Dassau plc, a quoted company, as follows.

	No of shares	Cost £
December 1985	1,000	2,000
April 1987 1 for 2 rights issue		£2 per share
15 November 2009	500	£1,500

On 1 November 2009 he sold 1,200 shares for £9,500.

Giles had capital losses brought forward from 2008/09 of £6,400.

You are required to calculate Giles's taxable gain for 2009/10.

11.5 Richard Price works for PB plc, a large UK quoted trading company. He has acquired shares in PB plc via a company share option plan in recent years as follows:

Date	Shares Acquired	Cost £
15.3.1990	2,000	2,000
17.12.1996	4,000	10,000

In May 1999 there was a 1:5 rights issue at £5 per share which Richard took up in full.

On 4 October 2009, Richard sold 1,800 shares at £7.50 each.

He still works for the company and his holding comprises less than 1% of the shares in issue.

You are required to calculate the gain on the disposal.

11.6 Julio has been resident and ordinarily resident in the UK for the last five years but has retained his Spanish domicile.

He makes the following disposals during 2009/10:

Transaction	Proceeds £	Cost £
Holiday villa in Portugal	319,000	65,000
10,000 shares in CommandN Plc	195,600	see below

CommandN Plc is a quoted UK company. Julio had purchased 7,000 shares in August 2000 for £157,220, a further 8,000 shares for £132,720 in January 2005 and 5,000 shares for £97,050 on 19 April 2010. He sold the shares on 1 April 2010.

The proceeds and cost of the Portuguese villa are shown at their sterling equivalents on the relevant dates. Julio has not brought any of the proceeds from the disposal of the villa to the UK.

You are required to calculate Julio's capital gains tax liability assuming that he makes any beneficial claims

11.7 George had purchased 10,000 shares in Rover Ltd on 12 August 1981 for £24,000. On 31 March 1982 they were worth £27,200.

On 12 April 2002 there had been a bonus issue of one share for every 4 held. The market value of the shares at that date was £3.25 per share.

On 17 January 2010 Rover Ltd was taken over by Moggie Plc. George received 2 shares and £0.75p for every share held. The Moggie Plc shares were worth £8.95 per share immediately after the takeover.

George sold half of his shares the day after the takeover.

You are required to calculate George's total chargeable gain arising in 2009/10. You should assume that he has never worked for either company and has always held less than 5% of the shares.

12.1 Lionel purchased a Victoria Cross medal in May 1983 for £3,000 and a vintage car in June 1985 for £4,000. He sold them both to a collector in April 2009 for £14,780 and £15,500 respectively.

Lionel also sold a painting for £90 in December 2009 which had cost £6,260 in January 1983.

You are required to calculate Lionel's total chargeable gains for 2009/10.

12.2 In August 2009 Miranda, a trader, disposed of three assets on which capital allowances have been claimed.

	Purchase Price £	Disposal Proceeds £
Motor car	8,000	4,000
Machinery: item 1	5,500	7,500
Machinery: item 2	4,000	3,500

All assets were purchased in October 2007.

You are required to calculate Miranda's chargeable gain or allowable loss.

12.3 Adrienne acquired a 90-year lease on 31 March 1981 for £20,000. On 31 March 2010 she granted a sublease of 55 years for £30,000. The reversionary interest is valued at £82,500. The value of the lease at 31 March 1982 was £40,000.

Adrienne also acquired a freehold property for £30,000 in March 1991. In November 2009 she granted an 11-year lease for a premium of £10,000 at which time the reversionary interest was valued at £50,000.

You are required to calculate Adrienne's 2009/10 taxable gain.

12.4 Doug sold the following items on 1 August 2009:

(1) A Leonardo cartoon bought in March 1984 for £7,200 and sold for £5,500.

(2) A lathe bought for use in his business in March 1985 which cost £4,300. The sales proceeds were £10,500. Doug had claimed capital allowances on this asset.

You are required to calculate Doug's chargeable gains for 2009/10 before the annual exempt amount and assuming he made no other disposals in the year.

12.5 (1) Joe acquired an 80 year lease on a property for £28,000 on 29 July 1983. He assigned the lease on 29 July 2009 for £79,000.

(2) As (1) except that it was a 57 year lease when it was acquired.

You are required to calculate the chargeable gain which would arise in situation (1) and (2).

12.6 Harold acquired the freehold of a property for £25,000 on 1 May 1990. On 1 October 2009 he granted a 20 year lease on the premises for a premium of £20,000, the value of the reversion being £17,000.

Charles, a trader who has been in business for many years making up accounts annually to 31 January, was granted a 25 year lease of business premises on 1 September 2009 at a premium of £12,000 and an annual rent of £3,000 payable monthly in advance.

You are required to calculate Harold's capital gain and show the deductions to be made in respect of the lease in Charles's accounts to 31 January 2010.

12.7 Evelyn exercised an option over an antique table in August 2009. The option had been granted to her in September 1996 for £2,000 and the option price was £3,500. Evelyn sold the table at auction in February 2010 for £8,000. The auctioneers' costs were 10% of the sale price.

You are required to compute the chargeable gains arising in respect of the above events in 2009/10.

13.1 Neil sold a house on 30 June 2009. He realised an £80,000 gain before taking account of any PPR relief. The house was originally purchased on 1 October 1980 and was occupied by Neil until 30 June 1986 at which date he purchased and moved into another residence, letting the original house until the date of sale.

You are required to calculate the chargeable gain arising on the sale of the house.

13.2 Robert owned a property with three storeys of equal value in Sheffield. He bought it on 30 June 1986 for £20,000. He used the top two storeys as his main residence. The ground floor was rented out to students. The ground floor has a separate access door. On 30 November 2009 Robert sold the whole property for £200,000.

You are required to:

(a) Calculate Robert's chargeable gain on the sale of the property.

(b) Give three examples of periods which are deemed occupation for the CGT principal private residence exemption.

13.3 Mr and Mrs Mackay bought their family home for £150,000 in August 1998. It has been occupied by them since purchase and they are now planning to sell the property in May 2009 for £560,000.

The Mackays plan to use the proceeds to purchase two new properties in May 2009.

Country house – cost £400,000
Flat in town   – cost £175,000

Mr Mackay will live in the flat in town during the week and spend weekends at the country house. Mrs Mackay will live in the country house. Mr Mackay plans to retire in 5 years and at that stage they will sell the flat and move permanently into the country house.

You are required to explain:

(a)   the Capital Gains Tax implications of selling the current family home.

(b)   the Capital Gains Tax implication of residing in two homes and any actions the Mackays should consider.

(c)   the likely Capital Gains Tax implications of selling the flat in town in 5 years time, assuming it rises in value.

13.4 On 2 May 1984 Peter Stamp, a retired solicitor, bought a private dwelling-house for £70,000, which he sold for £270,000 under a contract dated 3 July 2009. The house was situated in grounds of one half of a hectare.

He lived in this house as his only residence until 1 February 1987. It was then let for residential purposes until 1 December 1996. From that date until the date of sale the property was unoccupied.

You are required to compute the chargeable gain arising on the sale of the house.

13.5 On 4 April 2010, Mr Sinclair sold his house for £380,200. The house was originally purchased on 6 April 1986 for £110,000 and was used as his principal residence until 5 April 1987. From 6 April 1987 until 5 April 1992 the house was empty while Mr Sinclair was working abroad. Mr Sinclair is an architect and has always been treated as self-employed from when he started to practise in 1973.

On his return to the UK in April 1992 he moved back into the house. In April 1993 the house was converted to a flat upstairs (which Mr Sinclair used as his residence) and offices downstairs from which he ran his practice. He moved out of the flat on 5 October 2007 and the flat was empty until the whole property was sold on 4 April 2010. The flat occupied exactly half of the property. Mr Sinclair continued to use the offices for his practice until shortly before the sale.

You are required to calculate Mr Sinclair's chargeable gain on the sale of his home.

14.1 Arthur made the following investments in qualifying EIS companies in September 2006 and claimed the maximum available income tax relief:

Company   *Amount subscribed*
Galadriel Ltd   £40,000
Guinevere Ltd   £50,000
Mordred Ltd   £30,000

In 2009/10 Arthur disposes of his shares as follows:

Company   *Date of Disposal*   *Proceeds*
Galadriel Ltd   June 2009   £35,000
Guinevere Ltd   October 2009   £95,000
Mordred Ltd   November 2009   £20,000

You are required to calculate:

–   the amount of income tax relief withdrawn in 2009/10 (if any) as a result of the disposals, and
–   the chargeable gains or allowable losses arising on disposal.

14.2 **You are required to identify (with brief explanations) whether EIS income tax relief would be available on the following investments, based on the information given:**

(a) An employee invests £20,000 in newly issued shares of his employer company, which is an unlisted trading company.

(b) Bob subscribes £100,000 for newly issued shares in Brown Plc, an AIM listed company. Three years later the company obtains a full listing on the London Stock Exchange, although this was not envisaged at the time of Bob's investment.

(c) Jane subscribes £400,000 for a 55% shareholding in Tarzan Ltd, a UK manufacturing company.

(d) Juliet invests £10,000 in Capulet Ltd, a property development company with operations in London and Manchester.

(e) Hilda subscribes £600,000 for a 25% shareholding in Wagner Ltd, a London based clothing retail company.

14.3 Lola sold a holiday cottage for £350,000 in December 2009, having bought it for £180,000 in June 2001. She has capital losses brought forward of £15,000. She invested £200,000 in shares in Montez Ltd, a qualifying EIS company, in June 2009.

You are required to calculate the optimum amount of EIS deferral relief she should claim, assuming that she makes no other disposals in 2009/10.

14.4 Alan had been trading as a sole trader for a number of years. On 1 May 2009 he sold his business as a going concern to Bernard for £350,000.

The value of the assets of the business and the capital gains at the date of the transfer were as follows:

	Market value £	Cost £
Freehold land and buildings	250,000	70,000
Goodwill	85,000	–
Machinery and equipment	3,000	4,000
Stock	6,000	6,000
Debtors	7,000	5,000
Creditors	(1,000)	–
	350,000	

The land and buildings were acquired in June 1999.

Calculate Alan's capital gains tax liability for 2009/10 assuming he makes any beneficial claims.

14.5 Monty has been a director of a trading company in which he owns 30% of the shares for the last 4 years. On 1 August 2009 he disposed of his 30% holding in the company for £1,800,000, realising a gain of £1,700,000.

On 1 November 2009 Monty sold a painting for £12,000. He had acquired the painting for £1,000 on 1 May 2000.

Monty had capital losses brought forward of £15,000.

Calculate Monty's taxable gain for 2009/10 assuming he makes any beneficial claims.

14.6 Freda has run her fishing tackle shop since 1987. She sold the whole business as a going concern on 12 August 2009, realising a gain of £1,110,000.

Freda had not previously claimed any entrepreneurs' relief and had losses brought forward of £12,750.

She makes one other disposal in the year realising a gain of £24,000 on an investment asset.

You are required to calculate Freda's capital gains tax liability and state the date by which any claim for entrepreneurs' relief must be made.

15.1 Brandon has bought a flat in Essex with a view to letting it out at a rate of £1,200 per month from November 2009 onwards.

You are required to explain:

(a) The notification requirements to HMRC for income tax purposes;

(b) The penalty which will arise in the event of late notification;

(c) Whether Brandon is eligible to submit a simplified return in respect of his rental income and what needs to be recorded on the return.

15.2 Phyllis was issued with a notice to make a 2009/10 tax return on 15 May 2010. She filed her return electronically on 31 August 2011 and paid the tax payable of £160 on the same date.

Phyllis's 2008/09 income tax payable amounted to £140.

You are required to advise Phyllis on:

(a) The due dates for submission of her 2009/10 tax return and payment of her 2009/10 income tax.

(b) Any penalties and interest which she owes, assuming a rate of interest on overdue tax of 2.5%.

15.3 **You are required to explain the two situations where CGT may be paid in instalments, highlighting:**

- **the due dates/period of instalments;**
- **the deadline for making the claim to pay tax in instalments;**

15.4 Alicia was issued with a notice to make a 2009/10 return on 20 April 2010 and submitted her return on 18 February 2011. In the past she has always filed her tax returns on time.

On 25 February 2012 she receives a notice from HMRC advising her that they are opening an enquiry into her 2009/10 return and requesting various documents relating to expenses she has claimed against her self-employment income. Alicia believes it is too late for HMRC to enquire into her return and request documents.

You are required to advise Alicia on:

(a) Whether HMRC are still within the deadline for opening an enquiry into her 2009/10 return;

(b) How long she is expected to retain documents relating to her business;

(c) Whether HMRC can re-open returns from any earlier tax years.

15.5 John's income tax and CGT position for 2008/09 is as follows:

	£
Income tax liability	10,250
Tax deducted at source	(5,000)
	5,250
Class 4 NIC	1,000
CGT liability	8,200
Payments on account made re 2008/09	(5,000)
	9,450

You are required to:

(a) Calculate John's payments on account for 2009/10 stating the due dates.

(b) Explain what action John may take if he knows that his self-employment income will be significantly less in 2009/10 than in 2008/09 and any interest implications involved.

15.6 Ray's payments on account for 2009/10 based on his income tax liability for 2008/09 were £4,500 each. However when he submitted his 2008/09 income tax return in January 2010 he made a claim to reduce the payments on account for 2009/10 to £3,500 each. The first payment on account was made on 29 January 2010, and the second on 12 August 2010.

Ray filed his 2009/10 tax return in December 2009. The return showed that his tax liabilities for 2009/10 (before deducting payments on account) were income tax £10,000, capital gains tax £2,500. Ray paid the balance of tax due of £5,500 on 19 February 2011.

You are required to identify the time periods and amount(s) of tax on which interest will be charged.

15.7 Tabitha's income tax, NIC and CGT position for 2008/09 was as follows:

	£
Income tax liability	17,895
Class 4 NIC liability	2,808
CGT liability	32,455
Payments on account for 2008/09	15,500
Tax deducted at source	1,275

You are required to calculate the following:

(1) Tabitha's first payment on account for 2009/10.

(2) The interest and any other penalties due assuming Tabitha had paid her first payment on account on 25 May 2010.

Assume that the interest rate is 2.5% throughout 2009/10.

Ignore any balancing payment of tax for 2008/09.

Your answer should be to the nearest pound.

16.1 Tina commenced employment with Harrison Electrics Ltd on 1 November 2009. She was paid a salary of £1,000 per month and from 1 January 2010, was given the use of a new Ford Escort 1400cc with a list price of £15,000 with all private petrol paid for by the company. The emission rate is 170g/km.

You are required to calculate Tina's earnings for income tax purposes and the NIC payable by Tina and Harrison Electrics Ltd in respect of her 2009/10 remuneration.

16.2 Ruth is an director of Benson Ltd and earns a salary of £45,000 pa. Benson Ltd have loaned her £20,000 so she can redecorate her house. As at 5 April 2009 there was an outstanding balance of £15,000. On 5 January 2010 Ruth repaid a further £5,000. Ruth pays Benson Ltd interest at 3% pa on the loan. Assume that the official rate of interest throughout 2009/10 is 4.75%.

You are required to calculate the amount of Class 1 secondary and Class 1A contributions payable by Benson Ltd for 2009/10.

16.3 Natalie is a receptionist at Hospitality Hotel. She was provided with the use of a dinner set by the hotel on 6 October 2008. Its market value at that date was £2,000. On 6 October 2009 the hotel agreed to sell the dinner set to Natalie for £1,000, its market value at that date was £1,500.

You are required to calculate the Class 1A payable by Natalie's employer for 2009/10, stating the due date.

16.4 Judy is a director of Markham Ltd. She earns £25,750 pa and is provided with a company owned flat. The flat cost the company £60,000 when it was bought in 1994. Judy moved in 2001 when the flat had a market value of £100,000. The annual value of the flat is £3,000. Markham Ltd also pays for Judy's telephone bills, this costs the company £400 pa. Judy is also provided with furniture for use in her flat. The market value of the furniture was £2,500 in 2001.

Assume that the official rate of interest throughout 2009/10 is 4.75%.

You are required to calculate the NIC payable by Judy and Markham Ltd in respect of her 2009/10 remuneration.

16.5 The following people work for Dickens Ltd and are paid monthly:

Pip – a salesman who earns a salary of £28,000 pa with a bonus of £4,000 paid in August 2009.

Estella – a secretary who earned £16,000 pa up to 30 September 2009 and had a pay increase to £18,000 from 1 October 2009 onwards.

You are required to calculate the Class 1 primary contributions for 2009/10 payable by the above individuals and state the due date for payment.

16.6 **You are required to advise what types of NIC will be payable by Madison Plc and/or its employees in respect of the following remuneration in 2009/10. You should also state the due dates in each case.**

(a) Anna (age 67) works part-time for the company and earns a salary of £17,000 pa.

(b) Elaine, a manager, receives use of a company car and obtains reimbursement of the cost of her season ticket for Spurs football club.

(c) At Christmas the company provides a number of employees with a bottle of Champagne as a gift. Madison Plc has agreed with HMRC to settle the employees' personal tax liabilities in respect of these gifts.

16.7 Robert earns an annual salary of £65,000.

During 2009/10 his benefits, and expenses paid by his employer, were as follows:

	£
Mileage payments – 8,000 business miles	4,000
Other business related travel expenses	12,500
Interest free loan to purchase season ticket	1,784
Private medical insurance (contracted for by his employer)	450
Professional subscription	220
M&S vouchers	500
Gym membership (reimbursed by his employer)	1,020

You are required to calculate the total NIC due from Robert and his employer for 2009/10.

Your answer should be to the nearest pound.

17.1 Brash Ltd has 75 employees, who all earn in excess of £10,000 per annum. It provides a number of its employees with company cars which they are able to use for private purposes.

You are required to state which year end PAYE returns for 2009/10 Brash Ltd is required to submit and to state their due filing dates..

17.2 In 2009/10 Auster Ltd provided the following to a number of its employees, who all earned in excess of £8,500 p.a.

(1) Emily was made redundant by the company in May 2009. The company paid her statutory redundancy pay of £3,000 and an ex-gratia payment of £29,000.

(2) Patrick works in one of the company's restaurants. In 2009/10 he received tips of £1,000 directly from customers which the company allowed him to keep.

(3) Paul was provided with childcare vouchers of £50 per week.

You are required to explain whether Auster Ltd should apply PAYE to the above remuneration.

Solutions to exam style questions

1.1 Roger

	£
Allowances:	
Personal allowance (65 or over)	9,490
Restricted : ½ × (23,980 – 22,900)	(540)
PA	8,950
Blind person's allowance	1,890
Tax reductions:	
Married couple's allowance (75 or over, given based on age of older spouse) (relief restricted to 10%)	6,965

Vicky

PA (>75)	9,640

Some of this is being wasted as Vicky has income of only £4,500.

Roger's allowances have been restricted due to high net income. In order to maximise the benefit of allowances the interest generating bank account and/or the rental property could be held in joint names, leading to a 50:50 split of income for tax purposes. Splitting the rental property would be the most beneficial, as it would lead to £2,440 of the interest being taxed on Roger at the starting rate of 10%.

1.2 Charles

INCOME TAX COMPUTATION 2009/10

	Non-savings income £
Earnings	59,500
Less: qualifying interest (8% × 6,250)	(500)
Less: PA	(6,475)
Taxable income	52,525
Tax thereon:	

£		£
52,400 (W) @ 20%		10,480
125 @ 40%		50
Tax liability		10,530
Tax suffered at source (PAYE)		(13,800)
Tax repayable		(3,270)

Working.

Basic rate band extended by gross donation, ie (£12,000 × 100/80) = £15,000

1.3

	£
Trade profits	7,700
Discretionary trust income (£1,650 × 100/60)	2,750
	10,450
Less PA	(9,640)
Taxable income	810
Tax @ 20%	162
Less MCA (£6,965 × 2/12 × 10%)	(116)
Tax liability	46
Less tax deducted (£2,750 × 40%)	(1,100)
Repayable	(1,054)

Income from a discretionary trust comes with 40% tax credit.

Note: Interest on an ISA is exempt.

1.4

	Non savings income £	Dividend income £
Earnings	34,000	
Dividend income (£1,800 × 100/90)		2,000
Lottery winnings (exempt)	–	
	34,000	2,000
Less: PA	(6,475)	
Taxable income	27,525	2,000

Tax thereon:
£

	£
27,525 @ 20%	5,505
2,000 @ 10%	200
	5,705
Less: EIS IT relief (20,000 × 20%)	(4,000)
Tax liability	1,705
Less: PAYE	(7,200)
tax credit on dividends	(200)
IT repayable	(5,695)

Note: Legacy is capital and therefore excluded from the income tax computation.

Treatment of dividends

Income of a child (<18) arising out of a gift by her parents is treated as the income of the parent for income tax purposes, assuming that the income exceeds £100 gross per annum.

The dividends received by Philippa will not be taxed on Julie as Philippa is aged over 18.

1.5 (a) The value of the shares (£10,000) at the time of the gift may be deducted from the donor's gross total income.

(b) Interest on a loan to buy plant and machinery for use in a partnership is only deductible for three years from the end of the tax year in which the loan is taken out – hence, no deduction is available in this case.

(c) The royalties paid are grossed up by $^{100}/_{80}$ and deducted from the payer's total income. The basic rate tax of £390 must be added back to the payer's income tax liability.

(d) The donation is made net of 20% basic rate tax. Higher rate tax relief is given by extending the basic rate band by the gross donation of £2,500.

(e) Tax relief is only given for maintenance payments where the payer or recipient was born before 6 April 1935 – therefore, no relief is available here.

2.1 Mr Fairbanks

INCOME TAX COMPUTATION 2009/10

		Non-savings income £	Savings income £	Dividend income £
Earnings		6,000		
Dividends received	(£900 × $\frac{100}{90}$)			1,000
Building society interest	(£800 × $\frac{100}{80}$)		1,000	
Bank deposit interest	(£80 × $\frac{100}{80}$)		100	
Net income		6,000	1,100	1,000
Less: PA		(6,000)	(475)	
Taxable income		nil	625	1,000

Tax: £
£625 @ 10% 62
£1,000 @ 10% 100
Tax liability 162
Less: Tax suffered at source
    notional credit on dividend (100)
    Interest (£1,100 @ 20%) (220)
    PAYE (250)
Tax repayable (408)

2.2 Jonty

INCOME TAX COMPUTATION 2009/10

	Non-savings income £	Savings income £	Dividend income £
Earnings	45,000		
Building society interest £(80 × $\frac{100}{80}$)		100	
Dividends £(63 × $\frac{100}{90}$)			70
NS&I interest		142	
Net income	45,000	242	70
Less: PA	(6,475)		
Taxable income	38,525	242	70

Tax:
  £ £
37,400 @ 20% 7,480
  495 @ 20% (W) 99
  630 @ 40% = 252
  242 @ 40% = 97
   70 @ 32.5% = 23
Tax liability 7,951
Less: notional credit on dividend (7)
Less: tax suffered at source £(20 + 7,400) (7,420)
Tax payable 524

Working

Basic rate threshold extended by gross donation ie (£396 × 100/80) = £495

Note. Betting income is exempt.

2.3

	Non-savings income £	Savings income £	
Property income	23,900		
Interest (£4,400 × 100/80)		5,500	
Gilt interest		290	
Net income	23,900	5,790	Total = £29,690
Less: PAA (W1)	(6,475)		
Taxable income	17,425	5,790	

	£
Tax £17,425 @ 20%	3,485
£5,790 @ 20%	1,158
	4,643
Less: Married couples' allowance (W)	(674)
Tax liability	3,969
Less: Tax deducted:	
Interest	(1,100)
Tax payable	2,869

Working

	£
PAA (>75)	9,640
Less: ½ £(29,690 – 22,900) = £3,395	
Max 'restriction' £(9,640 – 6,475)	(3,165)
Allowance given	6,475
Unused restriction (£3,395 – 3,165)	230
MCAA (over 75)	6,965
Less: unused restriction	(230)
	6,735

Tax reducer @ 10% = 674

2.4

	Non-savings income £	Savings income £	Dividend income £
Trade profits	34,000		
UK dividends (£8,000 × 100/90)			8,889
Jersey bank interest		4,300	
Total income	34,000	4,300	8,889
Less: interest relief (W1)	(827)		
Net income	33,173	4,300	8,889
Less: personal allowance	(6,475)		
Taxable income	26,698	4,300	8,889

		£
Tax	£26,698 @ 20%	5,340
	£4,300 @ 20%	860
	£6,402 @ 10%	640
	£2,000 @ 10% (W2)	200
	£487 @ 32½ %	158
		7,198
Less: tax deducted on dividends		(889)
Tax payable		6,309

Workings

1 *Loan interest relief*

	£
£24,000 × 4% × 8/12	640
£14,000 × 4% × 4/12	187
	827

2 *Basic rate band extension:*

Gross gift aid donation £1,600 × 100/80 = £2,000

Notes: Premium Bond winnings are tax free.

2.5 Mildred

TAX COMPUTATION ON 2009/10

	Non-savings income £	Savings income £	Dividend income £
State pension	11,047		
Guernsey bank interest		13,450	
Dividends (£720 × 100/90 – see note)			800
Net income	11,047	13,450	800 Total = £25,297
Less: PAA (W1)	(8,754)		
Taxable income	2,293	13,450	800

	£
Tax: £2,293 @ 20%	459
£147 @ 10%	15
£13,303 @ 20%	2,661
£800 @ 10%	80
Tax liability	3,215
Less: Tax deducted:	
Dividends	(80)
Tax payable	3,135

Note. Mildred is taxed on the cash alternative to the stock dividend as this differs from the value of shares by less than 15%.

Workings

1 *Personal age allowance*

	£
PAA (>75)	9,640
Less: ½ £(24,672 – 22,900) (W2)	(886)
PAA given	8,754

2 *Adjusted net income*

	£
Actual net income	25,297
Less: gross donation to charity (£500 × 100/80)	(625)
Adjusted net income for age allowance purposes	24,672

Note. Do not need to extend the basic rate band as Mildred is not a higher rate taxpayer.

2.6 Loan

The company must pay tax of £20,000 (i.e. £80,000 × 25%) to HMRC by 1 October 2008.

The making of the loan has no tax consequences for Sylvia.

Write-off

The company will obtain a refund of the tax of £20,000 previously paid.

Sylvia will be treated as having received a gross dividend of £88,889 (i.e. £80,000 × 100/90). This will be taxable at 32.5%, less a notional tax credit of 10% of £8,889. The dividend should be included in her 2009/10 tax return and the income tax will be payable by 31 January 2011.

2.7

	Non Savings £	Savings £	Dividends £
Earnings	2,080		
Dividends: £122,850 × 100/90			136,500
Treasury stock interest		54,650	
Bank interest: £1,300 × 100/80		1,625	
NS&I account interest		600	
Total	2,080	56,875	136,500
Less: PA	(2,080)	(4,395)	
Taxable income	Nil	52,480	136,500
£2,440 @ 10%	244		
£34,960 @ 20%	6,992		
£12,500 @ 20% (W)	2,500		
£2,580 @ 40%	1,032		
£136,500 @ 32.5%	44,362		
Tax liability	55,130		
Less: Tax paid/ suffered			
Dividends £136,500 @ 10%	(13,650)		
Interest £1,625 @ 20%	(325)		
Tax payable	41,155		

Note: NS&I certificate is exempt from income tax

Working - Extension of basic rate band

Gift aid donation: £10,000 × 100/80 = £12,500

3.1

	£
Gross rents (£1,500 × 12) (accruals basis)	18,000
Less: Agent's fees	1,800
Interest (£60,000 × 7%)	4,200
Water rates	120
Insurance	500
Wear and tear allowance ((18,000 − 120) × 10%)	1,788
Property income	9,592

Tax relief may be obtained for the cost of furnishing a rental property in two ways:

(i) an annual 'wear and tear' allowance may be claimed, equal to 10% of rental income (less water rates and council tax if paid by the landlord), or

(ii) under the 'renewals basis', the cost of replacing items of furniture may be deducted.

Note: The cost of the new porch is capital and therefore not allowable.

3.2 The letting will meet the 'Furnished Holiday Letting' definition provided it is let furnished on a commercial basis and:

(i) it is available for letting at least 140 days in the year and actually let for at least 70 days, and
(ii) not more than 155 days may fall during periods of longer term occupation. Longer term occupation is a continuous period of more than 31 days during which the accommodation is in the same occupation.

Based on the facts given, it appears likely that Lizzie's cottage will qualify.

Capital allowances may be claimed on the cost of furnishings. In the year of expenditure, an annual investment allowance at 100% of £10,000 may be claimed.

Lizzie may claim the same losses as a trader – she may offset a 2009/10 loss against her other general income in 2009/10 and/or 2008/09. She may alternatively carry back the loss against her general income of 2006/07, 2007/08 and 2008/09. Finally, the loss may be carried forward against future profits from the letting business.

Lizzie should be aware that the favourable tax treatment for furnished holiday lettings has been withdrawn for 2010/11 onwards.

3.3

	Property A £	Property B £	Property C £
Rent	620	284 (W)	100
Agent's commission	(20)		
Advertising for tenants		(76)	
Repairs	(142)	(255)	(119)
Profit/(loss)	458	(47)	(19)

	£
Profit on A	458
Less loss on B and C	(66)
Property income assessment	392

Working

	£
April – Sept ($\frac{6}{12} \times £348$)	174
Dec – March ($\frac{3}{12} \times £440$)	110
	284

3.4 Property income:

	A £	B £
Income (3/12 × £2,400 + 6/12 × £1,600)	1,400	
(9/12 × £600)		450
Expenditure:		
Agent's commission:		
1.5.09	(25)	(10)
1.11.09	(25)	(10)
Repairs	–	(1,500)
Advertising	(50)	–
	1,300	(1,070)
Net rents		£230

Note. Installation of new kitchen equipment is a capital *not* a revenue expense.

Lease premium:

	£
Premium	5,000
Less: 2% × (10 – 1) × £5,000	(900)
Taxed as property income	4,100

Note The property income element of the lease premium may also be calculated using the formula: [s.277 ITTOIA 2005]

Premium paid × $\dfrac{50 - Y}{50}$ = Assessable property income

Y = the duration of the lease in complete years, ignoring the first year

Total property income assessment £230 + £4,100 = **£4,330**

3.5 (a)

October 1999 premium

	£
Premium	20,000
Less capital element:	
2% × (30 – 1) × 20,000	(11,600)
	8,400

Therefore, Brian's annual deductions amount to: £8,400 ÷ 30 years = £280 p.a.

October 2009 premium

	£
Premium received by Brian	8,000
Less capital element:	
2% × (5 – 1) × 8,000	(640)
	7,360
Less allowable deductions:	
£280 × 5 years	(1,400)
	5,960

(b)

Claire's allowable deductions

	£
Premium paid by Claire	8,000
Less capital element:	
2% × (5 – 1) × 8,000	(640)
	7,360

Therefore, Claire may claim a deduction from her trading income of £7,360 ÷ 5 yrs = £1,472 per annum for a period of 5 years.

This is time-apportioned in 2009/10 (year ended 31.12.09):

Deduction = £1,472 × 3/12 = **£368**

3.6 (a) The normal basis would be to assess Judy on her rental income less allowable expenses as follows:

	£
Rent (£600 × 12)	7,200
Less allowable expenses:	
Electricity	(1,200)
Gas	(1,400)
Wear & tear allowance (10% × 7,200)	(720)
	3,880

The alternative basis, for which Judy may elect would be to assess her on rental income less the 'rent a room' exemption (ignoring actual expenses):

	£
Rent	7,200
Less rent-a-room exemption	(4,250)
	2,950

(b) It will be more beneficial for Judy to elect for the alternative basis in 2009/10.

The deadline for the election for 2009/10 is 31 January 2012. The election will remain in force for future tax years unless it is withdrawn.

3.7 Seraphina is assessable on the net rental income for the period 1 June 2009 – 5 April 2010 as well as the income proportion of the lease premium.

	£
Rental income (W1)	3,896
Lease premium (W2)	36,000
2008/09 property income	39,896

Workings

(1) Rental income

	£
Rent (1.7.09 – 5.4.10): 9/12 × £42,000	31,500
Less: management fee: 15% × £31,500	(4,725)
Less: interest 5.25% × £685,000 × 50% × 10/12	(14,984)
Less: repairs	(7,895)
Net rental income	3,896

(2) Lease premium

	£
Premium	50,000
Less: capital element: 2% × (15-1) × £50,000	(14,000)
Income element	36,000

3.8 The grant of a lease for a premium is a disposal for CGT purposes.

This is the grant of a short lease (≤ 50 years) from a freehold so we need to use a modified part disposal formula:

	£
Capital element of premium (W)	14,000
Less: cost: $\dfrac{14,000}{50,000 + 565,000} \times £685,000$	(15,593)
Allowable loss	(1,593)

(W) Lease premium

	£
Premium	50,000
Less: capital element: 2% × (15-1) × £50,000	(14,000)
Income element	36,000

4.1

	Non savings Income £	Dividends £
Income :		
Employment income	95,000	
Dividends (3,000 × $\frac{100}{90}$)		3,333
Personal allowance	(6,475)	
Taxable income	88,525	3,333
Tax thereon:		
£37,400 @ 20%	7,480	
£51,125 @ 40%	20,450	
3,333 @ 32.5	1,083	
	29,013	
Less: EIS relief [Notes]		
(50,000 × 20%)	(10,000)	
Tax liability	19,013	
Less tax credits:		
Dividends	(333)	
PAYE	(27,000)	
IT repayable	(8,320)	

Notes:

(1) Patricia can claim to treat her 2010/11 EIS investment of £30,000 as if it were made in 2009/10.

(2) Interest on NS&I Certificates is exempt.

4.2 (a) An ISA may contain investments in cash and in stocks and shares (also including life insurance). The maximum subscription in 2009/10, for an individual who is less than 50 years old, is £7,200 pa overall, with no more than £3,600 pa in cash.

(b) Income and gains are both tax free within the ISA.

(c) The investor must be aged at least 18 (or 16 for a cash only ISA) and UK resident and ordinarily resident.

4.3 Any gain arising as a result of withdrawing funds from an ISA account is exempt from CGT.

LiteHead Ltd appears to be an EIS company. As a result, Maggie would have obtained income tax relief (at 20%) on making the investment, which will be withdrawn on the disposal (at the same rate) as sale takes place within three years of acquisition.

As the shares are sold at a gain, albeit within 3 years of their acquisition, the gain is calculated as normal ie ignoring any remaining EIS relief

	£
Proceeds £4.50 × 12,500	56,250
Less: cost	(12,500)
Gain	43,750

5.1

	£
Statutory redundancy pay	3,800
Ex-gratia cash payment	45,000
MV of car	12,000
Outplacement counselling (exempt)	–
	60,800
Less exempt amount	(30,000)
	30,800
Less foreign service exemption	
$(30,800 \times {}^{10}\!/_{30})$	(10,267)
Taxable	£20,533

5.2 Earnings:

	£
Salary	10,000
Car (£16,000 × 28%)	4,480
Second car (£12,000 × 20%)**	2,400
Fuel (16,900 × 28%)	4,732
Cost of wine	1,000
Earnings	22,612
Less: expenses	(600)
	22,012

The second car is assessed on Jim because his daughter receives it by virtue of *his* employment, not hers (would you expect a company car if you just worked on Saturdays?)

* $\dfrac{200 - 135}{5} = 13\%$ 15% + 13% = 28%

** $\dfrac{160 - 135}{5} = 5\%$ 15% + 5% = 20% (*Note.* Round down the emissions to 160)

5.3 Earnings – 2009/10

	£
Salary	30,000
Accommodation (W1)	1,925
Related expenses (W1)	4,950
	36,875

Workings

1   *Accommodation*

	£
Annual value	750
Additional charge: 4.75% × £(125,000 – 75,000)	2,375
less employee contribution	(1,200)
	1,925

Mr Thomas occupied the property for the first time more than 6 years after it was purchased in 1995, therefore the additional charge is based on the market value of the property when first occupied, not on cost plus alterations carried out prior to occupation.

Related expenses

	£
Household bills – light, heat, telephone £(750 + 250 + 350)	1,350
Council tax	1,400
Redecoration	700
Gardener	1,500
	4,950

5.4 (1) *Cheap taxable loan*

Average basis: $\dfrac{(10{,}000 + 9{,}000)}{2} \times \dfrac{10}{12} \times 4.75\% = \underline{£376}$

		£
Strict basis:	£10,000 × 2/12 × 4.75%	79
	£15,000 × 4/12 × 4.75%	237
	£7,500 × 2/12 × 4.75%	59
	£11,500 × 1/12 × 4.75%	46
	£9,000 × 1/12 × 4.75%	36
		457

HMRC may insist on the strict basis, although in practice the difference might be considered insignificant.

(2) *Cars*

Mercedes: £21,500 × 18% = £3,870 $\left(\dfrac{150-135}{5}\right) = 3 + 15 = 18\%$

Escort: £10,000 × 21% × 8/12 = £1,400 $\left(\dfrac{165-135}{5}\right) = 6 + 15 = 21\%$

5.5 Earnings

	£	£
Salary		32,600
Expenses allowance:		
Gross allowance (N1)	2,500	
Less business travel	(1,800)	
		700
		33,300
Benefits:		
Hi-fi equipment £(800 × 20%) (N2)	160	
Car £(15,000 × 24%) (N3)	3,600	
Medical insurance (N4)	300	
Clothing (N4)	400	
		4,460
Amount chargeable as earnings		37,760

Notes

(1) The expenses allowance is taxable, but Alf can claim the cost of business travel as an allowable deduction. Entertainment of clients is not deductible as this would not have been deductible for his employer.

(2) The annual value of the hi-fi equipment subject to tax is 20% of its cost.

(3) The emission rate is 45g/km greater than 135g/km. The percentage is 15% + 45/5% = 24%.

(4) The taxable value of the medical insurance and clothing is the cost to the company of providing the benefits.

5.6 Mr Bjork's benefits

	£	£	£
Jaguar: car (£20,000 × 32% × 4/12) (W1)			2,133
petrol (£16,900 × 32% × 4/12) (W1)			1,803
Mercedes: no private use (all business use)			–
Use of computer £6,000 × 20% × 6/12			600
Gift of compute			
Market value at acquisition		200	
Original market value	6,000		
Less assessed in respect of use:			
- 2007/08: £6,000 × 20% × 6/12	(600)		
- 2008/09: £6,000 × 20%	(1,200)		
- 2009/10: as above	(600)		
		3,600	3,600
Total benefits			8,136

Working

$$\left(\frac{220-135}{5}\right) = 17 + 15 = 32\%$$

5.7 EARNINGS INCOME FOR 2009/10

	£	£
Salary:		
April – June (3/12 × £31,000)	7,750	
July – March (9/12 × £36,000)	27,000	
		34,750
Bonus – paid in year		4,000
		38,750
Accommodation:		
Higher of (i) Rent paid £5,000 × 9/12 = £3,750	3,750	
(ii) Annual value 2,400 × 9/12 = £1,800		
Less contribution (£100 × 9 months)	(900)	
		2,850
		41,600
Less: pension contribution (covered in Chapter 7) (5% × £38,750)		(1,938)
Earnings		39,662

Note. Employers' contributions of up to £55 per week towards childcare provision are tax free therefore the £100 monthly payment is not taxable.

5.8

	£	£
Salary		30,000
Crèche [(200 – 55) × 52]		7,540
Parking space (exempt)		–
Mileage:		
Amount received (5,000 × 60p)	3,000	
Less authorised amount (5,000 × 40p)	(2,000)	
		1,000
		38,540
Less allowable deduction (club subscription)		(800)
Earnings		37,740

Note: Golf subscription is not allowable deduction.

5.9 *Employment income:*

	£
Salary: £52,000 × 8/12	34,667
Company car (W1) 25% × £23,000 × 8/12	3,833
Fuel 25% × £16,900 × 8/12	2,817
Termination package (W2)	13,990
Employment income:	55,307

Workings

(1) *Company car*

(189-135)/5 + 15% = 25%

(2) *Redundancy package*

	£	£	£
PILON			13,000
Discretionary payment		28,000	
Statutory redundancy		990	
Car	10,000		
Less: payment	(8,000)		
		2,000	
		30,990	
Less: exemption		(30,000)	
			990
Taxable			13,990

6.1

	Non savings income £	Savings £
Salary	60,000	
Exercise of EMI option (note)	5,000	
NS&I a/c interest		1,500
Net income	65,000	1,500
Personal allowance	(6,475)	
Taxable income	58,525	1,500
Tax thereon:		
£37,400 @ 20%	7,480	
£21,125 @ 40%	8,450	
£1,500 @ 40%	600	
	16,530	
Less PAYE	(15,000)	
IT payable	1,530	

Note: There are no income tax consequences at the time of grant of the option.

However, as the option was granted at a discount, there will be an income tax charge at the date of exercise on the amount of the discount i.e. 10,000 × (£2 − £1.50) = £5,000.

6.2 (a) If the scheme has been approved then there are no tax consequences on the grant or exercise of the options.

When Sue comes to sell the shares she will have a chargeable gain as follows:

	£
Sale proceeds = 5,000 × £10.40	52,000
Cost = 5,000 × £4.00	(20,000)
Gain	32,000

(b) As the scheme is unapproved, an employment income charge will arise on the exercise of the option as follows:

	£
Market value at date of exercise	10.00
Less exercise price	(3.00)
	7.00 per share

£7.00 × 5,000 shares = £35,000

Sale of shares

	£
Sale proceeds	52,000
Cost = MV at date of exercise	(50,000)
Chargeable gain	2,000

6.3 (i) As income tax charge would arise on the date of acquisition of the shares on the difference between the market value of the shares and the price paid.

i.e. 10,000 × (£5 − £2) = £30,000

(ii) There would be no income tax charge on grant of the option.

On exercise, there would be an income tax charge on the difference between the market value of the shares and the exercise price:

i.e. 10,000 × (£8 − £2) = £60,000

(iii) There would be no income tax charge on acquisition of the preference shares, as Sharon is paying market value for them.

On conversion of the preference shares, there would be an income tax charge on the difference between the market value of the preference shares and the ordinary shares.

i.e. 10,000 × (£8 − £2) = £60,000

6.4 These are unapproved share options, as Janet already holds options over shares worth £30,000 (the maximum in a CSOP scheme).

The difference between the exercise price (plus the cost of the options) and the market value at the exercise date is subject to income tax. The market value at the date of exercise is the base cost for CGT purposes.

Grant – no tax consequences

Exercise

	£
Market value at exercise: 5,000 × £12.50	62,500
Less: Exercise price: 5,000 × £2.75	(13,750)
Less: cost of options: 5,000 × 0.12p	(600)
Specific employment income	48,150
Tax @ 40%	19,260

Sale

	£
Proceeds: 5,000 × £13.95	69,750
Less cost (MV at exercise)	(62,500)
Chargeable gain	7,250
Less: Annual exempt amount	(10,100)
Taxable gain	Nil

7.1

	£
Earnings:	
Salary/bonuses	380,000
Medical insurance	1,500
Company car	12,000
Free parking (exempt)	–
Less: subscription	(500)
Relevant earnings	393,000

Jeremy can pay up to 100% of his earnings (i.e. £393,000) and obtain tax relief. He would pay 80% (i.e. £314,400) to the pension fund and the fund would reclaim 20% (£78,600) from HMRC.

However, as Jeremy would by paying more than the annual allowance of £245,000 into his pension, he will have to pay 40% on the excess:

40% × £148,000 = £59,200

7.2 (a) **Maximum contributions**

Ed and Joan can contribute any amount to their pension regardless of the level of their earnings. However tax relief will only be given for contributions up to the level of their earnings for the tax year.

The partnership profits for 2009/10 of £175,000 split 4:1 gives Ed earnings of £140,000 and Joan £35,000. Therefore Ed could contribute a maximum of £140,000 and Joan £35,000 and receive tax relief on their contributions.

They cannot obtain relief for 2008/09 as contributions cannot be carried back to a previous tax year.

(b) **Tax relief**

Basic rate tax relief is given through the pension holder paying contributions net of 20%. This means that they pay only 80% of the gross payment into the pension. HMRC pays the extra 20% on their behalf to the pension provider.

Ed will pay £112,000 (£140,000 × 80%) and Joan will pay £28,000 (£35,000 × 80%).

In addition Ed will be entitled to higher rate tax relief. This is given by extending the basic rate band for the tax year by the amount of the gross contribution ie £37,400 + £140,000 = £177,400.

(c) **No earnings**

There is no need for the individual to have earnings. Tax relief is available for a contribution of up to £3,600 per tax year into a pension regardless of the level of earnings.

7.3 INCOME TAX COMPUTATION 2009/10

	Non-savings income £
Earnings (W1)	54,871
Less: Personal allowance	(6,475)
Taxable income	48,396
Tax thereon:	
£39,650 @ 20% (W1)	7,930
£8,746 @ 40%	3,498
Tax liability	11,428
Less: tax deducted:	
PAYE	(6,000)
Tax due	5,428

Workings

1. *Earnings*

	£
Salary	
(£40,000 × 9/12)	30,000
(£44,000 × 3/12)	11,000
	41,000
Bonuses (note 1)	
Awarded 30.9.09	6,881
Awarded 31.3.10	6,990
Pension contributions by employer	Exempt
Total	54,871

2. *Personal pension contributions*

Dwaine pays £150 × 12	£1,800
× $\frac{100}{80}$	£2,250

Basic rate threshold: £37,400 + £2,250 = £39,650

Note: Bonus becomes taxable in the year in which a director is *entitled* to the payment (even if this is before actual receipt).

7.4 Alfred's earned income includes his salary, benefits and the FHL rental income. He can make contributions to his pension up to this amount. However, as this exceeds the annual allowance he will suffer a clawback charge at 40%.

	Non Savings £	Savings £	Dividends £
Earnings	244,000		
Rental income (incl FHL)	43,000		
Bank interest: £112,500 × 100/80 ÷ 2		70,313	
Dividends: £363,330 × 100/90			403,700
Total	287,000	70,313	403,700
Less: PA	(6,475)		
Taxable income	280,525	70,313	403,700
£37,400 @ 20%	7,480		
£269,000 @ 20% (W1)	53,800		
£44,438 @ 40%	17,775		
£403,700 @ 32.5%	131,202		
Tax liability	210,257		
Less: Tax paid/ suffered			
Dividends £403,700 @ 10%	(40,370)		
Interest £70,313 @ 20%	(14,063)		
	155,824		
Add: pension charge (W2)	9,600		
Tax payable	165,424		

Workings

(1) *Extension of basic rate band*

Pension contribution:

£244,000 + £25,000 (FHL) = £269,000

(2) *Pension tax charge*

	£
Contribution (above)	269,000
Less: annual allowance	(245,000)
Excess	24,000
Tax @ 40%	9,600

8.1 Mr Garcia will be resident and ordinarily resident but non-domiciled in the UK. Therefore, any UK income will be taxed on an arising basis, but he may claim the remittance basis for his overseas income. If he claims the remittance basis he will not be subject to the £30,000 remittance basis charge until he has been resident in the UK for at least 7 of the 9 preceding tax years. He will lose entitlement to the personal allowance.

(1) **The pension**

If Mr Garcia claims for the remittance basis to apply, the pension income will be taxable only when remitted to the UK. However, if he does not make a claim only 90% of the income from his Spanish pension will be taxable in the UK.

As it appears that he is planning to bring all of the pension income into the UK, he may decide not to make the claim for the remittance basis so that he is only taxed on 90% of the income. In this case, the income will be taxed at 20% and 40%.

(2) **Investment income**

If Mr Garcia makes a claim for the remittance basis to apply, his Spanish bank account interest and dividends will only be taxable when he brings the funds into the UK. It will be taxed as non-savings income, so even the dividends will be taxed at 40%.

Remittance planning

Assuming that Mr Garcia makes a claim for the remittance basis to apply to his overseas income, he should have any overseas income arising after he comes to the UK paid into a bank account in Spain separate from his existing savings. He can then bring his previous savings into the UK without giving rise to income tax, as this does not represent income arising while resident in the UK.

8.2 (a) Marco has become resident and ordinarily resident in the UK. However, he remains domiciled in Italy as he has not severed ties with his country of origin.

(b) As Marco came to the UK to take up an employment which is expected to last at least two years, he may by concession split the tax year of his arrival and be treated as a resident in the UK from the date of his arrival – i.e. from 5 August 2008.

(c) *Taxable income*

	£
Total employment earnings	80,200
Amount relating to the UK duties (80%)	64,160
Amounted enjoyed in the UK (£60,000 + £5,200)	65,200
Income from employment	65,200
Interest (£35 × $^{100}/_{80}$)	44
	65,244
Less PA	-
Taxable income	65,244

Marco is non-domiciled in the UK and can claim to be taxed on the remittance basis on his foreign income. He will not be subject to the £30,000 remittance basis charge as he has not been resident in the UK for 7 years of the preceding 9 tax years.

Individuals who claim the remittance basis are not entitled to a personal allowance.

8.3 (a) After 4 years of making regular visits to the UK which average 91 days or more per tax year, Steffen is then treated as resident from the start of the fifth tax year.

By the end of 2008/09 average visits from the last 4 tax years amount to:

(75 + 98 + 92 + 104) / 4 = 92.25

Hence, Steffen will be treated as a UK resident from 6 April 2009.

(b) Income tax 2009/10

	Non-savings £	Savings £
Offshore interest (£28,600 × $^{100}/_{55}$)		52,000
Rent (£57,800 × $^{100}/_{85}$)	68,000	
	68,000	52,000
Tax thereon:		
£37,400 @ 20%	7,480	
£30,600 @ 40%	12,240	
£52,000 @ 40%	20,800	
	40,520	
Less DTR on		
Rent: 68,000 × 15% (foreign tax clearly lower)	(10,200)	
Interest: 52,000 × 40% (UK tax clearly lower)	(20,800)	
Income tax payable	9,520	

Steffen is non-domiciled in the UK and can claim to be taxed on the remittance basis on his foreign income. He will not be subject to the £30,000 remittance basis charge as he has not been resident in the UK for 7 out of the preceding 9 tax years.

Individuals who claim the remittance basis are not entitled to a personal allowance.

9.1 (a) Matilda is a 'temporary non-resident' as her period of absence from the UK covers less than 5 complete tax years. As a result, gains made on assets which she owned before she left the UK and sold during her period of absence are taxable in the tax year of her return – i.e. 2009/10.

(b)

	£
Painting	55,000
Less CY loss (land)	(15,000)
Total chargeable gains	40,000

Note: The gain on the cottage is not chargeable because Matilda acquired it after she ceased UK residence.

10.1

	£
Gain: sales of shares	17,900
CY Loss (painting)	(7,000)
	10,900
Losses b/f (10,900 – 10,100)	(800)
	10,100
Less: annual exempt amount	(10,100)
Taxable gain	Nil

Losses c/f (5,000 – 800) = £4,200

The loss on the sale of a cottage to Mark's brother is a connected party loss. Therefore, it must be carried forward separately and can only be offset against future gains on disposal to Mark's brother.

10.2

	2009/10 £
Trade profits (y/e 31.12.09)	15,000
Property income	3,000
Original net income	18,000
s.64 loss relief	(18,000)
Revised net income	nil
Chargeable gains	16,000
s.261B TCGA 1992 loss relief (W)	(10,000)
Revised gains (covered by AE)	6,000

Loss memo

Loss incurred in 2010/11	28,000
s.64 against net income of 2009/10	(18,000)
	10,000
Relief against chargeable gain of 2009/10	(10,000)
	–

Working

Maximum offset of trading loss against chargeable gains:

Lower of: £

(i) trading loss remaining after s.64 10,000

and

(ii) net gains less any capital losses b/f 16,000

∴ £10,000

Module 1: Taxation of individuals

10.3

Asset	£
Proceeds	28,800
31.3.82 MV	(7,500)
Enhancement expenditure	(1,000)
Gain	20,300
Less Annual exempt amount	(10,100)
Taxable gain	10,200
CGT @ 18%	1,836

CGT due 31 January 2011

10.4 Computation of capital gains tax

	£
Total chargeable gains	98,000
Less: Annual exempt amount	(10,100)
Taxable gain	87,900
CGT @ 18%	15,822

Workings

1 Factory

	£	Gains £
Proceeds	225,000	
Less: cost	(150,000)	
Gain	75,000	75,000

2 Painting

Transfer to Emily on 1.7.01 on no gain/no loss basis

	£	
Cost to Arthur	50,000	
Becomes base cost for Emily		

Sale by Emily

	£	
Proceeds	73,000	
Less: cost	(50,000)	
Gain	23,000	23,000
		98,000

10.5

	£
Proceeds	45,000
Cost £8,000 × $\dfrac{45,000}{45,000+50,000}$	(3,789)
Gain	41,211
Less: Annual exempt amount	(10,100)
Taxable gain	31,111
CGT @ 18%	5,600

Note. No claim is available for a 'small part' disposal as proceeds > £20,000 and > 20% of MV of land.

10.6 (1) No s.23 claim made – part disposal

2000/01

	£	£
Proceeds		14,000
Less: cost: £40,000 × $\frac{14,000}{14,000 + 50,000}$		(8,750)
Gain		5,250

The cost remaining for future disposals is £31,250 (ie £40,000 – £8,750)

2009/10

	£	£
Proceeds		85,000
Less: Cost £(40,000 – 8,750)	31,250	
Restoration (enhancement) costs	14,000	(45,250)
Gain		39,750

10.7

	£
Insurance proceeds	17,000
Less: cost	(7,500)
	9,500

Restricted to proceeds not spent on replacement £(17,000 – 16,000) £1,000

Allowable expenditure of replacement asset is:

	£
Actual cost	16,000
Less: deferred (ie 'rolled-over') £(9,500 – 1,000)	(8,500)
Allowable expenditure	7,500

11.1

Share pool

	No of shares	Cost £
April 1985 acquisition	1,000	2,954
May 2005 acquisition	1,000	6,000
	2,000	8,954
August 2009 disposal		
$\frac{500}{2,000} \times £8,954$	(500)	(2,239)
	1,500	6,715

August 2009 disposal

	£
Proceeds	15,000
Less Cost	(2,239)
Chargeable gain	12,761

11.2

	Share pool	No of shares	Cost £
	April 1985 acquisition	5,000	5,605
	July 1999 bonus issue 1:5	1,000	–
		6,000	5,605
	December 2009 disposal	(3,500)	(3,270)
	Pool c/f	2,500	2,335

	£
Proceeds	6,250
Less cost	(3,270)
Gain	2,980

11.3 *Summary of gains:*

	£
Building (W1)	400,000
Forum Follies plc (W2)	5,000
Total chargeable gains	405,000
Less: Annual exempt amount	(10,100)
Taxable gain	394,900

Workings

1 *Building*

	£
Proceeds	600,000
Less 31.3.82 value	(200,000)
Gain	400,000

2 *The takeover of Forum Follies plc*

The elements in the takeover consideration have the following values:

	£
Ordinary shares (30,000 × £3.00)	90,000
Cash	10,000
Total consideration received	100,000

A gain only arises on the date of the takeover in respect of the cash element.

	£
Cash received (above)	10,000
Cost 50,000 × $\frac{10,000}{100,000}$	(5,000)
Gain	5,000

11.4 *Dassau plc shares*

(i) Acquisition 15 November 2009 (Acquired in following 30 days)

	£
Proceeds 500/1200 × £9,500	3,958
Cost	(1,500)
Gain	2,458

(ii) *Share pool (s.104 holding)*

	Shares	Cost £
December 1985	1,000	2,000
Rights issue April 1987 1:2 @ £2	500	1,000
	1,500	3,000
Disposal November 2009	(700)	(1,400)
	800	1,600

	£
Proceeds 700/1200 × £9,500	5,542
Less cost	(1,400)
Gain	4,142

Summary

	£
Total gains (£2,458 + £4,142)	6,600
less capital losses b/f (restricted)	–
	6,600
Less annual exempt amount	(10,100)
Taxable gain	–

11.5 *Gain*

	£
Proceeds	13,500
Less: Cost	(4,500)
Gain	9,000

Working

Share pool

	Shares	Cost £
March 1990	2,000	2,000
December 1996	4,000	10,000
	6,000	12,000
May 1999 rights issue 1: 5 @ £5	1,200	6,000
	7,200	18,000
October 2009 sale	(1,800)	(4,500)
C/f	5,400	13,500

11.6 Julio is taxable on his worldwide gains as he is UK resident. However, if he makes a claim to use the remittance basis he will only be taxed when he brings the overseas gain to the UK, although he will lose his annual exempt amount (and income tax personal allowances).

Since he has not yet remitted any of the gain he should make the claim. He will not be subject to the remittance basis charge of £30,000 as he has not been resident for seven years out of the last nine tax years.

CommandN Plc

The matching rules apply.

(i) Next 30 days

	£
Proceeds 5,000/10,000 × £195,600	97,800
Less: cost	(97,050)
Chargeable gain	750

(ii) Share pool

	£
Proceeds 5,000/10,000 × £195,600	97,800
Less: cost (W)	(96,647)
Chargeable gain	1,153

	£
Total gain £(750 + 1,153)	1,903
No Annual exempt amount as makes remittance basis claim	
Tax @ 18%	343

Working

Share pool

		Cost £
Purchase	7,000	157,220
Purchase	8,000	132,720
Total	15,000	289,940
Disposal	(5,000)	(96,647)
c/f	10,000	193,293

11.7 On the takeover there is an immediate charge to CGT in respect of the cash received:

	£
Cash proceeds (W1)	9,375
Less: cost (W1)	(1,094)
Chargeable gain	8,281

Disposal of ½ the shares

	£
Cash proceeds £8.95 × 12,500 (W2)	111,875
Less: cost (W2)	(13,053)
Chargeable gain	98,822
Total gains	107,103

Workings

(1) Takeover package

	Market value £	Cost £
Cash received: 75p × 12,500	9,375	1,094
Shares received: 12,500 × 2 × £8.95	223,750	26,106
Total	233,125	27,200

(2) Rover Ltd share pool

Detail	Number	Cost £
Purchase (use MV82)	10,000	27,200
Bonus issue 1:4	2,500	-
Total	12,500	27,200
Takeover 2:1	25,000	(1,094)
	25,000	26,106
Disposal (½)	(12,500)	(13,053)
c/f	12,500	13,053

12.1

	£
Victoria Cross:	
Proceeds	14,780
Less cost	(3,000)
	11,780

Chargeable gain not to exceed 5/3 × £(14,780 − 6,000) = £14,633

Note. Medals are only exempt if awarded for bravery or inherited.

Vintage car: Exempt

	Cost £
Paintings:	
Gross proceeds (deemed)	6,000
Cost	(6,260)
	(260)

	£
Gain	11,780
Less CY loss	(260)
Chargeable gains	11,520

12.2

Motor car: exempt

Machinery item 1:	£
Proceeds	7,500
Less cost	(5,500)
	2,000

Restrict to 5/3 £(7,500 − 6,000) = £2,500

Therefore gain = £2,000

Machinery item 2. There is never a capital loss on an item on which capital allowances have been claimed as a balancing allowance would be given instead through the capital allowances computation.

12.3

Grant of long lease:

	£
Proceeds	30,000
Less 31.3.82 MV	
£40,000 × $\dfrac{30,000}{30,000+82,500}$	(10,667)
Chargeable gain	19,333

Grant of short lease:	£
Proceeds (capital element of premium)*	2,000
Cost £30,000 × $\dfrac{2,000}{10,000+50,000}$	(1,000)
	1,000

* Premium	10,000
Less: 2% × (11-1) × £10,000	(2,000)
Assessed as property income	8,000

	£
Total chargeable gains (19,333 + 1,000)	20,333
Less: Annual exempt amount	(10,100)
	10,233

12.4

Summary

	£
Gain	6,200
Less: loss	(1,200)
Net gains	5,000

Workings

1. Leonardo cartoon:

	£
Proceeds (deemed)	6,000
Allowable cost	(7,200)
Allowable loss	(1,200)

2. Lathe

	£
Proceeds	10,500
Allowable cost	(4,300)
Gain	6,200

Restrict to $\frac{5}{3} \times £(10,500 - 6,000) = £7,500$ ∴ gain £6,200

12.5

(1) Assignment of long lease

	£
Proceeds	79,000
Cost	(28,000)
Chargeable gain	51,000

(2) Assignment of short lease

	Cost £
Proceeds	79,000
Cost: £28,000 × $\frac{88.371}{100.000}$ (31yrs) (57yrs)	(24,744)
Chargeable gain	54,256

12.6 Grant of short lease out of freehold

	£
Proceeds: capital element of premium = (2% × (20 − 1) × £20,000)	7,600
Cost: £25,000 × $\frac{7,600}{20,000+17,000}$	(5,135)
Gain	2,465

Charles

Assessable on landlord: £12,000 − [2% × (25 − 1) × £12,000] = £6,240

∴ allowable to Charles £6,240/25 yrs = £250 pa

In year to 31.1.10:

	£
Deduction for lease premium £250 × 5/12	104
Rent payable 5/12 × £3,000	1,250
	1,354

12.7 *Sale of table*

	£	£
Proceeds		8,000
Less: cost of disposal		(800)
		7,200
Less: cost – option	2,000	
– asset	3,500	(5,500)
Gain		1,700

Chattels rules ($5/3 \times £(8,000 - 6,000) = £3,333$) give a higher gain so do not apply.

13.1

		£
Gain		80,000
Exempt:		
1.4.82 – 30.6.86	51 months	
1.7.06 – 30.6.09	36 months	
	87 months	
Total period		
1.4.82 – 30.6.09	327 months	
∴ $\frac{87}{327} \times £80,000$		(21,284)
Letting gain		58,716
Less: letting relief		
Lowest of (i) £40,000		
(ii) PPR relief: £21,284		
(iii) letting gain (1.7.86 – 30.6.06 = 240m): £58,716		(21,284)
Chargeable gain		37,432

Note: Occupation and ownership prior to 1 April 1982 is ignored

13.2 (a)

	£
Proceeds	200,000
Less: cost	(20,000)
Gain	180,000
Less PPR exemption	
£180,000 × 2/3	(120,000)
Chargeable gain	60,000

Note. As the students occupy separate self-contained accommodation, the ground floor is treated as a separate residence, the gain on which is fully chargeable to CGT.

(b) **Any three** of:

(i) Any period employed outside the UK

(ii) Periods of up to four years working (employed or self-employed) elsewhere

(iii) Up to three years for any reason

(iv) The last three years of ownership where the property has been the principal private residence at some time.

(v) Any period whilst living in job related accommodation

(vi) First 12 months if not occupied due to building work or because unable to sell old home..

Note. (i) – (iii) must be preceded and followed by a period of actual occupation.

13.3 (a) On the sale of the current family home there will be no capital gains tax implications due to principal private residence (PPR) relief which ensures that the sale of a property which has been the taxpayer's only or main residence is exempt from capital gains tax.

(b) However, where a taxpayer owns two properties, even if he actually resides in both, PPR relief can only apply to one property. A husband and wife living together such as Mr and Mrs Mackay can only have one PPR between them ie it is not possible for the flat to be Mr Mackay's PPR and for the house to be Mrs Mackay's.

Instead, Mr and Mrs Mackay should elect which of the house and flat they wish to have treated as their main residence for the purposes of PPR relief. The election should be made within two years of residing in the two properties, in this case by May 2011 – otherwise the main residence will be determined as a question of fact.

Mr and Mrs Mackay do have a right to vary the election by a further written notice which can take effect for any period starting not more than two years before the date of the second notice.

(c) As Mr & Mrs Mackay are likely to sell the flat at a profit in 5 years time they should elect for the flat to be treated as the main residence. They should vary the election so that the house is treated as the main residence not more than three years before sale. The gain on the flat will then be exempt at the expense of a loss of approximately two years exemption on the house.

13.4 Computation of chargeable gain on sale of house

Period	Explanation	Occupation or deemed occupation (months)	Non occupation (months)
2.5.84 – 1.2.87	Actual occupation	33	
2.2.87 – 1.12.96	Letting		118
2.12.96 – 3.7.06	Absence		115
4.7.06 – 3.7.09	Last three years deemed occupation	36	
		69	233

Total ownership period = 302 months

	£
Proceeds (3.7.09)	270,000
Less: Cost	(70,000)
Gain	200,000
Less: Exemption for main residence $\frac{69}{302} \times £200,000$	(45,695)
	154,305
Less: letting exemption: lowest of	
£45,695 (gain exempted by private residence relief)	
£78,146 (chargeable gain attributable to letting) (W)	
£40,000 (maximum relief available for lettings)	(40,000)
Chargeable gain	114,305

Working

Gain in let period: $\frac{118}{302} \times £200,000 = £78,146$

13.5 Calculation of chargeable gain

	£
Proceeds	380,200
Less: Cost	(110,000)
Gain before PPR	270,200

	Flat £	Office £
Gain $\frac{17}{24} : \frac{7}{24}$	191,392	78,808
PPR	(191,392)	
Chargeable gain	Nil	78,808

PPR exemption

	Occupation	Non occupation	Total
6.4.86 – 5.4.87 (occupation)	1	–	1
6.4.87 – 5.4.91 (deemed 4 years)	4	–	4
6.4.91 – 5.4.92 (part of 3 years for any reason)	1	–	1
6.4.92 – 5.4.93 (occupation)	1	–	1
6.4.93 – 5.4.07 (14 years joint use)	7	7	14
6.4.07 – 4.4.10 (final 3 years deemed occupation)	3	–	3
	17	7	24

14.1 Galadriel Ltd

Income tax relief given 2006/07: 40,000 × 20% = £8,000

Income tax relief withdrawn in 2009/10: £8,000 × $\frac{35,000}{40,000}$ = £7,000

Capital loss:	£	£
Proceeds		35,000
Cost	40,000	
less IT relief not withdrawn	(1,000)	
		(39,000)
Allowable loss		(4,000)

Guinevere Ltd

No income tax relief withdrawn as sold more than 3 years after acquisition.

Gain on disposal is exempt.

Mordred Ltd

No income tax relief withdrawn as more than 3 years after acquisition.

Capital loss:	£	£
Proceeds		20,000
Cost	30,000	
less IT relief (30,000 × 20%)	(6,000)	
		(24,000)
Allowable loss		(4,000)

14.2 (a) EIS income tax relief will *not* be available, as the employee is 'connected' with the company.

(b) EIS income tax relief of £20,000 should be available as the company is unlisted (AIM listings being regarded as unlisted for this purpose) at the time of issue and there was no intention to obtain a full listing at that time.

(c) EIS relief will *not* be available as Jane is connected with the Company since she has a shareholding of over 30%.

(d) EIS relief will *not* be available as property development is not a qualifying activity.

(e) EIS income tax relief of £100,000 (i.e. £500,000 × 20%) will be available – this is the maximum relief available.

14.3

	£
Proceeds	350,000
Cost	(180,000)
	170,000
Less EIS deferral relief	(144,900)
Less capital losses	(15,000)
	10,100
AE	(10,100)
	Nil

The optimum EIS deferral relief claim is £144,900

14.4 Alan – Capital gains computation 2009/10

	£	£
1. *Land and buildings*		
Proceeds	250,000	
Less cost	(70,000)	
Chargeable gain		180,000
2. *Goodwill*		
Proceeds	85,000	
Less cost	-	
Chargeable gain		85,000
Total gains		265,000
Entrepreneur's relief £265,000 × 4/9		(117,778)
Chargeable gains		147,222
Annual exempt amount		(10,100)
Taxable gain		137,122
CGT @ 18%		24,682

14.5 Monty – Capital gains computation 2009/10

		£	£
1.	*Shares*		
	Gain	1,700,000	
	Less Entrepreneurs' relief (£1,000,000 x 4/9)	(444,444)	
	Chargeable gain		1,255,556
2.	*Painting*		
	Proceeds	12,000	
	Less cost	(1,000)	
	Gain	11,000	
	Restricted to 5/3 x (12,000 – 6,000)		10,000
	Total gains		1,265,556
	Less capital losses bfwd		(15,000)
	Total chargeable gains		1,250,556
	Annual exempt amount		(10,100)
	Taxable gain		1,240,456

14.6

This is a material disposal of whole or part of a business, so entrepreneurs' relief is available. Claim must be made by 31 January 2012.

	£
Gain	1,110,000
Less: entrepreneurs' relief 4/9 × £1,000,000	(444,444)
Chargeable gain	665,556
Add: other gains	24,000
Total gains	689,556
Less loss b/f	(12,750)
Chargeable gain	676,806
Less: Annual exempt amount	(10,100)
Taxable gain	666,706
CGT @ 18%	120,007

The lifetime limit of qualifying gains is £1,000,000.

15.1

(a) Brandon must notify HMRC of his new source of income by 5 October 2010.

(b) The failure to notify chargeability will arise after 1 April 2010. The penalty is therefore a percentage of the tax lost, depending on the behaviour of the taxpayer. The maximum percentage is 100% if Brandon deliberately failed to notify HMRC and concealed the need to notify. If the failure by Brandon was not deliberate the percentage is reduced to 30%. The maximum penalties can be reduced by the extent of disclosure to HMRC.

(c) Brandon may submit a simplified return for his rental income as the gross income is less than £68,000 for the year.

He is required to record three lines:

- Gross property income
- Total allowable expenses
- Net income

15.2 (a) As the notice was issued before 31 October 2010, Phyllis's 2009/10 tax return was due on 31 January 2011.

Her income tax payment for 2009/10 was also due on 31 January 2011. There were no payments on account required for 2009/10, as her 2008/09 income tax was below £1,000.

(b) *Penalty for late return*

It is reasonable to assume that as the return was not submitted until August 2011 then the Finance Act 2009 penalties for late payment and late filing will apply.

Late filing: Immediate penalty of £100. The return is more than 6 months late, but less than 12 months late. A daily penalty of £10 may be charged up to a maximum of 90 days. A tax geared penalty of 5% of the tax due will be charged. The tax geared penalty is subject to a minimum of £300, which will apply in this case.

Late payment penalty: As the return is more than 6 months late a penalty of 10% of the tax unpaid will be charged ie £16.

Interest on late tax payment:

Interest runs from 31 January 2011 to 30 August 2011:

i.e. £160 × 2.5% × $\frac{7}{12}$ = £2

15.3 Proceeds received in instalments

If proceeds are received in instalments over a period exceeding 18 months, the tax may be spread over the shorter of:

- the period of instalments, and
- eight years.

Gifts

The CGT on gifts which do not qualify for gift relief may be paid in instalments, provided the asset gifted is:

- land
- shares or securities out of a controlling holding, or
- unquoted shares or securities.

CGT is payable in ten yearly instalments, commencing on the normal due date of 31 January following the tax year.

The deadline for these elections is 4 years from the end of the tax year of disposal (5 years from 31 January following the tax year of disposal before 1 April 2010).

15.4 (a) As Alicia submitted her 2009/10 return late, HMRC have until 12 months following the next quarter day after submission to open an enquiry – i.e. until 30 April 2012.

(b) Alicia must keep records relating to her business for 5 years after 31 January following the tax year i.e. until 31 January 2016 for 2009/10.

(c) From April 2010 HMRC may raise a discovery assessment in respect of earlier years if:

- Alicia or her agent have carelessly or deliberately omitted information, or
- HMRC were not given sufficient information in the return to be able to identify the loss of tax.

From April 2010, the time limits for raising a discovery assessment are as follows:
- Ordinary time limit   4 years from the end of the tax year
- Where the omission is careless   6 years from the end of the tax year
- Where the omission is deliberate   20 years from the end of the tax year.

15.5 (a) POA

	£
Income tax liability	10,250
Class 4 NIC	1,000
Less: tax deducted at source	(5,000)
	6,250

POAs of £3,125 are due 31 January 2010 and 31 July 2010. Any balancing payment is due 31 January 2011.

(b) John may make a claim to reduce his payments on account for 2009/10.

He must state the reason for the reduction in his claim.

If John reduces the payments on account too far, so that there is a balancing payment for 2009/10, interest will run on the underpayment.

15.6 Ray has made an excessive claim to reduce his payments on account, and will therefore be charged interest on the reduction. The payments on account should have been £4,500 each based on the previous year's liability (not £5,000 each based on the current year's liability). He will be liable to interest as follows:

- 1st POA
  - on £3,500 – nil – paid on time
  - on £1,000 from due date of 31 January 2010 to day before payment, 18 February 2011

- 2nd POA
  - on £3,500 from due date of 31 July 2010 to day before part-payment of £3,500, 11 August 2010
  - on £1,000 from due date of 31 July 2010 to day before payment, 18 February 2011

- Balancing payment of income tax and CGT
  - on £3,500 from due date of 31 January 2011 to day before payment, 18 February 2011

15.7 (1) *Payment on account*

Payments on account are based on the previous year's income tax and Class 4 NIC only. The previous year's POAs are irrelevant here. CGT is never included.

	£
Income tax liability	17,895
Class 4 NIC liability	2,808
Less: tax deducted at source	(1,275)
	19,428
POA due 31 January (and July) 2010	9,714

(2) *Interest*

Interest is due from the due date to the day *before* payment:

31.1.10 – 24.5.10 = 114 days

2.5% × 114/365 × £9,714 = £76

There are no penalties on late paid payments on account.

16.1

	£
Salary (5 × £1,000)	5,000
Car benefit (£15,000 × 22% × 3/12)*	825
Fuel benefit (£16,900 × 22% × 3/12)*	929
Earnings for income tax	6,754

$* \dfrac{(17-135)}{5} = 7\%$

Percentage: 15% + 7% = 22%

Class 1 NIC primary (payable by Tina)

(1,000 –476) × 11% × 5 =   £288

Class 1 NIC secondary (payable by Harrison Electrics Ltd)

(1,000 – 476) × 12.8% × 5 = £335

Class 1A NIC (payable by Harrison Electrics Ltd)

(825 + 929) × 12.8% =   £225

16.2 *Class 1 secondary NIC*

(45,000 – 5,715) × 12.8% = £5,028

Class 1A

Loan benefit

	£
Average method: $\dfrac{15,000 + 10,000}{2} \times 4.75\%$	594
Less: interest paid 5/4/09 – 31/12/09: £15,000 × 3% × 9/12	(338)
1/1/10 – 5/4/10: £10,000 × 3% × 3/12	(75)
	181
Strict basis:	
5/4/09 – 5/1/10: £15,000 × (4.75% – 3%) × 9/12	197
6/1/10 – 5/4/10: £10,000 × (4.75% – 3%) × 3/12	44
	241

HMRC have the option to assess Ruth using the strict basis, giving a benefit of £241.

Class 1A: £241 × 12.8% = £31

[Credit also given if Class 1A calculated using benefit from 'average' method.]

16.3 Assessable benefit is the greater of

(a)

	£
Market value at acquisition	1,500
less price paid	(1,000)
	500

(b)

	£
Original market value	2,000
less assessed in respect of use (08/09)	
$^6/_{12}$ × 20% × £2,000	(200)
less assessed in respect of use (09/10) $^6/_{12}$× 20% × £2,000	(200)
less price paid	(1,000)
	600

∴ Benefit is £600 + £200 (use in 09/10) = £800

Class 1A = £800 × 12.8% = £102

Due date is 19 July 2010.

16.4

	£
Earnings	
Salary	25,750
Telephone bills	400
	26,150

Class 1 primary NIC (payable by Judy)

(26,150 − 5,715) × 11% = £2,248

Class 1 secondary NIC (payable by Markham Ltd)

(26,150 − 5,715) × 12.8% = £2,616

Class 1A (payable by Markham Ltd)

Benefits:	£
Flat (annual value)	3,000
Furniture (20% × £2,500)	500
	3,500

Class 1A = £3,500 × 12.8% = £448

Note: There is no additional charge for the accommodation as the original cost was less than £75,000.

16.5 *Pip: Class 1 primary contributions*

Normal months:

Earnings = £28,000 ÷ 12 = £2,333

Bonus month

Earnings = £4,000 + £2,333 = £6,333

Class 1 primary

		£
Normal month:	(2,333 − 476) × 11% × 11	2,247
Bonus month:	(3,656 − 476) × 11%	350
	(6,333 × 3,656) × 1%	27
		2,624

Estella: Class 1 primary contributions

		£
1st 6 months:	(1,333 − 476) × 11% × 6	566
Last 6 months:	(1,500 − 476) × 11% × 6	676
		1,242

Due dates: 19th following each tax month.

16.6 (a) Anna is not liable to Class 1 primary NIC as she is over the pensionable age.

Madison Plc will be liable to Class 1 secondary NIC - due on 19th following each tax month.

(b) The reimbursement of the season ticket will be subject to Class 1 primary contributions payable to Elaine and Class 1 secondary contributions payable by Madison Plc. Both are payable by 19th following each tax month.

The company car benefit will be subject to Class 1A NIC payable by Madison Plc. This is due by 19th July 2010.

(c) The benefits within the PAYE Settlement Agreement will be subject to Class 1B payable by Madison Plc. This is due by 19th October 2010.

16.7 Class 1 is due on salary and expense payments, unless the expense payment is contracted for by the employer, in which case Class 1A is due instead, from the employer only.

Class 1 is due on:	£
Salary	65,000
Mileage payments (W)	800
M&S vouchers	500
Gym membership (as reimbursed)	1,020
Total	67,320

Class 1A is due on:	£
Private medical insurance (as contracted for by employer)	450
Total	450

NIC due:

Employee	£	£
£(43,875 – 5,715) = 38,160 @ 11%	4,198	
£(67,320 – 43,875) = 23,445 @ 1%	234	
Total		4,432

Employer		
£(67,320 – 5,715) = 61,605 @ 12.8%		7,885

Class 1A		
Employer only: £450 @ 12.8%		58
Total NICs due		12,375

Other business related travel expenses and the professional subscription are exempt from NIC as they are deductible for Robert.

The beneficial loan is below the £5,000 threshold, so no (tax or) NICs are due.

Workings

Mileage payments

	£
Employer reimburses	4,000
Allowable under the HMRC scheme:	
8,000 × 40p	(3,200)
Excess	800

17.1 Year end returns:

- P35 – End of year summary return – due 19 May 2010
- P14 (P60 employee copy) – End of year return – due 19 May 2010
- P11D – Return of benefits for employees earning £8,500 or more) – due 6 July 2010
- P11Db – Class 1A return – due 6 July 2010

17.2 (1) The statutory redundancy pay and the ex-gratia payment are subject to income tax but the first £30,000 is exempt. PAYE should therefore be applied to £2,000 (3,000 + 29,000 – 30,000) of the ex-gratia payment.

(2) The company is not required to deduct PAYE from the tips as they are paid directly to Patrick by the customer and the company is not involved in any sharing out of the tips.

(3) The vouchers are tax free and therefore PAYE Is not required to be operated.

Awareness Paper
IHT, trusts and estates

Study Period Planner
Inheritance Tax, Trusts and Estates

Use this schedule and your exam timetable to plan the dates on which you will complete each Study Period. The letters 'H' and 'M' tell you whether the topic is high or medium priority.

Study Period	Topic		Due Date
1	Inheritance tax – basic principles	H	
2	Calculation of IHT on lifetime transfers	H	
3	IHT valuation/ BPR/APR	H	
4	Death estate	H	
5	Reliefs for falls in value on death	H	
6	IHT – additional aspects	M	
7	**Progress Test 1**	H	

Study Period	Topic		Due Date
8	Capital gains tax – basic principles	H	
9	IHT for trusts	H	
10	CGT for trusts	H	
11	Income tax for trusts	H	
12	Estates in administration	H	
13	**Progress Test 2**	H	

COURSE EXAM 1

A practice exam covering Study Periods 1 to 6

COURSE EXAM 2

A Practice exam covering all Study Periods

REVISION PHASE

Your revision phase will begin when **Course Exam 2** is complete. This should ideally be four months before the final exam.

TQT Note: The Course Exams contain questions for all FIVE of the awareness paper modules. In your exam you must answer questions from THREE modules. We suggest that you identify the THREE modules you will study and then work through the Study Period Planners for each of those modules until the point where you are told to take Course Exam 1. When you have completed all THREE modules to that point, sit Course Exam 1. Similarly, you should complete all THREE modules before you sit course exam 2. Course Exam 2 covers all of the Study Periods, although it is weighted towards the second half of your studies.

Study Period 1

Inheritance tax – basic principles

High Priority

Step 1 Exam Guidance

The contents of this study period are fundamental to any inheritance tax (IHT) question in the exam.

It introduces concepts and terminology that you must grasp and be able to use confidently to perform well in the exam.

These basic principles were tested in Question 12 of the May 2009 exam.

Step 2 Introduction to the session

In this period we begin our study of inheritance tax (IHT). This study period provides the background information, so that you can understand the rationale behind the charging of inheritance tax and identify situations when an inheritance tax liability will arise.

Step 3 Guidance through the Study Text

Read through Chapter 1 of the Inheritance Tax, Trusts and Estates Awareness Study Text after reading the following guidance:

In this chapter we learn the basics for calculating inheritance tax.

Read through Section 1. This should be fairly quick to read but is an **essential** section as it explains when a charge to IHT arises on a 'transfer of value' and sets out the types of property that are excluded from the IHT charge. Make sure you understand these basic principles before continuing.

Read through Section 2 which lists the exemptions available for lifetime transfers and those available for both lifetime and death transfers. Attempt Examples 2 and 3.

Finally, read through Sections 3 and 4. These sections are very brief, but very important. They explain the difference between the two types of lifetime transfers: chargeable transfers and potentially exempt transfers. You must be able to identify the types of transfer that fall into each category. Consolidate your understanding of the basics of IHT by ensuring that you understand the flow chart at the end of the chapter.

Step 5 i-Pass and Workbook Questions

Now attempt exam style questions (ESQs) 1.1 to 1.6 which will help to reinforce your knowledge of the topics covered in this study period and give you examples of the types of question you may see in the exam.

Your TQT's i-Pass CD Rom also contains some questions on the basics of IHT.

Step 4 Quick Quiz

Please attempt the quick quiz at the end of Study Text Chapter 1 to reinforce your understanding.

You may find it best to do this after a break, so that you can see what you remember and what you don't.

Study Period 2

Calculation of IHT on lifetime transfers

High Priority

Step 1 Exam Guidance

The calculation of inheritance tax on lifetime transfers of value is one of the key areas of IHT. Computations could cover lifetime tax or the IHT due as a result of a death.

You must be able to complete these calculations quickly and accurately. Remember, you only have one minute per mark in the exam.

Question 1 on the Sample Paper involved the calculation of tax on a lifetime gift.

Step 2 Introduction to the session

In this study period we continue to look at transfers of value and in particular at the tax on transfers of value made during lifetime.

By the end of this Study Period you will be able to calculate the IHT due in lifetime and on death on both chargeable lifetime transfers and on potentially exempt transfers.

Step 3 Guidance through the Study Text

Read through chapter 2 of the Study text, after reading the following guidance:

This Chapter is very structured. In the last period we learnt to identify chargeable lifetime transfers (CLTs) and potentially exempt transfers (PETs). In this study session we learn to compute the IHT arising as a result of making both CLT's and PETs.

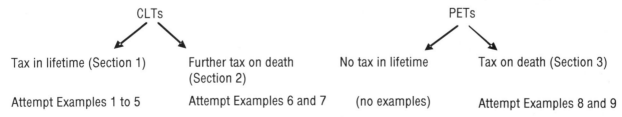

CLTs	PETs
Tax in lifetime (Section 1) Further tax on death (Section 2)	No tax in lifetime Tax on death (Section 3)
Attempt Examples 1 to 5 Attempt Examples 6 and 7	(no examples) Attempt Examples 8 and 9

These calculations are very examinable – take your time to work through the chapter and examples slowly to make sure you understand them fully.

Step 4 Quick Quiz

Please attempt the quick quiz at the end of Study Text Chapter 2 to reinforce your understanding.

You may find it best to do this after a break, so that you can see what you remember and what you don't.

Step 5 i-Pass and Workbook Questions

Now attempt ESQs 2.1 to 2.6 which will help to reinforce your knowledge of the topics covered in this study period and give you examples of the types of question you may see in the exam.

Your TQT's i-Pass CD Rom also contains some questions on the calculation of IHT on lifetime transfers.

Module 2: IHT, trusts and estates   99

Study Period 3

IHT valuation/BPR/APR

High Priority

Step 1 Exam Guidance

The topics covered in this Study Period are essential for the exam. You must be able to value assets for IHT purposes and identify the circumstances where agricultural property relief (APR) and/ or business property relief (BPR) are available.

These topics were tested in:

- The Sample paper in Q4 (Valuation of assets), Q8 (BPR) and Q12 (APR)
- The May 2009 exam in Q7 (BPR)

Step 2 Introduction to the session

Now that we know how to calculate IHT on lifetime transfers, in this Study Period we learn how to:

- Value a transfer for IHT purposes, with special rules for specific types of assets.
- Identify situations when APR and/ or BPR may be available and at what rate. These can reduce the value of a transfer to nil and apply before any other exemption (eg the annual exemption).

Step 3 Guidance through the Study Text

Read through Chapters 3 and 4 of the Study text after reading the following guidance:

Having learnt the loss to donor rule for valuing transfers, in this study period we learn more detailed valuation rules in Chapter 3:

Section 2: Related property rules – where the value of a transfer is determined by reference to the total value of related property and not just the property owned by the transferor. Try Example 2 to test your understanding of this principle.

Section 3: Special valuation rules for certain assets – there are special rules for a number of assets, most importantly quoted shares and securities (Section 3.2). Try Examples 3 and 4.

Chapter 4 considers business property relief (BPR) and agricultural property relief (APR). You must be aware of the conditions that need to be satisfied for the relief to be available (Sections 2 and 3). Locate them in the relevant part of your legislation. Then attempt Examples 2 and 3. Attempt Example 4 to test your understanding of the implications of the relief being withdrawn (Section 4).

This study period may take longer than the usual 3 hours.

Step 4 Quick Quiz

Please attempt the quick quizzes at the end of Study Text Chapters 3 and 4 to reinforce your understanding.

You may find it best to do this after a break, so that you can see what you remember and what you don't.

Step 5 i-Pass and Workbook Questions

Now attempt ESQs 3.1 to 3.6 and 4.1 to 4.7, which will help to reinforce your knowledge of the topics covered in this study period and give you examples of the types of question you may see in the exam.

Your TQT's i-Pass CD Rom also contains some questions on IHT valuation and BPR and APR.

Module 2: IHT, trusts and estates

Study Period 4

Death estate

High Priority

Step 1 Exam Guidance

The calculation of IHT on the death estate is a key IHT computation that can be examined in the same question with some other aspect (or aspects) of the syllabus, such as lifetime gifts, valuation rules or reliefs.

This topic has been tested as follows:

- Question 4 Sample exam paper
- Questions 1 and 10 of the May 2009 exam.

Step 2 Introduction to the session

In previous study periods we looked at the calculation of IHT on lifetime gifts, both during lifetime and as a result of death.

In this study period we learn how to value an individual's death estate and calculate any IHT due on their estate at death.

Step 3 Guidance through the Study Text

Read through Chapter 5 of the Study Text after reading the following guidance:

Section 1.2 sets out the different elements that could make up an individual's death estate. Note that all assets are valued at 'probate value' (ie the market value at the date of death) using the valuation rules we learnt in the previous study period.

At this point, refer to the death estate proforma in Section 1.4 so that you can see how all the possible components of the death estate fit together. Learn this proforma so that you know how and where to include each item. Also look at Sections 1.5 and 1.6 and note the treatement of debts, funeral expenses and proceeds from life assurance policies.

Go back to Section 1.3 where we learn how to calculate the tax due on the death estate. Attempt Examples 1 and 2 to reinforce your understanding of the calculation.

Section 2 covers the transfer of an unused nil rate band between spouses/civil partners on the second death where the nil rate band was not used on the first death.

Section 3 explains how 'quick succession relief' (QSR) is available where two deaths occur within a short time of each other and IHT is charged on both. The percentages you need for the formula are in your tax tables. Locate them now and try Example 4.

Step 4 Quick Quiz

Please attempt the quick quiz at the end of Study Text Chapter 5 to reinforce your understanding.

You may find it best to do this after a break, so that you can see what you remember and what you don't.

Step 5 i-Pass and Workbook Questions

Now attempt ESQs 5.1 to 5.9, which will help to reinforce your knowledge of the topics covered in this study period and give you examples of the types of question you may see in the exam.

Your TQT's i-Pass CD Rom also contains some questions on the death estate.

Module 2: IHT, trusts and estates   101

Study Period 5

Relief for falls in value on death

High Priority

Step 1 Exam Guidance

Reliefs and exemptions are essential knowledge for the exam. You will be covering a further two reliefs in this period. Your challenge is to ensure that you learn how to spot when each relief applies.

There were no questions on these reliefs in the sample paper or the May 2009 exam.

Step 2 Introduction to the session

Earlier we saw APR and BPR, which apply to both lifetime gifts and the death estate, and QSR which reduces death tax.

We now focus on two further reliefs that may apply when calculating death tax:

- Fall in value relief – where the value of an asset gifted during lifetime is lower at the date of death, and
- 'Post mortem relief' – where assets are sold from the death estate at a loss

Step 3 Guidance through the Study Text

Read through Chapter 6 of the Study Text after reading the following guidance:

In Section 1 we consider the relief available when an asset gifted during lifetime has *fallen in value* by the date of death. This can reduce the IHT due where the donor has died within seven years of making that gift. Attempt Example 1 to reinforce your understanding of the calculation.

Then read through Section 2, which covers relief for sales at a loss from the death estate of:

- Quoted shares
- Land and buildings
- Property valued using the related property rules.

There is no relief for any other assets.

Work through Examples 2 to 4 carefully, making sure you understand the slight difference in the rules depending on the asset being sold from the estate.

Step 4 Quick Quiz

Please attempt the quick quiz at the end of Study Text Chapter 6 to reinforce your understanding.

You may find it best to do this after a break, so that you can see what you remember and what you don't.

Step 5 i-Pass and Workbook Questions

Now attempt ESQs 6.1 to 6.6, which will help to reinforce your knowledge of the topics covered in this study period and give you examples of the types of question you may see in the exam.

Your TQT's i-Pass CD Rom also contains some questions on the death estate.

Study Period 6

IHT – additional aspects

Medium Priority

Step 1 Exam Guidance

There are four topics within this Study period. They broadly modify the basic IHT computation that we have already learnt in earlier study periods.

The following questions were set on these areas:

- Domicile: Sample Paper (Q2), May 2009 (Q2 and Q4)
- Pre-owned asset tax: Sample Paper (Q3)
- Gift with reservation: Sample Paper (Q9), May 2009 (Q9)

Step 2 Introduction to the session

In this study period we look at additional elements of the IHT computation:

1. The overseas aspects of IHT
2. Gifts with reservation of benefit
3. Conditional exemption for national heritage property
4. Jointly owned property

These topics are also important for IHT planning.

Step 3 Guidance through the Study Text

Read through Chapter 7 of the Study text after reading the following guidance:

This Chapter contains four different topics: Read through Section 1 – the overseas aspects of IHT to understand how overseas issues can affect who pays IHT and on what assets.

Then read carefully through Section 2 – gifts with reservation of benefit to understand the impact and consequences of retaining use of, or an interest in, an asset after it has been gifted. You should be able to identify when an income tax charge might apply instead of an IHT charge and how any tax liability is calculated. Attempt Examples 1 to 3.

Quickly read through Section 3 to understand the implications of making gifts of heritage property.

Finally read through Section 4 identifying how property can be held jointly, how such ownership affects the value entered into an individual's estate.

Step 4 Quick Quiz

Please attempt the quick quizzes at the end of Study Text Chapter 7 to reinforce your understanding.

You may find it best to do this after a break, so that you can see what you remember and what you don't.

Step 5 i-Pass and Workbook Questions

Now attempt ESQs 7.1 to 7.7, which will help to reinforce your knowledge of the topics covered in this study period and give you examples of the types of question you may see in the exam.

Your TQT's i-Pass CD Rom also contains some questions on the various aspects covered in this study period.

Progress Test 1

Study Period 7
High Priority

In order to reinforce what you have learnt so far, answer the following questions. Try to answer them without referring to your Study Text or notes. The test should take you no longer than one hour and covers Study Periods 1-6. Solutions start on page 117.

1. Jennifer makes the following lifetime transfers of value:

January 2005	£4,000 to her sister.
January 2009	£15,000 to her husband.
August 2009	£25,000 to her son on his wedding day.
February 2010	£5,000 to a discretionary trust.

    You are required to state how each of these transfers will be treated for IHT purposes and how Jennifer's annual exemptions will be allocated to the above gifts.

2. A lifetime gift can be categorised for IHT purposes as either exempt, a potentially exempt transfer or a chargeable lifetime transfer.

    You are required to define a potentially exempt transfer (PET) and to state the lifetime and death consequences of making a potentially exempt transfer.

3. Callum gifts £30,000 in cash to his daughter, on the occasion of her marriage in September 2006. Callum dies on 1 October 2009 leaving a death estate totalling £450,000.

    You are required to calculate the IHT due during lifetime and on Callum's death.

4. Steven made the following gifts during his lifetime:

1 August 2004	cash gift to a cousin of £343,000
1 January 2005	cash gift to a discretionary trust of £100,000

    Steven dies on 10 February 2010.

    You are required to calculate the IHT due in respect of the above gifts both in lifetime and on death.

5. Russell died owning 1,000 shares in Brand plc. These shares were quoted at 210p-230p on the date of Russell's death and there were marked bargains on that day of 200p, 210p and 220p.

    Calculate the value of Russell's shares in Brand plc for the purposes of inclusion in his death estate.

6. **State the four main conditions that must be satisfied for business property relief (BPR) to be available.**

7. **Explain when an individual is deemed to be domiciled in the UK for IHT purposes.**

Progress Test 1 (continued)

Study Period 7 — High Priority

8   Jean set up an investment company with her husband, Lewis, her brother, Eric and an unrelated person, Roy. The shareholdings were:

Jean   20% (valued at £80,000)
Lewis 10% (valued at £25,000)
Eric   40% (valued at £260,000)
Roy   30% (valued at £150,000)

Jean wants to give half of her shares to her son, William.

You are required to explain how the transfer will be valued for inheritance tax purposes and calculate the value of the transfer which may be chargeable to inheritance tax.

9   Sylvia died on 29 June 2009 leaving an estate valued at £432,000 to her daughter. Sylvia had received £30,000 (a tax free gift) on the death of her uncle Peter in May 2006. Uncle Peter's estate had settled the tax of £4,500.

You are required to calculate the IHT payable on Sylvia's death, assuming she had made no lifetime transfers.

10 Edna gifted a painting to her son, Albert, on 12 April 2004 when it was worth £75,000.

Edna had made gross chargeable transfers totalling £320,000 in 2001.

She died on 22 September 2009, leaving her estate worth £1.2 million to Albert. The painting was found to be a copy worth only £12,500 at the date of Edna's death.

You are required to calculate the IHT payable in respect of the gift and on Edna's death.

11 Wayne, who is now in poor health and has had to stop work, plans to transfer ownership of his house to his son James. He wishes to continue to live in the house.

You are required to set out the implications of Wayne's intentions for inheritance tax purposes and explain how can any potential problems be mitigated.

12 Jon who is resident, ordinarily resident and domiciled in the UK died on 3 December 2009. The following assets were included in his estate:

- His sole trader business, owned for the past 3 years and valued at £300,000
- Farm in Canada tenanted throughout the last 9 years with an open market value of £200,000 and an agricultural value of £70,000:
- 4,000 shares in Tin Ltd, an unquoted investment company, which he has owned for three years and are worth £120,000.

You are required to calculate the values of these assets to be included in the estate, after any available reliefs have been claimed.

You will find the answers to this test starting on page 117. If you answer more than 6 questions correctly, your performance is satisfactory; if you answer more than 8 correctly, you are doing well. Once you have reviewed how you have performed, go back over topics where you feel your understanding is poor.

Capital gains tax – basic principles

Study Period 8

High Priority

Step 1 Exam Guidance

The principles in this Study Period will not be examined in isolation. This chapter provides the fundamental information you need to be able to calculate capital gains tax (CGT) liabilities for trusts and their beneficiaries.

The topics in this chapter are likely to be examined as part of a trusts CGT question, as they were in Question 10 of the sample paper.

Step 2 Introduction to the session

To be in a position to deal with many tax issues relating to trusts, we must have some basic CGT knowledge. If you have already studied CGT for another paper of the CTA syllabus you may only need to review this Chapter, revising the basic principles.

The instructions given in Step 3 below presume you are studying this chapter **without** any previous knowledge and are based on Chapters 9 and 10 of the Taxation of Individuals module.

Step 3 Guidance through the Study Text

Read through Chapter 8 of the Study Text after reading the following guidance. After reading Section 1 for introduction turn to Chapters 9 and 10 of the '**Taxation of Individuals Awareness**' section of the text.

Sections 1 and 2 of Chapter 9 provide essential CGT background knowledge. Read through quickly but carefully.

Now turn to Chapter 10. Learn the proforma for calculating a capital gain in Section 1. Attempt Example 1. Read Sections 2.1 and 2.2 only on capital losses. Attempt Examples 2 to 4. You do not need to read the rest of this section. Then read through Section 3 which deals with assets acquired before 31 March 1982 and attempt Example 7.

Read Section 4 on valuation and try Examples 8 and 9. Quickly read through Section 5 on connected persons. Then cover Section 7.1 (but not 7.2) on part disposals and attempt Example 11. Then read Section 8 on compensation and work through Examples 13 and 14.

Next you need to study entrepreneurs' relief which is covered in detail in Section 4 of Chapter 10 of the Taxation of Unincorporated Businesses section of the text. Turn to this section and, after ensuring you understand when the relief applies, attempt Example 4.

Finally, turn back to Section 2.2 of Chapter 8 of the IHT, Trusts and Estates text. Gift relief is an **essential** topic for trusts and is considered again in a later study period.

Step 5 i-Pass and Workbook Questions

Now attempt ESQs 8.1 to 8.4 which will help to reinforce your knowledge of the topics covered in this study period and give you examples of the types of question you may see in the exam.

Your TQT's i-Pass CD Rom also contains some basic CGT questions.

Step 4 Quick Quiz

Please attempt the quick quiz at the end of Study Text Chapter 8 to reinforce your understanding.

You may find it best to do this after a break, so that you can see what you remember and what you don't.

Module 2: IHT, trusts and estates

Study Period 9

IHT for trusts

High Priority

Step 1 Exam Guidance

Trusts are a vital part of the IHT, Trusts and Estates Awareness syllabus. You cannot pass this module without a good knowledge of the different types of trusts that an individual may set up and how they are treated for inheritance tax, capital gains tax and income tax purposes.

This study period focuses on the IHT aspects of trusts. It is essential that you can differentiate between the different types of trust from the beginning of your study of trusts.

The topic was tested in:

- Sample exam paper (Q5)
- May 2009 exam (Q5 and Q11)

Step 2 Introduction to the session

In this Study period we consider the IHT treatment of trusts set up during lifetime and those set up on death. This can be very different depending on the type of trust.

We also look at the special IHT rules for certain trusts set up for children on the death of a parent.

Step 3 Guidance through the Study Text

Read through Chapter 9 of the Study Text, after reading the following guidance:

Read through Section 1 which covers the IHT rules for lifetime trusts. Make sure that you can distinguish between the different IHT charges (the 'exit' and 'principal' charges) and can calculate them accordingly using the proformas provided. Attempt Examples 1 to 5.

Section 1.7 is lower priority, so read through quickly and try the two examples, following through with the solution on this occasion.

Then read Sections 2.1 to 2.2 which deal with immediate post death interest trusts (IPDI trusts): special 'interest in possession' (IIP) trusts set up on death. Could you spot an IPDI trust in the exam? Work through Examples 8 and 9.

Section 2.3 covers trusts for children that have favourable IHT treatment. Again, make sure that you can distinguish between the different types as the IHT treatment for each differs. Attempt Example 10.

Read through Sections 3 to 6 quickly as these are lower priority. Do however read Section 7 carefully as this sets out the rules that applied to trusts before 22 March 2006 and are still potentially examinable, although the new rules are more important.

Step 5 i-Pass and Workbook Questions

Now attempt ESQs 9.1 to 9.7 which will help to reinforce your knowledge of the topics covered in this study period and give you examples of the types of question you may see in the exam.

Your TQT's i-Pass CD Rom also contains some questions covering IHT for trusts.

Step 4 Quick Quiz

Please attempt the quick quiz at the end of Study Text Chapter 9 to reinforce your understanding.

You may find it best to do this after a break, so that you can see what you remember and what you don't.

108 Module 2: IHT, trusts and estates

Study Period 10

CGT for trusts

High Priority

Step 1 Exam Guidance

CGT for trusts is very examinable.

It is possible that you will see trustees actually disposing of an asset. However, more likely is seeing the trustees passing out a trust asset to a beneficiary (a 'deemed' disposal). This will require the calculation of a gain and almost always the consideration of gift relief.

CGT for trusts was tested in:

- Sample exam paper (Q10)
- May 2009 exam (Q3 and Q6)

Step 2 Introduction to the session

In this Study period we consider the CGT treatment of trusts.

The CGT position for all trusts is the same in terms of the calculations required and rules that apply (contrast this with the IHT treatment). However, the gift relief position differs depending on what type of trust it is and entrepreneurs' relief is only available to trustees of IIP trusts.

This is a relatively short session, so spend any extra time you may have recapping the IHT and CGT treatment of trusts.

Step 3 Guidance through the Study Text

Read through Chapter 10 of the Study Text, which deals with the CGT consequences during the life of a trust, after reading the following guidance:

Read Section 1 which looks at the CGT consequences of setting up a trust from the settlor's perspective. Bear in mind the gift relief position as you are reading through.

Then read Section 2 which looks at actual disposals. Note the similarities between the computation for trustees and individuals and ensure you understand when entrepreneurs' relief is available. No gift relief to consider here as there is no gift.

Section 3 is extremely important as it deals with 'deemed disposals' by trustees (ie usually where the trustees give the assets to the beneficiaries) and capital losses. Note the different gift relief position depending on the type of trust. Attempt Example 1.

Quickly read through Sections 4 to 6 which are lower priority. Do however spend some time working through the summary table in Section 7. Try and see if you can reproduce this table without looking!

Step 4 Quick Quiz

Please attempt the quick quiz at the end of Study Text Chapter 10 to reinforce your understanding.

You may find it best to do this after a break, so that you can see what you remember and what you don't.

Step 5 i-Pass and Workbook Questions

Now attempt ESQs 10.1 to 10.7 which will help to reinforce your knowledge of the topics covered in this study period and give you examples of the types of question you may see in the exam.

Your TQT's i-Pass CD Rom also contains some questions on CGT for trusts.

Module 2: IHT, trusts and estates

Study Period 11

Income tax for trusts

High Priority

Step 1 Exam Guidance

The final area of trusts that could be examined in the IHT, trusts and estates Awareness module is income tax for trusts.

Income tax for trusts was tested as follows:

- Sample paper (Q6 and Q7)
- May 2009 exam (Q8)

Step 2 Introduction to the session

We now complete our study of trusts by considering the income tax treatment of trustees and beneficiaries.

The treatment depends on the type of trust, so you must be able to distinguish between a discretionary trust and an interest in possession (IIP) trust.

Step 3 Guidance through the Study Text

Read through Chapter 11 of the Study Text after reading the following guidance:

Skim read Section 1 on bare trusts.

Carefully read through Section 2 covering the income tax position of IIP trusts and their beneficiaries. Try Example 1. You should find the trust's tax calculation even easier to deal with than one for an individual.

Then read Sections 3.1 to 3.4 which set out the rules for discretionary trusts and their beneficiaries. Work through Examples 2 and 4.

A very important section is Section 3.5 which deals with the 'tax pool' that exists for discretionary trusts. Read it through carefully and then attempt Example 5.

Quickly read Section 4. You may wish to look back at your CGT notes on vulnerable beneficiary trusts so that you have a complete picture of the income tax and CGT treatment of them.

Finally read Section 5 on settlor interested trusts. Again you may wish to refer to your notes on the CGT implications for settlor interested trusts at this point.

Step 4 Quick Quiz

Please attempt the quick quiz at the end of Study Text Chapter 11 to reinforce your understanding.

You may find it best to do this after a break, so that you can see what you remember and what you don't.

Step 5 i-Pass and Workbook Questions

Now attempt ESQs 11.1 to 11.7 which will help to reinforce your knowledge of the topics covered in this study period and give you examples of the types of question you may see in the exam.

Your TQT's i-Pass CD Rom also contains some questions on income tax for trusts.

Study Period 12

Estates in administration

High Priority

Step 1 Exam Guidance

It is likely that at least one question will be set on some aspect of the taxation of a deceased person's estate whilst it is in 'administration'. A question could have an income tax or capital gains tax slant.

Question 11 on the Sample Paper tested the calculation of income tax for the personal representatives of an estate in administration.

Step 2 Introduction to the session

In this study period we consider the tax position of estates in administration. An estate is 'in administration' from the date the deceased dies after the value of the estate is worked out, all IHT is paid and the assets are distributed to beneficiaries of the estate.

You must understand the income tax and capital gains tax implications for both the personal representatives of the estate and any beneficiaries of the estate.

Step 3 Guidance through the Study Text

Read Chapter 12 of the Study Text after reading the following guidance:

Quickly read Section 1 for background.

Read Section 2 covering the PRs' income tax liability. Which type of trust is taxed in a very similar way? Discretionary or IIP? Attempt Example 1.

Then read Section 3 which sets out the income tax rules for the beneficiaries of an estate and work through Examples 2 to 4.

We then turn to the CGT aspects of estates in administration. Section 4 deals with the PRs' position and Section 5 with the beneficiaries. Try Example 5.

You have now completed your study of the **Inheritance Tax, Trusts and Estates Awareness** module.

Step 4 Quick Quiz

Please attempt the quick quiz at the end of Study Text Chapter 12 to reinforce your understanding.

You may find it best to do this after a break, so that you can see what you remember and what you don't.

Step 5 i-Pass and Workbook Questions

Now attempt ESQs 12.1 to 12.6 which will help to reinforce your knowledge of the topics covered in this study period and give you examples of the types of question you may see in the exam.

Your TQT's i-Pass CD Rom also contains some questions on estates in administration.

Study Period 13

Progress Test 2

High Priority

In order to reinforce what you have learnt so far, answer the following questions. Try to answer them without referring to your Study Text or notes. The test should take you no longer than one hour and covers Study Periods 8-12. Solutions start on page 121.

1. Mr Roberts died on 5 April 2008.

   Calculate the income tax payable by his estate for 2009/10 assuming the estate received the following income:

	£
Rents received from a furnished letting	9,000
Bank interest received	948
Dividends received	1,170

2. The Hick interest in possession trust received the following income in 2009/10:

	£
Bank interest	828
Dividends	1,215
Gross rental income	27,000

   And incurred the following expenses:

	£
Expenses re: rental property	2,700
Trust administration expenses	1,350

   Calculate the trust's income tax liability for 2009/10.

3. The Danston discretionary trust received the following income in the tax year 2009/10.

	£
Dividends	3,240
Gross rental income	32,400

   And, incurred the following expenses:

	£
Expenses re: rental property	2,700
Trust administration expenses	1,701

   No distributions were made during 2009/10.

   Calculate the trust's income tax liability for the tax year 2009/10.

4. Orinocho transferred an investment property worth £200,000 to a discretionary trust on 1 October 2004. The property had cost Orinocho £150,000 on 1 August 2004. Orinocho claimed gift relief on the transfer of the property into trust.

   The trustees sold the property on 1 February 2010 for £500,000. The property has never been occupied by a beneficiary of the trust.

   Calculate the trustee's chargeable gain on this disposal.

Module 2: IHT, trusts and estates

Progress Test 2 (continued)

Study Period 13 — High Priority

5 Petra created a discretionary trust on 1 September 2003, placing £380,000 of cash into the trust. Her cumulative total of gross chargeable lifetime transfers up to that point was £245,000 (relating to a transfer on 1 August 2000). Petra paid the IHT due on creation of the trust. On 31 March 2010, the trustees made an absolute appointment of trust capital to one of the beneficiaries of £100,000. The trustees bear the IHT payable.

Calculate the inheritance tax payable by the trustees on the exit from the trust.

6 Jimmy died on 12 September 1999 and under his will he set up a discretionary trust with £250,000 of cash with any IHT due being paid by his estate. The trust used the cash to buy shares in an unquoted trading company worth £150,000.

In the 7 years before his death he had made gross chargeable transfers totalling £208,000.

Calculate the first principle charge on the trust assuming that on 11 September 2009 the shares were worth £200,000 and the rest of the trust assets consisted of £140,000 in cash.

7 In 1989 Henry had set up a life interest trust for his niece Amy. A 5% holding of shares in Bramble Ltd (an unquoted company) had been settled and Henry had made a claim to hold over the gain of £20,000 on those shares. Holdings of quoted shares had also been settled at the same time.

Amy died in June 2009. At that time the trust assets consisted of:

Holding	Value at death £	Cost £	Date of acquisition
5% holding in Bramble Ltd	80,000	55,000	1989
1,000 Orange plc shares	15,000	6,000	1996
2,000 Apricot plc shares	25,000	9,000	1990

You are required to explain the CGT position of the trustees on Amy's death.

8 On 1 March 2000, Lisa transferred quoted shares valued at £709,000 into a discretionary trust, with Lisa paying any inheritance tax due.

On 1 August 2009, the trustees distributed half of the shares, worth £482,000, to Paul, a beneficiary. Paul paid any tax due. The remaining shares were worth £495,000 on 1 March 2010.

Lisa had made no other lifetime gifts.

You are required to calculate the inheritance tax payable:

(a) **When the trustees distribute the shares to Paul, and**
(b) **On 1 March 2010.**

9 From 22 March 2006 interest in possession (IIP) trusts set up during lifetime are relevant property trusts.

You are required to state the IHT position both before *and* after 22 March 2006:

(a) **When an individual set up an IIP trust during lifetime.**
(b) **When assets leave an IIP trust either during the lifetime of the life tenant or on the death of the life tenant.**

Progress Test 2 (continued)

Study Period 13 — High Priority

10   Stanley died on 15 August 2008. He left his entire estate worth £1,575,000, including an investment property with a probate value of £625,000, to his daughter Emily.

Emily requested the executors of her father's estate to sell the property on 12 May 2010. The executors received proceeds of £679,900 but had incurred £2,000 of legal fees in obtaining title to the property.

You are required to calculate the executors' gain on the sale of the property.

11   On 6 May 2009 all of the assets comprised in a discretionary settlement were advanced to Sally, one of the beneficiaries. The trustees made a capital loss on the advance of £5,000.

The trustees had made substantial capital gains in 2006/07 and 2007/08 but had made a capital loss in 2008/09 of £10,000.

You are required to explain what relief is available for the capital losses.

12   Beryl died on 1 April 2009 leaving her entire estate to her daughter, Janice.

During 2009/10 the personal representatives (PRs) of Beryl's estate received the following income:

	£
Rental income	30,000
Interest income (net)	9,600
Dividend income (net)	18,900

The PR's made a payment to Janice of £45,000 on 31 March 2010.

You are required to calculate the PR's income tax payable for 2009/10 and to explain how the payment to Janice will be treated.

You will find the answers to this test starting on page 121. If you answer more than 6 questions correctly, your performance is satisfactory; if you answer more than 8 correctly, you are doing well. Once you have reviewed how you have performed, go back over topics where you feel your understanding is poor.

Progress Test 1 — Solutions

1
January 2005 – PET	£4,000	
Less: AE of 2004/05	(3,000)	
Less: AE of 2003/04 (b/fwd)	(1,000)	Remaining £2,000 of AE lost
	Nil	

January 2009 – exempt transfer to husband does not use AE of 2008/09

August 2009 – PET	£25,000	
Less: Marriage exemption	(5,000)	
AE of 2009/10	(3,000)	
AE of 2008/09 (b/fwd)	(3,000)	
	14,000	

February 2010 – CLT	£5,000	
2009/10 AE already used against PET	(Nil)	
	£5,000	

2 A potentially exempt transfer (PET) is a transfer of value made during lifetime either from one individual to another or from one individual to a bare trust or a disabled person's trust.

During the lifetime of the transferor, a PET is treated as exempt from IHT.

It does, however, use the available annual exemption(s).

If the transferor dies more than seven years after making the PET, it becomes completely exempt.

If he dies within seven years of making the PET, it becomes chargeable.

3 In lifetime, the gift is a potentially exempt transfer (PET) and so no IHT is payable.

The value of the gift is:

		£
Gift		30,000
Less: marriage exemption (parent)		(5,000)
Less: annual exemption	2006/07	(3,000)
	2005/06	(3,000)
		19,000

As Callum dies within 7 years of the gift, there is tax to pay on death.

However, as Callum has made no other transfers of value, the gift of £19,000 is fully covered by his nil rate band and no tax is payable.

Tax on Death Estate

	£
Death estate value	450,000
Less: nil rate band remaining	
(£325,000 – £19,000)	(306,000)
	144,000
Tax due £144,000 × 40%	57,600

Progress Test 1 — Solutions

4 Lifetime tax:

Gift to cousin = PET, no tax due

Gift to discretionary trust – CLT, therefore tax due:

	£
Value of gift	100,000

No AE as used by PET
Covered by nil rate band of £263,000, therefore no tax to pay

Death tax:

	£	£
Gift to cousin:		343,000
Less AE 2004/05		(3,000)
2003/04		(3,000)
		337,000
Nil rate band at death	325,000	
Chargeable transfers in last 7 years	(Nil)	
NRB remaining		(325,000)
Taxable transfer		12,000
Tax @ 40%		4,800
Taper relief (5 – 6 years)		
60% × £4,800		(2,880)
Tax payable		1,920
Gift to discretionary trust:		
Value of gift		100,000
No nil band remaining		
£100,000 × 40%		40,000
Taper relief (5 – 6 years)		
60% × £40,000		(24,000)
Tax payable (no lifetime tax to deduct)		16,000

5 Share valuation

Lower of:

(a) Quarter-up valuation:

210p + (230p-210p/4) = 215p

(b) Average of highest and lowest marked bargains:

(220p + 200p)/2 = 210p

Therefore 210p 1,000 shares = £2,100

Progress Test 1 — Solutions

6 The conditions that need to be satisfied for BPR to be available are (ROSE):

   (a) *Relevant business property*: the property gifted must be relevant business property (eg a business, qualifying shares etc).

   (b) *Ownership*: The property must have been owned for two years or be replacement business property.

   (c) *Sale contract*: there must be no contract in place for the onward sale of the gifted asset

   (d) *Excepted assets*: when shares are gifted, relief is restricted where the company holds 'excepted' assets (ie investment assets such as rental property, shares, etc.)

7 An individual is deemed to be domiciled in the UK for IHT purposes:

   (a) If he has been resident in the UK for at least 17 out of the past 20 tax years.
   (b) For 36 months after ceasing to be domiciled in the UK for all other purposes.

   These rules only apply for IHT purposes and have no effect for income tax or capital gains tax purposes.

8 The transfer will be subject to the related property rules.

   The value of the transfer is:

	£
Before: 20/30 × £150,000	100,000
After: 10/20 × £80,000	(40,000)
Related value	60,000

   The related value will be used as it is higher than the isolated value which would be:

	£
Before: 20%	80,000
After: 10%	(25,000)
Unrelated value	55,000

9

	£	£
Sylvia's estate		432,000
Less: nil rate band	325,000	
Less: GCTs in last 7 years	(nil)	
		(325,000)
Chargeable estate		107,000
Tax @ 40%		42,800
Less QSR (W)		(1,565)
IHT payable		41,235

   Working
   QSR
   1st tax × net/gross × % (for 3-4 yrs)
   £4,500 × 30,000/34,500 × 40%   1,565

Solutions

Progress Test 1

10 The gift to Albert was a PET so no tax was due during Edna's lifetime. It did however use the annual exemptions of 2004/05 and 2003/04.

As Edna dies within seven years of making the gift the PET becomes chargeable.

The painting has fallen in value since the date of the gift so 'fall in value' relief is available to reduce the IHT due. The original value, however, remains in Edna's cumulative total.

	£	£
Transfer of value		75,000
Less: AE × 2		(6,000)
PET		69,000
Less: fall in value £(75,000 – 12,500)		(62,500)
		6,500
Less: nil rate band	325,000	
Less: GCTs in last 7 years	(320,000)	(5,000)
Chargeable		1,500
Tax @ 40%		600
Less: taper relief (5 – 6 yrs) 60%		(360)
IHT payable		240

Death estate

Estate		1,200,000
Less: nil rate band	325,000	
Less: GCTs in seven years before death (the 2001 GCT is before this)	(69,000)	(256,000)
		944,000
Tax @ 40%		377,600

11 As Wayne plans to give the house away but continue to enjoy the benefit of the house this would be a gift with reservation of benefit. Consequently:

(a) The transfer of ownership is a PET which will become chargeable if Wayne dies within seven years of the gift.

(b) The house will be counted as part of Wayne's estate on death

Whichever option collects the higher tax is chargeable.

The reservation of benefit rules can be avoided if Wayne pays a full commercial rent to James.

12 Jon's Estate

	£	£
Sole trader business	300,000	
less: 100% BPR	(300,000)	
		NIL
Canadian farm (no APR – not in UK or EEA)		200,000
Tin Ltd shares (no BPR – investment company)		120,000

Progress Test 2 — Solutions

		£		£
1	Rents from furnished let	9,000		
	Less: 10% furnished letting wear and tear allowance	(900)		
		8,100	× 20%	1,620
	Bank interest			
	Gross up (948 × 100/80)	1,185	× 20%	237
	Dividends (1,170 × 100/90)	1,300	× 10%	130
	IT liability			1,987
	Less taxed at source			
	Bank			(237)
	Dividends			(130)
	IT payable			1,620

2 The Hick interest in possession trust

	£
Bank interest (828 × 100/80) £1,035 @ 20% =	207
Dividends (1,215) × 100/90 £1,350 @ 10% =	135
Rental income (27,000 − 2,700) £24,300 @ 20% =	4,860
Liability	5,202

Note the trustees' expenses are not deductible

3 The Danston discretionary trust

	£
Rental income (32,400 − 2,700)	29,700
Dividends (3,240 × 10/90)	3,600
Gross income	33,300
Gross income	33,300
Less: expenses of trust (1,701 × 100/90)	(1,890)
Amount chargeable at 40%/32.5%	31,410
£1,000 @ 20% =	200
£28,700 @ 40% =	11,480
£1,710 (£3,600 − £1,890) @ 32.5% =	556
£1,890 @ 10% =	189
	12,425

		£	£
4	Proceeds		500,000
	Less: Cost	200,000	
	Less: gain held over (200,000 − 150,000)	(50,000)	
			(150,000)
	Trustees gain		350,000

Module 2: IHT, trusts and estates

Progress Test 2

Solutions

5   Petra Discretionary Trust

	£
Initial value	380,000
Nil rate band	325,000
Less: GCT of settler in 7 years prior to creation of trust	(245,000)
Available	80,000

£380,000 − £80,000 = £300,000 × 20% = £60,000

Effective rate on £380,000 is $\dfrac{60,000}{380,000} \times 100\% = 100\% = 15.789\%$

Number of quarter years from 1 September 2003 to 31 March 2010 = 26

Rate of IHT is therefore 30% × 26/40 × 15.789% = 3.0789%

Tax payable by the trustees is therefore £100,000 × $\dfrac{3.0789}{100 - 3.0789}$ = £3,177

6

	£	£
Shares (100% BPR)		Nil
Cash		140,000
Current value of trust		140,000
Nil band at PC date	325,000	
Settlor's transfers in 7 years prior to creation of trust	(208,000)	
		(117,000)
		23,000
Tax at 20%		4,600
Effective rate of tax 4,600/140,000 × 100% =	3.2857%	
IHT payable (3.2857% × 30% × £140,000)	£1,380	

7   When Amy's life interest terminates on death there is a tax free uplift to market value at the date of death. The exception is that if gains were held over when an asset was settled, the gain on that asset will be chargeable, but will be limited to the amount of the gain held over.

The chargeable gain accruing to the trustees on Amy's death is thus a maximum of £20,000, the gain held over when the Bramble Ltd shares were settled. It may be possible to make a further claim to hold over the gain against the base cost of the shares in the beneficiary's hands.

Progress Test 2 — Solutions

8 (a) *Exit charge*   £

Notional gift (initial value)   709,000
Less: nil rate band (no GCTs in 7 years before trust was set up)   (325,000)
    384,000
Tax @ 20%   76,800
Effective rate
76,800/709,000 × 100% = 10.83216%
Actual rate (complete quarters: 1.3.00– 1.8.09 = 37)
10.83216% × 37/40 × 30% = 3.00592%   318,000
Exit charge
3.00592% × £482,000   £14,488

(b) *Principal charge 1.3.10*   £   £

Notional gift (current value of remaining shares)   495,000
Less: nil rate band (no GCTs in 7 years before trust was set up)   325,000
 Less: amount subject to exit charge in previous 10 years   (482,000)
        Nil
        495,000
Tax @ 20%   99,000
Effective rate
99,000/495,000 × 100% = 20%
Actual rate
20% × 30% = 6%
Principle charge
6% × £495,000   £29,700

9 *Before 22 March 2006*

If an interest in possession (IIP) trust was set up before 22 March 2006, the transfer to the trust was treated as a potentially exempt transfer (PET) by the settlor.

If the trust ended during the life tenant's lifetime (ie the assets were distributed from the trust) the life tenant was (usually) treated as making a PET (if the assets went to another individual who was not the life tenant's spouse/ civil partner).

If the trust ended on the life tenant's death, the value of the assets in the trust would enter the life tenant's death estate as their 'settled property'.

After 22 March 2006

If an interest in possession (IIP) trust is set up after 22 March 2006, the transfer to the trust is treated as a chargeable lifetime transfer (CLT) by the settlor.

If the trust ends during the life tenant's lifetime or on their death there is an exit charge for IHT purposes as the trust is a relevant property trust.

Solutions

Progress Test 2

10

	£
Proceeds	679,900
Less: cost (probate value)	(625,000)
Less: legal fees (actual fees higher than scale charge allowed (W))	(2,000)
Chargeable gain	52,900

Working – scale charge

Probate value of assets sold/ PV of the total estate × £4,000 (SP 2/04)

£625,000/ £1,575,000 × £4,000   1,587

11 Where a loss accrues on the advance of property, that loss may be transferred to the beneficiary. The loss of £5,000 may be transferred to Sally, but it may only be set off against any gain arising on a disposal of the same property by Sally.

It is not possible for the trustees to carry the losses back against earlier gains. The loss in 2008/09 of £10,000 is unrelieved.

12

Income tax payable by PRs	Non- savings £	Savings £	Dividends £
Rental income	30,000		
Interest: £9,600 × 100/80		12,000	
Dividends £18,900 × 100/90			21,000
Taxable income	30,000	12,000	21,000

	£
Non-savings income: £30,000 @ 20%	6,000
Savings income: £12,000 @ 20%	2,400
Dividend income: £21,000 @ 10%	2,100
	10,500
Less: tax credits on	
Interest @ 20%	(2,400)
Dividends @ 10%	(2,100)
Income tax due	6,000

Janice will be treated as having received income of £45,000 net, which will be taxable on her in 2009/10. This is made up as follows:

	Net £	Tax £	Gross £
Rental income	24,000	6,000	30,000
Interest	9,600	2,400	12,000
Dividends (balance)	11,400	1,267	12,667
	45,000	9,667	54,667

Exam style questions

1.1 John has the following transactions in 2009/10:

   (1) On 1 May 2009 he sells a painting to an antique dealer for £8,000. He later discovers that the painting was actually worth £50,000 at the time of the sale.

   (2) He gifts cash of £50,000 to his spouse on 25 June 2009.

   (3) He donates £150,000 cash to Mencap on 18 August 2009.

   (4) He transfers his own main residence valued at £110,000 to a discretionary trust on 12 November 2009.

   (5) He gifts £5,000 to his father on the occasion of his second marriage on 1 February 2010.

   He has not made any other gifts during his lifetime.

   You are required to explain the inheritance tax treatment of these transactions.

1.2 Raymond and Sally married in December 2009.

   The following gifts were made:

	£
By Raymond's father	
To Raymond, cash of	20,000
To Sally, cash of	20,000
By Raymond (before marriage)	
To Sally, an engagement ring valued at	10,000
By Sally's sister	
To Sally, cash of	5,000

   You are required to explain the inheritance tax treatment of these gifts assuming the donors have already used their annual exemptions for 2009/10 and 2008/09.

1.3 Explain what is meant by the following terms for inheritance tax purposes and give an example of a common gift which falls into each category.

   (1) Chargeable lifetime transfer.
   (2) Potentially exempt transfer.
   (3) Exempt transfer.

1.4 Charles is domiciled in the UK. He made the following transfers to his wife Tamara:

31 January 2003	House in South Africa	£200,000
1 January 2010	Cash	£320,000.

   Charles dies on 12 February 2010. He had made no other lifetime transfers.

   You are required to explain the inheritance tax implications on the above transfers as a result of Charles's death ignoring annual exemptions and assuming:

   (i) **Tamara is domiciled in South Africa.**
   (ii) **Tamara is domiciled in the UK.**

   You are not required to calculate any IHT due.

1.5 In 2009/10 Spencer receives an annual salary of £150,000 and has the following transactions:

(1) He pays his two nieces' school fees which total £1,500. He has paid the fees for the last three years.

(2) He gifts cash of £50,000 to his civil partner, Simon, who is domiciled in Canada.

(3) He gives £100 to his three nephews for their birthdays and a further £100 at Christmas.

(4) He transfers his holiday home in Hawaii, valued at £120,000, to an interest in possession trust of which his sister is the life tenant.

(5) He makes a donation of £50,000 to the Labour Party.

He has not made any other gifts during his lifetime.

You are required to explain the inheritance tax treatment of these transactions.

1.6 Liam makes a number of dispositions during 2009/10.

You are required to state which two of the following dispositions are not transfers of value for Liam for IHT purposes, rather than falling within a specific IHT exemption.

For the purpose of the statements below you should assume that Liam is UK domiciled and is the life tenant of a qualifying interest in possession trust.

A   Liam sells a painting for £5,000. He later finds out that it was an original worth ten times what he sold it for.

B   Liam gives his three nieces £20 each for their birthdays and £25 each for Christmas.

C   The trustees of the life interest trust pass out half of the trust assets to Liam.

D   The trustees of the life interest trust pass out half of the trust assets to Liam's wife.

E   Liam gifts £5,000 to his god-daughter each year at Christmas. He has sufficient after-tax income to cover the payments.

2.1 Thomas made a gift of £283,000 to a discretionary trust in May 2004 and paid any tax due.

He made a further gift of £118,000 to the trust in July 2009, the trustees agreeing to pay any tax due.

You are required to calculate the inheritance tax due in respect of these lifetime transfers.

2.2 William gifted £361,000 to a discretionary trust on 1 June 2006, when the nil rate band was £285,000. William had made no earlier transfers of value.

On 15 August 2009 William died.

You are required to calculate the tax payable as a result of William's death if:

(i) The trustees agreed to pay the inheritance tax.
(ii) William paid the inheritance tax.

2.3 Andy put £363,000 into a relevant property trust on 3 April 2010 paying any tax due.

He dies on 17 September 2014.

His only other lifetime gift was a gross chargeable transfer of £139,500 on 14 June 2006.

You are required to calculate the IHT due on his death assuming that the nil rate band for 2009/10 continues to apply to all future years.

2.4 Walter gifted a painting he had owned for ten years to a discretionary trust in June 2009 when its value was £313,000. The trustees agreed to pay any tax arising.

His only other lifetime transfers had been a gift of £200,000 to the same discretionary trust when he set it up in March 2006 and a gift of £16,000 cash to his son in December 2008.

You are required to calculate the IHT due in respect of the gift of the painting.

2.5 Jake gave his daughter £84,000 on the event of her marriage in August 2006.

His only other lifetime transfer was the transfer of £265,000 into a discretionary trust, the beneficiaries of which were Jake's wife and their children, in May 2005.

Jake died on 25 November 2009.

You are required to calculate the inheritance tax due in respect of these lifetime transfers.

2.6 Sherry dies on 6 November 2009.

On 1 July 2004 she had given a car worth £32,000 to her daughter, Frances, and on 14 January 2005 she had set up a discretionary trust with cash of £428,000. Frances was one of the class of beneficiaries.

She had made no other lifetime gifts.

You are required to calculate the IHT due on Sherry's death.

3.1 Hazel owns 51% of the issued share capital of Oxford Ltd, an unquoted investment company. There are 10,000 £1 ordinary shares in the company.

The shares in the company are valued as follows:

51% holding	£150 per share
49% holding	£120 per share
2% holding	£ 50 per share

On 20 April 2009 Hazel gave 200 of her shares to a discretionary trust. She had set up the trust with cash of £163,000 on 15 May 2006.

You are required to calculate the IHT due in respect of the gift of shares.

3.2 The 10,000 issued shares in Brown Plc, an investment company, are held as follows:

	% holding	No of shares
Mr Brown	40	4,000
Mrs Brown (wife)	20	2,000
Jim Brown (son)	30	3,000
David Brown (nephew)	10	1,000

On 1 June 2006 Mrs Brown gave 1,500 shares to Jim. On that date the values of Brown Plc shares are agreed to be:

	£
0 – 25%	300
26 – 50%	600
51 – 75%	900
76 – 100%	1,200

Mrs Brown dies on 24 September 2009. She had made no other lifetime gifts.

You are required to calculate the IHT due in respect of the shares.

3.3 Shares in Finance Ltd, an investment company, with an issued share capital of 100 ordinary shares of £1 each, are held as follows:

Michael	45
Adrianne (his wife)	25
Unrelated third parties	30
	100

Current values for the shares are:

Shareholding	£
5%	20,000
40%	380,000
45%	420,000
65%	680,000
70%	740,000

Michael gifts a 5% holding to an interest in possession trust for his three children on 6 May 2009.

His only other lifetime gift was a gross chargeable transfer of £290,000 in June 2003.

You are required to calculate the IHT due in respect of the shares.

3.4 Conrad made a gift on 14 March 2010 of 10,000 shares in Minitip plc and 10,000 shares in Maxipack plc to a discretionary trust. The trustees agreed to pay the tax.

At the date of the gift the shares were valued as follows:

Minitip plc
Quoted at £21.80 – £22.25. Recorded bargains of £21.20, £21.75, £22.20 and £22.25.

Maxipack plc
Quoted at £12.00 – £12.80. There was only one recorded bargain of £12.25.

Conrad had made an earlier gross chargeable transfer of £175,000 in June 2008.

You are required to calculate the IHT due in respect of the shares.

3.5 Anya owns 12,000 Dale plc shares.

On 1 February 2010 the shares were quoted at 331.75 – 334.25, with bargains at 330, 333.25 and 334.

The shares had gone ex-dividend on 19 January 2010 and the dividend of 12.2p per share was paid on 5 February 2010.

You are required to explain and calculate the IHT value of the Dale plc shares if:

(i) Anya gifts the shares to a discretionary trust on 1 February 2010.
(ii) Anya dies on 1 February 2010 still owning the shares.

3.6 Sebastian made the following lifetime gifts:

(i) Villa in Spain to his brother, Richard on 12 August 2003.

At the date of the gift the villa is worth €468,000. The buying exchange rate on that day was €1.39 and the selling rate was €1.20.

(ii) 10,000 units in the Cosby Unit Trust to an interest in possession trust on 4 May 2008.

The bid price of units on that date was £3.58 and the offer price was £3.62.

Sebastian dies on 12 October 2009.

You are required to calculate the IHT due on his death in respect of his lifetime gifts.

4.1 Luke acquired 30% of Horace Ltd, a trading company, in July 2005. In February 2009 he gave the shares to his son, Marc, when they were worth £750,000. The value of the assets owned by Horace Ltd at the date of transfer were as follows:

	£
Office building	2,225,000
Goodwill	525,000
Net current assets	75,000
Cash (for day to day transactions)	20,000
Listed shares (<1% investments)	45,000
	2,890,000

Luke's only other transfer was a gross chargeable lifetime transfer of £500,000 in 2004.

Luke died on 12 March 2010. Marc still held the shares at the date of Luke's death which were then worth £795,000.

You are required to explain and calculate the IHT liability on Luke's death.

4.2 Jack has owned a newsagent since 1983. He sold it in February 2009, and reinvested the proceeds three months later in a health food store. He gave away the health food business in June 2010.

Olga inherited her husband's business when he died in June 2009. He had run the business since 2000. Olga gave the business away in December 2009, to her son.

Simon set up a trading business in January 2007. In July 2008 he gifted the business to his civil partner, John. John died in August 2009, leaving his estate to his niece, Amy.

You are required to explain on which of the above transfers business property relief be available and why.

4.3 Joan gave her entire 20% holding in ABC Ltd to her son on 4 June 2006. She had acquired these in 1999 for £40,000. Her husband, Alex owns 10% of the shares.

The assets of ABC Ltd at the date of the gift comprised:

	£
Land and buildings	300,000
Plant and machinery (exempt from CGT)	50,000
Investments	80,000
Net current assets	70,000
Total market value	500,000

The values of various shareholdings on 4 June 2006 are:

10% : £30,000
20% : £90,000
30% : £147,000

Joan dies on 21 March 2010. She had made one gross chargeable transfer of £427,500 in April 2001.

You are required to calculate the inheritance tax liability on Joan's death.

4.4 Arthur owned a factory for many years which was used for business purposes by Daley Ltd, an unquoted company wholly owned by Arthur.

In August 2009 Arthur gave the factory to his son when its value was £650,000. He had made no other gifts during his lifetime.

His son sold the factory in November 2009.

The factory was used throughout by Daley Ltd.

Arthur died on 25 December 2009.

You are required to calculate the inheritance tax liability on Arthur's death.

4.5 Arthur owned a factory for many years which was used for business purposes by Daley Ltd, an unquoted company wholly owned by Arthur.

In August 2009 Arthur gave the factory to an interest in possession trust for his son when its value was £676,000. He had made no other gifts during his lifetime.

The trustees sold the factory in November 2009.

The factory was used throughout by Daley Ltd.

Arthur died on 25 December 2009.

You are required to calculate the inheritance tax liability on Arthur's death.

4.6 Barney has had a 10% stake in his family's partnership for many years. His assets include:

(i) Partnership capital account valued at £60,000.

(ii) Land which he owns but which is occupied and farmed by the partnership under a 30 year agricultural tenancy dated October 1990. It is valued at £800,000, of which £600,000 is agricultural value. There is a mortgage of £200,000 on the property.

You are required to explain and calculate the APR and BPR available if Barney gifts both assets on 15 January 2010.

4.7 Barry died on 18 July 2009 leaving his entire estate to his wife, Melody.

During his lifetime he had made the following gifts:

14 May 2000 he made a cash gift of £91,000 to his nephew, Keith.

12 April 2004 he made a gross chargeable transfer of £238,000 to a discretionary trust.

25 June 2005 he gave £50,000 to his daughter, Francesca, in consideration of her marriage, which took place on that date.

3 October 2008 he transferred a 3% holding of unquoted trading company shares, valued at £750,000, to the discretionary trust created in April 2004 with his grandchildren as beneficiaries. The trustees had sold the shares by the date of Barry's death.

You are required to calculate the IHT due as a result of Barry's death.

5.1 Raoul, who is UK domiciled, dies in September 2009 leaving a house in France worth £125,000, personal property situated in France worth £30,000, a house in Scotland worth £180,000 and personal property situated in the UK worth £100,000.

His debts are a loan secured against the French house of £110,000, a loan secured against the Scottish house of £200,000 and a British Gas bill of £120.

Funeral expenses were £1,500.

You are required to calculate Raoul's death estate for IHT purposes.

5.2 Joe died on 10 August 2009.

His free estate was worth £293,000 which passed to his children. He was also the life tenant of a trust set up on his brother's death. The assets in the trust were worth £350,000 and passed to his son on his death.

Joe's only lifetime gift had been a gift to a discretionary trust of £380,000 in June 2000.

You are required to calculate the IHT liability arising as a result of Joe's death and state by whom it is payable.

5.3 Nicholas died in December 2004 leaving his whole estate of £130,000 to his brother David. IHT payable on Nicholas' death was £38,250.

David died on 1 December 2009 and his estate comprised:

Villa abroad	€260,000
Personal chattels (in UK)	£400,000

At the date of David's death the buying exchange rate was €1.5286 and the selling rate was €1.4086.

His personal representatives incurred additional costs in administering the foreign property of €15,750.

David had made no lifetime transfers.

You are required to calculate the IHT liability arising as a result of David's death.

5.4 Roberta died on 12 January 2006 leaving a UK property worth £250,000 to her brother Ronald. The IHT payable in respect of the property was £12,750. She left the rest of her estate to her daughter, Pearl.

Ronald died on 16 March 2010. He left his entire estate worth £500,000 to his niece, Pearl. He had made a gross chargeable transfer of £350,000 in October 2005.

You are required to calculate the IHT payable in respect of Ronald's estate.

5.5 Lionel was left a cottage in France on his uncle's death in August 2005. The cottage was worth £100,000 and the tax paid on it was £19,000.

Lionel sold the cottage in July 2007 for £263,000 and immediately gifted the entire proceeds to a discretionary trust. The trustees agreed to pay the tax.

Lionel dies in October 2009, leaving a free estate worth £500,000.

He also had a qualifying interest in possession in a trust, the capital assets of which are worth £105,000.

You are required to show the IHT payable in respect of Lionel's estate by the executors and the trustees.

5.6 Samantha died on 17 March 2010. She was UK resident, ordinarily resident and domiciled at the time of her death.

On that date her estate contained the following assets:

- The family home valued at £675,000. This was owned as joint tenants with her husband, Neil, who is also UK resident, ordinarily resident and domiciled.
- 15,000 shares in QuickTab Plc. On the date of death the shares were quoted at 562 – 568 with bargains at 562.5, 563, 565 and 567.5.
- A holiday home in Tuscany valued at €727,000. The selling rate €1.15 at the date of death was and the buying rate was €1.19. Expenses incurred in connection with administering the property came to €40,000.
- Personal chattels totalling £100,000.

There was an outstanding repayment mortgage of £175,000 on the UK property. Samantha's funeral costs were £15,675.

Samantha's will left everything to her three children equally.

You are required to calculate the value of Samantha's death estate.

5.7 Bart died on 7 August 2009 leaving a free estate valued at £800,000.

Bart was the life tenant of an IIP trust set up by his wife, Lily, on her death ten years ago. Lily had left her entire estate to the trust and had never made any lifetime gifts except within her annual exemptions.

The capital value of the assets in the trust at the date of Bart's death was £400,000. The remaindermen of the trust are Bart's two daughters.

Included in Bart's free estate was a holiday cottage in Cornwall that he had inherited on his grandfather's death on 12 September 2007. On that date the cottage was worth £215,000 and his grandfather's executors had paid inheritance tax of £42,000.

Bart left his estate to his two daughters.

Bart had made one gross chargeable transfer of £171,000 in May 2005.

You are required to calculate the Inheritance Tax due from:

(1)　Bart's PRs and
(2)　The trustees of the IIP trust

as a result of Bart's death, assuming all relevant claims are made.

5.8 Stuart Rumsfeld died on 14 November 2009 leaving his entire estate to his children. In his estate were the following assets:

(i)　25,000 shares in Aspen Ltd

Aspen Ltd is an unquoted trading company with 100,000 issued shares. Stuart has owned the shares since 1997.

The current values of the shares are as follows:

100% holding	£1,000,000
75% holding	£600,000
50% holding	£375,000
25% holding	£150,000

Stuart's second wife, Miranda, also owns 25% of the shares.

(ii)　Rumsfeld farm

The farm is located in the UK and includes a farmhouse, workers cottages and farm buildings. It is worth £2.6 million. Stuart inherited the farm on the death of his first wife, Doreen, on 1 May 1996. The farm is still rented to the same farmer on the 25 year lease that began on 1 January 1993.

(iii)　Cash and personal assets valued at £300,000.

Doreen had left most of her estate, including the farm, to Stuart in May 1996 but had left gifts that used up two thirds of the nil rate band at the time to her two children.

You are required to calculate the Inheritance Tax due on Stuart's death assuming all available reliefs are claimed and that Stuart had made no previous lifetime gifts.

5.9 Tasha has been UK resident and ordinarily resident since 1996. She is legally domiciled in Estonia.

In her estate she currently has the following assets:

Property in Estonia	£45,000
Shares in HB Plc, a UK incorporated company	£12,000
House in UK	£354,000
Deposits with HSBS Bank	
Estonian branch	£10,000
UK branch	£50,000
Jewellery and other personal assets in the UK	£7,500
Cash ISA accounts	£30,000
Car in the UK	£23,000

Tasha has never made any gifts during her lifetime, except to use her annual exemptions.

You are required to advise Tasha on her potential Inheritance Tax liability if she were to die during 2009/10 leaving her entire estate to her brother who lives in Estonia.

6.1 Andrew died on 10 May 2009.

His estate included a property in London worth £705,000, a car worth £35,000 and a villa in Portugal worth £120,000.

He also held a number of quoted shares at his death which were valued for probate purposes as follows:

	£
Lue Plc	15,000
Range plc	22,000
Reen plc	32,000

His personal representatives sold the shares as follows:

	Date of Sale	Gross Sale Proceeds £
Lue plc	14 November 2009	9,000
Range plc	15 January 2010	20,000
Reen plc	15 June 2010	30,000

The PRs acquired shares in Rown plc for £15,000 on 11 March 2010.

Andrew's only lifetime gift had been a gross chargeable transfer of £213,000 to a discretionary trust on 12 June 2004.

You are required to calculate the inheritance tax due assuming all available reliefs are claimed.

6.2 Tom died on 12 February 2010 owning personal assets worth £350,000.

The only transfers that he had made during his lifetime were as follows:

(i) 18 November 2002 – Gift of £155,000 cash to a discretionary trust.
(ii) 14 February 2007 – Gift of quoted investments worth £235,000 to his brother.

The investments transferred to his brother in 2007 were still owned by him at the date of Tom's death when they were worth £197,500.

You are required to calculate the inheritance tax due on Tom's death and state who is responsible for payment.

6.3 Keith died on 24 May 2009. His estate included 120,000 shares in Madden Ltd, an unquoted investment company. Keith's civil partner, Martin, owned the remaining 80,000 shares in the company.

HMRC Shares Valuation Division agreed the following values for the shares:

100% holding	£2,500,000
60% holding	£1,000,000
40% holding	£480,000

On 28 February 2012 the PRs sold the shares to an unconnected third party for £1,200,000.

Keith had made a gross chargeable lifetime transfer of £400,000 on 12 October 2004. The other assets in Keith's estate were valued at £325,000. He left his entire estate to his niece, Louise.

You are required to calculate:

(i) **The original IHT liability on the estate, and**
(ii) **The tax repayment obtained as a result of the sale of the shares.**

6.4 Maureen transfers land worth £700,000 into a discretionary trust. This is her only lifetime transfer and she paid the tax.

Almost four years later, Maureen dies.

Due to a fall in property values, the land is worth only £550,000 at the date of her death.

You are required to discuss briefly the IHT implications of the gift to the trust during Maureen's lifetime and on her death.

6.5 Serena died on 12 June 2009.

Her estate included the following:
(i) 10,000 shares in Regedit Ltd, an unquoted trading company, worth £540,000, that she had owned for six years.
(ii) Personal property worth £65,000.
(iii) A house in Lancashire worth £250,000.
(iv) A flat in London worth £750,000.

Serena's executors sold the flat on 18 July 2011 for £775,000. They paid legal fees of £15,000. They bought another flat for £565,000 on 28 September 2011.

On 24 November 2012 they sold the house in Lancashire for £195,000 (legal fees of £2,500).

Serena's only lifetime gift had been £450,000 to a discretionary trust in May 2002.

You are required to calculate the inheritance tax due on Serena's death assuming all available reliefs are claimed.

6.6 Charlotte died on 28 April 2009 leaving her entire estate, worth £1,895,000, to her only daughter, Emily. Her husband, Spencer, had died in 2001, leaving his assets to a nil band discretionary trust.

Included in the value of the estate were two properties, Moore Manor, valued at £750,000 and Crompton Hall, valued at £925,000.

On 16 June 2011 Charlotte's executors sold Crompton Hall for £888,000 and immediately purchased a much smaller property, Marston Mews, for £475,000.

Charlotte's only lifetime gift had been a gross chargeable transfer of £113,000 to a discretionary trust on 4 May 2004.

You are required to calculate the IHT due on Charlotte's death, assuming all available reliefs are claimed.

7.1 Mike and Sue have been married for many years. Mike is UK domiciled, but Sue is non-UK domiciled.

In January 2007, Mike gives Sue £40,000. He has previously used up his annual exemptions for 2006/07 and 2005/06. His only other lifetime transfer was a gross chargeable transfer of £120,000 in May 2003.

In July 2009 Mike dies leaving his estate, worth £320,000 to Sue.

You are required to explain, with calculations, the IHT position for Mike's estate.

7.2 Nikki is considering making a lifetime gift. She is deciding which of the following gifts she should make:

(i) Creation of a discretionary trust with herself as one of the beneficiaries.
(ii) Gift of an antique painting to her daughter. The painting will need to be kept in Nikki's house for insurance purposes.
(iii) Gift of her house to her son. Nikki will continue to live in it but will pay her son a market rent unless it is tax effective to live in it without any payment.

You are required to comment on the inheritance tax implications of each of the gifts.

7.3 For the whole of 2009/10 Lisa has the use of a vase that is within the Pre Owned Asset Tax (POAT) rules.

The current market value of the vase is £150,000.

Assume that the official rate of interest for 2009/10 is 4.75%

You are required to calculate Lisa's income tax liability for 2009/10 in respect of the vase and to advise her how she can avoid paying this income tax charge.

7.4 Serge dies on 17 April 2009. He came to England in 1983 and had been resident there ever since. His intention had always been to retire to his home country of Latvia.

Serge's estate included the following:
(i) Personal property in the UK worth £25,000.
(ii) A house in Surrey worth £650,000.
(iii) A property in Latvia worth £55,000.
(iv) 10,000 shares in BigTime Plc, a UK registered company, worth £15,000.
(v) An outstanding loan of £10,000 that he made to his brother, Dimitri, who still lives in Latvia.

There is a mortgage on the house in Surrey of £400,000.

Serge had made one lifetime gift of £58,000 cash to his brother on 6 June 2006.

You are required to calculate the IHT liability arising as a result of Serge's death.

7.5 Serge dies on 17 April 2009. He came to England in 1994 and had been resident there ever since. His intention had always been to retire to his home country of Latvia.

Serge's estate included the following:
(i) Personal property in the UK worth £25,000.
(ii) A house in Surrey worth £650,000.
(iii) A property in Latvia worth £55,000.
(iv) 10,000 shares in BigTime Plc, a UK registered company worth £15,000.
(v) An outstanding loan of £10,000 that he made to his brother, Dimitri, who still lives in Latvia.

There is a mortgage on the house in Surrey of £400,000.

Serge had made one lifetime gift of £58,000 cash to his brother on 6 June 2006.

You are required to calculate the IHT liability arising as a result of Serge's death.

7.6 Celia has owned a painting that HMRC has agreed qualifies as heritage property, important for its artistic interest. She has owned it for the last ten years and its current market value is £1,500,000.

Celia is considering placing the painting into a discretionary trust. She has made no other lifetime gifts.

You are required to advise Celia of the inheritance tax implications of the transfer assuming all beneficial claims are made.

7.7 Shamus gifted a painting, a Rembrandt original, to his daughter, Marian, on 7 May 2006. The painting was worth £2 million.

Shamus agreed with Marian that he would continue to hang the painting in his drawing room for the foreseeable future.

Shamus died on 21 October 2009 leaving his entire estate, worth £4.5 million, equally to Marian and his son, Bruce.

Shamus's only other chargeable lifetime transfer had been a gift of £500,000 to a discretionary trust in June 2000.

The Rembrandt painting had a value of £2.5 million by the date of Shamus's death.

You are required to calculate the IHT due as a result of Shamus's death.

8.1 Mary gifted an investment property worth £250,000 to a discretionary trust on 25 June 2009. It had cost her £157,500 in July 2000.

You are required to explain whether gift relief is available and, if so, how much. You should also state the base cost of the investment property for the trustees.

8.2 Bill bought 20 acres of land in 1996 as an investment for £20,000. He sold 5 acres in July 2009 for £30,000 when the remaining 15 acres were valued at £120,000. He has capital losses brought forward from 2008/09 of £12,000.

You are required to calculate the capital gains tax payable.

8.3 June buys a statue in July 1986 for £100,000.

It is destroyed in December 2008 and she immediately receives compensation of £230,000. It has no scrap value. She buys another statue for £180,000 in January 2010.

You are required to explain her CGT position, assuming she makes all relevant claims for relief.

8.4 Sam had been trading as a sole trader for a number of years. On 1 June 2009 he sold his business as a going concern to Angela for £1,500,000.

The value of the assets of the business and the capital gains at the date of the transfer were as follows:

	Market value £	Cost £
Freehold land and buildings	950,000	80,000
Goodwill	500,000	–
Machinery and equipment	6,000	4,000
Stock	50,000	50,000
Debtors	5,000	5,000
Creditors	(11,000)	–
	1,500,000	

The land and buildings were acquired in June 2002.

Calculate Sam's capital gains tax liability for 2009/10 assuming he makes any beneficial claims.

9.1 Linda created a discretionary trust on 1 November 2004, placing £200,000 of cash into the trust. Her cumulative total of chargeable lifetime transfers prior to that point was £208,000 (relating to a transfer on 16 September 2001) and she paid the tax due on the creation of the trust. On 21 March 2010 the trustees made an absolute appointment of capital of £50,000 to one of the beneficiaries.

You are required to calculate the inheritance tax on the exit from the trust assuming it is paid by the beneficiary.

9.2 On 18 November 1999 Anne, who had already used all available exemptions, settled £365,000 on a discretionary trust. She had made no previous chargeable transfers.

On 18 November 2007 the trustees distributed £125,000 to a beneficiary, who agreed to pay any tax. The trust fund had grown in value to £500,000 by that date.

By 18 November 2009 the discretionary settlement was valued at £650,000.

You are required to compute the exit and principal charges.

9.3 On 5 November 2009 Deanna set up a discretionary trust with cash of £650,000. She had made a previous gross chargeable lifetime transfer of £200,000 in August 2006.

On 7 January 2010 the trustees gave £25,000 from the trust to one of the beneficiaries, Lucy, Deanna's daughter.

You are required to explain the IHT consequences of both the gift to the trust and the distribution of cash to the beneficiary, assuming that the trustees pay any IHT liability.

9.4 Colin is the life tenant of an immediate post death interest trust. His daughter, Karen is the remainderman of the trust. The trust assets are currently worth £600,000.

Colin has made no lifetime transfers.

You are required to explain the IHT consequences if the trustees distribute all the trust assets to Karen:

(i) During Colin's lifetime, or
(ii) On Colin's death.

9.5 Fiona dies on 17 April 2008. Her will provides for a trust to be set up with £450,000 for her children Paul (date of birth 19 January 1993) and Stephanie (date of birth 14 June 1996). Fiona made no lifetime gifts.

The trust provides that the beneficiaries will become entitled to their share of the trust capital and income at age 25.

The trustees exercise their discretion on 19 January 2014 and distribute £35,000 to Paul for a deposit on a flat.

You are required to calculate the exit charge in January 2014 assuming 2009/10 tax rates and allowances continue to apply for later years.

9.6 Roger is considering a number of different trusts that he can possibly set up in his will for his three young children. On his shortlist are:

(i) A bereaved minor trust.
(ii) Age 18-25 trust.
(iii) Immediate post death interest trust.
(iv) Discretionary trust.

You are required to comment on the inheritance tax implications of each of the trusts.

9.7 Elizabeth set up a discretionary trust with £400,000 on 1 May 2001, the trustees agreeing to pay the tax. She had made one other gross chargeable transfer of £127,000 in June 1998.

On 15 August 2009 the trustees appointed £50,000 cash out of the trust capital to one of the beneficiaries.

You are required to calculate the Inheritance due:

(1) When the trust was set up, and
(2) When the trustees make the distribution in August 2009.

10.1 The Dibble Interest in Possession Trust was set up in May 2002 when unquoted shares worth £40,000 were transferred into the trust. The gain of £15,000 was deferred by gift relief (under s.165 TCGA 1993). The trust was to benefit Annie during her lifetime, with Jeremy becoming absolutely entitled on her death. Annie died in July 2009 when the shares were worth £65,000.

You are required to explain the capital gain tax consequences arising as a result of Annie's death.

10.2 Philippa bought an investment property for £100,000 in February 2002.

In April 2007 she settled the property into a discretionary trust for the benefit of her son, Angus, when it was valued at £150,000.

On 15 June 2008 Angus celebrated his thirtieth birthday. On that day he became absolutely entitled to the trust capital. Its value at that date was £575,000. Angus sold the property on 15 June 2009 for £650,000.

Angus is a higher rate taxpayer in all relevant years.

You are required to:

(1) Calculate Angus's CGT on the disposal, assuming that all relevant reliefs have been claimed where available.

(2) State whether it would it have been better, had the trust allowed it, for the trustees to retain the property until sale giving reasons for your decision.

10.3 Jane sets up a discretionary trust in March 1997 with an asset she acquired in July 1984. Her deferred gain was £12,000 and the value of the asset was £30,000.

The trustees sell the asset in January 2010 for £50,000.

You are required to calculate the trustees' capital gains tax liability for 2009/10.

10.4 In 1990 David had set up a life interest trust for his nephew Darren. A 5% holding of shares in Alpha Ltd (an unquoted company) had been settled and David had made a gift relief claim to defer the gain of £10,000 on those shares. Holdings of quoted shares had also been settled at the same time.

Darren died in August 2009. At that time the trust assets consisted of:

Holding	Value at death £	Cost £	Date of acquisition
5% holding in Alpha Ltd	60,000	45,000	1990
1,000 Beta plc shares	10,000	8,000	1996
2,000 Gamma plc shares	15,000	5,000	1990

You are required to explain the chargeable gains accruing to the trustees on Darren's death.

10.5 On 6 October 2009 all of the assets in the Jones Discretionary Trust were advanced to Cedric, one of the beneficiaries.

At that date the trustees had capital losses brought forward from the previous year of £2,000 and they made further capital losses on the advance of £3,000. The trustees had made substantial capital gains in 2006/07 and 2007/08.

You are required to briefly explain the reliefs available for the capital losses.

10.6 On 1 May 2002 Samuel gifted his entire 15% holding (1,500 shares) in Dockside Ltd, an unquoted trading company, to a discretionary trust for his son.

The other shares in the company are owned by his two brothers. The company was set up in July 1981 by all three brothers, when each subscribed £5,000 for his shares.

The 15% holding was worth £15,000 in March 1982 and £90,000 at the date it was transferred to the trust. A 100% holding would have been worth £1m.

On 2 November 2009 the trustees of the discretionary trust appoint the Dockside shares to Samuel's son, when they were worth £105,000. The son agrees to pay any IHT due.

You are required to show the CGT consequences of the gift and appointment of the Dockside shares, assuming any available reliefs are claimed.

10.7 The trustees of the Jameson life interest trust are considering distributing 150,000 shares in Jameson Ltd, an unquoted trading company, to the life tenant, Jeremy Jameson.

The shares were first subscribed for at par by Joyce Jameson, the settlor of the trust and Jeremy's aunt, in 1994 when the company was set up. The shares represent a 25% holding.

When Joyce put the shares into the trust in September 2001 they were worth £4.50 per share and a gain of £275,000 arose. She made a gift relief claim. At the time, 12% of the company's chargeable assets were investments.

The trustees would like to know their potential capital gains tax exposure if they distribute the shares to Jeremy in January 2010 when the estimated value will be £9.25 per share. The company's investments have increased to 17% of the total chargeable assets.

Jeremy has never worked for Jameson Ltd.

You are required to calculate the potential capital gains tax liability for the trustees. You should assume that all beneficial claims are made.

11.1 The Pritchard interest in possession trust received the following income in 2009/10:

	£
Bank interest (net)	460
Dividends (net)	675
Gross rents	15,000

The trustees incurred the following expenses:

	£
Expenses in respect of the rental property	1,500
Trust administration	450

You are required to calculate the income tax payable by the trustees and show the statement of income that the life tenant will receive.

11.2 The Young Discretionary Trust received the following income in 2009/10:

	£
Dividends	1,800
Gross rents	18,000

It incurred the following expenses:

	£
Expenses in respect of the rental property	1,500
Trust administration	945

A £500 distribution of income was made to a beneficiary during the year.

You are required to calculate the income tax payable by the trustees and show the statement of income that the beneficiary will receive.

11.3 You are preparing the Trust tax return for 2009/10 for the Elvin Discretionary Trust.

The trust's only income is net rental income of £8,500. Trust administration expenses of £882 were incurred.

In 2008/09, the year the trust was set up, tax of £650 was paid at 20% and 40%.

The first distribution was made in 2009/10 of £6,000.

You are required to calculate the income tax payable by the trustees in 2009/10.

11.4 Frazer is the trustee of an interest in possession trust. The income of the trust is paid to Miranda during her life. For the tax year 2009/10 the trust has the following income and expenses:

Rental income (gross)	£2,500
Dividends (net)	£1,800
Bank interest (net)	£960
Legal fees relating to income	£500
Letting expenses	£275

You are required to calculate the trust's total tax liability, how much tax the trust will have to pay under self-assessment and to show Miranda's statement of income from the trust.

11.5 The Foster Trust is a trust for a bereaved minor. In the year 2009/10, the trustee has the following income and expenses:

Bank interest (net)	£1,800
Dividends	£2,430
Rental income (net of allowable expenses)	£1,100
Expenses relating to income generally	£630

You are required to calculate the total tax liability of the trustee and the tax due under self assessment.

11.6 Assume that the Foster trust (question 11.5 above) has a balance brought forward on its tax pool at 6 April 2009 of £1,267.

The trust makes a net income payment of £1,000 to Peter, a beneficiary on 1 December 2009.

You are required to show the tax pool for 2009/10 and the tax deduction certificate that Peter will receive.

11.7 The trustees of the Percy Smythe discretionary trust received the following income during 2009/10:

Rental income	£16,800
Interest	£2,880
Dividends	£103,500

The trustees incurred revenue expenses of £520 relating to the letting of the trust's unfurnished rental property.

They made income payments of £5,000 to each of the five beneficiaries of the trust on 31 March 2010.

The trust pool carried forward at 6 April 2009 was £1,675.

You are required to:

(1) Calculate the income tax payable by the trustees, and
(2) Show the balance on the tax pool at 5 April 2010.

12.1 Bernard dies on 16 June 2009. Following his death his PRs had the following income and expenses for the rest of 2009/10:

Rental income (gross)	£2,500
Dividends (net)	£1,800
Bank interest (net)	£960
Letting expenses	£275
Administration expenses in relation to income	£500

You are required to calculate the PRs' income tax payable for 2009/10.

12.2 Bernard's estate (question 12.1) above is left equally to his two children, Jayne and Jack.

The administration of the estate is completed on 4 April 2010.

You are required to show the net income due to Jayne and Jack and the tax deduction certificate that each will receive from the PRs.

12.3 Mr Carr died on 30 June 2008. His estate had the following income and expenses during the period 6 April 2009 to 5 November 2009:

	£	
Rental income		
Tax adjusted property income	13,775	
Bank interest		
Credited 1 November 2009 (when account to be closed)	2,240	(net)
Dividends		
15 July 2009 (for the period ended 30.6.09)	2,812	
Professional expenses paid		
Interest on loan taken out to pay IHT (loan taken out 1 October 2008, ceased 1 November 2009)	95	per month
Accountancy fees	1,200	
Agents' fees re rental property	1,650	

You are required to calculate the income tax liability in respect of Mr Carr's estate for 2009/10.

12.4 Tanya dies on 12 December 2008 leaving her entire estate to her son, Jamie.

On 7 January 2010, the estate is still in administration and her executors sell 10,000 shares in Splendid Ltd, an unquoted trading company, from the estate for £156,000. The shares had cost Tanya £116,000 in April 2000 and had a probate value of £127,500.

You are required to calculate the executors' capital gains tax liability.

12.5 Tanya dies on 12 December 2008 leaving an estate worth £565,000.

On 7 January 2010, the estate is still in administration and her executors pass 10,000 shares in Splendid Ltd, an unquoted trading company, to Jamie. At that date they were worth £156,000. Jamie immediately sells the shares.

The shares had cost Tanya £116,000 in April 2000 and had a probate value of £127,500.

You are required to explain the capital gains tax consequences of the appointment of the shares to Jamie and calculate the CGT liability on the sale of the shares.

12.6 The personal representatives of Colin Holden's estate are preparing the tax deduction certificate (R185 (Estate income)) for his wife, Caroline Holden, the sole beneficiary of the estate.

Colin Holden died on 1 July 2009. Since that date the PRs have received the following income

Rental income	£9,900
Interest	£1,200
Dividends	£33,345

The PRs have incurred expenses of £575 so far in connection with the administration of the estate, which is still ongoing. They made an interim payment of £25,000 to Caroline on 12 December 2009.

You are required to calculate:

(1) The income tax payable by the PRs, and
(2) The net figures to be included on the R185 to be given to Caroline.

Solutions to exam style questions

1.1 The IHT treatment of the transactions are as follows:

(1) A sale of an asset at less than market value is not a transfer of value for inheritance tax purposes if there is no intention to confer a gratuitous benefit on the purchaser. Hence, this sale will not have any inheritance tax consequences.

(2) The gift to his spouse is exempt.

(3) The donation to the UK charity is exempt.

(4) The transfer of the main residence is a chargeable lifetime transfer (CLT):

	£
Gift	110,000
Less: AE 09/10	(3,000)
AE 08/09 b/f	(3,000)
Chargeable	104,000

(5) The gift to John's father is covered partly by the marriage exemption. There is no annual exemption left as it has been allocated to the CLT. The balance of the gift is a potentially exempt transfer, which means that it is exempt during John's life time and will only become chargeable if he dies within seven years of making the gift.

	£
Gift	5,000
Less: ME (child to parent)	(1,000)
PET	4,000

1.2 When a gift is made on the occasion of a marriage/ civil partnership ceremony at least £1,000 of the gift is always exempt regardless of who makes the gift and to whom it is made.

Higher exemptions apply depending on the relationship of the donor to the done.

Parent's gift on their child's wedding

A maximum of £5,000 is exempt. So, Raymond's father will be treated as making two potentially exempt transfers (PETs) as follows:

	£
To Raymond	20,000
Less: marriage exemption (ME)	(5,000)
PET	15,000
To Sally - PET	20,000

One party to the marriage making a gift to the other before the marriage

a maximum of £2,500 is exempt. As the couple are not yet married the spouse exemption cannot apply. So, Raymond will be treated as making a PET as follows:

	£
To Sally	10,000
Less: ME	(2,500)
PET	7,500

Any other individual making a wedding gift

A maximum of £1,000 is exempt. So, Sally's sister will be treated as making a PET as follows:

	£
To Sally	5,000
Less: ME	(1,000)
PET	4,000

1.3 IHT definitions:

(1) *Chargeable lifetime transfer.*

A chargeable lifetime transfer is a gift made during lifetime which gives rise to an immediate charge to IHT.

A gift to a relevant property trust during lifetime (ie any trust except a bare trust or a trust for a disabled person) is a CLT.

(2) *Potentially exempt transfer.*

A potentially exempt transfer is a gift made during lifetime which does not give rise to an immediate charge to IHT. There is only an IHT charge if the donor dies within seven years of making the gift.

A gift from one individual to another is a PET.

(3) *Exempt transfer.*

An exempt transfer is a gift made during lifetime or on death which is ignored for IHT purposes.

An example of a gift that is only exempt during lifetime is one that is within the annual exemption.

An example of a gift that is exempt both during lifetime and on death is a gift to a spouse or civil partner.

Note. Candidates may also have mentioned the following examples under (3):

Lifetime exemptions

- Small gifts under £250
- Normal expenditure out of income
- Marriage exemption

Exemptions during lifetime and on death

- Donations to UK charities
- Donations to certain political parties
- Gifts for national purposes (eg National Trust)

1.4

(i) *Tamara domiciled in South Africa*

Gifts from UK domiciled spouses to non-UK domiciled spouses are only exempt up to £55,000. This is a lifetime limit.

	£
Gift 31.1.03	200,000
Less: spouse exemption	(55,000)
PET	145,000

Charles survives more than seven years from making this gift so the PET is completely exempt and no IHT is due.

	£
Gift 1.1.10	320,000
Less: spouse exemption (used)	(nil)
PET	320,000

Charles dies within seven years of making this gift so the PET becomes chargeable and IHT will be due on £320,000.

(ii) *Tamara UK domiciled*

Gifts between UK domiciled spouses are completely exempt with no limit.

There is therefore no IHT due on either of the gifts.

1.5 The IHT treatment of the transactions are as follows:

(1) IHT is a tax on gifts out of capital, so if Spencer can show that the payments of his nieces' school fees come within the exemption for 'normal expenditure out of income' they could be completely exempt. To prove this he must show:

(i) The gifts are made out of his normal expenditure (ie are part of a pattern of giving)
(ii) They are made out of his income, and
(iii) They leave him with sufficient income to maintain his usual standard of living.

Based on the facts it is likely that the exemption will apply.

(2) The transfer to his civil partner is completely exempt as it is within the £55,000 limit for gifts from UK to non-UK domiciled spouses/ civil partners.

(3) The gifts to his nephews are exempt as they come within the small gift exemption. This allows gifts up to £250 each year to the same recipient to be completely exempt.

(4) The transfer of the Hawaii holiday home to the interest in possession trust is a chargeable lifetime transfer (CLT) because the trust is a relevant property trust:

	£
Gift	120,000
Less: AE 09/10	(3,000)
AE 08/09 b/f	(3,000)
Chargeable	114,000

(5) The gift to the Labour Party is exempt as it is a gift to a political party.

1.6 A Liam sells a painting for £5,000. He later finds out that it was an original worth ten times what he sold it for.
 C The trustees of the life interest trust pass out half of the trust assets to Liam.

Certain dispositions are exempt from an Inheritance Tax (IHT) charge, while others are not even transfers of value, so fall outside the scope of IHT.

When Liam sells the painting for less than it was worth, even though his estate has gone down in value considerably, Liam did not mean to make a 'gift' of the painting, ie he had no gratuitous intent. This is a bad bargain and is not caught by the IHT provisions.

When the trustees of the life interest trust pass out half of the trust assets to Liam, there is no transfer of value as before the 'gift' Liam was deemed to own the trust assets and after, he actually owns them, so his estate has not gone down in value.

The other dispositions fall within specific exemptions:

The gifts to his nieces fall within the small gifts exemption of £250 per recipient per tax year

When the trustees of the life interest trust pass out half of the trust assets to Liam's wife, it is treated as Liam making the gift directly, in which case it is exempt (by virtue of the spouse exemption).

The gift to his god-daughter is covered by the 'normal expenditure out of income' exemption.

2.1 When the donor pays the tax the rate must be grossed up.

May 2004

	£	£
Gift		283,000
AEs 2004/05 and 2003/04 b/f		(6,000)
		277,000
Nil rate band	263,000	
GCTs in the 7 years before the gift	–	
		(263,000)
		14,000
IHT @ 20/80		3,500
GCT = £(277,000 + 3,500) =		280,500

July 2009

	£	£
Gift		118,000
AEs 2009/10 and 2008/09 b/f		(6,000)
		112,000
Nil rate band	325,000	
GCTs in the 7 years before the gift	(280,500)	
		(44,500)
		67,500
IHT @ 20%		13,500

2.2 (i) Trustees pay the tax

	£
CLT	361,000
AE 06/07	(3,000)
05/06	(3,000)
Gross chargeable transfer	355,000
Tax payable on death	
40% £(355,000 – 325,000)	12,000
Less: taper relief (3-4 years) @ 20%	(2,400)
Less lifetime tax £(355,000 – 285,000) × 20%	(14,000)
Death tax payable	–

Note that lifetime tax is not repayable.

(ii) *William pays the tax*

	£
Lifetime tax:	
Gift less annual exemptions (see (i)) (361,000 – 6,000)	355,000
Lifetime tax (355,000 – 285,000) × 20/80	17,500
Gross chargeable transfer	372,500
Additional tax on death:	
GCT	372,500
Nil rate band on death	(325,000)
	47,500
Tax payable at 40%	19,000
Less taper relief (3 – 4 years) @ 20%	(3,800)
Less lifetime tax	(17,500)
Death tax payable	–

2.3 The lifetime tax is:

	£	£
Transfer of value	363,000	
Less: AE 2009/10		(3,000)
AE 2008/09 b/f		(3,000)
CLT		357,000
Less: nil rate band	325,000	
Less: GCTs in last 7 yrs	(139,500)	(185,500)
Chargeable		171,500
Tax @ 20/80 or 25%		42,875

The GCT is the total amount that leaves Andy's estate as a result of the gift (ie the gift PLUS the tax): £357,000 + £42,875 = £399,875.

The GCT in 2006 took place more than 7 years before death, so no further tax is due. The tax on the 2010 GCT is:

	£	£
GCT		399,875
Less: nil rate band	325,000	
Less: GCTs in the 7 yrs before the gift	(139,500)	(185,500)
Chargeable		214,375
Tax @ 40%		85,750
Less: taper relief		
(3.4.10 – 17.09.14) = 4 – 5 yrs: 40%		(34,300)
		51,450
Less: lifetime tax		(42,875)
IHT due		8,575

2.4

	£	£
Gift		313,000
AE 09/10		(3,000)
08/09 (used against PET)		nil
CLT		310,000
Less: nil rate band	325,000	
Less: GCTs in 7 yrs before gift		
£(200,000 - 6,000) (AEs 2005/06 and 2004/05)	(194,000)	(131,000)
		179,000
IHT @ 20%		35,800

Notes.

(i) The gift to the son is a PET and does not therefore use up any of the nil rate band whilst Walter is alive although it does use the available annual exemption(s).

(ii) The original transfer to the trust was covered by the nil rate band in that year.

2.5 Jake's gift into the relevant property trust is a chargeable lifetime transfer (regardless of who might benefit from the trust).

Lifetime tax

	£
CLT May 2005	
Transfer	265,000
Less: AE 05/06, 04/05 bf	(6,000)
	259,000

Covered by nil rate band

PET August 2006	
Transfer	84,000
Less: marriage exemption	(5,000)
AE 06/07	(3,000)
	76,000

Death tax

CLT – nil as covered by nil rate band

PET	76,000
Nil rate band available (325,000 – 259,000)	(66,000)
	10,000
Tax @ 40%	4,000
Less: taper relief (3-4 years) 20%	(800)
Death tax chargeable	3,200

2.6 (i) The gift to Frances is a PET, so no tax during lifetime. It does, however, use the available annual exemptions. A car is not an exempt asset for IHT purposes.

(ii) The gift to the discretionary trust is a chargeable lifetime transfer:

14.1.05

	£	£
Gift		428,000
AEs (used against PET)		(nil)
CLT		428,000
Nil rate band	263,000	
GCTs in the 7 years before the gift (PET does not use nil band during lifetime)	–	
		(263,000)
		165,000
IHT @ 20/80 (if the question is silent regarding who pays the tax assume the donor pays it)		41,250
GCT = £(428,000 + 41,250) =		469,250

Death tax: November 2009

(i) The PET becomes chargeable.

	£
Gift	32,000
AEs 2004/05 and 2003/04 b/f	(6,000)
PET	26,000

This is within the nil rate band so no tax is due.

(ii) There is additional tax due on the CLT:

	£	£
GCT		469,250
Less: nil rate band	325,000	
Less: GCTs in the 7 years before the gift (now includes the PET as it became chargeable)	(26,000)	(299,000)
		170,250
IHT @ 40%		68,100
Less: taper relief: 1.05 – 11.09 = 4-5 yrs: 40%		(27,240)
		40,860
Less: lifetime tax		(41,250)
IHT due		–

3.1 The loss to donor principle is used when valuing unquoted shares:

		£	£	£
Before the transfer	5,100 × £150			765,000
After the transfer	4,900 × £120			(588,000)
Transfer of value				177,000
Less: AE 2009/10				(3,000)
AE 2008/09 b/f				(3,000)
CLT				171,000
Less: nil rate band			325,000	
Less: GCTs in the 7 yrs before the gift		163,000		
Less: AEs 2006/07 and 2005/06 b/f		(6,000)	(157,000) (N)	
				(168,000)
Chargeable				3,000
IHT @ ²⁰/₈₀ / 25% (assume donor pays the tax as question is silent)				750

Note. The original gift to the trust was within the nil rate band at the time.

3.2 The gift to Jim is a PET, so there is no tax during Mrs Brown's lifetime, although the annual exemptions of 2006/07 and 2005/06 are allocated to it.

When Mrs Brown dies within seven years of making the gift, the PET becomes chargeable. The loss to donor principle is used when valuing unquoted shares. Where there is related property we must also take this into account.

		£
Before the transfer	2,000 × £900 (W1)	1,800,000
After the transfer	500 × £600 (W2)	(300,000)
Transfer of value		1,500,000
Less: AE × 2		(6,000)
PET		1,494,000
Less: nil rate band		(325,000)
Chargeable		1,169,000
IHT @ 40%		467,600
Less: taper relief 1.6.06 – 24.9.09 = 3-4 yrs: 20%		(93,520)
IHT due		374,080

Workings

(1) Mr B 40%
    Mrs B 20%
    60% ie value at £900 per share

(2) Mr B 40%
    Mrs B 5%
    45% ie value at £600 per share

Note The value of the transfer ignoring related property is £450,000 (1,500 × £300). As the value using the related property rules is higher (£1,500,000) this higher value is used.

3.3 The gift to the interest in possession trust is a chargeable lifetime transfer as all lifetime trusts (except to bare trusts and trusts for disabled persons) are relevant property trusts.

When valuing the shares we use the loss to donor and related property rules.

We are given the gross chargeable transfer amount for the earlier transfer which is the amount *after* annual exemptions.

		£
Before the transfer	$\frac{45}{45+25} \times £740,000$	475,714
After the transfer	$\frac{40}{40+25} \times £680,000$	(418,462)
Transfer of value		57,252
Less: AE 2009/10		(3,000)
AE 2008/09 b/f		(3,000)
CLT		51,252
Less: nil rate band £(325,000 – 290,000)		(35,000)
Chargeable		16,252
IHT @ 25% (assume Michael pays the tax as the question is silent)		4,063

Note The value of the transfer ignoring related property (£20,000 (5% holding)) is lower than the value using the related property rules then the related property valuation is used.

3.4

	£
Shares (W)	339,250
Less: AE 2009/10	(3,000)
AE 2008/09 (used against June 2008 transfer)	(Nil)
CLT	336,250
Less: nil rate band £(325,000 – 175,000)	(150,000)
Chargeable	186,250
IHT @ 20%	37,250

Working

Minitip: Lower of: ¼-up: £(22.25 – 21.80) ÷ 4 + 21.80 = £21.9125

and average: $£\dfrac{21.20 + 22.25}{2}$ = £21.725 × 10,000   217,250

Maxipack: Lower of: ¼-up: £(12.80 – 12.00) ÷ 4 + 12.00 = £12.20 × 10,000   122,000

and £12.25

Total   339,250

3.5   (i)   *Lifetime gift to discretionary trust*

The value of the shares is the lower of the ¼-up rule and the average.

¼-up: (334.25 – 331.75) ÷ 4 + 331.75 = 332.375p

average: $£\dfrac{330 + 334}{2}$ = 332p

ie 12,000 × 332p = £39,840

The price on the date of the gift reflects the fact that the shares have gone ex-div.

(ii)   *Shares held on death*

The value of the shares at the date of death is the lower of the ¼-up rule and the average.

However, because the dividend has gone ex-div and the dividend was paid after the date of death the net dividend must be added to the value.

	£
12,000 × 332p	39,840
Add net dividend: 12,000 × 12.2p	1,464
Total value	41,304

3.6   *Lifetime tax*

(i)   The gift to Richard is a PET, so no tax during lifetime. It does, however, use the available annual exemptions.

(ii)   The gift to the interest in possession trust is a chargeable lifetime transfer as the trust is a relevant property trust (lifetime trust set up after 21 March 2006):

4.5.08

	£	£
Gift: 10,000 × £3.58 (the bid price)		35,800
AEs 2008/09 and 2007/08 b/f		(6,000)
CLT		29,800
Nil rate band	312,000	
GCTs in the 7 years before the gift (PET does not use nil band during lifetime)	–	
		(312,000)
		Nil

Death tax: October 2009

(i) The PET becomes chargeable.

	£
Gift: €468,000 ÷ €1.39 (buying rate)	336,691
Less: AEs 2003/04 and 2002/03 b/f	(6,000)
PET	330,691
Less: nil rate band	(325,000)
	5,691
IHT @ 40%	2,276
Less: taper relief (12.8.03 – 12.10.09) 6-7 yrs: 80%	(1,821)
IHT due	455

(ii) There is additional tax due on the CLT:

	£	£
GCT		29,800
Less: nil rate band	325,000	
Less: GCTs in the 7 years before the gift (now includes the PET as it became chargeable)	(330,691)	(Nil)
		29,800
IHT @ 40%		11,920
Less: taper relief: <3yrs		(nil)
		11,920
Less: lifetime tax		(nil)
IHT due		11,920

4.1 The gift to Marc is a PET, so no tax during lifetime. BPR is potentially available at 100% for any level of shareholding in an unquoted trading company. The BPR is restricted by any 'excepted assets' held by the company (eg investments and surplus cash).

When Luke dies within seven years of gifting the shares the PET becomes chargeable.

BPR is available as Marc still holds the shares. It is, however, restricted by the investments held by the company (the cash is required for day-to-day transactions and is therefore not an excepted asset).

	£
Transfer	750,000
Less: BPR $\frac{2,845,000}{2,890,000} \times £750,000 \times 100\%$	(738,322)
	11,678
Less: AE 2008/09 and 2007/08 b/f	(6,000)
	5,678
IHT @ 40% (nil rate band fully used by other lifetime gifts)	2,271
Less: taper relief (< 3 yrs)	(nil)
IHT due	2,271

4.2 Business property relief (BPR) will be available on Jack's transfer. This is because the property that Jack is gifting replaced other relevant business property and the combined period of ownership is more than two years.

BPR will also be available on Olga's transfer. Olga inherited the business on the death of her husband and therefore the combined ownership period by her and her husband is taken into account.

Even though Simon has not run the business for more than two years, BPR is not relevant for the transfer from him to John as this is covered by the spouse/ civil partner exemption. When John dies BPR is not available for the business in his estate as he has not held the asset for long enough. Simon and John's periods of ownership cannot be combined as the asset was acquired on a lifetime gift and not inherited on death.

4.3 When Joan makes the gift to her son in 2006 it is a PET, so no tax due during her lifetime. BPR is potentially available. When she dies within seven years of making the gift the PET becomes chargeable.

When valuing the shares we must use the loss to donor and related property rules. The value of the shares is therefore based on Joan and Alex's combined shareholding of 30%.

BPR is available for any number of unquoted trading company shares, with a restriction for excepted assets.

		£
Value of holding before the transfer: 20/(20 + 10) × £147,000 (30% holding)		98,000
Less: value after the transfer (no shares left)		(nil)
Transfer of value		98,000
Less: BPR: 100% × £98,000 × $\frac{(500-80)}{500}$		(82,320)
		15,680
Less: AE 2006/07 and 2005/06 b/f		(6,000)
PET	£	9,680
Less: nil rate band	325,000	
Less: GCTs in 7 years before gift	(427,500)	(nil)
Chargeable		9,680
IHT @ 40%		3,872
Less: taper relief (4.6.06 – 21.3.10) = 3-4 yrs: 20%		(774)
IHT due		3,098

4.4 When Arthur makes the gift to his son in August 2009 it is a PET, so no tax due during his lifetime. BPR is potentially available.

When Arthur dies within seven years of making the gift the PET becomes chargeable. However, BPR is not available at the date of his death because his son no longer owns the factory (or replacement relevant business property).

The IHT due is therefore:

	£
Gift	650,000
BPR (not available as son no longer owns factory)	–
AE (09/10)	(3,000)
(08/09)	(3,000)
PET	644,000
Less: nil rate band (available in full)	(325,000)
	319,000
IHT @ 40% (no taper as owned for < 3yrs)	127,600

4.5 When Arthur makes the gift to the interest in possession trust for his son in August 2009 it is a CLT as the trust is a relevant property trust (not a bare trust or trust for disabled person(s)).

BPR is available at 50% as this is an asset used in a business.

The lifetime tax is therefore:

	£
Gift	676,000
Less: BPR @ 50%	(338,000)
	338,000
Less: AE (09/10)	(3,000)
(08/09)	(3,000)
	332,000
Less: nil rate band (available in full)	(325,000)
	7,000
IHT @ 25% (assume Arthur pays the tax as the question is silent)	1,750

The gross chargeable transfer is: £(332,000 + 1,750 =) £333,750

Module 2: IHT, trusts and estates

When Arthur dies within seven years of making the CLT there may be additional tax due. However, BPR is no longer available at the date of his death because the trustees no longer own the factory (or replacement relevant business property).

The IHT due is therefore:

	£
GCT	333,750
Add: BPR withdrawn	338,000
Total chargeable	671,750
Less: nil rate band (available in full)	(325,000)
	346,750
IHT @ 40% (no taper as owned for < 3yrs)	138,700
Less: lifetime tax	(1,750)
IHT due	136,950

4.6 The capital account is relevant business property for BPR purposes. BPR is available at 100%.

The mortgage on the land will reduce the IHT value of the land, which has agricultural value (AV) so APR will be available. The rate of APR is 50% because this is a pre-1.9.95 lease that has more than 24 months left to run.

Because the land is run as a business, BPR will be available on the remaining value. The farm is occupied and farmed by the partnership. The transfer of the farm will therefore reduce the net value of the partnership business and therefore the transfer will qualify for 100% BPR. [Nelson Dance Family Settlement v HMRC (2009) EWHC 71]

APR is given before BPR.

The IHT values are therefore:

	Capital account £	Land (AV) £	Land (balance) £
Assets	60,000	600,000	200,000
Less: mortgage (60:20)		(150,000)	(50,000)
	60,000	450,000	150,000
Less: APR @ 50%		(225,000)	
BPR @ 100%			(150,000)
BPR @ 100%	(60,000)		
IHT values	Nil	225,000	Nil

4.7 It is essential to calculate any lifetime tax on the gifts first, then any death tax on them.

Lifetime tax

14.5.00 – PET
12.4.04 – GCT within nil rate band, so no IHT
25.6.05 – PET – marriage exemption £5,000 available and annual exemption of 2005/06 (2004/05 used against GCT)
3.10.08 – CLT but BPR available at 100% so no lifetime tax

Death tax

14.5.00 – >7 yrs before death so no IHT implications
12.4.04 – Additional IHT but within nil rate band so no IHT due
25.6.05 – PET becomes chargeable

	£	£
Gift		50,000
Less: ME		(5,000)
Less: AE		(3,000)
PET		42,000
Less: nil rate band	325,000	
Less: GCTs in 7 yrs before gift	(238,000)	(87,000)
Taxable		Nil

3.10.08 – CLT – BPR withdrawn as trustees no longer hold the shares

	£	£
GCT		Nil
Add: BPR withdrawn	750,000	750,000
Less: AE 2008/09		(3,000)
Less: AE 2007/08 b/f		(3,000)
		744,000
Less: nil rate band	325,000	
Less: GCTs in 7 yrs before gift	(280,000)	(45,000)
£(238,000 + 42,000)		
Taxable		699,000
IHT @ 40%		279,600

No taper relief as < 3 years + no lifetime tax

5.1

	£	£
UK assets		
House in Scotland	180,000	
Less: Secured loan	(180,000)	nil
Other UK assets	100,000	
Less: Balance of secured loan £(200,000 – 180,000)	(20,000)	
Unsecured UK debt	(120)	
Funeral expenses	(1,500)	78,380
Non-UK assets		
House in France	125,000	
Less: Secured loan	(110,000)	15,000
Other Non-UK assets		30,000
Net estate for IHT		123,380

5.2 The gift to the discretionary trust took place more than seven years before Joe's death. There is therefore no additional IHT due on Joe's death and it can be ignored when considering the available nil rate band at the date of death.

			£
Free estate			293,000
Settled property (life tenant of qualifying interest in possession trust)			350,000
			643,000
Less: nil rate band remaining at death			(325,000)
			318,000
IHT @ 40%			127,200
Payable by:	Executors	293,000/643,000 × £127,200	57,962
	Trustees	350,000/643,000 × £127,200	69,238

5.3 David died within five years of inheriting the assets on his brother's death so quick succession relief (QSR) is available to reduce the IHT on his estate.

Because David was left the entire estate he had to pay the tax on it.

His death estate is:

	£	£
Free estate		
Personal chattels		400,000
Foreign property (€260,000 ÷ €1.5286 (buying rate))	170,090	
Less: costs: lower of: (i) €15,750 ÷ €1.5286 = £10,304		
(ii) 5% × £170,090 = £8,505	(8,505)	161,585
Value of estate		561,585
Less: nil rate band		(325,000)
		236,585
Tax @ 40%		94,634
Less: QSR £38,250 × $\frac{£91,750 *}{£130,000}$ × 20% (4 to 5 years)		(5,399)
IHT payable		89,235

* increase in David's estate (he paid the original IHT): £(130,000 – 38,250) = £91,750.

5.4 As Roberta and Ronald's deaths are within 5 years of each other, QSR applies to reduce the IHT payable on Ronald's death estate.

Because the asset left to Ronald was a specific gift of UK property it was tax-free (ie Ronald did not have to pay the tax on it, Roberta's residuary legatee, ie Pearl, did).

Consequently, the full value of the property is the 'net' amount in the QSR fraction.

	£
IHT on death estate:	
£500,000 × 40% (all nil band used)	200,000
Less: QSR(W)	(2,426)
IHT due	197,574
Working	
QSR: 1st tax × net gift/ gross gift @ % for 4 -5 years	
£12,750 × $\frac{250,000}{250,000 + 12,750}$ × 20% =	£2,426

5.5 Lionel's gift to the discretionary trust was a CLT. However there is no tax to pay as a result of Lionel's death as it is below the nil rate band.

Lionel's death estate

	£	£
Free estate		500,000
Settled property		105,000
Total estate		605,000
Less: nil rate band	325,000	
Less: GCTs in seven years before death		
(263,000 – 6,000 (2 × AEs))	(257,000)	(68,000)
		537,000
IHT @ 40%		214,800
Less: QSR (W)		(3,078)
Net tax due		211,722

Payable by executors

$\frac{500,000}{605,000}$ × £211,722 = £174,977

Payable by trustees

$$\frac{£105,000}{£605,000} \times £211,722 = \underline{£36,745}$$

Working

As the period between the uncle's and Lionel's deaths was less than five years (it was between 4 and 5 years) QSR is available (at 20%).

The cottage left to Lionel was a specific gift of non-UK property so it was tax-bearing, ie Lionel had to pay the tax on it. The net amount (ie the top figure) in the QSR fraction is therefore the value of the cottage *less* the tax.

QSR is therefore:

$$\frac{100,000 - 19,000}{100,000} \times £19,000 \times 20\% = \underline{£3,078}$$

5.6 The value of assets in the death estate is the probate value, ie the market value at the date of death.

Special rules apply for calculating the value of certain assets such as shares and overseas assets.

Total estate

	£
Family home (W1)	Nil
Shares (W2)	84,525
Tuscany property (W3)	580,378
Personal property	100,000
Total	764,903
Less: funeral costs	(15,675)
Death estate	749,228

Workings

(1) Family home

The family home is held as joint tenants with Samantha's husband. Her share of the property will pass automatically to Neil by operation of law, regardless of what it says in her will. Assets passing to a spouse are exempt from IHT. The value is therefore £Nil.

(2) Shares

Lower of:
(i) Quarter-up rule:
(568-562)/4 = 1.5 + 562   563.5p

(ii) Average
(562.5 + 567.5)/ 2   565p

ie 563.5p × 15,000   £84,525

(3) Tuscany villa

	£	£
€727,000 / 1.19 (buying rate)		610,924
Less: admin expenses		
Lower of:		
(i) €40,000 / 1.19	33,613	
(ii) 5% × £610,924	30,546	
		(30,546)
Probate value		580,378

5.7 The capital value of the IIP trust will be included in Bart's estate as his settled property as it is a qualifying IIP trust, having been set up before 22 March 2006.

Bart had made one lifetime gift in the seven years before his death, which was well within the nil rate band. No IHT is due but the gift does use up the nil rate band for the death estate.

Also, Lily had died having not used her nil rate band, so it is assumed that Bart's PRs will claim the unused amount (100%) to use against his death estate.

Death estate	£	£
Free estate		800,000
Settled property		400,000
Total estate		1,200,000
Less: own nil rate band	325,000	
Lily's unused nil rate band	325,000	
Less: GCT in 7 years before death	(171,000)	
		(479,000)
		721,000
Tax @ 40%		288,400
Less QSR (W)		(28,109)
IHT due		260,291

Split:

PRs $\frac{800,000}{1,200,000} \times £260,291$ 173,527

Trustees of IIP trust $\frac{400,000}{1,200,000} \times £260,291$ 86,764

Working - QSR

Relief is available

1st tax × net/ gross × % 1-2 years

£42,000 × 215,000/(215,000 + 42,000) × 80% = £28,109

5.8

Estate	£	£
Cash etc...		300,000
Shares (W)	187,500	
Less: BPR @ 100%	(187,500)	Nil
Farm (Note)	2,600,000	
Less: APR @ 50%	(1,300,000)	1,300,000
Total		1,600,000
Less: own nil rate band	325,000	
Add: spouse's unused nil rate band	108,333	
1/3 × £325,000		
		(433,333)
		1,166,667
Tax @ 40%		466,667

Note: The farm is eligible for APR on the full value @ 50% (pre 9.95 lease with more than 2 years left to run). There is no indication that there is any non-agricultural value from the facts.

Working - shares

The shares must be valued using the related property rules.

25,000/ 50,000 × £375,000 = £187,500

5.9 Tasha is not legally domiciled in the UK, and has only been resident for 13 years, so she is not deemed domicile. As a result she is only chargeable to IHT on her UK located assets.

Note: that ISA accounts and cars, although exempt for CGT, are chargeable for IHT.

	£
HB Plc shares	12,000
House in UK	354,000
Deposits with HSBS Bank UK	50,000
Jewellery and other personal assets	7,500
Cash ISA accounts	30,000
Car in the UK	23,000
Total	476,500
Less: nil rate band	(325,000)
	151,500
Tax @ 40%	60,600

6.1 As the PRs sold quoted shares from the death estate within one year of death at a loss, loss on sale relief (post mortem relief) is available. It is restricted by the purchase of replacement quoted shares within 2 months of the last sale.

	£	£
London house		705,000
Car		35,000
Portuguese villa		120,000
Quoted shares (W)		65,138
Total estate		925,138
Less: nil rate band	325,000	
Less: GCTs in 7 yrs before death	(213,000)	(112,000)
		813,138
IHT @ 40%		325,255

Working

	£	£
Original probate value of shares		69,000
Less: loss on sale relief		
Probate value of shares sold within 12 months £(15,000 + 22,000)	37,000	
Less: gross sale proceeds £(9,000 + 20,000)	(29,000)	
Loss	8,000	
Less: restriction $\frac{15,000}{29,000} \times £8,000$	(4,138)	(3,862)
Revised probate value		65,138

6.2

CLT 18.11.02

	£
Gift	155,000
AE 02/03	(3,000)
01/02	(3,000)
CLT	149,000

Below nil rate band so no IHT due.

PET 14.02.07

No lifetime tax, uses 06/07 & 05/06 annual exemptions

Death tax

CLT 18.11.02 > 7 yrs so no additional tax to pay

	£	£
PET 14.02.07: Gift		235,000
AE 06/07		(3,000)
05/06 b/f		(3,000)
GCT for cumulation purposes		229,000
Fall in value relief £(235,000 – 197,500)		(37,500)
		191,500
Nil rate band	325,000	
Less: CGTs in 7 yrs to gift	(149,000)	
		(176,000)
		15,500
Tax @ 40% (payable by brother)		6,200

No taper relief as < 3yrs

	£	£
Death estate		350,000
Nil rate band at death	325,000	
Less: GCTs in 7 yrs to death	(229,000)	
		(96,000)
		254,000
Tax @ 40% (Payable by PRs)		101,600

6.3 The shares are related property as Keith's civil partner also holds some of the shares.

The original value in the death estate would have been:

£2,500,000 × 120,000/200,000 = £1,500,000

No BPR is available as the shares are not qualifying business assets (shares in an investment company).

The spouse/civil partner exemption does not apply as the shares are not left to Martin – they are left to Keith's niece.

(i) *IHT liability*

The original IHT liability would therefore have been:

	£
Other assets	325,000
Madden Ltd shares	1,500,000
Total	1,825,000
Less: nil rate band (none remaining)	(nil)
Chargeable estate	1,825,000
IHT @ 40%	730,000

(ii) *Repayment*

As the shares are sold for less than £1,500,000 within three years of death, the original 'stand alone' value of the shares replaces the related property value in the death estate.

The revised value is therefore £1,000,000. We ignore the sales proceeds.

The tax repayment is:

(£1,500,000 - £1,000,000 =) £500,000 @ 40% = £200,000.

6.4 When Maureen made the gift to the discretionary trust it was a chargeable lifetime transfer (CLT). The annual exemption of £3,000 for the year of the transfer and the previous year (as she has made no other transfers) would have been available to reduce the value of the transfer.

The amount of the transfer within the nil rate band would have been chargeable at 0% and the balance taxable at lifetime rates (25% as Maureen paid the tax herself).

When Maureen dies four years after the gift, there is additional IHT due on the CLT.

The starting point for the death tax calculation is the gross chargeable transfer (the gift after annual exemptions plus the tax Maureen paid). However, relief is available for the fall in value of the land by reducing the GCT by the amount that the it has fallen in value, ie £150,000.

Tax is then charged at 40% (the death rate) and taper relief is available, based on the period between the gift and death. Maureen survived almost four years from making the gift so relief will be given at 20% (3-4 years).

Finally, a deduction is given for the lifetime tax paid.

It should be noted that fall in value relief applies only for the purposes of calculating the death tax payable on the lifetime transfer, it does not affect the cumulative total (ie the amount that uses up the nil rate band).

6.5 As the executors sold property from the death estate within three years of death, loss on sale relief (post mortem relief) is available. The loss in the 4th year can be netted off against the gain on the flat. The loss is restricted by the purchase in the period ending 4 months after the last sale in the three year period.

	£	£
Regedit Ltd shares	540,000	
Less: BPR @ 100%	(540,000)	Nil
Personal property		65,000
Property (W) (£1,000,000 – 12,526)		987,474
Total estate		1,052,474
Less: nil rate band	325,000	
Less: GCTs in 7 yrs before death (May 2002 gift outside period)	(nil)	(325,000)
		727,474
IHT @ 40%		290,990

Working	Probate value	Gross sale proceeds	(Loss)/ profit
	£	£	£
Lancashire house	250,000	195,000	(55,000)
London flat	750,000	775,000	25,000
	1,000,000	970,000	(30,000)
Less: restriction for purchases			
£30,000 × 565,000/970,000			17,474
Allowable loss			(12,526)

6.6 The GCT on 4 May 2004 is below the nil rate band at the date of death so there is no IHT due.

As Crompton Hall was sold at a loss within 3 years of Charlotte's death, post mortem relief is available (as restricted for the purchase of Marston Mews).

There is no transferable nil rate band available from Spencer's death as his remaining nil rate band at the date of his death would have been fully used by the nil rate band discretionary trust.

Estate	£	£
Chargeable estate	1,895,000	
Less: post mortem relief (W)	(17,208)	
Total		1,877,792
Less: nil rate band	325,000	
Less: GCTs in 7 yrs before death	(113,000)	
		(212,000)
		1,665,792
Tax @ 40%		666,317

Working – post mortem relief

	Probate value	Sale proceeds	Gain/ (loss)
	£	£	£
Crompton Hall	925,000	888,000	(37,000)
Net loss			(37,000)
Less: restriction for purchases:			
$\frac{475,000}{888,000} \times £(37,000)$			19,792
Allowable loss			(17,208)

7.1 Gifts between spouses (and civil partners) are usually exempt from IHT. However, only the first £55,000 of transfers from a UK domiciled spouse to a non-UK domiciled spouse are exempt. This exemption applies to the total of all transfers between spouse throughout lifetime and on death.

As Sue is not UK domiciled the lifetime gift of £40,000 will be covered by this spouse exemption.

Part of the death estate will be chargeable as only £15,000 (£55,000 – £40,000) of the exemption remains.

The GCT in May 2003 has no tax liability as it falls within the nil rate band.

The liability on the estate will be:

	£	£
Estate		320,000
Less: remaining spouse exemption (£55,000 – 40,000)		(15,000)
Chargeable estate		305,000
Less: Nil rate band	325,000	
Less: GCTs in seven years before death	(120,000)	(205,000)
		100,000
IHT @ 40%		40,000

7.2 (i) If Nikki sets up a discretionary trust this will be a chargeable lifetime transfer. Depending on the amount put into the trust and the level of Nikki's other lifetime gifts, if any, there may be IHT due. If she dies within seven years of making the gift there may be additional IHT due.

In addition, because Nikki will herself be a beneficiary of the trust this will be a gift with reservation of benefit (GWR). This means that the assets she places into the trust will continue to form part of her estate for IHT purposes, so when she dies they will be part of her death estate. There could therefore potentially be two charges to IHT on her death (the additional tax on the CLT and the death tax on the asset in the death estate). If this does happen, double charges relief should be available so that HMRC will only collect the higher of the two amounts.

(ii) If Nikki gifts the painting to her daughter this will be a potentially exempt transfer (PET) for IHT purposes. There is no tax during her lifetime but the annual exemption will be allocated to it. The PET will become chargeable if she dies within seven years of making the gift.

In addition, because Nikki will continue to keep the painting in her house this will also be a gift with reservation of benefit, so the painting will continue to form part of her estate for IHT purposes.

If she dies within seven years of making the gift there will be two IHT charges (the PET becoming chargeable and death tax on the painting in her death estate) in which case relief will be available so that HMRC will only collect the higher of the two amounts.

(iii) If Nikki gifts her house to her son this will again be a potentially exempt transfer (PET) for IHT purposes, with the same IHT consequences as outlines above.

In addition, if Nikki continues to live in the property and not pay a market rent this will also be a gift with reservation of benefit, so the house will continue to form part of her estate for IHT purposes, with the same IHT consequences as above if she dies within seven years of making the gift.

It is not therefore tax effective to live in the house and not pay rent. However, she can avoid the GWR rules by paying her son the market rent as suggested.

7.3 Where a chattel (ie a moveable tangible asset) is subject to the POAT rules, there is a tax charge equivalent to the market value of the asset multiplied by the official rate of interest.

The charge in respect the vase is:

4.75% × £150,000 = £7,125

To avoid an income tax charge Lisa can notify HMRC that the asset should come within the gift with reservation rules, usually by the self assessment return filing deadline (ie by 31 January 2011 for 2009/10).

Lisa should be aware that this does not avoid tax entirely as making the election brings the asset into her estate for IHT purposes.

7.4 Serge probably has not acquired a domicile of choice in the UK as he always intended to return to Latvia. However he is deemed domiciled in the UK for IHT purposes as he has been resident in the UK for at least 17 out of the last 20 years. Consequently he is chargeable on his worldwide assets.

The potentially exempt transfer to his brother becomes chargeable as he dies within seven years of making the gift.

	£	£
Personal property		25,000
Surrey house	650,000	
Less: mortgage	(400,000)	250,000
Latvia property		55,000
UK shares		15,000
Debt		10,000
Total estate		355,000
Less: nil rate band	325,000	
Less: GCTs in 7 yrs before death (£58,000 - £6,000 (2 × AEs))	(52,000)	(273,000)
		82,000
IHT @ 40%		32,800

7.5 Serge probably has not acquired a domicile of choice in the UK as he always intended to return to Latvia. He is not deemed domiciled in the UK for IHT purposes as he has not been resident in the UK for at least 17 out of the last 20 years. Consequently he is only chargeable to IHT on his UK assets. His non-UK assets are 'excluded property' and are outside the scope of IHT.

The potentially exempt transfer to his brother becomes chargeable as he dies within seven years of making the gift.

	£	£
UK personal property (UK assets)		25,000
Surrey house (UK asset)	650,000	
Less: mortgage	(400,000)	250,000
Latvia property (non-UK asset)		Nil
UK shares (UK asset)		15,000
Debt (non-UK asset)		Nil
Total estate		290,000
Less: nil rate band	325,000	
Less: GCTs in 7 yrs before death (£58,000 - £6,000 (2 × AEs))	(52,000)	(273,000)
		17,000
IHT @ 40%		6,800

7.6 Usually when an asset is placed into a discretionary trust there is a chargeable lifetime transfer. The annual exemption of £3,000 is available if no other gifts have been made in the current tax year and the previous year's exemption is also available if not used in that year. The amount of the gift that comes within the nil rate band is chargeable at 0% and the balance at 20% (or 25% if the donor pays the tax).

However, when the asset is classed as heritage property the transfer is 'conditionally exempt' for IHT purposes. A claim must be made within 2 years of the transfer.

This means that no IHT is due so long as certain conditions ('undertakings') are fulfilled by the donee (ie the trustees) regarding the property.

For example the trustees may be forbidden from taking the painting out of the UK and may have to make the painting available for public access.

IHT will be due if the undertakings are broken or the asset is sold or otherwise transferred without the undertakings being renewed by the new owner.

7.7 The June 2000 gift is more than 7 years before Shamus's death so there is no IHT due.

The gift to Marian in 2006 is a gift with reservation of benefit, ie it is a PET but the value of the asset also stays in Shamus's death estate.

On Shamus's death two calculations are required to ensure that there is no double taxation. The first taxes the PET and ignores the value in the death estate:

	£	£
PET becomes chargeable		
Gift		2,000,000
Less: AE × 2		(6,000)
PET		1,994,000
Less: nil rate band	325,000	
Less: GCTs in 7 years before gift	(500,000)	(Nil)
		1,994,000
Tax @ 40%		797,600
Less: taper relief (3-4 yrs): @ 20%		(159,520)
IHT due from Marian		638,080
Death estate		
Estate		4,500,000
Less: nil rate band	325,000	
Less: GCTs in 7 years before death	(1,994,000)	(Nil)
		4,500,000
Tax @ 40%		1,800,000
Total IHT		2,438,080

The second calculation ignores the PET and charges the current market value in the death estate:

	£	£
Death estate		
Estate	4,500,000	
Add: painting	2,500,000	7,000,000
Less: nil rate band	325,000	
Less: GCTs in 7 years before death	(Nil)	(325,000)
		6,675,000
Tax @ 40%		2,670,000

HMRC will collect the higher tax ie £2,670,000

8.1 As the gift is a chargeable lifetime transfer (CLT) for IHT purposes, gift relief is available for any asset.

	£
Deemed proceeds (MV)	250,000
Less: cost	(157,500)
Gain	92,500
The full gain can be deferred	£92,500
The base cost of the property for the trustees is:	
Cost (MV)	250,000
Less: gift relief claimed (ie gain deferred)	(92,500)
Cost c/f	157,500

Note. Effectively the trustees have taken over the donor's base cost.

8.2 Part disposal:

	£
Proceeds	30,000
Less: cost $\dfrac{30,000}{30,000 + 120,000} \times £20,000$	(4,000)
Gain	26,000
Capital losses bfwd	(12,000)
Total chargeable gains	14,000
Less: annual exempt amount	(10,100)
Taxable gain	3,900
CGT liability @ 18%	702

8.3 Gain on receipt of compensation:

	£
Proceeds	230,000
Less: Cost	(100,000)
Gain	130,000
Proceeds not reinvested and chargeable £(230,000 − 180,000)	50,000
Available for deferral £(130,000 − 50,000)	80,000
Base cost of new asset £(180,000 − 80,000)	100,000

8.4 Sam – Capital gains computation 2009/10

	£	£
1. *Land and buildings*		
Proceeds	950,000	
Less cost	(80,000)	
Chargeable gain		870,000
2. *Goodwill*		
Proceeds	500,000	
Less cost	−	
Chargeable gain		500,000
Total gains		1,370,000
Entrepreneur's relief £1,000,000 × 4/9		(444,444)
Chargeable gains		925,556
Annual exempt amount		(10,100)
Taxable gain		915,456
CGT @ 18%		164,782

Note The machinery and equipment are exempt as their cost and market value is less than £6,000

9.1

	£	£
Initial value		200,000
Nil rate band	325,000	
Less: b/f	(208,000)	
Available		(117,000)
		83,000
IHT @ 20%		16,600

Effective rate of tax $\dfrac{16,600}{200,000} \times 100$ = 8.3%

Actual rate of tax

8.3% × 30% × 21/40 = 1.30725%

IHT payable £50,000 × 1.49625% = £654

9.2 (i) *Exit charge*

	£
Pretend 'gift' 18.11.07	
Initial value of property on 18.11.99	365,000
Less: Nil rate band left 2007/08 (no previous transfers)	(300,000)
	65,000
Tax @ 20%	13,000

Effective rate $\dfrac{13,000}{365,000}$ = 3.56164%

Actual rate: $30\% \times 3.56164\% \times \dfrac{32}{40}$ = 0.85479%

Exit charge £125,000 × 0.85479% = £1,068

(ii) *Principal charge*

	£
Pretend 'gift' 18.11.09	
Current value of relevant property on 18.11.09	650,000
Less: Nil rate band left 2009/10 (325,000 – 125,000)	(200,000)
	450,000
Tax @ 20%	90,000

Effective rate $\dfrac{90,000}{650,000}$ = 13.84615%

Ten year charge rate 30% × 13.84615% = 4.153845%

Ten year anniversary charge £650,000 × 4.153845% = £27,000

9.3 When Deanna sets up the discretionary trust it is a chargeable lifetime transfer (CLT). The annual exemption of £3,000 for the year of the transfer and the previous year (as she made no other transfers in that year) will be available to reduce the value of the transfer.

The amount of the transfer within the remaining nil rate band (ie £325,000 – 200,000) will be chargeable at 0% and the balance taxable at lifetime rates (20% as the trustees agreed to pay the tax).

When the trustees distribute assets from the trust to beneficiaries this is usually a chargeable event for IHT purposes, an 'exit' charge. The charge is based on the value of what leaves the trust multiplied by a percentage calculated by reference to the settlor's lifetime transfers in the seven years before setting up the trust, adjusted for the number of complete quarters that have elapsed since the trust was set up.

However, as this 'exit' occurs within the first three months (ie full quarter) of the trust being set up, there is no exit charge.

9.4 The trust is a qualifying interest in possession trust. The IHT consequences are as follows:

(i) If the trustees distribute the trust assets to the remainderman (ie the capital beneficiary) during the life tenant's lifetime, this is treated as a transfer by the life tenant himself.

Consequently, Colin is treated as making a transfer of £600,000 to his daughter, which is a potentially exempt transfer (PET) for IHT purposes as this is a gift between individuals. There is no tax due during Colin's lifetime but the PET will become chargeable if he dies within seven years of making the gift.

Colin can request that his annual exemptions of the current and previous years are set against the transfer.

(ii) If the trustees distribute the trust assets as a result of the life tenant's death, the value of the trust assets enters the life tenant's death estate.

As a result, Colin's death estate will include settled property of £600,000. His nil rate band will cover part of this, and the balance will be taxable at 40%. The trustees will pay the tax.

9.5 The trust is an age 18-25 trust as it has been created on Paul and Stephanie's parent's death after 21 March 2007 and provides for them to receive the capital and income by age 25.

So, on 19 January 2014 when Paul turns 21 there will be an exit charge.

Exit charge

	£
Pretend 'gift' 19.1.14	
Initial value of property on 17.4.08	450,000
Less: Nil rate band left 2013/14 (no previous transfers)	(325,000)
	125,000
Tax @ 20%	25,000

Effective rate $\dfrac{25,000}{450,000}$ = 5.55556%

The complete number of quarters from Paul's 18th birthday to the exit is: 19.1.11 – 19.1.14 = 12

Actual rate: $30\% \times 5.55556\% \times \dfrac{12}{40}$ = 0.5%

Exit charge (gross up as trustees pay the tax):

£35,000 × $\dfrac{0.5\%}{100 - 0.5}$ %   = £176

9.6 (i) If Roger provides for a trust for bereaved minors (TBM) to be set up on his death, the assets that enter the trust will be chargeable in Roger's estate on his death.

The trustees will be able to exercise their discretion over the income and capital until the beneficiaries reach age 18.

When the beneficiaries receive the capital up to age 18 there will be no IHT consequences.

(ii) If Roger provides for an age 18-25 trust to be set up on his death, the assets that enter the trust will be chargeable in Roger's estate on his death.

The trustees can exercise their discretion over the income and capital until the beneficiaries reach age 25, at which time they must receive the capital and the income outright.

If they receive the capital up to age 18 there will be no IHT consequences (as for a TBM). If they receive the capital after 18 and up to age 25 there will be an IHT exit charge.

(iii) If Roger provides for an immediate post death interest trust to be set up on his death, again the assets that enter the trust will be chargeable in Roger's estate on his death.

The trustees can exercise their discretion over the capital of the trust but the beneficiaries will be entitled to an interest in possession, ie they will be entitled to receive the trust income (after expenses).

If assets leave the trust the transfer will be treated as a transfer by the life tenant(s).

(iv) If Roger provides for a plain discretionary trust to be set up on his death, again the assets that enter the trust will be chargeable in Roger's estate on his death.

The trustees can exercise their discretion over the capital and income of the trust until whatever age is specified in the trust deed, but there will be an exit charge every time assets leave the trust and a principal charge on every ten year anniversary of the trust being set up (ie Roger's death).

9.7 Setting up the trust is a chargeable lifetime transfer and the appointment out of trust capital is an exit charge.

CLT

	£	£
Gift		400,000
Less: AE 2001/02		(3,000)
Less: AE 2000/01 b/f		(3,000)
CLT		394,000
Less: nil rate band (2001/02)	242,000	
Less: GCT	(127,000)	(115,000)
		279,000
Tax @ 20%		55,800

Exit charge – the question is silent so assume the trustees pay the tax

	£	£
'Gift'		
Initial value of trust	400,000	
Less: tax paid by trustees	(55,800)	
		344,200
Less: nil rate band (2009/10)	325,000	
Less: GCTs in 7 years before trust set up	(127,000)	(198,000)
		146,200
Tax @ 20%		29,240

Effective rate
29,240/344,200 × 100 = 8.495061%

No of quarters since set up:
1.5.01 – 15.8.09 = 33

Actual rate
8.495061% × 30% × 33/40 = 2.102528%

Exit charge
$\frac{2.102528\%}{100 - 2.102528\%} \times £50,000$ £1,074

10.1 Ordinarily there is no CGT when a qualifying interest in possession trust comes to an end.

However, as gift relief was claimed when the trust was created, a chargeable gain will arise on the death of the life tenant.

The gain will be the lower of the gain arising using market value for proceeds and the original deferred gain ie the lower of:

(i) £(65,000 – 25,000 =) £40,000, and

(ii) £15,000

ie £15,000.

The gain may itself be deferred using gift relief as the assets are charged in the life tenant's death estate.

10.2 (1) The gain on settlement into the trust, and the gain on the property passing to Angus, would both have been held over under s.260 as both would have resulted in an IHT charge (CLT and exit charge respectively).

Angus's gain will be:

	£
Proceeds	650,000
Less: cost	(100,000)
Gain	550,000
Less Annual exempt amount	(10,100)
	539,900
Tax at 18%	97,182

(2) The trustees would have been taxable on the gain at the same rate as Angus, ie 18% although they would only be entitled to half the annual exempt amount. The tax due would have been:

	£
Proceeds	650,000
Less: cost	(100,000)
Gain	550,000
Less Annual exempt amount	(5,050)
	544,950
Tax at 18%	98,091

Therefore the tax will have increased by £909 if the trustees had sold it before distributing the cash proceeds. It therefore would not have been better for the trustees to have sold the property.

10.3 The deferred gain reduces the base cost of the asset in the hands of the trustees.

	£	£
Proceeds of sale		50,000
Less: Cost	30,000	
Less: Held over gain	(12,000)	(18,000)
Gain		32,000
Less: annual exempt amount		(5,050)
Taxable gain		26,950
CGT @ 18%		£4,851

10.4 When a qualifying life interest terminates on death there is no CGT for the trustees who obtain a tax free uplift to market value for the assets as at the date of death.

The exception to this is if gains were held over when an asset was put into the trust, the gain on that asset will be chargeable, but will be limited to the amount of the gain held over.

The chargeable gain accruing to the trustees on Darren's death is therefore a maximum of £10,000, the gain held over when the Alpha Ltd shares were settled.

It may be possible to make a further claim to hold over the gain against the base cost of the shares in the beneficiary's hands as death tax will be charged on the assets in Darren's estate as his settled property.

10.5 Trustees' capital losses can be used in the same way as an individual's, ie they can be used in the current year or carried forward against future gains.

Additionally, where a loss arises when an asset is advanced to a beneficiary, that loss may be transferred to the beneficiary.

So, the loss of £3,000 may be transferred to Cedric, but it may only be set off against any gain arising when Cedric comes to dispose of that same asset. He cannot use the losses against gains arising from any other asset.

It is not possible to carry losses back against earlier years' gains.

The brought forward losses of £2,000 are unrelieved and will be wasted as all the trust assets have been advanced.

10.6 *Gain on gift to trust (May 2002)*

	£
MV of shares	90,000
Less: 31.3.82 MV	(15,000)
Gain	75,000

A claim for gift relief can be made to defer the gain under s.260 TCGA 1992. The base cost of the shares for the trustees is £(90,000 − 75,000) = £15,000.

Gain on appointment to son

	£
MV of shares	105,000
Less: cost	(15,000)
Gain	90,000

This gain can be deferred using gift relief under s.260 TCGA 1992. The claim is made by the trustees and the son. The base cost of the shares for the son is £(105,000 − 90,000) = £15,000.

10.7 When the trustees distribute the shares there will be a deemed disposal at market value. The cost will be affected by the original gift relief claim made when the shares were put into the trust.

Gift relief will be available to defer the gain again (unquoted trading company shares)

	£
Proceeds £9.25 × 150,000	1,387,500
Less: cost (W)	(433,000)
Chargeable gain	954,500
Gift relief claim	
£954,500 × (100% − 17%)	(792,235)
Chargeable gain	162,265
Less: Annual exempt amount	(5,050)
Taxable gain	157,215
Tax @ 18%	28,299

Working

	£
Original gain	275,000
Less: gift relief	
£275,000 × (100% − 12%) (Note)	(242,000)
Chargeable gain	33,000
Base cost for trustees	
Market value: £4.50 × 150,000	675,000
Less: gift relief claimed	(242,000)
Cost c/f	433,000

Note The gift relief is restricted as 12% of the company's chargeable assets were non business assets (investments).

11.1

				£
Bank interest (£460 × 100/80)	£575	@ 20% =		115
Dividends (£675 × 100/90)	£750	@ 10% =		75
Rental Income £(15,000 – 1,500)	£13,500	@ 20% =		2,700
Tax liability				2,890
Less: tax credits				
Interest: 20% × £575				(115)
Dividends: 10% × £750				(75)
Tax due				2,700

R185 Statement of income	Net	Tax	Gross
	£	£	£
Non savings income	10,800	2,700	13,500
Savings Income	460	115	575
Dividend Income	225 (W)	25	250

Working
Net dividend income £(675 – 450) = £225

11.2

	£	£
Rental income (£18,000 –1,500)	16,500	
Dividends (£1,800 × 100/90)		2,000
Gross income	16,500	2,000
Less: trust expenses (£945 × 100/90)		(1,050)
Amount chargeable at trust rates	16,500	950
£ 1,000 @ 20% =		200
£16,500 – 1,000 = £15,500 @ 40% =		6,200
£ 950 @ 32.5% =		309
£ 1,050 @ 10% =		105
Tax liability		6,814
Less: tax credits on dividends: £2,000 @ 10%		(200)
Tax due		6,614

R185 Statement of income	Net	Tax	Gross
	£	£	£
Non savings income	500	333	833

11.3

The trustees will pay tax at the basic rate on their first £1,000 of income and also on any income used to pay expenses. The balance of income is taxable at the trust rate.

	£
Net rental income	8,500
Less: trust expenses (£882 × 100/80)	(1,103)
	7,397
Tax at 20% on £1,000	200
Tax at 40% on £6,397	2,559
Tax at 20% on £1,103	221
Tax due	2,980
Tax pool b/f	650
Add: current year tax paid @ 20%	421
@ 40%	2,559
	3,630
Less: tax credit needed to cover distribution to beneficiary (£6,000 × 40/60)	(4,000)
Additional tax payable	(370)
Total tax due (£2,980 + £370)	3,350

11.4 Trust's income tax liability 2009/10

	Non Savings Income £	Savings Income £	Dividend Income £
Rental income £(2,500 – 275)	2,225		
Bank interest £960 × 100/80		1,200	
Dividends £1,800 × 100/90			2,000
Taxable income	2,225	1,200	2,000

Total tax liability of trustee

	£
£2,225 × 20%	445
£1,200 × 20%	240
£2,000 × 10%	200
Total tax liability	885
Less: tax credits	
£1,200 × 20%	(240)
£2,000 × 10%	(200)
Tax to pay by self-assessment (ie the tax on rental income)	445

R185 Statement of income

	Net £	Tax £	Gross £
Non savings income	1,780	445	2,225
Savings income	960	240	1,200
Dividend income	1,300 (W)	144	1,444

Working
Net dividend income £(1,800 – 500) = £1,300

11.5

	Non-savings income £	Savings Income £	Dividend Income £	Income used for expenses £
Property income	1,100			
Bank Interest £1,800 × 100/80		2,250		
Dividends (2,430 – 630) × 100/90			2,000	
Dividends used for expenses £630 × 100/90				700
Taxable income	1,100	2,250	2,000	700

Tax on distributable income:

	£	£
NS: £1,000 × 20% (basic rate band)	200	
£ 100 × 40%	40	
NS: £1,100		
S: £2,250 × 40%	900	
D: £2,000 × 32.5%	650	
	1,790	
Basic rate tax on income used to meet expenses:		
£700 × 10%		70
Total tax liability	1,790	70
Less: notional tax credits on dividends		
£2,000 × 10%	(200)	
£700 × 10%		(70)
To tax pool	1,590	nil
Less: 'real' tax credits on savings income £2,250 × 20%	(450)	
Payable by trustees	1,140	

11.6

	£
Tax pool brought forward as at 6.4.09	1,267
Add: Tax for 2009/10 (see above)	1,590
Tax available for providing credits	2,857
Less: tax paid out as credit on payment £1,000 × 40/60	(667)
Carried forward at 5.4.10	2,190

Note

The £1,590 added into the tax pool can be analysed as follows:

	£
Tax paid at 40%	
£(100 + 2,250) × 40 %	940
Tax paid at 20% (basic rate band)	
£1,000 × 20%	200
Tax on dividend income effectively being paid at 22.5%	
£2,000 × (32.5 – 10%)	450
	1,590

Statement of income

Net	Tax @ 40%	Gross
£	£	£
1,000	667	1,667

11.7

	Non savings £	Savings £	Dividends £
Property income £(16,800 – 520)	16,280		
Interest £2,880 × 100/80		3,600	
Dividends £103,500 × 100/90			115,000
Total	16,280	3,600	115,000
£1,000 @ 20%	200		
£(15,280 + 3,600) @ 40%	7,552		
£115,000 @ 32.5%	37,375		
Tax liability	45,127		
Less: non-refundable tax credits on dividends	(11,500)		
Tax for tax pool	33,627		
Less: real tax credits	(720)		
IT payable	32,907		

Tax pool

	£
Tax pool c/f	1,675
Add: 2009/10 tax	33,627
Tax available to cover distributions	35,302
Less: required for distributions	(16,667)
5 × £5,000 × 40/60	
c/f	18,635

12.1   *PRs' income tax payable 2009/10*

	Non savings Income £	Savings Income £	Dividend Income £
Rental income £(2,500 – 275)	2,225		
Bank interest £960 × 100/80		1,200	
Dividends £1,800 × 100/90			2,000
Taxable income	2,225	1,200	2,000

PRs' total tax liability

	£
£2,225 × 20%	445
£1,200 × 20%	240
£2,000 × 10%	200
Total tax liability	885
Less: tax credits	
£1,200 × 20%	(240)
£2,000 × 10%	(200)
Tax due (ie the tax on rental income)	445

12.2   Jayne and Jack are the residuary beneficiaries of the estate. As the administration of the estate has been finalised, they are treated as receiving the income on the completion date.

The trust expenses are deductible when calculating the income due to the residuary beneficiaries and are deducted from dividend income in priority to other income.

The available net income is:

- Non-savings: £(2,225 – 445) = £1,780, ie £890 each
- Savings: £960 ie £480 each
- Dividends: £(1,800 – 500) = £1,300, ie £650 each.

The total income receivable by Jayne and Jack is £2,020 each.

R185 Statement of income (Estate)	Net £	Tax £	Gross £
Non savings income	890	223	1,113
Savings income	480	120	600
Dividend income	650	72	722

12.3   *Calculation of income tax liability*

	Non-savings £	Savings £	Dividends £	£
Property income	13,775			
Bank interest (£2,240 × 100/80)		2,800		
Dividends (£2,812 × 100/90)			3,124	
	13,775	2,800	3,124	
Less:				
Interest on loan to pay IHT (W)	(570)			
Net income	13,205	2,800	3,124	
Tax liability (@20%/20%/10%)	2,641	560	312	3,513

Working

Relief is only available for the loan interest paid in the 12 months from the date the loan was taken out. The first six months of interest would have been deductible in the previous year. No relief is available for the payment made on 1 October 2009:

6 × £95 = £570

12.4 The base cost of the shares is the probate value (ie value at the date of death).

PRs are entitled to the full annual exempt amount for the year of death and the two following years.

They pay CGT at 18%

The executors' gain will be:

	£
Proceeds	156,000
Less: cost (probate value)	(127,500)
Gain	28,500
Less Annual exempt amount	(10,100)
	18,400
Tax at 18%	3,312

12.5 The base cost of the shares for the executors is the probate value (ie value at the date of death).

When they pass the shares to Jamie, he effectively takes over the executors' CGT position, ie their base cost. There is no disposal for CGT purposes.

Jamie's gain will be:

	£
Proceeds	156,000
Less: cost (probate value)	(127,500)
Gain	28,500
Less Annual exempt amount	(10,100)
	18,400
Tax at 18%	3,312

12.6 (1) PRs

The PRs are taxable on the income received after the date of death, but receive no relief for any expenses of administration.

	Non savings £	Savings £	Dividends £
Property income	9,900		
Interest £1,200 × 100/80		1,500	
Dividends £33,345 × 100/90			37,050
Total	9,900	1,500	37,050
Tax @ 20%/20%/10%	1,980	300	3,705
Less: tax credit		(300)	(3,705)
IT payable	1,980	Nil	Nil

Note: that this is simply the tax due on the non savings income as the rest of the tax liability is covered by the tax credits.

(2) Caroline

Until the administration is finalised, Caroline is taxable on a receipts basis. The income is matched with non-savings, then savings and finally dividend income.

	Non savings £	Savings £	Dividends £
Gross income	9,900	1,500	37,050
Less: tax paid/ suffered	(1,980)	(300)	(3,705)
Net income	7,920	1,200	33,345
Less: expenses			(575)
Available for distribution	7,920	1,200	32,770
Matched with interim payment	(7,920)	(1,200)	(15,880)
c/f	Nil	Nil	16,890

R185 (Estate income)

	Gross £	Tax £	Net £
Non savings	9,900	1,980	7,920
Savings income	1,500	300	1,200
Dividends	17,644	1,764	15,880

Awareness Paper
Unincorporated businesses

Study Period Planner
Taxation of Unincorporated Businesses

Use this schedule and your exam timetable to plan the dates on which you will complete each Study Period. The letters 'H' and 'M' tell you whether the topic is high or medium priority.

Study Period	Topic		Due Date
1	Taxable income	H	
2	Taxable trade profits	H	
3	Capital allowances on plant and machinery	H	
4	Basis periods	H	
5	Trading losses	M	
6	**Progress Test 1**	H	

Study Period	Topic		Due Date
7	Partnerships	M	
8	National Insurance Contributions	M	
9	Outline of CGT/ Computing gains and losses	H	
10	Reliefs	H	
11	Partnerships and CGT	H	
12	Administration	H	
13	**Progress Test 2**	H	

COURSE EXAM 1

A Practice exam covering Study Periods 1 – 5

COURSE EXAM 2

A practice exam covering all Study Periods

REVISION PHASE

Your revision phase will begin when **Course Exam 2** is complete. This should ideally be four months before the final exam.

TQT Note: The Course Exams contain questions for all FIVE of the awareness paper modules. In your exam you must answer questions from THREE modules. We suggest that you identify the THREE modules you will study and then work through the Study Period Planners for each of those modules until the point where you are told to take Course Exam 1. When you have completed all THREE modules to that point, sit Course Exam 1. Similarly, you should complete all THREE modules before you sit course exam 2. Course Exam 2 covers all of the Study Periods, although it is weighted towards the second half of your studies.

Study Period 1

Taxable income

High Priority

Step 1 Exam Guidance

This study period introduces the topic of taxable income, which may or may not already be familiar to you.

It is unlikely that this topic will form the subject of an exam question in its own right but it is essential knowledge for the Taxation of Unincorporated Businesses Awareness Module.

Step 2 Introduction to the session

To understand how the topics in the remaining study periods of this Awareness module fit together, we require some background knowledge.

Although the topics studied in this chapter may not be examined in their own right, they underpin the rest of the syllabus and so are essential to your understanding of the module.

Step 3 Guidance through the Study Text

Read through Chapter 1 of the Taxation of Unincorporated Businesses Awareness Study Text after reading the following guidance:

In this chapter we learn the basics of income tax which are fundamental to our understanding of the Taxation of Unincorporated Businesses module.

Read quickly through Sections 1 and 2 for background. Then read carefully through Section 3, learning the proforma income tax computation in Illustration 1 and, noting, in particular, the position of trading income. The tax rates and allowances are in the Institute Tax Tables provided in the exam. Make sure you know where to find the relevant information. Work through Illustration 2 to check your understanding of the basic income tax computation.

Read quickly through Section 4 which covers the taxation of spouses (which includes civil partners) and introduces some simple planning issues.

Step 5 iPass and Workbook Questions

As this chapter is mainly background reading there is only one exam style question (ESQ) to attempt: Q 1.1.

Your TQT's i-Pass CD Rom also contains some questions to test your understanding of the topic of taxable income.

Step 4 Quick Quiz

Please attempt the quick quiz at the end of study text Chapter 1 to reinforce your understanding.

You may find it best to do this after a break, so that you can see what you remember and what you don't.

180 Module 3: Unincorporated businesses

Study Period 2

Taxable trade profits

High Priority

Step 1 Exam Guidance

In this study period we cover a number of topics that can form the basis of a whole question:

- The badges of trade.
- Adjusting accounting profit to reach taxable profit.

This area is very examinable and has been tested in:

- Sample Paper (Q1, Q2 and Q10)
- May 2009 exam (Q2 and Q3)

Step 2 Introduction to the session

In the previous study period we looked at how individuals are taxed on their income. In this period we cover how to turn a business's accounting profit into the self employed trader's taxable profit.

To complete the picture we will need to understand the calculation of capital allowances, covered in the next study period.

Step 3 Guidance through the Study Text

Read through Chapter 2 of the Study Text after reading the following guidance:

Read Section 1 quickly for background. Then read through Sections 2 and 3 on the badges of trade and self employment versus employment. Make notes on the key points as these are important areas.

Read through the rules in Section 4 for calculating the taxable profit of a self employed person, starting with the accounting profit. Follow through Illustration 1 and note the adjustments that are made to the accounting profit to arrive at the taxable profit. Attempt Examples 1 and 2 to check your understanding of the steps you need to go through to arrive at the taxable profit.

Section 5 gives you the opportunity to practise a comprehensive example of a profit adjustment calculation in Example 3. Work through this example carefully. This is an important area of the syllabus.

Finally, read quickly through Sections 6, 7 and 8 which are all quite brief.

Step 5 iPass and Workbook Questions

Now attempt ESQs 2.1 to 2.6 which will help to reinforce your knowledge of the topics covered in this study period and give you examples of the types of question you may see in the exam.

Your TQT's i-Pass CD Rom also contains questions testing the computation of an individual's taxable trade profits.

Step 4 Quick Quiz

Please attempt the quick quiz at the end of study text Chapter 2 to reinforce your understanding.

You may find it best to do this after a break, so that you can see what you remember and what you don't.

Module 3: Unincorporated businesses 181

Study Period 3

Capital allowances on plant and machinery

High Priority

Step 1 Exam Guidance

In this study period we look at the capital allowances available for expenditure on plant and machinery.

Look at the Institute's tax rates and allowances, which will be provided in the exam, to see how much information is given on capital allowances rates.

Capital allowances have been tested in:

- Sample Paper (Q3, Q4 and Q11)
- May 2009 exam (Q10)

Step 2 Introduction to the session

In the previous study period we learnt how to calculate the taxable profits of the self employed. In arriving at taxable profits we saw an entry in the proforma for the deduction of 'capital allowances'.

You can think of these as a form of tax depreciation.

Step 3 Guidance through the Study Text

Read through Chapter 3 of the Study text after reading the following guidance:

Read through Section 1 for background. Then read Section 2 which sets out the type of assets that qualify as plant. This is also background knowledge, so do not get bogged down in the detail. Instead, locate the rules in the legislation so that you can refer to them easily in the exam.

Read carefully through Sections 3 to 5 of the Chapter. These set out how to calculate capital allowances. Attempt Examples 1 to 3, making sure you know how to set out a capital allowances computation proforma. Section 5 is a useful summary of how to approach capital allowances computational questions.

The rest of the chapter deals with the calculation of plant and machinery capital allowances in special circumstances. Read these sections quickly. If you are short of time instead of working through the examples you could follow through with the solutions.

Step 4 Quick Quiz

Please attempt the quick quiz at the end of Study Text Chapter 3 to reinforce your understanding.

You may find it best to do this after a break, so that you can see what you remember and what you don't.

Step 5 iPass and Workbook Questions

Now attempt the ESQs 3.1 to 3.8 which will help to reinforce your knowledge of the topics covered in this study period and give you examples of the types of question you may see in the exam.

Your TQT's i-Pass CD Rom also contains questions testing the calculation of capital allowances.

182 Module 3: Unincorporated businesses

Study Period 4

Basis periods

High Priority

Examined: Sample Paper

Step 1 Exam Guidance

The allocation of taxable trading profits to the correct tax year's income tax computation is very examinable.

You will be expected to deal with three main situations:

- What happens in the opening years of a new trade? (Sample Paper Questions 2 and 11)
- What happens if an existing business changes its accounting date? (May 2009 Question 6)
- What happens when a business ceases? (Sample Paper Question 4).

Step 5 iPass and Workbook Questions

Now attempt the ESQs 4.1 to 4.9 which will help to reinforce your knowledge of the topics covered in this study period and give you examples of the types of question you may see in the exam.

Your TQT's i-Pass CD Rom also contains questions testing the basis period rules.

Step 2 Introduction to the session

In the first study period we learnt that income tax is calculated for tax years. However, we then saw in study periods 2 and 3 that taxable trading profit is calculated for accounting periods, which may or may not coincide with the tax year.

In this study period we learn how to allocate taxable trading profits for accounting periods to the appropriate tax year(s).

Step 4 Quick Quiz

Please attempt the quick quiz at the end of Study Text Chapter 4 to reinforce your understanding.

You may find it best to do this after a break, so that you can see what you remember and what you don't.

Step 3 Guidance through the Study Text

Read through Chapter 4 of the Study Text after reading the following guidance:

You must learn the rules for allocating taxable profits to tax years (ie identifying the correct basis period for a tax year) for:

- Continuing businesses – Section 1.1.
- Opening years of a business, including the identification of overlap profits – Sections 1.2 to 1.5.
- Closing years of a business, including the use of overlap profits – Section 1.6. Attempt Examples 1, 2 and 3.

Before attempting Examples 4 and 5 ensure you understand the order of approach required for examples where capital allowances need to be calculated.

Then read Section 2 which deals with existing businesses that change their accounting date. Can you identify the year of change and determine whether the change of accounting date leads to the creation or relief of overlap profits? Attempt Examples 6 to 8.

Module 3: Unincorporated businesses

Study Period 5

Trading losses — Medium Priority

Examined: Sample Paper

Step 1 Exam Guidance

You must be able to identify the amount of a trading loss and know how such losses can be used (ie when and against what the loss can be set off).

For the purpose of your exam, there are only eight ways in which an individual can use their trading losses: carry forward, current year, previous year, special extended carry back relief, against gains, special opening year relief, special final year relief and incorporation relief. Try and bear this in mind when deciding what loss relief is most appropriate.

Trading losses have been tested in:

- Sample Paper (Q5)
- May 2009 (Q5 and Q9)

Step 2 Introduction to the session

We use the same 'adjustment of profit' rules that we have already seen to calculate the tax adjusted loss. The trading profit figure in the income tax computation for a loss-making year is always nil. We then have to consider how any loss can be used to reduce other tax liabilities and the tax years in which any relief can be claimed.

Step 3 Guidance through the Study Text

Read through Chapter 5 of the study text, after reading the following guidance:

Read quickly through Section 1. The loss relief rules are in the Income Taxes Act 2007. Locate this and refer to it as you work through.

Sections 2 and 3 are **essential** for your understanding of the rest of the loss reliefs covered so concentrate on these in this session.

Read Section 2 on carrying forward losses (s.83). This happens automatically if no other claims are made. Try Example 1.

Carefully read Sections 3.1 to 3.3 which deal with setting losses off against general income (s.64). This claim can be made for the current loss-making year and/ or the previous year only and can lead to the individual wasting their personal allowance. Attempt Examples 2 and 3. Read quickly through Sections 3.4 and 3.5. However, do note (in Section 3.5) that if there is any loss left after a current or prior year claim it can be set against chargeable gains (which we deal with in a later study period).

Read Section 4 for the special temporary extension of loss carry back relief. Note that the carryback is only against the trading profits of the earlier years. Follow Illustration 2 carefully and try Example 4.

Read Section 5 and try Example 5 to consolidate your knowledge. Read Section 6 for the special loss relief rules that apply in the early years of a trade (s.72) and attempt Example 6. Then read Section 7 for the special 'terminal loss relief' rules that apply on the cessation of a trade (s.89) and attempt Examples 7 and 8. Read Section 8 which deals with the loss relief rules when an unincorporated business becomes a company (s.86) and, finally, Section 9 on restrictions on loss relief.

Step 4 Quick Quiz

Please attempt the quick quiz at the end of Study Text Chapter 5 to reinforce your understanding.

You may find it best to do this after a break, so that you can see what you remember and what you don't.

Step 5 iPass and Workbook Questions

Now attempt the ESQs 5.1 to 5.8 which will help to reinforce your knowledge of the topics covered in this study period and give you examples of the types of question you may see in the exam.

Your TQT's i-Pass CD Rom also contains questions testing trading losses.

Progress Test 1

Study Period 6

High Priority

In order to reinforce what you have learnt so far, answer the following questions. Try to answer them without referring to your Study Text or notes. The test should take you no longer than one hour and covers Study Periods 1-5. Solutions start on page 199.

1 Mr Matthews' accounts for his butchers shop for the year to 31 October 2009 show the following:

	£	£
Sales		50,000
Less cost of goods sold		(20,000)
Gross profit		30,0000
Less expenses:		
Depreciation	5,500	
Salary (note)	3,900	
Gift of 40 'Matthew Butchers' diaries	200	
Bank overdraft interest	500	
Utility bills	2,500	
		(12,600)
Net profit		17,400

Note. Salary was paid to Mr Matthews' daughter for working in the shop on a Saturday morning. Mr Matthews' previous Saturday girl would have been paid £1,500 for the same hours.

Calculate Mr Matthews' adjusted taxable trading profit before capital allowances for the year ended 31 October 2009.

2 For the year ended 31 March 2010, Mr Smith had the following transactions in capital assets in respect of his butchers shop business

		Cost/Proceeds £
1 May 2009	Purchase of equipment	45,000
28 June 2009	Sale of van	3,000
1 July 2009	Purchase of van	12,000
1 March 2010	Purchase of car for Mr Smith	10,000

The van sold on 28 June 2009 had originally cost Mr Smith £8,000. The car has CO_2 emissions of 172g/km and is used 20% for business and 80% privately.

The balance brought forward on the main pool at 1 April 2009 was £5,000.

Calculate the capital allowances in respect of Mr Smith's business for the year ended 31 March 2010.

Progress Test 1 (continued)

Study Period 6 — High Priority

3. Mr Harrowven started a new sole trader business on 1 October 2009. He made up his first set of accounts to 31 May 2010 and annually thereafter, until 1 December 2012 when he ceased in trade.

   His adjusted taxable trading profits, after capital allowances, for all accounting periods have been as follows:

	£
Period ended 31 May 2010	16,000
Year ended 31 May 2011	36,000
Year ended 31 May 2012	48,000
Period ended 30 November 2012	10,000

   Calculate the amount of taxable trading profit assessable to tax for all tax years affected by the profits above. You are required to identify and utilise overlap profits as part of your answer.

4. Mr Faragher had been trading for many years as a Fast Food Retailer. Due to trends in healthier eating he has had a difficult time trading in recent accounting periods and has made a trading loss.

   Details of his adjusted trading profits and losses for recent accounting periods are as follows:

Year ended 31 March 2008	Profit	£50,000
Year ended 31 March 2009	Loss	£(20,000)
Year ended 31 March 2010	Profit	£20,000

   Mr Faragher has no other taxable income or deductible expenses.

   You are required to state how the adjusted trading loss for the year ended 31 March 2009 can be used for income tax purposes.

5. Carol produces the following profit and loss account for her hairdressing business for the year ended 31 March 2010:

	£	£
Gross operating profit		30,000
Taxed interest received		860
		30,860
Wages and salary	7,000	
Rent and rates	2,000	
Depreciation	1,500	
Impairment of trade receivables	150	
Entertainment expenses	750	
Patent royalties	1,200	
Bank interest	300	
Legal expenses on acquisition of new factory	250	
		(13,150)
Net profit		17,710

   (a) Salaries include £500 paid to Bob, Carol's husband, who works full time in the business
   (b) No staff were entertained
   (c) Taxed interest and patent royalties (trade related) are shown gross

   You are required to calculate Carol's adjusted taxable trading profit before capital allowances for the year ended 31 March 2010.

Study Period 6

Progress Test 1 (continued)

High Priority

6. Spencer, a sole trader, incurred the following expenditure in his year ended 31 March 2010.

	£
Donation to the Labour Party	2,000
Patent royalty (paid for trade purposes)	780
Legal expenses relating to the creation of a 40 year lease	1,500
Lease payment on a BMW car (CO_2 emissions 175g/km, purchase price £23,000)	6,440
Client entertaining	2,500

   The lease agreement in respect of the BMW car was signed on 1 June 2009.

   You are required to state, with reasons, the amount that will be disallowed in arriving at trade profits.

7. **You are required to state five of the badges of trade and give a brief explanation of the application of each.**

8. Ralph began trading on 1 June 2009 and prepared accounts for the 14 month period to 31 July 2010. In the period to 31 July 2010 he made the following additions and disposals:

   1 July 2009   Spent £55,000 on a new heating system for his offices.

   12 August 2009   Purchased a new car for the production manager for £18,000. The car has CO_2 emissions of 100g/km.

   10 June 2010   Purchased a second hand lorry for £24,000.

   1 July 2010   Sold furniture for £5,000 which had cost £4,500 in May 2009.

   You are required to calculate the capital allowances computation for the period to 31 July 2010 assuming that Ralph claims the maximum allowances available.

9. David began trading on 1 October 2006 and prepared accounts to 30 September until he changed his accounting date by preparing accounts for the fifteen months to 31 December 2009.

   His results for the period were as follows:

	£
Year to 30 September 2007	24,000
Year to 30 September 2008	48,000
Fifteen months to 31 December 2009	75,000

   You are required to calculate David's taxable trade profits for his first four years of trade, stating any overlap profit carried forward.

10. Penelope began trading on 1 January 2010. In her first year of trading to 31 December 2010 she made trading losses of £52,000. Her projected loss for her second year is £36,000.

    You are required to show Penelope's allowable trading loss for her first two years of trade and to state how she can use the losses.

Module 3: Unincorporated businesses

Progress Test 1 (continued)

Study Period 6 — High Priority

11 Ray commenced trading in 2001 making up accounts to 31 January each year. He has unused overlap profits of £20,000.

Ray ceased to trade on 31 July 2009. His trading results in recent years have been:

	Profit/(Loss) £
Year to 31 January 2006	40,000
Year to 31 January 2007	30,000
Year to 31 January 2008	20,000
Year to 31 January 2009	8,000
6 months to 31 July 2009	(31,000)

Ray has taxable property income of £5,000 each year.

You are required to show Ray's net income for all periods affected by the above results assuming terminal loss relief is claimed.

12 Jane commenced trading on 1 January 2010 preparing her first set of accounts to 30 April 2010. In this period she generated £37,800 of profits before deducting capital allowances. On 1 January 2010 she bought a van for the business costing £20,000, a laptop and printer costing £3,000 and some office furniture costing £300. A month later she bought a car (CO_2 emissions 155g/km) for £18,000 which she would drive 80% of the time for business purposes.

You are required to calculate her trading income assessment for 2009/10.

You will find the answers to this test starting on page 199. If you answer more than 6 questions correctly, your performance is satisfactory; if you answer more than 8 correctly, you are doing well. Once you have reviewed how you have performed, go back over topics where you feel your understanding is poor.

Study Period 7

Partnerships

Medium Priority

Step 1 Exam Guidance

Partners in a partnership are effectively a group of self employed individuals working together. So, the rules that you have already learned in earlier study periods apply equally to partners.

Partnership income was examined in Question 8 of the Sample Paper and Question 1 of the May 2009 exam.

Step 2 Introduction to the session

In this study period you will use your knowledge of adjusted taxable profits and basis periods and apply it to the profits of a partnership business. You will learn how to split this profit between partners for income tax purposes, both in continuing partnerships and in situations where the composition of the partnership changes.

Step 3 Guidance through the Study Text

Read through Chapter 6 of the Study Text, after reading the following guidance:

Read Section 1 on how to split the profits of a partnership between the partners in a continuing partnership for income tax purposes, Follow through the Illustration and note the order of steps to follow. Then attempt Example 1.

Read Section 2, which deals with the profit split when there is a change in the membership of the partnership (eg new partner joins, partner retires), and work through Illustrations 2.2 and 2.3. Do not move on until you are confident with the calculations in these illustrations.

Section 3 deals with losses. No new rules to learn here as those we learnt in the last study period apply equally to partners. However, we need to know how much of the partnership's total loss should be allocated to each partner. Attempt Example 2.

Quickly read through the brief section on 'notional' profits and losses in Section 4, concentrating on working through Examples 3 and 4.

Finally read through Section 5 on Limited Liability Partnerships and attempt Example 5.

Step 4 Quick Quiz

Please attempt the quick quiz at the end of Study Text Chapter 6 to reinforce your understanding.

You may find it best to do this after a break, so that you can see what you remember and what you don't.

Step 5 iPass and Workbook Questions

Now attempt the ESQs 6.1 to 6.7 which will help to reinforce your knowledge of the topics covered in this study period and give you examples of the types of question you may see in the exam.

Your TQT's i-Pass CD Rom also contains questions testing partnerships.

Study Period 8

National Insurance Contributions

Medium Priority

Step 1 Exam Guidance

NICs are payable by the employed and the self employed. In addition, individuals who no longer have self employment income can make voluntary NI contributions.

You will **not** be examined on NIC for employees in the Taxation of Unincorporated Businesses Awareness module.

Question 9 of the Sample Paper and Question 7 of the May 2009 exam tested NICs.

Step 2 Introduction to the session

In this Study period we look at National Insurance Contributions (NIC). You must be able to identify and calculate the different classes of NIC payable by the self employed.

Look at the Institute's tax tables as you work through this chapter so that you know what information you will be given in the exam.

This is a very short study period so use any additional time to review any earlier period(s) that you may have struggled with.

Step 3 Guidance through the Study Text

Read through Chapter 7 of the Study Text after reading the following guidance:

Read quickly through Section 1 for background. Remember you are only examinable on NIC for self employed individuals and **not** employees.

Read Sections 2.1 and 2.2 carefully and follow through the Illustration. These are the essential NIC rules for the self employed and apply equally to partners, so once you are happy with them read Section 2.3 and attempt Example 1.

Read quickly through Section 3 which is not as important for the exam.

Step 5 iPass and Workbook Questions

Now attempt ESQs 7.1 to 7.7 which will help to reinforce your knowledge of the topics covered in this study period and give you examples of the types of question you may see in the exam.

Your TQT's i-Pass CD Rom also contains questions testing national insurance contributions.

Step 4 Quick Quiz

Please attempt the quick quiz at the end of Study Text Chapter 7 to reinforce your understanding.

You may find it best to do this after a break, so that you can see what you remember and what you don't.

Study Period 9

Outline of CGT/Computing gains and losses

High Priority

Step 1 Exam Guidance

The areas covered in the 'Outline of capital gains tax' (CGT) section of this study period are unlikely to be examined in their own right, but they are fundamental to any question involving CGT.

A likely exam scenario is a sole trader or partnership disposing of an asset and you will need to calculate the gain on disposal dealing with any reliefs that may be available.

The calculation of gains was examined in the Sample Paper as part of Question 6 on CGT reliefs.

Step 2 Introduction to the session

This study period covers the basic CGT knowledge that underpins any gains question in the exam.

If you have already studied CGT for another paper of the CTA syllabus you may only need to review this chapter, revising the basic principles.

The instructions given in Step 3 below presume you are studying this chapter **without** any previous knowledge.

Step 3 Guidance through the Study Text

Chapters 8 and 9 of the Study Text direct to you Chapters 9 and 10 of the '**Taxation of Individuals**' section of the text. You should read those chapters after reading the following guidance:

Chapter 9 provides essential CGT background knowledge. Read Sections 1.1 to 1.3 up to Example 1. Try this example to test your basic understanding. Then read through Section 2. Then read Section 3 on the administration of CGT and Section 4 on the overseas aspects.

Section 1 of Chapter 10 is fundamental to your study of CGT. Learn the proforma for calculating a capital gain. Attempt Example 1.

Read all of Section 2 on capital losses except Section 2.3 (year of death). Attempt Examples 2 to 4 and 6. Read through Sections 3, 4 and 5 which deals with assets acquired before 31 March 1982, valuations and connected persons.

Read through Section 7 on part disposals. It is important that you understand how to calculate the cost element of the CGT computation in this situation. Attempt Examples 11 and 12.

Finally read through Section 8 on compensation and insurance monies. This is less important than the other sections in this chapter.

Step 5 iPass and Workbook Questions

Now attempt ESQs 8.1 and 8.2 and 9.1 to 9.4 which will help to reinforce your knowledge of the topics covered in this study period and give you examples of the types of question you may see in the exam.

Your TQT's i-Pass CD Rom also contains questions testing the basics of CGT and computing gains and losses.

Step 4 Quick Quiz

Please attempt the quick quizzes at the end of Chapters 8 and 9 of the Unincorporated Businesses text to reinforce your understanding.

You may find it best to do this after a break, so that you can see what you remember and what you don't.

Reliefs

Study Period 10

High Priority

Examined: Sample paper

Step 1 Exam Guidance

Reliefs and exemptions are very important in any tax exam.

In the CGT part of the syllabus, you may be examined on how the payment of CGT on the disposal of an asset can be deferred (ie delayed) or reduced. This section covers a number of important reliefs, such as incorporation relief and rollover relief.

Rollover relief was examined in Question 6 of the Sample Paper and Question 4 of the May 2009 exam.

Incorporation relief was examined in Question 11 of the May 2009 exam.

Step 2 Introduction to the session

In this study period we learn about the CGT business reliefs that are available. We consider the situations in which gains can be deferred when the trader incorporates his business and when new business assets are bought to replace assets that have been sold (rollover relief).

In addition CGT gift relief is available when a trader gifts certain business assets or sells them at below their market value and entrepreneurs' relief also applies to reduce gains on certain business disposals.

Step 3 Guidance through the Study Text

Read through Chapter 10 of the Study Text after reading the following guidance:

Section 1 gives the background to this chapter, so read it quickly. Note that in all cases the gain on disposal is calculated as normal and then CGT reliefs are applied to reduce/defer the gain.

Read carefully through Section 2 which covers the basic principles of incorporation relief. Attempt Example 1

Then read Section 3 on rollover relief for replacement of certain business assets. Attempt Examples 2 and 3. The relief for 'depreciating' assets in Section 3.4 is a form of rollover but contrast the way in which the gain is deferred (it is 'frozen') with the way normal rollover applies (it is 'rolled over' into the base cost of the replacement asset).

Read Section 4 on entrepreneurs' relief noting to which type of disposals the relief applies. Attempt Examples 4 to 7.

Read Section 5 on gift relief, noting the types of assets for which the relief is available. In particular note the CGT position when some cash is received (sale at an undervalue) in Section 5.5. Attempt Examples 8 to 11.

Finally, read quickly through Section 6 which deals with the CGT consequences of an asset becoming part of trading stock.

Step 5 iPass and Workbook Questions

Now attempt ESQs 10.1 to 10.9 which will help to reinforce your knowledge of the topics covered in this study period and give you examples of the types of question you may see in the exam.

Your TQT's i-Pass CD Rom also contains questions testing the various CGT deferral reliefs.

Step 4 Quick Quiz

Please attempt the quick quiz at the end of Study Text Chapter 10 to reinforce your understanding.

You may find it best to do this after a break, so that you can see what you remember and what you don't.

192 Module 3: Unincorporated businesses

Study Period 11

Partnerships and CGT

High Priority

Examined: Sample Paper

Step 1 Exam Guidance

So far we have dealt with how partnerships are treated for income tax purposes. We now consider how CGT applies to partnerships.

You may be examined on the disposal of partnership assets, the distribution of assets to individual partners or the CGT implications of changes in partnership profit sharing arrangements.

The CGT aspects of partnership income was examined in Question 7 of the Sample Paper and Question 12 of the May 2009 exam.

Step 2 Introduction to the session

In this study period you will use your knowledge of capital gains tax and apply it to capital transactions carried out by partnerships.

You will learn how to deal with the disposal of partnership assets and the effects of changes in profit sharing ratios.

Step 3 Guidance through the Study Text

Read through Chapter 11 of the Study Text, after reading the following guidance:

Read Section 1 on how disposals of partnership assets are dealt with for CGT purposes. Note that on the sale of an asset to an outside party the partners are treated as disposing of their share of the asset. Attempt Example 1. Now read Section 1.4 which deals with the division of assets among partners. Try Example 2.

Read Section 2, which deals with changes in partnership sharing ratios, including when partners join and leave the partnership. Make sure you understand how the CGT treatment differs depending on whether partnership assets are revalued in the accounts. Try Examples 3 to 5.

Step 5 iPass and Workbook Questions

Now attempt the ESQs 11.1 to 11.3 which will help to reinforce your knowledge of the topics covered in this study period and give you examples of the types of question you may see in the exam.

Your TQT's i-Pass CD Rom also contains questions testing partnerships.

Step 4 Quick Quiz

Please attempt the quick quiz at the end of Study Text Chapter 11 to reinforce your understanding.

You may find it best to do this after a break, so that you can see what you remember and what you don't.

Module 3: Unincorporated businesses

Study Period 12

Administration

High Priority

Examined: Sample Paper

Step 1 Exam Guidance

The administrative provisions are essential knowledge for the exam. They can form part of a question or could be an entire question.

Learning where to find the relevant provisions in your legislation is crucial. Do not waste time learning details that you can easily locate in your open book.

Administration was tested in Question 12 of the Sample Paper and Question 8 of the May 2009 exam.

Step 2 Introduction to the session

This study period deals with the administrative requirements of the tax system for individuals. If you have already studied the Taxation of Individuals Awareness module some of this chapter will be familiar to you.

Here we concentrate on self assessment for individuals, ie the rules for income tax returns and paying tax.

Step 3 Guidance through the Study Text

Chapter 12 of the Study Text directs you to Chapter 15 of the Taxation of Individuals Awareness Study Text. Read that chapter through after reading the following guidance:

Section 1 is background knowledge only.

Read Section 2 carefully, noting the deadline for notifying HMRC of chargeability to income tax/capital gains tax (CGT). You should try and locate the rules in your legislation so that you can easily find and refer to them in the exam.

Read Sections 3 to 5 again locating the deadlines for submission of paper and electronic self assessment tax returns in the legislation. Whilst you are there, highlight any penalties and time limits/ periods mentioned in the section.

Read Section 6 and attempt Examples 1 and 2, then read Sections 7 to 9, noting HMRC powers, identifying the situations when penalties and interest are charged and noting the appeals procedure.

You have now completed your study of the **Taxation of Unincorporated Businesses Awareness** module.

Step 5 iPass and Workbook Questions

Now attempt the ESQs 12.1 to 12.6 which will help to reinforce your knowledge of the topics covered in this study period and give you examples of the types of question you may see in the exam.

Your TQT's i-Pass CD Rom also contains questions on the administration of income tax.

Step 4 Quick Quiz

Please attempt the quick quiz at the end of Study Text Chapter 8 to reinforce your understanding.

You may find it best to do this after a break, so that you can see what you remember and what you don't.

194 Module 3: Unincorporated businesses

Study Period 13

Progress Test 2

High Priority

In order to reinforce what you have learnt so far, answer the following questions. Try to answer them without referring to your Study Text or notes. The test should take you no longer than one hour and covers Study Periods 7-12. Solutions start on page 205.

1. Mr Buxton disposed of the following assets in 2009/10:

   (a) A vintage motor car, which had cost him £2,500 in 1997 was sold for £35,000 on 12 May 2009.

   (b) 1,000 shares in Matlock Ltd, an unquoted trading company, were gifted to his daughter on 11 August 2009. They were then worth £ 20,000 and had cost £3,000 in June 1985.

   (c) A piece of land was sold for £25,000 on 3 September 2009. This was part of a parcel of land which had been purchased in 1992 for £7,000. The land retained was valued at £55,000 in September 2009. Mr Buxton has capital losses brought forward of £1,000.

   You are required to calculate the capital gains tax payable by Mr Buxton for 2009/10 assuming all available reliefs are claimed.

2. Mr Paxton has a manufacturing business. He wants to sell one of his factories and buy a new one. He has heard there is a relief available to reduce the tax payable on the factory sale.

   You are required to explain the conditions that must be met in order for Mr Paxton to defer any chargeable gain arising on the disposal of the old factory.

3. Mrs Octagon has asked for your help in understanding how much income tax she must pay as payments on account of her 2009/10 self assessment tax liability.

   In 2008/09 she agreed her self assessment tax liability to be:

	£
Income tax due	5,500
Class 4 NIC due	500
CGT due	2,500

   She has not yet calculated her actual tax liability for 2009/10.

   You are required to calculate the payments on account due by Mrs Octagon for the 2009/10 tax year and state the due dates of payment for the payments on account and the final balancing payment for 2009/10.

4. Maurice runs a consultancy business. His taxable profits for the year ended 30 June 2009 are £95,400.

   You are required to calculate his NIC liability for 2009/10 and state when it is due.

5. Miss Johnson has been in partnership with Mr Smith for many years, sharing profits and losses equally, after deduction of a salary of £10,000 p.a. each. The partnership makes up accounts to 31 December each year. On 1 July 2009 the partners agreed to change the profit sharing agreement to reflect recent changes in the time each partner can dedicate to the business. From 1 July 2009 onwards the profit sharing agreement allowed for a salary of £20,000 p.a. to Miss Johnson and no salary for Mr Smith and the profits would be split 60:40 in favour of Miss Johnson.

   Adjusted trading profits for the year ended 31 December 2009 were £150,000.

   You are required to show how this profit would be allocated to the partners for this accounting period and state the tax year these profits would be taxed in.

Module 3: Unincorporated businesses

Progress Test 2 (continued)

Study Period 13 — High Priority

6   Oliver started receiving rental income in 2009/10. He was not aware that it was necessary to notify HMRC of this source of income but did so on 1 December 2010 as soon as he became aware of the need. His previous income had been employment income and taxed bank interest.

   HMRC issued a self assessment return on 15 January 2011.

   Oliver submitted his return, and paid the tax due of £10,000, on 25 June 2011.

   You are required to advise Oliver of any penalties, surcharges and interest due. Assume a rate of interest of 2.5%.

7   Reuben incorporated his sole trade business in August 2009. The gains arising on incorporation were:

   | Warehouse | £74,500 |
   | Goodwill | £12,000 |

   He received shares worth £225,000 from the company and cash of £75,000.

   You are required to calculate Reuben's gain after incorporation relief and entrepreneurs' relief and to state the base cost of the shares for any future disposal.

8   On 1 July 2009 Craig sold all of the assets of his business as a going concern for £1,200,000. He realised gains, before any reliefs, on a building and goodwill of £700,000 and £200,000 respectively.

   On 1 August 2009 Craig gave his 500 shares in Lambert plc (a quoted trading company) to his sister. He had acquired the shares for £1,000 in May 2000. They were worth £5,000 on 1 August 2009.

   You are required to calculate the capital gains tax payable by Craig for 2009/10 assuming he makes all beneficial elections.

9   Brianna has been trading for many years, preparing accounts to 31 March each year. She ceased trading on 30 June 2010. Her last set of accounts were for the three months to 30 June 2010.

   The main pool's written down value at 1 April 2009 was £25,260. Brianna's car, which she used 40% of the time for private use, had a written down value of £21,225.

   Brianna's capital transactions since 1 April 2009 were as follows:

Bought machinery	31 May 2009	£1,620
Bought machinery	14 April 2010	£1,740
Sold all pool items (below original cost)	30 June 2010	£25,295
Sold car	30 June 2010	£16,500

   You are required to calculate the balancing adjustment arising on cessation.

10 Tracey started trading on 1 November 2009, preparing accounts to 30 April each year. Her results are as follows:

	£
Period to 30 April 2010	36,000
Year ended 30 April 2011	96,000

   You are required to show Tracey's taxable profits for the tax years 2009/10 to 2011/12 inclusive, identifying any overlap profits.

Progress Test 2 (continued)

Study Period 13

High Priority

11. Jake bought a freehold property in 1970 for £80,000. In March 1982 it was worth £100,000. Throughout ownership he used the property 90% of the time for his business. He sold it in September 2009 for £400,000 replacing it with a slightly smaller property that he moved into in December 2009 for £370,000. He planned to use this new property 100% of the time for business use.

    You are required to calculate Jake's chargeable gain on the sale of the property, and state the base cost of the replacement property?

12. Basil and Sybil have been in partnership, preparing accounts to 31 December each year and sharing profits and losses equally. On 1 January 2009 Polly is admitted to the partnership and from that date profits are to be shared equally.

    The agreed profits are as follows:

Year to 31 December 2008	£72,000
Year to 31 December 2009	£84,000

    You are required to calculate each partner's trading income assessment for 2008/09 and 2009/10 and identify any overlap profits.

> You will find the answers to this test starting on page 205. If you answer more than 6 questions correctly, your performance is satisfactory; if you answer more than 8 correctly, you are doing well. Once you have reviewed how you have performed, go back over topics where you feel your understanding is poor.

Solutions

Progress Test 1

1   Mr Matthews

    Adjusted trading profit for the year ended 31 October 2009

	£
Net profit per accounts	17,400
Add:	
Depreciation	5,500
Salary (£3,900 – £1,500)	2,400
Taxable trading profit before capital allowances	25,300

    Note that the gifts of diaries were tax deductible as they carried and advert for his business, were not food, alcohol, tobacco or vouchers exchangeable for goods and cost less than £50 per donee.

2   Mr Smith

    Capital allowance computation

    Year ended 31 March 2010

	FYA £	Main pool £	Special rate car (PU 20%) £		Allowances £
TWDV Bfwd		5,000			
Additions qualifying for AIA/40% FYAs:					
Equipment	45,000				
Van	12,000				
	57,000				
AIA	(50,000)				50,000
	7,000				
FYA at 40%	(2,800)				2,800
	4,200				
Other additions:					
Car (special rate)			10,000		
Disposal		(3,000)			
		2,000	10,000		
WDA at 20%		(400)			400
WDA at 10%			(1,000)	× 20%	200
		1,600			
Transfer to main pool	(4,200)	4,200			
TWDV c/f		5,800	9,000		
Total allowances					53,400

Module 3: Unincorporated businesses   199

Progress Test 1 — Solutions

3   **Mr Harrowven: Taxable profits**

Starts to trade on 1 October 2009 – 'in' the 2009/10 tax year:

2009/10

Actual basis 1/10/09 to 5/4/10 = 6 months
6/8 × £16,000 =   £12,000

2010/11

Accounting period ending in tax year = 8 months to 31 May 2010. As < 12 months long, tax the profits of the first 12 months of trade:

	£
p/e 31 May 2010	16,000
Add: 4/12 x y/e 31 May 2011	
4/12 x 36,000	12,000
	28,000

2011/12

Accounting period ending in tax year = y/e 31 May 2011

CYB   £36,000

2012/13

	£
CYB y/e 31 May 2012	48,000
Period to cessation	
p/e 30 November 2012	10,000
	58,000
Less: overlap profits (W)	(24,000)
	34,000

Working

Overlap profits		£
09/10 and 10/11	1.10.09-5.4.10	12,000
10/11 and 11/12	1.6.10-30.9.10	12,000
Total		24,000

Check:

Taxed:		Profits used
£		£
12,000		16,000
28,000		36,000
36,000		
76,000		52,000

Difference £24,000

Solutions

Progress Test 1

4 Mr Faragher

Use of the loss for the year ended 31 March 2009.

The loss could be carried forward to use against the first available trading profits from the same trade, under S.83. This would mean that the loss of £20,000 would be deducted in full from the £20,000 of adjusted trading profit taxable in 2009/10, from the year ended 31 March 2010.

The loss could be relieved against general income in the accounting period of loss and/or the previous tax year. As the loss making period (the y/e 31 March 2009), ends in 2008/09, this loss relief could be used in 2008/09 and/or 2007/08. As he has no income in 2008/09, the loss could only be used in 2007/08, when there are adjusted trading profits of £50,000 to absorb the loss of £20,000.

5 Carol

Adjusted trading profit for the year ended 31 March 2010

	£	£
Net profit per accounts		17,710
Add:		
Depreciation	1,500	
Client entertaining	750	
Legal expenses	250	
		2,500
		20,210
Less: interest received (taxed as savings income not trading income)		(860)
Taxable trade profits		19,350

6 £6,966

Explanations:

	£
Political donations are never deductible	2,000
Legal expenses incurred in connection with the creation of a short lease are not allowable (expenses incurred in *renewing* the lease are allowable)	1,500
Expenditure on entertaining customers is never allowable	2,500
Car lease payment restricted as CO_2 emissions exceed 160g/km:	
Disallowable: £6,440 x 15%	966
	6,966

The patent royalty is allowed as a trade expense on the accruals basis

Solutions

Progress Test 1

7   Any five of the following badges of trade:

     (a)   Subject matter
             Is the asset the type of item that is usually held as an investment, eg works of art compared to one million toilet rolls! The former would usually indicate an investment and the latter would indicate trading.

     (b)   Frequency of transactions
             The more frequent the transaction the more likely it is going to be treated as a trading activity.

     (c)   Length of ownership
             The longer an item is held the more likely it is to be treated as a capital investment rather than trading stock.

     (d)   Supplementary work
             If work is done to an asset to make it more 'marketable' (ie attractive to a purchaser) it is more likely to be treated as trading stock and not an investment.

     (e)   Profit motive
             If the seller's motive is to make a profit it is likely he will be treated as trading.

     (f)   Way in which asset acquired
             If the asset has been inherited or received by way of gift there is a strong possibility any sale will be treated as a capital transaction rather than a trading activity.

8   Ralph - Capital allowances computation for the 14 months ending 31 July 2010

	FYA £	Main pool £	Special rate pool £	Allowances £
Additions qualifying for 100% FYA:				
Low emission car	18,000			
FYA at 100%	(18,000)			18,000
Additions qualifying for AIA/40% FYA:				
Furniture (May 2009)	4,500			
Heating system			55,000	
Lorry (no FYA post April 2010)		24,000		
AIA (Max £50,000 × 14/12) (Note)		(3,333)	(55,000)	58,333
FYA at 40%	(1,800)			1,800
Less disposal proceeds				
Furniture		(4,500)		
		16,167		
WDA at 20% × 14/12		(3,772)		3,772
Transfer balance to main pool	(2,700)	2,700		
TWDV c/f		15,095		
Total allowances				81,905

Note: The AIA is allocated to the additions in the special rate pool (WDA 10%) in priority to the additions in the main pool (WDA 20%) or additions which qualify for 40% FYA.

Module 3: Unincorporated businesses

Solutions

Progress Test 1

9 David

David's first year of trade is 2006/07.

His 'year of change' is 2009/10 where there is one long period ending in that tax year.

2006/07 (1.10.06 – 5.4.07)

| 6/12 × £24,000 | £12,000 |

2007/08 (1.10.06 – 30.9.07) £24,000

2008/09 (1.10.07 – 30.9.08) £48,000

Overlap profits = £12,000 (from 6 months to 5.4.07).

| *2009/10* – 15 months (1.10.08 – 31.12.09) | £75,000 |

Less: 3 months' overlap (so only 12 months taxed)

3/6 × £12,000	(6,000)
Taxable profit	£69,000
Overlap profits carried forward: £(12,000 – 6,000)	£6,000

10 Penelope

Penelope's first year of trade is 2009/10 (1.1.10 to 5.4.10).

2009/10

| 3/12 × £(52,000) | £(13,000) |

2010/11

Year ended 31.12.10
(do not double count losses)
£(52,000 – 13,000)   £(39,000)

Penelope can use the loss of 2009/10 as follows:

(a) Against her other current year income (before the personal allowance), and then against gains of that year.

(b) Against her income in the previous tax year (before personal allowance), and then against gains of that year.

(c) Against her income in the three tax years before the loss on a FIFO basis (ie 2006/07, 2007/08, 2008/09 in that order)

Penelope can use the loss of 2010/11 as follows:

(a) Against her other current year income (before the personal allowance), and then against gains of that year.

(b) Against her income in the previous tax year (before personal allowance), and then against gains of that year.

(c) Against her income in the three tax years before the loss on a FIFO basis (ie 2007/08, 2008/09, 2009/10 in that order)

Solutions

Progress Test 1

11 Ray - Taxable income computations

	2005/06 £	2006/07 £	2007/08 £	2008/09 £	2009/10 £
Trading income (Note)	40,000	30,000	20,000	8,000	-
Less: terminal loss relief (W1)		(19,000)	(20,000)	(8,000)	-
Property income	5,000	5,000	5,000	5,000	5,000
Net income	45,000	16,000	5,000	5,000	5,000

Note: 2009/10 trading income assessment: 6 months to 31 July 2009 - £31,000 loss thus assessment is £nil

(W1) Terminal loss

	£
2009/10	
6.4.09 – 31.7.09	
4 months to 31.7.09: 4/6 × (31,000)	20,667
Plus overlap profits	20,000
2008/09	
1.8.09 – 5.4.09	
6/12 × 8,000 + 2/6 × (31,000)	6,333
	47,000
Use of loss:	
Terminal loss	47,000
2008/09	(8,000)
2007/08	(20,000)
2006/07 – balance	(19,000)
	-

12 Jane – Taxable trading profit 2009/10

	£
Profit for 4 months to 30 April 2010	37,800
Less capital allowances	
Additions qualifying for 100% AIA: (20,000 + 3,000 + 300) = 23,300	
AIA, restricted to 4/12 × £50,000	(16,667)
Balance qualifies for 40% FYA (23,300 – 16,667) x 40%	(2,653)
Addition not qualifying for AIA:	
Main rate car (80% business use) £18,000 x 20% × 4/12 × 80%	(960)
Tax adjusted trading profit	17,520
2009/10 Trading income assessment	
1 Jan 2010 to 5 April 2010 ¾ × 17,520	13,140

Module 3: Unincorporated businesses

Solutions

Progress Test 2

1   Mr Buxton

    Gains:

    (a)   The sale of a motor car is an exempt disposal.

    (b)   Gift of shares in Matlock Ltd:

	£
Deemed proceeds (MV)	20,000
Less: Cost	3,000
	17,000
Less: Gift relief	(17,000)
Chargeable gain	–

    (c)   Land

	£
Sale proceeds	25,000
Less Cost £7,000 × £25,000/(25,000 + 55,000)	(2,188)
Chargeable gain	22,812

    CGT liability 2008/09:

Current year gains	22,812
Less brought forward losses	(1,000)
	21,812
Less: annual exempt amount	(10,100)
	11,712
Tax payable £11,712 × 18% =	£2,108

2   Mr Paxton:

    The relief that can be used to defer capital gains tax payable in these circumstances is rollover relief. The conditions that Mr Paxton must meet are as follows:

    - Mr Paxton must sell a qualifying asset (freehold land and buildings are qualifying assets).
    - The asset must have been used in Mr Paxton's trade.
    - Mr Paxton must reinvest the proceeds for the sale of the qualifying asset in another qualifying asset to be used in his trade.
    - The reinvestment must take place within the 12 months before and up to 36 months after the original qualifying asset was sold.

Progress Test 2 — Solutions

3 **Mrs Octagon**

Payments on account are based on the self assessment tax liability of the previous tax year. In this case, Mrs Octagon will pay two payments on account, each calculated as 50% of her 2008/09 self assessment tax liability. For these purposes her liability to income tax and Class 4 NIC is taken into account, but not her liability to capital gains tax.

The payments on account are therefore:

		£
31 January 2010	[(£5,500 +£500)/2]	3,000
31 July 2010		3,000

Any additional tax due for the year will then be due in a final payment on 31 January 2011.

4 **Maurice**

As Maurice is self employed he must pay both Class 2 and Class 4 NI contributions as follows:

Class 2

52 × £2.40 = £125

This is due monthly, usually via direct debit.

Class 4	£
£(43,875 – 5,715) @ 8%	3,053
£(95,400 – 43,875) @ 1%	515
Total Class 4 NIC due	3,568

This is due with the income tax liability, ie two payments on account of 50% × the previous year's Class 4 liability, on 31 January in the tax year and 31 July after the tax year, with any balancing payment on 31 January following the tax year.

5 The profits of the 31 December 2009 accounting period would be taxed in the tax year 2009/10, under the CYB rules.

Allocation of profit between the partners:

Year ended 31 December 2009:

	Total	Miss J	Mr S
Period 1/1/09 to 30/6/09	£	£	£
Salary £10,000 each × 6/12	10,000	5,000	5,000
Profit share (50:50)	65,000	32,500	32,500
Total £150,000 × 6/12	75,000	37,500	37,500
Period 1/7/09 to 31/12/09			
Salary £20,000 × 6/12/nil	10,000	10,000	Nil
Profit share (60:40)	65,000	39,000	26,000
Total £150,000 × 6/12	75,000	49,000	26,000
Total taxable in 2009/10		86,500	63,500

206 Module 3: Unincorporated businesses

Solutions

Progress Test 2

6   Oliver

    (a)   Late notification of chargeability

Oliver should have notified HMRC by 5 October 2010. He did not do so until 1 December 2010. As this was after 1 April 2010 the new late notification penalty regime applies. As Oliver was not deliberately trying to mislead HMRC the maximum penalty for late notification is 30%. As the disclosure was unprompted by HMRC and occurred within 12 months of the date the tax was payable (31 January 2011) HMRC are likely to reduce the penalty to nil.

    (b)   Late tax return

The tax return was due the later of 31 January 2011 and three months after issue, ie 15 April 2011.

Oliver did not submit the return until 25 June 2011 As the return is less than 3 months late there will only be an immediate £100 penalty (t is reasonable to assume that the Finance Act 2009 late filing penalties will apply by 2011).

    (c)   Interest

The tax was due on 31 January 2011. Late payment interest applies for the period 31.1.11 – 24.6.11 = 5 months

£10,000 × 5/12 × 2.5% = £104

    (d)   Late payment penalty

It is reasonable to assume that the Finance Act 2009 late filing penalties will apply by 2011. As the payment is more than 30 days but less than 6 months late the penalty 5% of the outstanding tax:

5% × £10,000 = £500

7   Reuben

Gain on incorporation

		£	£
Total gains	– warehouse	74,500	
	– goodwill	12,000	86,500
Less:	incorporation relief (automatic)		
	£86,500 × £225,000/£300,000		(64,875)
Gain			21,625
Less: entrepreneurs' relief £21,625 × 4/9			(9,611)
Chargeable gain			12,013
Market value of shares			225,000
Less: Incorporation relief			(64,875)
Base cost c/f			160,125

Solutions

Progress Test 2

8 Craig – Capital gains computation 2009/10

		£	£
1	Sale of business		
	Building	700,000	
	Goodwill	200,000	
	Total gains	900,000	
	Entrepreneurs' relief £900,000 x 4/9	(400,000)	
	Chargeable gain		500,000
2	Shares		
	Proceeds (Deemed MV)	5,000	
	Cost	(1,000)	
			4,000
	Total chargeable gains		504,000
	Less annual exempt amount		(10,100)
	Taxable gain		493,900
	CGT @ 18%		88,902

9 Brianna

	FYAs	Main pool	Old expensive car (60%)	Allowances
1.4.09 – 31.3109	£	£	£	£
TWDV b/f		25,260	21,225	
Addition qualifying for AIA/40% FYA:	1,620			
AIA	(1,620)			1,620
WDA @ 20%		(5,052)		5,052
WDA @ £3,000 restricted			(3,000) × 60%	1,800
TWDV c/f		20,208	18,225	
Total allowances				8,472
1.4.10 – 30.6.10				
Addition		1,740		
Disposals		(25,295)	(16,500)	
No allowances in year of cessation				
		(3,347)	1,725	
Balancing charge		3,347		(3,347)
Balancing allowance			(1,725) × 60%	1,035
Total balancing charge (additional profit)				(2,312)

Module 3: Unincorporated businesses

Progress Test 2 — Solutions

10
		£	£
2009/10			
01.11.09 – 05.04.10 (Actual)			
£36,000 × 5/6			30,000
2010/11			
01.11.09 – 31.10.10 (first 12 months)			
£36,000 + 6/12 × £96,000			84,000
2011/12			
01.05.10 – 30.04.11 (CYB)			96,000
Overlap			
01.11.09 – 05.04.10		30,000	
01.05.10 – 31.10.10		48,000	
		78,000	

11 Jake – Capital gains 2009/10

	BA £	NBA £
Proceeds (90:10)	360,000	40,000
Less: 1982 MV (90:10)	(90,000)	(10,000)
	270,000	30,000
Less rollover relief (Note)	(270,000)	
Chargeable gain	-	30,000
Base cost of new property		
Cost	370,000	
Less: rolled over gain	(270,000)	
	100,000	

Note: Business proceeds (£360,000) were fully reinvested (£370,000). Therefore gain can be deferred in full.

12 Basil, Sybil and Polly

	Total £	Basil £	Sybil £	Polly £
Y/e 31.12.08				
Profits (1:1)	72,000	36,000	36,000	
Y/e 31.12.09				
Profits (1:1:1)	84,000	28,000	28,000	28,000

Trading income assessments

Basil & Sybil - continue to be assessed on CYB
2008/09 £36,000 each
2009/10 £28,000 each

Polly - apply opening year rules
2008/09: 1.1 09 – 5.4 09 3/12 × 28,000 = £7,000

2009/10: CYB year to 31 December 2009 = £28,000

Overlap profits of £7,000 (1.1.09 to 5.4.09)

Exam style questions

1.1 During 2009/10 Edward, a married man aged 47, had trading income of £45,000 and property income of £5,000. On 1 June 2009 he took out a loan in order to contribute capital to the partnership in which he is a partner. On 1 December he paid interest on the loan of £600. Interest payable on the loan at 5 April 2010 was £400.

His wife, Pat's only income during 2009/10 was trading income of £10,000.

You are required to calculate Edward and Pat's income tax liability for 2009/10.

2.1 Albert's accounts for the year ended 31 March 2010 show a trading profit of £291,000. This is after deducting legal expenses of £2,816 and repairs of £26,600.

These comprised:

		£
1.	*Legal expenses*	
	Renewal of an existing short lease	424
	Unsuccessful application for planning permission	1,720
	Debt collection	672
		2,816

		£
2.	*Repairs*	
	Replacing the old slate roof on the office buildings with a new slate roof	8,900
	Overhauling a second-hand printing press purchased during the year but requiring repair before it could be used	5,200
	Demolishing an out-house and building new ladies' toilets	12,500
		26,600

You are required to calculate the adjustment to the trading profit which is required in respect of the above expenses for tax purposes.

2.2 The sundries account of Harry, a food wholesaler who employs 10 people, is as follows:

	£
Gifts to customers	2,700
Entertaining staff at Christmas party	300
Entertaining local customers at trade shows	140
Harry's annual subscription to food wholesaler's trade association	250
Charitable donation to fundraising event by local hospice for which the business received publicity	500
	3,890

The gifts were leather wallets, purchased wholesale at £45.00 each (retail value £55.00); all had an advertisement for Harry's business on the side.

You are required to state, with reasons, the amount which will be allowed in the computation of trading profits.

2.3 Paula, who has been trading for many years, makes up her accounts to 31 December.

She took goods for her own use costing £560 during the year ended 31 December 2009. Her normal mark-up is 40%. No adjustment had been made to the accounts for the goods.

In addition, she provided for impairments as follows:

	£
Debtors in liquidation	600
Specific debtors outstanding for more than six months	200
50% provision on other balances outstanding for between three and six months	350
Loan to John Williams, a former employee	125
	1,275

You are required to show the adjustments required to Paula's accounts for the year to 31 December 2009 in respect of the above items.

2.4 Mary's accounts for the year ending 30 June 2009 show the following:

	£	£
Fees (note 1)		90,000
Bank interest received		2,500
Total income		92,500
Less:		
Salaries (note 2)	30,000	
National Insurance (note 3)	4,800	
Utilities and telephone	2,700	
Case of wine to employee at Christmas	150	
Loan to former employee written off	500	
Bank overdraft interest	300	
		(38,450)
Net profit		54,050

Notes

(1) During the year Mary provided interior design consultancy services to her sister for free. She would normally charge £700 for such services.

(2) Salary costs for two employees.

(3) National Insurance costs represent Mary's Class 4 liability of £4,800.

You are required to calculate the tax adjusted trading profit before capital allowances for the year to 30 June 2009.

2.5 Richard commenced trading on 1 May 2009 and prepared his first accounts for 15 months ended 31 July 2010.

He incurred advertising costs of £500 on 1 April 2009.

On 1 May 2009 he leased a car, with a list price of £14,000 and CO_2 emissions of 163g/km, for use by one of his employees at a monthly rental of £300. The car is used 75% for business purposes and the employee makes no reimbursement for private use.

You are required to:

(a) State how (if at all) Richard can obtain income tax relief for the advertising costs.

(b) Calculate the deduction for car leasing costs that will be allowed in calculating his taxable trading profits for the period to 31 July 2010.

2.6 Olive is in business running a health food shop. Her accounts for the year to 30 June 2009 show a trading profit of £45,000, this is after deducting the following:

(1) Legal fees of £400 in connection with terminating an onerous trading contract.

(2) Gift of ten food hampers to local, loyal customers at Christmas, worth £30 each

(3) Cost of £500 for Olive to attend an IT course at the local college in order for Olive to acquire some basic IT skills. She had never used a computer prior to the course.

(4) Parking fine of £50 incurred by Olive's assistant while delivering food boxes to customers.

(5) Costs of running Olive's car of £8,000. She travels 10,000 miles a year of which 2,000 relate to travel from home to the shop each day, 5,000 relate to business journeys and the balance to private journeys.

You are required to calculate Olive's taxable trading profit for the year to 30 June 2009.

3.1 Wainwright, who owns a garage, incurred the following expenditure on plant and equipment:

	£
New light fittings for the offices	1,000
Canopy over the petrol filling station	10,500
Car ramp for the car repair workshop	3,800
Moveable partitions for the accounts offices moved from time to time	8,400
New display cabinets for the shop	2,000
	25,700

You are required to state, with reasons, how much is eligible for inclusion in the main plant and machinery capital allowance pool.

3.2 Fielding commenced trading on 1 May 2004 and prepares accounts to 30 April.

The tax written-down value of his plant and equipment on 1 May 2009 was £8,300.

On 4 September 2009, he sold a machine for £3,600 which had cost him £2,000 in August 2004.

On 4 April 2010, he purchased office equipment for £750 and a van for £8,000. He uses the van 20% of the time for private purposes.

You are required to calculate the total capital allowances available for the year to 30 April 2010.

3.3 John has been trading for many years, preparing accounts to 31 March. In the year ended 31 March 2010, his capital transactions were as follows:

1 May 2009	Purchased Volvo (CO_2 emissions 167g/km, for employee)	£16,000
4 May 2009	Purchased Ford Fiesta (CO_2 emissions 135g/km, used by John)	£6,500
10 May 2009	Sold Ford Cortina for (CO_2 emissions 145g/km, used by John)	£3,700

The tax written down value brought forward of the Cortina was £4,200. There was no balance on the main pool or special rate pool as at 1 April 2009.

All of the cars have 10% private use.

You are required to calculate the capital allowances available for the year ended 31 March 2010.

3.4 Maggie operates a chocolate-making business as an unincorporated trader. The following capital transactions took place in the year to 31 March 2010:

		£
Acquisitions		*Cost*
1 August 2009	Volvo car (CO_2 emissions 159g/km 30% private use)	22,000
1 September 2009	Vauxhall car (CO_2 emissions 105/km 25% private use)	11,000
1 March 2010	Delivery van	13,000
Disposals		*Proceeds*
1 August 2009	Old expensive car (CO_2 emissions 145g/km Audi) (30% private use)	13,000

The Volvo car acquired and the Audi car disposed of during the year were used by Maggie. The Vauxhall car was used by the production manager.

The original cost of the Audi car was £24,000.

The value of the capital allowance pools as at 1 April 2009 were:

| Main pool | £40,000 |
| Expensive car (Audi) | £18,000 |

You are required to calculate the capital allowances available to Maggie for the year to 31 March 2010.

3.5 On 1 June 2009 Robert commenced trading as a self-employed baker. His first set of accounts showed a tax adjusted trading profit, before capital allowances and hire purchase payments, of £65,000 for the 9 month period to 28 February 2010.

The following assets were acquired in the period to 28 February 2010:

		£
1 June 2009	Car (CO_2 emissions 172g/km, 25% private use)	11,000
3 June 2009	Equipment	44,240
1 July 2009	New electrical system for bakery	30,000

The car was used exclusively by Robert.

In addition on 1 July 2009 Robert acquired a photocopier on hire purchase. Robert agreed to pay 36 monthly instalments of £180, which included finance charges of £20. The hire purchase payments have not yet been reflected in Robert's accounts for the 9 month period.

You are required to calculate Robert's taxable trading profits for the period to 28 February 2010.

3.6 Tintin had been trading for many years preparing accounts to 30 November when he decided to cease trading on 31 July 2009.

On 1 May 2009 he acquired machinery for £1,500 and a car (CO_2 emissions 145g/km) for £6,000. He used the car 20% of the time for private purposes.

All items of plant and machinery were sold on 31 July 2009 for £3,000 (no item was sold for more than cost). The car acquired during the period was retained by Tintin. The market value of the car at 31 July 2009 was £5,000.

The tax written down value of the main pool at 1 December 2008 was £9,498.

You are required to calculate the capital allowances available to Tintin in the period to 31 July 2009.

3.7 Cameron is a self employed vet. His accounts for the year to 31 December 2009 show a trading profit of £125,000. He has recently moved into new premises.

He is unsure of the tax treatment of the following items that he has deducted in calculating his trading profit:

(1) Golf club membership of £2,500. Cameron has joined the club purely for business networking purposes.
(2) Legal fees of £750 in respect of a three year lease on the new premises.
(3) Lease payment of £4,520 on a Mercedes (CO_2 emissions 170g/km, purchase price £25,000)
(4) Parking fine of £60 incurred by one of Cameron's staff whilst picking up a delivery from a supplier.
(5) £24,000 on the purchase of new equipment on 1 August 2009.

The lease of the Mercedes car was taken out on 1 May 2009.

You are required to calculate Cameron's taxable trading profit for the year to 31 December 2009.

3.8 Anne has run her pony trail business for many years, drawing up accounts to 31 December each year.

In the year to 31 December 2009 she had the following capital transactions:

14 April 2009	£45,000 on an air conditioning system for the indoor paddock, which qualifies as an integral feature.
1 June 2009	Sold equipment for £13,500 which had originally been purchased for £12,000 in May 2008.
22 September 2009	Purchased a second hand van for £6,500. The van will be used by one of her employees and will have 20% private use.
1 November 2009	£24,000 on a Jeep 4 wheel drive vehicle (CO_2 emissions 180g/km) which she will use 40% of the time for private purposes.

The tax written down value of her main pool at 1 January 2009 was £136,733.

You are required to calculate the capital allowances that Anne can claim for her year ended 31 December 2009.

4.1 Stephen started trading as a landscape gardener on 1 July 2006. He prepared accounts to 30 April 2007 and annually thereafter.

You are required to state Stephen's basis periods for the first four tax years, identifying any overlap profits.

4.2 Avril has traded as a self-employed painter and decorator for a number of years. On 30 November 2009 she ceased to trade.

Avril's taxable trading profits had been as follows:

Year to 30 June 2008   £42,000
Year to 30 June 2009   £38,000

Her final accounts for the five months to 30 November 2009, show a tax adjusted trading profit before capital allowances of £16,000

The only assets used in the business were a van, which she retained for her personal use, and items of plant and machinery which she sold for £2,000. None of the individual items of plant and machinery were sold for more than their original cost.

Avril had only ever used the van for business purposes which had cost £13,000 in April 2001. It had a market value of £1,500 at 30 November 2009.

The tax written down value of the main capital allowances pool as at 1 July 2009 was £3,000.

Avril had overlap profits in respect of her opening tax years' of £2,500

You are required to calculate Avril's trading income assessment for 2009/10.

4.3 Wayne commenced trading on 1 May 2005. On 31 December 2009 he ceased trading. His trading results had been as follows:

Y/e 30 April 2006   £15,000
Y/e 30 April 2007   £21,000
Y/e 30 April 2008   £23,000
Y/e 30 April 2009   £24,000
P/e 31 December 2009   £14,000

You are required to calculate Wayne's trading income assessment for all tax years in which he was in business.

4.4 Martina commenced in business as a sports consultant on 1 August 2005. She made up accounts to 31 January 2006 and annually thereafter. Recent profits are as follows:

Y/e 31.1.09   £21,000

In order to change her accounting date to 30 June, Martina prepares accounts for the period to 30 June 2010, giving the appropriate notice to HMRC. The accounts show taxable profits of £34,000. She has two months worth of overlap profits of £2,000.

You are required to calculate her trading income assessments for 2009/10 and 2010/11.

4.5 Cecil commenced trading on 1 September 2008. He prepared accounts to 30 June 2009 and annually thereafter.

His tax adjusted trading profits for the first two periods were as follows:

	£
10 months ending 30 June 2009	52,500
Year ending 30 June 2010	71,500

On 1 September 2008 he acquired a machine for £5,000.

You are required to calculate Cecil's trading income assessments for the first three tax years.

4.6 Doug commenced trading 1 January 2009 and makes his first set of accounts up to 31 December 2009 and annually thereafter.

Results have been as follows:

Year ended	£
31 December 2009	18,000
31 December 2010	20,000
31 December 2011	28,000

You are required to:

(a) Calculate his trading income assessment for the first three tax years.

(b) Calculate his overlap profits and state how these can be used.

4.7 Olivia commenced business as a self-employed acupuncturist on 1 January 2009. Her results for her first set of accounts for the eighteen month period to 30 June 2010 are as follows:

	£	£
Gross operating profit		95,000
Less: Wages (Note 1)	45,750	
Rent and rates (Note 2)	12,000	
Depreciation	250	
Telephone and utilities	1,800	
Sundry expenses (all allowable)	425	
		(60,225)
Net profit		34,775

Notes:

(1) Olivia paid herself a salary of £30,000. She also employed a receptionist for £15,000 and her husband, Jake, to do the business's accounts for £750.

(2) Rent and rates relate to the whole of the practice building. The two rooms on the ground floor are used for the business. Olivia and her husband live above. Olivia uses one of the rooms as her office; the other two upstairs rooms are used for private purposes.

(3) In addition, she spends £950 on equipment during the period.

You are required to:

(1) Calculate Olivia's taxable trading profit for the eighteen month period to 30 June 2010.

(2) State the amount that will be taxed in 2009/10.

(3) State the amount of any overlap profits created in respect of the 18-month period to 30 June 2010.

4.8 Carrie has run her own 'personal shopper' business since 1 January 2001, when she prepared her first accounts to 30 September 2001 and then 30 September thereafter. Her overlap profits on commencement were £17,490.

In 2009 she decides to change her accounting date to 31 December.

Her recent taxable trade profits have been as follows:

	£
1.10.06 – 30.9.07	24,500
1.10.07 – 30.9.08	47,000
1.10.08 – 31.12.09	84,000

You are required to calculate Carrie's assessments for 2007/08, 2008/09 and 2009/10 and state the overlap profits carried forward

4.9 Chandler starts to trade on 1 January 2008, making up his first account to 30 June 2008.

His results, before capital allowances, are as follows:

	£
1.1.08 – 30.6.08	12,000
1.7.08 – 30.6.09	45,000

Capital allowances are calculated and claimed as follows:

	£
1.1.08 – 30.6.08	16,000
1.7.08 – 30.6.09	22,000

You are required to calculate the taxable trade profits and/ or losses for all relevant tax years and to state the overlap profits created, if any.

5.1 Sophie has been trading for many years making up accounts to 30 June. Her recent results were as follows:

		£
Year ended 30 June 2009	Profit	12,000
Year ended 30 June 2010	Loss	(14,000)

In addition she had a trading loss brought forward at 6 April 2009 of £3,000. In 2009/10 she also had property income of £1,000, and bank interest income of £500 (gross).

You are required to calculate the loss that will be carried forward to 2010/11, assuming maximum relief is taken in 2009/10. Show your workings.

5.2 Brenda commenced trading as a self-employed beautician on 1 January 2009. Her recent tax adjusted trading results have been as follows:

Six months to 30 June 2009	£(5,000) loss
Year to 30 June 2010	£12,000

You are required to calculate the trading income assessments for the first two tax years of trading.

5.3 Darren has run a hardware shop as a sole trader for a number of years.

He makes up his accounts to 30 September and his trading results for the last two years have been:

		£
Year ended 30 September 2008	Profit	5,000
Year ended 30 September 2009	Loss	(18,000)

Darren receives rental interest of £7,000 annually. In April 2009 he sold an investment property on which he realised a chargeable gain of £40,000.

You are required to state the ways in which Darren may utilise the trading loss.

5.4 Parker, who had traded since 2000, ceased to trade on 30 September 2009. His recent results have been:

		£
Year ended 31 December 2007	Profit	6,800
Year ended 31 December 2008	Profit	7,200
Period ended 30 September 2009	Loss	4,500

His overlap profits on commencement were £600.

Parker has no other income.

You are required to calculate Parker's terminal loss.

5.5 Keith incurs a loss of £9,000 in 2009/10, having commenced trading that year. His general income has been as follows:

	£
2005/06	5,000
2006/07	6,000
2007/08	2,000
2008/09	8,000

He wishes to claim relief available for losses in the opening years of a business against total income of earlier years.

You are required to state how much of the loss will be relieved and in which years and which order.

5.6 Pipchin commenced trading on 1 October 2004, making up his accounts to 30 September 2005 and annually thereafter. His recent results have been:

Year ended	£
30 September 2006	12,000
30 September 2007	(45,000)
30 September 2008	8,000
30 September 2009	14,000

He has received property income as follows:

	£
2006/07	10,400
2007/08	11,000
2008/09	11,000
2009/10	11,000

You are required to compute Pipchin's net income for 2006/07 to 2009/10, assuming maximum s.64 ITA 2007 claims are made to offset the loss against general income.

5.7 Bertie, whose has been trading as a sole trader for a number of years, made a trading loss of £70,000 in 2009/10.

In recent years his trading results have been as follows:

Year ended	£
31 July 2005	75,000
31 July 2006	55,000
31 July 2007	28,000
31 July 2008	4,000

Bertie has gross bank interest each year of £10,000 until 2009/10 when it is £5,000.

You are required to compute Bertie's net income for 2005/06 to 2009/10, assuming loss relief is taken in the most beneficial manner and against income as early as possible.

5.8 Alex has traded for many years making up accounts to 30 June each year. He has overlap profits brought forward from the beginning of the business of £24,000.

He ceased trading on 31 December 2009.

His recent trading results have been as follows:

	£
1.7.06 – 31.6.07	45,000
1.7.07 – 31.6.08	22,000
1.7.08 – 30.6.09	12,000
Period ending 31.12.09	(27,000)

You are required to calculate the terminal loss available for offset on the cessation of the trade and to state which years it can be set against, in the order in which they can be offset.

6.1 George is an employee of a partnership of solicitors and on 1 January 2010 will become an equity partner. It is envisaged that he will have a 10% share of income and capital profits. The firm's forecast trading profits are as follows:

Year ending 30 June 2010 £330,000
Year ending 30 June 2011 £420,000

You are required to calculate George's assessable income from the partnership for each of the tax years 2009/10, 2010/11 and 2011/12 and any overlap relief available to him.

6.2 Peter and Paul have been in partnership for many years, sharing profits equally.

From 1 July 2009 it was agreed that Peter and Paul would receive a salary of £30,000 and £35,000 per annum respectively. From this date Peter and Paul would share profits in the ratio 3:4.

The tax adjusted trading profits for the year to 31 December 2009 were £220,000.

You are required to calculate the trading income assessments for each of the partners for 2009/10.

6.3 Kenneth and Gail commenced trading on 1 January 2008, sharing profits and losses equally, until 1 January 2010 when they started sharing profits and losses 3:1 respectively.

Their results since they started trading have been:

	£
Year ended 31 December 2008	15,000 profit
Year ended 31 December 2009	28,000 loss
Year ended 31 December 2010	20,000 profit

You are required to:

(a) Calculate Kenneth's trading income assessments for the first four years of trading.
(b) State how the loss can be offset under s.72 ITA 2007 relief for losses in early years of trading.

6.4 A and B had been in partnership for many years sharing profits equally before C joined them on 1 June 2009. They agreed to continue sharing profits equally.

The profits were as follows:

Year ended 31.12.08	£60,000
Year ended 31.12.09	£72,000
Year ended 31.12.10	£84,000

You are required to calculate the trading income assessment for 2009/10 for all three partners.

6.5 Victor, Ann and Joan have been in partnership for a number of years sharing profits 20:30:50 after allowing for annual salaries of £35,000 for Victor and £25,000 for Ann.

Tax adjusted trading profits of the partnership for the year ended 31 December 2009 were £45,000.

You are required to calculate the trading income assessments for each of the partners for 2009/10.

6.6 Neil became a partner in a trading limited liability partnership on 1 January 2008.

He contributed capital to the partnership of £15,000 and £18,000 on 1 January 2008 and 1 January 2010 respectively.

Neil's share of the partnership's losses is as follows:

Year ended 5 April 2008	£10,000
Year ended 5 April 2009	£20,000
Year ended 5 April 2010	£11,000

You are required to state the amount of loss relief that Neil is entitled to in respect of the tax years 2007/08 to 2009/10 inclusive assuming he wishes to claim relief against other income under s.64 Income Tax Act 2007. State the amount of any unrelieved losses as at 5 April 2010.

6.7 Bill and Steve have been in partnership for many years, drawing up accounts to 31 March. They share profits equally after taking a salary of £36,000 each.

On 1 May 2009 Molly joined the partnership, from which time the profits were split 40:40:20 between Bill, Steve and Molly. None of the partners took a salary from this date.

The tax adjusted trading profit, before capital allowances, for the year ended 31 March 2010 was £275,000.

The tax written down value of the partnership's capital allowances main pool on 1 April 2009 was £116,500. On 15 April 2009 the partnership invested £45,000 in new plant and machinery.

You are required to calculate how much is taxed on each partner for 2009/10.

7.1 Steven has the following details for 2009/10:

	£
Taxable trade profits	49,000
Loss brought forward	3,000

In 2008/09 £2,000 of the trading loss had been offset against non-trading income.

You are required to calculate Steven's class 4 national insurance liability for 2009/10.

7.2 Charlie has been trading for many years. His profits per the accounts for the years to 30 June 2009 and 30 June 2010 were £4,000 and £6,500 respectively. These figures are after charging depreciation of £20,000 each year.

You are required to calculate Charlie's national insurance liability for 2009/10.

7.3 On 1 September 2009 Simon commenced trading as a self-employed decorator. His first set of accounts showed a tax adjusted trading profit before capital allowances of £70,000 for the 9 month period to 31 May 2010.

On 1 September 2009 Simon purchased equipment for £12,000 and on 1 October 2009 he purchased a car for £16,000. His mileage in the car was 70% for business purposes and 30% for private purposes and the CO_2 emissions of the car were 166g/km.

You are required to calculate Simon's trading income assessment and Class 4 National Insurance liability for 2009/10.

7.4 John and Fred have been in partnership for many years.

John and Fred receive an annual salary from the partnership of £35,000 and £20,000 respectively. Profits are shared in the ratio 2:3.

The tax adjusted trading profits for the year to 31 December 2009 were £90,000.

You are required to calculate the Class 4 National Insurance liability for each of the partners for 2009/10.

7.5 Lynne commenced trading as a sole trader on 1 March 2009. Her first set of accounts for the 15 months to 31 May 2010 showed a tax adjusted trading profit of £57,000.

You are required to calculate Lynne's Class 4 National insurance liability for 2009/10 and state when it is payable.

7.6 Malcolm, Pat and Rose have been in partnership for a number of years, sharing profits equally. Overlap profits on the commencement of trade were £20,000, £8,000 and £12,000 for Malcolm, Pat and Rose respectively.

On 1 December 2009 Rose retired from the partnership.

Recent tax adjusted profits of the partnership have been:

Year ended 30 April 2009   £240,000
Year ended 30 April 2010   £250,000

You are required to calculate the trading income assessment and the Class 4 National insurance liability for Rose for 2009/10.

7.7 Miranda is a self employed nail technician, drawing up accounts to 31 March.

Her accounting profits for the year ended 31 March 2010 show a profit before tax of £4,685. This is after drawing a salary of £5,435.

This accounting profit includes £150 for the cost of goods taken for her own use. The market value of the goods is £350.

The figure is also before making adjustments for depreciation of £280 and customer entertaining of £150.

The tax written down value on Miranda's capital allowances main pool was £900 at 1 April 2009.

You are required to calculate Miranda's total NIC liability for 2009/10.

8.1 **You are required to state which of the following assets are exempt for capital gains tax purposes.**

- a diamond brooch
- a thoroughbred racehorse
- a lease with an unexpired term of 25 years
- a micro-computer used in a business
- a limousine used by a car hire company

8.2 **You are required to state, with reasons, which of the following transactions are liable to UK capital gains tax:**

(1) Carl is resident in Germany but ordinarily resident in the UK. During 2009/10 he sold a house which is situated in Germany.

(2) Tracey is resident and ordinarily resident in Australia, During 2009/10 she sold her UK holiday home.

(3) Brad is resident and ordinarily resident in the UK. During 2009/10 he gave a part share in a greyhound to his daughter.

9.1 In August 1990, Jeremy bought a warehouse for £120,000 for use in his trade. He sold it for £220,000 in July 2009.

In August 2009 he sold an investment property for £500,000, that he had acquired in May 1981 for £50,000. He extended the property at a cost of £20,000 in May 1990. The property was valued on 31 March 1982 at £60,000.

You are required to calculate Jeremy's capital gains tax liability for 2009/10.

9.2 Julie owned a field which she purchased on 13 August 1987 for £8,000. On 10 September 2009, she sold a quarter of the field for development for £30,000. The remainder of the field was then worth £10,000.

Julie had made no other disposals in 2009/10. She had capital losses brought forward from 2008/09 of £15,000.

You are required to calculate Julie's capital gains tax liability for 2009/10 and state the amount of any losses carried forward.

9.3 Felicity invites the following people to dinner:

(1) Her husband
(2) Her mother-in-law
(3) Her business partner
(4) The civil partner of her business partner
(5) Her uncle
(6) Her step-father
(7) Her brother-in-law
(8) Her sister

You are required to state, with reasons, who is connected with Felicity for capital gains tax purposes.

9.4 Amber had the following transactions in the shares of Zingo Ltd:

		£
19.2.83	Purchased 2,000 shares, cost	10,000
20.9.90	Purchased 1,000 shares, cost	8,000
15.11.09	Sold 1,500 shares, proceeds	22,000

What is Amber's chargeable gain for 2009/10?

10.1 Luther sold a factory on 10 November 2009. He purchased the following assets for use in his business:

Date of purchase	Asset
21 September 2008	Freehold factory
4 June 2009	Fork lift truck
8 October 2011	Hovercraft
5 July 2013	Office block

You are required to explain, giving reasons, against which purchase(s) he may claim rollover relief.

10.2 Henry has run his own business for many years. In May 2009 he sold a factory for £100,000, which had cost £40,000 in May 1993. He bought another factory in January 2009 for £80,000.

You are required to calculate the chargeable gain arising on the sale of the factory and the base cost of the new factory assuming rollover relief is claimed.

10.3 Steven sold all of the assets of his unincorporated business, as a going concern to Carts Ltd on 1 January 2010. Details of the assets sold are as follows:

	Market value 1.1.10 £	Gain £
Goodwill	50,000	40,000
Freehold building	200,000	90,000
Stock	30,000	
Debtors	8,000	
	288,000	

Steven had purchased the building on 1 April 2008. He had acquired the goodwill when he purchased the trade and assets of a sole trader on 1 April 2001.

Steven received shares in Carts Ltd, with a value of £288,000, in consideration for the sale of the business.

You are required to:

(a) **Explain why the gains arising on the sale of the business will be rolled over into the base cost of the shares in Carts Ltd**

(b) **Calculate the base cost of the shares in Carts Ltd acquired by Steven in consideration for the sale of the business.**

10.4 Mr Terry transferred his sole trader business to a quoted company on 1 August 2009 realising gains of £46,000. The consideration comprised cash of £16,000 and shares with a nominal value of £50,000 and a market value of £60,000.

You are required to:

(a) **Calculate the chargeable gain on transfer and the base cost of the new shares for Mr Terry**
(b) **State the date by which Mr Terry must submit an election if he wishes to disapply incorporation relief.**

10.5 Jeremy Brett, who had run a manufacturing business for many years, decided to reduce the size of the operation in 2009/10. He therefore gave one of the factories (which had always been used for his business) to his son John although John persuaded his father to accept £50,000 in return.

The factory had been acquired on 2 January 1970 for £31,000. The market value in March 1982 was £42,000. It was worth £152,000 and was standing at a gain of £110,000 when it was passed to John in August 2009.

You are required to:

(a) Calculate Jeremy's chargeable gain, if any, for 2009/10 and state the base cost for John, on the assumption that all possible claims for relief are made

(b) State who needs to make the appropriate claim and the deadline for the claim.

10.6 Robert bought an 80% holding in an unquoted trading company on 10 July 2005 for £160,000. He gave the holding to his daughter, Lauren, on 13 December 2009, when it was worth £300,000. At that date, the assets of the company were:

	£
Factory	300,000
Quoted investments	50,000
Net current assets	25,000
	375,000

Robert has never worked for the company.

You are required to:

(a) Calculate the gain chargeable on Robert, after all available reliefs, but before the annual exemption.
(b) State the date that Robert's capital gains tax liability in respect of the above is payable.

10.7 In 2009/10 Arthur made the following disposals:

(1) On 1 June 2009 he sold a freehold warehouse for £850,000 which he had acquired in 1992 for £80,000. He had always used the building for the purposes of his unincorporated business until he ceased to trade in May 2008. The building has not been in use since May 2008.

(2) On 1 February 2010 he sold an unincorporated business, which he had established in May 2008, as a going concern. The following gains arose on the business's chargeable assets:

	Chargeable gain £
Goodwill	400,000
Business premises	800,000
Building held as an investment	180,000

Calculate Arthur's taxable gain in 2009/10 assuming he makes no other disposals and that he makes any beneficial claims.

10.8 Jen, a very successful hairdresser, sold her business as a going concern on 1 June 2009, realising a gain of £950,000.

On 1 September 2009 she sold 20,000 shares in Matted Ltd, an unquoted trading company with 400,000 shares in issue, to her sister for £190,000. The market value of the shares on the date of disposal was £800,000. Jen has been a non-executive director of Matted Ltd since she acquired her shares for £10,000 in July 2003.

You are required to calculate Jen's Capital Gains Tax liability for 2009/10 assuming that these are her only disposals and that she makes any beneficial claims.

10.9 Daryl had run his business as a sole trade since October 2000, at which date he purchased premises for £250,000 and goodwill for £100,000.

On 14 May 2009 he incorporated the business. The market value of the premises had increased to £790,000 and the value of the goodwill was now £500,000.

He received the following consideration from the company:

Cash	£200,000
Shares	£1,800,000

You are required to calculate Daryl's chargeable gain on incorporation, after all available reliefs, and to state the base cost of the shares for any future disposal.

11.1 Paul and Jason have been in partnership sharing profits equally for a number of years. In May 1999 the partnership acquired a freehold building for £500,000. In June 2009 Susan was admitted as a partner and thereafter profits were shared in the ratio 5:3:2. No adjustment for asset values have been made through the accounts.

In March 2010 the building was sold for £800,000.

You are required to explain the capital gains tax implications of the above and to calculate the chargeable gain arising for each partner in 2009/10.

11.2 Millie, Whisper and Brooke, have been in partnership for a number of years, sharing profits equally.

On 1 March 2010 the partners ceased trading. A building, with a market value of £300,000 was transferred to Millie at the date of cessation. The building had been acquired for £90,000 on 1 June 1999.

You are required to set out the capital gains tax implications of the transfer of the building on each of the partners.

11.3 Gary and Kevin have been in partnership for many years sharing profits equally. The only chargeable partnership asset is goodwill, which they purchased for £240,000 when they took over the partnership in September 2001.

On 7 August 2009 Veronica joined the partnership, from which time the profits were split 40:40:20 between Gary, Kevin and Veronica. The goodwill was revalued in the balance sheet at £585,000 on that date.

You are required to calculate the gain chargeable on each partner as a result of Veronica joining the partnership for 2009/10 and to show each partner's base cost carried forward. You should assume any available reliefs are claimed.

12.1 Jones, who has never received a tax return, commenced his first business on 5 May 2010.

You are required to:

(a) State by what date he must give notice that he is chargeable to income tax
(b) State the penalty for not notifying HMRC by this date.
(c) Give two situations where notification to HMRC of a new source of income is not required.

12.2 Percy has a final income tax liability for 2009/10 of £12,500 of which £3,000 has been deducted at source. He also has a CGT liability of £2,000. In 2008/09 his final income tax liability was £10,500 of which £3,500 was paid at source.

You are required to show how Percy's 2009/10 tax liability will be settled.

12.3 Jamie is in business as a sole trader. His 2009/10 tax return showed a balancing payment due of £2,000. He submitted his 2009/10 return and paid the tax due 7 months after the due filing date.

You are required to state:

(a) The penalties that will be payable by Jamie in respect of the late submission and payment of tax
(b) The date by which Jamie should have submitted his tax return for 2009/10.

12.4 Donald is in business as a sole trader. His tax position for the last two tax years is as follows:

	2008/09 £	2009/10 £
Income tax liability	22,000	25,000
Tax deducted at source	500	900
Capital gains tax liability	3,000	4,000
Class 4 NIC liability	5,000	5,500
Class 2 NIC liability	120	125
Payments on account	11,000	

You are required to state the amount of tax Donald should pay on 31 January 2010 to avoid any interest or penalties accruing.

12.5 Dan had an income tax and Class 4 NIC liability less tax deducted at source of £23,000 for 2008/09.

He made payments on account of his 2009/10 liability of £11,500 on 1 March 2010 and 1 October 2010. His 2009/10 income tax and Class 4 liability less tax deducted at source is £25,000. He paid the additional tax due on 31 January 2011.

You are required to show the interest and penalties due in respect of the payment of the 2009/10 income tax and Class 4 NIC liability. Assume a rate of interest of 2.5%. Ignore leap years.

12.6 You act for Roger who is concerned about the new penalties introduced for errors in tax returns.

You are required to state the range of penalties (in percentage terms) for Scenarios 1 to 3 below and to state what HMRC is likely to do in Scenario 4:

1. Roger submits his return and it is processed by HMRC. He had innocently forgotten to provide you with the tax deduction certificate from a new bank account he had opened during the year. HMRC find out about the account when processing the return.

2. Roger submits his return and it is processed by HMRC. He had deliberately omitted to provide you with the tax deduction certificate from a new bank account he had opened during the year. He advises you of the new account when you ask him about next year's return information and you advise HMRC at Roger's request.

3. Roger submits his return and it is processed by HMRC. He had deliberately omitted to provide you with the tax deduction certificate from a new bank account he had opened during the year. He does not tell you of the new account when you ask him about next year's return information. HMRC find out about the account when processing the return.

4. Roger submits his return and it is processed by HMRC. He had innocently forgotten to provide you with the tax deduction certificate from a new bank account he had opened during the year. He asks you to advise HMRC as soon as possible and to provide them with any information that they require in connection with the error.

Solutions to exam style questions

1.1 Edward and Pat

2009/10 Income tax liability

	Edward £	Pat £
Trading income	45,000	10,000
Property income	5,000	
Total income	50,000	10,000
Less Deductible payments:		
Qualifying interest (paid basis)	(600)	
Net income	49,400	10,000
Less personal allowance	(6,475)	(6,475)
Taxable income	42,925	3,525
Income tax		
£37,400 @ 20%	7,480	
£5,525 @ 40%	2,210	
£3,525 @ 20%		705
Income tax liability	9,690	705

2.1 Albert

Add back to trading profit:

	£
Unsuccessful application for planning permission	1,720
Overhaul of printing press	5,200
Ladies toilets	12,500
	19,420

Explanations:

1. Planning permission relates to expenditure of a capital nature and therefore is not allowed, irrespective of the outcome of the application.

2. The repair was required to the printing press before it could be used. The expense is therefore disallowed as capital expenditure.

3. The expenditure brings into place a new asset and is capital in nature.

2.2 Harry

£3,750 (ie 2,700 + 300 + 250 + 500)

Explanations:

1. Entertaining customers is never allowable.

2. Gifts to customers are allowable if the cost is less than £50 per person, they carry an advert and do not consist of food, drink, tobacco or vouchers.

3. Trade subscriptions are allowable.

4. Charitable donations to small local charities are allowable provided they benefit the business eg good publicity.

2.3 **Paula**

(a) Goods own use

$560 \times \dfrac{140}{100} = £784$ – add back to profit.

Explanation: Goods taken for own use treated as a sale.

(b) Impairments

	£
50% general provision	350
Loan to former employee	125
Add back to profit	475

Explanation: Specific provisions are allowed.

2.4 **Mary**

Tax adjusted trading profit for the year ending 30 June 2009

		£	£
Net profit			54,050
Less:	Bank interest received		(2,500)
Plus:	Class 4 NIC	4,800	
	Free services to sister	–	
	Gift to employee	–	
	Loan to former employee written off	500	
			5,300
			56,850

Note. No adjustments are required for gifts of services or gifts to employees. The latter are assessed on the employee as a benefit.

2.5 **Richard**

(a) The advertising costs will be treated as incurred on 1 May 2009 and deducting from the profit per the accounts for the period ended 31 July 2010.

The expenditure is allowable as it was incurred in the 7 years before trade started and it would have been allowable if it had been incurred after the commencement of trade.

(b) Allowable lease costs

$300 \times 15 \times 85\% = \underline{£3,825}$

Explanation: The allowable lease costs are restricted as the car has CO_2 emissions which exceed 160g/km. The % business use is irrelevant for the trader, where an employee uses the car.

2.6 **Olive**

Tax adjusted trading profit for the year ended 30 June 2009

	£
Profit per accounts	45,000
Legal fees (trade related)	–
Gifts (food disallowable)	300
IT course (disallowed as to acquire **new** skills)	500
Parking fine (allowed as employee)	–
Motor expenses (£8,000 x 5,000/10,000) (Note)	4,000
Tax adjusted trading profit	49,800

Note. Travel costs from home to place of business are not an allowable deduction.

3.1 Wainwright

Eligible for plant and machinery capital allowances:

	£
Car ramp	3,800
Partitions	8,400
Cabinets	2,000
	14,200

Explanation: The canopy and the light fittings are not eligible because they form 'part of the setting' in which the trade is carried on. The car ramp and cabinet perform a function in the business and therefore qualify. Also moveable office partitions were held to be plant in Jarrold v John Good & Sons Ltd. The light fittings, as part of an electrical system and so integral features, may be included in the special rate pool.

3.2 Fielding

Capital allowances – year to 30 April 2010

	FYA £	Main pool £	Van (PU 20%) £	Allowances £
TWDV B/F		8,300		
Additions qualifying for AIA/40% FYA:				
Additions	750		8,000	
AIA	(750)		(8,000) × 80%	7,150
Disposal (restrict to cost)		(2,000)		
		6,300		
WDA at 20%		(1,260)		1,260
				8,410
TWDV c/f		5,040		

3.3 John

Capital allowances – Y/e 31.3.10

			£		Allowances £
Volvo	Special rate car	Addition 1.5.09	16,000		
		WDA @ 10%	(1,600)		1,600
		TWDV c/f	14,400		
Cortina	PU car	TWDV b/f	4,200		
		Proceeds 10.5.09	(3,700)		
		Balancing allowance	500	× 90%	450
Fiesta	PU car Main rate car	Addition 4.5.09	6,500		
		WDA @ 20%	(1,300)	× 90%	1,170
		TWDV c/f	5,200		3,220

Explanation: The Volvo car would enter the special rate pool – there was a nil balance on the pool as at 1 April 2009. Separate calculations for the other cars because they are used privately. No AIA for cars. There is no restriction for private use by an employee.

3.4 Maggie

Capital allowances computation for the year to 31 March 2010

	FYA £	Main pool £	(PU 30%) £	(PU 30%) £	Allowances £
TWDV at 1.4.09		40,000	18,000		
Additions qualifying for 100% FYAs:					
New Vauxhall car	11,000				
100% FYA	(11,000)				11,000
Additions qualifying for AIA/40% FYA:					
Van	13,000				
AIA	(13,000)				13,000
Other additions:					
Volvo car (main rate)				22,000	
Disposal			(13,000)		
			5,000		
Balancing allowance			(5,000) × 70%		3,500
		40,000		22,000	
WDA @ 20%		(8,000)		(4,400)× 70%	11,080
TWDV cfwd		32,000	–	17,600	
Total allowances					38,580

3.5 Robert

Taxable trading profit for the 9 month period to 28 February 2010

	£
Adjusted trading profit	65,000
Less: HP finance charges (£20 x 8)	(160)
Capital allowances (W1)	(4,427)
Taxable trading profit	60,413

(W1) Capital allowances for the 9 months to 29 February 2010

	FYA £	Main pool £	Special rate pool £	Special rate car (PU 25%) £	Allowances £
Additions qualifying for AIA/40% FYA:					
3.6.09 Equipment	44,240				
1.7.09 Electrical system (AIA only)			30,000		
1.7.09 Photocopier (W)	5,760				
	50,000				
AIA (Max £50,000 x 9/12) (Note)	(7,500)		(30,000)		37,500
	42,500				
FYA @ 40%	(17,000)				17,000
	25,500				
Other additions:					
1.6.09 PU Car (special rate)				11,000	
				11,000	
WDA at 10% x 9/12				(825) x 75%	619
Transfer balance to main pool	(25,500)	25,500			
TWDV c/f		25,500		10,175	
Total allowances					55,119

230 Module 3: Unincorporated Businesses

(W) Cost of photocopier = 36 × £(180 − 20) = £5,760

Note: The AIA is allocated to the additions in the special rate pool (WDA 10%) in priority to the additions in the main pool (WDA 20%).

3.6 Tintin

Capital allowances – 8 months to 31 July 2009

	Main pool £	PU Car £		Allowances £
TWDV b/f	9,498			
Additions	1,500	6,000		
Disposals	(3,000)	(5,000)		
Balancing allowance	7,998	1,000	× 80%	8,798

Explanation: No AIA or WDAs are given in the final period of trading. The balancing allowance on the car is restricted by the private use.

3.7 Cameron

The tax adjusted trading profit for the year ended 31 December 2009 is:

	£
Profit per accounts	125,000
Add:	
Golf club membership	2,500
Legal fees (initial fees for short lease are disallowed)	750
Lease payment (£4,520 x 15%) (CO_2 emissions exceed 160g/km)	678
Parking fine (allowable as incurred by staff)	-
Tax adjusted trading profit	128,928

Note. The Annual Investment Allowance (Max £50,000) is available in respect of the £24,000 spent on the equipment on 1 August 2009 (assuming no other plant and machinery acquired in the year). This allows a 100% deduction to be taken for the £24,000 incurred on the equipment. As the full cost of the equipment has already been deducted from the trading profit no adjustment is therefore required in calculating the taxable trading profit.

3.8 Anne

The period spans 6 April 2008 when the new rules for capital allowances were introduced. Allowances must be time apportioned.

	FYA £	Main pool £	Special rate pool £	Special rate car (60%) £	Allowances £
TWDV b/f		136,733			
Additions eligible for AIA/40% FYAs:					
14.4.09			45,000		
22.9.09	6,500				
AIA: Max £50,000	(5,000)		(45,000)		50,000
	1,500				
FYA at 40%	(600)				600
Additions (Cars):					
1.11.09				24,000	
Disposal (restricted to cost)		(12,000)			
		124,733		24,000	
WDA @ 20% (W)		(24,947)			24,947
WDA @ 10%				(2,400) × 60%	1,440
Transfer to main pool	(900)	900			
c/f		100,686	−	21,600	
Total allowances					76,987

4.1 Stephen

	Basis periods	Basis of assessment
2006/07	1 July 2006 – 5 April 2007	Actual basis
2007/08	1 July 2006 – 30 June 2007	First 12 months of trade
2008/09	year ended 30 April 2008	CYB
2009/10	year ended 30 April 2009	CYB
Overlap profits	1 July 2006 – 5 April 2007	
	1 May 2007 – 30 June 2007	

4.2 Avril

2009/10 Trading income assessment

Basis of assessment: 17 month period to 30 November 2009

	£	£
Year ended 30 June 2009 – taxable profit		38,000
5 months to 30 November 2009 – Adjusted trading profit	16,000	
Plus: Balancing charge (W1)	500	
		16,500
Less: Overlap profits		(2,500)
Trading income assessment		52,000

(W1) Capital allowances for the 5 months to 30 November 2009

	Main pool £	Allowances £
TWDV bfwd	3,000	
Disposals:		
Van (MV)	(1,500)	
Plant and machinery	(2,000)	
	(500)	
Balancing charge	500	(500)

4.3 Wayne

		£	£	
2005/06	Actual 1.5.05 – 5.4.06			
	11/12 × £15,000		13,750	(overlap profits)
2006/07	Y.e. 30.4.06		15,000	
2007/08	Y.e. 30.4.07		21,000	
2008/09	Y.e 30.4.08		23,000	
2009/10	Y.e. 30.4.09	24,000		
	P/E 31.12.09	14,000		
	Overlap profits	(13,750)	24,250	

4.4 Martina

The year of change is 2009/10.

The relevant period is 1 February 2009 to 30 June 2009, a period of 5 months. As this is less than 12 months, the basis period for 2009/10 is the 12 months ending 30 June 2009.

		£	£
2009/10	12 months to 30.6.09		
	$^7/_{12} \times 21{,}000 + {}^5/_{17} \times 34{,}000$	22,250	
	Overlap profits created = $^7/_{12} \times 21{,}000 =$		12,250
2010/11	CYB (Y/e 30.6.10)		
	$^{12}/_{17} \times 34{,}000$	24,000	

4.5 **Cecil**

	Basis period	Basis of assessment	£
2008/09	1.9.08 – 5.4.09	Actual	
	£47,500 × 7/10		33,250
2009/10	1.9.08 – 31.8.09	First 12 months of trade	
	£47,500 + (£71,500 × 2/12)		59,417
2010/11	y/e 30.6.10	CYB	71,500

Taxable trading profits:

	£
10 months to 30.6.09: 52,500 – 5,000	47,500
Y.e. 30.6.10: 71,500	71,500

Capital allowances:	TWDV	Allowances
	£	£
10 months to 30.6.09	5,000	
AIA	(5,000)	
	-	5,000
Y.e. 30.6.10		
WDA 20%	-	-
	-	

4.6 **Doug**

(a) Trading income assessments

		£
2008/09	1.1.09 – 5.4.09 3/12 × £18,000	4,500
2009/10	CYB Y/E 31.12.09	18,000
2010/11	CYB Y/E 31.12.10	20,000

(b) Overlap profits

1.1.09 – 5.4.09
(3/12 × 18,000) = £4,500

Overlap profits are set off against the profits of the final tax year. In certain circumstances they can also be offset on a change of accounting date.

4.7 **Olivia**

(1) Tax adjusted trading profits for the eighteen months to 30 June 2010 are:

	£
Net profit per accounts	34,775
Add: Olivia's salary (appropriation of profit)	30,000
Rent and rates (private use £12,000 × 40%)	4,800
Depreciation	250
Less: capital allowances (pool < £1,000)	(950)
Tax adjusted trading profit	68,875

(2) 2009/10 Trading income assessment

The basis period for the 2009/10 trading income assessment is 6 April 2009 to 5 April 2010 (the actual basis as no accounting period ends in 2009/10).

12/18 × £68,875 = £45,917

(3) Overlap profits

Olivia's first year is 2008/09, when she will be taxed on 3 months' worth of the eighteen month period's profit.

Then in both 2009/10 and 2010/11 she will be taxed on 12 months of that same period's profit, ie 27 months in total. As the profit only relates to an 18 month period, 9 months' worth of profits will be taxed twice (ie overlap profits).

9/18 × £68,875 = £34,438

4.8 Carrie

The year of change is 2009/10.

The assessment for the years before the year of change are on the current year basis, ie 2007/08 = £24,500 and 2008/09 = £47,000.

The period of change is 15 months (1.10.08 – 31.12.09). Since we can never tax more than 12 months in any period we will need to relieve 3 months' worth of overlap profits. With an original accounts date of 30 September the business would have had 6 months' of overlap profits.

	£
15 m/e 31.12.09	84,000
Less: 3/6 × £17,490	(8,745)
Assessment	75,255

The overlap profits carried forward are £8,745 (£17,490 – £8,745)

4.9 Chandler

First, we need to deduct the capital allowances from the trade; we can then apply the opening year rules to determine the taxable trade profits.

	£	£
1.1.08 – 30.6.08	12,000	
Less: CAs	(16,000)	
		(4,000)
1.7.08 – 30.6.09	45,000	
Less: CAs	(22,000)	
		23,000

Opening year rules

2007/08

	£
1.1.08 – 5.4.08	
3/6 × £(4,000)	(2,000)
Trading assessment	Nil

2008/09

Period that ends in 2008/09 (ie 6 m/e 30.6.08) is < 12 months, so tax first 12 months of trade. Note that losses cannot be counted twice.

	£	£
1.1.08 – 30.6.08	(4,000)	
Less: already allowed	2,000	
	(2,000)	
1.7.08 – 31.12.08		
6/12 × £23,000	11,500	
		9,500

2009/10

	£
CYB – y/e 30.6.09	23,000

Overlap profits

The periods that are counted twice on commencement are:

		£
1.1.08 – 5.4.08 (3 months)		Nil
1.7.08 – 31.12.08 (6 months)		11,500
Total (9 months)		11,500

5.1 Sophie

2009/10

	£
Trade profits (y/e 30.6.09)	12,000
s.83 relief – trading loss b/fwd	(3,000)
	9,000
Other income:	
Property income	1,000
Bank interest	500
	10,500
s.64 relief	(10,500)
	NIL

Loss c/f 14,000 – 10,500 = £3,500

5.2 Brenda

Trading income assessments

		£	Assessment £
2008/09	Basis period: Actual 1.1.09 – 5.4.09		
	3/6 x £(5,000) = £2,500 Loss		Nil
2009/10	Basis period: First 12 months		
	Six months to 30.6.09	(5,000)	
	Less used in 2008/09	2,500	
	Six months to 31.12.09		
	£12,000 x 6/12	6,000	
			3,500

5.3 Darren

The loss arises in 2009/10 and may be utilised as follows:

(1) Against total income for the year of the loss (2009/10) and/or preceding year (2008/09)

(2) After an offset against total income for 2009/10 to relieve the rental income, the loss can be set against the capital gain arising in that year

(3) After an offset against total income for 2009/10 or 2008/09, the loss can be offset against any trading profits that arose in the three tax years prior to 2009/10 (LIFO basis) (FA09 temporary extended loss relief).

(4) Carry forward against the first available profits of the same trade.

5.4 Parker

Terminal loss:

	£
2009/10	
6.4.09 – 30.9.09 (6 April to date of cessation)	
$\frac{6}{9} \times 4,500$	3,000
Add: overlap profit	600
2008/09	
1.10.08 – 5.4.09 (12 months before cessation to 6 April)	
$(7,200 \times 3/12) - (3/9 \times 4,500)$ = profit thus take nil	–
	3,600

5.5 Keith

s.72 against total income

	£
2006/07	6,000
2007/08	2,000
2008/09	1,000
	9,000

Explanation: s.72 loss relieved against earlier years before later years, total income in all years must be reduced to nil to the extent that there is available loss.

5.6 Pipchin

		2006/07		2007/08		2008/09		2009/10
		£		£		£		£
Trade profits		12,000		Nil		8,000		14,000
s.83					(3)	(8,000)	(4)	(3,600)
						–		10,400
Property income		10,400		11,000		11,000		11,000
General income		22,400		11,000		11,000		21,400
s.64	(1)	(22,400)	(2)	(11,000)				
Net income		–		–		11,000		21,400

Loss Memo

		£
Loss in 2007/08		45,000
s.64: 2006/07	(1)	(22,400)
s.64: 2007/08	(2)	(11,000)
c/f under s.83		11,600
s.83: 2008/09	(3)	(8,000)
		3,600
s.83: 2009/10	(4)	(3,600)
		–

5.7 Bertie

	2005/06	2006/07	2007/08	2008/09	2009/10
	£	£	£	£	£
Trade profits	75,000	55,000	28,000	4,000	-
Bank interest	10,000	10,000	10,000	10,000	5,000
General income	85,000	65,000	38,000	14,000	5,000
s.64				(14,000)	
FA09 relief		(22,000)	(28,000)		
Net income	85,000	43,000	10,000	-	5,000

Loss Memo

		£
Loss in 2009/10		70,000
s.64: 2008/09	(1)	(14,000)
FA09 extended loss relief (against trading profits only)		
- 2007/08	(2)	(28,000)
- 2006/07 (max £50,000 - £38,000)	(2)	(22,000)
c/f under s.83		6,000

Notes:

(1) A s.62 claim must be made against other income in 2009/10 and or 2008/09 before an extended loss relief claim can be made. It would not be beneficial to make a claim in 2009/10 as other income is covered by the personal allowance.

(2) Extended loss relief enables the loss to be carried back against trading profits in the previous 3 years (LIFO basis). The offset in the earlier two years is restricted to a maximum of £50,000.

5.8 Alex

The year of cessation is 2009/10.

On the cessation of a trade the usual current and prior year loss reliefs against general income are available.

In addition, it is possible to calculate a 'terminal' loss, which can be set against the trading profits of the preceding 3 years on a LIFO basis.

The final year of trade (1.1.09 – 31.12.09) is 'split' around the tax year:

	£	£
Penultimate tax year (1.1.09 – 5.4.09):		
3/12 × £12,000 (ignore as profit)		Nil
Final tax year (6.4.09 – 31.12.09)		
(i) 6.4.09 – 30.6.09: 3/12 × 12,000	3,000	
(ii) 1.7.09 – 31.12.09	(27,000)	
Less: overlap profits	(24,000)	
		(48,000)
Terminal loss		48,000

This can be set against the trading profits of 2008/09, 2007/08 and 2006/07 in that order.

6.1 George

2009/10	Based on 1 January to 5 April 2010	
	3/12 × 330,000 × 10%	£8,250
2010/11	Based on first 12 months	
	1 January 2010 to 31 December 2010	
	(6/12 × £330,000 + 6/12 × £420,000) × 10%	£37,500
2011/12	Based on accounts year ended in 2011/12	
	ie 30 June 2011	
	£420,000 × 10%	£42,000
Overlap period		
	1 January to 5 April 2010	8,250
	1 July 2010 to 31 December 2010	
	(6/12 × £420,000 × 10%)	21,000
		£29,250

6.2 **Peter and Paul**

Allocation of profits to partners – year to 31 December 2009

	Peter £	Paul £	Total £
6 months to 30.6.09			
Trading profit £220,000 x 6⁄12			
– allocated equally	55,000	55,000	110,000
6 months to 31.12.09			
Salary (x 6/12)	15,000	17,500	32,500
Trading profit ((£220,000 x 6/12) – 32,500)			
– allocated 3:4	33,214	44,286	77,500
	103,214	116,786	220,000
Trading income assessment 2009/10			
Basis of assessment			
– year ended 31 December 2009	103,214	116,786	

6.3 **Kenneth & Gail**

(a) Trading income assessments

		£
07/08	1.1.08 – 5.4.08	
	15,000 × 3/12 × ½	1,875
08/09	ye 31.12.08	
	15,000 × ½	7,500
09/10	ye 31.12.09	
	(28,000) × 1/2 = (14,000)	–
10/11	ye 31.12.10	
	20,000 × ¾	15,000

(b) Loss relief

Kenneth's share of the loss = ½ × 28,000 = <u>14,000</u>

This can be c/back 3 years (FIFO) ie against total income of 2006/07, 2007/08 and 2008/09.

Explanation: Profits and losses split using PSR of *accounting period.*

6.4 **A, B and C**

2009/10 Trading income assessments

	A £	B £	C £	Total £
5 months to 31.5.09				
Trading profit £72,000 x 5/12				
– allocated equally	15,000	15,000	–	30,000
7 months to 31.12.09				
Trading profit (£72,000 x 7/12)				
– allocated equally	14,000	14,000	14,000	42,000
	29,000	29,000	14,000	72,000
Trading income assessment 2009/10				
Basis of assessment:				
CYB – year ended 31 December 2009	29,000	29,000		
Actual – 1.6.09 – 5.4.10				
£14,000 + (£84,000 x 1/3 x 3/12)			21,000	

6.5 Victor, Ann and Joan

2009/10 Trading income assessments

	Victor £	Ann £	Joan £	Total £
Year ended 31.12.09				
Salaries	35,000	25,000	–	60,000
Balance (20:30:50)	(3,000)	(4,500)	(7,500)	(15,000)
Profit	32,000	20,500	(7,500)	45,000
Reallocation of notional loss in ratio 32,000: 20,500	(4,571)	(2,929)	(7,500)	
Assessed in 2009/10	27,429	17,571	–	45,000

6.6 Neil

Loss relief available under s.64 ITA 2007

2007/08 £10,000 (unrelieved capital contribution £5,000) (Note 1)
2008/09 £5,000 (unrelieved loss £15,000) (Note 2)
2009/10 £18,000 (unrelieved loss £8,000) (Note 3)

Notes:

1. No restriction on loss relief as capital contributed (£15,000 exceeds loss)

2. Loss relief restricted to unrelieved capital contribution brought forward. Unrelieved loss of £15,000 is carried forward

3. Loss relief restricted to amount of capital contributed on 1 January 2010. Unrelieved loss carried forward are £8,000 (£15,000 + £11,000 − £18,000)

6.7 Bill and Steve

The accounting period must be time apportioned around the date that Molly joins the partnership.

First we need to calculate the partnership's taxable trade profits, after capital allowances.

	£
Trade profits	275,000
Less: CAs (W)	(68,300)
Taxable trade profits	206,700

Then we split this between the partners in their PSR:

1.4.09 – 30.4.09	Total £	Bill £	Steve £	Molly £
Salary × 1/12	6,000	3,000	3,000	
Balance 50:50	11,225	5,613	5,612	
Total: 1/12 × £206,700	17,225	8,613	8,612	
1.5.09 – 31.310 40:40:20				
Total: 11/12 × £206,700	189,475	75,790	75,790	37,895
Total	206,700	84,403	84,402	37,895

2009/10

Bill and Steve - £84,403 and £84,402 respectively (CYB)

Molly – opening year rules

1.5.09 – 31.3.10 (equivalent of 5.4.10 for exam purposes) = £37,895

Working

	FYA £	Main pool £	Allowances £
TWDV b/f		116,500	
Additions qualifying for AIA/40% FYA:	45,000		
AIA (max £50,000)	(45,000)		45,000
WDA @ 20%		(23,300)	23,300
c/f		93,200	
Total allowances			68,300

7.1 Steven

Class 4 profits:	£
Trade profits	49,000
less loss brought forward	(3,000)
less loss used against non-trading income in earlier years	(2,000)
	44,000

Class 4 liability
  (43,875 – 5,715) @ 8% — 3,053
  (44,000 – 43,875) @ 1% — 1
  — 3,054

7.2 Charlie

2009/10 National insurance liability

(1) Class 2 NICs

   Actual profits per the accounts for 2009/10:

	£
Year to 30 June 2009	
5.4.09 – 30.6.09 £4,000 x 3/12	1,000
Year to 30 June 2010	
1.7.09 – 5.4.10 £6,500 x 9/12	4,875
	5,875

   Profit exceeds lower threshold of £5,075.

   Class 2 payable: 52 x £2.40 = £125.

(2) Class 4 NICs

   Basis period for 2009/10: Tax adjusted profit for y.e. 30.6.09

	£
Profit per accounts	4,000
Add: Depreciation	20,000
Tax adjusted trading profit	24,000

   Class 4 payable: (£24,000 - £5,715) x 8% = £1,463.

   Total NIC liability £1,588 (£125 + £1,463)

7.3 Simon

Taxable trading profit for the 9 month period to 31 May 2010

	£
Adjusted trading profit	70,000
less: Capital allowances (W1)	(12,840)
Taxable trading profit	57,160

2009/10 Trading income assessment

	£
Basis period: 1 September 2009 to 5 April 2010	
7/9 x £57,160	44,458

2009/10 Class 4 National Insurance liability

	£
(£43,875 - £5,715) x 8%	3,053
(£44,458 - £43,875) x 1%	6
	3,059

(W1) Capital allowances for the 9 months to 31 May 2010

	FYA £	Special rate car (PU 30%) £		Allowances £
Addition qualifying for AIA/40% FYA:				
Equipment	12,000			
AIA	(12,000)			12,000
Addition not qualifying for AIA:				
Car (special rate)		16,000		
WDA x 10% x 9/12		(1,200)	x 70%	840
TWDV cfwd		14,800		
Total allowances				12,840

7.4 John and Fred

2009/10 Class 4 National Insurance liability

	John £	Fred £
(£43,875 - £5,715) x 8%	3,053	
(£49,000 - £43,875) x 1%	51	
(£41,000 - £5,715) x 8%		2,823
	3,104	2,823

Allocation of profits – Year ended 31 December 2009

	John £	Fred £	Total £
Salary	35,000	20,000	55,000
Trading profit (£90,000 – £55,000)			
– allocated 2:3	14,000	21,000	35,000
	49,000	41,000	90,000
Trading income assessment 2009/10			
Basis of assessment			
– year ended 31 December 2009	49,000	41,000	

7.5 Lynne

2009/10 Trading income assessment

	£
Basis period: 2nd year of assessment: No accounts ending in tax year:	
Actual basis 12/15 x £57,000	45,600

2009/10 Class 4 National Insurance liability

	£
(£43,875 – £5,715) x 8%	3,053
(£45,600 – £43,875) x 1%	17
	3,070

Payable under self-assessment rules:

- 31 January 2010: 50% of 2008/09 liability
- 31 July 2010: 50% of 2008/09 liability
- 31 January 2011: Balance of 2009/10 liability

7.6 Malcolm, Pat and Rose

Allocation of profits

	Rose £
Year to 30 April 2009	
£240,000 x 1/3	80,000
Year to 30 April 2010	
7 months to 30.11.09	
£250,000 x 7/12 x 1/3	48,611
5 months to 30.4.10	–
	48,611

Trading income assessment 2009/10

Basis of assessment – final year	
Y.e. 30.4.09	80,000
Period to 30.11.09	48,611
Overlap profits	(12,000)
	116,611

2009/10 Class 4 National Insurance liability

	£
(£43,875 – £5,715) × 8%	3,053
(£116,611 – £43,875) × 1%	727
	3,780

7.7 **Miranda**

Although Miranda's accounting profit is below the small earnings exemption of £5,075 it must be adjusted for her salary (drawings) and for the goods taken for own use for this purpose. It need not be adjusted for depreciation, provided capital allowances are not also deducted. The profit clearly exceeds the exception limit.

Class 2 payable: 52 x £2.40 = £125.

Her Class 4 contributions are based on the **taxable** profit:

	£
Profit per accounts	4,685
Add:	
Depreciation	280
Salary	5,435
MV of goods taken for own use £(350 – 150)	200
Customer entertaining	150
Less: CAs (small pool write off)	(900)
Tax adjusted trading profit	9,850

Class 4: £(9,850 – 5,715) @ 8% = £331

8.1 A racehorse is a wasting chattel and therefore is exempt from CGT.

The limousine is exempt as all cars are exempt.

8.2 **Carl**

(1) Carl is ordinarily resident in the UK and is therefore subject to UK capital gains tax on the disposal of assets situated anywhere in the world. The sale of the house will be subject to capital gains tax as it is a chargeable disposal (sale) of a chargeable asset (not an exempt asset).

(2) Tracey is neither resident nor ordinarily resident in the UK. She is not therefore subject to UK capital gains tax.

(3) A greyhound is a wasting chattel (tangible moving property with a life of 50 years or less) and is therefore an exempt asset.

9.1 **Jeremy**

Capital gains tax liability 2009/10

	£	£
Warehouse:		
Proceeds	220,000	
Less: cost	(120,000)	
Gain	100,000	100,000
Property:		
Proceeds	500,000	
Less: 31.3.82 MV	(60,000)	
Extension (May 1990)	(20,000)	
Gain	420,000	420,000
Total gains		520,000
Annual exempt amount		(10,100)
Taxable gain		509,900
CGT @ 18%		91,782

9.2 Julie

	£
Proceeds	30,000
Less: cost	
$\dfrac{30,000}{30,000 + 10,000} \times £8,000$	(6,000)
Gain	24,000
Less: Losses bfwd (restricted)	(13,900)
	10,100
Annual exempt amount	(10,100)
Taxable gain	NIL
Capital gains tax payable	£NIL
Losses cfwd (£15,000 – £13,900)	£1,100

9.3 Felicity

Felicity is connected with:

(1) Husband, sister (her relatives)
(2) Mother-in-law, step-father, brother-in-law (spouses of relatives or spouse's relatives)
(3) Business partner
(4) Civil partner of her business partner (Business partner's spouse/civil partner)

9.4 Amber

Share pool:

	No. of shares	Cost £
Purchase 19.2.83	2,000	10,000
Purchase 20.9.90	1,000	8,000
	3,000	18,000
Sale 15.11.09	(1,500)	(9,000)
c/f	1,500	9,000

Calculate gain:

	£
Proceeds	22,000
Cost	(9,000)
Chargeable gain	13,000

10.1 Luther

He can only claim the rollover relief against the purchase of the hovercraft as this is the only qualifying purchase.

Freehold factory: > 12 months before disposal

Forklift truck: not **fixed** P&M

Office: > 3 years after disposal.

10.2 Henry

Capital gain on sale of factory

	£
Proceeds	100,000
Cost	(40,000)
Gain	60,000
Less: Gain rolled over	(40,000)
Chargeable gain (proceeds not reinvested)	20,000
Base cost of new factory (£80,000 – 40,000)	40,000

10.3 Steven

(a) Steven has transferred **all** of the assets of the business, **as a going concern** in exchange for **consideration wholly in shares.**

Rollover relief for the transfer of a business to a company will therefore **automatically** apply unless Steven elects to disapply the relief.

(b) Base cost of shares in Carts Ltd

	£	£
Market value of shares		288,000
Less rollover relief on transfer of business:		
Gains arising on sale of business:		
Goodwill	40,000	
Freehold building	90,000	
		(130,000)
Base cost of shares		158,000

10.4 Mr Terry

(a) Gain on transfer of business

	£
Gain	46,000
Less: held-over $\dfrac{60,000}{16,000+60,000} \times £46,000$	(36,316)
Chargeable gain on transfer	9,684
Base cost of shares £(60,000 − 36,316) =	23,684

Explanation: s162 Incorporation relief available.

(b) Mr Terry must submit an election by 31 January 2013 (within two years of 31 January following the end of the tax year in which the business was transferred) if he wishes to disapply incorporation relief.

10.5 Jeremy Brett

(a) *Gain chargeable on Jeremy*

	£
Excess proceeds over 31.3.82 MV(50,000 − 42,000)	8,000
Base cost for John	
MV in August 2009	152,000
Less deferred gain (£110,000 − £8,000)	(102,000)
	50,000

(b) As the claim relates to the 2009/10 tax year it is assumed that the claim will be submitted after April 2010. In which case the claim must be made jointly by Jeremy and John on or before 5 April 2014 (ie 4 years from the end of the tax year of gift).

10.6 Robert

(a) *Chargeable gain*

	£
Proceeds (MV)	300,000
Less: cost	(160,000)
Gain	140,000
Gift relief (CBA/CA) $\dfrac{300}{300+50} \times £140,000$	(120,000)
Gain left in charge after gift relief	20,000

(b) Capital gains tax liability for 2009/10 is payable in full on 31 January 2011.

10.7 Arthur – Capital gains computation 2009/10

		£
1.	Gain on disposal of building	
	Proceeds	850,000
	Less cost	80,000
	Gain	770,000
	Entrepreneurs' relief £770,000 x 4/9	(342,222)
	Chargeable gain	427,778
2.	Sale of business	
	Gains:	
	Goodwill	400,000
	Business premises	800,000
		1,200,000
	Entrepreneurs' relief (£1m – £770,000) x 4/9	(102,222)
	Gains not qualifying for relief	180,000
	Chargeable gains	1,277,778
Total taxable gains (427,778 + 1,277,778)		1,705,556

10.8 Jen

The disposal of the business as a going concern is a material disposal for entrepreneurs' relief purposes.

The disposal of the Matted Ltd shares is eligible for gift relief (sale at an undervalue of a 5% holding in an unquoted trading company). Any gain remaining chargeable after gift relief is also a material disposal for entrepreneurs' relief purposes (she is an officer of the company in her capacity as non-executive director and has held 5% of the shares for at least a year).

Business

	£
Gain (per question)	950,000

Shares

	£
Proceeds (MV)	800,000
Less cost	(10,000)
Gain	790,000
Less: gift relief (balancing figure)	(610,000)
Gain remaining chargeable (W)	180,000

Total gains

Note. Entrepreneurs' relief is only available for up to £1 million of gains (lifetime limit).

	£
Business	950,000
Shares	180,000
Gain	1,130,000
Less: entrepreneurs' relief 4/9 × £1,000,000	(444,444)
Chargeable gain	685,556
Less: Annual exempt amount	(10,100)
Taxable gain	675,456
Tax @ 18%	121,582

Working

Gift relief - sale at an undervalue

	£
Actual proceeds	190,000
Less cost	(10,000)
Gain remaining chargeable	180,000

10.9 Daryl

Incorporation relief applies automatically when an individual incorporates their business (unless they elect to disapply the relief) to defer the gains arising into the base cost of any share consideration received.

Premises	£	£
Proceeds (MV)	790,000	
Less cost	(250,000)	
Gain		540,000
Goodwill		
Proceeds (MV)	500,000	
Less cost	(100,000)	
Gain		400,000
Total gains		940,000
Less: incorporation relief		
£940,000 × $\dfrac{1,800,000}{1,800,000 + 200,000}$		(846,000)
Gain before entrepreneurs' relief		94,000
Less: entrepreneurs' relief 4/9 × £94,000		(41,778)
Chargeable gain		52,222

Base cost of shares

	£
MV	1,800,000
Less incorporation relief	(846,000)
Cost c/f	954,000

11.1 Paul, Jason and Susan

Jason has effectively disposed of a 20% interest to Susan (reduced from 50% to 30%). There have been no adjustments in the accounts and the effective disposal takes place at no gain/no loss.

Susan acquires a base cost of £100,000 (£500,000 × 20%)

Jason is treated as disposing of part of the building for £100,000 on a no gain/no loss basis. His base cost for a future disposal is £150,000 (£250,000 - £100,000).

Sale of building:

	Paul	Jason	Susan
	£	£	£
Proceeds (5:3:2)	400,000	240,000	160,000
Less cost	(250,000)	(150,000)	(100,000)
Gain	150,000	90,000	60,000

11.2 Millie, Whisper and Brooke

Gain arising on transfer of building:

	Total	Each partner (1/3)
	£	£
Proceeds (Market value)	300,000	100,000
Less cost	(90,000)	(30,000)
Gain	210,000	70,000

The gain arising on Millie is not chargeable in 2009/10 but is deducted from the base cost of the building. The base cost of the building for future disposals is £ 230,000 (£300,000 – £70,000).

Entrepreneurs' relief is available to Whisper and Brooke on the disposal of their interest in the partnership and their share of the building transferred to Millie.

11.3 Gary and Kevin

When Veronica joins the partnership the existing partners make a disposal of 10% of their fractional ownership of the goodwill. Veronica is treated as acquiring each of their 10% fractions, giving a total of 20%. (W)

The disposal takes place at the balance sheet value. Entrepreneurs' relief is available as this is a material disposal (disposal of part of a business).

Chargeable gain		Gary	Kevin
Proceeds (10% × £585,000)		58,500	58,500
Less: cost: 10% × £240,000		(24,000)	(24,000)
Chargeable gain before entrepreneurs' relief		34,500	34,500
Less: entrepreneurs' relief			
4/9 × £34,500		(15,333)	(15,333)
Chargeable gain		19,167	19,167

Base costs c/f

	Gary £	Kevin £	Veronica £
Original (50% × £240,000)	120,000	120,000	
Less: used when Veronica joins	(24,000)	(24,000)	
c/f	96,000	96,000	
Veronica: £(58,500 × 2)			117,000

Working

Fractional entitlements

	Gary	Kevin	Veronica
Original	50%	50%	
After Veronica joins	(40%)	(40%)	20%
Disposal	10%	10%	

12.1 Jones

(a) By 5 October 2012 (within 6 months of the end of the tax year in which his trade commenced).

(b) The Sch 41 FA 2008 penalties for late notification will apply (apply from April 2010). The penalty is based on a percentage of the tax outstanding at the end of the tax year. The relevant percentage depends on the behaviour of the taxpayer. If the taxpayer has deliberately failed to notify HMRC the maximum penalty is 100% of the tax if the failure is concealed or 70% if it was not concealed. If the failure was not deliberate the maximum penalty is 30% of the tax.

(c) Notification is not required where:

(1) income tax has been suffered at source and there is no liability to higher rate tax and/or CGT; or

(2) where a tax return has been issued.

12.2 Percy

31.1.10	First payment on account for 2009/10 (W1)	£3,500
31.7.10	Second payment on account for 2009/10 (W1)	£3,500
31.1.11	Balancing payment for 2009/10 (W2)	£4,500

(W1) Payments on account
```
              10,500    IT
              (3,500)   deducted at source
               7,000    ÷ 2 = £3,500
```

(W2) Balancing payment
```
               2,000    CGT
              12,500    IT
              (3,000)   deducted at source
              (7,000)   POA
               4,500
```

12.3 **Jamie**

(a) It is reasonable to assume that, as the return relates to 2009/10 and it is submitted 7 months late, the FA 2009 late filing/payment penalties will apply.

There is an immediate £100 penalty. Daily penalties of £10 a day may be imposed as the return is more than 3 months late. The tax return was filed more than 6 months but less than 12 months late. A tax based penalty for late delivery of 5% of the tax outstanding at the end of the tax year will be charged, or £300 if greater.

As the tax was paid more than 30 days late a penalty of 5% of the tax unpaid will be charged. A further 5% penalty will be charged as the payment was more than 6 months late.

(b) The filing dates for the 2009/10 return depend on the filing method used by Jamie as follows:

- Paper return: later of 31 October 2010 and 3 months after the issue of a return
- Electronic return: later of 31 January 2011 and 3 months after the issue of a return.

12.4 **Donald**

Payment due on 31 January 2010

	£	£
2008/09		
Balance of income tax and Class 4 NIC liability :		
Income tax liability	22,000	
Class 4 NIC liability	5,000	
Less Tax deducted at source	(500)	
Income tax payable	26,500	
Less Payments on account	(11,000)	
		15,500
Capital gains tax liability		3,000
2009/10		
Income tax:		
First payment on account		
(50% of prior years income tax and Class 4 NIC payable)		
(£26,500 × 50%)		13,250
Payment due on 31 January 2010		31,750

12.5 **Dan**

2009/10 Income tax and Class 4 NIC liability

	£
Interest charges	
First payment on account due 31 January 2010. Paid 1 March 2010.	
Interest due: £11,500 × 1/12 × 2.5%	24
Second payment on account due 31 July 2010. Paid 1 October 2010	
Interest due: £11,500 × 2/12 × 2.5%	48
Balancing payment due 31 January 2011.	
Paid 31 January 2011. No interest charged.	–
	216

Penalties
Penalties do not apply to the late payment of payments on account.
The balancing payment was paid on time and therefore no penalties arise.

12.6 Errors in returns

The rates of penalties depend on the behaviour of the taxpayer in connection with the errors both when the error is made and when it is discovered.

In the first scenario Roger has not taken reasonable care and has made a careless error. As a result the penalty will be in the range 0% - 30%.

In the second scenario Roger has deliberately made the error but he has not concealed it when HMRC discovers it. As a result the penalty will be in the range 20% - 70%.

In the third scenario again Roger has deliberately made the error but he has concealed it. As a result the penalty will be in the range 30% - 100%.

In the 4th scenario there is a careless error which Roger tells HMRC about without being asked, and provides assistance in remedying the error. In this case HMRC have the power to "suspend" the penalty completely.

Awareness Paper
Corporation tax

Study Period Planner
Corporation Tax

Use this schedule and your exam timetable to plan the dates on which you will complete each Study Period. The letters 'H' and 'M' tell you whether the topic is high or medium priority.

Study Period	Topic		Due Date
1	Corporation tax basics (1)	H	
2	Corporation tax basics (2)	H	
3	Further CT/Land and buildings	M	
4	**Progress Test 1**	H	

Study Period	Topic		Due Date
5	Corporation tax losses	H	
6	Groups	H	
7	Special types of company/ Administration	M	
8	**Progress Test 2**	H	

COURSE EXAM 1

A practice exam covering Study Periods 1 – 3

COURSE EXAM 2

A practice exam covering all Study Periods

REVISION PHASE

Your revision phase will begin when **Course Exam 2** is complete. This should ideally be four months before the final exam

TQT Note: The Course Exams contain questions for all FIVE of the awareness paper modules. In your exam you must answer questions from THREE modules. We suggest that you identify the THREE modules you will study and then work through the Study Period Planners for each of those modules until the point where you are told to take Course Exam 1. When you have completed all THREE modules to that point, sit Course Exam 1. Similarly, you should complete all THREE modules before you sit course exam 2. Course Exam 2 covers all of the Study Periods, although it is weighted towards the second half of your studies.

Study Period 1

Corporation tax basics (1)

High Priority

Step 1 Exam Guidance

Any question on the calculation of corporation tax in the exam will rely on the background knowledge of the basic corporation tax computation in this study period.

A number of the topics covered in this period have been tested in:

- Sample Paper (Q2 and Q6)
- May 2009 exam (Q3 and Q10)

Step 2 Introduction to the session

The basics of the corporation tax computation are split across two study periods. Subsequent periods look at further aspects of this basic corporation tax computation.

In this study period we concentrate on calculating a company's taxable trade profit. In the next period we learn how to calculate the corporation tax liability.

Both are fundamental to your corporation tax studies so it is essential that you spend the time learning the basics.

Step 3 Guidance through the Study Text

Read through the relevant sections of Chapter 1 of the Study text after reading the following guidance:

Read Section 1 carefully. You will study further detail on the overseas aspects of corporation tax (CT) (briefly covered in Section 1.2) in a later study period. Note the terminology: a '**period of account**' is the period for which the company draws up its financial statements; an '**accounting period**' (AP) is the period for which the company pays CT (which can never be longer than 12 months). Try Example 1.

Section 2 is very important as it takes you through the different items that make up the basis of the corporation tax computation. Make sure you can quickly reproduce a proforma corporation tax computation.

Section 2.3 refers to adjusting a company's accounting profit to turn it into the taxable profit, including the deduction available for capital allowances. At this point you must look at Chapters 2 and 3 of the '**Taxation of Unincorporated Businesses**' part of the Text which covers the rules for both in detail. Note also the specific rules which relate to companies set out in Sections 2.3.2 and 2.3.3 of this corporation tax text.

There are further rules in Section 2.3.4 for short life assets that you must know for the Corporation Tax Awareness Module. Try Example 2 to check your understanding.

You should now be able to attempt most questions requiring the calculation of a company's taxable trading profit.

Step 5 iPass and Workbook Questions

Now attempt exam style questions (ESQs) 1.4 to 1.7, which will help to reinforce your knowledge of the topics covered in this study period and give you examples of the types of question you may see in the exam.

You may also try the ESQs in Chapters 2 and 3 of the Taxation of Unincorporated Businesses Text.

Your TQT's i-Pass CD Rom also contains some questions on the basic principles of corporation tax. However you will find it more useful to wait until you have completed the next study period before you attempt these.

Step 4 Quick Quiz

Attempt question 3 of the quick quiz at the end of Study Text Chapter 1 to reinforce your understanding.

You may also attempt the quick quizzes in Chapters 2 and 3 of the Taxation of Unincorporated Businesses Text.

You may find it best to do this after a break, so that you can see what you remember and what you don't.

Study Period 2

Corporation tax basics (2)

High Priority

Step 1 Exam Guidance

Remember that all questions in the exam will rely on your knowledge of the basic corporation tax computation.

A number of the topics covered in this period have been tested in:

- Sample Paper (Q4, Q9 and Q11)
- May 2009 exam (Q1, Q4 and Q12)

Step 2 Introduction to the session

In the previous study period we learned how to calculate the taxable trade profit that enters the company's corporation tax proforma.

This study period continues our study of the basics of the computation of corporation tax. It deals with how to calculate the corporation tax liability.

Step 3 Guidance through the Study Text

Read through the rest of Chapter 1 the Study text after reading the following guidance:

Read Section 3 which explains how CT is calculated. Pay particular attention to the 'marginal relief' formula in Section 3.5 and how to deal with an accounting period of less than 12 months (Section 3.7). Work through Examples 3 to 7.

Section 4 deals with a company's CT accounting period 'straddling' two financial years. Read through this quickly as it is not a high priority for the exam.

Then read Section 5 which explains how companies are taxed if a period of account is more than 12 months long. Remember: an AP can **never** be longer than 12 months.

We now turn to Corporate Gains. Section 6 refers you to Chapters 9 and 10 of the '**Taxation of Individuals**' part of the Text for essential CGT background knowledge. You only need to read through Section 2 of Chapter 9. In Chapter 10 read all sections except for Sections 2, 3 and 6. Work through the examples in those sections. Note that indexation allowance is available to companies (see Section 6.3 of the **Corporation Tax** Text). If you have already studied the Taxation of Individuals module you should note that the rules for assets held at 31 March 1982 and shares are different from those for companies.

Step 4 Quick Quiz

Please attempt questions 1 and 2 of the quick quiz at the end of Study Text Chapter 1 to reinforce your understanding.

You should also attempt questions 4 and 6 of the quick quiz at the end of Chapter 10 of the Taxation of Individuals Text.

You may find it best to do this after a break, so that you can see what you remember and what you don't.

Step 5 iPass and Workbook Questions

Now attempt ESQs 1.1 to 1.3 and 1.11 of this chapter, which will help to reinforce your knowledge of the topics covered in this study period and give you examples of the types of question you may see in the exam.

Your TQT's i-Pass CD Rom also contains some questions on the fundamentals of corporation tax.

Module 4: Corporation tax

Study Period 3

Further CT/Land and buildings

Medium Priority

Examined: Sample paper

Step 1 Exam Guidance

To succeed in the exam you must have a good knowledge of the principles covered in the first two study periods.

There may, however, be an additional mark or two, or sometimes a whole question on an area covered in this study period. These are additional aspects of the computation which you should only try to learn once you have completed the previous study periods.

The topics in this Study Period have been tested in:
- Sample Paper (Q1, Q3, Q8 and Q12)
- May 2009 exam (Q3, Q8 and Q11)

Step 2 Introduction to the session

In this session we consider a number of topics that could feature in the CT computation:

- Loan relationships
- Intangible fixed assets
- Research and Development expenditure
- Overseas aspects of CT
- Income from land and buildings.

Step 3 Guidance through the Study Text

Read Chapters 2 and 3 of the Study Text after reading the following guidance:

Read through Section 2 on the treatment of 'loan relationships'. The terminology here can make the topic seem tricky. Try and think of the loan relationship rules as the rules on how to treat interest paid and received by companies

Section 3 then deals with the treatment of 'intangible fixed assets' (ie intellectual property such as patents, copyrights etc...). Attempt Example 1. Example 2 is comprehensive but is too long to be an Awareness module question. However, do attempt this question as it is a good test of your understanding so far.

Read through Section 4 on the treatment of research and development expenditure and attempt Example 3. This is the one time that more than 100% of an expense can be deducted in the corporation tax computation.

Section 5 covers the overseas aspects of CT. Work through Examples 4 to 6.

Finally read Chapter 3. This is a very short chapter and there isn't a lot to learn! Do pay particular attention to the rules for the taxation of lease premiums. Work through Examples 1 and 2 thoroughly.

Step 5 iPass and Workbook Questions

Now attempt ESQs 2.1 to 2.9 and 3.1 to 3.4, which will help to reinforce your knowledge of the topics covered in this study period and give you examples of the types of question you may see in the exam.

Your TQT's i-Pass CD Rom also contains questions on the further aspects of the corporation tax computation.

Step 4 Quick Quiz

Please attempt the quick quizzes at the end of Study Text Chapters 2 and 3 to reinforce your understanding.

You may find it best to do this after a break, so that you can see what you remember and what you don't.

256 Module 4: Corporation tax

Study Period 4

Progress Test 1 — High Priority

In order to reinforce what you have learnt so far, answer the following questions. Try to answer them without referring to your Study Text or notes. The test should take you no longer than one hour and covers Study Periods 1–3. Solutions start on page 269.

1. Zac Ltd runs a manufacturing business. On 10 July 2009 the company sold an old office building for £250,000. The building had cost Zac Ltd £50,000 on 1 August 1981. It was extended in October 1981 at a cost of £10,000. Its value at 31 March 1982 was £80,000. After the sale the company rented office premises.

    Calculate the chargeable gain arising on the disposal of the office block.

2. Meacham Ltd was incorporated on 1 March 2009 and commenced to trade on 1 April 2009. It drew up its first set of accounts for the period to 31 July 2010.

    In its first period of trading it made an adjusted trading profit before capital allowances of £510,000 and made a gift aid payment of £30,000 on 1 July 2010. During the period it made the following capital additions:

    | 1 April 2009 | Equipment | £60,000 |
    | 1 April 2009 | Car for sales manager | £20,000 |

    The sales manager's car had CO_2 emissions of 100g/km and was used 20% of the time for private purposes.

    You are required to calculate the corporation tax liability of Meacham Ltd for the period to 31 July 2010. Assume that Finance Act 2009 rates and allowances continue into the future.

3. Rowan Ltd prepares accounts to 31 December each year.

    For the year ended 31 December 2009 the company had the following results:

	£
PCTCT	155,000
Gross dividends received	35,000
Profits	190,000

    The dividends were received in respect of a 20% holding of ordinary shares in a UK company.

    Rowan Ltd has two associates.

    Calculate Rowan Ltd's corporation tax liability for the year ended 31 December 2009.

4. Molly Ltd had always made up accounts to 31 December. However the company decided to change its accounting reference date to 31 March. The company made up accounts for the following periods:

    Year ended 31 December 2008
    Fifteen months to 31 March 2010

    State the corporation tax accounting periods for which Molly Ltd will prepare a corporation tax computation based upon the above accounting reference dates.

5. Unruly Ltd, a trading company, has owned 25% of the shares in Polite Ltd for many years. On 1 January 2007, Unruly Ltd disposed of a 20% holding in Polite Ltd and on 1 February 2010 the company disposed of the remaining 5% holding in the shares in Polite Ltd.

    Describe the tax implications of each of these transactions, making reference to the availability of any reliefs.

Progress Test 1 (continued)

Study Period 4 — High Priority

6 **State the categories of revenue expenditure on research and development that qualify as allowable expenditure for the additional research and development trading deduction for corporation tax purposes.**

7 In the year to 31 July 2010 Bramble Ltd received rental income from an overseas property and dividends in respect of a 20% holding of ordinary shares in an overseas trading company. The company is not resident in a tax haven.

The rental income received, net of 30% withholding tax, was £75,000.

The dividends received, net of 15% withholding tax, were £85,000.

Explain how the above overseas income will be treated for UK corporation tax purposes.

8 Wite-up Ltd received bank interest of £13,500 and debenture interest from Black-out Ltd of £45,400 during its year ended 31 December 2009

It also paid debenture interest of £40,000 to Grey Ltd on a loan of £1,000,000. It issued the debentures to Grey Ltd in May 2008 to raise £750,000 for the purchase of a factory to use in the trade and £250,000 to purchase an investment property.

You are required to show how these amounts will be treated for tax purposes assuming all figures are gross and are the amounts shown in the accounts.

9 Carlsway Ltd, which prepares accounts to 31 December each year, owns an investment property that it has let out on a five year lease to Doorling Ltd from 1 June 2009. The property was empty before Doorling Ltd took occupation.

Doorling Ltd was required to pay a premium of £35,000 and an annual rent of £14,400, payable monthly, in arrears, on the last day of the month.

Carlsway Ltd had the following expenses in connection with letting out the property:

Repairs and maintenance   £775
Loan interest   £2,800

You are required to calculate Carlsway Ltd's property income for the year ended 31 December 2009 and the deduction that Doorling Ltd can take against its trading income for its year ended 31 March 2010.

10 Splendour Ltd amortises its patents, which are valued at £235,000 and are not related to the company's trade, at a rate of 5% in its accounts. It receives patent royalties during the year in respect of these patents of £10,500.

You are required to calculate Splendour Ltd's loss and explain how it can be relieved.

Study Period 4

Progress Test 1 (continued)

High Priority

11 The following expense items were incurred by a company by XYZ Ltd:

    (a)   Entertaining overseas suppliers;
    (b)   Dividends paid;
    (c)   Interest paid in the UK on an overdraft with a UK bank;
    (d)   Entertaining staff;
    (e)   Expense in acquiring a trade related patent;
    (f)   Professional charges in raising medium term loan finance to acquire plant and machinery;
    (g)   Charitable covenant;
    (h)   Amortisation of goodwill acquired 1 June 2003;
    (i)   Revenue expenditure incurred 20 months before the start of trading;
    (j)   Interest paid in respect of a bank loan taken out to acquire a property which will be rented out.

You are required to state, with reasons, which of the above expenses will not be deductible from the company's trading profits.

12 G Ltd owns all the ordinary shares in P Ltd (a UK resident trading company), Q Ltd (a UK resident investment company acquired two months before the end of the accounting period), R Ltd (a UK resident dormant company) and S Ltd (a non-UK resident trading company).

G Ltd prepared accounts for 11 months to 31 March 2010. Its results were:

	£
Trading income	130,000
Chargeable gains	15,000

You are required to compute the corporation tax liability of G Ltd for the 11 months to 31 March 2010.

You will find the answers to this test at starting on page 269. If you answer more than 6 questions correctly, your performance is satisfactory; if you answer more than 8 correctly, you are doing well. Once you have reviewed how you have performed, go back over topics where you feel your understanding is poor.

Study Period 5

Corporation tax losses

High Priority

Examined: Sample paper

Step 1 Exam Guidance

The examiner can consider a loss making company's corporation tax computation as well as a profitable one.

Corporation tax losses questions can test your knowledge of:

- The different ways in which losses can be used against the company's other income or gains, and
- The company's decision on how to use the loss to achieve the best tax position.

Question 10 of the Sample Paper and Question 6 of the May 2009 exam tested corporation tax losses.

Step 5 iPass and Workbook Questions

Now attempt ESQs 4.1 to 4.8, which will help to reinforce your knowledge of the topics covered in this study period and give you examples of the types of question you may see in the exam.

Your TQT's i-Pass CD Rom also contains questions on corporation tax losses.

Step 2 Introduction to the session

In this Study Period, we consider the position of the loss making company.

If a company incurs a loss we must understand if and how any tax adjusted loss can be used for tax purposes.

We must also understand the company's decision making process for deciding which of a range of available loss reliefs it will use and in what order.

This is a brief chapter, but important, so take your time.

Step 4 Quick Quiz

Please attempt the quick quiz at the end of Study Text Chapter 4 to reinforce your understanding.

You may find it best to do this after a break, so that you can see what you remember and what you don't.

Step 3 Guidance through the Study Text

Read through Chapter 4 of the Study Text after reading the following guidance:

Read Section 1.1 for an overview of the treatment of a trading loss in the CT computation (ie the trading income assessment figure is 'nil').

Read through Sections 1.2 and 1.3 noting the main ways that a trading loss can be used including the temporary extension for losses in periods ending between 24 November 2008 and 23 November 2010. Focus on the accounting period(s) in which the loss can be used and where in the proforma the loss is deducted (ie after trading profits or after total profits?). Attempt Examples 1 to 3 to check your understanding. Section 1.4 deals with the use of the loss when a company ceases to trade.

Read Section 1.5 carefully. Do you understand the company's decision making process for using its loss(es)? Try and keep in mind that the company's main aim is to pay as little tax as possible and to obtain a refund if it has already unnecessarily paid tax in an earlier period. Try Example 4 to check your understanding.

Read Section 2 which covers the two main restrictions on the use of trading losses. Highlight the key ideas and terminology (eg 'major change in the nature or conduct of trade'). Finally read Sections 3 on first year tax credits.

Module 4: Corporation tax 261

Study Period 6

Groups — High Priority

Step 1 Exam Guidance

It can be very beneficial from a tax perspective for a company to be in a 'group' of companies. The examiner will expect you to understand the level of shareholding required for each group relationship and the implications where a group exists.

Groups have been tested in:

- Sample Paper (Q5 and Q11)
- May 2009 exam (Q5 and Q7)

Step 2 Introduction to the session

This is a very important Study Period. We look at the group aspects of corporation tax.

You should concentrate on the rules for group relief for trading losses and those for chargeable gains groups.

Once you have understood these fully you should move onto the anti-avoidance rules for transfer pricing transactions and controlled foreign companies.

This session may take longer than the usual 3 hours.

Step 3 Guidance through the Study Text

Read through the relevant sections of Chapter 5 of the Study text after reading the following guidance:

Read Section 1 for background, then Section 2 on associated companies. Note the two tax consequences of a company having associates and try Example 1.

Read Sections 3.1 and 3.2 which deal with 75% group relief group companies. Try Examples 2 and 3 to check your understanding. This is an essential topic for the exam.

The read Section 3.3 on tax planning for group relief. You must understand the decision making behind group relief claims. Attempt Example 4. Then read Section 3.4 which deals with companies joining and leaving a group and try Examples 5 and 6.

Read Section 4 which deals with 75% chargeable gains groups. Note how the definition is different from a group relief group. Try Examples 7 and 8. Note carefully the rules for group elections and companies leaving a group and try Example 9. Read the rest of the section quickly.

Read through Sections 5 and 6 on transfer pricing and controlled foreign companies, highlighting the key ideas and terminology. Attempt Examples 10 to 12. These are lower priority than the previous sections.

Step 5 iPass and Workbook Questions

Now attempt ESQs 5.1 to 5.8, which will help to reinforce your knowledge of the topics covered in this study period and give you examples of the types of question you may see in the exam.

Your TQT's i-Pass CD Rom also contains questions testing corporation tax groups.

Step 4 Quick Quiz

Please attempt the quick quiz at the end of Study Text Chapter 5 to reinforce your understanding.

You may find it best to do this after a break, so that you can see what you remember and what you don't.

262 Module 4: Corporation tax

Study Period 7

Special types of company/Administration

Medium Priority

Step 1 Exam Guidance

The topics covered in the previous study periods are highly examinable and you must be comfortable with those rules before you move onto this period where we learn to identify particular types of companies, for example an investment company, and the special rules that apply to them.

We also cover the corporation tax administration rules which can form part of or an entire question.

Question 9 of the May 2009 exam tested personal service companies.

Question 7 of the Sample Paper and question 2 of the may 2009 exam tested corporation tax administration.

Step 2 Introduction to the session

You have now covered the corporation tax rules that apply to mainstream companies. There are, however, a number of 'special' companies to which special rules apply. The rules you have already learnt do still apply to these 'special' companies but with some modification.

In this study period you learn to spot these companies in the exam and to apply the correct set of modified rules. You are also introduced to the administrative provisions that apply to companies.

Step 3 Guidance through the Study Text

Read through Chapters 6 and 7 of the Study text after reading the following guidance:

Start with Chapter 6. Read Section 1 on 'investment' companies and any companies with investments. Try Example 1 to test your understanding of the deductibility of management expenses.

Read Sections 2.1 to 2.3 for background on the Personal Service Company and Managed Service Company rules. Then read Section 2.4. Locate the relevant part of the legislation so that you can work through the proforma and Example 2.

Now turn to Chapter 7 on corporation tax administration. Read Section 1 on corporation tax returns and record keeping.

Now work through Section 2 on corporation tax payments for both large companies (ie those paying tax at the full rate of corporation tax) and non-large companies. It is essential that you know the different payment dates for each type of company. Carefully work Examples 1 to 4.

Finally read through Section 3 noting in your legislation the relevant penalties covered in this section.

You have now completed the technical material for the **Corporation Tax Awareness** module.

Step 5 iPass and Workbook Questions

Now attempt ESQs 6.1 to 6.7 and 7.1 to 7.5, which will help to reinforce your knowledge of the topics covered in this study period and give you examples of the types of question you may see in the exam.

Your TQT's i-Pass CD Rom also contains questions on special companies and corporation tax administration.

Step 4 Quick Quiz

Please attempt the quick quizzes at the end of Study Text Chapter 6 and 7 to reinforce your understanding.

You may find it best to do this after a break, so that you can see what you remember and what you don't.

Module 4: Corporation tax

Progress Test 2

Study Period 8 — High Priority

In order to reinforce what you have learnt so far, answer the following questions. Try to answer them without referring to your Study Text or notes. The test should take you no longer than one hour and covers Study Periods 5–7. Solutions start on page 275.

1. Badger Ltd submitted its form CT600, corporation tax return in respect of the year ended 31 December 2007 on 1 February 2010. Tax due on this return amounted to £35,000 and was also paid on 1 February 2010. Badger Ltd had received a notice requesting submission of a form CT600 for the year ended 31 December 2007 on 1 February 2008.

    State the penalties chargeable on Badger Limited for the failure to submit a corporation tax return, CT600, on time.

2. Matcham Ltd had the following profits for the year ended 31 March 2010:

Profits chargeable to corporation tax	295,000
Dividends received on 1 January 2010	9,000

    The dividends were received in respect of a 15% holding of ordinary shares in a UK trading company.

    Matcham Ltd has no associated companies.

    Calculate Matcham Ltd's corporation tax liability for the year ended 31 March 2010 and state the due date for payment of the tax due.

3. Palace Ltd has been making up accounts to 31 December for many years. On 1 January 2009 the company decided to change its accounting year end date to 31 March. The company can either make up:

    - A set of accounts for the 3 months to 31 March 2009 and thereafter for twelve months periods to 31 March, or
    - For the 15 months to 31 March 2010 and thereafter for twelve month accounting periods to 31 March.

    State the corporation tax accounting periods that will be taxed under each of the above options and state when the corporation tax will be payable assuming payment is not due by instalments.

4. Opera Ltd has been a large company for many years. The company makes up accounts to 31 December each year. For the year ended 31 December 2009, it estimates that its corporation tax liability will be £10 million.

    State the due date for the quarterly payments of corporation tax in respect of the accounting period ending on 31 December 2009 and state the amount due on each instalment date and explain how interest will be charged or paid if the corporation liability is greater or less than £10 million.

Progress Test 2 (continued)

Study Period 8

High Priority

5 D'Oyley Carte Ltd has been suffering poor trading conditions and has made a tax adjusted trading loss for the year ended 31 March 2009. Taxable profits and losses for recent accounting periods have been as follows:

	Trading Profit/(Loss) £
Year ended 31 March 2008	25,000
Year ended 31 March 2009	(50,000)
Year ended 31 March 2010 (estimated)	35,000

D'Oyley Carte Ltd has no other taxable income in any of the years concerned.

State the ways in which D'Oyley Carte Ltd could use the trading loss of the year ended 31 March 2009. Briefly advise on the most tax efficient use of the loss.

6 Ralph Ltd makes up accounts to 31 December each year and owns the following shareholdings in other companies:

100% of Buttercup Ltd
75% of Porter Ltd, a dormant company, and
51% of Corcoran Ltd a company purchased on 1 May 2009

State, with reasons, the number of associated companies in the Ralph Ltd group for the year ended 31 December 2009 and calculate the small companies' rate limits to be used by the group to calculate corporation tax for that year.

7 Ruth Ltd owns 75% of Badger Ltd, which in turn owns 75% of Bramble Ltd.

State which of these companies are:

- **In a 75% group relief for losses group**
- **In a 75% capital gains group.**

8 Metro Ltd owns 100% of the shares in Tropolis Ltd.

Metro prepares accounts to 31 December each year and in its accounting period ending 31 December 2009 it has a trading loss of £145,000.

Tropolis Ltd has taxable profits of £250,000 in its year ended 31 March 2009 and £60,000 in its year ended 31 March 2010.

You are required to calculate the amount of group relief that Tropolis Ltd can claim from Metro Ltd.

9 Sarah owns her own company through which she contracts her services to a number of clients.

During 2009/10 the company received £55,000 from relevant engagements performed by Sarah and a further £25,000 from other engagements.

Sarah received a salary of £10,000 and the company paid employer's NIC in respect of this salary of £548.

The company also paid £2,000 into Sarah's personal pension and reimbursed her business travelling expenses of £350.

You are required to calculate the deemed employment payment Sarah will be treated as receiving on 5 April 2010.

Study Period 8

Progress Test 2 (continued)

High Priority

10 Leopard Ltd has the following results for the 8 month period ending 31 March 2010:

PCTCT £296,000
Exempt dividend received 1 December 2009 £12,600

It has no associates.

You are required to calculate the corporation tax payable for the period ended 31 March 2010.

11 A Ltd has a wholly owned trading subsidiary B Ltd. In June 1986 A Ltd acquired a property for £50,000 which it transferred to B Ltd in July 2003, when its market value was £80,000. In May 2009 A Ltd sold all its shares in B Ltd to C Ltd an unconnected company. The property was then valued at £130,000.

You are required to explain how the above transactions will be treated for chargeable gain purposes. Your answer should include a calculation of any chargeable gains arising, stating in which company the gain arises, and when (ignore indexation allowance).

12 Widgets (UK) Ltd is a 100% subsidiary of Holdings Ltd. It has made trading losses over the past two years and expects to make a trading loss in the current accounting period.

Ventures Ltd intends to purchase Widgets (UK) Ltd. It is intended that the management of the company should be restructured, in which case the company will break even the following year and should then become profitable.

Widgets (UK) Ltd operates in the manufacturing side of the industry. Another of Ventures Ltd's subsidiaries runs a similar business and Ventures Ltd is considering diversifying Widgets (UK) Ltd's trade into the retail area.

You are required to comment briefly on the effects of these proposals on the use of the losses generated by Widgets (UK) Ltd.

You will find the answers to this test starting on page 275. If you answer more than 6 questions correctly, your performance is satisfactory; if you answer more than 8 correctly, you are doing well. Once you have reviewed how you have performed, go back over topics where you feel your understanding is poor.

Solutions

Progress Test 1

1 Gain on sale of old office building:

	Original cost £	31.3.82 MV £
Disposal proceeds	250,000	250,000
Less: cost 1981	(50,000)	
enhancement cost 1981	(10,000)	
31.3.82 MV		(80,000)
Unindexed gain	190,000	170,000
Less: indexation allowance to July 2009 on 31.3.82 MV:		
$\dfrac{209.3 - 79.44}{79.44}$ (= 1.635)		
1.635 × £80,000	(130,800)	(130,800)
Gain	59,200	39,200
Chargeable gain (lower gain)		39,200

2 Meacham Ltd

First AP: 1 April 2009 (commencement of trade) to 31 March 2010 (end of 12 month period)
Second AP: 4 months to 31 July 2010 (end of period of account)

	12 mths to 31.3.10 £	4 mths to 31.7.10 £
Adjusted trading profit: 12:4	382,500	127,500
Capital allowances (W1)	(74,000)	(400)
Trading profit	308,500	127,100
Charge on income: Gift Aid		(30,000)
PCTCT	308,500	97,100

Corporation tax liability (W2)

£308,500 × 28%	86,380	
7/400 × (1,500,000 − 308,500)	(20,851)	
£97,100 × 21% (assumes FY 09 rates apply)		20,391
	66,529	20,391

Progress Test 1 — Solutions

W1 Capital allowances

	FYA £	Main pool £	Allowances £
12 mths to 31.3.10			
Additions qualifying for 100% FYA:			
Low emission car	20,000		
FYA at 100%	(20,000)		20,000
Additions qualifying for AIA/40% FYA:			
Equipment	60,000		
AIA (Max £50,000)	(50,000)		50,000
	10,000		
FYA at 40%	(4,000)		4,000
Transfer to main pool	(6,000)	6,000	
TWDV c/f		6,000	
Total allowances			74,000
4 mths to 31.7.10			
WDA at 20% × 4/12		(400)	400
TWDV c/f		5,600	
Total allowances			400

W2 Corporation tax liability

4 month accounting period ended 31.7.10:

Profits limits: £1,500,000 × 4/12 = £500,000
£300,000 × 4/12 = £100,000

Company therefore pays tax at the small companies rate.

3 Rowan Ltd

Corporation tax Payable for the Year Ended 31 December 2009

The year spans FY08 and FY09 – however the rates and limits are the same in both FYs

155,000 × 28%	43,400
Less: Marginal relief	
(500,000 – 190,000) × 155,000/190,000 × 7/400	(4,426)
	38,974

Working

Limits for small company rate purposes

Upper limit   £1,500,000/3 = £500,000
Lower limit   £300,000/3 = £100,000

As profits are £190,000 (therefore > lower limit and < upper limit) Rowan Ltd is a marginal rate company.

Solutions

Progress Test 1

4   Molly Ltd will calculate corporation tax for the following periods:

   (a)   12 months to 31 December 2008
   (b)   12 months to 31 December 2009
   (c)   3 months to 31 March 2010

5   Unruly Ltd

The first disposal of shares in Polite ltd, on 1 January 2007 would have qualified for the substantial shareholdings exemption, as Unruly Ltd owned at least 10% of the shares in Polite Ltd for at least 12 months in the previous two years.

However, the substantial shareholding exemption would not apply to the sale of 5% of the shares in Polite Ltd on 1 February 2010, as Unruly Ltd had not owned at least 10% of the shares in Polite Ltd for a period of 12 consecutive months in the two previous years.

This sale would therefore result in a capital gain, or an allowable capital loss.

6   The categories of revenue expenditure qualifying for the additional trading deduction for companies are;

   (a)   Staff costs
   (b)   Consumables
   (c)   Computer software
   (d)   Fuel, power and water.

7   The rental income will be included gross (£75,000 x 100/70 = £107,143) as property income in the corporation tax computation. Double tax relief (DTR) will be available as the income has suffered UK and overseas tax. The DTR will be restricted to the lower of the UK tax and the overseas tax suffered (30%). As the highest marginal rate of UK corporation tax is 29.75% the DTR will be restricted to the amount of UK tax payable on the overseas rental income.

The dividends received will be exempt from UK tax. They will however be included as franked investment income (FII) in the calculation of profits, used to determine the rate of tax paid by Bramble Ltd. The amount included as FII is the amount received x 100/90. Any overseas tax suffered is irrelevant.

8   Wite-up Ltd

Companies that receive interest (other than companies such as banks) are treated as receiving income in respect of non-trading loan relationships.

Interest payable for trade purposes is allowable as a deduction against trading income.

Other interest payable for non-trade purposes is allowable as a deduction against the income in respect of non-trading loan relationships.

The debenture interest payable to Grey Ltd was used partly for trade purposes and partly for non-trade purposes and must be split:

Non-trade purposes: 40,000 × 250,000/1,000,000 = 10,000

Trade purposes: £40,000 × 750,000/1,000,000 = 30,000

Trading deduction: £(30,000)

Solutions

Progress Test 1

	£
Non-trading loan relationships	
Income (credits) receivable:	
Bank interest	13,500
Debenture interest	45,400
	58,900
Less: interest payable	(10,000)
Profit on non-trading loan relationships	48,900

9 Carlsway Ltd

	£
Lease premium (W)	32,200
Rental income (accruals basis)	
1.6.08 – 31.12.08 7/12 × £14,400	8,400
Less: expenses (Note)	(775)
	7,625
Property income	39,825

Note. The loan interest is dealt with under the loan relationship rules and will be a non-trading loan relationship debit.

Working

Lease premium

As the lease to Doorling Ltd is a short lease, part of the premium is taxable as income in the year it is received.

Premium	35,000
Less: capital element: 2% × (5 – 1) × £35,000	(2,800)
Taxable as property income	32,200

Doorling Ltd

Doorling Ltd can take a deduction for its monthly rent expense and the proportion of the lease premium that relates to the period (accruals basis).

Rent: 1.6.09 – 31.3.10 = 10/12 × £14,400	12,000
Lease premium: £32,200/ 5 × 10/12	5,367
Total deduction	17,367

10 Splendour Ltd

As the patents are not related to the company's trade, all debits and credits are dealt with as miscellaneous income in respect of intangible fixed assets.(IFAs).

	£
Miscellaneous income	10,500
Less: allowable debit: £235,000 × 5%	(11,750)
Deficit in respect of miscellaneous income (ie debit)	(1,250)

This loss can be relieved as follows:

(a) Set against current year total profits.
(b) Group relieve excess debit.
(c) Carry forward to next accounting period where it will be treated as if it were a non-trading debit arising in that period to be set against future profits on non-trading IFAs.

Solutions

Progress Test 1

11 Not allowable are (a),(b),(g) and (j).

(a) – Entertainment is only allowable if it is entertaining staff.
(b) – Dividends are not allowable as they are an appropriation of profit.
(g) – Deductible from total profits as a charge on income not as a trading expense.
(j) – Interest in respect of a non-trade related loan is deducted from income from non-trading loan relationships.

12 G Ltd – Corporation tax for 11 months to 31 March 2010

Three companies are associated, being P Ltd, Q Ltd and S Ltd. R Ltd is ignored as it is dormant.

Limits for small companies rate

	£
Upper limit $\times \dfrac{1,500,000}{4} \times \dfrac{11}{12}$	343,750
Lower limit $\times \dfrac{300,000}{4} \times \dfrac{11}{12}$	68,750

	£
Trading income	130,000
Chargeable gains	15,000
PCTCT	145,000
£145,000 × 28%	40,600
Less: Marginal relief	
7/400 × £(343,750 – 145,000)	(3,478)
Corporation tax due	37,122

Progress Test 2 — Solutions

1   Badger Ltd.

CT600 corporation tax return for the year ended 31 December 2007 was due to be submitted by 31 December 2008.

As the return was not submitted until 1 February 2010, the penalties would be;

£100 penalty for failing to submit a return on time, which would rise to £200 as the return was more than 3 months late.

As the return was more than six months late a tax geared penalty would arise of 10% of the tax unpaid six months after the return was due but as the return and tax were still outstanding 12 months after the return was due (31 December 2009) this penalty would rise to 20% of the tax unpaid. The penalty would therefore be £35,000 x 20% = £7,000.

This answer assumes that the Finance Act 2009 penalties for late filing/payment do not apply to a return filed in February 2010. Under the FA09 penalty regime the penalties would be:

Late filing: £100 immediate penalty. A daily penalty of £10 may be imposed for up to 90 days as the return is more than 3 months late. As the return is more than 12 months late tax geared penalties will apply depending on the behaviour of the company ranging from 10% of the tax due where the withholding of the return is not deliberate up to 100% of the tax due where the withholding of the return is deliberate and concealed.

Late payment: As the tax is paid more than 12 months late a penalty of 15% of the unpaid tax may be charged.

2   Matcham Ltd

	£
PCTCT	295,000
Add: Exempt dividends from non-associated companies (£9,000 × 100/90)	10,000
Profits'	305,000

Compared to the limits for small companies' rate purposes for the Financial Year 2009, this is a marginal rate company.

Corporation tax payable:

	£
295,000 x 28%	82,600
Less marginal relief	
(1,500,000 − 305,000) × 7/400 × 295,000/305,000	(20,227)
Corporation tax payable	£62,373

This is payable nine months and one day after the end of the accounting period, that is by 1 January 2011.

Solutions

Progress Test 2

3   Palace Ltd

Option 1 – 3 months accounts to 31 March 2009.

Corporation tax will be calculated for:
The 12 months to 31 December 2008, payable 1 October 2009.
The 3 months to 31 March 2009, payable 1 January 2010.
The 12 months to 31 March 2010, payable 1 January 2011.

Option 2 – 15 months accounts to 31 March 2010

Corporation tax will be calculated for:
The 12 months to 31 December 2008, payable 1 October 2009.
The 12 months to 31 December 2009, payable 1 October 2010.
The 3 months to 31 March 2010, payable 1 January 2011.

4   Opera Ltd

Payment dates:

14 July 2009
14 October 2009
14 January 2010
14 April 2010

The amount payable on each date will be £10,000,000/4 = £2,500,000.

If the liability is greater than £10 million, then interest will be charged on each underpaid instalment as if the due amount had been one quarter of the final liability. If the liability is less than £10 million, then interest will be paid by HMRC on each overpaid instalment on the same basis.

5   D'Oyley Carte Ltd

D'Oyley Carte Ltd could use its trading loss for the year ended 31 March 2009, as follows:

- Under S.393(1) the loss will be carried forward, if not used in any other way, against the next available trading profits of the same trade. In the year ended 31 March 2010 there are trading profits of £35,000 from which the loss can be deducted.

- Under S.393A(1)(a) the loss can be deducted total profits, before deduction of charges of the current accounting period (i.e. the year ended 31 March 2009). There are no profits of the current accounting period.

- Under S.393A (1)(b) the loss can be carried back and deducted from total profits of the twelve month period preceding the accounting period of loss provided a current year claim is made first. (i.e. the year ended 31 March 2008). There are profits of £25,000 in the year ended 31 March 2008, against which the loss could be used.

- As the loss arose in an accounting period ending between 24 November 2008 and 23 November 2010 it can be carried back against total profits (before deducting any charges) of the previous three years, provided a current year claim under S.393A is made first. The loss could therefore be carried back to year ended 31 Match 2008, then year ended 31 March 2007 and finally year ended 31 March 2006. There is no information provided in the question regarding the company's profits prior to the year ended 31 March 2008.

276   Module 4: Corporation tax

- The company is a small company throughout the three accounting periods for which information is available. If the loss is carried forward it will save tax at 21% compared to 20% if the loss is carried back to the year ended 31 March 2008. However, carrying the loss back would use the loss as early as possible. This will result in a repayment of tax, rather than just the reduction of a future liability that has yet to be paid. The most efficient use of the loss therefore depends on which factor is most important to the company's financial position, ie cashflow or amount of tax saved.

6 Ralph Ltd

There are three associates:

Ralph Ltd

Buttercup Ltd – own more than 50%

Porter Ltd – not counted as an associate, as, although own >50% the company is dormant.

Corcoran Ltd – is an associate. Own more than 50% and it is an associate throughout the year, even though it is acquired part way through the accounting period.

The small company limits for the group for the year ended 31 December 2009 are therefore:

£300,000/3 = £100,000

£1,500,000/3 = £500,000

7 Ruth Ltd

75% Group relief for losses group:

Ruth Ltd and Badger Ltd form one group and Badger Ltd and Bramble Ltd a separate group. All three companies cannot form one group relief for losses group, as for this purpose the effective interest held by the holding company needs to be at least 75%. In this case the effective interest is only 56.25% (75% x 75%).

75% capital gains group:

Ruth Ltd, Badger Ltd and Bramble Ltd all form one group for group capital gains purposes, as at each stage in the group structure there needs to be a 75% interest and the effective interest needs to be at least 51%.

8 Metro Ltd

Group relief can only be claimed for the current period. As Metro Ltd's and Tropolis Ltd's accounting periods are different we need to time apportion the loss to find the maximum relief available (ie the lower of Tropolis Ltd's profit and Metro Ltd's loss).

	£	£
Tropolis Ltd's y/e 31.3.09		
Profits: £250,000 × 3/12	62,500	
Metro Ltd's losses for that period:		
£(145,000) × 3/12	(36,250)	
Available loss		36,250
Tropolis Ltd's y/e 31.3.10		
Profits: £60,000 × 9/12	45,000	
Metro Ltd's losses for that period:		
£(145,000) × 9/12	(108,750)	
Available loss		45,000
Total loss available for group relief		81,250

Solutions

Progress Test 2

9   Sarah

	£
Income from relevant engagements only	55,000
Less: 5% flat rate deduction	(2,750)
	52,250
Less: other deductions	
Salary	(10,000)
NIC on actual salary	(548)
Pension contribution	(2,000)
Reimbursed expenses	(350)
Gross deemed payment	39,352
Less: Employer's NIC on deemed payment	
£39,352 × 12.8/112.8	(4,465)
Deemed employment payment	34,887

10 Leopard Ltd

8 m/e 31 March 2010

	£
PCTCT	296,000
Add: FII (gross dividend): £12,600 × 100/90	14,000
Profits'	310,000

'Profits' are above £200,000 (W) but below £1,000,000, so marginal relief applies

	£
PCTCT @ 28%	82,880
Less: marginal relief	
7/400 × (1,000,000 – 310,000) × 296,000/310,000	(11,530)
CT due	71,350

Working

CT Limits
£1,500,000 × 8/12	£1,000,000
£300,000 × 8/12	£200,000

11 A Ltd and B Ltd form a group for chargeable gains purposes. The transfer to B Ltd in July 2003 will take place at no gain/no loss.

When A Ltd sells its shares to C Ltd, B Ltd leaves the A Ltd gains group. As this happens within 6 years of the no gain/no loss transfer B Ltd will be assessed on a chargeable gain of £80,000 less £50,000 = £30,000. The gain is treated as arising at the start of the accounting period in which B Ltd leaves the group.

The disposal of B Ltd is likely to be exempt as the disposal of a substantial shareholding.

12 Widgets (UK) Ltd can only group relieve to the Ventures Ltd group any losses arising after the company joins the group.

Trading losses brought forward in Widgets (UK) Ltd (subject to any claim that the Holdings Ltd group makes for losses in the current accounting period but before Widgets (UK) Ltd leaves the group) can be carried forward in Widgets (UK) Ltd.

If however there is a major change in the nature or conduct of Widgets (UK) Ltd's trade within three years of being acquired by Ventures Ltd, the losses arising before the date of change of ownership will not be able to be carried forward and will therefore expire. Ventures Ltd should consider whether its proposals will be treated as a major change, in which case they could delay implementing them or restructure their plans.

Exam style questions

1.1 Buttercup Ltd, which makes up accounts to 31 March, purchased a 55% shareholding in an overseas company, Roote BV, and a 80% shareholding in a UK company, Petal Ltd, in 1988. In May 2009 it sold Petal Ltd and purchased 60% of another UK company, Stamen Ltd.

Buttercup Ltd produced the following results for the year ended 31 March 2010:

	£
Trading income	70,000
Dividend received	8,000

The dividend received was in respect of a 5% shareholding of ordinary shares in a UK company.

You are required to calculate the corporation tax payable for the year ended 31 March 2010.

1.2 Cal Limited had the following results for the year ended 30 September 2009:

	£
Trading income	600,000
Dividend received from Dal Limited	45,000
Dividend received from Thal Limited	90,000

Cal Limited owns 75% of the ordinary shares of Dal Limited and 35% of the ordinary shares of Thal Limited.

You are required to calculate Cal Limited's corporation tax liability for the year ended 30 September 2009.

1.3 Max Ltd has the following results for its 9 months ended 31 December 2009:

	£
Tax adjusted trading profits	62,000
Rental income	10,000
Bank interest received	23,000
Chargeable gain	9,000
Gift Aid paid (gross)	2,000
Dividend received from wholly owned subsidiary	28,000

As at 31 December 2009 accrued interest receivable was £5,000. No interest was accrued at 1 April 2009.

You are required to calculate Max Ltd's corporation tax liability for the period ended 31 December 2009.

1.4 Histon plc drew up accounts for the 15 month period to 30 June 2010. The trading profit figure for the 15 month period adjusted for tax but before capital allowances was £93,000. The company also had a chargeable gain of £20,000 in respect of a disposal on 1 February 2010 and made a payment under the Gift Aid scheme of £8,000 on 1 May 2010.

The balance on the capital allowances main pool as at 1 April 2009 was £20,000. On 1 June 2009 the company purchased a car (CO_2 emissions 164g/km) for £16,000 and a machine for £60,000.

You are required to calculate the profits chargeable to corporation tax for the period.

1.5 Ramble Ltd was incorporated in the UK on 1 March 2008 and commenced to trade on 1 April 2008. It drew up its first set of accounts to 30 April 2009. The shares are wholly owned by Robert Ramble. Robert works full time for the company.

In the year to 30 April 2010 the company acquired the following assets:

– car acquired on 1 June 2009 for £20,000. The car had CO_2 emissions of 158g/km and is used 20% of the time for personal purposes by Robert.
– a computer on 1 July 2009 for £65,000 including £800 for software.

Robert expects to sell both of the above assets for less than their original cost in 2 years time.

You are required to:

(a) State, with reasons, the corporation tax accounting periods arising in respect of the period from incorporation to 30 April 2010.

(b) Explain the capital allowances that will be available to Ramble Ltd in respect of the above assets and advise whether it would be appropriate to claim short life asset treatment in respect of the assets.

1.6 Overt Ltd prepares accounts to 31 March. An extract from the company's profit and loss account for the year to 31 March 2010 shows the following:

	£	£
Gross operating profit		5,600,000
Depreciation	65,000	
Rent, rates and utilities (Note 1)	105,000	
Repairs (Note 2)	40,000	
Professional fees (Note 3)	55,000	
Gain on sale of office building	(85,000)	
Sundry expenses (All allowable)	45,000	
		(225,000)
		5,375,000
Bank interest received		48,000
Profit before tax		5,423,000

Notes:

(1) Rent includes a premium of £50,000 which Overt Ltd paid on 1 April 2010 for the grant of a 30 year lease on office premises.

(2) Repairs includes £2,500 on replacing a rotten window in the factory.

(3) Professional fees includes £2,000 in connection with the 30 year lease acquired on the office premises and £5,000 in connection with setting up an Approved Share Incentive Plan to allow employees to acquire shares in the company.

(4) Capital allowances claimed for the year were £95,000.

You are required to calculate Overt Ltd's taxable trading income for the year to 31 March 2010.

1.7 Mariner Ltd prepares accounts to 31 December. During the year to 31 December 2009 the following transactions took place:

		Cost/Proceeds £
1 January 2009	Car sold (original cost £10,000)	4,000
15 April 2009	Van acquired	16,000
1 May 2009	Volvo car acquired	25,000
1 June 2009	Computer sold (original cost £25,000)	10,000

The car acquired on 1 May 2009 had CO_2 emissions of 171g/km and was for the use of the managing director. 30% of his annual mileage was for private purposes.

The balances on the capital allowance pools as at 1 January 2009 were:

Main pool	£85,000
Short-life asset (acquired 1 May 2005)	£24,000

You are required to calculate the capital allowances available to Mariner Ltd for the year ended 31 December 2009.

1.8 Albatross Ltd operates a manufacturing business and draws up its accounts to 30 September each year.

In the year to 30 September 2009 it made the following disposals:

(1) On 1 March 2009 it sold a 5% shareholding in Magpie Ltd, a trading company, for £80,000. It had acquired a 20% shareholding in Magpie Ltd for £60,000 on 1 June 2006.

(2) On 1 June 2009 it sold an office building for £1,200,000. The building had been acquired on 1 May 1993 for £200,000.

(3) On 1 July 2009 it sold 5 acres of a 15 acre piece of land for £50,000. The company had acquired the land for £10,000 on 1 April 2002. On 1 July 2009 the remaining 10 acres of the car park were valued at £120,000.

You are required to calculate the chargeable gains to be included in the company's corporation tax computation for the year ending 30 September 2009 in respect of the above transactions.

1.9 Angel Ltd, an unquoted trading company, prepares accounts to 31 December each year.

On 1 September 2006 Angel Ltd had purchased 20% of the shares in Scooby Ltd, an unquoted trading company for £17,000. On 1 November 2008 it had sold a 14% holding and it sold the remainder of the shares for £42,800 on 1 August 2009.

On 1 August 2009 Angel Ltd sold a factory for £1,850,000. It had purchased the factory in May 1999 for £575,000. On 1 June 2009 Angel Ltd had purchased a replacement factory in a less expensive area for £1,225,000.

You are required to calculate the company's total chargeable gains for its year ended 31 December 2009 and to state the base cost of the factory purchased on 1 June 2009 assuming all possible reliefs are claimed.

1.10 Specialty Suds Ltd prepares accounts to 30 September each year.

During the year ended 30 September 2009 it had the following capital transactions:

11 November 2008	Machinery purchased	£27,500
6 December 2008	Machinery sold (original cost £22,000)	£12,000
2 April 2009	Car purchased for employee (CO_2 emissions 152g/km)	£9,500
16 April 2009	Equipment purchased	£30,000

The tax written down value of the main pool at 1 October 2008 was £68,000 and of the long life asset pool was £119,000.

You are required to calculate the capital allowances available to Specialty Suds Ltd for the year ended 30 September 2009.

1.11 Seedy Ltd changed its accounting date and had the following results for the 8 month period ending 30 November 2009:

	£
Trading profit	910,000
Profit on non-trading loan relationships	40,000
Chargeable gains	32,000
Exempt dividends received from non-associated companies	22,500

Seedy Ltd paid tax at the full rate for its year ended 31 March 2009.

You are required to state the due date(s) for payment of the company's corporation tax liability for the 8 months ended 31 December 2009 and the amount(s) due.

2.1 Iron Ltd, a large company as defined for R&D purposes, spent £200,000 on qualifying research and development in the year to 31 March 2010. Tax adjusted profits before deducting any amount for research and development expenditure is £1,300,000 for the year.

Lead Ltd, a small company as defined for R&D purposes, spent £6,000 on qualifying research and development during the year to March 2010. Tax adjusted trading profits for the year before deducting any amount for research and development expenditure are £80,000.

You are required to:

(a) Calculated the taxable trading profits, after relief for research and development expenditure for both Iron Ltd and Lead Ltd for the year to 31 March 2010.

(b) Give three examples of the type of revenue expenditure which qualifies for research and development relief.

2.2 Plate Ltd buys goodwill for £50,000 on 1 May 2009. £5,000 is written off immediately to the profit and loss account. The goodwill is sold on 1 December 2009 for £65,000.

You are required to calculate the profit arising on the sale of the goodwill and to state how much of the gain will be eligible for rollover relief.

2.3 Muxton Ltd has charged the following items in arriving at its net profit per the accounts for the year ended 31 March 2010:

	£
Goodwill acquired 1 August 2008 written off	5,000
Interest on late payment of corporation tax (AP ended 31.3.08).	1,000
Interest payable on loan taken out to acquire machinery	10,000
Interest payable on loan taken out to acquire a rental property	8,000

You are required to explain how the above items will be treated in the company's corporation tax computation for the year ended 31 March 2010.

2.4 A Inc is incorporated overseas. In the year to 31 March 2010 it had tax adjusted trading income of £1,200,750 arising from its operations in the UK and tax adjusted trading income of £250,000 arising from its overseas manufacturing plants. Its only other income was a dividend of £50,000 it received from an overseas company in which it owns a 5% holding and rental income of £9,000 in respect of an overseas property.

15% withholding tax was suffered on both the dividend and rental income.

You are required to:

(a) State the rules for determining whether A Inc will be regarded as UK resident.

(b) Assuming that A Inc is UK resident calculate its UK corporation tax liability for the year to 31 March 2010.

Assume that the foreign dividend is an exempt dividend for UK corporation tax purposes.

2.5 B Inc, is incorporated overseas. It is wholly owned by a company resident overseas. On 1 January 2009 B Inc transferred its central management and control from the UK to Switzerland.

The company owned two chargeable assets as at the date of migration. The first was a factory situated in the UK, which was acquired for £200,000 in April 2002. The company continued to operate from this factory until 1 March 2010 when it was sold for £800,000. The market value of the factory on 1 January 2009 was £700,000.

The second asset was a factory in Switzerland, which was acquired on 1 June 2008 for £600,000. Its market value on 1 January 2009 was £900,000 and it was sold on 1 June 2010 for £1,100,000.

You are required to explain the UK corporation tax implications of the above events.

2.6   Bronco Ltd, a small company as defined for R&D purposes, had a trading loss of £200,000 and property income of £18,000 for the year ended 31 March 2010.

During December 2009 it spent £120,000 on qualifying research and development and its PAYE bill for the year was £25,000.

You are required to calculate Bronco Ltd's surrenderable loss and the R&D tax credit that the company may claim for the year to 31 March 2010. State the effect of the claim on the amount of any trading losses available to carry forward as at 31 March 2010.

2.7   Gerald Maine set up a company, Maine Ltd, on 1 December 2008 and commenced to trade on that date. He is the sole shareholder.

The company drew up its first accounts to 31 December 2009 and had the following results:

	£
Adjusted trading profits (before capital allowances)	156,000
Bank interest receivable	19,500
Loan interest payable (non trading)	13,000
Chargeable gain (disposal date 13 November 2009)	32,000

On 1 December 2008 the company acquired equipment for £55,000. On 1 December 2009 the company purchased a company car (CO_2 emissions 165g/km) for Gerald for £14,500 which he will use 40% of the time for private purposes.

Maine Ltd made a donation to charity under the Gift Aid scheme on 1 January 2009 of £10,000.

You are required to calculate the profits chargeable to corporation tax in respect of the period to 31 December 2009

2.8   Monulife Ltd makes up its accounts to 31 December each year.

In the year to 31 December 2009, Monulife Ltd received and paid the following:

	£
Bank interest	25
Interest on overpaid tax	157
Interest paid on bank loan taken out to acquire an investment property	3,250
Debenture interest paid	50,000

At 31 December 2009 there was interest accrued but not yet received on the bank account of £1,250.

Monulife Ltd had issued the debentures on 1 August 2006 to raise money to purchase equipment for the business. The amounts of interest paid are the amounts shown in the accounts.

You are required to calculate the taxable trading profit and the profit/deficit on non-trading loan relationships figures for Monulife Ltd for the year ended 31 December 2009

2.9   Amiable Ltd has the following income during its year ended 31 March 2010:

	£
Taxable trading profits	530,000
Chargeable gain	124,750
Profit on non-trading loan relationships	26,225
Rental income from overseas property (net of 25% tax)	250,000

It made a donation of £25,000 under the gift aid scheme on 21 January 2009.

You are required to calculate Amiable Ltd's corporation tax liability for the year ended 31 March 2010, stating the amount of double taxation relief available.

3.1 Alter Ltd owns a house which is let furnished at a rent of £1,500 per quarter payable in advance.

During the year ended 31 March 2010 Alter Ltd received the following rents:

	£
10 April 2009 – arrears of rent due on 31 March 2009	800
30 June 2009 – quarter commencing 1 July 2009	1,500
30 Sept 2009 – quarter commencing 1 October 2009	1,500

The tenants left on 31 January 2010 without paying the rent due on 31 December. Alter Ltd was unable to recover this from them and therefore wrote off the debt in the accounts

During the year the following expenses were incurred:

	£
Agent's commission	360
Mortgage repayments (including interest of £500)	800
Council tax	1,100
	2,260

You are required to calculate Alter Ltd's property income assessment for the year to 31 March 2010. Explain your treatment of the mortgage repayments.

3.2 Staple Ltd owns two rental properties. In the year to 31 December 2009 the company received the following rents and incurred the following expenses in connection with the properties:

Property 1 Furnished flat

Rent: Rented from 1 April 2009 for an annual rent of £10,000 payable quarterly in advance. Previous tenants moved out on 31 December 2008

Expenses: Professional fees in preparing rental agreement £1,000
Decorating prior to new tenants moving in £2,000

Property 2 Unfurnished office

Rent: Acquired 1 October 2009 and rented from 1 December 2009 for £15,000 per annum payable monthly in advance.

Expenses: Agent's fees £5,500
Insurance premium for the year to 30 September 2010 £1,500.

During the year to 31 December 2009 the company also had tax adjusted trading profits of £250,000 and chargeable gains of £8,000.

You are required to calculate Staple Ltd's profits chargeable to corporation tax for the year to 31 December 2009.

3.3 During the year to 31 December 2009 Aspen Ltd received the following income:

(1) Received a premium of £60,000 from Fairmount Ltd for the grant of a 25 year lease on an office property.

(2) Received a dividend from a Real Estate Investment Trust of £20,000 on 1 June 2009.

You are required to explain how the above income will be treated for corporation tax purposes in the tax computations of Aspen Ltd for the year to 31 December 2009.

3.4   Ghost Ltd received the following income during its year ended 31 December 2009:

	£
Rental income from 245 Main Street	30,000
Rental income from 134 George Street	18,720
Lease premium in respect of new 15 year lease of George St property	60,000

The company incurred expenses of £1,765 in connection with the Main Street property, which is let furnished, including £1,650 for council tax. It also incurred expenses of £3,000 in connection with the George Street property, which is let unfurnished.

Ghost Ltd's total annual interest payments in respect of both properties were as follows:

	£
245 Main Street	5,265
134 George Street	3,125

Ghost Ltd also received dividends of £33,750 from a REIT. The dividends were paid out of the REIT's tax exempt income.

You are required to calculate the company's property income figure for the year ended 31 December 2009.

4.1   Tunbridge Ltd has the following results:

Year ended	31 December 2006	31 December 2007	31 December 2008	31 December 2009
	£	£	£	£
Trading profit/(loss)	5,000	1,500	(10,000)	500
Interest received	1,500	500	2,000	1,000

The amount of interest received is the same as the amount accrued for each period.

The company claims relief for the loss sustained in 31 December 2008 as early as possible.

You are required to calculate the profits chargeable to corporation tax, after loss relief, for each of the above periods, and state the amount, if any, of unused losses carried forward at 31 December 2009. State by when the appropriate loss relief elections must be made.

4.2   Green Ltd has the following results for the year ended 31 March 2010:

	£
Trading income	175,000
Profit on non-trading loan relationships	30,000
Capital gains	20,000
Gift Aid donation paid (gross)	10,000
Exempt dividend received	15,000

The amount of interest received is the same as the amount accrued for the period. Green Ltd has no associated companies.

The company has trading losses brought forward of £210,000 and capital losses brought forward of £30,000.

You are required to calculate Green Ltd's corporation tax liability for the year ended 31 March 2010 and state the amount, if any, of unrelieved losses carried forward.

4.3 Montrelle Ltd has the following results for the three accounting periods to 31 December 2009:

Year ended:	31.12.07 £	31.12.08 £	31.12.09 £
Trading profit/(loss)	490,000	(550,000)	150,000
Property income	28,000	15,000	18,000
Chargeable gain	-	9,000	-
Charges on income – Gift Aid	5,000	10,000	10,000

You are required to show the profits chargeable to corporation tax for all years assuming that losses are set off under S.393A Income and Corporation Taxes Act 1988. Ignore the temporary extended loss carry back provisions of Finance Act 2009.

4.4 Tanui Ltd had always prepared accounts to 31 December until 2009 when it changed its accounting date to 30 June and prepared a six month set of accounts to 30 June 2009. On 30 June 2010 the company ceased to trade. The company has had the following results in recent accounting periods:

	Year to 31.12.06 £	Year to 31.12.07 £	Year to 31.12.08 £	6 mths to 30.6.09 £	Year to 30.6.10 £
Trading profit/(loss)	350,000	300,000	290,000	100,000	(950,000)
Bank interest income	12,000	10,000	18,000	5,000	2,000
Capital gain/(loss)	(10,000)	-	5,000	-	20,000
Charges on income – Gift Aid	8,000	8,000	8,000	4,000	-

You are required to show the profits chargeable to corporation tax for all years assuming that losses are set off as soon as possible under S.393A Income and Corporation Taxes Act 1988. Ignore the temporary extended loss carry back provisions of Finance Act 2009.

4.5 Mott Ltd commenced to trade on 1 April 2008 and has had the following results in recent accounting periods:

	Year to 31.3.09 £	Year to 31.3.10 £
Trading profits/(loss)	400,000	(80,000)
Bank interest income	20,000	8,000

The company is forecasting to make a profit of £100,000 in the year to 31 March 2011.

You are required to explain the loss relief options available to Mott Ltd and advise the company which option would be the most beneficial. Assume that tax rates for Financial year 2009 continue into the future.

4.6 Morvel Ltd, a highstreet retailer, has had the following results in recent accounting periods:

	Year to 31.12.08 £	Year to 31.12.09 £
Trading profit/(loss)	50,000	(180,000)
Bank interest income	5,000	2,000

On 1 March 2010 100% of the company's share capital was acquired by Amble Ltd, a UK trading company. Amble Ltd has considerable expertise in internet selling. Consequently after the acquisition 85% of Morvel Ltd's customers were obtained via the company's new website. Prior to the acquisition all sales had been made via highstreet retail stores. As a consequence of the change in selling method Morvel Ltd is forecasting to make a trading profit of £120,000 in the year to 31 December 2010.

You are required to explain the loss relief options available to Morvel Ltd.

4.7 Droma Ltd had the following results for the accounting periods to 31 March 2010.

	Y/e 31.3.06 £	Y/e 31.3.07 £	Y/e 31.3.08 £	Y/e 31.3.09 £	Y/e 31.3.10 £
Trading profits	45,000	60,000	41,000	55,000	(177,000)
Gains	10,000	–	2,000	–	15,000
Property income	5,000	7,000	4,000	16,000	32,000

You are required to explain how the trading losses could be utilised assuming Droma Ltd wishes to claim any loss relief as early as possible and compute the profits chargeable to corporation tax for all the above periods.

4.8 Cassel Ltd commenced to trade on 1 January 2009 and made up its first accounts to 31 December 2009. In 2010 it changed its year end to 31 March.

It has had the following trading results:

	£
y/e 31.12.09	88,000
p/e 31.3.10	24,500
y/e 31.3.11	(195,000)
y/e 31.3.12 (est)	116,000

Its only other income each year was £20,000 of interest income. It makes an annual gift aid donation of £10,000 on 1 June each year.

You are required to:

(1) **State how much loss is used in each relevant year assuming relief is taken as early as possible.**

(2) **Calculate the loss carried forward at 3 March 2011.**

(3) **State whether the loss, if any, can be set against PCTCT or trading profits only in the year ended 31 March 2012.**

5.1 Holding Ltd owns 100% of the ordinary share capital of Sub Ltd and there are no other companies in the group. Both companies have traded for several years. In the two years ended 31 March 2009 and 2010, the companies' tax adjusted trading profits and losses were

	2009 £	2010 £
Holding Ltd	109,000	(119,000)
Sub Ltd	95,000	268,000

You are required to explain how the loss of Holding Ltd should be utilised to maximise the group tax saving and to state the order in which the claims should be made.

5.2 Mr Phillips owns shares in the following UK resident companies:

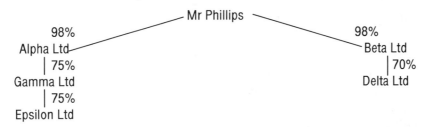

You are required to state which companies are associated with Alpha Ltd and which are within the same group for group relief and capital gains purposes.

5.3 James Ltd is a UK resident company and a member of a group. For the year to 30 September 2009, it has made profits of £700,000, and the group agrees that James Ltd should claim as much group relief as possible from other group companies. The following information is available about the other group companies:

(1) Edward Ltd is the parent company, and is an investment company. For the year ended 30 September 2009, its tax computations show:

	£
Chargeable gains	5,000
Management expenses	(20,000)

(2) Gordon Ltd joined on 1 January 2009, and has an accounting date of 31 March. In its year to 31 March 2009, its tax adjusted trading losses were £80,000. It was profit making in the year to 31 March 2010.

You are required to calculate the maximum amount of group relief which can be claimed by James Ltd.

5.4 Wind Ltd and Sail Ltd, its 85% owned subsidiary, prepare accounts to 31 March. In February 1993 Wind Ltd bought an asset for £80,000 and sold it to Sail Ltd in June 2009 for its market value of £200,000. On 1 April 2010 Sail Ltd sold the asset to an unconnected company for £300,000.

You are required to explain how the sale in June 2009 will be treated for corporation tax purposes and to calculate the chargeable gain arising on the sale on 1 April 2010.

5.5 Force Ltd owns 80% of the shares of Power Ltd. Force Ltd had acquired the 80% holding for £450,000 in April 2007. Both companies are UK resident trading companies with 31 March year ends.

On 1 June 2008 Force Ltd sold a factory to Power Ltd for £200,000 when its market value was £500,000. Force Ltd had acquired the factory on 1 June 2002 for £80,000.

On 1 March 2010 Force Ltd sold a 15% holding in Power Ltd to an unconnected company for £200,000.

You are required to explain, with calculations, the corporation tax implications of the above transactions. Ignore the gain, if any, arising on the sale of shares in Power Ltd.

5.6 Overseas Ltd is a company resident in Overseasland. It is owned 65% by Expansion Ltd, a company incorporated in the UK and 35% by Mr Offshore, who is non-UK resident.

The rate of corporation tax in Overseasland is 8%.

Overseas Ltd has not paid any dividends in the year to 31 March 2010.

You are required to explain with reasons how, if at all, the profits of Overseas Ltd will be taxed in the UK.

5.7 Tweet Ltd has the following shareholdings:

| Pounce Ltd | 100% |
| Feeder Ltd | 90% |

Feeder Ltd owns 80% of the shares in Booker Ltd.

The companies' results for the year ended 31 March 2010 are as follows:

	Tweet £	Pounce £	Feeder £	Booker £
Trading (profit/ loss)	875,000	(145,000)	189,000	21,000
Bank interest	12,000		8,000	400
Rental income		12,000		
Chargeable gains/ (loss)			65,000	(25,000)
Gift Aid payments	(25,000)	(2,500)	(12,000)	(1,000)

You are required to calculate the corporation tax payable by each company following any beneficial loss relief claims.

5.8 Chill Ltd has owned all of the share capital of Freeze Ltd since 15 May 2002 when it purchased the shares for £275,000. Both companies are unquoted trading companies and make up accounts to 31 December.

On 17 August 2009 Chill Ltd sold its entire holding in Freeze Ltd to an unconnected third party for £899,999.

On 21 April 2004 Chill Ltd had transferred a property to Freeze Ltd when its market value was £425,000. The property had originally cost Chill Ltd £219,000 in June 1999 and it was valued at £687,000 in August 2009.

You are required to calculate, in connection with the sale of the Freeze Ltd shares:

(1) The gain arising for Chill Ltd.

(2) The gain arising for Freeze Ltd.

You should assume that Freeze Ltd does not take any steps to mitigate its tax position in August 2009.

6.1 **You are required to explain how the following are treated for investment companies.**

(1) Incidental cost of raising loan finance
(2) Contributions to a training and enterprise council
(3) Accountants fees for preparation of annual accounts
(4) Capital allowances in respect of let properties
(5) Payment to registered occupational pension scheme.

6.2 Moriarty Ltd has one wholly owned subsidary Watson Ltd.

Watson Ltd results for the year ended 31 March 2010 were as follows:

	Moriarty Ltd £	Watson Ltd £
Trading profit	–	90,000
Expenses of management	(300,000)	–
Capital gain	–	10,000
Charges on income	–	(30,000)

Moriarty Ltd's expenses of management include £220,000 brought forward.

You are required to calculate how much group relief Watson Ltd can claim.

6.3 Carp Ltd, an investment company, had the following results for the year ended 31 December 2009:

	£
Rental income	300,000
Interest income	50,000
Management expenses:	
– Re property management	65,000
– General expenses	15,000
Interest payable re rental properties	22,000
Chargeable gains	264,000

The interest payable is in respect of loans taken out to fund the acquisition of rental properties.

Carp Ltd had unrelieved expenses of management of £25,000 as at 31 December 2008.

You are required to compute the profits chargeable to corporation tax for the year to 31 December 2009.

6.4 Albert owns all of the share capital of Sledge Consulting Ltd and works full-time for the company.

He was employed by Apollo plc as an IT manager until 1 March 2009 when he left the company and set up Sledge Consulting Ltd.

In 2009/10 Albert received a salary of £6,000 from Sledge Consulting Ltd on which employer's NIC of £36 was paid. He was also reimbursed business related travel expenses of £477. In addition Sledge Consulting Ltd paid £2,000 into a registered pension scheme for Albert.

In the year to 5 April 2010 Sledge Consulting Ltd received income of £85,000 from Apollo plc for IT consultancy services and £5,000 from sundry other clients.

You are required to calculate the deemed employment payment made to Albert on 5 April 2010.

6.5 The following is a summary of the main points arising from a telephone conversation you have recently had with one of your clients, Robert Archer.

1. Until recently he was employed as a proof reader by Robin Publications plc.

2. Robert has decided to resign from his employment on 6 April 2010 and set up a company, Archer Ltd, wholly owned by him, which will provide proofing reading services.

3. Robert is expecting that 80% of the company's income will be from services provided to Robin Publications plc.

4. Robert is planning to take a small annual salary of approximately £7,000 out of the company. Any other income that he receives from the company will be in the form of dividends.

You are required to briefly outline how the personal service companies legislation will affect Robert's plans.

6.6 Cheryl worked for five years at Argonaut Plc, an information technology (IT) firm.

She left Argonaut Ltd on 31 December 2008 and set up her own IT consultancy firm, Cherub Consulting Ltd, on 1 April 2009. She is the sole shareholder and the managing director.

In the year ended 31 March 2010, Cherub Consulting Ltd received £65,000 for a number of contracts completed for Argonaut Plc, on their premises, using Argonaut Plc's equipment.

Cherub Consulting Ltd also received £20,000 from other single-contract clients.

Cheryl receives a monthly salary of £1,000 from Cherub Consulting Ltd, on which £804 of employer's NIC was paid. The company also paid £5,000 into Cheryl's personal pension and reimbursed £1,250 of travel expenses.

Cherub Consulting Ltd incurred a further £3,600 of allowable business expenses in the year. It received no other income during the year.

HMRC has confirmed that the company is caught by the IR35 provisions.

You are required to calculate Cheryl's deemed employment payment for 5 April 2010 and to state the company's PCTCT for the year ended 31 March 2010.

6.7 Investalot Ltd is owned equally by Mr and Mrs Drake.

During its year ended 31 December 2009 it had the following results:

	£
Rental income	150,000
Chargeable gains	14,000
Interest	3,500
Dividends	119,000
Management expenses:	
Property management	41,040
General	68,000
Capital allowances:	
In connection with the property	1,500
General	2,225
Gift aid donation	15,000

Investalot Ltd had no unrelieved expenses of management brought forward at 1 January 2009.

In addition to the disposal that gave rise to the chargeable gain above, Investalot Ltd also sold its entire holding of 200,000 £1 shares in Enterprise Ltd for £120,000 on 14 May 2009. It had purchased the shares on 1 June 2005 at par. There are 1.5 million shares issued.

You are required to calculate Investalot Ltd's corporation tax liability for the year ended 31 December 2009 assuming any beneficial claims are made.

7.1 Jasmine Ltd prepares accounts to 31 December each year.

Its corporation tax liability for the year to 31 December 2008 was £2,600,000.

Its budgeted corporation tax liability for the year to 31 December 2009 was £3,400,000. Its actual corporation tax liability for the year ended 31 December 2009 was £3,550,000.

The company made the following payments on account of its corporation tax liability for the year to 31 December 2009:

	£
14 July 2009	650,000
14 October 2009	1,050,000
14 January 2010	850,000
14 April 2010	850,000
1 October 2010	150,000
	3,550,000

You are required to state how any interest charges will be calculated in respect of the tax liability for the year ended 31 December 2009.

7.2 New Venture Ltd commenced to trade on 1 April 2009 and prepared its first set of accounts for the 9 months to 31 December 2009.

In the 9 months to 31 December 2009 the company had a tax adjusted trading profit of £210,000 and a profit on non-trading loan relationships of £10,000. It received dividends of £10,000 from a 10% holding of ordinary shares in a UK company..

You are required to:

(a) **Calculate New Venture Ltd's corporation tax liability for the 9 month period to 31 December 2009 and state when it is payable.**

(b) **State by when the company's tax return for the period to 31 December 2009 must be submitted.**

7.3 Taranaki Ltd prepared accounts to 31 December each year until 2009 when it changed its accounting date and prepared a 7 month set of accounts to 31 July 2009.

The company's profits chargeable to corporation tax were £2,000,000 in the year to 31 December 2008 and £950,000 in the 7 months to 31 July 2009. The company did not receive any dividend income in either of the accounting periods.

You are required to state when Taranaki Ltd should pay its corporation tax liability for the 7 month period to 31 July 2009 in order to avoid any interest charges accruing.

7.4 Brooke Ltd commenced to trade on 1 January 2009 and prepared its first set of accounts for the 14 month period to 28 February 2010.

The company's only income in the period was trading income of £150,000.

You are required to:

(a) **State the due dates for filing the tax return and paying the corporation tax liability in respect of the 14 month period to 28 February 2010.**

(b) **State the penalty which would be payable if Brooke Ltd submitted a tax return 8 months late.**

7.5 Dynamo Ltd commenced trading on 1 October 2008 and prepared its first set of accounts for the 15 month period to 31 December 2009.

Its results for the period to 31 December 2009 were as follows:

	£
Trading profit	3,000,000
Chargeable gain	500,000

The chargeable gain arose on the sale of a piece of land on 1 December 2009.

You are required to:

(a) Calculate Dynamo Ltd's corporation tax liability for the 15 month period to 31 December 2009.

(b) State when the corporation tax liability for the period should be paid by Dynamo Ltd to avoid interest charges accruing.

Solutions to exam style questions

1.1 Buttercup Ltd

Buttercup Ltd has 3 associated companies.

Include companies bought and sold during the period.

Include non-resident companies.

FY09: Upper limit $\dfrac{1,500,000}{4} = 375,000$

Lower limit $\dfrac{300,000}{4} = 75,000$

	£
PCTCT	70,000
FII (8,000 × 100/90)	8,889
	78,889
GCT: 70,000 × 28%	19,600
7/400 (375,000 – 78,889) × $\dfrac{70,000}{78,889}$	(4,598)
	15,002

1.2 Cal Limited

Cal Limited is associated with Dal Limited

Upper limit 1,500,000/2 = 750,000   Lower limit 300,000/2 = 150,000

	£
PCTCT	600,000
FII (90,000 × 100/90) (Exclude dividend from associate)	100,000
Profits	700,000

FY08 (6m) and FY09 (6m): Rates and small companies limits are the same

£600,000 × 28%	168,000
7/400 × (750,000 – 700,000) × $\dfrac{600,000}{700,000}$	(750)
Liability	167,250

Note. 2 associated companies in the group.

1.3 Max Ltd

Corporation tax computation – 9 months to 31 December 2009

	£
Trading income	62,000
Property income	10,000
Profit on non-trading loan relationships (23,000 + 5,000)	28,000
Chargeable gain	9,000
Less Charges: Gift Aid	(2,000)
PCTCT	107,000
£107,000 × 21%	22,470

FY09 rates and limits apply:

Upper limit $\frac{1,500,000}{2} \times 9/12 = 562,500$

Lower limit $\frac{300,000}{2} \times 9/12 = 112,500$

1.4 Histon plc

Corporation tax – 15 months to 30 June 2010

	12m to 31.3.10 £	3m to 30.6.10 £
Trading income (W1)	14,800	17,140
Gain	20,000	–
Charge on income: Gift aid	–	(8,000)
PCTCT	34,800	9,140

(W1) Trading profit

	12m to 31.3.10 £	3m to 30.6.10 £
Tax adjusted profits before capital allowance (12.3)	74,400	18,600
Capital allowances (W2)	(59,600)	(1,460)
Tax adjusted trading profit	14,800	17,140

(W2) Capital allowances computation

	FYA £	Main pool £	Special rate pool £	Allowances £
Year ended 31.3.10				
TWDV at 1.4.09		20,000		
Additions qualifying for AIA/40% FYA:				
Machine	60,000			
AIA max £50,000	(50,000)			50,000
	10,000			
FYA @ 40%	(4,000)			4,000
Other additions:				
Special rate car			16,000	
WDA @ 20%		(4,000)		4,000
WDA @ 10%			(1,600)	1,600
Transfer to main pool	(6,000)	6,000		
TWDV cfwd		22,000	14,400	
Total allowances				59,600
3 months ended 30.6.10				
WDA @ 20%/10% x 3/12		(1,100)	(360)	1,460
TWDV cfwd		20,900	14,040	
Total allowances				1,460

1.5 **Ramble Ltd**

(a) **Accounting periods:**

- 1 April 2008 to 31 March 2009 – starts on commencement of trade and ends 12 months thereafter.
- 1 April 2009 to 30 April 2009 – starts after the end of the previous period and ends at the end of the company's period of account.
- 1 May 2009 to 30 April 2010 – starts after the end of the previous period and ends at the end of the company's period of account.

(b) **Capital allowances**

- *Car*

  CO_2 emissions are less than 160g/km. It is therefore a main rate car and will enter the main capital allowances pool qualifying for WDAs at 20% per annum. As the company is owned by a company there is no restriction for private use by Robert. Robert will be assessed to employment income on the private use of the car.

  Short life asset treatment is not available for cars.

- *Computer*

  Cost of computer and software is eligible for the 100% Annual Investment Allowance in the year to 30 April 2010 up to a maximum of £50,000. The balance of £15,000 is eligible for 40% FYAs as the asset was acquired in the period 1 April 2009 to 31 March 2010. The remaining balance (60%) enters the main pool and qualifies for WDAs at 20% in future years (but not in the year of acquisition).

  Short life asset treatment is available. However whether this treatment is beneficial depends on whether the company is expecting to dispose of the asset for less than its tax written down value, not its original cost. As the short life asset election does not need to be made until 30 April 2012 the company is likely to know whether it will be beneficial to make the election before the deadline for submitting the election.

1.6 **Overt Ltd**

Taxable trading income for the year ended 31 March 2010

	£	£
Profit before tax		5,423,000
Add back:		
Depreciation	65,000	
Lease premium	50,000	
Repairs (repair to part of building allowable)	-	
Professional fees re new lease (capital)	2,000	
Less:		
Lease premium allowable deduction (W1)	(700)	
Gain on sale of office building	(85,000)	
Bank interest (not trading income)	(48,000)	
Capital allowances	(95,000)	
		(111,700)
Taxable trading profit		5,311,300

(W1) Lease premium – allowable deduction

	£
Premium	50,000
Less 2% x (30 – 1) x £50,000	(29,000)
	21,000
Allowable deduction:	
£21,000/30	700

1.7 Mariner Ltd

Capital allowances computation for the year to 31 December 2009

	FYA £	Main pool £	Special rate pool £	Short life asset (SLA) £	Allowances £
TWDV at 1.1.09		85,000		24,000	
Additions qualifying for AIA/40% FYA:					
Van	16,000				
AIA	(16,000)				16,000
Other additions:					
Special rate car			25,000		
Disposals:					
Computer		(10,000)			
Car		(4,000)			
		71,000	25,000	24,000	
WDA at 20%		(14,200)		(4,800)	19,000
WDA at 10%			(2,500)		2,500
TWDV c/f		56,800	22,500	19,200	
Total allowances					37,500

Note: Prior to 1 April 2009 cars costing ≤ £12,000 were allocated to the main pool. Disposals of these cars after 1 April 2009 are also dealt with through the main pool.

1.8 Albatross Ltd

Chargeable gains – year ending 30 September 2009

(1) Sale of shares

Albatross Ltd, trading company, has disposed of shares out of a substantial shareholding (10% or more) in a trading company, which it has held for 12 months in the previous two years. The gain is therefore exempt.

(2) Office building

	£
Proceeds	1,200,000
Less: Cost (1 May 1993)	(200,000)
Unindexed gain	1,000,000
Less indexation allowance	
(209.8 – 141.1)/141.1 = 0.487 × £200,000	(97,400)
Indexed gain	902,600

(3) Land

	£
Proceeds	50,000
Less: Cost (April 2002)	
£10,000 × $\frac{£50,000}{£50,000 + £120,000}$	(2,941)
Unindexed gain	47,059
Less indexation allowance	
(209.3 – 175.7)/175.7 = 0.191 × £2,941	(562)
Indexed gain	46,497
Total chargeable gains	949,097

1.9 Angel Ltd

The disposal of the shares in Scooby Ltd comes within the substantial shareholding exemption as Angel had held at least 10% for 12 months out of the last 2 years.

Factory

	£
Proceeds	1,850,000
Less: cost	(575,000)
Less: IA	
208.8-165.6/165.6 = 0.261 × £575,000	(150,075)
Gain	1,124,925
Less: rollover relief	(499,925)
Chargeable now (W)	625,000

Base cost of new factory

	£
Cost	1,225,000
Less: rollover relief claimed	(499,925)
c/f	725,075

Working

Chargeable now = proceeds not reinvested

	£
Proceeds received	1,850,000
Less: proceeds spent	(1,225,000)
Chargeable now	625,000

1.10 Speciality Suds Ltd

1.10.08 – 30.9.09	FYA £	Main pool £	LLA pool £	Allowances £
TWDV b/f		68,000	119,000	
Additions qualifying for AIA/40% FYA:				
11.11.08 (no FYA)		27,500		
16.4.09	30,000			
AIA Max £50,000	(22,500)	(27,500)		50,000
	7,500			
FYA at 40%	(3,000)			3,000
Addition (Cars):				
2.4.09 Main rate car		9,500		
Disposal 6.12.08		(12,000)		
		65,500	119,000	
WDA @ 20%		(13,100)		13,100
WDA @ 10%			(11,900)	11,900
Transfer to main pool	(4,500)	4,500		
c/f		56,900	107,100	
Total allowances				78,000

1.11 **Seedy Ltd**

	£
Trading profit	910,000
Profit on non-trading loan relationships	40,000
Chargeable gains	32,000
PCTCT	982,000
Add FII £22,500 × 100/90	25,000
'Profits'	1,007,000
Tax @ full rate (W)	
£982,000 × 28%	274,960

The tax must be paid by quarterly instalments. The due dates with the due amounts are as follows:

	Explanation	£
14.10.09	Month 7 of AP (3/8 × PCTCT)	103,110
14.01.10	3 months after 1st payment (3/8 × PCTCT)	103,110
14.03.10	4 months after end of AP (Balance)	68,740
Total		274,960

Working

The corporation tax limits for the 8 month period are:

£1,500,000 × 8/12 = £1,000,000

£300,000 ×   = £200,000

2.1 **Iron Ltd**

(a) *Iron Ltd – year ended 31.3.10*

	£
Adjusted trading profits before R & D relief	1,300,000
Less R&D relief £200,000 × 130%	(260,000)
Tax adjusted trading profits	1,040,000

Lead Ltd – year ended 31.3.10

	£
Adjusted trading profits before R & D relief	80,000
Less R&D Expenditure	(6,000)
Tax adjusted trading profits	74,000

Lead Ltd is not be able to claim the additional 75% relief as it did not spend at least £10,000 in the year.

(b) Allowable revenue expenditure. Any three of:
- (i) Staff costs
- (ii) Consumables
- (iii) Computer software
- (iv) Fuel, power and water

2.2 **Plate Ltd**

Plate Ltd will have an accounting profit on sale of goodwill of:

	£	£
Proceeds		65,000
Cost	50,000	
Written off	(5,000)	(45,000)
		20,000

The profit taken to the P&L account will be £20,000.

The profit available for rollover is found by comparing proceeds to cost and not taking account of any write offs.

Eligible for rollover	£
Proceeds	65,000
Cost	(50,000)
	15,000

2.3 Muxton Ltd

(i) The goodwill is an intangible asset which has been acquired for the purpose of the trade. Under the IFA rules the amount written off is an allowable deduction from trading profits.

(ii) The interest on late payment of corporation tax is a non-trade related payment of interest. Under the loan relationship rules it is a non-trading loan relationship debit and is not deductible from trading profits.

(iii) The interest on the loan to acquire machinery is a trade related payment of interest. It is an allowable trading deduction on an accrual basis.

(iv) The interest on the loan to acquire a rental property is a non-trade related payment on interest. It is an allowable non-trading loan relationship debit. It is not an allowable deduction from property income.

2.4 A Inc

(a) A Inc is incorporated overseas. It will be deemed UK resident if it is controlled and managed from the UK.

(b) *Corporation tax computation – Year ended 31 March 2010*

	£	£
Trading income:		
– UK trade	1,200,750	
– Overseas trade	250,000	
		1,450,750
Property income (£9,000 x 100/85)		10,588
Profits chargeable to corporation tax		1,461,338
FII (£50,000 x 100/90)		55,556
'Profits'		1,516,894
Corporation tax payable @ 28%		409,175
Less DTR: Lower of:		
– UK tax (10,588 x 28%) = 2,965		
– Overseas tax = (10,588 x 15%) = 1,588		(1,588)
Corporation tax payable		407,587

Note: Exempt dividends from non-associated companies are included in FII. The amount received is grossed up by 100/90 (any overseas tax suffered is ignored).

2.5 B Inc

The company becomes non-UK resident when it transfers its central management and control overseas. On this date it is deemed to have disposed of and reacquired all of its chargeable assets at market value, thus giving rise to potential chargeable gains.

On 1 January 2009 a chargeable gain will arise on the factory situated in Switzerland calculated by reference to its market value at that date. When the factory is sold in June 2010 the company is not UK resident and no further chargeable gain will arise in the UK.

The factory situated in the UK continued to be used in a trade carried on in the UK for a period after migration. On 1 January 2009 there is no deemed disposal of the UK factory. The charge to tax is deferred until the factory is sold in March 2010. The gain on disposal is calculated in the usual way using sale proceeds and the original cost of the factory.

2.6 Bronco Ltd

Surrenderable loss

Lower of:

- Trading loss less amount set against other income £182,000 (200,000 – 18,000)
- 175% of R&D expenditure £210,000 (120,000 x 175%)

i.e. £182,000

R&D tax credit

Lower of:

- 14% of the surrenderable loss £25,480 (182,000 x 14%)
- PAYE bill of £25,000

The company can therefore claim £25,000.

Trading losses

The trading losses available to carry forward are reduced by £182,000, the amount of the surrenderable loss.

2.7 Gerald Maine

	1.12.08 – 30.11.09 £	1.12.09 – 31.12.09 £
Adjusted profits before CAs (12:1)	144,000	12,000
Less: CAs (W1)	(51,000)	(187)
Adjusted trading profit	93,000	11,813
Profit on non-trade loan relationship (W2) (12:1)	6,000	500
Chargeable gain	32,000	–
Less: Gift Aid	(10,000)	
PCTCT	121,000	12,313

Workings

(1) CAs

	Main pool £	Special rate car £	Allowances £
1.12.08 – 30.11.09			
Acquisition			
Equipment (no FYAs)	55,000		
AIA (Max £50,000)	(50,000)		50,000
	5,000		
WDA @ 20%	(1,000)		1,000
	4,000		
Allowances			51,000
1.12.09 – 31.12.09			
Acquisition		14,500	
WDA @ 20% × 1/12	(67)		67
WDA @ 10% × 1/12		(120)	120
c/f	3,933	14,380	
Total allowances			187

(2) Profit on non-trade loan relationship

	£
Interest receivable	19,500
Less: interest payable	(13,000)
	6,500

2.8 Monulife Ltd

Interest paid and receivable in connection with the trade is dealt with as trading items while that payable or receivable in connection with non-trade activities is dealt with under the 'loan relationship' rules.

Bank interest received and repayment supplement are always income from non-trading loan relationships. The amount receivable, including any accruals, is relevant.

The interest paid on the loan taken out to acquire the investment property also relates to a non-trading loan relationship, so is netted off against any income on non-trading loan relationships, while the debenture interest is paid in respect of a trading loan relationship, so is taken as a trading deduction.

	£
Bank interest £(25 + 1,250)	1,275
Repayment supplement on overpaid tax	157
Less: interest on loan to acquire property	(3,250)
Deficit on non-trading loan relationships	(1,818)
Trading deduction: debenture interest	(50,000)

Note: The figures shown in the accounts include any relevant accruals and are the figures also used for tax purposes.

2.9 Amiable Ltd

Rental income from an overseas property is taxed as property income. It is included in the computation gross and double taxation relief is available being the lower of the UK and the overseas tax suffered.

	Total £	UK £	Overseas £
Taxable trading profits	530,000	530,000	
Chargeable gain	124,750	124,750	
Profit on non-trading loan relationships	26,225	26,225	
Property income from overseas property net of 25% tax)			
£250,000 × 100/75	333,333		333,333
Less: Charge on income	(25,000)	(25,000)	
PCTCT/ profits	989,308	655,975	333,333
PCTCT @ 28%	277,006	183,673	93,333
Less: marginal relief (< £1.5m, > £300,000)			
7/400 × £(1,500,000 – 989,308)	(8,937)	(5,926)	(3,011)
CT liability	268,069	177,474	90,322
Less: DTR			
Lower of			
(i) UK tax : £90,322			
(ii) Overseas tax: 25% × £333,333 = £83,333	(83,333)		
CT due	184,736		

3.1 Alter Ltd

	£	£
Rent accrued: 1.4.09 – 31.1.10		
£6,000 × 10/12		5,000
Less bad debt relief		
£1,500 × 1/3		(500)
		4,500
Less expenses: Commission	360	
Council tax	1,100	
Wear and tear (10% × (4,500 – 1,100))	340	(1,800)
Property income assessment		2,700

Interest on loans taken out to purchase let property is relieved as a non-trading loan relationship debit.

3.2 **Staple Ltd**

Corporation tax computation – Year ended 31 December 2009

	£
Trading profit	250,000
Chargeable gains	8,000
Total profits	258,000
Property business losses (W1)	(875)
Profits chargeable to corporation tax	257,125

(W1) Property business loss

	Property 1 £	Property 2 £	Total £
Rent:			
9/12 x £10,000	7,500		7,500
1/12 x £15,000		1,250	1,250
	7,500	1,250	8,750
Less expenses:			
Wear and tear allowance (£7,500 x 10%)	(750)		(750)
Professional/agent's fees	(1,000)	(5,500)	(6,500)
Decorating	(2,000)	–	(2,000)
Insurance £1,500 x 3/12	–	(375)	(375)
Profit/(loss)	3,750	(4,625)	(875)

3.3 **Aspen Ltd**

(1) Lease premium

As the premium is received in respect of the grant of a short lease part of the premium will be assessed as property income in the year ended 31 December 2009.

	£
Premium received	60,000
Less: 2% (25 – 1) x 60,000	(28,800)
Property income	31,200

(2) Dividend from Real Estate Investment Trust (REIT)

Dividends paid out of a REIT's property income and gains are taxed as property income and not as dividends. Income of (£20,000) will be assessed as property income in the year ended 31 December 2009 (income tax is not deducted from distributions paid to other UK companies).

If the dividend is paid out of the REIT's other income (not property income or gains) the income will be treated as normal dividend income and will be treated as an exempt dividend for corporation tax purposes.

3.4 **Ghost Ltd**

	£
245 Main Street	25,400
134 George Street	58,920
REIT dividends	33,750
Property income	118,070

Notes:

(1) The loan interest paid is dealt with under the loan relationship rules.

(2) REIT dividends are paid gross to companies and come with a basic rate tax credit when paid from the REIT's tax-exempt income.

Workings

(1) 245 Main St

	£
Income	30,000
Less: expenses	(1,765)
Less: Wear & tear allowance (30,000 − 1,650) @ 10%	(2,835)
Property income	25,400

(2) 134 George St

	£	£
Income	18,720	
Less: expenses	(3,000)	
Rental income		15,720
Add: premium	60,000	
Less: 2% × (15−1) × £60,000	(16,800)	
		43,200
Total property income		58,920

4.1 Tunbridge Ltd

	y/e 31.12.06 £	y/e 21.12.07 £	y/e 31.12.08 £	y/e 31.12.09 £
Trading income	5,000	1,500	Nil	500
Profit on non-trading loan relationship	1,500	500	2,000	1,000
	6,500	2,000	2,000	1,500
S.393A(1)(a) – CY			(2,000)	
S.393A(1)(b) – PY		(2,000)		–
FA09 extended carry back	(6,000)			
PCTCT	500	Nil	Nil	1,500

Loss memo:	£
Trading loss – y.e 31.12.08	10,000
Current year offset	(2,000)
	8,000
Carry back	(2,000)
Extended loss carry back	(6,000)
Carried forward at 31 December 2009	–

The S.393A and FA09 elections must be submitted by 31/12/10. There are no losses to carry forward as at 31 December 2008.

4.2 Green Ltd

	£	£
Trading income		175,000
Loss carried forward (s 393(1))		(175,000)
		–
Profit on non-trading loan relationship		30,000
Gains	20,000	
Capital losses b/f	(20,000)	
		–
Gift Aid		(10,000)
PCTCT		20,000
FII (15,000 × 10/9)		16,667
Profits		36,667
Corporation tax payable		
£20,000 × 21%		4,200
Trading losses carried forward (210,000 − 175,000)		35,000
Capital losses carried forward (30,000 − 20,000)		10,000

4.3 Montrelle Ltd

Profits chargeable to corporation tax

Year ended	31.12.07 £	31.12.08 £	31.12.09 £
Trading income	490,000	–	150,000
Losses bfwd against trading profits			(8,000)
Property income	28,000	15,000	18,000
Chargeable gain	–	9,000	–
Total profits	518,000	24,000	160,000
Loss offset against total profits:			
– CY		(24,000)	
– PY	(518,000)		
Charges on income – Gift Aid	unrelieved	unrelieved	(10,000)
Profits chargeable to corporation tax	–	–	150,000

Loss memorandum

	£
Loss – y.e. 31.12.08	550,000
Offset against total profits:	
– CY – 31.12.08	(24,000)
– PY – 31.12.07	(518,000)
	8,000
Carried forward against trading profits:	
– y.e.31.12.09	(8,000)
	–

4.4 Tanui Ltd

Profits chargeable to corporation tax

	Year to 31.12.06 £	Year to 31.12.07 £	Year to 31.12.08 £	6 mths to 30.6.09 £	Year to 30.6.10 £
Trading income	350,000	300,000	290,000	100,000	–
Profit on non-trading loan relationship	12,000	10,000	18,000	5,000	2,000
Chargeable gain (20,000 – 5,000)	–	–	–	–	15,000
Total profits	362,000	310,000	308,000	105,000	17,000
Loss offset against total profits:					
– CY					(17,000)
– PY – 3 years	(181,000)	(310,000)	(308,000)	(105,000)	
Charges on income – Gift Aid	(8,000)	wasted	wasted	wasted	–
PCTCT	173,000	–	–	–	–

Loss memorandum

	£
Loss – y.e. 30.6.10	950,000
Offset against total profits:	
– CY – 30.6.10	(17,000)
– PY – 30.6.09	(105,000)
– 31.12.08	(308,000)
– 31.12.07	(310,000)
– 31.12.06 (6 mths)	(181,000)
Losses unrelieved	29,000

4.5 Mott Ltd

Loss relief options

(1) Relief against total profits of year ended 31 March 2010 followed by a carryback claim to 31 March 2009.

This would save tax at the small companies rate (21%) in the current year and at the small companies marginal rate (29.75%) in the prior year. It would also result in a tax repayment in respect of the year ended 31 March 2009.

(2) Relief against total profits of the current year and carry the balance forward against trading profits in the year ended 31 March 2011.

This would save tax at the small companies rate (21%) in both years and there would be a delay in obtaining relief for most of the loss until year ended 31 March 2011.

(3) Carry forward losses against trading profits in the year ended 31 March 2011.

This would save tax at the small companies rate (21%).

Recommendation

Option (1) is most beneficial as it saves the most tax and obtains relief as soon as possible.

4.6 Morvel Ltd

Loss relief options

(1) Offset against total profit of year ended 31 December 2009 and carry back to offset against total profits of prior year. Remaining losses are carried forward against future trading profits (see comments below).

(2) Offset against total profit of year ended 31 December 2009 and carry back to offset against total profits of previous three years under the temporary loss carry back relief in Finance Act 2009, if there are profits available to offset (not known from question). The offset in two earlier years is restricted to a maximum of £50,000. Remaining losses are carried forward against future trading profits (see comments below).

(3) Offset against total profit of year ended 31 December 2009 and carry forward against future trading profits.

It is likely however that there has been a major change in the conduct of the company's trade, due to the change in the method of selling the company's products. As this has occurred within 3 years of a change in ownership of the company the losses arising before the change in ownership cannot be carried forward to offset trading profits arising after the date of change in ownership. The losses can therefore only be offset against trading profits arising in the 2 months to 28 February 2010 i.e. £120,000 x 2/12.

(4) Carry forward against first available trading profits. This option is also subject to the change in ownership point set out in point (3).

4.7 Droma Ltd

As the loss arises in an accounting period ending between 24 November 2008 and 23 November 2010 it can be carried back against total profits (before deducting any charges) of the previous three years, subject to a maximum offset in the earlier two years of £50,000.

	Y/e 31.3.06 £	Y/e 31.3.07 £	Y/e 31.3.08 £	Y/e 31.3.09 £	Y/e 31.3.10 £
Trading profits	45,000	60,000	41,000	55,000	–
Gains	10,000	–	2,000	–	15,000
Property income	5,000	7,000	4,000	16,000	32,000
	60,000	67,000	47,000	71,000	47,000
CY					(47,000)
PY				(71,000)	
Extended c/b		(3,000)	(47,000)		
PCTCT	60,000	64,000	–	–	–

Loss memorandum:
Loss y/e 31.3.10	177,000
Less: current year	(47,000)
Less: prior year	(71,000)
Extended carry back claim:	
C/b to 31.3.08	(47,000)
C/b to 31.3.07 (Max £50,000 - £47,000)	(3,000)
Loss to c/f	9,000

4.8 Cassel Ltd

To carry a trading loss back, the company must first claim to set the loss against its current year income, even if this wastes a gift aid donation (as it does here).

The maximum loss that can be carried back to the year ended 31.12.09 is the lower of the available loss and nine month's worth of the profits of that period, as the loss can only be carried back against a total of 12 months worth of profits.

	y/e 31.12.09 £	p/e 31.3.10 £	y/e 31.3.11 £
Trading profits	88,000	24,500	–
Profit on non-trading loan relationships	20,000	20,000	20,000
PCTCT	108,000	44,500	20,000
Less: CY loss relief			(i) (20,000)
Less: CB loss relief	(iii) (81,000)	(ii) (44,500)	
Revised PCTCT	27,000	Nil	Nil
Less: charge on income	(10,000)	*	*
PCTCT	17,000	Nil	Nil

* Gift Aid is wasted

Loss memo

		£
Loss of y/e 31.3.11		195,000
(i) CY		(20,000)
(ii) p/e 31.3.10		(44,500)
(iii) y/e 31.12.09	9/12 × £108,000 = 81,000 (max)	(81,000)
c/f		49,500

The loss must be carried forward against future trading profits of the same trade.

The extended loss relief under FA09 is not available as the loss making accounting period ended after 23 November 2010.

5.1 Group relieve £118,000 to Sub Ltd to bring it down to lower limit of £150,000 (ie £300,000 ÷ 2). This saves tax at 29.75%.

Then choice between a carry back of the remaining loss of £1,000 to y/e 31.3.09 to save tax at 21% or group relief in y/e 31.3.10 to also save tax at 21%. Do the former to generate a cashflow advantage from obtaining a repayment in the prior year.

Only a group relief claim is required. Note that if a carry back claim were made technically the group relief claim should be made first, as the carry back claim is an 'all or nothing' claim.

5.2 **Mr Phillips**

Associates – all companies – as Mr Phillips has common control.

Group relief – Alpha & Gamma only as must have 75% relationship via other companies and the holding company must have an effective 75% holding in all sub-subsidiaries.

Capital gains – Alpha Ltd, Gamma Ltd and Epsilon Ltd. Group can include Epsilon Ltd as the principal company (Alpha Ltd) has a 56.25% holding in the company (i.e. at least 51%).

5.3 **James Ltd**

Group relief:

	£	£
From Edward = excess management expenses (20 – 5)		15,000
From Gordon – part of the group from 1.1.09 – 31.3.09		
Lower of:		
Loss 3/12 × £80,000	20,000	
Profits 3/12 × £700,000	175,000	20,000
		35,000

5.4 **Wind Ltd**

Transfer from Wind Ltd to Sail Ltd

Wind Ltd and Sail Ltd form a capital gains group as Wind Ltd owns 85% (at least 75%) of the ordinary share capital of Sail Ltd. The sale to Sail Ltd therefore automatically takes place at no gain/no loss. The deemed proceeds on the transfer will be the original cost plus indexation to the date of transfer (W1).

Chargeable gain – Sale of asset 1 April 2010

	£
Proceeds	300,000
Less: Cost (W1)	(120,960)
Unindexed gain	179,040
Less Indexation allowance	
(205.9 – 209.8)/209.8 = Nil × £120,960 (fall in RPI)	–
Chargeable gain	179,040

(W1) Cost

	£
Original cost (Feb 1993)	80,000
Indexation to June 2009	
(209.8 – 138.8)/138.8 = 0.512 × £80,000	40,960
Deemed proceeds/deemed cost to Sail Ltd	120,960

5.5 Force Ltd

Sale to Power Ltd

Force Ltd and Power Ltd form a capital gains group at the date of the sale of the factory as Force Ltd owns 80% (at least 75%) of the ordinary share capital of Power Ltd. The sale to Power Ltd therefore automatically takes place at no gain/no loss. The deemed proceeds on the transfer will be the original cost plus indexation to the date of transfer (W1).

Degrouping charge on leaving group

Power Ltd ceases to be a member of Force Ltd's capital gains group when Force Ltd reduced its shareholding to 65% on 1 March 2010.

As the factory was transferred to Power Ltd within 6 years of it leaving the group and it still owns the building at that date a degrouping charge will arise.

The degrouping charge will arise in Power Ltd in the year to 31 March 2010. It will be calculated by reference to the market value at the date of transfer and the original cost of the building as follows:

	£
Market value on 1.6.08	500,000
Less: Cost (W1)	(98,400)
Chargeable gain	401,600

(W1) Cost

	£
Original cost (June 2002)	80,000
Indexation to June 2008	
(216.8 − 176.2)/176.2 = 0.230 x £80,000	18,400
	98,400

5.6 Overseas Ltd

Overseas Ltd is likely to be a controlled foreign company (CFC) because it is:

(1) resident outside of the UK

(2) controlled by persons resident in the UK (Expansion Ltd, incorporated in the UK)

(3) subject to a lower level of taxation in Overseasland. A tax rate of 8% is likely to be lower than 75% of the tax which would be payable in the UK as the minimum UK tax rate is 21%.

If Overseas Ltd is a CFC the income profits (not gains) of the company will be apportioned to (65%) and taxed on Expansion Ltd. There are specified situations when the profits are not apportioned eg when the profits of the CFC for the accounting period do not exceed £50,000.

5.7 Tweet Ltd

Only Tweet Ltd, Pounce Ltd and Feeder Ltd are in a loss relief group, as Tweet Ltd's effective interest in Booker Ltd is only 72% (90% × 80%). Feeder and Booker Ltd are in a separate loss relief group, but Feeder Ltd cannot surrender any losses received from Pounce Ltd to Booker Ltd. Pounce Ltd does not have to use any of the losses itself.

All companies are in a gains group. It is preferable for Feeder Ltd's gain to be included in the results of the company with capital losses and/ or the lowest rate of tax. An election can be made to treat the asset as having been disposed of by that other company, in this case, Booker Ltd if the disposal was before 21 July 2009. If the disposal was on or after 21 July 2009 an election can be made to transfer the gain itself to Booker Ltd.

There are 4 associates, so the CT limits are:

£1,500,000 / 4 =   £375,000
£300,000/ 4 =   £75,000

	Tweet £	Pounce £	Feeder £	Booker £
Trading (profit/ loss)	875,000		189,000	21,000
Bank interest	12,000		8,000	400
Rental income		12,000		
Chargeable gains/ (loss)				40,000
Total income	887,000	12,000	197,000	61,400
CT rate	28%	21%	29.75% then 21%	21%
Total income	887,000	12,000	197,000	61,400
Less: CY loss				
Less: Group relief	(35,000)		(110,000)	
	852,000	12,000	87,000	61,400
Less: Gift Aid payments	(25,000)	(2,500)	(12,000)	(1,000)
PCTCT	827,000	9,500	75,000	60,400
CT due	231,560	1,995	15,750	12,684

Loss memo – Pounce Ltd

	£
y/e 31.3.10	145,000
To Feeder Ltd (note)	(110,000)
To Tweet Ltd	(35,000)
c/f	Nil

Note: Use sufficient loss to bring the PCTCT down to the level where the company only pays 21%. Remember to factor in the gift aid donation.

5.8 **Chilli Ltd**

Chill Ltd and Freeze Ltd are in a group for chargeable gains purposes (=75%). At the date of the original transfer of the property, the disposal took place at no gain/ no loss, ie Freeze Ltd took over Chill Ltd's original cost and indexation.

However, Freeze Ltd is sold within 6 years of that intra-group transfer so the gain that would have arisen at the date of the transfer becomes chargeable now on Freeze Ltd when it leaves the group (a 'de-grouping charge'). Freeze Ltd could elect to transfer the charge to Chill Ltd, but we are told that Freeze Ltd does not do anything to improve its tax position, so we can assume it does not make an election.

	£
Proceeds (MV)	425,000
Less: cost	(219,000)
Less: IA $\frac{185.7-165.6}{165.6}$ =0.121 x £219,000	(26,499)
Gain	179,501

As both Chill Ltd and Freeze Ltd are trading companies, the gain for Chill Ltd on the disposal of the Freeze Ltd shares is exempt (substantial shareholding exemption). This is because Chill Ltd has owned at least 10% of the shares for at least 12 months in the prior 2 years.

6.1 **Investment companies**

(1) The cost of raising loan finance will be a non-trading loan relationship debit. It is normally written off over the period of the loan

(2) The cost of contributions to a training and enterprise council, the accountant's fees and the pension payments are allowed as management expenses specifically.

(3) Capital allowances on let properties are relieved as expenses deductible from property income.

6.2 Moriarty Ltd

		£
Management expenses		300,000
Less bfwd		(220,000)
Current year available for group relief		80,000
Profits available in claimant	Trading income	90,000
	Gain	10,000
	Charges on income	(30,000)
		70,000

Only £70,000 can be surrendered.

6.3 Carp Ltd

Corporation tax computation – Year ended 31 December 2009

	£	£
Property income:		
Rent	300,000	
Less property management expenses	(65,000)	
		235,000
Profit on non-trading loan relationship (50,000 – 22,000)		28,000
Chargeable gains		264,000
		527,000
Less Expenses of management:		
General expenses	15,000	
Expenses of management brought forward	25,000	
		(40,000)
Profits chargeable to corporation tax		487,000

6.4 Albert

Deemed employment payment – 2009/10

	£
Income from relevant engagements	85,000
Less: Deduction at 5% (5% x 85,000)	(4,250)
Deductible travel expenses	(477)
Pension scheme contributions	(2,000)
Employer's NIC	(36)
Salary paid	(6,000)
Gross deemed employment income (gross of NIC)	72,237
Less: Employer's NIC	
72,237 x 12.8/112.8	(8,197)
Deemed employment payment	64,040

6.5 **Archer Ltd**

Implications of personal service companies legislation:

1. The services provided to Robin Publications plc will be regarded as a relevant engagement. If Robert had contracted directly with Robin Publications plc the relationship would have been deemed to be in the nature of an employment.

2. A deemed employment payment will arise in Archer Ltd on 5 April each year based on the income received from the relevant engagement.

3. The deemed employment payment is broadly based on the income received from the relevant engagement less the salary actually paid to Robert less a flat rate deduction of 5% of income plus other specified items.

4. PAYE and NIC is payable by Archer Ltd on the deemed employment payment.

5. Dividends paid to Robert in relation to income included in the deemed employment payment will not be taxable on Robert.

6.6 **Cheryl**

Cheryl is treated as receiving a deemed employment payment on 5 April 2010.

	£	£
Income from relevant engagements		65,000
Less : 5% flat rate deduction	3,250	
Salary	12,000	
Employers' NIC on actual salary	804	
Pension contribution	5,000	
Reimbursed expenses	1,250	
		(22,304)
Gross deemed employment payment		42,696
Less: Employer's NIC		
£42,696 × 12.8%/112.8%		(4,845)
Net deemed employment payment		37,851

Cherub Consulting Ltd's PCTCT:

	£	£
Trading profits: £65,000 + 20,000		85,000
Less : Salary	12,000	
Employers' NIC on actual salary	804	
Pension contribution	5,000	
Reimbursed expenses	1,250	
Other expenses	3,600	
		(22,654)
PCTCT		62,346

Note: The deemed employment payment and associated NIC cannot be deducted until the period in which the payment is deemed to be made, ie in the year ended 31 March 2011.

6.7 Investalot Ltd

Investalot Ltd is a close investment company. It is taxable at the full rate of corporation tax regardless of its level of profits.

Although the shares in Enterprise Ltd are a substantial shareholding the loss is allowed because Investalot Ltd is not a trading company and therefore the substantial shareholding exemption does not apply.. Had the shares been subscribed for the loss could have been offset against total profits, assuming Enterprise Ltd satisfied the criteria of the Enterprise Investment Scheme.

Any remaining loss will be carried forward against future gains.

CORPORATION TAX

	£	£
Property income	150,000	
Less: expenses	(41,040)	
Less: CAs	(1,500)	
		107,460
Profit on non-trading loan relationships		3,500
Gains (W)		–
Total		110,960
Less: Expenses of management		
General		(68,000)
Capital allowances		(2,225)
		40,735
Less: Gift aid donation		(15,000)
PCTCT		25,735
Tax:		
£25,735 × 28%		7,206

Loss on unquoted shares

	£
Proceeds	120,000
Less: cost	(200,000)
Loss	(80,000)

Net gains

	£
Gains	14,000
Current year loss	(14,000)
Net gains	nil

Capital loss carried forward

	£
Loss	(80,000)
Current year offset	14,000
	(66,000)

7.1 **Jasmine Ltd**

The level of Jasmine Ltd's corporation tax liability indicates that it pays tax at the full rate. Its tax liability is therefore payable in instalments, based on its actual tax liability for the year, as follows:

	Due £	Paid £	Shortfall/ (Over payment) £	Cumulative £
14 July 2009 £3,550,000 x ¼	887,500	650,000	237,500	237,500
14 October 2009	887,500	1,050,000	(162,500)	75,000
14 January 2010	887,500	850,000	37,500	112,500
14 April 2010	887,500	850,000	37,500	150,000
1 October 2010		150,000	(150,000)	
	3,550,000	3,550,000		

Interest will be charged as follows:

Interest period	Charged on £
14 July 2009 to 13 October 2009	237,500
14 October 2009 to 30 September 2010	75,000
14 January 2010 to 30 September 2010	37,500
14 April 2010 to 30 September 2010	37,500

7.2 **New Venture Ltd**

(a) *Corporation tax computation – 9 months ended 31 December 2009*

	£
Trading income	210,000
Profit on non-trading loan relationships	10,000
Profits chargeable to corporation tax	220,000
FII £10,000 x 10/9	11,111
'Profits'	231,111
Corporation tax payable:	
£220,000 x 28%	61,600
Less: Marginal relief	
FY09: 7/400 x (1,125,000 – 231,111) x 220,000/231,111	(14,891)
	46,709

Small companies limits:
Upper limit: £1,500,000 x 9/12 = £1,125,000
Lower limit: £300,000 x 9/12 = £225,000

Tax payable: 1 October 2010 (9 months and 1 day after the end of the accounting period.

(b) The company's tax return for the 9 months to 31 December 2009 must be submitted by 31 December 2010 (within 12 months of the end of the accounting period).

7.3 **Taranaki Ltd**

Payment due dates

Taranaki Ltd paid tax at the full rate in the year ended 31 December 2008 and the 7 months to 31 July 2009. The reduced upper small companies rate limit for a 7 month accounting period is £875,000 (1,500,000 x 7/12). The company's tax liability for the 7 month period to 31 July 2009 is therefore payable by instalments as follows:

	£
14 July 2009 £950,000 x 28% x 3/7	114,000
14 October 2009 £950,000 x 28% x 3/7	114,000
14 November 2009 (balance of liability)	38,000
Total liability (950,000 x 28%)	266,000

7.4 **Brooke Ltd**

(a) Filing and payment dates

There are two accounting periods in the 14 month period of account to 28 February 2010:

- Year to 31 December 2009
- Two months to 28 February 2010

	Filing date (12 months after end of period of account)	Payment date (9 months and one day after end of accounting period)
Year to 31 December 2009	28 February 2011	1 October 2010
Two months to 28 February 2010	28 February 2011	1 December 2010

(b) As the return will not be filed until late in 2011 it is reasonable to assume that the new Finance Act 2009 late filing penalties will apply.

The penalty for late filing would be an immediate £100 penalty. In addition daily penalties of £10 per day may be charged as the return is more than 3 months late (max 90 days). A tax geared penalty of 5% of the tax due (minimum £300) will also be charged as the return is more than 6 months but less than 12 months late.

7.5 **Dynamo Ltd**

(a) *Corporation tax computation – 15 month period to 31 December 2009*

	Year to 30.9.09 £	3 mths to 31.12.09 £
Trading income (12:3)	2,400,000	600,000
Chargeable gain (December 2009)		500,000
Profits chargeable to corporation tax	2,400,000	1,100,000
Corporation tax payable		
£2,400,000 × 28%	672,000	
£1,100,000 × 28% (Note 1)		308,000

(b) Due payment dates:
9 months after end of AP (Note 2)	1 July 2010	
Instalment basis (Note 3)		14 April 2010

Notes:

(1) Adjusted small companies upper limit £375,000 (1,500,000 × 3/12)

(2) In the first accounting period the company is large but its PCTCT does not exceed £10 million. Payment is therefore not due by instalments.

(3) Payment due on earlier of 14th day of month 7 from the start of the AP (14 April 2010) and 14th day of month 4 from the end of the AP (14 April 2010).

Awareness Paper
VAT and Stamp Taxes

Study Period Planner
VAT and Stamp Taxes

Use this schedule and your exam timetable to plan the dates on which you will complete each Study Period. The letters 'H' and 'M' tell you whether the topic is high or medium priority.

Study Period	Topic		Due Date
1	VAT basics	H	
2	Treatment of supplies	H	
3	Input tax	H	
4	Land and buildings	M	
5	**Progress Test 1**	H	

Study Period	Topic		Due Date
6	Overseas matters	M	
7	Miscellaneous VAT issues	H	
8	Administration	H	
9	Stamp Taxes	M	
10	**Progress Test 2**	H	

COURSE EXAM 1

A practice exam covering Study Periods 1 – 4

COURSE EXAM 2

A practice exam covering all Study Periods

REVISION PHASE

Your revision phase will begin when **Course Exam 2** is complete. This should ideally be four months before the final exam.

TQT Note: The Course Exams contain questions for all FIVE of the awareness paper modules. In your exam you must answer questions from THREE modules. We suggest that you identify the THREE modules you will study and then work through the Study Period Planners for each of those modules until the point where you are told to take Course Exam 1. When you have completed all THREE modules to that point, sit Course Exam 1. Similarly, you should complete all THREE modules before you sit course exam 2. Course Exam 2 covers all of the Study Periods, although it is weighted towards the second half of your studies.

Study Period 1

VAT basics — High Priority

Step 1 Exam Guidance

This study period considers the basics of VAT, ie the background information fundamental to your study of VAT.

These topics have examined in:

The contained the following questions covering these areas of the syllabus:

- Sample Paper (Q5 and Q7)
- May 2009 exam (Q1 and Q5)

Step 2 Introduction to the session

In this study period we begin our study of VAT by looking at the basics of VAT. These topics provide background information essential to your understanding of this syllabus.

Step 3 Guidance through the Study Text

Read through Chapter 1 of the VAT Awareness Study Text after reading the following guidance:

Sections 1 to 3 should be read through quickly, as background information. Follow through Illustrations 1 to 4. You need to know these details to understand the mechanics of VAT, but these areas might not be examined in their own right.

Read Section 4 on registration and deregistration carefully. You must be able to determine when a trader should or could register for VAT and identify the penalties for late registration. You must also be aware of the rules for deregistration from VAT. This is an important area of the syllabus. Work through the remaining illustrations and attempt Examples 1 to 3 to help reinforce your understanding of the section.

Step 4 Quick Quiz

Please attempt the quick quiz at the end of Study Text Chapter 1 to reinforce your understanding.

You may find it best to do this after a break, so that you can see what you remember and what you don't.

Step 5 i-Pass and Workbook Questions

Now attempt the VAT exam style questions (ESQs) 1.1 to 1.6 which will help to reinforce your knowledge of the topics covered in this study period and give you examples of the types of question you may see in the exam.

Your TQT's i-Pass CD Rom also contains some questions on VAT basics.

Study Period 2

Treatment of supplies

High Priority

Step 1 Exam Guidance

This Study Period covers background information to the calculation of VAT liabilities. It is the source of many potential exam questions.

Question 5 of the sample paper covers the VAT treatment of goods held at deregistration.

Step 2 Introduction to the session

In this study period we learn how to identify which rate of VAT applies to a particular supply. We must be able to determine when a supply has been made and whether it is:

- Exempt from VAT, or
- Zero rated, or
- Standard rated, or
- A lower rated supply.

Step 3 Guidance through the Study Text

Read through Chapter 2 of the Study Text, after reading the following guidance:

Read through Section 1 of the Chapter to understand the difference between zero rated and exempt supplies, working through Illustrations 1 and 2. This Section gives you the references within the legislation for the lists of zero rated, exempt and lower rated supplies. Take this opportunity to locate these lists in your copy of the legislation so that you can easily find and use them in the exam. There is no need to memorise the lists in the chapter. Try Example 1.

Read quickly through Section 2 to understand the circumstances in which supplies can be treated as having taken place.

Finally, read quickly through Section 3 to understand the VAT implications of transactions made by charities.

Step 5 i-Pass and Workbook Questions

Now attempt ESQs 2.1 to 2.6 which will help to reinforce your knowledge of the topics covered in this study period and give you examples of the types of question you may see in the exam.

Your TQT's i-Pass CD Rom also contains some questions on the treatment of supplies for VAT purposes.

Step 4 Quick Quiz

Please attempt the quick quiz at the end of Study Text Chapter 2 to reinforce your understanding.

You may find it best to do this after a break, so that you can see what you remember and what you don't.

Study Period 3

Input tax

High Priority

Step 1 Exam Guidance

This study period covers the recoverability of input VAT. It is the source of many potential exam questions.

These topics were tested in:

- Sample Paper (Q1 and Q8)
- May 2009 exam (Q6)

Step 2 Introduction to the session

In this study period we look at input VAT in detail.

You must be able to identify recoverable input VAT, which can be deducted when calculating the VAT liability, and irrecoverable input tax, which is 'blocked' from recovery (ie it cannot be deducted).

You must also be comfortable with the input VAT recovery position of traders who make both taxable and exempt supplies.

Step 3 Guidance through the Study Text

Read through Chapter 3 of the Study Text after reading the following guidance:

Quickly read Sections 1 and 2, which introduce the concept of input tax and then go on to set out the rules for the deductibility of input tax.

Read Section 3 carefully. This section deals with the situations when input tax is **not** recoverable and you must be able to identify these in the exam. Attempt Examples 1 and 2 as you work through this section.

Quickly read through Sections 4 and 5, but do pay particular attention to Section 4.2 on pre-registration input tax.

Carefully work through Section 6. This deals with 'partial exemption', which is one of the more complex (and examinable) VAT topics. You must be able to deal confidently with the VAT position of a partially exempt trader in the exam. Work through Examples 3 to 5 to reinforce your understanding.

Finally, read through Section 7 on the capital goods scheme, which deals with input VAT recovery for certain capital items (ie computers and land and buildings). Work through Illustrations 3 to 6 as you go along to test your understanding.

Step 4 Quick Quiz

Please attempt the quick quiz at the end of Study Text Chapter 3 to reinforce your understanding.

You may find it best to do this after a break, so that you can see what you remember and what you don't.

Step 5 i-Pass and Workbook Questions

Now attempt ESQs 3.1 to 3.11 which will help to reinforce your knowledge of the topics covered in this study period and give you examples of the types of question you may see in the exam.

Your TQT's i-Pass CD Rom also contains questions on input VAT.

322 Module 5: VAT and Stamp Duties

Study Period 4

Land and buildings — Medium Priority

Step 1 Exam Guidance

The VAT implications of transactions involving land and buildings can easily be examined as a whole question.

VAT on land and buildings was examined on the sample paper in Question 2.

Step 2 Introduction to the session

In this Study period we continue our study of VAT by looking at the rules for calculating VAT on transactions involving the supply of land and buildings.

Step 3 Guidance through the Study Text

Read through Chapter 4 of the Study text after reading the following guidance:

Section 1 sets out the general rules for zero rated transactions involving land and buildings. Work through Illustration 1 to test your understanding.

Section 2 covers the transactions involving land and buildings that are exempt, and the exceptions from the exemption. Work through Example 1 to check you have understood the section.

Quickly read Sections 3 and 4. Make sure you understand the general rule that leases are exempt supplies for VAT purposes and try Example 2.

Section 5 deals with the VAT position for transactions involving exempt commercial land and buildings if the trader 'opts to tax' them. Read through carefully to ensure that you are comfortable with the concept of the 'option to tax' and work through Illustration 2 to test your understanding.

Finally, read quickly through Section 6.

Step 4 Quick Quiz

Please attempt the quick quiz at the end of Study Text Chapter 4 to reinforce your understanding.

You may find it best to do this after a break, so that you can see what you remember and what you don't.

Step 5 i-Pass and Workbook Questions

Now attempt ESQs 4.1 to 4.6 which will help to reinforce and give you examples of the types of question you may see in the exam.

Your TQT's i-Pass CD Rom also contains questions on transactions involving land and buildings.

Module 5: VAT and Stamp Duties   323

Progress Test 1

Study Period 5 — High Priority

In order to reinforce what you have learnt so far, answer the following questions. Try to answer them without referring to your Study Text or notes. The test should take you no longer than one hour and covers Study Periods 1-4. Solutions start on page 335.

1. Mr Gillott is in business selling garden statues. He checks his turnover level regularly to ensure that he is still below the VAT registration threshold. At the end of October, his average monthly turnover of taxable supplies was £3,000. On 14 November 2009, he received a letter from a national magazine agreeing to use his products in reader offers, and ordering goods worth £69,000, to be supplied and invoiced within the next 28 days. The magazine intends to use his products in offers regularly from now on.

    State the dates by which Mr Gillott should notify HMRC of the need to register for VAT and which date the VAT registration will be effective from. Explain the penalty for late notification of registration.

2. **State the advantages and disadvantages of voluntarily registering for VAT.**

3. Betty opens a catering business on 1 September 2009. Her cumulative turnover for the five months to 31 January 2010 is £49,000. She is asked to cater for a large party in February 2010. The turnover from this alone will be £20,000.

    Explain when Betty will need to notify her liability to register for VAT and the date she will be registered from.

4. Kenwood Ltd incurred the following VAT-inclusive expenditure in the quarter to 31 March 2010:

    (a) £1,578 entertaining clients.

    (b) £294 entertaining employees.

    (c) £1,833 on repairs to a property occupied by one of its directors.

    (d) £899 on lease payments for a car provided to an employee. The employee uses the car 20% of the time for private purposes.

    You are required to calculate how much VAT input tax is not recoverable by the company.

5. Billy started trading on 1 October 2009 as a greeting cards designer and applied to register for VAT with effect from 1 December 2009. Prior to registration, he had incurred the following VAT inclusive expenditure:

	£
Computer for business use purchased new on 1 July 2009	700
Fees for market research on invoice dated 1 June 2009	400
Printing inks purchased on 1 August 2009	300

    Of the £300 of printing inks purchased on 1 August 2009, £200 (VAT inclusive) worth were still in stock on 1 December 2009.

    You are required to explain what input VAT Billy can reclaim in respect of these items.

Progress Test 1 (continued)

Study Period 5 — High Priority

6   Cradle Financial Services Ltd is partially exempt for VAT purposes and uses the standard method of apportioning input tax. Input tax for the quarter ended 31 December 2010 is:

Attributable to taxable supplies	Attributable to exempt supplies	Unattributable
£	£	£
800	1,200	600

The total amounts invoiced for the period were £22,800 (including VAT) of which £4,000 relates to exempt supplies.

What is the deductible input tax for the period?

7   **Briefly state the consequences for a trader who fails to register for VAT when required to do so.**

8   Zebra Ltd has been registered for VAT for many years and is partly exempt. Its partial exemption year ends on 31 March.

During the year ended 31 March 2010 Zebra Ltd incurs the following input tax:

	£
Attributable to taxable supplies	47,000
Attributable to exempt supplies	23,000
Residual input tax	14,000

The total value of supplies during the year was £700,000 of which £500,000 were taxable.

How much input tax is recoverable for the year ended 31 March 2010?

9   Treemendous Ltd purchased a computer for £57,500 (inclusive of VAT) on 1 May 2009. It used the computer 65% for taxable use in the quarter of purchase and 70% for taxable purposes in the year to 31 December 2009.

In the year to 31 December 2010 taxable use decreased to 60%.

Treemendous Ltd sold the computer for £10,000 plus VAT on 6 May 2011. Its taxable use in the period from 1 January 2011 to the date of sale was 60%.

You are required to calculate the initial input recovery and adjustments required for all other years.

10 Supplies of goods and services can be categorised as standard rated, exempt, zero rated or lower rated for VAT purposes.

You are required to state how the following are categorised for VAT purposes.

(a) **Investment advice**
(b) **Accountancy services**
(c) **Insurance**
(d) **Children's clothing**
(e) **Newspapers**
(f) **Fuel for domestic use**
(g) **Hot take-away meal**
(h) **Burial services**
(i) **Professional accountancy course**
(j) **Exports outside the EU**

Progress Test 1 (continued)

Study Period 5 — High Priority

11 The following transactions occurred in January 2010:

   1. Perky Ltd grants a 90 year lease from its freehold interest in a factory that was completed in early 2009.

   2. Jenny sells a factory for £340,000, excluding VAT, that she bought 12 years ago. She had been letting out part of the factory and so had previously opted to tax this building.

   3. Perred Ltd sells a 99 year lease in a new residential building that it had constructed.

   You are required to explain how these transactions are treated for VAT purposes.

12 A supply is acquired partly for business purposes and partly for the private use of an employee.

   You are required to describe how this should be dealt with for VAT.

You will find the answers to this test starting on page 335. If you answer more than 6 questions correctly, your performance is satisfactory; if you answer more than 8 correctly, you are doing well. Once you have reviewed how you have performed, go back over topics where you feel your understanding is poor.

Study Period 6

Overseas matters

Medium Priority

Examined: Sample Paper

Step 1 Exam Guidance

The VAT implications of overseas transactions is a topic which can be examined as a whole question.

VAT on overseas transactions is examined in Question 6 on the sample paper.

Step 2 Introduction to the session

In this study period we consider the VAT implications of buying goods and selling goods overseas, both within and outside the EU.

Step 3 Guidance through the Study Text

Read through Chapter 5 of the Study text after reading the following guidance:

Section 1 is a long and detailed Section which describes the VAT position of imports and exports of goods both inside and outside the EU. Make sure you are aware of the VAT implications of each of the different circumstances. Work through Illustration 1 and attempt Examples 1 and 2.

Section 2 considers international services. Note the general rule for supplies of services which depends on whether the customer is in business or not. Note the situations when the supply is treated as being made somewhere else. Follow through Illustrations 2 to 5. Use your legislation to help you as you read through this section, so that you know where to find the details in the exam.

Step 4 Quick Quiz

Please attempt the quick quiz at the end of Study Text Chapter 5 to reinforce your understanding.

You may find it best to do this after a break, so that you can see what you remember and what you don't.

Step 5 i-Pass and Workbook Questions

Now attempt ESQs 5.1 to 5.6 which will help to reinforce and give you examples of the types of question you may see in the exam.

Your TQT's i-Pass CD Rom also contains questions on overseas supplies of goods and services.

Module 5: VAT and Stamp Duties

Miscellaneous VAT issues

Study Period 7 — High Priority

Step 1 Exam Guidance

A number of the topics covered in this study period have been examined on the sample paper as whole questions and are essential for your exam.

These topics have been tested as follows:

- Transfer of a going concern: Sample Paper Q3, May 2009 Q9
- VAT groups: Sample Paper Q9, May 2009 Q4

Step 2 Introduction to the session

In this study period we consider a number of outstanding technical VAT issues. These are:

- The VAT position of traders who use certain VAT schemes
- The VAT treatment when a business is transferred as a going concern
- Group VAT registration for companies.

Step 3 Guidance through the Study Text

Read through Chapter 6 of the Study Text after reading the following guidance:

Sections 1 to 4 deal with various VAT schemes for certain traders. Carefully read Section 1, which covers the flat rate scheme, and work through Illustration 1. Quickly read through Section 2, which is a brief section that deals with the second-hand goods scheme, and Section 3, which deals with the farmers' flat rate scheme, working through Illustration 2. Then read through Section 4 on schemes for retailers. Try not to get bogged down with the detail, but work through slowly, using Illustrations 3 to 6 to help reinforce your understanding of the topic. Concentrate on understanding how the schemes work.

Section 5 deals with the VAT treatment when there is a disposal of a business as a going concern. Can you identify when a business is transferred as a going concern? Work through Illustrations 7 to 9 to help you learn the consequences of such a transfer.

Finally, read carefully through Section 6 ensuring you understand the VAT consequences of a group of companies registering as a single group entity for VAT purposes.

Step 4 Quick Quiz

Please attempt the quick quiz at the end of Study Text Chapter 6 to reinforce your understanding.

You may find it best to do this after a break, so that you can see what you remember and what you don't.

Step 5 i-Pass and Workbook Questions

Now attempt ESQs 6.1 to 6.10 which will help to reinforce and give you examples of the types of question you may see in the exam.

Your TQT's i-Pass CD Rom also contains questions covering the various topics in this study period, such as the transfer of a business as a going concern and group VAT registration.

Administration

Study Period 8

High Priority

Step 1 Exam Guidance

There are a number of administrative rules to learn in the VAT Awareness syllabus.

The examiner could tack an administrative point at the end of another question for, say, one mark, or make the topic the focus of a question.

These topics have been tested as follows:

- Sample Paper: Q4, Q10 and Q11
- May 2009 exam: Q4, Q7 and Q10

Step 2 Introduction to the session

In this Study Period we complete our study of VAT by looking at how a VAT return is completed, the records and returns that need to be maintained, the penalties imposed if traders do not comply with their obligations, bad debt relief and VAT accounting schemes to assist small businesses.

We also consider the system by which VAT assessments can be raised and the mechanism by which a VAT registered trader can appeal against a VAT assessment.

Step 3 Guidance through the Study Text

Read through Chapter 7 of the Study text, which covers a number of administrative topics, after reading the guidance below:

Read carefully through Section 1, which covers some basic administrative provisions, such as the period for which VAT returns are required, the contents of a VAT return and the determination of the tax point of a transaction. Follow through Illustrations 1 and 2 and attempt Example 1 to check your understanding of the section.

Read Section 2 covering the rules for keeping VAT records and the contents of a valid VAT invoice. Take this opportunity to locate the relevant part of the legislation referred to at the start of the section so that you can easily find and use it in the exam.

You can read quickly through Sections 3 to 7 on assessments and HMRC powers, interest, penalties and disclosure schemes. Section 4 refers you to Section 8 of Chapter 15 of the CTA Awareness Taxation of Individuals Study Text. You should study section 8 of that chapter before continuing with your study of this VAT and stamp taxes text. Again instead of learning the detail for these topics, learn where it is in your legislation.

Finally, work carefully through Sections 8 and 9, which deal with the relief available for bad debts and the two main schemes available to small businesses to help with VAT accounting: the cash accounting scheme and the annual accounting scheme. Use the examples and illustrations to check your understanding of these topics.

Step 4 Quick Quiz

Please attempt the quick quiz at the end of Study Text Chapter 7 to reinforce your understanding.

You may find it best to do this after a break, so that you can see what you remember and what you don't.

Step 5 i-Pass and Workbook Questions

Now attempt ESQs 7.1 to 7.10 which will help to reinforce and give you examples of the types of question you may see in the exam.

Your TQT's i-Pass CD Rom also contains questions covering the administrative areas of the VAT syllabus.

Module 5: VAT and Stamp Duties

Study Period 9

Stamp Taxes

Medium Priority

Examined: Sample Paper

Step 1 Exam Guidance

This Study Period covers the three stamp taxes: Stamp duty (SD), stamp duty reserve tax (SDRT) and stamp duty land tax (SDLT).

Stamp duty land tax was examined in Question 12 of the sample paper and Questions 11 and 12 of the May 2009 exam.

Step 2 Introduction to the session

In this study period we consider the stamp tax implications of transactions:
– involving shares (SD and SDRT) and
– land (SDLT)

Step 3 Guidance through the Study Text

Read through Chapter 8 of the Study text after reading the following guidance:

Section 1 is a useful brief summary of the scope of each of the stamp taxes. Read this for background information.

Read through Section 2 which covers stamp duty on share transactions where shares are transferred using a stampable instrument eg a stock transfer form. Section 2.5 covers an important relief from stamp duty for transactions involving groups of companies. This is an important section to study.

Read through Section 3 on stamp duty reserve tax. Make sure you understand the interaction of SD and SDRT. SDRT applies to all share transactions however the transfer of ownership is implemented, eg electronically as for quoted shares dealt with on the Stock Exchange or by a stock transfer instrument for private company shares. In the latter case SD is also payable on the stock transfer instrument and the SDRT liability is cancelled upon presentation of a stamped stock transfer form.

Stamp duty land tax is covered in Section 4. Read this and ensure you understand to what transactions it applies, who pays the tax and how the tax is calculated. Note in particular the treatment of leases and the relief available for groups of companies.

Finally quickly read through the administration of the taxes in Section 5.

Step 4 Quick Quiz

Please attempt the quick quiz at the end of Study Text Chapter 8 to reinforce your understanding.

You may find it best to do this after a break, so that you can see what you remember and what you don't.

Step 5 i-Pass and Study Text Questions

Now attempt ESQs 8.1 to 8.4 which will help to reinforce and give you examples of the types of question you may see in the exam.

Your TQT's i-Pass CD Rom also contains questions on Stamp Taxes.

Module 5: VAT and Stamp Duties

Progress Test 2

Study Period 10 — High Priority

In order to reinforce what you have learnt so far, answer the following questions. Try to answer them without referring to your Study Text or notes. The test should take you no longer than one hour and covers Study Periods 6-9. Solutions start on page 339.

1. Hamish, a VAT registered trader, owns a property in Edinburgh which is let to a builders merchant. He has made an option to tax in respect of the property. The following transactions take place in the quarter ended 31 March 2010:

    (a) Hamish charges quarterly rent of £3,000.
    (b) The tenant pays Hamish £10,000 for the surrender of his lease.

    All figures are exclusive of VAT.

    How much VAT will Hamish need to charge in respect of the above transactions for the quarter ended 31 March 2010?

2. **State how the time of supply of goods is determined for VAT purposes.**

3. Exceedingly Big Builders Ltd constructed a new bottling plant for Kipling Ltd. Work began on 1 August 2009. The construction work was completed on 17 April 2010. Payment was received on 12 April 2010 and a VAT invoice was issued on 3 May 2010, reflecting the full consideration already paid.

    State and explain the VAT tax point for the supply of the bottling plant.

4. Shadowplay Ltd has opted for cash accounting for VAT purposes. In the VAT quarter ended 31 December 2009 the following transactions take place:

    (a) Receipt of £5,000 as payment on account of invoice of £10,000 plus VAT issued on 30 September 2009.
    (b) Write off of a debt of £6,000 plus VAT which was due on 30 April 2009.
    (c) Payment of £350 against invoice of £2,000 plus VAT dated 28 November 2009 received from a supplier.

    What is the VAT payable/repayable for Shadowplay Ltd in respect of the quarter ended 31 December 2009? Calculate to the nearest pence.

5. White Horse Ltd is preparing its VAT return for the quarter ended 31 October 2009. This quarter, White Horse Ltd has written off the following bad debts:

Debtor	Date of supply	Amount (Inclusive of VAT) £	Payment received £
A Ltd	1 June 2009	1,150	Nil
B Ltd	1 November 2008	2,350	300
C Ltd	1 January 2009	2,300	Nil

    White Horse Ltd has already accounted to HM Revenue & Customs for all of the VAT charged on the supplies.

    How much VAT bad debt relief is due to White Horse Ltd for the quarter ended 31 October 2009?

Study Period 10

Progress Test 2 (continued)

High Priority

6 Cardart Ltd, a VAT registered trader, supplies a batch of greetings cards, on approval, to a new customer on 31 January 2010. The arrangement is that the customer will either pay for the goods on 31 March 2010 or return them intact. The cards are a great success and the customer pays Cardart Ltd for the cards on 28 February 2010. Cardart Ltd issues a VAT invoice dated 31 March 2010.

State and explain the tax point for the above sale by Cardart Ltd.

7 Silk Ltd manufactures textiles. The company is VAT registered and operates the cash accounting scheme. In the quarter to 31 March 2010 the company undertakes the following transactions:

   (a) Invoices sales of £4,000 plus VAT
   (b) Purchases raw materials for cash of £2,000 plus VAT
   (c) Receives cash from trade debtors of £3,525 in respect of invoices dated 1 February 2010.

How much VAT is due for payment by Silk Ltd in respect of the quarter to 31 March 2010?

8 Mr Dashwood submits his quarterly VAT return on time. He sent in his previous three returns late and had to pay a default surcharge. Unfortunately, although he has correctly calculated the VAT due as £1,520, he accidentally writes the cheque for £1,250 instead, when submitting his return. He does not realise his mistake in time to pay the balance before the deadline of 30 days after the return date.

How much default surcharge will HM Revenue and Customs be entitled to collect?

9 Frank is a sole trader who manufactures garden chairs. He is registered for VAT. He received an order for six chairs on 30 July 2009. The chairs were delivered to the customer on 20 August 2009 and an invoice was issued on 30 August 2009. Payment was made on 13 September 2009.

Explain what is the tax point for the sale of the garden chairs.

10 **You are required to state the three conditions that must be satisfied for a supply of goods to another EU member state to be zero rated for VAT purposes.**

11 XYZ Ltd is registered for VAT in the UK and has recently entered into the following transactions:

   - Sale of goods located in India which were delivered to America
   - Sale of goods located in Wales and delivered to Australia

Discuss the place of supply for VAT purposes and their subsequent treatment for VAT.

12 **You are required to explain the stamp taxes implications of the following transactions:**

   1. Ray sold 2,000 shares in Apple Ltd for £81,300 to Pear plc using a stock transfer form.
   2. Pluto Ltd sold some residential land to Saturn plc, an unconnected company, for £260,000.
   3. Sun Ltd paid £80,000 for the grant of a 30 year lease of a warehouse. The net present value of the rental was £510,000 and the annual rent was £10,000. The factory was not in a disadvantaged area.

You will find the answers start on page 339. If you answer more than 6 questions correctly, your performance is satisfactory; if you answer more than 8 correctly, you are doing well. Once you have reviewed how you have performed, go back over topics where you feel your understanding is poor.

Solutions

Progress Test 1

1. Turnover is expected to exceed £68,000 in 30 days following 14 November 2009 ∴ must notify HMRC by 13 December 2009 (end of 30 day period).

   He will be registered from 14 November 2009 (beginning of 30 day period).

   If Mr Gillot is late in notifying HMRC of his liability to register he will be charged a penalty of the greater of £50 and a percentage of the net tax due from the date when the trader should have been registered to the date of actual notification. The percentage starts at 5% if registration is no more than 9 months late and rises to 15% if registration is over 18 months late.

2. Voluntary registration for VAT:

   Advantages:

   - Can claim back input VAT incurred.
   - Improves the image of the business (can make the business look older and more established than it is).

   Disadvantages:

   - Increases prices to non VAT registered customers.
   - Burden of administration.

3. Betty's cumulative turnover in the preceding 12 months will exceed the £68,000 turnover limit on 28 February 2010. She needs to notify HMRC by 30 March 2010.

   She will be registered from the start of the following month (ie by 1 April 2010).

4. Kenwood Ltd

	£
The irrecoverable input VAT is as follows:	
Client entertaining: £1,578 × 7/47	235
Staff entertaining (all recoverable)	Nil
Director's accommodation services: £1,833 × 7/47	273
Leased car payment 50% × £899 × 7/47 (Note)	67
Total irrecoverable VAT	575

   Note. 50% of the lease payment is irrecoverable because there is private use of the vehicle. The level of private use is irrelevant.

5. Billy can reclaim all the input VAT suffered as follows:

   – Computer £91 – as a fixed asset and assumed still held at the date of registration.
   – Market research £52 – as a service provided within the 6 months prior to registration
   – Inks £26 – VAT recoverable on the stock still held at the date of registration

Solutions

Progress Test 1

6 Input tax

	Taxable supplies £	Exempt Supplies £
Directly attributable	800	1,200
Unallocated $\dfrac{16{,}000}{16{,}000 + 4{,}000} \Rightarrow 80\%$	480	120
	1,280	1,320

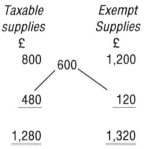
(600 split into 480 and 120)

- <£625pm
- > 50% of total input tax

  ∴ not de minimis

  ∴ £1,280 deductible

W: Net taxable supplies = (22,800 − 4,000) × 40/47 = £16,000

Tutorial note.

40/47 was used rather than the 7/47 in order to create a 1 step solution rather than a 2 step solution.

7
- The trader will be personally liable for output VAT due on taxable supplies from the due date of registration.
- Sales prices during the above period will be considered to have been VAT inclusive.
- A late registration penalty for the period of the default is payable unless there is a reasonable excuse for the delay. The amount of the penalty depends upon when the failure to register occurred.

  If it occurred prior to 1 April 2010 the penalty is the greater of £50 and a percentage (5%, 10% or 15%) of the net tax due depending on how late registration is.

  If the failure to register occurred after 1 April 2010 the penalty is a percentage of the potential lost tax depending on the behaviour of the taxpayer eg 70% where the failure is deliberate but not concealed. The penalty is reduced for the quality of disclosure by the taxpayer.

8 Partial exemption 500/700= 72% (round up) of residual input tax is recoverable.

47,000 + (72% x 14,000)

= £57,080

Note: The VAT relating to exempt supplies clearly exceeds the de minimis.

Progress Test 1 — Solutions

9   For the first VAT year to 31 December 2009, the recovery is:

£57,500 × 3/23 = £7,500 × 70% = £5,250.

For the second VAT year to 31 December 2010 the adjustment is:

£7,500 × 10% (ie 70% - 60%) × 1/5 = £150 payable to HMRC.

For the third VAT year to 31 December 2011 there are two adjustments:

(a)   £7,500 × 10% × 1/5 = £150, payable to HMRC

(b)   £7,500 × 30% (ie 100% - 70%) × 2/5 = £900, restricted to the VAT charged on the sale of the computer, ie £10,000 × 17.5% = £1,750. So, can recover the full £900 from HMRC.

The net adjustment for this third year is:

£(150) + £900 = £750 recoverable from HMRC.

10
(a)	Investment advice	Standard rated
(b)	Accountancy services	Standard rated
(c)	Insurance	Exempt
(d)	Children's clothing	Zero rated
(e)	Newspapers	Zero rated
(f)	Fuel for domestic use	Lower rated
(g)	Hot take-away meal	Standard rated
(h)	Burial services	Exempt
(i)	Professional accountancy course	Standard rated
(j)	Exports outside the EU	Zero rated

11 The grant of the lease is an exempt supply. Perky Ltd could opt to tax the grant, making it a standard rated supply.

The sale of the factory will be standard rated supply as Jenny has opted to tax the building. Output VAT will be £340,000 x 17.5% = £59,500

The grant of a major interest (freehold or lease exceeding 21 years) of newly constructed residential property is zero rated.

12 Generally the input tax should be apportioned between business and private use, and only the business proportion treated as deductible input tax.

The strict position under EU law, however, is that all of the input tax should be treated as recoverable but that there is a deemed supply of the private use, and output tax should be charged on the deemed supply.

Where the supply is of road fuel a scale rate is used to calculate the deemed supply.

Progress Test 2 — Solutions

1. Hamish

	£
Rent	3,000
Surrender	10,000
	13,000

   £13,000 @ 17.5% = £2,275.

   Tutorial note.

   Rent and payment for surrender are VATable.

2. Supply takes place on the date the goods are removed or made available to the customer. This is also known as the basic tax point.

   If an invoice is issued, or payment is received, **prior** to this date, then this earlier date becomes the tax point for the amount invoiced or payment received. The normal rule will apply to any balance.

   If an invoice is issued within 14 days *after* the basic tax point, then this becomes the tax point, unless the trader elects for this treatment not to apply. (This rule only applies if an 'earlier' date has not already fixed the tax point.) This period may be extended by HMRC to allow for, say, monthly invoicing.

3. The tax point is the earliest of

   (a) completion date = 17 April 2010

   (b) payment date = 12 April 2010

   (c) invoice date - if before the date of completion and payment. As it is later, then the tax point is 12 April 2010.

4. VAT only accounted for when cash is received or paid

   (a) Total invoice 10,000 + (15% × 10,000)   £11,500.00

   Receipt of $\frac{5,000}{11,500} \times £1,500$ £652.17

   (b) No cash involved

   (c) Total invoice £2,000 + (15% × 2,000) =   £2,300

   Payment of $\frac{350}{2,300} \times 300$ (£45.65)

   ∴ VAT payable to HMRC £652.17 – £45.65 =   £606.52

5. B Ltd (2,350 – 300) x 7/47 = £305

   C Ltd 2,300 x 3/23   = £300

   Total bad debt relief   = £605

   Tutorial note.

   Invoices over 6 months old are eligible for bad debt relief, ie B Ltd and C Ltd.

Solutions

Progress Test 2

6. Tax point is the date of receipt of the cash ie 28 February 2010.

   The 14 day rule only overrides the basic tax point if the invoice is dated within 14 days.

7.
	£	VAT £	
Received from debtors	3,525	525	(7/47 × 3,525)
Paid to suppliers	2,000	350	(17½% × 2,000)
VAT payable amounts to		175	

8. Greater of:

   £(1,520 − 1,250) = 270 @ 10% = £27

   (3rd default in notice period)

   Or minimum £30

   ∴ £30

9. Basic tax point = date goods removed 20.8.09.

   But invoice issued within 14 days of basic tax point therefore tax point is 30.8.09.

10. Conditions for despatch to be zero rated:
    - Supply must be made to a registered trader,
    - The supplier must quote the customer's VAT number on the invoice (to prove he is registered), and
    - The supplier must hold evidence that the goods were actually delivered to the other member state.

11. India to America: Goods located outside the UK and therefore outside the scope of UK VAT.

    Wales to Australia: Goods located within the UK and so UK supply liable to UK VAT, but zero rated as an export.

12. The stamp taxes implications are:

    1. Stamp duty of 0.5% × £81,300 rounded to the nearest £5 is payable by Pear plc i.e. £410. No stamp duty reserve tax will be payable if the stamp transfer document is presented within 6 years of the contract date.

    2. Stamp duty land tax (SDLT) of £7,800 (£260,000 × 3%) is payable by Saturn plc.

    3. SDLT payable by Sun Ltd:

       Premium: £80,000 × 1% = £800 − The zero rate is not available as the annual rent exceeds £1,000 and the property is non-residential.

       NPV of rents: (£510,000 − £150,000) × 1% = £3,600.

Exam style questions

1.1 In his first year of trading to 31 December 2008 Monty's turnover from his restaurant was £3,500 a month.

For the first seven months of 2009 his turnover was as follows:

	£
January 2009	4,000
February 2009	5,600
March 2009	7,000
April 2009	9,000
May 2009	10,000
June 2009	11,700
July 2009	12,000

You are required to state, with reasons, the date by which Monty is required to notify HMRC that he is liable to register for VAT.

Monty actually registers for VAT on 30 November 2009 and the net tax due on his first VAT return is £900.

You are required to outline what penalty Monty is liable for.

1.2 Big Ltd has acquired the rights to sell miniature televisions in the UK. The company was formed on 2 July 2009 and obtained the marketing rights on 3 July 2009. Its budgeted turnover for the first 12 months is:

Quarter ended	Turnover
	£
30 September 2009	2,000
31 December 2009	18,500
31 March 2010	210,000
30 June 2010	150,000

Turnover is expected to arise evenly within each quarter.

You are required to state:

By what date must the company inform HMRC of the need to register for VAT and from what date will registration be effective?

If the business terminates at a later date, within how many days must Big Ltd notify HMRC and when else must it notify HMRC that it must deregister?

1.3 Banbury plc issues an invoice on 1 February 2010 as follows:

	£	£
Goods		1,000
Less: trade discount	100	
cash discount	60	(160)
		840

The cash discount is only available if the invoice is settled within thirty days. The client pays within 10 days.

Banbury plc also sells an item on which standard-rated VAT is due on 1 March 2010. The item costs £600 excluding VAT before any discounts. The client is entitled to a 5% trade discount and a further 2.5% (on cost after trade discount) discount if he pays within 30 days. The client pays 60 days later.

You are required to state what VAT is due on both sales.

1.4 Richard commenced trading on 11 January 2009, and his first two years' monthly turnover (excluding VAT) is set out below. He does not wish to register unless he has to do so.

	2009 £	2010 £
January	2,200	10,420
February	2,690	10,700
March	3,590	10,630
April	4,690	12,290
May	5,370	14,980
June	4,960	12,990
July	5,240	11,920
August	6,920	12,540
September	6,380	9,300
October	7,060	12,230
November	9,410	11,920
December	9,930	13,440

You should assume that the registration thresholds are the same for 2010 as they are for 2009.

You are required to state the action Richard should take, and when, assuming all of his turnover is zero-rated.

1.5 Xilo Ltd made the following taxable supplies after its incorporation on 1 May 2009:

	2009 £	2010 £
January	nil	90,000
February	nil	102,000
March	nil	152,000
April	nil	170,000
May	8,000	
June	10,000	
July	17,000	
August	21,000	
September	24,000	
October	50,000	
November	60,000	
December	100,000	

You are required to outline (with explanations) the date on which the business should notify HMRC of its need to register for VAT and the date from which the business will be VAT registered.

1.6 Mr Cassell begins to run his own stationery shop on 1 November 2008. He makes the following supplies during his first year of trade:

	£
November 2008	1,200
December 2008	2,400
January 2009	3,800
February 2009	6,600
March 2009	8,250
April 2009	16,200
May 2009	18,900
June 2009	18,750
July 2009	19,100
August 2009	18,900
September 2009	19,600
October 2009	19,450

He incurred expenses of £3,000 (inclusive of standard rate VAT) each month.

You are required to:

(1) State the date by which Mr Cassell must notify HMRC of his liability to register for VAT.
(2) State the date from which he will be registered to charge VAT.
(3) The amount of any penalty if he does not notify HMRC until 1 November 2009.

2.1 You are required to discuss briefly the difference between a mixed supply and a compound supply. In your discussion give one example of each type of supply.

2.2 You are required to:

(a) explain the difference between zero-rated and exempt supplies.

(b) outline what type of supply are the following for VAT purposes?

    (i) Food sold for consumption away from the premises but where a microwave oven is made available to heat up the food either before or after the till point

    (ii) Pet food which is canned, packaged or prepared

    (iii) Santa flight to Lapland

    (iv) A coach excursion to a theme park

2.3 Ade Sleightholme is the managing director of one of your clients, Stimpson Group plc, which trades in the health sector owning and running two nursing homes for the elderly and infirm.

Stimpson Group plc has paid full rate VAT on all its fuel supplies since it commenced trading on 1 January 2000 and estimates that its costs, excluding VAT, are £30,000 per annum. A business contact has suggested to Ade that it should be possible for the Group to only pay the reduced rate of VAT on all its fuel supplies in the future and to recover the amount overpaid in full from the suppliers.

You are required to consider the proposition, commenting on the technical position with detailed reference to the legislation.

2.4 Iain is an employee of ABC Ltd. He has the use of a car with CO_2 emissions of 176g/km for one month and a car with CO_2 emissions of 208g/km for two months during the quarter ended 31 March 2010.

ABC Ltd pay all the petrol costs in respect of both cars without requiring Iain to make any reimbursement in respect of private fuel. Total petrol costs for the quarter amount to £300 (including VAT).

You are required to state what the VAT effect of the above on ABC Ltd is.

VAT Scale rates (VAT inclusive) for 3 month periods

	£
CO_2 emissions	
175	289
205	365

2.5 How would the following supplies be treated for VAT purposes?

(a) Plain, wholesome biscuits sold in a novelty 1940s biscuit tin.
(b) A subscription to a satellite TV provider which includes a weekly magazine.
(c) A ticket to fly to Rome which includes in-flight catering.

2.6 (a) Sale of a stamp by the post office.
    (b) Sale of a child's car seat.
    (c) A dentist's bill for a filling.
    (d) Sale of a mars bar.
    (e) A newspaper.

You are required to outline how the above supplies will be treated for VAT with legislative references to support your answer.

3.1 Ben commenced trading on 1 August 2010 repairing electrical equipment and applied to register for VAT with effect from 1 October 2010.

Prior to registration, he had incurred VAT as follows:

	£
Van purchased new on 3 May 2010	500
Accountancy fees on invoice dated 5 September 2010	30
Stock of spare parts as on 30 September 2010	240

Ben also incurred the following capital expenditure (including VAT) during his first VAT quarter:

	Net £	VAT £
Two cars for employees (available for private use)	14,234	2,135
Motor van	10,500	1,575
Second hand transit van	26,254	3,938

You are required to state how much VAT can be reclaimed by Ben in respect of the above items.

3.2 Kate's business was registered for VAT from 1 January 2010. The following transactions took place in the quarter ended 31 March 2010.

	£
Sales at standard rate (including VAT)	235,000
Sales at zero rate	50,000
Exempt sales	75,000

Sales are stated inclusive of VAT
Her input tax has been attributed as follows:

	£
Attributed to taxable supplies	60,000
Attributed to exempt supplies	17,000
Unattributed	73,000
	150,000

You are required to state what the recoverable input tax is.

3.3 Giles Ltd is a partially exempt trader for VAT purposes. The company makes up its accounts and VAT returns for the year to 31 March. The company's partial exemption recovery percentage for the year to 31 March 2009 was 79%.

During the quarter to 30 June 2009 the following amounts of VAT were charged on the company's purchases and other expenses.

	£
Wholly attributable to making taxable supplies	12,500
Wholly attributable to making exempt supplies	1,500
Non-attributable VAT	4,000

During the quarter the company made the following supplies.

	£
Standard rated supplies (excluding VAT)	140,000
Zero-rated supplies	20,000
Exempt supplies	40,000

You are required to compute the amount of input tax that can be reclaimed for the quarter assuming:

(1) The company chooses to use the recovery percentage for the previous year and

(2) The company does not use the previous years' recovery percentage.

3.4 Mr J Cake is a VAT registered trader. In the quarter to 31 August 2009 he makes net standard rated supplies of £40,000, zero-rated of £20,000 and exempt supplies of £23,000. His total input VAT is £45,000 of which £27,000 can be matched with taxable supplies and £9,000 with exempt supplies.

You are required to state how much input VAT Mr Cake can recover.

3.5 Nordon Ltd makes wholly taxable supplies and is registered for VAT. In the period ended 31 December 2009 it incurs the following input tax:

	£
re supplies for contracts to be fulfilled in the first quarter of 2010	15,200
re overheads in factory	3,300
re purchases of new company car for sales manager	5,100
re entertainment	
Clients	1,100
Employees	850

You are required to calculate the amount of deductible input tax for the quarter ended 31 December 2009.

3.6 Keith runs a large grocery store in a small village in Hertfordshire. The store sells all types of groceries and also has a post office counter, which is managed by his wife Julie.

Total input tax suffered by Keith's business was £35,000 for the year ended 30 April 2009.

This can be analysed as follows:

	£
Attributable to taxable supplies	20,000
Attributable to exempt supplies	10,000
Relating to general overheads and thus not directly attributable	5,000
	35,000

Turnover (VAT exclusive) can be analysed as follows:

	£
Groceries: standard rated	21,500
zero rated	80,200
Postal services	20,300
	122,000

You are required to calculate the amount of input tax recoverable for the year ended 30 April 2009.

3.7 Trusty Car Sales Ltd (TCS) is a car dealership, which also provides finance and insurance to customers on request.

On 19 May 2008 TCS purchased a computer to be used in the business for both operational and accounting purposes. The purchase invoice showed the total amount of VAT to be £26,250, of which £8,750 related to software.

TCS is partly exempt as a result of its services of arranging finance and insurance and it operates the partial exemption standard method. Its tax year ends on 31 March and the recovery rates in the tax years 2008 to 2010 were as follows:

2008	2009	2010
80%	70%	85%

You are required to:

(a) **Explain whether or not the purchase of the computer and the related software falls within the Capital Goods Scheme.**

(b) **Calculate, with explanations, the input tax which should have been recovered/paid in respect of the computer purchase in the tax years ending 31 March 2009 and 31 March 2010 and state on which return any adjustment required should have been made.**

3.8 Z Ltd purchased a computer for £100,000 + VAT on 1 January 2009. It used it 58% for taxable use in the quarter of purchase and 60% for taxable purposes in the year to 31 March 2009.

The taxable use in the year to 31 March 2010 was 50%. The computer was sold for £6,000 + VAT on 10 August 2010. The taxable use in the period 1 April 2010 to 10 August 2010 was 50%.

You are required to calculate the initial input recovery and adjustments required for all other years.

3.9 In her first VAT quarter to 31 March 2010 Alice made the following supplies:

Exempt supplies £86,000
Taxable supplies £325,000

Her input VAT for the period was as follows:

		£
Wholly attributable to:	Taxable supplies	1,895
	Exempt supplies	420
Overheads		1,545

You are required to calculate how much input VAT Alice can claim on her return for the quarter ended 31 March 2010.

3.10 Spice Ltd purchased a computer server for £75,000 (exclusive of VAT) on 1 May 2009. It used the server 61% for taxable use in the quarter of purchase and 68% for taxable purposes in the year to 31 March 2010.

The taxable use in the year ended 31 March 2011 was 49%.

Spice Ltd sold the server on 21 September 2011 for £19,000 (plus VAT). The taxable use for the period to the date of sale was 45%.

You are required to calculate the initial recovery and the adjustments required for all other years.

3.11 Patchwork Ltd makes widgets and made standard rated supplies of £247,000 (plus VAT) in the VAT year ended 31 December 2009.

The company also incurred the following VAT-inclusive expenditure during the year:

Client entertaining	£2,124
Staff entertaining	£2,258
Renovation work on property occupied by director	£15,575
Car with 80% business use	
Cost of the car	£16,800
Servicing costs	£3,021
Other wholly business expenses	£35,600

You are required to calculate the net VAT payable to HMRC by Patchwork Ltd.

4.1 **You are required to outline how the following supplies will be treated for VAT purposes:**

(a) Peter the plasterer sends an invoice to the builder BIG Homes Ltd for his work on 10 houses in a new housing estate the company is building.

(b) The services of a lawyer used by BIG Homes Ltd to draw up contracts for employees working on the development mentioned in (a).

(c) Juniper Ltd sells the freehold of a five year old restaurant to a property developer.

Give legislative references in your answer.

4.2 **You are required to state what type of supply the following are for VAT purposes. (Note that no options to tax have been made unless otherwise stated.)**

(a) Electrician's supply of services in relation to the conversion of a warehouse to luxury apartments.

(b) Supply of services of installing energy saving materials in residential accommodation or in a building intended for use solely for a relevant residential purpose.

(c) The grant of a 99-year lease in a new commercial building.

(d) The first grant of a major interest, by the person constructing, in a building designed as a dwelling.

(e) The sale of a freehold interest in a commercial building built in 1993 on which the landlord has 'opted to tax'.

4.3 Tim Clarke, a developer, is proposing to construct an office building for letting on land that he has recently purchased. Construction would commence on 1 July 2010. He is unsure whether to opt to tax the development or not. On completion of the development on 31 December 2011, Tim intends granting leases over one or more floors of the building to tenants.

The estimated costs of the development are as follows.

	Cost (excluding VAT) £	VAT £
Land	800,000	–
Construction costs	7,200,000	1,260,000
Professional costs	600,000	105,000
Interest costs	1,200,000	–

You are required to calculate the impact, both in terms of input tax recovery and its timing, of Tim deciding to opt to tax the development.

4.4 Mr Heart owns an eight storey office block in Manchester, which is currently let out to various tenants.

The building is in need of renovation and Mr Heart has been quoted a VAT inclusive cost of £750,000 to do this.

You are required to discuss Mr Heart's position in relation to the building outlining any planning point(s) which may benefit him.

4.5 **You are required to outline whether the option to tax can be made in relation to each of the following supplies:**

(a) **Sale of 20 acres of farmland**
(b) **Sale of a 30 year old house in Salford**
(c) **Lease of a one year old factory**
(d) **Freehold sale of a 1 year old office block**
(e) **99 year lease of a newly refurbished show room**

4.6 Girth Ltd purchases a new warehouse on 1 August 2009 and immediately decides to opt to tax the building.

Girth Ltd plans to purchase a number of other buildings in the future.

You are required to state:

(1) **The date by which the option to tax must be notified to HMRC.**
(2) **The date on which the cooling off period for revoking the option to tax ends.**
(3) **The earliest date on which the option to tax can be revoked if it is not revoked during the cooling off period.**
(4) **The name of the election that Girth Ltd can use to include any future properties within the option to tax.**

5.1 Jane Moss, a UK based designer registered for VAT in the UK, made the following supplies of hand made jewellery in the quarter ended 31 August 2009:

	£
to Canadian based purchasers	2,500
to Italian based purchasers	
registered for VAT in Italy	5,200
not registered for VAT in Italy	1,800

Jane also acquired £15,000 of ceramics and gem stones from a supplier based in Portugal.

You are required to state what the VAT implications are for Jane in respect of the above supplies and purchases.

5.2 ABC Ltd is registered for VAT in the UK and has recently sold the following.

(1) A set of furniture which was in India and was delivered from India to a customer in Australia;

(2) A table which was in Edinburgh and was delivered to a customer in America; and

(3) An armchair which was supplied to a customer in Hong Kong out of a batch of 100 received from China and re-exported.

You are required to:

(a) Outline the general rules in respect of the place of supply of goods;
(b) Discuss the place of supply of the goods supplied by ABC Ltd;

5.3 **You are required to state whether the following supplies are a dispatch, acquisition, export or import for VAT purposes.**

1 Sale of lamb to France
2 Purchase of lamb from New Zealand
3 Purchase of books from Brazil
4 Sale of children's clothes to Germany
5 Sale of chocolate to Italy
6 Purchase of wine from Australia
7 Purchase of wine from Germany
8 Sale of bird houses to USA
9 Purchase of green beans from Kenya
10 Sale of bacon to Portugal

5.4 On 1 March 2010 Alladyce Services Ltd instructs a firm of management consultants based in Jersey to perform a review of its business. The management consultants charge £100,000 to the company in respect of this service.

You are required to outline the VAT impact of the above scenario.

5.5 **You are required to briefly outline the difference between an export and a dispatch from a VAT point of view.**

5.6 Purse Ltd, a UK VAT registered business selling leather goods, recently had the following transactions:

(1) Sale of goods located in a warehouse in Canada which were delivered to the USA.
(2) Sale of goods located in a warehouse in Milton Keynes which were delivered to Mexico.

You are required to state whether the place of supply is inside or outside the UK in each instance and whether the transaction is:

(A) Zero rated, or
(B) Outside the scope of VAT.

6.1 Where the assets of a business are transferred in connection with all or part of the business as a going concern, the transfer is not treated as a taxable supply and no VAT is payable.

You are required to state four conditions that must be met in order for this treatment to apply.

6.2 Steve, an estate agent, undertakes work for individuals and for business clients. In the VAT year to 31 December 2009, the business client work amounted to £55,000 plus VAT. Turnover from work for individuals totalled £28,000 excluding VAT.

The flat rate percentage for an estate agency or property management business is 9.5%.

You are required to:

(1) Briefly describe the optional flat rate scheme.
(2) Calculate the VAT payable by Steve under the optional flat rate scheme for the year to 31 December 2009.

6.3 On 30 April 2009 Sparks Ltd ordered a new printing machine and on 16 May 2009 paid a deposit of £10,000. The machine was dispatched to Sparks Ltd on 31 May 2009. On 18 June 2009 an invoice was issued to Sparks Ltd for the balance due of £45,000. This was paid on 20 June 2009.

You are required to outline (and explain why you have reached this answer):

(a) **the tax point for the £10,000 deposit**
(b) **the tax point for the balance of £45,000**

6.4 Farmer Bard has an annual turnover of £70,000 from sales of potatoes grown on his land. He sells £65,000 to supermarkets and £5,000 from a roadside stall. In the year to 31 December 2009 he purchased seed potatoes costing £1,000 and manure for £5,000 from a neighbour, who is retired but runs a refuge for elderly horses. He also bought a new tractor for £40,000 (excl VAT) to replace his old tractor which had collapsed after 20 years of use and was towed away free of charge by the local scrap merchant.

Farmer Bard dreads completing his VAT return and finds VAT administration a 'real headache'.

You are required to explain how the flat-rate scheme would affect Farmer Bard.

6.5 Julip Cleaners operates a dry-cleaning outlet in Charlton undertaking work for individuals but also business clients such as a local hotel.

In the VAT year to 31 December 2009 the business client work amounts to £52,000 net of VAT and the individuals work has brought in cash takings of £72,000.

Julip Cleaners operates the flat rate scheme with an 9.5% flat rate applying.

You are required to outline how the flat rate scheme will apply to the business using the above figures.

6.6 The structure of Red Group is as follows:

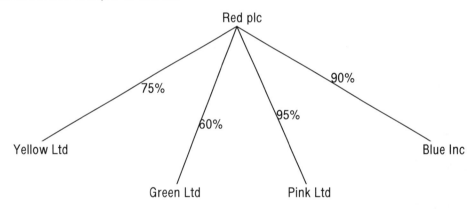

All the companies make electrical products except Yellow Ltd which is a finance company making only exempt supplies.

Blue Inc is an American company.

You are required to:

(a) **Discuss which companies are eligible to form a VAT group.**
(b) **Outline two effects of making a VAT group registration.**

6.7 Slick Tony sells prestige cars. He bought a Porsche from a member of the public for £8,000 in June 2010. He spent £550 plus VAT on restoration by a local garage he often uses. He sold the car to a member of the public for £12,500 in August 2010.

Slick Tony is preparing his quarterly VAT return to 31 August 2010.

You are required to:

(a) **outline briefly how the second hand goods scheme operates.**
(b) **state the output tax/input tax to be entered onto Tony's return in respect of the above car.**

6.8   Stan is an accountant. He provides his services to individuals and businesses.

During his VAT year to 31 December 2009 Stan provides services as follows:

Business clients   £78,000
Individual clients   £32,500

These figures are shown exclusive of VAT.

Stan also incurs expenses during the year of £11,745, inclusive of VAT at the standard rate.

The flat rate percentage for accountancy businesses is 11.5%.

You are required to calculate:

(1)   Stan's VAT due using the normal VAT rules.
(2)   Stan's VAT due using the flat rate scheme rules.

6.9   Jason had the following sales and purchases in his quarter ended 31 March 2010:

	£	
Standard rated sales	690,000	(inclusive of VAT)
Standard rated purchases	112,890	(plus VAT)
Zero rated purchases	95,750	

You are required to calculate the output VAT due for the quarter ended 31 March 2010, assuming Jason operates retail Apportionment Scheme 1.

6.10   Alone Ltd, which makes standard rated supplies, has the following shareholdings:

100% in Bone Ltd
80% in Clone Ltd
50% in Drone Ltd

It makes the following supplies of goods during its quarter ended 30 September 2009:

Amount	To
£54,000	Bone Ltd
£112,000	Clone Ltd
£99,000	Drone Ltd
£78,000	Individuals

All figures are exclusive of VAT. A VAT group registration is in effect which includes all those companies which are eligible to be included.

You are required to:

(1)   State which companies are eligible to be in a group for VAT purposes.
(2)   Calculate the output VAT to be shown on Alone Ltd's return for the quarter ended 30 September 2009.

7.1   Conway Ltd sends taxable goods to Payne Ltd on a sale or return basis. The goods are dispatched on 1 July 2009 and Payne Ltd accepts them on 30 September 2009. A tax invoice is issued on 23 October 2009 which is settled by Payne Ltd on 15 November 2009.

You are required to outline the tax point for this transaction giving your reasons.

7.2   Kindlyco Ltd sells goods to Meanieco Ltd on 12 June 2009 (VAT accounting period ended 31 July 2009) and raises an invoice for the supply on that day. The amount of the invoice is £2,600 including VAT and must be paid within 30 days. By December 2009, despite chasing, the invoice has not been paid.

You are required to state:

(a)   two of the conditions for a VAT registered trader to claim bad debt relief

(b)   on what VAT return Kindlyco Ltd can claim VAT bad debt relief, how much it can claim and where this should be included on the VAT return.

7.3 Derek submitted his recent VAT returns and payments as follows:

Period ended	Date submitted	Payment due
31 March 2009	15 May 2009	£17,500
30 June 2009	21 July 2009	£18,000
30 September 2009	20 December 2009	£22,000

A surcharge liability notice was issued on 10 June 2009.

Derek submitted his VAT return for the period ended 31 December 2009, 3 months late with tax outstanding of £25,000.

You are required to:

(a) state what the consequences are for the return for the period ended 30 September 2009 being submitted late.

(b) state the consequences of the December 2009 return being submitted late.

7.4 Peter Popper has an annual turnover of around £300,000. His VAT return for the quarter to 31 December 2008 is late. He then submits returns for the quarters to 30 September 2009 and 31 March 2010 late as well as making late payment of the tax due of £12,000 and £500 respectively.

Peter's VAT return to 31 March 2011 is also late and the VAT due of £1,100 is also paid late. All other VAT returns and VAT payments are made on time.

You are required to outline Peter Popper's exposure to default surcharge.

7.5 Jack is a VAT registered plumber. He submits his VAT return to 30 June 2010 on time showing VAT due of £14,000. However Jack deliberately increased the input tax deduction on this return by £3,000 of false invoices for purchases of plumbing supplies. HMRC initiate a review into Jack's return which prompts Jack to make a disclosure of his wrong doing.

State the maximum and minimum penalties that could be charged by HMRC on Jack.

7.6 The managing director of Charlie Ltd, Stanley Laurel, has written to you about various VAT matters. He has received notification of a control visit from the local VAT office and a review of the company's affairs prior to the visit has brought to light certain transactions which Mr Laurel suspects have not been correctly treated for VAT purposes. The transactions which he has queried are:

(1) Catering provided in the staff restaurant, where employees can purchase a two-course lunch for £2. The company subsidises the restaurant at a cost of approximately £1 per meal. No VAT has been accounted for on the restaurant sales.

(2) Bottles of whisky given to customers at Christmas. The cost to the company was £12 per bottle, although the full retail price would be £16. Again no VAT has been accounted for on these gifts.

(3) The company offers cash discounts for prompt payment, varying from 1.5% to 3.5%. Mr Laurel has discovered that the person who prepares the invoices has been calculating output tax on the full value of each invoice and then issuing a credit note if a discount is taken up.

(4) The company has sold two cars, formerly used by directors. The first is a BMW, which cost £22,000 and was sold to a private buyer for £15,000. The second is a Lotus which cost £30,000 and was sold, again to a private buyer, for £37,000. Mr Laurel has assumed that there is no VAT to account for on these sales, since no input tax credit was available when they were purchased.

You are required to briefly discuss the matters Stanley Laurel has raised. You are not required to deal with the interest or penalty implications of any errors made by the company. Assume a standard VAT rate of 17.5% applied where applicable.

7.7 Anthony Brown, who is registered for VAT, made the following supplies in 2009 to Jessica Heath. Ms Heath then moved away from the town but before she left she sent a note saying that she was unable to pay Anthony's bill in full but could only afford £5,200 and enclosed a cheque for that sum. She did not allocate the payment to any supply. The supplies made to her were as follows:

Tax point (date order)	Type of supply	Net value £	VAT £	Gross consideration £
2 April 2009	zero-rated	2,000	zero	2,000
4 May 2009	standard-rated	1,000	150	1,150
30 May 2009	standard-rated	5,000	750	5,750
12 June 2009	zero-rated	2,000	zero	2,000

Anthony has heard on the grapevine that he may receive a future payment in respect of the outstanding amount from her accountant in the future. His normal terms of business allow 30 days from the invoice date for payment and he submits returns to 31 May and quarterly thereafter.

You are required to calculate the VAT refund due to Anthony Brown and outline how Anthony would treat any future payment received in respect of the bad debt written off.

7.8 Dilatory Ltd has an annual turnover of approximately £1.2 million. The following is a summary of the last three VAT returns submitted by Dilatory Ltd.

	£	£	£
Output tax due	89,383	67,621	120,567
Input tax	20,396	32,564	79,972
Net tax due	68,987	35,057	40,595
Date due	30 June 2009	30 September 2009	31 December 2009
Date submitted and tax paid	19 July 2009	25 October 2009	14 February 2010

You are required to set out your calculations of the maximum default surcharge to which Dilatory Ltd is liable.

7.9 Rob Moore has an annual turnover of £450,000. His VAT return for the quarter to 30 September 2009 is late. He is late in submitting his return for the quarter ended 30 June 2010 and is late paying the VAT of £20,500. He is also late paying the VAT for the quarter to 31 December 2010 of £400 although he submits his return on time.

Rob's VAT return for the quarter ended 31 December 2011 is also late and the VAT due of £1,900 is also paid late. All other VAT returns and VAT payments are made on time.

You are required to:

(1) State the date to which the original surcharge liability notice will run and the amount of any penalty due on that date.

(2) Calculate the penalties due on each relevant date thereafter and state the date to which the penalty period will extend.

7.10 Deborah Hall runs a pet food distribution business. During her VAT quarter ended 31 March 2010 she ran a 10% discount promotion and one of her regular customers placed an order for £15,000 of goods on 21 March 2010.

Deborah always offers a 5% early payment discount regardless of any promotions being run. To obtain the discount, payment must be received within 30 days.

The goods arrived in Deborah's warehouse on 29 March 2010 and they were delivered to the customer on 30 March 2010. Deborah raised an invoice for the whole amount on 10 April 2010, which the customer paid in full on 1 June 2010.

You are required to:

(1) State the tax point for this transaction.
(2) State the return in which any output VAT must be reported.
(3) Calculate the amount of VAT due in respect of the transaction.

8.1 **You are required to explain the stamp taxes implications of the following transactions:**

1. Pat sold 200 shares in Bridge Ltd to Tom for £800 on 1 June 2009. The transfer was effected using a stock transfer form.

2. Plum Ltd sold 10,000 shares in Jam Ltd to Damson plc, an unconnected company, for £450,252 on 1 July 2009.

3. Peach Ltd acquired a warehouse from Albert for £280,000 on 1 June 2009. The warehouse was not in a disadvantaged area.

8.2 Samson Ltd paid £170,000 for the grant of a 20 year lease of a factory on 1 July 2009. The net present value of the rental was £620,000 and the annual rent was £30,000. The factory was not in a disadvantaged area.

You are required to explain the stamp taxes implications of the above transaction and state the due date for filing the stamp taxes return.

8.3 Beach Ltd owns 80% of Sand Ltd and 75% of Pebble Ltd. Pebble Ltd owns 60% of Shingle Ltd.

On 1 June 2009 Beach Ltd sold a factory to Shingle Ltd for £100,000 and a warehouse to Sand Ltd for £300,000.

On 1 October 2010 Beach Ltd sold the shares in Sand Ltd to an unconnected company for £1,200,000. Sand Ltd still owned the warehouse at this date.

You are required to explain the stamp taxes implications of the transfer of the properties.

8.4 Lionel granted a 25 year lease on a commercial property to Bill on 17 April 2009.

Bill paid a premium of £86,000 on 17 April 2009. The net present value of the rent is £154,000. Bill will also pay rent of £1,250 per month.

You are required to:

(a) **Calculate the Stamp Duty Land Tax payable on the grant of the lease.**
(b) **State the payment date.**
(c) **State who it is payable by.**

Exam style answers

1.1 When the value of taxable supplies in any previous twelve months exceeds £68,000 he is required to notify HMRC within 30 days ie 30 July 2009 (30 days after the 12 months to 30 June 2009).

Registration no more than nine months late so 5% penalty (ie £45) but subject to minimum limit of £50.

Note that the failure to register occurs before 1 April 2010 and therefore the Finance Act 2009 penalties for failure to notify do not apply.

1.2 Notification by 30 January 2010, ie 30 days after the start of a 30 day period (ie January 2010) in which turnover is anticipated to exceed £68,000. But registration will be effective from 1 January 2010.

If Big Ltd decides to terminate the business it must notify HMRC within 30 days.

Another occasion when Big Ltd would be required to notify HMRC of a need to deregister is when taxable supplies cease.

1.3 On first sale:

£147 (£840 × 17.5% = £147)

VAT based on fully discounted price (even if settlement discount not actually taken by the customer).

On the second sale VAT is due as follows:

£600 × 95% = 570   cost after trade discount
£570 × 97.5% = £556   after settlement discount
£556 × 17.5% = £97

All possible discounts are taken into account when calculating the VAT payable irrespective of when the customer actually pays.

1.4 All turnover zero-rated

Zero-rated supplies are taxable supplies and therefore taken into account in determining liability to registered. The first point at which past annual turnover exceeds the registration limit (then £68,000) is at the end of December 2009 (£68,440).

He must therefore notify HMRC of his liability by 30 January 2010 and is registered with effect from 1 February 2010.

Again the future 30 day turnover limit of £68,000 is not exceeded at any time in the period.

However, as Richard's turnover will be wholly zero-rated he may apply to HMRC to be exempted from the requirement to register (VATA 1994 Sch 1 para 14). His application should accompany the notice of liability to register (form VAT 1). If HMRC think fit, they will exempt him from registration.

It is however likely that being VAT registered will allow a significant reclaim of input VAT which will outweigh the administrative burden of registration.

1.5 Under the historic test cumulative taxable turnover at the end of August 2009 is £56,000 and at the end of September 2009 is £80,000.

Thus the registration limit is first exceeded at the end of September 2009.

HMRC must be notified of this within 30 days, so by 30 October 2009.

The business will be registered for VAT from 1 November 2009.

Although under the future test supplies of £100,000 in December alone would force the business to VAT register, an earlier registration date applies under the historic test – thus HMRC will use the earlier date.

1.6 Mr Cassell exceeds the VAT threshold of £68,000 in June. He must notify HMRC by 30 July 2009 and will be registered from 1 August 2009.

If he does not notify HMRC until 1 November 2009 he will have been no more than 9 months later so his penalty will be the higher of £50 and 5% × the net VAT due since the date he should have been registered, ie 5% × £6,385 (W) = £319

Working – net VAT due

	£
August 2009	18,900
September 2009	19,600
October 2009	19,450
Total	57,950
VAT @ 3/23	7,559
less: input VAT: £3,000 × 3 × 3/23	(1,174)
Net VAT due	6,385

2.1 A mixed supply is where there are individual elements within the supply that are treated separately for VAT. An example of this would be where a student enrols on a BPP revision course and has to purchase some books as part of the course. A course is standard rated and books are zero-rated. They are effectively treated as separate supplies, even though the student might purchase them together. The individual elements are treated separately for VAT. With a mixed supply, there is the need to perform some sort of apportionment to apportion the individual elements of the supply in order to calculate the VAT due.

A compound supply is just a single supply although it might be made up of several different things. A compound supply is a single supply with a single VAT liability. An example of this is a plane ticket. The traveller will also probably be provided with a meal on the flight. Air transport is zero-rated and catering is standard rated. However the traveller is buying a complete package and it is difficult to separate the two elements plus the meal is just a small insignificant piece of the overall larger flight. In such a case, this compound supply would just be treated as a single zero-rated supply of a flight ticket. With a compound supply only a single rate of VAT applies to the whole supply.

2.2 (a) Zero-rated supplies are taxable at 0%. A trader who sells taxable supplies, whether at the zero or standard rate, may reclaim VAT paid on related purchases.

Exempt supplies are not chargeable to VAT. A person making exempt supplies is unable to recover VAT on related purchases.

(b) VAT supply

(i) Standard-rated (supply is of hot food and must be standard-rated regardless of whether a charge is made for the use of the oven)

(ii) Standard-rated (excepted Item Group 1, Schedule 8, VAT Act 1994)

(iii) Zero-rated (Item 4, Group 8, Schedule 8, VAT Act 1994)

(iv) Zero-rated (Notice 744A)

2.3 The reduced rate of VAT, of 5%, is charged under VATA 1994 s.29A on any supplies falling within Sch 7A of that Act. Sch 7A Group 1 covers a wide range of fuel supplies, including, inter alia, electricity, gas, oil and coal. To obtain the reduced rate, Stimpson Group plc must be able to demonstrate that the fuel is supplied for 'qualifying use' (Group 1 Item 1) – as it is a commercial undertaking, this has to be for 'domestic use' (Note 3). In turn, as the premises in question are commercial, they must be 'used for a relevant residential purpose' (note 6).

'Relevant residential purpose' is defined in note 7 to include seven categories of premises; in addition there is an exclusion where the use is as a hospital, a prison or similar institution or an hotel or inn or similar establishment. Unfortunately the term 'residential accommodation' (note 7(1)) is not defined. The key issue to determine is whether or not the trading premises it runs come within any of the categories, and, if so, the impact of the exclusion.

Considering the nursing homes run by Stimpson Group plc these appear to fall clearly within note 7(1)(b), 'being a home… providing residential accommodation with personal care for persons in need of personal care by reason of old age, disablement ...'. Consequently the reduced rate of VAT should apply to all supplies of fuel made to the homes.

2.4 Value for the quarter:

	£
Car 1	
£289 × 1/3	96
Car 2	
£365 × 2/3	243
	339

Output tax: 7/47 × £339 = £50

Input tax: 7/47 × £300 = £45

2.5 (a) Biscuits sold in a fancy tin are a compound supply. This would be a single zero rated supply.

(b) The subscription to satellite TV with a monthly magazine was held in the *British Sky Broadcasting Ltd* case to be a compound supply with the supply of the zero rated magazine being only incidental to the main standard rated supply.

(c) An airline ticket is a compound supply – it is a zero rated supply of transport with an incidental (hence ignored) standard rated supply of catering.

2.6 (a) Postal services provided by the Post Office are exempt under Group 3 Schedule 9 VATA 1994.

(b) Children's car seats are charged to VAT at the reduced rate of 5% under Group 5 Schedule 7A VATA 1994.

(c) Services provided by registered medical practitioners such as Dentists are exempt under Group 7 Schedule 9 VATA 1994.

(d) Although food is normally zero rated under Group 1 Schedule 8 VATA 1994 sweets are specifically excluded from zero rating, so this supply will be a standard rated supply.

(e) Newspapers are zero rated for VAT under Group 3 Schedule 8 VATA 1994.

3.1 Regarding the pre-registration input tax Ben may recover £770 (all of it)

Stock – if unsold on registration date
Fixed assets – if within four years and still held and used in business
Services – if within six months prior to registration

When looking at the purchase of motor vehicles Ben may recover (1,575 + 3,938) = £5,513

VAT on cars with private use is not reclaimable. VAT on vans and lorries can be reclaimed

3.2 Taxable supplies = $235,000 \times \frac{100}{117.5} + 50,000 = £250,000$

Total supplies = 325,000
Share of unattributed input tax £
$\frac{250,000}{325,000} \times 100 = 77\%$ (rounded) × 73,000   56,210
Attributed to taxable supplies   60,000
     116,210

The input tax attributable to exempt supplies is not *de minimis*.

3.3 (1) Previous years' recovery percentage used

	£
Non attributable input VAT attributed to making taxable supplies	
79% × 4,000	3,160
Input VAT specifically attributable to making taxable supplies	12,500
Total input VAT reclaimed for the quarter	15,660

The VAT attributable to making exempt supplies (1,500 + 840), exceeds the de-minimis of £625 a month or £1,875 a quarter.

(2) Previous years' recovery percentage not used

	£
Non attributable input VAT attributed to making taxable supplies	
$\frac{160,000}{200,000}$ (80% × 4,000)	3,200
Input VAT specifically attributable to making taxable supplies	12,500
Total input VAT reclaimed for the quarter	15,700

The VAT attributable to making exempt supplies (1,500 + 800), exceeds the de-minimis of £625 a month or £1,875 a quarter.

3.4 Total taxable supplies: £40,000 + £20,000 = £60,000

Partial recovery fraction: $\frac{60,000}{60,000 + 23,000}$ = 72.289 rounded up to 73%

Input tax – taxable supplies

	£
Direct	27,000
Apportioned (45,000 – 27,000 – 9,000) × 73%	6,570
Total	33,570

Exempt VAT

	£
Direct	9,000
Apportioned (9,000 – 6,570)	2,430
Total	11,430

Exempt input VAT greater than £625 per month therefore irrecoverable.

3.5 Amount of deductible input tax:

	£
re supplies for contract to be fulfilled in first quarter of 2010	15,200
re overheads in factory	3,300
re employee entertainment	850
	19,350

3.6 Recoverable input tax

	£
Input tax attributed to taxable supplies	20,000
Unallocated input tax attributed to taxable supplies (£5,000 × 84 %) (W)	4,200
	24,200

Potentially not recoverable

	£
Input tax attributed to exempt supplies	10,000
Balance of unallocated £(5,000 – 4,200)`	800
	10,800

This amount of exempt input tax will be recoverable if it is small, ie, < £625 per month on average or £625 × 12 = £7,500 per annum. As the amount (£10,800) exceeds the de minimis limits it will not be recoverable. Thus, only £24,200 of input tax is recoverable.

Working

% of taxable to total supplies $\frac{21,500 + 80,200}{122,000} = 83.36\%$

Round up to next whole % = 84%

3.7 (a) The input tax incurred on the purchase of the computer was £17,500 (£26,250 – £8,750), giving the computer itself a VAT exclusive value of £100,000. The computer is therefore a capital item for the purposes of the Capital Goods Scheme as its value is £50,000 or more.

The Capital Goods Scheme (CGS) does not apply to the purchase of software.

(b) The computer was purchased on 19 May 2008 (which falls within the tax year ending 31 March 2009) which means the first interval for CGS purposes run from 19 May 2008 to 31 March 2009.

Input tax is recoverable in the first interval using the 2009 recovery rate of 70%. The calculation is therefore:

£17,500 × 70% = £12,250

Input tax incurred on the purchase of a computer within the capital goods scheme may be adjusted over five successive intervals. As there is a change in the level of partial exemption recovery, an adjustment is required in the second interval adjustment (ie year ended 31 March 2010) as follows:

$\frac{£17,500}{5} \times (70\% - 85\%) = £525$

The adjustment, ie additional input tax claim, should have been included on the VAT return for the second period after the end of the tax year ie in this case the period ended 30 September 2010.

3.8 For the first VAT year to 31 March 2009 the recovery (after the annual partial exemption adjustment) is £100,000 × 15% = £15,000 × 60% = £9,000.

For the second VAT year to 31 March 2010 the adjustment is £15,000 × 10% (ie 60%-50%) × 1/5 = £300, payable to HMRC.

For the third VAT year to 31 March 2011 there are two adjustments:

(a) £15,000 × 10% × 1/5 = £300, payable to HMRC.

(b) £15,000 × 40% (ie 100%-60%) × 2/5 = £2,400, restricted to the VAT charged on the sale of the computer ie £6,000 × 17.5% = £1,050, recoverable from HMRC.

The net adjustment for the third VAT year to 31 March 2011 is (£(300) + £1,050) = £750 recoverable from HMRC.

3.9 The partial exemption rules apply.

	£
Wholly attributable to taxable supplies	1,895
Partly attributable to taxable supplies	
$\frac{325,000}{325,000 + 86,000}$ = 79.08% rounded up to 80% × £1,545	1,236
Total	3,131
Add: exempt input VAT: £(420 + (1,545 – 1,236))	729
Total recoverable input VAT	3,860

ie all input VAT is recoverable (W)

Working – exempt input VAT

De minimis test:

Monthly average: $\dfrac{729}{3}$ = £243 ie not more than £625

Proportion of total $\dfrac{729}{3,860}$ = 18.9% ie not more than 50%

Therefore all the exempt input VAT can be recovered.

3.10 Computers costing at least £50,000 are inside the capital goods scheme and are dealt with over a 5 year period.

For the first VAT year to 31 March 2010, the recovery (after the annual partial exemption adjustment) is:

£75,000 × 15% = £11,250 × 68% = £7,650

For the second VAT year to 31 March 2011, the adjustment is:

£11,250 × (49% - 68%) × 1/5 = £427 payable to HMRC.

For the third VAT year to 31 March 2012 there are two adjustments:

(i)   £11,250 × (45% - 68%) × 1/5 = £517, payable to HMRC
(ii) £11,250 × (100% - 68%) × 2/5 = £1,440 recoverable from HMRC.

Note: The £1,440 is restricted to the VAT actually charged on the sale of the server, ie £19,000 × 17.5% = £3,325.

The net adjustment for the third VAT year to 31 March 2012 is:

£((517) + 1,440) = £923 recoverable from HMRC

3.11 Input VAT incurred on client (but not staff) entertaining is always disallowed as is expenditure on accommodation for directors. Input VAT on cars is also blocked, but the input VAT on the servicing costs can be reclaimed in full.

	£	£
Output VAT: £247,000 × 15%		37,050
Less: reclaimable input VAT		
Other expenses: £35,600 × 3/23	4,643	
Client entertaining	-	
Staff entertaining £2,258 × 3/23	295	
Renovation work on property occupied by director	-	
Car with 80% business use		
Cost of the car	-	
Servicing costs £3,021 × 3/23	394	
		(5,332)
Net VAT due		31,718

4.1 (a) Peter will be allowed to zero rate his services provided to BIG Homes Ltd as they are constructing new residential properties and Peter is a sub-contractor working on those properties. [Schedule 8 Group 5 VATA 1994]

(b) Services of lawyers are standard rated despite the overall project being zero rated. The lawyers' services do not fall with Schedule 8 Group 5 VATA 1994.

(c) The building is 'old' so the supply is exempt from VAT although Juniper Ltd may make an option to tax over the building and standard rate this supply. [Schedule 9 Group 1 and Schedule 10 VATA 1994]

4.2 VAT supply

(a) Reduced rate applies (item 1, Group 6, Schedule 7A, VAT Act 1994. Supply in the course of conversion not eligible for zero-rating under item 2, Group 5, Schedule 8, VAT Act 1994)

(b) Reduced rate applies (item 1, Group 2, Schedule 7A, VAT Act 1994)

(c) Exempt (item 1, Group 1, Schedule 9, VAT Act 1994)

(d) Zero-rated (item 1(a), Group 5, Schedule 8, VAT Act 1994)

(e) Standard-rated.

In general the supply would be exempt (Group 1 Schedule 9 VATA 1994) but the option to tax has been made (Schedule 10 VATA 1994) so that the supply becomes taxable at the standard rate.

4.3 If Tim opts to tax (under Sch 10 VATA 1994) the development at the outset, the VAT incurred by him will be recoverable in full as the project progresses. The net cost to him would therefore be £9.8 million. However, on letting the property he must charge VAT on any premium and rent received. Tim should be aware that this course of action might be unattractive to a potential tenant who is partially or completely exempt. He should also be aware that he will have to charge VAT on any future disposal of the building.

If Tim decides not to opt to tax the development and instead grants exempt leases, the VAT of £1.365 million charged on the supply will not be recoverable by Tim as it is directly attributable to the exempt supply of the lease on the building. Therefore the total cost of the development to Tim becomes £11.165 million.

Tim may be able to obtain a higher premium or rent for an exempt lease. However, whether this would be sufficient to give him the same yield from the increased capital cost of development, as he would achieve from a taxed building, is questionable. Therefore opting to tax may be the preferred route.

4.4 Since Mr Heart is leasing out a commercial property he is making an exempt supply of the office block.

The building needs renovation, costing £750,000. Renovating and building services are standard rated supplies so VAT will be charged on this supply to Mr Heart.

Because Mr Heart leases out the building and hence makes an exempt supply the £111,702 of input tax incurred on the renovation will relate to making an exempt supply of that office block and hence will be irrecoverable.

Mr Heart should consider making an option to tax over the property. If Mr Heart opts to tax the building he will make a taxable supply of that office building from the date of the option onwards. Thus, when the renovation occurs the £111,702 of input tax paid will relate to making a taxable supply of the building and hence will be recoverable in full.

Once the option to tax is made all future invoices for rent sent to the tenants must include VAT at 17.5%.

4.5 (a) The sale of land is an exempt supply and the option to tax can be made on this supply.

(b) The sale of a 30 year old house is an exempt supply. A house is a building in domestic rather than commercial use and so the option to tax cannot be made.

(c) The lease of a one year old factory is an exempt supply because although it is a new commercial property, the supply is of a lease rather than the freehold. Because the building is commercial the option to tax can be made.

(d) The freehold sale of a one year old office block being freehold, commercial and new is a standard rated supply. Since the supply is not exempt the option to tax does not apply here.

(e) A 99 year lease on a newly refurbished showroom is an exempt supply. The option to tax can be made over such a supply.

4.6 (1) Girth Ltd must notify HMRC that it has 'made' an option to tax by 30 August 2009.
(2) The cooling off period ends on 31 January 2010.
(3) The option to tax can only be revoked from 1 August 2029.
(4) Girth Ltd can make a 'Real Estate Election' (REE) to include all of its properties within the option to tax.

The option to tax must be notified within 30 days of being 'made'.

The company has a 6 month cooling off period.

After the cooling off period ends, the option to tax can only be revoked after 20 years.

5.1 Zero-rated export to Canadian customers – export evidence to be obtained and retained.

Zero-rated dispatch to VAT registered customer in Italy, provided customer's Italian VAT registration number is obtained and shown on the invoice and export evidence is obtained.

Standard-rated sale to non-registered customer.

Provided Jane gives the supplier her UK VAT registration number she will not be charged Portuguese VAT by the supplier. Instead, she will be required to account for output tax in her next VAT return and reclaim the same amount as input tax on the same return.

5.2 (a) *Place of supply of goods*

If the supply of any goods does not involve their removal from or to the UK they are treated as being supplied in the UK if they are in the UK at the time of the supply. If they are not in the UK at the time of the supply they are treated as being supplied outside the UK and the supply is therefore outside the scope of VAT.

Where the supply of any goods involves their removal from the UK, as, for instance, where they are exported, they are treated as being supplied in the UK.

If the supply involves the removal of goods to the UK, as where goods are imported, the place of supply is deemed to be outside the UK. However, the goods are subject to VAT on importation.

(b) *Place of supply for ABC Ltd*

The place of the supplies made by ABC Ltd is as follows:

(i) the furniture was supplied outside the UK because it was outside the UK when allocated to the supply;

(ii) the table was supplied in the UK because it was in the UK when allocated to the supply; and

(iii) the armchair was supplied in the UK because it was only allocated to the supply in the UK, ie once the stock had arrived from China.

5.3
1   Sale of lamb to France – dispatch
2   Purchase of lamb from New Zealand – import
3   Purchase of books from Brazil – import
4   Sale of children's clothes to Germany – dispatch
5   Sale of chocolate to Italy – dispatch
6   Purchase of wine from Australia – import
7   Purchase of wine from Germany – acquisition
8   Sale of bird houses to USA – export
9   Purchase of green beans from Kenya – import
10 Sale of bacon to Portugal – dispatch

5.4 Alladyce Services Ltd is a UK based company receiving services from management consultants based in Jersey, which is not in the UK and hence the UK company is receiving an international service. As the supply takes place after 1 January 2010 and the supply is between two businesses the place of supply is deemed to be where the customer (Alladyce Services Ltd) belongs i.e. the UK.

This means that Alladyce Services Ltd will have to apply the reverse charge procedure. The company will therefore account for output tax of £17,500, which is calculated as the £100,000 for the service at the standard rate of VAT. It will also account for input tax of £17,500. The normal input tax recovery rules apply to this input tax. So on the VAT return this will be output VAT of £17,500 and input VAT of £17,500, assuming that the input tax can be recovered in full by Alladyce Services Limited.

5.5 Exports are where a trader sells goods to a customer based in a country outside the UK but not in the European Union. An export is a zero-rated supply irrespective of what type of goods are being sold overseas. Exports of goods are always a zero-rated supply.

To apply zero rating to an export a trader must obtain the necessary evidence that the goods sold have been exported within three months of the time of the supply.

A dispatch is where a trader sells goods to a customer in the European Union. How the trader treats the dispatch depends on the status of his European customer. If the European customer is VAT registered in this EU member state and he gives the UK trader his VAT registration number, then the UK trader will zero-rate the supply of goods to his business customer.

If, however, the customer is not VAT registered in his EU member state, then the UK trader treats him in the same way as a UK customer and charges him UK VAT at the rate that would be appropriate to the goods being sold. Thus for example, if a trader is selling DVD players he would charge standard rate VAT. If he was selling wheat he would charge 0% VAT because food is zero-rated.

5.6 *Sale of goods from Canada to the USA*

The goods are located outside the UK so the place of supply is Canada, ie outside the UK. The supply is therefore outside the scope of UK VAT.

Sale of goods from Milton Keynes to Mexico

The goods are located inside the UK so the place of supply is the UK. The supply is therefore liable to UK VAT but it is an export so is zero rated.

6.1 The transfer of business assets is not treated as a taxable supply (it is treated as outside the scope of VAT) and no VAT is charged if the following conditions are met:

- The assets must be used by the transferee in carrying on the same kind of business as carried on by the transferor.
- Where the transferor is a taxable person, the transferee must be a taxable person or become one when the transaction takes place.
- If part of a business is transferred that part must be capable of separate operation.
- There should be no significant break in the normal trading pattern before or immediately after the transfer.

6.2 (1) The optional flat rate scheme is a simplification measure which enables businesses to calculate the net VAT due simply by applying a flat rate percentage to their tax-inclusive turnover ie the total turnover generated, including all reduced, zero-rated and exempt income.

The flat rate percentage will depend upon the trade sector into which a business falls for the purposes of the scheme. In the tax year to 31 December 2009 the percentages ranged from 2% for retailing food, confectionery, tobacco, newspapers or children's clothing to 11.5% for labour-only building construction services. The flat rate percentage for accountancy and book-keeping was 11.5% and for financial services was 10.5%.

Businesses using the scheme still need to issue VAT invoices to their VAT registered customers but do not have to record all the details of the invoices issued or purchase invoices received to calculate the VAT due. Invoices issued will show VAT at the normal rate rather than the flat rate.

(2) Gross sales:

		£
Business customers		
£55,000 × 115/100		63,250
Individuals		
£28,000 × 115/100		32,200
		95,450

VAT payable:

Flat rate 9.5% applies

9.5% × £95,450 = £9,068

6.3 (a) 16 May 2009

Date deposit is paid (as this is earlier than the dispatch date)

(b) 31 May 2009

Dispatch date (for the invoice date to apply it must have been issued within 14 days of the date of dispatch)

6.4 Farmer Bard (FB) made zero-rated sales of potatoes of £70,000. FB also made some purchases. The seed potatoes and manure will not have had the addition of VAT to their price but the tractor will have cost £40,000 plus £6,000 of VAT. His position over the whole year will thus have been a VAT recovery of £6,000.

If he joins the flat-rate scheme (FRS), he will not be able to recover the £6,000 of VAT on the tractor but will now charge 4% on the £65,000 of sales to his VAT registered customers (the supermarkets) totalling £2,600. No flat-rate is charged to the presumably non-VAT registered stall customers.

Comparing the two, the FRS has no VAT administration but only £2,600 is recovered, whereas when VAT registered £6,000 was recovered. However if FB is not planning any large asset purchases (and hence large input tax bills) in the next few years then the FRS will give him a better result in the future.

6.5 As business client work amounts to £52,000 Julip Cleaners will issue VAT invoices totalling £59,800 (£52,000 plus 15% VAT).

Individual work totals £72,000 (inclusive of VAT).

The total gross sales are £131,800.

VAT due to HMRC under the scheme will therefore amount to £12,521 (£131,800 × 9.5%).

VAT invoices are issued to customers in the normal way showing 15% VAT.

No input tax is recovered from purchases under the scheme unless a purchase costs over £2,000 (VAT inclusive).

6.6 (a) The companies eligible to form a VAT group are:

Red plc
Yellow Ltd
Green Ltd
Pink Ltd

Since Red plc controls all the companies the 'common control' definition is satisfied. However, a group can only consist of UK established companies so Blue Inc cannot be part of the VAT group.

Yellow Ltd may be included in the VAT group even if it makes exempt supplies. It may however impact the group as including it would make the group partially exempt.

(b) (i) The group is treated as a single taxable person for VAT with one company (the representative member) responsible for all VAT accounting.

(ii) All the members of the group are jointly and severally liable for the VAT liability of the whole group.

6.7 (a) The second hand goods scheme involves calculating a profit (known as the margin) made on each item that is bought or sold. The margin is effectively the difference between the price paid and the sale proceeds. Under the Scheme, the profit margin is VAT inclusive so, when multiplied by 7 over 47, gives the output VAT due on the individual sale. If the sale is made at a loss, in other words there is no profit margin, then there is no VAT due.

If the trader has incurred any costs, for example, repairing or improving the item before it is sold, these costs are not taken into account when calculating the profit margin. However, once all the output tax is calculated, any VAT incurred, for example on these costs, is treated as input tax and can be deducted from the output tax in the normal way.

A normal VAT invoice is not issued for sales under the Scheme. Thus any purchasers cannot reclaim any of the VAT charged. If a purchaser wants a VAT invoice and wants to recover any VAT charged, then the item must be accounted for outside of the scheme in the normal way.

(b) Margin

£(12,500 − 8,000) = £4,500

£4,500 × 7/47 = £670

Return to August 2010

Output tax = £670

Input tax

£550 × 17.5% = £96

The above entries would be made in respect of the Porsche on the VAT return to 31 August 2010.

6.8 Stan's VAT liability, using the normal VAT rules, is:

	£
Output VAT: £(78,000 + 32,500) × 15%	16,575
Less: input VAT: £11,745 × 3/23	(1,532)
Net VAT due	15,043

If he were to use the flat rate scheme, he would apply the flat rate percentage to his gross turnover (ie inclusive of VAT) and ignoring input VAT:

	£
£(78,000 + 32,500) × 115%	127,075
@ 11.5%	14,614

6.9 Apportionment scheme 1 is available to traders with VAT-exclusive annual sales of up to £1 million.

The estimated gross takings are split between the different types of turnover based on the types of expenditure incurred.

The fraction used is based on the VAT-inclusive standard rated purchases over the total purchases:

$$\frac{112{,}890 + 19{,}756 \text{ (VAT)}}{112{,}890 + 19{,}756 + 95{,}750} = \frac{132{,}646}{228{,}396} = 0.5807719$$

Standard rated supplies: £690,000 × 0.5807719 = £400,733

Output VAT is therefore: £400,733 × 7/47 = £59,684 due to HMRC

6.10　Companies can join a VAT group where there is common control, ie over 50%, so Alone Ltd, Bone Ltd and Clone Ltd are all eligible to be in the VAT group.

The output VAT due is:

	£
Output VAT (£99,000 + £78,000) @ 15%	26,550

7.1　30 September 2009.

The earlier of:

(a) Acceptance date
(b) Invoice date
(c) Cash received
(d) 12 months after dispatch

7.2　(a)　Two of the following:

(i) He must have supplied goods or services and accounted for and paid VAT on the supply.

(ii) All or part of the consideration must have been written off in the accounts.

(iii) Six months must have elapsed from the later of the date of supply and the time when the consideration became due and payable.

(b) VAT bad debt relief can be claimed on the VAT return for the period ended 31 January 2010 (payment outstanding for six months)

The amount of the claim will be 3/23 of £2,600 which equals £339

This sum should be added to the input tax figure claimed for the period (included in box 4 on the VAT return)

7.3　(a)　The surcharge liability notice (SLN) will be extended to the period ended 30 September 2010. Derek will be liable to a surcharge of £440 (£22,000 × 2%)

(b) The SLN will be extended to the period 31 December 2010 and a penalty of £1,250 (5% × £25,000) will be levied.

7.4　A surcharge liability notice will be issued after the late filing on the 31 December 2008 return outlining a surcharge period extending to 31 December 2009.

The late 30 September 2009 return is in the surcharge period so the period is extended to 30 September 2010. The late VAT payment triggers a 2% penalty. 2% × £12,000 = £240. Since £240 is less than the £400 de minimis limit it is not collected by HMRC.

The late 31 March 2010 return is in the surcharge period so the period is now extended to 31 March 2011. The late payment triggers a 5% penalty. 5% × £500 = £25. Since £25 is less than the £400 de minimis limit it is not collected by HMRC.

The late 31 March 2011 return is in the surcharge period. The period is extended to 31 March 2012. The late payment triggers a 10% penalty. 10% × £1,100 = £110. This is collected by HMRC since the £400 de minimis does not apply to penalties calculated at the 10% (and 15%) rate.

Peter will have to submit all four quarterly VAT returns to 31 March 2012 on time and pay the VAT on time to 'escape' the default surcharge regime.

7.5
The potential lost revenue as a result of Jack's error is;	£3,000
Jack's error was deliberate and concealed so the maximum penalty is £3,000 × 100% =	£3,000
However, Jack made a prompted disclosure so the minimum penalty is £3,000 × 50%	= £1,500

7.6 (1) Catering

The company should have accounted for output tax on the provision of catering to staff. The amount paid by the employee is treated as the VAT-inclusive value of the supply. Hence where the cost to the employee is £2, the amount of output tax due is 30p (£2 × 7/47).

(2) Gifts

Gifts of goods are generally deemed to be supplies on which output tax must be paid. There is however an exception, which applies to the present case, for small gifts which are made in the course or furtherance of business. A gift is small if the total cost of gifts given to the same person in a twelve month period is less than £50.

It seems likely that there will be no requirement for the company to account for tax on these gifts.

(3) Cash discounts

The current treatment is incorrect. Output tax should be accounted for on the amount due from the customer net of the maximum possible cash discount (provided that this is shown on the invoice), regardless of whether that discount is taken up.

(4) Sale of cars

Your assumption about the car sales is correct. For many years, sales of cars at above cost were thought to give rise to a VAT charge. However, a European Court ruling confirmed that no VAT should be charged on sales if no VAT was recovered on purchase. The sales are exempt from VAT. Thus no VAT is due on either the loss making sale or the profit making sale. Any input tax incurred in making the sales will be irrecoverable, subject to the de minimis rules.

7.7 Refund of VAT due to Anthony Brown

Tax point (date order)	Type of supply	Net value £	VAT £	Gross consideration £
2 April 2009	zero-rated	2,000	zero	2,000
4 May 2009	standard-rated	1,000	150	1,150
30 May 2009	standard-rated	5,000	750	5,750
12 June 2009	zero-rated	2,000	zero	2,000
		10,000	900	10,900

payment on account = £5,200

To calculate bad debt relief, the payment is allocated to the supplies on a 'first-in, first-out' basis. Thus, later debts are treated as bad rather than earlier ones. The bad debt of £5,700 (being £10,900 less £5,200) and the refund is identified as follows:

Tax point	Bad debt (gross consideration) £	VAT bad debt refund £
12 June 2009	2,000	zero
30 May 2009	3,700	483
	5,700	

The refund of VAT due under the bad debt relief legislation for Mr Brown is £483. This claim may be made once six months after the due date for payment of the debt has lapsed, ie in the return for the period to 28 February 2010.

Any bad debt refund must be repaid to HMRC to the extent of the VAT element of any full or part payment subsequently received (Value Added Tax Regulations 1995 (SI 1995/2518), reg. 171(1)). The claimant must include the VAT element on the VAT return for the period in which he received the payment. It is included in the box opposite the legend 'VAT due in this period on sales and other outputs'. A part payment would be treated as a part of £3,700 on which the VAT is £483, unless the debtor allocated the payment specifically to the zero-rated invoice which has not yet been included in any claim.

7.8   Computation of default surcharge

Quarterly Return to 31 May 2009:

No surcharge, but surcharge liability notice issued

Quarterly Return to 31 August 2009:

Default surcharge liability 2% × £35,057 = £701

Quarterly Return to 30 November 2009:

Default surcharge liability 5% × £40,595 = £2,030

7.9   If a business is late in submitting its return and/ or paying its VAT the surcharge liability notice (SLN) rules apply.

When Rob is late submitting his return for the quarter to 30 September 2009, the surcharge liability notice period will initially run to 30 September 2010. As the VAT is not paid late, no penalty is due.

As Rob is then late submitting his return and paying the tax for the quarter to 30 June 2010, which is within the SLN period, the period extends to 30 June 2011 and he will pay a penalty of £20,500 × 2% = £410.

The return for the quarter to 31 December 2010 is on time but the payment is late, so the SLN period is extended to 31 December 2011 and the penalty is now 5% × £400 = £20, which is below the de minimis limit of £400 so it is not collected by HMRC.

Rob's return for the quarter ended 31 December 2011 is late and the tax is paid late too. The SLN period is extended to 31 December 2012 and the penalty of 10% × £1,900 = £190 is due (the £400 limit does not apply to the 10% (or 15%) penalties).

Rob must submit four returns on time and pay the VAT on time before the SLN period can end.

7.10 The basic tax point for VAT purposes is the delivery date of the goods (ie when they are made available to the customer), ie 30 March 2010. However, as the invoice was raised within 14 days of this basic tax point, the invoice date, ie 10 April 2010, becomes the tax point. This amount will be reported on the June 2010 VAT return.

The VAT due is based on the discounted figure, even where the discount is not given:

	£
Value	15,000
Less: 10%	(1,500)
	13,500
Less: 5%	(675)
	12,825
Output VAT @ 17.5%	2,244

8.1   The stamp taxes implications are:

1. No stamp duty is payable as the transaction was after 13 March 2008 and the consideration was less than £1,000. There will be no stamp duty reserve tax charge if the stock transfer form is presented as being exempt from stamp duty.

2. Stamp duty reserve tax (SDRT) of 0.5% x £450,252 (£2,251) is payable by Damson plc. If the transfer of shares was effected using a stock transfer stamp duty of 0.5% x £450,252 rounded to the nearest £5 (£2,255) is payable. The SDRT liability will be cancelled when Damson plc provides a stamped stock transfer form provided this is within six years of the transfer.

3. Stamp duty land tax (SDLT) of £8,400 (£280,000 x 3%) is payable by Peach Ltd.

8.2   Stamp duty land tax (SDLT) is payable by Samson Ltd as follows:

Premium: £170,000 x 1% = £1,700 – The zero rate is not available as the annual rent exceeds £1,000 and the property is non-residential.

NPV of rents: (£620,000 - £150,000) x 1% = £4,700.

The SDLT return must be filed by 31 July 2009 i.e. within 30 days of the transaction.

8.3 Beach Ltd, Sand Ltd and Pebble Ltd form a group for stamp duty land tax purposes, as Sand Ltd and Pebble Ltd are 75% subsidiaries of Beach Ltd.

The sale of the warehouse to Sand Ltd therefore falls within the SDLT group relief exemption. However group relief will be withdrawn when Sand Ltd leaves the Beach Ltd group on 1 October 2010 still owning the land as Sand Ltd has left the group within three years of the transfer.

SDLT of £300,000 × 3% = £9,000 will therefore be payable.

Shingle Ltd is not part of the Beach Ltd SDLT group. SDLT is therefore payable on the sale of the factory. However no SDLT arises as the consideration of £100,000 falls within the zero rate band.

8.4 As the rent exceeds £1,000 and the land is non-residential property, the zero rate charge cannot apply.

The SDLT on the lease is:

	£
On premium: £86,000 × 1% (see above)	860
On rent: £(154,000 – 150,000) × 1%	40
Total	900

The due date is 30 days from completion, ie no later than 17 May 2009.

Bill must pay the SDLT.

Awareness Paper
Sample paper

You must tick in the boxes below which THREE Modules you have answered.

A ☐   B ☐   C ☐   D ☐   E ☐

The Chartered Tax Adviser Examination

Sample Paper

AWARENESS

TIME ALLOWED – 3 HOURS

- You should answer **THREE** out of the five following modules:

    Module A – VAT including Stamp Taxes
    Module B – Inheritance Tax, Trusts & Estates
    Module C – Corporation Tax
    Module D – Taxation of Individuals
    Module E – Taxation of Unincorporated Businesses

- Each module consists of 12 questions and each question carries 5 marks.

- You must answer all the questions from the modules you choose.

- You should answer questions in brief bullet points and/or summary computations where appropriate.

- You must answer questions in the spaces provided.

- You may not need all the space provided.

- You should make all calculations to the nearest month and pound unless stated otherwise.

NB In the actual examination candidates will be required to answer in the space under each question. There are no spaces shown in this sample paper.

You must tick the box below if you have answered this Module.

The Chartered Tax Adviser Examination

Sample Paper

AWARENESS

MODULE A – VAT INCLUDING STAMP TAXES

- Each question carries 5 marks.

- You must answer all the questions from the modules you choose.

- You should answer questions in brief bullet points and/or summary computations where appropriate.

- You must answer questions in the spaces provided.

- You may not need all the space provided.

- You should make all calculations to the nearest month and pound unless stated otherwise.

1   Alpha Developments owns a number of properties which it leases to tenants. The company purchased a mainframe computer for £140,000 plus VAT on 29 June 2007, and used this for its general business purposes.

Under Alpha Developments' partial exemption method, the level of taxable use has been determined as follows.

Year to 31 March	Rate
2007	80%
2008	70%
2009	85%
2010	75%

The computer was sold on 7 August 2009 for £47,000 inclusive of £6,130 VAT.

You are required to:

(1)   Compute the amount of input tax recoverable in respect of the purchase of the computer as well as any subsequent adjustments which must be made. (2)

(2)   Compute the additional input tax, if any, reclaimable from HMRC following the sale of the computer. (3)

Total (5)

2   (1)   The sale of the freehold in a warehouse built 18 months ago and used to store manufactured products since then.

(2)   Sale of 20 acres of land at the edge of his farm by Farmer Giles. The land has been in his family since 1800s.

(3)   Sale of the freehold of a semi-detached post WWII house by the current owner a VAT registered plumber.

(4)   24 month lease of newly built apartment by the builder Kimple Builders to Mr Smith.

(5)   99 year lease of a newly built office block by the builder Stats Construction.

You are required to categorise the above supplies of land and buildings for VAT and state whether an option to tax could be made. (5)

3   Horricks Ltd is selling its business as a going concern to a major competitor JL Industries Ltd on 1 January 2010.

The assets of the business comprise:

	£'000
Freehold interest in a two-year old warehouse	250
Goodwill	50
Plant and machinery	50
	350

You are required to:

(1)   State how the transfer will be treated for VAT assuming both businesses are VAT registered. (3)

(2)   Calculate the VAT due (if any) and state any planning points available to reduce the VAT chargeable. (2)

Total (5)

4   Lancashire Candles Ltd sells candles to both the wholesale and retail trade. The bad debts account at 30 June 2010 reflects the following:

Date of invoice	Debtor	Details	Amount £
30 June 2009	Scents Ltd	Retail sales	2,000
30 November 2009	Hope Ltd	Sale of now obsolete plant	10,000
20 December 2009	Dot Ltd (in liquidation)	Wholesale	5,000
15 April 2010	Jingle Ltd	Retail sales	3,000
30 April 2010	N/A	Increase in general provision	7,000
			27,000

Notes

(1) No adjustment has been made for any VAT relief.
(2) Lancashire Candles Ltd has terms requiring payment within 10 days of the invoice date.
(3) On 15 May 2010, a dividend of £1,500 was received from the liquidators of Dot Ltd.

In accordance with normal accounting practice, debtors are shown inclusive of VAT in the accounts.

You are required to calculate the amount of bad debt relief for VAT that can be claimed on the quarterly return to 30 June 2010. (5)

5   Charlie and Bella Royle have been in business as partners acting as Personal Trainers for over 10 years. However, due to their age, they decide to retire on 30 April 2010. On that date the assets held by the business (valued at replacement cost for identical items) are:

	£
Van	12,000
Motor car (owned outright and used for both business and private purposes)	14,000
Sports training equipment	1,000

The van and equipment items will be sold over the next few months. Charlie will keep the car for his own personal use.

You are required to outline for VAT purposes how Charlie and Bella must proceed following their decision to retire. (5)

6   In December 2010 Simply Bags Ltd made the following transactions of which the new chief accountant requires advice as to their VAT treatment.

(1) Sale of 600 ladies handbags to Cordes SARL – a company based in France.
(2) Purchase of fine leather from a supplier in Brazil.
(3) Purchase of 1,000 metal hinges for bags from a supplier in Italy.

You are required to discuss the VAT implications of the above three transactions. (5)

7   Hermione opened a clothes shop on 1 July 2008. Since then her sales have been consistent at £5,000 per month, apart from each December when, due to Christmas demand, turnover is £24,000. Hermione does not sell children's clothes.

Hermione didn't register for VAT until 29 March 2010. Her monthly input tax is £500.

You are required to calculate the penalty HMRC will charge for the late registration. (5)

8   Olivia runs a village post office and general store. In the quarter to 31 March 2010, she had the following:

	£
Standard rated supplies (excluding VAT)	53,000
Zero-rated supplies	7,000
Exempt supplies	12,500
Input tax:	
Attributable to taxable supplies	6,800
Attributable to exempt supplies	1,500
Residual	1,000

Taxable supplies include £4,000 (excluding VAT) for the sale of a computer, printer and scanner, which Olivia had previously used in her business.

You are required to calculate the VAT payable by/repayable to Olivia in her return for the quarter to 31 March 2010. (5)

9   The structure for the Marlowe Group is as below.

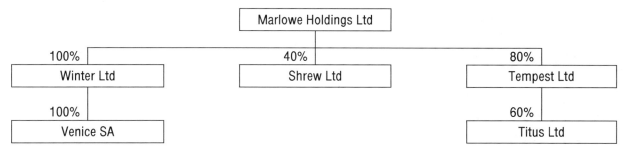

All companies except Venice SA have a place of business in the UK.

Titus Ltd runs children's day nurseries and makes wholly exempt supplies. All other companies make taxable supplies.

Which companies can be included in a VAT group registration and what are the effects of a group VAT registration? (5)

10 Tempest Ltd ordered a consignment of widgets from Caliban Ltd on 12 December 2009 paying a £2,000 deposit.

The widgets are dispatched from Caliban Ltd's factory on 15 January 2010.

An invoice is issued on 20 January 2010. Tempest Ltd paid the balance of £18,000 on 29 January 2010.

Briefly explain the VAT tax points for the deposit and for the balance? (5)

11 Gower Ltd submits its VAT returns and pays its VAT as follows:

Quarter ended	VAT due £	Date return submitted	Date VAT paid
30 June 2009	22,000	25 August 2009	25 August 2009
30 September 2009	28,000	25 October 2009	25 October 2009
31 December 2009	30,000	14 February 2010	14 February 2010
31 March 2010	(5,000)	31 May 2010	-
30 June 2010	7,000	29 July 2010	5 August 2010

You are required to outline how the default surcharge rules will apply to Gower Ltd. (5)

12 Harry granted a 45-year lease on a commercial property to Richard on 12 June 2010. The premium was £95,000 and the net present value of the rent is £180,000. Annual rents under the lease are £1,100 per month.

What is the Stamp Duty Land Tax payable on the grant of the lease and what is the due date for payment? (5)

You must tick the box below if you have answered this Module.

The Chartered Tax Adviser Examination

Sample Paper

AWARENESS

MODULE B – INHERITANCE TAX, TRUSTS & ESTATES

- Each question carries 5 marks.
- You must answer all the questions from the modules you choose.
- You should answer questions in brief bullet points and/or summary computations where appropriate.
- You must answer questions in the spaces provided.
- You may not need all the space provided.
- You should make all calculations to the nearest month and pound unless stated otherwise.

1   Paul gifts £275,000 to an interest in possession trust on 3 April 2010. The beneficiaries of the trust are his three teenage children.

His only other lifetime gifts have been a gross chargeable transfer of £115,500 on 14 June 2006 and gifts of £100 to each of his four nieces and nephew at Christmas every year since 2001.

Paul always pays any Inheritance Tax due in connection with his lifetime gifts.

You are required to calculate how much Inheritance Tax Paul must pay. You should also state Paul's gross chargeable transfer in respect of the April 2010 gift. (5)

2   Anne is a very wealthy 62 year old looking for Inheritance Tax advice.

She is UK domiciled and intends to leave all her assets to her husband, Gus, aged 47.

Gus was born in New Zealand. He moved to England when he married Anne, eleven years ago, and has told Anne that he intends to return to New Zealand if Anne dies before him.

Anne has no other relations and has made no other substantial gifts.

You are required to advise Anne on her Inheritance Tax position and any potential planning opportunities available to her. (5)

3   In May 2004 Lisa sold her family home for £650,000. She gave £400,000 to her son, David, who bought a property for Lisa to live in.

The property is currently worth £475,000 and has an annual rental value of £18,525. Lisa does not pay rent to David.

Lisa is a higher rate taxpayer.

You are required to calculate Lisa's tax liability for 2009/10 in respect of the property and to advise her how she can avoid paying this tax charge. (5)

4   Kari dies on 8 October 2009.

In her estate were the following assets:

(1)   *15,000 Smoky plc shares*

At the date of her death the shares were quoted at 230.25 – 235, with bargains at 231, 233.25 and 234.

The shares had gone ex-dividend on 28 September 2009 and the dividend of 19p per share was paid on 12 October 2009.

(2)   *Holiday home in France*

Kari had purchased the property for €127,500 when the buying exchange rate was €1.39 and the selling rate was €1.20. At the date of her death the villa is worth €622,000. The buying exchange rate is €1.51 and the selling rate is €1.32.

(3)   *1,000 shares in Fire Ltd*

Fire Ltd is an unquoted trading company valued at £725,000. Kari had owned the shares for ten years. The company does not hold any investments.

The costs of dealing with the overseas property came to €5,852.

Funeral expenses were £1,200.

Kari had made no gross chargeable lifetime transfers and left her entire estate to her son, Nick.

You are required to calculate the Inheritance Tax liability on Kari's estate. (5)

5   The trustees of the Conn Family Discretionary Trust pass a property worth £725,000 out of the trust to one of the beneficiaries on 1 June 2009. The trust had been set up by Janet Conn on 12 April 2003 with cash of £450,000.

Janet's only other lifetime gift had been a gift of £50,000 to her daughter on her wedding day on 25 April 2002.

You are required to calculate the exit charge when the property leaves the trust, assuming the beneficiary pays any Inheritance Tax due. (5)

6   The trustees of the Slocombe Discretionary Trust have a tax pool brought forward at the beginning of the tax year of £625.

They receive dividend income of £19,800 and have no trust management expenses.

They make an income payment of £9,000 to a beneficiary.

You are required to calculate the trustees' Income Tax liability and state the balance on the tax pool at the end of the year. (5)

7   Alan sets up a discretionary trust on 15 May 2009 for his two children, Samantha (age 12) and Jake (age 9).

The trust property consists of 50,000 shares in Loaded plc, a quoted trading company, and an investment property that is currently rented out. The annual trust income is expected to be in the region of £25,000 and expenses are expected to be approximately £1,500.

The plan is for the trustees to pay the children's school fees from trust income.

You are required to explain to Alan how the trust income will be taxed. You should ignore both Capital Gains Tax and Inheritance Tax. (5)

8   Henry acquired some shares in York Ltd (an unlisted trading company) in June 2008. In March 2010 he settled them on to a trust for his children and grandchildren.

Briefly explain the circumstances in which Business Property Relief will be available to reduce the transfer of value made by Henry to the trust. (5)

9   **Give five instances where a donor can give away an asset, be able to benefit from the use of the asset after the gift and not be caught by the rules regarding Gifts With Reservation of Benefit.** (5)

10   William is a company director earning £100,000 per annum. In June 2006, William created a discretionary trust for the benefit of his three minor children by settling an investment property (then worth £400,000). The chargeable gain of £120,000 on settlement was held over under S.260 TCGA 1992.

In March 2010 the trustees sold the property for £600,000. This was their only disposal in 2009/10.

You are required to explain (with appropriate calculations) the Capital Gains Tax position in respect of the above. (5)

11   Mrs Hathaway died on 5 April 2009 leaving her estate to her daughter Anne. The estate consisted of the family home, an investment property and a bank deposit.

The Executors completed the administration of the estate on 31 January 2010. The income and expenses during the administration period were as follows;

	£
Rental income	24,000
Bank deposit interest (net)	4,800
Letting expenses	(4,000)
Estate management expenses	(400)
Interest on short term loan to pay the IHT	(2,500)

You are required to show the entries required for form R185 (Estate Income) to be given to the residuary beneficiary. (5)

12   (1)   Small-holding of arable pasture in northern France. Farmed by a tenant under a long-lease since 1997.

    (2)   Cattle farm in North Yorkshire farmed by the taxpayer and his wife in partnership.

    (3)   Farmhouse (situated on the farmland) in which they live.

    (4)   Cattle herd.

    (5)   Tenanted land used by a sheep farmer in North Wales. 30-year lease signed in 1993 (due for renegotiation in 2013).

Briefly explain whether the above assets will qualify for agricultural property relief and (if so) at what rate. You should assume all assets have been held for many years. (5)

You must tick the box below if you have answered this Module.

The Chartered Tax Adviser Examination

Sample Paper

AWARENESS

MODULE C – CORPORATION TAX

- Each question carries 5 marks.

- You must answer all the questions from the modules you choose.

- You should answer questions in brief bullet points and/or summary computations where appropriate.

- You must answer questions in the spaces provided.

- You may not need all the space provided.

- You should make all calculations to the nearest month and pound unless stated otherwise.

1   Harrap Ltd recently acquired 100% of the shares in Overseas Inc, a company incorporated in a country which is not in the European Union. Following the acquisition, a number of directors of Harrap Ltd will join the board of directors of Overseas Inc.

Overseas Inc's main trading operations are outside of the UK but it operates a small manufacturing unit in the UK.

You are required to advise Harrap Ltd on how the UK residency position of Overseas Inc will be determined and the Corporation Tax implications of Overseas Inc being UK or non-UK resident. (5)

2   Gardener Ltd prepares accounts to 31 October. During the year to 31 October 2009 the following transactions took place:

		Cost/proceeds £
1 May 2009	Car acquired (CO$_2$ emissions 158g/km)	11,000
1 June 2009	Van acquired	13,000
1 June 2009	Mercedes car sold	15,000
1 July 2009	Machine sold (original cost £35,000)	40,000

The car acquired on 1 May 2009 was for the use of the sales manager and 25% of his annual mileage was for private purposes.

The balances on the capital allowance pools as at 1 November 2008 were:

	£
Main pool	45,000
Mercedes car (Old expensive car)	24,000
Short-life asset (acquired 1 May 2003)	4,000

You are required to calculate the capital allowances available to Gardener Ltd for the year ended 31 October 2009. (5)

3   Marine Ltd manufactures speedboats and prepares accounts to 31 March. In the year to 31 March 2010 the following transactions took place:

(1)   On 1 April 2009 the company issued £200,000 10% debentures. The funds were used to purchase an investment property which was rented out from 1 June 2009 at an annual rent of £25,000, payable quarterly in advance. The company incurred professional fees of £1,800 in connection with the issues of the debentures.

(2)   On 1 June 2009 the company took out a bank loan to fund the purchase of plant and machinery. Interest of £2,000 was paid during the year. Interest payable of £800 was accrued as at 31 March 2010.

You are required to explain how the above income and expenditure will be treated in the Corporation Tax computation of Marine Ltd for the year to 31 March 2010. (5)

4   Mammoth Ltd, an electrical engineering company, has always prepared accounts to 30 June. In 2009 it decided to change its accounting date and prepared accounts for the six months to 31 December 2009.

The company's trading profit for the six months to 31 December 2009 was £200,000. This figure is adjusted for tax purposes, with the exception of the following items:

(1)   An amortisation charge of £20,000 in relation to the goodwill of a business acquired in May 2007 has not yet been charged in the profit and loss account.

(2)   Capital allowances for the year have not yet been computed. The balance on the capital allowance main pool as at 1 July 2009 was £50,000.

On 1 August 2009 the company acquired plant and machinery for £15,000.

Mammoth Ltd has no other income in the period.

You are required to calculate Mammoth Ltd's Corporation Tax liability for the six months to 31 December 2009. (5)

5 Circle Ltd owns 100% of the share capital of Oblong Ltd and 80% of Square Ltd. Square Ltd owns 80% of the share capital of Triangle Ltd.

All companies are UK resident.

The results of Circle Ltd and Oblong Ltd for the year ended 31 December 2009 are as follows:

Year ended:	Circle Ltd £	Oblong Ltd £
Trading profit/(loss)	50,000	(220,000)
Chargeable gain/(loss)	15,000	(20,000)
Bank interest	10,000	5,000
Charges on income – Gift Aid	2,000	6,000

You are required to:

(1) State, giving reasons, whether Square Ltd and Triangle Ltd are in a group for group loss relief purposes with Circle Ltd and Oblong Ltd. (2)

(2) Calculate the amount of losses of Oblong Ltd which are available for group relief and the maximum amount of loss that Circle Ltd could claim from Oblong Ltd. (3)

Total (5)

6 Hotspur Ltd was incorporated on 1 January 2009. Its shares are wholly owned by Mr Percy.

Hotspur Ltd opened a bank account and began trading on 1 April 2009. The first accounts were drawn to 31 May 2010 and showed the following results;

	£
Adjusted trading profits before capital allowances	448,000
Bank interest receivable	7,000
Rental income (see below)	120,000

Plant and equipment was bought on 1 April 2009 for £53,000. Some equipment was sold in April 2010 for £1,600.

An investment property was acquired on 1 December 2009 and was immediately leased out at an annual rent of £120,000 payable in advance.

Compute the profits chargeable to Corporation Tax in respect of the period to 31 May 2010 and show the due date(s) for the submissions of forms CT 600. (5)

7 Verona Ltd (a large company) has traditionally drawn up accounts to 30 April. It joined the Swan plc group on 1 May 2009 and, to coincide with that of its new parent company, duly changed its accounting reference date to 31 December.

Verona Ltd estimated that its chargeable profits for the eight months to 31 December 2009 would be £5 million. At their board meeting on 6 April 2010, the directors signed off the accounts and provisional tax computations showing chargeable profits of £6 million.

You are required to calculate the Corporation Tax payment required to be made on 14 April 2010. (5)

8 **Give four ways in which a deficit on a non-trading loan relationship may be relieved.** (5)

9   Orsino Ltd incorporated a new wholly owned subsidiary (Viola Ltd) on 1 January 2009. Viola Ltd opened a bank account and started to trade on 1 February 2009. First accounts are drawn to 30 September 2009. Orsino Ltd has one other subsidiary.

The accounts of Viola Ltd for its first accounting period show the following:

	£
Tax adjusted profit	125,000
Bank interest receivable	8,000
Dividend received on quoted investment	1,000

Viola Ltd's only capital acquisition was a car, with CO_2 emissions of 163g/km, costing £9,000 on 1 May 2009.

You are required to calculate the Corporation Tax payable by Viola Ltd for the period ended 30 September 2009. (5)

10 **Briefly outline the circumstances in which the carry forward of trading losses could be denied on a change of ownership of a company.** (5)

11 Lysander Ltd is a property investment company, wholly owned by Theseus Ltd. Theseus Ltd had incorporated Lysander Ltd in 2002 when it subscribed for 100,000 £1 ordinary shares at par.

In 2010, Quince Ltd paid £10m for all of the share capital of Lysander Ltd.

The main asset of Lysander Ltd is an office block that it rents out to various third party tenants.

The office block was originally owned by Puck Ltd, another 100% subsidiary of Theseus Ltd. Puck Ltd had constructed the office block for £1 million in 2001. It was transferred to Lysander Ltd in 2007 for £3 million, when its market value was £6 million.

You are required to calculate the chargeable gains arising as a result of the above transactions, stating clearly which company will be chargeable. You should ignore indexation allowance. (5)

12 Cressida Ltd is a small company which manufactures paint. In its year ended 31 December 2009, it had the following income and expenditure:

	£	£
Income		
Paint sales		312,000
Patent royalty received from Mr Paris (UK trader)		8,000
		320,000
Expenses		
General manufacturing costs	120,000	
Research expenditure into new paint making methods	40,000	
Acquisition cost of business goodwill (Note)	100,000	
		(260,000)
Profit		60,000

Note: On 1 July 2009, Cressida Ltd paid £100,000 for the goodwill of a tin-making company. It will write the goodwill off over 5 years.

Calculate the Corporation Tax payable by Cressida Ltd for the year ended 31 December 2009. (5)

You must tick the box below if you have answered this Module.

The Chartered Tax Adviser Examination

Sample Paper

AWARENESS

MODULE D – TAXATION OF INDIVIDUALS

- Each question carries 5 marks.

- You must answer all the questions from the modules you choose.

- You should answer questions in brief bullet points and/or summary computations where appropriate.

- You must answer questions in the spaces provided.

- You may not need all the space provided.

- You should make all calculations to the nearest month and pound unless stated otherwise.

1. A new client, Reginald, has advised you that he purchased an investment property and started receiving rental income of £10,000 per month from 1 January 2010. He notified HMRC of this new source of income on 15 September 2010 and was issued with a 2009/10 tax return on 10 November 2010. He filed this return online on 13 February 2011.

   You are required to advise Reginald on the following matters, providing reasons for your conclusions:

   (1) Whether he notified HMRC of his new source of income on time
   (2) Whether he filed his 2009/10 tax return on time
   (3) The deadline for Reginald to make amendments to his tax return
   (4) The deadline for HMRC to open an enquiry into Reginald's 2009/10 tax return
   (5) Any penalties which Reginald may have incurred in respect of the above matters.

   (5)

2. Mr Falstaff is 76. In 2009/10 he received the following income:

	£
State pension	5,200
Employers pension (PAYE deducted £1,850)	14,000
Rental profits	4,800
Bank interest	750

   On 15 November 2009 he married Celia (63). Celia has self-employed trading profits of £30,000.

   On 1 January 2010 Mr Falstaff made a donation to charity of £500 under Gift Aid.

   You are required to calculate the Income Tax payable by Mr Falstaff for 2009/10. (5)

3. Antony joined Cleo plc as a HR manager on 1 July 2009 on a salary of £60,000. His benefits package included the following:

   (1) Company car, list price £20,000, CO_2 emissions 168 g/km, all petrol costs reimbursed by the company.

   (2) Use of an unfurnished company-owned flat until such time as he found suitable family accommodation in the area. The flat cost £250,000 in 2007 and has an annual rental value £1,000. Antony paid a notional rent of £200 per month for the use of the flat. He bought a family house on 31 January 2010 and duly moved out of the flat.

   You should assume HM Revenue & Customs' official interest rate is 4.75%.

   You are required to calculate the taxable benefits arising in 2009/10. Assume Cleo plc has paid other relocation costs for Antony in excess of £8,000. (5)

4. Eleanora was born in Australia, but moved to the UK 19 years ago to work for a UK company and has lived here ever since. She plans to return to Australia on her retirement in around five years' time.

   During 2009/10, Eleanora had the following income:

UK employment income	£70,000
Rent from letting out her house in Sydney	£12,000 (credited to her Australian bank account)
Dividend income from an overseas company	£20,000 (of which £11,000 was transferred to her UK account)

   You are required to discuss Eleanora's current residence and domicile status for UK tax purposes and explain the UK tax treatment of her various sources of income in 2009/10. You may assume that no overseas tax is payable on any of Eleanora's income and that she makes any beneficial claims. (5)

5   On 15 March 2007, Jemima was granted share options to acquire 5,000 shares in her employer company, Puddle plc, at a price equal to the March 2007 market value of £6.80 per share. The options were granted under the company's Enterprise Management Incentive scheme.

Jemima exercised her options in November 2009, by which time the shares were valued at £14.50 each. She sold the shares one month later for £14.70 per share.

Jemima's shareholding represents less than 1% of the company's shares.

You are required to explain (with supporting calculations where appropriate) Jemima's Income Tax, National Insurance Contributions and Capital Gains Tax position on grant and exercise of the options and on sale of the shares, assuming that she is a higher rate taxpayer and that she made no other chargeable gains during 2009/10. (5)

6   Roderigo sold some quoted shares in 2007 making a substantial capital gain. In 2008 he subscribed for shares in a qualifying EIS company and elected to defer the gain arising.

You are required to list five events which will result in the deferred gain becoming chargeable. (5)

7   Jamie lets out a furnished flat in the UK and receives the following rent:

	£
18 December 2008: Annual rental to 31 December 2009	15,000
22 December 2009: Annual rental to 31 December 2010	15,600

He also incurred the following expenditure on the property:

(1)   Insurance premiums paid in advance for the next 12 months: £3,600 on 1 August 2008 and £4,200 on 1 August 2009.

(2)   Council tax of £1,100 for the year to 31 March 2010.

(3)   Replacement of a chimney in November 2009 at a cost of £800, following damage in a storm.

(4)   Interest at 3% per annum on the outstanding loan of £200,000 which Jamie took out a few years ago in order to finance the purchase of the property.

You are required to calculate Jamie's taxable property income for the 2009/10 tax year. (5)

8   Emily is a director of Arcite Ltd with a salary of £50,000 per annum. During 2009/10 she also received the following remuneration:

(1)   Bonus of £36,000 for year ended 31 March 2009 paid on 20 July 2009.

(2)   Private medical insurance costing the company £480.

(3)   Free accommodation in a flat which has a market value of £180,000 and is rented by the company at a rate of £10,800 per annum.

(4)   Reimbursement of personal telephone bills totalling £650.

You are required to calculate the 2009/10 National Insurance Contributions payable by Emily and the company in respect of her remuneration, assuming that Emily is not contracted out of S2P. (5)

Question 9 has been amended to accommodate changes to capital gains tax legislation.

9   Maria made a number of disposals in February 2010, realising the following gains.

Date of purchase	Type of asset	Gain £
6 May 1971	Painting	Note
14 August 2007	Shares in West Ltd (20% shareholding)	45,000
2 November 2004	Shares in Coach plc (1% shareholding)	24,000

   Note

   The painting was acquired for £3,000. It was sold for £6,860, net of 2% auctioneers' fees. It was valued for insurance purposes at £4,000 in March 1982.

   Both West Ltd and Coach plc are trading companies. Maria has been employed by West Ltd since 2004. Maria had capital losses brought forward at 6 April 2009 of £5,000.

   You are required to calculate Maria's CGT payable for 2009/10. (5)

10 Henry Percy sold his house in Scotland on 30 September 2009 realising a gain (after selling expenses) of £272,000.

   He had bought the house in October 1978. On 1 April 1998 he bought a flat in Newcastle and elected for this property to be his main residence. He worked in Newcastle but continued to use the house in Scotland on occasional weekends. He sold the Newcastle flat in September 2008 and returned permanently to the house in Scotland.

   In 2009/10, Henry had self-employed trading profits of £37,500 and made no other gains.

   You are required to calculate Henry's Capital Gains Tax payable for 2009/10. (5)

11 Oswald gave the following assets to his family members in 2009/10:

   (1) In January 2010 he sold his shares in Shrew Ltd (an unlisted trading company) to his son Edmund for £40,000. He had bought the shares in February 2009 for £12,000 and they were worth £95,000 at the date of transfer. Oswald has never worked for Shrew Ltd.

   (2) On 3 February 2010 he sold a painting to his daughter Cordelia for £10,000. He had inherited it in 2006 when it has a probate value of £25,000. It was worth £20,000 at the date of the transfer.

   (3) In March 2010 he gave some shares in Southern Stone plc to his nephew Edgar. The shares had cost him £20,000 in May 2001 and were worth £8,000 at the date of the gift.

   You are required to calculate the net gains arising. Assume all appropriate claims are made. (5)

12 Miranda bought 10,000 shares in Tempest plc in June 2007 for £80,000. On 1 July 2008, Tempest plc was taken over by Prospero plc. For each of their Tempest plc shares, the shareholders received the following:

   Two new Prospero plc ordinary shares worth £4.75 each
   £10 of non-convertible loan stock (valued at par)
   £5.50 cash

   In December 2009, Miranda redeemed her loan stock and received £85,000.

   Miranda's shareholdings in Tempest plc and Prospero plc represented less than 1% of the companies' shares.

   You are required to calculate the chargeable gain / allowable loss on redemption of the stock. (5)

You must tick the box below if you have answered this Module.

The Chartered Tax Adviser Examination

Sample Paper

AWARENESS

MODULE E – TAXATION OF UNINCORPORATED BUSINESSES

- Each question carries 5 marks.

- You must answer all the questions from the modules you choose.

- You should answer questions in brief bullet points and/or summary computations where appropriate.

- You must answer questions in the spaces provided.

- You may not need all the space provided.

- You should make all calculations to the nearest month and pound unless stated otherwise.

1. Albert is in business running a café. His accounts for the year to 30 June 2009 show a trading profit of £35,000, this is after deducting the following:

   (1) Legal fees of £500 in respect of renewing the ten year lease on the cafe.

   (2) Repair costs of £200 in respect of a second-hand refrigeration unit which was acquired during the year. The repairs were required prior to using the unit in order to comply with health and safety regulations.

   (3) Cost of acquiring a delivery van on 1 June 2009 for £6,000. The van is used 20% of the time by Albert for private purposes.

   (4) Parking fine of £50 incurred by Albert whilst making a delivery of sandwiches to a local business.

   You are required to calculate Albert's taxable trading profit for the year to 30 June 2009 giving an explanation for your treatment of the repair costs. (5)

2. Maggie commenced business as a self-employed beautician on 1 February 2009. Her results for her first set of accounts for the fifteen month period to 30 April 2010 are as follows:

	£	£
Gross operating profit		120,000
Less : Wages (Note 1)	80,000	
Rent and rates (Note 2)	10,000	
Depreciation	2,000	
Telephone and utilities	2,500	
Sundry expenses (all allowable)	800	
		(95,300)
Net profit		24,700

   Notes

   (1) Wages includes £45,000 in respect of Maggie and £10,000 in respect of Maggie's daughter who works full-time in the business.

   (2) Rent and rates relate to the whole of the building. The beauty salon occupies three of its rooms; Maggie's son lives in the fourth room.

   (3) During the period Maggie used goods which had cost £500 for her own personal use. The usual retail price of these goods was £850. No adjustments have been made in the accounts for the goods removed.

   You are required to calculate Maggie's taxable trading profit for the fifteen month period to 30 April 2010 and to state the basis period for the trading income assessment in 2009/10. (5)

3. Karen operates a dress-making business as an unincorporated trader. The following capital transactions took place in the year to 31 August 2010:

		£
Acquisitions		*Cost*
1 October 2009	Jaguar car (CO_2 emissions 175g/km, 40% private use)	25,000
1 December 2009	Ford car (CO_2 emissions 145g/km, 20% private use)	10,000
1 March 2010	Delivery van	15,000
Disposals		*Proceeds*
15 September 2009	Expensive car (Volvo) (CO_2 emissions 175g/km, 40% private use)	12,000

   The Jaguar car acquired and the Volvo car disposed of during the year were used by Karen. The Ford car was used by the sales manager.

   The original cost of the Volvo car was £22,000.

The value of the capital allowance pools as at 1 September 2009 were:

Main pool	£25,000
Expensive car (Volvo)	£16,000

You are required to calculate the capital allowances available to Karen for the year to 31 August 2010. Assume tax rates and allowances for 2009/10 continue into the future. (5)

4 Gerald has traded as a self-employed carpenter for a number of years. On 31 December 2009 he ceased to trade.

Gerald's taxable trading profits had been as follows:

Year to 30 June 2008	£38,000
Year to 30 June 2009	£34,000

His final accounts for the six months to 31 December 2009 show a tax adjusted trading profit before capital allowances of £15,000.

The only assets used in the business were a van, which he retained for his personal use, and items of plant and machinery which he sold for £6,500. Gerald had only ever used the van for business purposes.

The van had cost £15,000 in April 2004 and had a market value of £8,500 at 31 December 2009. None of the individual items of plant and machinery were sold for more than their original cost.

The tax written down value of the main capital allowances pool as at 1 July 2009 was £4,000.

Gerald had overlap profits in respect of his opening years' assessments of £8,000.

You are required to calculate Gerald's trading income assessment for 2009/10. (5)

5 Brooke has been trading as a self-employed hairdresser for a number of years.

Her recent tax adjusted trading results have been as follows:

Year to 31 May 2007	£45,000
Year to 31 May 2008	£26,000
Year to 31 May 2009	£(10,000) loss

Brooke expects to have a tax adjusted trading profit of £500 for the year to 31 May 2010.

In addition to her trading income Brooke has other taxable income of £5,000 each year.

You are required to set out the options available to Brooke to utilise the loss arising in the year to 31 May 2009 and to explain the implications of each of the options. You do NOT need to quantify the amount of tax saved under each option. (5)

6 Richard sold a freehold building for £850,000 on 1 August 2009. The building had always been used for business purposes. Richard had acquired the building on 1 July 2002 for £400,000.

On 1 September 2009 he acquired a new freehold building, for use in his business, for £750,000.

You are required to:

(1) **Calculate the chargeable gain arising on the sale of the building assuming that Richard will not claim to rollover the gain into the cost of the building acquired on 1 September 2009.** (2)

(2) **Calculate the revised base cost of the building acquired on 1 September 2009 assuming that Richard elects to rollover the gain arising on the old building into the cost of the new building.** (3)

Total (5)

7 Antonio and Bassanio are in partnership sharing profits equally. Their only asset is the business goodwill, which they purchased in April 1991 for £200,000.

On 1 January 2010, Portia was admitted to the partnership and profits were thereafter split 50:30:20 between Antonio, Bassanio and Portia. No adjustment was made to the partnership accounts, although Portia made a direct payment of £80,000 to Bassanio for his share of the goodwill.

You are required to explain (with calculations) the capital gains consequences of Portia joining the partnership and show the base cost of her 20% share. (5)

8   Horatio and Claudius have been in partnership for many years drawing accounts annually to 30 November. Profits are split 3:2 after a salary of £15,000 to Claudius.

Horatio retired on 31 December 2009, so Claudius took the opportunity to move the accounts date to 31 December and thereafter continue as a sole trader. Profits for the period 1 December 2008 to 31 December 2009 were £260,000.

There were 4 months of overlap profits arising on the commencement of trade. These amounted to £15,000 and £10,000 for Horatio and Claudius respectively.

You are required to calculate the taxable trading profit for 2009/10 for Horatio and Claudius. (5)

9   Toby started trading on 1 May 2008. His results have been as follows:

	Profit/(loss) £
1 May 2008 to 31 January 2009	60,000
1 February 2009 to 30 April 2009	(30,000)
1 May 2009 to 30 April 2010	90,000

You are required to calculate the National Insurance Contributions payable by Toby for 2009/10. (5)

10 Florence owned a gift shop. She retired on 31 March 2010 and sold the business to an unconnected buyer, Oliver. Oliver paid Florence £400,000 for the business and the two parties agreed that this be broken down as follows.

	£
Business premises	220,000
Goodwill	100,000
Stock	60,000
Plant & machinery	20,000
	400,000

The stock cost £10,000 and had an estimated market value of £25,000. Florence has trading losses brought forward to offset any trade profits arising.

You are required to show the adjustment, if any, which should be made to Florence's final trading profits in respect of her stock. (5)

11 Warwick started trading as a wedding singer on 1 January 2009. His tax adjusted profits have been as follows;

| Year ended 31 December 2009 | 12,000 |
| Period ended 30 April 2011 | 30,000 |

His only asset is his car bought in December 2008 for £6,000, which he uses solely for business purposes.

You are required to calculate the taxable trading profits for 2010/11 and show any overlap profits to be carried forward. (5)

12. Morgan started trading on 1 May 2007. He notified his chargeability to Income Tax in July 2008 and was duly sent a 2007/08 tax return, which he filed on 29 January 2009. The Income Tax and Class 4 National Insurance Contributions due for 2007/08 was £16,000.

Within the return, Morgan made a claim to reduce his payments on account for 2008/09 to £5,500 each.

Morgan submitted his 2008/09 return on 27 February 2010 showing tax and National Insurance Contributions due for the year of £13,000. No claim was made to reduce his payments on account for 2009/10.

The following tax payments have been made;

	£
29 January 2009	21,500
30 September 2009	5,500
31 March 2010	8,500

Assume HM Revenue & Customs' official interest rate is 2.5%.

You are required to calculate the interest, surcharges and penalties for which Morgan is liable. You may do interest calculations on a monthly basis. Assume that the late filing/payment penalties in Finance Act 2009 do not apply. (5)

The Chartered Tax Adviser Examination

Sample Paper

Awareness

Suggested Answers

Module A – VAT including stamp taxes: answers

1 Alpha Developments

(1) Recovery on computer:

In year to 31 March 2008 (interval 1 – initial recovery): (70% £24,500) = £17,150
In year to 31 March 2009 (interval 2 – annual adjustment): 1/5 × £24,500 × (85% – 70%) = £735

In both cases, the input tax can be reclaimed.

(2) The sale of the computer is a taxable supply and the VAT on the remaining adjustment periods will be made on the basis that the computer was wholly used for taxable purposes (Regulations 115(3)).

In the year to 31 March 2010 the adjustment percentage is 75% (ie. taxable use of computer in period prior to sale).

Adjustment (credit) is (75 – 70)% × £24,500 × 1/5 = £245

For the years to 31 March 2011 and 2012 the adjustment is (100 – 70)% × 24,500 × 2/5 = £2,940

As the VAT charged on the sale of the computer is £6,130, the whole of the sale credit of £2,940 can be reclaimed (Regulation 115(3)).

Total adjustment (credit to business) = £3,185

2 Categorise

(1) Standard rated supply of the freehold of a 'new' (less than 3 years old) commercial building. As this supply is already standard rated an option to tax is not applicable.

(2) Exempt supply of land, however, Farmer Giles may make the option to tax prior to the sale to standard rate the supply.

(3) Exempt supply. Option to tax cannot apply to buildings which will be used as a dwelling.

(4) Exempt supply of lease. Zero rating does not apply since 'major interest' has not been supplied by constructor. Option to tax cannot apply to buildings which will be used as a dwelling.

(5) Exempt supply of a commercial lease. Option to tax can be made prior to sale by Stats Construction to standard rate the sale.

3 Horricks Ltd

(1) The sale of the business is a transfer of a going concern and is therefore outside the scope of VAT, assuming certain conditions are met, eg JL Industries Ltd uses the assets acquired from Horricks Ltd for the same kind of business, there is no significant break in trade, etc. However, unless JL Industries complies with additional obligations, TOGC treatment will not apply to the warehouse since it is 'new' (less than three years old) and if sold in isolation would be a standard rated supply.

(2) VAT due

Warehouse £250,000 × 17.5% = £43,750

Goodwill and plant/machinery are outside the scope of VAT on this transfer.

However, if JL Industries Ltd complies with certain additional obligations, the sale of the warehouse will fall within the TOGC and will therefore will not be subject to VAT. In order for this to be the case, JL Industries must:

- Opt to tax the warehouse
- Notify HMRC of this option to tax; and
- Notify Horricks that this option to tax will not be disapplied under special anti-avoidance rules

JL Industries must do all of this by the 'relevant date' (usually the date of completion).

If JL Industries Ltd does opt to tax, it will have to charge VAT on any supplies it makes in the future with respect to the warehouse (eg if it leases the building to another party).

4 Lancashire Candles Ltd

Scents Ltd

The debt is over six months old. VAT due is 3/23 × £2,000 = £261. This can be claimed as bad debt relief on next return to 30 June 2010 if debt is written off in company's accounts.

Hope Ltd

The VAT relating to the debt would have been £1,304 (£10,000 × 3/23). The date on which the debt can be written off for BDR purposes is 10 December 2009 so the debt is over six months old. As for Scents above bad debt relief is available if the debt is written off in the company's accounts.

Dot Ltd

£5,000 was due and £1,500 is repaid (by way of dividend) so £3,500 is outstanding. The debt is six months old (the date on which the debt can be written off for BDR purposes is 30 December 2009) so, as above, bad debt relief is due for £457 (£3,500 × 3/23) if the debt is written off in the company's books.

Jingle Ltd

The debt is not yet six months old (the date on which the debt can be written off for BDR purposes is 25 April 2010) so bad debt relief is not available on either the quarter ended June 2010 return or the quarter ended September 2010 return. The company must wait until the quarter ended 31 December 2010 return to claim £447 (£3,000 × 7/47).

General provision

Cannot satisfy the VAT bad debt conditions, so no bad debt relief is due.

5 Charlie and Bella Royle

The business must notify HMRC of a need to deregister by 30 May 2010 as it ceased to trade on 30 April 2010.

The following assets had input tax reclaimed on them and were in the business on the last day of registration.

	£
Van	12,000
Sports equipment	1,000
	13,000

Note: VAT was not recovered on the purchase of the car so it is ignored in the above calculation.

As this figure is not below the de minimis of £1,000, the partnership must account for output VAT in respect of the van and equipment on the final VAT return of the business.

When the van and equipment are later sold VAT is not charged as the business is no longer VAT registered.

6 Simply Bags Ltd

The VAT implications of the transactions are as follows:

(1) This is a dispatch to an EU customer in France. If Simply Bags Ltd has the French VAT registration number of Cordes SARL it may zero rate the sale of bags. If not it must charge VAT at the standard rate. It must also obtain and retain commercial evidence to show that the goods were despatched to another member state.

(2) This is an import. The goods will be held at the port of entry until Simply Bags Ltd pays the standard rate VAT (and other taxes) due to release the goods. This VAT is input tax and can be recovered in the normal way on the VAT return covering the date of importation.

(3) This is an acquisition from an EU supplier. If Simply Bags Ltd gave the supplier its UK VAT registration number the goods will arrive at the premises of the company VAT free. Simply Bags Ltd must charge itself standard rate VAT on these goods. This will be in the form of acquisition tax which must be declared on the VAT return covering the date of acquisition. Subject to the usual rules, Simply Bags may deduct this as input tax on the same VAT return.

7 Hermione

	£
2008	
July	5,000
August	5,000
September	5,000
October	5,000
November	5,000
December	24,000
2009	
January	5,000
February	5,000
March	5,000
April	5,000
Total	69,000

Hermione should have notified her liability to register for VAT by 30 May 2009 and should have charged VAT on sales from 1 June 2009. She is therefore 10 months late.

	£
Output tax	
£(6 × £5,000) + £(1 × 24,000) = £54,000 × 3/23 + (3 x £5,000 x 7/47)	9,278
Input tax (£500 × 10)	(5,000)
VAT due	4,278
Penalty @ 10%	£428

8 Olivia

$$\frac{\text{Taxable supplies}}{\text{Total supplies}} = \frac{60,000 - 4,000}{60,000 - 4,000 + 12,500} = 81.75\% \text{ (round to 82\%)}$$

Note: exclude supplies of capital items in partial exemption fraction.

	£
Input tax recoverable:	
Taxable supplies	6,800
Non-attributable (£1,000 × 82%)	820
Recoverable input tax	7,620
Exempt input tax is:	
Exempt	1,500
Non attributable £(1,000 – 820)	180
De minimis (< £625 per month and less than 50% of the total input VAT for the period) thus recoverable in this period)	1,680
VAT due:	
Output tax	£
£53,000 × 17.5%	9,275
Input tax recoverable £(7,620 + 1,680)	(9,300)
VAT repayable	(25)

9 Marlowe Group

The following companies CANNOT be within the VAT Group:

- Shrew Ltd (not under common control – ie < 50% owned)
- Venice SA (no UK place of business / fixed establishment in the UK)

The other companies can form a VAT Group (including the exempt company, Titus Ltd).

The main effects of group VAT registration are:

(a) The group is treated as one single taxable person.

(b) One company (the 'representative member') is responsible for all VAT accounting including the completion and submission of VAT returns.

(c) All the companies within the group registration are jointly and severally liable for any VAT due.

(d) Any supplies made between members of the VAT group are ignored (ie such supplies are outside the scope of VAT).

10 Tempest Ltd

Deposit

The basic tax point is the date the goods are dispatched – ie 15 January 2010.

However, a deposit is paid before this date, so the earlier date becomes the tax point but only to the extent of the deposit paid.

The tax point for the deposit is therefore 12 December 2009.

Balance

The basic tax point is the date the goods are dispatched – ie 15 January 2010.

An invoice is issued within 14 days of the basic tax point, so the invoice date becomes the tax point.

The tax point for the balance is therefore 20 January 2010.

The date of payment of the balance has no impact here.

11 Gower Ltd

30.6.09	Late return and VAT. SLN issued covering period from 1.7.09 to 30.6.10. No penalty charged.
30.9.09	Return & VAT on time.
31.12.09	Late return and VAT. 2% penalty applies. 2% × £30,000 = £600. Surcharge period extended to 31.12.10.
31.3.10	Return late. Repayment return so no penalty charged but surcharge period extended to 31.3.11.
30.6.10	Late payment of VAT. 5% penalty applies. 5% × £7,000 = £350. This is less than £400 so it will not be collected. Surcharge period extended to 30.6.11

12 Harry

The SDLT on the lease is:

	£
Duty on premium: £95,000 × 1% (note)	950
Duty on rent: £(180,000 – 150,000) × 1%	300
Total duty	1,250

Note

The zero rate charge does not apply because the annual rental exceeds £1,000 and the land is non-residential property.

The SDLT is payable by Richard no later than 12 July 2010 (30 days from completion).

Module B – Inheritance tax, trusts & estates: answers

1 Paul

Any gift to a trust during a person's lifetime (except to a bare trust or a trust for a disabled person) is a chargeable lifetime transfer as the trust is a relevant property trust. This trust cannot be a bereaved minor trust or age 18-25 trust as it is being set up during Paul's lifetime.

The tax due is:

	£	£
Transfer of value		275,000
Less: AE 2009/10 (Note)		(3,000)
AE 2008/09 b/f		(3,000)
CLT		269,000
Less: nil rate band	325,000	
GCT in previous 7 years	(115,500)	
		(209,500)
Chargeable		59,500
Tax @ 20/80 or 25%		14,875

Note. The full annual exemption for both 2009/10 and 2008/09 are available as the Christmas gifts to Paul's nieces and nephews come within the small gifts exemption as they are below £250.

The GCT is the total amount that leaves Paul's estate as a result of the gift (ie the chargeable gift PLUS the tax):

£269,000 + £14,875 = £283,875

2 Anne

Gifts between spouses are usually exempt from IHT. However, Gus has arguably retained his New Zealand domicile of origin because he intends to return to New Zealand if Anne dies before him, which is likely considering the age difference. He has no intention to make England his permanent home.

Since only the first £55,000 of transfers from a UK domiciled spouse to a non-UK domiciled spouse are exempt, only gifts up to this amount from Anne to Gus will be exempt.

Anne should consider making gifts up to this amount now. She will be able to use her annual exemption of £3,000 for the year of the gift and the exemption from the previous year as this has not already been used. The annual exemption is not available for transfers on death.

If she gifts more than the £55,000 limit, the excess will be a potentially exempt transfer (PET) for IHT purposes. A PET is exempt during the donor's lifetime and only becomes chargeable if they die within seven years of making the gift. So, if Anne survives more than seven years from making the gift, it will be completely exempt.

A final planning consideration could be for Anne to make regular gifts out of income. These are fully exempt from IHT so long as she can show a regular pattern of giving and that the gifts do not affect her standard of living.

3 Lisa

As Lisa provided the funds for the purchase of the property that she now lives in the property is caught by the Pre-Owned Asset Tax (POAT) rules.

There is an income tax charge equivalent to the annual value of the land less any amount paid by the individual for their use of it.

The charge in respect of Lisa's occupation of the property is:

£18,525 @ 40% = £7,410.

There are two possible ways in which Lisa can avoid an income tax charge:

(1) Lisa can pay David a market rent for her occupation of the property, or

(2) She can notify HMRC that the property should come within the gift with reservation rules. Notification should be made by the self assessment return filing deadline for the year the charge first applied, although HMRC may accept late notifications.

Lisa should be aware that this second option does not avoid tax entirely as making the election brings the asset into her estate for IHT purposes.

4 Kari

Death estate	£
Quoted shares (W1)	37,566
Holiday home (W2)	411,921
Unquoted shares (W3)	nil
Total	449,487
Less: administration costs	
$5,852 ÷ 1.51	(3,875)
	445,612
Less: reasonable funeral expenses	(1,200)
Death estate	444,412
Less: nil rate band	(325,000)
	119,412
Tax @ 40%	47,765

Workings

1 *Quoted shares*

Quoted shares are valued at the lower of the quarter-up and mid bargain values. As the shares had gone ex-div at the date of death, the value of the next dividend must be included in the value.

15,000 shares @ lower of:

(i) ¼-up:

(235 − 230.25) ÷ 4 + 230.25 = 231.4375

(ii) Mid bargain:

$$\frac{231 + 234}{2} = 232.50$$

	£
ie £2.314375 × 15,000 =	34,716
Add: dividend 15,000 × 19p	2,850
Probate value	37,566

2 Foreign property

Valued at the buying (ie the lower) exchange rate: €622,000 ÷ €1.51 =   £411,921

3 Unquoted shares

BPR is available for the shares as they are unquoted trading company shares that Kari has owned for more than two years.

	£
Shares:	725,000
Less: BPR @ 100%	(725,000)
	nil

5 Conn Family Discretionary Trust

	£
Exit charge	
Transfer to trust	450,000
Less: nil rate band (Note)	(325,000)
	125,000
Tax @ 20%	25,000

Effective rate:
25,000/450,000 × 100 = 5.55555%

Actual rate:
5.55555% × 30% × 24/40 = 0.99999%

Exit charge:
0.99999% × £725,000   £7,250

Note. The PET to her daughter on her wedding day does not use up any of the nil rate band as it is exempt during lifetime.

6 Slocombe Discretionary Trust

Income payments to discretionary trust beneficiaries come with a 40% tax credit. The trustees must have paid sufficient tax to cover this tax credit. They keep a tally of all the tax paid to HMRC in the 'tax pool'.

If there is insufficient tax paid to HMRC in the tax pool, the trustees have an additional liability that must be paid over with any other income tax liability. If there is sufficient tax, the balance is carried forward to cover payments in future years.

	£
Dividend income × 100/90	22,000
Taxable income	22,000
Basic rate band:	
£1,000 @ 10%	100
£21,000 @ 32.5%	6,825
Income tax liability	6,925
Less: 10% tax credit: £22,000 × 10%	(2,200)
Income tax due (and entering the tax pool)	4,725

The balance on the tax pool is:

	£
Tax pool b/f	625
Add tax paid in current year:	4,725
Available tax credits	5,350
Less: tax required to cover beneficiary's payment:	
£9,000 × 40/60	(6,000)
Additional tax liability	650
Total tax liability: £650 + £4,725	5,375
Tax pool c/f	nil

7 Alan

The first £1,000 of non-savings income will be taxed at the basic rate.

In addition any income used to pay trust expenses is also taxed at the basic rate depending on the type of income used to pay them (usually dividend income first).

The balance of non-savings income will be taxed at 40% and the dividends at 32.5%.

When the beneficiaries either receive income from the trust or funds are used for their benefit (eg when the trustees pays their school fees) that income is usually taxable on them. Such payments come with a 40% tax credit.

However, as Alan's unmarried minor children can benefit from the trust it is a settlor interested trust. This means that any income paid to or used for the benefit of the children will be taxed on Alan unless it is below the annual de minimis limit of £100 (gross).

It is unlikely that the school fees will be below this limit so the income used to pay the fees will not be taxed on the children but instead on Alan.

8 Henry

Where relevant business property has not been owned for 2 years, BPR will still be given if:

(a) 'Old' business property has been sold in the prior 3 years and replaced with the York Ltd shares. BPR will be given on the York Ltd shares if the aggregated ownership periods total at least two of the five years immediately preceding the transfer; or

(b) If Henry had acquired the York Ltd shares on the death of his spouse and the joint ownership period was at least 2 years; or

(c) Henry has acquired the shares on the death of a person within the last 2 years and that death transfer had qualified for BPR.

[see s.107 – 109 IHTA 1984]

9 Gifts with Reservation of Benefit

- Where the donor pays full consideration for the use of the asset;
- Where the donor gives away half of a house then shares that house with the donee (provided that the donor pays a reasonable share of all outgoings);
- Where the donor gives away a house and stays with the donee for less than one month a year in total (or less than 2 weeks if the donee is not present);
- Where the donor gives a house to a donee then stays with the donor for a short-term purpose (eg while convalescing after medical treatment);
- Where the donor gives away land then uses that land to walk dogs etc, as long as this does not restrict the donee's use.

(+ marks for other examples in HMRC Tax Bulletin November 1993).

10 William

Capital gain arising

	£	£
Proceeds		600,000
Cost	400,000	
Less: held over gain	(120,000)	
		(280,000)
Trustees gain		320,000
Less: Annual exempt amount		(5,050)
Taxable gain		314,950
CGT @ 18%		£56,691

11 Mrs Hathaway

2009/10	Non savings £	Interest £
Rental profit (£24,000 - £4,000)	20,000	
Interest (× 100/80)		6,000
Less: loan interest	(2,500)	
Taxable income	17,500	6,000
Less: tax suffered at 20%	(3,500)	(1,200)
Net income	14,000	4,800
Less: estate expenses		(400)
Net distributable income	14,000	4,400

R185 (Estate income)	Gross £	Tax £	Net £
Non-savings	17,500	3,500	14,000
Interest	5,500	1,100	4,400

12 Agricultural property relief

- Yes – APR available on land situated in UK, Channel Islands, Isle of Man or within the European Economic Area. Relief given at 100% x agricultural value, post 1.9.95 lease.

- Yes – relief given at 100% x agricultural value. BPR may be available on residual value.

- Yes – assuming that the farmhouse is 'of a character appropriate to the property', at 100% x agricultural value.

- No – livestock may qualify for BPR.

- Yes - relief given at 50% x agricultural value as lease signed pre 1.9.95 and has more than 2 years left to run.

Module C – Corporation tax: answers

1 Overseas Inc

Overseas Inc is incorporated outside of the UK. It will therefore only be resident in the UK if its central management and control is exercised in the UK. If the central management and control is exercised by the board of directors, the place where the board meetings are held will be an important factor in determining the residence of the company.

If Overseas Inc is deemed to be UK resident it will be subject to UK corporation tax on its worldwide profits. The profits arising from both the UK and overseas operations will therefore be taxed in the UK.

A non-UK resident company is only taxed in the UK on profits arising from a trade carried on through a permanent establishment in the UK, eg the manufacturing unit. If Overseas Inc is non-UK resident it will only be taxed in the UK on the profits arising from the UK manufacturing operations.

Double tax relief may be available for income which is taxed both in the UK and overseas.

2 Gardener Ltd

Capital allowances computation for the year to 31 October 2009

	FYA £	Main Pool £	Old Expensive Car £	Short life asset (SLA) £	Allowances £
TWDV at 1.11.08		45,000	24,000	4,000	
SLA transfer (held > 5 APs)		4,000		(4,000)	
Additions qualifying for AIA/40% FYA:					
1.6.09 Van	13,000				
AIA	(13,000)				13,000
Additions (Cars):					
1.5.09 Main rate car		11,000			
Disposals:					
1.7.09 Machine (limited to cost)		(35,000)			
1.6.09 Expensive car			(15,000)		
		25,000	9,000		
Balancing allowance			(9,000)		9,000
WDA @ 20%		(5,000)			5,000
TWDV cfwd		20,000	–	–	
Total allowances					27,000

3 Marine Ltd

(1) The debentures were issued to raise funds for non-trade related purposes and are therefore a non-trading loan relationship. The interest payable, on an accrued basis, of £20,000 will be a debit in respect of a non-trading loan relationship. The associated professional fees will be treated in the same way.

The accrued rent for the 10 months to 31 March 2010 of £20,833 (£25,000 × 10/12) will be taxed as property income.

(2) The bank loan was used for trading purposes and is therefore a trade related loan relationship. Interest payable is an allowable trading deduction. The interest is deductible on accrued basis and £2,800 will therefore be an allowable deduction from trading profits.

4 Mammoth Ltd

Corporation tax liability for the six months ended 31 December 2009

	£
Taxable trading income:	
Trading profit per accounts	200,000
Amortisation charge	(20,000)
Capital allowances:	
Pool WDA £50,000 × 20% × 6/12	(5,000)
Plant AIA £15,000 × 100%	(15,000)
Profits chargeable to corporation tax	160,000
Corporation tax liability (W):	
£160,000 × 28%	44,800
Less marginal relief:	
7/400 × (£750,000 − £160,000)	(10,325)
	34,475

Working

Rate of corporation tax

The accounting period is 6 months long. The limits used to determine the rate of corporation tax are therefore multiplied by 6/12:

Upper limit: £1,500,000 × 6/12	£750,000
Lower limit £300,000 × 6/12	£150,000

The company is therefore a small companies' marginal relief company for the period.

5 Circle Ltd

(1) Loss relief group

Circle Ltd owns at least 75% of Square Ltd. They therefore form a loss relief group.

Triangle Ltd is not in a loss relief group with Circle Ltd as Circle Ltd's indirect holding in Triangle Ltd is less than 75% ie 64% (80% × 80%).

Square Ltd and Triangle Ltd can form a separate loss relief group.

(2) Group relief – Year ended 31 December 2009

Oblong Ltd can surrender its current year trading loss of £220,000 and its excess charges on income of £1,000 (£6,000 − £5,000). Capital losses cannot be group relieved.

Circle Ltd can claim losses of £73,000 from Oblong Ltd, ie the amount of its profits chargeable to corporation tax (ie total profits (including gains) less charges on income).

6 Hotspur Ltd

	12 m/e 31.3.10 £	2 m/e 31.5.10 £
Adjusted profit before CAs (12:2)	384,000	64,000
CAs: AIA £50,000 (max)	(50,000)	
Balance £3,000 × 40% (FYA as acquired 1 April 2009)	(1,200)	
£(3,000 − 1,200 − 1,600) × 20% × 2/12		(7)
Taxable trading income	332,800	63,993
Profit on non-trading loan relationship (12:2)	6,000	1,000
Property income (4/12 : 2/12)	40,000	20,000
PCTCT	378,800	84,993
Due dates for CT 600	31.5.11	31.5.11

7 Verona Ltd

8 month CAP, therefore 3 payments on account required.

Initial payments based on profit estimate of £5m.

Instalment	Due	Working	£
1	14.11.09	£5m × 28% × 3/8	525,000
2	14.2.10	£5m × 28% × 3/8	525,000
			1,050,000
3	14.4.10	Balance required (N)	630,000
Total tax payable			1,680,000

N: Revised tax due = £6m × 28% = £1,680,000.

8 Non-trading loan relationship

(1) Against profits of the same accounting period before charges and s.393A loss relief.
(2) Surrendered as group relief.
(3) Carried back 12 months against profit on non-trading loan relationships.
(4) Against non-trading profits of the next accounting period.

9 Orsino Ltd

The chargeable accounting period is 1.2.09 to 30.9.09 (ie 8 months)

	£	£
Tax adjusted profit	125,000	
Less; capital allowances		
Special rate car: £9,000 × 10% x 8/12	(600)	
Trading profit		124,400
Profit on non-trading loan relationship		8,000
PCTCT		132,400
FII (£1,000 × 100/90)		1,111
Notional profits		133,511

There are 3 associated companies:

	£
Upper limit (£1.5 m × 1/3 × 8/12)	333,333
Lower limit (£300,000 × 1/3 × 8/12)	66,667

Marginal relief applies. CAP straddles FY 2008 and FY 2009 – but rates and limits are the same in each FY.

	£
CT due:	
£132,400 × 28%	37,072
$7/400 \times £(333,333 - 133,511) \times \dfrac{132,400}{133,511}$	(3,468)
Corporation tax payable	33,604

10 Trading losses

The carry forward of trading losses is denied where within a three year period there is BOTH

(1) a change of ownership of a company; AND
(2) a 'major change in the nature or conduct of the trade' carried on by the company.

A change will be 'major' if there is a change in any of the following:

- the type of property dealt in
- the type of services provided
- the facilities provided
- customers
- outlets
- markets

The carry forward of trading losses is also denied where:

(1) the company's activities had become small or negligible; and
(2) there is a change of ownership of the company; and
(3) following the change of ownership there is a considerable revival in the scale of activities.

11 Lysander Ltd

The sale of the shares in Lysander Ltd will result in a gain chargeable on Theseus Ltd.

	£
Proceeds	10,000,000
Less: cost 2002	(100,000)
Gain chargeable	9,900,000

The substantial shareholding exemption does not apply as Lysander Ltd is not a trading company.

There will also be a de-grouping charge as the office block had been transferred to Lysander Ltd in a NGNL transfer within 6 years of Lysander leaving the group:

	£
Market value at transfer in 2007	6,000,000
Less: Cost to group in 2001	(1,000,000)
Gain chargeable	5,000,000

This gain will be chargeable on Lysander Ltd.

12 Cressida Ltd

	£	£
Trading income:		
Paint sales		312,000
Patent royalty ($\times$ 100/80)		10,000
		322,000
Expenses:		
General manufacturing costs	120,000	
R&D expenditure (£40,000 $\times$ 175%)	70,000	
Amortisation of goodwill:		
£100,000 $\times$ 1/5 $\times$ 6/12	10,000	
		(200,000)
PCTCT		122,000

Small company. CAP straddles FY 2008 and FY 2009 – but rates and limits are the same in both FYs.

	£
Tax:	
£122,000 $\times$ 21%	25,620
Less: income tax suffered on patent royalty income	(2,000)
	23,620

Module D – Taxation of individuals: answers

1   **Reginald**

Reginald has notified chargeability on time. The deadline is 5 October 2010 for 2009/10.

As HMRC issued the tax return after 31 October, the deadline for filing online was 3 months after the tax return was issued ie by 10 February 2011. Therefore, Reginald filed his return late.

Reginald can amend his return within 12 months of the filing deadline – ie up until 10 February 2012.

If a return is filed late, HMRC has until the quarter day following the first anniversary of the actual filing date to open an enquiry ie 30 April 2012.

As Reginald filed his return less than six months late, he will incur a penalty of £100.

2   **Mr Falstaff**

	Non savings £	Savings £
State pension	5,200	
Employers pension	14,000	
Rental profits	4,800	
Bank interest (× 100/80)		937
Net income	24,000	937
Less: PAA (W1)	(8,934)	
Taxable income	15,066	937

Tax	
15,066 @ 20%	3,013
937 @ 20%	187
Tax liability	3,200
Less: PAYE	(1,850)
Tax on interest	(187)
Tax payable	1,163

Working

	£
Income	24,937
Less: gift aid (£500 × 100/80)	(625)
Income for PAA purposes	24,312
PAA (>75)	9,640
Less ½ × (24,312 – 22,900)	(706)
	8,934

Note: as marriage takes place after 5 December 2005, the married couples allowances goes to the one with the highest income (in this case this is Celia).

3 Antony

	£	£
Car:		
£20,000 × 21% × 9/12 $\frac{(165-135)}{5}$ + 15 = 21%		3,150
Fuel:		
£16,900 × 21% × 9/12		2,662
Accommodation:		
Annual value	1,000	
Additional yearly rent		
£(250,000 − 75,000) × 4.75%	8,312	
	9,312	
× 7/12	5,432	
Less: rents paid (£200 × 7)	(1,400)	
		4,032
Total taxable benefits		9,844

4 Eleanora

Eleanora is currently resident and ordinarily resident, but non-domiciled in the UK. Even though she has lived here for many years, she retains her non-domicile status because she has a clear intention to return to live in Australia.

Her UK employment income will be taxable in full in the UK on an arising basis.

As a non-domiciled individual, she may claim for her overseas rental income to be taxable in the UK only to the extent that it is remitted to the UK. So the rental income of £12,000 is not taxable in the UK.

The overseas dividend income will also only be taxable to the extent that it has been remitted to the UK (ie £11,000 × 100/90 (grossed up by a 10% non-repayable UK tax credit)). This amount will be taxed as non-savings income at a rate of 40%.

However, as Eleanora has been resident in the UK for at least 7 out of the preceding 9 tax years she will be subject to the £30,000 remittance based charge if she claims to be taxed on the remittance basis. This is in addition to the tax charged on her remitted income. It would not therefore be beneficial for Eleanora to claim the remittance basis in respect of 2009/10 and she will be taxed on all her foreign income on an arising basis. (The overseas dividends will be grossed up by the 10% non-repayable tax credit, but will only be taxed at the rate of 32.5%.)

5 Jemima

Grant

There is no tax or NIC on the grant of options under the EMI scheme.

Exercise

There is no tax or NIC on the exercise of the EMI options, because the exercise price was not less than the market value of the shares at the date of grant.

Sale of shares

The gain on the sale of shares is subject to CGT, as follows:

	£
Proceeds (£14.70 × 5,000)	73,500
Cost (£6.80 × 5,000)	(34,000)
	39,500
Annual exempt amount	(10,100)
	29,400
CGT @ 18%	5,292

6 Roderigo

The deferred gain will crystallise if;

(1) Roderigo disposes of the shares (other than by way of a gift to his spouse/civil partner);

(2) after transferring the shares to his spouse/civil partner, the spouse/civil partner then disposes of the shares;

(3) Roderigo becomes neither resident nor ordinarily resident within 3 years from the issue of the shares;

(4) after giving the shares to the spouse/civil partner, the spouse/civil partner becomes neither resident nor ordinarily resident within 3 years from the issue of the shares;

(5) the EIS shares cease to be eligible for relief.

7 Jamie

		£	£
Rent	(9/12 × £15,000)	11,250	
	(3/12 × £15,600)	3,900	
			15,150
Less allowable expenses:			
Insurance	(4/12 × £3,600)		(1,200)
	(8/12 × £4,200)		(2,800)
Council tax			(1,100)
Chimney replacement (Note)			(800)
Interest	(3% × £200,000)		(6,000)
Wear and tear allowance	(10% × (15,150 – 1,100))		(1,405)
Property income (2009/10)			1,845

Note: Replacement of a subsidiary part of an asset (eg chimney) is treated as revenue expenditure and therefore allowable.

8 Emily

Class 1 primary – payable by Emily

		£
Earnings		
Salary		50,000
Bonus		36,000
Telephone bills		650
		86,650
Class 1 primary:	(43,875 – 5,715) × 11%	4,198
	(86,650 – 43,875) × 1%	428
		4,626

Class 1 secondary – payable by Arcite Ltd

(86,650 – 5,715) × 12.8% = £10,360

Class 1A – payable by Arcite Ltd

		£
Accommodation	10,800	
Medical insurance	480	
	11,280 × 12.8%	£1,444

9 Maria

Capital gains tax computation 2008/09

		£	£
1	Painting		
	Proceeds	6,860	
	31.3.82 MV	(4,000)	
	Gain	2,860	
	Restricted to:		
	5/3 × (7,000 − 6,000) (Note gross proceeds used)		1,667
2	West Ltd		
	Gain before reliefs	45,000	
	Less Entrepreneurs' relief		
	£45,000 × 4/9	(20,000)	
	Gain		25,000
3	Coach plc		24,000
	Total gains		50,667
	Less losses brought forward		(5,000)
			45,667
	Less Annual exempt amount		(10,100)
	Taxable gain		35,567
	CGT at 18%		6,402

10 Henry Percy

	£
Gain	272,000
Less: PPR relief 19/27.5 × £272,000 (W1)	(187,927)
Gain	84,073
Less: Annual exempt amount	(10,100)
Taxable gain	73,973
CGT:	
£73,973 @ 18%	13,315

Working

	Occupied years	Absent years
1.4.82 – 31.3.98	16	
1.4.98 – 30.9.06		8.5
1.10.06 – 30.9.09	3	
(last 3 years)		
Total	19	8.5

11 Oswald

	£	£
Shares to son:		
MV	95,000	
Less: cost	(12,000)	
Gain	83,000	
Less: s.165 gift relief	(55,000)	
Chargeable gain £(40,000 – 12,000)	28,000	
		28,000
Painting to daughter:		
MV	20,000	
Less: cost	(25,000)	
Loss	(5,000)	
'Connected persons' loss so no relief against other gains		NIL
Shares to nephew:		
MV	8,000	
Less: cost	(20,000)	
Loss	(12,000)	
Nephew not a 'connected person' so general loss relief allowed		(12,000)
Net gains 2009/10		16,000

12 Miranda

Apportionment of consideration on takeover

	Value £	%
20,000 ordinary shares in Prospero plc	95,000	38%
£100,000 of loan stock in Prospero plc	100,000	40%
Cash	55,000	22%
Total	250,000	100%

Gain on receipt of loan stock in 2008/09 will be frozen until loan stock is sold / redeemed:

	£
Value of loan stock at takeover	100,000
Less: base cost	
£80,000 × 40%	(32,000)
Frozen gain	68,000

This gain crystallises in 2009/10 when the loan stock is redeemed.

The loss on redemption is not allowable as the loan stock is exempt from CGT.

Module E – Taxation of unincorporated businesses

1 Albert

Tax adjusted trading profit for the year ended 30 June 2009

	£
Profit per accounts	35,000
Add:	
Legal fees	–
Repair costs (Note)	200
Delivery van -cost	6,000
Parking fine	50
	41,250
Capital allowances (AIA) on van (W1) £6,000 × 100% × 80%	(4,800)
Tax adjusted trading profit	36,450

Note: The repair costs were initial repairs to a recently acquired asset and were necessary in order for the asset to be used in the business. The costs are therefore disallowed as capital.

2 Maggie

Tax adjusted trading profit for the fifteen months to 30 April 2010

	£
Net profit per accounts	24,700
Plus: Maggie's wages (appropriation of profit)	45,000
Rent and rates (private use £10,000 × ¼)	2,500
Depreciation	2,000
Goods own use	850
Tax adjusted trading profit	75,050

2008/09 Trading income assessment

The basis period for the 2009/10 trading income assessment is 6 April 2009 to 5 April 2010 (the actual basis as no accounting period ends in 2009/10).

3 Karen

Capital allowances computation for the year to 31 August 2010

	FYA £	Main pool £	Old expensive Car (PU 40%) £	Special rate Car (PU 40%) £	Allowances £
TWDV at 1.9.09		25,000	16,000		
Addition qualifying for AIA/40% FYA:					
Van	15,000				
AIA	(15,000)				15,000
Additions not qualifying for AIA:					
Jaguar car (special rate)				25,000	
Ford car (main rate)		10,000			
Disposal			(12,000)		
		35,000	4,000	25,000	
Balancing allowance			(4,000)× 60%		2,400
WDA @ 20%		(7,000)			7,000
WDA @ 10%				(2,500) × 60%	1,500
TWDV c/fwd	-	28,000	-	22,500	
Total allowances					25,900

4 Gerald

2009/10 Trading income assessment

Basis of assessment: 18 month period to 31 December 2009

	£	£
Year ended 30 June 2009 - taxable profit		34,000
6 months to 31 December 2009 - Adjusted trading profit	15,000	
Plus: Balancing charge (W)	11,000	
		26,000
Less: Overlap profits		(8,000)
Trading income assessment		52,000

Working

Capital allowances for the 6 months to 31 December 2009

	Main pool £	Allowances £
TWDV bfwd	4,000	
Disposals:		
Van (MV)	(8,500)	
Plant and machinery	(6,500)	
	(11,000)	
Balancing charge	11,000	11,000

5 Brooke

The loss arises in the tax year 2009/10.

Options available

(1) Carry forward against the first available future trading profits of the same trade.

Under this option £500 of the loss would be offset in 2010/11 (year ended 31 May 2010). The balance of £9,500 would be carried forward to future years. The benefit of the loss will therefore be delayed into the future.

(2) Offset against general income

The loss can be offset against general income of the current tax year (2009/10) and/or the previous tax year (2008/09).

In 2009/10 Brooke's other income is £5,000 which would be covered by the personal allowance. Offsetting the loss in this year would waste most of the personal allowance and is not therefore advisable.

In 2008/09 Brooke has trading income of £26,000 (year ended 31 May 2008) and other income of £5,000. The loss would be fully utilised, save tax at the basic rate and result in a repayment of tax.

6 Richard

(a) *Disposal of building – August 2009*

	£
Proceeds	850,000
Less: Cost (July 2001)	(400,000)
Chargeable gain	450,000

(b) *Base cost of new building - assuming rollover relief claimed*

	£
Rollover relief - restricted as proceeds are not fully reinvested.	
Proceeds not reinvested (£850,000 – £750,000)	100,000
Gain eligible to be rolled over (£450,000 – £100,000)	350,000
Cost of new building	750,000
Less: Gain rolled over	(350,000)
Revised base cost	400,000

7 Antonio, Bassanio and Portia

Portia is acquiring a 20% interest in the partnership goodwill on 1 January 2010.

Bassanio is disposing of a 20% interest in the partnership goodwill on 1 January 2010.

No adjustment is made via the partnership accounts, so the transaction takes place at no gain, no loss under SP D12 para 4.

As Portia makes a payment to Bassanio outside the accounts, this payment is treated as additional consideration.

Bassanio's CGT computation is therefore as follows:

	Bassanio £
Gain on 1.1.10:	
'Deemed proceeds' (20% share)	40,000
Less: cost (£200,000 × 20%)	(40,000)
Gain	NIL
Actual consideration paid	80,000
Gain	80,000

Bassanio is therefore deemed to have sold his 20% interest to Portia for £(40,000 + 80,000) = £120,000. This is Portia's CGT base cost for her 20% share.

8 Horatio and Claudius

	Total £	Horatio £	Claudius £
P/e 31.12.09 (13 m)	260,000		
Salary (× 13/12)	16,250		16,250
Balance (3:2)	243,750	146,250	97,500
	260,000	146,250	113,750
2009/10:			
P/e 31.12.09		146,250	113,750
Less: overlap relief (W)		(15,000)	(2,500)
Taxable profits		131,250	111,250

(W) Overlap: £

Horatio
Overlap profits arising on commencement 15,000

Claudius
Overlap profits arising on commencement (4 mths) 10,000
Used on change of accounts date:
£10,000 × ¼ 2,500

9 Toby

	£
2008/09:	
1.5.08 – 5.4.09	
£60,000 + £(30,000) × 2/3	40,000
2009/10:	
1.5.08 – 30.4.09	
£60,000 + £(30,000)	30,000
Add: losses taken in 2008/09	20,000
	50,000
NIC 2009/10:	
Class 2 (£2.40 × 52)	125
Class 4 £(43,875 – 5,715) × 8%	3,053
£(50,000 – 43,875) × 1%	61
	3,239

10 Florence

As stock is transferred along with other assets, under s.176 ITTOIA 2005, the value placed on stock has to be 'just & reasonable' to prevent manipulation of consideration to obtain a tax advantage.

HMRC will therefore expect the value to be placed on the stock at cessation to be its market value of £25,000.

As £60,000 has been accounted for in respect of the stock, £35,000 will therefore need to be deducted from the final trading profit.

The cost of the stock for Oliver will now be £25,000 (not £60,000 as agreed).

11 Warwick

	£	£	£ TWDV
Capital allowances:			
Year ended 31 December 2009	£6,000 × 20% (WDA) = £1,200	1,200	4,800
Period ended 30 April 2011	£4,800 × 20% × 16/12	1,280	3,520
Trading profits:			
Year ended 31 December 2009	£(12,000 − 1,200)	10,800	
Period ended 30 April 2011	£(30,000 − 1,280)	28,720	

Assessable profits & overlap

		£	£
2008/09	1.1.09 – 5.4.09		
2009/10	1.1.09 – 31.12.09		
Overlap	1.1.09 – 5.4.09		
	3/12 × £10,800	2,700	
2010/11	1.5.09 – 30.4.10		
	8/12 × £10,800		7,200
	+ 4/16 × £28,720		7,180
			14,380
Overlap	1.5.09 – 31.12.09		
	8/12 × £10,800	7,200	
2011/12	1.5.10 – 30.4.11		
Overlap c/f	From opening years		2,700
	Created on change of accounts date		7,200
			9,900

12   Morgan

Interest charges:

	£
2nd POA for 2008/09 (due 31.7.09)	
£5,500 × 2/12 × 2.5%	23
Balancing payment for 2008/09 (due 31.1.10)	
£2,000 × 2/12 × 2.5%	8
Over-reduction of POAs for 2008/09 (by £1,000 each)	
£1,000 × 12/12 × 2.5%	25
£1,000 × 6/12 × 2.5%	12
1st POA for 2009/10 (due 31.1.10)	
£6,500 × 2/12 × 2.5%	27
Total interest charges	95
Surcharge as 2008/09 balancing payment over 28 days late:	
£2,000 × 5%	100
Late return penalty for 2008/09	100
Grand total	295

CTA EXAMINATIONS
MAY AND NOVEMBER 2010
TAX TABLES

INCOME TAX

Rates	2009-10	2008-09
	%	%
Starting rate for savings income [1] [2]	10	10
Basic rate [3]	20	20
Higher rate [3]	40	40
Trust rate	40	40
	£	£
Savings income starting rate band [1] [2]	1 – 2,440	1 – 2,320
Basic rate band	1 – 37,400	1 - 34,800
Standard rate band for trusts	1,000	1,000

Notes
(1) Savings income is taxed at 10%, 20% or 40%.
(2) If an individual's taxable non-savings income exceeds £2,440, the 10% starting rate for savings will not apply.
(3) Dividend income is taxed at 10% up to the basic rate limit and at 32.5% thereafter.

Income Tax reliefs

	2009-10	2008-09
	£	£
Personal allowance	6,475	6,035
– age 65–74	9,490	9,030
– age 75 or over	9,640	9,180
Married couple's allowance [1] [2]		
– age under 75	NA	6,535
– age 75 or over	6,965	6,625
– Maximum income before abatement of relief - £1 for £2	22,900	21,800
– Minimum allowance	2,670	2,540
Blind person's allowance	1,890	1,800
'Rent-a-room' limit	4,250	4,250
Enterprise investment scheme relief limit [3]	500,000	500,000
Venture capital trust relief limit [4]	200,000	200,000
Employer supported childcare	£55 per week	£55 per week

Notes
(1) Relief restricted to 10%.
(2) Only available where at least one partner was born before 6 April 1935.
(3) Relief at 20%.
(4) Relief at 30%.

Pension contributions

	Annual allowance	Lifetime allowance
	£	£
2006-07	215,000	1,500,000
2007-08	225,000	1,600,000
2008-09	235,000	1,650,000
2009-10	245,000	1,750,000
2010-11 to 2015-16	255,000	1,800,000

Basic amount qualifying for tax relief   £3,600

Company cars and fuel

Car benefit   15% of list price for cars emitting 135g/km, increased by 1% per 5g/km over the limit
Capped at 35% of list price
10% of list price for cars emitting 120g/km or less
3% supplement on diesel cars
Fuel benefit - £16,900 multiplied by the percentage used in calculating the car benefit (ie based on CO_2 emission rating)

Van benefit   £3,000
Fuel benefit - £500

ITEPA Mileage Rates 2009-10 and 2008-09

Car or van[1]	First 10,000 business miles	40p
	Additional business miles	25p
Motorcycles		24p
Bicycles		20p
Passenger payments		5p

Note (1) For NIC purposes, a rate of 40p applies irrespective of mileage.

Official rate of interest

	2009-10	2008-09
	4.75%	6.10%

VALUE ADDED TAX

	From 1.1.10	1.12.08 to 31.12.09	To 30.11.08
Standard rate	17½%	15%	17½%
VAT fraction	7/47	3/23	7/47

Limits	From 1.5.09	1.4.08 to 30.4.09
Annual registration limit	£68,000	£67,000
De-registration limit	£66,000	£65,000

Thresholds	Cash accounting	Annual accounting
Turnover threshold to join scheme	£1,350,000	£1,350,000
Turnover threshold to leave scheme	£1,600,000	£1,600,000

CAPITAL ALLOWANCES

	6.4.09 – 5.4.10[1]	6.4.08 – 5.4.09[1]
Annual investment allowance (AIA)[2]	100%	100%
First year allowance (FYA)[3]	40%	N/A
WDA on plant and machinery in main pool[4]	20%	20%
WDA on plant and machinery in special rate pool[5]	10%	10%
Writing down allowance on patent rights and know-how	25%	25%

Notes (1) Dates for companies are 1 April - 31 March.

(2) 100% on the first £50,000 of investment in plant and machinery (except cars).

(3) A FYA is available for expenditure in the main pool. FYA is given after the AIA.

(4) A rate of 20% applies to cars with CO_2 emissions greater than 110g/km but not more than 160 g/km acquired on or after 6 April 2009 (1 April for companies).

(5) A rate of 10% applies to cars with CO_2 emissions greater than 160 g/km acquired on or after 6 April 2009 (1 April for companies).

(6) Cars acquired prior to 6 April 2009 (1 April for companies) continue to be written down based on cost rather than emissions.

100% First year allowances available to all businesses

1) New energy saving plant and machinery, and water efficient plant and machinery.
2) New cars registered between 16 April 2002 and 31 March 2013 if the car either emits not more than 110 g/km (120g/km prior to 1 April 2008) of CO_2 or it is electrically propelled.
3) Renovation or conversion of vacant business premises, in a designated Enterprise Area, for the purpose of bringing those premises back into business use.
4) Converting or renovating an empty or under-used space above a commercial property into qualifying residential accommodation.
5) Capital expenditure incurred by a person on research and development.

CORPORATION TAX

Financial year	2009	2008
Full rate	28%	28%
Small companies' rate	21%	21%
Profit limit for small companies' rate	£300,000	£300,000
Profit limit for small companies' marginal relief	£1,500,000	£1,500,000
Marginal relief fraction for profits between £300,000 and £1,500,000	7/400	7/400

Research and development expenditure

	SMEs From 1.8.08	From 1.1.05
Employees – less than	500	250
Turnover – not more than	€100m	€50m
Balance sheet assets – not more than	€86m	€43m

SMEs must meet the employees criteria and *either* the turnover *or* the balance sheet assets criteria.

NATIONAL INSURANCE CONTRIBUTIONS

	2009-10			2008-09		
Class 1 contributions	Annual	Monthly	Weekly	Annual	Monthly	Weekly
Lower earnings limit	£4,940	£412	£95	£4,680	£390	£90
Earnings threshold	£5,715	£476	£110	£5,435	£453	£105
Upper accruals point	£40,040	£3,337	£770	N/A	NA	N/A
Upper earnings limit	£43,875	£3,656	£844	£40,040	£3,337	£770

Employee's contributions in 2009-10 (2008-09)

Not contracted out:	11% (11%) on earnings between £110 (£105) and £844 (£770)
	1% (1%) above £844 (£770) per week
Contracted out:	9.4% (9.4%) on earnings between £110 (£105) and £770 (NA)
	11% (NA) on earnings between £770 (NA) and £844 (NA)
	1% (1%) on earnings above £844 (£770) per week
	1.6% rebate on earnings between £95 (£90) and £110 (£105)

Employer's contributions in 2009-10 (2008-09)

Not contracted out:	12.8% (12.8%) on earnings in excess of £110 (£105)
Contracted out:	
Salary related:	9.1% (9.1%) on earnings between £110 (£105) and £770 (£770)
	12.8% (12.8%) on earnings in excess of £770 (£770)
	3.7% (3.7%) rebate on earnings between £95 (£90) and £110 (£105)
Money purchase:	11.4% (11.4%) on earnings between £110 (£105) and £770 (£770)
	12.8% (12.8%) on earnings in excess of £770 (£770)
	1.4% (1.4%) rebate on earnings between £95 (£90) and £110 (£105)

	2009-10	2008-09
Class 1A contributions	12.8%	12.8%
Class 1B contributions	12.8%	12.8%
Class 2 contributions		
Normal rate	£2.40 pw	£2.30 pw
Small earnings exception	£5,075 pa	£4,825 pa
Class 3 contributions	£12.05 pw	£8.10 pw
Class 4 contributions		
Annual lower earnings limit (LEL)	£5,715	£5,435
Annual upper earnings limit (UEL)	£43,875	£40,040
Percentage rate between LEL and UEL	8%	8%
Percentage rate above upper earnings limit	1%	1%

CAPITAL GAINS TAX

	2009-10	2008-09
Annual exempt amount	£10,100	£9,600
CGT rate for individuals and trusts	18%	18%

Entrepreneurs' relief: Disposals in 2009-10 (and 2008-09)

Relevant gains (lifetime maximum)   £1,000,000
Reducing fraction   4/9

Lease percentage table

Years	Percentage	Years	Percentage	Years	Percentage
50 or more	100.000	33	90.280	16	64.116
49	99.657	32	89.354	15	61.617
48	99.289	31	88.371	14	58.971
47	98.902	30	87.330	13	56.167
46	98.490	29	86.226	12	53.191
45	98.059	28	85.053	11	50.038
44	97.595	27	83.816	10	46.695
43	97.107	26	82.496	9	43.154
42	96.593	25	81.100	8	39.399
41	96.041	24	79.622	7	35.414
40	95.457	23	78.055	6	31.195
39	94.842	22	76.399	5	26.722
38	94.189	21	74.635	4	21.983
37	93.497	20	72.770	3	16.959
36	92.761	19	70.791	2	11.629
35	91.981	18	68.697	1	5.983
34	91.156	17	66.470	0	0.000

Retail Prices Index

Where Retail Price Indices are required, it should be assumed that they are as follows.

	Jan	Feb	Mar	Apr	May	Jun	Jul	Aug	Sep	Oct	Nov	Dec
1982	–	–	79.44	81.04	81.62	81.85	81.88	81.90	81.85	82.26	82.66	82.51
1983	82.61	82.97	83.12	84.28	84.64	84.84	85.30	85.68	86.06	86.36	86.67	86.89
1984	86.84	87.20	87.48	88.64	88.97	89.20	89.10	89.94	90.11	90.67	90.95	90.87
1985	91.20	91.94	92.80	94.78	95.21	95.41	95.23	95.49	95.44	95.59	95.92	96.05
1986	96.25	96.60	96.73	97.67	97.85	97.79	97.52	97.82	98.30	98.45	99.29	99.62
1987	100.0	100.4	100.6	101.8	101.9	101.9	101.8	102.1	102.4	102.9	103.4	103.3
1988	103.3	103.7	104.1	105.8	106.2	106.6	106.7	107.9	108.4	109.5	110.0	110.3
1989	111.0	111.8	112.3	114.3	115.0	115.4	115.5	115.8	116.6	117.5	118.5	118.8
1990	119.5	120.2	121.4	125.1	126.2	126.7	126.8	128.1	129.3	130.3	130.0	129.9
1991	130.2	130.9	131.4	133.1	133.5	134.1	133.8	134.1	134.6	135.1	135.6	135.7
1992	135.6	136.3	136.7	138.8	139.3	139.3	138.8	138.9	139.4	139.9	139.7	139.2
1993	137.9	138.8	139.3	140.6	141.1	141.0	140.7	141.3	141.9	141.8	141.6	141.9
1994	141.3	142.1	142.5	144.2	144.7	144.7	144.0	144.7	145.0	145.2	145.3	146.0
1995	146.0	146.9	147.5	149.0	149.6	149.8	149.1	149.9	150.6	149.8	149.8	150.7
1996	150.2	150.9	151.5	152.6	152.9	153.0	152.4	153.1	153.8	153.8	153.9	154.4
1997	154.4	155.0	155.4	156.3	156.9	157.5	157.5	158.5	159.3	159.5	159.6	160.0
1998	159.5	160.3	160.8	162.6	163.5	163.4	163.0	163.7	164.4	164.5	164.4	164.4
1999	163.4	163.7	164.1	165.2	165.6	165.6	165.1	165.5	166.2	166.5	166.7	167.3
2000	166.6	167.5	168.4	170.1	170.7	171.1	170.5	170.5	171.7	171.6	172.1	172.2
2001	171.1	172.0	172.2	173.1	174.2	174.4	173.3	174.0	174.6	174.3	173.6	173.4
2002	173.3	173.8	174.5	175.7	176.2	176.2	175.9	176.4	177.6	177.9	178.2	178.5
2003	178.4	179.3	179.9	181.2	181.5	181.3	181.3	181.6	182.5	182.6	182.7	183.5
2004	183.1	183.8	184.6	185.7	186.5	186.8	186.8	187.4	188.1	188.6	189.0	189.9
2005	188.9	189.6	190.5	191.6	192.0	192.2	192.2	192.6	193.1	193.3	193.6	194.1
2006	193.4	194.2	195.0	196.5	197.7	198.5	198.5	199.2	200.1	200.4	201.1	202.7
2007	201.6	203.1	204.4	205.4	206.2	207.3	206.1	207.3	208.0	208.9	209.7	210.9
2008	209.8	211.4	212.1	214.0	215.1	216.8	216.5	217.2	218.4	217.7	216.0	212.9
2009	210.1	211.4	211.3	210.8*	210.3*	209.8*	209.3*	208.8*	208.3*	207.9*	207.5*	207.2*
2010*	206.8	206.5	206.2	205.9	205.7	205.5	205.4	205.4	205.5	205.6	205.7	205.9

* = assumed

STAMP DUTY / STAMP DUTY RESERVE TAX

Shares   0.5%

Stamp duty land tax

Rate (%)	Residential	Non-residential
Zero	Up to £125,000[1][2]	Up to £150,000[3]
1	Over £125,000[1][2] - 250,000	Over £150,000 - 250,000
3	Over £250,000 - 500,000	Over £250,000 - 500,000
4	Over £500,000	Over £500,000

Note
(1) A higher threshold of £150,000 applies to transactions in residential land in disadvantaged areas.
(2) From 3.9.08 to 31.12.09 a higher threshold of £175,000 applies unless it is a lease for less than 21 years.
(3) For non-residential property, where the land is a grant of a lease, the zero rate band is not available if annual rent exceeds £1,000.

New leases – Stamp duty land tax on rent

Rate (%)	Net present value of rent	
	Residential	Non-residential
Zero	Up to £125,000[1]	Up to £150,000
1%	Excess over £125,000[1]	Excess over £150,000

Notes (1) The higher threshold of £175,000 applies between 3.9.08 and 31.12.09 (unless the lease is for less than 21 years), however if exceeded SDLT is payable on the excess over £125,000.

INHERITANCE TAX

	Nil rate band		Nil rate band
6 April 1996 – 5 April 1997	up to £200,000	6 April 2003 – 5 April 2004	up to £255,000
6 April 1997 – 5 April 1998	up to £215,000	6 April 2004 – 5 April 2005	up to £263,000
6 April 1998 – 5 April 1999	up to £223,000	6 April 2005 – 5 April 2006	up to £275,000
6 April 1999 – 5 April 2000	up to £231,000	6 April 2006 – 5 April 2007	up to £285,000
6 April 2000 – 5 April 2001	up to £234,000	6 April 2007 – 5 April 2008	up to £300,000
6 April 2001 – 5 April 2002	up to £242,000	6 April 2008 – 5 April 2009	up to £312,000
6 April 2002 – 5 April 2003	up to £250,000	From 6 April 2009	up to £325,000

Death rate	40%	Wedding gifts – Child £5,000
Lifetime rate	20%	– Grandchild or remoter issue £2,500
Annual exemption	£3,000	– Other party to marriage £2,500
Small gifts	£250	– Other £1,000

Taper relief

		Quick succession relief	
Death within 3 years of gift	Nil%	Period between transfers less than one year	100%
Between 3 and 4 years	20%	Between 1 and 2 years	80%
Between 4 and 5 years	40%	Between 2 and 3 years	60%
Between 5 and 6 years	60%	Between 3 and 4 years	40%
Between 6 and 7 years	80%	Between 4 and 5 years	20%

OTHER INDIRECT TAXES

		2009-10	2008-09
Insurance Premium Tax[1]	Standard rate	5%	5%
	Higher rate	17.5%	17.5%
Landfill Tax[2]	Per tonne	£40	£32
	Qualifying material	£2.50 per tonne	£2.50 per tonne
Landfill Communities Fund (LCF)	Relief for 90% of qualifying contributions	6.0% × landfill tax liability	6.0% × landfill tax liability
Aggregates Levy[2]	Per tonne	£2.00	£1.95
Climate Change Levy[3]	Electricity	0.470p per kwh	0.456p per kwh
	Gas	0.164p per kwh	0.159p per kwh
	Liquid hydrocarbons	1.050p per kg	1.018p per kg
	Any other taxable commodity	1.281p per kg	1.242p per kg

Notes
(1) Premium is tax inclusive – IPT is 1/21 or 7/47 of the premium.
(2) Pro rated for part tonnes.
(3) Where the reduced rate applies it is 20% of the rate shown in the table.

Notes

Notes

CTA AWARENESS WORKBOOK (9/09)

REVIEW FORM & FREE PRIZE DRAW

All original review forms from the entire TQT range, completed with genuine comments, will be entered into a draw on 31 July 2010 and 31 January 2011. The names on the first four forms picked out will be sent a cheque for £50.

Name: _____   **Address:** _____

_____

How have you used this Workbook?
(Tick one box only)
☐ Home study (book only)
☐ On a course _____
☐ Other _____

Why did you decide to purchase this Workbook? *(Tick one box only)*
☐ Have used TQT Workbooks in the past
☐ Recommendation by friend/colleague
☐ Recommendation by a lecturer
☐ Saw advertising
☐ Other _____

During the past six months do you recall seeing/receiving either of the following?
(Tick as many boxes as are relevant)
☐ Our advertisement in *Tax Adviser*
☐ Our Publishing Catalogue

Which (if any) aspects of our advertising do you think are useful?
(Tick as many boxes as are relevant)
☐ Prices and publication dates of new editions
☐ Information on Workbook content
☐ Facility to order books off-the-page
☐ None of the above

Your ratings, comments and suggestions would be appreciated on the following areas of this Workbook.

	Very useful	Useful	Not useful
Study Period Planners	☐	☐	☐
Study Periods	☐	☐	☐
Progress Tests	☐	☐	☐
Course Exams	☐	☐	☐
Advice on Revision Phase	☐	☐	☐
Sample Paper	☐	☐	☐
Question abd Answer Bank	☐	☐	☐

	Excellent	Good	Adequate	Poor
Overall opinion of this Workbook	☐	☐	☐	☐

Do you intend to continue using TQT Products?   ☐ Yes   ☐ No

Please note any further comments and suggestions/errors on the reverse of this page. The TQT author of this edition can be e-mailed at: suedexter@bpp.com

Please return to: Sue Dexter, Tax Publishing Director, BPP Learning Media Ltd, FREEPOST, London, W12 8BR. BPP Learning Media Ltd is a member of the TQT joint venture.

CTA AWARENESS WORKBOOK (9/09)

REVIEW FORM & FREE PRIZE DRAW (continued)

TELL US WHAT YOU THINK

Please note any further comments and suggestions/errors below.

FREE PRIZE DRAW RULES

1 Closing date for 31 July 2010 draw is 30 June 2010. Closing date for 31 January 2011 draw is 31 December 2010.

2 Winners will be notified by post and receive their cheques not later than 6 weeks after the draw date.

3 The decision of the promoter in all matters is final and binding. No correspondence will be entered into.

NATURE'S MEDICINES

NATURE'S MEDICINES

A guide to herbal medicines
and what they can do for you

Reader's Digest

Contents

About this book	5
Nature's medicine chest	6
From plant to potent drug	8
Herbal medicine in the West	10
Herbs in Eastern medicine	12
Harnessing the healing power	14
Using herbal medicines safely	16
Cultivating your own herbs	18
Harvesting and preserving herbs	20
Make your own herbal remedies	22

A to Z of Plants 26

A to Z of Ailments 202

Addiction 204 • Ageing 206 • Allergies 208 • Blood, heart & circulatory problems 211 • Children's health problems 219 • Dental & gum problems 225 • Digestion 227 • Ear & eye problems 239 • Hair & nail problems 242 • Infections 245 • Metabolism & immune system disorders 251 • Muscles, bones & joints 256 • Nervous system & mental health 263 • Reproduction & sexuality 270 • Respiratory problems 279 • Skin problems 285 • Urinary tract & kidney problems 298

Glossary	302
Addresses and web sites	308
Index	309
Bibliography and picture credits	319

About this book

Nature's Medicines *is an introduction and practical guide to the properties of many plants used to treat illnesses and their symptoms in the Western world. The first part of the book outlines the history of herbalism and modern plant research, then explains how to find a qualified medical herbalist and the regulations governing the sale of herbal products. It also tells you how to cultivate and use your own herbs.*

A to Z of Plants

This section features 174 species, listed alphabetically according to common name, followed by their Latin and other names. We tell you how the plants are grown and harvested, which parts are used, each plant's chemical properties as demonstrated in scientific research, and what complaints the plants are used to treat. A section on preparation and dosage provides guidelines for self-medication (more uses are suggested in the 'A to Z of Ailments' section). Take note of the Cautions; these state clearly when the plant should not be used and lists possible side effects.

A to Z of Ailments

In this section more than 135 common illnesses are described, together with herbs that can be used to treat them. In each case, readers are advised not to use more than one herbal preparation at any given time without consulting a medical herbalist. It is also imperative not to exceed the dosages suggested here and in the 'A to Z of Plants' section.

Dosage and preparation

In order to be both safe and effective, a herbal medicine needs to be taken in the right way. Some herbs are best taken as infusions or decoctions (commonly referred to as teas), others as powders, tablets, capsules or liquid extracts. In all of these preparation types, the plant has undergone some degree of transformation to turn it into a medicine. Because manufacturing methods vary, some preparations are more concentrated than others.

For example, one herbal tablet may simply contain the powdered herb, compressed to form a tablet; however another tablet may contain an extract of the same herb, in a more concentrated form. Although both tablets may contain 1 g of medicine, the tablet produced from the concentrate may represent significantly more of the original starting material, and consequently, you would need to take fewer tablets to achieve the desired effect.

In order to reduce confusion, all doses in *Nature's Medicines* are listed according to the recommended dose when the herb is taken in its dried form (unless otherwise stated). In most cases, this will correspond with manufacturers' labelled dosage guidelines, but if you are unclear about which preparation to use, or how much of any herbal medicine to take, consult a medical herbalist before attempting self-medication.

Unless otherwise stated, all doses given are for adults. Consult a qualified medical herbalist for children's doses and treatment.

IMPORTANT

While the creators of this book have made every effort to be as accurate and up to date as possible, medical and pharmacological knowledge is constantly changing. Readers are advised to consult a qualified medical specialist for individual advice. Moreover, even though they are natural, herbs contain chemical substances that can sometimes have marked side effects. If used unwisely, they can be toxic. The writers, researchers, editors and publishers of this book cannot be held liable for any errors and omissions, or actions that may be taken as a consequence of information contained in this book.

ABOUT THIS BOOK 5

Nature's medicine chest

The plant world is an immense store of active chemical compounds. Nearly half the medicines we use today are herbal in origin, and a quarter contain plant extracts or active chemicals taken directly from plants. Many more have yet to be discovered, recorded and researched; only a few thousand have been studied. Across the globe, the hunt is on to find species that could form the basis of new medicines.

From the dawn of time

Humans have always used plants to ease their pains. They imbued them with magical powers and then gradually learnt to identify their properties. We can now enjoy the benefits of herbal medicines because, over thousands of years, our ancestors discovered which plants were beneficial and which were highly toxic.

Palaeobotanists, studying ancient burial sites, are confirming much of the herbal folklore handed down over the centuries. The preserved remains of seeds have substantiated what early doctors and herbalists wrote about the medicinal plants they used. In recent years, this folklore has been supported by scientific studies that confirm the safety and efficacy of many herbal treatments.

Thousands of years ago, the ancient Egyptians discovered simple ways to extract and use the active ingredients within plants. Egyptian papyrus manuscripts from 2000 BC record the use of perfumes and fine oils, and also that aromatic oils and gums were an essential part of the embalming process.

In ancient Greece in the 5th and 4th centuries BC, Hippocrates, known as the father of medicine, was already recommending asparagus and garlic for their diuretic qualities, poppy as a way of inducing sleep and willow leaves to relieve pain and fever. In the 1st century AD, another Greek doctor, Dioscorides, established the first collection of medicinal plants. His treatise on the subject was translated into Arabic and Persian. Centuries later, his work was also used by the Muslim scholars who influenced great universities of the period, particularly at Montpellier, Europe's most famous centre for the study of botany.

As a result of trade with Africa and Asia, the Western world's store of herbal medicines was enriched by the inclusion of camphor, cinnamon, ginger, ginseng, nutmeg, sandalwood, turmeric and senna.

For a long time, however, the use of both local plants and those with more distant origins was based solely on a collection of more or less fanciful beliefs. Throughout the

A miniature painting illustrating a 12th-century manuscript copy of *De Materia Medica* which shows a student with Dioscorides. Of the 500 plants included in the treatise written by this Greek doctor, who lived in the 1st century AD, 54 are still on the list of essential medicinal plants compiled by the World Health Organization in 1978.

At Abidjan, in the African country of Côte d'Ivoire, women pound plants that will be used to make medicines.

Middle Ages, herbal medicine consisted of a mixture of superstition, magic and empirical observation.

From the Renaissance onwards, scientists came to the fore, rejecting alchemists' elixirs and other magical remedies. Local plants were carefully collected and widely used to make infusions, decoctions and ointments. These plants make up the major part of the traditional cures that we in the modern world have inherited.

The active principles

In the late 1700s, Carl Wilhelm Scheele, a gifted Swedish chemist, obtained tartaric acid from grapes, citric acid from lemons and malic acid from apples. The techniques that he and his contemporaries used led to the isolation of the first purified compounds from plants that could be used as drugs.

First of all came the isolation of morphine from the opium poppy in

1803, then caffeine from coffee beans in 1819, quinine from cinchona bark and colchicine from meadow saffron, both in the year 1820, and atropine from deadly nightshade in 1835.

Similarly, Dr William Withering, an 18th-century English doctor and botanist, began to take an interest in the common foxglove, which was widely used in popular medicines as a treatment for water retention. In 1785 he published a paper on the plant, describing the foxglove's diuretic property and its beneficial effect on 'cardiac weaknesses'.

Clinical trials using extracts from the leaf began in 1809, but it was not until around 1835 that French chemist Claude Adolphe Nativel succeeded in isolating the plant's active principle, digitalin. Today, the related species woolly foxglove is the basis of numerous medicines and drugs that treat heart problems.

Aspirin from willow

One tree that generated great interest among scientists was the willow. In the early 1800s, chemists from Germany, Italy and France began the search for the compounds responsible for the widely known pain-relieving effects of its bark.

In 1828, the German pharmacist Johann Buchner was the first to obtain salicin, the major compound present in the bark, in a pure form. In 1838, the Italian chemist Raffaele Piria also obtained salicylic acid from the bark by various chemical processes. However, when ingested, these early compounds caused stomach upsets and blisters in the mouth.

In 1853, the French chemist Charles Frederic Gerhardt was able to synthesise a modified form of salicylic acid – acetylsalicylic acid. But it still wasn't further developed for more than 40 years until a German chemist, Felix Hoffman, working for Bayer, rediscovered Gerhardt's compound. Hoffman gave it to his father who suffered from arthritis and reported the beneficial effects.

Bayer decided to market the acetylsalicylic acid as a new drug for pain relief, and patented the compound acetylsalicylic acid in 1899. At last, from the willow, the first modern drug was born. Now, over 100 years later, aspirin remains one of the most important and most widely consumed drugs in the world.

A new era

From the 1930s onwards, advances in the science of chemistry have made it much easier to reproduce the active ingredients present in plants. However, plants will continue to have a medicinal importance in their own right.

Their active constituents may be slightly modified to improve their efficiency or to reduce undesirable side effects, but they are still the foundation of drugs that are vital for the treatment of disorders such as cancers and heart diseases, or as a means of combating malaria. They also remain the essence of herbal medicine – an area that is increasingly becoming a focus of medical attention and scientific research.

From plant to potent drug

There is a huge amount of collecting and research to be done if we are to benefit from the great diversity and therapeutic potential of plants. Many species have yet to be discovered, especially those growing in the lush forests of equatorial Africa, South America and South-East Asia, or on the Pacific islands. In Australia, research into the traditional Aboriginal use of plants may reveal valuable medicines.

Across the world, a wide range of experts is engaged in the search for new plant species. There are teams of ethnobotanists, phytochemists, pharmacognosists, ethnopharmacologists (scientists who study people and their plants) and herbalists. Hundreds of thousands of plants are collected, then analysed in high-tech research laboratories, where up to 50,000 plants a day are examined.

Some scientists target the species of a particular family of plants known to contain specific active substances. Attempts are made to collect plants from these families in order to find and compare their active constituents.

Others – the ethnobotanists – begin their search by talking to traditional healers, those members of a native population who understand the powers of plants. They select plants that seem promising, note their names in the local dialect, the parts used and what they are used for. This approach is proving particularly successful in uncovering evidence that may lead to new drugs, as such plants are already used medicinally and are therefore much more likely to contain active chemical constituents.

Scientists have also begun to observe which plants animals eat when they are ill. Swans with injured necks often eat willow leaves and twigs. Scientists know that this plant contains the pain-relieving compounds that are the basis of aspirin. When they are infested with lice, badgers dig holes under elder, the roots of which contain insecticidal compounds.

Known as zoopharmacognosy, this research area is also providing a means for discovering compounds and new herbal medicines.

A lengthy process

When samples have been identified and gathered in sufficient numbers, chemists take extracts from the raw materials to isolate a plant's pure chemical constituents. These extracts are tested, firstly to discover any possible toxicity, then to define their biological effects. The selection process is rigorous. It is estimated that, at this stage, only one out of every 10,000 plants analysed is kept.

Thorough clinical studies are then carried out. If the results are positive, the real work of preparing pharmaceutical medicines can begin as the active constituent is developed into a form suitable for ingestion, such as capsules, tablets or liquid solutions.

For the pharmaceutical laboratory, the final step is to apply to the appropriate authority for permission to put the medicine on the market. In Australia and New Zealand, from the middle of 2005, it is expected that this will be handled by the Trans-Tasman Therapeutic Products Agency, which will be accountable to both governments.

In total, 12–15 years, or even longer, may elapse between finding a promising plant in the wild and marketing the end product.

Nature's bounty

It is no accident that plants play an important role in contemporary pharmacological research, since the substances that interest us are those the plant itself uses to survive.

More than 100,000 of these special substances have been found in the plant world and, because of the effects on the human body of their complex chemicals, they form the basis of many medicines.

The struggle against malaria

Quinine, the active principle in the bark of the cinchona tree, first isolated in 1820, still has a role to play

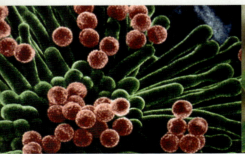 

Once used to bring down fevers in traditional Chinese medicine, artemisen, taken from *Artemesia annua*, is now the fastest and most effective antimalarial drug, and it has no adverse side effects.

The Madagascar periwinkle is cultivated on a large scale in Europe. Constituents have been extracted from it that have helped to create some of the most effective anticancer drugs.

8 NATURE'S MEDICINES

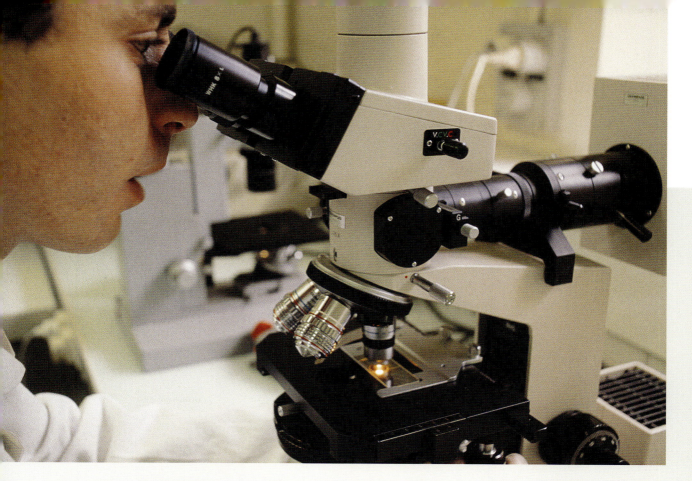

In the past few decades, increasingly sophisticated machines for analysing chemical substances have led to a significant advance in medical knowledge.

in the treatment of severe cases of malaria. But most strains of the parasites responsible for this illness have developed a resistance to the synthetic antimalarial drugs, modelled on quinine. The search for new chemicals is, therefore, a major medical priority, as some 300 million people contract malaria every year and 2 million die from it.

Qing hao or *Artemesia annua* (a species of wormwood used in traditional Chinese medicine) has recently given rise to a new class of antimalarial drug that is now used worldwide, especially in Africa and South-East Asia.

Fighting cancer

The Madagascar periwinkle was reputed to be a cure for diabetes in its native country, but the scientists who studied it noticed a reduction of white corpuscles in the blood of the animals involved and used the plant to treat leukaemia, in which white cells multiply abnormally. Two alkaloids with powerful effects, vinblastine and vincristine, were subsequently isolated in the periwinkle's leaf. A French team then created highly active derivatives from other constituents present in greater amounts in the plant. These drugs increased the life expectancy of patients suffering from Hodgkin's disease and acute leukaemia.

The anticancer property of an extract of bark from the Pacific yew tree was detected completely by accident in the mid-1960s. The active substance, taxol, was isolated a few years later. The clinical trials came to an abrupt halt, however, when it became clear that to get enough taxol to treat each patient, six 100-year-old trees would have to be felled. Fortunately, an answer was found in the needles of the European yew tree. A French team isolated a compound from it that could be chemically converted into products similar to and even more effective than taxol. They are widely used nowadays to treat certain breast and ovarian cancers.

The rhizome of the American mandrake contains anticancer substances similar to those in the alkaloids found in the Madagascar periwinkle. A substance extracted from *Camptotheca acuminata*, a tree found in southern China, was the source of two synthetic drugs: irinotecan, developed in Japan, and topotecan, developed in the United States. Both of these are used to treat certain forms of cancer.

Over the past few years, plants have played a role in some of the amazing advances made in all areas of medicine. Progress requires time, persistence and investment, but it is now generally recognised that plants hold great promise for the future health of humankind.

Herbal medicine in the West

Over thousands of years traditional ways of using plants medicinally have developed in different societies and in different countries all around the world. Today the study of herbs has become a medical science in its own right, and many new therapeutic uses for plants have been discovered, some of them as a result of brand new areas of interest being developed, like nutraceuticals and aromatherapy.

What is herbal medicine?

Herbal medicine, also known as phytotherapy, is the treatment of illnesses using measured doses of specific plants. A qualified medical herbalist can prescribe plants to be taken internally or used externally in various forms and concentrations, depending on the ailment.

The herbalist may suggest the addition of edible plants to the diet – such as celery, radish or cabbage – or may prescribe medicinal preparations, such as infusions, herbal tablets, capsules, powders or liquid extracts. The herbalist may also recommend the use of an essential oil derived from a medicinal plant.

Fresh lavender flowers undergo steam distillation to produce the essential oil. Large quantities of flowers are needed because the essential oil content is only about 1 per cent or even less.

A holistic approach

Conventional drug research tends to be focused on identifying a single, active constituent in a plant and this approach has yielded a significant number of blockbuster drugs. Herbalists take a holistic approach, believing that the whole of the plant should be used in a treatment, because all the constituents are important, not just the compounds that have been shown to be active.

Each herb may consist of hundreds of phytochemicals – plant-based compounds that herbalists believe interact in a 'synergistic' way. Together they achieve a greater effect than the sum of all their individual effects. An analogy can be made to music – we can appreciate that when single notes are played together in a certain way they make up the pleasing sound of a chord. The pharmaceutical industry is still focused on producing 'single notes', while herbalists argue that the 'chords' found in herbal medicines are more effective.

Recent studies have demonstrated this effect. For example, research carried out at Middlesex University, London, in 1999 showed that an extract of common sage was more potent as an inhibitor of acetylcholinesterase (so helping to maintain memory function) than any of the pure compounds that are found in the plant.

Using mixtures of compounds is an approach that is now also used in orthodox medicine. HIV/AIDS patients, for instance, are often given a 'cocktail' of drugs because the combination appears to work more effectively than using one single drug on its own.

New herbal trends

A recent development in herbal medicine is the creation of extracts with higher concentrations of certain active constituents. For example, St John's wort (*Hypericum*

> ### HEALING FLOWERS
>
> In the 1930s, the English physician Edward Bach developed a holistic system of healing based on plants. He believed that certain flowers give off 'vibrations' that directly influence the human spirit. Through trial and error, he established 38 remedies to be used to correct various states of emotional distress, which he believed were at the root of all illnesses. Since then, many other ranges of flower essences have been developed using flowers from many different countries. Among the most popular are the Australian Bush Flower Essences, which are used by herbalists and other natural health professionals around the world.
>
> The remedies are taken in the form of drops that contain a floral elixir. Bach flower remedies have no adverse side effects and many people find that they help them to regain inner harmony and balance. However, scientific research has yet to substantiate the effectiveness of the remedies.

perforatum) has been shown clinically to be beneficial in the treatment of mild to moderate depression, an effect that is believed to be at least partly due to a compound called hypericin. As a result, herbal manufacturers now produce extracts standardised to contain at least 0.3 per cent of hypericin.

Whether in fact these standardised extracts are more effective than traditional preparations is not absolutely certain. This is partly because clinical data is often available only for a standardised version of the herb – because a manufacturer has funded the study – and herbalists do not have the opportunity or resources to test traditional herbal preparations in the same way.

Several pharmaceutical companies have also started to research and develop pharmaceutical versions of herbal medicines. Like conventional synthetic drugs, these will have to undergo rigorous controls and testing that may take years and could cost millions of dollars.

Creating nutraceuticals

Herbal medicines are now also being incorporated into food. Plant extracts are being formulated to create food products that will help to cure ailments, prevent disease and maintain health. These so-called functional foods, or nutraceuticals, now enable people to take herbal medicines in a different way. Rather than swallowing a capsule, tablet or liquid extract, they can consume the herbs in yoghurt, soft drinks, fruit juices or chocolate bars.

Aromatherapy

For many people, one of the most pleasurable ways of enjoying the benefits of herbs is through aromatherapy. This involves the use of aromatic essential oils obtained from plants. The oils are usually produced by means of steam distillation. The practice of aromatherapy has gained widespread acceptance, and some conventional hospitals have even introduced it for their patients.

About 40 plant oils are currently in common use. Some, such as basil, cinnamon and rosemary, have a stimulating effect, while others, such as anise, neroli and chamomile, have a sedative effect. Some oils have a double effect, stimulating certain areas of the brain, while at the same time calming others.

Herbs in Eastern medicine

In most Asian countries, traditional forms of medicine are still widely practised. Plants play a crucial role, but they are used according to ways of thinking that are often very different from those in the West. These medicinal plants are now being intensively studied by scientists, which should help to clarify their role in various treatments, and perhaps to discover new applications for them.

India is the birthplace of Ayurvedic medicine, the oldest medical system known to humans. It is still in use today and takes a holistic approach, in which health is seen in terms of the whole being. Herbal remedies play a central role in it.

An enduring inheritance

Born on the banks of the river Indus, Ayurvedic medicine has been practised for over 5000 years, and was greatly influenced by Hindu philosophy. At first, the knowledge was passed on orally by spiritual teachers. But from around the 8th century BC, it was gradually set out in a number of medical treatises. Its use spread throughout Asia at the same time as Buddhism in the 1st and 2nd centuries AD, and has influenced a number of other medical traditions, particularly those in Tibet and China.

A holistic approach

In Ayurvedic medicine, it is thought that good health depends on a harmonious relationship between the three fundamental forces of energy, or *doshas*, which are regarded as governing all living processes. They are *vata* – the principle of air and movement, *pitta* – the principle of fire and transformation, and *kapha* – the principle of water, which ensures cohesion and support.

At birth all people are thought to receive a personal combination of *doshas*, which determines their basic physical constitution and susceptibility to illness. Ayurvedic medicine takes into account the temperament conferred by the *doshas*, as well as an individual's current emotional state and way of life.

Plants that cure

About 1250 plants are used in Ayurvedic medicine. Patients are given their own personal herbal mixture, to be taken, as appropriate, in the form of infusions, lotions, poultices or pills.

For example, someone with a *kapha* temperament – which is thought to lead to excess weight and lethargy – may be treated with ginger and capsicum. The *pitta* temperament may need andrographis or

China has the richest store of herbal medicines in the world and a vast legacy of experience, recorded over the centuries by its herbalist doctors.

dandelion root, plants that should not be given to the *vata* type. Instead, the latter will benefit from rosemary, which is too hot a plant for *pitta* individuals.

In the past, heavy metals have been detected in a number of Ayurvedic medicines. Certain plants have also been misidentified and the safety of some Indian herbal products has been questioned. It is important to ensure that any Ayurvedic products you buy have been approved for sale by the relevant government authority. (For more information, see p. 16.)

In China and Japan

Traditional forms of medicine, many based on the use of medicinal plants, have been practised for thousands of years in China and Japan. They now coexist side by side with Western medicine. Official plant research programs have been

For Ayurvedic doctors, taking the patient's pulse is essential before making a diagnosis.

In Ayurvedic medicine cayenne is used to treat those of a *kapha* temperament who might have a tendency to be overweight or prone to lethargy.

set up, and cooperation between practitioners of the old and the new is beginning to yield results.

Opposing principles

According to Taoist philosophy, everything in the universe depends upon the interplay of two opposing principles, *yin* and *yang*. Their interaction generates the life force, or *qi*, which circulates in the body through 12 key meridians. Illness is thought to be the result of a blockage or imbalance in this flow, and any treatment involves restoring the correct *yin–yang* balance.

Traditional Chinese medicine has also been influenced by another system of thought, based upon the theory of the five elements – fire, earth, metal, water and wood. Each of these elements is associated with specific emotions, tastes, bodily organs and plants.

'Hot' and 'cold' plants

In the 1st century AD, the herbal treatise *Shen Nong* recorded over 250 medicinal plants and also listed their 'temperature' and 'taste'. The combination of these two factors determines the healing potential of each plant. A plant that is 'hot' (*yang*), pungent, sweet and invigorating, like ginseng, is used to treat 'cold' conditions (*yin*). In order to reduce an excess of *yang*, 'cold', bitter and salty plants such as baical skullcap are needed.

The therapeutic qualities of plants also depend on where they grow. A low-altitude plant will have different healing powers to one that grows high up a mountain. The way they are prepared, whether with heat or water or a combination of the two, also has a bearing on their effects. The same is true of substances like honey, rice water and vinegar that are added to target the action on a particular organ.

A tradition that lives on

Traditional herbal medicines are still in widespread use in China and are now the subject of scientific study in many universities. More than 8000 plants have been investigated.

The research institute at the Academy of Beijing, the largest in China, has the task of establishing connections between the theories of traditional and modern medicine. Around 3000 scientists, doctors and technicians are working there on hundreds of projects.

Kampoh medicine

Chinese medicine was introduced into Japan in the 6th or 7th century AD and developed there under the name of *kampoh*, which means 'Chinese method'.

At the end of the 19th century, the Japanese government adopted Western medicine and gave up the teaching of *kampoh* but there has now been a significant change of policy. A research institute in traditional medicine has been set up in Tokyo, many universities have courses in herbalism and *kampoh* is again part of the medical school curriculum. Japan's state health insurance scheme will pay for plant-based preparations, and doctors often prescribe *kampoh* remedies.

Other Eastern traditions

Unani Tibb is a system of medicine that originated in ancient Persia around 980 AD, and developed throughout the Arab world and in India, where it is still practised today. The Ayurvedic system has its origins in Unani Tibb.

HERBS IN EASTERN MEDICINE 13

Harnessing the healing power

When you drink a cup of coffee, or sip mint tea, you are also taking a form of herbal medicine. The coffee gives you a lift, while the mint tea settles your stomach. Although these two beverages are often consumed simply for pleasure, they illustrate the principle on which herbal medicine is based – that plants can have a potent physiological effect on the body.

A plant's effect on the body varies according to its active constituents. Coffee beans, for example, contain caffeine, which stimulates the cardiovascular and nervous systems, making you more alert. Mint leaves contain menthol, which is calming and antispasmodic, relaxing the stomach and aiding digestion.

Coffee and mint are just two of the hundreds of plants that medical herbalists have at their disposal – each with its own properties. As a result of both training and experience, a good herbalist knows which herb or combination of herbs is best for treating a particular disorder.

Generations of herbalists have handed down that knowledge. In recent years scientific research has verified the actions of many plant extracts that now form the basis of thousands of modern drugs.

But herbalists do not simply look up an ailment and prescribe the corresponding herb – they take a holistic approach, looking at other less obvious factors that may be contributing to a problem. Their use of herbs is also holistic. Herbalists believe that the whole plant is more effective medicinally than any of its constituents in isolation.

A warning

Like many common herbs, coffee and mint tea are relatively harmless, but some herbs can have a more potent effect. Certain combinations of herbs can also have adverse side effects, and the action of some plants can interfere with that of conventional drugs. For example, St John's wort can reduce the effect of some of the drugs used to treat cardiac and circulatory disorders and has also been known to interfere with the contraceptive pill.

The 'Cautions' included in the 'A to Z of Plants' section of this book list the possible interactions and also which herbs should be avoided if you have a particular medical problem. If you are already taking prescribed medicines, it is imperative that you consult your doctor before trying any herbal remedy.

In the case of essential oils, you are advised never to ingest them unless you are under the supervision of a medical herbalist who has sufficient knowledge of their effects and possible toxicity.

Consulting a herbalist

It is always advisable to consult a qualified medical herbalist (see box left) before treating anything but the mildest of illnesses. It is also dangerous to diagnose illness in yourself or your family – what seems to be bronchitis for example, may be pneumonia or bronchial cancer.

Expect your first visit to a herbalist to be at least an hour long. As well as discussing your complaint, the herbalist will use the time to get to know you as an individual and take a full medical history, including lifestyle factors, such as whether you smoke and how much alcohol you drink – in confidence, of course, as in the case of a medical doctor. The prescription you are given can then be tailored to your specific needs. Herbalists use herbs in three ways: to cleanse and detoxify; to restore to normal function; and to maintain health. They often prepare their own formulations in the form of creams, ointments, liquid extracts or in a dry form (which will normally need to be boiled in water).

Many herbalists tailor-make customised medicines, specifically

---

HOW TO FIND A MEDICAL HERBALIST

It is best to choose a herbalist who is a member of one of the professional bodies listed below. These organisations have their own ethical codes and require their members to have a high standard of professional training. They should be able to give you details of herbalists in your area. In Australia and New Zealand, qualified naturopaths are also fully trained medical herbalists.

- **National Herbalists Association of Australia (NHAA)**. Incorporated in 1920, the NHAA is the oldest complementary medicine association in Australia.
- **The Australian Traditional Medicine Society (ATMS)**. The ATMS is Australia's largest professional association of complementary medicine practitioners, representing 65 per cent of the complementary health profession.
- **Australian Natural Therapists Association (ANTA)**. This association represents herbalists, naturopaths, traditional Chinese medicine practitioners and others in natural health care.
- **New Zealand Association of Medical Herbalists**. This is the professional body for medical herbalists in New Zealand.

For addresses, see p. 308.

> **TRAINING TO BECOME A HERBALIST**
>
> Australia and New Zealand are internationally regarded as leaders in the field of professional natural medicine training. However, it is still important to ensure that the course you enrol in provides a high standard of education.
>
> The professional bodies listed on p. 14 can supply details of accredited courses and training establishments. For instance, those recommended by the National Herbalists Association of Australia include the following:
> • **Nature Care College of Naturopathic and Life Studies, Sydney** (Advanced Diploma of Western Herbal Medicine, Advanced Diploma of Naturopathy).
> • **Southern School of Natural Therapies, Melbourne** (Advanced Diploma of Botanical Medicine).
> • **Southern Cross University, Lismore** (Bachelor of Naturopathy).

formulated for each patient's symptoms and case history. These medicines may be more effective than over-the-counter remedies. The herbalist will tell you how and when a remedy should be taken.

As with other holistic therapies, the effect of the herbs may not be immediately apparent and it may be a few months before you see any improvement. Chronic ailments that have been present for a long time generally take longer to treat.

Different strengths

The active principles contained in plants differ according to the medicinal form that is used. There is, for example, a big difference between the infusion, the liquid extract and the essential oil of the same plant. One preparation might treat digestive problems, the second insomnia, while the third may be used to relieve insect bites.

Qualified herbalists know, through training and experience, how a plant should be taken and the most effective dose. They should also be able to modify a treatment for a baby or young child or suggest a suitable alternative treatment.

Using a combination

Groups of plants can also be combined to treat the same illness, either because they have similar and complementary effects or because they have properties that are different but that work together to achieve the desired result.

For example, artichoke and turmeric both act upon the liver and the gall bladder in a similar way. Boldo, fumitory and peppermint, when combined in a treatment, have various beneficial effects – anti-inflammatory, antispasmodic, stimulating the secretion of gastric juices in the stomach – which all benefit the upper digestive tract. Finally, licorice, fennel and hyssop have different properties but when combined can effectively treat bronchial congestion.

A qualified herbalist will know which plants to combine to achieve the optimum effect and which might have conflicting effects.

It is then essential to keep to the herbalist's prescribed dosage, as in conventional medicine. Failure to do so can lead to adverse side effects or cause the treatment to fail. If you do experience difficulties with any prescribed herbal treatment, it is important to consult your healthcare practitioner as soon as possible.

HARNESSING THE HEALING POWER

Using herbal medicines safely

Many people who use herbal medicines assume that they must be completely safe because they are natural. In fact, they contain powerful, active organic compounds, and great care should be taken with their use. In many countries, including Australia and New Zealand, most forms of herbal medicine must comply with government regulations that prevent manufacturers from making unscrupulous claims about their products, and help to ensure that unsafe and dangerous herbs are not made available to the public.

Regulation: Australia

The regulation of medicines in Australia is overseen by the Therapeutic Goods Administration (TGA), a government body which uses the term 'complementary medicines' (sometimes also known as 'traditional' or 'alternative' medicines) to refer to vitamin, mineral, herbal, traditional, naturopathic and/or homoeopathic preparations.

Most products that are regarded as being a 'therapeutic good' must be entered on the Australian Register of Therapeutic Goods (ARTG) before they can be placed on the open market. This requirement has been in place since 1991, and includes all complementary medicines, over-the-counter medicines and prescription medicines.

Topical products that are intended for therapeutic (as opposed to cosmetic) use are also required to be entered on the ARTG.

Most medicines on the market in Australia, including complementary medicines, are legally required to be produced according to drug-standard Good Manufacturing Practice (GMP), regardless of whether they are produced in Australia or overseas. To ensure consumer safety, a licensing system is in place, and manufacturers must be licensed to perform the type of manufacturing they propose to undertake.

Those complementary medicines that are required to be entered onto the ARTG can be either 'listed' or 'registered' on the ARTG, depending on their ingredients and the indications and claims made.

The 'listed' category is for those medicines that are used for minor, self-limiting conditions and contain ingredients considered to be low risk. These ingredients must already be known to and pre-approved by the TGA for use in listed medicines. Manufacturers are limited as to the claims or statements that they are permitted to make about listed medicines, and must hold appropriate evidence (such as recent scientific study, or evidence of traditional use) to support any claims they make on actual product labels or in advertising of any form.

Where an ingredient is not currently allowable as an ingredient in a listable medicine, a dossier containing quality and safety data can be submitted for consideration by the authority in order that the ingredient can be added to the TGA's list of allowable ingredients.

It is important to be aware that Australian listed medicines are not 'approved' by the TGA; they are listed on the ARTG based on the manufacturer's assessment of compliance with specific criteria. Legislative control and industry codes of practice are in place and are co-regulated by industry and government authorities as well as complaints panels.

The Complementary Medicines Evaluation Committee (CMEC) is a panel of experts that is appointed to assist this process by advising government on issues pertaining to complementary medicines.

The 'registered' non-prescription complementary medicines category is for those medicines containing higher risk ingredients, those intended for more serious conditions and/or in cases where evidence of efficacy, quality and safety undergoes scientific evaluation.

Labelling: Australia

All complementary medicines, even those few types of complementary medicine not required to be on the ARTG, are subject to strict labelling requirements, which must list and quantify all the active ingredients in the product. Additionally, the purpose of the medicine must be detailed on the label, along with adequate directions for use, including advice as to whether the product is for adults or children.

Some complementary medicines are also required to include specific advisory or warning statements. For example, products containing St John's wort must carry a warning about potential interactions with certain pharmaceutical drugs.

All medicines must be labelled with the supplier's address, and medicines on the ARTG are labelled with an 'Aust L' or 'Aust R' number, which signifies whether the product is a listed or registered medicine. Additionally, all product labels must include a batch number and an expiry date. Any medicine that has passed its expiry date should be thrown away – your pharmacist can advise on safe medicine disposal.

Medicines not entered on the ARTG

Herbalists, naturopaths and other qualified practitioners commonly prepare medicines on a one-off basis after consultation with a particular client – herbal tonics and ointments are examples of this practice. The term used in the legislation to describe this process is 'extemporaneous dispensing', and medicines made under these circumstances are exempt from inclusion on

the ARTG. However, processed materials supplied to practitioners for these purposes (such as herbal liquid extracts) are still required to be produced in licensed premises compliant with drug-level GMP.

At the time of writing, herbs sold to the public in dried, crushed or powdered form, and without any directions for use, do not need to be processed at GMP–licensed premises. In other words, these (bulk) herbs currently fall outside the regulatory controls that apply to formulated products, and for this reason, the correct botanical identity of the herbs is not always assured. This has caused problems in the past with contamination or substitution of one plant for another, and reinforces the importance of taking care when choosing herbs for medicinal use.

Regulation: New Zealand

In New Zealand, medicines are required to be registered before they are placed on the market. However, unlike Australia, New Zealand has a category of products called 'dietary supplements', which are regulated under the Food Act.

The term 'dietary supplements' includes amino acids, minerals, herbs and nutrients sold in dosage forms such as sachets, capsules, liquids, lozenges, powders and tablets, which are intended to supplement the intake of those substances normally derived from food.

At the time of writing, pharmaceutical manufacturing standards such as the Australian GMP certification do not apply to dietary supplements sold in New Zealand. However, any New Zealand manufacturer exporting such products to Australia or to other world markets where this is a requirement would hold a drug-manufacturing licence issued by the New Zealand Medicines and Medical Devices Safety Authority (Medsafe).

Labelling: New Zealand

As in Australia, the quantities or proportions of the active ingredients are required to be stated on the label. So too are storage conditions, date marking, dosage instructions and the words 'Dietary Supplement'. Some nutrients are restricted to certain dosage levels.

While Australian complementary medicines are required to advise of their therapeutic purpose, New Zealand dietary supplements are generally not permitted to make a therapeutic claim.

Trans-Tasman treaty

In 2003, Australia and New Zealand signed a trans-Tasman treaty setting out the governance and accountability arrangements for a new agency that will replace both the Australian TGA and the New Zealand Medsafe agencies, and be accountable to both the Australian and New Zealand governments.

This single agency will regulate prescription, over-the-counter and complementary medicines and medical devices. The new agency is expected to commence operations sometime in mid-2005.

For the most part, it is expected that New Zealand will adopt regulatory controls similar to those currently in place in Australia, with likely changes to Australian–New Zealand food law to permit the sale of more 'medicinal foods' or dietary supplements of a foodlike nature.

For further information on the regulation of complementary medicines, visit the web sites of the relevant government authorities, which are listed on p. 308.

USING HERBAL MEDICINES SAFELY

Cultivating your own herbs

There are many advantages to growing your own herbs at home. Not only do they look pretty, but several can be used in cooking, and if you wish to use herbs medicinally you can be confident about their freshness and purity. Furthermore, many medicinal plants are becoming increasingly rare in the wild – some are even threatened with extinction – so growing your own herbs rather than gathering them will help to preserve those that remain.

Space no object
You do not need a lot of space to grow herbs. A successful herb garden can be grown in a container, hanging basket or window box.

You may like to dedicate a specific plot to your herb garden, or you may prefer to grow herbs among the flowers in a border.

It is important to plant herbs well away from busy roads, as they are prone to contamination by exhaust fumes. Do not use pesticides, again because of the risk of contamination. Fortunately, because they exude such strong aromas, herbs are targeted by very few insects. Make a note of what you have planted where – a simple diagram of the area and plant labels will help.

Soil and situation
Drainage is probably the most important single factor in successful herb growing. Few herbs will grow well in waterlogged soils, though marshmallow and peppermint do not mind wetter ground.

The soil does not have to be rich. In fact, highly fertile soils tend to produce plants with masses of foliage but a poor flavour. Instead of adding fertilisers, dig in homemade compost or buy organic compost. Most herbs do best in a sunny, sheltered spot.

Care with identification
Always take care to clearly identify any herb you harvest or plant for medicinal use. Do not rely on common names, which can vary from area to area. If necessary confirm the genus and species with a horticulturist or botanic gardens authority.

Growing from seed
Many herbs can be grown from seed. Be sure to buy seeds or seedlings from a reputable supplier so you can be confident of what you are planting and using. Seeds must be dry and free from mould. Sow seeds in trays in late winter, and transplant the seedlings outdoors in spring after the last frost.

Use fine seed-raising mix and do not cover the seeds too deeply. The smaller the seed, the shallower it should be sown. Cover fine seed with vermiculite.

Some seeds should be sown outdoors where they are to grow – dill and coriander, for example, do not like to be moved. If you can work your soil into a fine texture, your seeds will be happy. But if your garden is very stony or on heavy clay, it may be worth importing a layer of compost.

Sow seeds in very shallow drills and firm the soil over them. Mixing fine seeds such as oregano or thyme with sand will enable you to spread them more evenly. The soil needs to be kept moist in order for the seeds to germinate. A good way to stop the soil from drying out is to soak some sacking or newspaper in water and then spread it out over the seedbed.

Propagating by division

Some herbs spread so fast that division is an easy way to increase their numbers. Dig up the plant and ease it into several separate, smaller plants, making sure that each section has plenty of root attached to it. Lemon balm, lady's mantle and sweet violet are good candidates for division.

1 Dig up the plant, with all its roots, in spring or autumn. If it is young, divide the roots by hand.

2 If the plant is old, drive two garden forks, back to back, into the clump. Push the handles together, then pull them apart. Separate the roots into four pieces.

3 Cut away each woody centre. Split the remainder into pieces consisting of six buds or shoots. Remove any excess soil and unhealthy growth. Plant and water.

Growing from cuttings

Plants such as lavender and rosemary take a long time to grow from seed and are best propagated from cuttings. Pick a healthy young plant and choose shoots of the current year's growth – this will ensure that the tips of the shoots are soft and the lower stem is firm. Using a rooting hormone powder will help the cutting to root more quickly.

PROTECT FROM FROST

Perennial and biennial herbs are more likely to over-winter successfully if you protect them. In cold and frosty climates cover plants with mulch. Straw, leaves, sugar cane or evergreen prunings make a good blanket, which should be left in place until herbs show signs of growth.

1 Cut off 15–20 cm of non-flowering, leafy sideshoots. Remove the lower leaves.

2 Cut the shoot just below a leaf joint and remove the soft tip to leave cuttings 5–10 cm long.

3 Dip the base in hormone-rooting agent. Fill a pot with propagating mix (10 cm wide for five cuttings, 15 cm for ten).

4 Make widely spaced holes around the pot edge and insert the cuttings to one-third their length. Firm the soil. Water. Protect from frost.

CULTIVATING YOUR OWN HERBS

Harvesting and preserving herbs

All herbs have a peak harvesting time, when leaves, flowers, seeds or roots have their highest concentration of active constituents. Dry the herbs as soon as possible after cutting. Once dry, store them in sterilised, airtight, dark glass jars away from sunlight. Herbs will keep for about a year in a cool, dark place. Some remedies are made from bark or resins, and it is best to buy these from a herbalist as incorrect methods of collection can kill a shrub or tree.

Leaves

Pick leaves when the plant has enough foliage to keep growing. Collect them on a dry day when the dew has gone but before the sun gets too hot. Herbs like sage give off their fragrance, and thus lose their volatile oils, when it is hot. Choose young shoots of healthy plants, and take care not to crush or bruise them. Brush away any soil – do not wash the leaves. Spread them on kitchen paper in a warm, dark, dry place. Alternatively, tie them in small bunches and hang them away from direct sunlight in a sheltered but well-aired place. Most leaves will dry in 24–48 hours.

FRUIT AND BERRIES

Gather the fruit and berries just as they ripen. Line a baking tray with kitchen paper and spread the berries out on it in a thin layer. Put them in a warmed oven, switched off, with the door left just slightly open, for 3 hours. Afterwards, move the fruit or berries to somewhere dry, warm and dark – an airing cupboard is ideal if you have one – to finish off the drying process.

Flowers

Pick flowers as they start to bloom. Small flower heads can be dried whole. Spread them out evenly on a rack covered with kitchen paper or muslin in a warm, dry place, or hang them upside down over a sheet of muslin or a paper bag. Strip the petals from larger flower heads, such as those of calendulas, and dry them in a thin layer on a sheet of muslin or kitchen paper.

SEEDS

Collect fragile seed heads in late summer. When you pick them, leave on plenty of stalk so you can tie them in small, loose bunches. Hang the stems upside down in clean paper bags so that the seeds will be caught when they start to fall out. Once the seeds are dry, shake the bunch of seed heads gently to loosen any seeds that are still attached.

MICROWAVE DRYING

Herbs can be dried quickly in a microwave oven. Spread them out in an even layer on a length of kitchen paper, and dry at a low setting for 2–3 minutes. Check and rearrange them every 30 seconds or so to ensure that they are drying evenly.

Roots

Collect roots and rhizomes in autumn or winter once the plant has died down, but before the first frosts. Take what you need and replant the remaining underground plant. Wash the root and remove any soft parts or side roots. Slice thinly or chop into small chunks with a sharp knife and spread in a thin layer on kitchen paper on a baking tray. Dry for 2 hours in a warmed oven, switched off, with the door slightly open, and then keep in a warm place until completely dry.

HARVESTING WILD HERBS

DO

- Collect only where you have the landowner's permission to do so.
- Take a detailed plant guide for reference.
- Gather herbs in dry weather.
- Wear protective gloves when collecting plants that have bristles or caustic sap.
- Take only as much of the plant as you need.
- Make sure you take the correct medicinal part of the plant.

DON'T

- Collect rare or endangered species.
- Pick anything you are not sure about – some plants are poisonous.
- Pick plants damaged by disease or insects.
- Harvest from roadsides – exhaust fumes contaminate herbs.
- Mix different cut plant materials – you may not be able to identify them when you get home. Label as you go.
- Collect plants from national parks or protected areas.

Using fresh aloe vera

Aloe vera contains a thick, colourless gel at the centre of each leaf, which is useful for treating burns, wounds and dry skin conditions. Only use the gel when it is fresh because it is unstable and quickly loses its consistency. Do not use any of the gel that is tinged green.

2 Slice carefully along the leaf centre.

1 Cut off a healthy large leaf near its base.

3 Gently peel back the two cut edges. Using a blunt-edged knife, scrape the clear gel from the centre of the leaf.

HARVESTING AND PRESERVING HERBS 21

Make your own herbal remedies

Herbs can be used in a wide range of medicinal preparations. Some, such as syrups and liquid extracts, are made for internal use. Others, like creams and poultices, are for external application. Infusions and decoctions can often be taken internally or used externally – in gargles or on compresses, for example. It is not difficult to make your own remedies but it can be time consuming. The following step-by-step guides show you how to make simple herbal preparations at home.

Infusion

An infusion is a tea, and is made in the same way. Infusions are gentle remedies made from flowers and leaves and are best made fresh each day. Use the proportions of dried or fresh herb and water specified in the relevant sections of this book, multiplying quantities as required. The usual dose is 1 teacup three times a day. Infusions can also be used cold for gargles and mouthwashes, and hot or cold for a compress.

Compress

A compress is a pad of soft fabric soaked in a herbal infusion or decoction and applied to the painful area. A compress may be hot or cold. Hot compresses are useful to relieve cramp or muscle tension. Cold compresses are used when the skin feels hot to the touch. A cold compress can help to ease a headache.

1. **Soak a clean cotton pad in a herbal infusion or decoction.**
2. **Place pad over the affected part and cover with a towel.**
3. **Keep refreshing the compress to keep the area warm or cool as required.**

1. **Place the required amount of herb in a warmed china or glass (not metal) teapot or in a coffee plunger.**
2. **Pour on water that has been boiled, then left to stand for 30 seconds.**
3. **Leave to infuse for 5–10 minutes or as specified.**
4. **Strain and sip slowly. Sweeten with honey if desired.**

22 NATURE'S MEDICINES

Decoction

A decoction is a more vigorous way of extracting the active constituents from the tough parts of a herb, such as its bark, roots or seeds. For safety, use only the proportions of plant to liquid specified in the relevant sections of this book, multiplying quantities as required.

Decoctions are most effective if prepared fresh each day, but they can be kept for up to three days in a refrigerator.

1. Crush up seeds or bark in a mortar and pestle. If using fresh herbs, chop finely.

2. Put the required amount of water in a stainless steel or enamel saucepan. Add the broken dried herb or chopped fresh herb.

3. Bring to the boil, reduce heat and simmer for up to an hour, until the volume has reduced by about one-third.

4. Strain and add water to make up to the required amount. Sweeten with honey if desired.

Syrup

Syrups are a good way of making medicines more palatable. Sugar-based preparations soothe sore throats and other irritated mucous membranes. A standard syrup is made using 500 ml infusion or decoction and 500 g honey or unrefined sugar, but for home use you may prefer to make smaller quantities. The usual dose is 10 ml (5 ml for children) three times a day. Syrups keep for up to six months in a cool place.

1. Pour the infusion or decoction into a pan. An infusion should have been steeped for at least 10 minutes; a decoction should have been simmered for an hour.

2. Add the sugar or honey and heat gently until dissolved.

3. Remove from the heat and allow to cool.

4. Pour into sterilised glass bottles (use a funnel).

5. Stopper with a cork and apply a label. Note that syrups can ferment and a bottle sealed with a screw-top lid might explode.

MAKE YOUR OWN HERBAL REMEDIES

Making a tincture

Tinctures, such as rosehip, are made by steeping dried or fresh herbs in alcohol. For commercial tinctures, specific water-to-alcohol proportions are used for each herb. For homemade tinctures, vodka can be used, but it is safest to check the proportions first with a medical herbalist. Tinctures keep for up to three years if stored in a cool, dark cupboard.

Poultice

A poultice – usually used hot – is a herb paste applied directly to the skin on strips of gauze. Poultices are mainly used to draw pus from the skin, to reduce inflammation, heal boils and abscesses and draw splinters. Here the plant is calendula, an effective treatment for cracked skin, insect bites and sunburn.

1. Put 225 g of rosehips in a large glass jar. Pour in 700 ml of vodka and 300 ml of water and close the jar tightly.

2. Keep in a warm place for two weeks, shaking occasionally.

3. Strain through a muslin cloth, squeezing out the residue.

4. Discard the solids and pour the tincture into a dark glass bottle that is labelled with the herb's name and the date the tincture was made.

3. Apply a little olive oil to the skin to stop the poultice from sticking to it.

4. Spread the herb paste onto gauze or cotton strips and apply them to the skin.

5. Keep the poultice in place until it is cool and replace it as often as is required.

1 Finely chop 220 g of dried calendula.

2 Transfer the calendula to a bowl and mix with enough boiled water to make a paste.

Massage oils

The essential oil of some plants, such as sweet marjoram (see p. 178), can be used to make a massage oil to relieve aching bones and joints. Although a few essential oils, such as lavender, can be used neat, most should be diluted with a carrier oil, such as a cold-pressed apricot or almond oil, in the proportions specified in the 'Preparation and dosage' boxes in the 'A to Z of Plants' section. Do not keep for more than a few days. Some essential oils should not be used in pregnancy. Take care and consult a doctor or medical herbalist if in doubt.

Fragrant inhalations

Inhalations are used in the treatment of blocked nasal passages, catarrh, asthma and sinus infections. The simplest inhalations are infusions, but essential oils may also be used. Suitable herbs and essential oils include lavender, eucalyptus, pine and peppermint.

1 Put 2–4 teaspoons of dried lavender flowers into a bowl.

2 Pour boiling water over them. (For essential oils, add 3–5 drops to a bowl of freshly boiled water, rather than the other way around.)

3 Lean over the bowl with a towel covering both your head and the bowl.

4 Inhale the steam until it stops rising. Repeat twice a day or as needed.

5 If you are treating a child, allow the water to cool for 3–5 minutes before commencing the inhalation. Do not leave the child unattended.

MAKE YOUR OWN HERBAL REMEDIES

A to Z of Plants

Agrimony
Agrimonia eupatoria Rosaceae **Also called** Cockleburr, Church steeples, Sticklewort A slender hedgerow plant found throughout Europe, western Asia and northern Africa, agrimony grows up to 1 m in height. It has rough stems and large dark green leaves with whitish downy undersides. The spikes of yellow flowers have a spicy scent and appear in summer, followed by burrlike seed pods with hooked spines.

Parts used
FLOWER HEADS
- Flower heads are gathered in full flower in summer and dried in a warm place.
- For internal use, agrimony is usually made into an infusion, but it may also be used as a liquid extract, alone or in combination with a variety of other herbs. Externally, it is used in gargles, mouthwashes and compresses.

dried flower heads

Constituents
The flowers contain three types of active components: tannins – which have anti-oxidant, antimicrobial and anti-inflammatory properties; flavonoids – anti-oxidants believed to prevent cardio-vascular disease and fight cancer; and terpenes – the plant's volatile oils that give it its pleasing aroma.

Medicinal uses
The anti-inflammatory qualities of agrimony make it useful for treating a range of skin rashes and stomach upsets, as well as sore throats and rheumatism.

Weak infusions can be given to children with diarrhoea and mild tummy upsets. A Swedish study has confirmed that agrimony infusions can help to ease inflammatory skin conditions. A cooled infusion applied on a cloth soothes skin allergies and improves blood circulation, and a compress may help to reduce haemorrhoids.

Gargling with an infusion of agrimony may soothe sore throats, while rinsing is good for mouth ulcers and gum inflammations. Drinking infusions of agrimony improves digestion by stimulating the stomach and gall bladder. It can also soothe an irritable bowel.

Historically, agrimony was used to heal gunshot wounds, and research has shown that it helps to promote blood clotting.

Cultivation
Prefers well-drained soil in full sun with regular summer moisture. Agrimony is harvested when in flower.

PREPARATION AND DOSAGE

- **To treat mild diarrhoea, sluggish digestion, haemorrhoids**
  LIQUID EXTRACT 1–4 g dried herb equivalent, three times daily.
  INFUSION 2–4 g dried flowers infused in 1 cup of boiling water for 5 minutes before straining. Drink 3–4 cups a day.

- **To soothe sore throats and inflamed gums**
  GARGLE, MOUTHWASH Make an infusion as above, using approximately 2 g of dried flowers to 1 cup of boiling water. Cool and use as a mouthwash or gargle two or three times a day.

- **To treat haemorrhoids, skin problems**
  COMPRESS Use 10 teaspoons of the dried plant to 1 cup of cold water. Bring to the boil and let boil for 5 minutes. Cool and strain. Soak a soft cloth in the liquid and apply four or five times a day.

IF SYMPTOMS PERSIST, CONSULT A DOCTOR

CAUTIONS
- Do not use if pregnant or breastfeeding.
- Avoid exposure to bright sunlight when taking agrimony.

Albizia
Albizia lebbeck (syn. *Mimosa lebbeck*) Fabaceae **Also called** Women's tongue tree, East Indian walnut, Kokko, Lebbek tree, Siris, Shirisha *Albizia is a tall tree that is native to India and elsewhere in Asia. It seeds prolifically and is sometimes considered a weed. Albizia is renowned for it perfume, and for its clusters of greenish yellow pompom flowers. The flowers are formed by many long and conspicuous stamens forming balls, followed by long, brown, beanlike pods.*

Parts used
STEM BARK
- The stem bark is used to produce decoctions, tablets and liquid extracts.

Constituents
Albizia contains saponins, polyphenols, triterpenoids, alkaloids, glycosides and aromatic acids.

Medicinal uses
Albizia is a traditional Ayurvedic remedy for the treatment of asthma and allergies, and scientific research has confirmed its anti-allergic activity.

In a number of experiments, albizia has been shown to inhibit some of the immune processes that trigger or contribute to allergy symptoms. For example, albizia stabilises mast cells, which are responsible for much of the histamine release that occurs during allergic reactions. Histamine in turn is involved in many allergic symptoms, such as swollen tissues, itchy skin, tightening of the throat and asthma.

Herbalists prescribe albizia for the treatment of allergic conditions such as rhinitis, eczema and asthma. Research also indicates that albizia may offer some clues to the management of the most severe form of allergy, anaphylaxis. In animal research into experimentally induced anaphylactic reactions, albizia was found to exert a strong protective effect against anaphylactic shock, partially by enhancing adrenal activity and protecting against constriction of the airways.

Albizia may be particularly valuable for the treatment of asthma, although it appears that the duration of the condition may have an influence on the herb's effects. Consequently, treatment for asthma should ideally start within two years of symptoms developing.

Other indications that have been documented for albizia include bronchitis, gastric ulcer, inflammation of the gums, raised serum cholesterol, worm infestation, itchiness of the skin, antimicrobial activity and as a memory tonic.

Cultivation
Albizia is a deciduous tropical tree that tolerates dry and cold to frosty conditions when established. It grows readily from seed, however those with hard seed coats may need treatment to promote germination. Soaking for three minutes in boiling water followed by 24 hours in cold water is recommended. Water young plants regularly. Prune after flowering to remove pods and reduce weediness.

stem bark

PREPARATION AND DOSAGE
- Albizia should be taken only on the advice of a medical herbalist. Do not exceed the prescribed dosage

IF SYMPTOMS PERSIST, CONSULT A DOCTOR

CAUTIONS
- The safety of albizia has not been established during pregnancy or breastfeeding.
- If you are suffering from an acute allergic reaction, consult a doctor immediately.

THE A TO Z OF PLANTS   29

Alfalfa *Medicago sativa* Fabaceae **Also called** Lucerne

Although alfalfa is best known as a salad sprout, it is also used as a feed for livestock, and has medicinal applications as well. Reaching a height of 60–100 cm, alfalfa is a perennial herb that grows wild on the edges of fields. It bears purple-blue flowers in summer and its seed pods are coiled spirals.

Parts used

LEAVES
- The leaves are harvested up to five times every growing season, just as the plant starts to flower.
- The leaves are used to make teas, tablets and liquid extracts.

dried leaves

Constituents

Alfalfa is an excellent source of dietary nutrients, including protein, calcium and vitamins. It also contains saponins, isoflavones, coumarins, phenols, tannins and unsaturated fatty acids. The isoflavones and coumarins are phyto-oestrogens, and have similar – though milder – actions to oestrogen.

Medicinal uses

Due to its oestrogenic effects, alfalfa is reputed to regulate periods, and also to stimulate milk-flow in breast-feeding women. Experiments carried out by clinical nutritionists in 1982 showed that eating alfalfa helped to protect monkeys that were on a high-cholesterol diet from atherosclerosis. They also proved the effectiveness of alfalfa in decreasing blood-cholesterol levels.

There are some indications that alfalfa may help balance blood-sugar levels. This effect is yet to be confirmed, however it may be due to alfalfa's content of the mineral manganese, which is involved in the metabolism of glucose.

Alfalfa's fortifying and appetite-stimulating effects are well known, and so it is often given to induce weight gain and as a restorative tonic during convalescence. Alfalfa can help to reduce exhaustion and nervous agitation. In India, it is used in poultices to treat boils, and in Colombia it is used to treat coughs. It may have a therapeutic effect on gastric ulcers, and has been used in the treatment of kidney stones.

Cultivation

Plant in a sunny position in a light, well-drained soil. The blue flowers are rich in nectar and attract bees.

PREPARATION AND DOSAGE

- **As a tonic for exhaustion, convalescence, to improve appetite, and to increase body weight in children**

  LIQUID EXTRACT 3–10 g dried herb equivalent, three times a day.

  TABLETS, CAPSULES Tablets and capsules are available in varying doses up to approximately 1000 mg. Take them according to the manufacturer's instructions.

  INFUSION 2–4 g dried herb infused in 1 cup of boiling water for 5 minutes before straining; drink 3–4 cups a day.

IF SYMPTOMS PERSIST, CONSULT A DOCTOR

CAUTIONS

- Do not use to treat lupus (a chronic inflammatory disease that causes a scaly red rash on the face) or other autoimmune disorders or rheumatic conditions.
- If pregnant or breastfeeding, do not consume larger amounts than you would eat in a normal meal.
- Alfalfa may induce sensitisation to sunlight, so when using it, it is wise to avoid sunbathing.
- Do not exceed recommended doses.

Aloe vera   *Aloe vera, A. barbadensis*   Liliaceae   **Also called** Bitter aloe

A perennial succulent, aloe vera is native to the dry regions of eastern and southern Africa, and the Mediterranean basin. Its greeny grey, tightly packed, fleshy leaves have jagged, thorny edges and contain a cool, soothing gel which can be used to treat skin problems ranging from burns and minor wounds to itchy insect bites. The gel was believed to have been used as a beauty preparation by Cleopatra, Queen of Egypt.

Parts used

LEAF SAP AND GEL

- Leaves are used from two- to three-year-old plants.
- Gel exudes when the leaf is cut and sap comes from mucilage-rich cells inside the leaf.
- Available in skin preparations and drinks.

Constituents

Aloe vera contains anthraquinones such as aloin A and B, which are responsible for the plant's laxative and healing properties.

Medicinal uses

Aloe vera's medicinal properties have been known since ancient times. The laxative sap is dried and sold as 'resin'. The gel stimulates the immune system and has antibiotic, anti-inflammatory and antiseptic effects, which makes it useful in the treatment of skin problems such as eczema and psoriasis.

In the 1950s, aloe vera was renowned for treating radiation burns and was stored for use in a nuclear accident. It is now used for its soothing, moisturising and healing effects to treat wounds, burns, acne, anal fissures and haemorrhoids.

In 1996, investigations into aloe vera's effectiveness as an anti-inflammatory agent showed that it prevented swelling by inhibiting the migration of inflammatory cells and the chemicals that induce inflammation.

Aloe vera may also help rheumatic ailments. Research published in 1986 found that a cream containing aloe vera both prevented and acted as a treatment for rheumatoid arthritis in rats.

Because aloe vera is a powerful laxative, herbal practitioners advise that it should be used primarily as an external remedy. However, some commercial preparations can be taken internally and provide useful tonic action for the digestive system, as well as immune-stimulating properties. These immune-stimulant drinks have had aloe vera's laxative principles removed.

Cultivation

Grow in well-drained soil or potting mix in full sun or part shade, protected from frost.

leaf sap

PREPARATION AND DOSAGE

- **To treat a weak immune system**

  DRINKS (WITH POWERFUL LAXATIVE ELEMENT REMOVED) Follow manufacturer's instructions.

- **To treat wounds, burns, haemorrhoids, psoriasis, dermatitis**

  SKIN PREPARATIONS (CONTAINING 1% TINCTURE OR 2–3 PER CENT HYDRO-GLYCOLIC EXTRACT) Apply to the affected area two or three times a day.

IF SYMPTOMS PERSIST, CONSULT A DOCTOR

CAUTIONS

- Unless the powerful laxative component has been removed, taking aloe vera internally may cause diarrhoea, and this in turn may lead to low potassium levels. It may also trigger attacks of colitis.
- Aloe vera should not be taken by young children, or pregnant or breastfeeding women.
- Do not take if suffering from uraemia (excess urea in the blood) or disorders of the kidneys or liver.

Andrographis
Andrographis paniculata Acanthaceae **Also called** Chiretta, King of Bitters, Kirata, Kalmegh

Andrographis has been used as a traditional medicine in many parts of Asia, including Thailand, China and Vietnam. It also has a long history of use in Ayurveda for the treatment of both humans and livestock. Andrographis is an annual herb that produces small, white to pink flowers with brown or purple markings, followed by seed capsules that each contain numerous yellow-brown seeds.

Parts used

AERIAL PARTS

- Although the whole plant (including the root) has sometimes been used, use of the aerial parts is more common.
- The fresh juice of the leaf has been commonly used in Ayurvedic medicine.
- Dried plant preparations are also in use.

Constituents

Andrographis contains a group of diterpenoid lactones which are referred to as andrographolides. These are considered to be responsible for the major part of the plant's activity, and consequently preparations standardised for the herb's andrographolide content are considered to be the most effective.

Medicinal uses

In traditional Chinese medicine, this herb is considered to be bitter and cold. For this reason it is highly regarded for the treatment of what are thought of as hot conditions, such as acute infections and the fever that often accompanies them.

dried aerial parts

Clinical research has backed up this traditional application of the herb. For example, a number of trials have proven that when compared to placebos, andrographis helps to reduce the severity and duration of a range of respiratory infections, such as the common cold.

Andrographis has been documented to reduce or improve a wide variety of symptoms of acute respiratory infection, including fever, fatigue, sore throat, headache, cough, mouth ulcers, fatigue, insomnia, increased secretions from upper and lower respiratory tracts and earache. Additionally, it helps to reduce the incidence of colds when taken as a preventive. These effects are considered to be at least partially due to the presence of andrographolides.

Like many other extremely bitter herbs, andrographis has traditionally been prescribed to stimulate digestive activity and to exert a protective effect on the liver. It is indicated to improve appetite, reduce flatulence and enhance bile production. Andrographis is also used for infections and infestations of the bowel, and particularly for treating infective diarrhoea.

Andrographis has been taken for dermatological indications in a number of cultures, and has been recommended for itching, bites, abscesses, cold sores, shingles and a range of other skin conditions. In Malaysia, the herb has also been prescribed for the treatment of cardiovascular disease, and in Vietnamese medicine it is valued as a post-partum tonic.

Cultivation

Grow in a well-drained soil in sun or partial shade. Plants prefer warm climates with high humidity. Plants die down after flowering and seeding. Propagate annually by seed sown in spring into warm soil.

PREPARATION AND DOSAGE

- **To prevent colds, flu and respiratory infections; to stimulate appetite and improve digestion**

  LIQUID EXTRACT 500 mg–1.5 g dried herb equivalent, three times daily.
  TABLETS 500 mg–1 g three times daily, or follow maker's directions.

- **To treat colds, flu and other infections**

  LIQUID EXTRACT 1–2 g dried herb equivalent, three times daily.
  TABLETS 1–2 g, three times daily, or follow maker's instructions.

- **Where possible, choose a product standardised for its content of andrographolides**

IF SYMPTOMS PERSIST, CONSULT A DOCTOR

CAUTIONS

- Do not use andrographis if you are pregnant or breastfeeding.
- Do not take andrographis if you are suffering from heartburn or gastric ulcer, as it may aggravate the symptoms.
- Do not exceed the recommended dose as this may cause gastric discomfort and vomiting.
- At recommended doses, side effects (e.g. urticaria, headache) have only rarely been recorded. However, in those taking megadoses of andrographolides the incidence of side effects is much more common.

Angelica *Angelica archangelica* Apiaceae **Also called** Archangel

Known in the past as the Root of the Holy Spirit and the Angelic Herb, angelica is a striking architectural plant whose thick, hollow stalks can grow to 3 m tall. It has finely cut leaves and its oval fruits have wings like those of an angel, hence its name. In northern Europe during the Renaissance, angelica was thought to be able to cure all illnesses, particularly plague and pestilence.

Parts used

ROOTS
- The hard roots are collected from one- to two-year-old plants.
- Roots are washed, cut up and dried in the open air.
- They are used in decoctions, in capsules and in a drinkable solution.

Constituents

Angelica root has been found to contain 1 per cent essential oil. This consists mainly of beta-phellandrene, along with the aromatic coumarins angelicin, bergapten and osthole.

Medicinal uses

Angelica root is mainly used to treat common digestive problems such as indigestion and flatulence. It is also recommended for stomach pains and intestinal spasms.

dried roots

Angelica has long been used as a remedy for coughs, colds and influenza because it acts as an expectorant. It is particularly recommended for bronchitis.

A root extract may alleviate the painful symptoms of back pain, gout and rheumatism. In 1978, researchers demonstrated angelica's anti-inflammatory and pain-relieving properties. The root oil has also been found to be an antibacterial and antifungal.

In 1996 researchers found osthole to be an effective anticoagulant that may be useful in treating thrombosis. In 1998, researchers described bergapten as a photosensitising agent that may be of benefit to people suffering from psoriasis.

Angelica can be taken as a bitter tonic. It works by increasing appetite through stimulation of the salivary glands and digestive organs.

Cultivation

Angelica is a hardy biennial, best suited to moist soils and temperate climates. It is happy in sun or light shade.

PREPARATION AND DOSAGE

- **To treat digestive problems, coughs and colds**

  LIQUID EXTRACT 500 mg–2.5 g dried root equivalent taken three times a day.
  INFUSION 1–2 g dried root infused in 1 cup of boiling water for 10 minutes before straining. Drink 3 cups a day.
  DECOCTION Boil 1–2 g dried root in ¾ cup of water for 5 minutes before straining. Take as two doses during the course of a day.

IF SYMPTOMS PERSIST, CONSULT A DOCTOR

CAUTIONS

- Do not use angelica if pregnant or breastfeeding.
- Do not sunbathe when using, as it may cause sensitisation to sunlight in fair-skinned individuals.
- Avoid angelica if you are diabetic.

Anise *Pimpinella anisum* Apiaceae **Also called** Aniseed, Common anise

A highly aromatic low-growing plant, anise originated in the Middle East and was cultivated by the ancient Egyptians. Dainty yellow-and-white flowers on upright stems are followed by aromatic greyish fruits (known as seeds) that have a warm, sugary taste.

Parts used

SEEDS

- Seeds are gathered from late summer to autumn, after flowering.
- They are dried, and must then be stored in a dry, dark place.
- The essential oil is extracted and used in many pharmaceutical preparations, herbal medicines, foods and drinks.

Constituents

The seeds contain between 1 and 6 per cent essential oil. Up to 90 per cent of the oil is anethole, which gives anise its distinctive aroma. Other constituents are coumarins, including bergapten, flavonoids and sterols.

Medicinal uses

Anise has long been used in remedies to ease indigestion, bloating, belching, infant colic, and flatulence. The effectiveness of anise is largely due to its antispasmodic action, which is also thought to ease period pains. Anise increases fluid secretion in the intestine, stimulating digestion.

Anise has expectorant properties, making it useful in treating bronchitis. The expectorant action of both anise and its main active constituent, anethole, has been proven in animal studies cited in the *European Monographs on the Medicinal Uses of Plant Drugs*.

The *European Monographs* also mentions studies of the antibacterial, antifungal and insecticidal properties of the essential oil. Externally, the undiluted oil can be applied to get rid of head lice. It is also used in an ointment for treating scabies.

Anise seeds are thought to be mildly oestrogenic and have long been used in traditional medicine to ease childbirth, stimulate milk production in nursing mothers and regulate periods. Anise was also reputed to increase libido in both sexes. A study published in the *Journal of Ethnopharmacology* in 1980 showed that some anethole-based compounds are responsible for many hormone-mimicking effects.

Cultivation

Sow fresh seeds in early spring. Anise is a hardy plant that likes sun or light shade and rich, well-drained, sandy and slightly alkaline soil enriched with compost.

fruit

dried seeds

PREPARATION AND DOSAGE

- **To treat digestive problems and coughs**

  LIQUID EXTRACT 500 mg–1 g dried seed equivalent, three times a day.
  INFUSION 500 mg–1 g dried seeds infused in 1 cup boiling water for 5 minutes before straining. Drink 2–3 cups a day, after meals.
  POWDER Take 3 g daily in food.

- **To treat colic**

  DECOCTION Boil 2 teaspoons of seeds in 250 ml of milk; reduce to simmer for 10 minutes before straining. Drink two or three times daily after meals. Note that this preparation is unsuitable for those with dairy or lactose intolerance, especially infants.

IF SYMPTOMS PERSIST, CONSULT A DOCTOR

CAUTIONS

- Do not take iron supplements when taking anise.
- If pregnant or breastfeeding, do not consume larger amounts than you would in a normal meal.
- Do not sunbathe when taking anise as it may trigger sensitisation to sunlight.
- High doses of essential oil may cause nausea and vomiting.
- Avoid using any creams and lotions containing aniseed if you have an inflammatory skin condition or if you experience any allergic reaction.

Arnica

Arnica montana Asteraceae **Also called** Mountain tobacco, Leopard's bane A perennial, native to mountainous regions of Europe and naturalised in cooler parts of Australia and New Zealand, arnica is characterised by its yellow flowers borne on tall, hairy stems in summer. Its pointed leaves form a rosette around the base.

dried flowers

Parts used

FLOWERS

- Harvested in early summer and quickly dried, the flowers form the base of numerous preparations – most usually tinctures and creams.
- Mountain arnica *Arnica montana* is the only species that is used in herbal medicine. It should not be confused with its relative *Arnica chamissonis,* a plant with a similar appearance that is grown for ornamental purposes.

Constituents

Arnica contains anti-inflammatory sesquiterpenic lactones – of which the most important medically is helenalin. The plant has also been found to contain flavonoids, which strengthen blood vessels.

Medicinal uses

Arnica's primary use is for relieving bruising. Various lactones found in the plant inhibit the leakage of blood under the skin and also prevent the inflammation of the tissues surrounding an injured area.

Arnica is also used to relieve sprains and other minor injuries where there is swelling but no blood loss or broken skin. In studies carried out in 1979 and 1980 using sesquiterpenic lactones, helenalin was found to inhibit swelling and chronic arthritis in rats.

Arnica should never be taken internally except in its homeopathic form, which is very diluted in strength. The homeopathic remedy is generally used to treat those suffering from injuries, accident and shock.

Cultivation

This hardy plant needs a cool to mild climate and should be planted in a well-drained, acidic soil. It prefers to grow in a sunny location. Arnica is also reputed to be attractive to honey bees.

PREPARATION AND DOSAGE

- **To treat bruising, sprains, muscle aches**

    TINCTURE, OIL Use to make a compress and apply this to the affected area.
    CREAMS, GELS Massage into the affected area, as directed. If necessary, repeat two or three times a day.

IF SYMPTOMS PERSIST, CONSULT A DOCTOR

CAUTIONS

- Arnica is for external use only; preparations must never be used near the eyes or mouth, or on broken skin.
- If there is any contact with an open wound, it must be washed with plenty of distilled water.
- Under no circumstances should arnica be used to treat children under three years old.
- The sesquiterpenoid content may cause skin allergies for some people, especially those with a known allergy to other members of the Asteraceae family (such as daisies, chrysanthemums and echinacea). It is therefore sensible to carry out an initial patch test. Stop the treatment immediately if there is any sign of irritation, which should then gradually disappear.

THE A TO Z OF PLANTS

Asthma plant
Chamaesyce hirta formerly *Euphorbia hirta* Euphorbiaceae **Also called** Pill bearing spurge, Snakeweed, Queensland asthma plant Asthma plant has traditionally been used for asthma and other spasmodic conditions of the respiratory tract. It grows wild in many tropical and subtropical regions and thrives on roadsides and wastelands. This reddish green herb has stems that grow up to 40 cm long and tiny flowers that develop in late spring, followed by small, globular fruits.

Parts used
AERIAL PARTS
- Most herbal preparations are produced from the aerial parts of the plant, gathered while it is in flower. However, some research has also been conducted on the extract of the whole plant (including the root).
- In traditional Aboriginal medicine and also in Malaysia and India, the sap (or latex) was applied to warts, and in Malaysia it has also been used to treat eye conditions.

Constituents
Asthma plant contains flavonoids, polyphenols, tannins, triterpenes, phytosterols, shikimic acid and choline. The terpenes may be at least partly responsible for its anti-inflammatory activity, and some researchers have theorised that the antispasmodic actions traditionally associated with the plant may be due in part to the presence of shikimic acid and choline.

liquid extract

fruit

Medicinal uses
As its name suggests, asthma plant has traditionally been used by herbalists around the world to relieve asthma and other conditions associated with difficult breathing, such as emphysema and bronchitis. It is considered to improve breathing by bringing relaxation to the airways, and to have expectorant properties, helping to expel phlegm from the lungs.

This traditional usage has been supported to some degree by in vitro research showing that the whole plant extract has antispasmodic qualities.

In many parts of the world, including the Congo and India, asthma plant has been used to treat diarrhoeal conditions. Scientific research indicates that *Chamaesyce* extract is able to bring quick and effective relief to the acute symptoms of a range of protozoal bowel infections (such as amoebic dysentery).

Longer term (chronic) cases of amoebic dysentery were also responsive to treatment with asthma plant, and in one clinical trial, over 80 per cent of the 150 patients treated responded well to the herb, and had not experienced a relapse when they were followed up over five months later. (Some of this research used a fluid extract of the herb, and some used a tablet. It is important to be aware that the dosages used were much higher than those normally recommended by botanical herbalists, and have not been fully evaluated for safety.)

Cultivation
Grow from seed planted in well-drained to dry, sandy soil in sun.

PREPARATION AND DOSAGE
- **Asthma plant should be taken internally only on the advice of a medical herbalist**

IF SYMPTOMS PERSIST, CONSULT A DOCTOR

CAUTIONS
- There are no known contraindications or drug interactions, however, the safety of asthma plant has not been established in pregnancy or lactation. Since plants in the Euphorbiaceae family have been reported to have both contracting and relaxing actions in vitro, it is best avoided during pregnancy.
- No side effects should be expected if asthma plant is taken within the recommended dosage range, however large doses may cause gastrointestinal distress, nausea and vomiting. Note that in some instances, the research into the antiprotozoal activity of asthma plant has used very high doses, which have not been adequately evaluated for safety.
- Many species of Euphorbiaceae are toxic, and while *Chamaesyce hirta* is not, it is essential that great care is taken to ensure the correct species is used.
- This article refers only to *Chamaesyce hirta*. Asthma plant is sometimes confused with asthma weed *Parietaria judaica*, a dangerous plant that causes asthma rather than treating it.

Astragalus

Astragalus membranaceus, A. mongholicus, A. propinquus **Fabaceae** **Also called** Milk vetch, Huang qi

Astragalus is a native of Mongolia and parts of China and consequently has been used in traditional Chinese medicine for thousands of years. The Chinese believe that it tonifies the Qi (or inherent vitality of the body) and helps to overcome debility. In addition to being boiled in water to make a decoction, astragalus is sometimes added to soup or rice porridge to make a medicinal food.

Parts used

ROOTS

- Astragalus root is harvested in the autumn, once the plant is four years old.
- The roots are taken as a decoction, added to food or used as the basis for tablets, capsules or liquid extracts.
- Both the flowers and roots of astragalus are yellow, and traditionally those roots with stronger yellow colouring are regarded as being high quality and are thus more expensive to buy.

Constituents

Compounds that have been identified in astragalus root include saponins, flavonoids, polysaccharides, phytosterols and amino acids. The saponins and flavonoids have anti-oxidant properties, with the saponins also having a protective effect on the liver. The flavonoids are responsible for the root's yellow colouring. The role of the polysaccharide and saponin components has been investigated, and both of these constituents seem to help in stimulating and improving immunity.

dried roots

Medicinal uses

In traditional Chinese medicine, astragalus has been prescribed for a vast number of ailments, and scientific research has validated many of these applications. Most of the research has centred on the valuable role that the herb can play in preventing infection by viruses (such as the common cold) and helping to overcome long-standing viral infections.

Both of these effects seem to occur because astragalus is able to improve the function of the immune system, helping the body to fight the virus better. Astragalus has also been documented as helping cancer patients to recover from the side effects of their treatment with chemotherapy or radiotherapy. It seems likely that this effect is also at least partially due to the ability of the herb's active constituents to improve immunity.

Astragalus is a tonic or adaptogenic herb, helping to enhance the stamina and endurance of young people, and raising the vitality and improving the cardiac function of elderly people.

Other medicinal actions of astragalus include improving kidney function and acting as a mild diuretic, lowering blood pressure, aiding tissue repair and recovery from blood loss (including after childbirth), improving resistance to the cold and improving sperm motility in infertile men.

Cultivation

Astragalus seeds should be planted in autumn or spring. The herb prefers sun and well-drained, sandy soil.

PREPARATION AND DOSAGE

- **To treat chronic or longstanding viral infection; to raise vitality and stamina; to improve resistance to the cold**

  LIQUID EXTRACT 1–2.5 g dried herb equivalent, three times daily.
  TABLETS, CAPSULES Take according to manufacturer's instructions.
  DECOCTION Boil 3–10 g in ¾ cup of water for 10 minutes before straining. Drink in two doses during the day.

IF SYMPTOMS PERSIST, CONSULT A DOCTOR

CAUTIONS

- Astragalus is recommended for chronic (i.e. longstanding) infections, and is not recommended for acute illnesses.
- Do not use astragalus if you are pregnant or breastfeeding.
- If you are undergoing chemotherapy, radiotherapy or other treatment for cancer, do not use astragalus except under the supervision of your doctor or medical herbalist.

Baical skullcap *Scutellaria baicalensis* Lamiaceae **Also called** Huang quin

Baical skullcap is a native plant of Japan, Korea, Mongolia and China. Records unearthed from ancient Chinese tombs prove that it has been used in traditional Chinese medicine for nearly 2000 years. In its natural environment, the plant thrives in open, sunny areas at altitudes of up to 2000 m. It has erect stems that grow to 30–40 cm and each bears racemes of small, purple-blue hooded flowers.

Parts used

ROOTS

- The roots are harvested in spring, once the plant is three to four years old.
- They are used to make decoctions, liquid extracts, tablets and capsules.

dried roots

Constituents

Amongst the constituents of baical skullcap are flavonoids and flavone derivatives (including baicalin, baicalein, scutellarin and wogonin), which may contribute to its anti-inflammatory, anti-allergic and liver-stimulating actions. Sterols (including sitosterol) and benzoic acid are also present.

Medicinal uses

Flavonoids and flavone derivative constituents from baical skullcap have been demonstrated to inhibit the body's release of the inflammatory compound histamine, and may therefore be of assistance for the relief of allergic symptoms such as asthma, hay fever, eczema and urticaria (nettle rash). The herb also displays anti-inflammatory activity in chronic inflammatory disorders such as arthritis, where it may help prevent long-term destruction of bone.

In the gastrointestinal tract, baical skullcap is recommended to improve digestion, stimulate liver function and aid bile flow, so is prescribed for conditions associated with nausea, vomiting, diarrhoea and jaundice. It is specifically indicated for infective conditions of the digestive system, including chronic hepatitis and dysentery-like infections of the bowel.

In traditional Chinese medicine, baical skullcap is considered to be a cold and bitter remedy, and so is recommended for conditions associated with heat and damp heat. This makes it useful for infections accompanied by fever and thick mucus, including those of the respiratory tract. Typical indications include the common cold, bronchitis and pneumonia.

This cooling quality also makes baical skullcap an appropriate treatment for urinary tract infections which are accompanied by burning pain.

Other uses of the herb include as a sedative, diuretic, anti-oxidant and antihypertensive.

Cultivation

Grow from seed sown in autumn or spring or by division. Plants need full sun and well-drained soil with some additional watering during hot or dry summers.

PREPARATION AND DOSAGE

- To treat hay fever, allergic eczema, urticaria, feverish respiratory infections and as supportive therapy for allergic asthma; to stimulate liver function and help treat infections of the digestive tract

LIQUID EXTRACT 500 mg–1 g dried root equivalent taken three times daily.

DECOCTION Boil 500 mg–1 g dried root in 1 cup of water for 10 minutes before straining. Drink 3 cups per day.

IF SYMPTOMS PERSIST, CONSULT A DOCTOR

CAUTIONS

- In traditional Chinese medicine, baical skullcap is contraindicated in cold conditions, such as chills.
- Pregnant and breastfeeding women should not use baical skullcap.

Barberry *Berberis vulgaris* Berberidaceae

This thorny deciduous shrub is seen in hedgerows and scrubland in Europe, and is found worldwide in gardens in cool to temperate climates. The ancient Egyptians used barberry as a cure for fevers. It grows to a height of about 3 m and has grooved, yellow-grey bark, yellow wood and a yellow root. It bears bright yellow flowers in spring followed by elongated berries in various shades of pink or red.

Parts used

ROOT AND STEM BARK

- The root and stem bark are collected in spring or autumn and dried for use in powders, tinctures, decoctions as well as other extracts.

Constituents

The whole plant contains alkaloids, which are believed to possess anticancer properties. Some of the alkaloids are yellow, hence the plant's brightly coloured wood. The alkaloids berbamine and berberine are antibacterial; the root bark contains up to 3 per cent berberine.

Medicinal uses

Berberine accounts for several of the plant's properties. Animal studies have shown that this alkaloid reduces muscle spasms, which may explain why bitter-tasting barberry can aid digestion.

Because berberine is also a highly effective antibacterial, barberry is used to help combat infections such as *Helicobacter pylori,* which is associated with gastritis and peptic ulcers, and to treat yeast infections, such as thrush *(Candida albicans).*

Berberine also acts on the gall bladder to stimulate the secretion of bile, which carries waste products away from the liver. This supports the traditional use of barberry, which was to combat liver disorders such as jaundice and gallstones.

Externally, barberry's anti-inflammatory properties make it a useful treatment for sore or swollen eyes, eczema, psoriasis, rheumatism, hepatitis as well as a range of other inflammatory disorders. Recent laboratory studies carried out in

root bark

Bulgaria have confirmed the anti-inflammatory effect of berberine extracted from the barberry root.

Cultivation

Barberry prefers neutral or alkaline soil and grows best in full sunlight, although it will tolerate light shade in the right situations. It can be grown either from seeds or from cuttings, which are best taken in summer. However, it is generally not considered advisable to cultivate barberry for use in homemade herbal preparations.

PREPARATION AND DOSAGE

- **Barberry should be taken internally only on the advice of a medical herbalist**
- **To treat swollen eyes, skin inflammation**

  TINCTURE (1:3 IN 25 PER CENT ALCOHOL) Add 20 drops to 1 glass of water. Soak a cloth in this and squeeze out the excess. Apply to the closed eye for 15 minutes, two or three times a day.

IF SYMPTOMS PERSIST, CONSULT A DOCTOR

CAUTIONS

- Barberry should never be taken except under supervision and for no longer than a period of four to six weeks.
- Do not take more than advised by your medical herbalist.
- Barberry should not be taken during pregnancy.
- Do not take barberry to treat food poisoning or chronic heartburn.
- If using as an antibacterial, avoid vitamin B_6 and the amino acid L-histidine as they suppress barberry's efficacy.
- Berbamine and berberine have an anaesthetising effect, which can cause low blood pressure.

THE A TO Z OF PLANTS

Basil Ocimum basilicum Lamiaceae

Although native to south Asia, basil has long been grown in Europe as a culinary and medicinal herb. Its common name comes from the Greek word meaning 'royal'. Basil is an annual plant, growing to a height of about 40 cm. Its square stems and soft leaves are hairy and aromatic. Its flowers are white, crimson or multicoloured and form whorls on the plant's flower spike.

Parts used

LEAVES AND FLOWER HEADS

- Leafy, flowering stems are harvested when the flowers first appear in summer right through to autumn.
- The leaves and flower heads are then dried and blanched for use in infusions or decoctions.
- Alcoholic extracts from fresh flower heads are an ingredient in ointments used to help heal wounds.

Constituents

Basil contains an essential oil (up to 7 ml per kg), whose major chemical constituents differ according to where the plant has been cultivated. The essential oil of the variety grown on the islands of the Indian Ocean has an estragole content of 65–85 per cent. The variety that is cultivated in southern Europe and Egypt produces an essential oil whose main component is linalool. Basil also contains tannins.

dried leaves

Medicinal uses

Basil is known above all for its capacity to relieve spasms, especially stomach spasms. The leaves help digestion and improve the appetite. They are also used as a treatment for flatulence and stomach bloating.

Externally, the plant's astringent qualities make it a useful cold remedy. In a gargle it relieves sore throats, and as an inhalation it helps to clear the sinuses and air passages. As an ointment it can help to heal wounds and cuts, and is often combined with mint and caraway. The essential oil combats worms and germs. Clinical trials carried out in India and published in 1985 have demonstrated basil's antibacterial effects in helping to treat acne.

Cultivation

Basil should be grown in rich, light, well-drained or dry soil. It needs a warm, sunny position in the garden, but can also be grown in a pot on a sunny windowsill.

PREPARATION AND DOSAGE

- **To treat indigestion, loss of appetite, flatulence, bloating**

  INFUSION Put 4–6 g of dried leaves into 250 ml of boiling water. Cover and leave to infuse for 10 minutes and strain. Drink 1 cup without sugar a day. In cases of chronic bloating, drink 2–5 cups a day between meals. Stop the treatment after a week and then restart it a week later.

- **To treat inflamed throats**

  GARGLE Boil 4 teaspoons of dried leaves in 250 ml of water in a covered pan for 10–15 minutes. Strain and leave to cool. Use the liquid as a gargle two or three times a day.

- **To treat wounds, cuts**

  OINTMENT Apply to affected area two or three times a day.

IF SYMPTOMS PERSIST, CONSULT A DOCTOR

CAUTIONS

- Women who are pregnant or breastfeeding should avoid medicinal doses of basil.
- Basil should not be administered to babies or young children.
- Do not take medicinal doses of basil for long periods of time.

Bay   *Laurus nobilis*   Lauraceae   **Also called** Bay tree, Sweet bay, Laurel

This Mediterranean tree was revered in Roman times when leafy twigs were made into the laurel crowns worn by emperors. Male and female flowers are carried on separate trees, which can reach 20 m tall. In cultivation, however, bay trees rarely reach more than 8 m. The tough, oval leaves are aromatic and used as a culinary flavouring. The flowers are yellow and the fruit is a black berry containing one seed.

Parts used
LEAVES AND BERRIES
- The leaves are gathered from young branches during the summer and then dried for use in infusions. They also provide an essential oil.
- The berries are collected when ripe in late autumn and produce an oil called bay butter.

dried leaves

Constituents
Besides tannins and other active constituents, the leaves contain up to 3 per cent essential oil, which is composed of up to 70 per cent cineole. This oil is found in the berries, which also contain lauric, oleic, palmitic and linoleic acids.

Medicinal uses
The oil of the bay tree has antiseptic, antifungal and stimulant properties. Externally, the oil is excellent as a rub for easing aches and pains, rheumatism, sprains and bruises. It has been found to help in soothing mouth ulcers and inflammation, and in addition it can be used (but only under medical supervision) to treat a range of fungal infections.

When taken by mouth, bay has traditionally been used to treat digestive disorders, such as colic and stomach bloating. In 1997, studies published in the *Journal of Ethnopharmacology* showed that chemicals in the seeds helped to prevent the formation of certain types of stomach ulcers in laboratory rats.

Cultivation
Bay grows best in well-drained soil in sun or light shade. It is also quite suitable for growing in pots.

PREPARATION AND DOSAGE
- **To treat stomach disorders, colic, stomach bloating**
  INFUSION 5–10 g dried leaves infused in 1 litre of boiling water for 10 minutes before straining. Drink 2–3 cups a day.
- **To treat mouth ulcers and inflammation of the mouth**
  ESSENTIAL OIL Add 1 drop of essential oil to 10 ml of carrier oil. Apply three or four times a day.

IF SYMPTOMS PERSIST, CONSULT A DOCTOR

CAUTIONS
- Women who are pregnant or breastfeeding should avoid medicinal doses of bay.
- The essential oil should not be taken internally.
- External use may result in an allergic reaction. If it does, seek advice from a doctor or herbalist.

Bilberry
Vaccinium myrtillus Ericaceae **Also called** Blueberry, Blaeberry, Whortleberry

Preferring the damp, acidic soils of heaths, coniferous woods and moorland, bilberry is found throughout Europe and parts of North America, where it is harvested from the wild. It is a low-growing deciduous shrub with oval, serrated leaves. Its white or pinkish flowers are bell shaped and give way to purplish black, edible berries. Each berry is about the size of a small pea and, when ripe, has a clearly visible depression at the top.

Parts used
LEAVES AND BERRIES
- Both leaves and berries are used in infusions, tablets and liquid extracts, but the use of the berries is more common.
- The berries are gathered when ripe.

Constituents
The berries contain anthocyanins, which strengthen and protect the capillaries, and are also involved in bilberry's ability to improve vision in darkness or poor lighting. Polyphenols (catechin) and tannins are also present. The leaves contain phenolic acids (caffeic acid) as well as tannins and iridoids. Vitamin C and flavonoids are also present.

Medicinal uses
Bilberry is often prescribed for vein and lymphatic disorders and to strengthen the capillaries. Studies in 1976 revealed that the beneficial effect on the small blood vessels is due to the anthocyanins in the berries, which increase the strength of the capillaries while reducing their permeability.

The anthocyanins and vitamin C work together to protect against damage from free radicals (which are present in both the atmosphere and in food).

Bilberry has been shown to be useful in treating a number of problems that can affect good eyesight. It can, for example, improve the eye's ability to adapt to darkness. A clinical trial published in 1989 found that anthocyanins from bilberry, together with vitamin E, improved the symptoms of cataracts, a common complaint in older people.

Bilberry has been used to treat diarrhoea and inflammation of the digestive tract, as well as some other inflammatory conditions. The leaves have been indicated in the treatment of diabetes.

dried leaves and berries

Cultivation
Bilberry grows in moist, acid soil in sun or light shade and prefers cool to mild climates.

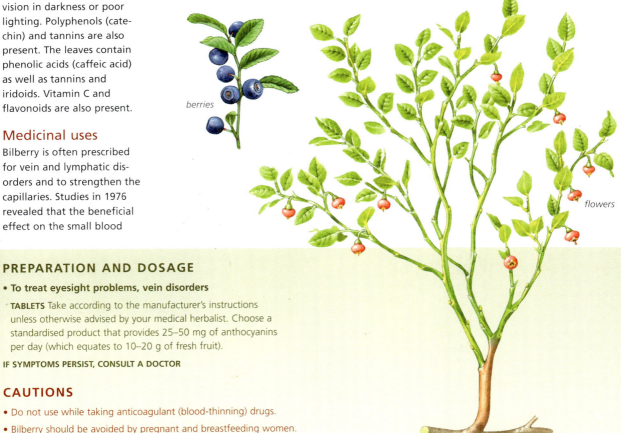
berries
flowers

PREPARATION AND DOSAGE
- **To treat eyesight problems, vein disorders**
  TABLETS Take according to the manufacturer's instructions unless otherwise advised by your medical herbalist. Choose a standardised product that provides 25–50 mg of anthocyanins per day (which equates to 10–20 g of fresh fruit).

IF SYMPTOMS PERSIST, CONSULT A DOCTOR

CAUTIONS
- Do not use while taking anticoagulant (blood-thinning) drugs.
- Bilberry should be avoided by pregnant and breastfeeding women.

Black cohosh *Cimicifuga racemosa* (syn. *Actaea racemosa*) Ranunculaceae

The Native Americans have long known about the medicinal properties of black cohosh. They call it squaw root and use it to alleviate menstrual problems and the pain of childbirth. Black cohosh originates from eastern North America, where it can be seen growing on hillsides and in shady places on the edges of woods and hedgerows. The plant reaches about 2–3 m in height.

Parts used
ROOTS
- In autumn, after the fruits have ripened, the root is dug up, then cut and dried.
- The dried root is used to make tablets and prepare liquid extracts.

Constituents
The root is rich in compounds that mimic the effects of oestrogen (a female sex hormone). Anti-inflammatory and anti-oxidant triterpenoid glucosides are also present as well as salicylic acid, which acts in a similar way to aspirin. The root contains tannins, which are anti-bacterial and aid in the healing of wounds.

Medicinal uses
In 1998, a German review documented the benefits of black cohosh in the treatment of menopausal problems such as hot flushes and depression. In a trial performed in 1987, tablets which contained black cohosh extract were found to improve menopausal symptoms to a significant extent.

Black cohosh is also prescribed for gynaecological problems, including periods (absent, painful or heavy) and premenstrual tension.

In 1998 Japanese scientists demonstrated the effects on blood vessels and arteries of piscidic acids – found in black cohosh – in vitro (laboratory tests). In earlier clinical studies in 1962 Italian researchers discovered that the plant could cause dilation of blood vessels without adversely affecting blood-pressure levels.

In traditional Chinese medicine, black cohosh is used to treat inflammation, pain and fever. The plant's anti-inflammatory properties, which suggest its potential use in the treatment of rheumatism, were reported in *Planta Medica* in 2000. Black cohosh also has a sedative effect and is beneficial in the treatment of anxiety. The plant has also been used to remedy coughs.

Cultivation
Grow in moist, rich soil, ideally in a position where there is some light shade.

dried roots

PREPARATION AND DOSAGE
- **Whether used in the form of a tablet or liquid extract, or in any other pharmaceutical preparation, a treatment based upon black cohosh should only ever be used in consultation with your doctor or medical herbalist**

IF SYMPTOMS PERSIST, CONSULT A DOCTOR

CAUTIONS
- Although no toxic side effects have been noted, it is important to take black cohosh only as prescribed by a medical herbalist.
- It should not be taken by women who are pregnant or breastfeeding, and women who have a history of breast cancer and other oestrogen-related cancers should also avoid it.
- Black cohosh should not be taken with drugs that lower blood pressure, except on the advice of a medical herbalist.
- It should not be taken if you are allergic to aspirin.
- It may cause gastrointestinal disturbances.

THE A TO Z OF PLANTS

Black mustard *Brassica nigra* Brassicaceae

This annual herb is widespread in Europe and Asia, where it has been grown for more than 2000 years. The leaves at the base of its stem are serrated; those at the top unserrated. Its flowers are yellow and the fruits are long seed pods, which contain spherical, blackish seeds.

seed pod

Parts used
FLOWER HEADS AND SEEDS
- The flower heads are harvested in early summer before they have bloomed fully. They are then dried, crushed and used for infusions.
- The seeds are harvested in late summer, then dried and crushed. The black mustard powder that results is used in poultices.

Constituents
Mustard seeds contain lipids that are rich in unsaturated fatty acids, such as erucic, oleic and linoleic acids. The seeds also contain glucosinolates, especially sinigrin, as well as different kinds of mucilage.

Medicinal uses
Black mustard seed has a warming effect since it improves the circulation by dilating the blood vessels. In the same way it is able to relieve the pain caused by inflammation. These properties lead to its use externally in poultices for the treatment of bronchitis, rheumatic and joint pains, and influenza.

When used internally, black mustard is recommended in small doses to restore lost appetite and cure indigestion. The glucosinolates in black mustard are currently being investigated for their potential as agents that inhibit the development of certain cancers. But it is not yet known if they are as effective as those present in other plants of the brassica family, such as broccoli.

Cultivation
Plant in well-drained, rich soil in a sunny location.

dried seeds

PREPARATION AND DOSAGE

- **To treat loss of appetite, indigestion**

    INFUSION 1.5 g (1 teaspoon) of dried flower heads infused in 1 cup of boiling water for 5 minutes before straining. Drink 3 cups a day before meals.

- **To treat bronchitis, rheumatic and joint pains, influenza**

    POULTICE Mix 50 g of fresh black mustard powder with 200 g of flax powder. Add enough lukewarm water to make a thick paste, then wrap in a cloth. Place the poultice on the affected area for about 10 minutes.

IF SYMPTOMS PERSIST, CONSULT A DOCTOR

CAUTIONS

- Use poultices with care. If they are applied with too high a dosage or for too long a time, they can cause intense pain, blisters and irreversible damage to skin.
- Do not use mustard if you have sensitive skin.
- Do not use mustard on broken skin or near the eyes.
- Patients with serious circulatory problems, respiratory diseases or vein disorders such as varicose veins should not use preparations containing mustard.
- Mustard preparations are not recommended for use with children.

Black pepper *Piper nigrum* Piperaceae

This woody perennial climber originates in South-East Asia, where its culinary and medicinal properties have been known for 4000 years. Its leaves are unlobed, thick and shaped like spearheads. The small lateral branches sprout roots, which enable the plant to grip as it climbs. Its small, white flowers form long spikes and are followed by green fruits that ripen to a reddish brown.

Parts used

FRUIT

- The fruit, or seeds, are picked when ripe from plants that must be at least three years old. After drying in the sun, they turn black.
- A pungent essential oil is extracted from the seeds. It is the oil that is usually used medicinally, although the seeds can also be used.

Constituents

As much as 2.5 per cent of the black pepper seed consists of the pungent, greeny yellow essential oil. The seed is rich in the alkaloid piperine (5–9 per cent).

Medicinal uses

Black pepper stimulates digestion and in Europe it is taken orally to treat sluggish digestion, flatulence, bloating and lack of appetite. Its antispasmodic properties make it useful for treating stomach cramps.

Black pepper has been used for many years to soothe rheumatic pains, a use that is supported by Indian research in 1990, which showed that piperine inhibits inflammation. Applied externally, black pepper produces a warming and reddening of the skin (and considerable temporary irritation), which leads to an anaesthetic effect.

In 2000, UK researchers found that black pepper had antibacterial properties since it was shown to be effective in combating the bacteria that are responsible for causing food poisoning.

Piperine can strengthen the effect of numerous other medicines, herbal remedies and spices. Therefore it is important to seek advice from a doctor or qualified herbalist before taking medicinal doses of black pepper in conjunction with other drugs.

Cultivation

The plant thrives in rich, moist soil and temperatures above 15°C.

dried fruit

PREPARATION AND DOSAGE

- **To treat sluggish digestion**

  INFUSION 3 g of pepper seeds infused in 150 ml of boiling water for 5–10 minutes before straining. Flavour with mint to taste, and drink two or three times a day before meals.

- **To treat rheumatism**

  CREAM (BASE CREAM WITH ADDED ESSENTIAL OIL) Rub into the painful areas two or three times a day.

IF SYMPTOMS PERSIST, CONSULT A DOCTOR

CAUTIONS

- Seek medical advice before using black pepper when taking other drugs. For example, it should not be taken together with blood-thinning (anticoagulant) drugs.
- It is not recommended for pregnant or breastfeeding women.
- Excessive intake can have an adverse effect on the liver.
- Do not take essential oil internally.

Blackberry *Rubus fructicosus* Rosaceae **Also called** Bramble

This sprawling perennial shrub with long, flexible, thorny stems grows wild in fields, along roadsides and in wasteland. Its leaves are made up of oval leaflets with serrated edges. Each leaflet has a vein running down the centre that is covered with fine prickles. Its white to pale pink flowers form clusters at the end of their stalks in summer. The sweet berries turn black as they ripen.

Parts used

LEAVES AND OCCASIONALLY ROOTS AND BERRIES

- Young tender leaves are gathered in spring before flowers appear.
- The leaves are dried and crushed for use in infusions and decoctions.
- Sometimes fresh leaves are used for external applications.
- The roots are collected in summer.
- The berries are collected as they ripen in late summer and autumn.

Constituents

The blackberry leaf is rich in tannins, organic acids, especially citric and isocitric acids, pentacyclic triterpenes and flavonoid glycosides of quercetin and kaempferol. The leaves and berries also contain vitamin C.

Medicinal uses

Blackberry has astringent, antiseptic, antifungal and tonic properties. The wealth of tannins provides its astringent qualities. It strengthens capillaries and is antibacterial. Blackberry leaves are taken internally to treat minor cases of diarrhoea. Blackberry is also indicated for vaginal discharge and is reputed to have expectorant properties. The tea is used for flu, colds and coughs.

Externally, a decoction of blackberry leaves is used as a gargle for sore throats, mouth ulcers and inflammation of the mouth and gums. It is also used to dress skin ulcers and wounds that are slow to heal. For these purposes blackberry leaves can be combined with agrimony and witch hazel.

Research published in *Planta Medica* in 1980 showed that blackberry reduces blood-sugar levels in both normal and diabetic rabbits, an effect partly due to its ability to stimulate the release of insulin.

Cultivation

Blackberry grows best in moist, well-drained soil in full sun and may become weedy. Blackberry is a noxious weed in many parts of Australia.

dried leaves

PREPARATION AND DOSAGE

- **To treat minor cases of diarrhoea**

  INFUSION Infuse 1.5 g of dried leaves in 1 cup of boiling water for 10 minutes and strain. Take 3 cups a day between meals.

- **To treat sore throats, mouth ulcers, mouth inflammation**

  MOUTHWASH/GARGLE Put 10 g of dried leaves into 100 ml of water. Bring rapidly to the boil and leave to infuse for 15 minutes. Strain and use as a mouthwash or gargle twice a day.

- **To treat skin ulcers, wounds**

  COMPRESS Soak a cloth in the infusion (see above) and apply to the affected area once or twice a day.

IF SYMPTOMS PERSIST, CONSULT A DOCTOR

CAUTIONS

- Pregnant or breastfeeding women should avoid blackberry leaves.

Blackcurrant *Ribes nigrum* Grossulariaceae

Blackcurrant is widely grown for its sweet black berries, which are one of the world's richest sources of vitamin C. The nutritional content of the berries varies according to where they are grown, and New Zealand is considered to offer optimal conditions because of its bright sunlight and frosty winters. New Zealand blackcurrants may contain significantly more vitamin C than blackcurrants from the United States.

Parts used

FRUIT AND LEAVES

- The leaves are gathered during the early part of summer, before flowering takes place.
- The berries are harvested during late summer when they are ripe, and are dried very carefully, because otherwise they tend to rot quickly.
- Blackcurrant is used as infusions, extracts and syrups. The berries and leaves are used to flavour numerous pharmaceutical products and foods.
- Blackcurrant seeds contain essential fatty acids.

Constituents

Aside from vitamin C, blackcurrant berries are also rich in sugars and organic acids; they contain polyphenols (in particular, flavonoids and anthocyanins), which have a beneficial effect on veins. The leaves possess a small amount of essential oil and flavonoids. The anthocyanins and flavonoids are likely to account for the anti-inflammatory properties of blackcurrant and its ability to protect the blood vessels; however the vitamin C content may also play a role.

Blackcurrant seeds are a rich source of the omega-6 fatty acid gamma-linolenic acid (GLA), which is also to be found in evening primrose oil.

Medicinal uses

Blackcurrant has long been used to treat rheumatism, and its anti-inflammatory effect has been demonstrated in research. In 1994 American researchers found blackcurrant seed oil to be a potentially effective treatment for rheumatoid arthritis, and previous studies had already shown that the seed oil may help to treat inflammatory disorders.

Research has highlighted the protective effect of blackcurrant fruit on the capillaries, giving them elasticity and strength – the fruit is often prescribed for vein and arterial ailments, including varicose veins. Furthermore, blackcurrant may help to improve circulation in the veins by keeping the blood thin.

Infections, including those of the urinary tract, can be treated with blackcurrant. Studies in 1976 found that anthocyanins in the fruit help to inhibit the growth of bacteria, and in 2001 scientists found that they had an antiviral action on the influenza virus.

Due to its functions on the immune system, vitamin C may also play a role in the anti-infective properties of blackcurrant berries.

Cultivation

Plant in well-drained soil enriched with compost, in sun or part shade.

dried leaves

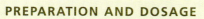

PREPARATION AND DOSAGE

- **As a source of vitamin C, to treat colds, influenza and throat infections**
  SYRUP Follow manufacturer's instructions.

- **To treat arthritis and rheumatism**
  CAPSULES (CONTAINING BLACKCURRANT SEED STANDARDISED FOR GLA CONTENT) Follow manufacturer's instructions.

  IF SYMPTOMS PERSIST, CONSULT A DOCTOR

CAUTIONS

There are no known cautions for the use of this plant.

Boldo *Peumus boldus* Monimiaceae

This evergreen shrub, related to the bay tree, is a native of Chile, though it is now cultivated in Italy and North Africa, particularly Morocco. It grows to 4–5 m in height and has rough, brittle, greyish green leaves, which give off a camphorlike smell when crushed. Clusters of pale yellow flowers are followed by small, black, fleshy berries. Boldo leaves are used by the indigenous peoples of South America in their cooking.

Parts used
LEAVES AND BARK
- The leaves are dried and then crushed for use in preparing infusions.
- Boldo leaves are also used in various pharmaceutical products that stimulate bile secretion.
- The bark is collected for boldine, the alkaloid substance it contains.

Constituents
The leaves are rich in the volatile oils ascaridole, cineole and camphor – which give the plant its distinctive aroma. Both leaves and bark contain flavonoids – cancer-fighting anti-oxidants, as well as a variety of alkaloids, the main one being boldine.

Medicinal uses
Boldo is widely used in herbal medicine to treat gallstones and for various liver, stomach and digestive disorders. The active constituent, boldine, stimulates bile secretion and reduces gall bladder inflammation.

Boldo has a soothing effect on the lining of the bladder, and antiseptic properties, and so can help cystitis sufferers. In Chile, the herb has long been used as a cure for syphilis and gonorrhoea and is also used to get rid of parasitic worms. In Brazil, the herb is taken to eliminate gas and bloating, for digestive and liver complaints and as a diuretic. It has also been used to treat rheumatism, gout, jaundice, colds and earaches.

Boldo has been clinically proven to aid digestion, and may sometimes be combined with a range of other plants, such as cascara, in the preparation of remedies for treating constipation.

dried leaves

Cultivation
Plant in sandy, well-drained soil. The shrub prefers a sunny position, an acidic soil and a mild climate.

PREPARATION AND DOSAGE
- **To treat dyspepsia (indigestion)**
  INFUSION Put 1 teabag into 200 ml of boiling water for up to 10 minutes. Drink up to 3 cups a day.
  IF SYMPTOMS PERSIST, CONSULT A DOCTOR

CAUTIONS
- Do not take boldo if you have severe liver disease or obstruction of the gall bladder.
- Boldo should not be used if you have an existing kidney condition.
- Boldo should not be used during pregnancy as it may be associated with a risk of miscarriage.

Borage
Borago officinalis Boraginaceae **Also called** Starflower

A rampant herbaceous annual, borage is the bane of many a gardener. It tends to grow on rough ground or at the roadside – but it loves flowerbeds too. The whole plant is covered with prickly hairs and grows 60–80 cm tall. The bright blue flowers appear in summer and are followed by little nutlike fruits, each containing a seed.

Parts used
SEEDS
- The seeds are commercially harvested and crushed for their oil.

dried seeds

Constituents
Borage oil is a rich source of the omega-6 fatty acid gamma-linolenic acid (GLA).

However, the leaves and flowers contain pyrrolizidine alkaloids, substances that are thought to damage the liver and cause cancer. Consequently, preparations containing flowers and leaves are no longer available to the public.

Medicinal uses
GLA, the essential fatty acid found in high quantities in borage oil, is also present in evening primrose oil, and hence the two plants have similar uses. For example, both are often used to help relieve the symptoms of premenstrual syndrome.

Borage oil is also believed to be beneficial for some skin ailments, such as eczema and the dryness and loss of elasticity that commonly affect ageing skin.

GLA may also have anti-inflammatory properties. In 1993, researchers in Pennsylvania found it to be an effective treatment for rheumatoid arthritis. Subsequently, a combination of borage oil and fish oil was shown to prevent inflammation caused by acute lung injury in rats.

Cultivation
This frost-hardy annual grows best from seeds planted in spring. It flowers quickly from seed and will then self-sow in the same spot. Choose a location with well-drained soil and plenty of sunshine.

PREPARATION AND DOSAGE
- **To treat PMS, dry skin, eczema, rheumatoid arthritis**

  CAPSULES Follow manufacturer's instructions.

IF SYMPTOMS PERSIST, CONSULT A DOCTOR

CAUTIONS
- Do not take borage leaves or flowers, or make an infusion from them, as they contain potentially harmful pyrrolizidine alkaloids.
- People suffering from epilepsy or schizophrenia, and those taking phenothiazine tranquillisers, should not use borage oil.
- The hairy leaves and stems may cause contact dermatitis.

Boswellia
Boswellia serrata Burseraceae **Also called** Frankincense, Indian frankincense, Indian olibanum tree, Mastic tree This deciduous tree from India has ash-coloured bark that peels away in flakes. The oval leaves are long and grow opposite one another, while white flowers grow in clusters. The resins (gum) of Boswellia species have long been used for incense, most famously the frankincense mentioned in the Bible. However, boswellia is also known for its medicinal properties.

Parts used
GUM
- The gum is collected all year round and can be used in fresh or dried form to make powders and decoctions.
- An essential oil is also extracted from the gum.

Constituents
The gum contains several triterpenoid acids known as boswellic acids, which are thought to impart the therapeutic actions of boswellia. Various sugars have also been found to be present in the gum. Ingredients of the essential oil, which is obtained from the gum, include pinene, phellandrene and sesquiterpene alcohols.

Medicinal uses
Boswellia has traditionally been used as an anti-inflammatory agent. A German review published in 2002 documents the effectiveness of boswellic acids in treating arthritis, chronic colitis, ulcerative colitis, Crohn's disease, bronchial asthma and reactive swelling around a brain tumour. The results of these clinical trials, coupled with the plant's antiseptic and expectorant properties, also explain its use in treating infections of the respiratory system.

Boswellia is also used to help skin problems and vaginal infections. In addition, it is believed to aid the digestive system and has been used to treat diarrhoea and intestinal infections.

Boswellia also stimulates blood circulation and has been used in the treatment of piles. The aroma of the essential oil is reputed to have sedative effects and can relieve anxiety.

In 2002, Swiss research suggested that extracts of boswellia may have the potential to destroy certain types of cancer cells.

Cultivation
Plant in moist but well-drained soil in a tropical climate. It requires full sun and temperatures above 15°C. The best gum is gathered in the hottest months from the driest areas.

dried gum

PREPARATION AND DOSAGE
- **To treat inflammatory conditions, including arthritis, colitis, Crohn's disease, asthma**

   CAPSULES Choose a product standardised for its content of boswellic acid, and with a dose equivalent to 2–4 g of resin. Take according to manufacturer's instructions.

IF SYMPTOMS PERSIST, CONSULT A DOCTOR

CAUTIONS
- Pregnant women should not use boswellia.
- Some individuals may experience heartburn or hot hands and feet.
- Boswellia is usually used for eight to twelve weeks at a time.

Brahmi
Bacopa monnieri Scrophulariaceae **Also called** Water hyssop, Thyme-leaved gratiola

Brahmi has a long history of use in Ayurvedic medicine and its use in India can be traced as far back as the 6th century. Brahmi is also native to Australia and other tropical countries, and grows in moist, wet places such as the banks of rivers and lakes. It is a small, prostrate plant with fleshy leaves and white or blue flowers. Brahmi is sometimes used as an ornamental plant in aquariums.

Parts used
WHOLE PLANT
- The whole dried plant is used in many traditional Ayurvedic formulations. It is also used in the manufacture of tablets and liquid extracts.

dried plant

Constituents
Brahmi contains saponins, triterpenes, alkaloids and flavonoids. The constituents considered most important are the dammarane-type saponins, including the bacosides and bacosaponins. High-quality commercial preparations of brahmi are sometimes standardised for their bacoside content.

Medicinal uses
Brahmi is prescribed as a brain tonic, and is understood to improve learning, concentration and memory, especially when used in stressful circumstances.

In 2001, a group of researchers in Australia conducted a double blind, placebo-controlled trial to investigate the effects of brahmi on mental performance. After three months, those taking brahmi showed significant improvements on tests measuring the speed and efficiency with which information processing took place, confirming the traditional usage of the plant as a memory tonic. This clinical trial also measured anxiety levels, and the results showed significant reductions in anxiety for those patients taking the brahmi, when compared to those taking a placebo.

Other research supports these traditionally recognised attributes of the herb, and have also reported lessening of mental fatigue and improvements in sleep quality, appetite and IQ.

In Ayurveda, brahmi is used as a tonic for the nervous system, and is prescribed in cases of nervous breakdown and exhaustion. It has also been used for a wide range of other complaints, such as indigestion, constipation, bronchitis and epilepsy, including in the treatment of animals.

Cultivation
Brahmi is grown in wet soil or shallow water in warm to tropical climates. It must be protected from frost. It is propagated by division.

PREPARATION AND DOSAGE
- **To treat anxiety and memory problems, and to improve concentration**
  LIQUID EXTRACT 1–2 g dried herb equivalent, three times a day.
  TABLETS, CAPSULES Up to 6 g per day, according to the manufacturer's instructions.

IF SYMPTOMS PERSIST, CONSULT A DOCTOR

CAUTIONS
- Side effects of nausea, dry mouth and fatigue may occur occasionally. If you experience these symptoms, discontinue the use of brahmi immediately.
- Do not use brahmi if you are pregnant or breastfeeding.
- This article refers only to *Bacopa monnieri*. The common name brahmi is also sometimes used in Ayurvedic textbooks to refer to *Centella asiatica*, which is detailed on page 107 of this book.

Broom
Cytisus scoparius **Fabaceae** **Also called** Common broom A native of Europe and North Africa, broom has become naturalised in south-eastern Australia and throughout New Zealand. Broom is a tough, tall, perennial shrub that thrives on scrubby moorland. Long, flexible branches grow in bundles from its stems. Sweetly scented bright-yellow flowers bloom in early summer, followed by downy seed pods.

Parts used
FLOWER HEADS
- Blooms are gathered just as they open in spring.
- Flowers are dried carefully to stop them from turning black and losing their active constituents.

dried flower heads

Constituents
The flowers are rich in carotenoids and flavonoids, both of which are anti-oxidants, known to help to prevent cardiovascular disease and fight cancer. The flowers also contain small amounts of some powerful alkaloids including a sedative called sparteine, as well as dopamine and tyramine.

Medicinal uses
Broom has long been held to be a diuretic and it is the flavonoid constituents that are responsible for this effect.

The alkaloid sparteine has a documented effect on heartbeat, and is known to decrease the conductivity of the heart. It is for this reason that the herb has sometimes been prescribed to help restore normal rhythm to the heartbeat.

The tyramine in broom constricts blood vessels. Preparations made using a combination of broom, black haw and juniper are used to treat varicose veins and poor circulation.

Cultivation
Sow ripe seeds in well-drained soil in a sunny position. Prune immediately after flowering to prevent seeding. Broom prefers a cool to mild climate and may become weedy. In New Zealand, broom is considered a troublesome pest, and in parts of Australia it has been declared a noxious weed.

PREPARATION AND DOSAGE
- Never try to make your own preparations of broom. The plant should only ever be taken as prescribed by a qualified medical herbalist

IF SYMPTOMS PERSIST, CONSULT A DOCTOR

CAUTIONS
- Use broom only under a medical herbalist's supervision. Its alkaloids can have toxic effects.
- Do not use if pregnant or breastfeeding.
- Do not use if you have high blood pressure.
- An overdose may cause dizziness, vomiting, diarrhoea and palpitations.
- The alkaloid tyramine can trigger a harmful interaction if used with certain antidepressants.

Buchu *Agathosma betulina* Rutaceae **Also called** Round buchu

A native of the mountainous regions of South Africa, the round buchu is a small, bushy shrub that grows up to 2 m tall. Its bright, greeny yellow oval leaves are covered in little depressions that hold the plant's aromatic, volatile essential oil, which has antiseptic properties. White or pink flowers and egg-shaped fruit appear when the leaves drop in autumn.

Parts used
LEAVES
- The leaves are harvested in summer, while the plant is in flower or fruit.
- They can be used alone or with other diuretic plants.

Constituents
The essential oil obtained from buchu leaves is rich in pulegone and diosphenol, colloquially known as 'buchu camphor'. These give it its strong, distinctive aroma, reminiscent of blackcurrant, but also similar to a combination of rosemary and peppermint. The oil also contains flavonoids and mucilage.

Medicinal uses
Buchu is mainly used to treat bladder problems and urinary tract infections such as cystitis, urethritis and prostatitis. The leaf also contains mucilage, which soothes inflamed mucous membranes, making it good for soothing the inflamed airways of chronic bronchitis sufferers. It is also used in the treatment of rheumatism and gout.

The leaf oil is well known for its diuretic and antiseptic qualities, which are attributed to the presence of the volatile oil diosphenol.

Buchu can help to ease digestive problems. British research in London demonstrated its antispasmodic properties in laboratory animal studies in 2001.

In traditional medicine, the leaf is used as a carminative, to expel wind from the gut. It also relieves the bloating associated with premenstrual syndrome. It is usually combined with other plants such as barberry, yarrow or marsh mallow.

Cultivation
Propagate buchu from seed or cuttings. Plant established shrubs in a well-drained, sunny position, ideally in an acid soil. Water on very hot days and during dry spells.

dried leaves

PREPARATION AND DOSAGE

- **To treat cystitis, bladder problems, mild fluid retention**

  LIQUID EXTRACT 500 mg–2 g dried leaf equivalent, three times a day.
  TABLETS, CAPSULES Doses up to approximately 600 mg are commercially available, usually in combination with other herbs. Take according to the manufacturer's instructions.
  INFUSION Place 1 teabag (approximately 2 g) into 1 cup of boiling water and infuse for 5 minutes. Drink 1 cup three times a day before meals.

IF SYMPTOMS PERSIST, CONSULT A DOCTOR

CAUTIONS

- Do not use buchu if you have a history of serious kidney disease.
- Pulegone, a constituent of the essential oil, is toxic in large doses.
- Avoid buchu if pregnant, since pulegone is a uterine stimulant.
- Do not use buchu if you are taking a blood-thinning (anticoagulant) drug, such as Warfarin.
- Diuretics cause potassium loss, but this can be offset by eating plenty of fresh fruit and vegetables.

Bupleurum
Bupleurum falcatum (syn. *B. chinense, B. scorzonaerifolium*) Apiaceae

Also called Hare's ear root, Sickle-leaved hare's ear, Chai hu, Saiko, Thorow-wax Bupleurum has been used medicinally for around 2000 years in China, where it is considered to balance the internal organs and energy. This slender, evergreen shrub is found growing wild in Asia and in much of central, southern and eastern Europe. It is characterised by tiny, yellow flowers on slender, hollow stems up to 30 cm high.

Parts used
ROOTS
- The roots are harvested in spring or autumn, as this is when their nutritional content is highest

dried roots

Constituents
Bupleurum contains flavonoids (including rutin), bupleurumol and triterpenoid saponins. The group of saponins known as the saikosaponins or saikosides are considered to be responsible for much of the herb's activity, and research has predominantly focused on these compounds.

Medicinal uses
Bupleurum has traditionally been prescribed for conditions associated with a sluggish or compromised liver function. Its indications include nausea, indigestion, liver enlargement and chronic liver diseases. Research carried out in Japan has confirmed that the saikosides exert a protective effect on the liver and are capable of lowering raised cholesterol levels.

Other scientific research has demonstrated that the saikosaponins have potent anti-inflammatory activity, stimulating the body's secretion of corticosteroids and enhancing their level of activity in the body. For this reason, herbalists prescribe bupleurum for the treatment of chronic inflammatory conditions such as hepatitis, and also for auto-immune diseases, which may develop.

Bupleurum is considered to be a cold and bitter remedy, and is therefore recommended to resolve conditions associated with heat, and for fevers. Bupleurum is particularly indicated for conditions in which fever symptoms alternate with chills (e.g. malaria), and when fever occurs as a symptom of influenza or a common cold.

In traditional Chinese medicine, bupleurum is indicated for menstrual irregularities, premenstrual syndrome and painful menstruation. It is also prescribed for haemorrhoids, and for prolapse of the uterus, rectum or bowel.

Cultivation
Propagated from seed in spring or by root division in autumn. Bupleurum prefers well-drained soil, sun and shelter from extremely cold winters. It is able to tolerate coastal conditions.

PREPARATION AND DOSAGE
- Bupleurum should be taken only on the advice of a medical herbalist

IF SYMPTOMS PERSIST, CONSULT A DOCTOR

CAUTIONS
- In sensitive patients bupleurum may cause nausea, reflux, flatulence and increased bowel movements. It has also been noted to have sedative activity in some people.
- Bupleurum is an ingredient in a traditional Chinese formula that has been associated with liver damage and inflammation of the lungs. Since there are several herbs in the formula, it is not clear whether bupleurum or another herb is responsible.
- It is important to note that most information pertaining to bupleurum is actually derived from research into the saikosaponins, and sometimes they were administered by injection. The activity of the whole root taken orally may differ from the information currently available in the medical literature.
- If you are taking steroid medication, do not take bupleurum except under the supervision of your doctor or medical herbalist.

Burdock *Arctium lappa* (syn. *A. majus*) Asteraceae **Also called** Great burdock

Common throughout the Northern Hemisphere, burdock is generally regarded as a weed. The plant thrives on roadsides and building sites and grows to almost 1 m tall. It has purple, thistlelike flowers that give way to fruits that are covered in spiny hooks that stick to fur and clothing. This action is said to have inspired the inventors of the Velcro fastening system. The seed heads ripen to release fawn-coloured seeds.

Parts used
ROOTS
- The wrinkled, greyish brown root is whitish and hard inside.
- The plant is harvested in summer just before the flowers appear.
- The root may be taken as a decoction or used to produce tablets and liquid extracts.

Constituents
Burdock root stores plant sugars known as inulin. The sweetness can be tasted when the root is chewed. It also contains antibacterial and antifungal compounds.

Medicinal uses
In traditional medicine, the root of burdock was used mainly to cleanse the blood and to treat eczema and psoriasis.

Today, the plant is still used for a range of skin disorders, with the root taken internally for ailments associated with oily skin, such as acne, boils and other types of spots.

The root has diuretic and purging effects, aiding the removal of the body's waste products and making it a useful detoxifier. For this reason, it is sometimes given for conditions associated with an accumulation of metabolic wastes, such as gout, which involves excessive amounts of uric acid.

Experiments have shown that the root has antibacterial and antifungal properties. It also lowers blood-sugar levels and may have potential in the treatment of diabetes.

Root extracts have oestrogenic effects which could prove useful in the treatment of menstrual disorders. However, further scientific research will be needed to see if this is the case.

dried roots

Cultivation
Sow seeds in spring in a wild part of the garden. Burdock does well on rough ground in a sunny location.

PREPARATION AND DOSAGE
- **To treat skin complaints (acne, spots, boils), gout**

  LIQUID EXTRACT 500 mg–1.5 g dried root equivalent, taken three times a day.
  DECOCTION Boil 6–12 g dried root equivalent in 1 litre of water for 10 minutes. Strain and drink 3 cups a day.

IF SYMPTOMS PERSIST, CONSULT A DOCTOR

CAUTIONS
- No toxicity or side effects have been recorded to date.
- Do not give to children under 15 years of age.
- Do not take during pregnancy.
- Do not use burdock if you are suffering from diarrhoea.

Butcher's broom *Ruscus aculeatus* Ruscaceae **Also called** Knee or Box holly

Butcher's broom is a low, woody shrub found in much of Europe and parts of Africa, with a long history of use as a medicinal plant. Butchers used to sweep their blocks with bundles of its branches, which is how the name originated. The evergreen 'leaves' are not true leaves but a widening of the stem. A tiny white flower appears in the middle of each leaf in spring, followed in autumn by a red, cherrylike berry.

Parts used

RHIZOMES

- Knotty rhizomes, grey and ringed with grooves, are dug up in autumn.
- Once dried, they are ground into powder or made into extracts.
- Powders and extracts are used in tablets, capsules, liquid extracts and creams.

Constituents

The active components of butcher's broom are substances known as steroidal saponins. These have beneficial effects on the veins, improving blood circulation, and they also possess anti-inflammatory properties.

Medicinal uses

When taken orally, the saponins in butcher's broom cause superficial blood vessels (the veins near the skin's surface) to contract.

Studies on human patients have shown that butcher's broom improves poor circulation in the veins of the lower limbs and reduces haemorrhoids. The plant is therefore recommended as a treatment for stiff, aching legs, varicose veins and piles. It can be combined with other plants that help to protect veins and capillaries, such as witch hazel.

Butcher's broom is a good remedy for oedema (fluid retention). German clinical trials published in 2002 found that extracts of butcher's broom reduced lower leg oedema in women who suffered chronic vein problems as a result of poor circulation. The study concluded that this was a safe and effective treatment for this condition. In 1988, Italian researchers reached the same conclusion, also highlighting the plant's beneficial effects on veins in the lower limbs. Butcher's broom can also help to combat vein problems associated with premenstrual syndrome and the oral contraceptive pill.

The rhizome is a mild laxative and a cure for cramp. It also has diuretic and anti-inflammatory properties.

dried rhizomes

Cultivation

Butcher's broom is frost-hardy. It thrives in sun and shade and likes a dryish soil. Grow from seed or divide the rhizomes in autumn.

roots and rhizomes

PREPARATION AND DOSAGE

- **To treat stiff, aching legs, varicose veins**

  CREAM Massage into the legs, as directed, once a day, starting at the ankles and moving up to the thighs.

  IF SYMPTOMS PERSIST, CONSULT A DOCTOR

CAUTIONS

- Do not use if pregnant or breastfeeding.
- Butcher's broom should be taken internally only on the advice of a medical herbalist.
- Do not exceed the dose recommended by your medical herbalist, as overdose may cause vomiting and low blood pressure.
- Do not use butcher's broom internally if you suffer from high blood pressure.
- Do not use if taking monoamine oxidase inhibitors (antidepressants), or drugs for high blood pressure or an enlarged prostate gland.

Calendula   *Calendula officinalis*   Asteraceae   **Also called** Marigold

Originally from the Mediterranean region, calendula has been cultivated for its ornamental, culinary and medicinal qualities for many centuries. The ancient Romans used to make a broth that was said to uplift the spirits, the Greeks flavoured food with it and in India it was used to decorate the altars in Hindu temples. It has vivid orange-gold flowers, soft green leaves and robust, angular stems.

Parts used

FLOWERS

- The flowers are gathered from early summer on, as they begin to bloom, and are then left to dry on racks in a dark, well-ventilated place.
- Dried calendula flowers are used in ointments, gargles and compresses.
- Calendula is also taken internally as an infusion or liquid extract.

Constituents

Calendula flowers contain flavonoids, carotenoid pigments which give them their orange colour, sterols, mucilage and an essential oil, rich in triterpenoids – thought to be responsible for its anti-inflammatory properties.

dried flowers

Medicinal uses

Applied externally, calendula – used in many cosmetics – is an effective treatment for skin problems such as cuts, cracked skin, sunburn and insect bites. It is also recommended as a treatment for mouth infections, and may be used as a douche in the treatment of vaginal thrush.

Calendula is also taken internally for gastric and duodenal ulcers.

Investigations into the healing powers of calendula flowers have highlighted not only their anti-inflammatory and antibacterial properties, but also their ability to fight off infection caused by viruses and parasites. Research in Italy in 1994 found that triterpenoids in the plant are responsible for its anti-inflammatory powers, and trials have shown that these can help to ease swelling caused by fluid retention.

Traditionally, calendula is considered to be a blood cleansing agent, and so is taken to treat acne and conditions associated with inflamed or congested lymph glands. It is also reputed to be capable of staunching bleeding, and of calming muscle spasms.

Cultivation

Calendula grows easily from seed sown in autumn and spring. It is best grown in well-drained neutral to alkaline soils, in sun or light shade. Deadhead plants for continuous flowering.

PREPARATION AND DOSAGE

- **To treat acne, lymphatic congestion, gastric or duodenal ulcers**

   FLUID EXTRACT 500 mg–1 g dried herb equivalent, three times daily.

   INFUSION Infuse 1–4 g dried flower heads in 1 cup of water for 5 minutes before straining. Drink 3 cups a day.

- **To treat acne, cracked skin, cuts, insect bites, sunburn**

   CREAM, OINTMENT Follow manufacturer's instructions.

- **To treat mouth infections, ulcers**

   GARGLE, MOUTHWASH Prepare the infusion as above, allow to cool, and use as a mouthwash or gargle two or three times a day.

IF SYMPTOMS PERSIST, CONSULT A DOCTOR

CAUTIONS

- Do not use calendula if you have a known allergy to other members of the Asteraceae family (e.g. daisies, chrysanthemums and echinacea).

Californian poppy *Eschscholzia californica* Papaveraceae

Although it is a native of the United States, Californian poppy also grows in Europe, Australia and New Zealand, where its attractive flowers have made it a favourite with gardeners. The erect stem grows to a height of 60 cm and is covered in long, serrated, bluish green leaves, and crowned with a solitary orange, yellow, pink or red flower in spring to autumn. The fruit, a lined capsule, splits itself open when ripe.

dried flowers and leaves

fruit

Parts used

STEMS, LEAVES AND FLOWERS

- The aerial parts – stems, leaves and flowers – are collected in summer.
- These are then dried and broken into fragments to be used for making infusions, liquid extracts, capsules and tinctures.
- Californian poppy is often used in combination with other sedative plants, such as passionflower and valerian.

Constituents

The Californian poppy, like all other members of the Papaveraceae family, contains a large number of alkaloids. It is also rich in flavonoids, including the various carotenoids, that are responsible for the bright colours of its flowers.

Medicinal uses

Californian poppy preparations are recommended for the treatment of nervous disorders, anxiety and for repeated bedwetting in children. Taken orally, they have long been used to help to induce sleep and to facilitate a deeper level of sleep – actions supported by animal research published in *Planta Medica* in 1991. Californian poppy is used either on its own or in conjunction with valerian, passionflower and olive tree.

The plant is also reputed to have anti-inflammatory as well as antispasmodic properties, and has traditionally been used to relieve various forms of pain.

Cultivation

A drought-hardy plant, the Californian poppy can be grown easily from seed, planted either from spring to early summer, or towards the end of summer and in autumn. It thrives in well-drained, sandy soil and prefers to be placed in a warm, sunny position. Plants usually self-seed.

PREPARATION AND DOSAGE

- **To treat sleeping problems, nervous exhaustion**

  LIQUID EXTRACT 1–2 g dried herb equivalent taken in a glass of water in the evening.

- **To treat bedwetting in children**

  Consult your medical herbalist for a dose that is appropriate for the age of your child.

IF SYMPTOMS PERSIST, CONSULT A DOCTOR

CAUTIONS

- It is advisable to consult a medical herbalist before taking Californian poppy, or giving it to children.
- Because of the sedative effect of Californian poppy, you should avoid operating machinery or driving a car while taking it.
- Californian poppy preparations should not be taken by women who are pregnant.

Caraway *Carum carvi* Apiaceae

With its feathery leaves and umbrella-like clusters of tiny white flowers, caraway is a pretty and popular garden herb with a culinary history that stretches back at least to the Stone Age. It is a biennial that grows to about 60 cm in height and bears deep brown seeds with a distinctive smell. Caraway is used to flavour digestive liqueurs and spirits, such as the German Kümmel, as well as confectionery.

Parts used

SEEDS
- Caraway seeds are gathered in summer just before they ripen.
- The seeds are often confused with cumin seeds.
- Caraway is used throughout Europe as infusions in herbal medicine.

Constituents

The volatile essential oil of caraway is largely composed of carvone (which is antiseptic and gives the plant its characteristic odour) and limonene. Flavonoids are also present in the plant.

Medicinal uses

People have been using caraway as a digestive herb for thousands of years. It stimulates the secretion of gastric juices and encourages the expulsion of wind.

In Europe, caraway has long been combined with fennel and anise in an infusion to treat intestinal cramps and bloating, as well as other uncomfortable ailments, such as flatulence.

Research published in 1985 found evidence for caraway's helpful effect on painful gut cramp. It proved that caraway oil relaxes intestinal muscles. It also has the same effect on uterine muscles, and as a result helps to relieve period pains.

Carvone's antibacterial properties help to fight off gut infections. In traditional Arabic medicine, caraway is a treatment for incontinence in children. As an expectorant, caraway can ease a chesty cough, and it is also used as a gargle for laryngitis. Its oil may help to clear up scabies.

Cultivation

Sow seeds or plant seedlings in a sunny spot with well-drained soil.

dried seeds

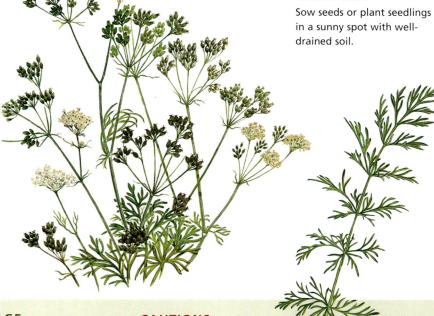

PREPARATION AND DOSAGE

- **To treat digestive problems**

  INFUSION Put 1 teaspoon of a mixture of equal parts caraway, fennel and anise seeds in 250 ml of boiling water. Leave to infuse for two or three minutes. Divide into two or three servings and drink over the course of the day before meals.

  Alternatively, take 1–5 g of ground caraway seeds and leave to infuse for 10–15 minutes in 1 cup of boiling water. Drink this amount over the course of the day in two or three smaller amounts before meals.

IF SYMPTOMS PERSIST, CONSULT A DOCTOR

CAUTIONS

- Like other plants in this family (such as coriander, cumin and dill), caraway may cause an allergic reaction such as a runny nose, watering eyes or diarrhoea. If you notice any side effects, stop using it.

Carob
Ceratonia siliqua Caesalpiniaceae **Also called** St John's bread, Locust bean

The 'locusts' on which John the Baptist is supposed to have survived in the desert are thought to have been carob beans, hence the popular name, St John's bread. The large, evergreen carob tree grows in the Mediterranean region and can reach 20 m in height. Its flowers are small, reddish, have no petals and form gleaming clusters. The bean is a large purple-brown pod in which 8 to 12 seeds lie in a fleshy pulp.

dried seeds

seed pod

Parts used
PODS AND SEEDS
- The seeds are soaked to soften them, then the outer coating and the germ are removed, leaving the albumen, which is ground to make carob gum – also known as locust bean gum.
- Carob flour is made by drying and grinding the pulp of the seed pods.

Constituents
Carob is largely made up of sugars and tannins. Almost 90 per cent of the bean is composed of sugar-type compounds, together with soluble fibre. It is also rich in mucilage, which acts to soothe inflamed mucous membranes. The seed pod pulp is also high in soluble sugars (40–50 per cent), as well as being rich in tannins.

Medicinal uses
Carob preparations are used for treating diarrhoea, indigestion and heartburn. Carob flour is mixed with sunflower seed and rice flours to make an absorbent preparation gentle enough to treat diarrhoea in babies. Tests carried out in Belgium in 1989 found that infants suffering with diarrhoea recovered more rapidly when they were given carob pod powder – possibly as a result of the tannins it contains, which not only bind to, and thus inactivate, toxins, but also help to inhibit the growth of bacteria.

In a Turkish teaching hospital study in 1998, carob bean juice was found to effectively combat diarrhoea in children. Carob helps to sooth intestinal irritation. The mucilage and gum are also both used in mild preparations as a treatment for vomiting, which is suitable for use with babies and pregnant women.

Carob bean gum is a useful ingredient in slimming foods and is widely used as a low-fat chocolate substitute. It lacks absorbable nutrients and can be used as a thickener, making food more substantial and filling – but not more fattening.

Cultivation
Carob is a slow-growing tree that thrives in dry and Mediterranean climates. It can be grown from seed or cuttings. It is drought-hardy when established.

PREPARATION AND DOSAGE
- **To treat diarrhoea**

  CAROB FLOUR Take 20–30 g a day mixed with lukewarm water or milk. To avoid irritating the throat, add a teaspoon of flour to the mixture. Consult a doctor before treating a baby with diarrhoea – hydration with a high electrolyte fluid is vital.

  IF SYMPTOMS PERSIST, CONSULT A DOCTOR

CAUTIONS
There are no known cautions for the use of this plant.

Cascara
Rhamanus purshianus Rhamnaceae **Also called** Cascara Sagrada

This evergreen tree is native to the west coast of the United States but is now cultivated in East Africa, where the climate is similarly hot and dry. Cascara grows to a height of 3–12 m and has oval, pointed leaves with numerous straight veins. Its fruit is a black, poisonous berry with a stone that contains a black seed. The bark of the tree is brownish and scattered with whitish pores.

Parts used
BARK
- Only cultivated trees are harvested, never those that grow wild. The bark is gathered in summer, preferably from three-year-old trees, then dried.
- The fresh bark is toxic.
- After drying and fragmentation, the bark is used in infusions and pharmaceutical preparations.

Constituents
The active principles in cascara bark are hydroxyanthraquinone glycosides, known as cascarosides, which exert a laxative effect.

Medicinal uses
Cascara bark has a laxative or purgative effect according to how much is taken. These effects are due to the way in which the plant affects the absorption of water and electrolytes and stimulates contractions within the intestine. Cascara bark is prescribed to help treat the symptoms of occasional bouts of constipation and must be taken strictly as recommended by the manufacturer, unless advised otherwise by a doctor or medical herbalist.

Cascara may also be beneficial in the treatment of liver disorders. Studies by Chinese scientists in 2000 found that the glycoside emodin reduced the development of fibrosis in rat livers. Further research is needed before this use can be suggested for humans.

Cultivation
Propagated by ripe seed, green-wood cuttings or layering, this species should be grown in well-drained soil in sun or light shade.

dried bark

PREPARATION AND DOSAGE
- **To treat constipation**

  CAPSULES Up to 400 mg per day, often combined with anti-griping herbs such as peppermint.

- **Cascara is not suitable for long-term use – if you have chronic constipation consult a doctor or medical herbalist to avoid aggravating the problem**

  IF SYMPTOMS PERSIST, CONSULT A DOCTOR

CAUTIONS
- Because of the strength of its action and possible side effects, cascara should not be used without medical supervision for more than eight to 10 days at a time.
- Never take more cascara than prescribed or in combination with other laxative products.
- Prolonged use can lead to laxative dependence, abdominal pains and an electrolyte imbalance.
- Cascara is not recommended for children under 15 or for women who are pregnant or breastfeeding.
- Cascara is not suitable for people with undiagnosed abdominal pain, inflammation or obstruction.

Cat's claw
Uncaria guianensis (left), *U. tomentosa* (below) Rubiaceae **Also called** Uña de Gato, Life-giving vine of Peru, Savéntaro Cat's claw is a giant climbing vine, native to the Amazon and other tropical parts of South and Central America. The hooklike thorns from which it takes its name grow to 2.5 cm and enable cat's claw to climb over other plants, reaching heights of up to 30 m. Cat's claw has been used medicinally in many parts of the region, especially in Peru, where its use dates back 2000 years.

Parts used
VINE BARK
- The bark is used in the production of tinctures, tablets and capsules.
- Traditionally a decoction was also used.

Constituents
Among the constituents of cat's claw are oxindole alkaloids, proanthocyanidins, glycosides, polyphenols, tannins and plant sterols, which include betasitosterol, stigmasterol and compesterol. The alkaloidal content of cat's claw varies from vine to vine, and may also vary over the lifetime of an individual plant – although they look the same to the naked eye, some specimens of the plant contain predominantly pentacyclic oxindole alkaloids, and others contain predominantly tetracyclic oxindole alkaloids. Medicinal products are produced from the pentacyclic oxindole variety.

Medicinal uses
In vitro research into cat's claw and certain oxindole alkaloids has shown that the plant can stimulate the function of the immune system in several ways, including enhancing phagocytosis (the process by which immune cells engulf invaders), and stimulating the production of immune compounds called interleukins.

Cat's claw is also believed to have antibacterial and antiviral properties, and was used by the Peruvians to treat infective diseases such as dysentery and diarrhoea. Herbalists prescribe it for infective diseases and conditions of depleted immune function, such as chronic fatigue syndrome. Although further research is needed, there is some indication that in the future cat's claw may play a valuable role in the fight against AIDS.

Similarly, although no clinical trials have yet been conducted to validate the traditional use of cat's claw for the treatment of cancer, in vitro research shows that the herb has some potential.

Cat's claw is recommended for the treatment of allergies and chronic inflammatory conditions, and was also traditionally used in this way. Indications include asthma, arthritis, rheumatism, gastric ulcers, inflammatory skin conditions and inflammation of the genito-urinary tract.

Cultivation
This tropical vine needs warm, frost-free conditions, shade and high humidity. It grows best in moist soil with added organic matter. Grow from seed or cuttings.

dried vine bark

PREPARATION AND DOSAGE
- **Cat's claw should be taken only on the advice of a medical herbalist. Do not exceed the prescribed dosage**

IF SYMPTOMS PERSIST, CONSULT A DOCTOR

CAUTIONS
- Some people experience side effects of diarrhoea and indigestion when taking cat's claw; the symptoms normally subside after around 10 days, however if you experience these symptoms, discontinue use of the plant.
- Cat's claw has documented antifertility properties and should not be taken by those trying to conceive, or by pregnant or breast-feeding women.
- Cat's claw should not be taken by children under three years old.
- Do not use cat's claw if you are taking other medicines, especially immunosuppressive medication, anticoagulant (blood thinning) and antihypertensive (blood pressure) drugs.
- There has been an isolated report of severe allergic reaction to cat's claw in one patient with auto-immune disease who was also taking several pharmaceutical medications.

Cayenne

Capsicum fructescens Solanaceae **Also called** Capsicum, Chilli, Hot pepper, Tabasco pepper, Spur pepper Native to tropical America, cayenne is now grown successfully as an annual in temperate parts of the world. This little, perennial shrub is no taller than 70 cm. Slender branches shoot out from the main stem, bearing oval leaves. The long, thin fruits, known as peppers, can reach 50 cm in length in certain varieties. The peppers are green at first, progressing to orange then bright red as they ripen.

Parts used

FRUIT (PEPPER)
- The peppers are harvested in summer, when ripe.
- They are dried at a temperature below 35°C, then used to make tinctures, powders, capsules, poultices and ointments.

Constituents

The hot, spicy taste is imparted by capsaicinoids, particularly capsaicin – first isolated from the plant in 1876. Carotenoids constitute 0.3–0.8 per cent of the pepper, and are responsible for its bright colour.

The peppers are also rich in vitamin C and contain saponins, which are thought to be able to kill bacteria.

Medicinal uses

Taken internally, cayenne stimulates the digestive system, and is used to treat indigestion, flatulence, colic and constipation.

Herbalists consider that its heating properties help to improve circulation, particularly bringing warmth to peripheral parts of the body, such as the hands and feet.

When applied to the skin, the capsaicin from the cayenne increases the area's blood flow, and promotes healing by transporting nutrients to the region and encouraging removal of toxins. It is used in this way to reduce pain and inflammation from lumbago, arthritis, muscle and joint pain and skin irritations.

Cayenne has also been applied to the scalp in poultices, aiming to prevent hair loss.

Due to the antiseptic and anti-inflammatory effects of saponins, cayenne is also used in a gargle for laryngitis.

Cultivation

Cayenne grows best in a greenhouse or on a sunny site, at temperatures above 18°C. Plant the seeds in a well-drained soil that is rich in nutrients.

powdered fruit

PREPARATION AND DOSAGE

- **To treat digestive problems, cold hands and feet**

  CAYENNE POWDER Sprinkle a very small amount (1–2 pinches) over food two or three times a day, or stir into juice.

- **To treat chronic laryngitis**

  GARGLE Mix a pinch of cayenne powder with 25 ml of lemon juice, add hot water and honey. Gargle two or three times a day.

- **To treat muscular and joint pain, skin irritations**

  CREAM, OINTMENT Apply according to manufacturer's instructions. Tincture of cayenne is only suitable for use when recommended by a medical herbalist. Do not exceed prescribed dose.

IF SYMPTOMS PERSIST, CONSULT A DOCTOR

CAUTIONS

- Cayenne should not be taken at the same time as drugs for lowering blood pressure or certain types of antidepressants. Take medical advice before using it.
- Avoid cayenne when pregnant or breastfeeding.
- Take care that cayenne does not come into contact with sensitive areas, such as the lips, mouth, eyes and genitalia.
- If you are suffering from gastric problems, consult a doctor or medical herbalist before using cayenne.
- Do not exceed the recommended dose.

Celery *Apium graveolens* Apiaceae **Also called** Smallage, Wild celery, Chinese celery

A biennial plant with a ridged, shiny stem, celery can grow to a height of 50–100 cm. The stalks of the wild plant have an unpleasant taste and should not be confused with those of the cultivated variety, traces of which have been found in ancient Egyptian tombs. The plant has indented, aromatic leaves and small, white flowers. The small, brown seeds have a characteristic celery odour and taste.

Parts used
SEEDS
- The seeds of the plant are collected during summer and autumn.

dried seeds

Constituents
Seeds contain 1.5–3 per cent of essential oil, mainly limonene. It is the pthalides present in the oil that impart celery's characteristic odour. The seeds also contain coumarins, flavonoids and furanocoumarins.

Medicinal uses
Celery seeds have traditionally been used to treat rheumatism. Tests performed in 1998 confirmed celery's anti-inflammatory and pain-killing qualities. Celery is also useful in treating arthritis and gout, perhaps as a result of its diuretic action, which may help to remove toxins associated with these conditions.

The diuretic and antiseptic qualities of the seeds indicate their use in treating cystitis and other urinary infections. The seeds are also reputed to expel trapped wind and so may act as a remedy for flatulence.

Celery is thought to lower blood pressure, and calm anxiety and tension. Studies published in *Fitoterapia* in 1985 document the sedative and antispasmodic effects of the phthalide compounds present in the essential oil.

Celery has also been used to reduce blood sugar, to treat coughs, bronchitis, asthma, muscle spasms, hiccups and bad breath.

Cultivation
Grow from seed sown in autumn or spring. Choose a nutrient-rich soil and a sheltered spot.

INFUSION 1 teaspoon of dried seeds infused in 1 cup of boiling water for 5–10 minutes before straining. Drink up to 3 cups a day.

IF SYMPTOMS PERSIST, CONSULT A DOCTOR

PREPARATION AND DOSAGE
- **To treat rheumatism, arthritis, gout and digestive disorders**
  LIQUID EXTRACT 2000 mg dried seed equivalent, three times daily.
  TABLETS, CAPSULES Follow manufacturer's instructions.

CAUTIONS
- Celery seeds are thought to stimulate the uterus, and so are not recommended for pregnant women.
- Celery is also inadvisable for people with an acute renal disorder.
- The furanocoumarins present may induce sensitivity to sunlight.
- Celery may sometimes provoke an allergic reaction.

Centaury *Centaurium erythraea*, formerly *Erythraea centaurium* Gentianaceae

Also called Feverwort The ability of this elegant little biennial to cure fever has been known for many hundreds of years, hence its other common name, feverwort. Its spindly stems are crowned in summer by clusters of pink, star-shaped flowers. Its long, pale leaves grow in a dense rosette around the base, but in pairs higher up the stem.

Parts used
LEAVES, STEMS AND FLOWERS
- The aerial parts are gathered in summer, as the flowers come into bloom.
- They are dried and crushed to be used in infusions, decoctions, powders and tinctures.
- Centaury is often combined with other herbs that stimulate the appetite, such as gentian and mugwort, and is an ingredient in the popular aperitif, vermouth.

Constituents
The aerial parts of centaury are rich in phenolic acids, flavonoids and xanthone derivatives. It also contains bitter principles, including a number of secoiridoids, also found in gentian.

Medicinal uses
The bitter secoiridoids stimulate the appetite by increasing the flow of gastric juices. Centaury is also taken to treat chronic digestive problems and flatulence. It is a diuretic and also stimulates bile flow, so is used to help in the elimination of toxins and treat various liver and gall bladder disorders.

The plant is frequently prescribed as a tonic in combination with anise, chamomile, peppermint and fennel, for extreme fatigue and during convalescence.

Experiments have shown that an aqueous extract of centaury helps to fight fever and is anti-inflammatory. These properties may be due to the phenolic acids.

Cultivation
Plant in sandy, neutral to alkaline soil, in a sunny spot. Grows best in cool climates.

dried leaves, stems and flowers

PREPARATION AND DOSAGE
- **To treat lack of appetite, indigestion, flatulence, fatigue**

  INFUSION 1 g dried herb infused in 1 cup of boiling water for 5 minutes before straining. Sip slowly before meals, three times a day.

  IF SYMPTOMS PERSIST, CONSULT A DOCTOR

CAUTIONS
- A course of treatment involving centaury should last no longer than 10 days, as the plant can irritate the lining of the stomach.
- Centaury is not suitable for people who suffer from peptic ulcers or inflammation in any part of the digestive tract.
- Do not use centaury preparations when pregnant or breastfeeding.

Chamomile, German *Matricaria recutita,* formerly *Chamomilla recutita*

Asteraceae Found throughout Europe, where it has a long history of use as a medicinal plant, chamomile grows wild in fields and along roadsides, and is cultivated in gardens. Commercial cultivation occurs in New Zealand and on a smaller scale in parts of Australia. The plant reaches a height of about 40 cm and its daisylike flowers have an aromatic scent.

Parts used

FLOWERS

- The flowers are gathered in full bloom, then dried.
- The dried flowers have a strong, distinctive smell and a bitter taste.
- Roman chamomile (*Chamaemelum nobile*) is used in medicines, but German chamomile (*Matricaria recutita*) is the preferred species.
- Chamomile is used in infusions, liquid extracts and a range of body and hair care products. Its distinctive blue oil is used in aromatherapy.

Constituents

Chamomile's bitter taste is due to substances called sesquiterpenoid lactones. Its essential oil contains azulenes, bisabols and flavonoids that give the herb its anti-inflammatory, antispasmodic and smooth muscle-relaxing properties, particularly in the gastro-intestinal tract.

Medicinal uses

Chamomile has been used for centuries as a medicinal plant, mostly for digestive disorders, where it acts to soothe inflamed or irritated gastrointestinal tissue and reduce the spasms of griping pain. It is also valuable as a mild sedative.

The essential oil has an anti-inflammatory effect on mucous membranes, and may help to reduce histamine-induced allergic reactions. A chamomile steam inhalation may help to ease sinusitis, asthma, hay fever and bronchitis. In 1979, German researchers determined that this anti-inflammatory effect is at least partly due to the plant's bisabol content.

The anti-inflammatory and antispasmodic properties of chamomile make it a good remedy for stomach-aches and period pains.

Externally, chamomile cream treats skin inflammation and promotes healing.

dried flowers

It is recommended for use with eczema, nappy rash and cracked nipples. It is also used as an eye bath and in antiseptic mouthwashes.

Cultivation

Sow seeds in spring in a well-drained, neutral to acid soil. Choose a spot in full sun or only light shade.

PREPARATION AND DOSAGE

- **To treat gastric or intestinal spasms, bloating, sluggish digestion, period pains, insomnia**

  LIQUID EXTRACT 1–3 g dried herb equivalent, three times a day.

  INFUSION Put 1 teabag or 5–8 g of loose chamomile into 1 cup of boiling water. Cover and leave to infuse for 10 minutes. For insomnia, drink 1–2 cups in the evening. For other conditions, drink 1 cup three times a day before meals.

  IF SYMPTOMS PERSIST, CONSULT A DOCTOR

CAUTIONS

- Do not use chamomile if you have a known allergy to any other of the members of the Asteraceae family (such as daisies, chrysanthemums or echinacea).
- Topical application may, in very rare cases, cause allergic reactions.
- Consult a doctor before use if you are taking anticoagulant (blood-thinning) drugs.

Chaste tree *Vitex agnus-castus* Verbenaceae **Also called** Monks' pepper

A native of the Mediterranean, chaste tree now grows in all the subtropical zones of the world. It reaches a height of 3–5 m and each of its graceful leaves is made up of between five and nine long, thin leaflets. Purple flower clusters are followed by a mass of red-and-yellow berries in autumn. These taste like a blend of sage and pepper, helping to explain why the plant is sometimes called monks' pepper.

Parts used
BERRIES
- The berries are picked when ripe, then dried and used in the preparation of liquid extracts, tablets and capsules.

dried berries

Constituents
The berries of the chaste tree contain essential oils, labdanes (diterpenic), iridoid glycosides (including agnuside), flavonoids, alkaloids and vegetable steroids, as well as fatty acids.

Medicinal uses
Chaste tree helps to correct problems arising from malfunctions of the pituitary gland, which secretes some of the hormones that help to control the menstrual cycle, stimulate ovarian function and produce sperm.

For these reasons, the herb is often used to treat premenstrual symptoms, including fluid retention, breast tenderness, period pain and mood swings. It may also be effective as a treatment for premenstrual aggravation of acne, cold sores and migraine.

Chaste tree is able to resolve many cases of menstrual cycle irregularity, and is recommended for amenorrhoea (absent cycle), oligomenorrhoea (prolonged cycle) and polymenorrhoea (shortened cycle), and to re-establish regular menstruation after taking the oral contraceptive pill.

By virtue of correcting these cyclical abnormalities, and the hormonal imbalances underlying them, chaste tree may offer the potential to overcome some instances of female infertility, as well as sometimes being helpful in the treatment of endometriosis and follicular ovarian cysts. It is also prescribed by herbalists to increase milk production in breastfeeding women.

Cultivation
Suited to rich, moist but well-drained soil, chaste tree prefers to be placed in a warm, sunny location. In hot or dry seasons, plants will need extra water. Propagate from seed or by cutting.

PREPARATION AND DOSAGE
- To treat pituitary gland problems that are causing periods to be absent or irregular, or premenstrual symptoms such as tension, breast tenderness and fluid retention

  LIQUID EXTRACT 500 mg–1 g dried fruit equivalent, three times daily, or as directed by your medical herbalist.

  TABLETS, CAPSULES Up to 1 g dried fruit equivalent, three times daily, or according to manufacturer's instructions.

- Note that effects may not be apparent for up to 12 weeks
- Infertility is a complex issue requiring professional care. If you are seeking treatment for infertility, it is recommended that you consult your medical herbalist before taking chaste tree

IF SYMPTOMS PERSIST, CONSULT A DOCTOR

CAUTIONS
- Chaste tree can sometimes cause allergic reactions such as itching. If this occurs, see a doctor.
- Excessive use of chaste tree preparations may affect the nervous system, causing a prickling sensation.
- Do not use chaste tree at the same time as the oral contraceptive pill, hormone replacement therapy or progesterone drugs. Also, do not use it if pregnant, except under the advice of a medical herbalist.
- Do not use chaste tree at the same time as antipsychotic drugs that block or boost the action of the neurotransmitter dopamine (e.g. anti-Parkinson's disease medication).

THE A TO Z OF PLANTS 67

Chickweed *Stellaria media* Caryophyllaceae

Chickweed's botanical name, Stellaria media, reflects the starlike shape of its delicate white flowers, which open in the sun, but may close on cloudy days. This sprawling annual plant is naturalised in temperate regions throughout much of the world, including Australia and New Zealand. It is a common and promiscuous garden invader, capable of producing five generations of offspring in a single year.

flower

Parts used

AERIAL PARTS, LEAVES AND STEMS

- The fresh aerial parts, leaves and stems are squeezed to produce a juice, known as a succus.
- The succus can be applied topically, or can be used in creams and ointments.
- The fresh leaves and stems are also used to make poultices.
- The roots of another species, *Stellaria dichotoma* (Yin chai hu), are used in Chinese medicine for fevers and to support undernourished children.

Constituents

Chickweed is a source of vitamins A and C and the mineral silica. These may explain the plant's traditional use as a nutritive tonic and a salad green. The plant also contains mucilage, triterpenoid saponins, coumarins, flavonoids, carboxylic acids and carotenoids.

Medicinal uses

Chickweed has a long history of use, but to date little scientific research is available to help explain the full extent of its actions.

It is mostly used topically to help relieve itchy and irritated skin, and this anti-inflammatory effect may be due to the plant's mucilage and saponin content.

Traditional indications for the topical use of chickweed include eczema, psoriasis, urticaria (nettle rash), skin rashes, boils, burns and slow-to-heal ulcers (including varicose ulcers). It has also been used to soothe haemorrhoids, and is gentle enough to use on babies' nappy rash. An infusion of chickweed is sometimes added to bath water to help relieve pain and inflammation in arthritic conditions.

Internally, the succus (fresh plant juice) is prescribed for the relief of gastrointestinal ulcers, to relieve coughs and as a gentle digestive stimulant.

It has also been used as a nutritive tonic for fatigue and lowered energy.

Cultivation

Chickweed likes moist soil, and tolerates either sun or shade. It is grown from seed, which may be sown at any time of the year. Plants may die down during hot summers without adequate moisture.

PREPARATION AND DOSAGE

- **To relieve itchy skin, eczema, psoriasis, varicose ulcers, nappy rash, haemorrhoids, burns and boils**

  SUCCUS/CREAM/OINTMENT Apply two or three times a day, or according to the manufacturer's instructions.

  POULTICE Chop 200 g fresh, washed fresh leaves and stems and mix with sufficient boiled water to make a paste. Spread the paste onto gauze or cotton strips and apply to the skin, keeping the poultice in place until it cools. To prevent the poultice sticking, apply a small amount of olive oil on the skin beforehand.

- **To soothe gastrointestinal ulcers and relieve coughs**

  SUCCUS 1–2 ml, three times a day, unless otherwise advised by your medical herbalist.

IF SYMPTOMS PERSIST, CONSULT A DOCTOR

CAUTIONS

- Do not exceed recommended dose, as this may cause diarrhoea and vomiting.
- Not suitable for internal use during pregnancy or breastfeeding.
- Allergic reactions (e.g. rashes) may sometimes follow topical use.

Chicory *Cichorium intybus* Asteraceae

Valued by the ancient Romans, who cultivated it as a vegetable, wild chicory is a common sight on waste ground and roadsides in Europe, New Zealand and parts of Australia. Growing up to 1 m tall, the hardy perennial has deeply indented leaves crowding around erect stems that are downy on the underside. Flower heads appear in summer to early autumn. Most are bright blue, but can be pink or white.

dried leaves and roots

Parts used

LEAVES, FLOWERS AND ROOTS

- The leaves are gathered when the plant is in flower and are used to prepare infusions, or eaten as a vegetable.
- The flowers and roots may be harvested at any time of the year if they are to be used fresh, or in late summer if they are to be dried. Roots are chopped up into small pieces before drying in the sun.
- Chicory roots are sometimes roasted and ground to be used as a substitute for coffee.

Constituents

The entire chicory plant contains a milky sap, of which the main constituent – about 45–60 per cent – is inulin. Phenol acid is also found in the flowers, while in the roots there are bitter sesquiterpene lactones.

Medicinal uses

For centuries it has been known that chicory has anti-inflammatory and antiseptic powers, because of which it was applied in poultices to ease swelling.

Its effectiveness is due to the phenol acid, which also acts as a diuretic, remedying any bloating caused by fluid retention. More recently, chicory has been shown to help ease the inflammation caused by rheumatism and gout.

The inulin encourages the growth of bacteria needed for the intestines to work properly. Chicory, therefore, can help to prevent and treat problems such as sluggish digestion, gastric ulcers and flatulence. It has also been shown that the inulin can help in lowering cholesterol levels in the blood.

Both inulin and the sesquiterpene lactones are bitter principles which stimulate the flow of digestive juices, including that of bile from the gall bladder. This allows the liver to work more efficiently. In 1998, scientists in India confirmed that the root had this effect.

Cultivation

Chicory grows well in almost any type of soil, especially if it is rich and well drained. The plant prefers sun.

PREPARATION AND DOSAGE

- **To treat liver and kidney problems, bloating, belching, sluggish digestion, flatulence**

  DECOCTION Put a 15–30 g mixture of root, leaves and flowers into 1 litre of water. Boil for 5 minutes. Strain and drink 1 cup before midday and evening meals.
  INSTANT DRINK PREPARATION Add 1 heaped teaspoon of instant chicory to a cup of boiling water. Add milk and sweeten to taste.

IF SYMPTOMS PERSIST, CONSULT A DOCTOR

CAUTIONS

- People suffering from an intestinal blockage or inflammation of the intestines should consult a medical herbalist before starting to use chicory.

THE A TO Z OF PLANTS 69

Cinnamon *Cinnamomum zeylanicum, C. cassia* Lauraceae

This tropical evergreen tree grows to a height of 5–8 m. It has tough, leathery leaves and clusters of small, white flowers followed by acornlike berries. The varieties most used are Ceylon cinnamon (*Cinnamomum zeylanicum*) and Chinese cinnamon (*C. cassia*). Cinnamon is an important element in Ayurveda – a traditional medicine that has been practised in India for more than 5000 years.

Parts used

BARK

- Trees that are eight years old or older are harvested every two years.
- The tubes of dried bark are used for infusions, tinctures and powders.
- A distillate of the bark produces an essential oil with a smell like pepper.

Constituents

Ceylon and Chinese cinnamon have constituents that vary slightly. Both types of bark contain up to 2 per cent essential oil, largely made up of cinnamic aldehyde. But Ceylon cinnamon also contains 1 per cent of eugenol, while only a trace of this substance occurs in Chinese cinnamon.

dried bark

Medicinal uses

The properties of the Ceylon and the Chinese varieties are very similar. Cinnamon bark is antispasmodic and it also stimulates the salivary glands and the mucous membranes of the stomach. It is used for digestive problems such as indigestion, poor appetite, trapped gas, nausea, belching, flatulence, diarrhoea and intestinal spasms.

The liquid extract has a soothing effect on gastro-duodenal ulcers. In 1989, Japanese scientists found that compounds in Chinese cinnamon acted as anti-ulcer agents in rats by improving gastric blood flow. However, in 2000, clinical trials in Israel found that cinnamon extract had no effect on *Helicobacter pylori*, a bacterium associated with many cases of gastric ulcer.

The oil is used externally to ease cramps, joint pains, rheumatism and neuralgia. The analgesic and anti-inflammatory properties of Chinese cinnamon are key constituents of Tiger Balm, a soothing liniment. And in 1994, Chinese scientists isolated the constituent cinnamophilin as an effective anti-inflammatory.

Cinnamon is antifungal. In 1995, Indian research showed cinnamic aldehyde to be potent against certain fungal organisms that cause respiratory tract infections.

The spice is a warming stimulant, and therefore is often prescribed for cold conditions, such as poor circulation, influenza and the common cold. It also stimulates the respiratory system, the uterus and the production of oestrogens.

Cultivation

Cinnamon trees cannot survive at temperatures below 15°C. They need a well-drained soil – they will even grow well in pure sand – and a spot with plenty of sun.

PREPARATION AND DOSAGE

- To treat gastritis, digestive problems, loss of appetite, colds, influenza, poor circulation

  LIQUID EXTRACT 500 mg–1 g dried bark equivalent, taken three times per day.

  INFUSION 500 mg–1 g dried bark infused in 1 cup of boiling water for 10 minutes before straining. Drink 3 cups a day.

IF SYMPTOMS PERSIST, CONSULT A DOCTOR

CAUTIONS

- The essential oil can trigger skin allergies and inflammation of the mucous membranes. If you are allergic to Peruvian balsam, you may also be allergic to cinnamon and should take particular care.
- Use cinnamon oil only when supervised by a medical herbalist.
- If pregnant or breastfeeding, do not consume more cinnamon than is normally present in food.

Cleavers *Galium aparine* Rubiaceae **Also called** Clivers, Goosegrass, Bedstraw, Catchweed

Cleavers is a common roadside and garden weed in Europe, North America, Australia, New Zealand and other temperate regions around the world. It is characterised by angular stems, whorls of lance-shaped leaves and clusters of small, white flowers. The fruit bears hooked prickles, and it is from these that cleavers takes its name, as it is renowned for attaching, or cleaving, itself to clothing and animals' fur.

Parts used

AERIAL PARTS

- The aerial parts of the plant are collected during flowering and fruiting.
- Cleavers is often taken as a fresh juice (or succus) preparation, or dried to form liquid extracts, tablets or infusions.

Constituents

Amongst the identified constituents are flavonoids (including hesperidin and quercetin), coumarins, sterols, tannins, phenolic acids and iridoid glycosides. Asperuloside is an iridoid glycoside, and may be at least partially responsible for the mild laxative actions of the herb. Although the root is not used in herbal medicine, it is interesting to note that it contains anthraquinone glycosides, compounds that are known to be strongly laxative and that are present in a number of other herbs, among them cascara and senna.

dried aerial parts

Medicinal uses

As is the case with many other herbal medicines, minimal scientific research has been conducted into cleavers and its medicinal potential at this stage. Instead, herbalists generally have to rely on empirical evidence to support its use.

Cleavers is largely used as a diuretic and as a tonic for the urinary tract. The fresh plant juice is considered to be more strongly diuretic than other preparations, and has traditionally been taken to relieve kidney stones and gravel, painful urinations, urinary tract infection and other causes of kidney and bladder inflammation.

Cleavers also has a reputation as a lymphatic tonic and mild detoxifier. It is indicated for the treatment of swollen or congested lymphatic tissue, and is thus often prescribed for a range of conditions, including tonsillitis, fibrocystic breast disease, glandular fever and lymphadenitis.

Skin conditions associated with sluggish lymphatic function or inefficient removal of body wastes may also respond well to cleavers, and the herb has often been taken to treat eczema, psoriasis and seborrheic dermatitis. It can also be used topically for skin conditions such as these, as well as for cases involving burns, grazes, ulcers and swollen lymph glands.

fruit with prickles (much enlarged)

Cultivation

Cleavers grows easily from seed sown in moist but well-drained soils in shady corners of the garden. It has a tendency to become weedy when introduced to gardens or pastures and needs care.

PREPARATION AND DOSAGE

- **To treat cystitis, urinary gravel, fluid retention, swollen or congested lymph glands (e.g. tonsillitis, glandular fever)**

  LIQUID EXTRACT 2–4 g dried plant equivalent, three times daily.
  EXPRESSED JUICE (SUCCUS) 5–15 ml, three times daily.
  INFUSION Infuse 2–4 g dried herb in 250 ml boiling water for 10 minutes before straining. Drink three cups a day.

- **To treat burns, grazes, ulcers, psoriasis, inflamed skin**

  COMPRESS Make the infusion as above, using 20 g of herb in 500 ml of water. Allow to cool, soak a clean cloth in the liquid, squeeze out excess moisture and apply to the affected area.

IF SYMPTOMS PERSIST, CONSULT A DOCTOR

CAUTIONS

- Do not take the fresh plant juice of cleavers if you are diabetic. Although it is yet to be validated, there is some evidence that the juice may affect blood-sugar levels.
- The safety of cleavers during pregnancy and lactation has not been established.

Cloves *Syzygium aromaticum* Myrtaceae

A native of the Spice Islands, now known as the Moluccas, this tall, slender evergreen can reach a height of 20 m. Its flowers grow in clusters and, if allowed to bloom, open into red-and-white bells. However, mature trees are not often in full bloom as the flower buds are picked for use as cloves. The tree does not produce these cloves until it is 20 years old. It is then productive for about 50 years.

Parts used
FLOWER BUDS
- Buds are harvested twice a year, in summer and winter.
- Cloves are the dried flower buds.

cloves

dried flower buds

fresh flower buds

Constituents
Clove oil consists largely of eugenol, a substance with anaesthetic and antiseptic properties. Cloves also contain tannins and flavonoids – cancer-fighting anti-oxidants that also help to strengthen the walls of veins.

Medicinal uses
Herbal practitioners use cloves to treat a range of digestive complaints, and oil of cloves for the relief of toothache.

The eugenol contained in cloves is the main active constituent. It is known to combat inflammation and bacterial and fungal infections and is also analgesic. Clove oil is the active ingredient in a wide range of mouthwashes and over-the-counter pain-relief remedies for toothache.

A paper published in 1999, in the *International Journal of Antimicrobial Agents*, reports on cloves' efficacy against both bacteria and yeasts. Chinese physicians have long used the herb to treat athlete's foot – a yeast (fungal) infection.

Studies performed in Taiwan showed that eugenol reduces blood clotting and is also effective as an anti-inflammatory. Research published in 1985 found clove oil to have a potent relaxant effect on the smooth muscle of the lungs and intestines. Because of this powerful sedative effect an overdose of eugenol can have a depressive effect on the central nervous system.

Cloves are often combined with other plants to treat bloating, gastritis, dyspepsia and rheumatic pains. They are also incorporated into various remedies to combat infections of the ear, nose and throat, as well as genito-urinary infections.

Cultivation
The tree needs a tropical or glasshouse environment.

PREPARATION AND DOSAGE

- **To treat gastritis, dyspepsia**

  DECOCTION Boil 1–2 cloves in 1 cup of water for 5 minutes before straining. Drink 1–2 cups a day.

- **To treat toothache**

  WHOLE CLOVES OR CLOVE OIL Chew a clove three or four times a day, or apply 3 drops of the essential oil on a cotton wool bud to the affected tooth and gum two or three times a day. See a dentist as soon as possible. It is important to be aware that repeated use of cloves in this way may cause damage to the gums, and this treatment should only be used as a first aid measure until you can see a dentist.

IF SYMPTOMS PERSIST, CONSULT A DOCTOR

CAUTIONS

- Dilute clove essential oil in vegetable oil before applying it directly to the skin, or it will burn.
- If pregnant or breastfeeding, do not consume more of the spice than is normally present in food.
- Do not swallow the essential oil. For the treatment of gastritis or dyspepsia use only the water-based decoction of the herb, as detailed on the left.
- Do not take cloves internally if you are using anticoagulant (blood-thinning) or antiplatelet medications.

Codonopsis
Codonopsis pilosula Campanulaceae **Also called** Bastard ginseng, Bellflower, Dan shen or Dang shen *Codonopsis takes its name from its distinctive flowers – the words 'kodon' and 'opsis' meaning 'resembling a bell'. The flowers of this hardy climbing perennial have green and purple markings, and are delicately patterned on the underside. Codonopsis is a native of China, where it is found especially in the Shanxi and Szechuan regions of the north and west.*

Parts used
ROOTS
- Codonopsis has traditionally been used as one of the ingredients in tonic foods, and may be cooked with rice or millet, or taken in teas, soups or pickles.
- The roots of plants more than three years old are harvested in the autumn, after the aerial parts have died back.

Constituents
The compounds that have been identified so far as being present in codonopsis include sterins, an alkaloid (perlolyrin), alkenyl and ankenyl glycosides, polysaccharides and tangshenoside.

Medicinal uses
Codonopsis has a reputation as a herbal adaptogen – a remedy that helps the body to cope with stressful circumstances, gently increasing energy, stimulating the body and enhancing concentration. It is regarded as having similar properties to another famous adaptogenic herb, Korean ginseng, but is considered to be milder in its action. In traditional Chinese medicine, symptoms of fatigue, headache, irritability, tense neck muscles and raised blood pressure are all considered to be among the stress-induced indications for codonopsis.

Codonopsis also has a tonic action in other areas of the body, including the digestive system – where it is indicated for ulcers, diarrhoea, vomiting and lack of appetite – and the cardiovascular system – where it is prescribed for coronary heart disease and hypertension. In the respiratory tract codonopsis is used to ease constricted airways and shortness of breath, and indications include asthma, chronic coughs and the presence of excessive mucus.

Codonopsis also acts as a blood and immune system tonic, and is taken particularly to enhance red blood cell levels and haemoglobin. It has traditionally been given to nursing mothers to improve lactation and strengthen the blood.

dried roots

Cultivation
Propagate from seed in spring or autumn or by cuttings of basal shoots in spring. Care is needed to avoid damaging the delicate taproots of the seedlings during transplanting. Codonopsis prefers light, well-drained slightly acid soil in semi-shade, and needs moist soil in summer. Codonopsis will twine, so provide a climbing frame.

PREPARATION AND DOSAGE
- To treat fatigue, shortness of breath, irritability, especially when due to stress

  LIQUID EXTRACT 750 mg–1.5 g dried root equivalent, three times a day, or as advised by your medical herbalist.
  DECOCTION Boil 20 g dried root in 750 ml of water for 15 minutes before straining. Drink ½ cup twice daily.

IF SYMPTOMS PERSIST, CONSULT A DOCTOR

CAUTIONS
- Although no adverse effects have been documented, codonopsis has not been assessed for safety during pregnancy.

Coffee *Coffea arabica* Rubiaceae

A native of Ethiopia, the evergreen coffee tree has dark green glossy leaves and can grow to 10 m tall. Its clusters of decorative white flowers are delicately perfumed with the scents of coffee and jasmine. The fruits are called cherries because they turn red as they ripen. Each cherry contains two coffee beans.

ripe fruit

Parts used

SEEDS (COFFEE BEANS)
- The cherries are picked when ripe, and contain the green, odourless raw seeds that are used in homeopathic medicine.
- The seeds gain their distinctive coffee bean aroma after they have been roasted.
- Caffeine is used in many medicines and as an additive for soft drinks.

Constituents

Phenolic acids, which constitute up to 5 per cent of coffee beans, possess stimulant and antiseptic properties. The caffeine content ranges from 0.6–3 per cent. Caffeine stimulates activity in all the major organs of the body. Roasting reduces caffeine content and adds pigments and aroma. The beans also contain small amounts of theobromine, tannin and trigonelline.

Medicinal uses

Caffeine causes people to feel more alert. One study published in 1987 in *Psychopharmacology* reported that a caffeine dose smaller than that found in a cup of coffee increased hearing and visual performance.

An Australian clinical study in 1996 demonstrated that coffee lessens the fall in blood pressure that normally occurs after eating. The researchers concluded that this stimulant action on the cardiovascular system was particularly beneficial for elderly people.

Because caffeine increases the metabolic rate, it maximises the pain-killing effect of analgesics like aspirin and paracetamol, and is added to them in 'ultra' versions.

Caffeine can alleviate nausea and vomiting, and some cases of headache and migraine. As a stimulant, it is used to prevent coma following collapse from narcotic poisoning. Other constituents of coffee also play a role: trigonelline may relieve migraine, while theophylline has stimulant, diuretic and cardiovascular properties. Research done in 2002 at Imperial College in London showed that theobromine relieves coughing.

raw coffee beans

Cultivation

Coffee will not survive where the temperature falls below 10°C. It likes well-drained soil and partial shade.

PREPARATION AND DOSAGE

- **To stimulate energy and alertness**

COFFEE Take as an instant beverage, or espresso-style. Note that coffee is more effective when taken infrequently, and that regular use may lead to withdrawal symptoms if you stop drinking it. This caution also applies to other sources of caffeine.

CAFFEINE TABLETS (50 MG) Take according to manufacturer's or pharmacist's instructions. Do not exceed recommended dose.

IF SYMPTOMS PERSIST, CONSULT A DOCTOR

CAUTIONS

- Classed as a stimulant, caffeine in preparations should be avoided by those involved in competitive sports.
- Avoid coffee if you are pregnant or breastfeeding.
- Coffee may aggravate or induce peptic ulcers and reflux problems.
- Coffee is not recommended for people with cardiovascular disease, or those receiving electro-convulsive therapy.
- Side effects can include increased heart rate, headaches, increased urination, insomnia and agitation.
- Expect caffeine-withdrawal headaches if you stop drinking coffee.

Coleus *Coleus forskohlii, Plectranthus forskohlii, Plectranthus barbatus* Lamiaceae

Coleus has traditionally been used in India as a pickled condiment, but was also valued for its medicinal activity, being used in Ayurvedic medicine to treat a range of complaints, including heart disease. It is an erect plant that grows to around 60 cm tall and smells like camphor. Coleus grows in sub-continental regions such as India, Nepal, Sri Lanka and Myanmar (Burma), but is now cultivated worldwide.

Parts used

ROOTS, LEAVES

- The leaves are picked fresh, and are used as an ingredient in pickles.
- The root is used for decoctions and liquid extracts.
- The active constituents are most concentrated in the root during autumn, the best time for harvesting.

liquid extract

Constituents

Most of the research has centred on the diterpene forskohlin, which was originally isolated in the 1970s, and is considered to be the main active constituent in coleus. The plant also contains a volatile oil.

Medicinal uses

Forskohlin has several actions on the circulatory system and is a valuable cardiac tonic. It has been shown to lower blood pressure and work against platelet aggregation. It is therefore used for certain heart conditions, especially congestive heart failure, as well as conditions associated with lack of oxygen to the heart muscle, such as angina.

Research indicates that the blood-pressure-lowering effect of forskohlin is at least partly due to its ability to relax the smooth muscles in the arteries, easing blood flow. Forskohlin is also able to increase the force of the heart muscle, and is thus able to improve blood flow to the heart (coronary blood flow) and to the brain.

Forskohlin also has relaxant effects on the smooth muscles in the airways, and is used as a treatment for asthma, bronchitis and shortness of breath.

Like other aromatic herbs, coleus is used to soothe digestive discomfort and symptoms such as wind and bloating. Its action on the digestive system is likely to be due to forskohlin, which increases secretions of digestive juices and has an antispasmodic effect on the gastrointestinal tract.

Topical applications containing small amounts of forskohlin may play a role in relieving the intraocular pressure of glaucoma.

In addition, coleus may also help to improve the symptoms of psoriasis.

Cultivation

Coleus is easy to grow in warm, frost-free climates. The plant grows in sun or partial shade in moist soil. Encourage bushy growth with regular tip pruning. Plants grow readily from cutting, but can also be grown from seed or by division.

PREPARATION AND DOSAGE

- **Coleus should be used only on the advice of a medical herbalist**

IF SYMPTOMS PERSIST, CONSULT A DOCTOR

CAUTIONS

- Do not use coleus (or forskohlin) if you have low blood pressure.
- Do not use coleus (or forskohlin) if you have a gastric (peptic or duodenal) ulcer.
- Since forskohlin has the potential to interact with many drugs, coleus should not be used at the same time as other medications unless supervised by your medical herbalist. Take particular care when combining coleus with antiplatelet and blood-pressure-lowering medications.
- It is important to note that most information pertaining to coleus is actually derived from research into forskohlin, which was sometimes administered by injection or inhalation. The activity of the whole root taken orally may differ from the information currently available in the medical literature.

Coriander *Coriandrum sativum* Apiaceae

Easily recognised by its distinctive scent, coriander is grown all over Europe, India and North Africa, as well as in Australia and New Zealand. The feathery fronds of this herbaceous annual reach heights of up to 60 cm, and in early summer the plants are covered in umbrella-shaped clusters of tiny, white or pink flowers. By late summer, these will have given way to small, round, wrinkled seeds.

Parts used

LEAVES AND SEEDS

- The seeds are collected as they start to turn yellow and ripen.
- Coriander seed heads are cut off in the early morning to preserve their beneficial properties. After drying in the sun, they are threshed and the individual seeds gathered.
- The seeds are dried, then crushed to a powder, which is used for infusions and tinctures.
- An essential oil can be extracted from the seeds.
- The aromatic leaves, when fresh, have antiseptic properties and can aid digestion, but are mainly used in cooking.

Constituents

Coriander's very oily seeds – comprising as much as 25 per cent fatty oil – contain phenolic acids and aliphatic aldehydes, which give the plant its scent. The essential oil extracted from the seeds contains a large quantity of linalool, which is antibacterial and controls spasms.

Medicinal uses

Various studies have shown that nearly all of coriander's medicinal properties are due to the essential oil in the plant's seeds, which can help to regulate gastric secretions and to release trapped wind. The seeds are therefore particularly effective in treating a range of digestive problems, and are also recommended for treating some common forms of diarrhoea that are due to infections, such as gastroenteritis.

Animal studies in India in 1997 demonstrated that preparations made from coriander seeds could help to lower blood cholesterol. The seeds are also believed to fight off bacterial and fungal infections.

Externally, coriander seed oil can be applied to help soothe the pain of haemorrhoids, as well as of joints affected by rheumatism.

Cultivation

Coriander seeds can be sown in any type of light, well-drained soil, during warm weather in spring and autumn. Plants grow best in a sheltered position, exposed to plenty of sunlight.

dried seeds

mature seed heads

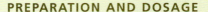

PREPARATION AND DOSAGE

- **To treat digestive problems, flatulence, griping**

  INFUSION 10–30 g crushed seeds infused in 1 litre of boiling water for 10 minutes before straining. Drink 1 cup after each meal.

IF SYMPTOMS PERSIST, CONSULT A DOCTOR

CAUTIONS

- Coriander can cause abdominal pain, poor appetite and an enlarged liver. Consult your doctor if you experience any abnormal symptoms.
- Avoid coriander if pregnant or breastfeeding.
- Never use pure extracted coriander essential oil internally.

Corn silk *Zea mays* Poaceae **Also called** Sweetcorn, Maize

A robust annual, corn is native to the Andes and Central America. Its stalk can grow as high as 3 m, with long, ribbonlike leaves. The female flowers, found halfway up the stalks, produce the cobs, which are long, cylindrical ears of corn, surrounded by a mass of silky styles then large bracts, and topped with a tuft of feathery styles. It is the styles that are used medicinally and referred to as corn silk.

Parts used
STYLES (CORN SILK) AND SEEDS OF FEMALE FLOWERS (CORN COBS)

- The corn cobs are picked during summer, before pollination, and the styles, which resemble fine strands of pale green silk and are hence known as corn silk, are carefully removed.
- The corn silk must be used fresh, or dried quickly, after which they turn dark brown. Preparations made from corn silk include infusions and extracts.
- Corn oil is extracted from the seeds. It is used for cooking, and in medicines and cosmetics.

Constituents
Corn silk contains saponins, tannins, phytosterols, mucilage, potassium and an essential oil. The oil from the seeds, or corn kernels, makes up about 20 per cent of their content and is rich in healthy, unsaturated fatty acids.

dried corn styles

Medicinal uses
Corn silk is mainly used for its anti-inflammatory and general healing powers, which have been confirmed by a number of scientific studies. It is because of these powers, coupled with corn silk's ability to act as a diuretic, that its preparations are most often used to treat urinary tract problems such as cystitis, water retention caused by kidney problems and kidney stones. The plant's ability to ease inflammation is sometimes employed in treating gout.

Corn silk preparations are also reputed to stimulate the secretion of bile, which is why they are often prescribed for liver and gall bladder disorders. It is also believed that corn silk can help to lower blood pressure and blood-sugar levels.

Oil from the seeds, or kernels, is an ingredient in cosmetics used to soften and moisturise the skin, and to combat wrinkles.

Cultivation
Corn can be grown from seeds. Plant them in late winter or spring in any rich, well-drained soil. The plant grows best in blocks (not rows) in full sun.

PREPARATION AND DOSAGE

- **To treat cystitis, inflammation of the urinary tract, fluid retention caused by kidney problems, kidney stones**

  LIQUID EXTRACT 2–8 g dried style equivalent, three times daily.

  INFUSION Put 1 teaspoon (2 g) of dried styles into 1 cup of water. Bring rapidly to the boil, then infuse for 5 minutes. Drink 1 cup three times a day.

IF SYMPTOMS PERSIST, CONSULT A DOCTOR

CAUTIONS

- Cosmetics containing corn oil have been known to induce contact dermatitis in people who have particularly sensitive skin.
- Women who are pregnant or breastfeeding should not consume large amounts of corn oil.
- Do not take more than the recommended dose, especially if you are taking drugs for diabetes, hypertension (high blood pressure) or hypotension (low blood pressure).

Cramp bark *Viburnum opulus* (syn. *Viburnum opulus* var. *americanus*) Caprifoliaceae

Also called Guelder Rose Cramp bark is a native of many regions of the Northern Hemisphere, and it also grows in gardens in Australia and New Zealand, where there are many varieties and named cultivars. This deciduous shrub has large maplelike leaves, each with three to five lobes. In late spring to early summer it bears clusters of white flowers, and in the autumn these produce sprays of distinctive red fruit.

Parts used

BARK

- The bark is collected by peeling it off in strips. This is best done in spring or early summer, when the plant is in flower.
- It is essential that the bark is not over-harvested or the tree will not survive.
- The berries are rich in vitamin C, however they should not be taken as they are poisonous.

Constituents

Among the constituents in cramp bark are tannins (3 per cent), resin, salicosides, hydroquinones (including arbutin) and coumarins (including scopoletin).

Medicinal uses

As the name implies, cramp bark is primarily used for conditions associated with spasm or cramping of the smooth or skeletal muscle. This usage has been known for many years – there are reports of Native American tribes using the bark in this way. The herb may be used to treat muscle tension in all forms, whether in the voluntary muscles (e.g. the limbs), or in involuntary (smooth) muscles such as those of the bowel, airways and female reproductive tract.

dried bark

Cramp bark is often prescribed to ease stomach cramps, back pain and other muscular symptoms associated with the menstrual cycle. It may be particularly useful where symptoms of stress or anxiety are present at the same time, as it has additional actions as a mild nervous system relaxant.

Cramp bark may also be beneficial for spasmodic conditions of the gastrointestinal tract, including irritable bowel syndrome, colic and constipation caused by tightness of the bowel.

In arthritis, the herb may bring relief by easing contracted muscles in the region of the inflamed joint, improving movement, blood flow and the removal of wastes from the affected tissue. Cramp bark is also useful for back pain, helping to relieve acute spasm and ongoing muscular tension.

In addition to these uses, cramp bark is sometimes prescribed for cardiovascular conditions, including poor peripheral circulation and high blood pressure. Due to its mild sedative actions, the bark's application in high blood pressure may be due to a calming effect.

Cultivation

Propagate from seed sown in autumn or from cuttings. Plants grow well in fertile, well-drained soil, preferably in full sun, and are an attractive addition to the garden.

PREPARATION AND DOSAGE

- **To treat period pain, musculoskeletal cramping, intestinal spasms, urinary or gall bladder colic**

    LIQUID EXTRACT 500 mg–1 g dried bark equivalent, taken three times a day.
    TABLETS Up to 1 g, taken three times a day; or follow the manufacturer's instructions.

IF SYMPTOMS PERSIST, CONSULT A DOCTOR

CAUTIONS

- The berries are poisonous and should not be eaten.
- Do not take cramp bark if you are pregnant or breastfeeding.

Cranberry *Vaccinium macrocarpon, V. oxycoccus* Ericaceae

Native to peat bogs and forests in North America and Europe, the cranberry is a slow-growing shrub. Now widely cultivated, the dark green leaves are topped by pinkish white flowers towards the beginning of summer. The flower and its stem were thought to resemble a crane, hence the name. The fruit – used in folk remedies since the 16th century or earlier – is a small, greenish berry that turns dark red as it ripens.

Parts used

FRUIT

- The berries are gathered when ripe in late summer.
- They are consumed as juice and are also used to make capsules and tablets.

Constituents

Cranberry berries contain glucose and fructose, many essential minerals and several organic acids, including vitamin C. They are also rich in anti-oxidant anthocyanins and proanthocyanins.

Medicinal uses

Cranberry is recommended to complement the use of antibiotics in the treatment of repeated urinary infections. Although it was originally thought that cranberry worked by making the urine more acidic, thus inhibiting the growth of bacteria, it is now known that this is not the case. Scientific tests have demonstrated that the proanthocyanins and fructose in cranberry juice prevent bacteria such as *E. coli* from causing infection by preventing their adherence to the mucous membranes lining the urinary tract.

In 2003, researchers in South Africa showed that drinking large quantities of cranberry juice may also help to prevent certain types of kidney stones. However, further research is required to confirm this theory.

Cultivation

Cranberries can be grown from cuttings or seeds, and they prefer moist, acidic soil in a cold climate. Although the plant can become dormant to survive extreme cold, frosts will kill off buds. Warmth and sun are needed to ripen the fruit fully.

dried berries

PREPARATION AND DOSAGE

- **To treat recurrent urinary infections**

    TABLETS, CAPSULES 10 g fresh fruit equivalent, three times a day, with plenty of water.

    FRESH UNDILUTED JUICE Drink 500 ml twice a day. This treatment must be prolonged.

    IF SYMPTOMS PERSIST, CONSULT A DOCTOR

CAUTIONS

- When using to treat a urinary infection, it is advisable to combine cranberry preparations with conventional pharmaceutical remedies, such as antibiotics.
- People who suffer from an enlarged prostate gland or from an obstruction of the urinary tract should always consult their doctor before using any preparations that contain cranberries.
- Due to the high natural sugar content of cranberry juice, and the large volume required to be effective, the tablets are more appropriate for patients with diabetes.

Cumin *Cuminum cyminum* Apiaceae

Native to Egypt and Asia, cumin was once widely used in Europe, enjoying particular popularity with ancient Roman cooks. Today, it is more popular in Asia and the Middle East. Cumin is a herbaceous annual that grows to a height of about 30 cm, its slender stem divided into long, slim secondary stalks. White or pinkish flowers give way to narrow, ridged seed pods, about 5 mm long, which contain the cumin seeds.

Parts used

SEEDS

- Cultivated in India and the Middle East, the seed pods appear in summer and are traditionally gathered by hand.
- The seeds are used, either whole or ground, in infusions. Its essential oil is colourless or pale yellow with a characteristic musky smell and a bitter, aromatic taste.
- In addition to its medicinal uses, cumin is an ingredient in many renowned spice mixtures, including Madras curry and ras-el-hanout – a combination of Moroccan spices.

Constituents

The essential oil constitutes 2–5 per cent of the seed and contains around 40 per cent cuminaldehyde. Cumin also contains flavonoids, which are beneficial in treating minor circulatory disorders and which also possess anti-inflammatory properties.

Medicinal uses

Used internally, cumin is considered to be highly effective in the treatment of indigestion, bloating and stomach infections. It can help to relieve flatulence and to relax the intestine. Research carried out in India in 1999 validated the use of cumin as a food preservative, disinfectant and astringent by demonstrating its action in combating various types of bacteria.

Cumin is available as an essential oil for external use and can also be added to creams and ointments used for massaging painful joints.

In 1989, Danish scientists found that cumin extracts helped to inhibit platelet aggregation and the generation of inflammatory mediators. These findings suggest that it might be beneficial in the treatment of thrombosis and inflammation.

Cumin is sometimes used during breastfeeding to relieve breast engorgement.

It can also stimulate menstruation and lactation. In addition, cumin is reputed to have aphrodisiac properties.

Cultivation

In spring, scatter seeds in a well-drained sunny spot. Harvest the seeds at the end of summer. They can be ground up or used whole.

dried seeds

PREPARATION AND DOSAGE

- **To treat indigestion, flatulence, intestinal infections**

  INFUSION Put 1 teaspoon of seeds into 250 ml of boiling water and infuse for 2–3 minutes. Alternatively, use 1–2 g of ground seeds and infuse for 10–15 minutes in a cup of boiling water. Strain and drink ½ cup before meals.

- **To treat painful joints**

  CREAMS, OINTMENTS Rub in slowly once or twice a day as directed.

  IF SYMPTOMS PERSIST, CONSULT A DOCTOR

CAUTIONS

- Large doses of the essential oil have proved to be harmful and have caused nervous tension.
- The essential oil is for external use only and should not be used during pregnancy.

Cypress
Cupressus sempervirens Cupressaceae **Also called** Italian cypress

An evergreen tree typical of Mediterranean countries, the cypress has reddish grey bark and small, opposed leaves that overlap and cover the whole branch. The female flowers produce fruits (cones), made of round, soft scales, which turn yellowy grey when ripe. The ancient Egyptians and Romans dedicated the tree to their gods of death and the underworld, which may be why it is often planted in cemeteries.

Parts used
CONES, LEAVES AND TWIGS
- The cones are gathered while still green, and used to make infusions, powders or extracts for capsules and tablets.
- The essential oil, commonly used in aromatherapy, may be distilled from the leaves and twigs, in addition to the cones.

Constituents
Cypress cones are composed mainly of dimeric proanthocyanidins, which have a strengthening effect on the veins, improving blood circulation particularly in the hands and feet. The cones contain tannins, a small quantity of essential oil and diterpenic acids.

Medicinal uses
As it can effectively treat all kinds of vein disorders, cypress is often prescribed for haemorrhoids and varicose veins. Formulations for both internal and external use may combine cypress with horsechestnut and witch hazel.

Cypress is antiseptic, sedative and diuretic, and also has an antispasmodic action, which may explain why it is used to ease coughs.

Aromatherapists recommend cypress essential oil as a massage oil or a bath additive to relieve tired, aching legs. They consider it to have drying properties and add it to foot baths for foot odour and excessive sweating.

Cultivation
Grow in well-drained, acid or alkaline soils in full sunlight. Cypress tolerates heat and dryness.

pieces of dried cones

PREPARATION AND DOSAGE

- **To treat varicose veins, haemorrhoids**

    INFUSION Put 2 teaspoons of crushed cones into 1 cup of boiling water. Drink 4–5 cups a day, before or between meals.

- **To treat varicose veins**

    GELS, OINTMENTS Gently apply to the affected areas. Massage in, working upwards. Do this in the evening just before going to bed, or as directed.
    AROMATHERAPY Dilute 2–4 drops in a carrier oil and massage into affected area, or add 5 drops to a foot bath or bathtub.

IF SYMPTOMS PERSIST, CONSULT A DOCTOR

CAUTIONS
- To date, no sign of toxicity has been recorded from the use of the cypress cone, even when taken over long periods.
- Caution should be taken by pregnant or breastfeeding women.
- Do not take the essential oil internally.

Damiana *Turnera diffusa, T. diffusa var. aphrodisiaca* Turneraceae

Damiana is an aromatic perennial that is native to tropical areas of the northern Caribbean and the Americas. In summer it produces yellow-orange flowers with five petals, which are followed by fruit containing many tiny seeds. The toothed leaves are pale green, with a furred undersurface. Apart from its medicinal uses, this herb is also used as the basis of a popular liqueur made in Mexico.

Parts used
LEAVES AND STEMS
- Leaves and stems are harvested in summer, when the plant is flowering.
- Although the dried leaves have traditionally been taken as an infusion, damiana is more commonly used as a liquid extract or in tablet form.

Constituents
Amongst the constituents of damiana are tannins, resins, gums, alkaloids, flavonoids, a volatile oil and damianin, a bitter principle. Arbutin (a key component of uva-ursi, see p.185) is present in low concentration, and may be partially responsible for the herb's activity. A glucoside called tetraphyllin B that contains cyanide is also present. However, the cyanide is safe at therapeutic doses.

dried leaves and stems

Medicinal uses
Damiana is traditionally regarded as an aphrodisiac, and was used by the Mayan Indians in this way. Herbalists still prescribe it as a male tonic, with particular regard to conditions affecting the male reproductive tract. Indications include impotence, premature ejaculation and situations where mental and emotional issues are considered to be affecting sexual performance.

These uses are difficult to validate in a clinical setting, however animal research has confirmed that damiana enhances sexual activity in male rats that were previously impotent or sexually underactive. The herb is also considered to have testosterone-like activity.

Damiana is predominantly prescribed for men. However, the Mayans also traditionally used it to aid childbirth and to treat menstrual disorders.

In both sexes, damiana is reputed to aid nervous exhaustion, anxiety and mild to moderate depression. Its stimulating action is traditionally considered to be of particular benefit in cases where anxiety and depression occur simultaneously, and where psychosexual issues are present.

Damiana is a mild diuretic and urinary antiseptic, and may be of assistance in the treatment of bacterial bladder infections. It is also a mild laxative and digestive stimulant. Research has shown it to have antibacterial activity against a number of organisms.

Cultivation
Damiana requires humid, warm, frost-free conditions, with full sun and a fertile, well-drained soil. In cold areas, plant in a greenhouse. Grows from seed or cutting.

PREPARATION AND DOSAGE
- **To treat impotence, premature ejaculation and psychosexual issues in men, for relief of nervous exhaustion and anxiety in both sexes**
  LIQUID EXTRACT 1–2 g dried herb equivalent, three times daily.
  IF SYMPTOMS PERSIST, CONSULT A DOCTOR

CAUTIONS
- Not recommended for pregnant or breastfeeding women.
- Do not take damiana if you are taking medication for diabetes, as it may affect your blood-sugar levels.
- Depression is a serious condition that is not suitable for self-treatment – do not stop taking prescribed antidepressants unless advised to do so by your doctor. Consult a doctor before using damiana for symptoms of depression.
- Damiana is not recommended for people with irritable bowel syndrome, or for those with an overactive nervous system.
- An overdose (200 g) of damiana has been known to cause tetany and convulsions. Do not exceed the recommended dose.

Dandelion *Taraxacum officinale* Asteraceae

Naturalised to all temperate regions of the world, where it is a common sight in gardens and lawns, dandelion is a herbaceous perennial that grows to about 10–30 cm in height. Deeply indented leaves spring up from around its base, with single yellow flowers appearing in spring. These are followed by seeds, each topped by a tuft of soft hairs that catch the wind, helping to disperse the plant far and wide.

Parts used

ROOTS AND LEAVES

- The root is collected in summer and autumn.
- Young leaves are gathered in spring.
- Both are dried for use in infusions, liquid extracts, tablets and capsules.
- The leaves may be eaten as a salad vegetable. The roasted roots may be used as a coffee substitute.

dried roots

Constituents

The root and leaves are rich in fructose and inulin and also contain bitter principles (sesquiterpene lactones), phenol acids and sterols. The leaves also contain flavonoids, potassium salts and coumarins.

Medicinal uses

The bitter principles give dandelion its strong diuretic powers, which have been confirmed in animal studies.

Dandelion leaf is therefore widely used to help stimulate urination in cases of water retention, kidney disorders, cellulite and obesity. It also contains potassium to replace that which is lost when urine production is increased.

Both the leaves and root are considered to act on the gall bladder and liver, and stimulate the secretion and excretion of bile, all of which can help to cleanse the body of toxins and waste matter. Traditionally, the roots are used more commonly to treat digestive, liver and gall bladder conditions, while the leaves are prescribed for urinary tract conditions.

In an exciting new development, animal studies in 2001 demonstrated that a herbal preparation containing dandelion could lower blood-sugar levels, suggesting its potential for treating diabetes.

Cultivation

Sow by seed in spring in moist to dry, neutral to alkaline soil in full sun.

PREPARATION AND DOSAGE

- **To treat fluid retention, kidney disorders, cellulite, obesity**

  LIQUID EXTRACT 4–10 g dried leaf equivalent, three times a day.
  TABLETS, CAPSULES Up to 1 g dried leaf equivalent, three times a day.
  INFUSION Put 1 teabag of dried leaves into 1 cup of boiling water and infuse for 10 minutes. Drink 2–3 cups a day.

- **To treat sluggish digestion, liver and gall bladder and mild constipation**

  LIQUID EXTRACT 500 mg–1 g dried root equivalent, three times a day.
  TABLETS Up to 500 mg, three times a day.
  DANDELION 'COFFEE' Follow manufacturer's instructions.

IF SYMPTOMS PERSIST, CONSULT A DOCTOR

CAUTIONS

- Those allergic to other members of the Asteraceae family (such as daisies and chamomile) may also be allergic to dandelion.
- Do not take dandelion root if you have gallstones.
- Do not use to improve the secretion of bile without consulting a doctor, as the problem may be a serious blockage of the bile duct, for which dandelion must not be used.
- Avoid plants from areas treated with pesticides or herbicides.
- Dandelion leaves should be avoided by those taking potassium-sparing diuretics or ACE inhibitors.

Devil's claw
Harpagophytum procumbens Pedaliaceae **Also called** Grapple plant

A native of southern Africa, particularly the Transvaal, where it has been used for centuries to treat a variety of ailments from indigestion and fever to skin cancer. Devil's claw gets its name from its strange capsulelike fruits that are covered in what look like miniature grappling hooks. In summer, this creeping perennial bears stunning deep red, trumpet-shaped flowers that can grow up to 6 cm in length.

Parts used
TUBERS
- The tubers, or swollen roots, are dug up in autumn, dried and cut into small round pieces.
- They are used for infusions, powders, drinkable solutions, ointments, gels and creams.
- Only wild plants are used in herbal medicines, which may endanger the survival of the species.

Constituents
The major constituents are iridoids (monoterpenic glucosides), which constitute 0.5–3 per cent of the dried drug. Since harpagoside is the most active of these medicinally, choose preparations that contain at least 1.5–2 per cent of harpagoside. Also present in the plant are phytosterols and flavonoids.

dried tubers

Medicinal uses
Studies have demonstrated that devil's claw can help to relieve pain, and in some cases improve mobility for people suffering from osteoarthritis or degenerative rheumatism. The anti-inflammatory powers conferred by harpagoside and the phytosterols are responsible for this, and the plant is often recommended for treating less serious cases of rheumatism. In recent years, trials have shown that the dose of devil's claw required to obtain relief from these conditions is higher than once thought. The plant is also used externally for joint pain.

Cultivation
This species has proved to be difficult to cultivate outside its native habitat.

PREPARATION AND DOSAGE
- **To treat rheumatism, arthritis, joint pain**

  TABLETS, CAPSULES 1–2 g dried tuber equivalent, three times a day between meals. For best results, choose a product standardised for its harpagoside content.

- **To treat minor joint pain**

  GELS, OINTMENT Massage in gently, twice a day.

IF SYMPTOMS PERSIST, CONSULT A DOCTOR

CAUTIONS
- Although generally well tolerated, devil's claw may cause diarrhoea.
- Never take devil's claw when pregnant or breastfeeding.
- Devil's claw is not recommended for people who suffer from duodenal or stomach ulcers or gallstones.

Dill *Anethum graveolens* Apiaceae

Native to the Mediterranean, where it still grows wild, dill was recognised as having medicinal properties by the ancient Egyptians, and it even rates a mention in the Bible. The dill plant sports a flourish of feathery leaves that fan out from the hollow, ridged stem. In midsummer it bears tiny, yellow flowers in umbrella-shaped clusters, followed by flat, oval, winged seeds, that are scattered on the wind.

Parts used
LEAVES AND SEEDS
- The leaves are used in poultices and compresses.
- The seeds are harvested when fully ripe, then dried in a shady place so that their constituent compounds remain active.
- They are used in infusions, tablets, tinctures and powders. An essential oil is also extracted.

Constituents
Dill seeds contain tannin and mucilage, resinous substances, aleurone and albuminoid fats. They are also rich in essential oil.

Medicinal uses
Dill was traditionally used to treat swelling and pain, and as a sedative. It has long been known that dill can also relieve flatulence and aid digestion, which partly explains its centuries-long use in cooking.

Dill seeds are effective for treating colic, indigestion and hiccups, particularly in infants and young children – probably because of their high concentration of essential oil. Research has also established the fact that the essential oil has antibacterial properties, which helps it to inhibit the growth of harmful intestinal bacteria.

Essential oil rubbed onto the skin can stop feelings of nausea, and dill seed preparations, applied externally in the form of a poultice, can be used to treat bruises and gum infections.

Cultivation
Dill can be grown by planting seeds in a well-drained, neutral to acid soil. The plant prefers a position in direct sunlight.

dried seeds

PREPARATION AND DOSAGE

- **To treat digestive problems**

  INFUSION Put 4–8 g of dried seeds into 1 litre of boiling water and infuse for 10 minutes. Drink 1 cup after meals. Follow maker's instructions with preparations for the treatment of colic in infants.

- **To treat bruises, blocked and overloaded breasts in women who are breastfeeding, gum infections**

  POULTICE Put 50–100 g of dried seeds into 1 litre of boiling water. Leave to infuse for 10 minutes. The leaves can also be used.

- **To treat nausea**

  ESSENTIAL OIL Rub a few drops onto the forearm two to three times a day.

IF SYMPTOMS PERSIST, CONSULT A DOCTOR

CAUTIONS
- Do not take the essential oil internally.
- Dill naturally contains high levels of salt, therefore any dried plant material or the water extract is not recommended for people who need to follow a salt-restricted diet.

Dong quai *Angelica sinensis* (syn. *A. polymorpha* var. *sinensis*) Apiaceae

Also called Dang qui, Tang kuei Dong quai is native to China, Korea and Japan, where it is found growing at high altitudes. Popularly known as the 'woman's herb', it has a long history of use in traditional Chinese medicine. Dong quai is a hardy upright perennial with greyish green leaves, and in summer produces clusters of between 12 and 36 rusty green flowers. It grows best in cool, damp areas.

Parts used

ROOTS

- The root is harvested in autumn.
- It is traditionally considered to consist of head and tail portions, and different properties are attributed to each of these root parts.
- The root is traditionally taken as a decoction or added to soups to form a medicinal food. In Western herbal medicine, the use of tablets or liquid extracts is more common.

dried roots

Constituents

Constituents of dong quai include phytosterols, ferulic acid, coumarins, vitamin B$_{12}$ and volatile oil. The volatile oil has a complex structure which includes sesquiterpenes, n-Butylene phthalide, ligustilide, safrol, isosafrol and carvacrol.

Medicinal uses

In traditional Chinese medicine, dong quai is considered to be the supreme women's herb for tonifying and strengthening the blood, and regulating the menstrual cycle. Herbalists recommend it to relieve period pain and rectify an irregular menstrual cycle, and to treat female infertility caused by blocked fallopian tubes. Dong quai is also popularly taken as a tonic during menopause, although research has not confirmed any reduction in symptoms of hot flushes.

Traditionally, dong quai is included as an ingredient in chicken soup taken to help recovery after childbirth. This reflects its reputation as a tonic herb for women, and also its specific application in Chinese medicine for blood deficiency and anaemia. Other conditions associated with deficient blood in traditional Chinese medicine include absent or scanty menses, poor memory and concentration, anxiety, pallor, insomnia, low vitality, poor circulation to the hands and feet, heart palpitations and restlessness.

In the cardiovascular system, dong quai is prescribed for the prevention of atherosclerosis, and may also be of benefit in angina, arrhythmia and as an antiplatelet agent. It is also used to treat bruising, contusions, swellings and similar injuries.

Dong quai is proven to stimulate aspects of immune function, including production of B- and T-lymphocytes, interferon and leukocytes.

Cultivation

Dong quai needs a cool climate to grow well and can be raised from seed. Plant in a semi-shaded situation and keep the soil moist.

PREPARATION AND DOSAGE

- **To treat menstrual irregularity, period pain, tinnitus, bruises and swollen tissues, and as a tonic for anaemia**

  LIQUID EXTRACT 500 mg–1 g dried root equivalent, taken three times a day.
  TABLETS, CAPSULES 500 mg–1 g dried root equivalent, three times a day, or according to manufacturer's instructions.
  DECOCTION Boil one whole uncut dong quai root in 1 cup of water. Divide into two doses, and take on an empty stomach in the morning and at bedtime.

IF SYMPTOMS PERSIST, CONSULT A DOCTOR

CAUTIONS

- Dong quai should not be used by pregnant or breastfeeding women.
- In traditional Chinese medicine, dong quai is contraindicated during acute viral infections, such as colds and flu, and for people with a tendency to heavy bleeding (e.g. heavy periods or haemorrhagic disease).
- Dong quai should not be taken with warfarin or other blood-thinning medications.
- Dong quai should not be taken by people with a history of oestrogen-sensitive tumours.

86 NATURE'S MEDICINES

Echinacea
Echinacea augustifolia, E. purpurea, E. pallida **Asteraceae** **Also called** Coneflower, Black Sampson, Snake root

A plant of the North American plains, echinacea was used by Native Americans to treat wounds and snakebites. European settlers were also quick to recognise its medicinal potential. Today, three species of this perennial herb are cultivated for medicinal purposes. Echinacea has a long flowering season and is a pretty and popular garden plant.

Parts used
ROOTS, LEAVES AND FLOWERS
- The root is more widely used than the aerial parts of the plant, and is considered to be more medicinally active.
- Roots must be from plants at least four years old.
- The root is cylindrical and scarred. It has a faint aromatic smell and tastes at first sweet, then bitter.
- Echinacea is used for liquid extracts, tablets and capsules, on its own or with other plants.

Constituents
Both the roots and the aerial parts contain alkylamides, caffeic acid esters, essential oil and polysaccharides. The aerial parts also contain flavonoids, while the roots contain non-toxic forms of pyrrolizidine alkaloids.

Medicinal uses
Echinacea is an effective remedy for influenza, colds, upper respiratory tract infections, genitourinary infections and other diseases. It is widely used to combat the common cold, restoring the body to health quickly while helping the immune system fight off other infections.

In 2002, scientists in Canada showed that, in vitro, echinacea was an effective antiviral agent against herpes simplex. In 1988, German researchers discovered that the herb produced a noticeable increase in phagocytosis, a process by which foreign bodies are engulfed by the body's immune cells.

Echinacea helps to strengthen the body's immune system and increases resistance to infection, particularly to influenza. This makes the herb especially useful for those with weakened immune systems. It may, therefore, be valuable as a supplementary treatment when the immune system is suppressed by drugs, for example, as a result of anticancer chemotherapy. However, this should be considered only in consultation with a doctor.

dried roots

Cultivation
Plant in a sunny spot in rich, well-drained soil.

PREPARATION AND DOSAGE
- **To treat colds, sore throat, influenza, bronchitis**

  LIQUID EXTRACT 1 g dried root equivalent, three times a day.

  TABLETS, CAPSULES 1 g dried root equivalent, or 3 g dried juice equivalent, three times a day.

- **As a preventive to keep infections from taking hold**

  LIQUID EXTRACT 500 mg dried root equivalent, twice a day.

  TABLETS, CAPSULES 500 mg–1 g dried root equivalent, once or twice a day.

IF SYMPTOMS PERSIST, CONSULT A DOCTOR

CAUTIONS
- Talk to your doctor before taking echinacea if you have an auto-immune illness such as lupus, or a progressive disease such as multiple sclerosis or HIV/AIDS.
- If you are allergic to flowers of the daisy family, you may be allergic to echinacea as well.
- Do not use to replace prescribed treatments. Antibiotics and other medicines may be needed as well.
- No toxic properties or adverse side effects have been reported.
- Talk to your medical herbalist before using echinacea for prolonged periods, as there is some controversy over whether extensive use weakens the herb's effects.

Elder
Sambucus nigra Caprifoliaceae **Also called** Elderberry, Black elder, Pipe tree

A native of Europe and North America, but now grown worldwide, the elder is reputed to have magical properties and therefore makes an appearance in the folklore of many countries. A deciduous tree, elder can grow up to 10 m tall. Its large, flat clusters of small, creamy flowers bloom in late spring, filling the air with a sweetly pungent scent. These are followed by small, black berries filled with dark purple juice.

Parts used
FLOWERS AND BERRIES
- The flowers are picked in late spring, when in full bloom.
- They are dried and used in the preparation of infusions and decoctions.
- The berries are picked when they are ripe in early autumn.

Constituents
Elderflower contains tannins, potassium, mucilage, phenols and flavonoids. The berries, traditionally used in syrups, jams and wines, are rich in anthocyanins, folic acid and vitamins A and C. They also contain flavonoids and cyanidin glucosides, which are poisonous in large doses.

dried flowers and berries

Medicinal uses
Elderflowers and berries are expectorant and also promote sweating, thus helping to reduce high temperatures, and to rid the body of toxins. These combined effects make elder a good choice for treating colds and flu.

In 1990, Bulgarian scientists found elderflowers to have antiviral action against herpes simplex Type I (the virus responsible for causing cold sores) and influenza types A and B. And recent clinical evidence from Israel also showed elderberry extract effectively inhibiting various strains of flu virus. If taken early enough in an infection, elder can greatly shorten recovery times.

Elder is also prescribed for the treatment of other respiratory conditions, especially those associated with catarrhal discharge, such as hay fever, sinusitis and pleurisy.

The results of a study conducted in France, published in 1983, found that elderflower preparations were diuretic. The berries are known to be mildly laxative.

An elderflower decoction makes an excellent anti-inflammatory mouthwash or gargle for swollen painful gums and sore throats.

The roots appear to be insecticidal – wild badgers have been observed rubbing their bodies vigorously against them to kill lice infestations in their fur. It therefore seems possible that a decoction used topically might help to eradicate an infestation of head lice.

Cultivation
Elder likes a rich, damp, neutral to alkaline soil and a sunny or lightly shaded location. Grow from seed sown in autumn.

fully open flower

unopened flower bud

PREPARATION AND DOSAGE

- **To treat influenza, colds, hay fever, catarrh**

  LIQUID EXTRACT 500 mg–1 g dried flower equivalent, three times a day.
  TABLETS, CAPSULES 500 mg–1 g dried flower equivalent, three times a day.
  INFUSION Put 2–5 g dried flowers into a cup of boiling water. Infuse for 5–10 minutes and strain. Drink at least 3 cups a day.

- **To treat sore throat, inflamed gums (gingivitis)**

  MOUTHWASH Put 50 g flowers into 1 litre boiling water. Boil for 5 minutes, then leave to cool. Use as a gargle or mouthwash four to six times a day, particularly after meals.

IF SYMPTOMS PERSIST, CONSULT A DOCTOR

CAUTIONS
- Do not eat raw fruit since it can cause nausea and vomiting.
- Do not use elder if pregnant or breastfeeding.
- Excessive or prolonged use causes excessive potassium loss via the urine.
- To date, there are no reported adverse side effects, despite the presence of small amounts of cyanidin glucosides.

Epilobium

Epilobium parviflorum, E. angustifolium Onagraceae **Also called** Willow-herb, Rosebay willowherb

Of the varieties of epilobium that grow in Europe, only two are used for their medicinal properties. One is E. parviflorum, *a small plant with tiny, pale pink flowers and hairy, spear-shaped leaves.* E. angustifolium, *the other variety, is a tall plant, with stems covered in long, narrow leaves and crowned by a spike of pink-purple flowers. Both can be found in woodland and on wasteland.*

Parts used
FLOWERS AND LEAVES
- The flowers and leaves are picked late in the summer, at the end of the flowering season.
- They are dried, and then used in infusions, powders and tinctures.

Constituents
The beneficial effects of epilobium stem largely from the flavonoids and tannins. The major flavonoid in *E. parviflorum* is myricitroside. The principal one in *E. angustifolium* is quercetolgluceronide. Both plants also contain betasitosterol and gallic acid. The tannins – oenotheines A and B – are present in both their flowers.

Medicinal uses
Epilobium is noted for its ability to reduce inflammation – largely as a result of its flavonoids and tannins. It is often prescribed to relieve the symptoms of benign prostate enlargement, although it is essential to have a thorough medical examination before using the plant for this purpose, to ensure that the prostate swelling really is benign. There is also some debate over which variety of the plant is best to prescribe for this condition. While *E. angustifolium* is known to contain some highly active inflammation-reducing tannins, those in *E. parviflorum* appear to be especially successful in the treatment of an enlarged prostate gland.

The plant's soothing powers have also been employed to treat irritable bowel syndrome, diarrhoea, sore throats, mouth ulcers and skin irritations such as eczema. The leaves are known to improve urinary flow and are beneficial in the treatment of cystitis and an irritable bladder.

Cultivation
Epilobium is a common weed, and is therefore not usually cultivated, but simply gathered from the wild. Occasionally, gardeners plant *E. angustifolium* because it is decorative.

dried flowers and leaves

PREPARATION AND DOSAGE
- It is not advisable to use any preparation made with epilobium, from simple infusions to more complex commercial products, unless they have been prescribed by a doctor or medical herbalist

IF SYMPTOMS PERSIST, CONSULT A DOCTOR

CAUTIONS
- Although no adverse side effects have been noted when using epilobium preparations, the plant should be used only under close medical supervision.

Eucalyptus *Eucalyptus globulus* Myrtaceae Also called Blue gum, Tasmanian blue gum

Native to Tasmania and small areas in southern Australia, but cultivated elsewhere in the world, the Tasmanian blue gum is a giant evergreen tree, usually 30–70 m tall, with a smooth, grey-blue trunk. The German botanist Ferdinand von Müller was the first European to recognise the medicinal powers of the fragrant oil in the long, narrow, leathery leaves growing on branches that are more than five years old.

Parts used

LEAVES

- There are several hundred species of *Eucalyptus*, but the preferred species for medicinal use is *Eucalyptus globulus*.
- Aromatic leaves from the older branches are collected, usually in summer.
- The leaves are either dried and ground into powder or distilled for their essential oil.

dried leaves

Constituents

The leaves contain flavonoids, and also large amounts of essential oil, which is rich in cineole and eucalyptol.

Medicinal uses

A number of studies have shown that eucalyptus can combat certain bacteria, and that it has antifungal and antiviral powers. Its antiseptic action, along with its ability to act as a decongestant, stems from the eucalyptol in the essential oil, making eucalyptus an effective treatment for respiratory ailments such as coughs and colds. For its antiseptic action, it is used to treat cuts and wounds, and has also been shown to be effective for burns.

The flavonoids in eucalyptus are known to help lower blood-sugar levels – an effect demonstrated in various clinical trials. One study has also shown its ability to ease the pain of aching muscles by increasing the blood flow to them.

Cultivation

Blue gum prefers a warm climate, but can grow at temperatures as low as -15°C. Plant seeds in a sunny position, in well-drained, fertile, acid to neutral soil.

PREPARATION AND DOSAGE

- **To treat bronchial ailments, sore throats, coughs, sinusitis**

  LOZENGES, COUGH MIXTURE Follow manufacturer's instructions.

- **To treat bronchial ailments, sore throats, coughs**

  BALM, OINTMENT, ESSENTIAL OIL Rub on chest and throat once or twice a day. Do not use eucalyptus balms, ointments or rubs on children under 2 years old without receiving medical advice first.

- **To treat colds, blocked noses**

  INHALATIONS Prepare an infusion of leaves and essential oil. While hot, inhale the steam through the nose or mouth, under a towel, for 10 minutes twice a day. Use as needed. If treating children, allow the water to cool for 5 minutes before commencing the inhalation. Do not leave the child unattended.

IF SYMPTOMS PERSIST, CONSULT A DOCTOR

CAUTIONS

- Eucalyptus should not be used by children under two years old, women who are pregnant or breastfeeding or people suffering from digestive or liver disorders.
- Never use eucalyptus preparations if you are taking any drugs to lower blood-sugar levels.
- Do not take the essential oil, except in commercial preparations.
- Keep the oil out of reach of children as it is toxic.

Evening primrose *Oenothera biennis* Onagraceae

Although a native of North America, the biennial evening primrose is very common in other parts of the world as well. Its large, short-lived yellow flowers appear clustered in spikes from summer to mid-autumn, and open only in the evenings to bloom by moonlight, hence the common name of the plant. Each fruit, a long, thick, erect stalkless capsule, contains about 600 small, round, beige seeds.

Parts used
SEEDS
- The seeds are collected when ripe.
- Oil is extracted from them and put into capsules for medicinal use.

Constituents
Twenty-five per cent of each seed is made up of an oil rich in essential fatty acids, including linolenic acid and gammalinolenic acid. The seeds also contain proteins, fibre and mineral materials rich in calcium.

Medicinal uses
Evening primrose oil has been remarkably effective as a treatment for premenstrual syndrome and, in particular, as a means of relieving breast pain.

This is because its fatty acids, mainly gammalinolenic acid, play an important role in the synthesis by the body of substances called prostaglandins (PGEs). PGEs are important because they help to regulate the action of several hormones – namely oestrogen, prolactin and progesterone – that are associated with the menstrual cycle. A good supply of the fatty acids found in evening primrose oil ensures a good supply of the PGEs that ensure these hormones will perform correctly in the body.

PGEs also help to maintain the suppleness and elasticity of the skin by helping to control the secretion of sebum, an oil that protects skin tissues. Evening primrose oil is therefore widely used in many ranges of cosmetics designed to help in preventing skin ageing.

In addition, research has shown that prostaglandin E_1 (PGE_1) controls the dilation of blood vessels and is anti-inflammatory. Evening primrose oil boosts the production of PGE_1 and is therefore recommended for the treatment of eczema, acne and arthritis.

Cultivation
The plant flourishes in well-drained, dry soil and sunny locations. Seeds should be sown in spring and the plants will then self-sow in good conditions.

seeds

PREPARATION AND DOSAGE
- **To treat premenstrual syndrome (PMS), breast tenderness, eczema, arthritis, ageing skin**

  CAPSULES 1 g taken three times a day. For PMS and breast tenderness, it may be enough to take evening primrose oil during the last 10 days of the menstrual cycle only. However, for severe symptoms, treatment throughout the month is recommended.

IF SYMPTOMS PERSIST, CONSULT A DOCTOR

CAUTIONS
- Evening primrose oil should not be taken by people who suffer from any form of epilepsy.

Eyebright *Euphrasia officinalis* Scrophulariaceae **Also called** Eufragia, Euphrasia

Native to chalky grasslands and meadows in England and Europe, eyebright has long been used in remedies for sore eyes – hence its name. This little plant grows up to 20 cm high and has downy leaves and small, lipped flowers whose white petals, tinged with mauve and yellow, appear from late summer to mid-autumn. There are species of eyebright native to alpine regions in both Australia and New Zealand.

Parts used

ALL PARTS ABOVE GROUND

- Plants are collected when they begin to flower, in late summer.
- The plant is cut off just above the root and then allowed to dry.
- Eyebright is used in a range of decoctions, tinctures, infusions and eye lotions.

Constituents

Eyebright contains tannins (making it astringent), antimicrobial iridoid glycosides that have anti-inflammatory properties, phenols (known to inhibit bacterial growth), an essential oil, flavonoids and resins.

Medicinal uses

The plant's astringent properties are known to be useful for treating eye problems. A compress soothes styes (infected eyelash follicles), inflamed corneas and conjunctivitis. The plant also cools tired and watering eyes and it is often an ingredient in eye lotions that are prescribed for these ailments.

In Icelandic medicine, juice squeezed from the plant is used for a variety of eye problems. People living in the Scottish Highlands used to make an infusion of eyebright in milk and paint it onto sore and irritated eyelids with a feather.

In 1994, a group of Spanish researchers demonstrated the anti-inflammatory properties of the iridoids in eyebright. Tannins in the herb improve resistance to infection by drying and contracting the body's tissues, while phenols assist by helping to inhibit the growth of bacteria.

An infusion of eyebright taken internally complements any topical eye treatment. It is also anti-catarrhal, making it useful in helping to clear runny noses, and in the treatment of middle ear infections and painful sinuses.

Cultivation

This frost-hardy plant is semi-parasitic, and for this reason, will thrive only when it is planted among grasses whose roots provide it with water and nourishment. Try sowing seed in a wild area of the garden, although you may need to experiment with various locations as this plant is difficult to grow.

dried aerial parts

PREPARATION AND DOSAGE

- **To treat colds, hay fever, sinusitis, middle ear infection**

  LIQUID EXTRACT 2–4 g dried herb equivalent, three times a day.
  INFUSION Infuse 2 g dried herb in 1 cup of boiling water for 10 minutes before straining. Drink 2–3 cups a day.

- **To treat inflamed eyelids, styes, conjunctivitis, tired or watery eyes**

  EYE LOTIONS, EYEWASHES, EYE COMPRESSES Proprietary products are available but should be used only under the supervision of a medical herbalist or doctor.

  IF SYMPTOMS PERSIST, CONSULT A DOCTOR

CAUTIONS

- Use eyebright preparations for eye problems only when under medical supervision.
- Protect your eyes with sunglasses when taking eyebright.
- Do not use internally if pregnant or breastfeeding.
- Overdose may cause itchy or inflamed eyes, breathing difficulties, nausea, insomnia and confusion.

Fennel
Foeniculum vulgare Apiaceae **Also called** Wild fennel, Bitter fennel, Sweet fennel

This tall perennial herb with feathery leaves is native to countries around the Mediterranean, where it was cultivated in ancient times. In many parts of the world it is a weed of wastelands and roadsides. All parts of fennel smell strongly of aniseed, and it has long been a popular culinary herb. Its tiny, greenish yellow flowers grow in large, flat heads. The small, yellow-brown seeds have an aromatic odour and taste.

Parts used
SEEDS
- Seeds are gathered in autumn, when yellow.
- They are used whole, or an essential oil may be extracted from them.
- The bulb at the base of the stem is used as a vegetable, although this use is normally confined to the variant *azoricum*.

Constituents
The essential oil – about 6 per cent of the seed – contains mainly anethole plus estragole and fenchone. Seeds contain phytosterols, flavonoids and coumarins.

Medicinal uses
Fennel has traditionally been used to ease problems of the digestive system, such as acid stomach, irritable bowel, constipation, flatulence, spasms, and may help to dissolve kidney stones. The plant is also a traditional remedy for the treatment of colic in infants.

dried seeds

Chewing the seeds is a pleasant remedy for bad breath, and since fennel also has anti-inflammatory and antimicrobial properties, it is frequently used in natural toothpaste products.

Fennel is further reputed to help those wishing to lose weight by suppressing the appetite while stimulating the metabolism. It is also thought to relieve motion sickness and other types of nausea, and it has been used to soothe inflamed eyes and sore throats. It is also an expectorant, and because of its antispasmodic action is used for coughs.

Fennel is thought to mimic the hormone oestrogen, which may explain why Indian women used it to stimulate lactation.

Cultivation
Plant in well-drained soil in an area with full sun.

PREPARATION AND DOSAGE

- **To treat digestive ailments**

  FENNEL WATER Take 5–15 drops in water once a day.
  LIQUID EXTRACT Take 10–40 drops in water once a day.
  INFUSION Add ½ teaspoon of crushed seeds to 1 cup of boiling water; cover and infuse for 10 minutes. Strain. Drink 1 cup three times a day.
  CAPSULES (300 MG) Take 2 capsules before meals.

- **To treat eye irritation**

  EYEBATH A cold infusion of fennel (see above) may be used, but it must be sterile. Otherwise use a commercial preparation.

IF SYMPTOMS PERSIST, CONSULT A DOCTOR

CAUTIONS
- Fennel may induce periods in menopausal women.
- Pregnant women should not consume amounts greater than those normally found in food.
- Women with breast or uterine cancer, or a history of these diseases, should avoid fennel.
- People who are allergic to carrots, celery or mugwort may have an adverse reaction when using fennel.
- Do not take the essential oil internally.

Fenugreek *Trigonella foenum-graecum* Fabaceae

Originally found beside the Black Sea, fenugreek is a widely grown annual in India, North Africa, the United States, Australia and New Zealand. The plant grows to a height of 50 cm and is strongly aromatic. It has oval leaves and triangular flowers, which range in colour from yellow to bright purple. The long, curved seed pods have many brown seeds, used in Indian cooking as a pungent curry spice.

Parts used

SEEDS
- The seed pods are picked in late summer when ripe.
- The pods are stripped away and the seeds are made into a liquid extract, or ground and sold as a powder or in tablet form.

dried seeds

Constituents
The main constituent of fenugreek is mucilage, a soluble fibre that soaks up water, forming a jellylike substance. The seeds also contain coumarins, steroidal saponins, an aromatic volatile oil and alkaloids.

Medicinal uses
Fenugreek has a tonic effect that combats tiredness and speeds convalescence. And because it is rich in mucilage, which coats mucous membranes protecting them from irritants, it soothes painful digestive disorders. Mucilage gives bulk to stools and lubricates the bowel, easing painful constipation.

In 2001, Indian researchers into diabetes noted that fenugreek lowers blood-sugar levels in Type 2 diabetes mellitus, reducing resistance to insulin and removing excess triglycerides in the blood. Also, Indian research published in the *Journal of Ethnopharmacology* in 2002 showed the seeds' anti-ulcer properties.

Fenugreek is prescribed to treat anorexia, but its bulking effects can aid dieting by making the stomach feel full. The fibre and saponin are known to reduce cholesterol and blood lipids, while its hormonal qualities are reported to combat loss of virility in men.

Since most of the research into fenugreek has used the seed, either in its natural state or with the bitter fats removed, these are preferred for medicinal use. The liquid extract does not contain the mucilage, which may be responsible for much of the plant's activity.

Externally, a poultice of fenugreek powder reduces skin inflammation and relieves pain.

Cultivation
Plant seeds in well-drained fertile soil, in a sunny position.

seed pod
seed

PREPARATION AND DOSAGE

- **To treat fatigue, weight loss, high blood lipids** (as an adjunct to other treatments)

  POWDER 2 g in a little water, three times daily.
  TABLETS, CAPSULES Follow manufacturer's instructions. Do not exceed 6 g per day.

- **To treat skin inflammation**

  POULTICE (USING THE POWDER) Apply to the affected part, changing the compress every 3–4 hours.

IF SYMPTOMS PERSIST, CONSULT A DOCTOR

CAUTIONS

- Do not use fenugreek, except under medical supervision, if you are diabetic, using hypoglycaemic drugs or taking monoamine oxidase inhibitors (MAOIs) or hormonal or anticoagulant (blood-thinning) medication.
- It contains steroid compounds and should not be taken by children before they reach puberty.
- Pregnant and breastfeeding women should not take more of the spice than is normally found in food.
- High doses or continual use may interfere with iron absorption.
- If you have an underactive thyroid gland, avoid taking high doses of fenugreek.

Feverfew *Tanacetum parthenium* Asteraceae

A hardy perennial, feverfew is native to Anatolia and has a long history of use as a medicinal herb. It was once planted near homes to ward off disease, and was used in the 17th century as an ingredient in a cosmetic cream to remove freckles. The plant grows to a height of 60 cm and looks like a cross between a daisy and chamomile. Its leaves and flowers exude a strong, quite bitter aroma.

Parts used
AERIAL PARTS
- Plants are collected in summer, when they are in full flower.
- They are dried and then stored away from sunlight and damp to prevent decomposition and any loss of efficacy.
- Fresh leaves can be picked and used whenever they are required.

Constituents
The main active constituents of feverfew are substances that are called sesquiterpene lactones, which have both anti-inflammatory and anti-spasmodic properties. The most important of these is known as parthenolide.

Medicinal uses
One of the staples of the herbal medicine chest, feverfew gives effective relief from headaches caused by dilation or contraction of blood vessels. It is used for migraine, period pain, fever, asthma and a range of other inflammatory disorders.

There has been much research into the plant's anti-inflammatory properties, and a compound called parthenolide appears to be its main active ingredient. Scientists in Canada, India and at King's College in the United Kingdom have all conducted experiments that demonstrate feverfew's anti-inflammatory effects.

Studies carried out at Nottingham University in 1988 found that the plant was effective in reducing the frequency and the severity of migraine attacks.

Cultivation
You can grow the plant in a pot, or sow seeds in spring in well-drained, stony soil in a sunny spot. Once established, plants will come back year after year.

dried flowers

PREPARATION AND DOSAGE
- **To prevent and treat tension headache and migraine**
  TABLETS, CAPSULES 50–200 mg dried herb equivalent, standardised to contain 200–600 mcg parthenolide per daily dose.

IF SYMPTOMS PERSIST, CONSULT A DOCTOR

CAUTIONS
- Avoid if allergic to the plant family Asteraceae (e.g. chamomile and yarrow). Allergic reactions occur more commonly when fresh feverfew leaf is taken, so standardised tablets and capsules are the preferred dosage form.
- Can cause stomach upsets in susceptible individuals.
- Avoid if pregnant or breastfeeding.
- Do not use if taking the contraceptive pill, or anticoagulant (blood-thinning) drugs.
- Discontinue use gradually to avoid withdrawal symptoms such as joint pain, headaches or insomnia.

Fig *Ficus carica* Moraceae

Often mentioned in the Bible, fig trees are found throughout the Mediterranean region. Athletes in ancient Greece gorged on figs, believing that they increased a man's speed and stamina. The deciduous tree can reach a height of 12 m. It has large, lobed leaves and its tiny flowers are hidden, clustered inside the green 'fruit', which ripen after being fertilised by insects crawling into the fleshy figs.

Parts used

FRUIT, LEAVES AND, RARELY, THE SAP

- Both figs and fig leaves are used in tinctures and decoctions.
- The fruit is eaten fresh or can be dried.
- Fig syrup is widely used as a mild laxative.

Constituents

Fresh, ripe figs may contain up to 50 per cent sugar (glucose). They also contain flavonoids, which possess an anti-inflammatory effect. Coumarins in the leaves are aromatic substances that aid digestion and have antiseptic properties. The coumarins include bergapten and psoralen, both of which are photosensitising agents.

dried leaves

Medicinal uses

People have eaten this nutritious, sugar-rich fruit for many thousands of years. The sugar and fibre in figs are responsible for their famous laxative effect.

Flavonoids and coumarins in both the fruit and leaves contribute to figs' digestive, soothing, calming and anti-inflammatory effects. Figs also help to clear catarrh from the nose and throat, and to remove poisons. Eating the fruit can ease coughs, sore throats and the pain of a range of inflammatory conditions.

Researchers have investigated the use of figs in treating diabetes. A clinical trial conducted in Spain and published in 1998 found that people with Type I (insulin-dependent) diabetes taking fig-leaf decoctions had lower blood-sugar levels after eating meals.

In traditional medicine, the milky sap of the fig tree was applied externally to help soothe minor aches, pains and insect bites, as well as to remove warts. However, the sap can burn and blister the skin and should therefore be used with some caution.

Cultivation

Figs grow best when planted in a warm, sunny and sheltered position. Plant ready-bought young plants or cuttings in well-drained, neutral to alkaline soil.

PREPARATION AND DOSAGE

- **To treat blocked nose, bronchial or wheezy chest, mild constipation**

  SYRUP OF FIGS Follow the directions on the bottle.

  DECOCTION Put 80–100 g dried figs into 1 litre of boiling water. Leave to soak for 20 minutes and strain. Drink the same day.

- **To treat coughs**

  GARGLE Use decoction described above.

IF SYMPTOMS PERSIST, CONSULT A DOCTOR

CAUTIONS

- Stay out of strong sunlight when using figs as the coumarins may induce photosensitisation.
- Due to their natural high sugar content, figs should not be used to treat diabetes, except under medical supervision.
- Do not take the sap internally.

96 NATURE'S MEDICINES

Flax Linum usitatissimum Linaceae Also called Linseed

The slender, graceful flax is a herbaceous annual that is cropped in most temperate regions around the world. Its seeds, also known as linseed, are widely used in herbal medicine and yield a valuable oil. The fibres of its stalks are used to make linen. Flax grows to about 1 m in height and bears beautiful sky-blue flowers. The pea-sized fruit contain 10 oily seeds.

dried seeds

Parts used
SEEDS
- Flax is a major arable crop in many parts of the world. It is harvested in late summer.
- The fruit is crushed to release the seeds, from which the oil (known also as linseed oil) is then extracted.
- Both whole and ground seeds are used in various herbal medicines.
- The meal – what is left of the seeds once the oil has been extracted – is also used.

Constituents
The seed consists of 35–45 per cent oil. Flax seed oil is rich in omega-3 unsaturated fatty acids, which protect against heart and circulation problems and are anti-inflammatory. It also contains proteins, mucilage, cholesterol-lowering phytosterols, anti-inflammatory lignans and cyanogenic glycosides, which are antispasmodic.

Medicinal uses
Flax seed is a gentle laxative. It is used to treat long-term constipation and colon disorders. It contains mucilage that lines and soothes the mucous membranes of an irritated digestive system and painful bowel.

The phyto-oestrogens in the seeds appear to have a beneficial effect on some breast and colon cancers. A paper published in the *American Journal of Kidney Disease* in 2001 reported flax seed's potential in the treatment of kidney disorders.

Research conducted in New Jersey, USA, in 1993 showed that flax seed reduced blood cholesterol in patients with high blood-cholesterol levels. In addition, an American paper published in 2000 suggested the seeds might benefit people with atherosclerosis.

Flax meal has long been used externally as a poultice for skin disorders such as spots and boils, itching, ulcers and bruising. It also helps soothe painful joints.

Cultivation
Sow seeds in spring in well-drained soil. Choose a sunny location in the garden.

PREPARATION AND DOSAGE
- **To treat chronic constipation, disorders of the colon, inflammation of the gastric and intestinal mucous membranes**
  MACERATION Put 15–20 g of seeds into 1 litre of cold water. Leave to soak overnight and strain. Drink 1 glass in the morning before eating and then 4–5 glasses during the day, but not at mealtimes.
  WHOLE SEEDS Take 15–20 seeds with water or in bread three times a day.
  OIL Follow manufacturer's instructions for liquid oil preparations.
- **To treat spots and boils, itching, bruising, painful joints**
  POULTICE Slowly pour water onto flax meal, stirring until it has become a smooth paste. Spread a 1-cm-thick warm layer onto gauze. Apply to the affected part one to three times a day.

IF SYMPTOMS PERSIST, CONSULT A DOCTOR

CAUTIONS
- Do not use if you have prostate cancer or an intestinal blockage.
- Do not combine with other drugs, laxatives or stool softeners.
- Do not use immature seeds, or meal past its use-by date. Its residual oil content causes it to go rancid.
- Since immature seeds are potentially toxic, flax is not suitable for self-harvesting. Use only commercially grown products.

Garcinia
Garcinia cambogia Clusiaceae **Also called** Brindleberry, Malabar tamarind

A native of South-East Asia and India, garnica is also distributed throughout west and central Africa. It is a tropical shrub found in moist forests and has glossy, dark green leaves. It bears yellow, pumpkin-shaped fruit the size of an orange. The fruit is used in traditional Thai and Indian cooking and has the effect of imparting a distinctive sour flavour to food, similar to that of tamarind.

Parts used
FRUIT INCLUDING RIND
- The fruit is split in half and the seeds removed.
- The halves are dried and then used to make dry extracts, drinks, chewing gum and tablets.
- Garcinia is also used in products for external use such as creams, ointments and lotions.

Constituents
Up to 50 per cent of the dry extract is made up of a fruit acid called hydroxycitric acid. This is the plant's main active ingredient, which is thought to help to control the formation of fat in the body. The fruit also contains other fruit acids that have anti-oxidant properties.

dried fruit

Medicinal uses
Garcinia has been used as a dietary aid for several thousand years in many parts of South-East Asia, where it has long been valued as an appetite suppressant.

This attribute seems to be due to the presence of hydroxycitric acid (HCA). Researchers think that HCA somehow affects the absorption and synthesis of fats, forcing the body to burn its own reserves.

In 2000, Japanese scientists found that hydroxycitric acid extracted from the rind of garcinia promoted lipid oxidation during exercise in mice. An American study published in the *Journal of Physiological Behaviour* in 2000 found that HCA failed to suppress the appetite. Another clinical study performed in New York in 1998 revealed that garcinia supplements produced neither significant weight loss nor loss of body fat.

Finally, British researchers reviewed all the available evidence on garcinia in 2004. In the paper that was published detailing their findings, they concluded that there was little evidence to support garcinia's use as a weight-loss remedy.

Cultivation
Garcinia is grown from seed. Out of tropical climates this plant needs damp warmth and thrives in a heated greenhouse.

fruit

PREPARATION AND DOSAGE
- **To treat cases of mild excess weight**

  CAPSULES (400 MG DRY EXTRACT) Take 1 capsule with 1 glass of water 30–60 minutes before main meals, three times a day. Your herbalist or doctor can advise you on whether this is an appropriate remedy for you.

IF SYMPTOMS PERSIST, CONSULT A DOCTOR

CAUTIONS
- Very occasionally, side effects of nausea and headache have been observed.
- Do not use if pregnant or breastfeeding.
- Do not give to children.
- Garnica may affect blood-sugar levels. It is therefore not recommended for diabetics.

Garlic *Allium sativum* Alliaceae

The long, slender leaves of garlic give the plant its name, which means 'spear plant' in Anglo-Saxon. Garlic is a small, herbaceous perennial and is part of the onion family. Its grasslike leaves encase the main stem, which bears umbrella-shaped clusters of flowers. The garlic bulb is made up of 10–15 cloves, each enclosed in a whitish, papery envelope. The cloves form the plant's underground food storage system.

cloves

Parts used
BULBS
- Garlic is harvested in summer or autumn.
- A piece of the plant stem is left attached to each bulb so that the bulbs can be strung into the familiar bunches.
- Once the outer parts are dried, garlic bulbs are stored in a dry place.
- The bulbs are eaten as part of the diet, or used pharmaceutically in a range of powders, extracts and tinctures.

Constituents
The main active component is the sulphur compound allicin, which is released when fresh garlic is crushed. In turn this produces other sulphides, which occur after the crushed bulb has been oxidised. The bulb also contains phenols – antiseptic and anti-inflammatory when taken internally – and flavonoids, known to have anticancer properties.

Medicinal uses
Garlic has been used since Biblical times for treating parasitic worms, as well as respiratory and digestive problems. It was vitally important as an antiseptic during World War I, and was in constant demand.

Garlic can also be used to prevent or treat infection. In 1999, Japanese scientists demonstrated its antibacterial action against *E. coli*, methicillin-resistant *Staphylococcus aureus* and salmonella infections.

Garlic has an antiseptic effect on the digestive and respiratory systems. It is also an immune stimulant. It makes the breath smell because its sulphur compounds evaporate rapidly. However, eating parsley will help to combat the odour.

By reducing fatty deposits on blood vessel walls, garlic may help to prevent hardening of the arteries. It tones the circulation and reduces the formation of blood clots. Garlic may also have the effect of dilating coronary blood vessels, helping to prevent angina.

Cultivation
Plant cloves in a rich, well-drained soil in autumn or spring, in a sunny spot. Each clove will form a bulb by mid-to late summer or early autumn.

PREPARATION AND DOSAGE
- To treat digestive and respiratory infections as well as intestinal worms, to improve circulation and help to prevent cardiovascular disease

FRESH CLOVES Take approximately 4 g (one clove) per day, raw. The garlic may be chopped and added to food. Eating parsley at the same time as the garlic may help to reduce breath odour.
TABLETS, CAPSULES Follow manufacturer's instructions, taking a maximum of 6 g dried clove equivalent per day. Note that the deodorised forms are considered to be less effective.

IF SYMPTOMS PERSIST, CONSULT A DOCTOR

CAUTIONS
- Individuals who are sensitive to garlic may experience heartburn, particularly if using fresh cloves.
- Those taking anticoagulant (blood-thinning) drugs or hypoglycaemics should check with their doctor before taking garlic.
- Anyone scheduled for surgery should tell the surgeon if they are taking garlic, and stop taking it two weeks before the operation.
- Garlic is safe and can be used by pregnant and breastfeeding women, although babies may not like the taste in milk.

THE A TO Z OF PLANTS

Gentian
Gentiana lutea Gentianaceae **Also called** Yellow gentian, Great yellow gentian, Bitterwort This large, upright perennial is commonly found in the Alps and other mountainous areas of Europe. Gentian's large leaves have five to seven prominent veins on the underside. The plant's flowers are a golden yellow and grow at the points where the leaves meet the stem. The thick, wrinkly roots have a bitter taste.

dried roots

Parts used
ROOTS
- At the end of summer the roots are collected from wild plants that are preferably 7–10 years old.
- The roots are washed, cut up and dried in the open.
- They are used to make powders, tinctures or extracts that are included in numerous medicinal products, such as liquid extracts, medicinal wines, tablets and capsules.

Constituents
The bitter taste of gentian root is due to secoiridoids, principally amarogentin and also gentiopicroside. When taken internally, these substances provoke a reflex action that stimulates salivary and gastric secretions.

Medicinal uses
The substances in gentian stimulate the flow of saliva and gastric juices even in very small amounts. A simple experiment will prove it: Merely grinding the root will cause one to salivate.

The root is traditionally used to remedy a lack of appetite and has long been an ingredient in aperitif drinks. It acts as a tonic on the whole digestive system, relieving gastric pains, improving sluggish digestion and stimulating bile secretions. A clinical study that was published in 1967 verified gentian's digestive qualities, observing that the herb promoted the secretion of gastric juices.

Gentian is also reputed to lower fevers and treat inflammation.

In spite of their extremely bitter taste, liquid extracts and infusions are preferred over tablets and capsules. The bitter sensation appears to trigger the plant's actions on the digestive system.

Cultivation
Plant in well-drained, humus-rich soil in a sunny or lightly shaded location.

PREPARATION AND DOSAGE
- **To treat gastric pains, sluggish digestion, loss of appetite**

  LIQUID EXTRACT 100–300 mg dried herb equivalent, taken three times a day before meals.
  INFUSION Add 0.6–2 g of dried root to 1 cup of boiling water. Infuse for 10 minutes, and then strain. Drink 3 cups a day before meals.

  IF SYMPTOMS PERSIST, CONSULT A DOCTOR

CAUTIONS
- Gentian could cause some side effects, such as headaches, if used in excess of prescribed doses.
- Pregnant or breastfeeding women should not use gentian.
- Individuals with gastroduodenal ulcers or high blood pressure should also avoid gentian.
- The plant should be harvested only by specialists because there is a danger of confusing it with white veratrum, and also because unsustainable harvesting has made it scarce in some areas.

Ginger *Zingiber officinale* Zingiberaceae

Originally from Asia, ginger is now cultivated in Africa, India, the West Indies, United States, Fiji and Australia. It is a tall, slender perennial with lance-shaped leaves and orchidlike flowers. The plant reproduces through its rhizome (rootstock) – the part used medicinally, in cooking, as a flavouring and in some confectionery. Ginger adds a spicy, hot and aromatic flavour to dishes from many Asian cuisines.

Parts used

RHIZOMES

- Rhizomes are gathered at least a year after planting but must be lifted carefully as they break easily.
- Root ginger is used fresh or dried.
- Dried ginger is used for infusions, extracts and tinctures and in many pharmaceutical products.

Constituents

Ginger is rich in aromatic volatile oils. These oils are its medically active constituents, and also give ginger its characteristic aroma and flavour. Ginger oil contains sesquiterpenes (known to be anti-inflammatory), particularly zingiberene. It also contains monoterpenes and aldehydes. These constituents have been shown by recent research to inhibit one of the most widespread common cold viruses. Pungent components called gingerols are thought to be responsible for ginger's antinausea effect.

Medicinal uses

Ginger is a strong circulatory stimulant. It has an anti-clotting effect and is also a vasodilator – so it can help to combat circulatory problems. It is also known to promote good digestion and is antispasmodic.

Ginger has a sedative effect. It also reduces nausea and vomiting, including travel sickness. A study in 1990 at St Bartholomew's Hospital, London, found that ginger reduced the incidence of nausea for post-operative patients. Its efficacy was comparable with metoclopramide, a widely used anti-emetic drug.

Research published in the *Journal of Nutrition* in 2000 showed that an extract of ginger reduced blood-cholesterol levels as well as inhibiting low-density lipoprotein (LDL) oxidation. This suggests that ginger could help to protect against the development of atherosclerosis and heart disease.

Ginger can help to sweat out a cold. It is an antiseptic expectorant and thus helpful for treating catarrhal coughs. It is also reputed to lower fever.

Australian studies that were carried out in 2000 revealed that several constituents of ginger had an anti-inflammatory effect and may, therefore, be helpful for chronic inflammatory conditions such as arthritis. The essential oil is prescribed for external use in a rub for the treatment of rheumatism and muscular pain.

Its antispasmodic effects make ginger a helpful remedy for treating period pains and digestive cramps. It can also help in curing flatulence and diarrhoea.

dried rhizome

Cultivation

Ginger is a tropical plant, but it will grow in a frost-free subtropical or warm temperate area. Plant rhizomes in a sunny position and keep well watered.

PREPARATION AND DOSAGE

- **To treat nausea and vomiting, morning sickness, poor digestion, period pains, flatulence, diarrhoea, colds**

    POWDER Take 0.5–1.5 g a day in water, or mixed with food.
    LIQUID EXTRACT Take up to 1 ml a day in a glass of water.
    TINCTURE (1:5 IN 60 PER CENT ALCOHOL) Take up to 30 drops a day in a glass of water.

- **To treat painful muscles or joints**

    CREAM (CONTAINING RHIZOME POWDER OR ESSENTIAL OIL) Apply to the affected parts two or three times a day (but not for acute joint inflammation).

IF SYMPTOMS PERSIST, CONSULT A DOCTOR

CAUTIONS

- Overdose can cause stomach upsets and drowsiness.
- Ginger can help pregnant women with morning sickness, but consult your doctor before using and do not take more than 2 g of dried ginger per day.
- Do not use if you are taking anticoagulant (blood-thinning) drugs or if you have gallstones.

Ginkgo *Ginkgo biloba* Ginkgoaceae **Also called** Maidenhair tree

Described by Charles Darwin as a living fossil, ginkgo is one of the world's oldest surviving tree species. It has grown in China, and elsewhere in the world, for more than two hundred million years – and individual trees live for a thousand years or more. Specimens have been found in the fossil record of both Australia and New Zealand. The ginkgo was brought to Europe in the 18th century as an ornamental tree.

Parts used

LEAVES
- Ginkgo is cultivated for the pharmaceutical industry in the Bordeaux region of France and South Carolina in the US.
- The crop is gathered by cutting branches from young trees.
- Ginkgo leaf is processed to produce liquid extracts, tablets and capsules.

Constituents

Ginkgo's active elements are ginkgolide terpenes and polyphenols – mainly flavonoids: anti-oxidants that strengthen blood vessels and improve the circulation. Many commercial preparations are standardised for these compounds, which are referred to on packaging as ginkgolides and bilobalides (terpenes) and ginkgo flavone glycosides (flavonoids). Ginkgo also contains ginkgolic acid, however many quality preparations are processed to reduce this constituent, which has a tendency to cause allergic headaches.

dried leaves

Medicinal use

Research carried out in 1999 showed that taking ginkgo extract counteracts declining mental faculties. A daily dose equivalent to 6–8 g dried leaf, given to elderly people for 12 weeks, improved concentration and memory and also reduced mood swings.

The extract's actions may be due to its effect on the circulation. Research has shown that ginkgo combats age-related deterioration of blood vessels in the brain. It also strengthens the veins and reduces bleeding in capillaries, and in addition can be used to remedy another age-related condition called acrocyanosis – what appears to be permanent bruising, especially on hands and feet.

In 1997, Chinese scientists found that ginkgolides had effects that may benefit asthma sufferers and help prevent conditions such as atherosclerosis. Herbalists prescribe ginkgo to enhance alertness in people of any age, and to treat impotence.

Cultivation

Place this cold-hardy but slow-growing plant in a rich, well-drained soil in sun.

PREPARATION AND DOSAGE

- **To treat mood swings and memory loss, to improve mental alertness and blood circulation**

  TABLETS 2 g standardised for content of ginkgo flavone glycosides and ginkgolides and bilobalides, taken three times a day. Do not exceed recommended dose unless supervised by a doctor.

IF SYMPTOMS PERSIST, CONSULT A DOCTOR

CAUTIONS

- Overdose can cause stomach upsets and dizziness. This appears to occur more commonly in patients who are frail, or have low body weight, indicating that a lower dose may be required.
- Do not give to children.
- Avoid if taking anticoagulant (blood-thinning) drugs, or if you have a bleeding disorder.
- Do not take if pregnant or breastfeeding.

Globe artichoke *Cynara scolymus* Asteraceae

Native to the Mediterranean, the globe artichoke is cultivated widely. Although enjoyed as a vegetable since the 15th century, its medicinal powers were not recognised until the 20th century. This herbaceous perennial grows up to 1.5 m tall, with a thick, ridged stem. The large, jagged leaves are grey-green, with a whitish down on their underside. Thistlelike, purple-green flowers appear in summer.

Parts used
LEAVES AND FLOWERS
- The leaves are picked, then dried and used in liquid extracts, capsules and decoctions.
- The unopened flower heads and fleshy bases are eaten as a vegetable.

Constituents
The leaves are rich in organic and phenolic acids, including cynarin, a bitter aromatic that is one of the most important constituents. They also contain sesquiterpene lactones, flavonoids, potassium salts, provitamin A and numerous enzymes.

Medicinal uses
Globe artichoke is mainly used to treat digestive problems, especially those linked to the liver and gall bladder, including indigestion, constipation and intolerance of fatty food. Globe artichoke is also useful for the treatment of nausea, abdominal distension and flatulence.

In 2001, German scientists noted that the flavonoids in the leaves could stimulate bile flow and encourage regeneration of liver cells. Earlier, the same team had also shown that the leaf extract can help to lower blood-cholesterol levels. The same effects were noted by Japanese researchers in 2002.

The flavonoids, assisted by the acids and potassium salts, also act as diuretics, easing kidney problems.

Cultivation
Globe artichoke thrives in moist, rich loam and warm temperatures. Sow seeds in early spring in well-drained soil in sun. Protect plants from frost. To get large heads, all lateral heads should be removed. Pick the unopened flower heads and leaves in early summer.

dried leaves

cross-section of an unopened flower head

PREPARATION AND DOSAGE

- **To treat indigestion, sluggish liver, constipation, fluid retention**

  LIQUID EXTRACT 0.5–1 g dried herb equivalent, three times a day.
  TABLETS, CAPSULES 0.5–1 g dried herb equivalent (standardised for cynarin content), three times a day.

- **To treat high cholesterol levels**

  LIQUID EXTRACT 1.5–3 g dried herb equivalent, three times a day.
  TABLETS, CAPSULES 1.5–3 g dried herb equivalent (standardised for cynarin content), three times a day.
  High doses for cholesterol reflect those used in clinical research.

IF SYMPTOMS PERSIST, CONSULT A DOCTOR

CAUTIONS

- Do not use any globe artichoke preparation if you have gallstones or an obstructed gall bladder.
- Taking globe artichoke is not recommended when breastfeeding, as it reduces the flow of milk.
- The sesquiterpene lactones can cause allergic reactions, in which case all globe artichoke preparations should be avoided.
- If you are allergic to other plants in the Asteraceae family, such as daisies, chamomile or echinacea, you may also be allergic to globe artichoke.

Goat's rue *Galega officinalis* Fabaceae **Also called** Galega, French lilac

Growing wild in southern Europe and parts of Asia, goat's rue is a bushy perennial that can reach a height of 1–1.5 m. If bruised, the leaves emit a goaty smell, possibly accounting for its name. The leaves consist of six to eight bright green leaflets, and blue, pink or white, butterfly-shaped flowers appear all summer. When ripe, its long seed pod twists and bursts open to scatter the seeds.

dried flowering tops

Parts used

FLOWERS
- The flowers are collected when they are in full bloom during summer.
- Once dried, they are used in making infusions, powders and tinctures.

Constituents

The alkaloid galegine and its derivatives are found throughout the plant. Goat's rue also contains chromium, flavonoids and tannins.

Medicinal uses

Goat's rue can be useful as a supplementary treatment for Type 2 (non-insulin dependent) diabetes, as it is rich in chromium, which helps to combat the body's inability to absorb glucose. Also, animal studies in Scotland have shown that its galegine can lower blood-sugar levels. While the herb is helpful, it is important that a diabetic patient also adheres to a strict diet and any prescribed regular medication.

In addition, the Scottish research noted the ability of galegine to reduce appetite, suggesting its potential for use in weight control.

Goat's rue is also recommended for digestive problems and is known to relieve chronic constipation. It is a diuretic, helping to prevent swelling resulting from fluid retention, and can increase perspiration as well. Galegine is also responsible for the plant's antibacterial powers, as shown by scientists in India in 2001. This, combined with the known anti-inflammatory effect of its flavonoids, may explain why goat's rue is sometimes used to treat fever.

Cultivation

Grow goat's rue from seed, planted in autumn, or by division. It is suited to deep, moist, well-drained soil, and should be positioned in the sun or a lightly shaded spot.

PREPARATION AND DOSAGE

- Preparations containing goat's rue should be taken only in consultation with a doctor or medical herbalist. As high doses are potentially toxic, it is very important to observe the exact dosages prescribed

IF SYMPTOMS PERSIST, CONSULT A DOCTOR

CAUTIONS

- As goat's rue can react adversely, especially with other drugs, it is essential to seek medical advice before using the plant.
- Prescribed doses of goat's rue must be adhered to since excessive consumption can lead to dangerous reductions in blood sugar.
- Although goat's rue preparations are sometimes prescribed to increase breast milk production, it is best to avoid them until toxicity studies have been undertaken. Toxicity has been reported in the milk of lactating sheep that have eaten excessive quantities of goat's rue.

Golden rod *Solidago virgaurea* Asteraceae **Also called** Woundwort

A common garden perennial, golden rod bears feathery yellow plumes that brighten up the autumn border. The plant grows widely in Europe, where its medicinal use extends back at least as far as the ancient Roman empire, and probably beyond. One of its most popular uses in traditional medicine was to promote wound-healing, which gave rise to the plant's nickname, 'woundwort'.

Parts used
AERIAL PARTS
- Plants are gathered in the autumn.
- They are dried and broken up into small fragments.
- Golden rod is used in the preparation of infusions and liquid extracts.

Constituents
The plant contains an essential oil, tannins that have astringent qualities, flavonoids such as quercetin and rutin, triterpenoid saponins and phenolic acids – antiseptic substances that assist in the reduction of inflammation.

Medicinal uses
Golden rod is a diuretic, as well as an expectorant. It also heals wounds, ulcers and other skin ailments.

The astringent tannins in golden rod contribute to its healing qualities and combat diarrhoea. Its flavonoids reduce the permeability of blood vessels and increase their strength, thus helping to improve circulation.

Golden rod is a remedy for inflammation and infection of the urinary tract – cystitis and urethritis, for example. The plant's analgesic and anti-inflammatory properties have been attributed to a phenolic acid called leiocarposide.

The herb has long been used to prevent and eliminate bladder stones and to stimulate urination. Its efficacy was proved by Polish studies carried out in 1986 and 1988 that showed the diuretic effects of leiocarposide, and its value in treating bladder stones.

Gargling with an infusion of golden rod can soothe a sore throat or a cough, while drinking the infusion will help with chronic nasal catarrh and hayfever.

The herb may also be prescribed for vaginal and oral thrush. German research published in 1987 backed this application by showing that virgaureasaponin, one of the plant's saponins, is an effective antifungal.

Cultivation
Grow from seed – it will spread by self-sowing once it is established. Golden rod likes well-drained soil in a sunny border.

dried aerial parts

PREPARATION AND DOSAGE
- **To treat cystitis, urethritis, bladder stones, insufficient urination, chronic nasal catarrh**

  LIQUID EXTRACT 0.5–1 g dried herb equivalent, taken with plenty of water, three times a day.

  INFUSION Put 1.5–3 g of herb into 1 cup of boiling water. Infuse for 10–15 minutes, then strain. Drink 3–5 cups a day.

- **To treat sore throat**

  GARGLE Make an infusion (as above), allow to cool and use as a gargle when required.

- **To treat wounds, ulcers**

  COMPRESS Put 50 g of the herb into 1 litre of boiling water. Leave to boil for 2 minutes. Soak a cloth with this decoction and apply twice a day.

IF SYMPTOMS PERSIST, CONSULT A DOCTOR

CAUTIONS
- To date, no side effects or toxicity have been recorded.
- People with chronic kidney disease should consult a doctor before using golden rod.

Golden seal
Hydrastis canadensis Ranunculaceae **Also called** Indian turmeric, Yellow puccoon, Yellowroot, Orangeroot Originating in North America, golden seal was used as a healing herb and an insect repellent by the Cherokee Indians. The plant belongs to the buttercup family, though it looks more like a miniature but inedible raspberry. Its dark yellow rhizome – which is short, thick and has many slender roots – spreads horizontally. Golden seal is endangered due to over-harvesting.

dried rhizome

rhizome

Parts used
RHIZOMES
- The rhizome is harvested in autumn after three years or more.
- The cut-up, dried rhizome is ground for capsules or made into liquid extracts.
- Golden seal is usually used as a liquid extract or a tincture, and may be combined with other plants.

Constituents
The main active components in the rhizome are alkaloids, including hydrastine and berberine. Hydrastine is known to constrict blood vessels and raise blood pressure. Berberine attacks bacteria and stimulates the immune system. Barberry contains very similar active constituents, and is often prescribed in place of golden seal, which is in short supply due to over-harvesting.

Medicinal uses
Golden seal has long been used in traditional medicine to stop bleeding, and is prescribed for blood loss between menstrual periods. The rhizome is good for blood circulation, making it useful for treating piles, varicose veins and oedema in the lower legs – when it may be combined with other plants such as witch hazel.

Golden seal is prescribed for catarrh, tinnitus, eczema, and eye and ear infections.

In 1999, American scientists found that golden seal increased immunoglobulin production, strengthening the immune system.

Studies published in 2001 in *Planta Medica* reported on the antibacterial activity of berberine, while Chinese scientists found that it restored a regular heartbeat, showing that the plant may be useful for arrhythmia.

Cultivation
Very hard to cultivate, golden seal needs a humus-rich, well-drained moist soil, preferably in shade.

PREPARATION AND DOSAGE
- **To treat period problems, chest infections, poor circulation**
  TABLETS, CAPSULES 250–500 mg dried rhizome equivalent, three times a day.
  LIQUID EXTRACT As prescribed by your medical herbalist.

IF SYMPTOMS PERSIST, CONSULT A DOCTOR

CAUTIONS
- The alkaloids in golden seal are toxic at high doses.
- Never take more than 2 g a day, except under supervision by a medical herbalist.
- Do not use for more than three weeks at a time, and take a two-week break between courses.
- Golden seal is not recommended for use by people with high blood pressure.
- Do not take during pregnancy or if you are breastfeeding.
- Do not give to children.

Gotu kola   *Centella asiatica* Apiaceae **Also called** Indian pennywort

A tropical perennial, gotu kola grows commonly in Madagascar, China, Indonesia, India, Sri Lanka, South Africa and the South Pacific. It thrives in damp, swampy habitats beside ponds and lakes or in paddy fields. It is a small, herbaceous plant, recognisable by its clusters of frilly, fan-shaped leaves. It bears white or purple to pink flowers beneath the foliage in summer, and these give way to small, oval fruit.

Parts used
WHOLE PLANT, LEAVES
- The whole plant or leaves are collected and used fresh or dried in infusions, decoctions and powders.
- The plant extract is used for tablets, capsules and ointments.

Constituents
The active compounds are triterpenoid saponins, including asiaticoside and brahmoside, which help to heal wounds. It also contains flavonoids, which help to strengthen the veins, and traces of essential oil.

Medicinal uses
Taken by mouth, gotu kola has a positive effect on vein and lymph disorders. It has reputed vasodilatory effects and is useful for strengthening veins and treating symptoms such as varicose veins, capillary bleeding and haemorrhoids. A review published in *Angiology,* in 2001, noted the effectiveness of gotu kola in treating chronic vein problems.

Gotu kola can help to treat skin disorders, including superficial wounds, minor burns, scars, psoriasis and ulcers. For all of these it may be taken internally and/or applied topically. In 1988, Italian researchers showed that its triterpenoids can stimulate the synthesis of connective tissue in human skin, which is likely to contribute to its wound-healing ability. Researchers in the UK found that the use of a cream containing gotu kola helps to reduce stretch marks during pregnancy.

The plant is also believed to have anti-inflammatory properties, and has been used to ease rheumatic complaints, and to treat eczema.

As a tonic, it is used to strengthen the nervous and immune systems, and to improve mental alertness and concentration.

dried plant

Cultivation
Gotu kola can be grown from seed, planted in spring, in a moist, sunny or lightly shaded plot. It needs temperatures above 10°C. It should not be confused with the widespread pennywort.

PREPARATION AND DOSAGE
- **To treat the immune system, the nervous system, poor circulation, vein and skin problems**

  LIQUID EXTRACT As prescribed by your medical herbalist.

  TABLETS, CAPSULES Up to 600 mg dried plant equivalent, three times a day.

- **To treat skin damage**

  OINTMENT Massage in thoroughly once or twice a day, as directed, after the damaged area has been disinfected.

IF SYMPTOMS PERSIST, CONSULT A DOCTOR

CAUTIONS
- A few cases of allergic reactions have been noted. Otherwise, the plant has caused no adverse side effects when used as prescribed.
- Do not take gotu kola internally during pregnancy.
- Do not confuse gotu kola with brahmi *Bacopa monnieri* (see p. 51).

Grape seed *Vitis vinifera* Vitaceae

For thousands of years the grape vine has provided fruit, wine and herbal medication. Grapes were cultivated in ancient Egypt, 4000 years ago, and it was the ancient Romans who first introduced them into France. Vines bear clusters of sweet-smelling pale green flowers followed by bunches of grapes, fruit which contains four seeds. The large, palmate leaves turn fiery red in autumn.

Parts used

SEEDS AND LEAVES

- The leaves and seeds are collected when the grapes ripen in autumn.
- The seeds are separated from the grape and used in tablets and capsules.
- Modern usage focuses on the seeds, however the leaves may also be used medicinally.
- The precise moment for harvesting the leaves is determined chemically, in order to maximise the amount of active constituents.
- The leaves are air-dried away from sunlight and are occasionally used to make infusions.

Constituents

The most important constituents of grape seed are anti-oxidant flavonoids that are collectively referred to as oligomeric proanthocyanidins (OPCs). The leaves are also rich in anthocyanins, in addition to organic acids, sugars, vitamins A, B_1, B_2 and C, and tannins.

Medicinal uses

Grape seed extract is one of the richest sources of anti-oxidant proanthocyanidins, and thus may be of great benefit to the circulatory system and heart. In 1994, Italian researchers showed that grape anthocyanins prevented free radical damage to tiny blood capillaries. Consequently, grape seed is often prescribed for the treatment of bruising and other conditions associated with bleeding under the skin.

dried leaves

Clinical trials carried out in Milan in 1999 also confirmed that anthocyanins are good for treating chronic (long-term) vein weakness. Grape seed is thus an appropriate treatment for oedema – heaviness and swelling in the lower legs. It is also prescribed for the treatment of varicose veins in addition to haemorrhoids.

Other therapeutic uses include the treatment of high blood pressure and high blood cholesterol levels. Additional actions of grape seed include anti-allergenic activity and a protective and supportive action for the anti-oxidant nutrient vitamin C. The anti-oxidants in grape seed may also offer protection against some cancers and heart disease.

Cultivation

Vines can be grown in any warm spot and are drought-tolerant when established. They make a quick cover for a pergola or fence. They grow best in well-drained, alkaline soils.

PREPARATION AND DOSAGE

- **To treat varicose veins and other vascular disorders, haemorrhoids, blood marks under the skin, high cholesterol**

  TABLETS, CAPSULES Up to 24 g dried seed equivalent per day. Choose a product that is standardised for its content of anthocyanins (sometimes called OPCs or proanthocyanidins), and follow the manufacturer's instructions.

  IF SYMPTOMS PERSIST, CONSULT A DOCTOR

CAUTIONS

- Grape seed is not recommended for use by pregnant or breastfeeding women.

Grapefruit seed *Citrus x aurantium (C. x paradisi)* Rutaceae

First described in the 18th century, the grapefruit tree, which grows up to 8 m in height, is thought to have developed as an accidental hybrid in the West Indies. It was probably derived by crossing the sweet orange with the pomelo *Citrus maxima*, which has a similar but larger fruit. It has been cultivated since 1823, when the first seeds were taken to Florida, and is now grown around the world.

Parts used

SEEDS
- The fruit is harvested from autumn to spring.
- It is commercially processed to obtain grapefruit seed extract.

Constituents

Grapefruit seed extract contains flavonoids and other phenolic compounds, amino acids, fatty acids and vitamins E and C.

Medicinal uses

Grapefuit is believed to possess antimicrobial properties and is indicated in the treatment of bacterial, fungal, viral and parasitic infections.

It can be used to combat colds, influenza and sore throats, as well as intestinal infections and diarrhoea.

In vitro studies on commercial grapefruit seed extract performed in Texas in 2002 demonstrated powerful antibacterial activity. But other studies that have confirmed the antimicrobial efficacy of commercial extracts have also detected the presence of synthetic preservatives, causing some researchers to doubt the natural plant's efficacy.

Although it is likely that the flavonoids and triterpenoids of natural grapefruit seed will be shown to display antibacterial effects, further research is necessary to clarify this issue. In the meantime, organically produced grapefruit seed extract is recommended.

Cultivation

Grapefruit is grown commercially in subtropical climates in a range of soils, using an appropriate rootstock. It needs full sun, well-drained soil and ample moisture.

liquid extract

PREPARATION AND DOSAGE
- Grapefruit seed should be used internally only on advice from a medical herbalist

IF SYMPTOMS PERSIST, CONSULT A DOCTOR

CAUTIONS
- Preparations made from grapefruit seed extract may irritate the digestive system.

Greater celandine
Chelidonium majus Papaveraceae **Also called** Celandine, Garden celandine, Swallow wort, Tetter wort

Greater celandine is native to Europe and Asia, where it colonises hedgerows, wasteland and damp areas such as ditches. It bears small, yellow flowers from spring to summer. The whole plant is covered in fine, bristly hairs. If you snap the stalk or root it exudes a dark orange sap that will leave yellow stains and has a foul odour.

Parts used
AERIAL PARTS
- The plant is harvested and dried when it is in flower.
- Although greater celandine has been used as a decoction in traditional Chinese medicine, Western herbalists prefer to use a liquid extract because it is thought to be a more effective way of extracting and using the active alkaloids.

Constituents
Greater celandine's active compounds are alkaloids, including chelidonine and protopine, both of which have been shown to have antispasmodic activity. In addition, greater celandine contains organic acids, flavonoids and carotenoids.

Medicinal uses
In traditional Asian medicine, greater celandine is used to calm the nervous system. Today, however, the herb tends to be prescribed more often for the treatment of liver problems.

The herb's antispasmodic action can ease spasms in the upper digestive tract and other digestive disorders, and is also helpful in treating coughs and asthma.

Greater celandine acts against bacteria and viruses. In addition, Korean scientists reported in 2002 that it may be an anticancer agent.

In vitro studies carried out in Germany in 1996 suggest that greater celandine could have a role to play in treating illnesses of the nervous system. The plant has mild analgesic and sedative qualities and can be used to ease rheumatic pain.

The sap has long been a remedy for wart removal.

Cultivation
Greater celandine likes moist soil and tolerates sun and shade. Propagate in spring, either from seed or by root division. It will self-sow in favourable conditions. Do not plant greater celandine in gardens used by children, or cultivate it for home use.

dried aerial parts

PREPARATION AND DOSAGE
- Greater celandine preparations should be taken internally only in consultation with a qualified medical herbalist
- To treat skins conditions such as warts, ringworm and eczema

  LIQUID EXTRACT OR FRESH SAP Apply to the affected area one to three times a day.

  IF SYMPTOMS PERSIST, CONSULT A DOCTOR

CAUTIONS
- Greater celandine is poisonous in large amounts, and can cause nausea and dysentery. Take this herb only under professional supervision.
- Pregnant or breastfeeding women should avoid this herb.
- Avoid greater celandine if you have low blood pressure.
- Do not give to children.
- Limit use to two weeks at a time.

Greater plantain
Plantago major, P. lanceolata **Plantaginaceae** **Also called** Common plantain, Ribwort plantain, Waybread

The flat rosette of leaves at the base of the greater plantain, *Plantago major*, blights many lawns. The leaves of the ribwort plantain, *P. lanceolata*, are spear shaped and upright. Both plants bear tiny flowers in cylindrical or egg-shaped spikes. Plantain is native to Europe and Asia, but is naturalised throughout New Zealand and much of Australia.

Parts used
LEAVES
- Leaves are collected during the summer, preferably before the plant flowers, and dried.
- Both species are used in soothing remedies, usually applied externally.
- They are also used in preparing infusions, liquid extracts and capsules.

dried leaves

Constituents
The leaves of both plantains contain an iridoid called aucubin, and flavonoids – anti-oxidants that strengthen blood vessels and are often anti-inflammatory. Plantain also contains mucilages.

Medicinal uses
Both forms of plantain have a long history of use in country lotions and potions to treat external complaints from itchy, chapped skin, cuts and grazes to insect bites or sore eyes.

Taken internally, the plant has a gentle expectorant action and the mucilage it contains soothes sore and inflamed mucous membranes, making it ideal for treating inflammation of the urinary tract, as well as for coughs and mild bronchitis.

Bulgarian research in 1982 showed plantain extract to be an effective way of treating chronic bronchitis, and in 1983 it was shown that plantain relieved constriction of the airways. Taken internally, it can ease asthma, catarrh, laryngitis, pharyngitis, hay fever and various allergic reactions that affect breathing.

The iridoids in plantain are anti-inflammatory. They were examined by scientists working in Spain in 2002, who found aucubin to have clearly demonstrable anti-inflammatory effects.

Plantain appears to have antibacterial properties. Norwegian studies in 2000 showed that a polysaccharide extract from the plant fought pneumococcal infection. Swedish research also suggested that polysaccharide injections could protect against streptococcus.

Cultivation
Plantain is an invasive plant and weed. Grow in a wild part of the garden, in sun or light shade.

PREPARATION AND DOSAGE
- **To treat irritated or inflamed urinary tract, bronchitis, pharyngitis, laryngitis, hay fever**
  INFUSION 1–4 g infused in 1 cup of boiling water for 5 minutes before straining. Drink 3 cups a day between meals.
- **To treat insect bites, chapped or cracked skin, grazes**
  CREAM Follow manufacturer's instructions.
  POULTICE Chop 200 g fresh, washed plantain and mix with sufficient boiled water to make a paste. Spread paste onto gauze or cotton strips and apply to skin, keeping in place until it cools. Apply olive oil to the skin to prevent the poultice from sticking.

IF SYMPTOMS PERSIST, CONSULT A DOCTOR

CAUTIONS
- No adverse side effects or toxicity have been reported to date, although an allergic reaction is possible.
- Do not use plantain from areas that may have been treated with a pesticide or herbicide.

Green tea, black tea *Camellia sinensis* Theaceae **Also called** Tea plant

Originating in China and India, tea is still a vitally important crop in both countries, although it is now grown elsewhere in the world, including Australia. Black and green tea are both prepared from the same plant – the leaves are simply cured in different ways. The shrub can reach a height of 10 m, but it is normally clipped to just 1 m. Tea flowers are white and sweet smelling, while fruits are round capsules.

Parts used

LEAVES

- The leaves, gathered all year round, usually by hand, are used to make green or black tea.
- The topmost leaves are more aromatic. Just the leaf bud and two adjacent young leaves are picked.
- Black tea is fermented, while green tea is gently steamed. The active constituents in green tea are stronger.
- Tea is drunk as an infusion, either on its own or blended with other plants such as mint or lemon.
- Tea leaf is used in medicinal preparations, including tablets and capsules.

Constituents

The main active constituent of both green and black teas is caffeine, which has a stimulating effect on the central nervous system. Tea contains phenolic acids, flavonoids and tannins. However, the fermentation alters the polyphenols in black tea, and green tea appears to be the more medicinally powerful.

Medicinal uses

Tea leaves have been used for thousands of years to make a thirst-quenching infusion and a medicinal beverage. In traditional Chinese medicine, green tea is prescribed for a wide range of ailments including headaches, depression and fatigue. It is also reputed to help prolong the lives of regular drinkers.

Research in recent years has focused on the cancer-fighting potential of green tea. Several animal studies have found that anti-oxidant polyphenols in green tea inhibit the growth of various cancers – particularly those of the prostate, pancreas, colon and rectum. These anti-oxidant compounds work by blocking the formation of cancer-causing compounds such as nitrosamines, suppressing the activation of carcinogens and neutralising cancer-causing agents.

The stimulant and diuretic effects of both green and black teas are largely due to their caffeine content. The stimulant action makes tea a good remedy for nervous exhaustion, and its diuretic effect is a useful complement for people following weight loss programs. Tea also has antibacterial properties, and its tannins make it an effective remedy for treating diarrhoea.

A cooled infusion of tea can be applied externally to soothe tired eyes and skin inflammation. Researchers working in America in 2002 confirmed that tea pigments definitely do have anti-inflammatory properties.

dried leaves

Cultivation

This tropical to subtropical plant grows best in warm, humid climates. It can be grown in a pot or garden, preferring a rich, acid soil.

PREPARATION AND DOSAGE

- **To treat nervous exhaustion, excess weight, diarrhoea**

  INFUSION Put 1 teaspoon of black or green tea into 1 cup of boiling water. Leave to infuse for 10 minutes. Drink 2 cups a day. For diarrhoea, make a stronger infusion of 1.5–2 teaspoons of tea per 1 cup of water.
  CAPSULES Up to 500 mg green tea extract. Choose a product standardised for its polyphenol content, and take according to the manufacturer's instructions.

IF SYMPTOMS PERSIST, CONSULT A DOCTOR

CAUTIONS

- Drinking tea in the evening may induce insomnia.
- A large intake of tea can cause constipation, indigestion and agitation, due to excessive caffeine.
- Pregnant women are advised to limit their intake of tea to 2 or 3 cups a day.

Guarana *Paullinia cupana* Sapindaceae

Native to the Amazon region of South America, guarana is a climbing woody vine with a fluted stem. Clusters of yellow flowers are followed by bright red fruits, each of which contains one bulky black seed surrounded by red, fleshy skin. The seeds contain caffeine, and were used by Amazonian Indians in a stimulant drink. This same property accounts for their inclusion in many modern 'energy' bars and drinks.

Parts used

SEEDS

- Seeds are collected when ripe, grilled, and their outer coating removed.
- They are ground in water to make a paste, rolled into bars and cured.
- The seeds can also be dried and roasted or powdered for capsules.
- Guarana is added to soft drinks and confectionery.

Constituents

Guarana has a high caffeine content: more than twice as much as coffee. Caffeine stimulates the central nervous system, increases the metabolic rate and is a mild diuretic. Guarana also contains small amounts of theobromine (a stimulant present in chocolate), theophylline and larger quantities of starch. Its bitter taste comes from astringent tannins.

Medicinal uses

Guarana is a traditional South American preparation, valued for the energising effect of its high caffeine content. It is used in stimulant drinks, as well as to treat nervous exhaustion. Its tannins make it a useful remedy for minor cases of diarrhoea. It is reputed to afford some protection against malaria.

Guarana is believed to increase the breakdown of fats, and is used to complement slimming diets. In 2001, a US clinical trial found that people taking a herbal preparation containing guarana lost significantly more weight than a group taking a placebo. Guarana was also found to reduce fats present in the blood.

In guarana's native Brazil, studies performed in 1988 found that it inhibited blood clotting. This suggests that guarana has potential in the treatment of thrombosis. Also, in 1997, Brazilian researchers found that guarana increased the stamina of mice during exercise.

seeds with outer covering removed

They also observed that guarana enhanced the animals' memories – they performed better in a maze – and appeared to reverse induced amnesia. However, these effects have not, so far, been replicated in human subjects.

Cultivation

Guarana is a native of the Amazon rainforest and requires a hot, humid, but shaded environment in order to thrive. It will not grow at temperatures below 18°C. Propagate from cuttings.

PREPARATION AND DOSAGE

- **To stimulate energy and alertness, aid weight loss**

  CAPSULES Up to 1000 mg of guarana, but not exceeding 50 mg caffeine. Take according to manufacturer's instructions.

- Note that guarana is more effective when taken infrequently, and that regular use may lead to withdrawal symptoms when you stop taking it. This also applies to other sources of caffeine

IF SYMPTOMS PERSIST, CONSULT A DOCTOR

CAUTIONS

- Do not exceed 100 mg of caffeine in an hour, or 600 mg in 24 hours.
- Guarana can cause rapid heart rate, upset stomach, headache, agitation and insomnia. Discontinue if these symptoms appear.
- Do not take if pregnant or breastfeeding.
- Avoid if you have cardiovascular disease or high blood pressure.
- Avoid excessive or prolonged use.
- If taking prescribed drugs, especially anticoagulants (blood-thinning drugs), consult a doctor before using guarana.

Gymnema
Gymnema sylvestre Asclepiadaceae **Also called** Gurmar (Hindi), Gurmabooti, Ram's horn, Meshasringi Gymnema is native to India, Sri Lanka and parts of Africa and Asia, although it is also found as far south as southern Australia. It is a liana – a large climbing vine – with small, yellow flowers and long, woody stems that may reach lengths of up to 8 m. It is found growing in tropical forests and in areas of bushland or woods, generally at altitudes of between 100 and 1000 m.

Parts used
LEAVES
- In traditional Ayurvedic medicine, the leaf is chewed to reduce the subject's ability to taste sweet foods.
- The roots and fruit have also been used in Ayurvedic medicine.
- In modern Western herbal medicine, usage centres mainly around liquid extracts made from the leaf. However, tablets are also available.

Constituents
Gymnema contains a polypeptide called gurmarin, which takes its name from the plant's Hindi name, Gurmar, meaning 'sugar destroyer'. Saponins, particularly gymnemasaponins and gymnemic acids, are also present, and these provide a significant part of the plant's activity. Other components include amino acids, an alkaloid, and the nutrients choline and betaine.

Medicinal uses
Gymnema has the peculiar property of decreasing the taste buds' ability to detect sweet tastes. This effect occurs after the leaf – or an infusion or liquid extract made from the leaf – has been held in the mouth for 30–60 seconds. Gymnema may offer valuable support for weight-loss programs, since research shows that appetite and kilojoule consumption are both reduced after pre-treatment with gymnema in this way.

Gymnema also has the potential to aid in the treatment of diabetes and other blood-sugar disorders. Indian research carried out in 1990 showed that gymnema offers benefits in both Type 1 and Type 2 diabetes.

After 18–20 months taking doses of a concentrated extract equivalent to about 8 g of dried gymnema leaf, patients were found to have improved levels of blood glucose and glycosylated haemoglobin (a measure used to assess blood sugar over time). Levels of cholesterol and other blood lipids were also reduced.

Gymnema has also been used in Ayurvedic medicine for a range of conditions that are not related to blood sugar, including urinary disorders, coughs, constipation and malaria.

dried leaves

Cultivation
Gymnema requires a tropical to subtropical climate. In its natural environment it grows in the wet season. Grow in sun to light shade in any well-drained soil, and water regularly. Provide a wire or trellis for support. Plants can be grown from seed or cutting.

PREPARATION AND DOSAGE
- **To aid weight loss and reduce sugar consumption**

  LIQUID EXTRACT 1–2 g dried leaf equivalent. Hold 1–2 ml of the liquid extract in the mouth for 30–60 seconds before swallowing with water. Repeat three to four times during the day.

- **As supportive treatment for diabetes**

  As prescribed by a doctor.

  IF SYMPTOMS PERSIST, CONSULT A DOCTOR

CAUTIONS
- Diabetes is a serious condition that requires medical management. If you are diabetic, do not take gymnema unless you are being supervised by your doctor, as it may affect the amount of insulin or other diabetes medication you require.
- Side effects of reflux and irritation of the gastric mucous membrane may occur, due to the herb's saponin content.
- Gymnema is not recommended for use by pregnant or breastfeeding women. Its safety has yet to be confirmed.

Hawthorn
Crataegus laevigata (syn. *C. oxyacantha*), *C. monogyna* Rosaceae

Also called May tree, Midland hawthorn Widely used as hedging throughout Europe, the bushy hawthorn, or may tree, also grows in Australia and New Zealand. Hawthorn can reach 10 m in height, and according to country folklore, the flowers' sweet but putrid scent was bequeathed by the Great Plague of London, which was raging at May-blossom time in 1665.

Parts used
FLOWERS AND BERRIES
- The flowers quickly spoil and must be picked while in bud, or just before they open in spring.
- The freshly picked flowers must not be allowed to lose their scent.
- They are spread out in thin layers on cloth and dried away from sunlight in a well-aired place.
- Both berries and flowers are used in infusions, capsules and tinctures.

Constituents
The hawthorn flower contains aromatic amines such as tyramine, which are known to be good for the heart. Flowers also contain flavonoids – anti-oxidants that dilate and protect blood vessels and help to prevent cardiovascular disease. The berries contain anthocyanins – pigments that are thought to be helpful in maintaining healthy blood vessels.

dried berries

Medicinal uses
The use of hawthorn for medicinal purposes dates back to the Middle Ages. At first, only the fruit was used, but today both fruit and flowers are known to have beneficial properties. Traditionally, hawthorn was recommended for angina, hardening of the arteries, high blood pressure and heart palpitations.

Hawthorn's effects on the heart and circulatory system have been the subject of extensive research – and scientists have proved its usefulness in the treatment of cardiovascular illnesses. It strengthens the heart and encourages a regular heart-beat. It improves the flow of blood to the heart and, by relaxing the involuntary muscles, helps to lower blood pressure. It dilates the blood cells and reduces the capillaries' resistance to blood flow. This latter effect was demonstrated in a series of animal trials conducted in France in 1985. Finally, by reducing heart palpitations, hawthorn exerts a general calming effect on the central nervous system.

Herbalists prescribe hawthorn for the treatment of rapid or irregular heart-beat. It is also recommended as a tonic for a weak heart – such as the tired heart of a very old person.

Cultivation
Hawthorn can be grown from cuttings. It is frost-hardy, likes full sun and tolerates most soils, but prefers an alkaline, rich, moist loam.

fruiting branch

flowering branch

PREPARATION AND DOSAGE
- **Hawthorn preparations should be taken only in consultation with a qualified medical herbalist**

IF SYMPTOMS PERSIST, CONSULT A DOCTOR

CAUTIONS
- Hawthorn is a long-term preventive remedy. Do not attempt to treat any form of heart disease without consulting a doctor, and do not take hawthorn if you are taking heart or blood pressure medication, except under medical supervision.
- Do not take hawthorn if you are pregnant or breastfeeding.
- Side effects have occasionally been documented for hawthorn. Symptoms include gastrointestinal disturbances, heart palpitations, insomnia, agitation and dizziness. If these occur, stop taking it.
- Large amounts may cause drowsiness, so avoid driving.

Heartsease
Viola tricolor Violaceae **Also called** Wild pansy, Johnny jump-up

A common sight in gardens, but also found wild in European hedgerows and on wasteland in summer, the wild pansy, or heartsease, grows to a height of around 40 cm. This herbaceous annual has angular, branching stems with spear-shaped, deeply indented leaves. A single, delicate flower – usually purple, yellow or white, but often a mix of all three – sits elegantly at the end of each stalk.

Parts used
FLOWERS, LEAVES AND STEMS
- The aerial parts are gathered from heartsease in summer, in the early morning before the flowers have opened.
- After drying quickly but gently, out of direct sunlight, the leaves, stems and flowers are all used to make infusions, liquid extracts and compresses.

Constituents
Salicylic acid and its derivatives have been identified in the aerial parts of heartsease, as well as mucilages, anthocyanosides, tannins, flavonoids and peptides.

Medicinal uses
The anti-inflammatory action of the salicylic acid in heartsease makes the plant highly effective when applied as a compress to ease skin problems such as acne, eczema, impetigo and seborrhoea (a scalp ailment caused by excessive secretion of sebum). An infusion of the aerial parts is also traditionally taken to treat these and similar conditions. Also, heartsease may be used to treat inflammation caused by rheumatism. Taken internally, it can treat respiratory tract infections and its mucilage also has a beneficial expectorant effect.

The plant's anthocyanosides and flavonoids help to keep blood vessels healthy and improve circulation. This is why it is sometimes prescribed for atherosclerosis (hardening of the arteries) and other heart conditions, which could account for the plant's name.

In addition, heartsease is known as a laxative and diuretic, helping to eliminate toxins and treat urinary tract infections. The tannins can boost immunity, and research in Norway has recently shown that the plant's peptides can help to fight infection.

Cultivation
Suited to any well-drained soil. Plant seeds in spring in a sunny or lightly shaded spot. It grows as a short-lived perennial in mild areas.

dried flowers, leaves and stems

PREPARATION AND DOSAGE
- **To treat eczema, impetigo, acne, pruritis**

  LIQUID EXTRACT 1–4 g dried herb equivalent, three times a day.
  INFUSION 1–4 g dried herb infused in a cup of boiling water for 10 minutes before straining. Drink 3 cups a day between meals.

- **To treat acne, seborrhoea, eczema (especially in children)**

  COMPRESS Add 20–30 g of fresh flowers to 500 ml of boiling water. Infuse for 15 minutes. Strain. Soak a compress in the infusion. Apply to affected areas in the morning and evening.

IF SYMPTOMS PERSIST, CONSULT A DOCTOR

CAUTIONS
- Raw or untreated heartsease can be slightly toxic, so avoid it.
- Never use heartsease internally for young children.
- Excessive use of heartsease can cause adverse skin reactions.

Hops *Humulus lupulus* Cannabaceae

A native of Europe, but now cultivated in New Zealand, Tasmania and parts of Victoria, hops is a climbing perennial. The tough, twisting stem bears heart-shaped leaves, divided into sharply indented lobes. Flowers of different sexes grow on separate plants. It is the female flowers that produce the decorative conelike 'hops' that have been used since ancient times in medicines and in brewing.

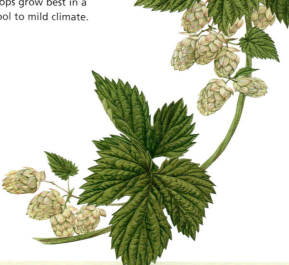

Parts used
FEMALE FLOWERS (CONES)
- The female flowers, or cones, are picked when they are yellowish green in colour in autumn.
- Once dried, the cones have an aromatic, bitter taste. They are mainly used in brewing, but are also made into infusions, powders and extracts for medicinal use. In balneotherapy (therapeutic use of baths), they are employed for their calming properties.

Constituents
The aromatic taste of the plant is due to the presence of an essential oil composed of mono and sesquiterpenoid hydrocarbons and oxygenated compounds. The compounds that cause its bitter taste include humulone and lupulone. Oestrogenic substances are also present.

dried cones

Medicinal uses
The sedative and sleep-inducing properties of hops, particularly of the essential oil and its oxygenated compounds, have been confirmed by various studies. Indeed, clinical trials in Germany showed a preparation of hops and valerian to be as effective as benzodiazepines in remedying sleep disorders. This combination was also demonstrated to be effective as a treatment for nervous problems.

The bitter compounds are known to help the digestive system to work more efficiently, and research has also revealed that the humulone and lupulone bitters can help in destroying bacteria and are antispasmodic.

Hops, along with several other plants that contain compounds with similar properties to the female hormone oestrogen, is being studied for its potential use in treating some problems relating to the menstrual cycle and menopause.

Cultivation
Cuttings taken in autumn can be planted out in spring in rich, well-drained soil, in sun or light shade. Otherwise, buy ready-grown young plants. Hops grow best in a cool to mild climate.

PREPARATION AND DOSAGE
- **To treat insomnia, nervous tension**

    LIQUID EXTRACT 0.5–1 g dried cone equivalent. For insomnia, take one dose shortly before bed. For nervous tension, take three to four doses a day.
    INFUSION 1–2 teaspoons of fresh dried hops infused in 1 cup of boiling water for 10 minutes. For insomnia, drink 1 cup shortly before bed. For nervous tension, drink 3 cups a day.
    BATH Prepare infusion as above, using 4–8 teaspoons of dried hops in 1 litre of water. Add to contents of a warm bath and soak in the water for 20 minutes. Repeat bath for several days.

IF SYMPTOMS PERSIST, CONSULT A DOCTOR

CAUTIONS
- Two of the bitters found in hops may have toxic side effects.
- Hops is not recommended for people who have a tendency to suffer from depression.
- Hops can cause contractions of the uterus, and is therefore not recommended during pregnancy.
- Women who are breastfeeding are advised to take only small amounts of any hops preparation.
- Some people have an adverse reaction to hops, which may take the form of respiratory allergy or contact dermatitis.
- Do not take hops if you are taking sedative medications.
- Avoid excessive alcohol intake when taking hops.

Horsechestnut
Aesculus hippocastanum **Hippocastanaceae** **Also called** Conker tree, Buckeye

A native of Anatolia, the horsechestnut is an elegant tree that can reach a height of 30 m. It is thought that the tree gets its name from the tiny, horseshoe-shaped marks – complete with what look like nail holes – that cover its branches. These are leaf scars, left behind when the leaves fall. The fruit, a prickly capsule, contains the large seeds, known to generations of children as conkers.

Parts used
SEEDS (CONKERS) AND BARK
- Seeds are collected in later summer when ripe.
- Seeds are used raw or stabilised by being soaked in alcohol.
- Seeds are used in infusions, powders and dry or soluble extracts. They may be used with other herbs, such as butcher's broom.
- Horsechestnut seeds are also made into ointments, creams and gels.
- The bark is also sometimes used, but the use of seeds is more common.

Constituents
Horsechestnut seeds contain a saponin known as aescin (sometimes referred to as escin), which constricts blood vessels, counteracting oedema (swelling) and inflammation. Many horsechestnut preparations are standardised for their aescin content. Flavonoids and sterols are also present.

crushed bark and conkers

Medicinal uses
Clinical trials have demonstrated that horsechestnut (standardised for its aescin content) is an effective treatment for chronic venous insufficiency, a cluster of conditions caused by reduced function of the veins in the legs that leads to impaired blood flow and decreased ability to pump blood from the legs back to the heart.

After two weeks of treatment, associated symptoms that may be relieved include pain, swelling, oedema, itchiness, fatigue and leg tension.

Horsechestnut seeds are also used to relieve other conditions associated with venous congestion, including haemorrhoids, varicose veins and bruising. For treating these conditions, it may be used topically in a cream or gel and/or taken orally.

Cultivation
This hardy tree can be grown from seed – a conker. Plant in a rich, well-drained soil in sun or light shade. It grows best in a cool climate.

seed pod splitting open

seed

PREPARATION AND DOSAGE
- **To treat vein and capillary disorders including leg oedema, haemorrhoids, leg ulcers and varicose veins**

  LIQUID EXTRACT As prescribed by your medical herbalist.
  TABLETS, CAPSULES 1.5 g dried seed equivalent (standardised to contain 50 mg aescin), two to three times per day.

IF SYMPTOMS PERSIST, CONSULT A DOCTOR

CAUTIONS
- Not suitable for children, or pregnant or breastfeeding women.
- Avoid if suffering from kidney disease or damage.
- Individuals taking anticoagulant (blood-thinning) drugs (warfarin or aspirin) should seek advice from a doctor before taking horsechestnut.
- Used externally, the plant may, in some very rare cases, cause an allergic reaction.

Horseradish *Armoracia rusticana* Brassicaceae

Horseradish has been used in Europe as a medicine for centuries. It is more familiar today in its role as a piquant condiment, a use which developed first in Germany and parts of Scandinavia and only spread to Britain in the 17th century. The plant has large leaves and a thick root with brown skin and white flesh. The root is rich in vitamin C, and sailors used to take it with them on long voyages to prevent scurvy.

Parts used

ROOTS

- The root – similar in appearance to a parsnip – is collected in autumn.
- It may be used fresh and can be kept for months in a refrigerator.
- It is also used in tablets.

Constituents

Horseradish contains an essential oil rich in sweet-smelling sulphur compounds known as glucosilinates. These compounds are found only in plants belonging to the mustard family. They can irritate the skin, causing blistering and burning. Horseradish contains twice as much vitamin C as lemon, and also contains B group vitamins and minerals, including potassium, calcium, iron and phosphorus.

dried roots

Medicinal uses

After they have been ingested, the glucosilinates help to flush the sinuses. This effect, combined with the herb's antimicrobial properties, expectorant action and high vitamin C content, makes horseradish a valuable remedy for the relief of hay fever, sinusitis, colds and other respiratory infections. The fact that it encourages perspiration means that it can also be used to help lower fevers.

Horseradish stimulates the appetite and digestive juices, meaning that animal and vegetable fats are more easily digested. Traditional herbalists prescribed horseradish for its strong diuretic properties, to treat kidney stones and urine retention, and it is still sometimes used for these conditions.

Horseradish is also a rubefacient, which means that it has the action of heating the skin temporarily. This property makes it useful in the treatment of a range of painful ailments such as arthritis, gout and chilblains.

Cultivation

Horseradish is easily grown from root cuttings, and it prefers a cool climate. Plant in well-drained, rich soil, in sun or partial shade.

PREPARATION AND DOSAGE

- **To relieve sinusitis, hay fever, respiratory infection**

  TABLETS Up to 1.5 g dried root equivalent, three times daily.

- **To treat rheumatic pain, arthritis, chilblains**

  POULTICE Spread fresh, grated root on a linen cloth. Lay on the affected area, with cloth against the skin, until a glowing sensation is felt. Discontinue use immediately if any discomfort is experienced.

IF SYMPTOMS PERSIST, CONSULT A DOCTOR

CAUTIONS

- Do not use pure, untreated juice or extract of horseradish as its caustic effects can irritate the digestive tract.
- Externally, horseradish may cause skin irritation and burning. Do not allow it to come into direct contact with skin or eyes.
- Do not give to children, and pregnant and breastfeeding women should not consume more than is contained in a normal meal.
- Those with gastric ulcers or thyroid disorders should avoid it.

THE A TO Z OF PLANTS

Horsetail *Equisetum arvense* Equisetaceae **Also called** Bottle brush

Thriving in swamps and marshes, where it can become weedy if allowed to spread, horsetail is found widely in Europe, the United States, Australia and New Zealand. Its fertile stem dies away and is replaced by a tall, sterile stem bearing several rings of leaves. The plant, which looks much like a baby's bottle brush, was once employed as an abrasive to scour pots and pans or to smooth rough wood.

Parts used

STERILE STEMS

- The stems are gathered in summer.
- Any stems with brown marks are rejected, as these indicate the presence of parasites.
- Once dried, stems are suitable for use only if they remain green.
- Horsetail is mainly used as a liquid extract or in tablet form.

Constituents

Horsetail is rich in minerals, especially silica, which has an anti-arthritic and connective tissue–strengthening effect. The stem also contains flavonoids – which have antioxidant and diuretic actions – as well as organic acids and nicotine.

Medicinal uses

Traditionally, extracts of horsetail have been used to treat a wide range of ailments including fluid retention, genito-urinary infections, kidney problems, prostate problems, obesity, arthritis, bleeding ulcers and tuberculosis. Horsetail is also prescribed to combat cellulite, a fatty deposit that collects around the thighs and buttocks.

The silica in horsetail is thought to strengthen connective tissue – in tendons, ligaments, cartilage and bone – which helps to explain its use in treating rheumatic complaints.

Horsetail also provides a valuable source of minerals for people prone to bone fractures, and is widely believed to help prevent osteoporosis.

Horsetail is prescribed for internal and external bleeding, and vaginal discharge.

Cultivation

Horsetail prefers swampy or marshy ground in the sun or light shade. It is a very invasive weed in the garden, and for that reason needs to be kept in check.

dried sterile stems

PREPARATION AND DOSAGE

- **To treat fluid retention, kidney problems, benign prostate conditions, cellulite and as a source of silica for bone health**

  DECOCTION Boil 1–4 g dried herb in 2 cups of water for 10–15 minutes before straining. Drink 2–3 cups a day. Avoid drinking horsetail at bedtime because of its diuretic action.

IF SYMPTOMS PERSIST, CONSULT A DOCTOR

CAUTIONS

- Do not use horsetail for more than six weeks at a time as it may irritate the digestive tract.
- Do not take horsetail if pregnant or breastfeeding.
- Do not take horsetail if you have heart or kidney disease.
- Be careful not to confuse horsetail with the poisonous marsh horsetail *Equisetum palustre*.
- If you experience bleeding from the bowel or urinary tract while taking it, consult a doctor.

Hyssop *Hyssopus officinalis* Lamiaceae

Used as a cleansing herb from Biblical times, the aromatic hyssop, a bushy evergreen shrub up to 60 cm in height, grows widely in the Mediterranean region. It is a constituent of scented liqueurs such as chartreuse, and imparts a fine flavour to honey when bees have access to its flowers.

dried aerial parts

Parts used

AERIAL PARTS
- Hyssop is picked at the beginning of the flowering period in summer.
- It is then dried for use in infusions.
- The flowers may be distilled and yield a pungent, spicy essential oil.

Constituents

Hyssop flowers contain a strongly aromatic essential oil composed of many compounds including camphor and terpenes. The plant also contains tannins and flavonoids, as well as caffeic and rosmarinic acids.

Medicinal uses

Hyssop has antispasmodic and expectorant actions, making it useful for the treatment of catarrhal coughs, asthma and bronchitis. It is a common ingredient in herbal cough mixtures. It can also soothe stomach cramps. This effect was demonstrated by Italian researchers in 2002, who found that the essential oil inhibited contraction of animal intestines.

Hyssop also raises blood pressure and stimulates perspiration – energising, tonic effects that can help to fight chronic fatigue.

The herb is antiseptic, antifungal and antiviral. A paper published in *Antiviral Research* in 1990 reports that leaf extracts demonstrate strong activity against HIV, the virus responsible for AIDS. Further research is required to clarify the herb's potential in this area, but scientists think that caffeic acid may contribute to hyssop's antiviral effect.

Externally, an infusion of hyssop leaves may be useful to treat bruises and aching muscles.

Cultivation

Sow seeds or plant cuttings in spring in well-drained, neutral to alkaline soil. Hyssop does best in a sunny border. Trim after flowering.

PREPARATION AND DOSAGE

- **To treat bronchitis, sore throat, colds and as a supportive therapy for asthma**

  INFUSION Put 1–2 teaspoons dried flowers into 1 cup of boiling water. Cover, infuse for 5–10 minutes and strain. Drink 3 cups a day while hot.

  COUGH MIXTURE Follow manufacturer's instructions.

  IF SYMPTOMS PERSIST, CONSULT A DOCTOR

CAUTIONS

- Do not exceed the recommended dose or take the essential oil internally.
- Do not take if pregnant or breastfeeding or if you have high blood pressure.
- Do not give to children.
- People allergic to oregano and thyme (members of the same plant family) may be allergic to hyssop.

Juniper *Juniperus communis* Cupressaceae

This evergreen shrub is found throughout Europe, where its blue-black berries have long been used for medicinal purposes. They were believed to protect against the plague. Juniper grows slowly, but can reach a height of 15 m. Whorls of evergreen leaves, like short, sharp needles, cover its erect stems. In spring, yellow or blue flowers appear on the male or female plants respectively.

Parts used

FRUIT

- Harvesting of juniper berries should not take place before the autumn of the third year of a tree's growth.
- The whole berry of the juniper is used, either crushed for infusions and decoctions or ground to a powder for capsules and tablets.
- Juniper is also available as a liquid extract and as an essential oil.
- Juniper berries are often used in combination with other diuretic plants, such as celery.

Constituents

About 0.5–2 per cent of a juniper berry is made up of an essential oil that is rich in monoterpenes. Juniper also contains some bitter elements, which assist in promoting digestion. Flavonoids, resin and tannins are also present.

Medicinal uses

Juniper berries are antiseptic and diuretic and are used to treat minor urinary problems. In 1987, Italian research showed that juniper is anti-inflammatory.

Juniper is often used to relieve pain and improve movement in cases of gout, arthritis and rheumatism.

The essential oil is also used to treat neuralgia and rheumatism, while an infusion added to a bath has a relaxing effect, relieving tendonitis and muscle pains.

Juniper berries are used to stimulate the appetite and to treat flatulence and other digestive disorders.

Juniper has also been shown to be active against viruses and, in addition, research conducted in 1994 suggested it may have potential for treating diabetes. More work will be needed to confirm these findings.

Cultivation

Juniper will grow in most soil types. Plant in sun or light shade from ripe seeds or cuttings taken in autumn.

berries

PREPARATION AND DOSAGE

- **To treat urinary problems, arthritis**

  DECOCTION Put 10 g of berries into 750 ml of boiling water. Leave to boil for 20 minutes, then strain. Drink 2–3 cups a day.

- **To treat digestive problems**

  INFUSION Put 0.5–2 g of crushed berries in 1 cup of boiling water. Infuse for 10 minutes, then strain. Drink 15 minutes before meals.

- **To treat muscle pains, rheumatism, neuralgia, tendonitis**

  INFUSION (AS ABOVE) Put 100–200 ml into the bath water.
  ESSENTIAL OIL Dilute, allowing 3 drops to 10 ml of carrier oil. Massage affected area two or three times a day.

IF SYMPTOMS PERSIST, CONSULT A DOCTOR

CAUTIONS

- Juniper must not be taken if you suffer from kidney disorders.
- Do not exceed the recommended dose as this may cause kidney and urinary tract dysfunction or cardiovascular complications. For these same reasons, juniper should not be taken for more than six weeks at a time.
- Some sensitive individuals may experience an allergic skin reaction to juniper.
- Juniper must not be taken by pregnant or breastfeeding women.

Kava *Piper methysticum* Piperaceae **Also called** Kava kava, Kava pepper

This evergreen, scrambling shrub is native to the islands of western Polynesia and parts of the South Pacific, where it still plays an important role in the traditional ceremonies, festivals and rituals of many indigenous peoples. The plant can reach 4 m in height, and has fleshy rhizomes, stems and heart-shaped leaves. Kava has male and female flowers on separate plants. It reproduces by underground runners.

Parts used

ROOTS

- In the Pacific Islands, kava has a long history of traditional use in rituals in which the powdered root is soaked in water to obtain a drink that creates feelings of calm and wellbeing.
- Rare but extremely serious side effects indicate that kava may be unsafe. At the time of writing, health authorities in many parts of the world have banned the sale of kava, or are carefully monitoring its use and side effects.

Constituents

The resin contains a group of compounds known as kava lactones, including kavain, methysticin, dihydromethysticin and yangonin. The amount of resin varies from 5–20 per cent, according to the variety and whether it has come from the main root or lateral roots.

dried roots

Medicinal uses

Research has shown the anti-inflammatory, sedative, antiseptic and analgesic effects of kava and its extracts.

Despite the documented medicinal effects, there are very real concerns about the safety of kava. Its use has been associated with severe liver damage and occasionally death. Experts have not determined the mechanism by which this occurs, or whether some people are more at risk than others.

Whilst it may be argued that liver toxicity has not been a feature of long-term traditional usage, it is also true that medicinal usage involves daily consumption, while traditional use is generally far less frequent.

Cultivation

Since it is a tropical plant, kava needs the warmth of a greenhouse in cool climates. Grow it in rich soil in partial shade for ornamental purposes only.

PREPARATION AND DOSAGE

- The medicinal use of kava should be avoided until the safety concerns have been clarified. Those who do decide to take the herb would be prudent to restrict their usage to short-term consumption of water-based preparations

IF SYMPTOMS PERSIST, CONSULT A DOCTOR

CAUTIONS

- Signs of liver toxicity that users should be aware of include unusual fatigue, mild fever, lack of appetite, nausea and vomiting, abdominal discomfort, unexplained bruising or bleeding, jaundice, dark urine and yellowing of the skin and eyes. Other side effects include dryness, pigmentation and scaliness of the skin (which reverses when intake is halted) and depression of nerve function.
- Kava should not be taken at the same time as alcohol, barbiturates, tranquillisers, antidepressants, sedatives or medicines for treating epilepsy.

Kelp *Fucus vesiculosus* Fucaceae **Also called** Bladderwrack

Found in abundance on the rocky coastlines of cold and temperate seas, kelp is characterised by its brownish green fronds that bear numerous fluid-filled bulges, or 'bladders'. The fronds can be up to 1 m long. Kelp is collected from the coasts of the English Channel and the Atlantic in early to midsummer. Some species grow around the shores of Australia and New Zealand.

Parts used

FRONDS OR THALLUSES

- Kelp is dried for use in capsules and tablets, and also used for liquid extracts.

Constituents

The main component of kelp is a polysaccharide called alginic acid. Other polysaccharides (including fucans) are also present, along with sterols, lipids and alginates. Kelp is an important source of iodine for people whose diet is deficient.

Medicinal uses

Several species of seaweed, including some that grow off the shores of Australia and New Zealand, are referred to as kelp. Most of these have not been fully investigated, and medicinal use should be restricted to *Fucus vesiculosus*.

Kelp is a source of iodine, other sources of which are eggs, seafood, low-fat milk products, iodised salt and seaweeds. Iodine deficiency is common in areas such as New Zealand, where the soil is deficient in the element.

Iodine is needed for the normal functioning of the thyroid gland, and is a component of the thyroid hormones. If iodine is deficient, the thyroid may become underactive, a condition known as hypothyroidism.

The thyroid controls the body's metabolic rate, so symptoms of iodine deficiency include low energy levels, sluggish digestion, constipation, a tendency to put on weight, heavy periods and sensitivity to the cold. Kelp has traditionally been used for the treatment of such symptoms, and may help to resolve them when iodine deficiency is the cause of the problem.

Cultivation

Kelp is gathered from the wild rather than cultivated.

dried thalluses

PREPARATION AND DOSAGE

- **To treat mild thyroid underactivity, as an aid to weight loss**

  LIQUID EXTRACT 1.5–2.5 g dried thallus equivalent, taken three times a day.
  TABLETS, CAPSULES Follow manufacturer's instructions. Do not exceed recommended dose.

IF SYMPTOMS PERSIST, CONSULT A DOCTOR

CAUTIONS

- Kelp should not be taken by children, people with hyperthyroidism (overactive thyroid), or pregnant or breastfeeding women.

- Do not exceed recommended dose or take kelp for an extended period of time, except under medical supervision.

- Prolonged use can lead to intolerance, the main symptoms being the painful dilation of the thyroid gland. This should disappear after you stop taking kelp, however consult a doctor if you experience this, or any symptoms of hyperthyroidism.

- Kelp may aggravate acne.

- Do not take kelp with aspirin or other anticoagulant (blood-thinning) preparations, or with prescribed thyroid medications.

Korean ginseng
Panax ginseng Araliaceae **Also called** Asiatic ginseng, Chinese ginseng, Man root, Ren shen

Korean ginseng has been used as a medicine in China for several thousand years, and continues to be one of the most commonly used herbal medicines in the world. The name 'ginseng' is Chinese for 'man-shape', reflecting the human form of the root. 'Panax' is from the Greek word 'panakos', or 'panacea', and indicates Korean ginseng's reputation as a cure for all ills.

dried roots

root

Parts used
ROOTS
- The rootstock, consisting of main and lateral roots, with small root hairs, may be 60 cm long. The roots are harvested during autumn from plants that are six to seven years old.
- Ginseng that has been harvested from the wild is considered to be particularly potent and is probably the most expensive medicinal plant in the world. Most ginseng is commercially cultivated.
- 'White ginseng' is a term that refers to roots that have been peeled and sun-dried, while the more potent 'red ginseng' roots have been steamed prior to drying.
- Korean ginseng has traditionally been used dried (and powdered) for decoctions, or eaten fresh in a food such as soup. Ginseng is also taken in tablets and capsules, and as a liquid extract.

Constituents
The group of saponins that is collectively referred to as ginsenosides is widely considered to be responsible for much of the medicinal action, and many commercial preparations are standardised for their ginsenoside content. The main root and lateral branches have optimal ratios of ginsenosides, whilst the root hairs are regarded as inferior.

Medicinal uses
Korean ginseng has been the subject of much research. It helps to improve stamina, concentration, alertness, work efficiency, mood, sleep and an individual's sense of wellbeing. It is also indicated as a reproductive tonic, and has been shown to improve sperm motility and testosterone levels in infertile men. It is particularly recommended when stress and emotional states are affecting sexual performance.

High doses of ginseng have been shown to reduce cholesterol and other blood lipids. It also normalises both high and low blood pressure and has a hypoglycaemic action in diabetic and non-diabetic patients.

Korean ginseng stimulates several aspects of immune function, and in future may be shown to play a role in the treatment of people with HIV. Based on widespread consumption of ginseng tea over long periods of time, researchers have identified a protective effect against certain cancers.

In traditional Chinese medicine, Korean ginseng is regarded as a tonic for the Qi, or 'vital force'.

Cultivation
Grow in warm, humid conditions in a rich, moist, well-drained soil. Propagate by seed or division of tuber. Germination is slow and may take two years.

PREPARATION AND DOSAGE
- **To enhance stress coping, mood, energy levels, to aid male fertility and stamina in young healthy individuals and as a tonic in old age**
  TABLETS, CAPSULES (250–500 mg dried root equivalent). Take twice daily, one dose in the morning and one dose around midday. Choose a product standardised for its ginsenosides content. **LIQUID EXTRACT, DECOCTION** As prescribed by a medical herbalist. This treatment should be taken for a maximum of three weeks at a time, with a minimum of two weeks' break between courses.

IF SYMPTOMS PERSIST, CONSULT A DOCTOR

CAUTIONS
- Do not exceed the recommended dose or combine with stimulants.
- Ginseng is contraindicated in pregnancy, breastfeeding, acute infection, haemorrhage, acute inflammatory conditions, blood clots, acute asthma, depression, anxiety, mental illness and for those taking monoamine-oxidase inhibitors, antipsychotics, hormonal therapy, insulin (or other hypoglycaemic drugs) or warfarin.
- If you have cardiac disease, diabetes or high or low blood pressure, do not take Korean ginseng unless supervised by a doctor or medical herbalist.
- Ginseng should be avoided by individuals who are highly energetic, nervous or prone to hysteria, and by women who experience heavy periods.
- Occasional side effects have included headache, disturbed sleep and oestrogenic symptoms (breast tenderness and vaginal bleeding).

Kuzu   *Pueraria lobata*   Fabaceae   **Also called**   Kudzu, Japanese arrowroot

Native to semi-tropical regions of Asia, kuzu is a climber that can reach 30 m. Its dark green leaves are composed of three lobes and are held on long leafstalks. Kuzu has been used in Chinese medicine since at least 200 BC, but it is more often grown these days as a cooking ingredient and as a fodder crop. Its yellowish, light brown roots are cylindrical. Its fruit consists of seed pods containing black seeds.

Parts used

ROOTS
- The roots are harvested in spring or autumn.
- The dried, powdered roots have similar qualities to cornstarch and arrowroot, hence the plant's primary use is as a thickening agent in cooking.

Constituents

The plant contains numerous active elements including isoflavonoids (daidzein, daidzin, puerarin), coumarins and saponins.

Medicinal uses

Kuzu protects the liver and helps the body to metabolise alcohol. Japanese research published in 1998 verified this, suggesting that the protective action on the liver was due to several saponins.

Kuzu is also reputed to suppress the craving for alcohol. American research published in 1998 showed that puerarin, daidzin and daidzein decreased alcohol consumption in a group of alcohol-preferring rats.

It has been demonstrated that the plant affects the hormonal system in a similar way to oestrogen and it is recommended for balancing hormones during menopause.

Kuzu is a popular remedy in macrobiotic medicine, and is considered to have alkalising qualities that help to treat acidic conditions, particularly in the digestive system. The plant is also reputed to ease muscular aches and pains, and is beneficial in the treatment of colds and flu. It increases blood flow to the heart and brain and is indicated in the treatment of angina and high blood pressure.

Cultivation

Plant in well-drained soil, preferably in the sun. Sow seeds – soaked are best – in spring at 13–18°C.

crushed roots

PREPARATION AND DOSAGE

- **To treat diarrhoea, acidic digestive conditions, symptoms of menopause, liver ailments, alcohol cravings**

  DECOCTION Put 10 g of kuzu powder or granules into 2–3 teaspoons of cold water and stir to dissolve. Add 1 cup of water to the dissolved kuzu and heat over a medium flame, stirring constantly until the liquid becomes clear. Drink 2–3 cups a day, whilst hot. In macrobiotic medicine, chopped umeboshi plum may be added to the simmering kuzu drink.

IF SYMPTOMS PERSIST, CONSULT A DOCTOR

CAUTIONS

- There are no known cautions for the use of this plant.

Lady's mantle *Alchemilla vulgaris* Rosaceae **Also called** Alchemilla

This perennial plant occurs throughout Europe and is easily recognised by its large, fan-shaped leaves made up of 8 to 10 serrated lobes. Its genus name Alchemilla means alchemy, and stems from the medieval alchemists' fascination with the plant. They collected the dew from the concave leaves, believing it to have magical powers. Lady's mantle bears clusters of little, green flowers and its yellow fruit contains one seed.

Parts used
FLOWERS AND LEAVES
- The flowers and leaves are picked in summer, while the plant is in flower, and dried in a shady place.
- The plant is used in preparing infusions, tinctures and liquid extracts.

flower

Constituents
Lady's mantle contains large amounts of tannins (6–8 per cent). It also contains flavonoids (2 per cent) and some salicylic acid.

Medicinal uses
Due to its tannin content, lady's mantle has astringent and coagulant properties, and is therefore able to tighten the tissues and stop bleeding. Traditionally it has been used in compresses to be placed over wounds in order to speed healing.

Taken internally, lady's mantle is a valuable herb for treating irregular or excessive menstrual bleeding. A strong infusion taken often also treats mild diarrhoea.

When applied externally, the plant helps to relieve itching and inflammation, and is used to treat cellulitis (a skin infection), gingivitis, insect bites and (in a sitz bath) ailments affecting the vulva such as itching and vaginal discharge.

A 1986 French study showed that lady's mantle inhibits the breakdown of the skin's elastic and connective tissues, supporting its use to treat stretch marks and ageing skin.

dried flowers and leaves

Cultivation
Sow seeds in moist, well-drained soil in a sunny or slightly shady position in early spring. Plants will self-seed in subsequent years. Lady's mantle grows best in a cool to mild climate.

PREPARATION AND DOSAGE

- **To treat menstrual disorders, diarrhoea**

  LIQUID EXTRACT 1–2 g dried herb equivalent, three times a day.

  INFUSION 1–2 g dried herb infused in 1 cup of boiling water for 10 minutes before straining. Drink 3 cups a day for menstrual disorders or 5–6 cups a day for mild diarrhoea.

- **To treat cellulitis, stretch marks, gingivitis**

  COMPRESS Boil 40 g of dried leaves in 1 litre of water. Soak a cloth in this decoction and apply three times a day.

- **To treat vaginal discharge**

  SITZ BATH Use 1 litre of infusion per bath. Bathe twice a day.

IF SYMPTOMS PERSIST, CONSULT A DOCTOR

CAUTIONS
- Pregnant and breastfeeding women should avoid lady's mantle.
- Seek medical advice if also taking aspirin or anticoagulant (blood-thinning) medications.

Lavender *Lavandula angustifolia* (syn. *L. officinalis*) Lamiaceae

This small, bushlike shrub, a native of the Mediterranean region, grows to a height of 30–60 cm. Its stems are erect and its leaves are narrow and silvery green. All parts of the plant are aromatic, but its flowers particularly so. The Romans used lavender to perfume their washing water, and it remains one of the most popular and well-known herbs. The tiny purple flowers appear on spikes above the foliage in summer.

Parts used

FLOWERS

- After being gathered in spring and summer, the flowers are dried for use in infusions and capsules, or they may be processed to extract the essential oil.
- Ointments, creams and gels are made with a base of the essential oil.
- Traditionally a product of France, lavender is now also farmed in Australia and New Zealand.

dried flowers

Constituents

Lavender contains an essential oil (fresh flower, 0.1–1 per cent and dry, 1–3 per cent). There are over 40 constituents, including linalyl acetate, linalool and terpinene-4-ol.

Medicinal uses

Lavender is well known for its sedative and calming effects. In 2001, Japanese researchers found that the scent of lavender reduced mental stress, indicating its use for treating depression, anxiety and tension headaches. It has other properties, such as easing spasms, helping digestion, relieving flatulence and aiding the passage of bile. It may also help some types of asthma.

Lavender is antiseptic and antibacterial and soothes minor skin infections, insect bites and burns.

Lavender is used in therapeutic baths to treat blood circulation problems, and it can ease rheumatic pains as well as lowering fevers.

Cultivation

Plant seeds in spring in well-drained, neutral to alkaline soil in full sun. Grows best in cool to mild climates.

PREPARATION AND DOSAGE

- **To treat nervous agitation, anxiety, stress, gastrointestinal spasm, mild insomnia**

  LIQUID EXTRACT As prescribed by a medical herbalist.

  INFUSION 2–3 g dried flowers infused in 1 cup of boiling water for 5–10 minutes before straining. For stress, 3–4 cups a day; for digestive conditions, 0.5 cup a day; for insomnia, 1 cup at bedtime.

- **To treat period pains, tension headaches**

  MASSAGE OIL Add 3 drops of lavender oil to 10 ml of carrier oil. For period pain, massage into the abdomen and lower back. For tension headache, massage into neck, shoulders and temples.

IF SYMPTOMS PERSIST, CONSULT A DOCTOR

CAUTIONS

- Pregnant or breastfeeding women should avoid using lavender, although many midwives advocate its use during labour.
- The essential oil must not be ingested, although small amounts may be applied to the skin for the almost instantaneous relief of minor burns. Keep the oil away from the eyes.

Lemon balm *Melissa officinalis* Lamiaceae **Also called** Balm, Bee balm, Melissa

This perennial herb is native to the eastern Mediterranean, but it grows wild all over Europe, as well as in New Zealand and southern Australia. Its stems are erect and form dense clumps about 70 cm high. All parts of lemon balm are hairy and have a strong lemon scent. Its pointed, oval leaves have rounded indentations and prominent veins. Lemon balm has white or pinkish flowers and small, brown fruit.

Parts used

LEAVES

- After collection in summer (when flowering begins) the leaves are dried in the open air.
- Lemon balm is used mainly for infusions or powder capsules. The plant may also be processed to release its essential oil.
- The plant has a traditional use in liqueurs such as benedictine.

Constituents

Lemon balm contains flavonoids, tannins and phenol acids, including rosmarinic acid. An essential oil – melissa oil – is also present in the plant in small amounts. This is one of the most expensive essential oils available, reflecting the low yield from each plant. The oil consists mainly of citrals.

Medicinal uses

Lemon balm is most often prescribed to treat morning sickness and intestinal problems such as sluggish digestion, bloating and flatulence.

A number of experiments have clearly shown the plant's capacity to relieve stomach spasms and aid digestion. In 2001, a German trial found that a herbal preparation containing lemon balm improved the symptoms of dyspepsia.

The plant is also used to treat minor sleep problems as well as nervousness and mild depression. For these purposes it is combined with several other plants, such as lime flower, hawthorn and passionflower.

A Spanish review published in 2001 also documents the use of lemon balm for treating attention deficit disorder, as well as hyperactivity in infants.

Earlier research has demonstrated the antiviral properties of lemon balm, which is used topically to treat herpes and cold sores.

dried leaves

It also appears to have an effect on the thyroid gland.

Cultivation

Plant seeds or cuttings in moist soil in a sunny or lightly shaded location.

PREPARATION AND DOSAGE

- **To treat digestive problems, nervousness, depression, minor sleep problems**

    LIQUID EXTRACT 500 mg–1 g dried leaf equivalent, three times daily.
    INFUSION 2–3 g dried leaves infused in 1 cup of boiling water for 5 minutes before straining. Drink 2–3 cups a day, or 1 cup at bedtime for sleep problems.

IF SYMPTOMS PERSIST, CONSULT A DOCTOR

CAUTIONS

- It is best not to use lemon balm over a long period of time, in excess of one to three months.

Lemon verbena *Aloysia triphylla (Lippia citriodora)* Verbenaceae

A native of North and South America, lemon verbena is a shrub that can grow to a height of 1.5 m. It was introduced into Europe from Chile in the late 18th century. It has long, thin leaves that grow in groups of three or four. Its small, whitish flowers have four petals and are followed by fleshy fruits. The dried lemon-scented leaves became popular in pot pourri.

Parts used

LEAVES

- The leaves are collected twice a year, once in mid-summer and again in mid-autumn, and then spread out in a thin layer to dry.
- Once dry, the leaves give off a pleasant lemony scent if crushed. They are used to make delicious infusions or are processed to release the essential oil, which is often combined with other plants to produce a natural sedative.

Constituents

Lemon verbena contains flavonoids and a small quantity of essential oil, whose main component is citral, responsible for the plant's characteristic scent.

Medicinal uses

Although research carried out on lemon verbena has concentrated mainly on its sedative properties, no absolute conclusion has yet been reached on its efficacy.

dried leaves

The opposite may, in fact, be the case, since one study seemed to demonstrate that an infusion of the plant had no sedative and calming effects at all.

Lemon verbena is reputed to possess antispasmodic properties, and is therefore indicated in the treatment of indigestion, flatulence, diarrhoea and colic. It is also used to help relieve asthma and lower fevers.

In addition, the plant possesses antibacterial and insecticidal properties. In 2002, a Portuguese study demonstrated the anti-oxidant properties of an infusion of the leaves.

The leaves are used in herbal medicine – like the aerial parts of peppermint and lime – as stimulants to help digestion. They can be found in both pharmacies and food shops.

Cultivation

Plant in light, well-drained soil in a sunny location. Cuttings should be planted in summer and watered regularly.

PREPARATION AND DOSAGE

- **To treat digestive problems**

  INFUSION Put 1 sachet into a cup of boiling water. Leave to infuse for 5 minutes, then strain. Drink 2 cups a day after main meals.

  IF SYMPTOMS PERSIST, CONSULT A DOCTOR

CAUTIONS

- Those with kidney disorders should avoid excessive doses of the herb.
- Pregnant or breastfeeding women should not take lemon verbena.

Licorice *Glycyrrhiza glabra* Fabaceae **Also called** Sweetwood

This perennial shrub is native to southern Europe, although several other species with medicinal properties are found elsewhere in the world. It has upright branched stems to about 1 m high, bearing alternate leaves made up of 7 to 17 bright green leaflets. Its small, pale blue to lilac flowers grow in spikes. It has thick, woody roots and creeping stems that can reach 2 m in length. The fruit is a reddish brown pod.

Parts used

ROOTS

- The roots are collected in autumn from plants at least three years old.
- Once washed, the roots are dried in the sunshine.
- The roots are used in segments, in powders (for infusions and macerations) or as a juice.

Constituents

A large proportion of the root is composed of polysaccharides. Other components include coumarins, a small amount of phytosterols (mainly oestriol), flavonoids, saponins (in particular glycyrrhizin and glycyrrhizinic acid) and some traces of essential oil that give the plant its aroma and sweet taste. The pharmacological activity is due to the flavonoids and saponins.

dried roots

Medicinal uses

The glycyrrhizin and glycyrrhizinic acid in licorice impart several medicinal properties. It can be used to treat gastric ulcers and inflammation. It releases phlegm and soothes coughs, eases asthma, stimulates the immune system and helps to fight dental plaque and tooth decay, as well as mouth and throat infections.

Licorice root is also used to treat digestive problems such as bloating, spasms, sluggish digestion, belching and flatulence. The plant has a slight oestrogenic effect and its flavonoids can help to protect liver cells and combat free radicals.

Licorice can also be used to treat skin inflammation and infections. Research published in 1980 demonstrated the anti-inflammatory effects of glycyrrhizinic acid against erythema (reddening of the skin) caused by exposure to ultraviolet light. Licorice is traditionally prescribed as an adrenal tonic, restoring energy levels after periods of stress and exhaustion. It stimulates the secretion of aldosterone, a hormone that causes water and sodium retention, but prevents retention of potassium. Licorice can therefore have adverse side effects if taken in large doses, particularly by those with heart or liver problems.

Cultivation

Plant in rich, well-drained soil in a sunny location. The seeds should be sown in spring. It thrives in a cool to mild climate.

PREPARATION AND DOSAGE

- **To treat gastric inflammation, bloating, coughs, low energy**

  LIQUID EXTRACT As prescribed by a medical herbalist.

  DECOCTION Boil 1–4 g dried root in 1 cup of water for 10–15 minutes before straining. Drink 2–3 cups a day.

IF SYMPTOMS PERSIST, CONSULT A DOCTOR

CAUTIONS

- Any treatment using licorice must be accompanied by a low-salt diet and should never last longer than four to six weeks.
- The maximum daily dose of glycyrrhizin is 100 mg. Care should be taken not to consume too many drinks or sweets containing licorice during the treatment.
- The plant should not be taken during pregnancy or if suffering from high blood pressure, heart problems requiring the use of the drug digitalis or any illnesses that hinder the elimination of salts from the body, such as liver disorders.
- Licorice is not recommended for people with kidney disorders, or those taking steroid medications.

Lime flower
Tilia cordata, T. platyphyllos (and their hybrids) Tiliaceae **Also called** Linden tree, Tilia, Small-leaved lime

Lime tree is native to Europe, and is widely grown as a street or garden tree in cool to mild climates. It reaches 20–40 m in height, and has a smooth, grey bark that cracks with age. Its leaves are an asymmetric heart shape with serrated edges. The sweetly scented, light yellow flowers grow in clusters and have long, greenish yellow bracts that are joined to the flower stalk.

Parts used
FLOWERS AND BRACTS
- The flowers are collected from both wild and cultivated trees at a stage when two-thirds of the flowers have bloomed. The flowers are then dried in thin layers away from sunlight.
- The flowers are used in preparing infusions.

Constituents
The flowers have been found to contain phenolic acids, proanthocyanadins, tannins, flavonoids, mucilages and a small quantity of essential oil that has a sedative effect.

Despite the name, lime flower is not a member of the genus *Citrus*, which includes the more familiar oranges, lemons and limes.

Medicinal uses
Taken internally, the flowers are prescribed for a range of minor sleep problems and nervous conditions, such as anxiety and restlessness.

A hybrid of *Tilia cordata* and *T. platyphyllos* was shown by Portuguese scientists in 2001 to possess sedative effects.

The antispasmodic effects have so far only been demonstrated by in vitro research, but the plant has also been found to possess diuretic qualities.

Lime flowers have been recommended for the treatment of hypertension, for fatty deposits in blood vessels (since they have the effect of dilating the vessels) and also to help in the relief of migraines.

Lime flowers are traditionally considered to be particularly beneficial when any of the conditions described above are caused or aggravated by stress or anxiety

Used externally in a solution, lime flowers can help soothe cracked and chapped skin, insect bites and other skin irritations.

Cultivation
Plant in moist, well-drained soil in a sunny location. Trees can be grown from seed planted when ripe, and will thrive in a cool climate.

dried flowers and bracts

PREPARATION AND DOSAGE
- **To treat minor sleeping problems, anxiety, stress**

    INFUSION 2–4 g dried flowers infused in 1 cup of boiling water before straining. For stress and anxiety, drink 3 cups a day. To aid sleep, drink 1 cup at bedtime.

- **To treat cracked or chapped skin, insect bites**

    SOLUTION (WITH A BASE OF LIME FLOWERS) Apply to the affected area several times a day.

    IF SYMPTOMS PERSIST, CONSULT A DOCTOR

CAUTIONS
- Do not exceed the stated dose as this may affect heart function.
- Lime flowers should not be taken by anyone with a heart disorder, except as directed by a medical herbalist.
- Pregnant or breastfeeding women should not take lime flowers.

Mallow
Malva sylvestris Malvaceae **Also called** Blue mallow, Common mallow The mallow is a robust plant with a thick stem and downy, lobed leaves. It grows wild throughout Europe and in parts of Australia and New Zealand. The showy, mauvish flowers are streaked with crimson veins. The fruit is a circle of small nuts, each containing a single seed.

dried flowers and leaves

Parts used
LEAVES AND FLOWERS
- The leaves are collected in spring, before the plant is in bloom. Flowers are gathered from summer to early autumn.
- Both flowers and leaves are arranged in thin layers and then left to dry in a dark place, so as not to destroy their anthocyanic pigments.
- Once dried, the leaves and flowers are used to prepare infusions, decoctions and powders.

Constituents
Both the leaves and flowers are rich in soothing mucilages. Anthocyanin pigments, responsible for the colour of mallow flowers, also contain polysaccharides and flavonoids.

Medicinal uses
Mallow is well known for its soothing effect on the bronchial tubes, and is most frequently used to help in easing bronchial ailments as well as coughs.

The plant can also be taken to calm inflammation in the digestive tract and to treat the symptoms of constipation and colitis.

Externally, mallow soothes skin irritations and, as a gargle, is good for oral problems. The decoction can also be applied to babies' gums to soothe teething pain.

Japanese studies in 1989 have shown that mallow's anti-inflammatory action is due to its mucilage content.

Scientific researchers are now exploring new uses for the plant because recent studies have revealed the fact that the polysaccharides contained in mallow – also found in the related marshmallow root (see p.135) – can help in strengthening the immune system.

Cultivation
Mallow is grown from seed. Plant seeds in late spring, in a sunny or lightly shaded spot. Mallow grows in any well-drained soil and thrives in poor soils. In many areas, mallow can become weedy.

PREPARATION AND DOSAGE
- **To treat coughs, bronchial conditions, colitis, irritable bowel syndrome and constipation**

  INFUSION 5–10 g dried leaves and flowers infused in 1 litre of boiling water for 5–10 minutes before straining. For coughs, drink up to 3 cups a day. For digestive complaints, drink up to 4 cups a day.

- **To treat inflammation of the mouth**

  MOUTHWASH Make an infusion as above, using 30 g of dried flowers and leaves in 1 litre of water. Use as a mouthwash or gargle several times a day.

IF SYMPTOMS PERSIST, CONSULT A DOCTOR

CAUTIONS
- Very high doses of preparations that contain mallow have been known to have a laxative effect.

THE A TO Z OF PLANTS

Manuka
Leptospermum scoparium Myrtaceae **Also called** New Zealand tea tree, Red tea tree, Kahikatoa Tea made from the leaves of manuka was used by James Cook as a remedy against scurvy during his second voyage in 1773. Thus manuka became the first 'tea tree', a name that is now applied to numerous other trees. Although Cook first found manuka in New Zealand, it is also native to Australia, where it is common in the southeast.

Parts used
AERIAL PARTS, HONEY
- Many parts of the manuka tree were used in traditional Maori medicine, including the leaves, bark, sap, gum and seeds.
- The essential oil is produced from the leaves and end branches.
- Modern usage centres on topical application of the essential oil, and the use of honey from bees foraging on manuka flowers.

Constituents
Manuka contains an essential oil with a very complex structure. Constituents include tannins, flavonoids, triterpene acids and their derivatives, and an antibacterial agent leptospermone. Like other honeys, manuka honey contains a percentage of hydrogen peroxide (which is antiseptic), however the superior antimicrobial activity of manuka honey is attributed to a second, non-peroxide, substance.

honey and dried aerial parts

Medicinal uses
To Maori, manuka was an important medicinal plant, and different parts were used to treat a wide variety of ailments, including fevers, urinary complaints, dysentery, diarrhoea, burns and coughing. In Australia, the leaves were often infused to produce an aromatic tea during the early colonial era.

Research in New Zealand confirms that manuka, particularly its essential oil, is strongly antimicrobial. As a result, modern usage centres on topical applications for the treatment or prevention of infection. The essential oil has been proven to be effective against a wide range of organisms, including some bacteria that are resistant to antibiotic therapy, and some fungi. The pure essential oil is recommended for the treatment of acne, fungal infections of the nail bed and skin and athlete's foot. The diluted essential oil is applied to open wounds and used as a mouthwash or gargle for oral infections.

The essential oil is also considered to be an anti-inflammatory, and is used to treat eczema, burns and insect bites, encouraging skin repair and helping to prevent infection. For rheumatic conditions, the essential oil is rubbed into the affected muscles and joints.

Manuka honey has been the subject of extensive research and offers great potential for the treatment of ulcers and other wounds.

Cultivation
Manuka is grown in sun to part shade in any well-drained soil and is propagated from seeds or cuttings.

seed capsules

PREPARATION AND DOSAGE
- **To treat acne, fungal infections such as ringworm and athlete's foot, insect bites, cuts, non-infected wounds**

  ESSENTIAL OIL For infections, apply a few drops of oil to affected area twice daily for at least 5 days after infection has cleared up. For non-infected sites, swab with essential oil diluted in water.

- **To treat infected wounds and ulcers that are slow to heal**

  ACTIVE MANUKA HONEY Apply honey to an absorbent wound dressing and place over the affected area, with a second dressing to prevent the honey from leaking. Change dressings regularly. Medical management of the wound may be required.

IF SYMPTOMS PERSIST, CONSULT A DOCTOR

CAUTIONS
- Do not take the essential oil or manuka preparations internally.
- Do not use the essential oil if you are pregnant or breastfeeding.
- When taken internally over a long period, manuka may impair nutrient absorption due to its highly astringent nature. Users are therefore advised to take manuka preparations at least 30 minutes before or after meals.

Marshmallow *Althaea officinalis* Malvaceae

Found on damp ground all over Europe, the marshmallow can reach a height of 1 m. The down on its stems and large leaves gives the plant a velvety look, and in late summer delicate pinky white flowers appear briefly, followed by flat, round fruits. However, the marshmallow is mainly valued for its thick, white, fibrous roots, which the ancient Romans considered a delicacy.

Parts used
ROOTS AND LEAVES
- The roots are dug up in the autumn, two years after first planting. They are dried, then used in the preparation of infusions, powders, extracts and syrups.
- The leaves are sometimes picked in summer and used for infusions.

Constituents
A large proportion of the root consists of mucilage. Some phenolic acids and flavonoids are also present.

Medicinal uses
Marshmallow is well known for having soothing and anti-inflammatory properties, and it is widely prescribed to calm dry coughs and treat other respiratory ailments, including sore throats and bronchitis. It is also very effective in soothing mouth ulcers, dental abscesses, boils, acne and burns, when applied to the affected area on a compress.

Tests have shown that the high level of mucilage in marshmallow root is responsible for its power to reduce inflammation and ease the discomfort of coughs.

Other research has confirmed the antiseptic powers of marshmallow, as well as its ability to combat infection by stimulating the immune system.

For these reasons, herbalists prescribe marshmallow to soothe the inflammation and pain of complaints such as cystitis and urethritis, as well as a range of other urinary tract infections.

dried roots

Cultivation
Marshmallow can be propagated from seeds gathered in late summer or by division in late autumn. Plant in any type of moist to wet soil, in an area where the plants will receive plenty of sunshine.

PREPARATION AND DOSAGE

- **To treat coughs, sore throat, bronchitis, urinary tract infection**

  LIQUID EXTRACT 2–5 g dried root equivalent, three times a day.
  INFUSION 2–3 g dried root infused in 1 cup of boiling water for 10 minutes before straining. Drink 2–3 cups a day.

- **To treat mouth inflammation, dental abscesses**

  MOUTHWASH Make an infusion as above, using 10 g of dried root, and use as a mouthwash or gargle several times a day.

- **To treat boils, acne**

  COMPRESS Make an infusion as for the mouthwash above, and apply as a compress to the affected area several times a day.

IF SYMPTOMS PERSIST, CONSULT A DOCTOR

CAUTIONS

- If you are taking other medicines, check with your doctor before using a marshmallow extract, as it can affect their absorption.
- Marshmallow has been shown to lower blood-sugar levels. Therefore, It may interfere with the action of other therapies or medications being used to control blood-sugar levels, such as insulin for diabetes.

Maté   *Ilex paraguariensis*   Aquifoliaceae   **Also called** Yerba maté, Paraguay tea

A South American evergreen, the maté tree grows wild near streams, but is cultivated on a large scale in Brazil, Paraguay, Uruguay and Argentina. Maté tea, made by infusing the leaves, is regarded as the national drink throughout much of South America. The tree can reach a height of 10–15 m when fully mature, and bears oval, leathery leaves, similar to those of holly – but without thorns.

Parts used

LEAVES

- Where grown commercially, the maté tree is pruned low to make the job of harvesting the leaves easier.
- Leaves are picked from trees that are at least four years old.
- They are dried rapidly over a fire and chopped into small pieces.
- The dried leaf, known as green maté, is used in drinks and infusions.

Constituents

The chemical composition of maté is complex. Once dried, up to 10 per cent of the leaf is composed of phenol acids, and there are also saponins, flavonoids, a little resin and some traces of essential oil. The main active compounds, however, are caffeine and theobromine, a diuretic and cardiac stimulant.

Medicinal uses

Because maté contains high levels of caffeine, a potent stimulant, it is used to combat fatigue. Maté is also a diuretic and is widely used for kidney problems.

All the research conducted on caffeine shows that it increases alertness and intellectual capacity and generally stimulates the central nervous system. It has been shown that caffeine can raise the base metabolic rate by about 10 per cent. Together with the caffeine in maté, the theobromine, phenol acids, flavonoids and saponins all contribute to this energising effect.

Research published in *Planta Medica* in 1988 showed that maté can also suppress the appetite. That finding, and a 1995 study demonstrating the ability of maté infusions to break down fats in the blood, suggest that the herb may be useful for those following a weight-loss regime.

Recent French research has indicated that maté may help to protect against hardening of the arteries, a cause of many major heart and circulatory disorders. It is also sometimes prescribed to alleviate the pain of tension headaches and rheumatism.

Cultivation

Maté is a tropical tree and needs protection when temperatures fall below 7°C. In cool areas is can be grown indoors or in a greenhouse.

dried leaves

PREPARATION AND DOSAGE

- **To treat lethargy, nervous exhaustion, kidney problems**

  INFUSION 2–3 g dried leaves infused in 1 cup of boiling water before straining. Drink 1–3 cups a day, preferably before 5 pm to avoid any difficulty in falling asleep at night. Maté is more effective when taken infrequently.

IF SYMPTOMS PERSIST, CONSULT A DOCTOR

CAUTIONS

- Excessive use of maté tea can overstimulate the nervous system.
- Do not take if you have sleep problems.
- Do not take maté if you suffer from heart or circulatory problems.
- Use of maté should be avoided when pregnant or breastfeeding.
- Maté is on the list of banned stimulants for sports participants.
- Recent South American studies suggest a possible link between drinking large amounts of maté tea and an increased risk of developing cancer of the lungs or oesophagus.
- Regular use of maté may lead to withdrawal symptoms when you stop drinking it, as is the case with other sources of caffeine.

Meadowsweet *Filipendula ulmaria* (syn. *Spirea ulmaria*) Rosaceae **Also called** Queen of the meadow

Growing in temperate parts of Europe and Asia, meadowsweet loves damp places, where it grows up to around 2 m tall. The fernlike leaves, made up of three to nine pairs of leaflets, grow alternately along the hollow, red-veined stem. Clusters of sweet-smelling, creamy white flowers blossom in summer. Their fragrance made them a popular flavouring for beers and wines in the Middle Ages.

Parts used

STEMS, LEAVES AND FLOWERS

- The aerial parts are picked in early summer, as the first flowers appear.
- They are dried in a shady, well-aired place, until they turn yellow, then used for infusions and tinctures.

Constituents

Meadowsweet is rich in tannins, hence its sharp, astringent taste. It also contains flavonoids and a fragrant essential oil, largely made up of salicylates, which have an anti-inflammatory effect.

Medicinal uses

Meadowsweet is highly effective in treating flu symptoms, headaches, toothache and joint pain caused by rheumatism and gout. It can also stimulate sweating. Its salicylates confer its anti-inflammatory and pain-relieving powers and the flavonoids also contribute to this effect, as well as helping to soothe muscle spasms and digestive tract problems, including gastric ulcers and acid stomach complaints, such as indigestion. Studies in the Ukraine have confirmed the plant's benefits in ulcer treatment.

Meadowsweet has antibacterial and healing powers, in which its tannins and flavonoids play a major role. For centuries, it has been prescribed for urinary tract infections and as a diuretic – often being recommended for excess weight and bloating due to water retention.

dried stems, leaves and flowers

Cultivation

Meadowsweet can be grown by division or from seeds. Plant in spring in moist, rich, water-retentive, alkaline soil, in sun or light shade.

PREPARATION AND DOSAGE

- **To treat indigestion, gastric ulcer, influenza, headache, fluid retention, rheumatism**

  LIQUID EXTRACT 2–5 g dried herb equivalent, three times a day.
  INFUSION Put 1 tablespoon of herb into 1 cup of water that is just beginning to simmer. Cover, infuse for 10 minutes and strain. Drink 3–4 cups a day, the first on an empty stomach.

- **To treat joint pains, wounds, ulcers**

  COMPRESS Make the infusion as above, simmering for about 20 minutes. Apply on a compress to the affected area, three to four times a day.

IF SYMPTOMS PERSIST, CONSULT A DOCTOR

CAUTIONS

- Avoid if allergic to aspirin.
- Do not use meadowsweet in combination with standard 300 mg aspirin tablets, to avoid overdose. It can, however, be taken by those on low-dose aspirin (75 mg a day).
- Meadowsweet may constrict the airways, and should never be taken by people with asthma.
- Do not take when pregnant or breastfeeding.

Milk thistle
Silybum marianum (Carduus marianus) Asteraceae **Also called** St Mary's thistle, Blessed thistle, Variegated thistle A tough, herbaceous plant that thrives on wasteland, milk thistle is found in many parts of the world. Its shiny leaves are fringed with spines and have white veins, the result, according to myth, of milk from the Virgin's breast falling onto the plant. Crimson-mauve flowers made up of hundreds of florets crown the tops of stems in summer. These are followed by tufted seeds.

Parts used
SEEDS & LEAVES
- The seeds may be used fresh or dried.
- They are collected in autumn, dried and used in tablets, capsules and liquid extracts.
- Milk thistle is often combined with other plants that are used to treat bile problems, such as globe artichoke.
- The leaves are also sometimes used, but the use of the seeds is more common.
- The leaves are picked at the end of summer. They are then dried, cut into small pieces or crushed into a powder, and then used in the preparation of infusions.

dried seeds and leaves

Constituents
The seeds contain silymarin, a mixture of several compounds that are known to protect the liver. The leaves contain flavonoids – antioxidants that are good for circulation – and b-sitosterol, a substance that emulsifies fats and helps to break down cholesterol deposits.

Medicinal uses
In a number of studies, the silymarin in milk thistle has been shown to have antioxidant properties which help to protect the liver and other parts of the body from damage by free radicals. This is why milk thistle is recommended as a supplementary treatment for chronic hepatitis and cirrhosis. Spanish studies have also noted silymarin's anti-inflammatory action, and its soothing powers are sometimes employed to treat piles.

In addition, milk thistle is known to calm muscular spasms and stimulate the flow of bile from the gall bladder. It is therefore recommended as a treatment for bile flow and minor digestive problems, such as sluggish liver function. The plant is also reputed to stimulate menstruation.

Cultivation
Milk thistle grows readily from seed. Plant in a wild part of the garden in a sunny, well-drained spot. This plant tends to become weedy, and is considered to be a noxious weed in some parts of Australia and New Zealand.

PREPARATION AND DOSAGE
- To treat minor digestive problems, bile problems, chronic hepatitis, cirrhosis and improve liver function

LIQUID EXTRACT 4–9 g dried seed equivalent, three times a day.
TABLETS, CAPSULES 4–9 g dried seed equivalent, three times a day. Where possible, choose a product standardised for its content of silymarin (sometimes called silybin on product labels). Tablets and capsules are the preferred dosage form for those who are unable to tolerate alcohol.

IF SYMPTOMS PERSIST, CONSULT A DOCTOR

CAUTIONS
- Milk thistle can be allergenic. Stop using if you have a reaction.
- Do not use to treat problems caused by an obstruction to the flow of bile, such as gallstones.
- It is not advisable to use the plant when pregnant or breastfeeding.
- An overdose of any milk thistle preparation can cause vomiting.

Mistletoe *Viscum album* Viscaceae

Common in Europe, Viscum album *is a parasitic shrub that sinks its roots into the branches of trees with soft bark, such as ash, poplar and old apple trees. Its smooth, branched stems bear leathery, evergreen leaves. In spring, it bears clusters of yellowish flowers. The fruit, a sticky white berry, ripens in early winter. The medicinal qualities of mistletoes native to Australia and New Zealand have not been investigated.*

Parts used
LEAVES AND FRUIT (BERRIES)
- The leaves are gathered in spring and autumn and are dried rapidly until they turn a yellowy green.
- Despite their unpleasant bitter taste, the leaves are used in preparations that are taken internally. These include infusions, extracts, capsules and other pharmaceutical products.
- Sometimes the berries are picked for medicinal use.

Constituents
The significant active compounds in mistletoe are viscotoxins and lectins, poisonous substances, which, in tiny doses, are believed to help boost the immune system.

Medicinal uses
Mistletoe's capacity to lower blood pressure has been verified by experimental data, and seems to be due to the combined effects of a group of compounds rather than to one specific active agent.

Research in Germany has shown that mistletoe has a stimulating effect on the immune system and inhibits the growth of tumours – an effect attributed to its viscotoxins and lectins. This could make mistletoe useful in fighting cancer, if the toxicity of these components can be controlled.

It has also been claimed that the plant can help in treating hardening of the arteries, but the results of human clinical trials have so far proved disappointing.

Cultivation
Mistletoe is a parasitic plant associated with mature trees and is usually spread by birds. Rubbing its berries into crevices in the underside of the bark of a suitable soft-barked tree, such as apple, willow, ash, or poplar, can encourage mistletoe to grow there.

dried leaves

PREPARATION AND DOSAGE
- **Whether used in a simple infusion or in any other pharmaceutical preparation, only a medical herbalist or doctor can decide if mistletoe is a safe or suitable treatment in any individual case**

IF SYMPTOMS PERSIST, CONSULT A DOCTOR

CAUTIONS
- Because mistletoe leaves and berries contain several poisonous substances, no preparation of the plant should be taken unless under the supervision of a qualified medical herbalist or doctor.

Mugwort *Artemisia vulgaris* Asteraceae

Throughout Europe and around the Mediterranean, tufts of mugwort grow wild beside woodland paths and streams. Its upright stems often have reddish marks and can reach a height of 1.5 m. The deeply indented leaves are dark green on the top and white beneath. Tiny heads of small yellow or reddish brown flowers cluster around the stems in summer.

dried leaves and flowers

Parts used
LEAVES AND FLOWER HEADS
- Leaves and flowers are gathered in early summer, just as the plant comes into bloom. Flowers taken from dry areas are said to have more beneficial properties than those from a damp location.
- The dried plant is used to make infusions, powders, extracts, tinctures and a tonic wine.

Constituents
The presence of sesquiterpene lactones accounts for the bitter taste of mugwort. It also contains a little essential oil, flavonoids that have an anti-oxidant effect, coumarins and some phytosterols, which appear to mimic the action of the female hormone, oestrogen.

Medicinal uses
Though few of its properties are scientifically proven, mugwort is prescribed to treat a range of digestive problems, including slow digestion, indigestion and loss of appetite.

Mugwort is also reputed to be antispasmodic, so can help to ease intestinal cramps, and is an effective remedy for period pains. It is sometimes prescribed to bring on late periods.

There are centuries-old references to the effectiveness of mugwort in warding off disease and in 1989, in studies in China, scientists demonstrated the plant's antibacterial powers.

The herb is still prescribed to fight bacterial and fungal infections, and can be of great benefit when treating fevers, skin inflammation and rheumatism. It is also used to eliminate worms, an ability attributed to its essential oil and sesquiterpene lactones.

Mugwort has a long history of use in traditional Chinese medicine, and is one of the principle herbs used to make moxa, a treatment in which burning rolls of chopped herbs are used to warm acupuncture points.

Cultivation
Grow from seed, planted in spring. Mugwort likes sun, and does best in well-drained, neutral to alkaline soil.

PREPARATION AND DOSAGE
- **To treat digestive problems, delayed periods, menstrual pain, intestinal worms**

    LIQUID EXTRACT 500 mg–2 g dried herb equivalent, three times daily.
    INFUSION 5–10 g dried herb infused in 500 ml of boiling water for 10 minutes before straining. Drink in two doses during the day, preferably between meals. For period pains, this treatment should be taken for eight to ten days prior to menses.

IF SYMPTOMS PERSIST, CONSULT A DOCTOR

CAUTIONS
- Mugwort should not be used when pregnant or breastfeeding.
- People who are taking anticoagulant (blood-thinning) drugs such as warfarin should not use mugwort.
- Because of its sesquiterpenic lactones, contact with mugwort can cause allergic reactions such as dermatitis and conjunctivitis.
- Do not exceed the recommended or prescribed dose of mugwort.
- Moxabustion (the use of moxa) should be attempted only by trained professionals.

Mullein *Verbascum thapsus* Scrophulariaceae **Also called** Great mullein, Aaron's rod

Widely cultivated in Egypt and in central and southern Europe, mullein is a herbaceous biennial that is now naturalised in Australia and New Zealand. The plant is covered in yellowish down, which was once used for making wicks for candles – hence it is sometimes known as the 'candlewick plant'. From spring to autumn, it sports densely packed spikes of bright yellow flowers, which are often over 1 m tall.

Parts used
FLOWERS AND LEAVES
- The flowers must be picked when in full bloom and then dried rapidly in order to preserve their effectiveness.
- The leaves are collected when the plant is about two years old, and they should be harvested before flowering begins.
- Flowers and leaves are used in infusions, liquid extracts and also in tablets, capsules and infused oil.

Constituents
Mullein contains tannins, sugars, mucilage, flavonoids, iridoids, saponins and yellow colourants.

Medicinal uses
The mucilage in mullein helps to soothe irritation, while its saponins and flavonoids combine to reduce inflammation. The saponins also contribute expectorant properties, helping to remove mucus and phlegm from the respiratory tract. Consequently, a syrup made from mullein is used to ease a range of respiratory tract infections, such as colds, sore throats, asthma, bronchitis and laryngitis, as well as the symptoms of influenza.

In addition, the plant's anti-inflammatory and soothing abilities have long been recognised as effective in treating digestive problems, such as diarrhoea, gastritis, enteritis and colitis, and in helping to ease gout.

Applied externally, mullein will help to heal cuts and leg ulcers and to soothe skin irritations. Olive oil infused with the dried flowers is sometimes used to ease the pain of earache and haemorrhoids.

Cultivation
Mullein grows easily from seeds, planted in a sunny position in any type of well-drained soil. It is considered to be a weed in most parts of New Zealand and Australia. In some parts of Australia, landowners are legally compelled to take steps to eradicate it.

dried flowers

PREPARATION AND DOSAGE
- **To treat sore throats, colds, flu, laryngitis, bronchitis, tracheitis, gastritis, enteritis, colitis**

  LIQUID EXTRACT 500 mg–1.5 g dried herb equivalent, taken three times a day.
  INFUSION 1.5–2 g dried herb infused in 1 cup of boiling water for 15 minutes before straining. Drink 3 cups a day.

- **To treat cuts, leg ulcers, skin irritations**

  COMPRESS Soak 3 teaspoons of dried plant in 300 ml of cold water for 30 minutes. Gently bring to the boil. Strain. Soak a cloth in the solution. Apply twice a day.

IF SYMPTOMS PERSIST, CONSULT A DOCTOR

CAUTIONS
- Mullein should not be taken when pregnant or breastfeeding.

Myrrh *Commiphora myrrha, C. molmol* Burseraceae

Found mainly in East Africa and Somalia, the myrrh tree has a thick, twisted trunk that can grow to around 5 m high. The tiny leaves are made up of two leaflets, each with a spine at its tip. Small yellow-red flowers grow on the spiny branches in summer. Myrrh was greatly valued in ancient times, and in the Bible was one of the gifts presented at the birth of Jesus. It is also used in traditional Chinese and Ayurvedic medicine.

Parts used

RESIN

- During the rainy season, cuts are made in the bark of the tree, through which the resin oozes. This is white at first, then it turns yellow and finally a brownish red.
- The resin solidifies to form cracked translucent pieces of varying shapes and sizes. This is the precious myrrh mentioned in the Bible. It has a strong aroma and a bitter taste – 'myrrh' is Hebrew for bitterness.
- The myrrh pieces break up easily, and are used to make tinctures.

Constituents

The essential oil of myrrh contains furano-sesquiterpenes, which have an anti-inflammatory effect and give the wood a rich, characteristic scent. The resins are rich in alcohols and triterpenic acids.

Medicinal uses

Myrrh is one of the earliest plants to be put to medicinal use. Its healing powers were widely appreciated in the ancient world, and more recently studies have confirmed its antiseptic, anti-inflammatory, fever-reducing and analgesic actions. These are often employed to treat minor wounds as well as oral problems, such as inflammation, gum infections and damage caused by dentures.

Myrrh is also known to have the ability to relieve nasal congestion, and may help ease digestive problems due to trapped wind and muscle spasms.

Cultivation

Myrrh is hard to cultivate. It needs a warm, frost-free climate with distinct wet and dry seasons. In cooler or wetter areas, grow it in a heated greenhouse with temperatures above 10°C. Sow seeds in spring, or take cuttings at the end of the growing season.

resin

PREPARATION AND DOSAGE

- **To treat inflammation in the mouth, gum infections, damage from dentures**

  TINCTURE (1:5 in 90 per cent alcohol) Put 1 teaspoon into a glass of water. Use up to three times a day as a mouthwash, or applied directly to the affected area.

  IF SYMPTOMS PERSIST, CONSULT A DOCTOR

CAUTIONS

- Do not use myrrh internally, except when being supervised by a medical herbalist, and even then only for a short time.
- Prolonged use of myrrh is not recommended, because it can cause allergic reactions in some people.
- Individuals who suffer from any thyroid disorder should always seek the advice of a medical herbalist before using myrrh.
- Women who are pregnant or breastfeeding are advised to use myrrh sparingly, if at all.

Myrtle *Myrtus communis* Myrtaceae

Native to scrubland around the Mediterranean, but widely grown in Australia and New Zealand, myrtle is an evergreen shrub with erect, hairy stems and shiny, pointed oval leaves covered in tiny pits. White, sweet-smelling flowers are followed by purple-black fruits, or berries, about the size of a pea. Myrtle featured widely in myth and legend, symbolising Venus and love for the ancient Greeks.

Parts used

LEAVES AND BERRIES

- The leaves are gathered in spring, then dried in the shade so that they remain green.
- They are used in infusions and powders, as well as for their essential oil.
- The berries are picked in autumn. Fresh ones are sometimes chewed. In Corsica and Sardinia, a popular drink is made by steeping the berries in alcohol.

Constituents

Myrtle leaves contain a small quantity of essential oil. The berries contain more oil as well as tannins, and a number of organic acids.

Medicinal uses

Recent research has confirmed the antiseptic and decongestant powers of myrtle, which traditionally made it a valued treatment for respiratory and intestinal problems. It is also used occasionally to treat genital and urinary tract infections.

For its emollient and healing powers, it is recommended for treating skin infections, such as abscesses and boils, and the essential oil will kill lice infestations.

The berries are also sometimes chewed as an appetite stimulant, because they are said to help in promoting gastric function.

In addition, myrtle may have a new use in the treatment of diabetes. Preliminary tests have shown that it can help to reduce high blood-sugar levels.

Cultivation

Myrtle can be grown from seeds in autumn, a young nursery plant or woody cuttings taken in spring to autumn. It does best in a cool climate, in well-drained, neutral to alkaline soil.

dried leaves

berries

PREPARATION AND DOSAGE

- **To treat respiratory disorders**

   As prescribed by a medical herbalist.

- **To treat abscesses, boils**

   COMPRESS Boil 10 g dried leaves in 1 litre of water for 10 minutes, ensuring the pot is covered, and soak a clean cloth in the solution. Apply this to the affected area, two or three times a day. Alternatively, use a cloth soaked in diluted myrtle essential oil.

IF SYMPTOMS PERSIST, CONSULT A DOCTOR

CAUTIONS

- Because certain components in the essential oil can irritate the digestive system, it is highly advisable to take myrtle preparations internally only in close consultation with a doctor or medical herbalist.

Nettle *Urtica dioica* Urticaceae **Also called** Stinging nettle

Until the 17th century, nettle stalks were widely used for their fibres, which make a hardwearing, linenlike fabric. The German army used nettle fabric to make uniforms in World War I when cotton ran short. The word 'nettle' comes from an old Scandinavian word, noedl, meaning needle, from the plant's needle-sharp stinging hairs. Nettles colonise ditches, clearings and wasteland.

Parts used

LEAVES AND ROOTS

- The plant is harvested in spring and early summer, before flowering, when the stinging hairs are rich in histamine and serotonin.
- The leaves are used fresh, or dried to make infusions.
- The roots may be dried and powdered for capsules or used fresh.
- Both leaves and roots are crushed to yield juices.

Constituents

The leaves contain both iron and vitamin C – which aids iron absorption. They also contain other minerals, especially the elements calcium and potassium, as well as phenols and flavonoids. The stinging hairs consist largely of silicon, and contain histamine, serotonin and acetylcholine.

The roots are rich in polysaccharides, lecithin, phenolic compounds and sterols.

Medicinal uses

'Urtication', or flogging the affected parts of the body with nettles, was an old remedy for painful rheumatic joints.

Today, treatment is less brutal. Nettle is prescribed internally as a diuretic, as it can increase elimination of sodium and urea, thus helping to ease rheumatic and arthritic conditions. In addition, the leaves are also strongly anti-inflammatory, as shown by some in vitro studies carried out in Germany in 1999.

A nettle infusion is a good tonic that helps to stimulate the appetite, providing iron and fighting fatigue.

The root may help some prostate and urination problems. This was confirmed by German research published in *Planta Medica* in 2000, which observed that the root inhibited the growth of prostate tissue. Italian research carried out in 2002 suggests that root extracts may be useful in reducing blood pressure.

Externally, nettle is used for the treatment of acne, eczema, greasy skin and dandruff.

dried leaves

Cultivation

Grow nettles from seed planted in spring in a moist, loamy soil. Choose a spot with sun or light shade. Nettles are regarded as a weed in some areas.

PREPARATION AND DOSAGE

- **To treat rheumatic pain, fatigue, poor appetite**

  LIQUID EXTRACT 2–3 g dried herb equivalent, three times a day.
  TABLETS, CAPSULES Up to 2 g, three times a day.
  INFUSION 3–6 g dried herb infused in 1 cup of boiling water for 10 minutes before straining. Drink 3 cups a day.

- **To treat urine difficulties linked to benign prostate problems**

  LIQUID EXTRACT 1–2 g dried root equivalent, three times a day.
  CAPSULES Up to 6 g dried root equivalent, three times a day, or according to manufacturer's instructions.

- **To treat skin and scalp conditions**

  POULTICE Stew the leaves or roots and apply twice a day.

IF SYMPTOMS PERSIST, CONSULT A DOCTOR

CAUTIONS

- If taken over a long period, nettle leaves can cause skin rashes.
- May cause gastric inflammation.
- Do not self-prescribe for prostate problems – seek medical advice.
- Do not use if taking medication to treat diabetes, high or low blood pressure, or to depress the central nervous system.
- Do not take if pregnant or breastfeeding.

New Zealand flax *Phormium tenax* Phormiaceae **Also called** Harakeke

The curious flowers and long leaves of New Zealand flax make this plant a distinctive part of the New Zealand landscape. The stiff, sword-shaped leaves, up to 3 m long, grow from the base of this clump-forming plant, and an abundance of tubular, dull red flowers are borne on the long stalks in summer. It was introduced to Britain early in the 19th century, and was later used there for making twine and rope.

Parts used

LEAVES, ROOTS, GEL, SAP

- In traditional Maori medicine, a range of poultices and topical preparations were prepared from the roots, gel and sap. The roots and sap were sometimes taken internally.
- The leaves yield sap when cut open, while the gel is collected from between the bases of the young leaves.

Constituents

Laxative anthraquinones are present in the rhizomes. The gel is considered to have similar characteristics to that of *Aloe vera*, and this may help to explain the plant's traditional usage as a remedy for burns.

gel

Medicinal uses

In New Zealand, Maori used the plant for its fibre, but they also found it to be a valuable source of medicine. Various preparations were used to treat wounds, skin complaints, broken limbs, digestive problems and genito-urinary ailments.

The gel is considered to have antiseptic and mild pain-relieving properties, and the ability to help stop bleeding. Burns and wounds were treated with the gel, which was also used topically to relieve rheumatic pain and toothache. The flax root was applied if a wound needed disinfecting, and was also sometimes roasted on hot stones and then used to make a poultice to treat abscesses and ulcers. Wound dressings were made from the matted leaves, which were also used to bind broken limbs.

Curiously, New Zealand flax seems to have been used as a remedy for both diarrhoea and constipation. Leaf sap and chewed roots were taken for diarrhoea, whilst the roots were pounded to produce a juice with purgative, laxative properties that was used to expel intestinal worms.

Mixed with other plants, New Zealand flax was also used for treating female complaints, including bringing on menstruation and treating painful periods. Some Maori tribes used the leaf sap for the treatment of gonorrhoea.

Cultivation

New Zealand flax enjoys full sun and regular moisture. When planting, allow space for the clump to grow in width, and for the tall, bird-attracting flower spike, which can reach 3 m or more in height. Once established, flax plants are drought tolerant. Propagate from seed or by division in early spring. Potted plants are available for planting year round.

flower

PREPARATION AND DOSAGE

- **To treat burns, minor skin irritations**
  Apply the gel to the affected area.

IF SYMPTOMS PERSIST, CONSULT A DOCTOR

CAUTIONS

- Caution is advised when taking New Zealand flax preparations internally, as there is little information available regarding potential interactions with other medications.
- Repeated or long-term use as a laxative is not advised.

Nutmeg *Myristica fragrans* Myristicaceae

Found in tropical countries, such as Brazil, Indonesia and the West Indies, the nutmeg tree can grow to a height of 20 m. It has shiny, evergreen foliage, but its clusters of delicate, yellow flowers do not appear until the tree is around seven years old. The fleshy, pale yellow fruits each contain one large seed – the 'nut' – enclosed first in a hard, woody casing, then in a red or orangey membrane, known as mace.

Parts used

SEEDS (NUTS)
- The fruit is picked when ripe and beginning to split, and the seed is then removed.
- Using steam, about 8–15 per cent of the essential oil is extracted, together with nutmeg butter (used in the pharmaceutical industry).

Constituents
Nutmeg's essential oil, which has a sharp taste and a peppery smell, is composed mainly of camphene and pinene, but also contains myristicin, which is toxic.

Medicinal uses
Although nutmeg essential oil is reputed to be a tonic and aphrodisiac, it is seldom used for these purposes because of the toxicity of its myristicin content. Instead, it is reserved almost exclusively for use externally, as an anti-inflammatory remedy for joint pains, muscular injuries, rheumatism and tendonitis.

However, scientists in India have shown that the essential oil can help to lower blood cholesterol and to decrease fatty deposits around the liver, heart and aorta. In addition, Nigerian studies have shown that the essential oil can inhibit the formation of blood clots. All this evidence suggests that nutmeg could be useful in protecting against blockages and hardening of the arteries and associated heart and circulatory problems. Studies have also shown that it can lower harmful cholesterol.

One reason that nutmeg is used as a spice is because it aids digestion, and clinical studies have discovered that it can help treat diarrhoea.

Cultivation
Grow from seeds when ripe, or woody cuttings at the end of the growing season. Best in a humid, tropical climate in rich, well-drained sandy soil. In cool climates, grow in a humid greenhouse heated to a minimum of 15–18°C.

nuts

nut still encased in mace

PREPARATION AND DOSAGE

- **To treat joint pains, muscle injuries, rheumatism, tendonitis**

  ESSENTIAL OIL Dilute, using 3 drops of essential oil to 50 ml carrier oil. Apply directly to the affected area up to three times a day, or add to a daily bath.

IF SYMPTOMS PERSIST, CONSULT A DOCTOR

CAUTIONS

- Nutmeg's essential oil must never be ingested. The myristicin in it is toxic, and can cause dizziness, headaches and hallucinations, and irritates the digestive system.
- Externally, the essential oil must only be used sparingly for short periods, as it can irritate the skin.
- Consult a medical herbalist before considering internal use.

Oak *Quercus robur* Fagaceae **Also called** English oak

Venerated by the Druids, the oak was well known in the ancient world for its medicinal powers. The long-lived tree can grow to over 50 m tall, with boughs spreading to a circumference of nearly 100 m. In spring, dense clusters of oval, lobed leaves appear along with dangling male flowers, or catkins. Female flowers are barely visible, turning to the familiar brown, egg-shaped fruits, or acorns, by autumn.

Parts used

BARK FROM YOUNG BRANCHES

- The bark is collected in the spring, then cut up or crushed.
- It is used in infusions, liquid extracts and compresses, and may be added to foot and hand baths.
- Oak bark is also used in combination with other astringent plants, such as witch hazel.

Constituents

Tannins make up about 10–20 per cent of oak bark. These include epicatechin, gallocatechin and catechin. The highest concentration of tannins is found in trees that are about 10 years old.

Medicinal uses

Oak bark is known for its ability to combat various viruses, and the tannins give it astringent properties. For these reasons, when taken internally in small doses, it can help to relieve non-specific, acute diarrhoea and indigestion.

Applied externally, it can treat inflamed or chapped skin, chilblains, wet eczema, minor bleeding and haemorrhoids. It can also be added to baths to combat excessive foot odour.

Gargles and mouthwashes made with oak bark are used to soothe inflammation of the gums and the lining of the mouth, as well as for sore throats.

Tests have recently shown that the tannins in oak are able to limit tissue damage in people suffering from rheumatic disease. This discovery may eventually result in a new medicinal use for the oak bark.

Cultivation

Plant acorns in well-drained soil in sun or partial shade, or propagate by grafting in autumn or late winter.

female flowers between the leaves; male flowers dangling

bark from young branches

PREPARATION AND DOSAGE

- **To treat non-specific acute diarrhoea**

    LIQUID EXTRACT 500 mg–2 g dried bark equivalent, taken three times a day.

    INFUSION 2 g dried bark infused in 1 cup of boiling water for 10 minutes before straining. Drink 3–4 cups a day.

- **To treat foot odour, inflamed or chapped skin, chilblains, wet eczema, light bleeding, haemorrhoids**

    BATHS AND COMPRESSES Put 100 g of bark powder into 1 litre of water. Boil for 20 minutes and filter. Bathe feet or hands three or four times a day, or apply soaked compresses to the area affected.

    LIQUID EXTRACT (diluted to 10 per cent strength) Add to a bath or apply on a compress three or four times a day.

IF SYMPTOMS PERSIST, CONSULT A DOCTOR

CAUTIONS

- Oak bark preparations should not be taken internally for more than four weeks at a time.
- Do not use oak bark baths if you have dermatitis or a cut. Also avoid them if you have an infectious illness or feel feverish.
- Make sure an oak bark bath does not come into contact with your eyes.

Oats *Avena sativa* Poaceae

Grown in all temperate regions of the world, oats are an important cereal crop. Long, slender leaves grow along stalks, which can reach a height of around 1.5 m. Clusters of flowers are followed by the tiny ears that enclose the seeds, or grain.

Parts used

SEEDS (GRAIN) AND STEMS

- After harvesting, which generally takes place in late summer, the seeds and stems are dried.
- When gathered for medicinal uses, the grain is removed from the husk and pressed, then used along with the dried stalks in the preparation of infusions, tablets and liquid extracts.

Constituents

Oat grains contain gluten, vitamins B_2, B_5 and E, the minerals calcium, iron, manganese and zinc, a soothing oil and a small quantity of alkaloids. The stems also contain flavonoids.

Medicinal uses

Herbalists have long considered oats to be an excellent nervous system tonic, one particularly suited for use in situations where long-term stress has led to exhaustion. They also regard it as a valuable restorative in some instances of depression.

Vitamin B_5 and other B vitamins are known for their ability to ease depression, stress and fatigue, and alkaloids are said to soothe the nerves. Their presence in oats may help to explain why the herb is frequently prescribed in this way.

In some controlled trials, athletes placed on an oat-based diet demonstrated an increase in stamina of approximately 4 per cent.

Herbalists have long used oats to help ease indigestion and to soothe the intestinal inflammation associated with diarrhoea. This anti-inflammatory action, probably due to the flavonoids, can also bring relief from rheumatism and gout.

In the ancient world, oats were used to treat skin problems, such as boils and impetigo, and recent clinical trials carried out in France have confirmed their efficacy in this regard. The addition of rolled porridge oats to bathwater has long been a popular remedy to relieve the itch of chickenpox and other skin conditions.

Oats have also been shown to lower cholesterol. In a Mexican study, men given oat-enriched cookies over an 8-week period showed a drop of around 26 per cent in their cholesterol levels.

Cultivation

Sow the seeds in spring in well-composted, well-drained soil in a sunny position.

grains

PREPARATION AND DOSAGE

- **To treat stress, insomnia, exhaustion, minor nervous problems, mild depression, rheumatism, gout**

  LIQUID EXTRACT 1–4 g dried herb equivalent, three times a day.
  TABLETS Follow manufacturer's instructions.
  INFUSION 3 g dried herb infused in 1 cup of boiling water for 5 minutes before straining. Drink 3–4 cups a day. For insomnia, drink 1 cup at bedtime.

- **To treat skin ailments**

  COMPRESS Make up the infusion (see above) and soak a clean cloth in it before applying to the affected area.
  DECOCTION Put 20 g of dried plant into 1 litre of water. Allow to boil for 3 minutes, then leave for 10–20 minutes. Strain, then add to bathwater. Alternatively, tie ½ cup of rolled porridge oats into a handkerchief or stocking to form a loose ball, and then use in the bath as a sponge.

IF SYMPTOMS PERSIST, CONSULT A DOCTOR

CAUTIONS

- Like many other cereals, oats are rich in gluten and therefore should be avoided by people suffering from coeliac disease.

Olive *Olea europaea* Oleaceae

Widely cultivated in the Mediterranean region, and more recently in wine-growing areas of Australia and New Zealand, the olive tree has a grey, twisted trunk and grows to a height of about 10 m. Its spear-shaped, evergreen leaves are grey-green on top and silvery white beneath. Its flowers are white and grow in erect clusters. Its oval fruit, the olive, is green at first, ripening to black, with a hard stone at its centre.

Parts used

LEAVES AND FRUIT

- Mature leaves are gathered in spring, before the flowers come into bud.
- They are dried, broken into fragments and used for infusions, extracts and tinctures, or combined with other plants in preparations that lower blood pressure.
- Olives are picked in autumn and winter. Their oil is expressed cold from the ripe fruit for culinary use and for creams and liniments.

Constituents

The leaves of the olive tree contain secoiridoids, in particular oleuropein, which reduces blood pressure. They also contain triterpenes and flavonoids. Olive oil, which is obtained from the fruit, is rich in monounsaturated (oleic acid) and polyunsaturated fatty acids (linoleic and linolenic acids) as well as the anti-oxidant vitamin E.

Medicinal uses

Thanks mainly to the oleuropeoside, olive leaves have several beneficial effects. They are useful in helping to reduce blood pressure, dilate coronary blood vessels, regulate heartbeat, lower blood-sugar levels and they also act as a diuretic.

Olive leaves, often in combination with hawthorn (see p. 115), are considered an effective treatment for mild cases of high blood pressure. Their ability to lower blood pressure was demonstrated by Egyptian researchers in animal studies carried out in 2002.

The extract can also be used as a supplementary treatment for less serious forms of Type 2 (non-insulin dependent) diabetes. The results of Spanish studies performed in 1992 showed that oleuropeoside lowered blood-sugar levels in in vitro models of diabetes.

Applied externally, olive oil softens and soothes the skin, which is why it is an ingredient in many protective sunscreens and liniments used to soothe burns.

dried leaves

Cultivation

Olive trees are grown from seed sown in autumn, or cuttings. They are frost-hardy and need a well-drained soil and plenty of sunshine. Depending on the variety, olives differ greatly in flavour, and those that make the best eating do not necessarily produce the finest oil.

PREPARATION AND DOSAGE

- **To treat mild cases of high blood pressure, mild forms of Type 2 diabetes**

  LIQUID EXTRACT 500 mg–1 g dried leaf equivalent, taken three times a day.
  TABLETS, CAPSULES Follow manufacturer's instructions.
  INFUSION Put 20 dried leaves in 300 ml of water. Boil for 30 seconds and leave to infuse for 10 minutes. Strain. Drink at least 3 cups a day during meals.

- **To treat sunburn, burns**

  OLIVE OIL–BASED CREAMS AND LINIMENTS Apply as directed several times a day.

IF SYMPTOMS PERSIST, CONSULT A DOCTOR

CAUTIONS

- To date, when used as directed or prescribed, neither olive leaf nor olive oil has any known adverse side effects.

Oregano *Origanum vulgare* Lamiaceae **Also called** Wild marjoram

A perennial that can reach a height of 30–80 cm, oregano is grown worldwide. Its pointed, oval leaves grow in pairs opposite each other along the woody, reddish stems. Between mid-summer and mid-autumn, round clusters of pinkish crimson flowers appear at the top of the plant, offering passing bees an abundance of nectar. As well as having medicinal value, the aromatic plant is also a popular culinary herb.

Parts used

AERIAL PARTS

- The best time to gather oregano is in early to mid-summer, just as the first flowers appear.
- Once picked, the aerial parts are dried and used for infusions or to extract the essential oil.

Constituents

Oregano is rich in flavonoids, and the essential oil contains thymol and carvacrol, both of which have strong antiseptic and antispasmodic properties.

Medicinal uses

Researchers have demonstrated the ability of thymol and carvacrol in the essential oil to act against bacterial and fungal infections. For example, in 2001, American studies showed the power of the essential oil to act against the fungus *Candida albicans*, which can cause thrush. The essential oil is also beneficial in helping to treat a range of urinary, intestinal and lung infections, and is known to have a stimulating, tonic effect.

Scientists have also demonstrated the antispasmodic powers of thymol and carvacrol, and oregano infusions are recommended for coughs and bronchitis, as well as for indigestion and stomach spasms, with the volatile oils helping to settle flatulence and stimulate the flow of bile.

Oregano can also be applied externally in ointments and massage oils to help ease rheumatic pain, period pain and headaches.

Cultivation

Oregano can be grown from seed, sown in autumn or spring. It thrives in dryish, well-drained, neutral to alkaline soil and needs warmth and full sun for its true flavour to develop.

dried aerial parts

PREPARATION AND DOSAGE

- **To treat abdominal wind, stomach upsets, candida (thrush)**

  CAPSULES Follow manufacturer's instructions.

- **To treat rheumatic pain, headaches**

  MASSAGE OIL Soak 100 g of aerial parts in 500 ml of warmed olive oil for 30 minutes. Strain and apply three or four times a day to painful areas, including, if necessary, the forehead and temples. Otherwise apply a mixture of 3 drops of essential oil to every 10 ml of carrier oil.

IF SYMPTOMS PERSIST, CONSULT A DOCTOR

CAUTIONS

- In large doses oregano may cause excitability and irritability.
- Applied externally, the essential oil may cause skin irritations.
- Never ingest the essential oil, unless prescribed by a doctor or medical herbalist, as it can irritate the mucous membranes.
- Avoid oregano when pregnant, as it can stimulate the uterus.

Papaya *Carica papaya* Caricaceae **Also called** Pawpaw

Characterised by a tall, slender trunk crowned with a clump of leaves, the papaya tree grows in many tropical and subtropical regions and can reach a height of 3–10 m. The greenish male flowers are small, and cluster under the leaves. The female flowers are bigger and grow singly or in groups of two or three near the top of the trunk. The fruit is a large berry, packed with orange flesh when ripe.

Parts used

FRUIT SAP

- Sap is collected by means of tap-holes inserted in the unripe fruit when it is still on the trees.
- The sap, a white liquid or latex, has to be dried in order to preserve it, and this is done in the sunshine.
- The dried sap ranges in colour from yellow to brown and smells like meat extract.
- Each fruit provides about 10 g of fresh sap, which will produce up to 2 g of raw, dried papain in powder form. Papain is used for tablets, capsules and elixirs. It is also included in a range of pharmaceutical products.

Constituents

The sap contains a mixture of enzymes that are proteolytic (able to break down proteins). These include papain, chymopapain and papayaproteinases.

Medicinal uses

Papain kills stomach parasites as well as having a calming, soothing effect on the digestive system. Its proteolytic enzymatic activity helps stomach acids to break down proteins.

The plant is used to treat stomach and pancreatic disorders, abdominal bloating and nausea caused by migraine. It is also used to treat various intestinal parasites, such as threadworms, ascaris (roundworms) and ancylostoma, as well as various blood vessel problems, such as varicose veins, ulcers and haemorrhoids. Studies performed in Italy in 1996 demonstrated that the sap exerted antifungal activity against *Candida albicans*, the microbe that is responsible for thrush.

Used externally, papaya acts against water retained in the tissues, and is beneficial in the treatment of oedema, abscesses and wounds. Clinical studies performed in 1969 found that papaya may possess anti-inflammatory properties that would benefit patients recovering from operations or injuries.

Cultivation

Papaya can be grown from seed, planted in moist, rich soil in spring. Seeds produce male and female plants. Remove excess males, leaving only 1 per 50 females. Papaya needs warmth and sunshine and will not tolerate frost. In cold climates, it must be grown in a heated greenhouse.

fruit

powder

PREPARATION AND DOSAGE

- **To treat digestive ailments**

  TABLETS Take as directed on the label, as constituents vary according to brand. Papain is sometimes prescribed with bromelain, from pineapple (see p.156).

- **To treat wounds**

  RAW FRUIT OR JUICE Apply to the affected area, two to three times a day, for up to a week.

IF SYMPTOMS PERSIST, CONSULT A DOCTOR

CAUTIONS

- Medicinal use of papaya is not recommended for pregnant or breastfeeding women.
- Papaya preparations may trigger allergies in some susceptible individuals.
- Prolonged use should be avoided.
- Papainous injections may induce a fatal allergic reaction.

Passionflower *Passiflora incarnata* Passifloraceae **Also called** Maypops, Apricot vine

This climbing shrub is native to South America and can grow to 9 m. It has three-lobed, indented leaves and climbs by means of tendrils. Its showy flowers grow singly and have white petals, surmounted by a crown of violet or pink filaments, and large stamens with orange-coloured sacs. This medicinal plant must not be confused with the cultivated variety that produces passionfruit.

Parts used

AERIAL PARTS

- The aerial parts of the plant are gathered at the end of summer.
- After drying, passionflower is used for infusions, tinctures, liquid extracts and powders.

Constituents

In addition to a tiny percentage of maltol, passionflower contains traces of indole alkaloids and up to 2.5 per cent of various flavonoids.

Medicinal uses

Passionflower is used to treat insomnia, anxiety, muscle spasms, palpitations and digestive problems that have a nervous origin. It is a gentle remedy, and is particularly suitable for use with children. Its properties produce a relaxing effect, making it a mild, non-addictive tranquilliser, similar in some respects to valerian. It has also been used traditionally as a painkiller for toothache, period pain and headaches.

Scientific studies carried out in 1974 suggest that maltol and ethyl maltol impart the sedative effects. In addition, the flavonoids are likely to have a sedative action as well.

Cultivation

Plant potted vines or sow seeds in spring, or take cuttings in summer. Grow in full sun in well-drained soil.

dried aerial parts

PREPARATION AND DOSAGE

- **To treat insomnia, anxiety, nervous agitation**

  LIQUID EXTRACT 500 mg–1 g dried herb equivalent. For insomnia, take one dose at bedtime. For anxiety and agitation, take one dose three times a day.

  TABLETS, CAPSULES Follow manufacturer's instructions.

IF SYMPTOMS PERSIST, CONSULT A DOCTOR

CAUTIONS

- To date, no side effects have been recorded for the use of passionflower in therapeutic doses. However, pregnant and breastfeeding women should avoid the plant until more information is available about its safety in these circumstances.

Pau d'arco *Tabebuia impetiginosa* Bignoniaceae **Also called** Lapacho

Pau d'arco is a large tree that is native to mountainous regions of South America. Its medicinal use is believed to have originated in Brazil at least 1000 years ago, and from there it spread to other regions of South America before gaining international prominence as a reputed cancer cure. The tree has smooth, greyish bark, papery grey-green leaves and attractive flowers that range from rose-pink to deep purple.

Parts used

INNER BARK

- The wood and inner bark are dried for use in preparing decoctions, tablets and liquid extracts.
- Traditionally, decoctions were used for topical applications. For these, the herb was boiled in water. However, it is not known whether alcohol-based processes are more efficient for the extraction of key active constituents.

Constituents

Key constituents of pau d'arco include naphthoquinones and furanonaphthoquinones, flavonoids, anthraquinones, coumarins and iridoids. Although most research has focused on lapachol, a naphthoquinone, it is considered likely that other constituents also contribute to the herb's actions.

inner bark

Medicinal uses

The traditional Brazilian use of pau d'arco for the treatment of cancer is supported by in vitro research that shows that lapachol and other constituents are able to inhibit the growth and activity of tumour cells. Immune-stimulating activity has also been documented for some constituents. Further research is required before the effects of the plant on cancer are fully understood, and conclusive results with human cancer patients are not yet available.

Pau d'arco and some of its individual constituents have documented antibacterial, antiviral, antifungal and antiparasitic effects. Amongst the affected organisms are the herpes virus, Epstein-Barr virus (the virus that causes glandular fever) and penicillin-resistant *Staphylococcus aureus*. The herb is also prescribed for the treatment of thrush and is considered an important natural antibiotic for bacterial and viral infections, especially of the mouth and throat.

In traditional Brazilian medicine, topical applications of pau d'arco were used to treat psoriasis, eczema, skin cancer and snake bite. The plant was also taken for dysentery, intestinal inflammation and other digestive conditions, as well as for sore throats, inflamed joints and degenerative disorders.

Cultivation

Grow in moist, well-drained fertile soil, preferably in full sun and in a tropical to subtropical climate. In cool areas, grow plants in containers and provide winter warmth. Plants may not flower when grown in cool areas. Pau d'arco can be grown from seed, cutting or by layering.

PREPARATION AND DOSAGE

- Pau d'arco should be used only on the advice of a medical herbalist

IF SYMPTOMS PERSIST, CONSULT A DOCTOR

CAUTIONS

- Pau d'arco should not be used by pregnant or breastfeeding women, or in conjunction with anticoagulant (blood-thinning) medications, such as warfarin.
- Do not exceed the recommended dose.
- Do not rely on pau d'arco as the sole treatment for cancer or infection. The effects are not fully understood, and may be mild.

Peppermint Mentha x piperita Lamiaceae

The peppermint we know today is a perennial cultivated as a cross between water mint and spearmint. It has square, purplish or crimson stems and its aromatic leaves are oval shaped with pointed tips. The plant bears whorls of crimson flowers in late summer. Peppermint, along with spearmint, is one of the most popular flavourings in the world, being used in everything from ice-creams to liqueurs.

Parts used
LEAVES
- The leaves are harvested in summer when the plant is flowering and at its most aromatic.
- Fresh or dried, the leaves are used for infusions. The essential oil is used externally or professionally prescribed in enteric-coated capsules.
- Peppermint has a wide variety of uses as a flavouring.

Constituents
Peppermint is rich in phenolic compounds (7 per cent), the properties of which include antiviral, anti-inflammatory and antioxidant actions. It also contains generous amounts of flavonoids and tannins. The yield of essential oil is very high: 10–30 ml per kg of the dried plant.

The composition of the oil varies according to weather and when it is harvested. The oil's main constituents are menthol (30–50 per cent), menthone (15–35 per cent) and menthyl acetate (10 per cent).

dried leaves

Medicinal uses
Peppermint has digestive, antispasmodic properties due mainly to its essential oil and flavonoids. It is therefore taken internally to treat problems such as bloating, sluggish digestion, belching, flatulence and inadequate bile secretion.

Taiwanese trials in 1997 verified the oil's carminative effect when it was found to relieve the intestinal cramps suffered by individuals with irritable bowel syndrome (IBS). In 2001, American research also found it to be effective in children with IBS. In small doses it has a sedative effect and in large doses a tonic effect.

Externally, the essential oil helps to soothe skin irritations and insect bites. Taken as an inhalation, it is useful in the treatment of colds and flu since the menthol component acts as a nasal decongestant. It can also be used as a mouthwash to treat oral infections, and it may remedy headaches. Commercially, the largest use of peppermint oil is as a chewing-gum flavour.

Cultivation
Suited to rich, moist soil. Place in a sunny or lightly shaded location.

PREPARATION AND DOSAGE
- **To treat bloating, sluggish digestion, belching, flatulence, inadequate bile secretion, colic**
  INFUSION Put 1 teaspoon dried leaves into 150 ml of boiling water. Infuse for 10–15 minutes, then strain. Drink 1 cup after meals.
  ENTERIC-COATED PEPPERMINT CAPSULES As prescribed by a doctor or medical herbalist.
- **To treat headache**
  ESSENTIAL OIL Dilute, allowing 3 drops per 10 ml of carrier oil. Massage into forehead, temples and base of skull. Avoid eyes.
- **To treat colds, oral infections**
  INHALATIONS, MOUTHWASH Put a handful of leaves into a bowl of boiling water. Inhale the steam, or cool and use as a mouthwash.

IF SYMPTOMS PERSIST, CONSULT A DOCTOR

CAUTIONS
- Use of the leaf poses no risk, but the essential oil must be taken internally only under medical supervision. Avoid prolonged use.
- The essential oil should not be taken by small children or pregnant or breastfeeding women.
- The essential oil may exacerbate acid reflux problems.

Pine
Pinus sylvestris Pinaceae **Also called** Scot's pine

Native to the mountainous regions of Europe and north and west Asia, the pine can reach a height of 30 m or more. In the Scottish Highlands, the trees were once used as dramatic markers for the burial places of warriors, heroes and chieftains. Druids used to light large bonfires of pine at the winter solstice to celebrate the passing of the seasons and to draw back the sun.

Parts used
CONES, RESIN AND NEEDLES
- Cone buds are picked in the spring. The essential oil is extracted or the buds are dried.
- The needles are the source of essential oils used in disinfectants.
- The resin, collected from cuts in the trunk, is distilled and provides turpentine.

Constituents
The pine cone buds contain an essential oil that is rich in pinene, limonene and resin. Pine-needle oil is distilled from the fresh needles and branch tips. The needles also contain flavonoids and a small amount of vitamin C.

dried cone buds

Pine resin is rich in terpenes, which give it its aroma.

Medicinal uses
Pine has long been recognised as being a powerful bronchial disinfectant. According to Egyptian papyruses, physicians to the pharaohs used to prescribe pine resin for pneumonia and lung problems. It has a soothing effect on mucous membranes, making it a good inhalant for respiratory problems.

Pine has antiseptic, diuretic and antirheumatic properties. It exerts a decongestant effect on the upper respiratory tract and is often prescribed for the treatment of chronic (long-term) bronchitis, coughs and laryngitis.

Its powerful antiseptic action helps to eliminate respiratory and urinary tract infections. Finnish studies performed in 2000 found pine to be effective against several species of bacteria as well as *Candida albicans*, the fungus that is responsible for causing thrush.

Externally, turpentine oil rubbed well into the skin stimulates circulation in the peripheral blood vessels, which helps to remove toxins and supplies vital nutrients to the cells.

Pine-needle oil is used in vapour rubs that are recommended as a supplementary treatment for colds and chills. Drops of the essential oil added to boiling water make a refreshing decongesting steam vapour for blocked nose or sinuses.

Cultivation
Pines can grow very tall. In good conditions, in a cool climate, a 30 m pine can quickly dominate a small garden, so think carefully before planting. Pine trees like any well-drained, neutral to acid soil (although they will also tolerate alkaline conditions) and a sunny spot.

PREPARATION AND DOSAGE

- **To treat bronchitis, coughs, laryngitis**

  INFUSION Put 20 g of buds into 1 litre of boiling water. Infuse for 10 minutes and strain. Drink 4–5 cups a day.

- **To treat laryngitis**

  GARGLE Make up the infusion (see above) and use as a gargle four or five times a day.

- **To treat colds, chills, respiratory congestion**

  INHALANT Make up the infusion (see above) and inhale the steam from it three or four times a day.
  BATH Put 250 g of dried pine needles in a fabric bag into a warm bath. Or put about 250 g of pine needles into 2 litres of boiling water and infuse for 20 minutes. Strain and add to a warm bath.

To treat rheumatic pains

OINTMENT, LINIMENT Apply several times a day as directed.
ESSENTIAL OIL Dilute, allowing 3 drops of essential oil per 10 ml of carrier oil, and massage into affected areas.

IF SYMPTOMS PERSIST, CONSULT A DOCTOR

CAUTIONS
- No adverse side effects from the use of pine buds have been recorded to date.
- Do not use essential oils internally.
- Do not use pine oil externally if you are prone to skin allergies.

Pineapple *Ananas comosus* Bromeliaceae

Native to South America, but grown worldwide in areas with a suitable climate, the pineapple is a perennial with a large stem that can grow to 1 m in height. Its fleshy, spiny leaves are shaped like spearheads. The flowers form a dense spike on the top of the stem. The fruit, topped by a crown of leaves, is made up of yellow or reddish yellow berries, which seem to be welded to one another.

Parts used

RIPE AND UNRIPE FRUIT AND STEM

- The best way of consuming pineapple is to eat the ripe, raw fruit or to drink its juice.
- The stems are collected after the fruit has been harvested.
- Bromelain – an enzyme found in pineapple – is made into tablets.

Constituents

The fruit and the stem of the pineapple plant both contain an enzyme called bromelain, which is proteolytic (it breaks down proteins). The fruit is also a source of vitamins A and C.

Medicinal uses

Bromelain is the key to pineapple's medicinal uses. This enzyme breaks down proteins and also has anti-inflammatory and healing properties. It is prescribed for the treatment of swelling following injury or surgery.

Research published in 1986 suggests that bromelain works by inhibiting the synthesis of inflammatory mediators as well as inhibiting platelet aggregation. Separate research performed in Germany in 1999 confirmed this antiplatelet activity, indicating its use in the treatment of thrombosis.

The unripe fruit has the effect of stimulating the appetite, and is an effective treatment for indigestion. The ripe fruit helps in reducing stomach acidity and flatulence.

Cultivation

Pineapple is suited to both tropical and subtropical environments. In cooler zones, grow against a north-facing masonry wall where there is plenty of sun or in a heated greenhouse.

fresh fruit

PREPARATION AND DOSAGE

- **To treat indigestion, inflammation**

  BROMELAIN TABLETS, CAPSULES Up to 2000 mg per day, in divided doses, before meals. Higher doses may be taken if prescribed by a medical herbalist. Bromelain is sometimes prescribed with papain from papaya (see p.151).

IF SYMPTOMS PERSIST, CONSULT A DOCTOR

CAUTIONS

- Pineapple fruit and juice normally cause no side effects, but should not be given to children under six, as bromelain can irritate the digestive mucous membranes.
- Excessive pineapple intake can cause stomach-ache, diarrhoea and allergic reactions.
- Pregnant women should not drink large quantities of pineapple juice since it may induce uterine contractions.
- Pineapple should not be used while taking anticoagulant (blood-thinning) drugs, and may enhance the effects of some drugs. Check first with a medical herbalist.

Poppy, common
Papaver rhoeas Papaveraceae **Also called** Corn poppy, Field poppy, Flanders poppy

Characterised by their blood red, papery flowers and delicate hairy stems, poppies are annuals often seen growing wild on the edges of fields throughout Europe. The leaves are highly serrated and form large rosettes at the base of the flower stems. The fruit is an oval-shaped capsule enclosing hundreds of tiny black seeds.

Parts used
PETALS
- After the petals have been gathered and dried in spring and early summer, they are used to make liquid extracts and syrups.
- The flowers may be mixed with other plants with similar qualities, such as lime flowers and lavender.

Constituents
Poppy petals contain mucilage, anthocyanins and a small amount of alkaloids, which constitute 0.07 per cent of the plant, the main one being rhoeadine. These exert similar but milder effects than those found in the opium poppy. The seed capsules of the plant are not used medicinally because they contain toxic alkaloids, but are used in cooking, and are safe in small amounts.

Medicinal uses
The mucilage content of the petals has a soothing effect on the lining of the throat. Preparations with a base of poppy petals, often combined with blue mallow and marshmallow, provide an effective treatment for dry coughs and hoarseness.

Poppy possesses sedative and antispasmodic effects, and is prescribed to treat the symptoms of nervous tension, particularly mild insomnia, in adults and children. It is also reputed to aid digestion and possesses mild analgesic qualities.

A French study in 2001 demonstrated the sedative effects of the plant. Analysis of the extract used showed the presence of anthocyanins, but no alkaloids.

Traditionally, the common poppy has been used to treat cardiac rhythm abnormalities in adults whose hearts are otherwise healthy.

Cultivation
Grow from seed planted in autumn or early spring. Suited to well-drained soil and a sunny location.

dried petals

PREPARATION AND DOSAGE
- **Poppy should be taken only on the advice of a medical herbalist**

IF SYMPTOMS PERSIST, CONSULT A DOCTOR

CAUTIONS
- It is best to consult a medical herbalist before taking the plant.
- Keep out of reach of children. Cases of poisoning after ingesting poppy syrup have been recorded.

Psyllium   *Plantago ovata* Plantaginaceae **Also called** Ispaghula, Blond psyllium

Native to western Asia and India, psyllium is a small annual herb with many erect stems and narrow, lance-shaped leaves that are indented and hairy with a vertical, parallel vein. The white flowers grow in cylindrical spikes. The size and shape of the plant's pink or greyish brown seeds – 2 mm long and shaped like small, oval boats – gave rise to the name, derived from the Greek word *psylla, meaning flea.*

dried seeds

Parts used
SEEDS AND HUSKS
- When ripe, the seeds are harvested, threshed and dried in the sun.
- The seeds are then used to make bulk-forming laxatives, which may be in the form of powders, drinkable solutions and granules.

Constituents
Up to around 30 per cent of the seed is composed of mucilage, which is responsible for its laxative effects. In addition, the seed also contains proteins, lipids and sterols.

Medicinal uses
The mucilage present in psyllium helps to bulk out the stools by absorbing water. As the mucilage is not absorbed by the digestive tract, the result is a marked improvement in both the movement and the softness of the stools. Due to this gentle action, psyllium is a popular remedy for both constipation and diarrhoea.

Psyllium should be used on its own, and not combined with stimulant laxatives such as senna. A clinical trial performed in Germany in 1994 documents the efficacy of psyllium husk in treating irritable bowel syndrome. Psyllium is also reputed to soothe gastric inflammation, as well as urinary tract infections.

It has also been suggested that psyllium mucilage may reduce both blood-sugar and cholesterol levels. A Spanish study performed in 2001 demonstrated the ability of psyllium husk to lower blood-glucose levels after eating.

Cultivation
Plant in well-drained soil in an area that receives some light shade. The seeds are obtained at the beginning of autumn, and some can then be saved for sowing the following spring.

PREPARATION AND DOSAGE
- **To treat constipation, high cholesterol**

  POWDER SACHET (3–6 g) Take 1 sachet with a main meal, diluted in a large glass of water.
  GRANULES Follow manufacturer's instructions.

IF SYMPTOMS PERSIST, CONSULT A DOCTOR

CAUTIONS
- Do not take laxatives for prolonged periods without the consent of a doctor.
- Psyllium should never be used by anyone with undiagnosed abdominal pains, intestinal blockage or a diagnosed intestinal illness.
- While taking the laxative, you should eat a healthy, high-fibre diet, drink plenty of fluids and take physical exercise.
- Do not take other medications at the same time of day as psyllium.

Puha *Sonchus oleraceus* Asteraceae **Also called** Smooth sow thistle

Puha is common throughout New Zealand and much of Australia, and is generally regarded as a weed. It grows in a wide variety of habitats, including coastal and damp places, gardens, paddocks and roadsides. The plant is tall and lush, with distinctive grey-green leaves with irregular margins. The stems are tough and hollow with a milky sap, while the flowers are pale yellow and resemble those of the dandelion.

Parts used
LEAVES
- The leaves are used as both a medicine and a nutritious vegetable.

Constituents
The constituents of puha include several phenols and the triterpene taraxerol – chemicals with anti-infective and purgative properties. Nutrients include vitamin C, together with calcium, phosphorus and iron.

Medicinal uses
Some think that puha was one of the plants used by Captain Cook as a remedy for scurvy. However, it seems more likely that it was introduced into Australia and New Zealand, probably from Europe. The Greek physician Dioscorides noted in his 1st-century herbal that smooth sow thistle was a remedy for 'burning stomach' and scorpion bites.

A related New Zealand native species, the prickly sow thistle, or puwha (*Sonchus kirkii*), was used by Maori for food, but they soon found that the smooth sow thistle was more palatable than the prickly variety. It was not long before the plant was used for medicinal as well as culinary purposes.

Preparations of the thistle were prescribed by Maori for stomach complaints, wounds and carbuncles, while a combination of juices from puwha and other plants was used after childbirth to expel the placenta and reduce bleeding. Puha was also traditionally used to bring on late menses, and to treat diarrhoea. The leaves were used as a poultice to treat inflammatory swellings.

In Australia, some groups of Aboriginal people ate the raw leaves to soothe pain and induce sleep. The plant was also used as part of an emetic concoction.

In Africa, puha has been used to expel intestinal worms and as a treatment for wounds and ulcers.

Although it is predominantly used as a vegetable, puha is still sometimes prescribed by herbalists as a laxative and skin healer. Its leaves are considered to have similar properties to those of dandelion, acting as a diuretic and liver tonic.

Cultivation
Puha grows easily from seed. However, it tends to become weedy, and is often infested by aphids. The plant thrives in a variety of habitats, but it prefers moist, fertile soils with sun or partial shade. Avoid growing puha in areas where cattle graze, as it may cause photosensitisation.

fresh leaves

PREPARATION AND DOSAGE
- Use as a nutritious vegetable. Puha leaves are steamed, in the same way as spinach

IF SYMPTOMS PERSIST, CONSULT A DOCTOR

CAUTIONS
- There are no known cautions regarding the culinary or medicinal use of puha.

Pumpkin   *Cucurbita pepo*   Cucurbitaceae   **Also called** Summer squash

Grown in Central America for at least 9000 years, pumpkin is now cultivated all over the world for its enormous, globular fruit. The name pumpkin derives from 'pepon', a Greek word meaning mellow or sun ripened. A long, prickly stem bears large, downy leaves and deep yellow funnel-shaped flowers. These are followed by orange fruits containing numerous flat, white seeds.

Parts used

SEEDS AND FRUIT FLESH

- The flesh is eaten fresh, or dried for medicinal use.
- The seeds may be hulled and eaten whole, crushed for oil or used in tinctures.
- The vegetables grown and sold in Australia and New Zealand as pumpkins are the species *C. maxima*. The flesh and seed of *C. pepo* is described here.

dried seeds

Constituents

The flesh is a good source of beta carotene and contains vitamin E, both cancer-fighting anti-oxidants. The seeds contain around 30 per cent unsaturated oil – mainly linoleic acid – and are rich in iron, phosphorus and zinc, known to benefit prostate problems and acne.

Medicinal uses

Pumpkin seeds are prescribed to treat ailments of the prostate gland. In particular, the seeds' high zinc content and diuretic effect make them a good remedy for non-cancerous prostate enlargement. A Swedish clinical trial found that a substance called curbicin, obtained from pumpkin seeds and dwarf palms, noticeably improved the symptoms of enlarged prostate.

Pumpkin seed oil is also reputed to be beneficial in ailments of the urinary system. A paper published in 1994 describes the effectiveness of the seed oil in improving the function of the bladder and urethra.

Pumpkin seeds have long been used to get rid of roundworms. The seeds are still a popular de-worming remedy, especially for children, as they are nontoxic and safe. A Taiwanese study looking at purging the body of tapeworms found a combination of pumpkin seeds and areca nuts to be safe and effective. The amino acid cucurbitine has known anti-tapeworm properties.

Egyptian research published in 1995 found that pumpkin seed oil improved arthritic conditions, while a decoction of the seeds is used to remedy intestinal inflammation. Pumpkin flesh is high in fibre and acts as a gentle laxative. For external use, the flesh can be pulped and applied as a poultice to treat burns, while the oil is a soothing emollient.

Cultivation

Pumpkin thrives in warm and temperate climates. Grow from seed in a rich, well-drained soil in a sunny spot.

PREPARATION AND DOSAGE

- **To treat prostate and urinary problems in men**

  CAPSULES Follow manufacturer's instructions.

- **To treat worms**

  SEEDS Eat 60–100 g hulled seeds (pepitas) a day to prevent or eliminate worms. Follow with a purgative such as castor oil.

IF SYMPTOMS PERSIST, CONSULT A DOCTOR

CAUTIONS

- Do not take pumpkin with warfarin or other anticoagulant (blood-thinning) medications. In rare instances, pumpkin has been reported to lengthen bleeding time.
- Do not self-prescribe for prostate enlargement, as this could be due to prostate cancer. Consult a doctor.
- Do not take if pregnant or breastfeeding.
- Excessive use of diuretics can lead to cramps and cardiovascular or renal problems.
- Do not exceed recommended doses of pumpkin seeds, as excessive intake may cause liver damage.

Raspberry *Rubus idaeus* Rosaceae **Also called** Garden raspberry, European red raspberry

Native to both Asia and Europe – where its history as a food and medicinal plant stretches back at least to ancient Greece and Rome – raspberry is highly prized for its sweet, red berries. This deciduous biennial shrub with pale green leaves can reach a height of 2 m. Drooping clusters of small, white flowers appear in the second year of growth, to be followed by juicy, red fruit.

Parts used
LEAVES AND FRUIT
- The leaves are used in preparing infusions, liquid extracts and tablets.
- The berries, used in decoctions, are ready from summer to early autumn.

Constituents
The leaves contain polypeptides, flavonoids and tannins including anthocyanins, while the fruit contains pectin, fruit sugars and acids, and vitamins A, B_1 and C.

Medicinal uses
A tea made from the leaves can be taken to treat diarrhoea, urinary problems, kidney stones, gallstones and fluid retention. Traditionally, the leaves have been used during the last trimester of pregnancy to tone the uterus and aid childbirth. However, there is little research to validate this use.

The leaves are applied externally to treat skin irritations and wounds, and excessive vaginal discharge. The berries also have an astringent action which helps to heal wounds. This may be due to the anthocyanins, which studies have shown could inhibit enzymes involved in the body's inflammatory response.

Cultivation
Place young plants in moist, well-drained soil, in sun or partial shade. Raspberries prefer a cool climate.

dried leaves

PREPARATION AND DOSAGE

- **As a *partus praeparator* (to prepare the uterus for childbirth)**
  As prescribed by a doctor, midwife or medical herbalist.

- **To treat diarrhoea, urinary infections**
  INFUSION Steep 1 teaspoon of dried leaves in 1 cup of boiling water for 10 minutes, strain and drink three times a day.
  LIQUID EXTRACT Take 4–8 mg of dried herb equivalent in water three times a day.
  TABLETS Follow manufacturer's instructions.

- **To treat skin ailments**
  COMPRESS Soak a cloth in the infusion (see above) or diluted tincture and apply to the affected area.

IF SYMPTOMS PERSIST, CONSULT A DOCTOR

CAUTIONS
- Not recommended in pregnancy, except during the third trimester, and then only under the supervision of a doctor, midwife or medical herbalist. Do not take raspberry in the early stages of pregnancy and do not exceed the prescribed dose.
- Do not combine with drugs that lower blood-sugar levels or with the drug Antabuse (disulfiram).

Red clover Trifolium pratense Fabaceae Also called Purple clover, Wild clover, Trefoil

A short-lived perennial that grows to a height of 40 cm, red clover is common throughout Europe, particularly in sandy meadowland, and has become naturalised in Australia and New Zealand. It has long-stalked leaves along its hairy stems, usually made up of three, pointed, oval leaflets marked with a white crescent. Its fragrant, globular, pink-purple flowers appear in late spring and summer.

Parts used
FLOWER HEADS
- The flower heads are picked as soon as they open, in late spring and early summer.
- The flower heads are dried and then used in the preparation of infusions, liquid extracts, tinctures and ointments.

dried flower heads

Constituents
Red clover contains isoflavones that mimic the action of oestrogen. Anti-inflammatory salicylates and phenolic glycosides and saponins are also present. Another constituent found in the plant is sitosterol, which research indicates may be useful in helping to treat certain cancers.

Medicinal uses
Red clover is used both externally and internally. Externally, it is used for skin ailments, such as the inflammatory conditions eczema and psoriasis. Internally, the plant is known to be helpful in relieving the discomfort of a range of ailments such as sore throats, mouth ulcers and coughs.

However, the most popular medical use for red clover these days is as a supplement to prevent or reduce the symptoms of menopause.

The isolated isoflavones in the plant are similar in molecular structure to that of human oestrogen, and clinical trials suggest that they can help in reducing hot flushes, as well as some of the other common symptoms of menopause.

Unlike synthetic oestrogen, the isoflavones obtained from red clover do not appear to produce any significant side effects.

Cultivation
Red clover can be grown from seeds, sown in autumn or spring, or by division, also in spring. Plant in a moist, well-drained soil in a spot that gets plenty of sun. In some parts of Australia, red clover is planted as a pasture crop and for bee forage.

PREPARATION AND DOSAGE

- To treat skin ailments, coughs

  LIQUID EXTRACT 2–4 g dried herb equivalent, three times a day.
  INFUSION 2 teaspoons dried flower heads infused in 1 cup of boiling water for 10 minutes before straining. Drink 3 cups a day.

- To treat or prevent hot flushes and other symptoms of menopause

  TABLETS (containing isoflavones from red clover) As prescribed by a doctor or medical herbalist, or according to manufacturer's instructions.

IF SYMPTOMS PERSIST, CONSULT A DOCTOR

CAUTIONS
- Red clover should be avoided by women trying to conceive, as research on livestock has shown that it can act as a contraceptive.
- Until further research is available, red clover is not recommended for people with a history of tumours that are stimulated by the presence of the hormone oestrogen, and it should not be taken at the same time as drugs that thin or inhibit the clotting of blood.
- Avoid fermented clover, which can cause internal bleeding.

Rehmannia

Rehmannia glutinosa Scrophulariaceae **Also called** Chinese foxglove, Glutinous rehmannia Rehmannia is a hairy perennial with a rosette of scalloped leaves. It bears purplish, tubular flowers with yellow to brown markings. The tuberous orange root has been used in traditional Chinese medicine since at least the 4th century, and probably for much longer. Regarded as one of the 50 most important Chinese medicinal herbs, it was prized as a longevity tonic.

Parts used
ROOTS
- The cultivated roots are harvested in the autumn or early winter. Wildcrafted roots are collected in early spring.
- Fresh, dried or cured roots are taken as decoctions or liquid extracts.
- To cure the fresh root, it is washed in millet wine and steamed and dried several times.
- Different Chinese names are used for the cured and uncured roots: the uncured root is referred to as *shen di huang*, whilst the cured root is called *shen di hung*.

Constituents
Rehmannia contains phytosterols including sugars, beta stigmasterol, iridoid glycosides, as well as a number of other glycosides.

Medicinal uses
In traditional Chinese medicine, the uncured root is regarded as sweet, cold and slightly bitter, and is prescribed to reduce heat in feverish conditions characterised by thirst and scarlet tongue. It is also considered to nourish the blood and generate fluids, so is recommended for dryness of the mouth and for constipation caused by poor lubrication of the stool. The cured root is considered to promote blood production, and is indicated for anaemic states, haemorrhage and general menstrual irregularities.

Rehmannia is considered to have immunostimulant characteristics that are applicable to inflammatory, allergic and auto-immune conditions such as asthma, urticaria and rheumatoid arthritis. It has been shown to have a protective effect on the liver, and consequently is prescribed for hepatitis and other degenerative liver conditions.

Rehmannia is recommended for the treatment of chronic nephritis, and is a tonic to the kidneys. It also acts as an adrenal tonic, and helps in limiting the suppressive effects of corticosteroids and chemotherapy.

dried roots

Cultivation
Grow rehmannia in a moist but well-drained soil that's rich in humus. Plant in an area that receives partial shade. The climate should be cool to mild and frost free. In frost-prone regions, plants should be lifted or sheltered over winter. Propagate by seed sown in late winter, root cuttings taken in late autumn, or by softwood basal cuttings taken in spring.

PREPARATION AND DOSAGE
- **Rehmannia should be taken internally only on the advice of a medical herbalist**

IF SYMPTOMS PERSIST, CONSULT A DOCTOR

CAUTIONS
- Rehmannia should not be taken by anyone with renal failure or a history of kidney disease.
- Diarrhoea may occur if rehmannia is taken to excess.
- Side effects of mild oedema (fluid retention) have been reported.

Rhubarb Rheum palmatum Polygonaceae Also called Chinese rhubarb

Native to north-east Asia, this species of rhubarb – unlike the more familiar garden variety – is used as a herbal remedy. A tall, herbaceous plant, it has very thick, fleshy leaf stalks and wide, jagged, palm-shaped leaves. Loose clusters of tiny, star-shaped, white, greenish or reddish flowers are followed by dry, winged fruits. Only the bulky rhizome is of medicinal value.

Parts used

RHIZOMES

- Although grown in temperate regions around the world, the rhizome used in herbal medicine usually comes from either China or Korea.
- Rhizomes of plants between six and ten years old are dug up in autumn.
- Dried rhizome is used to prepare infusions, decoctions, liquid extracts and powders, or is sold in fragments.

Constituents

The components present in Chinese rhubarb that are responsible for its laxative action are anthracene derivatives, mainly consisting, in the dried rhizome, of anthraquinone glycosides. Flavonoids and tannins are also present. The latter are thought to be responsible for the constipation sometimes induced by low doses of rhubarb.

dried rhizomes

Medicinal uses

Rhubarb is an extremely effective laxative, although very low doses have sometimes been known to cause constipation. Numerous studies have revealed that the plant stimulates the intestinal muscles and increases the absorption of water and electrolytes. However, rhubarb preparations should not be used for longer than 10 consecutive days, because of the danger of developing laxative-induced illnesses, such as colitis, diarrhoea, electrolyte imbalances and hypokalaemia (a reduction of potassium in the blood).

Recent studies in China have shown that rhubarb preparations can actually help to cleanse the blood by reducing excessive amounts of urea and other nitrogenous waste products in it. It is thought that this is due to direct action by the plant on the kidneys, an action which further research has revealed may also help to limit inflammation in cases of chronic renal failure.

Chinese scientists have also shown that the plant can inhibit the chain of reactions in the body that leads to the constriction of blood vessels.

Rhubarb is also used to stimulate the appetite and improve digestion, as well as to treat gall bladder and liver problems.

Cultivation

Chinese rhubarb can be grown from seeds, sown in late winter, or from root cuttings planted in late autumn. The plant prefers a moist, well-drained soil, rich in humus, and exposure to plenty of sunshine.

PREPARATION AND DOSAGE

- **To treat constipation**

  LIQUID EXTRACT As prescribed by a medical herbalist.
  DECOCTION Boil 20 g of dried or 40 g of fresh rhubarb rhizome in 750 ml water and simmer to reduce to around 500 ml. Take 50–100 ml in the early evening.

- **To treat lack of appetite**

  DECOCTION Take 10 ml of the decoction (see above) twice a day.

IF SYMPTOMS PERSIST, CONSULT A DOCTOR

CAUTIONS

- Chinese rhubarb should not be taken at the same time as other laxatives, and it is advisable to combine the treatment with exercise and changes in diet.
- People suffering from an intestinal obstruction, arthritis, kidney disease or urinary problems should not use Chinese rhubarb preparations.
- The plant is not recommended as a laxative for children aged between 10 and 15, and should never be given to children under 10 years of age.
- It is not advisable to take rhubarb when pregnant or breastfeeding.
- People with known allergies should be cautious when using Chinese rhubarb preparations.
- Do not use rhubarb leaves, which are known to be toxic.

164 NATURE'S MEDICINES

Rosehip *Rosa canina* Rosaceae **Also called** Common briar

Rosehips are gathered from the dog rose, a bushy shrub that grows wild in most temperate regions of the world. It can reach a height of 1–3 m, and in spring to summer bears pretty, bright pink or whitish flowers on its thorny branches. Once the petals have fallen, the flower's receptacle starts to ripen, becoming red and pulpy. This is the rosehip, and the seed pods are found in its pulp.

Parts used

ROSEHIPS

- Ripe rosehips are gathered in late summer to autumn, then dried and broken into fragments or crushed into powder.
- Both fragments and powder are used to make infusions, decoctions, tinctures and tablets.
- Rosehips are often combined with other tonic plants, such as stinging nettle and echinacea.

Constituents

Rosehips are rich in vitamins C and B_2 and contain substantial amounts of pectins, some organic acids – particularly malic and citric acids – and tannins. They also contain proanthocyanidins, which have a protective anti-oxidant effect.

Medicinal uses

Because rosehips have such a high vitamin C content, preparations with a base of rosehip have a tonic effect and can help to boost the immune system. They are given as a general pick-me-up during illnesses and convalescence, and to help increase resistance to infections such as common colds and influenza.

In addition, the tannins confer astringent powers that ease diarrhoea, particularly if caused by fever. The pectins and organic acids have a diuretic effect, and the organic acids help to stimulate the gastric juices, relieving gastritis.

Research carried out recently has also suggested that rosehip may help to ease the pain and improve the mobility of joints affected by arthritis.

Cultivation

Dog rose can be grown from cuttings or seeds in moist, well-drained soil that is rich in nutrients. It is best suited to a neutral to mildly acidic soil and should be placed in a sunny spot.

rosehips

dried rosehips

PREPARATION AND DOSAGE

- **To treat chills, influenza, vitamin C deficiency, general fatigue**

  INFUSION Put 2–2.5 g of fragmented rosehips into 1 cup of boiling water. Leave to infuse for 10 minutes and then filter. Drink 3–4 cups a day.
  TABLETS, CAPSULES (usually combined with vitamin C) Follow manufacturer's instructions.

- **To treat diarrhoea**

  DECOCTION Put 30–50 g of fragmented rosehips into 1 litre of boiling water. Boil gently for 5 minutes. Leave to infuse for 15 minutes and filter. Take regularly, particularly at breakfast.

IF SYMPTOMS PERSIST, CONSULT A DOCTOR

CAUTIONS

- Until further safety information is available, preparations made with a base of rosehips are not recommended for women who are pregnant or breastfeeding.

Rosemary *Rosmarinus officinalis* Lamiaceae

From medieval times, rosemary – a symbol of love and fidelity – was often worn in bridal wreaths and given to wedding guests. Rosemary is a bushy, aromatic evergreen shrub found all around the Mediterranean. Spikes of pale blue or lilac flowers bloom from spring to early summer. They yield an essential oil that is one of the ingredients of eau de cologne.

Parts used
FLOWERS AND LEAVES
- The flowers are gathered when they are in full bloom and then dried.
- The evergreen leaves can be collected at any time of year.
- The leaves are scalded and then dried.
- Rosemary is used in infusions, liquid extracts and as an essential oil.

Constituents
Rosemary contains many active constituents. Its flavonoids are stimulant and anti-oxidant. Its phenols – in particular rosmarinic acid – are antiseptic and reduce inflammation. Its astringent tannins fight infection, while rosmaricine has been shown to have both stimulant and analgesic properties. The plant's volatile oil has a sharp, stimulating fragrance and contains a range of active compounds including cineole and camphor.

dried leaves

Medicinal uses
The flavonoids in rosemary stimulate the circulation by strengthening the capillaries and improving venous blood flow. All of these are benefits that justify rosemary's traditional medicinal application, which was to improve memory and concentration, ease headaches and stimulate hair growth.

The herb also calms the digestion, and is prescribed for gut problems such as dyspepsia, stomach cramps, bloating and constipation.

A series of animal studies conducted in 1987 found that an extract of rosemary increased the flow of bile, important in the digestion of fats. In addition, research published in 1995 found the plant to be diuretic and to have a detoxifying effect on the liver.

Rosemary has expectorant and antibacterial properties and can be used to treat bronchial, ear, nose and throat infections. It is also a good tonic for people suffering from general fatigue.

Externally, rosemary oil is diluted in a neutral oil, such as sunflower oil, and used as a rub to ease muscular pain, sciatica and rheumatic pain and inflammation. An infusion added to bath water is also said to help to ease the pain of rheumatism.

Rosemary extract also stimulates hair follicles and scalp circulation, and is applied to the scalp as a treatment for dandruff.

Cultivation
Rosemary is easily grown from cuttings. Once rooted, plant in a warm, sheltered, sunny spot, ideally in well-drained neutral to alkaline sandy soil. Rosemary does not thrive in wet, cold areas, and will need shelter if the weather is generally cool.

PREPARATION AND DOSAGE

- **To treat dyspepsia, stomach cramps, bloating, constipation, respiratory infections, headache, poor concentration**

  LIQUID EXTRACT As prescribed by a medical herbalist.
  INFUSION 2–4 g of dried herb infused in 1 cup of boiling water for 10 minutes before straining. Drink 3 cups a day (not at bedtime).

- **To treat rheumatism, muscle aches**

  INFUSION Put 50 g of herb into 1 litre of boiling water. Cover and leave to infuse for 30 minutes and add to the bath water.
  ESSENTIAL OIL Dilute, allowing 3 drops to 10 ml of carrier oil. Rub on painful joints.

IF SYMPTOMS PERSIST, CONSULT A DOCTOR

CAUTIONS
- The essential oil should not be taken, and should not be used topically by pregnant or breastfeeding women, children or those with hypersensitive skin.
- If pregnant or breastfeeding, do not consume more rosemary than would normally be found in the diet.
- Do not take the herb if anaemic, and avoid taking rosemary and iron supplements at the same time.

Sage and clary sage *Salvia officinalis* and *S. sclarea* Lamiaceae

Native to the Mediterranean, common sage is a woody, aromatic shrub. Its small, grey-green leaves are thick and downy. Clary sage looks different, having much larger leaves, but has similar medicinal properties. German wine merchants used to add extracts of clary sage to Rhine wines to improve their aroma, and its essential oil is used in perfume manufacture and aromatherapy.

Parts used

LEAVES

- The leaves are collected in summer, just before the flowers bloom, or in autumn.
- The leaves are dried under cover and away from the daylight.
- Both forms of sage yield an aromatic essential oil.
- Sage is used in the preparation of infusions, decoctions, liquid extracts and tinctures.

dried leaves

Constituents

The leaves of sage plants contain flavonoids (anti-oxidants that help to improve the circulation) in addition to phenols such as caffeic and rosmarinic acid, and tannins which have been found to have antimicrobial and anti-inflammatory properties.

The main constituents of sage essential oil are substances called thujones, along with terpenes, cineole and camphor. Clary sage oil has a scent similar to ambergris and contains linalyl acetate and linalool.

Medicinal uses

Sage suppresses sweat secretion and is especially useful for reducing night sweats, hot flushes and other symptoms of menopause. Common sage and clary sage are prescribed for digestive ailments such as indigestion and bloating.

In vivo tests published in *Planta Medica* in 1988 found sage oil to be antispasmodic. It may, therefore, prove to be beneficial for the treatment of period pains and stomach cramps. Clary sage is often used in massage oil for this purpose. In an interesting development, researchers at Middlesex University and at King's College, London, are studying the use of sage for treating Alzheimer's disease.

Used externally, a strong infusion of the fresh herb makes a soothing antiseptic mouthwash and gargle.

Cultivation

Sage is easily grown from cuttings or seed. Plant in full sun in a well-drained, neutral to alkaline soil.

Sage

Clary sage

PREPARATION AND DOSAGE

- **To treat digestive problems, fatigue, night sweats**

    INFUSION Put 20 g of dried leaves of sage or clary sage into 1 litre of boiling water. Leave to infuse for 10 minutes and strain. Drink 1–2 cups a day.

    LIQUID EXTRACT As prescribed by a medical herbalist.

- **To treat sore gums, sore throat**

    MOUTHWASH, GARGLE Make a strong infusion and use when required.

IF SYMPTOMS PERSIST, CONSULT A DOCTOR

CAUTIONS

- Sage leaves should not be used over a long period of time.
- Do not take the essential oil internally.
- Do not give to children.
- Avoid if pregnant or breastfeeding.
- Sage may interfere with hypoglycaemic and anticonvulsant therapy.

St John's wort *Hypericum perforatum* Clusiaceae

The scent of St John's wort was thought by the ancient Greeks to ward off evil spirits. The plant grows wild throughout Europe and elsewhere, thriving in woods, hedgerows, roadsides and meadows. It is considered to be a weed in parts of Australia and New Zealand. Its bright yellow flowers bloom from summer to autumn. St John's wort has been used as a remedy for nervous disorders for more than 2000 years.

Parts used

FLOWERING TOPS

- The flowers are gathered during the summer and dried in bunches.
- There are many similar-looking plants, but St John's wort can easily be distinguished by the black spots on its petals and translucent spots on its leaves.
- St John's wort is used in the preparation of infusions, tablets and liquid extracts.

Constituents

The yellow flowers of St John's wort yield a deep red oil – the colour of which is derived from hypericin, a red pigment thought to be responsible for many of the plant's medicinal effects. The oil also contains flavonoids and tannins.

Medicinal uses

As a result of its wound-healing properties, St John's wort has traditionally been used to treat burns and skin irritations. However, it has also been shown to have a positive effect on mild to moderate depression, and is now widely prescribed as a mild antidepressant.

The mechanism by which the plant exerts its antidepressant action remains unclear, despite extensive clinical research.

In vitro studies conducted in 1984 suggested that hypericin acted in a similar way to monoamine oxidase inhibitor antidepressants (more commonly known as MOAIs). German research published in 1998 documents the antidepressant activity of a substance in the plant named hyperforin, which seems to have a beneficial effect on serotonin activity in the brain.

St John's wort is also prescribed for depressive symptoms including anxiety, nervous fatigue, negativity and sleeping difficulties.

Externally, St John's wort is recommended for minor burns and scalds and to ease neuralgia, sciatica and other painful inflammations.

dried flowering tops

Cultivation

St John's wort is a perennial weed, and is a particular problem in parts of Australia and New Zealand. Once established, it is hard to get rid of. Plant seeds in a well-drained soil in a sunny or lightly shaded location.

PREPARATION AND DOSAGE

- **To treat anxiety, nervous fatigue, insomnia**

  TABLETS 1800 mg dried flowering herb equivalent, standardised for hypericin content. Take three times a day (see Cautions).
  LIQUID EXTRACT As prescribed by a medical herbalist.

IF SYMPTOMS PERSIST, CONSULT A DOCTOR

CAUTIONS

- Depression is a serious condition, not suitable for self-treatment. Do not stop taking prescribed antidepressants, unless advised to do so by a doctor. Consult a doctor before using St John's wort for treating the symptoms of depression.
- St John's wort is known to interact with a large number of medications. If you are taking any other medicine, including an oral contraceptive, talk to a doctor before taking this herb.
- Avoid sunbathing, as external use may occasionally cause photosensitivity and a consequent skin rash. Other side effects have occasionally been documented, including gastrointestinal upset, fatigue and restlessness.
- Do not take St John's wort if pregnant or breastfeeding.

Sandalwood *Santalum album* Santalaceae

A small tree grown mainly in India, sandalwood is the source of a valuable oil used in perfumes, soaps and incenses. Sandalwood oil has long been used – particularly in the East – to scent and purify the air in the home and in places of worship. When burned as joss sticks or in an oil burner it releases a sweet, soothing aroma. The wood itself is highly prized for woodcarving.

Parts used
HEART OF THE TRUNK
- The heartwood of the sandalwood tree is yellowish in colour and has a subtle scent.
- It can be gathered at any time of year, but is at its best in summer.
- Powdered sandalwood is widely used in the perfume industry and in aromatherapy.
- The plant's essential oil is an ingredient in many creams and balms.

Constituents
Sandalwood contains a pigment called santalene, which is the source of its red colour. Its essential oil is rich in terpenes – in particular santalol – which give it its pleasing aroma and are thought to have sedative properties. Sandalwood also contains resins, which have antiseptic and antifungal actions and stimulate the immune system to fight infection. Its astringent

pieces of heartwood

tannins have anti-oxidant, antibacterial and anti-inflammatory properties.

Medicinal uses
Sandalwood's essential oil was taken for a long time as a cure for gonorrhoea, cystitis and other urinary infections. It was also prescribed for skin diseases and acne. Traditional Chinese practitioners use sandalwood oil as a sedative.

Today, antibiotics are used to treat most genito-urinary infections, however, modern herbalists still prescribe sandalwood as a diuretic to help combat water retention and oedema (swelling) in the lower legs. In addition, Chinese practitioners sometimes use it as a pain-killer for the treatment of gum pain, toothache, gastric problems and migraines.

Japanese studies published in 2000 found that the terpene known as santalol had analgesic effects on rats. It is believed to help relieve abdominal and chest pain.

The scent of sandalwood is reputed to calm the mind, and it is often used in Buddhist monasteries as an aid to meditation.

Sandalwood may also have cancer-fighting properties. American research carried out in 1997 suggested that the oil slows down the development of skin tumours. It also inhibits the proliferation of viruses. An in vitro study conducted in Argentina in 1999 showed that sandalwood oil acted against the herpes viruses responsible for genital herpes and cold sores.

Cultivation
Sandalwood, which is rarely cultivated outside the tropics, is parasitic and needs a host tree nearby for its roots to feed on. It likes light shade and a moist, well-drained, fertile soil.

wood

PREPARATION AND DOSAGE
- **To treat abdominal and chest pains**
  ESSENTIAL OIL Dilute, allowing 3 drops to 10 ml of carrier oil. Massage into affected areas.
- **To treat skin infections**
  ESSENTIAL OIL Dilute a few drops in 180 ml of water and apply to the affected area three times a day.

IF SYMPTOMS PERSIST, CONSULT A DOCTOR

CAUTIONS
- Do not take sandalwood essential oil internally unless advised to do so by a medical herbalist or doctor, and then for no longer than a period of six weeks.
- Internal use is not recommended for people with kidney disorders, for children or for pregnant or breastfeeding women.

Saw palmetto *Serenoa repens* Arecaceae **Also called** Shrub palmetto, Sabal

A small, palmlike plant, saw palmetto is native to North America. Native Americans and early American settlers used the berries to treat genito-urinary problems. Its therapeutic effect on the neck of the bladder and the prostate in men was so effective that it became known as the 'plant catheter'. Its fruit is an oval, fleshy purplish black berry.

Parts used
BERRIES
- Berries are gathered in autumn when they ripen.
- They are used to make capsules, tablets and liquid extracts.

Constituents
The active constituents of saw palmetto are a volatile oil, steroidal saponins, tannins, flavonoids, free fatty acids and polysaccharides. The plant is a tonic, and is one of the few herbal remedies considered to be anabolic – which means that it helps to strengthen and build body tissues.

Medicinal uses
Saw palmetto extract is prescribed for benign enlargement of the prostate gland in men, as long as the growth is not large enough to need surgery. In 1996, French scientists demonstrated saw palmetto's effectiveness in reducing benign prostate enlargement. It works by preventing testosterone from being converted into dihydrotestosterone, the hormone that is thought to cause prostate cells to multiply, leading to an enlarged prostate gland.

In clinical trials conducted over the past 20 years, men taking saw palmetto felt less urgency and got up less often at night to urinate, or had greater urine flow. Research suggests that, while the conventional prescription drug finasteride is better at increasing the rate of urine flow and shrinking the prostate, saw palmetto causes fewer problems with sex drive and performance.

Most of the research carried out so far has used a special liposterolic extract of saw palmetto that retains many of the oil-based active constituents, such as esters, phytosterols and free fatty acids.

Saw palmetto has also been prescribed for men to treat reduced sex drive and impotence.

Cultivation
Saw palmetto enjoys tropical and subtropical conditions. If temperatures fall below 10°C, provide shelter or grow in a greenhouse.

dried berries

berries

PREPARATION AND DOSAGE
- **To treat benign enlargement of the prostate**
  CAPSULES (standardised for their free fatty acid content) Follow manufacturer's instructions.

IF SYMPTOMS PERSIST, CONSULT A DOCTOR

CAUTIONS
- Do not self-prescribe for prostate enlargement, as the condition could be due to prostatic cancer. Consult a doctor.
- No adverse side effects or interactions with other drugs have been recorded to date.
- Saw palmetto has hormonal effects and may interfere with oral contraceptives and hormone replacement therapy.
- Do not take if pregnant or breastfeeding.
- Do not use if you are also taking prescribed prostate drugs.

Schisandra *Schisandra chinensis* Schisandraceae **Also called** Chinese magnolia vine

Native to north-east China, schisandra is a woody climbing plant with fragrant, pink flowers that are followed by small, red berries. Known and valued in Chinese herbal medicine for at least 2000 years, the berries are known as the 'fruit with five flavours'. These flavours correspond to major human organs: sour to liver, bitter to heart, sweet to spleen, pungent to lungs and salty to the kidneys.

Parts used
BERRIES
- Berries are gathered when they ripen in autumn.
- They are dried and used to make powders, dry extracts and tinctures.

Constituents
Schisandra contains several compounds, including essential oils, phenols and lignans. Several of the active components are lignan derivatives, thought to help protect against prostate, colon and breast cancers. Vitamins C and E are also present.

Medicinal uses
Schisandra is valued in Chinese medicine as a youth tonic, and is used to treat weakness, exhaustion and infertility. It is considered to be a warming herb, and is traditionally indicated for asthma, chronic cough, night sweats and diarrhoea.

Schisandra is also traditionally used as a liver tonic with a cleansing action.

Research has shown that schisandra helps to promote liver regeneration and detoxification, and to protect against the oxidation of lipids in the liver. Chinese researchers have also observed that the extract enhances concentration and may be helpful in improving memory. In addition, it strengthens and quickens the reflexes and increases efficiency in stress-related tests.

Recent research suggests that the berries also have protective effects against certain forms of cancer. In 1992, Japanese scientists showed that a lignan isolated from schisandra protected against inflammation and chemically induced tumour development.

Schisandra has an overall protective effect on cells and muscles, and can help to lower blood cholesterol.

Cultivation
For berries, you will need male and female plants. Grow in rich, well-drained, moist soil, with roots in the shade and the top in sun.

dried berries

berries

PREPARATION AND DOSAGE
- To treat high blood-cholesterol levels, stress
- To improve liver function, memory, concentration

  LIQUID EXTRACT, TABLETS 500 mg–1.5 g dried fruit equivalent, three times daily.

IF SYMPTOMS PERSIST, CONSULT A DOCTOR

CAUTIONS
- Schisandra should not be taken during pregnancy, except under professional supervision.
- Mild, transient gastrointestinal symptoms and headaches have occasionally been reported.
- Schisandra is traditionally contraindicated in the early stages of colds and coughs.

THE A TO Z OF PLANTS

Senna *Senna alexandrina* (syn. *Cassia angustifolia*) Caesalpiniaceae

The laxative effects of senna were first discovered by Arab physicians in the 10th century. The shrub, which grows to about 1 m in height, is native to hot, barren regions and is cultivated in India and Pakistan. Its yellow flowers are followed by flat, papery pods containing six to eight seeds.

Parts used
LEAVES AND PODS
- The leaves are picked before the plant flowers.
- The pods are harvested in the autumn.
- Leaves and pods are both sun dried.
- They are used for decoctions, laxative medicines and tablets.

Constituents
Senna's main laxative components are anthraquinones known as sennosides. The plant also contains flavonoids and mucilage.

Medicinal uses
Senna is a powerful laxative and the main active ingredient in many proprietary brands of constipation remedy. It works by stimulating rhythmic intestinal contractions known as peristalsis, and starts to work about 10–12 hours after ingestion. However, it is better to deal with the cause of constipation, rather than relying on laxatives. This usually involves eating high-fibre foods such as fruit, vegetables and whole grains (for example, wholemeal bread or brown rice), drinking plenty of fluids and taking exercise.

A clinical study conducted in the UK in 1993 found senna to be more effective than the commonly prescribed laxative, lactulose, in treating chronic constipation in elderly individuals.

Cultivation
Senna can be grown from seeds, planted in well-drained soil. It will not tolerate frost, but needs a warm location with plenty of sun.

dried pods

seed pod

PREPARATION AND DOSAGE

- **To treat constipation**
  DECOCTION Steep 3–6 pods in 150 ml of water for 6–12 hours. Drink one dose a day, preferably at bedtime.
  LIQUID EXTRACT As prescribed by a medical herbalist.
  TABLETS, COMMERCIAL PREPARATIONS Follow manufacturer's instructions. Do not exceed recommended dose.
  IF SYMPTOMS PERSIST, CONSULT A DOCTOR

CAUTIONS
- Do not take senna for more than eight to ten days at a time. Excessive or prolonged use can cause severe digestive problems.
- Repeated use of strong laxatives may aggravate constipation.
- Do not give senna to children under 12 years of age.
- Do not take senna at the same time as drugs that contain anthraquinones.
- Do not take senna when pregnant or breastfeeding.
- Consult a doctor before use if taking the heart drug digitalis.
- Do not take senna if you have any intestinal blockage or inflammation, or suffer from haemorrhoids.

Shepherd's purse *Capsella bursa-pastoris* Brassicaceae

Originally from Europe, shepherd's purse is a weed that thrives in wastelands throughout the world, including Australia and New Zealand. Fragile, upright stems bear clusters of little, white flowers followed by seed pods shaped like small pouch purses – from which the plant gets its name. As well as having medicinal properties, shepherd's purse also has a long history of use as a food plant.

Parts used

AERIAL PARTS

- The plant may be harvested at any time throughout the year.
- Its active components lose some of their potency when stored for any length of time.
- It is used in the preparation of liquid extracts, infusions and tablets.

Constituents

Shepherd's purse contains a powerfully active essential oil, in addition to choline, acetylcholine and tyramine, as well as flavonoids.

Medicinal uses

Traditionally, shepherd's purse was used to treat haemorrhaging after childbirth and for all forms of internal bleeding. In World War I, it was employed to staunch bleeding when supplies of other styptic medicines, such as ergot, ran low. Today, it is prescribed as a gentle remedy for heavy periods, and can also be used to stop nosebleeds.

The plant has antiseptic, diuretic and urinary properties, which make it a useful remedy for cystitis. It is also astringent and anti-inflammatory, making it useful for the treatment of haemorrhoids.

Shepherd's purse can also cause the uterus to contract. This effect was demonstrated in 1969 in a study that observed the stimulating effect of the plant's alkaloids on the uterus.

Cultivation

Shepherd's purse will flourish in even the poorest soils. Plant in a sunny or lightly shaded spot.

dried aerial parts

PREPARATION AND DOSAGE

- **To treat heavy or painful periods, haemorrhoids**

  LIQUID EXTRACT 500 mg–1 g dried herb equivalent, taken three times daily.
  INFUSION 1–3 g dried herb infused in 1 cup of boiling water for 10–15 minutes before straining. Drink 3 cups a day.

- **To treat nose bleeds**

  INHALATION Make an infusion (see above) and allow it to cool. Use as a nasal douche, snorting it up through the nostrils.

IF SYMPTOMS PERSIST, CONSULT A DOCTOR

CAUTIONS

- No toxicity or undesirable side effects have been recorded to date, but shepherd's purse may have a sedative effect, and should not be used by pregnant or breastfeeding women.
- Do not used the herb at the same time as anticoagulant (blood-thinning) drugs.
- Consult a doctor before use if you are taking drugs for blood pressure, heart problems or thyroid disorders.

Siberian ginseng *Eleutherococcus senticosus* Araliaceae

This deciduous, thorny shrub is native to eastern Russia, as its name suggests, and also China, Korea and Japan. It forms a bush 2–3 m in height, its grey stems and branches bearing palmate leaves. The small, globular flowers are held singly or in groups of two or three on smooth leaf stalks. The female flowers are yellow, while the male flowers are purple.

dried roots

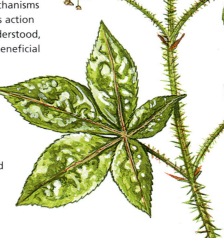

Parts used

ROOTS
- The roots are collected when they are rich in active constituents, either in autumn just before the leaves fall, or in spring as new growth begins.
- Some researchers advocate the use of the leaves as well, but this is under debate currently.
- The root is used to make liquid extracts and tablets.

Constituents

The constituents in the root of Siberian ginseng include polysaccharides and eleutherosides A to G and I to M, which are thought to stimulate the immune system.

Medicinal uses

Siberian ginseng first came to prominence in the 1950s, when Russian scientists identified it as a more economical and abundant alternative to Korean ginseng. It is described as an 'adaptogen' because it helps the body to adapt to physical and psychological stress, an effect that is largely due to the plant's tonic action on the adrenal glands.

Siberian ginseng is often prescribed for fatigue and nervous exhaustion, and may be particularly useful for people who are subject to environmental and occupational stress, and for sportspeople, who may experience better physical endurance.

Siberian ginseng enhances the functioning of the immune system in several ways, including improving resistance to infection and increasing numbers of certain types of immune cells. Herbalists frequently prescribe it for recurrent viral infections and for patients with compromised immune systems, including those with chronic fatigue syndrome.

Anticancer activity has been noted in animal studies, and this is thought to be due to the herb's immuno-stimulating properties. Some research has also shown that this improved immune function helps to reduce the side effects experienced by cancer patients who are undergoing chemotherapy, radiation and surgery.

Although the mechanisms of Siberian ginseng's action are not yet fully understood, it is likely that it is beneficial in maintaining overall good health rather than treating specific illnesses.

Cultivation

Propagate from seed sown in spring or autumn. Plant in a well-drained, rich soil in a sunny or slightly shady spot.

PREPARATION AND DOSAGE

- **To treat stress, fatigue, viral infections**

  LIQUID EXTRACT As prescribed by a medical herbalist.
  TABLETS, CAPSULES 300 mg–1 g dried root equivalent, taken three times a day.

IF SYMPTOMS PERSIST, CONSULT A DOCTOR

CAUTIONS

- It would be best to see a doctor or medical herbalist before using the plant. Do not use it for more than a month at a time, taking a break of at least two months before restarting.
- It is not suitable for children before they reach puberty, pregnant and breastfeeding women or women taking oral contraceptives.
- It is not suitable for people who are suffering from insomnia, high blood pressure, nervous tension, obesity, heart palpitations and benign breast lumps.
- Hyperactive, schizophrenic or manic individuals should avoid it.
- Stimulants, alcohol and spicy foods should all be avoided while using Siberian ginseng.

Skullcap

Scutellaria lateriflora Lamiaceae **Also called** Helmet flower, Virginia skullcap, Mad dog skullcap

Skullcap is found in the swampy areas and damp woods of North America's temperate regions. It is an erect perennial with thin, toothed leaves, and grows to around 90 cm. The flowers are usually blue, but occasionally pink or white, and are produced along one side of the stem in summer. They are followed by seed capsules with a shape reminiscent of a military helmet called a skullcap.

Parts used

AERIAL PARTS

- Skullcap is harvested late in the flowering season, after the seed pods have started to appear.
- The dried herb is used in preparing tablets and liquid extracts.
- In the past, skullcap preparations have been contaminated by plants from the *Teucrium* genus, some of which are toxic. Manufacturers are now aware of this issue and guard against it. However, it is important to choose quality preparations of skullcap from a reputable manufacturer.
- The related species baical skullcap is also used in herbal medicine.

Constituents

Amongst the constituents of skullcap are the phenols baicalein and wogonin, and a complex volatile oil with at least 70 constituents, 26 of which are sesquiterpenes.

Medicinal uses

Skullcap is regarded as a relaxant for the nervous system, and is commonly taken to relieve anxiety, nervous tension and mild depression. Herbalists also recommend it for other conditions where stress and anxiety are causative factors, particularly those of a cardiac nature.

Until recently, there has been no clinical research to support this use. However, in 2003 the results of a small-scale, double-blind, placebo-controlled clinical trial were published in the journal *Alternative Therapies*.

The researchers reported that when compared to a placebo, skullcap preparations caused a significant reduction in feelings of stress and anxiety. Further research is needed to validate this finding and expand our understanding of the way the herb works.

Skullcap has been extensively prescribed as a herbal sedative, and is reputed to induce restful sleep. The herb has also traditionally been used to relieve epilepsy, headache, menstrual problems and the pain of teething. In 19th-century America, it was regarded as a cure for rabies.

dried aerial parts

Cultivation

Skullcap grows in any well-drained soil that is not too heavy. Grow in a sunny to partially shaded position. The plant dies back completely in winter and can be grown from seed or by cuttings taken in spring or summer.

PREPARATION AND DOSAGE

- **To relieve nervous tension, stress, anxiety, insomnia**

  LIQUID EXTRACT, TABLETS, CAPSULES 500 mg–2 g dried flowering plant equivalent. For tension, stress and anxiety, take three times a day; for insomnia, take one dose at bedtime.

  IF SYMPTOMS PERSIST, CONSULT A DOCTOR

CAUTIONS

- Do not exceed the recommended dose – symptoms that have been observed in overdose include giddiness, stupor, confusion and seizures.
- Although no problems have been reported, it would be best not to operate machinery or drive whilst taking skullcap.
- Pregnant and breastfeeding women should avoid taking skullcap until more information is available regarding its safety under those circumstances.

Slippery elm *Ulmus rubra (syn. U. fulvus)* Ulmaceae **Also called** Red elm

Slippery elm, a native of Central and North America, grows in forests near streams, reaching 20 m in height. The pointed, toothed leaves have rough, dark green upper surfaces, but are paler and downy underneath. Small, inconspicuous clusters of flowers are followed by reddish brown fruits, each consisting of a single seed. Populations of this valuable herb have declined due to the impact of Dutch elm disease.

Parts used

INNER BARK

- The fibrous inner bark is harvested in spring from the tree trunk and larger branches of trees that are around 10 years old. It is 2–4 mm thick and is available in flat or folded oblong pieces.
- It is taken internally as a powder, normally mixed with water. Tablets and capsules are also available.

Constituents

The main component of slippery elm is a form of carbohydrate called mucilage, which can absorb a large amount of water. The other constituents include tannin, phytosterols (including beta sitosterol), and sesquiterpenes.

powder

Medicinal uses

Due to its high mucilage content, slippery elm has a soothing and emollient effect wherever it comes into contact with irritated or inflamed tissue.

In the digestive tract, it is used to relieve indigestion and soothe and heal ulcerated mucous membranes. It protects the bowel wall in inflammatory bowel disease, irritable bowel syndrome and haemorrhoids. It is also used to help in relieving constipation, where it acts to lubricate the stool, making it easier to pass.

These soothing properties have also led to its use as an ingredient in lozenges for sore throats and as a drawing poultice to be applied to boils and splinters.

Traditionally, slippery elm has also been recommended to relieve inflammation and irritation in the urinary tract and respiratory system. It is also considered to be a nutritious and easily assimilated food, and consequently the powder has traditionally been used to make a gruel designed to nourish debilitated and convalescing patients.

Cultivation

Grow slippery elm in deep, moist soil in full sun in a cool to mild climate. As an elm, this species is vulnerable to Dutch elm disease. It is grown from seed sown in autumn or by summer cuttings. Plants can also be grown from suckers, or you can purchase bare-rooted plants in winter.

PREPARATION AND DOSAGE

- **To treat inflammation and irritation of the digestive system, constipation, sore throat**

  POWDER Mix 1 teaspoon with ¼ cup of water and drink three times a day before meals, along with an additional glass of water. It may also be mixed with mashed banana or grated apple, but it is important that at least one glass of water is also consumed.
  TABLETS, CAPSULES Take according to manufacturer's instructions, with a full glass of water.

- **To draw boils to a head**

  POWDER Mix 1 teaspoon of powder with 2–3 teaspoons of water to form a paste. Apply to the affected area once daily.

  IF SYMPTOMS PERSIST, CONSULT A DOCTOR

CAUTIONS

- There are no known safety issues when taken as directed.

Star anise
Illicium verum Illiciaceae **Also called** Chinese anise

Native to southern China and northern Vietnam, this evergreen can grow to a height of 18 m. Star anise has white, aromatic bark and its leaves taper to a point. The single flowers are greenish or whitish yellow and followed by star-shaped fruit, hence its common name. The fruit has a strong aroma and a sweet, sugary flavour. A single fruit is made up of 8 to 12 seed pods, each containing a brown, shiny seed.

Parts used
FRUIT
- The tree can live for 80 years, but the fruit is not harvested during the first 10 years. The fruit is picked when still green and not fully ripe.
- After being dried in the sun, the fruit turns a reddish brown colour.

Constituents
The fruit contains a large quantity of essential oil (5–10 per cent), which is rich in anethole. This is mainly in the form of E-anethole.

Medicinal uses
Anethole is thought to be the source of a good many of the therapeutic properties associated with star anise. Traditionally, the plant is used to relieve digestive and intestinal problems and is regarded as particularly useful for treating colic.

The effects of the fruit vary in accordance with the amount of anethole present. In small doses, it stimulates the appetite, promotes digestion, helps to expel wind and calms intestinal spasms. In excessive doses, it can stimulate the central nervous system to such a degree that it causes trembling and convulsions.

Like anise, star anise possesses oestrogenic effects. It promotes menstruation, eases childbirth and stimulates milk secretion. A study published in the *Journal of Ethnopharmacology* in 1980 suggests that the active ingredients are based on anethole polymeric units. Star anise is also believed to increase the libido of both men and women.

The plant is reputed to possess both stimulant and diuretic properties, and can be beneficial in conditions such as lumbago. Like anise, it is sometimes present in cough remedies. Japanese and Indian researchers have found that star anise is effective against various strains of bacteria, yeasts and fungi and could therefore be useful in fighting off many types of infections.

dried fruit

Cultivation
Plant in moist, well-drained, neutral to acid soil in a slightly shaded position.

fruit

PREPARATION AND DOSAGE
- **To treat digestive problems**
  INFUSION 1 teaspoon of dried fruit infused in 1 cup of boiling water for 10 minutes before straining. Drink 2 cups a day before meals.

IF SYMPTOMS PERSIST, CONSULT A DOCTOR

CAUTIONS
- Do not confuse the fruit of star anise with the poisonous fruit of Japanese anise *Illicium anisatum*. Although they are quite similar in appearance, the fruit of Japanese anise is smaller and more irregular than that of star anise. The fruit of Japanese anise also has a sharp, bitter odour, whereas star anise smells and tastes like aniseed.
- Do not exceed the recommended dose.

Sweet marjoram *Origanum majorana* Lamiaceae

A woody perennial, sweet marjoram grows to a height of about 60 cm. Small, velvety, oval leaves crowd its stems, with tight spikes of white or pinkish flowers opening all summer. Apart from its medicinal uses, the sweet aroma makes the plant a popular culinary herb. It is widely cultivated in Hungary, Spain and North Africa, as well as being picked from the wild in its native Portugal.

Parts used

STEMS, LEAVES AND FLOWERS

- Aerial parts are collected from mid-summer to mid-autumn, while the plant is in flower.
- The stems and leaves are dried for both culinary and medicinal use.
- A yellowy green essential oil is extracted from fresh flowers. It has a very penetrating, camphorated smell.

Constituents

Sweet marjoram contains bitters, tannins, flavonoids, manganese and zinc. Its essential oil is rich in cavacrol and thymol. Sabinene, linalool and terpenes are also present.

Medicinal uses

Sweet marjoram is recognised as a useful plant for treating digestive problems, such as intestinal spasms, nausea, bloating, loss of appetite, flatulence and diarrhoea. It can also act as a sedative, so is effective in cases where indigestion is due to a nervous problem, as well as being an effective remedy for insomnia. Research recently carried out in Korea has shown that the plant's ursolic acid (a terpene) is responsible for its power to calm.

Sweet marjoram is also known for its ability to stimulate lactation and perspiration. The latter action, coupled with the plant's diuretic powers, helps to expel toxins from the body.

Applied externally, the essential oil will help to soothe joint and muscle aches, and can be helpful in easing the pain of toothache and mouth ulcers.

dried stems, leaves and flowers

Cultivation

Sweet marjoram will grow from seed. Plant in a warm, sunny position in spring. Plants thrive in a nutrient-rich, well-drained, neutral to alkaline soil.

PREPARATION AND DOSAGE

- **To treat flatulence, abdominal bloating, nausea, minor nervous problems**

  INFUSION Add 1–2 teaspoons dried herb to 1 cup of boiling water and infuse for 15 minutes before straining. Drink 3 cups a day.

- **To treat joint and muscle ache**

  ESSENTIAL OIL Dilute, allowing 3 drops of essential oil per 10 ml of carrier oil. Massage into affected areas as required.

IF SYMPTOMS PERSIST, CONSULT A DOCTOR

CAUTIONS

- Do not use sweet marjoram essential oil internally.
- Pregnant and breastfeeding women should not use sweet marjoram essential oil, and should not consume more of the herb than would be present in a normal meal.

Sweet violet *Viola odorata* Violaceae **Also called** English violet, Blue violet

A herbaceous perennial, sweet violet can be found in damp, shady places in most temperate regions of the world. About 10–15 cm high, its bright green leaves form a rosette around the base of the long, erect flower stems. The young leaves are kidney shaped, taking on their familiar heart shape and becoming slightly downy as they mature. During autumn, single, fragrant violet-blue to whitish flowers open.

Parts used
LEAVES AND FLOWERS
- The leaves are picked in spring and used to prepare liquid extracts.
- The flowers are sometimes used in fragrant syrups, mostly for culinary purposes, but also to help relieve coughs.

dried leaves and flowers

Constituents
The sweet violet plant contains phenolic glycosides, together with saponins, flavonoids and mucilage.

Medicinal uses
Sweet violet has long been used to treat respiratory tract illnesses, as well as inflammation of the intestines. Various research projects have demonstrated the anti-inflammatory, analgesic and expectorant powers of the plant's constituents in helping to dissolve mucus, loosen phlegm, reduce fever and ease pain.

These soothing powers have also been harnessed to treat mouth infections and certain skin conditions, such as cracked skin.

Recent studies carried out in Sweden suggest that sweet violet may also have the potential to treat cancer. Peptides from the plant have been shown to have a cytotoxic effect, inhibiting the growth of certain types of malignant tumours.

Cultivation
Sweet violet can be grown in several ways: by dividing a mature plant, from seeds sown in spring, or from cuttings planted in autumn. The plant thrives in a moist, well-drained soil in a sunny location. However, it is important to provide some shade in summer.

PREPARATION AND DOSAGE

- **To treat congestion of the respiratory tract**

   INFUSION Add 2–4 g of dried flowers to 1 cup of boiling water. Cover and infuse for 10 minutes. Drink 3 cups a day.
   SYRUP Heat together 100 g of dried flowers, 500 g of sugar and 300 g of water until boiling, then leave to cool. Take 2 teaspoons, two or three times a day at mealtimes.
   LIQUID EXTRACT As prescribed by a medical herbalist.

- **To treat cracked skin, including cracked nipples**

   CREAMS, OINTMENTS Apply products containing 3 per cent sweet violet to the affected area.

IF SYMPTOMS PERSIST, CONSULT A DOCTOR

CAUTIONS
- When taken in large doses, preparations containing sweet violet rhizome can cause vomiting.

Tamarind *Tamarindus indica* Caesalpiniaceae **Also called** Indian date

Native to Madagascar, the tamarind tree is cultivated in numerous other tropical regions. It can reach a height of 20–25 m, with branches that often touch the ground. The fragrant, golden yellow flowers are streaked with red. Following them are long, dangling seed pods, that start grey-green, ripening to a rusty brown. They contain a sweet, brownish yellow pulp in which sit five to ten shiny, reddish brown seeds.

Parts used

FRUIT PULP

- The fruit is picked from summer to autumn. The pulp is then extracted and the seeds removed and discarded.
- The pulp can be used fresh, or to prepare a powder or dry extract.
- Sometimes the juice is used. This is obtained by soaking the pulp in hot water and then pressing it.
- An infusion of the leaves is sometimes used for topical applications, such as for leg ulcers.

Constituents

Tamarind pulp is rich in pectin, simple sugars and organic acids, including tartaric and citric acid. Its slightly aromatic scent is due to terpene compounds.

Medicinal uses

Tamarind pulp is a potent laxative, and is recommended as a treatment for constipation in both adults and children. In addition, it can be of help in remedying other digestive ailments, such as sluggishness, flatulence, nausea and morning sickness.

In India, tamarind is used to fight infections, particularly those of the intestines, as well as colds and catarrh. This use is backed up by research showing that various isolated constituents have immunostimulant properties. Additionally, extracts of tamarind have been proven to have antibacterial, antifungal and antiviral activity. Susceptible organisms include *Salmonella typhimurium*, *E. coli*, *Staphylococcus aureus* and the rubella virus.

Cultivation

Tamarind can be grown from seeds planted in spring. It needs a tropical to subtropical climate to thrive, with temperatures above 18°C. In colder zones, it will need to be grown in a heated greenhouse. It will tolerate poor soil, but needs good light.

dried fruit pulp

fruit

PREPARATION AND DOSAGE

- **To treat constipation**

  FRESH SEEDLESS PULP Eat 10–50 g a day, adjusting the dose as necessary.
  CAPSULES (200 mg) Take 1–2 capsules with a large glass of water after the evening meal.
  POWDER Add 1–2 g to 1 cup of boiling water, then leave for 10 minutes. Drink this after the evening meal.

IF SYMPTOMS PERSIST, CONSULT A DOCTOR

CAUTIONS

- Tamarind may interact adversely with aspirin, as well as other non-steroidal anti-inflammatory drugs.
- Take only the recommended therapeutic dose of the plant, and avoid long-term use.

Tea tree *Melaleuca alternifolia* Myrtaceae **Also called** Snow in summer

Native to northern New South Wales, southern Queensland and parts of Papua New Guinea, tea tree was used by some Aboriginal groups as a medicinal plant before the arrival of white settlers. This evergreen shrub or small tree has pale, papery bark and narrow, pointed leaves. In summer it bears dense spikes of unusual, feathery, white flowers, which are followed by woody, cup-shaped seed capsules.

Parts used

LEAVES AND TWIGS

- The leaves and twigs have a characteristic tea tree odour when crushed.
- The leaves and twigs are distilled and used to produce the essential oil, which is applied topically and also added to creams, ointments and other products for topical use.
- There are more than 60 different tea tree species native to Australia, but it is *Melaleuca alternifolia* that is famous for its essential oil.

Constituents

Compared to other species of tea tree, *Melaleuca alternifolia* has a high proportion of terpenes, and particularly of terpinen-4-ol, which is considered to be a gentle but extremely effective antiseptic. Cineol is an undesirable constituent of tea tree that is irritating to the skin. The best-quality tea tree oil preparations are considered to be those containing cineol at levels below 10 per cent.

Medicinal uses

The remarkable healing properties of tea tree oil have been known in Australia since the 1920s, when it was first used in surgery and dentistry. It was also used in World War II munitions factories, where it helped to the heal skin injuries caused by metal filings and turnings.

The essential oil is a remarkable antiseptic that effectively kills bacteria and fungi. It is used for all varieties of skin infections, including acne and tinea, as well as to prevent cuts and wounds becoming infected. It is an ingredient in preparations used to treat insect bites, thrush and other vaginal infections, and also to help relieve sunburn.

Tea tree oil kills bacteria when they are propelled through air-conditioning ducts, and is also used as a steam inhalation to help relieve sinus congestion in upper respiratory tract infections.

Cultivation

Tea tree prefers moist soils, and will tolerate poor drainage. Additional water is essential in dry times. It will grow in sun to shade. Grow from seed or cuttings.

essential oil

seed capsules

PREPARATION AND DOSAGE

- **To treat acne, skin infections, cuts**

  ESSENTIAL OIL Dilute the essential oil (1 part essential oil to 15 parts water) and apply to the affected area, avoiding eyes.

- **To treat tinea, vaginal infections, sunburn**

  CREAM Follow manufacturer's instructions.

IF SYMPTOMS PERSIST, CONSULT A DOCTOR

CAUTIONS

- Do not take the essential oil internally, except in commercial preparations such as throat lozenges, where the dose has been carefully controlled.
- Do not use undiluted tea tree oil as it may irritate the skin. For sensitive areas such as the genitals, use a commercial preparation that has been specially formulated for the purpose.
- Do not use tea tree oil if you have a known sensitivity or allergy to it. If redness or burning occurs, wash the area with water immediately.
- Pregnant and breastfeeding women should avoid using tea tree oil.

Thyme, common *Thymus vulgaris* Lamiaceae

A low-lying, perennial shrub, common thyme grows on arid hillsides around the Mediterranean. This plant was a symbol of courage to the ancient Greeks. Tiny, greyish green leaves cover the many wiry branches of the erect, woody stems. From spring until late summer, spikes of small white or pink flowers appear. The pungent taste and rich aroma of the leaves make them a popular flavouring in a wide range of dishes.

Parts used

LEAVES AND FLOWER STALKS

- The leaves and flower stalks are gathered at the beginning of the flowering season and dried carefully away from sunlight.
- The dried thyme is used in the preparation of infusions, powders for capsules and in pharmaceutical products, such as soothing cough syrups.
- An essential oil is also extracted from the dried leaves and flower stalks. This is used in antiseptic creams and ointments.

Constituents

The dried leaves and flower stalks of common thyme contain flavonoids and 0.5–2 per cent essential oil. The composition of the essential oil varies. Thymol, methylchavicol, cineole and borneol are all present, with other compounds. Thymol is known to be an extremely effective antimicrobial agent, and is an ingredient in commercial mouthwashes.

Medicinal uses

Research has shown that the flavonoids in thyme, methylchavicol and thymol have a muscle-relaxing effect. As a result, the plant is sometimes used as an antispasmodic to treat digestive problems, such as bloating, belching, flatulence and sluggish digestion.

Thyme is also effective for soothing coughs and can help to treat respiratory infections and relieve nasal congestion due to colds, hay fever and asthma.

Studies have demonstrated that thyme's essential oil is antiseptic, and it is sometimes recommended for minor cuts and wounds, as well as for insect bites and stings. The plant is also prescribed as a mouthwash or gargle to treat gum disease and tonsillitis.

Cultivation

Grow from seed, sown in spring, or summer cuttings. A warm, sunny plot with rich, dry, light soil is ideal.

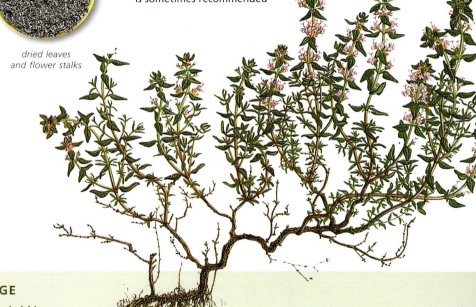

dried leaves and flower stalks

PREPARATION AND DOSAGE

- **To treat sluggish digestion, bloating, belching, flatulence, inadequate bile flow, coughs**

  INFUSION Infuse 2 g dried plant in 1 cup of boiling water for 5 minutes before straining. Drink 3 cups a day. For best results, keep the infusion covered while the herb is steeping.
  LIQUID EXTRACT As prescribed by a medical herbalist.

- **To treat gum disease or tonsillitis**

  MOUTHWASH, GARGLE Prepare an infusion as above and use as a mouthwash or gargle twice a day.

IF SYMPTOMS PERSIST, CONSULT A DOCTOR

CAUTIONS

- To date, common thyme has shown no adverse side effects, but excessive use is not advisable.
- Use the plant sparingly when pregnant or breastfeeding.
- Use the essential oil only under professional supervision.

Tribulus *Tribulus terrestris* Zygophyllaceae **Also called** Caltrop, Goatshead, Puncture vine

Tribulus is found throughout the world. It has a long history of use in Ayurvedic and traditional Chinese medicine. However, it is a weed in many countries and is classified as noxious in most states of Australia. This sprawling, hairy annual has many creeping stems, and from summer to autumn bears solitary yellow flowers. These are followed by the sharp, spiny fruits that give the plant its common names.

Parts used

FRUIT

- Each fruit splits into five spiny nuts when ripe, each of which contains several seeds. Although the roots and other parts of the plant have also been used in herbal medicine, the modern Western usage centres on the fruit, which is available as tablets and liquid extracts.

Constituents

Much of the research has concentrated on a group of saponins called furanosterolic glycosides, which include protodioscin and protogracillin. Many commercial products are standardised for these, and some experts have warned against the use of non-standardised preparations, as they may not exert the same effects that are documented in the research.

dried fruit

Medicinal uses

A significant body of research is accumulating to confirm the use of tribulus as a tonic herb for the male reproductive system, with specific application to male infertility. In open clinical trials, the herb was found to improve sperm function, and had a beneficial effect on sperm profile in men with low sperm count. Animal research has shown similar effects, including increased plasma testosterone levels, libido and sexual activity.

Tribulus may also be of benefit to female infertility in certain circumstances, and may help to relieve the symptoms of menopause.

In Ayurvedic medicine, the herb is used in a similar way – it is considered to be an aphrodisiac, and the seeds were sometimes used to increase female fertility and lactation. Other traditional Ayurvedic and Chinese uses of tribulus include the treatment of a wide variety of urinary complaints – such as kidney stones, cystitis and painful urination – and to relieve skin complaints including psoriasis, scabies and leprosy. It is also used to treat swollen, painful eyes.

Cultivation

Tribulus is a noxious weed in most parts of Australia, as it is poisonous to livestock. Check with your local council before sowing seeds. It thrives in full sun and moist but well-drained soils.

PREPARATION AND DOSAGE

- **To improve male sexual function; to treat symptoms of menopause, urinary tract complaints**

    TABLETS (standardised for their protodioscin content) Follow the manufacturer's instructions.

- **To treat male or female infertility**

    As advised by a medical herbalist.

IF SYMPTOMS PERSIST, CONSULT A DOCTOR

CAUTIONS

- Tribulus should not be taken during pregnancy, and should be discontinued as soon as pregnancy is suspected.
- Do not exceed the recommended dose.
- Tribulus has been documented to cause liver damage and other symptoms in livestock.

Turmeric *Curcuma longa* Zingiberaceae

Cultivated in Asia, Africa and the West Indies, turmeric is a tropical perennial. Its pointed, lance-shaped leaves can grow up to 70 cm long. Low clusters of flowers spring up from the middle of the plant in summer. The rhizome is cylindrical, often with fingerlike protuberances, and is a rich yellowy orange on the inside. It has a warm, slightly acrid taste. When powdered, it is widely used to colour and flavour food.

Parts used

RHIZOMES

- The rhizome is dug up in winter, when it is dormant. It is cut into pieces, boiled and then dried.
- In herbal medicine, turmeric rhizome is mainly used in the preparation of powders, tinctures and occasionally infusions.

dried rhizomes

Constituents

Turmeric rhizome contains a number of curcuminoids, which are mainly responsible for its colour and are known to be anti-inflammatory. It is also rich in essential oil.

Medicinal uses

Scientists have demonstrated that the curcuminoids have powerful anti-inflammatory activity, supporting the herb's traditional use in the treatment of rheumatism, arthritis, eczema, asthma, psoriasis and other inflammatory conditions.

Turmeric rhizome is often prescribed for liver and gall bladder problems, and has been found to protect the liver and stimulate the secretion of bile – an effect that is attributed to the essential oil. It has also been prescribed as a treatment for lack of appetite, indigestion and stomach acidity.

Turmeric displays antioxidant and antibacterial properties, and it is believed to help in lowering blood cholesterol and also in inhibiting blood clotting. This suggests that it could be beneficial in preventing hardening of the arteries and heart attacks.

There is also evidence that it may be useful in the treatment of some circulatory and menstrual disorders.

Cultivation

Turmeric can be grown from seeds planted in autumn, or rhizome cuttings planted in early summer. It thrives in moist, well-drained soil in tropical and subtropical areas with temperatures above 15°C and high humidity. In cold and frost-prone areas, plants need warmth and shelter in winter.

PREPARATION AND DOSAGE

- **To treat digestive problems, inflammatory conditions (arthritis, eczema, psoriasis), high cholesterol; to act as an anti-oxidant**

  CAPSULES (standardised for their curcuminoid content) Follow manufacturer's instructions to a maximum of 5 g a day.
  LIQUID EXTRACT As prescribed by a medical herbalist.

IF SYMPTOMS PERSIST, CONSULT A DOCTOR

CAUTIONS

- High doses of turmeric can irritate the stomach, causing nausea.
- The plant should not be taken at the same time as anticoagulant (blood-thinning) drugs.
- Do not use for gall bladder problems caused by a blocked bile duct.
- Turmeric should not be taken in medicinal doses by pregnant women or those trying to conceive.

Uva-ursi *Arctostaphylos uva-ursi* Ericaceae **Also called** Bearberry

Found in the mountainous parts of Europe, Asia and America, uva-ursi is a small, low-growing shrub with woody, branching stems that trail along the ground. Its leathery, evergreen leaves are spatula shaped, and are joined in early summer by clusters of pretty, waxy-looking flowers that are white, lightly marked with red. Glossy, bright red berries follow the flowers in autumn.

Parts used

LEAVES

- As they are evergreen, the leaves can be picked at any time, though only the youngest are chosen.
- Once dried in the open air, the leaves are used in the preparation of infusions, liquid extracts, tablets and capsules.

Constituents

Uva-ursi contains phenolic glycosides, mainly arbutin, which the body converts into antibacterial hydroquinones. Tannins, allantoin and diuretic flavonoids are also present in the plant.

Medicinal uses

A number of recent research projects have clearly demonstrated that when the phenolic glycosides in uva-ursi, especially arbutin, are converted in the body to hydroquinone, they have the ability to act as a powerful antibiotic. Uva-ursi has been shown to be effective for treating urinary tract infections, such as cystitis and urethritis, boils and abscesses infected with the *Staphylococcus aureus* bacterium, and also food poisoning and diarrhoea.

Uva-ursi is thought to be more effective in fighting the bacteria that cause urinary infections when the patient's urine is more alkaline than acidic: in other words, the efficacy of uva-ursi is likely to increase if it is taken in conjunction with a vegetable-based diet. Therefore, during treatment with the plant, it is advisable to follow a strict diet, containing plenty of fresh fruit and vegetables and only a small quantity of meat and dairy products. An alternative would be to take a regular dose of bicarbonate of soda.

Recent animal research into uva-ursi has also shown its ability to reduce swelling and inflammation.

dried leaves

Cultivation

Uva-ursi can be grown from seeds planted in autumn, or from cuttings planted in summer. Choose a moist, peaty to sandy soil. The plant will thrive in a sunny or lightly shaded plot, and grows best in areas that have a cool climate.

PREPARATION AND DOSAGE

- **To treat urinary infections**

  LIQUID EXTRACT 1.5–2.5 g dried herb equivalent, three times daily.
  CAPSULES, TABLETS Up to 700 mg three times a day. May be standardised to contain as much as 10 per cent (70 mg) arbutin. Follow manufacturer's instructions.

  IF SYMPTOMS PERSIST, CONSULT A DOCTOR

CAUTIONS

- Uva-ursi is rich in tannins, which can cause liver damage when taken in high doses. Therefore, any course of treatment using the plant should not last longer than a week. Also, no more than five such courses should be taken in a single year.
- The plant is not recommended as a treatment for people suffering from kidney disease.
- The high tannin content of the plant can cause nausea, vomiting, constipation and cramping if taken in excessive doses.
- Avoid uva-ursi when pregnant or breastfeeding, and do not give it to children under 12 years of age.

Valerian *Valeriana officinalis* Valerianaceae

Native to Europe and north Asia, valerian is grown as a garden plant in cooler parts of Australia and New Zealand. It prefers damp places, but can survive in dry ground. The erect stems can grow as tall as 2 m, with indented leaves forming a rosette around the base of the plant. Throughout the summer, clusters of white, pink or red flowers open at the very top of the main stems.

Parts used

RHIZOMES

- Only the rhizomes of plants over two years old are used.
- They are washed, then left to dry at a low temperature to preserve their active constituents.
- The dried rhizome is used in the preparation of tablets, capsules, infusions and liquid extracts.

Constituents

The main compounds in valerian are valepotriates, valerenic acid and valeranone, which have a sedative effect and can calm muscle spasms. Gamma-aminobutyric acid (GABA), which can block the transmission of signals in the brain, is also present.

Medicinal uses

Valerian is one of the best-known herbal tranquillisers, and is frequently prescribed as a remedy for minor nervous disorders and sleeping difficulties. Because of this, it has been the subject of a number of studies in many parts of the world. These have confirmed the sedative and antispasmodic powers of the valepotriates and valerenic acid in the plant. The plant's antispasmodic action may be the basis of its purported ability to lower blood pressure.

Recent clinical trials conducted by researchers in Brazil demonstrated clearly that valerian was not only highly effective in remedying insomnia, but could also help to improve the quality of sleep enjoyed. In addition, extracts from the plant showed great potential in the treatment of disorders caused by extreme anxiety.

Cultivation

Valerian can be grown from seeds planted in early spring or by division of existing clumps in autumn to winter. Valerian grows best in moist, rich soil, preferably in a sunny or lightly shaded spot.

dried rhizomes

fruit

PREPARATION AND DOSAGE

- **To treat minor nervous disorders and sleeping difficulties**

  TABLETS, CAPSULES Up to 2000 mg dried herb equivalent, preferably standardised for its valerenic acid content. For nervous disorders, take up to three times a day. For insomnia, take 1 dose an hour before bed.
  LIQUID EXTRACT As prescribed by a medical herbalist.

IF SYMPTOMS PERSIST, CONSULT A DOCTOR

CAUTIONS

- Avoid if pregnant or breastfeeding.
- Do not use at the same time as other drugs that have a sedative effect.
- Do not drive, or engage in any activity where lack of concentration could be dangerous, for up to two hours after ingesting.
- Overdose may cause headache, nausea, altered heartbeat, blurred vision and restlessness.
- For some people, valerian may act as a stimulant rather than as a sedative.

Vervain *Verbena officinalis* Verbenaceae **Also called** Verbena, Simpler's joy, Turkey grass

This herbaceous perennial, which grows to a height of 30–70 cm, is found in many parts of the world, including Australia and New Zealand. Pairs of lobed, oval leaves grow opposite each other along the erect, branched stems. Long, slender spikes of pale lilac flowers hang from the top of the plant in summer. Sometimes known as verbena, the plant should not be confused with lemon verbena (*Aloysia triphilla*).

Parts used
LEAVES, STEMS, FLOWERS
- The aerial parts are picked in summer, when the flowers are in bloom.
- Vervain must be dried promptly to preserve the power of its active compounds. It is used mostly to prepare infusions and liquid extracts.

Constituents
Vervain flowers and stems contain iridoid glycosides, including verbenalin and aucubin, which are known to be both anti-inflammatory and antispasmodic. Other constituents include volatile oils, mucilage, bitter principles, saponin, polyphenols, beta carotene and tannin.

Medicinal uses
Vervain has been used for centuries for a variety of infections, especially colds, influenza and other conditions associated with fever. This traditional application is supported by new research that indicates the herb has immune-boosting properties.

As a nervous system tonic, herbalists prescribe it for fatigue, tension and mild depression. It is also helpful during convalescence and for lack of appetite.

Vervain has antispasmodic activity, and is used to relieve muscle cramps, colic and period pain. It increases certain hormonal secretions, including those involved in breast-milk production.

Topically, the plant will treat sunburn, nappy rash and cracked or chapped skin.

Cultivation
Vervain can be grown from seed. Plant in any moist, well-drained soil in spring or autumn, in a sunny spot.

dried leaves, stems and flowers

PREPARATION AND DOSAGE
- **To treat nervous tension, cramps, fatigue, influenza; to stimulate breast-milk production**

  LIQUID EXTRACT 500 mg–1 g dried herb equivalent, three times daily.
  INFUSION Infuse 1–4 g dried herb in 1 cup of boiling water for 10 minutes before straining. Drink 3 cups a day.

- **To treat rashes, sunburn, cracked and chapped skin**

  COMPRESS Add a handful of dried plant to 150 ml of boiling water. Infuse for 10 minutes and apply on a cloth, two or three times a day.

IF SYMPTOMS PERSIST, CONSULT A DOCTOR

CAUTIONS
- Vervain preparations should not be taken during pregnancy.
- It is not advisable to use vervain when taking any drugs to raise or lower blood pressure, or with any form of hormonal therapy.
- Do not take with the medication levodopa (L-dopa).

THE A TO Z OF PLANTS 187

Walnut *Juglans regia* Juglandaceae

Native to Anatolia, walnut trees are now found worldwide. They grow to 25 m in height, with a massive trunk and widely spreading boughs. In early spring, long male flowers hang from the previous year's branches, while the new branches sport female flowers. The leaves, at first red, gradually turn green, while the fruit – a woody nut – has a smooth coating that changes from green to brown as it ripens.

Parts used

LEAVES
- The leaves are picked in spring and early summer, then dried rapidly at a temperature of 40°C.
- The dried leaves are used for making infusions, tinctures and liquid extracts. Each must contain at least 2 per cent of the flavonoid hyperoside.

dried leaves

Constituents

Walnut leaves are rich in healing tannins. Juglone, napthaquinone and the flavonoids hyperoside and quercetin are also present, together with ascorbic acid and essential oil.

Medicinal uses

Eating walnuts may help to protect the heart – research shows that daily consumption of walnuts (or their oil) helps to improve the levels of triglycerides in the blood.

The tannin content of walnut leaves renders them astringent and healing, while juglone has strong antimicrobial properties. For these reasons, leaf preparations are used for diarrhoea and intestinal infections.

Research indicates that walnut leaves may also have anti-inflammatory properties and may reduce the side effects of chemotherapy in cancer treatment.

The hulls of *Juglans nigra* (black walnut) are sometimes recommended for treating cancer and HIV/AIDS, but there is no research to substantiate its effectiveness.

Cultivation

Buy a small tree or plant seeds under cover in rich, well-drained acidic soil. The trees thrive in full sunlight, in a cool to mild climate.

PREPARATION AND DOSAGE

- **To treat diarrhoea, disorders involving the bacteria of the intestinal tract**

    INFUSION Infuse 10 g dried leaves in 1 litre boiling water for 15 minutes before straining. Drink 3 cups a day.

IF SYMPTOMS PERSIST, CONSULT A DOCTOR

CAUTIONS

- Although walnut has no known toxic side effects, it is not advisable to exceed the recommended dosage.

White horehound
Marrubium vulgare Lamiaceae **Also called** Horehound, Common horehound

A native of the Mediterranean, white horehound is seen throughout Australia and New Zealand, preferring warm, sunny locations. Its erect stems reach 30–60 cm in height and bear wrinkly leaves with scallop-shaped indentations. In summer, small, white flowers appear where the leaves join the stem. The plant has an applelike smell.

Parts used
FLOWERING TOPS
- Harvesting occurs in spring and in early summer, when the plant is in bloom.
- After drying and fragmentation, the plant is used in infusions, decoctions, tinctures and extracts.

Constituents
The flowers contain bitter diterpenes, including marrubiin, premarrubiin and marrubic acid. Other constituents include flavonoids, alkaloids and a small amount of essential oil.

Medicinal uses
The plant is traditionally used to treat coughs, and it is one of the most effective herbal expectorants known. It is commonly prescribed by herbalists to relieve colds and flu, as well as other conditions associated with respiratory congestion. It works by breaking up and releasing phlegm, exerting an antispasmodic action and relieving inflammation in the respiratory tract. This expectorant activity of white horehound was verified by a number of experiments performed in 1976.

Because of its bitter constituents (in particular the marrubiin), white horehound has the effect of stimulating the appetite and thus aids digestion.

An animal study in 2001 highlighted the potential of white horehound for treating high blood pressure.

Cultivation
Plant in a well-drained, neutral to alkaline soil in a sunny location. Choose a wild part of the garden, as the plant can be invasive. Growers should be aware that white horehound is considered to be a noxious weed in parts of Australia and New Zealand.

dried flowerering tops

PREPARATION AND DOSAGE
- To treat coughs and colds, flu, respiratory congestion, minor digestive problems

  LIQUID EXTRACT 1–2 g dried herb equivalent, three times daily.

IF SYMPTOMS PERSIST, CONSULT A DOCTOR

CAUTIONS
- High doses of marrubiin can adversely affect the heart.
- Pregnant women should avoid this herb, while those who are breastfeeding should limit consumption to small amounts, as advised by a medical herbalist.

White peony   *Paeonia lactiflora (albiflora)*   Paeoniaceae   **Also called** Bai shao

The large, showy flowers of this herbaceous perennial can be bright red, red-purple or white, and appear against the brilliant green leaves in early summer. The peony family has a long history of medicinal use – it even takes its name from Paeon, the physician of the Greek gods – and it is cultivated for its ornamental qualities as well. The source of the peony's medicinal properties lies in its swollen, tuberous roots.

Parts used

ROOTS
- Harvesting of the roots takes place in late autumn from plants that are four or five years old.
- The roots are dried, broken into fragments and used for infusions, decoctions and liquid extracts.

Constituents

White peony contains the monoterpene glycosides paeoniflorin and albiflorin. Paeoniflorin is considered to be an important active constituent, and much of the research has focused on this compound. Benzoic acid, asparagine and pentagalloyl glucose have also been identified.

Medicinal uses

In traditional Chinese medicine, white peony is regarded as a tonic herb for the blood, liver and spleen, and considered to be bitter, astringent and cooling. It is indicated to help dispel congealed blood and to clear heat from the body.

White peony is one of the most important women's herbal tonics in traditional Chinese medicine. It is prescribed for several menstrual complaints, including premenstrual syndrome, heavy bleeding, bleeding between periods and the absence of periods. Herbalists also recommend it for polycystic ovarian syndrome, uterine fibroids and some types of female infertility, often in combination with licorice or other herbs. It has antispasmodic actions, and is used for menstrual pain, cramping of the skeletal muscles and gastrointestinal griping. Research indicates that paeoniflorin may work by helping to normalise some types of female hormonal imbalance.

In 2001, Chinese scientists showed that paeoniflorin prevented blood clot formation. It may also be effective in the treatment of eczema, high blood pressure, fever and as a sedative. The herb's anti-inflammatory properties make it useful in treating rheumatism and other inflammatory conditions.

Cultivation

Plant in a rich, well-drained soil in a sunny or lightly shaded location in a cool climate. Do not use in home preparations.

dried roots

root

PREPARATION AND DOSAGE

- White peony preparations should be taken only on the advice of a medical herbalist

IF SYMPTOMS PERSIST, CONSULT A DOCTOR

CAUTIONS

- This herb should only be taken under professional supervision.
- Do not exceed the recommended dose.
- Women who are pregnant or breastfeeding should avoid peony.
- Do not take white peony if you are taking warfarin or any other anticoagulant (blood-thinning) medications.

Wild cherry *Prunus serotina* Rosaceae **Also called** Rum cherry, Black cherry

Wild cherry is a large tree, native to North America and cultivated in Europe for its timber. The shiny, fine-toothed leaves turn yellow or red before falling from the tree in autumn. Fragrant, white flowers are borne in late spring and early summer in long spikes, and are followed by small, purple-black fruit. The bark is smooth, glossy and reddish brown when the tree is young, turning darker and rougher as it ages.

Parts used
INNER BARK
- The inner bark may be curved, flat or ridged, and usually occurs in pieces about 4 mm thick (larger pieces are considered to have inferior medicinal properties).
- The bark is used to make the liquid extracts prescribed by herbalists.

Constituents
Amongst the constituents of wild cherry bark are coumarins, tannins, sugars, benzaldehyde, resins and eudesmic acid. Prunasin, a cyanogenic glycoside, is also present, and is considered to be largely responsible for the herb's action as a cough suppressant.

Medicinal uses
Wild cherry bark has a long history of use as a cough suppressant or 'anti-tussive' herb, and was listed for this use in the United States *Pharmacopoeia* of 1820. Traditionally, it was taken to relieve the coughs that resulted from common ailments such as tuberculosis and whooping cough.

Modern herbalists still use the herb for the same actions, prescribing it in syrups for the relief of colds, flu, bronchitis, tracheitis, pneumonia and pleurisy, especially when the cough is dry, unproductive, irritating or spasmodic. It is sometimes recommended to prevent spasms of the airways, such as occur in asthma patients.

Due to the presence of tannins, wild cherry bark also has astringent properties, and has been used to treat diarrhoea and haemorrhoids. It was traditionally used by women of the Cherokee tribe to aid childbirth, and has also been taken as a mild sedative and to stimulate the appetite.

liquid extract

Cultivation
Wild cherry grows best in a cool to mild climate in a well-drained soil, with reliable moisture and full sun. Plant bare-rooted plants in winter, or grow from seed.

PREPARATION AND DOSAGE
- Wild cherry bark should be taken only on the advice of a medical herbalist

IF SYMPTOMS PERSIST, CONSULT A DOCTOR

CAUTIONS
- Wild cherry bark is highly toxic when taken to excess, and should only ever be used under the supervision of a medical herbalist or doctor.
- Do not exceed the recommended dose.
- Wild cherry bark should not be taken by children, or by pregnant or breastfeeding women.

Wild indigo *Baptisia tinctoria* Fabaceae **Also called** Rattle weed, Horsefly weed

Wild indigo is a bushy plant found in open woodlands and fields of North America, especially near sandy coastlines. Its yellow flowers resemble those of lupins, and appear in summer at the top of the plant's tallest branches. The blue-green leaves are divided clover-fashion into three leaflets, each about 2 cm long. They turn black when dried.

Parts used

ROOTS

- The rootstock consists of a crown root with extending branch roots.
- The rough, wrinkled and warty surface comes away easily to reveal a fibrous, yellowish brown core.
- The roots are lifted in autumn and dried to use in tablets and liquid extracts, which are usually prescribed in conjunction with other herbs, such as echinacea.

Constituents

The constituents of wild indigo include flavonoids, alkaloids, coumarins, polysaccharides, glycosides and resin. Oestrogenic flavonoids such as genistein and biochanin A are also present.

Medicinal uses

Wild indigo is considered to be an immune system stimulant, with particular use in the prevention and treatment of upper respiratory tract infections such as colds, pharyngitis and sinusitis. In vitro research supports this use, and has shown immune-enhancing activity for some of the herb's constituents. However, the few clinical trials that have been conducted have combined wild indigo with other immunostimulant herbs, and have not used therapeutic doses.

In addition to its actions on the immune system, herbalists regard it as a lymphatic tonic, and often prescribe it with echinacea to help patients overcome tonsillitis, glandular fever and other infections affecting glandular tissue.

Traditionally, wild indigo was used as an antiseptic, and applied topically to wounds, boils and ulcers. It was used as a mouthwash or gargle to treat mouth ulcers, gum disease, and tonsillitis, and used as a douche in female complaints. These uses have now largely been discontinued, although the herb is sometimes prescribed internally as a blood cleanser for the treatment of boils, acne and a variety of other skin infections.

liquid extract

Cultivation

Grow wild indigo in any well-drained soil in a sunny spot. Tall plants may need staking. Sow ripe seed or divide existing plants when they are dormant, in late autumn or early spring.

PREPARATION AND DOSAGE

- **Wild indigo should be taken internally only under the supervision of a medical herbalist**

IF SYMPTOMS PERSIST, CONSULT A DOCTOR.

CAUTIONS

- Wild indigo is taken in very small doses, and is consequently only recommended for use by those under the supervision of a medical herbalist.
- Do not exceed the recommended dose or continue the treatment for an extended period of time. Symptoms of nausea and vomiting have been observed when the herb is taken to excess.

rootstock

Wild yam *Dioscorea villosa* Dioscoreaceae **Also called** Colic root, Rheumatism root

A relative of the edible yam, wild yam is native to Mexico and the southern United States, where it can be found growing wild in woodlands. It has now become naturalised in semi-tropical and temperate climates around the world. A large climbing plant with dense, tuberous roots and twining stems that can reach a height of 6 m, it has heart-shaped leaves and tiny, yellowy green flowers.

Parts used
RHIZOMES
- The rhizome is 5–10 cm in diameter. Once cleaned, it is dried, crushed or ground to a powder.
- Wild yam is most frequently used in liquid extracts and creams.

Constituents
Wild yam's rhizome contains steroidal saponins (dioscin, gracillin), tannins, phytosterols and starch. Wild yam is also the source of diosgenin, which is processed to form hormones for medical use, including progesterone.

Medicinal uses
Wild yam has been used to treat arthritis and rheumatism. This anti-inflammatory action is thought to be imparted by dioscin. Wild yam is also antispasmodic and is used to treat colic, irritable bowel syndrome and other painful muscular spasms. As a result of this, wild yam is also used to relieve menstrual cramps and labour pains.

There is much folklore connected with wild yam's use to treat women's hormonal problems, but there is no evidence to prove this. In clinical trials performed in 2001, patients were given a wild yam–based cream to rub onto their bodies, while other patients received a placebo. The researchers did not observe any relief of menopausal symptoms in either group.

Cultivation
Wild yam can be propagated from seed or root division. Plant in a well-drained, nutrient-rich soil in full sun or light shade.

dried rhizomes

PREPARATION AND DOSAGE
- To treat spasmodic and cramping pain of the gastrointestinal tract, the musculoskeletal system or the female reproductive tract

    LIQUID EXTRACT As prescribed by a medical herbalist.

    IF SYMPTOMS PERSIST, CONSULT A DOCTOR

CAUTIONS
- Women who are pregnant or breastfeeding should avoid using wild yam.

THE A TO Z OF PLANTS

Willow *Salix alba* Salicaceae **Also called** White willow, Willow bark

This deciduous tree is characterised by its graceful branches bearing silky, lance-shaped leaves. It grows to a height of 10–15 m, and has been introduced into southern Australia and New Zealand, where it is found in damp places, especially along riverbanks. Its flowers are catkins that appear in spring. The supple young twigs are traditionally used as a material for fences and basketwork.

Parts used

BARK

- The bark is taken from young branches collected in late winter and spring from trees that are two to five years old.
- The bark is cut into small pieces or crushed for use in decoctions.
- It is also used in capsules and tablets, often in combination with other anti-inflammatory plants, such as devil's claw.

dried bark

Constituents

Willow bark contains salicin, which the body converts into salicyl alcohol and subsequently into the known anti-inflammatory agent salicylic acid (a natural form of aspirin). It also contains flavonoids and proanthocyanidins (condensed tannins) that are well known for their astringent and wound-healing properties.

Medicinal uses

Willow bark combats inflammation, rheumatism, pain, headaches and fever. Japanese scientists carried out experiments in 2002 which demonstrated that salicylic acid (produced from the conversion of salicin in the intestines) reduced fever without damaging the stomach.

Willow bark is also known to have an antiseptic effect and is used externally to treat wounds and ulcers. It has been used in the treatment of diarrhoea and for intestinal infections. For its ability to reduce fever, it is also indicated in the treatment of influenza.

A trial that was carried out by researchers in Germany in 2001 found that a preparation containing willow exerted a moderate analgesic effect on a group of people suffering from osteoarthritis.

Cultivation

Suited to a moist or wet soil and a sunny location. Propagate from cuttings taken in summer. Before planting a tree, bear in mind that willow will take up a lot of space in a smaller garden. *S. alba* has been declared a noxious weed in some parts of Australia, including New South Wales, where many river systems are infested.

PREPARATION AND DOSAGE

- **To treat fever, flu, headaches, pains, rheumatism**

  DECOCTION Boil 1–3 g dried bark in 1 cup of water for 10 minutes before straining. Drink 1 cup three times a day before food.
  CAPSULES, TABLETS Up to 9 g per day in divided doses. Follow manufacturer's instructions.

- **To treat ulcers, wounds**

  COMPRESS Soak a cloth in the decoction (see above). Apply two or three times a day.

  IF SYMPTOMS PERSIST, CONSULT A DOCTOR

CAUTIONS

- Willow may occasionally cause side effects of nausea, gastrointestinal discomfort, dizziness and a rash. Similar effects are likely if excessive amounts are consumed.
- Willow bark is not recommended for pregnant or breastfeeding women, or for people with asthma, stomach ulcers, diabetes or kidney or liver disorders.
- Anyone allergic to aspirin or salicylates must not take willow.
- Willow should not be taken in combination with diuretics, drugs that lower blood pressure or thin the blood, or non-steroidal anti-inflammatory drugs.
- Excessive use of a decoction of the plant can cause mouth sores.

Winter savory *Satureja montana* Lamiaceae

This small, woody perennial grows wild as a small bush in well-drained, chalky areas of southern Europe and bears tough, shiny, lance-shaped leaves. One of the oldest of the popular culinary flavourings, winter savory has been grown in Britain since the Middle Ages, and is now widely grown in gardens in Australia and New Zealand. Its flowers are pure white or speckled with pink.

Parts used

NON-WOODY FLOWERING TOPS

- The herb is harvested just after the flowers come into bloom in summer.
- The crop may be dried for use as a seasoning or infusion, or may be processed for its essential oil.

Constituents

The essential oil is rich in carvacrol and thymol, but also contains some other monoterpenes. The exact mix of compounds varies according to the time of year and the weather.

Medicinal uses

The ancient Greek physician Dioscorides defined winter savory as being 'heating and drying' and likened it to thyme in its uses. Winter savory owes its therapeutic properties mainly to its essential oil. The plant is traditionally used for its tonic and digestive qualities, which include relief of intestinal spasms as well as relief from the effects of fungal and bacterial infections.

Externally, the herb's antiseptic properties mean it is useful for treating minor wounds, fungal skin infections, mouth ulcers, thrush and sore throats.

In 1998, in vitro studies found that winter savory demonstrated potent activity against HIV Type 1. However, further research is needed before winter savory can be recommended for this use.

Cultivation

Plant seeds in spring in a well-drained, alkaline soil. Choose a warm, sunny spot. Winter savory is commonly cultivated as a garden herb, both for its practical applications and decorative appearance.

dried flowering tops

PREPARATION AND DOSAGE

- **To treat belching, flatulence, diarrhoea**

  INFUSION Infuse 5 g dried flowering tops in 1 cup of boiling water for 10 minutes, ensuring that the infusion is covered while the herb is steeping. Strain and drink 3 cups a day.

- **To treat minor wounds**

  INFUSION Put 30 g of dried flowering tops into 1 litre of boiling water. Infuse for 10 minutes, then strain. Apply directly onto the wound to clean it.

- **To treat fungal skin infections**

  COMPRESS Soak a cloth in the infusion (see above) and apply to the affected areas two times a day.

- **To treat mouth ulcers, thrush, sore throats**

  GARGLE Use the infusion (see above) three or four times a day.

IF SYMPTOMS PERSIST, CONSULT A DOCTOR

CAUTIONS

- Take the essential oil internally only under the supervision of a medical herbalist or doctor.
- When the essential oil is used externally, there is a risk that it will irritate the skin.
- Winter savory is not recommended in any form for women who are pregnant.

Witch hazel *Hamamelis virginiana* Hamamelidaceae

A native of North America, witch hazel was used by a number of Native American tribes as a medicinal herb before European settlement. It is now widely grown in cool climates for the ornamental appeal of its spidery flowers and large, oval leaves. Its yellowish flowers grow in clusters at the junction of branches and leaf stalks in winter. It bears brown fruit consisting of small capsules, which split to release the seeds.

Parts used

LEAVES AND BARK

- The leaves are gathered during summer, before they turn brown.
- The bark is harvested in autumn or spring.
- Once dried, witch hazel leaves and bark are used for infusions, powders, dry and liquid extracts and tinctures.
- Witch hazel is an ingredient in mouthwashes, gels and ointments.

Constituents

Tannins constitute more than 10 per cent of the dried leaf. They impart vasoconstrictive and anti-inflammatory effects. Witch hazel also contains flavonoids, which are anti-inflammatory and strengthen the blood vessels, and a small proportion of essential oil.

Medicinal uses

Experiments have demonstrated that the extract made from witch hazel leaves strengthens veins, reduces the permeability of capillaries and has anti-inflammatory properties. It has also been shown to constrict blood vessels. In 2002, German trials showed that witch hazel can reduce erythema, which is the reddening of the skin due to dilated blood vessels. The plant's anti-inflammatory activity supports its use in treating eczema.

Witch hazel can be taken orally or applied as an ointment to treat circulation problems such as heavy, aching legs, varicose veins and haemorrhoids.

Further German research carried out in 2002 has demonstrated the plant's antimicrobial activity. A compound containing witch hazel was found to be effective against the bacterium *Staphylococcus aureus* and the yeast *Candida albicans*.

The plant's antibacterial and soothing qualities account for its use in mouthwashes and eye drops.

Cultivation

Place young plants in moist, rich, neutral to acid soil. Does best in cold climates.

dried leaves

PREPARATION AND DOSAGE

- **To treat circulation problems, haemorrhoids**

  LIQUID EXTRACT 2 g dried bark or leaf equivalent, taken three times a day.
  CAPSULES (dried leaf) Take 2 g, three times a day.

- **To treat circulatory problems, haemorrhoids, inflammation**

  GELS, OINTMENTS Massage into affected area once a day.
  WITCH HAZEL WATER Apply once or twice a day.

IF SYMPTOMS PERSIST, CONSULT A DOCTOR

CAUTIONS

- Witch hazel appears to have no toxic effects, but it might cause contact allergies.
- Pregnant or breastfeeding women should avoid taking witch hazel internally.

Withania
Withania somnifera Solanaceae **Also called** Ashwagandha, Winter cherry

A native of tropical India, withania forms a bush that can reach 1.2 m in height. The plant has been used in traditional Indian medicine for more than 2000 years. Its Sanskrit name means 'the thing that has the smell of a horse' – a reference to the horse's strength and vitality rather than its odour. It is also said to be an aphrodisiac, and beneficial in infertility. Its yellowy green flowers give way to gleaming red berries.

dried roots

root

Parts used
ROOTS
- The roots are harvested in autumn, dried, then cut up for use in decoctions, capsules, tablets and liquid extracts.

Constituents
The withania root is notable for a steroid called withanolide, which is anti-inflammatory. It also contains alkaloids, particularly withasomnine, that are responsible for the root's sedative qualities.

Medicinal uses
Withania has traditionally been prescribed as a tonic. This use was supported by a paper in the *Journal of Ethnopharmacology*, published in 2000, which described how the plant helps the body to cope with and adapt to stressful situations. It also lowers blood pressure, slows the heart rate and boosts the immune system. In Indian medicine, withania is commonly prescribed to help convalescing patients to overcome fatigue. The plant is also used to treat anxiety and a variety of nervous problems, and in large doses is capable of inducing sleep.

Research performed in America in 1991 found that withania contains components that act in the same way as the main inhibitory neurotransmitter in the central nervous system. It is this that is likely to account for its sedative and sleep-inducing qualities.

Painful rheumatic joints respond to the plant's anti-inflammatory properties, and its high iron content makes it useful in the treatment of anaemia.

Cultivation
Plant in dry, stony soil, preferably in the sun or light shade. It is considered a weed in parts of Australia.

PREPARATION AND DOSAGE
- **To treat fatigue, anxiety, stress, insomnia, rheumatic joints**

    LIQUID EXTRACT, TABLETS 1–2 g dried root equivalent, taken three times a day.
    DECOCTION Allow 1–2 g of root per cup of water. Boil in a saucepan for 15 minutes, leave to infuse for 10 minutes, then strain. Take 2 cups a day.

    IF SYMPTOMS PERSIST, CONSULT A DOCTOR

CAUTIONS
- Avoid using withania when pregnant or breastfeeding.
- Those taking barbiturates and other tranquillisers should avoid taking withania.

Wormwood
Artemesia absinthium Asteraceae **Also called** Absinthe, Green ginger

Wormwood is a shrubby, aromatic perennial with grey-green leaves covered in fine, white, silky hairs. Tiny, yellow flower heads are borne in loose clusters on the upper ends of the branches in spring and summer. A popular garden plant in many parts of the world, wormwood is native to parts of Europe, Africa and Asia, and is found on roadsides and wasteland in Australia and New Zealand, where it has become naturalised.

Parts used
LEAVES AND OTHER AERIAL PARTS

- The leaves, stems and flowers are dried for use in the preparation of infusions and tinctures.
- Wormwood is one of the most bitter herbs known, and is used in minute doses in some alcoholic beverages, such as absinthe and vermouth.

dried leaves

Constituents
Amongst the constituents of wormwood are essential oil, flavonoids, lignans, sesquiterpene lactones and phenolic acids. As much as 35 per cent of the essential oil may consist of thujone, which is known to be both addictive and neurotoxic when taken in excess.

Medicinal uses
As its name suggests, wormwood has traditionally been used to clear worms and other parasites from the bowel. Wormwood and related species are still used in this way to treat humans and animals in many parts of the world – an ability that is thought to be due to the presence of the sesquiterpene lactones.

The herb's extremely bitter taste stimulates receptors in the tongue, and this in turn triggers the secretion in the digestive system of gastric juices, pancreatic enzymes and bile. For this reason, herbalists prescribe wormwood in low doses to bring about an overall improvement in digestive function, and specifically to stimulate the appetite, improve absorption of nutrients and treat indigestion.

In recent years, research has validated the traditional Chinese medicinal use of the related species *Artemesia annua* (Chinese wormwood, or *qing hao*). The active constituent artemesinin has been demonstrated to prevent and cure malaria in a large percentage of cases, and is considered to be particularly useful for the treatment of drug-resistant strains of malaria.

Cultivation
Wormwood needs well-drained soil and full sun. It thrives in hot or dry areas and in coastal gardens, and is drought tolerant when established. Prune in spring or to remove unwanted flowers at other times. Plants grow readily from cuttings.

flower head

PREPARATION AND DOSAGE
- Wormwood should be taken internally only on the advice of a medical herbalist.

IF SYMPTOMS PERSIST, CONSULT A DOCTOR

CAUTIONS
- Do not take wormwood except under the advice of a medical herbalist, and do not exceed the recommended dose. Thujone and certain other constituents are toxic, and may cause severe harm in overdose.
- Wormwood should not be taken by children, pregnant or breastfeeding women, or anyone with digestive hyperacidity.
- Do not take wormwood if you have a known allergy to other members of the Asteraceae family, such as echinacea or chamomile.

Yarrow *Achillea millefolium* Asteraceae **Also called** Milfoil, Achillea

Native to Europe and western Asia, this herb grows on rough ground in fields and on roadsides in Australia and New Zealand, often as a garden escapee. Its thin, dark green leaves are divided into many segments, reflected in its species name of *millefolium*, which means 'a thousand leaves'. Flat heads of numerous, tiny, white, or sometimes pink, flowers appear in summer.

Parts used

FLOWER HEADS, NON-WOODY PARTS OF THE PLANT AND SEEDS

- The plant is harvested just after the completion of flowering, during summer and autumn.
- Yarrow is usually dried for use in the preparation of an infusion, but it can also be used fresh. It is sometimes available as a liquid extract.

Constituents

The flowers contain around 0.2–0.5 per cent essential oil, whereas the leaves contain 0.02–0.07 per cent. Anti-inflammatory flavonoids are also present in the plant, as well as tannins, alkaloids and bitter compounds.

dried flower heads

Medicinal uses

As a result of its numerous active components, yarrow has many medicinal uses. It is antispasmodic, carminative (it is able to relieve the build-up of trapped wind), anti-inflammatory and anthelmintic (able to deal with intestinal worms). These actions are mostly due to the presence of the plant's essential oil.

Yarrow is also traditionally used to reduce fevers, and consequently is often taken at the onset of infections such as colds and flu, where it is often combined with elder or peppermint. It may also be of assistance in the reduction of phlegm.

Yarrow is diuretic, lowers blood pressure and eases palpitations. It is regarded as a circulation remedy, with the capacity to relax blood vessels that are too tightly constricted and constrict those that are too flaccid. Consequently, it is often prescribed for the treatment of varicose veins and ulcers, venous stasis, phlebitis and haemorrhoids. It is also used to relieve digestive disorders, including stomach ailments, inflammation of the intestinal walls, constipation and flatulence.

The plant has traditionally been used to soothe the pain of uterine cramps during menstruation and childbirth. Taken regularly in small doses, it can also help to regulate the menstrual cycle, particularly in those cases where menstruation is scant or infrequent.

When used externally, yarrow's anti-inflammatory action helps in the relief of rheumatic aches and pains.

flower head

Cultivation

Propagate in spring, either from seed or by division. Plant in a well-drained soil and choose a sunny location. This plant can be invasive.

PREPARATION AND DOSAGE

- **To treat fevers, colds, flu, flatulence, digestive ailments**

  LIQUID EXTRACT 1–2 g dried herb equivalent, three times a day.
  INFUSION 2–4 g dried herb infused in 1 cup of boiling water for 5 minutes before straining. Drink 3 cups a day.

- **To treat uterine pains**

  SITZ BATH Put 100 g of the dried plant into 20 litres of hot water.

IF SYMPTOMS PERSIST, CONSULT A DOCTOR

CAUTIONS

- Yarrow may cause contact allergies, particularly in those people allergic to other members of the Asteraceae family, such as echinacea and chamomile.
- It is not advisable to use yarrow when pregnant or breastfeeding.
- Exposure to sunlight is not recommended. Yarrow may act as a photosensitiser.
- Large doses may produce vertigo and headaches.

Yellow dock *Rumex crispus* Polygonaceae **Also called** Curled dock

Native to Europe and North Africa, yellow dock is now found worldwide. It is naturalised in New Zealand and eastern and southern Australia, and is common in paddocks, on stream banks and near drains. Growing up to 1.5 m tall, yellow dock has stout stalks that bear large, curly-edged leaves. Tiny, greenish flowers sprout in dense clusters at the top of the plant. The seed capsules are papery discs 3–6 mm in length.

Parts used

ROOTS

- The roots are harvested in autumn and dried to make decoctions and liquid extracts.
- The leaves can be eaten steamed as a nutritious vegetable, similar to spinach, and are popularly applied as a poultice to relieve nettle stings.

Constituents

Yellow dock contains tannins (including catechol), bitter principles, resin, anthraquinone glycosides, rumicin, chrysophanic acid and a complex volatile oil. Like spinach, it also contains iron and oxalates.

Medicinal uses

Yellow dock is considered to have a mildly stimulating action on the liver and gall bladder, and to stimulate the flow of bile. It is recommended for treating a wide variety of digestive symptoms, including indigestion, flatulence and sluggish bowel function. The presence of anthraquinone glycosides in the plant confer laxative properties, although this effect is gentler than that observed in several other anthraquinone-containing herbs, such as senna and cascara.

By supporting the digestive system, and in particular the body's excretion of wastes, yellow dock is traditionally believed to act as a blood cleanser. It is recommended for a variety of skin conditions, including acne, psoriasis and eczema, as well as for chronic enlargement of the lymph glands and for the treatment of rheumatism. The herb is considered to be specifically indicated if constipation accompanies any of these complaints.

dried roots

Cultivation

Yellow dock thrives in moist soils in sun or partial shade. It grows easily from seed sown in spring. In some parts of Australia it is considered a noxious weed and should not be grown (check with your local agriculture department). The green fruit is considered poisonous to cattle.

PREPARATION AND DOSAGE

- To treat indigestion, flatulence, constipation, acne, psoriasis, eczema

    LIQUID EXTRACT 2–4 g dried root equivalent, three times a day.
    DECOCTION Boil 2–4 g dried root in 1 cup of water for 10 minutes before straining. Drink three cups a day.

    IF SYMPTOMS PERSIST, CONSULT A DOCTOR

CAUTIONS

- Do not rely on yellow dock or other laxative herbs for more than 8–10 days at a time. The best treatment for constipation is more dietary fibre, adequate water intake and regular exercise.
- Do not exceed the recommended dose. Overuse may cause abdominal cramps, diarrhoea and loss of potassium.
- Yellow dock should not be used by pregnant or breastfeeding women, or anyone with obstruction of the bowel or gall bladder.

Ziziphus *Ziziphus jujuba* (syn. *Z. vulgaris*)   Rhamnaceae   **Also called** Jujube, Chinese date

This small tree grows to a height of 6–8 m and is common throughout the Mediterranean region and in China, where it has been grown for some 3000 years. The bark on its trunk is brown and covered in small cracks, and its branches are thorny. Ziziphus leaves are oval and fluted and the flowers are yellowish green and grow in small clusters. Its fruit is a berry that contains a single seed.

Parts used

FRUIT, SEEDS

- The berries, called jujubes, are harvested in autumn, as soon as they turn brown.
- They are then dried and their seeds are removed. The dried flesh is used in preparing decoctions and a flour that is mixed to a paste.
- The seeds are also used medicinally.
- Ziziphus can be combined with other plants with soothing qualities, such as carob and marshmallow.

Constituents

The flesh of the berry is rich in mucilages, which have soothing properties. It also contains flavonoids, saponins (such as ziziphus saponins I, II and III), as well as vitamins A, B and C.

Medicinal uses

Ziziphus is one of the four 'pectoral' fruits that are especially good for chest ailments – the others being dates, figs and raisins. In traditional Chinese medicine, ziziphus is used to rebuild strength and stamina when the body is in a weakened state, such as during convalescence or chronic fatigue syndrome. It has been shown to be effective against bacteria, inflammation, fevers and diabetes.

Ziziphus is believed to modify the immune response and reduce allergic reactions. In 1997, for example, Japanese scientists showed that triterpene oligoglycosides isolated from ziziphus prevented the release of the inflammatory mediator histamine in vitro.

Ziziphus also has a sedative effect and can help with insomnia. In 2002, it was found that the glycoside jujuboside inhibited stimulation of the brain's hippocampus, which may account for the plant's sedative effects.

Taken orally, the jujube fruit is used to relieve hoarseness, voice loss, inflammatory throat infections, coughs and bronchitis.

Its astringent, binding action makes it an effective remedy for diarrhoea, taken on its own or with other soothing plants.

Cultivation

Best in a warm climate, protected from frosts. Grow in a well-drained, moist or dry soil in a sunny spot. Ziziphus can be grown from seed, suckers or cuttings. The plant is considered a weed in parts of northern Australia.

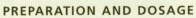

dried fruit

PREPARATION AND DOSAGE

- **To treat voice loss, sore throat, cough, bronchitis, diarrhoea, insomnia, recovery during convalescence**

  DECOCTION Put 30–50 g of ground fruit into 1 litre of water. Boil for 30 minutes and strain. Drink as required.
  LIQUID EXTRACT As prescribed by a medical herbalist.

IF SYMPTOMS PERSIST, CONSULT A DOCTOR

CAUTIONS

- No harmful side effects have been associated with the consumption of jujube berries.
- Pregnant or breastfeeding women should not take ziziphus as a herbal medicine.

A to Z of Ailments

ADDICTION

Alcohol dependence

The National Health and Medicine Research Council (NHMRC) of Australia advises that men who drink more than four standard drinks a day, and women who have more than two drinks a day are at risk of long-term harm from their alcohol consumption, with an even greater risk associated with alcohol intake above these levels. Lower levels of intake are recommended for pregnant and breastfeeding women, people with liver disease and those with mental health problems. All adults should aim to have at least two alcohol-free days each week. A standard drink is defined as 30 ml spirits (40% alc. vol.); 60 ml sherry or port (20% alc. vol.); 100 ml wine (12% alc. vol.); 285 ml beer (4.9% alc. vol.) or 425 ml light beer (2.7% alc. vol.).

There is no specific volume of use that defines alcoholism. Instead, alcohol dependence is identified by the occurrence of at least three of the following in the previous 12 months:
- A strong compulsion to use alcohol
- Difficulties controlling the onset of use, the amount of alcohol consumed or the termination of drinking
- Withdrawal symptoms when alcohol is withheld, or the use of alcohol to prevent such symptoms
- Increasing alcohol tolerance – i.e. the need to use more alcohol to create the same effect
- Continuing alcohol use despite clear evidence of harm
- Neglect of social or occupational activities to allow for alcohol use
- Prior unsuccessful attempts to quit

Symptoms
- Inability to cope with daily life without alcohol
- Trembling – sometimes known as DTs (delirium tremens) – which only ceases when an alcoholic drink is consumed
- Enlarged capillaries and redness of the face
- Weight loss
- Blackouts and memory problems
- Aggressive behaviour
- Emotional behaviour: excessive or inappropriate laughing or crying
- Pain (polyneuritis) in the legs
- Sexual impotence

CONSULT YOUR DOCTOR OR MEDICAL HERBALIST
- Withdrawal from excessive alcohol consumption should be carried out under medical supervision and may even require hospitalisation.

Causes

Alcohol dependence is often caused by social or psychological problems, such as depression. Some racial groups are considered to have lowered tolerance to alcohol, and so are at higher risk. In addition to the situations discussed above, binge drinking can also be damaging to the health, and authorities are concerned about its effects – particularly in young people.

WHICH PLANTS?

WARNING Use only one of the following at any given time.

INTERNAL USAGE
For anxiety and depression
LEMON BALM 2–3 g dried leaves infused in 1 cup of boiling water for 5 minutes before straining. Drink 2–3 cups a day.

As a sedative
VALERIAN Tablets, up to 2 g dried herb equivalent; take one dose an hour before bed.

For liver support
MILK THISTLE Tablets, up to 9 g dried herb equivalent, three times a day.

As advised by a medical herbalist
- Bupleurum

Other measures
- Join a society such as Alcoholics Anonymous and consider individual or group psychotherapy.
- Take supplements of the vitamins B_1, B_2, B_6, nicotinamide, C, D and E, with the mineral zinc to correct the deficiencies linked to alcoholism.

See also Hepatitis

> **DID YOU KNOW?**
>
> **Alcoholism**
> Kuzu can aid withdrawal from alcohol. A number of studies have shown that saponins in the plant protect the liver and also combat alcohol cravings. Kuzu is also reputed to help treat symptoms of drug withdrawal.

Drug withdrawal problems

Withdrawal from certain drugs that act on the brain (such as sleeping tablets or antidepressants) is especially difficult because physical dependency may have developed. If they are withdrawn too quickly, anxiety may recur, either because the condition is still present and the drugs have been withdrawn too soon, or because withdrawal itself provokes an acute reaction.

Symptoms
- Rapid aggravation of the condition that is being treated (anxiety, depression, insomnia)
- Aches and pains that have no apparent cause
- Insomnia, or an overwhelming desire to sleep
- Shaking, sweating and the inability to concentrate
- Fatigue, irritability, depression, greatly increased or decreased sexual urges
- Convulsions (if a long-term sedative treatment is suddenly discontinued)

ADDICTION

CONSULT YOUR DOCTOR OR MEDICAL HERBALIST
- Patients should never discontinue a course of treatment on their own initiative, even though they may feel normal for 24 hours before experiencing symptoms of withdrawal syndrome. Some treatments must be followed for a specified period of time in order to be effective.
- Only the prescribing doctor can help a patient to get through a successful withdrawal.
- A two-week washout period is recommended between stopping one drug and starting another medication, regardless of whether it is herbal or pharmaceutical.

WHICH PLANTS?

WARNING Use only one of the following at any given time.

A qualified medical herbalist can advise on the time scale for the withdrawal, and will usually prescribe specific doses of plant-based treatments to help in easing the process.

INTERNAL USAGE
To support the nervous system during withdrawal from tranquillisers or opiates
PASSIONFLOWER Liquid extract, 500 mg–1 g dried herb equivalent, twice during the day and at bedtime.
LAVENDER 2–3 g dried flowers infused in 1 cup of boiling water for 5–10 minutes. Drink 3–4 cups a day, between meals.

For liver support
MILK THISTLE Tablets, up to 9 g dried herb equivalent, three times a day.

As advised by a medical herbalist
- Bupleurum, St John's wort

Other measures
- Reduce your stress levels by maintaining a healthy lifestyle and a regular exercise program.
- Acupuncture and yoga have helped some people to get through this difficult period.

Nicotine addiction

Nicotine addiction results from the habitual use of tobacco. Its dangers are linked to both the components of the tobacco and their adverse chemical effects on the human body.

Heavy smoking can cause premature ageing of the skin, cancers of the mouth, lung and bladder, cardiovascular diseases (atherosclerosis, deterioration of the cardiac muscle, cerebral haemorrhage), respiratory diseases (chronic bronchitis, emphysema) and impotence. It can also cause pre- and post-natal problems, such as miscarriage, complications in pregnancy, foetal growth defects, sudden infant death syndrome and increased susceptibility to infection.

Symptoms
- An urge to smoke, especially after a meal, or when consuming another stimulant such as coffee
- Symptoms you may experience when quitting smoking include difficulty in concentrating, irritability, a sense of deprivation, increased appetite, sleep disorders

CONSULT YOUR DOCTOR
- Sometimes medical treatment is advised to support you as you quit smoking – this is more likely to be necessary if there is any kind of associated problem.
- Your doctor or pharmacist can help you with advice about nicotine replacement therapy.

Causes
The nicotine in tobacco is the main cause of the addiction. It modifies the chemistry of the brain and has both stimulatory and relaxing effects. But smoking may also have become a habit because of pleasurable associations with, for example, the first cup of tea or coffee of the day, or a sociable evening or meal with friends.

WHICH PLANTS?

WARNING Use only one of the following at any given time.

A program for giving up smoking, which above all requires very strong motivation, must be adapted to each individual case by the herbalist, and take particular account of the individual's personality and lifestyle.

INTERNAL USAGE
To treat nervous anxiety and sleep disorders
VALERIAN Tablets, up to 2 g dried herb equivalent; take one dose an hour before going to bed.

To improve ability to cope with stress
SIBERIAN GINSENG Tablets, capsules, 300 mg–1 g dried root equivalent, three times a day.

EXTERNAL APPLICATION
To prevent voice loss, hoarseness and sore throat associated with giving up smoking
MYRRH Tincture (1:5), 1 teaspoon in water. Use as a gargle three times a day.

See also **Bronchitis**

AGEING

Ageing is a natural process that begins to take effect as soon as we reach adulthood. It usually becomes more noticeable after the age of 60 due to the progressive degeneration of the non-renewable tissues throughout the body. However, it is important to be aware that with a healthy lifestyle it is perfectly possible for many people to retain extremely good health well into their older years.

Symptoms
- Skin loses tone and firmness
- Insomnia
- Blood, heart and circulatory problems may develop
- Deterioration associated with the brain and nervous system may cause memory loss, mental fatigue and reduced psychomotor skills
- Breathing difficulties, chronic coughs, frequent mouth infections and eye ailments are common
- Kidney function may deteriorate
- Decreased appetite, ability to digest food and assimilate nutrients
- Osteoporosis and reduction of muscular mass
- Reduced resistance to cold
- Fear of confronting new situations, irritability

CONSULT YOUR DOCTOR OR MEDICAL HERBALIST
- It is important to see your doctor about any symptoms that are troubling you. An annual check-up is also advised. Your doctor will perform the necessary investigations to reveal the underlying cause of any problems.
- A medical herbalist may be able to help you manage the ageing process by reducing symptoms and addressing risk factors for more serious conditions.

Causes
Disorders associated with ageing are a result of general wear and tear on the body, the ageing of tissues as cellular proteins break down and a gradual decrease in the body's metabolic rate.

WHICH PLANTS?

WARNING Use only one of the following at any given time.

INTERNAL USAGE
To improve energy levels
KOREAN GINSENG Tablets, capsules, 250–500 mg dried root equivalent, twice a day; take one dose in the morning and one dose around midday; choose a product standardised for its ginsenosides content. (See Cautions, p. 125.)
ROSEHIPS 2–2.5 g fragmented dried rosehips infused in 1 cup of boiling water for 10 minutes before straining. Drink 3–4 cups a day.
FENUGREEK Powder, 2 g in a little water, three times a day.

To prevent cardiovascular disorders
GINKGO Tablets, up to 2 g, standardised for ginkgo flavone glycosides, and ginkgolides and bilobalide. Take up to three times a day. (See Cautions, p. 102.)

To alleviate anxiety and insomnia
LIME FLOWERS Infuse 2–4 g of dried flowers in 1 cup of boiling water for 5 minutes, before straining. Drink 1 cup twice a day and another in the evening.
VALERIAN Tablets, up to 2 g dried herb equivalent; take one dose an hour before going to bed.

To prevent digestive disorders
CHAMOMILE Infuse 1 sachet of chamomile flowers in 1 cup of boiling water for 5–10 minutes. Drink 3 cups a day, before meals.
ANISE Infuse 500 mg–1 g dried seeds in 1 cup of boiling water for 5 minutes before straining and cooling. Drink 3 cups a day, after meals.

To relieve chronic coughs
WHITE HOREHOUND Liquid extract, 1–2 g dried herb equivalent, taken three times a day.
HYSSOP 1–2 teaspoons dried herb infused in 1 cup of boiling water for 5–10 minutes before straining. Drink 3 cups a day.

As advised by a medical herbalist
- Gentian, hawthorn, wild cherry bark

EXTERNAL APPLICATION
For mouth infections
MYRRH Tincture (1:5), 1 teaspoon in water. Use as a mouthwash three times a day.
CALENDULA Put 5 g dried flower heads in 1 litre of boiling water, infuse for 5 minutes, strain and cool. Use as a gargle and mouthwash two or three times a day.

Other measures
- Eat small, regular meals that are nutritionally balanced and not too spicy or rich. Be sure to chew your food well, as this helps trigger the release of digestive juices and will help to make it easier for your food to be digested.
- Eat plenty of red fruit (blackberries, raspberries, mulberries) and fruit containing vitamin C (oranges, mandarins, lemons, mangoes, kiwi fruit). Many fruits are rich in antioxidants (thought to slow the destructive action of free radicals), vitamins, calcium and iron.
- Take regular gentle exercise to promote good circulation – joining a tai chi class is particularly recommended. Having regular massages will also help to improve your circulation.
- Keep your mind and memory active. Read, do the crossword puzzle, take up a hobby and join in with social activities whenever possible.
- Try to reduce your stress and anxiety levels with the help of relaxation classes and other techniques. Stress can have a number of adverse effects on your health.

AGEING

See also Ageing skin, Osteoporosis, Prostate disorders

> **DID YOU KNOW?**
>
> ### Ageing
> In traditional Chinese medicine, Korean ginseng is regarded as an important tonic for older people. Several clinical trials have researched this aspect of its traditional use and suggest that in older patients it may help to improve concentration and mental function, REM sleep and depression.

Ageing skin

As a person ages, the structures of the skin begin to change, the surface loses moisture, and tone and elasticity are reduced. The pace at which these changes occur varies from person to person depending on genetic make-up and lifestyle factors, such as smoking and exposure to the sun.

Symptoms
- Skin becomes more wrinkled and acne rosacea may develop
- Age spots may appear on the face and hands
- Skin becomes finer, more transparent and may turn a yellowish grey colour
- Skin becomes drier due to a lack of sebum, and may appear dehydrated, flabby, flaky or itchy

Causes
Skin ageing is a normal part of the general ageing process. It can be accelerated by dehydration caused by exposure to the sun or wind, by a lack of the vitamins A, C and D and by excessive alcohol consumption and smoking.

WHICH PLANTS?

WARNING Use only one of the following at any given time.

INTERNAL USAGE
To improve skin condition
EVENING PRIMROSE OIL Capsules, 1000 mg, three times a day with meals.

EXTERNAL APPLICATION
To treat dry, rough skin
EVENING PRIMROSE Pierce a capsule of evening primrose oil and mix with 10 ml of carrier oil. Apply once or twice a day.
CALENDULA Apply a calendula-based cream as directed on the label.

Other measures
- Reduce your use of alcohol and stop smoking altogether.
- Prevent dehydration by drinking 1.5–2 litres of water every day and avoiding diuretics such as tea, coffee or dandelion.
- Take cod liver oil capsules (1 capsule a day) and consider taking an antioxidant supplement.
- Avoid sun exposure and sunbeds and protect your skin against ultraviolet radiation by wearing sunscreen and a hat when outdoors.

Memory loss

Your memory is the product of a network of millions of neurones communicating with each other and transmitting information received through your senses. There are two kinds of memory: short-term memory retains practical information that is useful more or less immediately (the time of an appointment, for example), whilst long-term memory stores recollections of past events. Each type of memory loss has different consequences for the sufferer. Memory loss can affect anyone over 60, and in some cases younger people too.

Symptoms
- Short-term memory loss: inability to recall recent events; poor attention span; appearing withdrawn; disturbed sleep patterns
- Long-term memory problems: no sense of time or place; difficulty in recognising others, or of remembering past events; depression

CONSULT YOUR DOCTOR OR MEDICAL HERBALIST
- Consult your doctor if the symptoms occur persistently. Medical advice is essential to rule out the development of Alzheimer's disease or other causes of dementia.

Causes
Ageing is one of many factors that can cause memory problems. Other causes include: stress, certain medications (such as antidepressants), arterial hypertension, hypothyroidism, alcoholism, lack of sleep, deficiency of vitamins B_1 and B_{12}, epilepsy, concussion, stroke and head trauma.

WHICH PLANTS?

WARNING Use only one of the following at any given time.

INTERNAL USAGE
To help improve the blood supply to the brain
GINKGO Tablets, up to 2 g, standardised for ginkgo flavone glycosides, and ginkgolides and bilobalide. Take up to three times a day. (See Cautions, p. 102.)

EXTERNAL USE
Sage and lemon balm (essential oils) have both been shown to inhibit an enzyme that causes the breakdown of acetylcholine (a key chemical involved in memory storage). Recent research in Britain has shown that sage and lemon balm have great potential for reducing memory loss, and it is possible that both essential oils from the plant could be used to beneficial effect in an aromatherapy massage.

AGEING

Other measures
- Keep up your intellectual and social activities.
- Take regular physical exercise to help you to relax, improve your sleep and develop your concentration.
- Take care to eat a healthy, well-balanced diet.

See also Ageing, Alzheimer's disease

Wrinkles & Bags under the eyes

The first visible signs of ageing usually appear on the face, and take the form of wrinkles and shadows under the eyes. There may also be swelling and reddening of the upper eyelids.

Symptoms
- Wrinkles: creases of varying depths in the skin
- Bags under the eyes: puffy, darkened skin below the eyes

Causes
Wrinkles occur because the skin loses elasticity as it ages. Premature wrinkling can be caused by overexposure to the ultraviolet rays in sunlight. The first lines to appear are usually 'crow's feet', which occur at the corners of the eyes as a result of repeatedly contracting the facial muscles. Frown lines may occur between the eyebrows and furrows may crease the forehead. Bags under the eyes are due to congestion of the lymphatic circulation in the area beneath the lower eyelid. They often appear in cases of acute or long-term insomnia. Stress, headaches and fatigue may accentuate the problem.

WHICH PLANTS?

WARNING Use only one of the following at any given time.

INTERNAL USAGE
To combat wrinkles
EVENING PRIMROSE OIL Capsules, 1000 mg, three times a day, with meals.

EXTERNAL APPLICATION
To combat wrinkles
EVENING PRIMROSE Pierce a capsule of evening primrose oil and mix with 10 ml of carrier oil. Apply once or twice a day.
CALENDULA Apply a calendula-based cream as directed on the label.

To treat bags under the eyes
GREEN/BLACK TEA Infuse 2 sachets of dried tea leaves in boiling water for 5 minutes, allow to cool and then place one over each eye for 5–10 minutes.
CHAMOMILE Follow directions for green/black tea (see above).

Other measures
- Don't smoke, and maintain a low to moderate alcohol intake.
- Avoid stress and learn to relax.
- Eat a healthy diet, rich in fruit, vegetables and whole grains.
- Drink 2 litres of water a day, and reduce your consumption of tea, coffee and other diuretics.

ALLERGIES

Allergies are the result of the body's immune system having an abnormal reaction to an otherwise innocuous substance that does not provoke the same reaction among other (non-allergic) people. Allergic reactions may occur soon after contact with the allergen or may be delayed by several hours.

Symptoms
- Difficulty breathing, wheezing (asthma), coughing
- Eczema, itching, urticaria (nettle rash)
- Runny nose, blocked nose, sneezing
- Conjunctivitis: sore, red eyes that are watery and/or itchy
- Diarrhoea (as a consequence of food allergies)
- In rare cases, a person may be so sensitive to a substance that they suffer anaphylactic shock when they come into contact with it. This life-threatening condition is characterised by swelling of the lips, tongue and throat. The airway may become blocked and there may be a loss of consciousness. Amongst the most common triggers are insect stings, shellfish and nuts

CONSULT YOUR DOCTOR
- A doctor may suggest skin or blood testing to try to identify the allergen.
- Seek immediate emergency medical attention for cases of swelling of the lips, throat and upper body, or if there is any difficulty in breathing.
- Some susceptible people are advised to carry adrenaline injections or antihistamine tablets for protection against future attacks.

Causes
Some allergic reactions occur when the sufferer comes into physical contact with the allergen – common triggers are dishwashing liquid, plants, metals and fabrics. Respiratory allergies such as hay fever and asthma are triggered by pollen, animal hair, mould and house dust. Food allergies may be caused by numerous types of food and by certain food colourings and other additives.

ALLERGIES

Allergies to different substances tend to manifest in different parts of the body – e.g. it is common for people who are sensitive to lactose to experience diarrhoea and other digestive symptoms. Susceptibility to allergies often runs in families. Stress and alcohol intake may sometimes aggravate the symptoms of an allergy.

WHICH PLANTS?

WARNING Use only one of the following at any given time.

INTERNAL USAGE
To reduce inflammation
BAICAL SKULLCAP Liquid extract, 500 mg–1 g dried root equivalent, three times a day.

To ease digestive allergic reactions
GLOBE ARTICHOKE Tablets, capsules, 500 mg–1 g dried herb equivalent, standardised for cynarin content, three times a day.
PEPPERMINT 1 teaspoon dried leaves infused in 150 ml of boiling water for 10–15 minutes before straining. Drink 1 cup after every meal.

To combat nasal symptoms
ELDER Liquid extract, 500 mg–1 g dried flower equivalent, three times a day.

As advised by a medical herbalist
- Albizia

EXTERNAL APPLICATION
To combat eye symptoms
CHAMOMILE Make an infusion with 2 sachets of chamomile – one for each eye – and allow to cool. Squeeze out the excess liquid, then place a sachet over each closed eye and leave it in place for 10 minutes. Repeat two or three times a day.

Other measures
- Avoid all possible contact with any known allergens.
- Pay attention to your diet: milk, tomatoes, chocolate and eggs are foods frequently implicated in chronic food allergies. Shellfish and nuts are commonly associated with violent and sudden allergic reactions.
- Talk to your doctor or medical herbalist about an elimination diet to help identify allergens.
- Some nutritional supplements can ease the symptoms of allergic reactions – e.g. vitamin C, bioflavonoids, vitamin E, B vitamins (particularly vitamin B_5, also known as pantothenic acid), and also calcium, magnesium and especially manganese, which are often deficient in people who have allergies. The omega-3 and omega-6 essential fatty acids are important, as are vitamin A and zinc.

See also Asthma, Eczema, Hay fever, Urticaria

Hay fever (allergic rhinitis)

One of the most common allergies is triggered by pollen and affects the respiratory tract and eyes. The allergy tends to start during adolescence or early adulthood and is associated with a family history of allergies (including eczema and asthma).

Symptoms
- Frequent sneezing
- Blocked nose and/or nasal discharge
- Itching in the eyes, throat and nasal area
- Sometimes wheezing in the chest, or the worsening of an already existing asthma

CONSULT YOUR DOCTOR
- Seek immediate medical attention if breathing becomes difficult, asthma symptoms worsen or there is swelling of the lips, mouth or throat.

Causes
Hay fever occurs because of a hyper-sensitive reaction to grass, flower and tree pollens, or sometimes the spores of certain fungi. The histamine released from the lining of nasal, eye or lung tissue leads to inflammation and swelling, and excessive production of mucus.

WHICH PLANTS?

WARNING Use only one of the following at any given time.

INTERNAL USAGE
To address nasal discharge from nose and eyes
ELDER Liquid extract, 500 mg–1 g dried flower equivalent, three times a day.
GOLDEN ROD Infusion, 1.5–3 g dried herb infused in 1 cup of boiling water for 10–15 minutes before straining. Drink 3–5 cups a day.

To reduce inflammation
BAICAL SKULLCAP Liquid extract, 500 mg–1 g dried root equivalent, three times a day.

As advised by a medical herbalist
- Albizia

Other measures
- Increase your fluid intake to maintain hydration of the mucous membranes.
- A series of tests to try to isolate the offending allergen can be arranged through your GP. A course of desensitising injections is sometimes recommended, but these occasionally produce dramatic reactions, and are not always effective.

ALLERGIES

- Try to avoid areas where there is a lot of your particular allergen in flower, especially when the pollen count is particularly high (as announced by the Weather Bureau).

See also Allergies, Asthma, Eye disorders

Urticaria

Urticaria (hives) is characterised by raised white or yellow areas surrounded by red inflammation. The weals are extremely itchy and vary in size. Normally urticaria lasts a few hours, but it can be persistent. If it lasts longer than six weeks, it is termed chronic.

Symptoms
- Weals form rapidly and may cover the entire body
- Inflamed, sensitive skin with raised itchy white or yellow lumps
- General malaise

CONSULT YOUR DOCTOR
- Urticaria can spread rapidly in a very short time and should always be medically investigated.

Causes

Urticaria can be caused by an allergy to food (such as lemons, nuts and tomatoes), medication or an insect bite or sting. It can arise after contact with a wide variety of plants, including primulas and, of course, nettles.

Urticaria can also be caused by certain viral and parasitic infections, or it can occur as part of an auto-immune disorder or as a response to stress. In some cases, it may be a reaction to cold, water or sunlight.

WHICH PLANTS?

WARNING Use only one of the following at any given time.

INTERNAL USAGE
To reduce inflammation
BAICAL SKULLCAP Liquid extract, 500 mg–1 g dried root equivalent, three times a day.
CHAMOMILE Infuse 1 sachet of chamomile flowers in 1 cup of boiling water for 5–10 minutes. Drink 3 cups a day, before meals.

To soothe the liver
MILK THISTLE Tablets, up to 9 g dried herb equivalent, three times a day.
GLOBE ARTICHOKE Tablets, capsules, 500 mg–1 g dried herb equivalent, standardised for cynarin content, three times a day.
BAICAL SKULLCAP Liquid extract, 500 mg–1 g dried root equivalent, three times a day.

EXTERNAL APPLICATION
To soothe the rash
CHAMOMILE Add 2 drops of chamomile essential oil to a bowl of tepid water. Soak a cloth in the water and then apply as a compress, three times a day.
LAVENDER Prepare a compress as for chamomile (see above).
THYME Prepare a compress as for chamomile (see above).

As advised by a medical herbalist
- Albizia, greater plantain, licorice

Other measures
- Try to identify a trigger for the urticaria and avoid contact with it.
- Consult an acupuncturist. Chronic urticaria may respond to this therapy.

See also Allergies, Asthma, Eczema

BLOOD, HEART & CIRCULATORY PROBLEMS

Anaemia

When the level of oxygen-carrying haemoglobin in the blood is below normal, a person is said to be anaemic. Iron is required for haemoglobin formation, and iron-deficiency anaemia is the most prevalent form. However, anaemia may also be a symptom of some other underlying disorders.

Symptoms
- Fatigue, exhaustion
- Pale or grey-tinged skin
- Dizziness when moving from a seated to a standing position
- Rapid heart rate and breathlessness after mild exertion
- Headaches

CONSULT YOUR DOCTOR
- Although anaemia is extremely common (especially among women), it should not be taken lightly. Cases should always be medically investigated, since it may signify the presence of serious underlying illness.

Causes

Women are more prone to anaemia than men, due to their menstrual blood loss. Pregnancy also increases the risk of iron-deficiency anaemia by draining the body's iron reserves. Vegetarians and those with low intake of animal foods are also more likely to develop anaemia. Disorders of the intestine in which there is blood loss or malabsorption of iron and other nutrients may lead to anaemia. It can also result from long-term, usually inflammatory diseases such as rheumatoid arthritis, in which case the anaemia cannot be treated by diet or vitamin supplements alone.

WHICH PLANTS?

WARNING Use only one of the following at any given time.

INTERNAL USAGE
As a blood tonic
NETTLE 2–4 g dried leaves infused in 1 cup of boiling water for 10 minutes before straining. Drink 3 cups a day.
FENUGREEK Powder, 2 g in a little water, three times a day.

Other measures
- As a preventive measure, adopt a diet that is rich in iron and vitamins.
- Reduce your consumption of foods known to impair iron absorption, including bran, foods rich in phosphorus (such as soft drinks), and stimulants (tea and coffee).

See also Endometriosis, Fibroids

Angina

A strangling or constrictive pain in the chest is a classic symptom of angina. It is caused by a temporary lack of oxygen in the heart muscle, usually due to an insufficient blood supply. The pain commonly occurs at times when the heart is working hard (such as during exercise), and diminishes with rest. However, attacks may also occur at times of inactivity or even during sleep. Angina is sometimes an indication of increased risk of heart attack (myocardial infarction) – especially if the pattern of the attacks increases in frequency or becomes more irregular.

Symptoms
- Intense and varying pain in the chest around the sternum (breastbone), radiating up to the neck and face, as well as the shoulders and arms (commonly the left arm)
- Dizziness, with a tendency to faint
- Palpitations (rapid heartbeat)
- Breathlessness from mild exertion
- Nausea, sometimes accompanied by vomiting
- Anxiety caused by the symptoms experienced

CONSULT YOUR DOCTOR
- Consult a doctor if you experience any of the above symptoms, especially if there is a history of cardiovascular disease in your family.
- Herbal remedies should only be used to complement conventional treatments, and cannot replace regular medical supervision.

Causes

The most frequent causes are stress, tobacco, alcohol and excess blood cholesterol. Angina pectoris can also be caused by poor blood supply due to a lesion on a coronary artery (arteritis), or may occur following the constriction of an artery as a result of stress.

WHICH PLANTS?

WARNING Use only one of the following at any given time.

The following may be recommended as a complementary treatment to conventional medicine:

As advised by a medical herbalist
- Coleus, garlic, ginger, ginkgo, hawthorn, valerian

Other measures
- Eat a diet that is rich in foods that contain anti-oxidants (which includes most fruit and fresh vegetables) and low in cholesterol.
- Stop smoking (see Nicotine addiction).
- Avoid stressful situations.
- If you have a sedentary lifestyle, talk to your doctor about a gentle exercise program. Bear in mind that it will be important to progress gradually if you have been suffering with angina – walking, yoga or tai chi may be among the exercises recommended.

See also Heart disease prevention

BLOOD, HEART & CIRCULATORY PROBLEMS

Arrhythmia

Abnormalities in the rhythm or rate at which the heart beats are collectively termed arrhythmia. The rhythm of the heart is created by the contractions of the cardiac muscle, which has a normal frequency of about 70–75 contractions a minute. When the heartbeat is faster than normal, the arrhythmia is termed tachycardia, and when it is slower than normal it is termed bradycardia.

Symptoms
- Difficulty in breathing, breathlessness
- Blue lips and extremities (cyanosis)
- A trembling feeling beneath the sternum, or a feeling that the heart is pounding or beating too fast in the chest
- Tiring easily
- Oedema (fluid retention)
- A cough may sometimes be present

CONSULT YOUR DOCTOR
- An abnormal heartbeat rhythm can constitute a medical emergency. There are several types of arrhythmia, of varying degrees of severity, and only a GP or a specialist can determine the correct form of treatment.

Causes
Abnormal heartbeat rhythms are caused by a disruption of the electrical impulses within the heart muscle. Causes of abnormal rhythms include heart conditions such as coronary artery disease, myocardial infarction (heart attack) or disorders of the heart valves, and hormonal disorders (such as hyperthyroidism).

WHICH PLANTS?

WARNING Use only one of the following at any given time.

Some of the following plants may be recommended as a supplement to conventional medicine:

As advised by a medical herbalist
- Hawthorn, St John's wort, lemon balm, passionflower, valerian

Other measures
- Learn to control anxiety, which increases heartbeat rhythms.
- Avoid all unnecessary fatigue and take time out to rest.
- Take trace elements – especially selenium – daily as directed by your doctor or medical herbalist.
- Reduce stimulants such as tea, coffee and chocolate, and avoid smoking.

Atherosclerosis & Arteritis

Atherosclerosis is characterised by the build-up of fatty deposits, complex starches, blood platelets and fibrous and calcium-containing tissue on the artery walls. The arteries gradually harden and are eventually obstructed by the accumulation of the deposits.

Arteritis is the term given to inflammation of the arterial walls causing a narrowing or complete obstruction. Although the symptoms of arteritis are similar to atherosclerosis, treatment differs and usually involves strong anti-inflammatory medication or steroids. Complementary herbal medicine for the condition is best taken as advised by a competent medical herbalist.

Symptoms
- Symptoms tend to appear only when the condition is serious enough to affect blood flow, and vary according to the area of the body affected
- Intermittent pain in the calf occurring, for example, after walking a limited distance on level ground or climbing a short flight of stairs
- Pins and needles in the legs, cold feet
- In very extreme circumstances, angina, heart attack, circulatory problems of the brain or renal failure may eventuate
- Dead tissue, poorly healing wounds or leg ulcers and risk of gangrene

CONSULT YOUR DOCTOR
- It is best to consult a doctor about treatment, although herbal medicines can play a useful complementary role.
- Atherosclerosis is a natural part of ageing, but it can be delayed, and the severity of accompanying symptoms can be reduced by following a special diet and with the aid of a competent medical herbalist. He or she will prescribe the appropriate herbs for your condition and symptoms.

Causes
Atherosclerosis is partly due to the natural ageing of the arteries, but is also associated with obesity, diabetes, high blood pressure and high cholesterol. Those with poor diets and those who smoke or drink alcohol to excess are most at risk.

WHICH PLANTS?

WARNING Use only one of the following at any given time.

The aim of the treatment is to rejuvenate the arteries and tackle problems caused by high blood cholesterol, high blood pressure or diabetes. Other heart disease risk factors should also be addressed at the same time (see Heart disease prevention).

212 NATURE'S MEDICINES

BLOOD, HEART & CIRCULATORY PROBLEMS

INTERNAL USAGE
As a preventive measure
GARLIC Tablets, capsules, follow manufacturer's instructions, to a maximum of 6 g dried garlic clove equivalent per day.
GINKGO Tablets, up to 2 g, standardised for ginkgo flavone glycosides, and ginkgolides and bilobalide. Take up to three times a day. (See Cautions, p. 102.)
BILBERRY Tablets, up to 20 g fresh fruit equivalent per day.
GLOBE ARTICHOKE Tablets, capsules, 500 mg–1 g dried herb equivalent, standardised for cynarin content, three times a day.
PSYLLIUM Take 1 sachet of psyllium powder in a large glass of water, with a main meal.
GRAPE SEED Tablets, capsules, up to 24 g dried seed equivalent per day, standardised for anthocyanidin content.

Other measures
- Make sure your diet contains large quantities of fresh fruit and vegetables, along with complex carbohydrates, and 'good' oils from nuts, seeds and cold-pressed vegetable oils. Choose low-fat forms of protein, and favour fish and vegetable protein sources over red meat.
- Avoid a sedentary lifestyle. A brisk daily walk of at least half an hour is recommended.
- Limit your intake of processed foods, especially deep fried and sugary foods.
- Consider taking a supplement of antioxidant nutrients such as vitamins C and E, and the mineral selenium.
- Limit your consumption of alcohol, and give up smoking if you haven't done so already.

See also Angina, Diabetes, Heart disease prevention, Hypertension, Lipid disorders, Obesity

> **DID YOU KNOW?**
>
> ## Atherosclerosis
> Garlic is believed to help combat hypertension and atherosclerosis by reducing the level of lipids in arterial blood. It also acts on the arterial walls, causing the smooth arterial muscles to relax so that the blood vessels dilate.

Chilblains

Excessive constriction of blood vessels just beneath the skin during cold weather can lead to the itchy, purple-red swellings known as chilblains. The condition generally affects the extremities (nose, hands, feet and ears).

Symptoms
- Initially, the skin loses feeling and becomes white and stiff
- Next, the skin turns intensely red or purple and is very painful
- Blisters and cracks appear

CONSULT YOUR DOCTOR
- In extreme cases, when sores or ulcers develop, for example, it is best to consult your GP.
- For minor cases, a medical herbalist, pharmacist or chiropodist will be able to advise which lotions or creams will help circulatory problems, prevent itching and promote healing.

Causes
Exposure to natural or artificial cold, or contact with a very cold surface such as ice or snow may inhibit the circulation. If this continues, it can lead to the death of the affected skin and to deep sores. Those most at risk include elderly people with circulatory problems and people suffering from anaemia.

WHICH PLANTS?

WARNING Use only one of the following at any given time.

INTERNAL USAGE
GINGER Tincture (1:5), take 20–30 drops in a glass of water three times a day.
CAYENNE Sprinkle a pinch or two over food, three times a day, or stir into juice such as tomato juice.
GINKGO Tablets, up to 2 g, standardised for ginkgo flavone glycosides, and ginkgolides and bilobalide. Take up to three times a day. (See Cautions, p. 102.)

EXTERNAL APPLICATION
BLACK MUSTARD Mix 50 g of fresh black mustard powder with 200 g of flax powder (also known as linseed meal). Add enough lukewarm water to make a thick paste, then wrap it in a thick cloth and place the poultice wherever the pain occurs for about 10 minutes. When treating a child, do not apply the poultice for more than 3–5 minutes.
CAYENNE Apply a cayenne-based ointment to the affected area three to four times a day, as directed on label.

Other measures
- Protect the most exposed parts of your body from the cold with the help of gloves, socks etc.
- Ensure that your home is adequately and comfortably heated.
- Take regular aerobic exercise to promote the circulation.
- A course of physiotherapy may be required to help regain mobility in the affected areas, particularly if the chilblains are severe.

See also Raynaud's disease

A TO Z OF AILMENTS   213

BLOOD, HEART & CIRCULATORY PROBLEMS

Haemorrhoids

Haemorrhoids (or 'piles') are swollen varicose veins that occur in the lining of the anus. They tend to cause pain when stools are passed, and may bleed or protrude outside the anus (prolapsed haemorrhoids).

Symptoms
- Pain and/or rectal bleeding on defecation
- Inflammation of the anus, with swelling and the formation of soft, swollen veins in the lining
- Mucus discharge and itching around anal opening (prolapsed haemorrhoids)
- Hard haemorrhoids and extreme pain, as a result of thrombosis in the veins – termed 'thrombosed external haemorrhoids'
- Occasionally, sharp pain caused by a fissure (tear) of the anus

CONSULT YOUR DOCTOR
- It is important to seek medical investigation to rule out other, more serious disorders that produce similar symptoms (such as anal fistulae). More serious cases, including prolapsing haemorrhoids, may require medical treatment, and sometimes surgery.

Causes
Often hereditary, haemorrhoids are linked to chronic complaints that increase the pressure inside the abdomen (such as constipation, a chronic cough or bronchitis, obesity, pregnancy, recurrent heavy lifting and prolonged sitting). A diet lacking in fibre and containing digestive irritants (such as spicy food) may also contribute.

WHICH PLANTS?
WARNING Use only one of the following at any given time.

INTERNAL USAGE
To strengthen and help tone the blood vessels
GRAPE SEED Tablets, capsules, up to 24 g dried seed equivalent per day, standardised for anthocyanidin content.
HORSECHESTNUT Tablets, 1.5 g dried seed equivalent, standardised for aescin content. Take 2–3 tablets a day.
BILBERRY Tablets, up to 20 g fresh fruit equivalent per day.

To soothe an inflamed and irritated digestive tract
SLIPPERY ELM 1 teaspoon slippery elm powder mixed with ¼ cup of water and drunk three times a day before meals, along with an additional glass of water.

EXTERNAL APPLICATION
HORSECHESTNUT Apply horsechestnut-based cream or gel two or three times a day, as directed on the label.
WITCH HAZEL Apply witch hazel–based ointment once a day.

Other measures
- Avoid external irritants (such as tight-fitting clothes) and internal ones (spices, alcoholic drinks).
- Observe strict hygiene.
- Avoid sitting for extended periods and avoid carrying or lifting heavy weights.
- Calm the inflammation with ice cubes wrapped in a fine cloth.
- If constipation occurs, follow an appropriate dietary regime or take gentle medication, as recommended by your medical herbalist.

See also Constipation, Vein disorders

Heart disease prevention

Heart disease is one of the major causes of death and disability in the developed world. However, many of the risk factors are well understood and able to be addressed. The term 'heart disease' includes conditions such as angina, arrhythmia, heart attack and congestive heart failure.

Congestive heart failure is the inability of the heart to pump the blood around the body adequately – it is a serious, life-threatening condition, and is the leading cause of hospitalisation in the Western world for people over 65 years of age.

Symptoms
- The symptoms of heart attacks and angina are very similar. However, the pain of a heart attack is more severe, and lasts for longer. The pain of heart attack is normally described as a strong pressure or squeezing pain felt in the middle of the chest. The pain may also extend to the jaw, neck or shoulder, or down the arm. It is often accompanied by shortness of breath. Unlike angina, heart attack pain does not resolve with rest
- Symptoms of congestive heart failure include fatigue, shortness of breath, oedema (fluid retention and swelling) and the failure of other organs such as the kidneys. The symptoms may develop slowly or suddenly, depending on the speed at which the heart failure is occurring

CONSULT YOUR DOCTOR
- It is important to seek emergency medical help if you experience symptoms of heart attack, or suspect someone else is having one – the

BLOOD, HEART & CIRCULATORY PROBLEMS

sooner treatment is commenced, the better the chances of recovery. You should also seek medical help if you experience other symptoms of heart disease. Regular check-ups are advised for anyone at high risk of developing heart disease and especially for those with a family history of cardiac conditions.

Causes

- High blood pressure damages the heart and blood vessels, and consequently is a major risk factor for heart disease.
- High cholesterol levels predispose you to heart disease by causing atherosclerosis, a condition in which fatty plaques are deposited on the artery walls, narrowing the blood vessels and restricting blood flow. Factors such as cigarette smoking, high blood pressure and diabetes also contribute to the development of atherosclerosis, which is a strong risk factor for angina and heart attack, as well as stroke.
- People who have a family history of cardiac problems, are obese, physically inactive, drink to excess or smoke are also at increased risk of heart disease, as are people with diabetes.
- People who feel depressed, anxious, hostile or socially isolated are more likely to develop heart disease than other people. Stress – especially work stress accompanied by feelings of being under pressure, but having little control – has also been established as a risk factor.

WHICH PLANTS?

WARNING Use only one of the following at any given time.

It is best to consult a doctor about treatment, although herbal medicines can play a useful complementary role, and may assist in preventing heart disease.

INTERNAL USAGE
To help reduce the risk of cardiovascular disease
GARLIC Tablets, capsules, follow manufacturer's instructions, to a maximum of 6 g dried garlic clove equivalent per day.

As a supportive therapy for high cholesterol levels
GLOBE ARTICHOKE Tablets, capsules, 500 mg–1 g dried herb equivalent, standardised for cynarin content, three times a day.
PSYLLIUM Take 1 sachet of psyllium powder in a large glass of water, with a main meal.
GRAPE SEED Tablets, capsules, up to 24 g dried seed equivalent per day, standardised for anthocyanidin content.

As nervous system support during times of stress
LIME FLOWERS Infuse 2–4 g of dried flowers in 1 cup of boiling water for 5 minutes, before straining. Drink 1 cup twice a day and another in the evening.
PASSIONFLOWER Liquid extract, 500 mg–1 g dried herb equivalent, twice during the day and at bedtime.
OATS Liquid extract, 1–4 g dried herb equivalent, two or three times a day.

As advised by a medical herbalist
- Coleus, ginkgo, hawthorn

Other measures

- Dietary anti-oxidants play a valuable role in protecting against heart disease by combating damaging free radicals that enhance disease processes. Eat at least 5 serves of fresh fruit and vegetables every day, and consider taking an anti-oxidant supplement as well.
- Stop smoking, and limit your alcohol intake to a maximum of one or two standard drinks a day (red wine seems to be the best for heart health).
- Eating a high-fibre diet helps your body to excrete cholesterol, while reducing your salt intake may help to reduce your blood pressure.
- Maintain a healthy body weight, and take regular aerobic exercise (but if it's been a while since you exercised, talk to your doctor before you start).
- Take steps to improve your ability to cope adequately with stress – consider meditation, hypnotherapy or relaxation classes.

See also Angina, Arrhythmia, Atherosclerosis & Arteritis, Excess weight & Obesity, High blood pressure, Lipid disorders

High blood pressure

Your blood pressure is recorded as two numbers, e.g. 110/60, with the higher number (systolic blood pressure) indicating the pressure in your arteries as the heart squeezes out blood during each beat, and the lower number (diastolic pressure) indicating the pressure as it relaxes before the next heartbeat. Your blood pressure varies to meet your body's needs, but a permanent resting blood pressure of more than 140/90 mmHg is considered high, and is a risk factor for stroke, heart attack and kidney problems. You may be symptom free or you may experience one or more of the following symptoms.

Symptoms

- Tiredness, breathlessness following physical effort
- Buzzing in the ears
- Occasional dizzy spells

CONSULT YOUR DOCTOR

- If you experience the above symptoms, consult your doctor to find out if you suffer from hypertension (high blood pressure). If your blood pressure is higher than 140/90 mmHg, it is wise to arrange to have it checked regularly.

A TO Z OF AILMENTS 215

BLOOD, HEART & CIRCULATORY PROBLEMS

Causes

High blood pressure may have hereditary or metabolic causes, or it may be associated with atherosclerosis. It is also linked to obesity, as well as to high alcohol intake.

WHICH PLANTS?

WARNING Use only one of the following at any given time.

The following plants may be recommended as a complementary treatment to conventional medicine:

As advised by a medical herbalist
- Black cohosh, blackcurrant, celery, coleus, elder, garlic, hawthorn, valerian

Other measures

- Pay attention to your diet – especially if you suffer from obesity, gout, diabetes or atherosclerosis.
- Aim to be within 10 per cent of your ideal body weight.
- Avoid tobacco and reduce your alcohol consumption.
- Take regular physical exercise and practise a relaxing hobby such as yoga or meditation.
- Ensure that your diet contains as much fresh fruit and as many vegetables as possible.
- Reduce the amount of salt you add to your food, and avoid processed foods, which may contribute as much as 75 per cent of the salt in your diet.

See also Angina, Atherosclerosis & Arteritis, Heart disease prevention, Lipid disorders

Lipid disorders

This term covers all anomalies in the balance of fatty substances (lipids) such as cholesterol, phospholipids and triglycerides that circulate in the blood. An excess of these fats overloads the blood vessels and causes circulatory problems that can lead to serious illness. Blood tests are needed to identify abnormal levels of lipids in the blood. Symptoms appear as a result of circulatory problems.

Symptoms

- Dizziness, buzzing in the ears
- Pain in the chest or legs on walking (see Angina, Atherosclerosis & Arteritis)
- Fatty patches in the skin under the eyes or elsewhere

CONSULT YOUR DOCTOR
- Monitoring and prevention are very important in this type of ailment. It is therefore essential to consult a doctor, who will make an accurate diagnosis and prescribe the appropriate tests and treatment.

Causes

Lipid problems can be due to genetics, diabetes, obesity, age, alcohol intake, tobacco and menopause. Although dietary habits may also be involved, they are not necessarily a causative factor. Lipid disorders can also be brought on by medication (contraceptives and some anti-HIV medicines).

WHICH PLANTS?

WARNING Use only one of the following at any given time.

INTERNAL USAGE
GLOBE ARTICHOKE Tablets, capsules, 500 mg–1 g dried herb equivalent, standardised for cynarin content, three times a day.
MILK THISTLE Tablets, up to 9 g dried herb equivalent, three times a day.

As advised by a medical herbalist
- Bupleurum

Other measures

- Stop smoking and limit your alcohol intake to 1–2 glasses of wine a day for men, or 1 glass of wine for women.
- Drink green tea.
- Take regular exercise.
- Adopt a diet that is low in saturated fats and sugar.
- Reduce your consumption of meat and dairy products.

> **DID YOU KNOW?**
>
> **Blood lipids & grape seed**
> Studies in the USA have shown that consuming a small amount of grape seed oil every day, combined with following a low-fat diet, may help to increase your 'good' (HDL) cholesterol and reduce your 'bad' (LDL) cholesterol.

Low blood pressure

The medical term for blood pressure that is well below average is 'hypotension'. It is most often noticed by a sufferer on moving from a seated position to standing, when they may experience temporary dizziness. The normal response of the body is to raise the blood pressure a little on standing, in order to maintain a good flow of oxygen to the brain.

Symptoms

- Dizzy spells, giddiness, blurred vision, headache
- Dizziness sometimes experienced by older men when they are passing urine during the night (known as micturition syncope)

BLOOD, HEART & CIRCULATORY PROBLEMS

CONSULT YOUR DOCTOR
- Only a doctor can measure blood pressure accurately and determine the appropriate treatment for cases of hypotension.

Causes

Hypotension may be brought on by a fall in the blood pressure of the lower limbs (perhaps due to varicose veins). It often occurs on rising, following a prolonged spell of sitting or lying down; this is known as postural hypotension.

The drop in pressure on changing position is common among the elderly. More rarely, hypotension can be caused by cardiac or kidney problems, or sometimes by dehydration due to medication, especially diuretics.

WHICH PLANTS?

WARNING Use only one of the following at any given time.

Some of the following plants may be recommended as a complementary treatment to conventional medicine:

As advised by a medical herbalist
- Ginger, hawthorn, rosemary, winter savory

Other measures

- Wear support stockings to avoid varicose veins, which will cause circulatory problems.
- Get up slowly, gently moving to a sitting position first to avoid sudden falls in blood pressure. Be sure that you have some support while standing or walking.

Lymphoedema

Lymph is a clear fluid that bathes all the body's cells, removing waste products and fighting infection. It circulates around the body via an extensive network of lymphatic vessels. A malfunction anywhere in this network causes characteristic swelling in one or several limbs due to an accumulation of lymph in the tissues – this condition is referred to as 'lymphoedema'.

Symptoms

- Swollen arm (following radical surgery such as a mastectomy, for example)
- Permanent, whitish swelling of the leg
- Tension and feeling of tiredness in the limbs
- Swelling
- Pains, cramp

CONSULT YOUR DOCTOR OR MEDICAL HERBALIST
- Lymphoedema requires medical treatment in which herbal medicine can play a helpful complementary role. Medical intervention should be sought as soon as lymphoedema strikes any part of the body.

Causes

Lymphoedema is the result of a breakdown in the lymphatic drainage. The problem may be caused by poor blood circulation, vein disorders, complications following surgical removal of a vein or when blood flow is obstructed in some way, as in arthritis of the knee or if cancer spreads through the lymphatic system. It may also occur after surgical removal of lymph nodes or following a course of radiotherapy.

WHICH PLANTS?

WARNING Use only one of the following at any given time.

EXTERNAL APPLICATION
For use in massage
WITCH HAZEL Apply a witch hazel–based cream, always working towards the heart. Use the cream as directed on the label.

In the bath
CYPRESS Add up to 8 drops of essential oil to running bath water. Bathe for 10–20 minutes.
ROSEMARY Add up to 8 drops of essential oil to running bath water. Bathe for 10–20 minutes.

As advised by a medical herbalist
- Cleavers, dandelion

Other measures

- To dissipate the swelling, consult a physiotherapist who can give the appropriate advice and suggest suitable exercises.
- Manual drainage (gentle massages) by a physiotherapist may help.
- Moderate exercise, such as using an exercise bicycle, gentle walking or swimming, can be effective.
- Support bandages, in layers or spread out, are often a relief, but are best applied by a nurse.

See also **Fluid retention**

A TO Z OF AILMENTS 217

BLOOD, HEART & CIRCULATORY PROBLEMS

Raynaud's disease or phenomenon

This circulatory disorder affects the fingers and toes. In sufferers, the blood vessels that supply the fingers and toes contract suddenly when exposed to cold, cutting off the blood supply. This leads to pallor and then cyanosis (blueness from lack of oxygen) in the extremities for a few minutes. The phenomenon is sometimes limited to two or three fingers or toes.

Symptoms
- First stage: the fingertips (or toes) become pale, then blue. This is accompanied by intense, almost unbearable pain
- Second stage: the fingertips turn red, swell and become painful again
- Tingling and numbness in the skin

CONSULT YOUR DOCTOR
- Medical advice is essential for this sometimes severe disorder, which can mask more serious conditions, such as scleroderma and rheumatoid arthritis.

Causes
Raynaud's disease or phenomenon is caused either by the effects of cold followed by sudden warming or by some form of strong emotion, such as anxiety. It can be a sign of atherosclerosis of the extremities, blood-clotting disorders or a hormonal imbalance (thyroid). It is sometimes caused by certain medications and treatments such as beta-blockers, adrenaline or chemotherapy.

It mainly affects people who are between 20 and 40 years old, smokers, and is five times more common in women than men. There also seems to be a higher incidence among people who handle vibratory tools such as pneumatic drills.

WHICH PLANTS?

WARNING Use only one of the following at any given time.

INTERNAL USAGE
To improve circulation
GINKGO Tablets, up to 2 g, standardised for ginkgo flavone glycosides, and ginkgolides and bilobalide. Take up to three times a day. (See Cautions, p. 102.)
GARLIC Tablets, capsules, follow manufacturer's instructions, to a maximum of 6 g dried garlic clove equivalent per day.

As advised by a medical herbalist
- Cayenne, ginger

Other measures
- Stop smoking.
- Avoid getting cold – wear double pairs of gloves or socks.
- Warm hands and feet gently.

Vein disorders

The term 'chronic venous insufficiency' (CVI) is used to describe a cluster of conditions caused by reduced function of the veins in the legs, leading to impaired blood flow and decreased ability to pump blood from the legs back up to the heart. Other conditions that affect the veins and are associated with impaired blood circulation include haemorrhoids, phlebitis and deep vein thrombosis (DVT).

Symptoms
- Heaviness in the legs
- Discomfort, pain and cramps in the calves and the legs
- 'Pins and needles' and restless leg syndrome
- Swelling in the thighs and/or calves
- Swollen, painful veins in the cases of varicose veins and haemorrhoids
- Changes to the texture and quality of skin on the leg

CONSULT YOUR DOCTOR
- Vein disorders can be serious, so it is important to consult your doctor to determine an appropriate treatment.

Causes
Inadequate flow of blood from the feet towards the heart is generally caused by damage to the veins of the legs and failure of the small valves in the veins that help to keep the blood moving upwards. Many factors can contribute to this problem, including genetic factors, obesity, hormonal treatment, prolonged standing and raised pressure inside the abdomen. Some people are particularly prone to vein disorders, including those with a family history of varicose veins, women who are pregnant or taking the contraceptive pill and those whose professions involve a great deal of standing or lifting heavy weights.

WHICH PLANTS?

WARNING Use only one of the following at any given time.

INTERNAL USAGE
To act as a vein tonic, strengthening the veins and exerting an anti-inflammatory action
HORSECHESTNUT Tablets, 1.5 g dried seed equivalent, standardised for aescin content. Take 2–3 tablets a day.

To improve blood circulation
GINKGO Tablets, up to 2 g, standardised for ginkgo flavone glycosides, and ginkgolides and bilobalide. Take up to three times a day. (See Cautions, p. 102.)
GRAPE SEED Tablets, capsules, up to 24 g dried seed equivalent per day, standardised for anthocyanidin content.

As advised by a medical herbalist
- Broom, ginger

EXTERNAL APPLICATION
Horsechestnut Apply horsechestnut-based cream or gel two or three times a day as directed on the label.
Cypress Add 3 drops of essential oil to 10 ml sweet almond oil and massage into the affected area.
Witch hazel Gently massage in witch hazel–based gel or ointment once a day as directed on the label.

Other measures
- As far as possible, wear support stockings, and avoid prolonged standing or sitting.
- Aid circulation and maintain a healthy weight by taking regular physical exercise and walking for at least 30 minutes a day.
- Try not to lift heavy weights.

CHILDREN'S HEALTH PROBLEMS

Bronchiolitis in babies

A viral disease that mainly affects babies, bronchiolitis causes inflammation of the smallest of the lungs' airways – the bronchioles – and can cause fever, cough and breathing difficulties. The disease is more prevalent in winter, sometimes in epidemic proportions.

Symptoms
- Begins like a cold, with blocked or runny nose, sneezing and a dry cough
- Cough worsens within two days, and wheezing develops, along with rapid or difficult breathing. The baby may grunt while breathing, signifying that the airways are blocked
- Fever
- Appetite may be reduced and the child may be irritable
- In severe cases, a bluish tinge to the skin due to lack of oxygen – call for emergency medical help immediately

CONSULT YOUR DOCTOR
- Consult your doctor urgently if you notice any problems at all with your baby's breathing.
- In severe cases, your baby may need to be admitted to hospital for oxygen and physiotherapy. If the baby's mouth has a bluish tinge, or if it is having severe difficulty breathing, seek medical assistance immediately.

Causes
Most cases of bronchiolitis are caused by the respiratory syncytial virus, commonly known as RSV, which is transmitted by means of airborne droplets, usually when an adult or child nearby coughs or sneezes.
  The infection affects babies because their bronchioles are still very tiny, and are therefore easily blocked by mucus or inflammation.

WHICH PLANTS?
WARNING Use only one of the following at any given time.

INTERNAL USAGE
Do not give preparations to infants without the advice of a qualified medical herbalist or a doctor.

For a cough and fever
Thyme 2 g dried herb infused in 1 cup of boiling water for 5 minutes before straining and cooling. For babies 6–12 months, give 20 ml of the infusion, three times a day.
Elder 2 g dried herb infused in 1 cup of boiling water for 10 minutes before straining and cooling. For babies 6–12 months, give 20 ml of the infusion, three times a day.
Sweet violet 2 g dried flowers infused in 1 cup of boiling water for 10 minutes before straining and cooling. For babies 6–12 months, give 20 ml of the infusion, three times a day.

EXTERNAL APPLICATION
Massage preparation
Lavender Add 3 drops of essential oil to 10 ml carrier oil and massage 1 teaspoon of this mixture into the chest, back and throat.

Other measures
- Massage may help to clear mucus from the baby's bronchioles.
- Ensure the baby drinks regularly to avoid dehydration.
- Keep the room humid by boiling an electric kettle with the lid off for a few minutes every hour, or use a steam vapouriser to which a few drops of tea tree or eucalyptus oil have been added.
- At night, elevate the head of the cot by 30–40 degrees to ease breathing.

CHILDREN'S HEALTH PROBLEMS

> **DID YOU KNOW?**
>
> **Infant bronchiolitis and asthma**
>
> Bronchiolitis generally clears up in around a week. It is a viral infection and does not respond to treatment with antibiotics. Sometimes, the infection can lead to asthma, and this may be indicated by the presence of a persistent cough.

Colic

Colic is the term used to describe the griping pain of trapped wind in babies. It is extremely common, and although it is distressing for both the child and the parents, is relatively harmless, and usually passes by six months of age.

Symptoms

- Loud and continuous crying that regularly starts soon after a feed and persists for up to 4 hours. The crying may make the baby's face appear red and flushed
- Knees may be drawn up towards the abdomen or, alternatively, may be held straight and rigid
- Abdomen may feel rigid, and may be bloated and distended
- Bowel movements or wind may signal the start or end of the crying episode
- Smiling (in young babies) or blueness around the mouth
- Hands may be clenched

CONSULT YOUR DOCTOR

Consult your doctor as soon as your baby develops colic – it is important to rule out more serious conditions, including intestinal obstruction, hernia and abdominal infections. Especially if:

- The symptoms of colic are accompanied by fever, diarrhoea, vomiting or constipation
- The crying sounds as though the baby is in pain (as opposed to just making a fuss)
- Your colicky child is not gaining weight and is not hungry

Causes

Colic may be a reaction to unsuitable food – the common culprits include undiluted fruit juice, food allergies (e.g. to dairy products) and foods that contain large quantities of sugar. The breastfeeding mother's diet may also contribute to colic in her baby.

Other factors include emotional stress, exposure to antibiotics at a young age (damaging the fragile microflora in the developing bowel), hormonal compounds in breast milk, overfeeding and swallowing excessive quantities of air (e.g. during crying, or because the teat of the bottle is the wrong size).

WHICH PLANTS?

WARNING Use only one of the following at any given time.

Do not give preparations to infants without the advice of a qualified medical herbalist or a doctor.

As advised by a doctor or medical herbalist
- Anise, dill, fennel

Other measures

- A lactation consultant can assist you in understanding the best way to feed your baby.
- Breastfeeding mothers should reduce or restrict their intake of caffeine, onions, garlic, broccoli, beans and dairy products.
- If your baby is bottle-fed, experiment with specially formulated low-allergen products, and ensure the hole of the teat is large enough to prevent the baby from swallowing an excess amount of air. To enlarge the hole, pass a needle through it.
- A specially formulated children's probiotic supplement may be of assistance – talk to your medical herbalist about it.

Common childhood illnesses

Today, most children are vaccinated against measles, mumps and rubella. All of these infections confer immunity on sufferers – it is very rare to catch them more than once.

Mumps causes a tender swelling of the parotid glands beneath the jaw. In adolescent and adult males, mumps may lead to testicular inflammation.

Measles is a viral illness that causes a rash and a fever. It is potentially dangerous because it can cause complications, including ear infections and encephalitis.

Rubella (German measles) is a mild infection that causes a rash and slight fever. If a mother contracts rubella in the first four months of pregnancy, her unborn child is at increased risk of developing a deformity.

Chickenpox causes a rash of itchy spots that turn into blisters. When the blisters dry, scabs form, disappearing after 12 days or so. Scratching the spots may lead to bacterial infection and permanent scarring.

CONSULT YOUR DOCTOR

Consult a doctor without delay if:

- Your child has a fit
- Your child has a stiff neck
- Dark red blotches appear on the skin
- Your child has a high fever for more than two days, or if the temperature rises above 38.5°C
- Your child cries constantly or has difficulty breathing
- Your child is confused, delirious or excessively sleepy

Causes

All the childhood illnesses listed are viruses, usually spread by airborne droplets. Children who go to school or kindergarten are more likely to be exposed than those who are usually at home. Vaccination confers immunity, and breastfeeding helps to protect babies from infection.

WHICH PLANTS?

WARNING Use only one of the following at any given time.

INTERNAL USAGE
Do not give preparations to infants without the advice of a qualified medical herbalist or a doctor.

To keep the fever down
ELDER 2 g dried herb infused in 1 cup of boiling water for 10 minutes before straining and cooling. For babies aged 6–12 months, give 20 ml of the infusion, three times a day; for children aged 1–6 years, give 50 ml, three times a day; and for children aged 7–12 years, give 75 ml, three times a day.

SWEET VIOLET 2–4 g dried flowers infused in 1 cup of boiling water for 10 minutes before straining and cooling. For babies aged 6–12 months, give 20 ml of the infusion, three times a day; for children aged 1–6 years, give 50 ml, three times a day; and for children aged 7–12 years, give 75 ml, three times a day.

To boost the immune system
ECHINACEA Echinacea syrups are available in formulations specifically made for children. Follow manufacturer's instructions according to the child's age.

EXTERNAL APPLICATION
To dry up chickenpox blisters
LAVENDER Essential oil, apply 1 drop of pure essential oil to the spots, twice a day, before scabs form. For babies and smaller children, dilute 3 drops of oil in 1 teaspoon of carrier oil.

To soothe an itchy rash
OATS Tie ½ cup of rolled porridge oats into a handkerchief or stocking to form a loose ball, and use it in the bathtub as a sponge.

CHICKWEED Apply a chickweed-based cream as directed on the label.

Other measures

- Ensure the child drinks plenty of liquids to prevent dehydration – a specially formulated electrolyte drink may be required. Talk to your doctor or pharmacist.
- Keep the child lightly covered.
- Keep the atmosphere in the sick child's room humid, and the temperature at 18–20°C.

Coughs, Colds & Throat infections

For the first few months of life, infants are largely protected from coughs and colds by their mother's antibodies. Thereafter, children build up their own defences against disease. One of the ways that this occurs is from exposure to a wide variety of bacteria, viruses and other pathogens, particularly at school. Consequently, it is quite common for young children to experience repeated coughs, colds and throat infections.

Symptoms

- The symptoms of a common cold include a runny nose, cough and a slight fever
- Tonsillitis causes a fever, sore throat and pain on swallowing
- Sinusitis causes a headache (especially on bending forward), a runny nose and a reduced sense of smell and therefore a poor appetite
- Fever may also occur

CONSULT YOUR DOCTOR

- If a child's cold does not clear up quickly, consult a doctor. It is important that a simple viral infection is not allowed to develop bacterial complications, which may infect the middle ear, the tonsils, chest or sinuses, and may require antibiotic treatment.

Causes

The common cold is widespread all year round, but especially in winter. Most coughs, colds and throat infections are spread by airborne droplets when an infected person coughs or sneezes. A healthy immune system will help your child's defence against infection.

WHICH PLANTS

WARNING Use only one of the following at any given time.

INTERNAL USAGE
Do not give preparations to infants without the advice of a qualified medical herbalist or a doctor.

To boost the immune system
ECHINACEA Echinacea syrups are available in formulations specifically made for children. Follow manufacturer's instructions according to the child's age.

For a dry cough
MARSHMALLOW 2–3 g dried root infused in 1 cup of boiling water for 10 minutes before straining and cooling. For babies aged 6–12 months, give 20 ml of the infusion, three times a day; for children aged 1–6 years, give 50 ml, three times a day; and for children aged 7–12 years, give 75 ml, three times a day.

For a cough with phlegm
MULLEIN 1.5–2 g dried herb infused in 1 cup of boiling water for 15 minutes before straining and cooling. For babies aged 6–12 months, give 20 ml of the infusion, three times a day; for children aged 1–6 years, give 50 ml, three times a day; and for children aged 7–12 years, give 75 ml, three times a day.

ELDER 2 g dried herb infused in 1 cup of boiling water for 10 minutes before straining and cooling. For babies aged 6–12 months, give 20 ml of the infusion, three times a day; for children aged 1–6 years, give 50 ml, three times a day; and for children aged 7–12 years, give 75 ml, three times a day.

THYME 2 g dried herb infused in 1 cup of boiling water for 5 minutes before straining and cooling. For babies aged 6–12 months, give 20 ml of the infusion, three times a day; for children aged 1–6 years, give 50 ml, three times a day; and for children aged 7–12 years, give 75 ml, three times a day.

Other measures
- Clear a baby's nose with saline nose drops, available from the chemist.
- Put your baby to sleep on his or her back, but raise the head of the cot by placing books under the legs – this will help make it easier to breathe.
- Keep the room humid by boiling an electric kettle with the lid off for a few minutes every hour, or use a steam vapouriser to which a few drops of tea tree or eucalyptus oil have been added.
- If you child is unwell, let him or her stay home from kindergarten or school for a few days – this will aid recovery, and reduce the transmission of the virus to other children.

Croup & Tracheitis

Croup is a viral infection of the airways that usually affects young children (three months to three years). Tracheitis is a similar condition, but with a bacterial cause and more severe consequences. In severe cases it may obstruct the airways.

Symptoms
- Deep cough that is reminiscent of the bark of a seal or dog
- Hoarse or raspy voice
- Noisy, rapid, difficult breathing
- Symptoms change from hour to hour, tending to be better in the morning and worsening as the day progresses (or following a sleep)
- Usually resolves after three to five days, although cough may persist
- The child may be in severe and rapidly worsening respiratory distress, as signified by difficulty breathing, marked contraction of the ribcage and abdominal muscles to support breathing and bluish tinge to the skin. Call for emergency medical help immediately
- Obstructed airway – difficulty in breathing that worsens with time
- High fever
- Child looks and feels very ill and worsens very quickly

CONSULT YOUR DOCTOR
- If your child is having difficulty breathing or has bluish skin, immediate medical help is needed. Take them to the hospital or call an ambulance.
- Bacterial tracheitis is diagnosed in approximately 2 per cent of cases.

Causes
Croup is a viral infection, often caused by the parainfluenza virus. The most common cause of tracheitis is bacterial infection with *Staphylococcus aureus* following an upper respiratory tract infection. A membrane of mucus may develop across the airway, making it more difficult to breathe. Children are more susceptible than adults to these diseases due to the narrow dimensions of their airways.

WHICH PLANTS?

WARNING Use only one of the following at any given time.

Croup and tracheitis require medical management. Herbal medicine may be able to boost the immune system and ease breathing, but should always be regarded as complementary to medical treatment.

As advised by a medical herbalist
- Echinacea, elder, marshmallow, thyme

Other measures
- Ensure your child drinks plenty of fluids.
- Take steps to reduce fever (see Fever).
- Some children find it easier to breathe in cool air – try taking them outside.

Ear infections

Medically known as otitis media, middle ear infection mainly affects young children. The infection causes inflammation of the cavity between the eardrum and the inner ear. It tends to follow a common cold, as poor mucus drainage from the upper respiratory tract may provide an environment that is hospitable to microbes and allows them to thrive.

Symptoms
- Intense pain in the ear
- High temperature
- Headache
- Hearing may be impaired
- Pus may discharge from the ear

CONSULT YOUR DOCTOR
- Research has shown that taking antibiotics does not significantly reduce the pain or duration of an ear infection, or its possible longer-term consequences.
- Many doctors advise giving paracetamol or ibuprofen to relieve pain and letting the infection run its course. However, if a discharge is present, antibiotics may need to be prescribed.

Causes

Most ear infections are caused by the bacteria or viruses that spread via the Eustachian tubes to infect the middle ear. Less common causes include hay fever and other allergies, passive smoking and poor diet. Research has shown that children who have been breastfed are less likely to get ear infections than those fed on formula.

WHICH PLANTS?

WARNING Use only one of the following at any given time.

INTERNAL USAGE
Do not give preparations to infants without the advice of a qualified medical herbalist or a doctor.

To boost the immune system
ECHINACEA Echinacea syrups are available in formulations specifically made for children. Follow manufacturer's instructions according to the child's age.
ROSEHIPS 2–2.5 g fragmented dried rosehips infused in 1 cup of boiling water for 10 minutes before straining and cooling. For babies aged 6–12 months, give 20 ml of the infusion, three times a day; for children aged 1–6 years, give 50 ml, three times a day; and for children aged 7–12 years, give 75 ml, three times a day.

As an anti-inflammatory
MULLEIN 1.5–2 g dried herb infused in 1 cup of boiling water for 15 minutes before straining and cooling. For babies aged 6–12 months, give 20 ml of the infusion, three times a day; for children aged 1–6 years, give 50 ml, three times a day; and for children aged 7–12 years, give 75 ml, three times a day.

Other measures
- Unblock the nose. Children need to be taught how to blow their nose effectively. Your doctor can advise you.

Eczema, childhood

The most common type of eczema in children is atopic eczema. It causes itchy, red, scaly patches and small, fluid-filled blisters that weep when scratched, releasing liquid that then dries into crusts. Atopic eczema is usually found in skin folds – at elbow creases, behind the ears and behind the knees. Most children grow out of eczema after about three to five years.

Symptoms
- Red, puffy areas of skin
- Raw, scabbed or flaking skin
- Dry skin
- Persistent scratching may cause the skin to thicken

CONSULT YOUR DOCTOR
- Consult a doctor as soon as symptoms appear to ensure that there is no viral or bacterial infection.

Causes

Eczema tends to run in families, especially where there is a history of other allergies – asthma or hay fever, for example. Other trigger factors include wearing wool next to the skin, and living in a household where people smoke. Breastfed children are less likely to suffer from eczema.

Sometimes, eczema is caused by food allergies such as to milk, eggs or fish. Airborne allergens include cat or dog hair, house dust mites and pollen.

WHICH PLANTS?

WARNING Use only one of the following at any given time.

INTERNAL USAGE
Do not give preparations to infants without the advice of a qualified medical herbalist or a doctor.

HEARTSEASE 1–4g g dried herb infused in 1 cup of boiling water for 10 minutes before straining and cooling. For babies aged 6–12 months, give 20 ml of the infusion, three times a day; for children aged 1–6 years, give 50 ml, three times a day; and for children aged 7–12 years, give 75 ml, three times a day.

EXTERNAL APPLICATION
CALENDULA Apply a calendula-based cream as directed on the label.
CHICKWEED Apply a chickweed-based cream as directed on the label.
HEARTSEASE Add 20–30 g fresh flowers to 500 ml boiling water. Infuse for 15 minutes, then strain and cool. Soak a cloth in this infusion and apply to the affected areas morning and evening.

Other measures
- Air and vacuum clean the child's room frequently.
- Keep the house warm and the atmosphere humid.
- Do not allow smoking in the house.
- Avoid woollen clothing worn next to the skin.
- Take your child outdoors whenever possible, since sunlight helps to heal the scabs.
- As a preventive measure, try to breastfeed a newborn baby for at least six months before introducing other foods.

See also **Eczema**

CHILDREN'S HEALTH PROBLEMS

A TO Z OF AILMENTS 223

CHILDREN'S HEALTH PROBLEMS

Sleeping problems

Almost a third of infants below the age of three have sleeping problems, either when first being put to bed or at some time during the night.

It is important to remember that some babies and children need more sleep than others. Anything from 10 to 15 hours in every 24 is 'normal'. You may find that you need to sacrifice a toddler's daytime nap in order to enjoy a good night's sleep yourself.

Symptoms
- The child resists going to bed and, once put down, remains awake
- After sleeping for 1–3 hours, the child awakes disorientated from a deep sleep and may cry, talk or even sleepwalk
- Nightmares

CONSULT YOUR DOCTOR
- Persistent sleep disturbance should be investigated by your doctor.
- Family history, environment, previous episodes and the child's behaviour can all provide clues as to the source of the problem.

Causes
Sleep problems are often related to something that is happening during the child's waking hours – something in the diet, stress or emotional anxiety, for example. Trouble getting to sleep is often simply the result of external stimulus – the room may be too light, too noisy or too hot.

WHICH PLANTS?

WARNING Use only one of the following at any given time.

INTERNAL USAGE
Do not give a child sedative herbs except in cases of minor sleep problems or to complement medical treatment. Do not give preparations to infants without the advice of a medical herbalist or a doctor.

LEMON BALM 2–3 g dried leaves infused in 1 cup of boiling water for 5 minutes before straining and cooling. For babies aged 6–12 months, give 20 ml of the infusion, at dinner and bedtime; for children aged 1–6 years, give 50 ml, at dinner and bedtime; and for children aged 7–12 years, give 75 ml, at dinner and bedtime.

CHAMOMILE 5–8 g dried herb infused in 1 cup of boiling water for 10 minutes before straining and cooling. For babies aged 6–12 months, give 20 ml of the infusion, at dinner and bedtime; for children aged 1–6 years, give 50 ml, at dinner and bedtime; and for children aged 7–12 years, give 75 ml, at dinner and bedtime.

Other measures
- Keep to a regular timetable for the child's meals.
- Establish a regular bedtime and a standard routine for settling down for the night. This will help a child to understand what is expected, and provide the security of knowing when things are going to happen. Similarly, wake your child up at a certain set time, which will also encourage the development of a routine.

Teething

The term 'teething' is used to describe the eruption of a baby's teeth. Teething can sometimes be very painful and is often accompanied by gum inflammation and a tummy upset.

Symptoms
- Red, swollen gums and a red cheek on the side the tooth is emerging
- Pain, causing the child to refuse food and drink
- Dribbling
- Fever
- Diarrhoea

CONSULT YOUR DOCTOR
- If a fever that you suspect is caused by teething lasts longer than two days, see a doctor. The child may have an unrelated bacterial or viral infection.

Causes
Before it erupts, the budlike tooth is encased in a small sac in the jawbone. When the tooth erupts, it pierces the gum, which causes inflammation and pain. Teething pain mainly affects children aged between six months and two years.

WHICH PLANTS?

WARNING Use only one of the following at any given time.

EXTERNAL APPLICATION
LAVENDER Add 3 drops of essential oil to 10 ml carrier oil. Apply a little externally to the cheek on the side where the tooth is aching.

MALLOW 3 g dried herb infused in 100 ml of boiling water for 10 minutes before straining. Dip your finger in the cooled infusion and apply to sore gums.

Other measures
- Give children something hard to chew on – a teething ring if they can hold one.
- Gently massage the gum with one of your fingers.

DENTAL & GUM PROBLEMS

Gum disease

People who have been unwell, those who have a poor diet and anyone who does not observe scrupulous oral hygiene may be susceptible to gum disorders such as gingivitis and periodontitis. The term 'gingivitis' is used to describe inflammation of the gums, medically referred to as the gingivae or gingival tissues. The word periodontitis is used to refer to inflammation of the periodontal tissues, which is found around the roots of the teeth.

Symptoms
- Healthy gum tissue tends to be pink, with a firm texture and well-contoured margins around the necks of the teeth. In gingivitis, the gums become red, swollen and spongy, with a tendency to bleed when brushing the teeth or when gently probing during a dental examination
- Over time, gums affected by gingivitis decrease in size, which may expose the delicate cementum on the surface of the root of the tooth, rendering it liable to damage during brushing. This, in turn, may expose the sensitive dentine beneath the cementum, causing the teeth to become sensitive, especially to cold
- Ongoing inflammation of the gingival tissues may lead to the formation of a pocket in the gums around the root of the tooth. This allows both plaque and bacteria to accumulate, and over time may lead to resorption of bone in the area, or to increasing mobility of the teeth

CONSULT YOUR DOCTOR OR DENTIST
- If symptoms persist for more than a week, see a doctor or dentist. Gum disease that does not clear up fairly rapidly may indicate a more serious underlying condition.

Causes
Gingivitis may be caused by poor dental hygiene, allowing plaque to build up around the necks of the teeth. The plaque bacteria produce a variety of toxins, and the body's response to these determines the extent of the subsequent inflammation, and whether it affects only the gums or spreads to the periodontal region.

Risk factors for the development of gum disorders include having crowded or crooked teeth that are difficult to keep clean, smoking, hormonal imbalances, some prescription drugs, and conditions such as diabetes, epilepsy, anaemia and leukaemia.

WHICH PLANTS?

WARNING Use only one of the following at any given time.

EXTERNAL APPLICATION
CALENDULA Infuse 5 g dried flower heads in 1 cup of boiling water for 5 minutes. Strain, cool and use as a mouthwash or gargle three times a day.
THYME 2 g dried herb infused in 1 cup of boiling water for 5 minutes before straining. Cool and use as a mouthwash two or three times a day.
ECHINACEA Liquid extract, 1 g dried root equivalent, three times a day in 15 ml water. Use as a mouthwash before swallowing. Repeat three times a day for up to a week.

Other measures
- Brush your teeth and gums after every meal.
- Use floss or interdental brushes between the teeth once a day.
- Use an antibacterial mouthwash containing tea tree or manuka.
- Avoid smoking, especially a pipe.
- Don't chew toothpicks.
- See your dentist regularly – most gingivitis will resolve quickly and easily if the plaque is removed from around the necks of the teeth.

See also Mouth ulcers

Halitosis

Bad breath, known medically as halitosis, is an embarrassing condition. You rarely know that you have it – and friends are usually too polite to tell you.

Symptoms
- Unpleasant odour from the mouth
- May be accompanied by bad taste in the mouth

CONSULT YOUR DOCTOR
- If you suffer from persistent bad breath, consult your doctor to determine the underlying cause.

Causes
Halitosis has many causes including smoking, eating strong-smelling foods (such as garlic and onions) and having an empty stomach. Other causes include gum infection, dental caries, decayed food caught between the teeth and infection of the stomach or digestive tract.

WHICH PLANTS?

WARNING Use only one of the following at any given time.

INTERNAL USAGE
In all cases and as a preventive
ANISE Liquid extract, 500 mg–1 g dried seed equivalent, three times a day. Use as a mouthwash before swallowing.
CORIANDER Infuse 10–30 g crushed seeds in 1 litre of boiling water for 10 minutes before straining. Drink 1 cup after each meal.
PEPPERMINT 1 teaspoon of dried leaves infused in 150 ml of boiling water for 10–15 minutes before straining. Cool and use as a mouthwash two or three times a day.

To prevent gum infection
ECHINACEA Liquid extract, 1 g dried root equivalent, three times a day in 15 ml water. Use as a mouthwash before swallowing. Repeat three times a day for up to a week.

DENTAL & GUM PROBLEMS

To cleanse the digestive tract
STAR ANISE 1 teaspoon dried fruit infused in 1 cup of boiling water for 10 minutes before straining. Take 2 cups a day before meals.
CLOVES Boil 1–2 cloves in 1 cup of water for 5 minutes before straining. Drink 1–2 cups a day.
CINNAMON Infuse 1 g cinnamon bark in 1 cup of boiling water for 10 minutes before straining. Drink 3 cups a day.

To settle poor digestion
TURMERIC Capsules, standardised for curcuminoid content; follow manufacturer's instructions up to 5 g a day.
ROSEMARY 2–4 g dried herb infused in 1 cup of boiling water for 10 minutes before straining. Drink 3 cups a day, but avoid drinking at bedtime.
LAVENDER 2–3 g dried flowers infused in 1 cup of boiling water for 5–10 minutes. Drink 3–4 cups a day between meals.

EXTERNAL APPLICATION
SAGE 20 g dried leaves infused in 1 litre of boiling water for 10 minutes before straining. Drink 1–2 cups a day.
BASIL Boil 2 tablespoons dried leaves in 250 ml of water for 10–15 minutes. Strain and cool. Use as a mouthwash and gargle two or three times a day.

Other measures
- Maintain good oral hygiene by brushing and flossing your teeth three times a day – try a toothpaste containing tea tree or eucalyptus oil.
- Use an antibacterial mouthwash containing tea tree or manuka.
- Visit the dentist regularly.
- Stop smoking, and limit your intake of coffee, garlic and other strong-smelling foods.

See also Acid reflux, Gastritis, Gum disorders, Indigestion

Mouth ulcers

Ulcers are painful, raw lesions on the gums or elsewhere in the mouth.

Symptoms
- A small white sore with red edges
- The ulcer may be preceded by a tingling sensation in the affected region, or it may just seem to appear out of nowhere
- The lesions tend to be acutely sensitive to acidic or salty foods
- They may resolve quickly and with no treatment, but sometimes persist for an extended period of time

CONSULT YOUR DOCTOR
- If symptoms persist for more than a week, see a doctor. Gum disease that does not clear up may indicate a more serious underlying condition.

Causes
A large number of triggers for mouth ulcers have been identified, and it is likely that the causes differ from person to person. Sufferers of recurrent or persistent mouth ulcers should consider the following factors, all of which have been linked to mouth ulcers:
- Dental hygiene: not brushing teeth and gums regularly.
- Food allergies: eating foods that can promote ulcers.
- Mechanical injury: repeated friction between the teeth, dentures or braces and the gums or tongue.
- Nutritional deficiencies: amongst other nutrients, dietary deficiencies of iron, zinc, folic acid, vitamin B_{12}, and the amino acid l-lysine.
- Stress, infection or fatigue, or underlying illnesses such as hormonal imbalance, Crohn's disease and HIV.
- Digestive function: gastric acid imbalance.

WHICH PLANTS?

WARNING Use only one of the following at any given time.

INTERNAL USAGE
To support immune function
ANDROGRAPHIS Tablets, 500 mg–1 g dried herb equivalent, standardised for andrographolides, three times a day.

As advised by a medical herbalist
- Gentian

EXTERNAL APPLICATION
SAGE 20 g dried leaves infused in 1 litre of boiling water for 10 minutes before straining. Cool and use as a mouthwash two or three times a day.
CALENDULA Infuse 5 g dried flower heads in 1 cup of boiling water for 5 minutes. Strain, cool and use as a mouthwash three times a day.
MYRRH Tincture (1:5), 1 teaspoon in water. Use as a gargle three times a day.

Other measures
- Brush your teeth and gums thoroughly after every meal.
- Use floss or interdental brushes between the teeth once a day.
- An antibacterial mouthwash containing tea tree or manuka is recommended. However, if it aggravates the pain, it is best used only at times when no ulcers are present.
- Cut out foods that can promote ulcers, such as certain fatty foods, chocolate, nuts, dried fruit and spices.
- Avoid acidic foods such as tomatoes, citrus and pineapples when the ulcers are present, as these may cause aggravation. Other foods to be wary of include chewing gum, coffee, salty and vinegary foods (e.g. pickles, salad dressing, olives) and crunchy foods such as potato chips.
- Stop smoking, especially if you smoke a pipe.

DIGESTION

- Try taking a regular multivitamin and mineral supplement for a month or two, and observe whether your mouth ulcers seem to improve.

Tooth decay

A small cavity in the protective enamel of the tooth can lead rapidly to tooth decay. If left untreated, the tooth beneath the enamel will begin to rot, eventually causing toothache.

If the infection spreads to neighbouring tissue, it can cause an abscess.

Symptoms
- Noticeable sensitivity of the affected tooth to cold and heat
- Pain on contact with sugary or acid foods, and in response to pressure
- Throbbing pain – coinciding with the pulse

CONSULT YOUR DENTIST
- Consult a dentist at the onset of toothache in order to minimise the risk of infection.

Causes
Tooth decay, known medically as dental caries, is often exacerbated by diet (too much sugar) or by eating predominantly soft food. Poor dental hygiene encourages invasion by the bacteria that cause caries. Other risk factors for tooth decay include too few minerals in the diet, poor general health, stress and menopause.

WHICH PLANTS

WARNING Use only one of the following at any given time.

EXTERNAL APPLICATION
To cleanse the naturally occurring bacteria in the mouth
CALENDULA Infuse 5 g dried flower heads in 1 cup of boiling water for 5 minutes. Strain, cool and use as a mouthwash or gargle three times a day.
THYME 2 g dried herb infused in 1 cup of boiling water for 5 minutes before straining. Cool and use as a mouthwash two or three times a day.
MYRRH Tincture (1:5), 1 teaspoon in water. Use as a gargle three times a day.

For toothache
CLOVES Chew a clove three or four times a day. Alternatively, rub 1 drop of neat essential oil onto the painful tooth two to three times a day for three days.
CAYENNE Mix a pinch of cayenne powder with 25 ml lemon juice, then add hot water and honey to taste. Wash around the mouth twice a day.
PEPPERMINT 1 teaspoon of dried leaves infused in 150 ml of boiling water for 10–15 minutes before straining. Cool and use as a mouthwash two or three times a day.

Other measures
- Maintain good oral hygiene by brushing and flossing your teeth three times a day – try a toothpaste containing tea tree or eucalyptus oil.
- Use an antibacterial mouthwash containing tea tree or manuka.
- Visit the dentist regularly.
- Eat a balanced diet, avoiding sugary snacks and soft drinks.
- Don't leave the remains of acidic food, such as apples, in the mouth after eating. Rinse the mouth with water or brush the teeth afterwards.
- Chew your food well.
- Be aware that although a small amount of fluoride helps to protect the teeth, an excess of fluoride may promote tooth decay. The amount present in fluoridated toothpaste appears to be both safe and effective; however, fluoride supplements (except in homoeopathic form) are not recommended.

See also Gum disease

Acid reflux

The regurgitation of acid from the stomach into the oesophagus is termed gastro-oesophageal, or 'acid', reflux. It occurs when the muscular valve that controls the entrance to the stomach is weak or inefficient. Persistent acid reflux may lead to oesophagitis (inflammation of the oesophagus).

Symptoms
- Painful burning sensation in the oesophagus, sometimes extending into the mouth
- Undigested food or gastric juices may be regurgitated into the mouth.
- Reflux may occur when lying down, especially after meals
- Cough, chronic inflammation of the pharynx

CONSULT YOUR DOCTOR
- Your doctor can usually diagnose gastro-oesophageal reflux by carrying out an examination, although sometimes an X-ray or even endoscopy (fibre-optic camera passed down the oesophagus) is required.

Causes
Gastro-oesophageal reflux is often associated with a hiatus hernia. However, other factors may be significant, such as anxiety, stress, gall bladder disorders, disordered production of the gastric juices, habitually eating excessively large meals and wearing tight clothing.

WHICH PLANTS?

WARNING Use only one of the following at any given time.

INTERNAL USAGE
MEADOWSWEET Liquid extract, 2–5 g dried herb equivalent, three times a day.
FENNEL Infuse ½ teaspoon of crushed seeds in 1 cup of boiling water for 10 minutes before straining. Drink 3 cups a day.

A TO Z OF AILMENTS   227

DIGESTION

Papaya Papain tablets, take according to manufacturer's instructions.
Basil Infuse 4–6 g of dried leaves in 250 ml of boiling water for 10 minutes. Strain. Drink 1 cup without sugar a day.
Chamomile Infuse 1 sachet of chamomile flowers in 1 cup of boiling water for 5–10 minutes. Drink 3 cups a day, before meals.
Turmeric Capsules, standardised for curcuminoid content. Follow manufacturer's instructions up to 5 g a day.

As advised by a medical herbalist
- Gentian

Other measures

- Eat smaller, more frequent meals, taking time to chew your food well.
- Drink slightly sparkling mineral water.
- Don't lie down or go to bed straight after a meal.
- Raise the head of the bed a few centimetres to allow gravity to assist the function of the stomach valve.
- Stop smoking (which loosens the valve and therefore increases reflux of acid back up into the oesophagus) and reduce your alcohol consumption.

See also Peptic ulcer

Constipation

One of the most important methods that the body uses to excrete its wastes is via the stool. Consequently, passing a bowel motion regularly and easily is vital for good health. Stools are produced from fibre, an indigestible component of grains, fruit, vegetables and other plant foods. As it passes through the digestive tract to the bowel, fibre absorbs cholesterol, fats and a variety of other waste substances, and transports them to the bowel, where they can be excreted.

The term 'constipation' is used when stools are passed infrequently, or are hard and difficult to pass. Although there are differing opinions as to exactly how often one should go to the toilet, one bowel motion a day is generally considered 'normal'.

Symptoms

- Stools that are dry, hard and infrequent
- Bloating and wind
- Colic and cramping pain may also occur

CONSULT YOUR DOCTOR
- Constipation usually passes in a few days, but if you have been unable to pass a motion for a week, then see a doctor. It is also important to consult a doctor if you experience alternating bouts of diarrhoea and constipation.

Causes

Constipation is usually the result of a lack of dietary fibre and low intake of fluids. Other factors include a lack of exercise, stress or a reluctance to empty the bowels – perhaps because piles or an anal fissure make it painful to do so. Certain drugs, such as those containing codeine, can also cause constipation. Women suffer from constipation at times of hormonal change, especially during pregnancy and menopause, and sometimes also as a symptom of premenstrual syndrome.

WHICH PLANTS?

WARNING Use only one of the following at any given time.

Stools can be made softer and bulkier – and therefore easier to pass – by taking plants containing mucilage, such as psyllium, slippery elm and flax seeds.

The laxative plants suggested below can irritate the intestine and are not recommended for repeated or long-term use. Seek the advice of a medical herbalist or a doctor before taking any of these herbal remedies for more than a few days at a time.

Internal usage
To provide mucilage
Flax (linseed) Capsules, take according to manufacturer's instructions.
Psyllium Take 1 sachet of psyllium powder in a large glass of water, with a main meal.
Slippery elm 1 teaspoon slippery elm powder mixed with ¼ cup of water and drunk three times a day before meals, along with an additional glass of water.

As a laxative
Yellow dock Liquid extract, 2–4 g dried root equivalent, three times a day.

As advised by a medical herbalist
- Cascara, senna

Other measures

- Drink plenty of fluids, at least 2 litres of water a day.
- Take regular exercise.
- Eat more dietary fibre in the form of whole grains (brown rice, wholemeal bread), vegetables, fruit and legumes.
- Try to train your bowel by going to the toilet at a regular time every day.
- Always go to the toilet as soon as you feel the need to empty your bowels – avoid delays wherever possible.

Crohn's disease

Crohn's disease is a chronic inflammatory condition of the intestines that usually affects the end of the small intestine (ileum) at its junction with the large intestine. It is associated with chronic (long-term) diarrhoea, ulceration of the intestinal mucous membranes and severe abdominal pain.

Crohn's disease can occur at any age, but it mostly afflicts adolescents and young adults, and also has a tendency to run in families.

Symptoms
- Painful abdominal spasms and cramps. Pain may be worse in the lower right-hand region of the abdomen
- Diarrhoea, sometimes with the passage of blood or mucus. Blood loss may lead to anaemia
- Weight loss due to malabsorption. Nutritional deficiencies may also occur for the same reason
- Ulcers that progressively tunnel through the affected area into the surrounding tissue are called fistulae, and may become infected

CONSULT YOUR DOCTOR OR MEDICAL HERBALIST
- At this time, Crohn's disease is considered to be incurable, although many patients experience long periods of remission. Most patients need ongoing medical supervision, and surgical removal of a portion of the intestine is sometimes required.
- Many of the orthodox medical treatments are associated with significant side effects, and medical herbalism may help to reduce these, as well as to manage the symptoms of the disease. Your medical herbalist will develop a treatment plan for you, aimed at reducing diarrhoea, inflammation and pain, stopping rectal bleeding, enhancing tissue repair and correcting nutritional deficiencies.

Causes
It is not known what causes Crohn's disease. It could be due to an abnormal allergic response to cereals or to milk-based products, or to a bacterium or virus in the intestine. Crohn's disease is not caused by emotional stress or anxiety, however, many sufferers do find that stressful episodes may trigger the symptoms.

WHICH PLANTS?
WARNING Use only one of the following at any given time.

INTERNAL USAGE
To relieve inflammation
SLIPPERY ELM 1 teaspoon slippery elm powder mixed with ¼ cup of water and drunk three times a day before meals, along with an additional glass of water.
MARSHMALLOW 2–3 g dried root infused in 1 cup of boiling water for 10 minutes before straining. Drink 2–3 cups a day.
CHAMOMILE Infuse 1 sachet of chamomile flowers in 1 cup of boiling water for 5–10 minutes. Drink 3 cups a day, before meals.

For diarrhoea
OAK BARK Liquid extract, 500 mg–2 g dried bark equivalent, three times a day.

As advised by a medical herbalist
- Peppermint oil (enteric-coated capsules), rehmannia

Other measures
- Eat a balanced diet, avoiding foods likely to upset digestion.
- Drink plenty of fluids in order to avoid dehydration as a result of diarrhoea.
- Take fish oil, which is rich in omega-3 fatty acids, for its anti-inflammatory properties.
- Talk to your doctor or medical herbalist about appropriate nutritional supplements for your case.

Detoxification

We are exposed to toxins through our air, food, water and drugs. Our bodies and the bacteria within them also produce toxic compounds.

The main organs of detoxification are the liver and bowel, and the kidneys and urinary tract, with the skin and lungs involved to a lesser extent. If these organs become unable to keep pace with the body's toxic load, your natural health professional may recommend a period of detoxification to improve the body's functions and vitality, and to treat physical symptoms that you may be experiencing.

Symptoms
- Sluggish bowel function; nausea; indigestion
- Fatigue
- Headaches
- Skin problems (acne, dermatitis, eczema, psoriasis)
- Inability to tolerate alcohol and/or fatty foods
- High cholesterol and blood lipid levels
- Other symptoms may also occur according to the type of toxin you have been exposed to and your body's individual ability to deal with it

CONSULT YOUR DOCTOR OR MEDICAL HERBALIST
- Before commencing a detoxification program – detoxing is best done under professional supervision.
- If you experience unpleasant effects during the detoxification process.

Causes
Causes of overload include excessive consumption of alcohol, fat, food additives and use of recreational drugs. Certain pharmaceutical drugs may also build up in the body, as may environmental and industrial pollutants, and heavy metals.

DIGESTION

Environmental pollutants may include air pollution, leaded petrol fumes, agricultural pesticides and herbicides, and compounds from cigarette smoke. Industrial pollutants may include such substances as dry cleaning fluid and gases given off by new carpets.

WHICH PLANTS?

WARNING Use only one of the following at any given time.

As advised by a medical herbalist
- Baical skullcap, bupleurum, cleavers, dandelion, globe artichoke, milk thistle, psyllium, turmeric, wild indigo, yellow dock

Other measures
- Although strict fasting is an effective means of detoxifying, it is also unnecessarily harsh and is not recommended. Most health-care professionals recommend a slower and gentler detoxifying program.
- Since you may experience transient headaches, changes to bowel habits and fatigue while detoxing, start the program at a time when you can take plenty of rest.
- Drink large quantities of filtered water whilst on your detox program.
- Avoid alcohol, caffeine, smoking, recreational drugs, sugar and fatty or processed foods.

Diarrhoea

The frequent passage of loose bowel motions, often accompanied by stomach cramps, is a symptom of an underlying illness or irritation. Most people experience diarrhoea at some time and it often clears up without the need for intervention. Chronic diarrhoea, however, can stem from the inefficient absorption of water from the stools by the colon. Severe or prolonged bouts of diarrhoea can lead to dehydration.

Symptoms
- Abdominal cramps, often preceding the passage of loose or liquid stools
- Bloating and flatulence

Causes
Acute diarrhoea can be caused by anxiety, food allergy, some medicines, bacterial food poisoning and some tropical infections. It can also be symptomatic of a general viral infection. Chronic diarrhoea is usually a symptom of an intestinal disorder.

CONSULT YOUR DOCTOR OR MEDICAL HERBALIST
- In small children and old people, dehydration caused by diarrhoea can be serious so a doctor should be consulted.
- Chronic (long-term) diarrhoea should also be investigated and herbal preparations can help to treat it.

WHICH PLANTS?

WARNING Use only one of the following at any given time.

INTERNAL USAGE
To soothe the bowels
CAROB Take 20–30 g carob flour a day, mixed with lukewarm water or milk.

To ease stomach cramps
LEMON BALM 2–3 g dried leaves infused in 1 cup of boiling water for 5 minutes before straining. Drink 2–3 cups a day.
THYME 2 g dried herb infused in 1 cup of boiling water for 5 minutes before straining. Drink 3 cups a day.

To ease intestinal gases
STAR ANISE 1 teaspoon dried fruit infused in 1 cup of boiling water for 10 minutes before straining. Take 2 cups a day, before meals.

To ease diarrhoea
OAK BARK Liquid extract, 500 mg–2 g dried bark equivalent, three times a day.

As advised by a medical herbalist
- Cat's claw, grapefruit seed

Other measures
- Maintain your fluid intake. Rehydration fluid (available from pharmacies) is recommended for those at risk of dehydration, especially children and the elderly.
- Avoid foods that may irritate the bowels, such as dairy products, wholegrain cereals, too much sugar and raw vegetables.
- Choose grilled lean meat, fish, ham, pasta, rice, dry biscuits and stewed fruit.

See also Crohn's disease, Ulcerative colitis

Gall bladder, inflammation of

Cholecystitis is the medical term for inflammation of the gall bladder. The gall bladder swells and becomes tender, and infection usually follows. The condition may be acute, where the attack is sudden and severe and requires immediate hospitalisation; or it can be chronic, with repeated, milder attacks. Women over the age of 50 are the most commonly affected. Acute cholecystitis is usually caused by gallstones.

Symptoms
- Painful abdominal contractions
- Tenderness and pain on the right side of the abdomen, just beneath the rib cage
- A temperature above 38°C, often accompanied by shivering
- Sudden fatigue and loss of appetite
- Nausea and vomiting

CONSULT YOUR DOCTOR
Suspected gall bladder problems require prompt medical attention as cholecystitis may become serious and lead to perforation of the gall bladder involving peritonitis. If acute cholecystitis is suspected, immediate hospital attention is required.

In chronic cases, medical herbalism may help to address the symptoms and improve gall bladder function.

DIGESTION

Causes
Cholecystitis is usually caused by a gallstone blocking the bile duct and trapping the bile in the gall bladder. Other causes may include bacterial infection, reduced blood supply to the gall bladder (usually in diabetic patients) and tumours.

As advised by a medical herbalist
- Andrographis, centaury, cinnamon, lavender, rosemary, turmeric

Other measures
- Follow a diet that reduces cholesterol levels (see Lipid disorders, p. 216) as most gallstones are cholesterol-based.
- During attacks of cholecystitis, take rest lying down rather than sitting.

See also Detoxification, Gallstones, Lipid disorders

Gallstones

Thickened bile in the gall bladder may solidify into gallstones (lithiasis), which are usually asymptomatic. Pain develops if the stone blocks the bile duct, preventing the normal passage of bile into the intestine, and leads to inflammation of the gall bladder.

Symptoms
- Intermittent pain under the ribs on the right side of the abdomen, usually commencing a few hours after eating, and sometimes accompanied by flatulence
- The pain may also be felt in the back or the right shoulder, causing symptoms similar to those of a heart attack
- Nausea, sometimes vomiting
- Inability to digest fatty foods
- Stools may be light-coloured and fatty if the stone is completely obstructing the bile duct. The skin and whites of the eyes then become yellow
- Symptoms suggesting inflammation of the gall bladder (see above)

Causes
The gall bladder acts as a storage vessel for bile, which dissolves fats in the small intestine into smaller particles to enable them to be digested. The contents of the bile include cholesterol, lecithin and bile salts.

In most cases, stones are formed when an excess or thickening of the bile occurs, and the contents of the bile (especially the cholesterol component) become solid instead of remaining in their normal liquid state. The characteristic pain occurs if the stone becomes lodged in a biliary duct leading into or out of the gall bladder.

Risk factors for the development of gallstones include being overweight, suffering with gastrointestinal conditions such as Crohn's disease, and being over 40 years old. Women are more likely than men to get gallstones. Being vegetarian appears to reduce the risk, as does consuming large amounts of calcium.

CONSULT YOUR DOCTOR OR MEDICAL HERBALIST
- Only a doctor can establish a diagnosis and prescribe the necessary treatment, which may be either medical or surgical. A medical herbalist can assist with supportive therapy.

WHICH PLANTS?

WARNING Use only one of the following at any given time.

Plants that stimulate the production of bile are called choleretic. Several are also cholagogic – they stimulate the gall bladder to contract and expel bile.

As advised by a medical herbalist
- Boldo, globe artichoke, lemon balm, peppermint, turmeric

Other measures
- Avoid foods high in fat, and instead eat a high-fibre diet.
- Reduce your intake of refined carbohydrates (such as white sugar and flour).
- After a suitable interval, follow your meals with some physical activity.
- Acupuncture may help.

See also Detoxification, Gall bladder, inflammation of, Lipid disorders,

Gastritis & Oesophagitis

In gastritis the lining of the stomach becomes inflamed. It can be either acute, occurring suddenly, or chronic, developing slowly over several years. Oesophagitis is the inflammation of the lining of the oesophagus (sometimes referred to as the gullet).

Symptoms
- Burning and discomfort in the chest with oesophageal spasms
- Flow-back of stomach contents into the oesophagus accompanied by acid regurgitation into the mouth (acid reflux)
- Bad breath during the episodes of discomfort
- Nausea and spasms of the empty stomach
- Mouth ulcers and inflammation of the tongue may occur
- Sputum may be speckled with blood if gastric bleeding is present
- Loss of appetite and weight loss
- Chronic cough may sometimes occur due to throat irritation

A TO Z OF AILMENTS

DIGESTION

CONSULT YOUR DOCTOR OR MEDICAL HERBALIST
Gastritis or oesophagitis may be due to a lack of vitamin B_{12} or iron. They can also be associated with disorders such as an ulcer, hiatus hernia or even cancer. A medical examination will reveal the cause of the inflammation.

Causes
Gastritis can be due to excessive or insufficient gastric acid in the stomach. It is particularly associated with stress, excessive alcohol consumption, smoking, a diet that is low in vitamins or a diet that is high in fatty or acidic food. Certain drugs such as aspirin and anti-inflammatories (like ibuprofen) can cause irritation leading to inflammation of the stomach lining. Gastritis is also more common in people who have irregular eating habits.

Oesophagitis is primarily related to acid reflux, but also commonly occurs when people do not wash down certain types of tablets properly (such as aspirin and anti-inflammatories), or go to bed immediately after taking such medication.

WHICH PLANTS?

WARNING Use only one of the following at any given time.

INTERNAL USAGE
SLIPPERY ELM 1 teaspoon slippery elm powder mixed with ¼ cup of water and drunk three times a day before meals along with an additional glass of water.
GINGER Tincture (1:5), take 20–30 drops in a glass of water three times a day.
CHAMOMILE Infuse 1 sachet of chamomile flowers in 1 cup of boiling water for 5–10 minutes. Drink 3 cups a day, before meals.
MEADOWSWEET Liquid extract, 2–5 g dried herb equivalent, three times a day.
LEMON BALM 2–3 g dried leaves infused in 1 cup of boiling water for 5 minutes before straining. Drink 2–3 cups a day.

PEPPERMINT 1 teaspoon dried leaves infused in 150 ml of boiling water for 10–15 minutes before straining. Drink 1 cup after every meal.
ROSEMARY 2–4 g dried herb infused in 1 cup of boiling water for 10 minutes before straining. Drink 3 cups a day, but avoid drinking at bedtime.

As advised by a medical herbalist
- Gentian, wormwood

Other measures
- Eat slowly, chewing well.
- Avoid tobacco, alcohol, aspirin and anti-inflammatories, which irritate the stomach.
- Avoid spicy, fatty or 'rich' foods, and try to eat small, frequent meals. Leave at least a couple of hours between eating and going to bed.
- Always take tablets or capsules with plenty of water.

See also Acid reflux, Indigestion

Gastroenteritis

With this condition, there is inflammation of the stomach and intestines. Gastroenteritis may occur quite suddenly, often causing violent vomiting and diarrhoea. It is usually accompanied by severe spasmodic abdominal pains. For most people, gastroenteritis is not a serious illness and it clears up within a few days.

Symptoms
- Loss of appetite, intense thirst from dehydration
- Vomiting, spasms, colic and abdominal cramps
- Shivering
- Diarrhoea, sometimes leading to anal irritation and acute rectal pains
- Flatulence
- Weakness

CONSULT YOUR DOCTOR OR MEDICAL HERBALIST
- If a young or elderly person with these symptoms also has a fever or traces of blood in the stools, consult a doctor immediately.
- The same applies for people who have an impaired immune system, or those who have recently returned from travelling abroad.

Causes
Gastroenteritis is commonly caused by viruses, bacteria and other micro-organisms, which are transferred via contaminated water or food. Viral gastroenteritis may be passed on from person to person in much the same way as the common cold or flu.

The ailment can also be caused by taking too much alcohol, eating highly spiced dishes or certain drugs (including antibiotics).

WHICH PLANTS?

WARNING Use only one of the following at any given time.

INTERNAL USAGE
To ease vomiting and reduce inflammation
GINGER Tincture (1:5), take 20–30 drops in a glass of water three times a day.
CHAMOMILE Infuse 1 sachet of chamomile flowers in 1 cup of boiling water for 5–10 minutes. Drink 3 cups a day, before meals.

For intestinal spasms
THYME 2 g dried herb infused in 1 cup of boiling water for 5 minutes before straining. Drink 3 cups a day.
LEMON BALM 2–3 g dried leaves infused in 1 cup of boiling water for 5 minutes before straining. Drink 2–3 cups a day.

To ease intestinal gas
ANISE Liquid extract, 500 mg–1 g dried seed equivalent, three times a day.
PEPPERMINT 1 teaspoon dried leaves infused in 150 ml of boiling water for 10–15 minutes before straining. Drink 1 cup after every meal.

To prevent infection
GARLIC Tablets, capsules, follow manufacturer's instructions, to a maximum of 6 g dried garlic clove equivalent per day.
GINGER Tincture (1:5), take 20–30 drops in a glass of water, three times a day.

Other measures
- Stay in bed and get plenty of rest.
- Drink plenty of fluids to make up for water lost through vomiting and diarrhoea. Add 4 teaspoons of sugar and ½ teaspoon of salt to each litre of water. Sip throughout the day. Rehydration fluid (available from pharmacies) is recommended for those at risk of dehydration, especially children and the elderly.
- Take a probiotic supplement containing *Lactobacillus acidophilus* and *Bifidobacterium lactis*, or similar probiotic organisms.
- Avoid dairy products. Plain white boiled rice is suitable when the appetite first returns.

See also Diarrhoea

Hepatitis & Cirrhosis

The term 'hepatitis' refers to the inflammation of the liver, which is commonly caused by a virus (hepatitis A, B, C, D or E), but can also occur after taking certain drugs or poisons. It damages liver cells and may lead to cirrhosis, in which the function of the liver is seriously and irreversibly impaired.

Symptoms
- Asthaenia (tiredness unconnected to any effort)
- Loss of appetite, nausea
- General poor health accompanied by weight loss
- Oedema (swelling) of the lower limbs
- Whites of the eyes and skin and tissue of the eyelids turn yellow (jaundice)
- Swelling (oedema) of the abdomen
- Cirrhosis and hepatitis tend to have similar symptoms. However, in cirrhosis, the symptoms may not be evident until the disease process has been occurring for several years

CONSULT YOUR DOCTOR OR MEDICAL HERBALIST
- Consult your doctor immediately if you have one or several of the above symptoms; rapid detection offers the best chance of a cure.
- A full examination should be made in order to eliminate similar conditions requiring different treatment (such as gallstones and cancer of the liver, gall bladder or pancreas).
- Diagnosis can be confirmed by means of a blood test.

Causes
Most cases of hepatitis are caused by viruses, which produce infections that vary in gravity and prognosis. Certain kinds of hepatitis can lead to cirrhosis of the liver (whereby liver cells are progressively destroyed).

Cirrhosis can also be caused by alcohol abuse as well as a range of drugs and chemicals.

WHICH PLANTS?

WARNING Use only one of the following at any given time.

These plants should not be taken without consulting the doctor in charge of the case.

INTERNAL USAGE
To protect and rejuvenate the liver
MILK THISTLE Tablets, up to 9 g dried herb equivalent, three times a day.
BAICAL SKULLCAP Liquid extract, 500 mg–1 g dried root equivalent, three times a day.
GLOBE ARTICHOKE Tablets, capsules, 500 mg–1 g dried herb equivalent, standardised for cynarin content, three times a day.

To support the immune system
ASTRAGALUS Liquid extract, 1–2.5 g dried herb equivalent three times a day.

As advised by a medical herbalist
- Bupleurum, rehmannia

Other measures
- Stop all alcohol consumption and recreational drug use.
- Make a point of eating dried fruit, grapes, figs, spinach, watercress, potatoes, carrots, artichokes, rice, wholemeal bread, yoghurt, chicory (in salad), sunflower oil, olive oil, brewer's yeast, sesame seeds.
- If you belong to a high risk group for hepatitis B or C (sex with different partners, intravenous drug use, health worker), regular testing for the presence of these viruses increases the chances of successful treatment.
- Vaccinations are available against hepatitis A and B.
- In the acute stages of the disease, adopt a protein-free diet.

See also Alcoholism, Drug withdrawal, Liver problems

Indigestion

The medical term for indigestion is dyspepsia, which covers heartburn and the variety of symptoms associated with difficulty digesting foods.

DIGESTION

Symptoms

- An uncomfortable feeling of heaviness in the stomach
- Pain experienced in the sternum region of the chest
- Nausea, belching and flatulence
- Vomiting sometimes occurs, and tongue may be white and furry
- In cases of digestive poisoning, fever and/or diarrhoea may occur

CONSULT YOUR DOCTOR

- If the dyspepsia is frequent, chronic or involves weight loss. If jaundice (yellowing of the skin and whites of the eyes) is present, or repeated vomiting occurs, it is imperative to find out the underlying cause.
- The symptoms of indigestion can be similar to those of a heart attack – call for an ambulance immediately if your symptoms are accompanied by a pain that radiates down the arm or up the neck (towards the jaw and teeth), or by dizziness, weakness, sweating or shortness of breath.

Causes

Dyspepsia is caused by digestive problems of the stomach or the intestines. It is frequently the result of overindulgence in excessively fatty or spicy foods. It may also be related to a problem in the gall bladder or the pancreas, or to the under- or overproduction of stomach acids.

WHICH PLANTS?

WARNING Use only one of the following at any given time.

INTERNAL USAGE

MEADOWSWEET Liquid extract, 2–5 g dried herb equivalent, three times a day.
CARAWAY Infuse 1–5 g ground seeds in 1 cup of boiling water for around 10–15 minutes. Divide this amount into 3 doses and drink before meals.
CHAMOMILE Infuse 1 sachet of chamomile flowers in 1 cup of boiling water for 5–10 minutes. Drink 3 cups a day before meals.

GINGER Tincture (1:5), take 20–30 drops in a glass of water three times a day.
PEPPERMINT 1 teaspoon dried leaves infused in 150 ml of boiling water for 10–15 minutes before straining. Drink 1 cup after every meal.
STAR ANISE 1 teaspoon dried fruit infused in 1 cup of boiling water for 10 minutes before straining. Take 2 cups a day before meals.
TURMERIC Capsules, standardised for curcuminoid content; follow manufacturer's instructions up to 5 g a day.
PAPAYA Papain tablets, take according to manufacturer's instructions.

As advised by a medical herbalist
- Gentian

Other measures

- Avoid carbonated drinks, such as soda water, soft drinks and beer. Avoid these completely in cases of flatulence.
- Avoid any foods that you have trouble digesting.
- Never overload the stomach. Eat smaller meals more frequently.
- Take 1 teaspoon of bicarbonate of soda in water in order to neutralise stomach acids.

See also Acid reflux, Gastritis & Oesophagitis

DID YOU KNOW?

Digestive problems

Mint and caraway essential oils can help to relieve chronic dyspepsia. Double-blind studies were carried out on patients suffering from various digestive disorders (but not gastroduodenal ulcers) using a commercial preparation containing 90 mg of mint and 50 mg of caraway essential oils.

After four weeks the pain disappeared in 63 per cent of patients, while 94 per cent of patients experienced an improvement in symptoms. Both essential oils are antispasmodic.

Irritable bowel syndrome

Irritable bowel syndrome is the name given to a cluster of symptoms that cause abdominal pain and uncoordinated function of the digestive system, in particular the intestines. Women are more likely to be affected than men.

Symptoms

- Abdominal pain that is often colicky – it comes in waves, and is associated with at least two of the other symptoms below
- Pain may be relieved by passing wind or a bowel movement
- At the onset of pain, stools may be harder or looser than normal, and may be passed more or less frequently than normal (diarrhoea or constipation may occur)
- Bloating of the abdomen
- Mucus may be passed from the rectum
- Patient may feel that the bowel has not been completely emptied
- In addition to these symptoms, nausea and lack of appetite may occur

CONSULT YOUR DOCTOR

The symptoms of irritable bowel syndrome are similar to those of many other gastrointestinal conditions, so it is important to see your doctor, who can arrange for the necessary investigations to rule out more serious disease.

Causes

In spite of considerable research, the cause of irritable bowel syndrome has still not been established. However, several triggers and aggravating factors have been identified. These include prior infection of the bowel, food sensitivity and allergy, stressful episodes and anxiety, overuse of laxatives, low intake of dietary fibre, smoking and salicylates (e.g. aspirin).

DIGESTION

WHICH PLANTS?

WARNING Use only one of the following at any given time.

INTERNAL USAGE
To relieve cramping pain
FENNEL Infuse ½ teaspoon of crushed seeds in 1 cup of boiling water for 10 minutes before straining. Cool and drink 3 cups a day (infants, 2–3 teaspoons three times a day).
CARAWAY Infuse 1–5 g ground seeds in 1 cup of boiling water for about 10–15 minutes. Divide this amount into 3 doses, cool and drink before meals.
STAR ANISE 1 teaspoon dried fruit infused in 1 cup of boiling water for 10 minutes before straining. Take 2 cups a day, before meals.

To provide mucilage
FLAX (LINSEED) Capsules, take according to manufacturer's instructions.
PSYLLIUM Take 1 sachet of psyllium powder in a large glass of water, with a main meal.
SLIPPERY ELM 1 teaspoon slippery elm powder mixed with ¼ cup of water and drunk three times a day before meals, along with an additional glass of water.

As a laxative
YELLOW DOCK Liquid extract, 2–4 g dried root equivalent, three times a day.

To ease diarrhoea
OAK BARK Liquid extract, 500 mg–2 g dried bark equivalent, three times a day.

To support the nervous system
PASSIONFLOWER Liquid extract, 500 mg–1 g dried herb equivalent, twice during the day and at bedtime.

As advised by a medical herbalist
- Cascara, peppermint oil (enteric-coated capsules), senna

Other measures
- Keep a food diary over a few weeks and try to identify any foods that trigger your symptoms.
- Eat a balanced diet, with an emphasis on soluble fibre such as oats and lentils. Avoid hot spicy foods, dairy products and processed foods, all of which are aggravating factors for many sufferers.
- Take plenty of exercise and try to have a relaxed lifestyle.
- Stop or reduce smoking and alcohol consumption.

See also Wind, Bloating & Belching

Liver problems

The liver has three major roles in the body: it filters the blood, removing toxins, bacteria and other particles from the circulation; it synthesises and secretes the bile; and it is involved with the metabolism of food, the storage of vitamins and minerals, and the detoxification of hormones and toxins.

Conditions that may affect the liver include 'sluggish liver', infection, alcohol damage and reactions to pharmaceutical drugs. Acute liver failure affects previously healthy people, and requires immediate medical help. Cirrhosis is the term used to describe chronic liver failure, in which there is irreversible damage to the liver, with a progressive reduction of function.

Symptoms
- Sluggish liver is the term used when the liver is underfunctioning, although no damage may have occurred. Symptoms include constipation, acne and other skin conditions, headache, fatigue and inability to tolerate fats and alcohol
- Symptoms of hepatitis include extreme fatigue, lack of appetite, weight loss, oedema of the lower limbs and abdomen, and jaundice. Cirrhosis tends to have the same or similar symptoms, which may not appear for several years after the disease process commences, becoming more evident as the liver becomes progressively disabled

CONSULT YOUR DOCTOR
- Consult your doctor immediately if you have one or several of the symptoms of hepatitis or cirrhosis. Rapid detection offers the best chance of a cure.
- A full examination should be made in order to eliminate similar conditions requiring different treatment (such as gallstones and cancer of the liver, gall bladder or pancreas).
- Diagnosis can be confirmed by means of a blood test.

Causes

Sluggish liver function is predominantly associated with poor eating habits (especially excess dietary fat), and may also be due to exposure to environmental and industrial toxins. It is believed that sluggish bile flow plays a causative role in the development of the symptoms of sluggish liver.

Hepatitis is most commonly caused by viral infection, but may also be due to direct toxic effects of certain pharmaceutical drugs – one of the most common causes of hepatitis from drugs is excess paracetamol, especially when combined with alcohol.

Amongst the causes of acute liver failure are viral hepatitis, adverse reactions to certain medicines and poisoning. The most common cause of chronic liver failure (cirrhosis) is alcohol abuse, but it may also be due to diseases that cause ongoing liver injury and inflammation, such as chronic viral hepatitis, cystic fibrosis and haemochromatosis (in which excess iron is accumulated).

A TO Z OF AILMENTS 235

DIGESTION

WHICH PLANTS?

WARNING Use only one of the following at any given time.

These plants may offer valuable support to a sluggish liver; however, liver disease requires professional treatment. Do not use these plants as supportive therapy in liver disease without consulting the doctor in charge of the case.

Internal usage
To protect and rejuvenate the sluggish liver
Milk thistle Tablets, up to 9 g dried herb equivalent, three times a day.
Baical skullcap Liquid extract, 500 mg–1 g dried root equivalent, three times a day.
Globe artichoke Tablets, capsules, 500 mg–1 g dried herb equivalent, standardised for cynarin content, three times a day.

To aid bowel function
Psyllium Take 1 sachet of psyllium powder in a large glass of water, with a main meal.

As advised by a medical herbalist
- Astragalus, bupleurum, rehmannia, St John's wort

Other measures
- Support your liver by avoiding alcohol, caffeine, smoking and recreational drugs.
- Follow a diet that is low in fats, sugars and processed foods, but which contains large quantities of fresh fruit and vegetables, fibre and filtered water.
- Get plenty of rest.

See also Gall bladder, inflammation of, Gallstones, Hepatitis

Nausea

The term 'nausea' actually derives from the Greek word for 'ship', and was originally used to describe seasickness, but has now come to describe the sensation that one is going to vomit.

Symptoms
- Pallor
- Headache
- Sudden fatigue
- Cold sweats, dizziness
- Nausea and possibly vomiting

CONSULT YOUR DOCTOR OR MEDICAL HERBALIST
Although most instances of nausea and vomiting are transient, it is important to remember that these symptoms may also be indicative of serious underlying disease. A doctor should be consulted under the following circumstances:
- If a head injury precedes the symptoms
- If lethargy, confusion, headache, stiff neck or severe abdominal pain accompanies the nausea or vomiting
- If there is a danger of dehydration (especially if the patient is a child). Symptoms of dehydration to look out for include dry lips and mouth, sunken eyes, decreased urination and rapid pulse
- If the vomiting persists for more than several hours in a child, or a day in an adult
- If vomiting and diarrhoea are both present
- If blood is present in the vomit (this may look like coffee grounds)
- If rapid breathing or pulse is present

Causes
Nausea has a wide variety of causative factors, including hormonal change (as in pregnancy), food poisoning and motion sickness. It may also occur as a side effect of certain drugs (such as chemotherapy) and as a symptom of underlying disease, such as viral infections and gall bladder problems.

For susceptible people, motion sickness may occur during road, sea or air travel. It is caused by the effects of movement on the delicate organs of balance in the inner ear, and is made worse by unpleasant fumes, anxiety or travelling on a full stomach.

Morning sickness is caused by the hormonal changes that occur during pregnancy.

WHICH PLANTS?

WARNING Use only one of the following at any given time.

The following should ideally be started 12–24 hours before travel to ensure good blood levels at the onset of travel and during the journey, if it is long.

Internal usage
For general nausea
Ginger Tincture (1:5), take 20–30 drops in a glass of water three times a day, or in tablet form, following manufacturer's instructions.
Fennel Infuse ½ teaspoon of crushed seeds in 1 cup of boiling water for 10 minutes before straining. Drink 3 cups a day.
Peppermint 1 teaspoon dried leaves infused in 150 ml of boiling water for 10–15 minutes before straining. Drink 1 cup after every meal.
Slippery elm 1 teaspoon slippery elm powder mixed with ¼ cup of water and drunk three times a day before meals, along with an additional glass of water.

DIGESTION

To relieve morning sickness
GINGER Tincture (1:5), take 20–30 drops in a glass of water three times a day, or in tablet form, following manufacturer's instructions.

Other measures
- When travelling, avoid leaning forward and closing your eyes, and try to keep your eyes focused on the horizon. Try to move to the centre of the ship, or to the front – rather than the back – of the car, as this lessens movement. Some people find relief by stimulating acupuncture points, and special wrist bands are available for this purpose.
- For morning sickness, try eating a piece of dry toast (or some other bland food) as soon as you wake up – even before you get out of bed.

Peptic ulcer

A raw area, about 10–25 mm across, in the lining of the oesophagus, stomach or duodenum, is known as a peptic ulcer. The stomach lining is specially designed to be tolerant to hydrochloric acid and other compounds present in the digestive juices. But if the lining is damaged, exposing the more delicate underlayer to the acid, a painful ulcer may develop.

Peptic ulcers are less common now that a wider range of antacid medications are available over the counter.

Symptoms
- Epigastric pain below the sternum, in the pit of the stomach, between 30 minutes and an hour after meals
- Heartburn (dull, burning pain in the centre of the chest)
- Nausea and vomiting
- Blackened stools may indicate the presence of bleeding in the stomach (the blood appears black because it has been digested – more visible blood in the stools indicates that the bleeding is occurring further down the digestive tract)

CONSULT YOUR DOCTOR OR MEDICAL HERBALIST
- A consultation with your GP is recommended to correctly diagnose and treat the condition.

Causes
The development of a peptic ulcer has been associated with many factors, including overwork, anxiety, smoking, eating spicy foods and infection by the bacterium *Helicobacter pylori*. Certain types of medication, including aspirin and other non-steroidal anti-inflammatories (NSAIDS) and cortisone, have also been implicated.

WHICH PLANTS?

WARNING Use only one of the following at any given time.

INTERNAL USAGE
MEADOWSWEET Liquid extract, 2–5 g dried herb equivalent, three times a day.
SLIPPERY ELM 1 teaspoon slippery elm powder mixed with ¼ cup of water and drunk three times a day before meals, along with an additional glass of water.
CHAMOMILE Infuse 1 sachet of chamomile flowers in 1 cup of boiling water for 5–10 minutes. Drink 3 cups a day, before meals.

Other measures
- Fatty or acidic food may worsen the symptoms.
- Take the time to chew your food well, especially if the food is raw.
- Eat little meals more often – food is the best way to mop up excess acid.
- If you like spicy food, always use powdered rather than fresh spices in cooking, as they are less of an irritant for the stomach.
- Try to avoid stressful situations.

See also Acid reflux, Gastritis & Oesophagitis, Indigestion

DID YOU KNOW?

Peptic ulcers
The discovery that peptic ulcers are associated with the presence of *Helicobacter pylori* marked the beginning of a new phase in treatment.

Research showed that plant-based substances could inhibit the bacterium. This led to the development of non-antibiotic treatments for peptic ulcers. The range of plants that inhibit *H. pylori* includes garlic, cinnamon, chamomile, calendula, golden seal and a blend of mint and caraway.

Ulcerative colitis

Ulcerative colitis is a chronic disease associated with chronic inflammation and ulceration of the rectum and colon. It is very similar to Crohn's disease, and is characterised by bloody diarrhoea, which may also contain pus and mucus. Its first manifestation is usually the most severe. Thereafter, its development is characterised by remissions and relapses over a period of years. Ulcerative colitis usually affects young adults, but it can also occur in elderly people.

Symptoms
- Diarrhoea containing blood, pus and mucus
- Fever, extreme fatigue
- Abdominal pain, general malaise
- Loss of appetite, weight loss

CONSULT YOUR DOCTOR
Any appearance of blood or mucus in the stool warrants medical investigation. If you experience symptoms such as these, it is crucial to seek medical advice. Once the condition has been diagnosed, regular medical supervision is required to avoid complications. However, medical herbalism may help to relieve the symptoms of the disease.

DIGESTION

Causes

The cause of ulcerative colitis is a subject of debate. It may be an inherited auto-immune disorder, whereby the body produces antibodies that attack its own cells in the gut. It is frequently associated with other diseases whose genetic origins have been proven or suspected (rheumatoid arthritis).

It often affects people who have a diet that is low in fibre and too rich in refined sugars, while non-smokers and ex-smokers are more likely to be affected than smokers. Emotional stress, an associated infection, gastroenteritis or a course of antibiotics can cause a flare-up of the disease.

WHICH PLANTS?

WARNING Use only one of the following at any given time.

INTERNAL USAGE

To relieve inflammation and soothe the gut
SLIPPERY ELM 1 teaspoon slippery elm powder mixed with ¼ cup of water and drunk three times a day before meals, along with an additional glass of water.
MARSHMALLOW 2–3 g dried root infused in 1 cup of boiling water for 10 minutes before straining. Drink 2–3 cups a day.
CHAMOMILE Infuse 1 sachet of chamomile flowers in 1 cup of boiling water for 5–10 minutes. Drink 3 cups a day before meals.

To ease spasms
CRAMP BARK Liquid extract, 500 mg–1 g dried bark equivalent, three times a day.

For diarrhoea
OAK BARK Liquid extract, 500 mg–2 g dried bark equivalent, three times a day.

To prevent anxiety
LIME FLOWERS Infuse 2–4 g of dried flowers in 1 cup of boiling water for 5 minutes before straining. Drink 1 cup twice a day and another in the evening.
PASSIONFLOWER Liquid extract, 500 mg–1 g dried herb equivalent, twice during the day and at bedtime.
OATS Liquid extract, 1–4 g dried herb equivalent, two or three times a day.

As advised by a medical herbalist
- Peppermint oil (enteric-coated capsules), rehmannia

Other measures

- Prevent stress by practising yoga or relaxation techniques.
- Avoid milk, dairy products, yeast, raw fruit and vegetables.
- Ongoing diarrhoea increases your risk of nutritional deficiencies – eat a diet high in protein, iron and potassium, and take a multivitamin and mineral supplement to help replace what has been lost through diarrhoea. A probiotic supplement containing the good bacteria *Lactobacillus acidophilus* and *Bifidobacterium lactis* is also recommended to help maintain bowel function.

See also Crohn's disease, Diarrhoea, Gastroenteritis

Wind, Bloating & Belching

The presence of gas in the stomach or intestines is experienced as wind, bloating and belching.

Symptoms

- Bloating: a painful, distended stomach and difficulty in expelling the gas
- Belching (or 'burping'), which is the expulsion of gas from the stomach, via the mouth
- Flatulence (or 'wind'), which is the expulsion of gas from the bowel – it may be accompanied by colicky pain

CONSULT YOUR DOCTOR OR MEDICAL HERBALIST
- Whilst some level of belching and flatulence is considered normal, and related to your diet, these symptoms may also be indicative of underlying disease – a full check-up is advised.

Causes

Wind and bloating occur when you eat too quickly and swallow air at the same time as the food, or if you have a fizzy drink with a meal. They may also be due to poor chewing habits. People who are anxious and swallow their food awkwardly are particularly susceptible.

Some foods produce more gastro-intestinal gas than others – common culprits include garlic and other sulphur-containing vegetables (e.g. onions); peas, legumes and pulses; cabbage and other cruciferous vegetables (e.g. broccoli); sugary foods; and quantities of raw vegetables or fruit.

Flatulence can also be the result of excessive bacterial activity in the colon. Equally, intestinal infections, bacterial proliferation and the start of gastro-enteritis can often be the cause. Flatulence can also follow constipation and intestinal blockage or paralysis. It is common among people who are anxious or stressed.

WHICH PLANTS?

WARNING Use only one of the following at any given time.

INTERNAL USAGE

FENNEL Infuse ½ teaspoon of crushed seeds in 1 cup of boiling water for 10 minutes before straining. Cool and drink 3 cups a day (infants, 2–3 teaspoons up to three times a day).
CARAWAY Infuse 1–5 g ground seeds in 1 cup of boiling water for about 10–15 minutes. Divide this amount into 3 doses, cool and drink before meals.
CORIANDER Infuse 10–30 g crushed seeds in 1 litre of boiling water for 10 minutes before straining. Drink 1 cup after each meal.
CUMIN Infuse 1 teaspoon of seeds in 250 ml of boiling water for 2–3 minutes. Drink ½ cup before main meals.
LEMON VERBENA Infuse 1 sachet of dried leaves in 1 cup of boiling water for 5 minutes. Drink 2 cups a day after main meals.
PEPPERMINT 1 teaspoon dried leaves infused in 150 ml of boiling water for 10–15 minutes before straining. Drink 1 cup after every meal.
ROSEMARY 2–4 g dried herb infused in 1 cup of boiling water for 10 minutes before straining. Drink 3 cups a day, but avoid drinking at bedtime.
SWEET MARJORAM 1–2 teaspoons dried herb infused in 1 cup of boiling water for 5–10 minutes before straining. Drink 3 cups a day.
ANDROGRAPHIS Liquid extract, 500 mg–1.5 g dried herb equivalent, three times a day.
PAPAYA Papain tablets, take according to manufacturer's instructions.

Other measures

- Eat small quantities of food at a time, chewing well before swallowing.
- Avoid soft drinks and chewing gum.
- Soaking beans, lentils and other legumes overnight in water before they are cooked reduces their gas-producing tendencies.
- Reduce consumption of sugary and starchy food.
- Eliminate excess air by taking charcoal tablets.
- Fibre is very important for your health, so it is vital that you do not avoid it just because it produces gas. Experiment with different types of fibre; some may suit your system more than others. Try starting with a small amount of fibre every day and building the quantity up as you become better able to tolerate it.
- Take some regular physical exercise, such as walking.

See also Irritable bowel syndrome

EAR & EYE PROBLEMS

Ear disorders

Infection of the middle ear (otitis media) is the most common type of ear disorder, particularly in children (see Ear infections, p. 222). In adults, another common disorder is otitis externa – which causes inflammation of the outer ear, and is also often the result of an infection.

Outer and middle ear disorders can also be the result of injury, a boil in the ear canal or a blockage caused by ear wax. Earache may also be an accompanying symptom of the common cold, sinusitis or tooth decay and other dental problems.

Symptoms

- Mild to severe earache
- Inflammation of the ear
- Discharge of pus from the ear
- Slight hearing loss

CONSULT YOUR DOCTOR

- If the pain is severe, see your doctor immediately to determine the cause. Antibiotics may be prescribed or an antifungal drug if a fungal infection is the cause.

Causes

Otitis externa can be caused by a bacterial, viral or fungal infection. It is quite common among swimmers, as moisture in the ear can encourage infection.

Earache can be caused by a blockage of the ear, and is sometimes worsened by attempts to clear the ear using a cotton bud, as this may push the obstruction deeper into the ear canal. Rarely, painful blisters in the ear may be caused by a herpes infection.

EAR & EYE PROBLEMS

WHICH PLANTS?

WARNING Use only one of the following at any given time.

INTERNAL USAGE
To fight infection and reduce inflammation
MULLEIN 1.5–2 g dried herb infused in 1 cup of boiling water for 15 minutes before straining. Drink 3 cups a day.
ECHINACEA Liquid extract, 1 g dried root equivalent, three times a day.
GOLDEN SEAL Tablets, capsules, 250–500 mg dried rhizome equivalent, three times a day. Do not take if you have high blood pressure.

As advised by a medical herbalist
- Tea tree oil

See also Tinnitus

Eye disorders

Problems affecting parts of the eye such as the retina or macula can produce a variety of sight defects.

Symptoms
- Reduced vision
- Inability to see in poor light (night blindness)
- Black specks in the field of vision (scotoma)
- Runny or painful eyes after prolonged visual effort

CONSULT YOUR DOCTOR
- Visual disorders should always be taken seriously. Always see a GP or optician before consulting a medical herbalist.
- Early detection of macular degeneration is the best way to prevent or minimise vision loss. Adults over 50 years and individuals with a family history of macular degeneration are advised to have eye checks at least every two years.

Causes

Eye disorders can be due to problems affecting the veins and arteries within the eye, or deterioration of the ophthalmic nerve. They may also be linked to high blood pressure or diabetes. They are also often part of the ageing process that affects the retina and ocular tissues.

Macular degeneration is a major cause of irreversible sight loss and is associated with damage to the macula, the central region of the retina. Risk factors for its development include: being over 75, having a family history of the disease, smoking and being female. Free radical damage to the blood vessels of the retina may also be involved.

WHICH PLANTS?

WARNING Use only one of the following at any given time.

INTERNAL USAGE
To treat eye problems
BILBERRY Tablets, up to 20 g fresh fruit equivalent per day.

As an anti-oxidant
GRAPE SEED Tablets, capsules, up to 24 g dried seed equivalent per day, standardised for anthocyanidin content.

EXTERNAL APPLICATION
To prevent eye fatigue, irritation and soreness
EYEBRIGHT Infuse 1 heaped teaspoon of dried flowers in 1 cup of boiling water for 15 minutes. Soak two clean cotton pads in the infusion and place one over each closed eye for 10 minutes.
CHAMOMILE Make an infusion with 2 sachets of chamomile – one for each eye – and allow to cool. Squeeze out the excess liquid, then place a sachet over each closed eye and leave it in place for 10 minutes. Repeat two or three times a day.

Other measures
- Sudden loss of eyesight or rapid changes in vision require immediate medical investigation.
- Have your eyesight checked by an optician.
- Protect your eyes from sun and smoke.
- Give up smoking.
- Eat fresh fruit and vegetables (berries, tomatoes, carrots) for their circulatory and anti-oxidant properties.
- Regular consumption of fresh, raw nuts (e.g. almonds, brazil nuts, hazelnuts – not peanuts) has been associated with delayed progression of macular degeneration. Similarly, regularly eating fish decreases your likelihood of developing the condition.
- Vegetable oils and margarine have been associated with increased risk of developing macular degeneration.
- Consider taking a nutritional supplement specially formulated to help reduce the likelihood that your eyesight will be affected by macular degeneration. Look for those that contain anti-oxidants, zinc and the carotenoids lutein and zeaxanthin.

See also Ageing

Eye infections

Infectious conditions of the eye include conjunctivitis, inflammation of the tear sac, inflammation of the uvea or middle layer covering the eyeball (uveitis), infection of the eyelids (blepharitis) and styes. Retinal infection (retinitis) can also occur in people with a compromised immune system.

Symptoms
- Bloodshot eyes
- Itching or pain
- Impaired vision (cloudiness or blurring)
- Over-sensitivity to light
- Inflammation or infection along the rim of the eyelid, often with scaling
- Painful red swelling under the eye can herald inflammation of the tear duct

EAR & EYE PROBLEMS

CONSULT YOUR DOCTOR
- If any of these infections do not respond to anti-inflammatory treatment, or if itching or pain persist for more than 24 hours.
- If suffering vision loss, go straight to a hospital casualty department.

Causes

Although the causes of eye inflammation may be environmental (wind, cold, dust, pollen), they can lead to, or be caused by, a viral or bacterial infection. An inflamed eye can also be due to seborrhoeic dermatitis (see Scalp problems, p. 244) that usually affects the scalp and eyebrows.

WHICH PLANTS?

WARNING Use only one of the following at any given time.

INTERNAL USAGE
To support the circulation to the eye region
BILBERRY Tablets, up to 20 g fresh fruit equivalent per day.

To help fight infection
ECHINACEA Liquid extract, 1 g dried root equivalent, three times a day.
GOLDEN SEAL Tablets, capsules, 250–500 mg dried rhizome equivalent, three times a day. Do not take if you have high blood pressure.

EXTERNAL APPLICATION
BARBERRY Tincture (1:3 in 25 per cent alcohol), soak a cloth in a glass of water to which 20 drops have been added, and then squeeze out the excess. Apply to affected closed eye for 15 minutes. Repeat two to three times a day.
CHAMOMILE Make an infusion with 2 sachets of chamomile – one for each eye – and allow to cool. Squeeze out the excess liquid, then place a sachet over each closed eye and leave it in place for 10 minutes. Repeat two or three times a day.

EYEBRIGHT Infuse 1 heaped teaspoon of dried flowers in 1 cup of boiling water for 15 minutes. Soak two clean cotton pads in the infusion and place one over each closed eye for 10 minutes.
CALENDULA Infuse 5 g of dried flower heads in 1 litre of boiling water for 5 minutes. Allow to cool, then soak a cloth in the infusion, squeeze out the excess, and apply to closed eyes for 15 minutes. Repeat three or four times a day.

Other measures

- Wear dark glasses to protect your eyes from sunlight.
- Have any ear, nose and throat problems treated promptly.
- Blepharitis (infection of the rim of the eyelids) can be relieved by daily washes using cotton buds soaked in sodium bicarbonate solution or baby shampoo, wiped repeatedly along the eyelashes.

DID YOU KNOW?

Eye infections
Native Americans used many plants medicinally. They are known to have treated eye infections with an infusion of golden seal and also with willow ash. Some of their plant remedies were adopted by European pioneers.

Tinnitus

An auditory sensation in the ear that is not caused by any external noise characterises this stressful condition. Subjective tinnitus refers to buzzing, roaring, ringing or whistling in the ear that may be continuous or intermittent, but is perceived only by the sufferer. Objective tinnitus is caused by vascular sounds in the head and neck, or muscular contractions of the middle ear or the soft palate in the mouth. Upon examination, the noise can be heard by the specialist as well as by the patient.

Symptoms

- Intermittent or continuous thudding, felt in the arteries of the neck, the temples and in the rear part of the head
- A whistling sound in the ear
- Reduced ability to hear external sounds
- Reduced ability to hear certain sounds (high- or low-pitched sounds, for example)

CONSULT YOUR DOCTOR
- A visit to the doctor is vital in order to identify the origin of the problem. The treatment will vary according to the type of tinnitus diagnosed.

Causes

Certain problems of the middle or inner ear can lead to tinnitus, including ear infections, partial deafness, Ménière's disease, or damage of the acoustic nerve or the auditory centres in the brain. A blockage in the external ear canal and vascular problems (hypertension, atherosclerosis or congested Eustachian tubes) can also result in tinnitus.

Tinnitus can be extremely frustrating for the sufferer, since in many cases the causes cannot be determined.

EAR & EYE PROBLEMS

WHICH PLANTS?

WARNING Use only one of the following at any given time.

INTERNAL USAGE
For stress
PASSIONFLOWER Liquid extract, 500 mg–1 g dried herb equivalent, twice during the day and at bedtime.

For circulatory problems
GINKGO Tablets, up to 2 g, standardised for ginkgo flavone glycosides, and ginkgolides and bilobalide. Take up to three times a day. (See Cautions, p. 102.)
BILBERRY Tablets, up to 20 g fresh fruit equivalent per day.

For infections
MULLEIN 1.5–2 g dried herb infused in 1 cup of boiling water for 15 minutes before straining. Drink 3 cups a day.
ECHINACEA Liquid extract, 1 g dried root equivalent, three times a day.
GOLDEN SEAL Tablets, capsules, 250–500 mg dried rhizome equivalent, three times a day. Do not take if you have high blood pressure.

EXTERNAL APPLICATION
For congestion in the Eustachian tubes and sinuses
EUCALYPTUS Add 2–3 drops of eucalyptus essential oil to a bowl of freshly boiled water. Cover your head with a towel and place head over bowl. Inhale deeply for 10 minutes.

PINE Follow instructions for eucalyptus oil inhalation (see above).
TEA TREE Follow instructions for eucalyptus oil inhalation (see above).

Other measures
- If possible, treat the disorder responsible for the tinnitus.
- If a blockage of ear wax is the cause, consult your doctor about its removal.
- Protect your hearing from any very high noise levels that you may experience during the course of your day.
- Acupuncture may help.
- Consider relaxation techniques.

See also Ear disorders, Hypertension

DID YOU KNOW?

Tinnitus & ginkgo
A number of clinical trials have shown that ginkgo helps to relieve tinnitus. However, other trials have not shown positive results – it may be that these trials used inadequate doses of ginkgo. Whatever the case, some further research will be required before this effect is fully understood.

HAIR & NAIL PROBLEMS

Hair loss

Hair is continually falling out and regrowing in cycles that last several months. However, the discovery of an excessive amount of hair on the pillow, or hair that comes out in clumps during brushing, may be a cause for some concern. The appearance of several small, coin-shaped bald patches on the scalp indicates a condition known as alopecia areata.

Symptoms
- Excessive loss of hair, with or without the roots
- General thinning of the hair

CONSULT YOUR DOCTOR
Both men and women should seek a doctor's advice if hair loss is sudden and excessive, as there may be a more serious underlying cause.

Causes

Although baldness in men is usually hereditary, it may also reflect changes in the male hormones (androgens). Hormonal factors are also commonly involved in hair loss in women, e.g. the reduced oestrogen levels of menopause may lead to thinner hair in the post-menopausal years. Excessive loss of hair may also be due to a deficiency of certain minerals and proteins. It is sometimes connected to anaemia, fatigue or to problems with the endocrine glands. It can also be caused by alcoholism or by certain drugs (notably anticancer medication). Well-defined patches of complete baldness surrounded by normal hair (alopecia areata) may be related to other auto-immune conditions (such as some thyroid disorders), but usually resolves itself eventually. Sometimes there is a psychological cause behind hair loss, as in trichotillomania (hair loss due to habitual pulling out of hair).

242 NATURE'S MEDICINES

HAIR & NAIL PROBLEMS

WHICH PLANTS?

WARNING Use only one of the following at any given time.

INTERNAL USAGE
EVENING PRIMROSE OIL Capsules, 1000 mg, three times a day with meals.
HORSETAIL Boil 1–4 g dried herb in 2 cups of water for 10–15 minutes before straining. Drink 2–3 cups a day.
GINKGO Tablets, up to 2 g, standardised for ginkgo flavone glycosides, and ginkgolides and bilobalide. Take up to three times a day. (See Cautions, p. 102.)

EXTERNAL APPLICATION
To stimulate circulation to the scalp
PEPPERMINT Add 3 drops of essential oil to 10 ml carrier oil. Massage into scalp once a week. Shampoo out after 10–15 minutes application.
ROSEMARY Infuse 50 g dried herb in 1 litre of boiling water for 30 minutes. Strain, cool and then massage into the scalp. Shampoo out after 10 minutes. Repeat once a week.

To act as a scalp tonic
NETTLE 20 g dried herb boiled in 750 ml water until it is reduced to roughly 500 ml. Strain, cool and rub into the scalp twice a week, rinsing after 15 minutes. If using fresh herb, twice the amount will be required.

As a male hormonal tonic
SAW PALMETTO Capsules, standardised for their content of free fatty acids. Follow manufacturer's instructions.

Other measures
- Ensure you eat a balanced diet.
- Ask your doctor to check if you have anaemia – you may need to take an iron supplement.
- Other minerals may also be beneficial, especially zinc and silica.
- If you live in a climate with low levels of sunlight, consider taking a course of vitamin D (cod liver oil is a good source, and will also provide vitamin A).
- Do not panic about generalised hair loss – the hair will usually begin to stop falling out and grow back more thickly again after a few months.

DID YOU KNOW?

Hair
The Sioux of North America made a lotion from nettle leaves that helped hair to regrow. When scientists analysed this hair preparation they found that the irritant substances contained in the stinging part of the leaves stimulated the blood circulation of the scalp. It is the increased blood supply that encourages cells to produce new hair.

Nail disorders

The main disorders affecting the nails are fungal infections, ingrown toenails and structural damage, such as brittleness. Paronychia is a skin infection that affects the area around a fingernail or toenail.

Symptoms
- Fungal infections are associated with yellowish discolouration of the nails, which may also become brittle and thick, and may peel. The surrounding skin may be swollen and itchy, and the nails and skin may become tender or painful to the touch
- Ingrown nails can be extremely painful, especially if they happen to become infected
- In paronychia, the cuticles are red, swollen and painful. Pus may form beneath the cuticle
- Longitudinal ridges (i.e. parallel to the fingers)
- Dry, brittle nails that snap easily
- Soft nails that split or peel away in fine layers

CONSULT YOUR DOCTOR
Whilst the majority of nail problems are relatively harmless, brittle nails and fungal infections can sometimes signify more serious conditions. Ask your doctor to examine your nails to rule out any underlying illness that requires medical treatment.

Causes
Brittle nails can be due to nutritional deficiencies (e.g. zinc, iron, vitamin A, silica, biotin); a disorder of the digestive tract or endocrine glands; or localised trauma of the nail. Fungal infections of the nails tend to arise when a person's immune system is weakened due to stress or other illness. Psoriasis may mimic fungal infection of the nails.

WHICH PLANTS?

WARNING Use only one of the following at any given time.

INTERNAL USAGE
For fungal infections
ECHINACEA Liquid extract, 1 g dried root equivalent, three times a day.

As advised by a medical herbalist
- Barberry, golden seal, pau d'arco

For brittle nails
EVENING PRIMROSE OIL Capsules, 1000 mg, three times a day with meals.
HORSETAIL Boil 1–4 g dried herb in 2 cups of water for 10–15 minutes before straining. Drink 2–3 cups a day.

A TO Z OF AILMENTS 243

HAIR & NAIL PROBLEMS

EXTERNAL APPLICATION
For fungal infections
TEA TREE Apply a tea tree–based cream or gel, as directed on the label.
THYME 2 g dried herb infused in 1 cup of boiling water for 5 minutes before straining. Allow to cool and soak affected nails in the liquid for 15 minutes twice a day.

Other measures
- To strengthen your nails, take a multivitamin and mineral supplement.
- Keep the nails cut short. Disinfect the scissors or clippers after cutting infected nails in order to avoid infecting the others.
- Avoid immersing your hands in water for long periods of time, and when this is unavoidable, wear cotton-lined latex gloves.
- Avoid exposure to harsh chemicals, including nail polish remover.
- Don't wear false nails.
- Don't wear shoes that put pressure on your toenails.

See also Fungal infections

DID YOU KNOW?
Discoloured nails
Yellow or green nails may signal infection (fungal or bacterial), but yellow colouring may also be due to nicotine staining.

Injury to the nail may cause black or blue markings, or small splinterlike flecks (although these may also be due to serious cardiovascular disease, as may blue-grey nails).

In anaemia, the nails are commonly very pale or white.

Nutritional disorders may be indicated by white spots (commonly zinc deficiency).

Scalp problems

The two main problems affecting the scalp are dandruff (the excessive flaking of the skin of the scalp) and seborrhoeic dermatitis of the scalp (an excessive production of sebum).

Symptoms
Dandruff
- Flakes may be small, white and shiny, or large, greasy, moist and yellowish
- Scalp may or may not be itchy and tends to be greasy
- Large, thick flakes that are yellowish and moist

Seborrhoeic dermatitis
- Hair tends to be lank, and to become greasy rapidly
- Itchiness causing lesions
- An unpleasant smell from the scalp
- Redness around the edges of the scalp, which may become inflamed
- Sometimes dermatitis spreads to the eyebrows and eyelids

CONSULT YOUR DOCTOR
- Although dandruff is not a serious disorder, a doctor should be consulted if it becomes severe.
- Other conditions that resemble dandruff include: eczema, psoriasis, ringworm (a fungal infection), the presence of lice, and ichthyosis (a predominantly genetic condition that is associated with extremely scaly skin).

Causes
Dandruff results from an accelerated shedding of dead skin cells. It can be caused by a fungus, anxiety or hair products that contain too much detergent (or which are used too frequently).

Seborrhoeic dermatitis arises from an excessive secretion of sebum, and is often accompanied by a widespread fungal infection. The condition may come and go but is usually aggravated during periods of stress.

WHICH PLANTS?
WARNING Use only one of the following at any given time.

INTERNAL USAGE
To treat seborrheic dermatitis
EVENING PRIMROSE OIL Capsules, 1000 mg, three times a day with meals.
FLAX (LINSEED) Capsules, take according to manufacturer's instructions.
ROSEMARY 2–4 g dried herb infused in 1 cup of boiling water for 10 minutes before straining. Drink 3 cups a day, but avoid drinking at bedtime.
SAGE 20 g dried leaves infused in 1 litre of boiling water for 10 minutes before straining. Drink 1–2 cups a day.

EXTERNAL APPLICATION
To prevent dandruff
NETTLE 20 g dried herb boiled in 750 ml water until it is reduced to roughly 500 ml. Strain, cool and rub into the scalp twice a week, rinsing after 15 minutes. If using fresh herb, twice the amount will be required.
ROSEMARY Add 3 drops of essential oil to 10 ml carrier oil and massage into the scalp. Leave for 15 minutes and then shampoo out. Repeat once or twice a week.

To treat seborrhoeic dermatitis
SAGE 20 g dried leaves infused in 1 litre of boiling water for 10 minutes before straining. Cool, then massage the liquid into the scalp. Rinse after 15 minutes and repeat twice a week.
HEARTSEASE Add 20–30 g fresh flowers to 500 ml boiling water and infuse for 15 minutes before straining. Massage the cooled liquid into the scalp and rinse out after 15 minutes. Repeat twice a week.
MARSHMALLOW 20 g dried root infused in 500 ml boiling water for 10 minutes before straining. Rub the cooled liquid well into the scalp and rinse off after 15 minutes. Repeat twice a week.

INFECTIONS

ROSEMARY Add 3 drops of essential oil to 10 ml carrier oil and massage into the scalp. Leave in place for 15 minutes and then shampoo out. Repeat treatment twice a week.

NETTLE 20 g dried herb boiled in 750 ml water until it is reduced to roughly 500 ml. Strain, cool and rub into the scalp twice a week, rinsing after 15 minutes. If using fresh herb, twice the amount will be required.

WITCH HAZEL Apply witch hazel water to the scalp and rinse off after 15 minutes. Repeat twice a week.

Other measures

- Use mild shampoo, or shampoo that is suitable for your scalp condition.
- Try avoiding shampoo altogether – after an initial phase of increased greasiness, the scalp will usually settle back to a normal state, requiring only regular washing with warm water.
- Avoid scratching or picking at the scalp, which may aggravate any inflammation that is present.
- Take a multivitamin and mineral supplement.

Fever

Although not in itself an illness, a fever may arise from a wide range of medical problems. It can also be the first sign that something is wrong. Any sustained rise in body temperature above 37.5°C should always be taken seriously.

Symptoms

- Severe shivering, followed by drenching sweats and/or chills; alternating between these two states
- Lengthy or serious fevers are often accompanied by a rapid pulse, shortness of breath, a dry mouth and feeling faint
- Confusion, especially in the elderly

CONSULT YOUR DOCTOR OR MEDICAL HERBALIST

- Except in cases where the cause is obviously benign (such as with a common cold), a doctor should be consulted if a fever lasts for more than 12 hours.
- If in doubt, do not try to reduce the fever quickly with medication. Fever indicates the progress of the illness that provoked it. To lower it can actually impede the immune system's fight against the virus.
- Instead, call your doctor as soon as possible if the temperature rises suddenly and severely (above 41°C in adults).
- Get help right away if your child has a temperature of 38.5°C or more, has a seizure or if the fever is accompanied by dark red blotches on the skin.

Causes

In general, fevers arise because of a bacterial, viral or parasitic infection or an inflammatory condition. They can also result from general metabolic problems, such as hyperthyroidism, or from simply being overtired.

WHICH PLANTS?

WARNING Use only one of the following at any given time.

INTERNAL USAGE

To support the body during fever

ELDER Liquid extract, 500 mg–1 g dried flower equivalent, three times a day.

YARROW 2–4 g dried herb infused in 250 ml of boiling water for 5 minutes before straining. Drink 3 cups a day.

ANDROGRAPHIS Tablets, 1–2 g dried herb equivalent, standardised for andrographolides, three times a day.

To support the immune system

ANDROGRAPHIS Tablets, 1–2 g dried herb equivalent, standardised for andrographolides, three times a day.

ECHINACEA Liquid extract, 1 g dried root equivalent, three times a day.

EXTERNAL APPLICATION

JUNIPER Add 3 drops of essential oil to every 10 ml carrier oil. Rub over the forehead and chest two or three times a day.

CHAMOMILE As for juniper (see above)

LAVENDER As for juniper (see above)

Other measures

- Remove all but a light layer of clothing from the patient, and ensure that the room is well ventilated.

INFECTIONS

Fungal infections

The term 'mycosis' describes various types of infection of the skin and mucous membranes caused by microscopic fungi. These include candidiasis (thrush) and various forms of tinea (such as ringworm and athlete's foot).

They tend to occur in warm, damp folds of skin, such as in the armpit and groin area. They can also affect the scalp or elsewhere on the body, appearing as crusty round patches, gradually enlarging and leaving a healed centre.

Symptoms
- Red or brown patches partially covered with vesicles (tiny blisters) or small scabs, which sometimes gradually enlarge as described above
- Sore, creamy yellow raised patches in the mouth
- White, cracking, itching inflamed areas in the groin
- Thickened, itchy, scaly patches on the scalp
- Thickening of the skin on the sides of the toes, followed by cracking and flaking

CONSULT YOUR DOCTOR
- Do not treat these infections before asking your doctor to confirm that this is a fungal skin infection and not another type of skin problem, such as eczema or psoriasis.

Causes
Candidiasis is caused by a group of fungi similar to yeast, the most common of which is *Candida albicans*. Naturally present in the intestinal flora, these fungi sometimes undergo an abnormal development, especially in areas such as in folds of skin, in the mouth or in the vagina, following a course of antibiotics or due to an immune deficiency.

People with diabetes and people with HIV/AIDS are more susceptible to fungal skin infections than other people, and indeed all other types of infection.

Athlete's foot, groin infections and ringworm are usually caused by such fungi as *Epidermophyton* and *Trichophyton*. As the name suggests, athlete's foot – associated with wearing shoes and sweating – is found widely among sportsmen and women, and spreads easily on floors of showers and change rooms.

WHICH PLANTS?

WARNING Use only one of the following at any given time.

INTERNAL USAGE
ECHINACEA Liquid extract, 1 g dried root equivalent, three times a day.

As advised by a medical herbalist
- Barberry, grapefruit seed, pau d'arco

EXTERNAL APPLICATION
For antifungal action
TEA TREE Apply a tea tree–based cream or gel, as directed on the label.

To heal the skin
CALENDULA Infuse 5 g dried flower heads in 1 litre boiling water for 5 minutes. Cool, strain and apply to the affected area as a compress three times a day.

Other measures
- Prevent athlete's foot by wearing sandals, shoes and cotton socks that allow your feet to breathe. Ensure that your feet are clean, drying your feet and toes well after a bath or shower. Keep your toenails short and disinfect scissors and other instruments used for foot care.
- Similarly, for tinea infections in the groin, dry the area well and wear loose cotton clothes.
- Scalp infections may be helped by keeping the hair short and using the treatments described (see Scalp problems p. 244).

Glandular fever & Chronic fatigue syndrome

Glandular fever (infectious mononucleosis) is an infectious viral disease characterised by tiredness combined with fever, swollen glands, pharyngitis (inflammation of the throat) and sometimes jaundice. It mainly affects adolescents and young adults and is transmitted via saliva, which is why it is known as the 'kissing disease'.

Chronic fatigue syndrome (CFS) is sometimes referred to as myalgic encephalitis (ME). It is a complex group of symptoms that can affect the body in many different ways, and may mimic other diseases.

Symptoms
Glandular fever
- General symptoms can be mild or severe: general malaise, loss of appetite, shivering, headaches, muscle pains
- Fever
- Extreme tiredness
- Swollen glands
- Sore throat
- Jaundice (sometimes)
- Rash similar to scarlet fever
- Spleen may be swollen, producing tenderness in the upper left side of the abdomen
- Symptoms last around three weeks
- If these symptoms are present but the sore throat is not, the infection may be cytomegalovirus (CMV) rather than glandular fever. When this is the case, the glandular swelling is likely to be a less prominent symptom

Chronic fatigue syndrome
- Overwhelming tiredness, unrelated to any activity, and not relieved by sleep or rest
- Flulike symptoms: swollen lymph glands, sore throat, headache, aches and pains

- Other symptoms may include concentration difficulties, memory problems, depression
- Sleeping for long periods (or conversely, insomnia)
- Reduced resistance to infection
- Food allergies and inability to tolerate exposure to chemicals
- Symptoms must be present for at least six months before a diagnosis of CFS is made

CONSULT YOUR DOCTOR OR MEDICAL HERBALIST
- If you experience the symptoms above, seek medical advice to make sure you do not have a more serious illness. A clinical diagnosis of glandular fever can be easily confirmed with a blood test, but a diagnosis of CFS is more difficult to establish.

Causes
Glandular fever is usually caused by the Epstein-Barr virus, which is primarily transmitted by saliva. Adolescents represent 70 per cent of those affected and incidence peaks at between 14 and 16 for girls, and 16 and 18 for boys.

No single cause of CFS has been established, and it is likely that the disease occurs for a number of reasons, possibly due to interaction of certain environmental and physiological factors (e.g. lowered immunity at the same time as exposure to agricultural pesticides). In a significant percentage of patients, infection with glandular fever, CMV or other viral illnesses may precipitate CFS.

WHICH PLANTS?

WARNING Use only one of the following at any given time.

INTERNAL USAGE
To strengthen the body's immune system and resistance to secondary infections
ECHINACEA Liquid extract, 1 g dried root equivalent, three times a day.
ASTRAGALUS Liquid extract, 1–2.5 g dried herb equivalent, three times a day.
GARLIC Tablets, capsules, follow manufacturer's instructions, to a maximum of 6 g dried garlic clove equivalent per day.
SIBERIAN GINSENG Tablets, capsules, 300 mg–1 g dried root equivalent, three times a day.

As a lymphatic tonic
CLEAVERS Liquid extract, 2–4 g dried plant equivalent, three times a day.

As advised by a medical herbalist
- Cat's claw, grapefruit seed, pau d'arco

Other measures
- Rest as much as possible. If you are able to tolerate exercise, take a gentle walk, but don't push yourself.
- Avoid alcohol and cigarettes, and minimise your exposure to chemicals (e.g. bleach, dry cleaning fluid, cleaning products, food additives).
- Eat plenty of fresh fruit and vegetables.
- Take as much time off work or school as you need – trying to return to your previous level of activity too soon may hinder your recuperation.

See also **Fatigue**

Herpes

Herpes is a recurrent and extremely contagious viral disease. It can infect the mucous membranes, including those of the eye. There are several variants: labial herpes – cold sores being the most common – and genital herpes, a sexually transmitted disease.

Symptoms
- Tiny white 'fever spots' or blisters, filled with yellowish liquid and outlined in red
- Lesions may occur singly or in groups, appearing around the corners of the lips or inside the lower lip, eventually spreading to the cheek or the tongue
- A burning sensation, followed by eruption of the blisters
- A yellowish scab forms, falling off after a few days
- Itching and a burning sensation
- In the case of genital herpes, fever, painful swelling of the lymph glands of the groin
- In labial herpes in children, small ulcerations appear on the lips, palate, inside the cheeks, with painful underarm swelling

CONSULT YOUR DOCTOR
- In cases of swelling, fever or recurring symptoms, consult a doctor without delay.
- If herpes reaches the eyes, it is important to consult an ophthalmologist.
- Genital herpes should be reviewed in a sexual health clinic.
- Pregnant women with genital herpes should discuss the issue with their doctor, so that special care can be taken to protect the baby.

Causes

The virus responsible for herpes is *Herpes simplex*, which is very contagious via skin contact until scabs are formed. It affects adults and children, especially those with weakened immune systems. Influenza, cold, sunlight, overwork, stress or the onset of menstruation can bring on herpes. Genital herpes is contracted via anal, vaginal or oral sex.

WHICH PLANTS?

WARNING Use only one of the following at any given time.

INTERNAL USAGE
ECHINACEA Liquid extract, 1 g dried root equivalent, three times a day.
LEMON BALM Liquid extract, 500 mg–1 g dried leaf equivalent, before meals three times a day.
LICORICE 1–2 teaspoons root powder steeped in 1 cup of boiling water for 10 minutes before straining. Drink 2–3 cups a day, for no more than four to six weeks.
ASTRAGALUS Liquid extract, 1–2.5 g dried herb equivalent, three times a day.

EXTERNAL APPLICATION
LEMON BALM Infuse 20 g dried flower heads in 500 ml of boiling water for 10 minutes. Cool, strain and apply to the affected area as a compress three times a day.
CALENDULA Infuse 5 g dried flower heads in 1 litre boiling water for 5 minutes. Cool, strain and apply to the affected area as a compress three times a day.

As advised by a medical herbalist
- Pau d'arco, St John's wort

Other measures
- During a herpes (cold sore) attack and for several days afterwards, refrain from all physical contact (kissing and sexual relations) to avoid infecting your partner.
- Even when the virus is latent (i.e. no sores are present), wear condoms to avoid infecting your sexual partner.
- To prevent subsequent attacks, strengthen your immune system with regular courses of immune-enhancing herbs such as echinacea.

See also Shingles

Influenza

Influenza is a contagious viral infection of the respiratory tract. It is often mild, but can be epidemic. Complications due to bacterial secondary infection can be serious, sometimes fatal.

Symptoms
- Muscular aches, shivering, headache
- High temperature (up to 40°C)
- Sore throat, dry cough
- Chest pains
- Tiredness and general debility

CONSULT YOUR DOCTOR
- It is important to consult a doctor in the case of those most vulnerable (children, the elderly or those whose immune systems are weak) or if symptoms persist beyond a few days.

Causes

Influenza is caused by a virus, influenza A, B or C. The A virus is the most dangerous, and has caused the great pandemics; the C virus is the most benign. It occurs more often in winter because cold temperatures lower the body's resistance to the virus. Stress, tiredness and certain conditions, such as diabetes, corticosteroid treatment or chemotherapy, also weaken the immune system.

WHICH PLANTS?

WARNING Use only one of the following at any given time.

INTERNAL USAGE
To boost the immune system
ECHINACEA Liquid extract, 1 g dried root equivalent, three times a day.
ANDROGRAPHIS Tablets, 1–2 g dried herb equivalent, standardised for andrographolides, three times a day.
ASTRAGALUS Liquid extract, 1–2.5 g dried herb equivalent, three times a day.

To support the body during fever
ELDER Liquid extract, 500 mg–1 g dried flower equivalent, three times a day.
YARROW 2–4 g dried herb infused in 250 ml of boiling water for 5 minutes before straining. Drink 3 cups a day.
ANDROGRAPHIS Tablets, 1–2 g dried herb equivalent, standardised for andrographolides, three times a day.

To soothe a cough
WHITE HOREHOUND Liquid extract, 1–2 g dried herb equivalent, three times a day.
MARSHMALLOW 2–3 g dried root infused in 1 cup of boiling water for 10 minutes before straining. Drink 2–3 cups a day.
MULLEIN 1.5–2 g dried herb infused in 1 cup of boiling water for 15 minutes before straining. Drink 3 cups a day.
ELDER Liquid extract, 500 mg–1 g dried flower equivalent, three times a day.

EXTERNAL APPLICATION
EUCALYPTUS Mix 3 drops essential oil to every 10 ml carrier oil. Rub into the chest, back, throat and temples every 2–4 hours.
TEA TREE Follow instructions for eucalyptus (see above).

As advised by a medical herbalist
- Wild cherry bark

INFECTIONS

Other measures
- Drink plenty of water or other liquids (fruit juices, vegetable bouillon, etc.).
- Stay indoors and rest in bed as much as possible.
- Ask your doctor about an annual vaccination against the flu.

See also Bronchitis, Common cold, Fever, Viral infection

Shingles

Shingles *(Herpes zoster)* is a viral infection very similar to herpes. It is characterised by a skin eruption in the form of groups of red plaques or blisters that appear along certain nerve segments. It tends to appear on a narrow area of skin, which may be located over the ribs, in a strip on the neck and arm, on the face, or on one side of the lower part of the body.

Symptoms
- First phase: a dull aching and burning sensation along the nerve segment; intense pain is sometimes present, and the skin may become very sensitive
- Second phase: appearance of red plaques interspersed with blisters and accompanied by a slight fever
- Third phase: after two to three days, the blisters dry up to be replaced by scabs that fall off after about 10 days, leaving a white scar
- Pain sometimes persists for several years after the first attack (this occurs more often in people over 50 years of age)

CONSULT YOUR DOCTOR
- If you experience symptoms such as those listed above, see your doctor, who can accurately identify the specific painful rash caused by shingles, and may be able to prevent possible complications. For example, shingles on the face is particularly dangerous when it affects the skin of the eyelids, as it may also affect the cornea.

Causes
Shingles is caused by the chickenpox virus, a member of the *Herpes* family of viruses. After an initial attack of chickenpox, the virus remains in the spinal cord, but is suppressed by the immune system. During an attack of shingles, the virus moves out along the nerves that supply the skin, causing the hypersensitivity and painful rash. Consequently, only people who have previously had chickenpox are at risk of shingles.

An attack of shingles tends to occur when the immune system has been weakened by a serious illness, such as flu, cancer or tuberculosis, or simply by mental or physical fatigue or stress. The area of the attack may also be linked to a weakness in the corresponding internal organ. People who have not previously had chickenpox may contract the virus from a shingles patient.

WHICH PLANTS?

WARNING Use only one of the following at any given time.

INTERNAL USAGE
To strengthen the body's resistance
ECHINACEA Liquid extract, 1 g dried root equivalent, three times a day.
ELDER Liquid extract, 500 mg–1 g dried flower equivalent, three times a day.
LICORICE 1–2 teaspoons of root powder steeped in 1 cup of boiling water for 10 minutes before straining. Drink 2–3 cups a day for no more than four to six weeks.
ASTRAGALUS Liquid extract, 1–2.5 g dried herb equivalent, three times a day.

EXTERNAL APPLICATION
LEMON BALM Infuse 20 g dried flower heads into 500 ml of boiling water for 10 minutes. Cool, strain and apply to the affected area as a compress three times a day.
CALENDULA Infuse 5 g dried flower heads in 1 litre boiling water for 5 minutes. Cool, strain and apply to the affected area as a compress three times a day.

As advised by a medical herbalist
- Cayenne (ointment), pau d'arco, St John's wort

Other measures
- Eat meat, fish and dairy products, which are rich in amino acids, and nuts, beans, seeds and oily fish, which contain essential fatty acids. These nutrients help to repair cells.
- Take vitamins B and C, and the mineral zinc.
- Due to a high risk of contagion, avoid contact with other people, especially those who have not previously had chickenpox and are likely to have a low resistance.
- Ensure that the infected areas remain clean and dry.
- Although they may itch, do not rub or scratch the plaques as the blisters may become infected if they burst.
- Apply a cool, wet flannel or ice cubes to reduce pain and soothe itching.
- Pregnant women are more at risk from the consequences of shingles, and should consult their midwife, GP or antenatal clinic if they have been exposed to the virus.
- Take plenty of rest.

See also Herpes

Thrush

Thrush (often referred to as *Candida*) is a fungal infection that most commonly affects the internal and external regions of the female genitals, and may extend to the surrounding area and anus. Thrush affects 75 per cent of women at least once in their life and becomes chronic in 45 per cent of cases. The symptoms can be extremely irritating and painful.

A TO Z OF AILMENTS

INFECTIONS

Symptoms
- An odourless white vaginal discharge that looks like curdled milk
- Itching and burning of the vulva and vagina
- A cracking and splitting sensation
- Redness and swelling of the vulva
- Dryness and pain, making sexual relations difficult or impossible
- Frequent burning on urination

CONSULT YOUR DOCTOR OR MEDICAL HERBALIST
- Consult a gynaecologist or doctor if you experience excessive discharge, burning, pain or dryness of the vulva and vagina.
- Consult a doctor or medical herbalist if you experience repeated episodes of thrush, or if the infection is present for long periods of time.

Causes
The fungus *Candida albicans* causes 90 per cent of thrush infections. Naturally present in the intestines, it passes into the vagina via the blood, lymph glands or skin when there is an imbalance in the intestinal flora. Upon reaching the vaginal mucosa, it finds favourable conditions (acidic environment, moisture, warmth and high levels of glycogen) that allow it to develop rapidly. HIV, diabetes and the use of antibiotics, corticosteroids and other immunosuppressants may encourage the development of thrush.

Thrush can be contracted during sexual relations, and women are particularly susceptible to this form of transmission. Infection by the *Candida* fungus may also occur in conjunction with nappy rash in infants.

WHICH PLANTS?

WARNING Use only one of the following at any given time.

Medicinal plants should be used in conjunction with the standard treatments for thrush prescribed immediately by the doctor.

INTERNAL USAGE
To stimulate the immune system
ECHINACEA Liquid extract, 1 g dried root equivalent, three times a day.
SIBERIAN GINSENG Tablets, capsules, 300 mg–1 g dried root equivalent, three times a day.
ASTRAGALUS Liquid extract, 1–2.5 g dried herb equivalent, three times a day.

As advised by a medical herbalist
- Barberry, grapefruit seed, pau d'arco

EXTERNAL APPLICATION
TEA TREE Apply a tea tree–based cream or gel, as directed on the label. Choose a product that has been specially formulated for the genital area.
CHAMOMILE Infuse 1 sachet of dried chamomile flowers in 1 cup of boiling water for 10 minutes. Use the liquid to bathe the vagina once or twice a day.
LAVENDER 2–3 g dried flowers infused in 1 cup of boiling water for 10 minutes before straining. Use the liquid to bathe the vagina and genital area once or twice a day.
CALENDULA Infuse 5 g dried flower heads in 1 litre boiling water for 5 minutes. Cool, strain and use the liquid to bathe the vagina and genital area once or twice a day.

Other measures
- As far as possible, avoid taking the oral contraceptive pill, antibiotics or corticosteroids. If this is impossible, use complementary (topical and oral) antifungal treatment.
- Wear cotton underwear and avoid restrictive clothing.
- Avoid perfumed soaps, bubble baths and other bath products. Do not use scented vaginal deodorants.
- If you have chronic thrush, use a neutral pH soap for personal hygiene.

See also **Fungal infections**

Viral infections

Viruses are infective microscopic organisms that differ from bacteria in that they penetrate the cell, forcing the cellular DNA to create thousands more viruses that are released to infect neighbouring cells. The body's only defence is a healthy immune system. The majority of the common respiratory, gastrointestinal and hepatic infections are viral in origin.

Symptoms
- Symptoms differ according to the type of virus and the illnesses that they cause

CONSULT YOUR DOCTOR
- Viral infections that are obviously benign (such as the common cold) can be treated at home. In all other cases it is imperative to seek medical advice. Treatment of viral infections is largely restricted to alleviating symptoms and boosting the body's immune system.

Causes
Viruses can enter the body by a variety of transmission routes, including via food and drink, through punctured skin or during sexual intercourse. Some invade cells near the site of entry or pass into the bloodstream, or move along nerve fibres to target specific organs. Factors such as immune deficiency, chronic fatigue syndrome or ongoing stress make the body more vulnerable to viruses. A weakened immune system may also be caused by an inadequate or unbalanced diet.

METABOLISM & IMMUNE SYSTEM DISORDERS

WHICH PLANTS?

WARNING Use only one of the following at any given time.

Internal usage
To strengthen the body's resistance
ECHINACEA Liquid extract, 1 g dried root equivalent, three times a day.
LICORICE 1–2 teaspoons root powder steeped in 1 cup of boiling water for 10 minutes before straining. Drink 2–3 cups a day for no more than four to six weeks.
ASTRAGALUS Liquid extract, 1–2.5 g dried herb equivalent, three times a day.
ANDROGRAPHIS Tablets, 1–2 g dried herb equivalent, standardised for andrographolides, three times a day, or according to manufacturer's instructions.

To aid convalescence
ROSEHIPS 2–2.5 g fragmented dried rosehips infused in 1 cup of boiling water for 10 minutes before straining. Drink 3–4 cups a day.
OATS Liquid extract, 1–4 g dried herb equivalent, two or three times a day.
SIBERIAN GINSENG Tablets, capsules, 300 mg–1 g dried root equivalent, three times a day.

Other measures
- To boost immunity, eat a well-balanced diet that is rich in foods containing flavonoids, tannins and proanthocyans (coloured fruits and vegetables such as carrots, broccoli, blackcurrants and blueberries). Garlic and onions may also be particularly beneficial.
- Avoid excessive consumption of caffeine and alcohol, which weaken the body's natural defences.
- Try not to get too tired or stressed.

See also **Herpes, Shingles**

Diabetes

Diabetes mellitus is caused by an excess of glucose in the blood (hyperglycaemia) due to the reduced effectiveness or lack of insulin (the hormone that is responsible for the absorption of blood sugar into the body's cells). There are two types of diabetes mellitus: insulin-dependent (Type 1), which usually occurs in people under the age of 35; and the more prevalent non-insulin dependent diabetes (Type 2), which occurs mainly in people over 40. Diabetes mellitus tends to run in families.

Symptoms
- Extreme thirst with frequent need to urinate
- Weight fluctuations
- Fatigue
- Slow healing of wounds and infections
- Vision problems
- Poor circulation (may present as pins and needles in the hands and feet, impotence and a range of other circulatory symptoms)
- Cravings for sugary foods and refined carbohydrates, and increased appetite in general may be symptomatic of diabetes, but may also indicate a less severe form of blood-sugar imbalance, sometimes referred to as hypoglycaemia. Other symptoms associated with hypoglycaemia include fatigue, mood swings and difficulty concentrating. It is considered that symptoms such as these may be an indication of increased risk of diabetes in later life

CONSULT YOUR DOCTOR
- In many people, diabetes goes unnoticed until it has been present for some time.
- If you have any doubts about the origins of one or several of the symptoms described above, consult your doctor who can arrange a blood-sugar test.

Causes
Insulin-dependent diabetes (Type 1) occurs when the insulin-producing cells in the pancreas are destroyed (probably during a viral illness), resulting in a complete lack of insulin. It tends to occur in children and adolescents, the onset worsening swiftly over several days to a serious illness.

Non-insulin dependent diabetes (Type 2) is effectively the result of exhaustion of the pancreatic cells that produce insulin, or of the inability of the body to use insulin properly. Those most at risk are obese people over the age of 40, with a family history of diabetes. However, as obesity in younger people increases, non-insulin dependent diabetes is becoming more common at an earlier age. High dietary intake of sugar and refined carbohydrates is also considered to be a contributory factor. Non-insulin dependent diabetes is usually treated by dietary modification and drugs to stimulate increased production or effectiveness of insulin. Sometimes, however, non-insulin dependent diabetes becomes so difficult to control with tablets and diet that insulin injections are required.

WHICH PLANTS?

WARNING Use only one of the following at any given time.

Medical herbalism is not suitable treatment for Type 1 diabetes, and should be used to treat only mild cases of Type 2 diabetes, under the supervision of your doctor.

A TO Z OF AILMENTS 251

METABOLISM & IMMUNE SYSTEM DISORDERS

As advised by a medical herbalist or doctor
- Bilberry, fenugreek, goat's rue, gymnema

Other measures
- Follow a sensible, balanced diet. Reduce your consumption of fats and refined foods (white sugar, flour, bread and white rice).
- Incorporate more complex carbohydrates into your diet. Aim for a daily intake of 25–40 g of fibre from sources such as wholegrain bread and pasta, oat bran and brown rice. The body digests these complex carbohydrates slowly, leading to a steady level of sugar in the blood. High consumption of fibre has been associated with reduced risk of developing Type 2 diabetes.
- Maintain or achieve a healthy body weight. This will make your diabetes much easier to control or reduce your risk of developing it in the first place.
- Take regular exercise, unless your doctor advises against it.

See also Excess weight & Obesity, Heart disease prevention

DID YOU KNOW?
Diabetes
Diabetes is considered to be the fastest growing disease in the world – an alarming statistic when you consider that many cases could be prevented through good nutrition. In Australia, it is estimated that there are over 1 million sufferers, although as many as half of these may be undiagnosed. The statistics are similar in New Zealand, where around 20 new cases are diagnosed every day.

Excess weight & Obesity

People are technically obese – rather than simply overweight – when they weigh 20 per cent or more above the normal weight for their height, as measured on standard weight charts such as the Body Mass Index (BMI).

Alternatively, the waist measurement may be used to provide an indication of whether being overweight is predisposing an individual to increased risk of heart problems, diabetes, lipid disorders or high blood pressure. For men, a waist measurement of more than 94 cm indicates increased risk, with 102 cm suggesting that the risk is substantial. For women, a waist measurement of 80 cm or more indicates increased risk, whilst a measurement above 88 cm suggests substantial risk.

Obesity is becoming increasingly common in children and young people, and is already leading to serious problems that were previously seen at a much later age, such as Type 2 diabetes.

Symptoms
- Excess weight
- Bulky physical appearance
- Abundant fat in the subcutaneous tissues
- Breathlessness when any form of physical exertion is involved

CONSULT YOUR DOCTOR OR MEDICAL HERBALIST
- If you are obese, your doctor will be able to determine whether it is due to overeating or the result of a physical dysfunction. You should consult your doctor before undertaking any form of treatment, including changes to your current level of exercise.

Causes
Becoming overweight – the first step to obesity – is the result of absorbing more calories than are expended in energy. It can be caused by a range of factors, such as lack of physical exercise, an unbalanced diet, heavy drinking, compulsive eating, and physical disorders including diabetes and hypothyroidism.

WHICH PLANTS?

WARNING Use only one of the following at any given time.

INTERNAL USAGE
To detoxify the system and support liver health
DANDELION Liquid extract, 500 mg–1 g dried root equivalent, three times a day.
GLOBE ARTICHOKE Tablets, capsules, 500 mg–1 g dried herb equivalent, standardised for cynarin content, three times a day.
MILK THISTLE Tablets, up to 9 g dried herb equivalent, three times a day.

For fluid retention
DANDELION Liquid extract, 4–10 g dried leaf equivalent, three times a day.

As a lymphatic tonic
CLEAVERS Liquid extract, 2–4 g dried plant equivalent, three times a day.

As advised by a medical herbalist
- Cayenne, kelp

METABOLISM & IMMUNE SYSTEM DISORDERS

Other measures
- Ask your doctor or medical herbalist to refer you to a nutritionist or dietary consultant who can develop a special eating plan for you.
- Eat balanced meals including plenty of fibre, vegetables and fruit and lean protein foods.
- Avoid sugars, refined foods and saturated fats.
- Be more energetic. Use the stairs instead of taking lifts, and take up physical activities and sports, after consultation with your doctor.

See also Hypothyroidism

> **DID YOU KNOW?**
>
> **Obesity in New Zealand**
> New Zealanders have one of the highest daily kilojoule intakes in the world, on a par with America, and higher than Australia. The average New Zealander consumes an amazing 13,000–16,000 kJ (3100–3800 calories) per day. One in every two New Zealanders is now considered overweight or obese.

Fatigue

Many people feel that they do not have the energy to keep pace with their daily lives. In some cases fatigue may be symptomatic of underlying disease, but in others, it is likely to be lifestyle induced.

Symptoms
- Desire or need to sleep
- Lack of energy to perform desired activities
- Difficulty concentrating
- Irritability and mood swings; decreased ability to tolerate stress
- Muscular fatigue

CONSULT YOUR DOCTOR
- If fatigue is intense and persistent, it is important to consult a doctor who can help to determine its precise nature and also eliminate underlying illness.

Causes
Fatigue can be caused by lack of sleep, excessive physical or mental activity, stress and poor dietary habits. It is a feature of many diseases, including depression and other psychiatric illness, infection, anaemia and other dietary deficiencies, kidney or liver disorders, cancers and metabolic disorders such as thyroid insufficiency and diabetes.

WHICH PLANTS?

WARNING Use only one of the following at any given time.

INTERNAL USAGE
OATS Liquid extract, 1–4 g dried herb equivalent, two or three times a day.
ROSEMARY 2–4 g dried herb infused in 1 cup of boiling water for 10 minutes before straining. Drink 3 cups a day, but avoid drinking at bedtime.
KOREAN GINSENG Tablets, capsules, 250–500 mg dried root equivalent, twice daily. Take one dose in the morning and one dose around midday. Choose a product standardised for its ginsenosides content. (See Cautions, p. 125.)
SIBERIAN GINSENG Tablets, capsules, 300 mg–1 g dried root equivalent, three times a day.
GREEN TEA 1 teaspoon of green tea infused in 1 cup of boiling water for 10 minutes before straining. Drink 2–3 cups a day.
ASTRAGALUS Liquid extract, 1–2.5 g dried herb equivalent, three times a day.

Other measures
- Ensure you get all the sleep your body requires.
- If stress is a factor, take steps to improve your ability to cope. Exercise, hypnotherapy and meditation classes may all offer some benefit.
- Eat a balanced diet containing daily serves of protein, and lots of fresh fruit, vegetables, nuts and seeds. Drink at least 2 litres of filtered water every day, and avoid alcohol, caffeine, fatty and sugary foods and smoking.

See also Glandular fever & Chronic fatigue syndrome, Stress

Hyperthyroidism

Hyperthyroidism is a malfunction of the thyroid gland, in which thyroid hormone is overproduced, increasing the body's metabolic rate. It affects five times more women than men, generally between 30 and 60 years of age.

Symptoms
- Swelling of the thyroid gland (goitre) at the front of the neck
- Protruding eyeballs (exophthalmia), retraction of the lids, excessive watering, limited vision
- Raised red or purple patches on the shins (pretibial myxoedema)
- Cardiovascular complications: accelerated heart rate (tachycardia), irregular heartbeats (auricular fibrillation), shortness of breath
- Weight loss despite increased appetite and energy intake
- Fatigue, muscle weakness
- Thinning hair
- Diarrhoea
- Nervousness, irritability, tremor, anxiety, insomnia, dislike of heat
- Menstrual flow tends to be light or scanty

A TO Z OF AILMENTS 253

METABOLISM & IMMUNE SYSTEM DISORDERS

CONSULT YOUR DOCTOR
- If you experience swelling of the neck and any of the other symptoms listed above, consult your doctor.
- If you have hyperthyroidism and become pregnant, consult your doctor.

Causes

In 90 per cent of cases where the patient is under 40 years old, hyperthyroidism is caused by Grave's disease. This is an auto-immune condition in which the body's own antibodies stimulate the production of thyroid hormones. It can occur at any age, but rarely before puberty and generally between 20 and 50 years old. It manifests through eye disorders, pretibial myxoedema (see p. 253) and goitre.

In other cases, hyperthyroidism may be caused by a tumour of the pituitary gland or thyroid cancer that has developed from secondary growths.

WHICH PLANTS?

Consult your doctor before commencing any alternative therapy.

WARNING Use only one of the following at any given time.

Hyperthyroidism is not suitable for self-treatment. The following plants may help to relieve anxiety.

INTERNAL USAGE
To relieve anxiety
LAVENDER 2–3 g dried flowers infused in 1 cup of boiling water for 5–10 minutes. Drink 3–4 cups a day between meals.
LIME FLOWERS 2–4 g dried flowers infused in 1 cup of boiling water for 5 minutes before straining. Drink 1 cup twice a day and another in the evening.
VALERIAN Tablets, up to 2 g dried herb equivalent, take up to three times a day.

As advised by a medical herbalist
- Hawthorn, lemon balm

Other measures
- Take vitamins C, E and B-complex, which are important for maintaining the health of the thyroid gland.

See also Low body weight

> **DID YOU KNOW?**
>
> ### Hyperthyroidism
> Vegetables of the *Brassica* genus (including cabbage and broccoli) contain glucosinolate, a substance that prevents the synthesis of certain thyroid hormones. Peanuts and soy beans also contain this substance, which means they are all recommended in cases of hyperthyroidism.

Hypothyroidism

The term 'hypothyroidism' refers to underactivity of the thyroid gland and underproduction of thyroid hormone, causing the body's metabolism to be slowed down. It can be congenital or acquired, and affects six times more women than men. There may be a family history of thyroid disease or other auto-immune conditions (such as pernicious anaemia or rheumatoid arthritis).

Symptoms
- Tiredness, sleepiness, depression
- Low blood pressure
- Weight gain that is unrelated to energy intake
- Goitre (swelling in the front of the neck)
- Aversion to the cold
- Hoarseness
- Slow pulse (bradycardia)
- Muscular aches and pains
- Anaemia
- Dry, scaly skin with vitiligo (white patches ringed by overpigmented skin)
- Dry, unruly hair
- Irregular or heavier periods
- Sterility, impotence, constipation

CONSULT YOUR DOCTOR OR MEDICAL HERBALIST
- If you experience swelling of the thyroid gland or the appearance of one or more of the above symptoms, see your doctor, who can diagnose the disorder and prescribe appropriate medication. He or she will also be able to eliminate the possibility of other conditions, including cancer.
- Regular monitoring of your medication and thyroid hormone levels is also important.
- If you have been taking thyroid medication and still have the symptoms listed above, or conversely, if you develop any symptoms of an overactive thyroid (see Hyperthyroidism, p. 253), the dosage of your medicine may need to be adjusted.
- If you have hypothyroidism and become pregnant, consult your doctor.

Causes

Hypothyroidism can be caused by spontaneous atrophy of the thyroid gland, or, if there is a goitre, brought on by an inflammatory reaction of the thyroid linked with hormonal underproduction, taking certain drugs or excessive iodine intake.

In some cases, hypothyroidism develops following radioactive iodine treatment or surgical removal of part of the thyroid gland as a treatment for hyperthyroidism. Several auto-immune diseases can facilitate its development.

WHICH PLANTS?

WARNING Use only one of the following at any given time.

Hypothyroidism is not suitable for self-treatment. Consult your doctor before starting any alternative therapy.

INTERNAL USAGE
For dry skin
EVENING PRIMROSE OIL Capsules, 1000 mg, three times a day with meals.

As advised by a medical herbalist or doctor

To stimulate thyroid activity
- Kelp

Other measures
- Ask your GP or medical herbalist about additional mineral supplements, such as iodine, zinc and selenium.
- Take vitamins C and E, as well as B complex vitamins, which are important for maintaining the health of the thyroid gland.
- Be aware that herbal treatment may interact with your medication – always seek professional help.

See also Excess weight & Obesity

Immune system deficiency

Immune system deficiency occurs when the body is in a state of low resistance to foreign micro-organisms, such as viruses, bacteria or parasites. The body becomes less capable of mobilising its immune defences, the innate collection of cells and proteins it normally activates to overpower the invaders.

Symptoms
- Recurrent infections
- Infection by organisms that are generally considered harmless
- Slow recovery from infections
- Excessive tiredness

CONSULT YOUR DOCTOR OR MEDICAL HERBALIST
- If any of the above symptoms is persistent enough to suggest that the immune system is impaired, it is imperative to seek medical advice.

Causes
A weakened immune system may indicate numerous disorders, ranging from allergies to HIV/AIDS. It can be due to exposure to toxins – medications and other synthetic substances – or may also be related to zinc deficiency, Crohn's disease, anorexia nervosa or to a state of depression or anxiety.

WHICH PLANTS?

WARNING Use only one of the following at any given time.

As advised by a medical herbalist

To strengthen the body's immune defences
- Andrographis, astragalus, echinacea, golden seal, Siberian ginseng, withania

For tiredness and fatigue
- Cinnamon, oats, rosehip, rosemary, Siberian ginseng

Other measures
- Eat a balanced diet, with particular emphasis on fresh fruit and vegetables, and with at least 1–2 serves of lean protein every day.
- Consider taking a supplement of key immune system nutrients, such as vitamins A and C, and the minerals zinc and selenium.
- Avoid stress, cigarette smoking and junk food.
- Make sure you get enough sleep.

See also Common cold, Fungal infections, Herpes, Influenza, Shingles, Viral infections

Low body weight

A person is usually considered underweight if they are significantly below the weight appropriate for their height and age, as measured by charts such as the Body Mass Index (BMI). The BMI chart, however, is appropriate only for adults, and has limitations because it cannot distinguish between body fat and muscle, which can make very muscular people appear overweight. Equally, the chart may make people who have lost muscle mass, such as the elderly, appear excessively underweight.

Some individuals are genetically disposed to be underweight. In other cases, if someone is more than 20 per cent below the standard weight for their height, disease, stress or poor diet may be the cause.

If substantial weight loss occurs suddenly or progressively, it is almost certainly a symptom of a serious disorder.

Symptoms
- Failing to put on weight, despite eating well
- General lack of fatty tissue
- Tiredness, muscular pains, headaches and hypotension (low blood pressure)

CONSULT YOUR DOCTOR
- Any unexplained weight loss should be investigated by your doctor, regardless of whether it occurs suddenly or progressively.

Causes
Genetic factors are often at play when a person is underweight. However, it may also be due to inadequate diet and a lack of nutrients; poor intestinal absorption; pancreatic dysfunction; stress; overexercising; hyperthyroidism or eating disorder.

METABOLISM & IMMUNE SYSTEM DISORDERS

In young girls, unexplained weight loss may mask anorexia or Turner's syndrome (a chromosomal abnormality that affects growth in approximately 1 in 3000 females).

WHICH PLANTS?

WARNING Use only one of the following at any given time.

Medical herbalism can aid in a limited way by helping to relax and nourish the body and by improving appetite and digestion where appropriate.

INTERNAL USAGE
To nourish
FENUGREEK Powder, 2 g in a little water, three times a day.
OATS Liquid extract, 1–4 g dried herb equivalent, two or three times a day.

To stimulate appetite and aid digestion
PEPPERMINT 1 teaspoon dried leaves infused in 150 ml of boiling water for 10–15 minutes before straining. Drink 1 cup after every meal.
GENTIAN Liquid extract, 100–300 mg dried herb equivalent, three times a day before meals.

For anxiety
LAVENDER 2–3 g dried flowers infused in 1 cup of boiling water for 5–10 minutes. Drink 3–4 cups a day between meals.
LIME FLOWERS 2–4 g dried flowers infused in 1 cup of boiling water for 5 minutes, before straining. Drink 1 cup twice a day and another in the evening.

Other measures
- Do not embark upon any treatment without medical advice.
- Eat dishes you enjoy, in pleasurable circumstances.
- Work towards a balanced diet, and add foods that have a positive medical effect such as dried fruit, rolled oats, rosehip syrup and soy beans.
- Use spices such as ginger and cinnamon, which stimulate digestion.
- If necessary, learn relaxation techniques to improve your ability to cope with stress.
- Learn to accept the body you were born with – for many people, being underweight is a matter of genetics.

See also Fibromyalgia, Neuralgia

DID YOU KNOW?

Body Mass Index
The formula to calculate your Body Mass Index is: weight (kg) $\div$ height^2 (metres).
For a person 150 cm tall and weighing 60 kg, this works out to $60 \div (1.5 \times 1.5) = 26.7$

WHAT YOUR BODY MASS INDEX (BMI) MEANS
Below 18.5: Underweight
18.5–24.9: Normal weight
25–29.9: Overweight
30.0 and above: Obese

MUSCLES, BONES & JOINTS

Back pain & Neck pain

Back and neck pain affect most people at some time in their life, and are common reasons for lost working days. The causes are many and varied, and require careful diagnosis.

Symptoms
- Intense, unbearable stabs of sharp pain, aggravated by the slightest effort (coughing, sneezing, defecation)
- Acute painful muscle contraction at the base of the neck, often waking to find the head twisted to one side
- Painful twisting of the neck (torticollis), which remains in a fixed position
- Lumbago (acute muscular contraction in the lower back or lumbar region)
- Intense lumbar pain on one side, often associated with a 'blocked' feeling
- Pain in part, or along the whole, of the sciatic nerve (the main nerve in each leg and the largest nerve in the body). Back pain may be present too, but is often less intense than the leg pain
- A reduction in muscular strength, or in feeling, making walking difficult or almost impossible
- Reduced range of movement

CONSULT YOUR DOCTOR OR MEDICAL HERBALIST
- Back pain generally indicates a minor muscular strain or overuse injury, and usually passes after a few days. However, it can also be a sign of infection, inflammation, tumour, arthritis, osteoporosis or damage to the intervertebral disc ('slipped disc') that only your doctor can diagnose.

MUSCLES, BONES & JOINTS

Causes

Back and neck pain can be caused by inefficient functioning of the spinal column or the muscles or ligaments that support it. It can arise from the physical demands of work, poor posture, housework, gardening or lumbar strain as a result of long and tiring journeys. Sometimes it is stress related.

WHICH PLANTS?

WARNING Use one of the following at any given time.

Medical herbalism may offer symptom relief, but takes second place to treatments such as physiotherapy, acupuncture, osteopathy or chiropractic.

INTERNAL USAGE
DEVIL'S CLAW Tablets, capsules, 1–2 g dried tuber equivalent, three times a day. For best results choose a product standardised for its harpagoside content.

EXTERNAL APPLICATION
CAYENNE Apply cayenne-based ointment to the affected area three to four times a day, as directed on the label.
CINNAMON Apply cinnamon-based ointment to the affected area three to four times a day, as directed on the label.
ROSEMARY Add 3 drops of essential oil to 10 ml carrier oil. Rub in two or three times a day.
NUTMEG Add 3 drops of essential oil to 50 ml carrier oil. Apply one to three times a day, or use in one bath a day.

Other measures

- Consult a physiotherapist, osteopath, chiropractor or acupuncturist.
- As a preventive, try to avoid lifting heavy weights.
- Avoid any activities that put too much strain on the back (such as squash, judo and tennis), and maintain good posture.
- Try gentle, supervised muscle building in the gym to help to strengthen your back and reduce the severity and frequency of attacks – improving the strength of your abdominal muscles may reduce the load on your back.
- Wear appropriate footwear, possibly with orthopaedic soles.
- Watch your weight and try to achieve a healthy weight for your height.

See also Neuralgia

DID YOU KNOW?

Backache

Devil's claw is the herb usually prescribed for backache. Medical herbalists consider it to be a highly effective anti-inflammatory, and it has an analgesic effect on non-sciatic, non-inflammatory back pain. This was shown in trials conducted in Leipzig, Germany, when 117 patients were given 480 mg of dried extract twice a day. The treatment did not produce toxic effects in any of the cases studied.

Cramp

An involuntary, painful spasm in a muscle is known as cramp. It is a common occurrence, and seldom lasts more than a few moments.

Symptoms

- Muscular pain, usually of the toes or calf muscle; occurs more often at rest or during the night
- Hardening and contraction of a muscle
- Abdominal muscle cramps are a feature of premenstrual syndrome and some bowel conditions

CONSULT YOUR DOCTOR OR MEDICAL HERBALIST

- Cramp is usually relieved by massage. However, if it occurs regularly at night and interrupts the sleep pattern, a doctor may be able to prescribe a drug to prevent its recurrence.
- If cramp persists for an hour or more, urgent medical attention should be sought.
- Cramping pain in the chest area warrants urgent medical assistance. Call for medical help immediately.

Causes

Cramp is a muscular spasm that has a variety of causes, including simple muscular fatigue and sitting or lying in an awkward position. It often occurs during or after exercise due to lactic acid build-up in the muscles, and may also be due to a temporary circulatory problem.

Cramp may also be caused by dietary deficiency of the minerals calcium, magnesium and/or potassium, and sometimes occurs as a side effect of certain pharmaceutical medications, particularly those that increase potassium and magnesium excretion.

In many cases, the true cause of the problem remains unclear.

WHICH PLANTS?

WARNING Use only one of the following at any given time.

INTERNAL USAGE
CRAMP BARK Liquid extract, 500 mg–1 g dried bark equivalent, three times a day.

EXTERNAL APPLICATION
CINNAMON Apply cinnamon-based ointment to the affected area three to four times a day, as directed on the label.
NUTMEG Add 3 drops of essential oil to 50 ml carrier oil. Apply one to three times a day or use in the bath once a day.

A TO Z OF AILMENTS 257

MUSCLES, BONES & JOINTS

Other measures
- Consume plenty of fluid before, during and after exercise – you may also like to consider an electrolyte replacement drink if you sweat a lot, or are exercising in hot weather.
- Massage the muscles to relax them. During a cramp, get out of the chair or bed and stretch the affected muscle hard.
- Regular stretching of the affected area can considerably reduce the frequency and severity of subsequent attacks. Stretch the muscle for 10 seconds repeatedly over 3 minutes, three times a day – especially before and after exercise. For example, to stretch the calf muscles, straighten the knee and use the muscles of the front of the shin to pull your toes up towards you.
- If you suspect your medication may be causing your cramps, talk to your doctor about it.

Fibromyalgia

The symptoms of fibromyalgia, involving painful stiff joints and muscles, resemble those found in some other illnesses. The disorder is chronic and varies in intensity according to the individual. In its most severe forms, it can limit all the activities of those afflicted. Fibromyalgia affects around 2 per cent of the population.

Symptoms
- Pains in all areas of the body, and particularly at certain tender spots on the back, neck, chest, hips, sternum and limbs
- Joint and muscle stiffness
- Sleeplessness
- Constant tiredness
- Symptoms may be worse when the patient is under stress
- The patient may also experience irritable bowel syndrome, headaches, premenstrual syndrome, depression and other symptoms

CONSULT YOUR DOCTOR OR MEDICAL HERBALIST
- If neglected, fibromyalgia can become a chronic problem. It is therefore essential, if one or several of the symptoms appear, to seek medical advice.

Causes
The precise origin of the syndrome is unknown, but it often appears after a traumatic shock. Even if all clinical examinations give normal results, it is important not to assume that fibromyalgia is psychosomatic in origin.

WHICH PLANTS?
WARNING Use only one of the following at any given time.

Orthodox medicine may not be particularly helpful. But with medical herbalism, treatment can be individually tailored to the symptoms of each particular case.

INTERNAL USAGE
For pain and inflammation
CRAMP BARK Liquid extract, 500 mg–1 g dried bark equivalent, three times a day.
DEVIL'S CLAW Tablets, capsules, 1–2 g dried tuber equivalent, three times a day. For best results choose a product standardised for its harpagoside content.

To improve sleep
PASSIONFLOWER Liquid extract, 500 mg–1 g dried herb equivalent, twice during the day and at bedtime.

To reduce anxiety
ST JOHN'S WORT Tablets, 1.8 g dried flowering herb equivalent, standardised for hypericin content, take three times a day or as professionally prescribed. St John's wort is known to interact with a large number of pharmaceutical medications and should be used under professional supervision. (See Cautions, p. 168.)

For fatigue and tiredness
WITHANIA Liquid extract, 1–2 g dried root equivalent, three times a day.
OATS Liquid extract, 1–4 g dried herb equivalent, two or three times a day.
SIBERIAN GINSENG Tablets, capsules, 300 mg–1 g dried root equivalent, three times a day. Take for up to one month at a time.

EXTERNAL APPLICATION
To relax the muscles
CINNAMON Apply cinnamon-based ointment to the affected area three to four times a day, as directed on the label.

To treat inflammation
NUTMEG Add 3 drops essential oil to 50 ml carrier oil. Apply one to three times a day or use in one bath a day.

Other measures
- Take physical exercise that builds up muscle strength – this is likely to be one of the most important components of your treatment.
- Consider physiotherapy, osteopathy, chiropractic or acupuncture.
- Some patients find it helpful to take a magnesium supplement.
- Try to adapt your lifestyle to your state of health.
- Avoid tobacco and excessive alcohol.

See also **Glandular fever & Chronic fatigue syndrome, Psychosomatic disorders**

MUSCLES, BONES & JOINTS

Gout

This painful condition is caused by deposits of uric acid crystals in the joints. The uric acid is a by-product of the breakdown of proteins in the body. The joint in the big toe is commonly the first to be affected. Men are much more likely to suffer from gout than women. There is a family history in about a third of cases.

Symptoms
- Sudden, sharp pain in the affected joint (often starting with the big toe)
- The affected joint may be red, swollen and warm. It is also likely to be extremely tender when touched
- Deposits of uric acid crystals around the affected joint may cause it to become deformed
- Incidence is increased in those with diabetes or high blood pressure

CONSULT YOUR DOCTOR
- Only a doctor can diagnose gout. Your doctor may use a combination of medical examination, X-rays and blood tests to distinguish between gout, pseudogout (a similar condition, in which the crystals are of calcium rather than uric acid), rheumatoid arthritis, osteoarthritis, a deep abscess, phlebitis and other conditions.

Causes
Gout is caused by a combination of two phenomena: excessive breakdown of proteins, and the failure of the kidneys to eliminate uric acid. In many cases, there is a genetic disorder in metabolising proteins.

Otherwise, the problem may relate to anticancer drugs, some blood pressure drugs and aspirin. It is also associated with psoriasis and some blood cancers.

For those at risk, symptoms can be brought on by overindulgence in alcohol, red meat, game, offal, alcohol, protein-rich plants such as peas, lentils and beans, and by drinking too little water. Amongst the other known triggers for gout attacks are illness, surgery and severely restricted diets.

WHICH PLANTS?

WARNING Use only one of the following at any given time.

INTERNAL USAGE
CELERY Liquid extract, 2 g dried seed equivalent, three times a day.
JUNIPER 10 g dried berries boiled in 750 ml of water for 20 minutes. Drink 3 cups of this decoction per day.
DEVIL'S CLAW Tablets, capsules, 1–2 g dried tuber equivalent, three times a day. For best results, choose a product standardised for its harpagoside content.

EXTERNAL APPLICATION
JUNIPER Make the decoction above, and add 100 ml to a warm bath.

Other measures
- Drink plenty of water – this helps to dilute the quantity of uric acid present in your urine.
- Do not drink alcohol, as it affects your body's ability to process uric acid.
- Go on a protein-free diet for at least one week, eliminating even vegetable proteins such as lentils and soy milk. Avoid offal at all times, as well as sardines, anchovies and herring.

See also Osteoarthritis, Rheumatoid arthritis

DID YOU KNOW?

Gout
A traditional remedy for gout was eating cherries. It has now been discovered that the consumption of 225 g of cherries a day (fresh or tinned) lowers levels of uric acid in the blood, which may well explain why they can be so effective in treating the disorder.

Osteoarthritis

Osteoarthritis is characterised by inflammation of and structural change to the cartilage that lines the ends of the joints – especially the hips, knees and spine. Over time – and usually in people aged over 60 – progressive destruction of the cartilage leads to degradation of the bone beneath the cartilage, and of the membrane containing synovial fluid that lubricates the joint. As a result, joints become painful and swollen, and their function declines.

Symptoms
- Pain in the joints during activity, relieved by rest
- Swelling and stiffness that gets worse over time
- Joint may be deformed, and range of motion may be reduced
- Where pain reduces use of the joint, weakness and shrinkage of surrounding muscles may occur

CONSULT YOUR DOCTOR OR MEDICAL HERBALIST
- A consultation with a doctor is required in order to diagnose osteoarthritis.
- Do not use herbal medicines until the diagnosis has been confirmed, as other diseases have similar symptoms but require different treatments.

A TO Z OF AILMENTS 259

MUSCLES, BONES & JOINTS

Causes

The natural wear and tear that occurs with age can lead to the development of osteoarthritis. An old joint fracture, a congenital joint deformity and damage to the cartilage may cause it earlier in life. Overweight people are more at risk, as are sports players and those whose work involves repetitive movement or the use of vibratory machinery.

WHICH PLANTS?

WARNING Use only one of the following at any given time.

INTERNAL USAGE

To treat inflammation and pain
DEVIL'S CLAW Tablets, capsules, 1–2 g dried tuber equivalent, three times a day. For best results choose a product standardised for its harpagoside content.
MEADOWSWEET Liquid extract, 2–5 g dried herb equivalent, three times a day.
CELERY Liquid extract, 2 g dried seed equivalent, three times a day.
JUNIPER 10 g dried berries boiled in 750 ml of water for 20 minutes. Drink 3 cups of this decoction per day.

EXTERNAL APPLICATION

CAYENNE Apply cayenne-based ointment to the affected area three to four times a day, as directed on the label.
DEVIL'S CLAW Apply a devil's claw–based cream or ointment twice a day as directed on the label.
GINGER Add 3 drops of essential oil to 10 ml of carrier oil and massage into affected area two or three times a day.
JUNIPER Add 3 drops of essential oil to 10 ml vegetable oil. Rub in two or three times a day.

Other measures

- Take regular gentle exercise that does not strain the joints, such as swimming. It will not worsen the disease, and may gradually reduce pain and stiffness.
- Support painful joints with a special bandage, available from the chemist or a sports shop.
- The nutritional supplements glucosamine and chondroitin supply the building blocks of cartilage, and may help to reduce the pain and progression of osteoarthritis.

See also Gout, Rheumatoid arthritis

Osteoporosis

The body's bone mass is at its peak at the age of 30. After the age of 45, it starts to decrease, three times faster in women than in men, particularly after menopause. The term 'osteoporosis' refers to the biological decalcification of the normal bony mass, accompanied by an increased risk of fractures, particularly of the hip, wrist and vertebrae, leading to arthritic pain and compression of the spinal column.

Symptoms

- Back pain and, less commonly, pain in the chest, hip, wrist and pelvic area
- Pain that is mechanical in nature, although it may appear spontaneously, or be caused by effort or trauma
- Loss of height (due to compression of the spinal column)
- Increased risk of fractures from falls

CONSULT YOUR DOCTOR OR MEDICAL HERBALIST

- Although osteoporosis is an extremely common feature of ageing, it may be prevented or its progress slowed if it is caught early enough. Your doctor can advise on measures to minimise bone loss.
- Do not embark on a course of self-treatment without consulting your doctor.

Causes

Osteoporosis occurs due to the physiological ageing of the bony mass (which reduces the volume of the bones by 40 per cent in a 20 year period). It develops more rapidly after menopause due to declining oestrogen levels, and may also be precipitated by long-term immobility of a limb.

Adequate levels of dietary calcium over the full course of life are essential for the maintenance of bone health into old age, and deficiency of calcium is a key contributory factor to the development of osteoporosis.

Other factors that increase the risk of developing osteoporosis include taking cortisone over a long period, Cushing's disease, hyperthyroidism, periods of anorexia or intense athletic activity in women (such as marathon running), and cancer. Smoking and heavy drinking also increase the risk.

WHICH PLANTS?

WARNING Use only one of the following at any given time.

INTERNAL USAGE

To treat inflammation and pain
DEVIL'S CLAW Tablets, capsules, 1–2 g dried tuber equivalent, three times a day. For best results choose a product standardised for its harpagoside content.
MEADOWSWEET Liquid extract, 2–5 g dried herb equivalent, three times a day.
WILLOW Tablets, capsules, up to 9 g dried herb equivalent per day, in divided doses.

260 NATURE'S MEDICINES

Other measures

- The best treatment for osteoporosis is prevention. Ensure everyone in the family eats calcium-rich foods on a daily basis. Those at risk should also consider taking a calcium supplement (choose one that also includes important co-factors, such as vitamin D, and the minerals magnesium and silica).
- Avoid inactivity: walk regularly, do a work-out, go swimming. Weight-bearing exercise throughout life is particularly important as it offers some protection against osteoporosis.
- Reduce alcohol and caffeine, and stop smoking.
- If you think you may be at risk of osteoporosis, discuss the possibility of bone density scanning with your GP.
- Amenorrhoea (an absence of menstrual periods) is associated with reduced oestrogen levels and increased risk of osteoporosis. If you are affected, work with your GP and medical herbalist to identify the cause and rectify any problems.

See also Ageing, Menopause

DID YOU KNOW?

Are you getting enough calcium?

Osteoporosis can largely be prevented by maintaining adequate calcium intake, and yet dietary surveys indicate that as many as 70 per cent of Australian women may consume less than the recommended daily amount.

Dairy foods are an easy way to maintain your calcium intake – if you eat just one tub of low-fat yoghurt every day, and have 300 ml of high-calcium milk on your breakfast cereal, you'll get most of the recommended daily intake. Non-dairy sources include hummus, tahini, tinned salmon and sardines, dried figs and almonds.

Rheumatoid arthritis

Rheumatoid arthritis is one of the most severe forms of arthritis. It is an auto-immune disease that affects the synovial membranes of the joints. Typically, the inflammation initially affects an individual joint of the hands, knees or feet, spreading over time to affect other joints, and may also affect many other organs.

Women are three times more likely to suffer from the condition than men, with symptoms usually appearing between the age of 25 and the peri-menopausal period.

Symptoms

- Tiredness and flulike symptoms may be the first signs of the disease
- Then joint symptoms develop, with intermittent or constant pain in the joint area
- Pain may be severe enough to disturb sleep and to drastically affect quality of life
- Joints are normally affected in a symmetrical pattern (e.g. both wrists)
- Stiffness and swelling of the affected joints, particularly after resting – consequently stiffness may be severe in the morning
- Joints become deformed as the condition progresses, and may be puffy, red and swollen. They may also fuse together, further restricting range of motion (this is termed ankylosis)
- Anaemia, fatigue, weight loss, poor appetite, fever and aching muscles are amongst other features of the disease. Other organs that may be affected include the eyes, lungs, heart, blood vessels, spleen, skin and lymphatic tissue

CONSULT YOUR DOCTOR OR MEDICAL HERBALIST

- Rheumatoid arthritis must be diagnosed by a doctor, who can talk to you about your treatment options.
- If you want to complement this with herbal remedies, consult your doctor or a medical herbalist, who will ensure there is no adverse reaction between the prescribed medication and the medicinal plants.

Causes

As with other auto-immune diseases, rheumatoid arthritis is caused by the body attacking part of its own tissue (in this case the synovial membrane), mistakenly thinking it is foreign, and culminating in severe damage to the joint tissue and tendons. It is not known why this occurs, but it can be triggered by a bacterial or viral infection in those who are susceptible. There is often a family history of auto-immune disease.

WHICH PLANTS?

WARNING Use only one of the following at any given time.

The treatment of rheumatoid arthritis combines prescribed medicines (often based on corticosteroids) with rest (to protect the joints) and physiotherapy (to prevent stiffening). Medicinal plants can complement this treatment.

INTERNAL USAGE

DEVIL'S CLAW Tablets, capsules, 1–2 g dried tuber equivalent, three times a day. For best results choose a product standardised for its harpagoside content.
MEADOWSWEET Liquid extract, 2–5 g dried herb equivalent, three times a day.
TURMERIC Capsules, standardised for curcuminoid content. Follow manufacturer's instructions up to 5 g a day.
WILLOW Tablets, capsules, up to 9 g dried herb equivalent per day, in divided doses.

MUSCLES, BONES & JOINTS

EXTERNAL APPLICATION
CAYENNE Apply cayenne-based ointment to the affected area three to four times a day, as directed on the label.
CINNAMON Apply cinnamon-based ointment to the affected area three to four times a day, as directed on the label.
GINGER Add 3 drops of essential oil to 10 ml of carrier oil. Massage into the affected area two or three times a day.
JUNIPER Add 3 drops of essential oil to 10 ml vegetable oil. Rub in two or three times a day.

Other measures
- Avoid unnecessary fatigue.
- Acupuncture may help to relieve the symptoms.
- Nutritional supplements that may support the bony tissue include vitamin B and the minerals copper, manganese, silica and sulphur.
- Eat oily fish from cold regions, which are rich in anti-inflammatory essential fatty acids and have a beneficial effect on arthritis. Fish oil supplements are also available, and may offer some benefit.
- Try to maintain your weight within the normal range to reduce pressure on your musculoskeletal system.
- Regular exercise when the joints are not acutely inflamed will help to maintain the strength of the muscles around the joints. Swimming is ideal as it is not weight-bearing.

See also Gout, Osteoarthritis

Sprains

A sprain is an injury to the ligaments that hold together the bone ends of the joint. In a mild sprain, these are stretched, and in more severe cases they are torn. Sprains cause painful swelling around the joint, which cannot be moved without considerable discomfort.

Symptoms
- Sharp pain at the moment of trauma, followed by intense pain over at least 24 hours
- Swelling of the joint
- Bruising
- Restricted mobility of the joint

CONSULT YOUR DOCTOR OR MEDICAL HERBALIST
- Early attention is important in order to ensure a rapid cure. If joint movement is very painful for more than 18 hours, consult a doctor, who can X-ray the joint to make sure there is no fracture.
- A benign sprain can be treated simply by rest and topical creams or ointments. In more serious cases, the joint may need the support of a splint or plaster.

Causes
Sprains are usually caused by sudden, excessive force on a joint, such as tripping and twisting an ankle or wrist as the body's full weight falls on the joint. In elderly people, unsteadiness or weakness in the ligaments may lead to this kind of trauma.

WHICH PLANTS?

WARNING Use only one of the following at any given time.

Taken homoeopathically, arnica is excellent for this type of trauma. Ask your medical herbalist for more information.

INTERNAL USAGE
DEVIL'S CLAW Tablets, capsules, 1–2 g dried tuber equivalent, three times a day. For best results choose a product standardised for its harpagoside content.
WILLOW Tablets, capsules, up to 9 g dried herb equivalent per day, in divided doses.

EXTERNAL APPLICATION
ARNICA Gently massage arnica cream or gel into the affected area two or three times a day.
ROSEMARY Add 3 drops of essential oil to 10 ml vegetable oil. Rub in two or three times a day.

Other measures
- Rest the affected joint in a supported position while acutely painful, but try to exercise it as soon as possible, since this increases the speed and strength of healing.
- If an ankle is affected, wear supportive shoes with laces.
- Apply cold compresses.
- Consider laser treatment or physiotherapy if healing is slow, or the range of motion remains restricted.

DID YOU KNOW?

Sprains
Arnica has been used in ointments to treat sprains and bruises for hundreds of years. One early proponent was the 12th-century German saint Hildegard of Bingen, who wrote treatises on medicinal plants. Nowadays, arnica is sometimes used by plastic surgeons to help reduce postoperative pain and swelling.

Tendonitis

Tendons are the connective tissues that transmit the mechanical effort of the muscles to the bones. Tendonitis is an inflammation of the sheaths of the tendons. It can be traumatic or rheumatic in origin and can last between a week and six months.

Symptoms
- Intense joint pain, usually in the arm or leg
- Limited movement
- Extension of pain to the entire limb
- Waking in pain during the night

CONSULT YOUR DOCTOR
Only your doctor can diagnose tendonitis, which can be confused with other conditions with similar symptoms.

Causes
Inflammation of the tendons may occur after overexertion, or as a result of a pulled tendon. It can also be linked to muscle fatigue caused by repetitive tasks at work, unaccustomed movement or intense athletic training. Sometimes, no causative reason for the inflammation can be determined.

WHICH PLANTS?

WARNING Use only one of the following at any given time.

INTERNAL USAGE
To treat inflammation and pain
FEVERFEW Tablets, capsules, 50–200 mg dried herb equivalent, standardised to contain 200–600 mcg parthenolide per daily dose.
WILLOW Tablets, capsules, up to 9 g dried herb equivalent per day, in divided doses.
TURMERIC Capsules, standardised for curcuminoid content. Follow manufacturer's instructions up to 5 g a day.
DEVIL'S CLAW Tablets, capsules, 1–2 g dried tuber equivalent, three times a day. For best results choose a product standardised for its harpagoside content.

EXTERNAL APPLICATION
CAYENNE Apply cayenne-based ointment to the affected area three to four times a day, as directed on the label.
CINNAMON Apply cinnamon-based ointment to the affected area three to four times a day, as directed on the label.
NUTMEG Add 3 drops of essential oil to 50 ml carrier oil. Apply one to three times a day or use in one bath a day.

Other measures
- At the first sign of tendonitis, stop using the affected limb.
- Place an ice pack on the affected joint.
- Use a strong support bandage on the affected joint.
- Other effective therapies include laser treatment and manipulation.
- After healing, try to strengthen the affected muscles, perhaps at a gym or with physiotherapy.

NERVOUS SYSTEM & MENTAL HEALTH

Alzheimer's disease

A disease that attacks the cells, nerves and transmitters in the brain, Alzheimer's is the most common form of dementia. Most patients are over the age of 65. The disease is often accompanied by a reduction in the flow of blood to the brain, and as this happens at different rates from one individual to another, the rate of memory loss varies between individuals.

Symptoms
- Impairment of short-term memory
- Loss of a sense of time
- Depression, anxiety
- Mood swings
- Difficulty in processing information, leading to confusion

CONSULT YOUR DOCTOR OR MEDICAL HERBALIST
- It is vital that you consult a doctor if you experience short-term memory difficulties, and if there is a history of Alzheimer's disease within your family.

Causes
The causes of Alzheimer's disease are still little understood. Age is the greatest risk factor, followed by a genetic predisposition. It is now believed that the disease develops due to a combination of reduced levels of the neurotransmitter acetylcholine and the death of brain cells.

Factors that have been linked to Alzheimer's disease include repeated strokes, dietary deficiency of fatty acids, stress and a lack of oestrogen. People who smoke and those who have high blood pressure or high cholesterol levels are at increased risk of developing Alzheimer's disease.

NERVOUS SYSTEM & MENTAL HEALTH

WHICH PLANTS?

WARNING Use only one of the following at any given time.

Certain herbs may help to slow down or prevent the onset of Alzheimer's disease, improve the circulation, and alleviate the mood swings, anxiety and sleep problems experienced by sufferers of the disease.

INTERNAL USAGE

As a preventive treatment
SAGE 20 g dried leaves infused in 1 litre of boiling water for 10 minutes before straining. Drink 1–2 cups a day.

To improve memory, blood circulation and mental well-being
GINKGO Tablets, up to 2 g, standardised for ginkgo flavone glycosides, and ginkgolides and bilobalide. Take up to three times a day. (See Cautions, p. 102.)
SCHISANDRA Liquid extract, tablets, 500 mg–1.5 g dried fruit equivalent, three times a day.
BRAHMI Tablets, capsules, up to 6 g per day, according to manufacturer's instructions.

To reduce anxiety
LEMON BALM Liquid extract, 500 mg–1 g dried leaf equivalent, before meals three times a day.
PASSIONFLOWER Liquid extract, 500 mg–1 g dried herb equivalent, twice during the day and at bedtime.
CALIFORNIAN POPPY Liquid extract, 1–2 g dried herb equivalent, twice during the day and at bedtime.

Other measures

- Eat a balanced diet, making sure you include plenty of oily fish and cold-pressed vegetable oils, such as extra virgin olive oil, as well as fresh vegetables and fruit.
- Take vitamins A, C and E, as well as zinc and selenium.
- Take regular exercise.
- Exercise your memory: play card games, recite poems and talk to others about events from your past.

See also Ageing, Memory

Anxiety

Anxiety is a state of fear usually arising from a particular cause or threat, even if the reason for the perceived threat is not obvious to the sufferer. It is accompanied by a feeling of unease that can include physical symptoms and may vary in intensity from slight anxiety to terror, and can be acute or chronic.

Panic disorder is a state that occurs when anxiety becomes so acute and intense that it paralyses the sufferer. Panic attacks are recurrent, unpredictable anxiety attacks that are of short duration but very intense, occurring among people who would otherwise not necessarily feel as anxious in the same circumstances. Anxiety also takes the form of phobias, such as agoraphobia and claustrophobia. Phobias are an intense fear of, and attempt to avoid, certain objects or specific situations. Obsessive-compulsive disorders, withdrawal syndrome, psychoses and mental disorders also accompany anxiety, varying from slight to very intense.

Symptoms

- Sweating
- Desire to urinate and defecate
- Sensation of suffocation
- Palpitations
- Dry mouth or copious amounts of saliva
- Feeling hot or cold
- Pain
- Dizziness
- Insomnia
- Tremor or tics
- Desire to escape
- Anxious thoughts
- In the most serious cases, a feeling of utter helplessness and inability to perform normal everyday activities

CONSULT YOUR DOCTOR
- If the symptoms are severe or long term it is essential to consult a doctor to confirm that they are a result of anxiety and to determine its origin.

Causes

Anxiety is frequently linked to a psychological or emotional problem. It can be caused by an emotional conflict, a feeling of insecurity or stress, or can indicate depression. It can also be a sign of serious mental illness.

WHICH PLANTS?

WARNING Use only one of the following at any given time.

Medical herbalism can be used to treat moderate anxiety, when insomnia, palpitations and slight dizziness are the most common symptoms.

INTERNAL USAGE
LAVENDER 2–3 g dried flowers infused in 1 cup of boiling water for 5–10 minutes. Drink 3–4 cups a day between meals.
LEMON BALM Liquid extract, 500 mg–1 g dried leaf equivalent, before meals three times a day.

264 NATURE'S MEDICINES

Lime flowers Infuse 2–4 g of dried flowers in 1 cup of boiling water for 5 minutes before straining. Drink 1 cup twice a day and another in the evening.
Passionflower Liquid extract, 500 mg–1 g dried herb equivalent, twice during the day and at bedtime.
Valerian Tablets, up to 2 g dried herb equivalent, take up to three times a day.
St John's wort Tablets, 1.8 g dried flowering herb equivalent, standardised for hypericin content, take three times a day or as professionally prescribed. St John's wort is known to interact with a large number of pharmaceutical medications and should be used only under professional supervision. (See Cautions, p. 168.)

Other measures
- Talk to your GP about seeing a psychotherapist or clinical psychologist.
- Take regular physical exercise and take up relaxation exercises, such as yoga.
- Consult an acupuncturist.

See also Depression, Stress

Depression

Sadness, pessimism, reduced self-esteem and lack of interest are among the symptoms of depression. It is considered a serious mental condition if it persists without obvious cause, or intensifies and affects behaviour, becoming itself a symptom of a psychiatric illness.

Symptoms
- Feeling sad and tired
- Crying at inappropriate times
- Difficulty in concentrating, and in forming and carrying out plans and ideas (low motivation)
- Self-criticism, lack of self-esteem, even self-loathing
- Lack of appetite and spirit and inability to take pleasure in life
- Weight fluctuation
- Insomnia, particularly waking up frequently during the small hours of the night, or alternatively sleeping to excess
- Thoughts of death or suicide

CONSULT YOUR DOCTOR
- For people with a history of psychological fragility, getting over a disappointment or an emotional setback can lead to depression.
- If prescribed a chemical or herbal antidepressant, do not discontinue it suddenly without medical advice. For some medications, a period of gradual withdrawal will be advised.

Causes
Depression can affect people who have experienced great emotional loss, such as the death of someone close, a disappointment in love or a social problem. However, there may be no single obvious cause.

Depression can occasionally be triggered by viral illnesses, disorders such as hypothyroidism or by hormonal changes after childbirth. Some people also suffer from Seasonal Affective Disorder (SAD), triggered by the darkness of winter.

As an illness, it is more common where there is a history of depression within the family.

WHICH PLANTS?

WARNING Use only one of the following at any given time.

Depression is not suitable for self-treatment. Always consult your doctor or medical herbalist before taking any of these plants.

Internal usage
St John's wort Tablets, 1.8 g dried flowering herb equivalent, standardised for hypericin content, take three times a day or as professionally prescribed. St John's wort is known to interact with a large number of pharmaceutical medications and should be used only under professional supervision. (See Cautions, p. 168.)
Damiana Liquid extract, 1–2 g dried herb equivalent, three times a day.
Californian poppy Liquid extract, 1–2 g dried herb equivalent, twice during the day and at bedtime.
Lavender 2–3 g dried flowers infused in 1 cup of boiling water for 5–10 minutes. Drink 1 cup at bedtime.

Other measures
- Take a trace element treatment containing magnesium and potassium.
- Consult your GP, a trained counsellor, clinical psychologist or psychotherapist.
- Take some rest; if possible, go away on holiday.
- Maintain an exercise program, which stimulates production of endorphins that raise mood.

See also Anxiety, Stress

NERVOUS SYSTEM & MENTAL HEALTH

Insomnia

The term 'insomnia' encompasses a range of problems that affect sleep. Most people experience it at some time in their life, but as sleeping patterns differ from one individual to another, its symptoms vary and tend to be characterised by the discomfort suffered as a result of not being able to fall asleep or stay asleep.

Symptoms
- Difficulty in getting to sleep or staying asleep
- Premature wakening with a feeling of sleep deprivation
- Night-time wakefulness at the slightest external stimulus, and prolonged nocturnal wakefulness
- Daytime tiredness, possibly accompanied by a strong desire for sleep

CONSULT YOUR DOCTOR
- If insomnia persists for any length of time, consult your doctor.

Causes
Insomnia is commonly due to a state of stress, psychological tension, anxiety and various fears, including the fear of sleep. It often accompanies the onset of depression, but it can also be caused by ailments such as atherosclerosis, Alzheimer's disease or digestive or respiratory problems. Overuse of coffee, tea, tobacco or even vitamin C can also contribute to insomnia.

WHICH PLANTS?

WARNING Use only one of the following at any given time.

INTERNAL USAGE
CALIFORNIAN POPPY Liquid extract, 1–2 g dried herb equivalent, twice during the day and at bedtime.
HOPS 1–2 teaspoons fresh or dried hops infused in 1 cup of boiling water for 10 minutes. Alternatively, 10 g dried flowers infused in 1 litre of boiling water for 10 minutes before straining. Drink 1 cup just before bedtime.
LAVENDER 2–3 g dried flowers infused in 1 cup of boiling water for 5–10 minutes. Drink 3–4 cups a day between meals.
LEMON BALM Liquid extract, 500 mg–1 g dried leaf equivalent, before meals three times a day.
LIME FLOWERS Infuse 2–4 g of dried flowers in 1 cup of boiling water for 5 minutes, before straining. Drink 1 cup twice a day and another in the evening.
PASSIONFLOWER Liquid extract, 500 mg–1 g dried herb equivalent, twice during the day and at bedtime.
VALERIAN Tablets, up to 2 g dried herb equivalent, take one dose an hour before bed.

Other measures
- Try relaxing exercises such as yoga.
- Take trace elements, notably magnesium.
- Make a point of going for a walk every evening, but avoid stimulating physical or mental exercise just before retiring.
- Try to go to bed and get up at the same time every day, including weekends. If you need to be up at a certain time, avoid anxiety about oversleeping by using an alarm clock.
- If you cannot get to sleep, get out of bed and sit in a chair to read, returning to bed again only when you feel sleepy – this avoids the brain associating the bed with wakefulness.
- Self-hypnosis can help to break the cycle of repetitive thoughts. Imagine yourself in a room or garden that you know intimately. Walk very slowly around it in your mind, carefully noticing and examining the details of everything that is in it.
- Don't use day-time naps to catch up on sleep.

See also Anxiety, Stress

Migraine

The main symptom of migraine is a severe headache, often accompanied by nausea or vomiting. A migraine can last from four hours to three days. The disorder generally starts around puberty and diminishes by middle age. Migraines are often related to menstrual periods or to specific foods. The condition affects more women than men.

Symptoms
- Sharp, debilitating headache, felt on one side of the head or face, or all over the head, and described as throbbing
- Nausea and vomiting
- Strong aversion to bright light or loud noise
- About 60 per cent of sufferers experience some symptoms in the hours or days before the headache occurs (this is called a 'prodrome'). These symptoms may include mood alterations, sensitivity to light or smells, fatigue, gastrointestinal disturbance and increased thirst
- The term 'aura' is used to describe visual disturbances (such as flashes of light) that may be experienced in the 20 minutes immediately before the migraine (these occur in about one in five cases)
- Many patients also experience symptoms after the headache has passed. These may range from fatigue and irritability to euphoria

CONSULT YOUR DOCTOR
- If you experience the symptoms above, consult your doctor who can arrange the necessary investigations to determine the cause, and rule out other causes.
- If you have more than three or four attacks in a month, you may need long-term medical treatment.
- If your headache was caused by an injury or trauma to the head.

NERVOUS SYSTEM & MENTAL HEALTH

- If your headache is accompanied by a rash, fever, stiff neck or numbness of a limb.
- If the headache has different characteristics to your normal symptoms, and especially if it is more severe than normal.
- If the headache is very severe, and comes on extremely quickly (under 5 minutes).

Causes

Most migraines occur for no apparent reason. The condition can run in families, and may be related to blood flow in the brain and/or abnormalities in serotonin metabolism. Sufferers can often pinpoint trigger factors. Some foods, for example, can set off a migraine. The four 'Cs' – citrus, cheese, chocolate and coffee – as well as red wine, peanuts and fried food are all known to be common culprits.

Other causes include bright lights, loud noises, a change in the weather, stress, tiredness and hormonal changes. An attack is more likely just before the menstrual period, or when the sufferer is relaxing after a stressful day. Natural therapists associate migraines with liver dysfunction, and consequently your medical herbalist may recommend a detoxification program as part of your treatment plan (see Detoxification, p 229).

WHICH PLANTS?

WARNING Use only one of the following at any given time.

Herbs can help to prevent migraines, but once a migraine has begun, it will run its course.

INTERNAL USAGE
For long-term preventive treatment
FEVERFEW Tablets, capsules, 50–200 mg dried herb equivalent, standardised to contain 200–600 mcg parthenolide per daily dose.

For migraines that accompany the onset of periods
CHASTE TREE Tablets, capsules, up to 1 g dried fruit equivalent, three times a day, or according to manufacturer's instructions.

Other measures

- Follow a balanced diet, avoiding known trigger foods.
- Practise relaxation exercises.
- Drink lots of water, especially before, during and after exercise.

See also Tension headache

DID YOU KNOW?

Migraine
Analgesics (pain-killers) are best taken at the onset of a migraine headache. Once the migraine attack has taken hold, it tends to be resistant to all forms of pain-killing medication.

Neuralgia

Pain associated with a nerve, whatever the cause, is known as neuralgia. Related conditions include neuritis – the inflammation of a nerve, and polyneuritis – the inflammation of several nerves.

Symptoms

- Sharp, shooting pain along the path of the affected nerve. For example, sciatic pain tends to shoot down the back of the leg
- Reduced sensitivity and abnormal sensations
- Heightened sensitivity to touch and other stimuli, sometimes to the point of pain
- Paralysis of one or a group of motor nerves
- In cold weather, facial nerve pain

CONSULT YOUR DOCTOR
- The symptoms of neuralgia or neuritis require immediate medical attention. Treatment is often difficult and needs regular medical supervision.

Causes

The main causes of neuralgia, neuritis and polyneuritis are injury to the nerve, nerve abnormality or infections, especially by viruses. Postural and structural changes can also cause neuralgia by causing pressure on the nerve.

They can also be exacerbated by toxic substances, such as tobacco and alcohol, by certain types of medication (especially those used in the treatment of HIV) and by conditions such as diabetes and uraemia (an accumulation of waste products in the blood).

WHICH PLANTS?

WARNING Use only one of the following at any given time.

EXTERNAL APPLICATION
NUTMEG Add 3 drops of essential oil to 50 ml carrier oil. Apply once to three times a day, or add some diluted oil to a warm bath.
CAYENNE Apply cayenne-based ointment to the affected area three to four times a day, as directed on the label.
ST JOHN'S WORT Apply St John's wort cream or oil to the affected area three to four times a day, as directed on the label.

Other measures

- Consult an osteopath, chiropractor or acupuncturist.

See also Back pain

A TO Z OF AILMENTS 267

NERVOUS SYSTEM & MENTAL HEALTH

Psychosomatic disorders

The repeated manifestation of physical symptoms that seem to have been caused, or worsened, by psychological factors such as anxiety or stress are called psychosomatic disorders (sometimes 'somatic disorders').

Symptoms
- Headache, especially at the top of the skull
- A dry mouth or overproduction of saliva
- Visual disorders
- Nausea, belching, bloated stomach
- Flatulence, abdominal swelling in the region of the hypochondrium (upper abdomen, below the ribs)
- Tachycardia (palpitations)
- A throbbing sensation in the carotid arteries that supply blood to the head and neck
- Twinges of pain in the side
- Isolated instances of diarrhoea
- Yawning, fatigue
- Frequent but sparse urination
- A feeling of feverishness, burning ears
- Sudden hypotension (low blood pressure), accompanied by feelings of malaise (sweating, buzzing in the ears, clouded vision)
- Tearfulness and emotional disorders

CONSULT YOUR DOCTOR
- If one of these apparently ordinary symptoms is repeated, consult your doctor. He or she will be able to determine whether the cause is psychosomatic or related to a more serious condition.

Causes
Certain minor nervous disorders and some forms of annoyance or slight anxiety can trigger physical symptoms. Psychosomatic disorders may also be symptomatic of depression.

WHICH PLANTS?

WARNING Use only one of the following at any given time.

INTERNAL USAGE
To support the nervous system
CHAMOMILE 1 sachet of chamomile flowers infused in 1 cup of boiling water for 5–10 minutes. Drink 3 cups a day before meals.
LAVENDER 2–3 g dried flowers infused in 1 cup of boiling water for 5–10 minutes. Drink 3–4 cups a day between meals.
DAMIANA Liquid extract, 1–2 g dried herb equivalent, three times a day.
OATS Liquid extract, 1–4 g dried herb equivalent, two or three times a day.

Other measures
- Maintain a regular exercise routine and practise yoga or some other relaxation exercises.
- Take trace elements, especially magnesium, manganese and potassium.
- Discuss with your GP the idea of seeing a clinical psychologist or psychiatrist to try to establish the cause of the disorder, and alleviate the symptoms.

See also Anxiety, Depression, Fibromyalgia, Stress

Stress

People experience stress in response to a variety of mental, physical and emotional triggers, which vary from one person to the next.

Prolonged stress can lead to the development of secondary health problems.

Symptoms
- Anxiety, irritability, quick temper
- Fatigue
- Difficulty in sleeping
- Emotional upset and weepiness
- Shaking, palpitations and vertigo
- Poor memory, distraction, difficulty in finding words
- Recurrent infections
- An aggravation of diabetes, premature ageing, arrhythmia and other heart problems
- Weight gain or weight loss may also occur, depending on the individual's constitution

CONSULT YOUR DOCTOR OR MEDICAL HERBALIST
- Most people recover from short-term stress relatively quickly. However, if you are under chronic stress, or if your stress is causing mental or physical symptoms, it should be recognised and addressed as soon as possible.
- A person suffering from stress should not take too many stimulants but, rather, some form of medication that enables the body to adapt to stress.

Causes
There are many different causes of stress: excessive or extended effort without rest almost automatically leads to physical stress, as does working under unpleasant conditions. Similarly, family worries, money difficulties or the death of a loved one lead to mental stress.

Prolonged stress weakens the immune system and may be responsible for persistent or recurrent infections. It may also increase your risk of developing serious conditions such as heart disease.

NERVOUS SYSTEM & MENTAL HEALTH

WHICH PLANTS?

WARNING Use only one of the following at any given time.

INTERNAL USAGE
To improve energy, stamina and endurance under stress
KOREAN GINSENG Tablets, capsules, 250–500 mg dried root equivalent, twice daily. Take one dose in the morning and one dose around midday. Choose a product standardised for its ginsenosides content. (See Cautions, p. 125.)
SIBERIAN GINSENG Tablets, capsules, 300 mg–1 g dried root equivalent, three times a day.
DAMIANA Liquid extract, 1–2 g dried herb equivalent, three times a day.
CODONOPSIS Liquid extract, 750 mg–1.5 g dried root equivalent, three times a day.

To support the nervous system and adrenal glands
OATS Liquid extract, 1–4 g dried herb equivalent, two or three times a day.
LICORICE 1–2 teaspoons root powder steeped in 1 cup of boiling water for 10 minutes before straining. Drink 2–3 cups a day for a period of no more than four to six weeks.

To boost the immune system
ECHINACEA Liquid extract, 1 g dried root equivalent, three times a day.
ELDER Liquid extract, 500 mg–1 g dried flower equivalent, three times a day.

Other measures
- Take plenty of rest, interspersed with regular, moderate exercise (such as walking).
- Practise yoga, deep-breathing exercises or tai chi.
- Eat a balanced, nutritious diet, with plenty of fresh fruit and vegetables, nuts and seeds and lean sources of protein.
- Avoid caffeine, alcohol, recreational drug use and sugary and fatty foods.
- Nutritional supplements that have been associated with improved ability to handle stress include magnesium, potassium and the B group vitamins

See also Anxiety, Depression, Insomnia, Tension headache

Tension headache

Tension headaches are the most common form of headache. They usually commence around middle age.

Symptoms
- Headache is described as feeling like a tight band around the head and/or neck
- May be mild, severe or intermittent
- The onset of the headache is late in the day
- Duration of symptoms varies from a few minutes to constant pain that may persist for as long as a few years
- Stress may also be present. This type of headache occurs more commonly in people who are depressed or anxious
- Sleeping difficulties may occur – the headache may be strong enough to stop you falling asleep, but is not normally strong enough to wake you

CONSULT YOUR DOCTOR
- Talk to your doctor about your headaches – he or she will arrange the necessary investigations to determine their cause. These may include food allergy tests, eye tests and an examination of your sinuses.
- If your headache was caused by an injury or trauma to the head.
- If your headache is accompanied by a rash, fever, stiff neck, visual changes or numbness of a limb.
- If your headache has different characteristics to your normal symptoms, and especially if it is more severe than normal.
- If your headache is very severe, and comes on extremely quickly (under 5 minutes).

Causes
The causes of tension headache have not been determined. Triggers that have been identified include grinding the teeth, excessive caffeine, noise pollution, eyestrain and poor posture. The nature of the pain indicates that muscular tension is at least partly to blame.

WHICH PLANTS?

WARNING Use only one of the following at any given time.

INTERNAL USAGE
To relieve muscular tension
CRAMP BARK Liquid extract, 500 mg–1 g dried bark equivalent, three times a day.
VALERIAN Tablets, up to 2 g dried herb equivalent, take up to three times a day.

To support the nervous system
OATS Liquid extract, 1–4 g dried herb equivalent, two or three times a day.
PASSIONFLOWER Liquid extract, 500 mg–1 g dried herb equivalent, twice during the day and at bedtime.

A TO Z OF AILMENTS

NERVOUS SYSTEM & MENTAL HEALTH

EXTERNAL APPLICATION
CINNAMON Apply cinnamon-based ointment to the shoulders, neck and base of the skull, three to four times a day, as directed on the label.

Other measures

- Try keeping a symptom diary to help you identify what may be triggering your headaches.
- Maintain a regular exercise program, which should include both aerobic nd relaxation exercises, such as tai chi or yoga.
- Take a magnesium supplement, which may assist with stress-coping mechanisms and muscular stress. A vitamin B complex supplement may also offer some assistance.

See also Migraine, Stress

Vertigo

The term 'vertigo' describes the sensation of objects whirling around you horizontally or vertically. Vertigo is caused by a problem in the inner ear, which controls balance. Vertigo may clear up on its own without treatment, but it can also be symptomatic of other more serious conditions, such as multiple sclerosis.

Symptoms

- Unsteadiness, especially on turning the head suddenly, lifting it from the pillow, or bending it back to look upwards – this sensation generally passes within a minute or two
- Nausea, vomiting
- Falling to the ground
- Whistling in the ears together with impaired hearing
- Eyes may move from side to side

CONSULT YOUR DOCTOR

- If vertigo continues, consult your doctor, who will determine the cause and prescribe an appropriate treatment to prevent complications, such as permanent deafness.

Causes

Vertigo can be triggered by infections, such as influenza or ear infections. Diseases such as Ménière's disease and atherosclerosis may also cause vertigo. It can be the result of taking certain medications, or it can simply arise while watching a film with exaggerated special effects, or when taking a spinning amusement park ride.

WHICH PLANTS?

WARNING Use only one of the following at any given time.

Consult a medical herbalist, who will be able to advise you as to the best course of treatment for your particular symptoms. Where poor circulation is a contributory factor, these herbs may be useful.

INTERNAL USAGE
GINKGO Tablets, up to 2 g, standardised for ginkgo flavone glycosides, and ginkgolides and bilobalide. Take up to three times a day. (See Cautions, p. 102.)

Other measures

- If an attack of vertigo occurs suddenly, as a result of an infection, it should be treated with bed rest and appropriate medication.
- If it persists for several days, walk as much as you can to allow the body to adjust and cope with the condition.
- If your vertigo is position-related, your doctor may recommend that you see a physiotherapist, chiropractor or osteopath.

REPRODUCTION & SEXUALITY

Breast disorders

Breast pain or lumps are associated with various anomalies in the structure of the breast – usually benign. Disorders include cysts (tumours which contain fluid), zones of fibrous tissue and glandular nodules.

Breast problems often affect women between the ages of 40 and 50, and can increase in severity just before the onset of menopause, following which they lessen. Breast pain is one of the most common symptoms of PMS.

Symptoms

- Breasts may be swollen, tender, hard, painful
- Many small bumps and easily movable lumps may be felt beneath the surface of the breast
- Breast lumps may or may not fluctuate with the menstrual cycle
- These symptoms warrant immediate medical attention as they may indicate breast cancer: breasts may appear dimpled (like orange peel) or indented when the arms are held above the head; nipples may become inverted or retracted; discharge or bleeding from the nipples

CONSULT YOUR DOCTOR

- Any lump, whether painful or not, should be assessed by your GP. A biopsy may be required to determine whether or not it is benign.
- Bleeding or discharge from the breast, changes to the contour of the breast (e.g. dimpling, retracted nipple, indentation) or the new development of eczema around the nipple all warrant immediate medical attention.
- If breast pain is disabling, consult your doctor.
- Many breast complaints are related to problems with the cervical and dorsal vertebrae. In such cases, you should consult a physiotherapist or an osteopath.

Causes

Breast pain or lumps can be caused by several factors – they can be due to overproduction of oestrogen (and other hormonal imbalances), circulatory problems, cancerous growths or psychological factors. Hormonal and emotional balances are closely linked, and stress can exacerbate the problem.

Breast tenderness is a common occurrence in pregnancy, and as a side effect of the oral contraceptive pill.

WHICH PLANTS?

WARNING Use only one of the following at any given time.

INTERNAL USAGE
For benign, premenstrual breast tenderness
EVENING PRIMROSE OIL Capsules, 1000 mg, three times a day with meals during the last 10 days of the cycle.
CHASTE TREE Liquid extract, 500 mg–1 g dried fruit equivalent in a little cold water every morning, for up to six months. Effects may not be apparent for three months.

Other measures

- The vast majority of breast disorders are benign, but it is important to perform regular breast checks so that if more serious disease does develop it is detected and treated quickly. our doctor can teach you the techniques required to perform an efficient self-examination.
- Have regular mammograms, especially: if you or other women in your family have a history of breast cancer; if you have never had a baby; if you have used oestrogen therapy (the oral contraceptive pill or hormone replacement therapy) for long periods of time; or if you started your periods early or finished them late (first period before age 12, last period after 55 years old).
- Give up smoking.

See also Premenstrual syndrome

DID YOU KNOW?

Mastitis & breast pain

The breasts represent an important part of a woman's self image and sexuality. Although pain is a common symptom of a breast disorder, there is often no relation between the intensity of the pain and the gravity of the illness. Breast cancer is often not very painful. However, fear of breast cancer can give rise to pains in the breasts.

Breastfeeding problems

Problems with breastfeeding can be caused by lack of milk, the appearance of cracks in the nipple, engorgement of the breast, mastitis (inflammation of the lymphatic vessels in the breast) or by an abscess.

Symptoms

- Lack of milk – the baby cries abnormally and does not put on weight
- Lesions on the nipple, ranging from fine to more severe cracks
- Engorged, swollen, hard and painful breasts
- Mastitis – the breast is taut, hot, painful and has a mottled appearance
- Breast abscess – mother's temperature rises, milk and pus leak from the nipple and an abscess forms

---

REPRODUCTION & SEXUALITY

CONSULT YOUR DOCTOR
- It is imperative that a doctor is consulted if you have a temperature, sharp pain or pus from the nipple.
- In the case of mastitis, a course of anti-inflammatory drugs may be prescribed for the first 24 hours, but usually not antibiotics.
- For an abscess, antibiotics and anti-inflammatories will often be prescribed.
- If you are having difficulty feeding, ask your doctor to refer you to a lactation consultant.

Causes

Lack of milk can be linked to emotional causes. Cracked nipples can be caused by the baby failing to suck in the correct position, poor hygiene or by nipples that are too short or concave in shape. Engorgement of the breast usually indicates difficulty with the milk flow rather than an overfull breast. Mastitis is the result of an inflammation of the lymphatic mammary vessels due to the presence of bacteria infecting the breast, either via the nipple or the areola, or via blood from another infection in the body. An abscess develops if inflammation of a milk duct or cracked nipples remains untreated.

WHICH PLANTS?

WARNING Use only one of the following at any given time.

It is advisable to seek advice from a professional herbalist or a doctor before starting treatment.

INTERNAL USAGE
To improve milk flow
ANISE Liquid extract, 500 mg–1 g dried seed equivalent, three times a day.
CUMIN Infuse 1 teaspoon of seeds in 250 ml of boiling water for 2–3 minutes. Drink ½ cup before main meals.

A TO Z OF AILMENTS 271

REPRODUCTION & SEXUALITY

As advised by a medical herbalist
- Fenugreek

EXTERNAL APPLICATION
For cracked nipples
CALENDULA Infuse 5 g dried flower heads in 1 litre boiling water for 5 minutes. Cool, strain and apply to the affected area as a compress three times a day.

Other measures

- To prevent cracked nipples, draw out the nipples during pregnancy to prepare them for breastfeeding. During the ninth month of pregnancy, smear a thick coating of petroleum jelly (40 g) and lanolin (40 g) on the nipples three times a week.
- For effective feeding, ensure you are comfortable, and position the baby so that it takes the entire areola into its mouth.
- Wash the nipples carefully with clean, boiled water.
- Wash your hands before and after each feed. Dry the areola with a clean pad or warm air.
- Insert a soft pad in your bra.

Endometriosis

The uterus is a hollow organ lined with endometrial tissue, which undergoes changes during the menstrual cycle and, unless conception takes place, is shed during the monthly menstruation. In endometriosis, deposits (or cysts) of endometrial tissue are found in abnormal locations. The most common sites for the cysts to be located are on the surface of the Fallopian tubes, uterus and uterine ligaments, pelvic cavity, or intestines or within the Fallopian tubes. The presence of an endometrial cyst may cause damage or displacement to the organ it rests on, leading to dysfunction and pain.

Although endometriosis is considered to be the reason for as many as one in four cases of female infertility, it is also important to note that not all women with endometriosis will be infertile.

Symptoms

- Severe menstrual pain, starting just before the period commences, and resolving after menstruation
- Heavy menstrual bleeding, with clots. Bleeding may also occur between periods
- Anaemia due to heavy blood loss
- Lower back pain, pelvic congestion and pain may also occur during sexual intercourse and defecation
- Diarrhoea and constipation may occur
- The type of pain and dysfunction depends on the location of the cysts and the displacement and dysfunction of the organs they have adhered to
- Infertility may occur. Sometimes the disease is completely asymptomatic and is not suspected until investigations are performed to determine the cause of infertility
- Symptoms usually disappear after menopause and during pregnancy

CONSULT YOUR DOCTOR
- In cases of intense pain, severe bleeding or infertility, consult your GP.
- Although symptoms such as those listed above may cause a diagnosis of endometriosis to be suspected, the only way it can be confirmed is by laparoscopy.

Causes

The origin of endometriosis is unknown, but a number of theories have been proposed. For example, endometriosis may be the result of a menstrual dysfunction called retrograde menstruation, in which blood and endometrium tissue move back up into the Fallopian tubes and abdominal cavity instead of flowing down to the vagina for excretion. It is unclear whether this is due to a structural defect of the uterus, or is caused by uterine contractions when expelling the uterine tissue. Not all women with retrograde menstruation have endometriosis.

Other factors that have been identified include genetic factors (daughters of women with endometriosis have roughly a 50 per cent chance of developing it themselves) and hormonal issues, in particular the production of oestrogens. The daughters of women who were prescribed Stilboestrol® (synthetic oestrogen) during pregnancy are predisposed to endometriosis.

WHICH PLANTS?

WARNING Use only one of the following at any given time

Endometriosis should be treated by a doctor or medical herbalist. The plants listed below are recommended as complementary therapies to help ease the symptoms. Talk to your doctor before taking any medicines.

INTERNAL USAGE
For menstrual pain
CRAMP BARK Liquid extract, 500 mg–1 g dried bark equivalent, three times a day.
GINGER Tincture (1:5), take 20–30 drops in a glass of water three times a day.

REPRODUCTION & SEXUALITY

To ease heavy bleeding
SHEPHERD'S PURSE Liquid extract, 500 mg–1 g dried herb equivalent, three times a day.
LADY'S MANTLE Liquid extract, 1–2 g dried herb equivalent, three times a day.

External application
LAVENDER Add 3 drops of essential oil to 10 ml carrier oil and massage in enough of this mixture to cover the lower abdomen and lower back. Apply twice a day.
CLARY SAGE Essential oil, follow instructions for lavender oil given above.

As advised by a medical herbalist
- Chaste tree, white peony

See also Female infertility, Menstrual problems, Premenstrual syndrome

Female infertility

The inability to conceive is known as primary infertility if a woman has never had a baby. If the woman has been pregnant in the past it is referred to as secondary infertility, even if the pregnancy was ectopic, terminated or resulted in a miscarriage.

Symptoms
- An inability to become pregnant, despite regular intercourse over a period of one to two years

CONSULT YOUR DOCTOR
- It is important to consult a specialist, who will carry out various examinations to try to determine the cause.
- The fertility of your partner also needs to be checked.

Causes
There may be a physical reason for infertility, e.g. a malformation of the uterus, Fallopian tubes or ovaries following a genital infection or endometriosis. It can also be due to a hormonal imbalance or an ovarian or other type of disorder (thyroid, adrenal). It may even be the result of medication.

Female and male causes of infertility each account for about one-third of cases where a couple fails to conceive. In the remaining third, infertility either involves both partners, or no clear cause can be established.

Where no cause is identified, doctors may suggest relaxation techniques and the elimination of stress. Your medical herbalist can prescribe herbs to help in this area, and also to help maintain hormonal balance.

WHICH PLANTS?

WARNING Use only one of the following at any given time.

Infertility requires professional treatment by a doctor or medical herbalist. Talk to your doctor before you start any form of treatment.

As advised by a medical herbalist
- Chaste tree, white peony

Other measures
- Maintain a normal body weight (BMI of 18.5 to 30 – see Excess weight & Obesity, p. 252.)
- Both partners should stop smoking, reduce caffeine consumption and avoid drinking heavily.
- Start taking a folic acid (folate) supplement at least three months before you hope to conceive – this helps to reduce your baby's risk of spina bifida. Additionally, deficiency of folic acid is associated with reduced egg production, and so may be contributing to your conception difficulties. You need to take 400 mcg per day, unless your doctor advises you to take a higher dose.
- Zinc is essential for the regulation of the female cycle, so many natural therapists recommend that those trying to conceive take a supplement (15 mg per day).
- A wide range of other nutritional imbalances can also affect fertility levels, so it's worthwhile taking a multivitamin during the pre-conception period and throughout pregnancy. Your pharmacist can advise you about a product that has been specially formulated for use before, during and after pregnancy.

See also Endometriosis, Fibroids, Male Infertility

Fibroids

Fibroids are non-malignant uterine tumours which may be as small as a pea or as large as a grapefruit. They take their name from their fibrous, rubbery consistency. Fibroids tend to grow slowly until menopause, thereafter decreasing in volume.

While benign in itself, a fibroid may cause infertility, and presents a risk of anaemia if it causes increased bleeding. They are very common, affecting 20 per cent of 30-year-old women and 40 per cent of 50-year-olds.

Symptoms

- Abnormally long or heavy periods, with clotting
- Painful periods
- Bleeding between periods
- Discomfort and heaviness, depending upon the size of the fibroid
- In some cases fibroids will be asymptomatic, while in others the location and size determine the symptoms, and the consequences for other organs. For example: fibroids in or on the uterus tend to produce heavy bleeding and cramping pain; fibroids pressing against the bowel or urinary tract may disrupt the function of these organs, causing constipation or increased urinary frequency; fibroids putting pressure on the Fallopian tubes may interfere with the ability to conceive. Talk with your doctor about your individual case
- Pain may be worse during pregnancy

CONSULT YOUR DOCTOR

- In cases of infertility, urinary problems, constipation and especially where there is heavy bleeding or serious discomfort, consult your GP.

Causes

Fibroids are caused by hormonal imbalance, insufficient progesterone production and excessive oestrogen production. Stress, emotional shock, obesity or pre-menopause may all contribute.

WHICH PLANTS?

WARNING Use only one of the following at any given time.

Fibroids should be treated by a doctor or medical herbalist. The plants listed below are recommended as complementary therapies to help ease the symptoms. Talk to your doctor before taking any medicines.

INTERNAL USAGE
To normalise the menstrual cycle
EVENING PRIMROSE OIL Capsules, 1000 mg, three times a day with meals during the last 10 days of the menstrual cycle.

For menstrual pain
CRAMP BARK Liquid extract, 500 mg–1 g dried bark equivalent, three times a day.
GINGER Tincture (1:5), take 20–30 drops in a glass of water three times a day.

To ease heavy bleeding
SHEPHERD'S PURSE Liquid extract, 500 mg–1 g dried herb equivalent, three times a day.
LADY'S MANTLE Liquid extract, 1–2 g dried herb equivalent, three times a day.

EXTERNAL APPLICATION
LAVENDER Essential oil, add 3 drops to 10 ml of carrier oil. Massage into the lower abdomen and lower back. Apply twice a day.

Other measures

- Avoid all sporting activities likely to aggravate the pelvis, such as tennis, jogging and skipping.
- Avoid wearing high heels.

See also Menstrual problems, Premenstrual syndrome

> **DID YOU KNOW?**
>
> **Fibroids**
> Avoid plants that stimulate oestrogen levels (e.g. red clover, black cohosh, dong quai), as these may enlarge the fibroids.

Impotence

The term 'impotence' refers to both the inability of a man to achieve an erection, and also to premature or delayed ejaculation. It is sometimes referred to as erectile dysfunction.

Symptoms

- Inability to achieve an erection, with or without libido
- Loss of the erection during sexual intercourse
- Premature ejaculation, that is, before penetration or shortly afterwards
- Delayed ejaculation: erection is achieved but impossible to bring to completion by ejaculation

CONSULT YOUR DOCTOR

- While often psychological in origin, impotence may be caused by other factors, and consequently a doctor should be consulted.

Causes

In many cases, impotence springs from psychological problems. These may include: stress, anxiety, depression, fatigue, lack of desire for a partner, anxiety about the sexual act or uncertainty about sexual orientation. Previous episodes of impotence or bad experiences may reinforce the anxiety of it happening again.

Chronic tobacco or alcohol abuse may also be factors. However, sometimes there may be physiological causes: vascular problems, diabetes, high blood pressure, problems affecting the blood reservoirs of the penis that control erection, neurological disorders, low levels of the male hormone testosterone, or the side effects of medication.

REPRODUCTION & SEXUALITY

WHICH PLANTS?

WARNING Use only one of the following at any given time.

Presuming your doctor has confirmed that there is no physical cause for the impotence, the following plants may be of assistance.

INTERNAL USAGE
As a tonic for the male reproductive system
SAW PALMETTO Capsules, standardised for their content of free fatty acids, follow manufacturer's instructions.
KOREAN GINSENG Tablets, capsules, 250–500 mg dried root equivalent, twice daily. Take one dose in the morning and one dose around midday. Choose a product standardised for its ginsenosides content. (See Cautions, p. 125.)
DAMIANA Liquid extract, 1–2 g dried herb equivalent, three times a day.

To improve blood flow
GINKGO Tablets, up to 2 g, standardised for ginkgo flavone glycosides, and ginkgolides and bilobalide. Take up to three times a day. (See Cautions, p. 102.)
GRAPE SEED Tablets, capsules, up to 24 g dried seed equivalent per day, standardised for anthocyanidin content.

For depression, stress and anxiety
WITHANIA Liquid extract, 1–2 g dried root equivalent, three times a day.
KOREAN GINSENG Tablets, capsules, 250–500 mg dried root equivalent, twice daily. Take one dose in the morning and one dose around midday. Choose a product standardised for its ginsenosides content. (See Cautions, p. 125.)
DAMIANA Liquid extract, 1–2 g dried herb equivalent, three times a day.

As advised by a medical herbalist
- Tribulus

Other measures

- If there are no apparent physiological causes, ask your GP or sexual health clinic about counselling. Talking to your partner is also important, and may help to relieve anxiety and clear the air for both of you.
- Avoid smoking and recreational drug use, and limit your alcohol intake.
- Regular physical exercise is highly recommended – it improves the circulation, helps to maintain your overall health and improves your mood.

See also Libido, problems, Prostate disorders

Libido problems

The libido, or sexual drive, can be disturbed by psychological or physiological factors. This occurs in both men and women.

Symptoms
- Lack of sexual desire
- A feeling of tiredness, migraine or other symptoms of discomfort before sexual relations
- Anxiety at the thought of having sex

CONSULT YOUR DOCTOR OR MEDICAL HERBALIST
- In many cases, low libido is related to general health, stress or energy levels. Relationship issues are also understandably likely to affect the desire of either partner to have sex.
- However, sometimes a prolonged decline in the libido can be one of the first signs of nervous depression, of a serious nervous illness, of Alzheimer's disease or of other serious mental affliction. A doctor's advice is essential.

Causes

Lack of interest in one's partner, the focusing of this interest on someone or something else, fatigue, stress and an emotional problem can all affect the libido. In 90 per cent of cases, loss of libido is psychological in origin.

However, chronic alcohol or tobacco abuse can cause problems, as well as medicines such as beta-blockers, medication for prostate disease, certain antidepressants and immunosuppressants.

WHICH PLANTS?

WARNING Use only one of the following at any given time.

The role of plants is limited to complementing psychotherapy by their stimulating action on the nervous system.

INTERNAL USAGE
DAMIANA Liquid extract, 1–2 g dried herb equivalent, three times a day.
KOREAN GINSENG Tablets, capsules, 250–500 mg dried root equivalent, twice daily. Take one dose in the morning and one dose around midday. Choose a product standardised for its ginsenosides content. (See Cautions, p. 125.)
WITHANIA Liquid extract, 1–2 g dried root equivalent, three times a day.

As advised by a medical herbalist
- Tribulus

Other measures

- Do not try to force desire.
- Avoid stress (go on holiday, if possible).
- Consult a GP, or ask at the nearest sexual health clinic for a referral to a counsellor or clinical psychologist. If relationship issues are to blame, couples counselling may offer some benefit.

See also Impotence, Stress

A TO Z OF AILMENTS 275

REPRODUCTION & SEXUALITY

Male infertility

Issues relating to male fertility account for around a third of cases where a couple fails to conceive after trying for a year. Many of these issues relate to the production of viable sperm.

Symptoms

- An inability to conceive a child, despite regular intercourse over a period of one to two years
- Failure to sustain an erection, making intercourse difficult or impossible
- Failure to ejaculate
- In many cases, sexual function is normal, and no symptoms are present

CONSULT YOUR DOCTOR

- It is important to consult a specialist, who will carry out various examinations to try to determine the cause.
- The fertility of your partner also needs to be checked.

Causes

Conception is more difficult if the sperm count is low, if the sperm clump together (agglutination) or if their motility is poor (i.e. they are not mobile enough to fertilise the egg — for example due to abnormal shape). Impotence may also prevent conception.

Male infertility may also be a consequence of a number of diseases, including diabetes, sexually transmitted infection, orchitis (inflammation of the testicles), varicoceles (varicose veins in the scrotum) and a history of testicular cancer.

WHICH PLANTS?

WARNING Use only one of the following at any given time.

Infertility requires professional treatment by a doctor or medical herbalist. Talk to your doctor before starting a treatment.

As advised by a medical herbalist

- Astragalus, damiana, ginkgo, grape seed, Korean ginseng, saw palmetto, tribulus, withania

Other measures

- Do not use alcohol, marijuana, cocaine or cigarettes, which all have negative effects on sperm.
- Do not wear tight or constrictive clothing.
- Maintain a regular exercise program, but don't overexert yourself, as this may reduce sperm production.
- Avoid cycling for long periods of time as this may restrict the blood supply to the testes.
- Zinc is especially important for male reproductive health and for sperm production. Maintain adequate dietary intake by eating seafood, meat, oysters, wheat germ, sunflower seeds and other sources, and consider taking a supplement containing 15 mg per day — especially if you're vegetarian.
- Anti-oxidant nutrients are also important — talk to your doctor or medical herbalist about supplementing with selenium, vitamin C and vitamin E.

See also Female infertility, Impotence

DID YOU KNOW?

Nutrition for healthy sperm

In one clinical trial of sub-fertile men, a daily supplement of zinc and vitamin C increased sperm production by nearly 75 per cent. In another study, sperm health and conception rates were improved when men who were enrolled in an IVF program took vitamin E supplements.

Menopause & Peri-menopause

The term 'menopause' describes the period of time in which a woman's menstruation ceases, signalling the ending of her fertile years. This may occur suddenly or over a period of several years in which the time between the periods gets progressively longer, until they finally stop altogether. Because this is likely to occur over a protracted period, it is impossible to tell when menopause has occurred until after the event. The term 'peri-menopause' describes the extended period of time when changes relating to menopause occur.

Some diseases become more prevalent after menopause (e.g. osteoporosis and heart disease), and the question of whether menopause should be medically 'treated' remains controversial, especially as hormone replacement therapy increases the risk of other diseases (such as breast cancer).

Symptoms

- Some women experience no symptoms other than lengthening or absence of the monthly cycle
- Period problems: cycles irregular, shorter or longer; bleeding may become heavier or scanty, and may occur between periods
- The appearance or worsening of premenstrual syndrome or of breast problems
- Hot flushes
- Mood swings
- Vaginal dryness
- Tiredness
- Libido changes may occur

276 NATURE'S MEDICINES

CONSULT YOUR DOCTOR OR MEDICAL HERBALIST
- If you have heavy bleeding or unbearable hot flushes and sweats, consult your GP.
- Herbs can help, but ask about any possible contraindications to phyto-oestrogens (naturally occurring oestrogens in plants), especially if you have a history of breast cancer.
- Never take oestrogenic essential oils (notably sage or mugwort) since they can have a toxic effect on the nervous system.

Causes
Menopause concludes the reproductive phase of a woman's life – she has few eggs left in her ovaries, and blood levels of the naturally occurring sex hormones oestrogen and progesterone start to decline. The end of ovulation causes a lack of oestrogens and progesterone, indicating menopause. While not totally replacing the sex hormones, herbal medicines can often help to lessen the symptoms of menopause.

WHICH PLANTS?

WARNING Use only one of the following at any given time.

If you have a history of oestrogen-dependent tumours (e.g. breast cancer), do not take herbal medicines except under the supervision of your doctor and medical herbalist.

INTERNAL USAGE
For hot flushes and other symptoms of menopause
RED CLOVER Tablets, standardised for their isoflavone content. Follow manufacturer's instructions unless otherwise advised by your doctor or medical herbalist.
SAGE 20 g dried leaves infused in 1 litre of boiling water for 10 minutes before straining. Drink 1–2 cups a day.

As advised by a medical herbalist
- Black cohosh, chaste tree, dong quai, lady's mantle, St John's wort

EXTERNAL APPLICATION
To treat breast pain
CALENDULA Infuse 5 g dried flower heads in 1 litre boiling water for 5 minutes. Cool, strain and apply to the affected area as a compress three times a day. Or apply a calendula-based cream as directed on the label.

To treat vaginal dryness
ALOE VERA Gel, apply aloe vera gel to the vagina, once daily at bedtime.

Other measures
- Make sure you eat plenty of fruits and vegetables that are rich in vitamins A, C and E, and high in anti-oxidants.
- Talk to your doctor about increasing your intake of soy and other dietary sources of phyto-oestrogens.
- Eat fish that are rich in omega-3 fatty acids at least three times a week (such as salmon, mackerel, tuna, sardines, halibut, herring and anchovies).
- Talk to your GP about a bone-density scan to determine your risk of developing osteoporosis.
- Stop smoking, and reduce your intake of alcohol and caffeine.
- Don't stop taking prescribed hormone replacement therapy (HRT) without talking first to your health-care professional. It is important to weigh up the risks and benefits in your particular case. Furthermore, stopping HRT suddenly may cause a rebounding of your symptoms.

See also Osteoporosis

Menstrual problems

Common menstrual irregularities include amenorrhoea (the absence of periods) and dysmenorrhoea (painful periods). Amenorrhoea can occur in a girl who is of an age to have started menstruation but has not yet done so, or in a woman who is already menstruating.

Dysmenorrhoea may appear at an early stage in puberty or as a secondary complaint, occurring after several years of pain-free cycles. The pains can take the form of simple cramps or may be so incapacitating that the sufferer is forced to take to her bed.

Menstrual problems mainly affect young girls, women who are stressed, anxious or nervous and pre-menopausal women. They may also be a symptom of underlying disease.

Symptoms
- Amenorrhoea (absence of periods)
- Non-appearance of periods at puberty, known as primary amenorrhoea
- The absence of menstruation for at least three months in a woman who is menstruating, known as secondary amenorrhoea
- Dysmenorrhoea
- Abdominal pains during periods, frequently severe, which may start several hours before the onset of a period and may continue for one to two days
- Sometimes accompanied by diarrhoea, nausea, vomiting, fainting

REPRODUCTION & SEXUALITY

CONSULT YOUR DOCTOR
- Whatever the nature of the problem, it is best to have a clinical examination to confirm the cause before embarking on any form of herbal treatment.
- Amenorrhoea may require several forms of investigation, including radiological and hormonal assessments. An ultrasound scan of the uterus and ovaries and sometimes an X-ray of the pituitary gland can detect any possible tumour.
- In cases of severe or persistent pain, consult your GP.

Causes

Primary amenorrhoea can be due simply to the delay of the onset of puberty, particularly if there is a family history of this. Much more rarely, it may be caused by genital malformation. Secondary amenorrhoea can be caused by psychological problems, excessively intensive sporting activity, extremely low body weight, a tumour on the ovary or pituitary gland or certain drugs.

Dysmenorrhoea may be due to circulatory problems, infection, fibroids, endometriosis or polyps. But hormonal problems are the most common cause – possibly as a result of excessive oestrogen or insufficient progesterone and probably stress related, although the exact cause is not known. Period problems may also be caused by infection, an intra-uterine device (IUD), other forms of contraceptive, certain types of medication, systemic diseases such as hypothyroidism and blood disorders.

WHICH PLANTS?

WARNING Use only one of the following at any given time.

INTERNAL USAGE

To treat absent or irregular periods
CHASTE TREE Liquid extract, 500 mg–1 g dried fruit equivalent, in a little cold water every morning, for up to six months. Effects may not be apparent for three months.

To reduce cramping pain
CRAMP BARK Liquid extract, 500 mg–1 g dried bark equivalent, three times a day.
MUGWORT Liquid extract, 500 mg–2 g dried herb equivalent, three times a day.
GINGER Tincture (1:5), take 20–30 drops in a glass of water three times a day.

To treat blood loss between periods
GOLDEN SEAL Tablets, capsules, 250–500 mg dried rhizome equivalent, three times a day. Do not take if you have high blood pressure.

EXTERNAL APPLICATION
LAVENDER Add 3 drops of the essential oil to 10 ml carrier oil and massage in enough of this mixture to cover the lower abdomen and lower back. Apply twice a day.
CLARY SAGE Essential oil, follow instructions for lavender oil given above.

As advised by a medical herbalist
- White peony

Other measures

- If menstrual problems are stress related, relaxation techniques, breathing exercises, yoga and massage can be useful.
- If appropriate, to help you to control your emotions better, consider psychotherapy.
- Reducing your intake of caffeine may help to decrease symptoms of dysmenorrhoea.

See also **Premenstrual syndrome**

DID YOU KNOW?

Menstrual problems
In the Middle Ages, feverfew was widely used for menstrual problems, and was known as 'the herb of mothers and the mother of herbs'.

Premenstrual syndrome

The term 'premenstrual syndrome' (PMS), also known as premenstrual tension (PMT), is applied to a group of physical and emotional symptoms linked to the menstrual cycle. These symptoms occur just before the period starts and end once it has begun. They can last for between two days and two weeks (the latter coinciding with the start of ovulation) and affect 40 per cent of women.

Symptoms

There are about 150 physical and emotional symptoms that can occur separately or together.

Physical symptoms including
- Tender, swollen breasts
- A bloated abdomen that can range from merely uncomfortable to extremely painful
- Urinary disorders
- Weight gain
- A general feeling of bloatedness, with swollen hands and feet and vascular disorders
- Cravings for sugar and refined carbohydrates

Emotional symptoms including
- Unpredictable moods, irritability, aggression, tearfulness, anxiety, depression, nervousness and headaches
- Insomnia, sleepiness and hypersomnia (sleeping for unusually long spells)
- Lack of concentration, memory disorders
- Loss of appetite or libido problems

CONSULT YOUR DOCTOR OR MEDICAL HERBALIST
- If symptoms prevent you from leading a normal life, or are severe enough to cause you to take time off work.

Causes

Premenstrual symptoms are likely to be the result of imbalance in the complex fluctuation of the different hormones that regulate the female cycle. However, no single cause has been identified.

Some symptoms appear to be the result of increased capillary permeability, which causes the swelling of tissues of the breasts, abdomen and brain. In some cases, this may be due to the increased production of oestrogen, triggered by a number of factors, including stress and nutritional deficiencies.

WHICH PLANTS?

WARNING Use only one of the following at any given time.

INTERNAL USAGE
To regulate the cycle and reduce symptoms of PMS
CHASTE TREE Liquid extract, 500 mg–1 g dried fruit equivalent in a little cold water every morning, for up to six months. Effects may not be apparent for three months.

For stress, anxiety, depression and sleep problems
WITHANIA Liquid extract, 1–2 g dried root equivalent, three times a day.
CALIFORNIAN POPPY Liquid extract, 1–2 g dried herb equivalent, twice during the day and at bedtime.
LAVENDER 2–3 g dried flowers infused in 1 cup of boiling water for 5–10 minutes. Drink 3–4 cups a day between meals.
LIME FLOWERS Infuse 2–4 g of dried flowers in 1 cup of boiling water for 5 minutes, before straining. Drink 1 cup twice a day and another in the evening.
PASSIONFLOWER Liquid extract, 500 mg–1 g dried herb equivalent, twice during the day and at bedtime.
VALERIAN Tablets, up to 2 g dried herb equivalent, take up to three times a day.

To relieve breast pain
EVENING PRIMROSE OIL Capsules, 1000 mg, three times a day with meals during the last 10 days of the menstrual cycle.

As advised by a medical herbalist
- Dong quai, lady's mantle, white peony

Other measures

- Increase your fibre intake (fresh and dried vegetables, fruit and whole cereals). Eat fewer foods with refined sugars, and more foods containing slow-release glucose, such as wholemeal bread and pasta, and Basmati rice.
- Reduce your intake of animal fats, such as red meat and full-fat dairy products, and replace them with oils that are monounsaturated or poly-unsaturated (sunflower and olive oils).
- Eat less animal protein and more vegetable protein of various types (such as tofu and other forms of soy). Cut down on salt.
- Reduce your consumption of stimulants such as cigarettes, coffee and tea.
- Take vitamins B (especially B_6), C and E (anti-oxidants), and the minerals magnesium, chromium and zinc.

RESPIRATORY PROBLEMS

Asthma

During an asthma attack, the mucous membranes of the airways become inflamed, swollen and go into spasm, reducing the available space for the air to flow through. Excessive mucus may be produced, further obstructing the passage of air. The attack may resolve itself spontaneously, or it may need medical treatment.

Symptoms
- Difficulty breathing in and out (especially out)
- Spasmodic coughing in children, not accompanied by a fever
- A feeling of suffocation or shortness of breath
- Wheezing
- Nocturnal attacks, with or without copious production of mucus
- Fear, especially in children
- Rapid heartbeat, light-headedness, sweating

CONSULT YOUR DOCTOR
- Asthma can be severe and is responsible for hundreds of deaths a year. A medical consultation will be needed to distinguish between bronchial asthma, a smoker's cough, a chest infection and other breathing difficulties, such as the simple viral bronchitis that often follows a common cold.
- Cardiac asthma – caused by fluid retention in the lungs during heart failure – can mimic bronchial asthma. The doctor will decide upon the treatment with the patient. Hospitalisation could be necessary.
- Talk to your doctor about an asthma management plan for your specific case. This will most likely encompass medications to take prophylactically and during an attack, as well as a safe exercise regime and a program to ensure regular ongoing monitoring of your case.

A TO Z OF AILMENTS

RESPIRATORY PROBLEMS

Causes

Asthma can be a reaction to environmental allergens such as smoke, pollen, perfume and pollution, and to food allergies (especially to nuts, eggs and shellfish, but may also be due to other foods). Smokers, the elderly and those who have already had an allergic reaction, such as eczema or allergic rhinitis, are particularly susceptible to asthma. Some medications, such as aspirin, beta-blockers and anti-inflammatories, can also trigger asthma in predisposed people.

Asthma can also occur after physical exercise, sudden floods of emotion or after rapid changes of temperature, such as moving from a warm house to outdoor temperatures. Asthma is more likely to occur during a viral infection such as a cold or flu. There may also be an inherited predisposition to asthma.

WHICH PLANTS?

WARNING Use only one of the following at any given time.

Asthma is not suitable for self-treatment. Herbal medicines as prescribed by your medical herbalist should be viewed as complementary therapy, and should not be taken without prior consultation with your doctor.

As advised by a medical herbalist
- Albizia, asthma plant, boswellia, licorice, mullein, wild cherry

Other measures

- Take regular exercise according to the asthma management plan discussed with your doctor. You may need to take prophylactic medication before exercising in order to prevent an attack. Follow your GP's advice.
- Take minerals such as copper, magnesium, manganese and sulphur.
- Ask your GP about a referral to an allergy clinic.
- Try acupuncture treatment.
- Taking breathing lessons from a physiotherapist can sometimes help.
- Ask your GP about getting flu and pneumococcal vaccinations.
- Eat lots of oily deep-sea fish, which contain anti-inflammatory omega-3 fatty acids and may help to protect against asthma.

See also Bronchitis, acute & chronic

DID YOU KNOW?

Asthma

Australia and New Zealand have some of the highest incidences of asthma in the world, with as many as one in four children experiencing the symptoms of asthma at some point in their lives. In New Zealand alone, asthma is believed to account for over half a million lost school days per year.

Bronchitis, acute & chronic

Acute bronchitis is an inflammatory infection of the large bronchi and generally follows an infection of the upper respiratory tract or another illness, such as measles or whooping cough.

The disease is described as chronic when the infection is present for at least three months a year and for more than two years. With chronic bronchitis, there is widespread inflammation of the bronchial tubes with an excessive production of clear or green mucus.

The term 'chronic obstructive pulmonary disease' (COPD) is used to describe chronic bronchitis and emphysema, which both cause progressively reduced lung function and are strongly associated with a history of smoking.

Symptoms

Acute bronchitis
- Chesty cough, producing mucus
- Possible fever
- Fatigue
- Wheezing and shortness of breath
- Dry, hacking cough may persist for several weeks after other symptoms have resolved, and are caused by ongoing irritation of the mucous membrane
- Secondary bacterial infection and pneumonia may complicate acute bronchitis and require medical treatment. The presence of yellow-green mucus indicates that this may have occurred

RESPIRATORY PROBLEMS

Chronic bronchitis
- The presence of a productive cough for most days of the month, in at least three months a year for the previous two years
- Breathlessness or shortness of breath – the patient becomes increasingly less mobile and may require oxygen
- Oedema (fluid retention), especially in the ankles and abdomen
- Lips may appear blue due to low levels of oxygen in the blood
- Increased risk of developing pneumonia, heart failure and pulmonary hypertension

CONSULT YOUR DOCTOR OR MEDICAL HERBALIST
- If your fever is severe or lasts longer than three days, or if you experience difficulty breathing.
- If the mucus is bloody or smells foul.
- If the patient is elderly, frail, a child or has existing heart or lung disease or compromised immune function.
- The doctor will make a diagnosis by listening to your lungs and may also send some sputum away for analysis.

Causes
Acute bronchitis usually develops after a viral infection of the upper respiratory tract, and usually clears up within five days. However, secondary bacterial infection may also occur, and if allowed to continue unchecked, this may progress to pneumonia. Those most likely to be affected (and also most at risk of pneumonia) include people with poor immunity, such as the elderly, children, smokers and people with existing illness. (See Immune system deficiency, p. 255).

Chronic bronchitis is not caused by infection. The strongest contributing factor is tobacco smoking. The ongoing irritation caused by the smoke causes a number of changes in the respiratory tract – e.g. reducing the ability to expectorate excess mucus. The continual presence of large amounts of mucus provides an environment that is hospitable to bacteria, and increases the tendency to develop infection.

WHICH PLANTS?

WARNING Use only one of the following at any given time.

Herbal medicines can be taken to relieve the chesty symptoms and support the immune system in acute bronchitis, but this treatment should be complementary to the treatment prescribed by your doctor and taken only as advised by a qualified herbalist.

Chronic bronchitis requires professional treatment by your doctor and medical herbalist.

INTERNAL USAGE
Acute bronchitis
THYME 2 g dried herb infused in 1 cup of boiling water for 5 minutes before straining. Drink 3 cups a day.
WHITE HOREHOUND Liquid extract, 1–2 g dried herb equivalent, three times a day.
HYSSOP 1–2 teaspoons dried herb infused in 1 cup of boiling water for 5–10 minutes before straining. Drink 3 cups a day
MARSHMALLOW 2–3 g dried root infused in 1 cup of boiling water for 10 minutes before straining. Drink 2–3 cups a day.
ANDROGRAPHIS Tablets, 1–2 g dried herb equivalent, standardised for andrographolides, three times a day, or according to manufacturer's instructions.
ECHINACEA Liquid extract, 1 g dried root equivalent, three times a day.

As advised by a medical herbalist
- Asthma plant, ziziphus

EXTERNAL APPLICATION
As a chest rub
EUCALYPTUS Mix 3 drops of essential oil in 10 ml carrier oil and rub into the chest and back.
LAVENDER Essential oil, follow instructions for eucalyptus given above.

Inhalation
EUCALYPTUS Add 2–3 drops of eucalyptus essential oil to a bowl of freshly boiled water. Cover your head with a towel and place head over bowl. Inhale deeply for 10 minutes.
PINE Follow instructions for eucalyptus oil inhalation given above.
TEA TREE Follow instructions for eucalyptus oil inhalation given above.

Other measures
- Stop smoking.
- Do breathing exercises or have respiratory physiotherapy.
- Ask your GP about having flu and pneumococcal vaccinations.
- Drink plenty of fluids, to liquefy the phlegm and make it easier to expel.
- Keep the room humid by boiling an electric kettle with the lid off, or use a steam vapouriser to which a few drops of tea tree or eucalyptus oil have been added.

See also Asthma

Common cold

The common cold, referred to medically as rhinitis or upper respiratory tract infection (URTI), is extremely common – most people experience at least two colds a year, with an increased incidence in the winter months. It is an inflammation of the lining of the respiratory tract, in particular the nasal passages.

Symptoms
Symptoms commence within two to three days of being infected, and generally resolve within five days of appearing.
- Sore throat
- Blocked or runny nose; frequent sneezing
- Nasal discharge, initially runny and clear and then thick and coloured greenish yellow
- Dry cough
- Fever, eye irritation, headache, fatigue, and generalised aches and pains

A TO Z OF AILMENTS 281

RESPIRATORY PROBLEMS

CONSULT YOUR DOCTOR
- Consult your doctor if a cold is persistent, or if you experience symptoms consistent with acute bronchitis or sinusitis (see Bronchitis, acute & chronic p. 280, Sinusitis p. 283).

Causes

More than a hundred different viruses are capable of causing rhinitis, and since each of them is different, our bodies don't develop immunity to them. It is possible to catch several in a year, especially if a lowered immune system increases your vulnerability. Children tend to catch colds more often because their immune systems are still developing.

Colds are passed from person to person via droplets that are dispersed into the atmosphere by the sneezing or coughing of infected people. Hand-to-hand contact and handling contaminated objects can also spread the virus.

WHICH PLANTS?

WARNING Use only one of the following at any given time.

INTERNAL USAGE
To prevent and combat infection
ECHINACEA Liquid extract, 1 g dried root equivalent, three times a day.
ANDROGRAPHIS Tablets, 1–2 g dried herb equivalent, standardised for andrographolides, three times a day, or according to manufacturer's instructions.
ASTRAGALUS Liquid extract, 1–2.5 g dried herb equivalent, three times a day.
GARLIC Tablets, capsules, follow manufacturer's instructions, to a maximum of 6 g dried garlic clove equivalent per day.

To soothe irritation
THYME 2 g dried herb infused in 1 cup of boiling water for 5 minutes before straining. Drink 3 cups a day.
MARSHMALLOW 2–3 g dried root infused in 1 cup of boiling water for 10 minutes before straining. Drink 2–3 cups a day.

ROSEMARY 2–4 g dried herb infused in 1 cup of boiling water for 10 minutes before straining. Drink 3 cups a day, but avoid drinking at bedtime.
WHITE HOREHOUND Liquid extract, 1–2 g dried herb equivalent, three times a day.

EXTERNAL APPLICATION
EUCALYPTUS Add 2–3 drops of eucalyptus essential oil to a bowl of freshly boiled water that has been allowed to cool a little. Cover head with a towel and place over the bowl. Inhale deeply for 10 minutes.
TEA TREE Essential oil, follow the instructions for eucalyptus oil inhalation given above.

Other measures
- Increase your intake of vitamin C and zinc.
- Eating garlic and onions may help your immune system to fight the infection.
- Drink plenty of fluids to liquefy the phlegm and make it easier to expel.
- Keep the room humid by boiling an electric kettle with the lid off, or use a steam vapouriser to which a few drops of tea tree or eucalyptus oil have been added.

See also Bronchitis, acute & chronic, Hay fever, Immune system deficiency, Sinusitis, Viral infection

Hoarseness & Voice loss

The larynx is responsible for voice production. If it becomes inflamed through irritation or infection, the result is hoarseness (dysphonia) or complete voice loss (aphonia).

Symptoms
- Hoarseness
- Some throat soreness
- Partial or complete voice loss
- Occasionally, a slight cough

CONSULT YOUR DOCTOR
- In cases of chronic hoarseness, ask for an ear, nose and throat examination by your doctor or a specialist.
- Sudden hoarseness accompanied by breathing difficulties may be a symptom of severe laryngitis requiring urgent medical intervention.

Causes

Inflammation of the larynx may be caused by infection, allergies, irritation by toxic agents such as tobacco smoke or alcohol or overuse of the vocal cords. Other less obvious causes of hoarseness, which should be checked if the infection resists medical treatment, include secondary effects of acid reflux, psychological problems or possibly cancer.

WHICH PLANTS?

WARNING Use only one of the following at any given time.

INTERNAL USAGE
THYME 2 g dried herb infused in 1 cup of boiling water for 5 minutes before straining. Drink 3 cups a day.
GREATER PLANTAIN 1–4 g dried leaves infused in 1 cup of boiling water for 5 minutes. Drink 3 cups a day.
MULLEIN 1.5–2 g dried herb infused in 1 cup of boiling water for 15 minutes before straining. Drink 3 cups a day.
MARSHMALLOW 2–3 g dried root infused in 1 cup of boiling water for 10 minutes before straining. Drink 2–3 cups a day.
SLIPPERY ELM 1 teaspoon slippery elm powder mixed with ¼ cup of water and drunk three times a day before meals, along with an additional glass of water.

RESPIRATORY PROBLEMS

External application
Agrimony Infuse 2 g dried herb in 1 cup of boiling water for 5 minutes before straining. Cool and use as a gargle two or three times a day.
Eucalyptus Mix 3 drops of essential oil to 10 ml of carrier oil and rub 5 ml into the throat and chest area twice a day. Or add 2–3 drops of eucalyptus essential oil to a bowl of freshly boiled water. Cover your head with a towel and place head over bowl. Inhale deeply for 10 minutes.
Tea tree Essential oil, follow instructions for eucalyptus given above.
Sage 20 g dried leaves infused in 1 litre of boiling water for 10 minutes before straining. Use as a gargle two or three times a day.

Other measures
- Talk as little as possible to rest the vocal cords.
- Avoid irritants such as cigarette smoke.
- Increase your fluid intake.

See also Laryngitis

Laryngitis

A common affliction of the voice box, laryngitis may be acute or chronic and can result in hoarseness and voice loss.

Symptoms
- A cough that is initially dry, later producing phlegm
- Coughing on inhalation
- Pain while coughing (rare)
- Altered or hoarse voice, to the point of loss of voice (aphonia)

CONSULT YOUR DOCTOR OR MEDICAL HERBALIST
- Laryngitis will often disappear spontaneously, and medical herbalism may help it to do so.
- If symptoms persist, see your doctor to exclude the possibility of any serious underlying condition.

Causes
Laryngitis is very often the result of a viral infection. However, chronic cases may also be caused by persistent irritation from tobacco smoke, alcohol or fumes or overuse of the voice. (See Hoarseness & Voice loss p. 282).

WHICH PLANTS?

WARNING Use only one of the following at any given time.

Internal usage
For coughs and catarrh
Mullein 1.5–2 g dried herb infused in 1 cup of boiling water for 15 minutes before straining. Drink 3 cups a day.
Thyme 2 g dried herb infused in 1 cup of boiling water for 5 minutes before straining. Drink 3 cups a day.
Elder Liquid extract, 500 mg–1 g dried flower equivalent, three times a day.
Greater plantain 1–4 g dried leaves infused in 1 cup of boiling water for 5 minutes. Drink 3 cups a day.
Marshmallow 2–3 g dried root infused in 1 cup of boiling water for 10 minutes before straining. Drink 2–3 cups a day.
White horehound Liquid extract, 1–2 g dried herb equivalent, three times a day.

For loss of voice
Mullein 1.5–2 g dried herb infused in 1 cup of boiling water for 15 minutes before straining. Drink 3 cups a day.

To boost the immune system and fight infection
Echinacea Liquid extract, 1 g dried root equivalent, three times a day.
Andrographis Tablets, 1–2 g dried herb equivalent, standardised for andrographolides, three times a day, or according to manufacturer's instructions.
Astragalus Liquid extract, 1–2.5 g dried herb equivalent, three times a day.
Garlic Tablets, capsules, follow manufacturer's instructions, to a maximum of 6 g dried garlic clove equivalent per day.

External application
Eucalyptus Mix 3 drops essential oil to every 10 ml carrier oil. Rub into the chest, back, throat and temples every 2–4 hours.
Pine Follow instructions for eucalyptus oil given above and use as inhalation.
Tea tree Follow instructions for eucalyptus oil given above and use as inhalation.

Other measures
- Talk as little as possible to rest the vocal cords.
- Avoid irritants such as cigarette smoke.
- Increase your fluid intake.

Sinusitis

The sinuses are hollow cavities in the facial bones, adjoining and linked to the nose. There are four pairs of sinuses: maxillary, frontal, ethmoidal and sphenoidal. Sinusitis is an inflammation of one or more of these sinuses, due to a bacterial infection. The blocked sinuses associated with the common cold are often misdiagnosed as sinusitis, which can lead to the unnecessary prescription of antibiotics.

Symptoms
- Generalised headache, often worse in the mornings
- Pain on the affected side when you lean forward or press on the affected sinuses
- Discharge and obstruction of the affected nasal passage
- Fever (sometimes)
- Coughing at night (post-nasal drip)
- Loss of sense of smell (and therefore also of taste to some extent)
- Sometimes pain on chewing

CONSULT YOUR DOCTOR
- Only a doctor can determine the exact cause of sinusitis.

Causes

Sinusitis often follows infections of the ear, nose and throat such as the common cold. It can also be caused by the presence of polyps in the nose or sinuses, or by dental procedures such as tooth extractions and fillings.

Some forms of sinusitis are the result of allergies linked to atmospheric pollution (smoke, pollen, dust).

WHICH PLANTS?

WARNING Use only one of the following at any given time.

INTERNAL USAGE
HORSERADISH Tablets, up to 1.5 g dried root equivalent, three times a day.
ECHINACEA Liquid extract, 1 g dried root equivalent, three times a day.
GARLIC Tablets, capsules, follow manufacturer's instructions, to a maximum of 6 g dried garlic clove equivalent per day.
GOLDEN SEAL Tablets, capsules, 250–500 mg dried rhizome equivalent, three times a day. Do not take if you have high blood pressure.
THYME 2 g dried herb infused in 1 cup of boiling water for 5 minutes before straining. Drink 3 cups a day.
ELDER Liquid extract, 500 mg–1 g dried flower equivalent, three times a day.

Other measures

- Try to control the quality of the air you breathe. Avoid smoky or dusty atmospheres.
- Place an air humidifier in rooms where you spend several hours at a time. A vapouriser containing a few drops of eucalyptus or tea tree essential oil may also help.

Throat infections

Tonsillitis and pharyngitis are among the most common throat infections. With tonsillitis, the tonsils are inflamed, while pharyngitis (commonly referred to as sore throat) is an infection of the pharynx.

Symptoms
Tonsillitis
- Soreness when swallowing
- Redness of the throat and tonsils, often accompanied by white or creamy patches or spots
- Ulcerations (small sores) on one tonsil (trench mouth)
- Blisters on the throat
- Sometimes a slight fever (and chills) may occur
- Sometimes a slight cough
- Swollen, tender lymph nodes under the jaw

Pharyngitis
- Pain in the back of the throat
- Soreness when swallowing
- Often a runny or blocked nose (as in the common cold)
- Fever

CONSULT YOUR DOCTOR
- Medical advice should be sought if a sore throat lasts for more than two days, becomes very severe, or you have an immune deficiency or a history of heart or kidney infections.
- Tonsillitis is occasionally troublesome, with a very small risk of complications such as otitis media, sinusitis, abscess on the tonsil (quinsy), rheumatic fever and kidney infections. However, antibiotics are not very effective at preventing these complications.
- Recurrent episodes of tonsillitis should be investigated by your doctor.

Causes

Tonsillitis and pharyngitis are usually caused by infection with viruses or bacteria, such as *Streptococcus* ('strep throat') and other organisms. If allowed to proceed untreated, a *Streptococcus* infection may cause kidney problems and rheumatic fever.

Tonsillitis can be a manifestation of herpes, glandular fever and other less common infections.

WHICH PLANTS?

WARNING Use only one of the following at any given time.

INTERNAL USAGE
MULLEIN 1.5–2 g dried herb infused in 1 cup of boiling water for 15 minutes before straining. Drink 3 cups a day.
ECHINACEA Liquid extract, 1 g dried root equivalent, three times a day.
MARSHMALLOW 2–3 g dried root infused in 1 cup of boiling water for 10 minutes before straining. Drink 2–3 cups a day.
SLIPPERY ELM 1 teaspoon slippery elm powder mixed with ¼ cup of water and drunk three times a day before meals, along with an additional glass of water.
ANDROGRAPHIS Tablets, 500 mg–1 g dried herb equivalent, standardised for andrographolides, three times a day.
THYME 2 g dried herb infused in 1 cup of boiling water for 5 minutes before straining. Drink 3 cups a day.
ELDER Liquid extract, 500 mg–1 g dried flower equivalent, three times a day.

EXTERNAL APPLICATION
CALENDULA Put 5 g dried flower heads in 1 litre of boiling water, infuse for 5 minutes, strain and cool. Use as a gargle and mouthwash two or three times a day.
SAGE 20 g dried leaves infused in 1 litre of boiling water for 10 minutes before straining. Use as a gargle two or three times a day, before swallowing.

SKIN PROBLEMS

Other measures
- Increase your intake of fluids.
- Take regular lukewarm baths to help to reduce any fever.
- Increase your intake of vitamin C and zinc.
- If the doctor prescribes antibiotics for a strep throat, it is vital that you finish the course, even if the symptoms have gone and you are feeling better. This is to ensure that the infection is completely eradicated and to reduce the risk of complications.
- Gargle with an antibacterial mouthwash containing tea tree or manuka.

See also Hoarseness & Voice loss, Laryngitis

DID YOU KNOW?

Pharyngitis
In 2003, researchers studied the effects of a herbal tea containing slippery elm, licorice, and marshmallow (along with other herbs) on the symptoms of pharyngitis. The results showed that when compared to a placebo, the tea containing these herbs quickly resulted in significantly improved symptoms.

Abscess

An abscess is a localised pocket of infection or pus that can occur anywhere in the body, but commonly affects the skin. It is most frequently caused by a bacterial infection.

Symptoms
- A thin membrane enclosing pus, cellular debris, dead tissue and micro-organisms
- Sharp pain in the affected area of the skin, with swelling, tenderness and intense reddening. In other locations they may cause fever, lethargy and other symptoms of generalised infection
- Feeling of a painful build-up under the skin

CONSULT YOUR DOCTOR OR MEDICAL HERBALIST
- Herbal treatment can help to bring an abscess to a head. However, because a chronic abscess may indicate deep-seated illness, you should always consult a doctor.
- Your doctor may need to lance the abscess in order to release purulent matter and encourage healing.

Causes
An abscess of the skin is caused by an infection being introduced through a break in the skin. This can be the result of a splinter, a bite or a non-sterile injection. An abscess can also form after scraping the skin or having hair removal carried out under unhygienic conditions.

WHICH PLANTS?

WARNING Use only one of the following at any given time.

INTERNAL USAGE
To boost the immune system
ECHINACEA Liquid extract, 1 g dried root equivalent, three times a day.
GARLIC Tablets, capsules, follow manufacturer's instructions, to a maximum of 6 g dried garlic clove equivalent per day.
ANDROGRAPHIS Tablets, 500 mg–1 g dried herb equivalent, standardised for andrographolides, three times a day.

As advised by a medical herbalist
- Barberry

EXTERNAL APPLICATION
To treat the infection and promote healing
ACTIVE MANUKA HONEY Apply honey to an absorbent wound dressing and place it over the affected area, with a second dressing over the entire area to prevent the honey from leaking. Change dressings regularly – adhesion of the dressing to the wound indicates that more frequent changes are required. Medical management of the wound may be required.
TEA TREE Apply a tea tree–based cream or gel, as directed on the label.
LAVENDER Apply 1 drop of pure essential oil to the abscess, once a day.

To bring the abscess to a head
SLIPPERY ELM Mix 1 teaspoon of slippery elm powder with 2–3 teaspoons of water to form a paste. Apply to the affected area once a day.

Other measures
- Follow the rules of basic hygiene and wash your hands and nails thoroughly before treating the abscess or touching your skin.

See also Skin infections

SKIN PROBLEMS

Acne

The simplest form of acne affects around 90 per cent of adolescents, appearing as red or white pimples and blackheads that can leave temporary scars on the face, chest and back. More serious forms leave the face pockmarked. A rare form is fulminant acne, that combines fever with pain in the joints and muscles.

Symptoms
- Greasy look to the face, chest, back and scalp
- Appearance of blackheads
- Presence of whiteheads, in which the follicle opening is clogged with trapped sebum and sealed by normal-coloured skin, resulting in infection and inflammation.
- Acne may worsen premenstrually

CONSULT YOUR DOCTOR
- A visit to the doctor is recommended, unless acne is very mild.

Causes

During adolescence, the oil-producing glands in the skin produce increased amounts of sebum, the oily secretion that protects and lubricates the skin. Acne occurs when sebum blocks the sebaceous ducts, forming a plug. Then bacteria on the surface of, or just beneath, the skin start to proliferate.

The eruption of acne is activated by heat, after exposure to the sun (which may seem to improve the condition of skin but in reality has a negative effect), or before periods in women. It can also be triggered by some medicines, such as certain corticosteroids, hormonal treatments, the contraceptive pill, anti-epileptic drugs and antidepressants.

WHICH PLANTS?

WARNING Use only one of the following at any given time.

INTERNAL USAGE
DANDELION Liquid extract, 500 mg–1 g dried root equivalent, three times a day.
BURDOCK Liquid extract, 500 mg–1.5 g dried root equivalent, three times a day.
YELLOW DOCK Liquid extract, 2–4 g dried root equivalent, three times a day.
CLEAVERS Liquid extract, 2–4 g dried plant equivalent, three times a day.
EVENING PRIMROSE OIL Capsules, 1000 mg, three times a day with meals.

EXTERNAL APPLICATION
ALOE VERA Gel, apply aloe vera gel twice a day, as directed on the label.
LAVENDER Add 3 drops of the essential oil to 10 ml carrier oil. Apply to the affected area three times a week, in the early evening.
CALENDULA Infuse 5 g dried flower heads in 1 litre boiling water for 5 minutes. Cool, strain and apply to the affected area as a compress three times a day. Alternatively, apply a calendula-based cream as directed on the label.
NETTLE 20 g dried herb boiled in 750 ml water until it is reduced to roughly 500 ml. Strain, cool and use to wash the face once a day, three times a week.

As advised by a medical herbalist
- Chaste tree

Other measures
- Cleanse the skin in the morning and evening with gentle, non-aggressive products. Try to avoid soap, instead using just plain warm water.
- Never squeeze the pimples.
- Avoid very greasy cosmetics and moisturisers – look for oil-free formulations.
- Avoid topical astringents, as they only encourage the skin to produce yet more oil.
- Supplementation with zinc and vitamin A may help to balance sebum production and reduce scarring.

DID YOU KNOW?

Acne
Burdock is a medicinal plant that has been rather neglected. Yet its leaves, and especially its roots, have known antibacterial and antifungal properties. Recent studies have even shown that they contain compounds that remain active after exposure to ultraviolet rays.

Acne rosacea

Identified by a persistent redness of the skin and dilation of the blood vessels, and also through the appearance of pimples, acne rosacea afflicts older people. Fair women, with menopausal flushes, are the most susceptible. It can also affect men in middle life, with the nose growing large and warty. Acne rosacea may also be referred to as simply 'rosacea'.

Symptoms
- Redness spread over the face
- Enlargement of the nose
- Appearance of a fine network of tiny red/mauve spider veins across the cheeks, nose and chin
- Pimples and pustules

CONSULT YOUR DOCTOR
- It is important to consult a doctor as soon as possible to avoid disfiguring effects on your appearance.

Causes

The cause of rosacea remains unclear, although there is some evidence that it may be caused by a skin infection called *Demodex folliculorum* and the immune system's reaction to it. Ultra violet light from sunbeds or sunshine may also provoke it.

Natural therapists also consider that food intolerance and deficient digestive acid production may play a role.

SKIN PROBLEMS

WHICH PLANTS?

WARNING Use only one of the following at any given time.

INTERNAL USAGE
To relax
WITHANIA Liquid extract, 1–2 g dried root equivalent, three times a day.
LIME FLOWERS Infuse 2–4 g of dried flowers in 1 cup of boiling water for 5 minutes, before straining. Drink 1 cup twice a day and another in the evening.
PASSIONFLOWER Liquid extract, 500 mg–1 g dried herb equivalent, twice during the day and at bedtime.

To fight infection
ECHINACEA Liquid extract, 1 g dried root equivalent, three times a day.
GARLIC Tablets, capsules, follow manufacturer's instructions, to a maximum of 6 g dried garlic clove equivalent per day.
BURDOCK Liquid extract, 500 mg–1.5 g dried root equivalent, three times a day.

For dilated blood vessels on the face
BURDOCK Liquid extract, 500 mg–1.5 g dried root equivalent, three times a day.
HEARTSEASE Liquid extract, 1–4 g dried herb equivalent, three times a day.

To improve blood circulation
GRAPE SEED Tablets, capsules, up to 24 g dried seed equivalent per day, standardised for anthocyanidin content.

To detoxify the liver and promote digestion
DANDELION Liquid extract, 500 mg–1 g dried root equivalent, three times a day.
GLOBE ARTICHOKE Tablets, capsules, 500 mg–1 g dried herb equivalent, standardised for cynarin content, three times a day.
PAPAYA Papain tablets, take according to manufacturer's instructions.

EXTERNAL APPLICATION
ALOE VERA Gel, apply aloe vera gel twice a day, or as directed on the label.
LAVENDER Apply 3 drops of essential oil to 10 ml carrier oil and use to cover the face. Apply three times a week, in the early evening.
CALENDULA Infuse 5 g dried flower heads in 1 litre boiling water for 5 minutes. Cool, strain and apply to the affected area as a compress three times a day.
WITCH HAZEL Massage in a witch hazel–based ointment once or twice a day.

Other measures
- Adopt a diet that is low in animal fats, chocolate and refined sugar.
- Avoid all stimulants (coffee or tea), as well as spicy food.
- Reduce alcohol consumption.
- Take a course of vitamins A, B, C and E.
- Avoid scented or oily soaps. Use soap-free dermatological cleansers to wash the face, and skin-care products that are suited to your skin type.
- Avoid exposure to bright sunlight and strong winds.

See also Indigestion

Bedsores

Also known as pressure sores, bedsores are the destruction of the skin and underlying tissues due to a lack of oxygenation allied to poor circulation. They can form very rapidly.

Symptoms
- First sign: the skin is discoloured, light or dark red and painful
- The skin then turns black, hardens and becomes dead to the touch
- The dead skin sloughs off, leaving an open sore, which reveals the underlying tissue
- The most common sites are those that are in contact with the bed, chair or wheelchair – heels, buttocks, the base of the spine, hips and elbows

CONSULT YOUR DOCTOR
- Medical or nursing advice is essential in the case of all sores of unknown origin, or those showing any sign of a secondary infection.

Causes
In general, bedsores are caused by poor oxygen supply to the skin, and commonly affect those who are bedridden or have reduced mobility and are unable to change position (due to a limb in plaster, for example). The elderly or diabetics are most at risk, as well as those suffering from circulatory problems in the legs.

WHICH PLANTS?

WARNING Use only one of the following at any given time.

INTERNAL USAGE
To improve the circulation
GINKGO Tablets, up to 2 g, standardised for ginkgo flavone glycosides, and ginkgolides and bilobalide. Take up to three times a day. (See Cautions, p. 102.)
GRAPE SEED Tablets, capsules, up to 24 g dried seed equivalent per day, standardised for anthocyanidin content.

For healthy skin
EVENING PRIMROSE OIL Capsules, 1000 mg, three times a day with meals.

To prevent infection
ECHINACEA Liquid extract, 1 g dried root equivalent, three times a day.
GARLIC Tablets, capsules, follow manufacturer's instructions, to a maximum of 6 g dried garlic clove equivalent per day.

SKIN PROBLEMS

EXTERNAL APPLICATION
ACTIVE MANUKA HONEY Apply honey to an absorbent wound dressing and place it over the affected area, with a second dressing over the entire area to prevent the honey from leaking. Change the dressings regularly – adhesion of the dressing to the wound indicates that more frequent changes are required. Medical management of the wound may be required.

LAVENDER Add 3 drops of essential oil to 10 ml carrier oil and apply to the affected area once a day, three to four times a week.

CALENDULA Infuse 5 g dried flower heads in 1 litre boiling water for 5 minutes. Cool, strain and apply to the affected area as a compress three times a day.

Other measures
- Change garments and bed linen immediately if damp.
- Help the patient to change position as often as possible – at least every two hours when awake.
- Give local massage alternating with hot and cold applications. For instance, apply ice cubes then dry the damp area with a hair dryer set to warm.
- Use cushions to relieve pressure on affected areas.
- Ensure the patient eats a nutritious diet. A vitamin and mineral supplement is advised, and additional zinc may also be recommended.

Bruises

A blow to the body with a hard object, a fall or other physical trauma will result in bruising or contusion. Bruises can range from a small, bluish mark, in the case of minor bruises, to large, black swellings in more severe cases.

Symptoms
- A bump or swelling
- Redness or a bluish colour, with a burning pain
- Colour fades to yellow as the bruise gradually heals
- Accumulation of blood in pockets beneath the skin

CONSULT YOUR DOCTOR
- It is recommended that you consult a doctor if you are worried about any bruising, or feel that it may be accompanied by a fracture or sprain, or if the bruising is on the abdomen and is the result of a severe impact (such as a car crash).
- A doctor should also intervene if the swelling does not go down, or if bruising is extensive.
- Unexplained bruising, or bruising that occurs after very mild trauma may be symptomatic of a bleeding disorder, and should be medically investigated.

Causes
The underlying tissues or deeper layers of skin at the site of a bruise become swollen and taut because of the accumulation of blood that has leaked from damaged blood vessels.

WHICH PLANTS?
WARNING Use only one of the following at any given time.

Taken homoeopathically, arnica is excellent for this type of trauma. Ask your medical herbalist for more information.

INTERNAL USAGE
To encourage healing and address inflammation
PINEAPPLE Bromelain tablets, capsules, up to 2 g per day in divided doses before meals.

To aid circulation and protect blood vessels
GINKGO Tablets, up to 2 g, standardised for ginkgo flavone glycosides, and ginkgolides and bilobalide. Take up to three times a day. (See Cautions, p. 102.)
GRAPE SEED Tablets, capsules, up to 24 g dried seed equivalent per day, standardised for anthocyanidin content.
GREEN TEA Capsules, up to 500 mg extract, standardised for polyphenol content. Take according to manufacturer's instructions.
HORSECHESTNUT Tablets, 1.5 g dried seed equivalent, standardised for aescin content. Take 2–3 tablets a day.

EXTERNAL APPLICATION
ARNICA Cream, gently massage arnica cream or gel into the affected area two or three times a day.
WITCH HAZEL Apply a witch hazel–based ointment or gel once or twice a day, or as directed.
HORSECHESTNUT Apply a horsechestnut-based cream or gel two or three times a day, as directed on label.

Other measures
- Place an ice pack on the affected area.
- Take a bath of salt water.

Burns & Erythema

Burns are lesions on the skin or the mucous membrane, due to intense heat (or also intense localised cold). They are classified according to their severity. Erythema is the term used for superficial redness of an area of skin.

Symptoms
First-degree burn
- Superficial lesions on the outer layer of the skin
- Localised redness (erythema)

SKIN PROBLEMS

Second-degree burn
- More serious damage to the outer layer of skin and tissue below, in the form of blisters
- Intense pain

Third-degree burn
- Very severe damage
- Skin has a brown or burnt appearance
- Irreversible lesions and the destruction of nerve endings
- In contrast to second-degree burns, pain may disappear
- State of shock (fainting, pale skin, sweating)
- This type of burn always requires urgent medical attention and hospitalisation.

CONSULT YOUR DOCTOR
- All severe and extensive burns, particularly if they are not painful (indicating third-degree burns), require immediate medical attention.

Causes

A burn is caused by exposure to extreme heat or cold. Erythema can have several different causes: irritation, friction, sunburn, infection, viral disease.

WHICH PLANTS?

WARNING Use only one of the following at any given time.

Before attempting any treatment to help a wound to heal over, make sure that it is clean and that there is no deep-seated inflammation or infection.

INTERNAL USAGE
GOTU KOLA Capsules, up to 600 mg dried herb equivalent, three times a day.

EXTERNAL APPLICATION
MANUKA For non-infected sites, dilute the essential oil in water and swab the affected area.
GOTU KOLA Massage in cream, ointment or lotion based on gotu kola once or twice a day, as directed on the label.

ALOE VERA Gel, apply aloe vera gel three times a day, or as directed on the label.
LAVENDER Apply 1 drop of pure essential oil twice a day.
CALENDULA Infuse 5 g dried flower heads in 1 litre boiling water for 5 minutes. Cool, strain and apply to the affected area as a compress three times a day.

Other measures

- Except for severe burns, try to cool the skin and underlying tissue by running cold water over it for some minutes – this may help to limit the damage.

See also Sunburn

Cellulite

Cellulite is the term given to dimpled and lumpy skin. It affects 90 per cent of women after puberty, and afflicts both those who are plump and those who are slim. It usually appears on the skin of the arms, the thighs, the buttocks and the abdomen.

Symptoms
- 'Orange peel' appearance to the skin, with small dimples
- An increase in fatty mass around the hips and the thighs, down to the knees. It may also affect the upper arms
- If cellulite extends as far as the knees, poor circulation may be the cause

CONSULT YOUR DOCTOR
- The problem of cellulite is purely cosmetic, but you may wish to consult your GP if you are concerned.

CAUSES

The tendency towards cellulite may be hereditary. It is caused by the storage of fat under the skin, complicated by fluid retention and ageing connective tissue, and can also be provoked by weight gain. Hormonal imbalance may be a factor, particularly at puberty and during menopause.

WHICH PLANTS?

WARNING Use only one of the following at any given time.

INTERNAL USAGE
For fluid retention
DANDELION Liquid extract, 4–10 g dried leaf equivalent, three times a day.
CLEAVERS Liquid extract, 2–4 g dried plant equivalent, three times a day.
HORSETAIL Boil 1–4 g dried herb in 2 cups of water for 10–15 minutes before straining. Drink 2–3 cups a day.

To support detoxification
GLOBE ARTICHOKE Tablets, capsules, 500 mg–1 g dried herb equivalent, standardised for cynarin content, three times a day.
MILK THISTLE Tablets, up to 9 g dried herb equivalent, three times a day.
DANDELION Liquid extract, 500 mg–1 g dried root equivalent, three times a day.

To improve the circulation
GOTU KOLA Capsules, up to 600 mg dried herb equivalent, three times a day.
GRAPE SEED Tablets, capsules, up to 24 g dried seed equivalent per day, standardised for anthocyanidin content.
HORSECHESTNUT Tablets, 1.5 g dried seed equivalent, standardised for aescin content. Take 2–3 tablets a day.

As advised by a medical herbalist
- Cayenne, gymnema, kelp

A TO Z OF AILMENTS   289

SKIN PROBLEMS

Other measures
- Discuss your hormonal balance with your herbalist.
- If you need to lose weight, follow a slimming regime.
- Take regular exercise.

See also Excess weight & Obesity, Hypothyroidism

Eczema

A common skin condition, eczema can occur almost anywhere on the body. There are many variants, and the irritation is often spread by blisters. Eczema generally goes through several stages.

Symptoms
- Redness, inflammation and swelling
- The appearance of very small blisters, at first oozing, then dry and cracked
- Itching, which can lead to compulsive scratching, spreading any infection and worsening the condition
- Skin is coarse or scaly, and may be thicker than in unaffected areas

CONSULT YOUR DOCTOR OR MEDICAL HERBALIST
- If the cause of the eczema is not obvious, consult a doctor to get the correct diagnosis and treatment.
- Treatment of eczema should not be confined to topical therapy, but should address the causes.
- Long-term treatment is often essential in order to avoid relapses, and to prevent the condition becoming chronic.

Causes
In adults, eczema is often triggered by the skin reacting to contact with irritating substances, such as dishwashing detergent or nickel and other metals. This is called contact eczema or contact dermatitis. It may also occur as a reaction to stress, infection, eating certain foods, as well as overeating, intoxication and extremes of temperature.

Along with asthma and hay fever, eczema is an atopic disease – an inherited form of allergy. If you have eczema as a child, you are more likely to develop hay fever or asthma as you get older. (Note that childhood eczema requires different treatment.)

WHICH PLANTS?

WARNING Use only one of the following at any given time.

INTERNAL USAGE
EVENING PRIMROSE OIL Capsules, 1000 mg, three times a day with meals.
BURDOCK Liquid extract, 500 mg–1.5 g dried root equivalent, three times a day.
YELLOW DOCK Liquid extract, 2–4 g dried root equivalent, three times a day.
HEARTSEASE Liquid extract, 1–4 g dried herb equivalent, three times a day.

For diet-related eczema
BAICAL SKULLCAP Liquid extract, 500 mg–1 g dried root equivalent three times a day.

For stress-induced eczema
WITHANIA Liquid extract, 1–2 g dried root equivalent, three times a day.
PASSIONFLOWER Liquid extract, 500 mg–1 g dried herb equivalent, twice during the day and at bedtime.

EXTERNAL APPLICATION
To treat inflammation
ALOE VERA Gel, apply aloe vera gel three times a day, or as directed on the label.
GREATER PLANTAIN Rub fresh leaves directly onto the affected area, or apply a cream containing 4 per cent of the extract.
CALENDULA Infuse 5 g dried flower heads in 1 litre boiling water for 5 minutes. Cool, strain and apply to the affected area as a compress three times a day. Alternatively, apply a calendula-based cream as directed on the label.
CHICKWEED Apply a chickweed-based cream as directed on the label.
WITCH HAZEL Apply a witch hazel–based ointment or gel, once or twice a day, as directed.

To prevent secondary infection
TEA TREE Apply a tea tree–based cream or gel as directed on the label.

As advised by a medical herbalist
- Albizia

Other measures
- Replace soaps that are harsh, acidic, perfumed or detergent-based with some that are oil- or cream-based.
- Take vitamins (especially vitamin A) to improve skin health and reduce itching, as well as trace elements such as zinc and sulphur to help to prevent scarring.

See also Asthma, Eczema, childhood, Hay fever

Insect stings & bites

When insects sting or bite, the wound can vary from a small skin lesion to a large, angry swelling – as the body reacts against the irritant or toxin.

Symptoms
- Redness
- Bruising (haematoma)
- Swelling
- Appearance of blisters
- Itching

CONSULT YOUR DOCTOR OR MEDICAL HERBALIST
- If you or your child has been bitten by a spider or snake, immediate medical help may be required. In Australia, call the Poisons Information Centre on 13 11 26 for advice. In New Zealand, call the National Poisons Centre on 0800 764 766. These advice lines are staffed 24 hours a day.

SKIN PROBLEMS

- If the person who has been stung has previously had an anaphylactic reaction to a bite or sting (e.g. of an ant, bee, wasp or jellyfish), call for an ambulance immediately.
- Even if the person has never had an anaphylactic reaction before, be alert to the symptoms. These include breathing difficulties, rapid swelling of areas away from the bite (especially the eyes and lips) and feeling faint. Call for emergency help immediately.

Causes
In most cases insect bites are innocuous, causing only a localised reaction. The insect may also inject poison through its sting, further irritating the skin.

WHICH PLANTS?

WARNING Use only one of the following at any given time.

Only follow the recommendations below in non-emergency situations.

EXTERNAL APPLICATION
TEA TREE Apply a tea tree–based cream or gel, as directed on the label.
LAVENDER Apply 1 drop of pure essential oil to the affected area, once a day.
THYME Add 5 drops essential oil to 10 ml carrier oil. Apply to the affected area two to three times a day.
CALENDULA Infuse 5 g dried flower heads in 1 litre boiling water for 5 minutes. Cool, strain and apply to the affected area as a compress three times a day.

Other measures
- Wash the bitten area with soap and water before applying any other substance to it.
- Apply a cold pack to the area.
- Wear clothes that cover most of your body when you are in a badly infested area.
- Use an insect repellent.
- Take a first aid course to help you understand more about serious bites and stings and their treatment.

Itching

Itching is a common symptom, with a wide variety of causes. It is associated with the desire to scratch, and is commonly (but not always) accompanied by redness or irritation of the skin.

Symptoms
- Desire to scratch
- Redness of the skin
- Skin may display small spots or blisters, weals, eczema or psoriasis, or bites

CONSULT YOUR DOCTOR
- If your face is swollen, or you have difficulty in breathing, consult a doctor urgently.
- The rapid appearance of an itchy rash may indicate an infectious disease such as chickenpox – consult your doctor for advice.

Causes
The body reacts to substances it is allergic to by producing antibodies that release histamine, which in turn cause redness and itching. The allergenic substance can be external, such as soap or a dye, or internal. Certain foods, such as strawberries, milk, soy beans or kiwi fruit are common culprits. Some drugs, notably antibiotics, can also cause an allergic reaction.

Stress, dietary excess, ageing or hereditary factors all increase the risk of an allergic reaction.

More rarely, itching is caused by diseases such as scabies or chickenpox, by systemic disease such as kidney or liver disease, or as a side effect of chemotherapy. It may also be caused by insect bites or stings, or by contact with certain plants.

WHICH PLANTS?

WARNING Use only one of the following at any given time.

Many itchy skin conditions respond well to internal and external treatment with herbal medicines, but a complete diagnosis is required first.

EXTERNAL APPLICATION
TEA TREE Apply a tea tree–based cream or gel, as directed on the label.
MULLEIN 3 teaspoons dried herb soaked in 300 ml cold water for 30 minutes. Gently bring to the boil. Strain. Soak a cloth in this liquid and apply to the affected area as a compress twice a day.
CHAMOMILE Infuse 5 g dried flower heads in 1 cup of boiling water for 10 minutes. Cool and apply to the affected area as a compress three times a day.
LAVENDER Apply a lavender-based cream, ointment or lotion, as directed on the label.
CALENDULA Infuse 5 g dried flower heads in 1 litre boiling water for 5 minutes. Cool, strain and apply to the affected area as a compress three times a day.

SKIN PROBLEMS

Other measures
- Avoid foods that you suspect may give you an allergic reaction.
- Discuss with your GP the possibility of blood and skin tests to identify the substances that are causing the allergies or a condition that might be causing the itching.
- Do not scratch. This merely worsens the condition and develops into a vicious cycle. Cutting your nails will help to stop them damaging the skin. Cotton mittens or gloves will reduce the risk of children scratching themselves in their sleep.
- Try to identify any particular clothes or washing materials that aggravate it. Start with wool, soap and biological washing powders. Try using no soap or shampoo at all to wash with – just warm water. This will leave the natural oils undisturbed on the skin.

See also Eczema, Psoriasis, Urticaria

Perspiration & Body odour

Some people perspire excessively without the slightest physical exertion. The condition, known as hyperhydrosis, can affect localised areas or the entire body. The skin can also release an unpleasant odour, whether or not it is sweating, in spite of adequate personal hygiene.

Symptoms
- Excessive perspiration, independent of physical effort
- Sticky perspiration that is difficult to eliminate from the armpits
- Unpleasant skin odour

CONSULT YOUR DOCTOR
- This type of skin disorder can be symptomatic of an internal condition that needs to be diagnosed. Only a doctor can determine whether it is a common disorder or may be something more serious.

Causes
Certain body odours are defined as idiopathic, which means that their cause is unknown. In some cases, the condition is genetic and several members of the same family are affected. Body odour and excessive perspiration problems also frequently affect people who are obese, anxious, very tired or who suffer from digestive, renal and metabolic disorders.

WHICH PLANTS?

WARNING Use only one of the following at any given time.

INTERNAL USAGE
To reduce excessive sweating
SAGE 20 g dried leaves infused in 1 litre of boiling water for 10 minutes before straining. Drink 1–2 cups a day.

For stress and anxiety
WITHANIA Liquid extract, 1–2 g dried root equivalent, three times a day.
LAVENDER 2–3 g dried flowers infused in 1 cup of boiling water for 5–10 minutes. Drink 3–4 cups a day between meals.
LIME FLOWERS Infuse 2–4 g of dried flowers in 1 cup of boiling water for 5 minutes before straining. Drink 1 cup twice a day and another in the evening.

For digestive problems
CHAMOMILE Infuse 1 sachet of chamomile flowers in 1 cup of boiling water for 5–10 minutes. Drink 3 cups a day before meals.
PEPPERMINT 1 teaspoon dried leaves infused in 150 ml of boiling water for 10–15 minutes before straining. Drink 1 cup after every meal.

To detoxify
DANDELION Liquid extract, 500 mg–1 g dried root equivalent, three times a day.
GLOBE ARTICHOKE Tablets, capsules, 500 mg–1 g dried herb equivalent, standardised for cynarin content, three times a day.

As advised by a medical herbalist
- Ziziphus

EXTERNAL APPLICATION
CORIANDER Infuse 10–30 g crushed seeds in 1 litre of boiling water for 10 minutes before straining. Spray on the affected area twice a day.
HEARTSEASE Add 20–30 g fresh flowers to 500 ml boiling water. Infuse for 15 minutes, then strain. Soak a cloth in this infusion and apply to the affected areas morning and evening.
SANDALWOOD Mix 3 drops of the essential oil to 10 ml carrier oil and rub into the affected areas. Leave for 15 minutes before washing off.

Other measures
- Use talcum powder after taking a shower and drying your skin carefully.
- Try to limit stress. Consider taking relaxation therapy.

Psoriasis

Psoriasis is an extremely common chronic skin disorder associated with severe itching and the presence of well-defined, reddish plaques covered with scales that turn white and flake off, especially when scratched.

The condition is often hereditary and tends to affect adolescents and young adults. It usually develops in clearly defined areas of the body, such as the elbows, knees and scalp, but it may cover the entire body.

Symptoms
- Reddish plaques covered with whitish scales and with a clearly marked border. They usually occur in the bend of the elbow, at the back of the knee or on the scalp
- Itching, which may be unbearable
- Scratching and flaking of scales leaves skin red, sometimes causing bleeding

SKIN PROBLEMS

- Complaint erupts and subsides for no apparent reason
- Sometimes plaques occur under the nails, causing them to lift off and become deformed
- Arthritis and joint pain may accompany the skin symptoms in 5 per cent of patients (psoriatic arthritis)

CONSULT YOUR DOCTOR
- Psoriasis should be medically diagnosed as it can resemble eczema or mycosis (a fungal skin disorder) in the initial stages, which are not treated in the same way.

Causes

In many cases, psoriasis is hereditary and several members of the same family are affected. Large numbers of sufferers have been found to have difficulty in the assimilation of fats, or suffer from diabetes. The condition occurs when the skin cells multiply more than normal but are not sloughed off at the same pace, causing the thickened plaques and scaling. Stress is believed to play a role, since the appearance of psoriasis is often triggered by strong emotion.

Alcohol and some medications (especially certain anti-inflammatories and beta-blockers) may be culprits too. One type of spotty psoriasis (guttate psoriasis) may be triggered by a bacterial infection, especially in the throat.

Plaques are more likely to develop over the sites of previous skin injuries.

WHICH PLANTS?

WARNING Use only one of the following at any given time.

INTERNAL USAGE
For healthy skin
EVENING PRIMROSE OIL Capsules, 1000 mg, three times a day with meals.
GOTU KOLA Capsules, up to 600 mg dried herb equivalent, three times a day.

For stress and anxiety
WITHANIA Liquid extract, 1–2 g dried root equivalent, three times a day.
LAVENDER 2–3 g dried flowers infused in 1 cup of boiling water for 5–10 minutes. Drink 3–4 cups a day between meals.
LIME FLOWERS Infuse 2–4 g of dried flowers in 1 cup of boiling water for 5 minutes before straining. Drink 1 cup twice a day and another in the evening.
PASSIONFLOWER Liquid extract, 500 mg–1 g dried herb equivalent, twice during the day and at bedtime.

To aid digestion
CHAMOMILE Infuse 1 sachet of chamomile flowers in 1 cup of boiling water for 5–10 minutes. Drink 3 cups a day before meals.
PEPPERMINT Infuse 1 teaspoon dried leaves in 150 ml of boiling water for 10–15 minutes before straining. Drink 1 cup after every meal.
TURMERIC Capsules, standardised for curcuminoid content. Follow manufacturer's instructions up to 5 g a day.

To treat infections
GOLDEN SEAL Tablets, capsules, 250–500 mg dried rhizome equivalent, three times a day. Do not take if you have high blood pressure.

For inflammation
LICORICE 1–2 teaspoons root powder steeped in 1 cup of boiling water for 10 minutes before straining. Drink 2–3 cups a day for no more than four to six weeks at a stretch.

To support the liver and aid detoxification pathways
DANDELION Liquid extract, 500 mg–1 g dried root equivalent, three times a day.
GLOBE ARTICHOKE Tablets, capsules, 500 mg–1 g dried herb equivalent, standardised for cynarin content, three times a day.
MILK THISTLE Tablets, up to 9 g dried herb equivalent, three times a day.

As advised by a medical herbalist
- Barberry

EXTERNAL APPLICATION
For itch, pain and inflammation
ALOE VERA Gel, apply aloe vera gel two to three times a day, or as directed on the label.
GOTU KOLA Massage in cream, ointment or lotion based on gotu kola, once or twice a day, as directed on the label.
CALENDULA Infuse 5 g dried flower heads in 1 litre boiling water for 5 minutes. Cool, strain and apply to the affected area as a compress three times a day.
CHICKWEED Apply a chickweed-based cream or gel, as directed on the label.
OATS Boil 20 g in 1 litre of water for 3 minutes, then leave to soak for 10–20 minutes before straining. Add the liquid to bath water and bathe for 15–20 minutes.

Other measures

- Sunbathing can help, but consult your doctor first about the risk of skin cancer.
- PUVA treatment (ultraviolet radiation treatment) may also be beneficial.
- Stop smoking and reduce alcohol intake.
- Adopt a low-fat diet, but include plenty of oily, deep-sea fish, which contain anti-inflammatory essential fatty acids (omega-3s). Long-term supplementation with omega-3 fatty acids may also offer some benefit.
- Take steps to improve your tolerance of stress.

SKIN PROBLEMS

> **DID YOU KNOW?**
>
> **Psoriasis**
> Every square centimetre of normal human skin produces around 1250 new cells per day, while skin affected by psoriasis may produce nearly 30 times this number. Psoriatic plaques build up to such an extent since there is no corresponding increase in the pace at which the cells peel off naturally.

Skin conditions

The skin is the largest organ of the human body. It acts as a protective barrier from the outside world and helps to regulate the body's water content.

Dry skin can lead to flaking and discomfort. It can be exacerbated by climatic conditions or contact with irritants such as detergents or the salt in sea water. Greasy skin is associated with acne and other skin problems.

Symptoms
Dry skin
- A dull, fine-grained appearance
- Extremely fragile, itchy and flaky
- Feelings of tautness
- Rough to the touch

Greasy skin
- Shiny, moist appearance
- Coarseness, with subcutaneous fat
- Blocked or open pores, with blackheads present

CONSULT YOUR DOCTOR
- If you are concerned about the health of your skin, consult your doctor, who can diagnose eczema, seborrheic dermatitis, acne, psoriasis or other skin conditions.

Causes
Dry skin is usually caused by the inefficiency of the natural oil-producing glands. If they fail to produce enough sebum, the skin is left without protection from outside irritants.

Greasy skin is caused by overproduction of sebum, and may be due to extreme nervousness, obesity, an over-rich diet, hormonal changes or the use of oral contraceptives.

WHICH PLANTS?

WARNING Use only one of the following at any given time.

INTERNAL USAGE
Dry skin
EVENING PRIMROSE OIL Capsules, 1000 mg, three times a day with meals.
GOTU KOLA Capsules, up to 600 mg dried herb equivalent, three times a day.
GRAPE SEED Tablets, capsules, up to 24 g dried seed equivalent per day, standardised for anthocyanidin content.

Greasy skin
BURDOCK Liquid extract, 500 mg–1.5 g dried root equivalent, three times a day.

EXTERNAL APPLICATION
Dry skin
CHAMOMILE Add 3 drops of chamomile essential oil to 10 ml carrier oil and massage into the affected area two to three times a day.
CALENDULA Infuse 5 g dried flower heads in 1 litre boiling water for 5 minutes. Cool, strain and apply to the affected area as a compress three times a day. Alternatively, apply a calendula-based cream as directed on the label.
OATS Boil 20 g of dried herb in 1 litre of water for 3 minutes, then leave to soak for 10–20 minutes before straining. Add the liquid to bath water and bathe for 15–20 minutes.

Greasy skin
NETTLE 20 g dried herb boiled in 750 ml water until it is reduced to roughly 500 ml. Strain, cool and wipe over the face with a cotton wool pad. Leave on for 15 minutes, then rinse off. Repeat two to three times a week.
WITCH HAZEL Apply witch hazel water once or twice a day, as directed on the label.

Other measures
- Protect your skin from environmental damage caused by cold, heat (including saunas), sun, sea water and atmospheric pollution.
- Keep your skin moist with a pure water spray.
- Take supplements of zinc, vitamin A and also vitamin E.

Skin infections

Some skin infections are viral in origin (herpes, warts, *Molluscum contagiosum*, chickenpox and shingles), some are bacterial (boils, cellulitis, erysipelas and impetigo) while others are fungal (athlete's foot and ringworm).

Skin infections can have serious complications. In the case of impetigo, they can lead to kidney disease or to a general organic infection (septicaemia). In boils, the spread of infection can lead to a type of carbuncle.

Symptoms
Impetigo
- Reddened skin
- Fluid-filled blisters, which burst leaving yellowish scabs
- Fever and swellings (lymph nodes) in serious cases

SKIN PROBLEMS

Boils and carbuncles
- Rounded nodules appear
- Inflammation (redness, heat and swelling) with pain on contact
- Swelling of nodules, which fill with pus
- A white spot appears in the centre (the head of the boil)

CONSULT YOUR DOCTOR
- In case of complications, such as swollen lymph nodes, fever or general poor health, it is important to consult your doctor as soon as possible.

Causes
Impetigo is a bacterial infection. It is a common and very contagious ailment that frequently affects children.

Boils develop when hair follicles become infected. The infection spreads to surrounding tissues which fill up with pus. Diabetes can also cause boils.

Skin infections are spread by scratching the infected areas and by poor personal hygiene. Those susceptible are primarily infants in crèches and schools, and those with low immunity who are already suffering from dermatitis.

WHICH PLANTS?

WARNING Use only one of the following at any given time.

INTERNAL USAGE
For infection
ECHINACEA Liquid extract, 1 g dried root equivalent, three times a day.
GARLIC Tablets, capsules, follow manufacturer's instructions, to a maximum of 6 g dried garlic clove equivalent per day.

To detoxify the liver and kidneys
DANDELION Liquid extract, 500 mg–1 g dried root equivalent, three times a day.
GLOBE ARTICHOKE Tablets, capsules, 500 mg–1 g dried herb equivalent, standardised for cynarin content, three times a day.
BURDOCK Liquid extract, 500 mg–1.5 g dried root equivalent, three times a day.
YELLOW DOCK Liquid extract, 2–4 g dried root equivalent, three times a day.

EXTERNAL APPLICATION
TEA TREE Add 1 ml essential oil to 15 ml water and apply to the affected area, avoiding the eyes.
SLIPPERY ELM Mix 1 teaspoon of slippery elm powder with 2–3 teaspoons of water to form a paste. Apply to the affected area once a day to bring the boil to a head.
CHICKWEED Apply a chickweed-based cream as directed on the label.
THYME Infuse 2 g dried herb in 1 cup of boiling water for 5 minutes before straining. Soak a cloth in this infusion and apply to the affected area for 15 minutes, three to four times a day.
LAVENDER Add 3 drops of the essential oil to 10 ml carrier oil and cover the affected area. Repeat two or three times a day.

As advised by a medical herbalist
- Barberry, wild indigo

Other measures
- Avoid scratching – this will reduce the chance of the infection spreading to other areas.
- Never squeeze a boil to remove the pus. It should be left to clear up, untouched, although poultices may be used to bring it to a head.
- Support your immune system by avoiding fatty and sugary foods whilst the infection is present.

See also Abscess

Stretch marks

When there is a significant increase in weight, often as a result of pregnancy, the skin is distended and tissues may rupture. This occurs more commonly on the skin of the breasts, stomach and buttocks, and takes the form of fine stretch marks of unequal lengths, but generally ranging up to 20 cm.

Symptoms
- Pink or purplish red raised lines that after a few months usually become flattened and pale

CONSULT YOUR DOCTOR OR MEDICAL HERBALIST
- Herbal treatments are only complementary and should not replace regular medical supervision, especially in cases of extreme weight variation.

Causes
Stretch marks are usually caused by thinning and lack of elasticity in the skin, at a time of weight increase. They can sometimes be linked to an endocrine disorder such as hyperthyroidism or to the use of steroid medications such as prednisone. Body-builders may also develop them, because of the extra muscle bulk, the stretching of the skin during exercising or even the alteration of adrenal or testicular hormones.

WHICH PLANTS?

WARNING Use only one of the following at any given time.

It is difficult to treat stretch marks. However, medicinal plants can help by stimulating the rebuilding of the elasticity of the skin, and by improving both the quality of the collagen in the connective tissue and blood circulation.

INTERNAL USAGE
For healthy skin
EVENING PRIMROSE OIL Capsules, 1000 mg, three times a day with meals during the last 10 days of the menstrual cycle.

To improve blood circulation
GINKGO Tablets, up to 2 g, standardised for ginkgo flavone glycosides, and ginkgolides and bilobalide. Take up to three times a day. (See Cautions, p. 102.)
GOLDEN SEAL Tablets, capsules, 250–500 mg dried rhizome equivalent, three times a day. Do not take if you have high blood pressure.

A TO Z OF AILMENTS   295

SKIN PROBLEMS

GRAPE SEED Tablets, capsules, up to 24 g dried seed equivalent per day, standardised for anthocyanidin content.

EXTERNAL APPLICATION
GOTU KOLA Massage in cream, ointment or lotion based on gotu kola once or twice a day, as directed on the label.
LADY'S MANTLE Boil 40 g of dried leaves in 1 litre of water. Leave to infuse for 10 minutes, soak a cloth in the liquid and apply three times a day.

Other measures

- Along with other symptoms, stretch marks may be an indication of zinc deficiency. Talk to your doctor or medical herbalist about taking a zinc supplement. Vitamins A, C and E and the minerals iron and silica may also be indicated.
- Immerse the lower part of your body in cold and then hot baths.
- Have massages.
- Follow a sensible weight-loss program – crash dieting and sudden changes in weight may worsen the problem.

See also Excess weight & Obesity

Sunburn

Depending on its severity, sunburn can cause anything from an acute inflammation of the skin to severe blistering.

Symptoms

- Redness of the skin with a sharp burning sensation
- Blisters, then peeling of the skin
- In severe cases, fever, nausea and headaches (sunstroke)

CONSULT YOUR DOCTOR OR MEDICAL HERBALIST

- If you have several or all of the above symptoms, you should consult a doctor. All cases of serious sunburn need rapid medical attention.

Causes

The principle cause of sunburn is sun exposure, including exposure to reflected sun rays from the snow or sea. It is possible to get sunburnt even on cloudy days. Prolonged or repeated sun exposure is a major risk factor for the development of skin cancers.

Certain drugs can also make you more susceptible to sunburn (some antibiotics and acne treatments in particular, but also some herbal medicines).

PUVA therapy (the technique of using the sun's rays to treat certain skin complaints, such as psoriasis) can also have the same effect.

WHICH PLANTS?

WARNING Use only one of the following at any given time.

INTERNAL USAGE
GOTU KOLA Capsules, up to 600 mg dried herb equivalent, three times a day.
GRAPE SEED Tablets, capsules, up to 24 g dried seed equivalent per day, standardised for anthocyanidin content.
PINEAPPLE Bromelain tablets, capsules, up to 2 g per day in divided doses before meals.

EXTERNAL APPLICATION
ALOE VERA Gel, apply aloe vera gel two to three times a day, or as directed on the label.
LAVENDER Add 3 drops of essential oil to 10 ml carrier oil and apply to the affected area two to three times a day.
CALENDULA Infuse 5 g dried flower heads in 1 litre boiling water for 5 minutes. Cool, strain and apply to the affected area as a compress three times a day.
WITCH HAZEL Apply witch hazel water to the affected skin once or twice a day, as directed on the label.

Other measures

- Protect your skin before any exposure to the sun, and do not sunbathe for very long without sun protection. The sun's rays are likely to be strongest between noon and 3 pm.
- If your skin is fair or delicate, use a strong sunscreen, cover up and wear a hat.
- Drink plenty of fluids whilst in the sun, and avoid consuming alcohol, which can contribute to dehydration.
- If blisters occur, do not pierce them.

Warts

Warts are a common but unpleasant skin condition. They are small, benign skin tumours that appear as growths of varying shape and are extremely common. They tend to develop slowly and haphazardly, can disappear quickly for no apparent reason and may be slightly contagious.

Symptoms

- Discolouration of the skin, in raised patches
- Appearance of one or more small, rough growths
- In some cases, itching or bleeding, which may signify a bacterial or fungal infection
- Occurring on the sole of the foot, a plantar wart may be painful when standing or walking

CONSULT YOUR DOCTOR

- Ask your doctor to check any warts to confirm that they are not skin cancers.

Causes

Warts are caused by the human papilloma class of viruses (HPV), which provoke an abnormal growth of cells in a given place. Warts have different appearances, depending on their location. The most frequently seen varieties are common warts, which generally occur on the hands, and plantar warts (verrucas) that occur on the feet.

SKIN PROBLEMS

Cervical warts are sexually transmitted by certain strains of HPV and may be precursors of cervical cancer.

Genital warts *(Condyloma acuminata)* are caused by a different type of virus, as is *Molluscum contagiosum*, a harmless but highly contagious infection which is often found among children, and which is characterised by shiny papules on the skin's surface.

Scratching, warm, damp feet and fungal skin infections encourage the development of warts as the virus enters the skin via small cuts or scratches. Fatigue and stress can increase susceptibility to warts.

WHICH PLANTS?

WARNING Use only one of the following at any given time.

The following plants may be used to treat common and plantar warts, and Molluscum contagiosum. Genital and cervical warts are not suitable for self-treatment, and require medical help.

INTERNAL USAGE
For infection
ELDER Liquid extract, 500 mg–1 g dried flower equivalent, three times a day.
ECHINACEA Liquid extract, 1 g dried root equivalent, three times a day.
GARLIC Tablets, capsules, follow manufacturer's instructions, to a maximum of 6 g dried garlic clove equivalent per day.
LICORICE 1–2 teaspoons root powder steeped in 1 cup of boiling water for 10 minutes before straining. Drink 2–3 cups a day for no more than four to six weeks.
ASTRAGALUS Liquid extract, 1–2.5 g dried herb equivalent, three times a day

EXTERNAL APPLICATION
For their antiviral properties
MULLEIN Soak 3 teaspoons dried herb in 300 ml cold water for 30 minutes. Gently bring to the boil. Strain. Soak a cloth in this liquid and apply to the affected area as a compress twice a day.

GREATER CELANDINE Apply liquid extract to the affected area one to three times a day.
LEMON BALM Infuse 20 g dried flower heads in 500 ml of boiling water for 10 minutes. Cool, strain and apply to the affected area as a compress three times a day.
CALENDULA Infuse 5 g dried flower heads in 1 litre boiling water for 5 minutes. Cool, strain and apply to the affected area as a compress three times a day.

As advised by a medical herbalist
- Pau d'arco

Other measures
- Avoid walking barefoot in public places (especially swimming pools and locker rooms).
- Try not to touch the infected area(s), and avoid contact with anyone who has warts.
- Some warts resolve spontaneously or with appropriate herbal treatment. Others are more stubborn.
- Have regular pap smears, especially if you have a history of cervical warts.

Wounds & Grazes

Wounds are cuts, punctures or tears in the skin or other tissues. They vary in depth and are more or less clearly defined. Grazes are wounds that only affect the superficial skin tissues.

Symptoms
Wounds
- A cut or tear with either 'clean' or irregular edges
- A puncture injury
- Bleeding, often profuse

Grazes
- An abrasion or scratch on the outer layer of the epidermis
- Short-lived bleeding

CONSULT YOUR DOCTOR
- You can treat simple grazes yourself, provided they have not become infected or inflamed.
- For wounds, see your doctor or go to the emergency department at the local hospital, especially if they contain foreign bodies such as pieces of glass or gravel, or are infected or inflamed.
- A wound with irregular edges cannot be stitched or drawn together, and usually has to be dressed. Ensure that your tetanus injections are up to date and, if necessary, ask for an injection or booster.
- If a wound begins to throb and grow hot, or to discharge pus, it may be infected – see your doctor.

Causes
Like bruises, wounds and grazes are localised damage caused by some form of violent contact with a sharp or heavy object. Cuts usually create wounds with clean edges, unlike contusions and tears, which can be external or internal.

WHICH PLANTS?

WARNING Use only one of the following at any given time.

Only use medicinal plants if your tetanus injections are up to date and if the wound is not serious.

INTERNAL USAGE
To prevent infection
ECHINACEA Liquid extract, 1 g dried root equivalent, three times a day.
GARLIC Tablets, capsules, follow manufacturer's instructions, to a maximum of 6 g dried garlic clove equivalent per day.

EXTERNAL APPLICATION
To disinfect the affected area and encourage healing
TEA TREE Add 1 ml essential oil to 15 ml water and apply to the affected area, avoiding the eyes.

A TO Z OF AILMENTS 297

SKIN PROBLEMS

ACTIVE MANUKA HONEY Apply honey to an absorbent wound dressing and place it over the affected area, with a second dressing over the entire area to prevent the honey from leaking. Change the dressings regularly – adhesion of the dressing to the wound indicates that more frequent changes are required. Medical management of the wound may be called for.

To cover an infected wound
LAVENDER Add 1–2 drops of essential oil to the compress used as a dressing.

For inflammation
ALOE VERA Gel, apply aloe vera gel two to three times a day, or as directed on the label.
CALENDULA Infuse 5 g dried flower heads in 1 litre boiling water for 5 minutes. Cool, strain and apply to the affected area as a compress three times a day.

Other measures
- Always clean grazes and wounds with a disinfectant.
- Use a sticking plaster to draw the edges of a wound together.
- Put a light dressing on a graze to keep out infection.

URINARY TRACT & KIDNEY PROBLEMS

Cystitis & Urethritis

Cystitis is an inflammation of the bladder, and urethritis is an inflammation of the urethra or passage through which the bladder is emptied. Attacks can be sudden and acute, or chronic and long term. Cystitis is very common in women, but occurs rarely in men.

Symptoms
- Burning pain when urinating, more intense in the case of urethritis
- Frequent urge to urinate, often without a real need to do so
- Urine is dark, and blood or pus may be present
- Often shivering and fever

Causes
Cystitis and urethritis are caused by a bacterial infection of the bladder, which can be linked to constipation, diarrhoea or sexual relations. In women, poor personal hygiene can sometimes be a cause of cystitis. Most cases of cystitis are caused by the bacterium *E. coli*.

CONSULT YOUR DOCTOR OR MEDICAL HERBALIST
- Despite the fact that most women are able to identify cystitis themselves, a doctor's diagnosis should still be sought to ensure that there is no other disease present.
- A simple examination of the urine is usually sufficient. Cystitis may not appear to be a serious complaint, but without correct treatment even a benign inflammation is at risk of becoming more serious.

WHICH PLANTS?

WARNING Use only one of the following at any given time.

INTERNAL USAGE
CRANBERRY Tablets, capsules, 10 g fresh juice equivalent, three times a day, with plenty of water. Or drink 500 ml of fresh juice twice a day.
BUCHU Infuse 1 sachet in 1 cup of boiling water for 5 minutes. Drink 1 cup three times a day before meals.
DANDELION Liquid extract, 4–10 g dried leaf equivalent, three times a day.
CLEAVERS Liquid extract, 2–4 g dried plant equivalent, three times a day.
GOLDEN ROD Infusion, 1.5–3 g dried herb infused in 1 cup of boiling water for 10–15 minutes before straining. Drink 3–5 cups a day.
CORN SILK Liquid extract, 2–8 g dried corn silk equivalent, three times a day.
UVA-URSI Liquid extract, 1.5–2.5 g dried herb equivalent, three times a day.
MARSHMALLOW 2–3 g dried root infused in 1 cup of boiling water for 10 minutes before straining. Drink 2–3 cups a day.

As advised by a medical herbalist
- Barberry

Other measures
- Drink plenty of fluids: 1.5–2 litres a day of water, infusions or juice.
- Ensure you urinate regularly, at least four or five times a day, emptying the bladder completely each time.
- If you are constipated, eat fresh fruit and green vegetables, take meals at regular times and drink plenty of fluids with them.
- Avoid wearing tight clothes.
- After going to the toilet, wipe yourself from front to back and not vice versa.
- If bouts of cystitis occur after sexual activity, get into the habit of urinating immediately after intercourse.

URINARY TRACT & KIDNEY PROBLEMS

- Avoid substances that can be irritants, such as tea, coffee, spices and alcohol.
- Avoid vaginal deodorants, douches or underwear made of artificial fibres.

DID YOU KNOW?

Urinary infection

Golden rod, which was used in urology in ancient times, is enjoying a revival and appears to be particularly effective for treating urinary infections.

It is an anti-inflammatory, a diuretic, a urinary antiseptic and it stimulates the immune system, as has been recently discovered. Its action is both local (on the urinary passages) and general, thanks to its effect on the pituitary gland, which influences the working of the adrenal glands. It can be employed to treat practically all urinary problems.

Fluid retention

When too much water is stored in the body it causes swelling, known medically as oedema – or fluid retention. It can affect any part of the body, including the lungs and the abdominal cavity. Localised swelling, of the ankles or fingers, for example, is usually only temporary and often corrects itself.

Symptoms

- Swollen tissues in the area affected, such as the lower legs, abdomen, face, arms and fingers
- Pressing the skin leaves an indentation for a few moments
- Shortness of breath, particularly when lying down
- Symptoms may only occur premenstrually, or in hot or humid weather

CONSULT YOUR DOCTOR OR MEDICAL HERBALIST

- Anyone with symptoms of fluid retention – not to be confused with obesity – should consult a doctor to establish the cause.
- The condition is usually treated with diuretic drugs that increase urinary output. When a large amount of fluid has collected, such as in the abdomen, this may need to be drained via a tube under a local anaesthetic.

Causes

Generalised fluid retention can be caused by conditions that affect protein levels in the blood. These include kidney disease, liver disease and malnutrition. It can also be caused by anything that increases the leakiness of blood capillaries, such as an injury or burn. Hormonal imbalances, as in premenstrual syndrome, may also cause fluid retention.

When an individual suffers from heart failure, fluid retention occurs because the heart is unable to pump blood round fast enough to clear fluid from the tissues.

Common, everyday causes of fluid retention include a sedentary lifestyle as well as bad posture – for example, prolonged standing or sitting with your legs crossed. Swollen ankles are common in hot weather, or when flying, especially if movement is restricted.

WHICH PLANTS?

WARNING Use only one of the following at any given time.

Fluid retention can be a symptom of a serious medical problem. Seek advice from your doctor. A medical herbalist can advise which of the following herbs is best to help alleviate your symptoms.

If caused by a kidney disorder
- Barberry, cleavers, corn silk, dandelion leaf, horsetail, meadowsweet

If caused by a liver disorder
- Boldo, corn silk, globe artichoke, lime flowers, milk thistle, rosemary

If due to poor circulation
- Agrimony, butcher's broom, grape seed, horsechestnut

If cardiac in origin
- Hawthorn

Other measures

- Reduce salt intake, as sodium encourages fluid retention.
- Eat foods that stimulate the elimination of water, such as horseradish, celery, nettle, beetroot and sorrel.
- Put your feet up during the day, with heels higher than your hips.
- Raise the foot of the bed a few centimetres – using a phone book, for example.
- Walk as much as possible to help the muscles to pump fluid back up to the heart more effectively.
- For congested lungs, sleep propped up on pillows. This will ease breathing, as well as help the kidneys to excrete more fluid.

See also Kidney infection, Premenstrual syndrome

A TO Z OF AILMENTS 299

URINARY TRACT & KIDNEY PROBLEMS

Kidney infection

Kidney infection, also known as pyelonephritis, is an acute inflammation of the urinary tract and kidneys.

It tends to affect pregnant women; however, it can also be chronic and start in childhood.

Symptoms
- Burning sensation when passing urine
- Pain and a sense of heaviness in the lower back (generally this occurs only on one side)
- Fever that escalates rapidly and is preceded by shivering
- Sometimes nausea and vomiting
- Infrequent urination and dark-coloured urine, or conversely, a frequent need to urinate
- Repeated infections may cause scar tissue to develop, leading to serious kidney damage
- Occasionally, severe complications may ensue, including kidney failure, blood infection (bacteraemia) and high blood pressure

CONSULT YOUR DOCTOR
- Acute pyelonephritis should be treated immediately. The diagnosis can be determined by tests carried out on the urine, which will reveal the nature of the bacteria involved.
- In the event of repeated urinary problems, medicinal plants can have a preventive effect.

Causes
Acute kidney infection is usually a complication of cystitis or of a benign urinary infection that has migrated up the ureter to the kidneys. It is more likely to occur under circumstances where the flow of urine is obstructed.

It can also be the result of a massive bacterial invasion of the urinary system, particularly in a hospital environment. It also occurs when there is a previous history of urinary disorders.

WHICH PLANTS?

WARNING Use only one of the following at any given time.

INTERNAL USAGE
For inflammation and pain
CORN SILK Liquid extract, 2–8 g dried corn silk equivalent, three times a day.
MARSHMALLOW 2–3 g dried root infused in 1 cup of boiling water for 10 minutes before straining. Drink 2–3 cups a day.

To increase urination
DANDELION Liquid extract, 4–10 g dried leaf equivalent, three times a day.

To treat infection
GARLIC Tablets, capsules, follow manufacturer's instructions, to a maximum of 6 g dried garlic clove equivalent per day.
GOLDEN ROD Infusion, 1.5–3 g dried herb infused in 1 cup of boiling water for 10–15 minutes before straining. Drink 3–5 cups a day.

As advised by a medical herbalist
- Barberry, grapefruit seed

Other measures
- Increase your fluid intake to facilitate urination, bring down the fever and reduce inflammation.
- Avoid alcohol, tea and coffee.

See also Cystitis & Urethritis, Fluid retention

Kidney stones

When urates, calcium or phosphates (present in urine) become concentrated in the kidneys, stones can form, which migrate towards the bladder or the ureter, producing severe pain.

Symptoms
- Sharp, recurring pain in the kidney area, from the lower back and side of the abdomen, into the pelvis
- Possibly, blood in the urine
- Fever in cases of secondary infection

CONSULT YOUR DOCTOR
- If you suffer any of the symptoms above, it is important to consult a doctor and possibly a urologist.

Causes
Kidney stones may be caused by metabolic disorders allied to a diet too rich in proteins and calcium. But an excess of calcium in the blood may also be caused by osteoporosis, hyperthyroidism, excessive levels of vitamin D, or uric acid in those suffering from gout. Stones can also form following an infection or the slowdown of kidney function. Dehydration may also be a factor.

Men are three times more likely than women to develop kidney stones, and they tend to be a recurrent problem.

URINARY TRACT & KIDNEY PROBLEMS

WHICH PLANTS?

WARNING Use only one of the following at any given time.

Kidney stones can be extremely painful, and always require professional medical treatment. Herbal medicines, as prescribed by a medical herbalist, may play a valuable complementary role in reducing the symptoms.

As advised by a medical herbalist
- Corn silk, golden rod, marshmallow

Other measures
- Eat fruit such as melon and grapefruit, and especially watermelon and citrus fruit.
- Drink lots of water (if you live in an area with hard water, use filtered or bottled water instead of tap water).
- Ask your medical herbalist whether he or she would advise a course of minerals in your case.

Prostate disorders

It is estimated that by the age of 50, at least 50 per cent of men will experience prostate symptoms.

Benign prostatic hyperplasia (BPH) causes an enlargement of the prostate gland, which restricts the urethra (urinary canal) that passes through the prostate, causing urinary obstruction and retention. Because enlargement of the prostate gland is also a symptom of prostate cancer, a medical examination is essential in every case.

Prostatitis, an infection or inflammation of the prostate gland, may be either chronic or acute.

Symptoms
Prostatic enlargement
- Frequent urge to urinate, especially during the night
- A feeling of not being able to empty the bladder (an ultrasound scan usually confirms the presence of a residue)
- Reduction in the force or volume of urinary flow
- May be difficult to start urinating (hesitancy), or once started, the stream may be intermittent
- Incontinence and blood in the urine may also occur
- Sometimes tightness and burning in the bladder

Prostatitis
- A feeling of heaviness and pain in the groin and above the base of the penis
- Pain when urinating, with urgency and frequency. Also painful ejaculation
- Fever in cases of serious infection

CONSULT YOUR DOCTOR
- Only a medical examination can make the distinction between BPH, a prostate or urinary infection, and prostate cancer.
- Some forms of BPH require surgical intervention. Prostatitis is also potentially serious – it can lead to sterility and requires medical treatment.

Causes
Prostatic enlargement may be caused by a hormonal imbalance. This is a common development in men from the age of 45 into old age.

Prostatitis is usually the result of an infection of the urinary tract, possibly caused by ureteritis, cystitis or sexually transmitted diseases.

WHICH PLANTS?

The following treatment is only for prostate conditions which have been medically confirmed as benign.

Internal usage
SAW PALMETTO Capsules, standardised for their content of free fatty acids, follow manufacturer's instructions.

Other measures
- Do not take decongestants or any over-the-counter cold remedies since they may aggravate the symptoms.
- If you are having trouble urinating, consult your doctor.
- Consider taking a zinc supplement, and include pumpkin seeds (also known as pepitas) in your diet.

See also **Cystitis & Urethritis**

A TO Z OF AILMENTS 301

GLOSSARY

Type in **bold** indicates entry in glossary

acid Having a pH value below 7, pH being a measure of the acidity or alkalinity of a substance (such as soil) or a solution.

acute Arising suddenly, and usually of short duration.

aerial parts The parts of a plant that grow above the ground.

aggregation of platelets Coagulation of blood **platelets** causing the formation of a blood clot, involved in the healing of wounds.

AHA Acronym for alpha-hydroxy-acid, a substance composed of fruit acids.

alcoholate An alcohol-based preparation of a plant.

alkaline Having a pH value of more than 7, pH being a measure of the acidity or alkalinity of a substance (such as soil) or solution.

alkaloids Organic compounds of plant origin, with a marked pharmacological action, whose molecules contain at least one nitrogen atom.

allergen A substance or molecule that can trigger an allergic reaction in those sensitive to that substance.

allergenic Provoking an allergic reaction.

analgesic Prevents or reduces the perception of pain.

anethole A compound found in volatile oils with an odour of anise. It is extracted from, for example, anise (*Pimpinella anisum*) and star anise (*Ilicium verum*) and used in flavourings.

annual A plant that lives for one year, during the course of which it grows from a seed, reproduces and dies.

anorexia Loss of appetite. Anorexia nervosa is a psychological condition related to the fear of becoming fat.

anthelmintic or vermifuge Acting to expel or destroy intestinal worms.

anthocyanins Plant pigments found mainly in plants that are blue, mauve or purple. They form part of the **polyphenol** group.

anthraquinones Quinones (molecules with a cyclical structure) deriving from anthracene that have laxative properties.

antibiotic Kills bacteria or prevents their proliferation.

antifungal Kills microscopic fungi or prevents their proliferation.

anti-inflammatories Class of drug designed to relieve inflammation in the body. Common examples are ibuprofen, aspirin and paracetamol.

anti-oxidant Combats the actions of free radicals, which are produced naturally by the body during cell metabolism, but when produced to excess can sometimes have a harmful degenerative effect.

antipruritic Acts against itchiness.

antipyretic Reduces fever.

antiseptic Destroys or weakens micro-organisms, such as bacteria, microscopic fungi, parasites.

anxiolytics, tranquillisers, sedatives Drugs or herbal medicines that reduce anxiety or nervousness.

aphrodisiac Substance that stimulates or intensifies sexual desire.

aqueous extract Preparation obtained after treating a plant with water, at which point the solution obtained is concentrated.

arrhythmia Irregularities of the heartbeat.

asthenia General fatigue, weakening of the body.

astringent Tightens tissue, in particular the skin. An example is tannin.

auricles The two small chambers of the heart that receive blood back from the rest of the body, before pumping it into the ventricles. Also known as atria.

autoimmune disease The body's allergic reaction to part of itself, mistaking it for a foreign agent or chemical. Rheumatoid arthritis is an example, where the body attacks the synovial tissue of its own joints.

Ayurvedic medicine Ancient system of holistic medicine originating in India.

bacterium (plural, bacteria) Infectious agents usually comprising a single cell, living and reproducing on living or dead organic matter, sometimes capable of causing disease in humans. Staphylococcus and streptococcus are examples of bacteria.

benign Not very serious. Not cancerous.

berberine A bitter-tasting yellow alkaloid, obtained from barberry and other plants, and used in medicine as a tonic.

betacarotene Orange-coloured pigment from the **carotenoid** group, used by the body to produce vitamin D.

biennial Plant whose life cycle is two years. The first year the plant forms leaves and builds up reserves, and in the second produces an upright stem that carries flowers.

bile duct Canal that links the gall bladder to the small intestine, through which bile flows during digestion.

bitter principles A range of organic compounds, characterised by their bitter taste, that stimulate the secretion of saliva and digestive juices.

blood platelets *See* **platelets**.

blood serum Clear liquid that separates from a blood clot after coagulation.

bract A leaflike structure situated at the base of a flower or a group of flowers (inflorescence). Often smaller than the other leaves, it can, however, be well developed and brightly coloured in certain species.

bronchodilator Increases the diameter of the bronchi (airways in the lungs).

calcareous Containing calcium – alkaline, chalky.

calculus Hard, stonelike mass that can form in the kidneys, the salivary glands or the gall bladder.

capillaries Tiny vessels with very thin walls that ensure the body's cells are supplied with fluids and nutrients. Blood capillaries carry blood, and lymphatic capillaries transport lymph.

GLOSSARY

capsule Dry fruit that opens when ripe to disperse its seeds via a cap of small holes (pores) or a transversal slit, such as the fruit of the poppy.

carbohydrate Sugars and starches. Foods such as flour, potatoes, rice and bread consist mostly of carbohydrates. Used to produce energy in the body.

carcinogenic Potentially causing cancer.

cardiovascular system The parts of the body relating to the flow of blood. This includes the heart, arteries, capillaries and veins.

carminative Facilitates the expulsion or absorption of intestinal gas.

carotenoids Group of orange, red or yellow-coloured pigments, very common in vegetables and present in the animals that consume them.

catecholamines Group of organic molecules that are the body's neurotransmitters (messengers from the nervous system) or hormones, and which include adrenaline.

catkin In botany, a collection of very small flowers (inflorescence) in a simple spike, generally drooping, e.g. the inflorescence of the poplar.

cholesterol In the body, blood cholesterol – a fatlike waxy material that is a component of all cells – is manufactured by the liver. It is also involved in the creation of some hormones and helps to make vitamin D and bile acids to aid digestion. High levels of blood cholesterol (inherited, or associated with poor diet and obesity) are a major risk factor for heart disease. Dietary cholesterol is the cholesterol contained in food. It is now not generally considered to affect blood cholesterol levels to any significant degree in healthy people, although the debate continues.

chronic Persistent, long-term

colic Abdominal pain that waxes and wanes in a rhythmic fashion.

collagen Fibrous protein that is an important constituent of skin in particular, which improves its elasticity.

connective tissue Tissue such as collagen that fills and supports the body's organs.

corm A swollen underground stem, similar to a bulb, having papery rather than fleshy scale leaves. It is used by the plant for storage and propagation.

cornea The clear convex part of the front of the eye which allows the passage of light.

corticosteroids Hormones produced by the adrenocortex (outer region of the adrenal gland) from cholesterol, and their synthetic equivalents. Cortisone is a corticosteroid.

cortisone Corticosteroid hormone that plays an important role in the regulation of the metabolism, including the processing of fats, sugars and proteins.

coumaric (derivative) Plant compounds derived from coumarins.

coumarins Aromatic compounds with various properties. Often acting as an anticoagulant in the blood, they are commonly used as a venous tonic.

decoction Water-based preparations, made from the tough parts of herbs, such as seeds, barks and roots, that release their active constituents only when cut or broken into small pieces and simmered.

demulcent Soothing, usually mucilaginous or oily substance, used especially to relieve pain in inflamed or irritated mucous surfaces.

depurative Encouraging elimination of waste products from the body.

dermatitis Inflammation of the skin. Also known as eczema.

dermis Lower layer of skin covered by the epidermis (outer layer) consisting of tissue composed of blood vessels, nerves, the base of hair follicles and sweat glands.

DEXA-scan An X-ray used to measure bone density.

diuretic Increases the production of urine.

division Type of propagation in which a plant is split into parts, one or more of which can be replanted.

dopamine Molecule acting as a neurotransmitter (substance that transmits messages between nerves). Found largely in the brain.

double-blind study or trial Experiment in which neither the patient nor the doctor knows whether the patient is taking the real substance under evaluation (for example, a new drug or herbal medicine), or a placebo (ineffective substance, often a sugar pill). Thought to be the most objective and reliable way to test the effectiveness of new medicines or treatments.

dried extract Formed when a plant is extracted with a solvent (aqueous extract if extracted only with water). The resulting solution is filtered and the solvent removed to produce a solid or semi-solid dry extract.

dyspepsia Indigestion.

emollient Softens tissue, notably the skin.

encephalitis Inflammation or infection of the brain.

endocrine Relating to the organs and tissues that secrete hormones.

ENT Acronym for ear, nose and throat.

enzyme Protein that accelerates the biochemical reactions that occur in living organisms.

epidermis Outer layer of the skin.

erythema Redness of the skin.

Escherichia coli Parasitic bacterium that lives in the intestine, not virulent in its normal state, but which, in certain cases, can cause various ailments (infections of the urinary or biliary tracts, septicaemia, etc). Synonym: colibacillus or coliform.

essential oil Volatile, highly aromatic oil contained in certain plants that have medicinal properties. Obtained by steam distillation.

excitant Causing stimulation.

expectorant Aids evacuation of any secretions that have accumulated in the air passages, by encouraging coughing.

fatty acids Organic molecules that are the principal constituents of lipids (fats). Fatty acids are known as **saturated** when all the carbon–carbon links are single. They are known as unsaturated when at least two carbon atoms are linked by a double bond.

GLOSSARY

fissure Split in the skin or membrane, for example, an anal fissure – split in the skin of the anus.

fistula Abnormal channel linking two hollow organs, or one of them and the skin, often caused by ulceration or congenital malformation (such as an anal fistula).

flavones Plant compounds belonging to the flavonoid group, present in vegetables, fruit, wine or tea.

flavonoids Plant pigments with diuretic, anti-inflammatory and anti-spasmodic properties.

flora (intestinal, buccal, skin) The types of microbes that live in or on a particular part of the body – mostly bacteria. They are often harmless and can be protective, if they prevent other more pathological microbes from establishing themselves.

flower heads A flower cluster (inflorescence) which, when gathered, includes petals, sepals, bracts, small leaves and flower stalks.

follicle Name given to various anatomical structures, such as a cluster of cells (ovarian follicle) or a structure in the form of a small cavity (hair follicle). All generally have a secretory, excretory or protective function.

free radicals Atoms or group of atoms produced during cell **metabolism** and by the action of certain rays (especially light rays). They are highly reactive and unstable. When they occur in large numbers, they are liable to degrade cell membranes and are thought therefore to represent a potential risk of heart disease, cancer and other serious conditions. **Anti-oxidants** help to limit their harmful effects.

fungi Infectious agents that, unlike plants, have no green chlorophyll, stems, roots or leaves. They live in, or off, living or dead organic material, sometimes causing disease. Examples include yeasts, tinea, moulds, mushrooms, *Candida*. They reproduce through spores.

glomerulus Small knot of blood vessels in the kidneys whose role is to filter waste matter from the blood into the urine. Each kidney contains about a million glomeruli.

glucosides Plant substances consisting of compounds that have at least one glucose molecule attached.

glucosinolates Sulphurated vegetable compounds that are mainly found in plants of the *Brassica* genus (such as horseradish), and which have expectorant properties.

glycerides Category of lipids composed of a fatty acid combined with one or more glycerine molecules.

glycogen A carbohydrate found in the liver and muscles, which is used by the body as an energy store.

gullet See **oesophagus**.

haematoma Accumulation of blood in tissue, often following a blow and commonly called a bruise.

haemoglobin Major oxygen-bearing protein in red blood cells that gives blood its red colour. It is made up of an iron-containing compound haem (approx. 6 per cent) and the protein globin (approx. 94 per cent). It carries oxygen in the blood and supplies it to the body's tissues.

haemorrhage Bleeding.

Helicobacter pylori Bacterium suspected of causing chronic gastritis and stomach ulcers.

hepatic Relating to the liver.

herb Term used to describe a plant used in medical herbalism, without its roots, but with or without flowering tops.

herbaceous (plant) Plant characteristic of a herb and without a woody stem.

hermaphrodite In botany, a flower that has both male (stamen) and female (pistil) organs.

heteroside Complex sugar composed of a glucose molecule combined with a non-sugar molecule.

histamine Compound in plant and animal tissue, notably released during allergic reactions, causing characteristic inflammation and itching.

hormone Substance secreted by an endocrine gland which, after having been transported through the blood supply to a target organ, modifies that organ's activity.

hyperglycaemia Higher than normal level of sugar in the blood.

hyperparathyroidism Condition caused by overactive parathyroid gland (glands situated behind the thryroid).

hypersensitivity Condition of heightened sensitivity of the immune system when in contact with an allergen already experienced, which causes an allergic reaction.

hypertension High blood pressure.

hypotension Low blood pressure.

immune system The organs, tissues, cells and molecules that protect the body against invading pathogens or abnormal body cells.

immunodeficiency Weakness of the immune system.

immunosuppression Abnormally weak activity of the immune system following a disease such as HIV/AIDS or leukaemia, or chemotherapy for tumours or organ transplants, or removal of the spleen.

inflammation A protective reaction by the body to injury, infection, allergy or cancer. The affected tissue becomes hot, red, swollen and painful.

in vitro Designating biological processes or experiments conducted in an artificial environment outside a living organism.

in vivo Designating biological processes or experiments conducted or occurring within the living organism.

iridoids Plant compounds belonging to the terpene group with various medicinal properties, such as anti-inflammatory.

ischaemia Reduced blood supply to an area of the body, resulting in inadequate oxygenation of the tissues.

isoflavones Plant compounds belonging to the flavonoid group that have an action in the body similar to that of **oestrogen**.

GLOSSARY

keratin Fibrous protein that is the principal constituent of nails and hair.

ketones Substances produced in the body as a by-product of the burning of fats to produce energy – often found in people who can't use, or don't have, any glucose as an energy source, such as in diabetes or starvation.

latex The usually milky, viscous sap of certain trees and plants, containing substances such as alkaloids, mineral salts, starch and sugars.

laxative, purgative A substance that stimulates evacuation of the bowels.

leaflets Division of a compound leaf.

lesion Any visible abnormality, caused by disease. Most common on the skin.

linalool (or linalol) A colourless, fragrant compound found in many volatile oils, which is used in the manufacture of perfume.

liniment A fluid preparation used externally on the skin.

lipids Any of numerous fats and fatlike substances which, with carbohydrates and proteins, constitute the principal structural material of living cells.

lymphatic Concerning the lymph fluid. The lymphatic system includes lymph nodes and all the capillaries and vessels that transport the lymph fluid.

lymphocyte Type of white blood corpuscle, which plays a part in the working of the immune system.

malignant Of disease, a tumour or other disorder that tends to become progressively worse and results in death.

medicinal wine Preparation obtained by macerating medicinal plants in wine.

meningitis Inflammation or infection of the outer covering of the brain.

metabolism All the biochemical reactions that take place in the body and keep it supplied with energy.

monoterpenes Plant compounds containing 10 carbon atoms from the **terpene** group, whose molecules have one cycle (or none), with medicinal properties, present in most essential oils.

mucilage Sticky carbohydrate substance present in many plants, such as slippery elm.

mucous membrane Membrane lining the ducts or cavities of the digestive tube, the urogenital and respiratory systems and the interior of the eye socket that ensures they keep moist through the production of mucus.

myxoedema Thickening and roughening of the skin, a symptom of hypothyroidism (an underactive thyroid gland) when generalised, and of hyperthyroidism (an overactive thyroid gland) when limited to the shins.

narcotic A substance that dulls the senses, induces sleep and with prolonged use becomes addictive.

necrosis Death of tissue.

nervous system Body's control system. The central nervous system (brain and spinal column) works with the peripheral nerve system (consisting of billions of nerve cells) to relay sensory and motor impulses through the body.

neuropathy Generic term describing all illnesses of the central nervous system.

neurotoxic Toxic to the body's central nervous system.

neurotransmitters Chemicals produced in the body to enable communication between one nerve cell and another, or between a nerve and a muscle.

neutral Having a pH value of 7, so neither acid or alkaline, pH being a measure of the acidity or alkalinity of a substance (such as soil) or solution.

node In botany, the point at which a leaf's stalk (petiole) joins a stem.

noradrenaline Substance that acts on the sympathetic nervous system (that stimulates the body's involuntary functions: digestive, respiratory, cardiac and urogenital) as a neurotransmitter (messenger from the nervous system) Also referred to as norepinephrine.

oedema Abnormal accumulation of fluid in the tissues of the body, causing swelling.

oesophagus Tube linking the mouth to the stomach, also known as gullet.

oestrogen Female sex hormone secreted by the ovaries that play a major role in the regulation of the menstrual cycle.

oestrogenic Having an action similar or identical to that of oestrogen.

officinal Designating a plant used in medicine (from Latin *officinalis* 'used or kept in a [medical] workshop'), and apparent in many plant names such as dandelion (*Taraxacum officinale*) or sage (*Salvia officinalis*).

oilcake The solid residue that remains after the oil has been extracted from the fruits and seeds of oleaginous plants.

opiate Derived from opium.

opposite In botany, describing leaves, opposite each other on the same node (point at which the leaf joins the stem).

organic Relates to the constituents of living organisms, for example organic acids, organic compounds.

osteo-densitometry An X-ray used to measure bone density, sometimes also called a DEXA-scan.

palmate Describes a leaf divided into elongated leaflets arranged like the fingers of an open hand.

papule A skin lesion forming a small, firm elevation.

pathological Causing disease.

pectin An organic substance, produced by plants and abundant in fruits such as plums. Its structure is similar to that of starch. Pectin is the substance that makes jams and jellies set.

perineum Area between the anus and the genitalia.

periodontal disease Any disease affecting the tissues that surround and support the teeth, such as gums and bones.

peristalsis Involuntary, wavelike muscular contractions that propel undigested food and digestive wastes along the alimentary canal.

petiole The small stem (leafstalk) that forms the narrow part of a leaf and attaches it to the stem of the plant.

GLOSSARY 305

GLOSSARY

phenols A family of organic plant compounds. They include salicylic acid (found in willow) and thymol (found in thyme).

photosensitivity Sensitivity to sunlight caused by certain substances known as photosensitisers.

physiological Relating to the way the body functions.

phytochemicals The chemical components of plants.

phyto-oestrogens Organic compounds with a structure and action similar to that of oestrogens.

phytoprogesterone An organic compound with a similar structure and action to progesterone.

phytosterols Sterols that are produced by plants.

pituitary gland Small gland situated at the base of the brain (beneath the hypothalamus) that secretes several hormones that are very important for the functioning of the body.

platelets The smallest of the three types of blood cell, responsible for clotting the blood when there is an injury or inflammation in a blood vessel.

pod In botany, dry fruit that opens into halves on maturity, with seeds being born in each of the two halves.

polyp The medical term for a benign tumour that develops on a mucous membrane in the body.

polyphenols Compounds that contain phenol groups, often with antibacterial and anti-oxidant properties.

polysaccharide A class of complex carbohydrates, whose molecules contain several monosaccharide molecules. Examples include starch and cellulose.

polyunsaturated fats The oils largely found in plants (such as sunflower, safflower) consisting of long chains of carbon connected with multiple bonds. They are less likely to be made into cholesterol in the body, so less likely to cause atherosclerosis. Olive oil is monounsaturated, so it contains only one multiple bond.

proanthocyanins, proanthocyanidins Polymeric, phenolic compounds that are often referred to as condensed tannins or **polyphenols**.

probiotics Beneficial bacteria used as dietary supplements or food additives to replace or promote the development of normal intestinal flora.

progesterone Female sex hormone secreted during the second phase of the ovarian cycle and during pregnancy.

prolactin Hormone secreted by the pituitary gland after giving birth, and while the new baby continues to suckle at the breast. It stimulates the production of progesterone from the ovary, so preventing menstruation, and maintains the milk flow.

prolapse The displacement of an organ (womb, rectum, bladder) due to a weakness in the structures that hold it in place within the body.

prostaglandins Any of various substances composed of fatty acids that have a hormone-like activity and are found especially in mammals.

protein Molecule used by the body as building blocks (for example, in muscle, skin, hormones or enzymes) and made up of various amino acids.

proteolytic Describes an enzyme that hydrolyses proteins.

provitamin A substance such as carotene from which vitamins are made within the body.

prurigo An inflammatory disease of the skin characterised by the formation of **papules** and intense itching.

pruritis Intense itching.

psychomotor skills Muscular activity related to mental processes, such as driving a car.

psychosomatic Describes physical symptoms that result from emotional states, either repressed or excessive.

purgative (See **laxative, purgative**)

pyrrolizidine alkaloids A group of plant alkaloids that are found in herbs such as borage (*Borago officinalis*), some of which can cause liver damage if taken in excess.

red cells The cells in the blood responsible for carrying oxygen, through its constituent haemoglobin.

remission Marked improvement or temporary absence of symptoms in a disorder (such as cancer or multiple sclerosis), sometimes ending in relapse.

renal Related to the kidneys.

respiratory system The parts of the body related to breathing, which allow the exchange of oxygen and carbon dioxide with the inhaled air. This includes the diaphragm, lungs, bronchi and the trachea.

retina The lining of the back of the eye, which perceives light and images.

rhizome A bulbous underground stem, which usually grows horizontally, and bears roots and aerial stems.

saponins Organic compounds (found in the roots, rhizomes and bulbs of plants) that foam like soap when shaken with water. The term derives from the Latin *saponis* meaning 'soap'.

saturated fats Animal fats, containing single bonds between the atoms. Excess saturated fats in the diet can lead to atherosclerosis. Dairy products, eggs and meat all contain saturated fats.

sebaceous gland A small gland at the base of the hair follicle that produces the oily secretion known as sebum.

seborrhoea Greasiness of the skin due to the over-production of sebum by the sebaceous glands of the skin and hair follicles.

secoiridoids Plant substances based on the **iridoid** group of compounds.

sedatives (See **anxioltics, tranquillisers, sedatives**)

senescence The ageing of body tissue.

serotonin A compound that occurs in the brain and acts as a neurotransmitter.

sesquiterpenes Organic compounds that have medicinal – especially anti-inflammatory – properties and are found in certain essential oils.

spasm A muscular contraction which is both involuntary and painful.

GLOSSARY

sphincter (muscle) Ring of muscle under the control of the autonomic nervous system, which opens or closes to regulate the passage of material in the body (for example, the anal sphincter opens to allow the passage of stools).

spike Cluster of flowers (inflorescence) attached without petioles (stalks) along a central axis called a raceme.

spore A cell ensuring the dispersal and reproduction of fungi and ferns.

stamen The male organ of a flower that produces pollen.

staphylococcus A bacterium found commonly on the skin, often benign, but sometimes pathological, causing boils and abscesses. *S. aureus* (Latin for 'gold') is responsible for impetigo, an infection of the skin with yellow crusts.

sternum The breastbone.

steroids Organic compounds belonging to the larger **sterol** group and including corticosteroid hormones, cholesterol and certain of the sex hormones (oestradiol, testosterone).

sterols Alcohols of the steroid group, such as cholesterol and ergosterol, found in animals and plants and that have various physiological effects.

stigma The upper part of the pistil (the female organs of a flower) that receives the pollen.

succulent A plant, usually native to arid areas, that has fleshy leaves or stems that can store water.

syndrome A group of symptoms which, considered as a whole, are characteristic of a particular disease or condition.

synovial Relating to synovia or synovial fluid, the viscous liquid that lubricates the joints. It is secreted by the synovial tissue, which forms the membrane that surrounds the joints.

tannins Phenolic, organic compounds that can combine with proteins and are used in herbal remedies for their medicinal (especially astringent) actions. The name derives from the fact that they were originally used to tan hides.

terpenes Organic compounds, the molecules of which are usually characterised by a ring system. They are generally aromatic and are found in essential oils.

testosterone A male sex hormone secreted by the testicles (and in smaller quantities by the ovaries in women).

thiamine Another name for vitamin B_1.

thujone A volatile oil found in plants including sage *(Salvia officinalis)*, that has carminative and antiseptic effects in therapeutic doses. Higher amounts of the oil can cause convulsions in people susceptible to epilepsy.

tic The regular or recurrent twitching or spasm of a muscle or group of muscles.

toxin Poisonous substance, secreted by certain organisms, that can cause adverse effects in the body.

trace elements Chemicals that are vital for the healthy functioning of the body, but are only needed in very small quantities, such as selenium and zinc.

tranquillisers (See **anxioltics, tranquillisers, sedatives**)

triglycerides Basic building blocks of fats, linked to glycerol and constituting a storage medium for lipids (fats) in the body's adipose tissues.

triterpenes Organic compounds belonging to the larger group of **terpenes** whose molecules comprise 30 carbon atoms and one or more ring systems. They have medicinal properties such as anti-inflammatory and are found in certain essential oils.

tryptophan One of the 20 amino acids involved in the composition of proteins.

tuber A large, usually underground stem that stores food reserves for the growth of the plant, such as the potato, and is involved in its propagation.

uraemia The accumulation in the blood of urea – usually excreted in the urine – due to kidney failure.

urea A toxic ammoniac compound produced by protein **metabolism** and excreted in non-toxic form in urine.

ureter The canal that conveys urine from the kidney, where it is produced, to the bladder, where it is stored.

urethra The canal that conveys urine from the bladder out of the body.

urethritis Inflammation of the urethra.

vascular system The network of blood vessels in the body.

vasodilator An agent, drug or nerve that causes the walls of a blood vessel to dilate.

veinotonic A substance that strengthens the walls of blood vessels.

venous Related to the veins and venous system generally.

ventricles (heart) The two major chambers of the heart that pump blood around the body.

vermifuge (See **anthemintic, vermifuge**)

virus Infectious agent comprising a genetic core (DNA or RNA) and an outer coat made of protein, only able to live and reproduce within the cells of another living organism, sometimes causing disease in humans. The common cold, warts, flu, glandular fever and HIV are all examples of fairly common viral infections.

volatile oils Fragrant oils extracted or distilled from plants, and thought to be produced by the plant to attract pollinating insects and to deter animals and predatory insects. They are commonly known as essential oils.

white cells The blood cells produced by the immune system, to help protect the body against infection and cancer. The main types are neutrophils and lymphocytes. Some of them produce antibodies, molecules that also help to ward off infection and cancer.

xanthone A bright yellow substance with fungicidal properties that is found in several plants, including St John's wort and centaury.

ADDRESSES & WEB SITES

Addresses and contact details

National Herbalists Association of Australia
13 Breillat Street
Annandale, NSW 2038
Tel: (02) 9555 8885
www.nhaa.org.au

Australian Traditional Medicine Society
PO Box 1027
Meadowbank, NSW 2114
Tel: (02) 9809 6800
www.atms.com.au

Australian Natural Therapists Association
Tel: 1800 817 577
Email: anta1955@bigpond.com
www.anta.com.au

Australian Integrative Medicine Association
Locked Bag 29
Clayton, VIC 3168
Tel: (03) 9594 7561
www.aima.net.au

Australian Acupuncture and Chinese Medicine Association
Suite 5
28 Gladstone Road
Highgate Hill, QLD 4101
Tel: 1300 725 334
www.acupuncture.org.au

New Zealand Association of Medical Herbalists
Tel: (07) 855 6724
www.nzamh.org.nz

New Zealand Society of Naturopaths
PO Box 90–170
Auckland Central Post Office
Auckland
www.naturopath.org.nz

Web sites

The Internet is a valuable resource for anyone interested in alternative or complementary therapies. Many sites are devoted to herbs and their uses, and most sell herbal remedies online.

www.botanical.com
Online version of the definitive reference work *A Modern Herbal* by Mrs. M. Grieve, first published in 1931. Fascinating folklore and history of herbs, as well as their medicinal and culinary uses. Many of the entries contain advice on cultivation.

www.holisticonline.com
This US site has a huge database of herbs (go into the site and click 'herbs' in the 'most popular destinations' box), listed both by their scientific names and their common names. A typical entry will give the plant's other names, its application in herbal medicine – European, Chinese or Indian uses may be listed – and safety advice. Some entries give a short history of the herb and list its active components.

www.rain-tree.com
Raintree is a well-designed site specifically about tropical plants found in the Amazon rainforest. Plants are listed by their scientific and their common names. The site is run by Raintree Nutrition Inc, a US company that markets medicinal plants, and aims to prevent further destruction of the rainforests.

www.nhaa.org.au
The National Herbalists Association of Australia is an association of professional practitioners of herbal medicine. You can use the site to find a qualified herbalist, to keep up to date on the politics of herbal medicine, and to find information about accredited herbal medicine courses.

www.nicsl.com.au/cochrane/index.asp
Free access to the Cochrane Library for all Australian residents. This brings together research examining the effectiveness of different health-care treatments and interventions, including some herbal medicines. It is the best single source of information on the effects of health care.

www.herbmed.org
HerbMed is an electronic herbal database with useful links to other relevant sites. The US-based site is clearly laid out and easy to use. It describes itself as 'an evidence-based information resource for professionals, researchers and general public'.

www.tga.gov.au
The Therapeutic Goods Administration (TGA) is part of the Australian government Department of Health and Ageing. It monitors the sale, promotion and manufacture of therapeutic goods in Australia, including herbal medicines.

www.medsafe.govt.nz
The New Zealand Medicines and Medical Devices Safety Authority provides information on medicines and their regulation in New Zealand.

http://holisticmed.com/www/herbalism.html
Herbal Medicine Internet Resources is a US site compiled by the Holistic Medicine Resource Center. It has numerous links to herbal medicine web sites, organisations, practitioner databases, training, publications and discussion groups.

www.jtaproject.com
The Trans-Tasman Therapeutic Products Agency should be operating by mid-2005, and will replace the Australian TGA and Medsafe in New Zealand.

www.everybody.co.nz
Up-to-date and useful information on a wide variety of health topics, specifically written for New Zealanders.

www.blackmores.com.au/expert
Free service from Blackmores providing general information regarding the treatment of self-limiting conditions using herbal and nutritional medicines.

www.ncbi.nlm.nih.gov/entrez/query.fcgi
PubMed is a US-based service run by the National Library of Medicine that enables extensive researching of clinical trials and other medical papers.

http://bio.waikato.ac.nz/honey
Provides information about the medicinal properties of honey, with particular emphasis on manuka honey.

INDEX

Page numbers in **bold** print refer to main entries. Where possible, plants are indexed under their common name.

A

Aaron's rod see mullein
abscesses, 135, 143, 185, 271, 285
absinthe see wormwood
acid reflux, **227–8**, 231, 232
acne
 aloe vera for, 286
 basil for, 40
 burdock for, 55, 286
 calendula for, 57, 286
 chaste tree for, 67, 286
 cleavers for, 286
 dandelion for, 286
 evening primrose for, 91, 286
 heartsease for, 116
 lavender for, 286
 manuka for, 134
 marshmallow for, 135
 nettle for, 286
 overview of, **286**
 tea tree for, 181
 yellow dock for, 200, 286
acne rosacea, 207, **286–7**
acrocyanosis, 102
acute bronchitis, **280–1**
addiction, 126, **204–5**, 207, 235
ageing, **206–8**, 212
agrimony (Agrimonia eupatoria), 28, 283, 299
AIDS see HIV/AIDS
albizia (Albizia lebbeck), **29**, 209, 210, 280, 290
alcohol dependence, 126, **204**, 207, 235
alfalfa (Medicago sativa), **30**
allergic rhinitis see hay fever
allergies
 agrimony for, 28
 albizia for, **29**
 baical skullcap for, **38**, 209
 cat's claw for, 62
 chamomile for, 209
 ear infections &, 223
 elder for, 209
 German chamomile for, 66
 globe artichoke for, 209
 greater plantain for, 111
 overview of, **208–10**
 peppermint for, 209
 ziziphus for, 201
 see also asthma; eczema; food allergies; hay fever
aloe vera (Aloe vera, A. barbadensis), **21**, **31**, 277, 286, 287, 289, 290, 293, 296, 298
alopecia areata, 242
Alzheimer's disease, 167, **263–4**, 266
American mandrake, 9
amoebic dysentery, 36
anaemia, 86, 163, **211**
anaphylactic shock, 29, 291
andrographis (Andrographis paniculata), **32**, 226, 231, 239, 245, 248, 251, 255, 281, 282, 283, 284, 285
angelica (Angelica archangelica), **33**
angina, 75, 86, 99, 115, 126, **211**, 214, 215

anise (Pimpinella anisum), **34**, 206, 220, 225, 233, 271
anorexia, 94
anxiety
 black cohosh for, 43
 boswellia for, 50
 brahmi for, 51
 Californian poppy for, 58, 264, 279
 celery for, 64
 damiana for, 82
 dong quai for, 86
 lavender for, 128, 254, 256, 264, 279, 292, 293
 lemon balm for, 204, 264
 lime flower for, 132, 206, 238, 254, 256, 265, 279, 292, 293
 oats for, 238
 overview of, **264–5**
 passionflower for, 152, 238, 264, 265, 279, 293
 St John's wort for, 168, 258, 265
 skullcap for, 175
 valerian for, 186, 205, 206, 254, 265, 279
 withania for, 197, 279, 292, 293
appetite loss
 alfalfa for, 30
 basil for, 40
 black mustard for, 40
 centaury for, 65
 cinnamon for, 70
 gentian for, 100
 mugwort for, 140
 nettle for, 144
 rhubarb for, 164
 sweet marjoram for, 178
 wormwood for, 198
appetite suppression
 fennel for, 93
 garcinia for, **98**
 maté for, 136
apricot vine see passionflower
archangel see angelica
arnica (Arnica montana), **35**, **262**, 288
aromatherapy, **11**
arrhythmia, **212**
arteritis, **212–13**
arthritis
 baical skullcap for, 38
 blackcurrant for, 47
 boswellia for, 50
 cayenne for, 63, 262
 celery for, 64
 cinnamon for, 262
 cramp bark for, 78
 devil's claw for, 84, 261
 evening primrose for, 91
 ginger for, 262
 horseradish for, 119
 juniper for, 122, 262
 meadowsweet for, 261
 turmeric for, 184, 261
 willow for, 261
 see also rheumatoid arthritis
ashwagandha see withania
asthma, 208
 albizia for, **29**, 280
 asthma plant for, **36**, 280
 baical skullcap for, 38
 boswellia for, 50, 280
 children &, 220
 codonopsis for, 73
 coleus for, 75

hyssop for, 121
lemon verbena for, 130
licorice for, 280
mullein for, 141, 284
overview of, **279–80**
thyme for, 182
wild cherry for, 280
asthma plant (Chamaesyce hirta), **36**, 280, 281
asthma weed (Parietaria judaica), 36
astragalus (Astragalus membranaceus, A. mongholicus, A. propinquus), **37**, 233, 236, 247, 248, 249, 250, 251, 253, 255, 276, 282, 283, 297
atherosclerosis, 30, 97, 101, 102, 116, **212–13**, 215, 216, 218
athlete's foot, 72, 134, 246
Australian Natural Therapists Association, 14
Australian Register of Therapeutic Goods, **16**, 17
Australian regulations, **16**
Australian Traditional Medicine Society, 14
Ayurvedic medicine, **12**

B

babies, **219–20**, 222
back pain
 angelica for, 33
 cayenne for, 257
 cinnamon for, 257
 cramp bark for, 78
 devil's claw for, **257**
 nutmeg for, 257
 overview of, **256–7**
 rosemary for, 257
bacterial infections, 245, 255
 cloves for, 72
 coriander for, 76
 cumin for, 80
 garlic for, 99
 grapefruit for, 109
 mugwort for, 140
 oregano, for, 150
 pau d'arco for, 153
 pine for, 155
 tamarind for, 180
 tea tree for, 181
 uva-ursi for, 185
 winter savory for, 195
 witch hazel for, 196
 see also under particular infection e.g. sinusitis
bad breath, 93, **225–6**
baical skullcap (Scutellaria baicalensis), 13, **38**, 209, 210, 230, 233, 236, 290
balm see lemon balm
barberry (Berberis vulgaris), **39**, 240, 243, 246, 250, 285, 293, 295, 298, 299, 300
basil (Ocimum basilicum), **40**, 226, 228
bastard ginseng see codonopsis
bay (Laurus nobilis), **41**
bearberry see uva-ursi
bedsores, **287–8**
bedstraw see cleavers
bedwetting, 58
bee balm see lemon balm
belching
 andrographis for, 239

anise for, 34
caraway for, 239
chicory for, 69
cinnamon for, 70
coriander for, 239
cumin for, 239
fennel for, 239
lemon verbena for, 239
papaya for, 239
peppermint for, 154, 239
rosemary for, 239
sweet marjoram for, 239
thyme for, 182
winter savory for, 195
bellflower see codonopsis
benign prostatic hyperplasia, 301
bilberry (Vaccinium myrtillus), **42**, 213, 214, 240, 242, 252
bile problems, 138, 154
bitter aloe see aloe vera
bitter fennel see fennel
bitterwort see gentian
black cherry see wild cherry
black cohosh (Cimicifuga racemosa), **43**, 216, 277
black elder see elder
black mustard (Brassica nigra), **44**, 213
black pepper (Piper nigrum), **45**
black sampson see echinacea
black tea see tea
black walnut (Juglans nigra), 188
blackberry (Rubus fructicosus), **46**
blackcurrant (Ribes nigrum), **47**, 216
bladder stones, 105
bladderwort see kelp
blaeberry see bilberry
blepharitis, 240, 241
blessed thistle see milk thistle
bloating, stomach
 andrographis for, 239
 basil for, 40
 bay for, 41
 black pepper for, 45
 caraway for, 59, 239
 chicory for, 69
 coriander for, 239
 cumin for, 80, 239
 fennel for, 239
 German chamomile for, 66
 lemon verbena for, 239
 licorice for, 131
 papaya for, 239
 peppermint for, 154, 239
 rosemary for, 166, 239
 sage and clary sage for, 167
 sweet marjoram for, 178, 239
 thyme for, 182
blonde psyllium see psyllium
blood clotting
 agrimony for, 28
 cloves for, 72
 garlic for, 99
 ginger for, 101
 guarana for, 113
 Raynaud's disease &, 218
blood disorders
 dong quai for, 86
 fenugreek for, 211
 globe artichoke for, 216
 grape seed for, 216
 milk thistle for, 216
 nettle for, 211
 rehmannia for, 163

INDEX 309

INDEX

see also anaemia; lipid disorders
blood pressure
 ageing &, 207
 black cohosh for, 216
 blackcurrant for, 216
 celery for, 64, 216
 coffee for, 74
 coleus for, 75, 216
 corn silk for, 77
 cramp bark for, 78
 elder for, 216
 garlic for, 213
 ginger for, 217
 hawthorn for, 115, 216, 217
 Korean ginseng for, 125
 mistletoe for, 139
 olive for, 149
 overview of, **215–17**
 rosemary for, 217
 valerian for, 186, 216
 white horehound for, 189
 winter savory for, 211
 withania for, 197
blood sugar
 burdock for, 55
 fig for, 96
 gymnema for, 114
 olive for, 149
blue gum *see* eucalyptus
blue mallow *see* mallow
blueberry *see* bilberry
Body Mass Index, 232, 255, **256**
body odour, **292**
boils
 burdock for, 55, 295
 chickweed for, 68, 295
 dandelion for, 295
 echinacea for, 295
 flax for, 97
 garlic for, 295
 globe artichoke for, 295
 lavender for, 295
 marshmallow for, 135
 myrtle for, 143
 oats for, 148
 overview of, **295**
 slippery elm for, 176, 295
 tea tree for, 295
 thyme for, 295
 uva-ursi for, 185
 yellow dock for, 295
boldo (*Peumus boldus*), 15, **48**, 231, 299
bone disorders, 260
bone health, 120
borage (*Borago officinalis*), **49**
boswellia (*Boswellia serrata*), **50**, 280
bottle brush *see* horsetail
box holly *see* butcher's broom
brahmi (*Bacopa monnieri*), **51**, 264
bramble *see* blackberry
breast abscess, 271
breast disorders, 71, 85, 91, **270–1**, 277, 278, 279
breast engorgement, 80
breastfeeding problems, **271–2**
brindleberry *see* garcinia
brittle nails, 243
bronchiolitis, **219–20**
bronchitis
 albizia for, 29
 andrographis for, 281
 asthma plant for, 36
 black mustard for, 44
 buchu for, 53

echinacea for, 87, 281
eucalyptus for, 281
fig for, 96
greater plantain for, 111
hyssop for, 121, 281
lavender for, 281
mallow for, 133
marshmallow for, 135, 281
mullein for, 141
overview of, **280–1**
pine for, 155, 281
tea tree for, 281
thyme for, 281
white horehound for, 281
ziziphus for, 201
broom (*Cytisus scoparius*), **52**, 218
bruising
 arnica for, 35, 288
 dill for, 85
 dong quai for, 86
 flax for, 97
 ginkgo for, 288
 grape seed for, 108, 288
 green tea for, 288
 horsechestnut for, 118, 288
 hyssop for, 121
 overview of, **288**
 pineapple for, 288
 witch hazel for, 288
buchu (*Agathosma betulina*), **53**, 298
buckeye *see* horsechestnut
bupleurum (*Bupleurum falcatum*), **54**, 204, 205, 216, 230, 233, 236
burdock (*Arctium lappa*), **55**, 286, 287, 290, 294, 295
burns
 aloe vera for, 31, 289
 calendula for, 289
 chickweed for, 68
 cleavers for, 71
 gotu kola for, 107, 289
 lavender for, 128, 289
 manuka for, 134, 289
 New Zealand flax for, 145
 olive for, 149
 overview of, **288–9**
 St John's wort for, 168
burping *see* belching
butcher's broom (*Ruscus aculeatus*), **56**, 299

C

caffeine, 7, 14, 74, 112, 113, 136, 230
calcium, 260, **261**
calendula (*Calendula officinalis*), 20, 24–5, **57**, 206, 207, 208, 223, 225, 226, 227, 237, 240, 246, 248, 249, 250, 272, 277, 284, 286, 287, 288, 289, 290, 291, 293, 294, 297, 298
Californian poppy (*Eschscholzia californica*), **58**, 264, 265, 266, 279
caltrop *see* tribulus
Camptotheca acuminata, 9
cancer, 9, 44, 50, 52, 62, 97, 112, 125, 139, 153, 169, 171, 174, 179
cancer treatment side effects
 astragalus for, 37
 echinacea for, 87
 Siberian ginseng for, 174

walnut for, 188
Candida albicans see thrush
candidiasis, 246, **249–50**
caraway (*Carum carvi*), **59**, 234, 237, 239
carbuncles, **295**
carob (*Ceratonia siliqua*), **60**, 230
cascara (*Rhamanus purshianus*), **61**, 228, 235
cataracts, 42
catarrh, nasal
 elder for, 88, 283
 golden rod for, 105
 golden seal for, 106
 greater plantain for, 283
 hyssop for, 121
 marshmallow for, 283
 mullein for, 283
 thyme for, 283
 white horehound for, 283
catchweed *see* cleavers
cat's claw (*Uncaria guianensis, U. tomentosa*), **62**, 230, 247
cayenne (*Capsicum fructescens*), **63**, 213, 227, 249, 252, 257, 260, 262, 263, 267
celandine *see* greater celandine
celery (*Apium graveolens*), **64**, 216, 259, 260
cellulite
 cleavers for, 289
 dandelion for, 83, 289
 globe artichoke for, 289
 gotu kola for, 289
 grape seed for, 289
 horsechestnut for, 289
 horsetail for, 120, 289
 lady's mantle for, 127
 milk thistle for, 289
 overview of, **289–90**
centaury (*Centaurium erythracaea*), **65**, 231
Ceylon cinnamon, 70
chai hu *see* bupleurum
chamomile, German (*Matricaria recutita*), **66**, 206, 208, 209, 210, 224, 228, 229, 232, 234, 237, 238, 240, 245, 250, 268, 291, 292, 293, 294
chamomile, Roman (*Chamaemelum nobile*), 66
chaste tree (*Vitex agnus-castus*), **67**, 267, 271, 273, 277, 278, 279, 286
cherries, 259
 see also wild cherry
chickenpox, 148, 220, 221, 249, 291
chickweed (*Stellaria media*), **68**, 221, 223, 290, 293, 295
chicory (*Cichorium intybus*), **69**
chilblains, 119, 147, **213**
children
 asthma &, 220
 bronchiolitis &, **219–20**
 chickenpox &, 220, 221
 colic &, **220**
 common health problems of, **220–1**
 coughs, colds & throat infections in, **220–1**
 croup &, **222**
 diabetes in, 251
 ear infections &, 220, **222–3**
 eczema &, **223**
 fever in, 219, 221, 245
 labial herpes in, 247

measles &, 220
mumps &, 220
rubella &, 220
sleeping disorders of, **224**
teething &, 133, 175, **224**
throat infections &, **221–2**
tracheitis &, **222**
viruses &, **219**, **220–1**, **222**, 223
chilli *see* cayenne
Chinese anise *see* star anise
Chinese celery *see* celery
Chinese cinnamon, 70
Chinese date *see* ziziphus
Chinese foxglove *see* rehmannia
Chinese herbal medicine *see* traditional Chinese medicine
Chinese magnolia vine *see* schisandra
Chinese rhubarb *see* rhubarb
Chinese wormwood (*Artemesia annua*), 8, 9, 198
chiretta *see* andrographis
cholecystitis, 230–1
cholesterol
 chicory for, 69
 coriander for, 76
 fenugreek for, 94
 flax for, 97
 ginger for, 101
 globe artichoke for, 103, 215, 216
 grape seed for, 108. 215
 Korean ginseng for, 125
 milk thistle for, 216
 oats for, 148
 psyllium for, 158, 215
 schisandra for, 171
 turmeric for, 184
chronic bronchitis, 280, **281**
chronic fatigue syndrome, 62, 174, 201, **246–7**, 250
chronic venous insufficiency, **218–19**
church steeples *see* agrimony
cinnamon (*Cinnamomum zeylanicum, C. cassia*), **70**, 226, 231, 237, 255, 257, 258, 262, 263, 270
circulatory problems
 agrimony for, 299
 bilberry for, 213, 242
 black cohosh for, 216
 blackcurrant for, 47, 216
 boswellia for, 50
 brahmi for, 264
 broom for, 52
 butcher's broom for, 56, 299
 cayenne for, 63
 celery for, 216
 cinnamon for, 70, 226
 coleus for, 75, 216
 cramp bark for, 78
 cypress for, 217, 219
 elder for, 216
 garlic for, 99, 213, 216, 218
 ginger for, 217
 ginkgo for, 102, 213, 218, 242, 264, 275, 288
 globe artichoke for, 213
 golden rod for, 105
 golden seal for, 106
 gotu kola for, 107, 289
 grape seed for, 213, 218, 275, 287, 288, 289, 299
 hawthorn for, 216, 217
 heartsease for, 116

310 NATURE'S MEDICINES

INDEX

horsechestnut for, 218, 219, 288, 289, 299
lavender for, 128
psyllium for, 213
rosemary for, 166, 217
schisandra for, 264
valerian for, 216
winter savory for, 217
witch hazel for, 196, 217, 219
yarrow for, 199
see also arteritis; atherosclerosis; chilblains; lymphoedema; Raynaud's disease; vein disorders
cirrhosis, 138, **233**, 235
clary sage *(Salvia sclarea)*, **167**, 273, 278
cleavers *(Galium aparine)*, **71**, 217, 230, 247, 252, 286, 289, 298, 299
clivers *see* cleavers
cloves *(Syzygium aromaticum)*, **72**, 226, 227
cockleburr *see* agrimony
cod liver oil, 207
codonopsis *(Codonopsis pilosula)*, **73**, 269
coffee *(Coffea arabica)*, 7, 14, **74**, 207
cold, common
  andrographis for, 32, 282
  angelica for, 33
  astragalus for, 282
  baical skullcap for, 38
  basil for, 40
  blackberry for, 46
  blackcurrant for, 47
  bupleurum for, 54
  children &, **221**
  cinnamon for, 70
  echinacea for, 87, 282
  elder for, 88
  eucalyptus for, 90, 282
  eyebright for, 92
  garlic for, 282
  ginger for, 101
  grapefruit seed for, 109
  hyssop for, 121
  kuzu for, 126
  marshmallow for, 282
  mullein for, 141
  overview of, **281–2**
  peppermint for, 154
  pine for, 155
  rosemary for, 282
  tea tree for, 282
  thyme for, 182, 282
  vervain for, 187
  white horehound for, 189, 282
  wild indigo for, 192
  yarrow for, 199
  see also influenza
cold sores, 169, 247, 248
coleus *(Coleus forskohlii, Plectranthus barbatus, P. forskohlii)*, **75**, 211, 215, 216
colic
  anise for, 34
  bay for, 41
  cayenne for, 63
  cramp bark for, 78
  fennel for, 93
  lemon verbena for, 130
  overview of, **220**
  peppermint for, 154
  vervain for, 187
  wild yam for, 193

colic root *see* wild yam
colitis, 50, 133, 141, **237–8**
common briar *see* rosehip
common broom *see* broom
common horehound *see* white horehound
common plantain *see* greater plantain
common poppy *(Papaver rhoeas)*, **157**
common thyme *(Thymus vulgaris)*, **182**, 210, 219, 222, 225, 227, 230, 232, 244, 281, 282, 283, 284, 291, 295
Complementary Medicines Evaluation Committee, 16
compresses, **22**
concentration
  brahmi for, 51
  dong quai for, 86
  ginkgo for, 102
  gotu kola for, 107
  Korean ginseng for, 125
  rosemary for, 166
  schisandra for, 171
  see also memory problems
coneflower *see* echinacea
conjunctivitis, 92
conker tree *see* horsechestnut
constipation
  cascara for, 61
  cayenne for, 63
  cramp bark for, 78
  fennel for, 93
  fenugreek for, 94
  fig for, 96
  flax for, 97
  globe artichoke for, 103
  goat's rue for, 104
  mallow for, 133
  overview of, **228**
  psyllium for, 158
  rehmannia for, 163
  rhubarb for, 164
  rosemary for, 166
  senna for, **172**
  slippery elm for, 176
  tamarind for, **180**
  yellow dock for, 200
contact allergies, 208, 290
coriander *(Coriandrum sativum)*, 18, **76**, 225, 239, 292
corn silk *(Zea mays)*, **77**, 298, 299, 300, 301
corn poppy *see* common poppy
coughs
  angelica for, 33
  anise for, 34
  black cohosh for, 43
  blackberry for, 46
  bronchiolitis &, 219
  chickweed for, 68
  children &, **221–2**
  codonopsis for, 73
  common poppy for, 157
  cypress for, 81
  elder for, 219, 222, 248, 283
  eucalyptus for, 90
  fennel for, 93
  fig for, 96
  ginger for, 101
  greater plantain for, 283
  hyssop for, 206
  licorice for, 131
  mallow for, 133
  marshmallow for, 135, 221, 248, 283
  mullein for, 221, 248, 283

pine for, 155
red clover for, 162
sweet violet for, 219
thyme for, 182, 219, 222, 283
white horehound for, 189, 206, 248, 283
wild cherry for, 191
ziziphus for, 201
cracked nipples, 179, 271, 272
cramp bark *(Viburnum opulus)*, **78**, 238, 257, 258, 269, 270, 274, 278
cramps
  caraway for, 59, 235
  cinnamon for, 257
  cramp bark for, 78, 257
  fennel for, 235
  hyssop for, 121
  lemon balm for, 230
  mugwort for, 140
  nutmeg for, 257
  overview of, **257–8**
  rosemary for, 166
  sage and clary sage for, 167
  star anise for, 235
  thyme for, 230
  vervain for, 187
  yarrow for, 199
cranberry *(Vaccinium macrocarpon, V. oxycoccus)*, **79**, 298
Crohn's disease, 50, **228–9**, 231, 255
croup, **222**
cultivation, **18–19**
cumin *(Cuminum cyminum)*, **80**, 239, 271
curled dock *see* yellow dock
cuts
  basil for, 40
  calendula for, 57
  eucalyptus for, 90
  manuka for, 134
  mullein for, 141
  tea tree for, 181
  thyme for, 182
  see also wounds
cypress *(Cupressus sempervirens)*, **81**, 217, 219
cystic fibrosis, 235
cystitis
  boldo for, 48
  buchu for, 53, 298
  celery for, 64
  cleavers for, 71, 298
  corn silk for, 77, 298
  cranberry for, 298
  dandelion for, 298
  epilobium for, 89
  golden rod for, 105, 298
  marshmallow for, 135, 298
  overview of, **298–9**
  sandalwood for, 169
  shepherd's purse for, 173
  tribulus for, 183
  uva-ursi for, 185, 298
cytomegalovirus, 246, 247

D

damiana *(Turnera diffusa)*, **82**, 265, 268, 269, 275, 276
dandelion *(Taraxacum officinale)*, 12, **83**, 207, 217, 230, 252, 286, 287, 289, 292, 293, 295, 298, 299, 300
dandruff, **244**
dang quai *see* dong quai

dan(g) shen *see* codonopsis
deadly nightshade, 7
decoctions, **23**
delirium tremens, 204
dementia, **263–4**
Demodex folliculorum, 286
dental and gum problems, 28, 29, 46, 85, 88, 127, 133, 135, 142, 167, 169, 182, **225–7**
  see also mouth infections/inflammation
depression
  Californian poppy for, 265, 279
  damiana for, 275
  Korean ginseng for, 275
  lavender for, 128, 265, 279
  lemon balm for, 129, 204
  oats for, 148
  overview of, **265–6**
  St John's wort for, 11, 168, 265
  vervain for, 187
  withania for, 275, 279
dermatitis *see* eczema
detoxification, 14, 55, **229–30**, 289, 292, 293, 295
devil's claw *(Harpagophytum procumbens)*, **84**, 257, 258, 259, 260, 261, 262, 263
diabetes, 246, 295
  bilberry for, 42, 252
  blackberry for, 46
  burdock for, 55
  fenugreek for, 94, 252
  fig for, 96
  goat's rue for, 104, 252
  gymnema for, 114, 252
  Korean ginseng for, 125
  myrtle for, 143
  olive for, 149
  overview of, **251–2**
diarrhoea
  agrimony for, 28
  andrographis for, 32
  asthma plant for, 36
  bilberry for, 42
  blackberry for, 46
  boswellia for, 50
  carob for, **60**
  cinnamon for, 70
  coleus for, 75
  coriander for, 76
  fennel for, **93**
  fenugreek for, 94
  ginger for, 101
  golden rod for, 105
  grapefruit seed for, 109
  green tea for, 112
  guarana for, 113
  kuzu for, 126
  lady's mantle for, 127
  lemon verbena for, 130
  mullein for, 141
  oak bark for, 147, 229, 230, 235, 238
  oats for, 148
  overview of, **230**
  raspberry for, 161
  rosehip for, 165
  sweet marjoram for, 178
  tea for, 112
  walnut for, 188
  winter savory for, 195
  ziziphus for, 201
'dietary supplements' (NZ), 17
digestive problems
  agrimony for, 28

INDEX

andrographis for, 32, 239
angelica for, 33
anise for, **34**, 206, 233
baical skullcap for, 38, 233
basil for, 40, 226, 228
bay for, 41
bilberry for, 42
black pepper for, 45
boldo for, 48
boswellia for, 50
buchu for, 53
caraway for, **59**, 234, 235, 239
carob for, 230
cascara for, 228
cayenne for, 63
celery for, 64
centaury for, 65
chamomile for, 206, 228, 229, 232, 234, 237, 238, 292, 293
chicory for, 69
cinnamon for, 70, 226
cloves for, 72, 226
codonopsis for, 73
common poppy for, 157
coriander for, 76, 239
cumin for, 80, 239
dill for, 85
fennel for, 235, 236, 239
flax for, 97, 228, 235
garlic for, 99, 233
gentian for, 100
German chamomile for, 66
ginger for, 101, 232, 233, 234, 236, 237
globe artichoke for, 103, 209, 233
goat's rue for, 104
greater celandine for, 110
hops for, 117
juniper for, 122
kuzu for, 126
lavender for, 128, 226
lemon balm for, 129, 234, 232
lemon verbena for, **130**, 239
licorice for, 131
marshmallow for, 229, 238
meadowsweet for, 137, 232, 239, 234, 237
milk thistle for, 138, 233
mugwort for, 140
mullein for, 141
oak bark for, 229, 230, 235, 238
oats for, 148
overview of, **227–39**
papaya for, 151, 228, 234, 239
passionflower for, 235
peppermint for, 154, 209, 229, 232, 233, 234, 236, 239, 292, 293
pineapple for, 156
psyllium for, 228, 235
rehmannia for, 229
rosemary for, 166, 226, 232, 239
sage and clary sage for, 167, 226
senna for, 228
slippery elm for, **176**, 228, 229, 232, 235, 236, 237, 238
star anise for, **177**, 226, 230, 234, 235
sweet marjoram for, 178, 239
tamarind for, 180

thyme for, 182, 230, 232
turmeric for, 184, 226, 228, 234, 293
white horehound for, 189
wormwood for, 198
yarrow for, 199
yellow dock for, 200, 228, 235
see also indigestion; liver problems
dill (Anethum graveolens), 18, **85**, 220
dock see yellow dock
dong quai (Angelica sinensis), **86**, 277, 279
drug–herb reaction, 14
drug withdrawal problems, **204–5**
dry skin, 49, 255, **294**
drying herbs, 20, **21**
duodenal ulcers, 57, 70
dysmenorrhoea see menstrual pain
dyspepsia see indigestion

E

E. coli, 180, 298
ear disorders
 children &, 220, **222–3**
 echinacea for, 223, 241, 242
 eyebright for, 92
 golden seal for, 241, 242
 mullein for, 223, 241, 242
 overview of, **241**
 rosehip for, 223
 see also tinnitus; vertigo
East Indian walnut see albizia
Eastern herbal medicine, **12–13**
 see also traditional Chinese medicine
echinacea (Echinacea augustifolia, E. purpurea, E. pallida), **87**, 221, 222, 223, 225, 240, 241, 242, 243, 245, 246, 247, 248, 249, 250, 251, 255, 269, 281, 282, 283, 284, 285, 287, 295, 297
eczema
 albizia for, 290
 aloe vera for, 31, 290
 baical skullcap for, 38, 289
 borage for, 49
 burdock for, 55, 290
 calendula for, 290
 chickweed for, 68, 290
 cleavers for, 71
 evening primrose for, 91, 244, 290
 gotu kola for, 107
 greater celandine for, 110
 greater plantain for, 290
 heartsease for, 116, 244, 290
 manuka for, 134
 oak for, 147
 overview of, **223**, **290**
 passionflower for, 290
 red clover for, 162
 tea tree for, 290
 witch hazel for, 196, 245, 290
 withania for, 290
 yellow dock for, 200, 290
elder (Sambucus nigra), **88**, 209, 216, 219, 221, 222, 245, 248, 249, 269, 283, 284, 297
elderberry see elder
emphysema, 36

encephalitis, 220
endometriosis, **272–3**
energy and alertness, 113, 125, 206
English oak see oak
English violet see sweet violet
enteritis, 141
Epidermophyton, 246
epilepsy, 207
epilobium (Epilobium parviflorum, E. angustifolium), **89**
Epstein-Barr virus, 153
erectile dysfunction, **274–5**
erythema, 288, **289**
essential oils, 14, 15, 25
eucalyptus (Eucalyptus globulus), 25, **90**, 242, 248, 281, 282, 283
eufragia see eyebright
European red raspberry see raspberry
European yew, 9
evening primrose (Oenothera biennis), **91**, 207, 208, 243, 244, 255, 271, 274, 279, 286, 287, 290, 293, 294, 295
eye disorders and infections
 barberry for, 39, 240
 bilberry for, 42, 240
 calendula for, 208, 209, 240
 chamomile for, 209, 240
 echinacea for, 240
 evening primrose for, 208
 eyebright for, **92**, 240
 fennel for, 93
 golden seal for 240
 grape seed for, 240
 green tea for, 208
 overview of, **239–41**
 tea for, 208
 tribulus for, 183
eyebright (Euphrasia officinalis), **92**, 240

F

fasting, 230
fatigue
 astragalus for, 253
 centaury for, 65
 cinnamon for, 255
 codonopsis for, 73
 fenugreek for, 94
 green tea for, 253
 hyssop for, 121
 Korean ginseng for, 253
 maté for, 136
 nettle for, 144
 oats for, 148, 253, 258
 overview of, **253**
 rosehip for, 165, 255
 rosemary for 166, 253, 255
 sage and clary sage for, 167
 St John's wort for, 168
 Siberian ginseng for, 174, 253, 255, 258
 vervain for, 187
 withania for, 197, 258
 ziziphus for, 201
 see also chronic fatigue syndrome
female infertility
 chaste tree for, 67, 273
 dong quai for, 86
 overview of, **273**
 tribulus for, 183

white peony for, 190, 273
fennel (Foeniculum vulgare), 15, 93, 220, 236, 239
fenugreek (Trigonella foenumgraecum), **94**, 206, 211, 252, 256
fever
 andrographis for, 245, 248
 bronchiolitis &, 219
 bupleurum for, 54
 chamomile for, 245
 echinacea for, 245
 elder for, 219, 221, 245, 248
 juniper for, 245
 lavender for, 245
 rehmannia for, 163
 sweet violet for, 219, 221
 thyme for, 219
 vervain for, 187
 willow for, 194
 yarrow for, 199, 245, 248
feverfew (Tanacetum parthenium), **95**, 263, 267, 278
feverwort see centaury
fibroids, 190, **273–4**
fibromyalgia, **258**
fig (Ficus carica), **96**
flatulence
 andrographis for, 32, 239
 angelica for, 33
 anise for, 34
 basil for, 40
 black pepper for, 45
 caraway for, 59, 239
 cayenne for, 63
 celery for, 64
 centaury for, 65
 chicory for, 69
 cinnamon for, 70
 coriander for, 76, 239
 cumin for, 80, 239
 dill for, 85
 fennel for, 93, 239
 ginger for, 101
 juniper for, 122
 lavender for, 128
 lemon balm for, 129
 lemon verbena for, 130, 239
 papaya for, 239
 peppermint for, 154, 239
 rosemary for, 239
 sweet marjoram for, 178, 239
 tamarind for, 180
 thyme for, 182
 winter savory for, 195
 yarrow for, 199
 yellow dock for, 200
flax (Linum usitatissimum), **97**, 228, 235, 244
flax, New Zealand (Phormium tenax), **145**
fluid retention
 agrimony for, 299
 barberry for, 299
 boldo for, 299
 buchu for, 53
 butcher's broom for, 56, 299
 chaste tree for, 67
 cleavers for, 71, 289, 299
 corn silk for, 77, 299
 dandelion for, 83, 252, 289, 299
 globe artichoke for, 103, 299
 goat's rue for, 104
 golden seal for, 106
 grape seed for, 299
 hawthorn for, 299
 horsechestnut for, 118, 299

INDEX

horsetail for, 120, 289, 299
lime flowers for, 299
meadowsweet for, 137, 299
milk thistle for, 299
overview of, **299**
raspberry for, 161
rosemary for, 299
sandalwood for, 169
sweet marjoram for, 178
food allergies, 208, 209, 210, 223, 229, 230, 290
food poisoning, 45, 185, 230, 236
foot odour, 147
foxglove, 7
frankincense *see* boswellia
French lilac *see* goat's rue
fumitory, 15
fungal infections
 bay for, 41
 calendula for, 246
 cinnamon for, 70
 cloves for, 72
 coriander for, 76
 echinacea for, 243, 246
 golden rue for, 105
 grapefruit seed for, 109
 manuka for, 134
 mugwort for, 140
 oregano for, 150
 overview of, **246**
 pine for, 155
 tamarind for, 180
 tea tree for, 181, 244, 246
 thyme for, 244
 winter savory for, 195

G

gall bladder disorders, 77, 83, 103, **230–1**, 236
gallstones, 39, 48, 161, 231
garcinia (*Garcinia cambogia*), **98**
garden celandine *see* greater celandine
garden raspberry *see* raspberry
garlic (*Allium sativum*), **99**, 211, 213, 215, 216, 218, 233, 237, 247, 282, 283, 284, 285, 287, 295, 297, 300
gastric spasms, 66, 193
gastric ulcers
 albizia for, 29
 barberry for, 39
 calendula for, 57
 chickweed for, 68
 chicory for, 69
 cinnamon for, 70
 meadowsweet for, 137
gastritis, 72, 141, **231–2**
gastroenteritis, 76, **232–3**
gastrointestinal problems
 anise for, 233
 baical skullcap for, 38
 chamomile for, 232
 cinnamon for, 70
 cramp bark for, 78
 gentian for, 100
 ginger for, 232, 233
 lavender for, 128
 lemon balm for, 232
 licorice for, 131
 meadowsweet for, 232
 peppermint for, 232, 233
 psyllium for, 158
 rosemary for, 232
 slippery elm for, 232

thyme for, 232
gastro-oesophageal reflux, 227–8
genital herpes, 169, 247, 248
genito-urinary infections, 120
gentian (*Gentiana lutea*), **100**, 206, 226, 256
German chamomile (*Matricaria recutita*), **66**, 206, 208, 209, 210, 224, 228, 229, 232, 234, 237, 238, 240, 245, 250, 268, 291, 292, 293, 294
German measles, 220
ginger (*Zingiber officinale*), **101**, 211, 213, 217, 218, 232, 233, 234, 236, 237, 260, 262, 272, 274, 278
gingivitis, 88, 127, **225**
ginkgo (*Ginkgo biloba*), **102**, 206, 207, 211, 213, 215, 218, **242**, 243, 264, 275, 276, 287, 288, 295
ginseng *see* Korean ginseng; Siberian ginseng
glandular fever, 71, **246**, **247**
glaucoma, 75
globe artichoke (*Cynara scolymus*), **103**, 209, 210, 213, 215, 216, 230, 231, 233, 236, 252, 287, 289, 292, 293, 295, 299
glutinous rehmannia *see* rehmannia
goat's rue (*Galega officinalis*), **104**, 252
goatshead *see* tribulus
goitre, 253, 254
golden rod (*Solidago virgaurea*), **105**, 209, 298, 299, 300, 301
golden seal (*Hydrastis canadensis*), **106**, 237, 240, 241, 242, 243, 255, 278, 284, 293, 295
gonorrhoea, 58, 169
Good Manufacturing Practice, **16**, 17
goosegrass *see* cleavers
gotu kola (*Centella asiatica*), **107**, 289, 293, 294, 296
gout
 angelica for, 33
 burdock for, 55
 celery for, 64, 259
 cherries for, 259
 chicory for, 69
 corn silk for, 77
 devil's claw for, 259
 horseradish for, 119
 juniper for, 259
 meadowsweet for, 137
 mullein for, 141
 oats for, 148
 overview of, **259**
grape seed (*Vitis vinifera*), **108**, 213, 214, 215, 216, 218, 240, 275, 276, 287, 288, 289, 294, 296, 299
grapefruit seed (*Citrus x aurantium, C. x paradisi*), **109**, 230, 246, 247, 250, 300
grapple plant *see* devil's claw
Grave's disease, 254
grazes
 aloe vera for, 297
 calendula for, 297
 cleavers for, 71
 echinacea for, 297

garlic for, 297
greater plantain for, 111
manuka for, 297
overview of, **297–8**
tea tree for, 297
greasy skin, 55, **294**
great burdock *see* burdock
great mullein *see* mullein
great yellow gentian *see* gentian
greater celandine (*Chelidonium majus*), **110**, 297
greater plantain (*Plantago major, P. lanceolata*), **111**, 210, 282, 283, 290
green ginger *see* wormwood
green tea (*Camellia sinensis*), **112**, 208, 216, 253, 288
guarana (*Paullinia cupana*), **113**
guelder rose *see* cramp bark
gum disorders/problems
 agrimony for, 28
 albizia for, 29
 blackberry for, 46
 calendula for, 227
 dill for, 85
 echinacea for, 225
 elder for, 88
 lady's mantle for, 127
 mallow for, 133
 marshmallow for, 135
 myrrh for, 142
 overview of, **225**, **226–7**
 sage and clary sage for, 167
 sandalwood for, 169
 thyme for, 182, 225
 see also teething
gurmabooti *see* gymnema
gurmar *see* gymnema
guttate psoriasis, 293
gymnema (*Gymnema sylvestre*), **114**, 252

H

haemochromatosis, 235
haemorrhoids *see* piles
hair problems, 166, **242–3**, **244–5**
halitosis, 93, **225–6**
harakeke *see* New Zealand flax
hare's ear *see* bupleurum
harvesting and preserving herbs, 20–1
hawthorn (*Crataegus laevigata, C. monogyna*), **115**, 206, 211, 212, 215, 216, 217, 254, 299
hay fever, 208
 baical skullcap for, 38
 elder for, 88, 209
 eyebright for, 92
 golden rod for, 209
 greater plantain for, 111
 horseradish for, 119
 overview of, **209–10**
 thyme for, 182
headache
 chaste tree for, 267
 cinnamon for, 270
 cramp bark for, 269
 feverfew for, **95**, 267
 lavender for, 128
 maté for, 136
 meadowsweet for, 137
 oats for, 269
 oregano for, 150

passionflower for, 269
peppermint for, 154
rosemary for, 166
valerian for, 269
willow for, 194
see also migraine
heart conditions
 broom for, 52
 codonopsis for, 73
 coleus for, 75, 211, 215
 common poppy for, 157
 garlic for, 211, 213, 215
 ginger for, 211
 ginkgo for, 206, 211, 215
 globe artichoke for, 215
 grape seed for, 215
 hawthorn for, 115, 211, 212, 215, 299
 heartsease for, 116
 lemon balm for, 212
 lime flowers for, 215
 maté for, 136
 oats for, 215
 overview of, **214–15**
 passionflower for, 212, 215
 psyllium for, 215
 St John's wort for, 212
 valerian for, 211, 212
 walnut for, 188
 see also angina; arrhythmia
heartsease (*Viola tricolor*), **116**, 223, 244, 287, 290, 292
Helicobacter pylori, 39, 237
helmet flower *see* skullcap
hepatitis, 235
 astragalus for, 233
 baical skullcap for, 233
 barberry for, 39
 bupleurum for, 54, 233
 globe artichoke for, 233
 milk thistle for, 138, 233
 overview of, **233**
 rehmannia for, 163, 233
herb cultivation, **18–19**
herbal medicine
 Eastern, **12–13**
 home made, **22–5**
 Western, **10–11**
 see also traditional Chinese medicine
herbalist consultations, **14–15**
herbalist training, **15**
Herpes simplex, 87, 88, 248
herpes viruses, 153, 169, 241, **247–8**, **249**
Herpes zoster, **249**
HIV/AIDS, 10, 62, 121, 125, 188, 195, 246
hives *see* urticaria
hoarseness and voice loss, 201, 205, **282–3**
holistic approaches, **10**, **12**, 14
homemade herbal remedies, **22–5**
honey *see* manuka
hops (*Humulus lupulus*), **117**, 266
horehound *see* white horehound
horsechestnut (*Aesculus hippocastanum*), **118**, 214, 218, 219, 288, 289, 299
horsefly weed *see* wild indigo
horseradish (*Armoracia rusticana*), **119**, 284
horsetail (*Equisetum arvense*), **120**, 243, 289, 299
hot flushes, 276

INDEX 313

INDEX

black cohosh for, 43
dong quai for, 86
red clover for, 162, 277
sage and clary sage for, 167, 277
hot pepper *see* cayenne
huang quin *see* baical skullcap
hung qi *see* astragalus
hyperhydrosis *see* perspiration and body odour
hypertension *see* blood pressure
hyperthyroidism, 245, **253–4**, 255, 300
hypothyroidism, **124**, 207, **254–5**
hyssop (*Hyssopus officinalis*), 15, **121**, 206, 281

I

immune system
  aloe vera for, 31
  andrographis for, 245, 248, 255, 283, 285
  astragalus for, 233, 247, 248, 250, 255, 283
  cat's claw for, 62
  dong quai for, 86
  echinacea for, **87**, 221, 245, 247, 248, 250, 255, 269, 283, 285
  elder for, 248, 269
  eucalyptus for, 248
  garlic for, 247, 283, 285
  golden seal for, 106, 255
  gotu kola for, 107
  Korean ginseng for, 125
  marshmallow for, 135, 248
  mistletoe for, 139
  mullein for, 248
  overview of, **251–6**
  Siberian ginseng for, 174, 247, 250, 255
  tea tree for, 248
  white horehound for, 248
  wild indigo for, 192
  withania for, 197, 255
  yarrow for, 248
impetigo, 116, 148, **294**, 295
impotence, 82, **274–5**
Indian date *see* tamarind
Indian frankincense *see* boswellia
Indian herbal medicine, **12**
Indian olibanum tree *see* boswellia
Indian pennywort *see* gotu kola
Indian turmeric *see* golden seal
indigestion
  basil for, 40
  black mustard for, 44
  boldo for, **48**
  bupleurum for, 54
  caraway for, 234
  cayenne for, 63
  centaury for, 65
  chamomile for, 234
  cloves for, 72
  cumin for, 80
  ginger for, 234
  globe artichoke for, 103
  lemon verbena for, 130
  meadowsweet for, 137, 234
  mugwort for, 140
  oats for, 148
  overview of, **233–4**
  papaya for, 234
  peppermint for, 234
  pineapple for, 156
  sage and clary sage for, 167
  star anise for, 234
  sweet marjoram for, 178
  turmeric for, 234
  wormwood for, 198
indigo *see* wild indigo
infections, **245–51**
infective diarrhoea, 32
infertility
  female
    chaste tree for, 67, 273
    dong quai for, 86
    overview of, **273**
    tribulus for, 183
    white peony for, 190, 273
  male
    Korean ginseng for, 125, 276
    overview of, **276**
    tribulus for, 183, 276
inflammatory bowel disease
  anise for, 233
  caraway for, 235
  carob for, 230
  chamomile for, 232, 238
  cramp bark for, 238
  fennel for, 235
  flax for, 235
  garlic for, 233
  ginger for, 232, 233
  lemon balm for, 230, 232
  marshmallow for, 238
  oak bark for, 229, 230, 238, 235
  peppermint for, 233
  psyllium for, 235
  slippery elm for, 176, 238, 235
  star anise for, 235
  thyme for, 230, 232
  yellow dock for, 235
inflammatory disorders
  baical skullcap for, 38, 209, 210
  chamomile for, 210
  cramp bark for, 258
  cumin for, 80
  devil's claw for, 258
  feverfew for, 95
  nutmeg for, 258
  turmeric for, 184
  see gall bladder disorders; osteoarthritis; rheumatoid arthritis
influenza
  andrographis for, 32
  angelica for, 33
  black mustard for, 44
  blackberry for, 46
  blackcurrant for, 47
  bupleurum for, 54
  cinnamon for, 70
  echinacea for, 87
  elder for, 88
  grapefruit seed for, 109
  meadowsweet for, 137
  mullein for, 141
  rosehip for, 165
  vervain for, 187
  white horehound for, 189
  willow for, 194
  yarrow for, 199
  see also cold, common
infusions, 15, **22**
inhalations, fragrant, **25**
insect bites/stings
  calendula for, 57, 291
  greater plantain for, 111
  lady's mantle for, 127
  lavender for, 128, 291
  lime flower for, 132
  manuka for, 134
  overview of, **290–1**
  peppermint for, 154
  tea tree for, 181, 291
  thyme for, 182, 291
intestinal spasms, 66, 193
iodine deficiency, **124**
irritable bowel syndrome, 78, 93, 133, 154, 158, 176, 193, **234–5**
ispaghula *see* psyllium
Italian cypress *see* cypress
itching, 68, 97, **291–2**, 293

J

Japanese anise (*Illicium anisatum*), 177
Japanese arrowroot *see* kuzu
Japanese herbal medicine, **12–13**
jaundice, 39, 246
Johnny jump-up *see* heartsease
joint aches and pains
  cayenne for, 63
  cumin for, 80
  devil's claw for, 84
  flax for, 97
  ginger for, 101
  meadowsweet for, 137
  nutmeg for, 146
  sweet marjoram for, 178
  see also arthritis; rheumatism
jujube *see* ziziphus
juniper (*Juniperus communis*), **122**, 245, 259, 260, 262

K

Kahikatoa *see* manuka
kalmegh *see* andrographis
kampoh medicine *see* Japanese herbal medicine
kava (*Piper methysticum*), **123**
kelp (*Fucus vesiculosus*), **124**, 252, 255
kidney infection, **300**
kidney problems
  barberry for, 299, 300
  chicory for, 69
  cleavers for, 299
  corn silk for, 77, 299, 300, 301
  dandelion, for, 83, 299, 300
  flax for, 97
  garlic for, 300
  golden rod for, 300, 301
  horsetail for, 120, 299
  marshmallow for, 300, 301
  maté for, 136
  meadowsweet for, 299
  overview of, 299, **300–1**
kidney stones, 71, 77, 79, 93, 119, 161, 183, **300–1**
king of bitters *see* andrographis
kirata *see* andrographis
kokko *see* albizia
Korean ginseng (*Panax ginseng*), **125**, 206, 207, 253, 269, 275, 276
kuzu (*Pueraria lobata*), **126**, 204

L

labelling, **16**, 17
lady's mantle (*Alchemilla vulgaris*), 19, **127**, 273, 274, 277, 279, 296
lapacho *see* pau d'arco
laryngitis
  cayenne for, 63
  elder for, 283
  eucalyptus for, 283
  greater plantain for, 111, 283
  marshmallow for, 283
  mullein for, 141
  overview of, **283**
  pine for, 155
  tea tree for, 283
  thyme for, 283
  white horehound for, 283
lavender (*Lavandula angustifolia*), 10, 19, 25, **128**, 205, 210, 219, 221, 224, 226, 231, 245, 250, 254, 256, 264, 265, 266, 268, 273, 274, 278, 279, 281, 285, 286, 287, 288, 289, 291, 292, 293, 295, 296, 298
lebbek tree *see* albizia
lemon balm (*Melissa officinalis*), 19, **129**, 204, 207, 212, 224, 230, 231, 232, 248, 249, 254, 264, 266, 297
lemon verbena (*Aloysia triphylla*), **130**, 239
leopard's bane *see* arnica
leprosy, 183
libido problems, 34, **275**, 276
lice infestations, 143
licorice (*Glycyrrhiza glabra*), **131**, 15, 210, 248, 249, 251, 269, 280, 285, 293, 297
life-giving vine of Peru *see* cat's claw
lime flower (*Tilia cordata*, *T. platphyllos*), **132**, 206, 215, 238, 254, 256, 265, 266, 279, 287, 292, 293, 299
linden tree *see* lime flower
linseed *see* flax
lipid disorders (blood), **216**
liquid extracts, 15
liver problems
  baical skullcap for, 210, 233, 236
  boldo for, 48, 299
  bupleurum for, 54
  chicory for, 69
  corn silk for, 77, 299
  dandelion for, 287, 293
  globe artichoke for, 103, 210, 233, 236, 287, 293, 299
  kuzu for, 126
  lime flowers for, 299
  milk thistle for, 138, 204, 205, 210, 233, 236, 293, 299
  overview of, **235–6**
  papaya for, 287
  psyllium for, 236
  rehmannia for, 163
  rosemary for, 166, 299
  schisandra for, 171
  see also cirrhosis
locust bean *see* carob
lucerne *see* alfalfa
lumbago, 63
lymphatic disorders
  bilberry for, 42
  calendula for, 57

INDEX

cleavers for, 71, 247, 252
gotu kola for, 107
yellow dock for, 200
lymphoedema, **217**

M

macular degeneration, 239, 240
mad dog skullcap *see* skullcap
Madagascar periwinkle, 8, **9**
maidenhead tree *see* ginkgo
maize *see* corn silk
malabar tamarind *see* garcinia
malaria, **8–9**, 113, 198
male infertility
  Korean ginseng for, 125, 276
  overview of, **276**
  tribulus for, **183**, 276
male sexual function
  damiana for, 82
  ginkgo for, 275
  Korean ginseng for, 275
  saw palmetto for, 275
  tribulus for, 183
mallow (*Malva sylvestris*), **133**, 224
manuka (*Leptospermum scoparium*), **134**, 285, 288, 289, 298
marigold *see* calendula
marsh horsetail (*Equisetum palustre*), 120
marshmallow (*Althaea officinalis*), 18, **135**, 221, 222, 229, 238, 244, 248, 281, 282, 283, 284, 285, 298, 300, 301
massage oils, **25**
mastic tree *see* boswellia
mastitis, 271
maté (*Ilex paraguariensis*), **136**
may tree *see* hawthorn
maypops *see* passionflower
meadow saffron, 7
meadowsweet (*Filipendula ulmaria*), **137**, 227, 232, 234, 237, 260, 261, 299
measles, 220
memory problems
  ageing &, **207–8**
  brahmi for, 51, 264
  dong quai for, 86, 277
  ginkgo for, 102, 207, 264
  guarana for, 113
  lemon balm for, 207
  rosemary for, 166
  sage for, 10, 207
  schisandra for, 171, 264
  see also Alzheimer's disease; concentration
menopausal problems
  aloe vera for, 277
  black cohosh for, 43, 277
  calendula for, 277
  dong quai for, 86
  hops for, 117
  kuzu for, 126
  overview of, **276–7**
  red clover for, 162, 277
  sage and clary sage for, 167, 277
  tribulus for, 183
menstrual pain, 277, 278
  anise for, 34
  chaste tree for, 67
  cramp bark for, 78, 272, 274, 278
  dong quai for, 86
  feverfew for, 95

German chamomile for, 66
ginger for, 101, 272, 274, 278
lavender for, 128
mugwort for, 140, 278
sage and clary sage for, 167
shepherd's purse for, 173
vervain for, 187
white peony for, 190
wild yam for, 193
yarrow for, 199
menstrual problems
  black cohosh for, 43
  burdock for, 55
  caraway for, 59
  chaste tree for, **67**, 278
  clary sage for, 278
  dong quai for, 86
  feverfew for, 278
  golden seal for, 106
  hops for, 117
  lady's mantle for, 127, 273, 274
  lavender for, 278
  mugwort for, 140
  overview of, **277–8**
  rehmannia for, 163
  shepherd's purse for, 273, 274
  white peony for, 190
  wild yam for, 193
  yarrow for, 199
  see also premenstrual tension/syndrome
mental health and nervous system, **263–70**
meshasringi *see* gymnema
metabolism & immune system disorders, **251–6**
middle ear infection, 92
midland hawthorn *see* hawthorn
migraine
  chaste tree for, 267
  coffee for, 74
  feverfew for, 95, 267
  sandalwood for, 169
milfoil *see* yarrow
milk thistle (*Silybum marianum*), **138**, 204, 210, 216, 230, 233, 236, 252, 289, 293, 299
milk vetch *see* astragalus
mint, 14, 234, 237
  see also peppermint
mistletoe (*Viscum album*), **139**
monk's pepper *see* chaste tree
morning sickness, 101, 129, 180, 236, 237
motion sickness, 93, 236, 237
mountain tobacco *see* arnica
mouth infections/inflammation
  bay for, 41
  blackberry for, 46
  calendula for, 57, 206
  mallow for, 133
  manuka for, 134
  marshmallow for, 135
  myrrh for, 142, 206
  sweet violet for, 179
  see also dental and gum problems
mouth ulcers
  andrographis for, 226
  bay for, 41
  blackberry for, 46
  calendula for, 57, 226
  myrrh for, 226
  overview of, **226–7**
  red clover for, 162
  sage for, 226

sweet marjoram for, 178
winter savory for, 195
mugwort (*Artemisia vulgaris*), **140**, 278
mullein (*Verbascum thapsus*), **141**, 221, 223, 241, 242, 248, 280, 282, 283, 284, 291, 297
mumps, 220
muscle aches and pains
  arnica for, 35
  cayenne for, 63, 257
  cinnamon for, 257, 258
  cramp bark for, 258
  devil's claw for, 257, 258
  juniper for, 122
  nutmeg for, 146, 257
  rosemary, for, 166, 257
  sweet marjoram for, 178
  see also sprains; tendonitis
muscle spasms
  barberry for, 39
  cinnamon for, 257
  cramp bark for, 257
  meadowsweet for, 137
  nutmeg for, 257
  passionflower for, 152
musculoskeletal cramp, 78
myrrh (*Commiphora myrrha, C. molmol*), **142**, 205, 206, 226, 227
myrtle (*Myrtus communis*), **143**

N

nail disorders, **243–4**
nappy rash, 68, 187
nasal catarrh, 88, 105, 106, 121, 283
National Herbalists Association of Australia, 14
Nature Care College of Naturopathic and Life Studies, Sydney, 15
nausea
  dill for, 85
  fennel for, 236
  ginger for, 101, 236, 237
  overview of, **236–7**
  peppermint for, 236
  slippery elm for, 236
  sweet marjoram for, 178
  tamarind for, 180
neck pain, **257**
nervous disorders
  brahmi for, 264
  Californian poppy for, 264, 265, 266
  cayenne for, 267
  chamomile for, 268
  chaste tree for, 267
  cinnamon for, 270
  codonopsis for, 269
  common poppy for, 157
  cramp bark for, 269
  damiana for, 265, 268, 269
  echinacea for, 269
  elder for, 269
  feverfew for, 267
  ginkgo for, 264, 270
  hops for, 117, 266
  Korean ginseng for, 269
  lavender for, 264, 265, 266, 268
  lemon balm for, 129, 264, 266
  licorice for, 269
  lime flower for, 265, 266
  nutmeg for, 267

oats for, 268, 269
passionflower for, 152, 264, 265, 266, 269
sage for, 264
St John's wort for, 265, 267
schisandra for, 264
Siberian ginseng for, 269
skullcap for, 175
valerian for, 186, 265, 266, 269
vervain for, 187
withania for, 197
nervous exhaustion
  Californian poppy for, 58
  damiana for, 82
  green tea for, 112
  guarana for, 113
  maté for, 136
  oats for, 148
  Siberian ginseng for, 174
  tea for, 112
nervous system and mental health, **263–70**
nettle (*Urtica dioica*), **144**, 211, 243, 244, 245, 286, 294
nettle rash, 38
neuralgia, 122, **267**
New Zealand Association of Medical Herbalists, 14
New Zealand flax (*Phormium tenax*), **145**
New Zealand Medicines and Medical Devices Safety Authority, 17
New Zealand regulations, 17
New Zealand tea tree *see* manuka
nicotine addiction, **205**
night sweats, 167
nipples, cracked, 179, 271, 272
nose bleeds, 173
nutmeg (*Myristica fragrans*), **146**, 257, 258, 263, 267
nutraceuticals, **11**

O

oak (*Quercus robur*), **147**, 229, 230, 235, 238
oats (*Avena sativa*), **148**, 215, 221, 238, 251, 253, 255, 256, 258, 268, 269, 293, 294
obesity, 83, **252–3**
oedema *see* fluid retention
oesophagitis, 227, **231–2**
oily skin, 55, **294**
olive (*Olea europaea*), **149**
orangeroot *see* golden seal
oregano (*Origanum vulgare*), **150**
osteoarthritis, 84, **259–60**
osteoporosis, 120, **260**, 300
otitis externa, 241
otitis media, **222–3**, 241
overweight and obesity, 83, **252–3**

P

Pacific yew, 9
papaya (*Carica papaya*), **151**, 228, 234, 239, 287
Paraguay tea *see* maté
parasitic infections, 109, 151, 245, 255
paronychia, 243

INDEX 315

INDEX

partus praeparator, 161
passionflower *(Passiflora incarnata)*, **152**, 205, 212, 215, 235, 238, 242, 258, 264, 265, 266, 269, 279, 287, 293
pau d'arco *(Tabebula impetiginosa)*, **153**, 243, 246, 247, 248, 249, 250, 297
pawpaw *see* papaya
peony *see* white peony
peppermint *(Mentha x piperita)*, 15, 18, 25, **154**, 209, 225, 227, 229, 231, 232, 233, 234, 235, 236, 238, 239, 243, 256, 292, 293
peptic ulcers, 39, **237**
perimenopause, **276–7**
period pain *see* menstrual pain
period problems *see* menstrual problems
periodontitis, 225
perspiration and body odour, **292**
pharmaceuticals, **7**, **8–9**, 10
pharyngitis, 111, 192, 284, 285
phytochemicals, 10
piles
 agrimony for, 28
 aloe vera for, 31
 bilberry for, 214
 boswellia for, 50
 butcher's broom for, 56
 chickweed for, 68
 coriander for, 76
 cypress for, 81
 gotu kola for, 107
 grape seed for, 108, 214
 horsechestnut for, 118, 214
 oak for, 147
 overview of, **214**
 shepherd's purse for, 173
 slippery elm for, 176, 214
 witch hazel for, 196, 214
 yarrow for 199
pill bearing spurge *see* asthma plant
pine *(Pinus sylvestris)*, 25, **155**, 242, 281, 283
pineapple *(Ananas comosus)*, **156**, 288, 296
pipe tree *see* elder
pituitary gland problems, 67
pneumococcal infection, 111
pneumonia, 38
polycystic ovarian syndrome, 190
poppy, common *(Papaver rhoeas)*, **157**
poultices, **24–5**
premenstrual tension/syndrome
 black cohosh for, 43
 borage for, 49
 buchu for, 53
 butcher's broom for, 56
 Californian poppy for, 279
 chaste tree for, 67, 271, 279
 evening primrose for, **91**, 271, 279
 lavender for, 279
 lime flowers for, 279
 overview of, **278–9**
 passionflower for, 279
 valerian for, 279
 white peony for, 190
 withania for, 279
preserving and harvesting herbs, **20–1**
pressure sores *see* bedsores

probiotic supplements, 233, 238
propagation, **19**
prostaglandins, **91**
prostate conditions
 epilobium for, 89
 horsetail for, 120
 nettle for, 144
 overview of, **301**
 pumpkin for, 160
 saw palmetto for, **170**, 301
prostatitis, 53, 301
protozoal bowel infections, 36
pruritis, 116
pseudogout, 259
psoriasis
 aloe vera for, 31, 293
 burdock for, 55
 calendula for, 293
 chamomile for, 293
 chickweed for, 68, 293
 cleavers for, 71
 coleus for, 75
 dandelion for, 293
 evening primrose for, 293
 globe artichoke for, 293
 golden seal for, 293
 gotu kola for, 107, 293
 lavender for, 293
 licorice for, 293
 lime flowers for, 293
 milk thistle for, 293
 oats for, 293
 overview of, **292–4**
 passionflower for, 293
 peppermint for, 293
 red clover for, 162
 turmeric for, 293
 withania for, 293
 yellow dock for, 200
psoriatic arthritis, 293
psychosomatic disorders, **268**
psyllium *(Plantago ovata)*, **158**, 213, 215, 228, 230, 235, 236
puha *(Sonchus oleraceus)*, **159**
pumpkin *(Cucurbita pepo)*, **160**
puncture vine *see* tribulus
purple clover *see* red clover
pyelonephritis, **300**

Q

qing hao *(Artemesia annua)*, 8, 9, 198
queen of the meadow *see* meadowsweet
Queensland asthma plant *see* asthma plant

R

ram's horn *see* gymnema
raspberry *(Rubus idaeus)*, **161**
rattle weed *see* wild indigo
Raynaud's disease, **218**
red clover *(Trifolium pratense)*, **162**, 277
red elm *see* slippery elm
red tea tree *see* manuka
regulation of herbal medicines, **16**, **17**
rehmannia *(Rehmannia glutinosa)*, **163**, 229, 233, 236, 238
reproduction and sexuality, **270–1**

respiratory disorders
 agrimony for, 283
 andrographis for, **32**, 248, 281, 282, 283, 284
 asthma plant for, **36**
 astragalus, 248, 283
 baical skullcap for, 38
 boswellia for, 50
 bronchiolitis, **219–20**
 calendula for, 284
 codonopsis for, 73
 coleus for, 75
 echinacea for, 87, 248, 281, 282, 283, 284
 elder for, 88, 248, 283, 284
 eucalyptus for, 90, 248, 281, 282, 283
 garlic for, 99, 282, 283, 284
 golden seal for, 106, 284
 greater plantain for, 282, 283
 heartsease for, 116
 horseradish for, 119, 284
 hyssop for, 121, 281
 lavender for, 281
 mallow for, 133
 marshmallow for, **135**, 248, 281, 282, 283, 284
 mullein for, 141, 248, 282, 283, 284
 myrtle for, 143
 peppermint for, 154
 pine for, 155, 281, 283
 rosemary for, 166, 282
 sage for, 283, 284
 slippery elm for, 176, 282, 284
 sweet violet for, **179**
 tea tree for, 181, 248, 281, 282, 283
 thyme for, 182, 281, 282, 283, 284
 white horehound for, 189, 248, 281, 282, 283
 wild cherry for, 191
 wild indigo for, 192
 yarrow for, 248
 see also cold, common; coughs; influenza
respiratory syncytial virus, 219
rheumatism
 black mustard for, 44
 black pepper for, 45
 blackcurrant for, 47
 celery for, 64
 devil's claw for, 84
 gotu kola for, 107
 heartsease for, 116
 horseradish for, 119
 juniper for, 122
 lavender for, 128
 manuka for, 134
 meadowsweet for, 137
 mugwort for, 140
 nettle for, 144
 nutmeg for, 146
 oats for, 148
 oregano for, 150
 pine for, 155
 rosemary for, 166
 turmeric for, 184
 willow for, 194
 withania for, 197
rheumatism root *see* wild yam
rheumatoid arthritis, 47, 49, 163, 211, 238, **261–2**
rhubarb *(Rheum palmatum)*, **164**
ribwort plantain *see* greater plantain

ringworm, 110, 134, 246
Roman chamomile *(Chamaemelum nobile)*, 66
rosacea *see* acne rosacea
rosebay willowherb *see* epilobium
rosehip *(Rosa canina)*, 24, **165**, 206, 223, 252, 255
rosemary *(Rosmarinus officinalis)*, 12, 19, **166**, 217, 226, 231, 232, 239, 243, 244, 245, 253, 255, 257, 262, 282, 299
round buchu *see* buchu
roundworms, 160
rubella (German measles), 180, 220
rum cherry *see* wild cherry

S

sabal *see* saw palmetto
safe usage, **16–17**
sage *(Salvia officinalis)*, 10, 20, **167**, 207, 226, 244, 264, 277, 283, 284, 292
saiko *see* bupleurum
St John's bread *see* carob
St John's wort *(Hypericum perforatum)*, 10–11, 14, **168**, 205, 212, 236, 248, 249, 258, 265, 267, 277
St Mary's thistle *see* milk thistle
Salmonella typhimurium, 180
sandalwood *(Santalum album)*, **169**, 292
savéntaro *see* cat's claw
saw palmetto *(Serenoa repens)*, **170**, 243, 275, 276, 301
scabies, 183, 291
scalp problems, **244–5**
scarlet tongue, 163
schisandra *(Schisandra chinensis)*, **171**, 264
sciatica, 166, 168
Scot's pine *see* pine
seaweed *see* kelp
seborrhoeic dermatitis, 71, 240, **244–5**
seborrhoea, 116
seeds, **18**, **20**
senna *(Senna alexandrina)*, **172**, 228, 235
sex drive, **275**
sexual function, male
 damiana for, 82, 275
 ginkgo for, 275
 Korean ginseng for, 275
 saw palmetto for, 275
 tribulus for, **183**
shepherd's purse *(Capsella bura-pastoris)*, **173**, 273, 274
shingles, 249
shirisha *see* albizia
shrub palmetto *see* saw palmetto
Siberian ginseng *(Eleutherococcus senticosus)*, **174**, 205, 247, 250, 251, 253, 255, 258, 269
sickle-leaved hare's ear *see* bupleurum
simpler's joy *see* vervain
sinusitis
 echinacea for, 284
 elder for, 284

INDEX

eucalyptus for, 90
eyebright for, 92
garlic for, 284
golden seal for, 284
horseradish for, 119, 284
overview of, **283–4**
tea tree for, 181
thyme for, 284
wild indigo for, 192
siris *see* albizia
skin infections, **294–5**
skin problems
  ageing &, 206, **207**
  agrimony for, 28
  albizia for, 29, 290
  aloe vera for, 31, 286, 287, 289, 290, 293, 296
  andrographis for, 32, 285
  arnica &, 35, 288
  baical skullcap for, 38, 290
  barberry for, 39, 285, 295
  borage for, 49
  boswellia for, 50
  burdock for, **55**, 286, 287, 290, 294
  calendula for, 57, 207, 208, 246, 286, 287, 288, 289, 290, 291, 293, 294, 296
  cayenne for, 63
  chamomile for, 66, 210, 291, 293, 294
  chaste tree for, 286
  chickweed for, **68**, 290, 293, 295
  cleavers for, 71, 286, 289
  corn silk for, 77
  dandelion for, 286, 287, 289, 295
  echinacea for, 246, 285, 287, 295
  epilobium for, 89
  evening primrose for, 91, 207, 208, 255, 286, 287, 290, 293, 294, 295
  fenugreek for, 94
  flax for, 97
  garlic for, 285, 287, 295
  ginkgo for, 287, 288, 295
  globe artichoke for, 287, 289, 295
  golden rod for, 105
  golden seal for, 107, 293, 295
  gotu kola for, 289, 293, 294, 296
  grape seed for, 287, 288, 289, 294, 296
  greater celandine for, 110
  greater plantain for, 111, 290
  green tea for, 208, 288
  heartsease for, 116, 287, 290
  horsechestnut for, 288, 289
  horsetail for, 289
  lady's mantle for, 127, 296
  lavender for, 128, 210, 285, 286, 287, 288, 289, 291, 293, 295, 296
  licorice for, 293
  lime flower for, 132, 287, 293
  manuka for, 134, 285, **288**, 289
  marshmallow for, 135
  milk thistle for, 289
  mugwort for, 140
  mullein for, 141, 291
  myrtle for, 143
  nettle for, 144, 286, 294
  New Zealand flax for, 145
  oak for, 147

oats for, 148, 293, 294
papaya for, 287
passionflower for, 287, 290, 293
pau d'arco for, 153
peppermint for, 293
pineapple for, 288, 296
raspberry for, 161
red clover for, 162
St John's wort for, 168
sandalwood for, 169
slippery elm for, 285, 295
sweet violet for, 179
tea for, 208
tea tree for, **181**, 246, 285, 290, 291, 295
thyme for, 210, 291, 295
tribulus for, 183
turmeric for, 293
vervain for, 187
wild indigo for, 295
winter savory for, 195
witch hazel for, 196, 287, 288, 290, 294, 296
withania for, 287, 290, 293
yellow dock for, 200, 286, 290, 295
see also under particular problem e.g. psoriasis
skin ulcers
  blackberry for, 46
  cleavers for, 71
  golden rod for, 105
  gotu kola for, 107
  horsechestnut for, 118
  manuka for, 134
  meadowsweet for, 137
  mullein for, 141
skullcap *(Scutellaria lateriflora)*, **175**
sleeping problems
  Californian poppy for, 58, 266, 271
  chamomile for, 66, 224
  childhood, **224**
  common poppy for, 157
  hops for, 117, 266
  lavender for, 128, 266, 279
  lemon balm for, 129, 224, 266
  lime flower for, 132, 206, 266, 279
  oats for, 148
  overview of, **266**
  passionflower for, 152, 258, 266, 279
  St John's wort for, 168
  skullcap for, 175
  sweet marjoram for, 178, 239
  valerian for, 186, 204, 205, 206, 266, 279
  withania for, 197
  ziziphus for, 201
slippery elm *(Ulmus rubra)*, **176**, 214, 228, 229, 232, 235, 236, 237, 238, 282, 284, 285, 295
small-leaved lime *see* lime flower
smallage *see* celery
smoking *see* nicotine addiction
smooth sow thistle *see* puha
snake root *see* echinacea
snakeweed *see* asthma plant
snow in summer *see* tea tree
sore throat
  agrimony for, 28
  basil for, 40
  blackberry for, 46
  echinacea for, 87

elder for, 88
eucalyptus for, 90
golden rod for, 105
grapefruit seed for, 109
hyssop for, 121
marshmallow for, 135
mullein for, 141
myrrh for, 205
red clover for, 162
sage and clary sage for, 167
slippery elm for, 176
winter savory for, 195
ziziphus for, 201
Southern Cross University, Lismore, 15
Southern School of Natural Therapies, Melbourne, 15
sprains, 35, **262**
spur pepper *see* cayenne
Staphylococcus aureus, 153, 185, 222
star anise *(Illicium verum)*, **177**, 226, 230, 234
star flower *see* borage
sticklewort *see* agrimony
stinging nettle *see* nettle
stomach problems
  bay for, 41
  cumin for, 80
  hyssop for, 121
  lemon balm for, 129
  meadowsweet for, 137
  rosemary for, 166
  see also bloating, stomach; gastric ulcers; peptic ulcers
streptococcus infection, 111, 284, 285
stress
  codonopsis for, 73, 269
  damiana for, 269, 275
  echinacea for, 269
  elder for, 269
  Korean ginseng for, 269, 275
  lavender for, 292, 293
  licorice for, 269
  lime flower for, 132, 215, 292, 293
  oats for, 148, 215, 269
  passionflower for, 215, 242, 290, 293
  schisandra for, 171
  Siberian ginseng for, 174, 205, 269
  skullcap for, 175
  withania for, 197, 275, 279, 290, 292, 293
stretch marks, **295–6**
styes, 92
summer squash *see* pumpkin
sun exposure and ageing, 207, 208
sunburn
  aloe vera for, 296
  calendula for, 57, 296
  gotu kola for, 296
  grape seed for, 296
  lavender for, 296
  olive for, 149
  overview of, **296**
  pineapple for, 296
  tea tree for, 181
  vervain for, 187
  witch hazel for, 296
swallow wort *see* greater celandine
sweet bay *see* bay
sweet corn *see* corn silk
sweet fennel *see* fennel

sweet marjoram *(Origanum majorana)*, 25, **178**, 239
sweet violet *(Viola odorata)*, 19, **179**, 219, 221
sweetwood *see* licorice
syrups, **23**

T

tabasco pepper *see* cayenne
tamarind *(Tamarindus indica)*, **180**
tang kuei *see* dong quai
tapeworms, 160
Tasmanian blue gum *see* eucalyptus
tea *(Camellia sinensis)*, **112**, 207, 208, 211, 212, 216, 253, 266, 279, 287, 288, 299, 300
tea tree *(Melaleuca alternifolia)*, **181**, 241, 242, 244, 246, 250, 281, 282, 283, 285, 290, 291, 295, 297
teething, 133, 175, **224**
tendonitis, 122, 146, **262–3**
tension headache, **269–70**
tetter wort *see* greater celandine
Therapeutic Goods Administration, 16, 17
thorow-wax *see* bupleurum
throat infections
  agrimony for, 28
  andrographis for, 284
  basil for, 40
  blackberry for, 46
  calendula for, 284
  echinacea for, 87, 284
  elder for, 88, 284
  eucalyptus for, 90
  golden rod for, 105
  grapefruit seed for, 109
  hyssop for, 121
  marshmallow for, 135, 284
  mullein for, 141, 284
  myrrh for, 205
  overview of, **284–5**
  red clover for, 162
  sage and clary sage for, 167, 284
  slippery elm for, 176, 284
  thyme for, 284
  winter savory for, 195
  ziziphus for, 201
thrush *(Candida albicans)*, 39, 105, 150, 153, 155, 181, 195, 196, 246, **249–50**
thyme, common *(Thymus vulgaris)*, **182**, 210, 219, 222, 225, 227, 230, 232, 244, 281, 282, 283, 284, 291, 295
thyme-leaved gratiola *see* brahmi
thyroid problems *see* hyperthyroidism; hypothyroidism
tinctures, **24**
tinea, 181, 246
tinnitus, 86, 106, **241–2**
tonsillitis, 71, 182, 221, **284**
tooth decay, **227**
toothache
  cayenne for, 227
  cloves for, 72, 227
  meadowsweet for, 137
  peppermint for, 227
  sandalwood for, 169

INDEX   317

INDEX

sweet marjoram for, 178
see also teething
tracheitis, 141, **222**
traditional Chinese medicine
  andrographis &, 32
  artemisen &, 8, 9
  astragalus &, 37
  baical skullcap &, 38
  black cohosh &, 43
  bupleurum &, 54
  chickweed &, 68
  Chinese wormwood &, 198
  codonopsis &, 73
  dong quai &, 86
  green tea &, 112
  Korean ginseng &, 125
  mugwort &, 140
  overview of, **12–13**
  rehmannia &, 163
  sandalwood &, 169
  white peony &, 190
  ziziphus &, 201
Trans-Tasman Therapeutic Products Agency, 8
travel sickness *see* motion sickness
trefoil *see* red clover
tribulus (*Tribulus terrestris*), **183**, 275, 276
Trichophyton, 246
trichotillomania, 242
tuberculosis, 120
turkey grass *see* vervain
turmeric (*Curcuma longa*), **15**, 184, 226, 228, 230, 231, 234, 261, 263, 293

U

ulcerative colitis, **237–8**
ulcers, 57, 70, 194
  see also gastric ulcers; mouth ulcers; peptic ulcers; skin ulcers
Uña de Gato *see* cat's claw
Unani Tibb, 13
urethritis, 53, 105, 135, 185, **298–9**
urinary tract disorders
  baical skullcap for, 38
  buchu for, 53, 298
  cleavers for, 71, 298
  corn silk for, 77, 298
  cranberry for, 79, 298
  dandelion for, 298
  golden rod for, 105, 298, 299
  greater plantain for, 111
  heartsease for, 116
  juniper for, 122
  marshmallow for, 135, 298
  meadowsweet for, 137
  nettle for, 144
  overview of, **298**, **301**
  psyllium for, 158
  pumpkin for, 160
  raspberry for, 161
  sandalwood for, 169
  saw palmetto for, 301
  slippery elm for, 176
  tribulus for, 183
  uva-ursi for, **185**, 298
  see also fluid retention; kidney problems
urine retention, 119
urticaria, 38, 68, **210**

uterine fibroids, 190, **273–4**
uva-ursi (*Arcostaphylos uva-ursi*), **185**, 298

V

vaginal discharge/infections
  blackberry for, 46
  boswellia for, 50
  calendula for, 250
  chamomile for, 250
  golden rod for, 105
  horsetail for, 120
  lady's mantle for, 127
  lavender for, 250
  raspberry for, 161
  tea tree for, 181, 250
vaginal dryness, 276, 277
valerian (*Valeriana officinalis*), **186**, 204, 206, 211, 212, 216, 254, 265, 266, 269, 279
varicose ulcers, 68
varicose veins, 217, 218
  blackcurrant for, 47
  broom for, 52, 218
  cypress for, 81
  golden seal for, 106
  gotu kola for, 107
  grape seed for, 108
  horsechestnut for, 118
  witch hazel for, 196
  yarrow for, 199
variegated thistle *see* milk thistle
vein disorders
  bilberry for, 42, 214
  broom for, 52, 218
  cypress for, 81, 219
  ginger for, 218
  ginkgo for, 218
  golden seal for, 106
  gotu kola for, 107
  grape seed for, 108, 214, 218
  horsechestnut for, 118, 196, 214, 218, 219
  overview of, **218–19**
  papaya for, 151
  rosemary for, 166
  slippery elm for, 214
  witch hazel for, 196, 214, 219
  yarrow for, 199
verbena *see* lemon verbena; vervain
vertigo, **270**
vervain (*Verbena officinalis*), **187**
violet *see* sweet violet
Virginia skullcap *see* skullcap
viruses, 245, 255
  andrographis for, 248, 251
  astragalus for, **37**, 247, 248, 251
  calendula for, 248
  cleavers for, 247
  echinacea for, 221, 222, 247, 248, 251
  elder for, 219, 221, 222, 248
  eucalyptus for, 248
  garlic for, 247
  grapefruit seed for, 109
  lemon balm for, 248
  licorice for, 248, 251
  marshmallow for, 221, 222, 248
  mullein for, 221, 248
  oak for, 147
  oats for, 251

overview of, **250–1**
pau d'arco for, 153
rosehip for, 251
sandalwood for, 169
Siberian ginseng for, 174, 247, 251
sweet violet for, 219, 221
tamarind for, 180
tea tree for, 248
thyme for, 219, 222
white horehound for, 248
yarrow for, 248
see also under particular virus e.g. influenza
voice loss and hoarseness, 201, 205, **282–3**

W

walnut (*Juglans regia*), **188**
warts, 110, **296–7**
water consumption, 207, 208, 209, 228, 230, 233
water hyssop *see* brahmi
waybread *see* greater plantain
weight
  excess body, 83, 252–3
  low body, **255–6**
weight loss
  green tea for, 112
  guarana for, 113
  gymnema for, 114
  horsetail for, 120
  kelp for, 124
  maté for, 136
  meadowsweet for, 137
  tea for, 112
Western herbal medicine, **10–11**
white horehound (*Marrubium vulgare*), **189**, 206, 248, 281, 282, 283
white peony (*Paeonia lactiflora (albiflora)*), **190**, 273, 278, 279
white willow *see* willow
whortleberry *see* bilberry
wild celery *see* celery
wild cherry (*Prunus serotina*) **191**, 206, 248, 280
wild clover *see* red clover
wild fennel *see* fennel
wild indigo (*Baptisia tinctoria*), **192**, 230, 295
wild marjoram *see* oregano
wild pansy *see* heartsease
wild yam (*Discorea villosa*), **193**
willow (*Salix alba*), **7**, **194**, 260, 261, 262, 263
willowherb *see* epilobium
winter cherry *see* withania
winter savory (*Satureja montana*), **195**, 217
witch hazel (*Hamamelis virginiana*), **196**, 214, 217, 219, 245, 287, 288, 290, 294, 296
withania (*Withania somnifera*), **197**, 255, 258, 275, 276, 279, 287, 292, 293
withdrawal problems, 126, **204–5**
women's tongue tree *see* albizia
worm infestations, 29, 40, 48, 99, 140, 160, 198, 199
wormwood (*Artemesia absinthium*), **198**
wormwood, Chinese (*Artemesia annua*), 8, 9, 198

wounds, 31, 40, 46, 90, 107, 134, 137, 151, 161, 181, 182, 194, 195, **297–8**
woundwort *see* golden rod
wrinkles, 77, 207, **208**

Y

yam *see* wild yam
yarrow (*Achillea millefolium*), **199**, 245, 248
yellow dock (*Rumex crispus*), **200**, 228, 230, 235, 286, 290, 295
yellow gentian *see* gentian
yellow pucoon *see* golden seal
yellowroot *see* golden seal
yerba maté *see* maté

Z

zinc, 204, 209, 243, 255, 273, 276, 282, 284, 286, 301
ziziphus (*Ziziphus jujuba*), **201**, 281, 292

CREDITS

Bibliography

The doses used in *Nature's Medicines* have been recommended by our scientific consultants with reference to the books listed below:

British Herbal Pharmacopoeia
(British Herbal Medicine Association, 5th edition, 1995)

A Clinical Guide to Blending Liquid Herbs
(K. Bone. Churchill Livingstone, 1st edition, 2003)

The Complete Guide to Herbal Medicines
(C.W. Fetrow, J.R. Avila. Springhouse Corporation, 1st edition, 2000)

The Complete Medicinal Herbal
(P. Ody. Dorling Kindersley, 1st American edition, 1993)

Concise Medical Dictionary
(Oxford University Press, 6th edition, 2002)

The Encyclopedia of Herbal Medicine
(T. Bartram. Grace Publishers, 1st edition, 1995)

The Encyclopedia of Medicinal Plants
(A. Chevallier. Dorling Kindersley, 1st edition, 1996)

The Harvard Medical School Family Health Guide
(A. L. Komaroff, ed. Cassell, 1st UK edition, 2003)

The Herb Book
(J. Lust. Benedict Lust Publications, 2nd edition, 1974)

Herbal Medicines
(J. Barnes, A.A. Anderson, J.D. Phillipson. Pharmaceutical Press, 2nd edition, 2002)

Magic & Medicine of Plants
(Reader's Digest Australia, 1st edition, 1994)

Major Herbs of Ayurveda
(E. M. Williamson, ed. Compiled by The Dabur Research Foundation & Dabur Ayurvet Ltd, Ghaziabad, India. Churchill Livingstone, 1st edition, 2002)

Pharmacognosy, Phytochemistry, Medicinal Plants
(J. Bruneton. Lavoisier Publishing, 2nd edition, 1993)

Potter's New Cyclopaedia of Botanical Drugs and Preparations
(R.C. Wren. The C.W. Daniel Company Ltd, 2nd edition, 1994)

Principles and Practice of Phytotherapy
(S. Mills, K. Bone. Churchill Livingstone, 1st edition, 2000)

The Royal Horticultural Society New Encyclopedia of Herbs and Their Uses
(Deni Bown. Dorling Kindersley, 2nd edition, 2003)

The Publishers wish to thank Living Nature and Rachel Heldon for their assistance.

Picture credits

The following abbreviations are used throughout the picture credits: *l* left; *r* right; *t* top; *c* centre; *b* bottom. RD indicates images that are copyright of The Reader's Digest Association Limited.

Front cover Adlibitum/RD. **Back cover** *l* Forest & Kim Starr/United States Geological Survey; *c* Photodisc; *r* John Freeman/RD. **Endpapers** Sarah Cuttle/RD. **2-3** Michael Peuckert/Flowerphotos. **4** Sarah Cuttle/RD. **6** *tr* C. Boisseaux-Chical-Lavie/REA; *bl* G. Dagli Orti/Topkapi Palace Museum Library. **7** Sarah Cuttle/RD. **8** *l* Biophoto/Photo Researchers/Cosmos; *r* BSIP. **9** BSIP/Auscape. **10** Paul Felix. **11** *t* Garden World Images; *b* RD. **12** *tr* O. Franken/Corbis; *bl* L. Hebberd/Corbis. **13** Sarah Cuttle/RD. **15** Sarah Cuttle/RD. **17** RD. **18-20** *all images* Debbie Patterson/RD. **21** *t all images* Debbie Patterson/RD; *b all images* John Freeman/RD. **22-25** *all images* John Freeman/RD. **26-27** Sarah Cuttle/RD. **28** F. Merlet/Colibri. **29** *t* Hugh Nicholson/Terania Rainforest Publishing; *b* Oxford Scientific Films/Photolibrary.com. **30** P. Nief/Colibri. **31** *t* D. Ellinger/Foto Natura/Bios; *b* Sarah Cuttle/RD. **32** Professor Kazuo Yamasaki. **33** *t* M. Greff/Bios; *b* Sarah Cuttle/RD. **34** E. Morell/Okapia/Bios. **35** P. Nief/Jacana. **36** Tony Rodd. **37** *both* Steven Foster. **38** *t* Professor Kazuo Yamasaki; *b* Steven Foster. **39** *t* D. Bringard/Bios; *br* Sarah Cuttle/RD. **40** F. Merlet/Bios. **41** *t* Gayo/Bios; *b* Sarah Cuttle/RD. **42** M. Rauch/Bios. **43** PPVW Zilverrkaars/Foto Natura/Bios. **44** G. Pölkins/Okapia/Bios. **45** H. Fougere/Bios. **46** P. Nief/Jacana. **47** F. Renard/Bios. **48** D. Bown/Oxford Scientific Films/Bios. **49** H. Lenain/Bios. **50** Reproduced with permission of Krystal Colloids. **51** *both* Forest & Kim Starr/United States Geological Survey. **52** H. Ausloos/Bios. **53** Reproduced with permission of ARC-Roodeplaat (Elsenburg). **54** Georgia Glynn-Smith/Garden Picture Library. **55** *t* B. Gibbons/Oxford Scientific Films/Bios; *b* Sarah Cuttle/RD. **56** J. Mayet/Bios. **57** *t* B. Laurier/Bios; *b* Sarah Cuttle/RD. **58** E. Morell/Okapia/Bios. **59** H. Reinhard/Okapia/Bios. **60** F. Strauss/Map. **61** Steven Foster. **62** Deni Bown/Oxford Scientific Films/Photolibrary.com. **63** D. Heuclin/Bios. **64** *t* Michael Howes/Garden Picture Library; *b* Sarah Cuttle/RD. **65** D. Boag/Oxford Scientific Films/Bios. **66** Tony Rodd. **67** H. Reinhard/Okapia/Bios. **68** RD. **69** *t* D. Bringard/Bios; *b* Sarah Cuttle/RD. **70** S. Schall/Map. **71** Lynn Watson. **72** D. Heuclin/Bios. **73** *t* RD; *b* Steven Foster. **74** *t* M. Gunther/Bios; *b* Sarah Cuttle/RD. **75** *t* Deni Bown/Oxford Scientific Films/Photolibrary.com; *b* Henriette Kress. **76** D. Bringard/Bios. **77** G. Lopez/Bios. **78** *t* RD; *b* Steven Foster. **79** H. Reinhard/Okapia/Bios. **80** *t* H. Reinhard/Okapia/Bios; *b* Sarah Cuttle /RD. **81** Klein-Hubert/Bios. **82** *t* Steven Foster; *b* D. Harms/Wildlife Bildagentur. **83** J.-P. Delobelle/Bios. **84** Oxford Scientific Films/Bios. **85** *t* G. Sommer/Jacana; *b* Sarah Cuttle/RD. **86** *tl* Professor Kazuo Yamasaki; *br* Steven Foster. **87** M. Harvey/Bios. **88** G. Böttger/Naturbild/Okapia/Bios. **89** B. Marcon/Bios. **90** *tl* L. Tarnaud/Jacana; *br* Sarah Cuttle/RD. **91** J.-C. Malausa/Bios. **92** P. Nief/Map. **93** *t* Christopher Fairweather/Garden World Images; *b* Garden World Images. **94** Dr K.J. Strank/Freundeskreis Botanischer Garten, Aix-la-Chapelle. **95** H. Reinhard/Okapia/Bios. **96** J. Frebet/Bios; *b* Sarah Cuttle/RD. **97** N. Le Roy/Jacana. **98** Alex Moffett/Renaissance Herbs. **99** Face & Cie/Bios. **100** H. Reinhard/Okapia/Bios. **101** antphoto.com.au. **102** *t* M. Gunther/Bios; *b* Sarah Cuttle/RD. **103** W. Layer/Jacana. **104** H. Reinhard/Okapia/Bios. **105** Ch. Testu/Colibri. **106** D. Bown/Oxford Scientific Films/Bios. **107** *both* A–Z Botanical Collection. **108** F. Strauss/Map. **109** *t* Sunniva Harte/Garden Picture Library; *b* Garden World Images. **110** D. Barthélemy/Bios. **111** A.& J.-C. Malausa/Bios. **112** *tl* E. Schacke/Naturbild/Okapia/Bios; *br* Sarah Cuttle/RD. **113** J. Sauvanet/Bios. **114** *tl* Professor Kazuo Yamasaki; *br* Jenny Grinlington. **115** P. Nief/Colibri. **116** J.-L. Le Moigne/Bios. **117** Y. Noto-Campanella/Bios. **118** G. Lopez/Bios. **119** *t* B. Laurier/Bios; *b* Sarah Cuttle/RD. **120** B. Dubreuil/Bios. **121** N.& P. Mioulane/Map. **122** S. Schall/Map. **123** Steven Foster. **124** *t* Michel Paris; *b* Paul Kay/Photolibrary.com. **125** Corbis/Australian Picture Library. **126** MNHM. **127** Y. Thonnerieux/Bios; *b* Sarah Cuttle/RD. **128** *tl* Klein-Hubert/Bios; *br* Sarah Cuttle/RD. **129** *t* G. Ken/Horizon; *b* Sarah Cuttle/RD. **130** H. Reinhard/Okapia/Bios. **131** Klein-Hubert/Bios. **132** PPVW/Foto Natura/Bios. **133** T. Lafranchis/Bios. **134** Konrad Wothe/Oxford Scientific Films/Photolibrary.com. **135** *t* R. Cavigneaux/Bios; *b* Sarah Cuttle/RD. **136** M. Gunther/Bios. **137** *t* F. Renard/Bios; *b* Sarah Cuttle/RD. **138** M. Chadirac/Bios. **139** H. Reinhard/Okapia/Bios. **140** P. Nief/Colibri. **141** D. Halleux/Bios. **142** M. Viard/Horizon. **143** D. Bringard/Bios. **144** H. Reinhard/Okapia/Bios. **145** RD. **146** D. Heuclin/Bios. **147** J.-Y. Grospas/Bios. **148** R. Toulouse/Colibri. **149** *t* M. Gunther/Bios; *b* Sarah Cuttle/RD. **150** J. Mayet/Bios. **151** JMC/Bios. **152** Denis-Huot/Bios. **153** Gerald D. Carr. **154** *tl* D. Halleux/Bios; *br* Sarah Cuttle/RD. **155** *t* D. Chipot/Bios; *b* Sarah Cuttle/RD. **156** J.-C. Malausa/Bios. **157** E. Vialet/Bios. **158** Michel Paris. **159** Dick Roberts/NSIL. **160** *tl* Richard Surman/RD; *br* Jerry Parva/Garden Picture Library. **161** *t* Jonathan Buckley/RD; *b* Garden World Images. **162** *tl* Heather Angel/Biofotos; *br* Sarah Cuttle/RD. **163** *t* Photolibrary.com; *b* RD. **164** G. Maclean/Oxford Scientific Films/Bios. **165** G. Lopez/Bios. **166** Michel Paris. **167** *t* M. Viard/Horizon; *c & b* Sarah Cuttle/RD. **168** *t* A.& J.-C. Malausa/Bios; *b* Sarah Cuttle/RD. **169** Harry Smith Collection. **170** Klein-Hubert/Bios. **171** Photo Lamontagne. **172** Michel Paris. **173** *t* H. Reinhard/Okapia/Bios; *b* Sarah Cuttle/RD. **174** Photo Lamontagne. **175** Henriette Kress. **176** *both* Steven Foster. **177** Photo Lamontagne. **178** *tl* N.& P. Mioulane/Map; *br* Sarah Cuttle/RD. **179** *t* H. Reinhard/Okapia/Bios; *b* Sarah Cuttle/RD. **180** D. Bown/Oxford Scientific Films/Bios. **181** Michael Maconachie/Auscape. **182** G. Lopez/Bios. **183** *t* Photolibrary.com; *b* Henriette Kress. **184** Gayo/Bios. **185** *t* G. Lopez/Bios; *b* Sarah Cuttle/RD. **186** P. Nief/Colibri. **187** *t* Henriette Kress; *b* RD. **188** *tl* D. Bringard/Bios; *br* Sarah Cuttle/RD. **189** G. Villareal/Bios. **190** *tl* Steven Foster; *b* Didier Willery/Garden Picture Library. **192** Steven Foster. **193** A. Descat/Map. **194** *tl* Martin B. Withers/Corbis/Australian Picture Library; *br* RD. **195** D. Halleux/Bios. **196** *tl* H.G. Heyer/Naturbild/Okapia/Bios; *br* Sarah Cuttle/RD. **197** D. Bown/Oxford Scientific Films/Bios. **198** Dick Roberts/NSIL. **199** *both* Sarah Cuttle/RD. **200** Dick Roberts/NSIL. **201** M. Gunther/Bios. **202-203** Sarah Cuttle/RD. **204-301** all images occur elsewhere in this book and are hence credited elsewhere on this page.

Illustrations

Françoise Bonvoust **92, 118, 141, 186** Luc Bosserdet **115** Pierre Brochard **28** Jean Coladon **71, 89** Marjorie Crosby-Fairall **32, 54, 62, 125, 153, 190** *b* Brian Delf **147** Maurice Espérance **59, 68, 199** William Fraschini **1, 30, 34** *r*, **40, 43, 45, 48, 53, 56, 58, 60, 61, 63, 67, 70, 72, 74, 76, 77, 79, 81, 84, 87, 91, 95, 97, 98, 99, 103, 106, 108, 120, 121, 123, 126, 130, 132, 133, 136, 138, 142, 146, 148, 151, 152, 156, 158, 164, 169, 170, 171, 172, 174, 177, 180, 184, 189, 190** *t*, **193, 197, 201** Ian Garrard **117, 131** Odette Halmos **111** Madeleine Huau **52, 122** Mette Ivers **41, 49, 83, 104** Mary Kellner **175, 192** Josiane Lardy **46, 116** Annie Le Faou **65, 105, 113** Nadine Liard **44** David Mackay **36** Guy Michel **47, 94, 100, 139, 144, 157** Britt-Mari Norberg **34** Nicola Oram **101, 134, 145, 159, 181, 200** Charles Pickard **42, 143** Reproduced with permission of the Trustees of the Royal Botanic Gardens, Kew **50** Jean-Paul Turmel **66** Denise Weber **35, 88, 127, 140, 150, 166, 182, 195, 198**.

CREDITS 319

Consultants for Australia and New Zealand
Chief Australian Natural Health Adviser Jayne Tancred, ND, Dip Bot Med, Dip Nut, Dip Hom
Australian Natural Health Adviser Pamela Allardice, BA (Comm)
Horticultural Adviser Jennifer Stackhouse, MAIH, BA, Ass Dip Hort
Regulatory Adviser Sue Akeroyd, PhCMPS
New Zealand Natural Health Adviser Lynda Wharton, BA, ND, Dip Acu, MNZRA

Scientific Consultant
John Wilkinson, BSc PhD DIC MRSC C Chem
Senior lecturer in phytochemistry and pharmacognosy, Middlesex University, London

Medical Consultant
Andrew Dunford, MSc MRCGP MNIMH
Dr Dunford is a GP and medical herbalist

Project Management Limelight Press Pty Ltd
Art Direction Mark Thacker
Senior Designer Stephen Smedley
Designers Donna Heldon, Alex Stafford, Heidi Helyard
Picture Researcher Annette Crueger
Copy Editor Edwin Barnard, Capricorn Press Pty Ltd
Senior Editor Samantha Kent
Assistant Editor Françoise Toman
Proofreader Bronwyn Sweeney
Indexer Diane Harriman
Production Controller Janelle Garside

READER'S DIGEST GENERAL BOOKS
Executive Editor Elaine Russell
Managing Editor Rosemary McDonald
Art Director Sue Rawkins

Nature's Medicines is published by Reader's Digest (Australia) Pty Limited
80 Bay Street, Ultimo, NSW 2007
www.readersdigest.com.au

First Australian and New Zealand edition 2005
Copyright © Reader's Digest (Australia) Pty Limited 2005
Copyright © Reader's Digest Association Far East Limited 2005
Philippines Copyright © Reader's Digest Association Far East Limited 2005

All rights reserved. No part of this book may be reproduced, stored in a retrieval system, or transmitted in any form or by any means, electronic, electrostatic, magnetic tape, mechanical, photocopying, recording or otherwise, without permission in writing from the publishers.

® Reader's Digest, The Digest and the Pegasus logo are registered trademarks of The Reader's Digest Association, Inc., of Pleasantville, New York, USA.

National Library of Australia Cataloguing-in-Publication data:
Nature's medicines.
Includes index.
ISBN 1 876689 16 1.

1. Medicinal plants. 2. Botany, Medical. 3. Materia medica, Vegetable. I. Tancred, Jayne.
II. Reader's Digest Association.

615.321

Prepress by Sinnott Bros, Sydney
Printed and bound by Tien Wah Press (Pte) Ltd, Singapore

We are interested in receiving your comments on the contents of this book.
Write to: The Editor, General Books Editorial, Reader's Digest (Australia) Pty Limited,
80 Bay Street, Ultimo, NSW 2007 or email us at bookeditors.au@readersdigest.com

To order additional copies of *Nature's Medicines* call 1300 303 210 (Australia)
or 0800 540 032 (New Zealand) or email us at customerservice@au.readersdigest.com

Concept code US3570/IC
Product code 041-2941